Sample stanza from Einarr Skúlason, *Geisli*

16. Ok hagliga hugðisk
hrøkkviseiðs ins døkkva
lyngs í lopt upp ganga
látrs stríðandi síðan.

Lét, sás landfolks gætir,
líknframr himinríki
umgeypnandi opnask
alls heims fyr gram snjǫllum.

Ok stríðandi látrs ins døkkva hrøkkviseiðs lyngs hugðisk síðan ganga hagliga upp í lopt. Líknframr umgeypnandi alls heims, sás gætir landfolks, lét himinríki opnask fyr snjǫllum gram.

And the enemy of the lair of the dark coiling fish of the heather [SNAKE > GOLD > GENEROUS MAN] thought then that he went easily up into the air. The outstandingly merciful encompasser [*lit.* holder in hand] of the whole world [= God], who watches over the people of the country, caused the kingdom of heaven to open before the clever king.

Mss: **Flat**(2ra), Bb(117rb); R(35v), T^x(37r), W(81), U(68), A(12v) (*SnE*, ll. 5-8).

Readings: [1] hagliga: *so* Bb, hverlofaðr Flat [2] -seiðs: baugs Bb [4] látrs: látr Bb [5] landfolks: *so* Bb, R, T^x, W, U, A, lands folk Flat [6] líknframr: líknsamr Bb, A, líkbjartr R, T^x, W, líknbjartr U [7] umgeypnandi: umgeypnanda T^x; opnask: opna R, T^x, W, U, A.

Editions: *Skj* Einarr Skúlason, 6. *Geisli* 16: AI, 462, BI, 431, *Skald* I, 213; *Flat* 1860-8, I, 2, Cederschiöld 1873, 3, Chase 2005, 66, 137-8; *SnE* 1848-87, I, 450, *SnE* 1931, 159, *SnE* 1998, I, 78.

Context: Lines 5-8 occur in several mss of the *Skm* section of *SnE* among examples of kennings for Christ. Snorri comments: 'Here kennings become ambiguous, and the person interpreting the poetry has to distinguish from the context which king is being referred to. For it is normal to call the emperor of Constantinople king of the Greeks, and similarly the king that rules Palestine, to call him king of Jerusalem ... And the kenning that was quoted above, calling Christ king of men, this kenning can be applied to any king.' (Faulkes 1987, 127-8; cf. *SnE* 1998, I, 78). Snorri was aware of Einarr's use of *double entendre* to associate Óláfr with Christ. — *Notes*: [2] hagliga 'easily': The Bb reading is necessary for the rhyme with hugðisk. — [6] líknframr 'outstandingly merciful': The reading of the *SnE* mss R, T^x and W, líkbjartr 'bright in body' offers a viable alternative here, as does U's líknbjartr 'bright of (?shining in) mercy'. — [7, 8] umgeypnandi alls heims 'encompasser [*lit.* holder in hand] of the whole world': Ps. XCIV.4 (*in manu eius fines terrae* 'in his hands are all the ends of the earth') is probably the inspiration for this kenning, understood here to refer to God even though Snorri Sturluson (see Context) apparently understood it to refer to Christ. Cf. similar periphrases in Anon *Mgr* 2/5, Kálf *Kátr* 36/3, Gamlkan *Has* 29/7-8 and 64/6.

POETRY IN *FORNALDARSÖGUR*

SKALDIC POETRY OF THE SCANDINAVIAN MIDDLE AGES

I Poetry from the Kings' Sagas 1: From Mythical Times to c. 1035
II Poetry from the Kings' Sagas 2: From c. 1035 to c. 1300
III Poetry from Treatises on Poetics
IV Poetry on Icelandic History
V Poetry in Sagas of Icelanders
VI Runic Poetry
VII Poetry on Christian Subjects
VIII Poetry in *fornaldarsögur*
IX Bibliography and Indices

Editorial Board under the auspices of the
Centre for Medieval Studies, University of Sydney
Margaret Clunies Ross (University of Sydney and University of Adelaide)
Kari Ellen Gade (Indiana University)
Guðrún Nordal (Háskóli Íslands)
Edith Marold (Universität Kiel)
Diana Whaley (University of Newcastle upon Tyne)
Tarrin Wills (University of Aberdeen and University of Copenhagen)
Hannah Burrows (for Bibliography; University of Aberdeen)

The General Editors gratefully acknowledge major funding from the following bodies:
Australian Research Council
Social Sciences and Humanities Council of Canada
Western Universiy, Canada

This print edition is published in parallel with an electronic edition containing additional and
interactive features created by Tarrin Wills

VOLUME VIII

POETRY IN *FORNALDARSÖGUR*
Part 1

Edited by

Margaret Clunies Ross

BREPOLS

A catalogue record for this book is available from the British Library

© 2017, Brepols Publishers n.v., Turnhout, Belgium

All rights reserved. No part of this publication may be reproduced, stored in a retrieval system, or transmitted, in any form or by any means, electronic, mechanical, photocopying, recording, or otherwise, without the prior permission of the publisher.

D/2017/0095/209
ISBN: 978-2-503-51900-5 (in 2 vols)

Contents

Contents	v
Volume Editor's Preface and Acknowledgements	ix
General Abbreviations	xi
Sigla used in this Volume	xvii
Sigla for Skaldic Poems and Stanzas	xvii
Sigla for Manuscript Collections	xxxix
Sigla for Manuscripts used in the Editions of this Volume	xl
Sigla for Sagas, *Þættir* and Compendia	xlii
Technical Terms	xlv
The Contributors	li
Introduction	lv
Skaldic Poetry of the Scandinavian Middle Ages – a New Edition	lv
The Icelandic *fornaldarsaga*	lvi
The poetry in this volume	lxi
Manuscripts	lxii
Editions	lxix
Metre	lxxi
Structure, style and diction of *fornaldarsaga* poetry	lxxix
Normalisation	xci
How to use this edition	xciii

Poetry in *fornaldarsögur*: The Corpus

PART 1

Áns saga bogsveigis — Edited by Beatrice La Farge	3
Ásmundar saga kappabana — Edited by Peter Jorgensen	15
Bósa saga — Edited by Wilhelm Heizmann	25
Breta saga	38
Gunnlaugr Leifsson —Russell Poole	38
Merlínusspá I — Edited by Russell Poole	38
Merlínusspá II — Edited by Russell Poole	134

Friðþjófs saga ins frækna — Edited by Margaret Clunies Ross	190
Starkaðr gamli Stórvirksson — Margaret Clunies Ross	241
Gautreks saga — Edited by Margaret Clunies Ross	241
Gríms saga loðinkinna — Edited by Beatrice La Farge	288
Gǫngu-Hrólfs saga — Edited by Margaret Clunies Ross	298
Hálfs saga ok Hálfsrekka — Edited by Hubert Seelow	303
Hervarar saga ok Heiðreks — Edited by Hannah Burrows	367

Part 2

Hjálmþés saga ok Ǫlvis — Edited by Richard L. Harris	489
Hrólfs saga kraka — Edited by †Desmond Slay	540
Ketils saga hœngs — Edited by Beatrice La Farge	549
Máguss saga jarls — Edited by Margaret Clunies Ross	597
Orms þáttr Stórólfssonar — Edited by Peter Jorgensen	603
Ragnars saga loðbrókar — Edited by Rory McTurk	617
Krákumál — Edited by Rory McTurk	707
Ragnars sona þáttr — Edited by Rory McTurk	778
Sturlaugs saga starfsama — Edited by Margaret Clunies Ross	782
Sǫrla þáttr — Edited by Rory McTurk	786
Vǫlsunga saga — Edited by Margaret Clunies Ross	791
Þjalar-Jóns saga — Edited by Philip Lavender	799
Ǫrvar-Odds saga — Edited by Margaret Clunies Ross	805

Poem recorded outside a saga context

Svartr á Hofstöðum — Kari Ellen Gade	951
Skaufhala bálkr — Edited by Kari Ellen Gade	951
Bibliography — Edited by Hannah Burrows	987
Index of First Lines	1039

Indices of Names and Terms	1059
Mythical, Biblical and Legendary Names	1059
Personal Names	1070
Nicknames	1070
Ethnic and Regional Names (including names of royal dynasties)	1071
Place Names	1072
Miscellaneous Names	1076
Indigenous Terms	1076

VOLUME EDITOR'S PREFACE AND ACKNOWLEDGEMENTS

My first acknowledgement, as editor of the present volume, is to Rory McTurk for saving me and the other General Editors of the series *Skaldic Poetry of the Scandinavian Middle Ages* from the serious mistake of omitting the contents of this volume from our new edition. It surprises and slightly shames me now, in retrospect, given all I have learned about *fornaldarsaga* poetry over the years that Volume VIII has been in active preparation, that we had originally planned to omit this large, important and somewhat under-researched corpus of verse. When we announced the format of the new edition to participants at the Eleventh International Saga Conference at the University of Sydney in July 2000, Rory stood up and persuaded us to reconsider our decision. I am very pleased that we heeded his advice, as I have come to realise how much we still have to learn about this body of poetry, which, along with the prose texts in which it has been transmitted, has been somewhat neglected until recently and treated as a lesser type of eddic verse, an *Eddica minora*, to use the title of a well-known early twentieth-century anthology of poems and extracts from *fornaldarsögur*.

Much of what is new in this volume is attributable to the expertise and dedication of the editors of the individual texts within it, and I am grateful to them all for the exacting work of editing and the background knowledge that they have brought to the task. In many cases new research has underpinned their work, whether in terms of a fresh examination of the manuscript sources, new knowledge about the textual and literary background of the poetry, and/or the preparation of a new English translation of the poems or stanzas.

The quality of the editions in Volume VIII depends in the first instance on the work of the eleven Contributing Editors, but is also very much dependent on the contributions made by the General Editors in the process of Quality Control for each edition. Without their knowledge and expertise I could not have produced this volume and I am deeply grateful to them for the time and effort they have spent on it. I would like to thank especially Kari Ellen Gade, Edith Marold and Diana Whaley for saving me from many an egregious error.

Thanks are also due to Hannah Burrows, the Bibliography editor, for all her painstaking checking of the references in this edition and for her advice on how to present some of them, and to Tarrin Wills for assistance and advice about everything related to the database and for producing the final versions of Volume VIII for export to Brepols. I would also like to thank Guy Carney, our consultant editor at Brepols, for his patience and sound advice at all stages of preparation of this and other volumes in the *SkP* series.

Helen Appleton, currently of Balliol College Oxford, is someone without whose assistance this volume could not have been produced. I employed Helen with funds provided from a Discovery Research Grant awarded to me by the Australian Research Council between 2013-16 to enter all the editions in this volume into the skaldic database. She has done so with great skill and accuracy and put up with my many interventions and alterations to the editions. Her expertise and intuitive understanding of how the database works have been remarkable and I thank her very much. I must also express my gratitude to the Australian Research Council for awarding me the grant that allowed me to employ Helen.

Thanks are also due to other bodies or to individuals: Russell Poole is grateful to the Social Sciences and Humanities Council of Canada (SSHRC) and Western University Canada for research funding enabling him to prepare his editions of *Merlínusspá I* and *II*; the volume editor would also like to thank Anders Andrén for advice and information on archaeological questions and the Kungliga bibliotek, Stockholm, for permission to reproduce in the edition of *Þjalar-Jóns saga* an image of a wolf-like creature biting a man's arm from the lower margin of fol. 121v of Holm perg 6 4°.

The Introduction to Volume VIII sketches a new approach to *fornaldarsaga* poetry in terms of subject-matter, structure, style, and diction, but, being a general work of a defined length, it can only be suggestive of ways in which the observations within it can be taken further. An exception to this observation concerns Section 6 on metres, which has been specially written by Kari Ellen Gade. This uses the editions in the volume as the basis for a series of analyses of the metres of *fornaldarsaga* poetry, something not previously attempted in any detail, and then applies the results of that analysis to three test cases within the corpus. I am most grateful to Kari for undertaking this work and thank her also for her many other acts of assistance to me in the preparation of this volume for publication.

Margaret Clunies Ross,
Adelaide, South Australia and Wivenhoe, Essex,
June 2017

GENERAL ABBREVIATIONS

Note that sigla for all Old Norse-Icelandic poetry, sagas, compendia and *þættir* referred to in this edition are to be found the Lists of Sigla below, with the exception of abbreviations for poems of the Poetic Edda (which are listed in this section), while abbreviated references to editions, facsimiles and secondary sources are to be found listed in alphabetical order in the Bibliography. All other abbreviations are listed here.

Abbreviations are used in all parts of the edition, except at the beginnings of sentences and in most sections of the Introduction as well as in discursive sections (Introduction, Context) in the individual editions. Note that plurals of abbreviated words are written in full, e.g. 'infinitives', 'adverbs' unless plural forms are listed below, e.g. 'll.', 'sts'.

1. Grammatical and Linguistic Abbreviations

acc. — accusative
adj. — adjective
adv. — adverb
comp. — comparative
conj. — conjunction
cpd — compound
dat. — dative
def. art. — definite article
e-m — *einhverjum*
e-n — *einhvern*
e-s — *einhvers*
e-t — *eitthvat*
e-u — *einhverju*
f. — feminine
gen. — genitive
imp. — imperative
indef. — indefinite
indic. — indicative
inf. — infinitive
instr. — instrumental
interrog. — interrogative
m. — masculine

m. v. — middle voice, mediopassive
n. — neuter
nom. — nominative
pers. n. — personal name
pers. pron. — personal pronoun
pl. — plural
p. n. — place name
poss. — possessive
p. p. — past participle
prep. — preposition
pres. part. — present participle
pret. — preterite
pron. — pronoun
refl. — reflexive
rel. — relative
sg. — singular
subj. — subjunctive
sup. — superlative
1st pers. — first person
2nd pers. — second person
3rd pers. — third person

2. Abbreviations for Languages

Dan. — Danish
Engl. — English
Ger. — German
Gk — Greek
Gmc — Germanic
Goth. — Gothic
Icel. — Icelandic
IE — Indo-European
Lat. — Latin
LG — Low German
ME — Middle English
MHG — Middle High German
MLG — Middle Low German
ModDan. — Modern Danish
ModEngl. — Modern English
ModIcel. — Modern Icelandic
ModIr. — Modern Irish
ModNorw. — Modern Norwegian
ModSwed. — Modern Swedish

New Norw. — New Norwegian (*nynorsk*)
Norw. — Norwegian
ODan. — Old Danish
OE — Old English
OFr. — Old French
OHG — Old High German
OIcel. — Old Icelandic
OIr. — Old Irish
ON — Old Norse (used where differentiation between individual early Nordic [*norrœn*] languages is not necessary or possible)
ONorw. — Old Norwegian
OS — Old Saxon
OSwed. — Old Swedish
OWN — Old West Norse
Swed. — Swedish
WGmc — West Germanic

3. Abbreviated References to Poems of the Poetic Edda in this Edition

Akv — Atlakviða
Alv — Alvíssmál
Am — Atlamál
Bdr — Baldrs draumar
Brot — Sigurðarkviða in meiri (Brot af)
Fáfn — Fáfnismál
Fj — Fjölsvinnsmál
Ghv — Guðrúnarhvǫt
Grí — Grímnismál
Gríp — Grípisspá
Grott — Grottasǫngr
Guðr I — Guðrúnarkviða I
Guðr II — Guðrúnarkviða II
Guðr III — Guðrúnarkviða III
Hamð — Hamðismál
Hárb — Hárbarðsljóð
Hávm — Hávamál
Helr — Helreið Brynhildar
HHj — Helgakviða Hjǫrvarðssonar
HHund I — Helgakviða Hundingsbana I
HHund II — Helgakviða Hundingsbana II
Hym — Hymiskviða
Hyndl — Hyndluljóð

Lok — *Lokasenna*
Oddrgr — *Oddrúnargrátr*
Reg — *Reginsmál*
Rþ — *Rígsþula*
Sigrdr — *Sigrdrífumál*
Sigsk — *Sigurðarkviða in skamma*
* Skí* — *Skírnismál*
Vafþr — *Vafþrúðnismál*
Vsp — *Vǫluspá*
Vǫl — *Vǫlundarkviða*
Þry — *Þrymskviða*

4. Other Abbreviations and Notations

c. — circa
C10th — tenth century (and similarly for references to other centuries)
ch. — chapter
chs — chapters
d. — died
ed. — editor, edited (by)
edn — edition
eds — editors, editions
fol. — folio
fols — folios
hap. leg. — *hapax legomenon* (pl. *legomena*) – unique word(s)
l. — line
ll. — lines
lit. — literally (used in translations [italicised] and notes [roman])
Lv — *lausavísa*, pl. *lausavísur* 'loose stanza(s)', free-standing stanzas
ms. — manuscript
mss — manuscripts
n. — note (but e.g. Anm. if notes are labelled as such in the source)
nn. — notes
no. — number
nos — numbers
p. — page
pp. — pages
r. — reigned (of regnal dates of kings, jarls, etc.)
S. — Saint
s. a. — *sub anno* 'under year'– for references to materials in annals
sby — somebody
st. — stanza
sth. — something

sts — stanzas
vol. — volume
vols — volumes
* — reconstructed form, e.g. hypothetical etymon, no longer extant text
† — obelos symbol for textual material that is impossibly corrupt or cannot be made sense of. One † is placed immediately before the beginning of the piece of corrupt text and another immediately after it.

Sigla used in this Volume

Sigla for Skaldic Poems and Stanzas

Aðils Lv (*Hrólf*) — *Hrólfs saga kraka* (Aðils konungr, Lausavísa)
    See individual stanza(s) for *Skj* references
Alrekr Lv (*Hálf*) — *Hálfs saga ok Hálfsrekka* (Alrekr konungr, Lausavísa)
    See individual stanza(s) for *Skj* references
Angantýr Lv (*Heiðr*) — *Hervarar saga ok Heiðreks* (Angantýr Arngrímsson, Lausavísur)
    See individual stanza(s) for *Skj* references
AngH Lv (*Heiðr*) — *Hervarar saga ok Heiðreks* (Angantýr Heiðreksson, Lausavísur)
    See individual stanza(s) for *Skj* references
Anon *Alpost*[VII] — Vol. 7. Anonymous, *Allra postula minnisvísur* (852-71)
    Skj: [Anonyme digte og vers XIV]: [B. 9]. Allra postula minnisvísur (AII, 509-11; BII, 559-62)
Anon *Bjark*[III] — Vol. 3. Anonymous, *Bjarkamál in fornu* (495)
    Skj: Anonyme digte og vers [X]: II. A. Bjarkamál en fornu (AI, 180-1; BI, 170-1)
Anon *Brúðv* 13[VII] — Vol. 7. Anonymous, *Brúðkaupsvísur*, 13 (538-9)
    Not in *Skj*
Anon *Brúðv* 27[VII] — Vol. 7. Anonymous, *Brúðkaupsvísur*, 27 (548-9)
    Not in *Skj*
Anon *Darr*[V] (*Nj*) — Vol. 5. *Njáls saga* (Anonymous, *Darraðarljóð*)
    Skj: Anonyme digte om historiske personer og begivenheder [XI]: [1]. Darraðarljóð (AI, 419-21; BI, 389-91)
Anon *Eirm*[I] — Vol. 1. Anonymous, *Eiríksmál* (1003)
    Skj: Anonyme digte og vers [X]: I. A. [1]. Eiríksmál (AI, 174-5; BI, 164-6)
Anon (*FoGT*) 13[III] — Vol. 3. Anonymous, *Stanzas from the* Fourth Grammatical Treatise, 13 (586)
    Skj: Anonyme digte og vers [XIII]: [C]. D. Religiøse og moraliserende vers af den 4. grammatiske afhandling 5 (AII, 164; BII, 181)
Anon (*FoGT*) 24[III] — Vol. 3. Anonymous, *Stanzas from the* Fourth Grammatical Treatise, 24 (601)
    Skj: Anonyme digte og vers [XIII]: D. 3. Vers af den 4. grt. afhandling 18 (AII, 217; BII, 235)
Anon (*Gautr*) (*Gautr*) — *Gautreks saga* (Anonymous, Lausavísa *from* Gautreks saga)
    See individual stanza(s) for *Skj* references
Anon *Gát*[III] — Vol. 3. Anonymous, *Gátur* (631)
    Skj: Anonyme digte og vers [XIII]: D. 5. [b]. Andre gåder (AII, 228-9; BII, 247)
Anon *GnóðÁsm* 1[III] — Vol. 3. Anonymous, *Gnóðar-Ásmundar drápa*, 1 (626)
    Skj: Anonyme digte og vers [XII]: A. 5. Gnóðar-Ásmundardrápa (AI, 591; BI, 591)

Anon *Grf*^V (*Gr*) — Vol. 5. *Grettis saga Ásmundarsonar* (Anonymous, *Grettisfærsla*)
Not in *Skj*
Anon *Gyð*^{VII} — Vol. 7. Anonymous, *Gyðingsvísur* (515-26)
Skj: [Anonyme digte og vers XIV]: [B. 13]. Af et digt om en rig mand, der gav alt sit bort (AII, 539-41; BII, 597-9)
Anon *Harst*^{II} — Vol. 2. Anonymous, *Haraldsstikki* (807-8)
Skj: Anonyme digte om historiske personer og begivenheder [XI]: [5]. Haraldsstikki (AI, 424; BI, 394)
Anon *Harst* 1^{II} — Vol. 2. Anonymous, *Haraldsstikki*, 1 (807-8)
Skj: Anonyme digte om historiske personer og begivenheder [XI]: [5]. Haraldsstikki (AI, 424; BI, 394)
Anon (*Hálf*) — Anonymous, *Lausavísur* from *Hálfs saga ok Hálfsrekka*
Skj: Anonyme digte og vers [XIII]: E. 6. Vers af Fornaldarsagaer: Af Hálfssaga (AII, 256-69; BII, 276-91)
Anon (*Heiðr*) (*Heiðr*) — *Hervarar saga ok Heiðreks* (Anonymous, *Lausavísur* from *Hervarar saga ok Heiðreks*)
Skj: Anonyme digte og vers [XIII]: E. 5. Vers af Fornaldarsagaer: Af Hervararsaga (AII, 242-56; BII, 262-76)
Anon (*HjǪ*) (*HjǪ*) — *Hjálmþés saga ok Ǫlvis* (Anonymous, *Lausavísur* from *Hjálmþérs saga ok Ǫlvis*)
Skj: Anonyme digte og vers [XIII]: E. 16. Vers af Fornaldarsagaer: Af Hjálmþérs saga ok Ǫlvis (AII, 333-41; BII, 353-63)
Anon (*Hrólf*) (*Hrólf*) — *Hrólfs saga kraka* (Anonymous, *Lausavísa* from *Hrólfs saga kraka*)
Skj: Anonyme digte og vers [X]: II. B. 1. Kong Rolf i Adilses hal (AI, 181; BI, 171)
Anon (*HSig*) 4^{II} — Vol. 2. Anonymous, *Lausavísur* from *Haralds saga Sigurðarsonar*, 4 (818)
Skj: Anonyme digte om historiske personer og begivenheder [XI]: [7]. Lausavísur 9 (AI, 426 (ll. 1-4), 360 (ll. 5-8); BI, 396 (ll. 1-4), 331 (ll. 5-8))
Anon *Hsv*^{VII} — Vol. 7. Anonymous, *Hugsvinnsmál* (358-449)
Skj: Anonyme digte og vers [XIII]: [C. E/5]. Hugsvinnsmál (AII, 167-97; BII, 185-210)
Anon *Krm* (*Ragn*) — *Ragnars saga loðbrókar* (Anonymous, *Krákumál*) (706)
Skj: Anonyme digte og vers [XII]: H. Krákumál (AI, 641-9; BI, 649-56)
Anon (*LaufE*) 5^{III} — Vol. 3. Anonymous, Stanzas from *Laufás Edda*, 5 (642)
Skj: Anonyme digte og vers [XII]: C. Vers om ubestemmelige personer og begivenheder 37 (AI, 601; BI, 601)
Anon *Leið*^{VII} — Vol. 7. Anonymous, *Leiðarvísan* (137-78)
Skj: Anonyme digte og vers [XII]: G [2]. Leiðarvísan (AI, 618-26; BI, 622-33)
Anon *Liðs*^I — Vol. 1. Anonymous, *Liðsmannaflokkr* (1014)
Skj: Anonyme digte om historiske personer og begivenheder [XI]: [2]. Liðsmannaflokkr (AI, 422-3; BI, 391-3)

Anon *Lil*^{VII} — Vol. 7. Anonymous, *Lilja* (544-677)
  Skj: Eysteinn Ásgrímsson: Lilja (AII, 363-95; BII, 390-416)
Anon *Líkn*^{VII} — Vol. 7. Anonymous, *Líknarbraut* (228-86)
  Skj: Anonyme digte og vers [XIII]: C. 1. Líknarbraut (AII, 150-9; BII, 160-74)
Anon (*Mberf*) 2^{II} — Vol. 2. Anonymous, *Lausavísur* from *Magnúss saga berfœtts*, 2 (829-30)
  Skj: Anonyme digte om historiske personer og begivenheder [XI]: [7]. Lausavísur 15 (AI, 427-8; BI, 397-8)
Anon *Mey*^{VII} — Vol. 7. Anonymous, *Heilagra meyja drápa* (891-930)
  Skj: [Anonyme digte og vers XIV]: [B. 12]. Af heilogum meyjum (AII, 526-39; BII, 582-97)
Anon *Mhkv*^{III} — Vol. 3. Anonymous, *Málsháttakvæði* (1213)
  Skj: Anonyme digte og vers [XIII]: A. [1]. Málsháttakvæði (AII, 130-6; BII, 138-45)
Anon *Nkt*^{II} — Vol. 2. Anonymous, *Nóregs konungatal* (761-806)
  Skj: [Anonyme digte og vers XII]: [2]. Nóregs konunga-tal (AI, 579-89; BI, 575-90)
Anon (*OStór*) (*OStór*) — *Orms þáttr Stórólfssonar* (Anonymous, *Lausavísa* from *Orms þáttr Stórólfssonar*)
  Skj: Anonyme digte og vers [XIII]: E. 18. Vers af Fornaldarsagaer: Af Orms þáttr Stórólfssonar (AII, 342-4; BII, 364-7)
Anon *Ól*^I — Vol. 1. Anonymous, *Poem about Óláfr Tryggvason* (1061)
  Skj: [Anonyme digte og vers XIV]: A. 9. Af et digt om Olaf Tryggvason (AII, 462-3; BII, 494-5)
Anon *Óldr*^I — Vol. 1. Anonymous, *Óláfs drápa Tryggvasonar* (1031)
  Skj: [Anonyme digte og vers XII]: [1]. Óláfs drápa Tryggvasonar (AI, 573-8; BI, 567-74)
Anon (*ÓTHkr*) 1^I — Vol. 1. Anonymous, *Lausavísa* from *Óláfs saga Tryggvasonar in Heimskringla*, 1 (1073)
  Skj: Anonyme digte og vers [X]: I. A. [3]. Et niddigt om kong Harald blåtand (AI, 176; BI, 166)
Anon *Pét*^{VII} — Vol. 7. Anonymous, *Pétrsdrápa* (796-844)
  Skj: [Anonyme digte og vers XIV]: [B. 7]. En drape om apostlen Peder (AII, 500-8; BII, 545-58)
Anon *Pl*^{VII} — Vol. 7. Anonymous, *Plácitusdrápa* (179-220)
  Skj: Anonyme digte og vers [XII]: G [1]. Plácítúsdrápa (AI, 607-18; BI, 606-22)
Anon (*Ragn*) (*Ragn*) — *Ragnars saga loðbrókar* (Anonymous, *Lausavísur* from *Ragnars saga loðbrókar*)
  Skj: Anonyme digte og vers [XIII]: E. 2. Vers af Fornaldarsagaer: Af Ragnarssaga loðbrókar (AII, 232-42; BII, 251-61)
Anon *Run*^{VI} — Vol. 6. Anonymous, *Norwegian Rune Poem*
  Skj: Anonyme digte og vers [XIII]: D. [6]. Runedigt (AII, 229-30; BII, 248-9)

Anon *RunI*^{VI} — Vol. 6. Anonymous, *Icelandic Rune Poem*
    Not in *Skj*
Anon (*SnE*) 9^{III} — Vol. 3. Anonymous, *Stanzas from Snorra Edda*, 9 (519)
    Skj: Anonyme digte og vers [X]: II. B. 6. En troldkvinde (AI, 182; BI, 172)
Anon (*SnE*) 11^{III} — Vol. 3. Anonymous, *Stanzas from Snorra Edda*, 11 (522)
    Skj: Anonyme digte og vers [X]: III. A. Om skjaldskab 2 (AI, 184; BI, 173)
Anon *Sól*^{VII} — Vol. 7. Anonymous, *Sólarljóð* (287-357)
    Skj: Anonyme digte og vers [XII]: G [6]. Sólarljóð (AI, 628-40; BI, 635-48)
Anon *Stríðk* 1^{III} — Vol. 3. Anonymous, *Stríðkeravísur*, 1 (628)
    Skj: Anonyme digte og vers [XII]: A. 3. Stríðkeravísur (AI, 590; BI, 591)
Anon (*StSt*) (*StSt*) — *Sturlaugs saga starfsama* (Anonymous, *Lausavísur* from *Sturlaugs saga starfsama*)
    Skj: Anonyme digte og vers [XIII]: E. 17. Vers af Fornaldarsagaer: Af Sturlaugs saga starfsama (AII, 341-34; BII, 364)
Anon (*Stu*) 23^{IV} — Vol. 4. Anonymous, *Lausavísur from* Sturlunga saga, 23
    Skj: Anonyme digte og vers [XIII]: B. Anonyme løse vers angående bestemte historiske begivenheder 22 (AII, 142; BII, 152)
Anon *Sveinfl* 1^I — Vol. 1. Anonymous, *Flokkr* about Sveinn Álfífuson, 1 (1029)
    Skj: Anonyme digte om historiske personer og begivenheder [XI]: [3]. Flokkr om Sven Alfifassön (AI, 423; BI, 393)
Anon *Sǫrl* (*Sǫrla*) — *Sǫrla þáttr* (Anonymous, *Sǫrlastikki*)
    Skj: Anonyme digte og vers [XIII]: E. 4. Vers af Fornaldarsagaer: Af Sǫrlaþáttr (AII, 242; BII, 262)
Anon (*TGT*) 35^{III} — Vol. 3. Anonymous, *Stanzas from the* Third Grammatical Treatise, 35 (561)
    Skj: Anonyme digte og vers [XII]: G [5]. Andre religiøse vers og herhen hørende digtbrudstykker 2 (AI, 627; BI, 635)
Anon (*Vǫls*) (*Vǫls*) — *Vǫlsunga saga* (Anonymous, *Lausavísur* from *Vǫlsunga saga*)
    See individual stanza(s) for *Skj* references
Anon (*Vǫlsa*)^I — Vol. 1. Anonymous, *Lausavísur* from *Vǫlsa þáttr* (1089)
    Skj: Anonyme digte og vers [XIII]: D. 4. Vers af Vǫlsaþáttr (AII, 219-21; BII, 237-9)
Anon (*Ǫrv*) (*Ǫrv*) — *Ǫrvar-Odds saga* (Anonymous, *Lausavísa* from *Ǫrvar-Odds saga*)
    Skj: Anonyme digte og vers [XIII]: E. 10. Vers af Fornaldarsagaer: Af Ǫrvar-Oddssaga (AII, 289-319; BII, 310-39)
Arn *Frag* 4^{III} — Vol. 3. Arnórr jarlaskáld Þórðarson (biog. vol. 2), *Fragments*, 4 (6)
    Skj: Arnórr Þórðarson jarlaskáld: 7. Vers af ubestemmelige digte, samt én lausavísa 3 (AI, 354; BI, 326)
Arn *Hardr*^{II} — Vol. 2. Arnórr jarlaskáld Þórðarson, *Haraldsdrápa* (260-80)
    Skj: Arnórr Þórðarson jarlaskáld: 6. Erfidrápa om kong Harald hårdråde (AI, 349-53; BI, 322-6)

Arn *Hryn*^{II} — Vol. 2. Arnórr jarlaskáld Þórðarson, *Hrynhenda, Magnússdrápa* (181-206)
    Skj: Arnórr Þórðarson jarlaskáld: 2. Hrynhenda, Magnúsdrápa (AI, 332-8; BI, 306-11)
Arn *Magndr*^{II} — Vol. 2. Arnórr jarlaskáld Þórðarson, *Magnússdrápa* (206-29)
    Skj: Arnórr Þórðarson jarlaskáld: 3. Magnúsdrápa (AI, 338-43; BI, 311-15)
Án Lv (*Án*) — *Áns saga bogsveigis* (Án bogsveigir, Lausavísur)
    Skj: Anonyme digte og vers [XIII]: E. 11. Vers af Fornaldarsagaer: Af Áns saga bogsveigis (AII, 319-20; BII, 339-40)
Árm Lv^{II} — Vol. 2. Ármóðr, Lausavísur (620-3)
    Skj: Ármóðr: Lausavísur (AI, 530-1; BI, 511-12)
Ásb Lv (*OStór*) — *Orms þáttr Stórólfssonar* (Ásbjǫrn, Lausavísur)
    See individual stanza(s) for *Skj* references
Ásb *Ævkv* (*OStór*) — *Orms þáttr Stórólfssonar* (Ásbjǫrn, *Ævikviða*)
    See individual stanza(s) for *Skj* references
Ásm Lv (*Frið*) — *Friðþjófs saga ins frœkna* (Ásmundr, Lausavísa)
    See individual stanza(s) for *Skj* references
Ásmk Lv (*Ásm*) — *Ásmundar saga kappabana* (Ásmundr kappabana, Lausavísur)
    See individual stanza(s) for *Skj* references
Bbreiðv Lv^V (*Eb*) — Vol. 5. *Eyrbyggja saga* (Bjǫrn breiðvíkingakappi Ásbrandsson, Lausavísur)
    Skj: Bjǫrn Ásbrandsson, Breiðvíkingakappi: Lausavísur (AI, 133-4; BI, 125-6)
Bjarmij Lv (*Heiðr*) — *Hervarar saga ok Heiðreks* (Bjarmi jarl, Lausavísa)
    See individual stanza(s) for *Skj* references
Bjarni Frag^{III} — Vol. 3. Bjarni ...ason, *Fragments* (20)
    Skj: Bjarni ason (el. a sk).: Brudstykker af digte (AI, 542; BI, 523)
Bjbp *Jóms*^I — Vol. 1. Bjarni byskup Kolbeinsson, *Jómsvíkingadrápa* (954)
    Skj: Bjarni Kolbeinsson: Jómsvíkingadrápa (AII, 1-10; BII, 1-10)
BjHall *Kálffl*^I — Vol. 1. Bjarni gullbrárskáld Hallbjarnarson, *Kálfsflokkr* (877)
    Skj: Bjarni Hallbjarnarson gullbrárskáld: Kalfsflokkr (AI, 393-6; BI, 363-5)
Bjhít *Grám*^V (*BjH*) — Vol. 5. *Bjarnar saga Hítdœlakappa* (Bjǫrn Hítdœlakappi Arngeirsson, *Grámagaflím*)
    Skj: Bjǫrn Arngeirsson hítdœlakappi: 1. Grámagaflím (AI, 300; BI, 276)
Bjhít Lv^V (*BjH*) — Vol. 5. *Bjarnar saga Hítdœlakappa* (Bjǫrn Hítdœlakappi Arngeirsson, Lausavísur)
    Skj: Bjǫrn Arngeirsson hítdœlakappi: 2. Lausavísur (AI, 300-5; BI, 277-83)
BjRagn Lv (*Ragn*) — *Ragnars saga loðbrókar* (Bjǫrn Ragnarsson, Lausavísur)
    See individual stanza(s) for *Skj* references
Bjǫrn Lv (*Frið*) — *Friðþjófs saga ins frœkna* (Bjǫrn, Lausavísur)
    See individual stanza(s) for *Skj* references
Blakkr Lv^{II} — Vol. 2. Blakkr, Lausavísur (649-51)
    Skj: Blakkr: 2. Lausavísur (AI, 538; BI, 519)

Bragi Frag 2^{III} — Vol. 3. Bragi inn gamli Boddason, *Fragments*, 2 (56)
   Skj: Bragi enn gamli: 1. Ragnarsdrápa 20 (AI, 4; BI, 4)
Bragi Lv^{IV} — Vol. 4. Bragi inn gamli Boddason, Lausavísur
   Skj: Bragi enn gamli: (AI, 5; BI, 5)
Bragi *Rdr*^{III} — Vol. 3. Bragi inn gamli Boddason, *Ragnarsdrápa* (27)
   Skj: Bragi enn gamli: 1. Ragnarsdrápa (AI, 1-4; BI, 1-4)
Bragi *Troll* 1^{III} — Vol. 3. Bragi inn gamli Boddason, An exchange of verses between Bragi and a troll-woman, 1 (64)
   Skj: Bragi enn gamli: 3. Lausavísur 2 (AI, 5; BI, 5)
Bragi *Þórr*^{III} — Vol. 3. Bragi inn gamli Boddason, Þórr's fishing (46)
   Not in *Skj*
Bragi *Þórr* 2^{III} — Vol. 3. Bragi inn gamli Boddason, Þórr's fishing, 2 (48)
   Skj: Bragi enn gamli: 1. Ragnarsdrápa 16 (AI, 4; BI, 4)
Brúni Lv (*Ket*) — *Ketils saga hœngs* (Brúni, Lausavísa)
   See individual stanza(s) for *Skj* references
Busla *Busl* (*Bós*) — *Bósa saga* (Busla, Buslubœn)
   Skj: Anonyme digte og vers [XIII]: E. 14. Vers af Fornaldarsagaer: Af Bósasaga (AII, 330-2; BII, 350-3)
Bǫðmóðr Lv (*Ket*) — *Ketils saga hœngs* (Bǫðmóðr Framarsson, Lausavísur)
   See individual stanza(s) for *Skj* references
Bǫlv *Hardr*^{II} — Vol. 2. Bǫlverkr Arnórsson, *Drápa* about Haraldr harðráði (286-93)
   Skj: Bǫlverkr Arnórsson: Drape om Harald hårdråde (AI, 385-7; BI, 355-7)
Edáð *Banddr*^{I} — Vol. 1. Eyjólfr dáðaskáld, *Bandadrápa* (454)
   Skj: Eyjólfr dáðaskáld: Bandadrápa (AI, 200-2; BI, 190-2)
Egill^{V} — (Egill Skallagrímsson)
   Skj: Egill Skallagrímsson (AI, 34-60; BI, 30-53)
Egill *Arkv*^{V} (*Eg*) — Vol. 5. *Egils saga Skalla-Grímssonar* (Egill Skallagrímsson, Arinbjarnarkviða)
   Skj: Egill Skallagrímsson: 4. Arinbjarnarkviða (AI, 43-8; BI, 38-41)
Egill *Hfl*^{V} (*Eg*) — Vol. 5. *Egils saga Skalla-Grímssonar* (Egill Skallagrímsson, Hǫfuðlausn)
   Skj: Egill Skallagrímsson: 2. Hǫfuðlausn (AI, 35-9; BI, 30-3)
Egill Lv^{V} (*Eg*) — Vol. 5. *Egils saga Skalla-Grímssonar* (Egill Skallagrímsson, Lausavísur)
   Skj: Egill Skallagrímsson: 7. Lausavísur (AI, 48-59; BI, 42-53)
Egill *St*^{V} (*Eg*) — Vol. 5. *Egils saga Skalla-Grímssonar* (Egill Skallagrímsson, *Sonatorrek*)
   Skj: Egill Skallagrímsson: 3. Sonatorrek (AI, 40-3; BI, 34-7)
EGils^{IV} — Vol. 4. Einarr Gilsson
   Skj: Einarr Gilsson (AII, 397-411; BII, 418-40)
EGils *Guðkv*^{IV} — Vol. 4. Einarr Gilsson, *Guðmundarkvæði*
   Skj: Einarr Gilsson: 1. Et digt (drape?) om Guðmund Arason, biskop (AII, 397-404; BII, 418-29)

EGils Selv^{IV} — Vol. 4. Einarr Gilsson, *Selkolluvísur*
    Skj: Einarr Gilsson: 3. Selkollu-vísur (AII, 408-11; BII, 434-40)
Eil Þdr^{III} — Vol. 3. Eilífr Goðrúnarson, *Þórsdrápa* (68)
    Skj: Eilífr Goðrúnarson: 2. Þórsdrápa (AI, 148-52; BI, 139-44)
EirRagn Lv (*Ragn*) — *Ragnars saga loðbrókar* (Eiríkr Ragnarsson, Lausavísur)
    See individual stanza(s) for *Skj* references
Elg-Fróði Lv (*Hrólf*) — *Hrólfs saga kraka* (Elg-Fróði, Lausavísa)
    See individual stanza(s) for *Skj* references
ESk Elfv^{II} — Vol. 2. Einarr Skúlason, *Elfarvísur* (565-7)
    Skj: Einarr Skúlason: 10. Elfarvísur (AI, 477; BI, 449)
ESk Eystdr^{II} — Vol. 2. Einarr Skúlason, *Eysteinsdrápa* (559-61)
    Skj: Einarr Skúlason: 8. Eysteinsdrápa (AI, 475; BI, 447)
ESk Frag^{III} — Vol. 3. Einarr Skúlason, Fragments (151)
    Skj: Einarr Skúlason: 12. Ubestemmelige vers, tilhørende forskellige fyrstedigte eller lausavísur (AI, 479-82; BI, 451-4)
ESk Geisl^{VII} — Vol. 7. Einarr Skúlason, *Geisli* (5-65)
    Skj: Einarr Skúlason: 6. Geisli (AI, 459-73; BI, 427-45)
ESk Hardr I^{II} — Vol. 2. Einarr Skúlason, *Haraldsdrápa I* (542-4)
    Skj: Einarr Skúlason: 2. Haraldsdrápa I (AI, 456-7; BI, 424-5)
ESk Lv 14^{III} — Vol. 3. Einarr Skúlason (biog. vol. 2), Lausavísur, 14 (177)
    Skj: Einarr Skúlason: 11. Lausavísur 13 (AI, 485; BI, 457)
ESk Run^{II} — Vol. 2. Einarr Skúlason, *Runhenda* (551-9)
    Skj: Einarr Skúlason: 7. Runhenda (AI, 473-5; BI, 445-7)
ESk Sigdr I^{II} — Vol. 2. Einarr Skúlason, *Sigurðardrápa I* (538-42)
    Skj: Einarr Skúlason: 1. Sigurðardrápa (AI, 455-6; BI, 423-4)
ESk Øxfl^{III} — Vol. 3. Einarr Skúlason, *Øxarflokkr* (140)
    Skj: Einarr Skúlason: 11. Øxarflokkr(?) (AI, 477-9; BI, 449-51)
Eskál Vell 4^I — Vol. 1. 18. Einarr skálaglamm Helgason, *Vellekla*, 4 (287)
    Skj: Einarr Helgason skálaglamm: 3. Vellekla 2 (AI, 122; BI, 117)
Eskál Vell 7^I — Vol. 1. 18. Einarr skálaglamm Helgason, *Vellekla*, 7 (291)
    Skj: Einarr Helgason skálaglamm: 3. Vellekla 8 (AI, 124; BI, 118)
Eskál Vell 26^I — Vol. 1. 18. Einarr skálaglamm Helgason, *Vellekla*, 26 (315)
    Skj: Einarr Helgason skálaglamm: 3. Vellekla 27 (AI, 129; BI, 122)
Eystk Útkv (*Hálf*) — *Hálfs saga ok Hálfsrekka* (Eysteinn konungr, Útsteinskviða)
    See individual stanza(s) for *Skj* references
Eyv Hák^I — Vol. 1. Eyvindr skáldaspillir Finnsson, *Hákonarmál* (171)
    Skj: Eyvindr Finnsson skáldaspillir: 1. Hákonarmál (AI, 64-8; BI, 57-60)
Eyv Hál^I — Vol. 1. Eyvindr skáldaspillir Finnsson, *Háleygjatal* (195)
    Skj: Eyvindr Finnsson skáldaspillir: 2. Háleygjatal (AI, 68-71; BI, 60-2)
Eyv Hál 2^I — Vol. 1. 13. Eyvindr skáldaspillir Finnsson, *Háleygjatal*, 2 (199)
    Skj: Eyvindr Finnsson skáldaspillir: 2. Háleygjatal 3-4 (AI, 68; BI, 60)

Eyv *Hál* 9[I] — Vol. 1. 13. Eyvindr skáldaspillir Finnsson, *Háleygjatal*, 9 (207)
   Skj: Eyvindr Finnsson skáldaspillir: 2. Háleygjatal 11 (AI, 69-70; BI, 61)
Eyv *Hál* 10[I] — Vol. 1. 13. Eyvindr skáldaspillir Finnsson, *Háleygjatal*, 10 (208)
   Skj: Eyvindr Finnsson skáldaspillir: 2. Háleygjatal 12 (AI, 70; BI, 61-2)
Eyv Lv[I] — Vol. 1. Eyvindr skáldaspillir Finnsson, Lausavísur (213)
   Skj: Eyvindr Finnsson skáldaspillir: 3. Lausavísur (AI, 71-4; BI, 62-5)
Feima Lv (*GrL*) — *Gríms saga loðinkinna* (Feima Hrímnisdóttir, Lausavísa)
   See individual stanza(s) for *Skj* references
Fjǫl Lv (*Gautr*) — *Gautreks saga* (Fjǫlmóðr Skafnǫrtungsson, Lausavísur)
   See individual stanza(s) for *Skj* references
Forað Lv (*Ket*) — *Ketils saga hœngs* (Forað, Lausavísur)
   See individual stanza(s) for *Skj* references
Framarr Lv (*Ket*) — *Ketils saga hœngs* (Framarr víkingakonungr, Lausavísur)
   See individual stanza(s) for *Skj* references
FriðÞ Lv (*Frið*) — *Friðþjófs saga ins frœkna* (Friðþjófr Þorsteinsson, Lausavísur)
   See individual stanza(s) for *Skj* references
Gamlkan *Has*[VII] — Vol. 7. Gamli kanóki, *Harmsól* (70-132)
   Skj: Gamli kanóki: 2. Harmsól (AI, 562-72; BI, 548-65)
Gauti Lv (*Gautr*) — *Gautreks saga* (Gauti konungr, Lausavísa)
   See individual stanza(s) for *Skj* references
Gestumbl *Heiðr* (*Heiðr*) — *Hervarar saga ok Heiðreks* (Gestumblindi, *Heiðreks gátur*)
   Skj: Anonyme digte og vers [XIII]: D. 5. Heiðreks gátur (AII, 221-8; BII, 240-7)
Gill Lv (*Gautr*) — *Gautreks saga* (Gillingr Skafnǫrtungsson, Lausavísur)
   See individual stanza(s) for *Skj* references
GizGrý Lv (*Heiðr*) — *Hervarar saga ok Heiðreks* (Gizurr Grýtingaliði, Lausavísur)
   See individual stanza(s) for *Skj* references
Gísl *Magnkv*[II] — Vol. 2. Gísl Illugason, *Erfikvæði* about Magnús berfœttr (416-30)
   Skj: Gísl Illugason: 1. Erfikvæði um Magnús berfœtt (AI, 440-4; BI, 409-13)
Glúmr *Gráf* 4[I] — Vol. 1. 15. Glúmr Geirason, *Gráfeldardrápa*, 4 (252)
   Skj: Glúmr Geirason: 2. Gráfeldardrápa 3 (AI, 76; BI, 66)
Glúmr *Gráf* 5[I] — Vol. 1. 15. Glúmr Geirason, *Gráfeldardrápa*, 5 (254)
   Skj: Glúmr Geirason: 2. Gráfeldardrápa 4 (AI, 76; BI, 66)
Glúmr *Gráf* 12[I] — Vol. 1. 15. Glúmr Geirason, *Gráfeldardrápa*, 12 (262)
   Skj: Glúmr Geirason: 2. Gráfeldardrápa 11 (AI, 77-8; BI, 68)
Glúmr Lv 1[I] — Vol. 1. 15. Glúmr Geirason, Lausavísa, 1 (266)
   Skj: Glúmr Geirason: 3. Lausavísa (AI, 78; BI, 68)
GOdds Lv[IV] — Vol. 4. Guðmundr Oddson, Lausavísur
   Skj: Guðmundr Oddson: Lausavísur (AII, 79-81; BII, 90-2)
Grett[V] — (Grettir Ásmundarson)
   Skj: Grettir Ásmundarson (AI, 309-13; BI, 287-90)
Grett Lv 6[V] (*Gr* 14) — Vol. 5. *Grettis saga Ásmundarsonar* 14 (Grettir Ásmundarson, Lausavísur, 6)

Skj: [Anonyme digte og vers XIV]: A. 1. Vers af sagaer: Af isl. slægtsagaer: Af Grettissaga 12 (AII, 433-4; BII, 465)

Grett Lv 9^V (*Gr* 18) — Vol. 5. *Grettis saga Ásmundarsonar* 18 (Grettir Ásmundarson, Lausavísur, 9)

Skj: [Anonyme digte og vers XIV]: A. 1. Vers af sagaer: Af isl. slægtsagaer: Af Grettissaga 16 (AII, 435; BII, 466)

Grett Lv 31^V (*Gr* 63) — Vol. 5. *Grettis saga Ásmundarsonar* 63 (Grettir Ásmundarson, Lausavísur, 31)

Skj: Grettir Ásmundarson: 2. Lausavísur 9 (AI, 313; BI, 290)

Grett *Ævkv I*^{V} (*Gr*) — Vol. 5. *Grettis saga Ásmundarsonar* (Grettir Ásmundarson, *Ævikviða I*)

Skj: Grettir Ásmundarson: 1. Ævikviða (AI, 309-11; BI, 287-8)

Grett *Ævkv II* 1^V (*Gr* 39) — Vol. 5. *Grettis saga Ásmundarsonar* 39 (Grettir Ásmundarson, *Ævikviða II*, 1)

Skj: Grettir Ásmundarson: 1. Ævikviða 4 (AI, 310; BI, 287)

Gríml Lv (*GrL*) — *Gríms saga loðinkinna* (Grímr loðinkinni, Lausavísur)

See individual stanza(s) for *Skj* references

GSúrs Lv^V (*Gísl*) — Vol. 5. *Gísla saga Súrssonar* (Gísli Súrsson, Lausavísur)

Skj: Gísli Súrsson: Lausavísur (AI, 101-9; BI, 96-104)

GSvert *Hrafndr*^{IV} — Vol. 4. Guðmundr Svertingsson, *Hrafnsdrápa*

Skj: Guðmundr Svertingsson: Hrafnsdrápa (AII, 46-9; BII, 55-7)

GunnHám^V — (Gunnarr Hámundarson)

Not in *Skj*

GunnHám Lv 14^V (*Nj* 29) — Vol. 5. *Njáls saga* 29 (Gunnarr Hámundarson, Lausavísur, 14)

Skj: Anonyme digte og vers [XII]: F b. Uægte vers i sagaer: I Njálssaga 1 (AI, 604; BI, 604)

GunnLeif *Merl I* (*Bret*) — *Breta saga* (Gunnlaugr Leifsson, *Merlínusspá I*) (38)

Skj: Gunnlaugr Leifsson: Merlínússpá II (AII, 22-36; BII, 24-45)

GunnLeif *Merl II* (*Bret*) — *Breta saga* (Gunnlaugr Leifsson, *Merlínusspá II*) (134)

Skj: Gunnlaugr Leifsson: Merlínússpá I (AII, 10-21; BII, 10-24)

Gusi Lv (*Ket*) — *Ketils saga hængs* (Gusi finnakonungr, Lausavísur)

See individual stanza(s) for *Skj* references

Gyðja Lv (*Ǫrv*) — *Ǫrvar-Odds saga* (Gyðja, Lausavísur)

See individual stanza(s) for *Skj* references

Halli XI *Fl*^{II} — Vol. 2. Halli stirði, *Flokkr* (337-43)

Skj: Halli stirði: Flokkr (AI, 401-2; BI, 370-1)

Hallm *Hallkv*^{V} (*Bergb*) — Vol. 5. *Bergbúa þáttr* (Hallmundr bergbúinn, *Hallmundarkviða*)

Skj: Anonyme digte og vers [XIII]: D. 2. [2]. Drömmevers: Af Bergbúaþáttr (AII, 210-13; BII, 226-9)

HallmGr *Hallkv*[V] (*Gr*) — Vol. 5. *Grettis saga Ásmundarsonar* (Hallmundr, *Hallmundarkviða*)
    Not in *Skj*
HallmGr *Hallkv* 1[V] (*Gr* 51) — Vol. 5. *Grettis saga Ásmundarsonar* 51 (Hallmundr, *Hallmundarkviða*, 1)
    Skj: [Anonyme digte og vers XIV]: A. 1. Vers af sagaer: Af isl. slægtsagaer: Af Grettissaga 37 (AII, 441; BII, 472)
HallmGr *Hallkv* 6[V] (*Gr* 56) — Vol. 5. *Grettis saga Ásmundarsonar* 56
    Skj: [Anonyme digte og vers XIV]: A. 1. Vers af sagaer: Af isl. slægtsagaer: Af Grettissaga 42 (AII, 442; BII, 473)
Hallvarðr *Frag* (*Frið*) — *Friðþjófs saga ins frœkna* (Hallvarðr, *verses*)
    See individual stanza(s) for *Skj* references
Hást Lv[IV] — Vol. 4. Hásteinn Hrómundarson, *Lausavísur*
    Skj: Hásteinn Hrómundarson halta: Lausavísur (AI, 97-8; BI, 91-2)
HaukrV *Ísldr*[IV] — Vol. 4. Haukr Valdísarson, *Íslendingadrápa*
    Skj: Haukr Valdísarson: Íslendingadrápa (AI, 556-60; BI, 539-45)
Hálfr Innkv (*Hálf*) — *Hálfs saga ok Hálfsrekka* (Hálfr Hjǫrleifsson, *Innsteinskviða*)
    See individual stanza(s) for *Skj* references
Hástigi Lv (*HjǪ*) — *Hjálmpés saga ok Ǫlvis* (Hástigi, *Lausavísa*)
    See individual stanza(s) for *Skj* references
Hbreiðm Lv 1[II] — Vol. 2. Hallr Þórarinsson breiðmaga, *Lausavísa*, 1 (610-11)
    Skj: Hallr Þórarinsson breiðmaga: Lausavísa (AI, 528; BI, 508-9)
Heiðr Lv (*Ǫrv*) — *Ǫrvar-Odds saga* (Heiðr, *Lausavísur*)
    See individual stanza(s) for *Skj* references
Heiðrekr *Heiðr* (*Heiðr*) — *Hervarar saga ok Heiðreks* (Heiðrekr, *Heiðreks gátur*)
    Skj: Anonyme digte og vers [XIII]: D. 5 [38]. Heiðreks gátur [38] (AII, 228; BII, 247)
Heiðv Lv (*Hrólf*) — *Hrólfs saga kraka* (Heiðr vǫlva, *Lausavísur*)
    See individual stanza(s) for *Skj* references
Hergunnr Lv (*HjǪ*) — *Hjálmpés saga ok Ǫlvis* (Hergunnr, *Lausavísur*)
    See individual stanza(s) for *Skj* references
Herv Lv (*Heiðr*) — *Hervarar saga ok Heiðreks* (Hervǫr, *Lausavísur*)
    See individual stanza(s) for *Skj* references
HervH Lv (*HjǪ*) — *Hjálmpés saga ok Ǫlvis* (Hervǫr Hundingjadóttir, *Lausavísur*)
    See individual stanza(s) for *Skj* references
Hfr *ErfÓl*[I] — Vol. 1. Hallfreðr vandræðaskáld Óttarsson, *Erfidrápa Óláfs Tryggvasonar* (400)
    Skj: Hallfrøðr Óttarsson vandræðaskáld: 3. Óláfsdrápa, erfidrápa (AI, 159-66; BI, 150-7)
Hfr *ErfÓl* 24[I] — Vol. 1. 28. Hallfreðr vandræðaskáld Óttarsson, *Erfidrápa Óláfs Tryggvasonar*, 24 (434)

Skj: Hallfrøðr Óttarsson vandræðaskáld: 3. Óláfsdrápa, erfidrápa 17 (AI, 163; BI, 154)

Hfr *Hákdr*^III — Vol. 3. Hallfreðr vandræðaskáld Óttarsson, *Hákonardrápa* (212)
  Skj: Hallfrøðr Óttarsson vandræðaskáld: 1. Hákonardrápa (AI, 155-6; BI, 147-8)

Hfr *Hákdr* 5^III — Vol. 3. 28. Hallfreðr vandræðaskáld Óttarsson (biog. vol. 1), *Hákonardrápa*, 5 (219)
  Skj: Hallfrøðr Óttarsson vandræðaskáld: 1. Hákonardrápa 3 (AI, 155; BI, 147)

Hfr Lv^V — Vol. 5. Hallfreðr vandræðaskáld Óttarsson, Lausavísur
  Skj: Hallfrøðr Óttarsson vandræðaskáld: 5. Lausavísur (AI, 166-73; BI, 157-63)

Hfr *Óldr*^I — Vol. 1. Hallfreðr vandræðaskáld Óttarsson, *Óláfsdrápa* (387)
  Skj: Hallfrøðr Óttarsson vandræðaskáld: 2. Óláfsdrápa (AI, 156-9; BI, 148-50)

Hfr *Óldr* 1^I — Vol. 1. 28. Hallfreðr vandræðaskáld Óttarsson, *Óláfsdrápa*, 1 (392)
  Skj: Hallfrøðr Óttarsson vandræðaskáld: 2. Óláfsdrápa 3, 4/1-4 (AI, 157; BI, 149)

Hfr *Óldr* 6^I — Vol. 1. 28. Hallfreðr vandræðaskáld Óttarsson, *Óláfsdrápa*, 6 (398)
  Skj: Hallfrøðr Óttarsson vandræðaskáld: 2. Óláfsdrápa 8/5-8, 9/1-4 (AI, 158-9; BI, 150)

Hharð Lv 8^II — Vol. 2. Haraldr harðráði Sigurðarson, Lausavísur, 8 (49-50)
  Skj: Haraldr Sigurðarson harðráði: Lausavísur 13 (AI, 359; BI, 330-1)

Hharð Lv 10^II — Vol. 2. Haraldr harðráði Sigurðarson, Lausavísur, 10 (51-2)
  Skj: Haraldr Sigurðarson harðráði: Lausavísur 15 (AI, 359; BI, 331)

Hhárf Lv 1^I — Vol. 1. 2. Haraldr hárfagri Hálfdanarson, Lausavísa, 1 (71)
  Skj: Haraldr hárfagri: 2. Lausavísa (AI, 6; BI, 6)

Hildibrandr Lv (*Ásm*) — *Ásmundar saga kappabana* (Hildibrandr, Lausavísur)
  See individual stanza(s) for *Skj* references

Hildigunnr Lv (*Ǫrv*) — *Ǫrvar-Odds saga* (Hildigunnr, Lausavísa)
  See individual stanza(s) for *Skj* references

Hildr Lv^I — Vol. 1. Hildr Hrólfsdóttir nefju, Lausavísa (139)
  Skj: Hildr Hrólfsdóttir nefju: Lausavísa (AI, 31; BI, 27)

Hjálm Lv — Hjálmarr inn hugumstóri, Lausavísur
  See individual stanza(s) for *Skj* references

Hjþ Lv (*HjǪ*) — *Hjálmþés saga ok Ǫlvis* (Hjálmþér Ingason, Lausavísur)
  See individual stanza(s) for *Skj* references

Hjǫrleifr Lv (*Hálf*) — *Hálfs saga ok Hálfsrekka* (Hjǫrleifr konungr, Lausavísa)
  See individual stanza(s) for *Skj* references

HlǫðH Lv (*Heiðr*) — *Hervarar saga ok Heiðreks* (Hlǫðr Heiðreksson, Lausavísur)
  See individual stanza(s) for *Skj* references

Hregg Lv (*GHr*) — *Gǫngu-Hrólfs saga* (Hreggviðr konungr, Lausavísur)
  See individual stanza(s) for *Skj* references

Hringrk Lv (*Frið*) — *Friðþjófs saga ins frœkna* (Hringr konungr, Lausavísur)
  See individual stanza(s) for *Skj* references

Hróksv Hrkv (*Hálf*) — *Hálfs saga ok Hálfsrekka* (Hrókr inn svarti, Hrókskviða)
  See individual stanza(s) for *Skj* references

Hskv *Útdr*^{II} — Vol. 2. Halldórr skvaldri, *Útfarardrápa* (483-92)
    Skj: Haldórr skvaldri: 2. Útfarardrápa (AI, 486-8; BI, 458-60)
HSt *Rst*^I — Vol. 1. Hallar-Steinn, *Rekstefja* (893)
    Skj: Hallar-Steinn: 1. Rekstefja (AI, 543-52; BI, 525-34)
Humli Lv (*Heiðr*) — *Hervarar saga ok Heiðreks* (Humli konungr, Lausavísur)
    See individual stanza(s) for *Skj* references
Hundk Lv (*HjǪ*) — *Hjálmpés saga ok Ǫlvis* (Hundingi konungr, Lausavísur)
    See individual stanza(s) for *Skj* references
HvítRagn Lv (*Ragn*) — *Ragnars saga loðbrókar* (Hvítserkr Ragnarsson, Lausavísa)
    See individual stanza(s) for *Skj* references
HǫrðG Lv 7^V (*Harð* 14) — Vol. 5. *Harðar saga* 14 (Hǫrðr Grímkelsson, Lausavísur, 7)
    Skj: [Anonyme digte og vers XIV]: A. 2. Vers af sagaer: Af isl. slægtsagaer: Af
    Harðar saga Grímkelssonar 14 (AII, 448; BII, 480)
HǫrðG Lv 8^V (*Harð* 15) — Vol. 5. *Harðar saga* 15 (Hǫrðr Grímkelsson, Lausavísur, 8)
    Skj: [Anonyme digte og vers XIV]: A. 2. Vers af sagaer: Af isl. slægtsagaer: Af
    Harðar saga Grímkelssonar 15 (AII, 448; BII, 480)
Hǫrðr Lv (*HjǪ*) — *Hjálmpés saga ok Ǫlvis* (Hǫrðr/Hringr, Lausavísur)
    See individual stanza(s) for *Skj* references
Ill *Har*^{II} — Vol. 2. Illugi bryndœlaskáld, Poem about Haraldr harðráði (282-5)
    Skj: Illugi Bryndœlaskáld: 1. Et digt om Harald hårdråde (AI, 384; BI, 354)
Ingimarr Lv 1^{II} — Vol. 2. Ingimarr af Aski Sveinsson, Lausavísa, 1 (497-8)
    Skj: Ingimarr af Aski: Lausavísa (AI, 494; BI, 466)
Innsteinn *Innkv* (*Hálf*) — *Hálfs saga ok Hálfsrekka* (Innsteinn Gunnlaðarson,
    Innsteinskviða)
    See individual stanza(s) for *Skj* references
Innsteinn Lv (*Hálf*) — *Hálfs saga ok Hálfsrekka* (Innsteinn Gunnlaðarson, Lausavísur)
    See individual stanza(s) for *Skj* references
Íms Lv (*Gautr*) — *Gautreks saga* (Ímsigull Skafnǫrtungsson, Lausavísa)
    See individual stanza(s) for *Skj* references
Ív^{II} — Vol. 2. Ívarr Ingimundarson (501-27)
    Skj: Ívarr Ingimundarson (AI, 495-502; BI, 467-75)
Ív *Sig*^{II} — Vol. 2. Ívarr Ingimundarson, *Sigurðarbálkr* (501-27)
    Skj: Ívarr Ingimundarson: Sigurðarbǫlkr (AI, 495-502; BI, 467-75)
ÍvRagn Lv (*Ragn*) — *Ragnars saga loðbrókar* (Ívarr Ragnarsson, Lausavísa)
    See individual stanza(s) for *Skj* references
Kári Lv 5^V (*Nj* 50) — Vol. 5. *Njáls saga* 50 (Kári Sǫlmundarson, Lausavísur, 5)
    Skj: Anonyme digte og vers [XII]: F b. Uægte vers i sagaer: I Njálssaga 9 (AI, 606;
    BI, 606)
Keth Lv (*Ket*) — *Ketils saga hœngs* (Ketill hœngr, Lausavísur)
    See individual stanza(s) for *Skj* references
Ketilr Lv 1^V (*Vígl* 2) — Vol. 5. *Víglundar saga* 2 (Ketilríðr Hólmkelsdóttir, Lausavísur,
    1)

Skj: [Anonyme digte og vers XIV]: A. 7. Vers af sagaer: Af isl. slægtsagaer: Af Víglundarsaga 2 (AII, 455; BII, 488)

Kleima Lv (*GrL*) — *Gríms saga loðinkinna* (Kleima Hrímnisdóttir, Lausavísa)
See individual stanza(s) for *Skj* references

Kolb Lv^{IV} — Vol. 4. Kolbeinn Tumason, Lausavísur
Skj: Kolbeinn Tumason: 2. Lausavísur (AII, 38-40; BII, 47-9)

KormǪ^V — (Kormákr Ǫgmundarson) (272)
Skj: Kormákr Ǫgmundarson (AI, 79-91; BI, 69-85)

KormǪ Lv^V (*Korm*) — Vol. 5. *Kormáks saga* (Kormákr Ǫgmundarson, Lausavísur)
Skj: Kormákr Ǫgmundarson: 2. Lausavísur (AI, 80-91; BI, 70-85)

KrákÁsl Lv (*RagnSon*) — *Ragnars sona þáttr* (Kráka/Áslaug Sigurðardóttir, Lausavísur)
See individual stanza(s) for *Skj* references

Margerðr Lv (*HjǪ*) — *Hjálmþés saga ok Ǫlvis* (Margerðr, Lausavísa)
See individual stanza(s) for *Skj* references

Mark *Eirdr* 4^{II} — Vol. 2. Markús Skeggjason, *Eiríksdrápa*, 4 (436-7)
Skj: Markús Skeggjason: 1. Eiríksdrápa 5 (AI, 445; BI, 414-15)

Mark *Eirdr* 6^{II} — Vol. 2. Markús Skeggjason, *Eiríksdrápa*, 6 (438-9)
Skj: Markús Skeggjason: 1. Eiríksdrápa 8 (AI, 446; BI, 415)

Mark *Eirdr* 17^{II} — Vol. 2. Markús Skeggjason, *Eiríksdrápa*, 17 (447)
Skj: Markús Skeggjason: 1. Eiríksdrápa 19 (AI, 448; BI, 417)

Mark *Eirdr* 22^{II} — Vol. 2. Markús Skeggjason, *Eiríksdrápa*, 22 (450-1)
Skj: Markús Skeggjason: 1. Eiríksdrápa 24 (AI, 449; BI, 418)

Mark *Eirdr* 23^{II} — Vol. 2. Markús Skeggjason, *Eiríksdrápa*, 23 (452-3)
Skj: Markús Skeggjason: 1. Eiríksdrápa 25 (AI, 449; BI, 418)

Mark *Eirdr* 24^{II} — Vol. 2. Markús Skeggjason, *Eiríksdrápa*, 24 (453-4)
Skj: Markús Skeggjason: 1. Eiríksdrápa 26 (AI, 450; BI, 418-19)

Mark Lv^{III} — Vol. 3. Markús Skeggjason, Lausavísur (295)
Skj: Markús Skeggjason: 4. Lausavísur (AI, 452-453; BI, 421)

Marm Lv (*Hálf*) — *Hálfs saga ok Hálfsrekka* (Marmennill, Lausavísur)
See individual stanza(s) for *Skj* references

Mágj Lv (*Mág*) — *Máguss saga jarls* (Mágus jarl, verses)
Skj: [Anonyme digte og vers XIV]: A. 8. Vers af sagaer: Af isl. slægtsagaer: Af Mágus saga (AII, 461; BII, 493-4)

Mgóð Lv^{II} — Vol. 2. Magnús inn góði Óláfsson, Lausavísur (5-7)
Skj: Magnús Óláfsson enn góði: Lausavísur (AI, 330; BI, 304)

Neri *Frag* (*Gautr*) — *Gautreks saga* (Neri, verses)
See individual stanza(s) for *Skj* references

Okík *Magn*^{II} — Vol. 2. Oddr kíkinaskáld, Poem about Magnús góði (31-4)
Skj: Oddr kíkinaskáld: 1. Et digt om Magnus d. gode (AI, 354-5; BI, 327)

Ormarr Lv (*Heiðr*) — *Hervarar saga ok Heiðreks* (Ormarr, Lausavísur)
See individual stanza(s) for *Skj* references

OSnorr^I — Vol. 1. Oddr Snorrason (890)
    Not in *Skj*
Ólhv *Hák* 1^II — Vol. 2. Óláfr hvítaskáld Þórðarson, *Poem about Hákon*, 1 (657-8)
    Skj: Óláfr Þórðarson hvítaskáld: 1. Et digt om kong Hákon (AII, 92-3; BII, 104)
ÓTr^I — Vol. 1. Óláfr Tryggvason (383)
    Skj: Óláfr Tryggvason (AI, 152; BI, 144-145)
Ótt^I — Vol. 1. Óttarr svarti (335)
    Skj: Óttarr svarti (AI, 289-99; BI, 267-75)
Ótt *Hfl*^I — Vol. 1. Óttarr svarti, *Hǫfuðlausn* (739)
    Skj: Óttarr svarti: 2. Hǫfuðlausn (AI, 290-6; BI, 268-72)
Ótt *Knútdr*^I — Vol. 1. Óttarr svarti, *Knútsdrápa* (767)
    Skj: Óttarr svarti: 3. Knútsdrápa (AI, 296-8; BI, 272-5)
Ótt *Knútdr* 10^I — Vol. 1. 38. Óttarr svarti, *Knútsdrápa*, 10 (779)
    Skj: Óttarr svarti: 3. Knútsdrápa 8 (AI, 297-8; BI, 274)
Refr *Ferðv*^III — Vol. 3. Hofgarða-Refr Gestsson, *Ferðavísur* (243)
    Skj: Hofgarða-Refr Gestsson: 4. Et rejsedigt (AI, 320-1; BI, 296-7)
Reginn Lv (*Hrólf*) — *Hrólfs saga kraka* (Reginn, Lausavísa)
    See individual stanza(s) for *Skj* references
Rloð Lv (*Ragn*) — *Ragnars saga loðbrókar* (Ragnarr loðbrók, Lausavísur)
    See individual stanza(s) for *Skj* references
Run N B252^VI — Vol. 6. 3. Middle Ages, *Hordaland*, 9
    Not in *Skj*
Run *Ög*^VI — Vol. 6. Viking Age, *Östergötland*
    Not in *Skj*
Rv Lv^II — Vol. 2. Rǫgnvaldr jarl Kali Kolsson, Lausavísur (575-609)
    Skj: Rǫgnvaldr jarl kali Kolsson: Lausavísur (AI, 505-12; BI, 478-87)
RvHbreiðm *Hl*^III — Vol. 3. Rǫgnvaldr jarl and Hallr Þórarinsson, *Háttalykill* (1001)
    Skj: Rǫgnvaldr jarl og Hallr Þórarinsson: Háttalykill (AI, 512-28; BI, 487-508)
RvHbreiðm *Hl* 9-10^III — Vol. 3. Rǫgnvaldr jarl and Hallr Þórarinsson, *Háttalykill*, 9-10 (1017)
    Skj: Rǫgnvaldr jarl og Hallr Þórarinsson: Háttalykill 5a (AI, 514; BI, 489)
RvHbreiðm *Hl* 15^III — Vol. 3. Rǫgnvaldr jarl and Hallr Þórarinsson, *Háttalykill*, 15 (1022)
    Skj: Rǫgnvaldr jarl og Hallr Þórarinsson: Háttalykill 8a (AI, 515; BI, 490-1)
RvHbreiðm *Hl* 21^III — Vol. 3. Rǫgnvaldr jarl and Hallr Þórarinsson, *Háttalykill*, 21 (1029)
    Skj: Rǫgnvaldr jarl og Hallr Þórarinsson: Háttalykill 11a (AI, 516; BI, 492)
RvHbreiðm *Hl* 43^III — Vol. 3. Rǫgnvaldr jarl and Hallr Þórarinsson, *Háttalykill*, 43 (1051)
    Skj: Rǫgnvaldr jarl og Hallr Þórarinsson: Háttalykill 22a (AI, 520; BI, 497-8)

RvHbreiðm *Hl* 44^{III} — Vol. 3. Rǫgnvaldr jarl and Hallr Þórarinsson, *Háttalykill*, 44 (1052)
   Skj: Rǫgnvaldr jarl og Hallr Þórarinsson: Háttalykill 22b (AI, 520; BI, 498)
RvHbreiðm *Hl* 45^{III} — Vol. 3. Rǫgnvaldr jarl and Hallr Þórarinsson, *Háttalykill*, 45 (1053)
   Skj: Rǫgnvaldr jarl og Hallr Þórarinsson: Háttalykill 23a (AI, 521; BI, 498)
RvHbreiðm *Hl* 49^{III} — Vol. 3. Rǫgnvaldr jarl and Hallr Þórarinsson, *Háttalykill*, 49 (1057)
   Skj: Rǫgnvaldr jarl og Hallr Þórarinsson: Háttalykill 25a (AI, 521; BI, 499)
RvHbreiðm *Hl* 53^{III} — Vol. 3. Rǫgnvaldr jarl and Hallr Þórarinsson, *Háttalykill*, 53 (1060)
   Skj: Rǫgnvaldr jarl og Hallr Þórarinsson: Háttalykill 27a (AI, 522-3; BI, 500)
RvHbreiðm *Hl* 54^{III} — Vol. 3. Rǫgnvaldr jarl and Hallr Þórarinsson, *Háttalykill*, 54 (1061)
   Skj: Rǫgnvaldr jarl og Hallr Þórarinsson: Háttalykill 27b (AI, 523; BI, 500)
RvHbreiðm *Hl* 55^{III} — Vol. 3. Rǫgnvaldr jarl and Hallr Þórarinsson, *Háttalykill*, 55 (1063)
   Skj: Rǫgnvaldr jarl og Hallr Þórarinsson: Háttalykill 28a (AI, 523; BI, 500-1)
RvHbreiðm *Hl* 57^{III} — Vol. 3. Rǫgnvaldr jarl and Hallr Þórarinsson, *Háttalykill*, 57 (1066)
   Skj: Rǫgnvaldr jarl og Hallr Þórarinsson: Háttalykill 29a (AI, 522; BI, 501)
SigHálf Lv (*Hrólf*) — *Hrólfs saga kraka* (Signý Hálfdanardóttir, Lausavísa)
   See individual stanza(s) for *Skj* references
Sigmund Lv 2^V (*Nj* 16) — Vol. 5. *Njáls saga* 16 (Sigmundr Lambason, Lausavísur, 2)
   Skj: Anonyme digte og vers [XIII]: D. 1. [1]. Uægte vers af slægtsagaer: Af Njálssaga 14 (AII, 201; BII, 214)
Sigoa Lv (*Ragn*) — *Ragnars saga loðbrókar* (Sigurðr ormr í auga, Lausavísa)
   See individual stanza(s) for *Skj* references
Sigurðr Lv (*Ǫrv*) — *Ǫrvar-Odds saga* (Sigurðr, Lausavísur)
   See individual stanza(s) for *Skj* references
Sigv^I — Vol. 1. Sigvatr Þórðarson (347)
   Skj: Sigvatr Þórðarson (AI, 223-75; BI, 213-54)
Sigv *Austv*^{I} — Vol. 1. Sigvatr Þórðarson, *Austrfararvísur* (578)
   Skj: Sigvatr Þórðarson: 3. Austrfararvísur (AI, 233-40; BI, 220-5)
Sigv *Berv*^{II} — Vol. 2. Sigvatr Þórðarson, *Bersǫglisvísur* (11-30)
   Skj: Sigvatr Þórðarson: 11. Bersǫglisvísur (AI, 251-6; BI, 234-9)
Sigv *Berv* 15^{II} — Vol. 2. 37. Sigvatr Þórðarson (biog. vol. 1), *Bersǫglisvísur*, 15 (27)
   Skj: Sigvatr Þórðarson: 11. Bersǫglisvísur 18 (AI, 256; BI, 238-9)
Sigv *ErfÓl*^{I} — Vol. 1. Sigvatr Þórðarson, *Erfidrápa Óláfs helga* (663)
   Skj: Sigvatr Þórðarson: 12. Erfidrápa Óláfs helga (AI, 257-65; BI, 239-45)
Sigv *Erlfl*^{I} — Vol. 1. Sigvatr Þórðarson, Flokkr *about* Erlingr Skjálgsson (629)
   Skj: Sigvatr Þórðarson: 7. Flokkr om Erlingr Skjalgsson (AI, 244-7; BI, 228-31)

Sigv *Knútdr*^{I} — Vol. 1. Sigvatr Þórðarson, *Knútsdrápa* (649)
    Skj: Sigvatr Þórðarson: 10. Knútsdrápa (AI, 248-51; BI, 232-4)
Sigv Lv 5^I — Vol. 1. 37. Sigvatr Þórðarson, Lausavísur, 5 (705)
    Skj: Sigvatr Þórðarson: 13. Lausavísur 6 (AI, 267; BI, 247)
Sigv Lv 18^I — Vol. 1. 37. Sigvatr Þórðarson, Lausavísur, 18 (722)
    Skj: Sigvatr Þórðarson: 13. Lausavísur 21 (AI, 271-2; BI, 251)
Sigv Lv 26^I — Vol. 1. 37. Sigvatr Þórðarson, Lausavísur, 26 (732)
    Skj: Sigvatr Þórðarson: 13. Lausavísur 28 (AI, 274; BI, 253)
Sigv *Nesv*^{I} — Vol. 1. Sigvatr Þórðarson, *Nesjavísur* (555)
    Skj: Sigvatr Þórðarson: 2. Nesjavísur (AI, 228-32; BI, 217-20)
Sigv *Nesv* 7^I — Vol. 1. 37. Sigvatr Þórðarson, *Nesjavísur*, 7 (566)
    Skj: Sigvatr Þórðarson: 2. Nesjavísur 6 (AI, 229-30; BI, 218)
Sigv *Nesv* 9^I — Vol. 1. 37. Sigvatr Þórðarson, *Nesjavísur*, 9 (569)
    Skj: Sigvatr Þórðarson: 2. Nesjavísur 8 (AI, 230-1; BI, 218)
Sigv *Nesv* 15^I — Vol. 1. 37. Sigvatr Þórðarson, *Nesjavísur*, 15 (578)
    Skj: Sigvatr Þórðarson: 2. Nesjavísur 14 (AI, 232; BI, 220)
Sigv *Vestv*^{I} — Vol. 1. Sigvatr Þórðarson, *Vestrfararvísur* (615)
    Skj: Sigvatr Þórðarson: 5. Vestrfararvísur (AI, 241-3; BI, 226-8)
Sigv *Víkv*^{I} — Vol. 1. Sigvatr Þórðarson, *Víkingarvísur* (532)
    Skj: Sigvatr Þórðarson: 1. Víkingarvísur (AI, 223-8; BI, 213-16)
Sjólfr Lv (*Ǫrv*) — *Ǫrvar-Odds saga* (Sjólfr, Lausavísur)
    See individual stanza(s) for *Skj* references
Skall Lv^V (*Eg*) — Vol. 5. *Egils saga Skalla-Grímssonar* (Skallagrímr Kveldúlfsson, Lausavísur)
    Skj: Skallagrímr Kveldúlfsson: Lausavísur (AI, 30; BI, 26-27)
Skinnhúfa Lv (*HjǪ*) — *Hjálmþés saga ok Ǫlvis* (Skinnhúfa/Hildisif, Lausavísa)
    Skj: Anonyme digte og vers [XIII]: E. 16. Vers af Fornaldarsagaer: Af Hjálmþérs saga ok Ǫlvis (AII, 333-41; BII, 353-63)
Skúli Lv 1^{III} — Vol. 3. Skúli Þorsteinsson, Lausavísa, 1 (367)
    Skj: Skúli Þórsteinsson: 2. Lausavísa (AI, 306; BI, 284)
Skúli *Svǫlðr*^{III} — Vol. 3. Skúli Þorsteinsson, Poem about Svǫlðr (360)
    Skj: Skúli Þórsteinsson: 1. Digt om Svolderslaget (AI, 305-6; BI, 283-4)
SnH Lv^{II} — Vol. 2. Sneglu-Halli, Lausavísur (323-32)
    Skj: Sneglu- [Grautar-] Halli: 2. Lausavísur (AI, 388-90; BI, 358-60)
SnSt^{III} — Vol. 3. Snorri Sturluson (370)
    Skj: Snorri Sturluson (AII, 52-79; BII, 60-90)
SnSt *Ht*^{III} — Vol. 3. Snorri Sturluson, *Háttatal* (1094)
    Skj: Snorri Sturluson: 2. Háttatal (AII, 52-77; BII, 61-88)
Snæbj Lv^{III} — Vol. 3. Snæbjǫrn, Lausavísur (376)
    Skj: Snæbjǫrn: Lausavísur (AI, 211; BI, 201)

Sóti Lv 1^V (*Harð* 8) — Vol. 5. *Harðar saga* 8 (Sóti, Lausavísur, 1)
  Skj: [Anonyme digte og vers XIV]: A. 2. Vers af sagaer: Af isl. slægtsagaer: Af Harðar saga Grímkelssonar 8 (AII, 447; BII, 478-9)
Sóti Lv 2^V (*Harð* 10) — Vol. 5. *Harðar saga* 10 (Sóti, Lausavísur, 2)
  Skj: [Anonyme digte og vers XIV]: A. 2. Vers af sagaer: Af isl. slægtsagaer: Af Harðar saga Grímkelssonar 10 (AII, 447; BII, 479)
StarkSt Frag 1^{III} — Vol. 3. Starkaðr gamli Stórvirksson (biog. vol. 8), *Fragment*, 1 (382)
  Not in *Skj*
StarkSt Vík (*Gautr*) — *Gautreks saga* (Starkaðr gamli Stórvirksson, *Víkarsbálkr*)
  See individual stanza(s) for *Skj* references
Steinarr *Woman*^{III} — Vol. 3. Steinarr, Poem about a woman (384)
  Skj: Steinarr: Af et digt om en kvinde (AI, 417; BI, 386)
Steing^V — (Steingerðr Þorkelsdóttir)
  Skj: Steingerðr Þórkelsdóttir (AI, 91; BI, 85)
Steinn *Óldr* 13^{II} — Vol. 2. Steinn Herdísarson, *Óláfsdrápa*, 13 (378-9)
  Skj: Steinn Herdísarson: 3. Óláfsdrápa 14 (AI, 412; BI, 382)
Steinunn Lv^V — Vol. 5. Steinunn Refs (Dálks)dóttir, Lausavísur
  Skj: Steinunn Refs (Dálks)dóttir: Lausavísur (AI, 135-6; BI, 127-8)
Steinþ Frag 1^{III} — Vol. 3. Steinþórr, *Fragment*, 1 (390)
  Skj: Steinþórr: Af et ubestemmeligt digt (AI, 417; BI, 387)
StjOdd Geirdr 9^V (*StjǫrnODr* 14) — Vol. 5. *Stjǫrnu-Odda draumr* 14 (Stjǫrnu-Oddi Helgason, *Geirviðardrápa*, 9)
  Skj: Anonyme digte og vers [XIII]: D. 2. [1]. Drömmevers: Af Stjǫrnu-Oddadraumr II 9 (AII, 210; BII, 225)
Sturl^{II} — Vol. 2. Sturla Þórðarson (392)
  Skj: Sturla Þórðarson (AII, 101-29; BII, 112-36)
Sturl *Hákkv*^{II} — Vol. 2. Sturla Þórðarson, *Hákonarkviða* (699-727)
  Skj: Sturla Þórðarson: 4. Hákonarkviða (AII, 108-19; BII, 118-26)
Sturl *Hrafn*^{II} — Vol. 2. Sturla Þórðarson, *Hrafnsmál* (727-45)
  Skj: Sturla Þórðarson: 5. Hrafnsmál (AII, 119-24; BII, 126-31)
Sturl *Hryn*^{II} — Vol. 2. Sturla Þórðarson, *Hrynhenda* (676-98)
  Skj: Sturla Þórðarson: 3. Hrynhenda (AII, 102-8; BII, 113-18)
Svart *Skauf* — Svartr á Hofstöðum, *Skaufhala bálkr* (948)
  See individual stanza(s) for *Skj* references
SvB Lv 3^V (*Gr* 35) — Vol. 5. *Grettis saga Ásmundarsonar* 35 (Sveinn á Bakka, Lausavísur, 3)
  Skj: [Anonyme digte og vers XIV]: A. 1. Vers af sagaer: Af isl. slægtsagaer: Af Grettissaga 27 (AII, 438; BII, 469)
Svtjúg Lv 1^I — Vol. 1. 26. Sveinn tjúguskegg Haraldsson, Lausavísa, 1 (379)
  Skj: Anonyme digte og vers [X]: Tillæg [3]. Sveinn tjúguskegg (AI, 186; BI, 175-6)
Tindr *Hákdr*^{I} — Vol. 1. Tindr Hallkelsson, *Hákonardrápa* (336)
  Skj: Tindr Hallkelsson: 1. Drape om Hakon jarl (AI, 144-7; BI, 136-8)

Tóki Lv (*HjǪ*) — *Hjálmþés saga ok Ǫlvis* (Tóki víkingr, Lausavísa)
    See individual stanza(s) for *Skj* references
Úlfrauð Útkv (*Hálf*) — *Hálfs saga ok Hálfsrekka* (Úlfr inn rauði, Útsteinskviða)
    See individual stanza(s) for *Skj* references
ÚlfrU[III] — Vol. 3. Úlfr Uggason (402)
    Skj: Ulfr Uggason (AI, 136-9; BI, 128-30)
ÚlfrU *Húsdr*[III] — Vol. 3. Úlfr Uggason, *Húsdrápa* (402)
    Skj: Ulfr Uggason: 1. Húsdrápa (AI, 136-8; BI, 128-30)
Útsteinn Innkv (*Hálf*) — *Hálfs saga ok Hálfsrekka* (Útsteinn Gunnlaðarson, Innsteinskviða)
    See individual stanza(s) for *Skj* references
Útsteinn Lv (*Hálf*) — *Hálfs saga ok Hálfsrekka* (Útsteinn Gunnlaðarson, Lausavísa)
    See individual stanza(s) for *Skj* references
Útsteinn *Útkv* (*Hálf*) — *Hálfs saga ok Hálfsrekka* (Útsteinn Gunnlaðarson, Útsteinskviða)
    See individual stanza(s) for *Skj* references
Valg[II] — Vol. 2. Valgarðr á Velli (300-10)
    Skj: Valgarðr á Velli (AI, 390-3; BI, 360-3)
Valg *Har*[II] — Vol. 2. Valgarðr á Velli, Poem about Haraldr harðráði (300-10)
    Skj: Valgarðr á Velli: Et digt om Harald hårdråde (AI, 390-3; BI, 360-3)
Vargeisa Lv (*HjǪ*) — *Hjálmþés saga ok Ǫlvis* (Vargeisa/Álfsól, Lausavísur)
    See individual stanza(s) for *Skj* references
Vetrl Lv 1[III] — Vol. 3. Vetrliði Sumarliðason, Lausavísa, 1 (425)
    Skj: Vetrliði Sumarliðason: Lausavísa (AI, 135; BI, 127)
VíglÞ Lv 1[V] (*Vígl* 3) — Vol. 5. *Víglundar saga* 3 (Víglundr Þorgrímsson, Lausavísur, 1)
    Skj: [Anonyme digte og vers XIV]: A. 7. Vers af sagaer: Af isl. slægtsagaer: Af Víglundarsaga 3 (AII, 455-6; BII, 488)
VSt *Erf*[III] — Vol. 3. Vǫlu-Steinn, *Ǫgmundardrápa* (427)
    Skj: Vǫlu-Steinn: (AI, 98-9; BI, 93)
Ýma Lv (*HjǪ*) — *Hjálmþés saga ok Ǫlvis* (Ýma trǫllkona, Lausavísur)
    See individual stanza(s) for *Skj* references
Þfagr *Sveinn*[II] — Vol. 2. Þorleikr fagri, *Flokkr* about Sveinn Úlfsson (313-22)
    Skj: Þórleikr fagri: En flokk om Sven Ulfssön (AI, 396-9; BI, 365-8)
Þhorn *Gldr*[I] — Vol. 1. Þorbjǫrn hornklofi, *Glymdrápa* (73)
    Skj: Þórbjǫrn hornklofi: 1. Glymdrápa (AI, 22-4; BI, 20-1)
Þhorn *Harkv*[I] — Vol. 1. Þorbjǫrn hornklofi, *Haraldskvæði (Hrafnsmál)* (91)
    Skj: Þórbjǫrn hornklofi: 2. Haraldskvæði (Hrafnsmál) (AI, 24-9; BI, 22-5)
ÞjJ Lv (*ÞJ*) — *Þjalar-Jóns saga* (Þjalar-Jón Svipdagsson, Lausavísur)
    See individual stanza(s) for *Skj* references
Þjóð *Haustl*[III] — Vol. 3. Þjóðólfr ór Hvini, *Haustlǫng* (431)
    Skj: Þjóðólfr ór Hvini, enn hvinverski: 2. Haustlǫng (AI, 16-20; BI, 14-18)

Þjóð Lv^I — Vol. 1. Þjóðólfr ór Hvini, Lausavísur (64)
  Skj: Þjóðólfr ór Hvini, enn hvinverski: 4. Lausavísur (AI, 21; BI, 19)
Þjóð Yt^I — Vol. 1. Þjóðólfr ór Hvini, *Ynglingatal* (3)
  Skj: Þjóðólfr ór Hvini, enn hvinverski: 1. Ynglingatal (AI, 7-15; BI, 7-14)
ÞjóðA Frag 1^{II} — Vol. 2. Þjóðólfr Arnórsson, Fragments, 1 (159)
  Skj: Þjóðolfr Arnórsson: 4. Lausavísur 9 (AI, 379; BI, 349)
ÞjóðA *Har*^{II} — Vol. 2. Þjóðólfr Arnórsson, Stanzas about Haraldr Sigurðarson's *leiðangr* (147-58)
  Not in *Skj*
ÞjóðA *Har* 5^{II} — Vol. 2. Þjóðólfr Arnórsson, Stanzas about Haraldr Sigurðarson's *leiðangr*, 5 (155-6)
  Skj: Þjóðolfr Arnórsson: 4. Lausavísur 22 (AI, 382; BI, 352)
ÞjóðA *Magn* 12^{II} — Vol. 2. Þjóðólfr Arnórsson, Stanzas about Magnús Óláfsson in *Danaveldi*, 12 (99-100)
  Skj: Þjóðolfr Arnórsson: 4. Lausavísur 6 (AI, 378; BI, 348)
ÞjóðA *Magnfl*^{II} — Vol. 2. Þjóðólfr Arnórsson, *Magnússflokkr* (61-87)
  Skj: Þjóðolfr Arnórsson: 1. Magnúsflokkr (AI, 361-8; BI, 332-8)
ÞjóðA *Run*^{II} — Vol. 2. Þjóðólfr Arnórsson, *Runhent* poem about Haraldr (103-7)
  Skj: Þjóðolfr Arnórsson: 2. Runhent digt om Harald hårdråde (AI, 368; BI, 338-9)
ÞjóðA *Sex*^{II} — Vol. 2. Þjóðólfr Arnórsson, *Sexstefja* (108-47)
  Skj: Þjóðolfr Arnórsson: 3. Sexstefja (AI, 369-77; BI, 339-46)
ÞjóðA *Sex* 15^{II} — Vol. 2. Þjóðólfr Arnórsson, *Sexstefja*, 15 (127-8)
  Skj: Þjóðolfr Arnórsson: 3. Sexstefja 14 (AI, 372; BI, 342)
ÞjóðA *Sex* 20^{II} — Vol. 2. Þjóðólfr Arnórsson, *Sexstefja*, 20 (134-5)
  Skj: Þjóðolfr Arnórsson: 3. Sexstefja 19 (AI, 373; BI, 343-4)
ÞjóðA *Sex* 21^{II} — Vol. 2. Þjóðólfr Arnórsson, *Sexstefja*, 21 (135-6)
  Skj: Þjóðolfr Arnórsson: 3. Sexstefja 20 (AI, 373-4; BI, 343-4)
ÞjóðA *Sex* 29^{II} — Vol. 2. Þjóðólfr Arnórsson, *Sexstefja*, 29 (144-5)
  Skj: Þjóðolfr Arnórsson: 3. Sexstefja 30/1-4 (AI, 376; BI, 346)
ÞjóðA *Sex* 31^{II} — Vol. 2. Þjóðólfr Arnórsson, *Sexstefja*, 31 (146-7)
  Skj: Þjóðolfr Arnórsson: 3. Sexstefja 29 (AI, 376; BI, 345)
Þjsk *Jarl*^{I} — Vol. 1. Þorleifr jarlsskáld Rauðfeldarson, *Jarlsníð* (372)
  Skj: Þórleifr jarlsskáld Rauðfeldarson: 3. Jarlsníð (AI, 142; BI, 133)
Þjsk *Jarl* 1^I — Vol. 1. 24. Þorleifr jarlsskáld Rauðfeldarson, *Jarlsníð*, 1 (372)
  Skj: Þórleifr jarlsskáld Rauðfeldarson: 3. Jarlsníð (AI, 142; BI, 133)
Þjsk Lv^I — Vol. 1. Þorleifr jarlsskáld Rauðfeldarson, Lausavísur (375)
  Skj: Þórleifr jarlsskáld Rauðfeldarson: 4. Lausavísur (AI, 142-3; BI, 133-4)
Þloft *Tøgdr* 4^I — Vol. 1. 51. Þórarinn loftunga, *Tøgdrápa*, 4 (857)
  Skj: Þórarinn loftunga: 2. Tøgdrápa 5 (AI, 323; BI, 299)
Þorm Lv^V (*Fbr*) — Vol. 5. *Fóstbrœðra saga* (Þormóðr Kolbrúnarskáld, Lausavísur) (820)
  Skj: Þórmóðr Bersason Kolbrúnarskáld: 2. Lausavísur (AI, 281-8; BI, 260-6)

Þorm *Þorgdr*^{V} (*Fbr*) — Vol. 5. *Fóstbrœðra saga* (Þormóðr Kolbrúnarskáld, *Þorgeirsdrápa*)
  Skj: Þórmóðr Bersason Kolbrúnarskáld: 1. Þorgeirsdrápa (AI, 277-81; BI, 256-6)
Þórðh Lv^V (*Þórð*) — Vol. 5. *Þórðar saga hreðu* (Þórðr hreða, Lausavísur)
  Not in *Skj*
Þórhunds Lv (*Hrólf*) — *Hrólfs saga kraka* (Þórir hundsfótr, Lausavísa)
  See individual stanza(s) for *Skj* references
ÞSjár *Þórdr* 2^I — Vol. 1. 14. Þórðr Særeksson (Sjáreksson), *Þórálfs drápa Skólmssonar*, 2 (238)
  Skj: Þórðr Særeksson: 2. Þórolfs drápa Skolmssonar 3 (AI, 328; BI, 302-3)
ÞSkall *Valfl*^{II} — Vol. 2. Þorkell Skallason, *Valþjófsflokkr* (382-4)
  Skj: Þórkell Skallason: Valþjófsflokkr (AI, 414; BI, 383-4)
Þskúm Lv 1^I — Vol. 1. 21. Þorleifr skúma Þorkelsson, Lausavísa, 1 (360)
  Skj: Þórleifr skúma Þórkelsson: Lausavísa (AI, 117; BI, 111-12)
Þul *Ara*^{III} — Vol. 3. Þulur, *Ara heiti* (949)
  Skj: Anonyme digte og vers [XII]: IV. vv. Ara heiti (AI, 687; BI, 676)
Þul *Ara* 1^{III} — Vol. 3. Þulur, *Ara heiti*, 1 (950)
  Skj: Anonyme digte og vers [XII]: IV. vv. Ara heiti (AI, 687; BI, 676)
Þul *Á*^{III} — Vol. 3. Þulur, *Á heiti* (838)
  Skj: Anonyme digte og vers [XII]: IV. v. Á heiti (AI, 669-70; BI, 666-7)
Þul *á hendi*^{III} — Vol. 3. Þulur, *Heiti á hendi* (967)
  Skj: Anonyme digte og vers [XII]: IV. öö. Heiti á hendi (AI, 689; BI, 678)
Þul *Ása I*^{III} — Vol. 3. Þulur, *Ása heiti I* (754)
  Skj: Anonyme digte og vers [XII]: IV. e. Ása heiti (I) (AI, 657; BI, 660)
Þul *Ásynja*^{III} — Vol. 3. Þulur, *Ásynja heiti* (762)
  Skj: Anonyme digte og vers [XII]: IV. h. Ásynja heiti (AI, 658-9; BI, 661)
Þul *Boga*^{III} — Vol. 3. Þulur, *Boga heiti* (821)
  Skj: Anonyme digte og vers [XII]: IV. p. Boga heiti (AI, 666; BI, 665)
Þul *Dœgra*^{III} — Vol. 3. Þulur, *Dœgra heiti* (914)
  Skj: Anonyme digte og vers [XII]: IV. mm. Dœgra heiti (AI, 683; BI, 674)
Þul *Dœgra* 1^{III} — Vol. 3. Þulur, *Dœgra heiti*, 1 (914)
  Skj: Anonyme digte og vers [XII]: IV. mm. Dœgra heiti (AI, 683; BI, 674)
Þul *Dverga*^{III} — Vol. 3. Þulur, *Dverga heiti* (692)
  Skj: Anonyme digte og vers [XII]: IV. ii. Dverga heiti (AI, 679-80; BI, 672)
Þul *Elds*^{III} — Vol. 3. Þulur, *Elds heiti* (920)
  Skj: Anonyme digte og vers [XII]: IV. pp. Elds heiti (AI, 684; BI, 674-5)
Þul *Eyja*^{III} — Vol. 3. Þulur, *Eyja heiti* (972)
  Skj: Anonyme digte og vers [XII]: IV. bbb. Eyja heiti (AI, 689-90; BI, 678-9)
Þul *Fiska*^{III} — Vol. 3. Þulur, *Fiska heiti* (852)
  Skj: Anonyme digte og vers [XII]: IV. x. Fiska heiti (AI, 670-1; BI, 667)
Þul *Fjarða*^{III} — Vol. 3. Þulur, *Fjarða heiti* (982)
  Skj: Anonyme digte og vers [XII]: IV. ccc. Fjarða heiti (AI, 690; BI, 679)

Þul *Fjarða* 1[III] — Vol. 3. Þulur, *Fjarða heiti*, 1 (983)
  Skj: Anonyme digte og vers [XII]: IV. ccc. Fjarða heiti (AI, 690; BI, 679)
Þul *Galtar* 1[III] — Vol. 3. Þulur, *Galtar heiti*, 1 (900)
  Skj: Anonyme digte og vers [XII]: IV. dd. Galtar heiti (AI, 677; BI, 670)
Þul *Grýlu* 1[III] — Vol. 3. Þulur, *Grýlu heiti*, 1 (966)
  Skj: Anonyme digte og vers [XII]: IV. ææ. Grýlu heiti (AI, 688; BI, 678)
Þul *Hana* 1[III] — Vol. 3. Þulur, *Hana heiti*, 1 (947)
  Skj: Anonyme digte og vers [XII]: IV. uu. Hana heiti (AI, 686-7; BI, 676)
Þul *Hesta*[III] — Vol. 3. Þulur, *Hesta heiti* (935)
  Skj: Anonyme digte og vers [XII]: IV. rr. Hesta heiti (AI, 685-6; BI, 675-6)
Þul *Hjálms*[III] — Vol. 3. Þulur, *Hjálms heiti* (828)
  Skj: Anonyme digte og vers [XII]: IV. s. Hjálms heiti (AI, 667-8; BI, 665-6)
Þul *Hrafns*[III] — Vol. 3. Þulur, *Hrafns heiti* (944)
  Skj: Anonyme digte og vers [XII]: IV. tt. Hrafns heiti (AI, 686; BI, 676)
Þul *Hugar ok hjarta*[III] — Vol. 3. Þulur, *Hugar heiti ok hjarta* (964)
  Skj: Anonyme digte og vers [XII]: IV. zz. Hugar heiti ok hjarta (AI, 688; BI, 678)
Þul *Jǫtna I*[III] — Vol. 3. Þulur, *Jǫtna heiti I* (706)
  Skj: Anonyme digte og vers [XII]: IV. b. Jǫtna heiti (I) (AI, 654-5; BI, 658-9)
Þul *Jǫtna II*[III] — Vol. 3. Þulur, *Jǫtna heiti II* (718)
  Skj: Anonyme digte og vers [XII]: IV. f. Jǫtna heiti (II) (AI, 657-8; BI, 660)
Þul *Kálfv*[III] — Vol. 3. Þulur, *Kálfsvísa* (663)
  Skj: Anonyme digte og vers [XII]: I. II. Þulur: Kálfsvísa (AI, 650; BI, 656-7)
Þul *Konunga*[III] — Vol. 3. Þulur, *Konunga heiti* (687)
  Skj: Anonyme digte og vers [XII]: IV. hh. Konunga heiti (AI, 679; BI, 671)
Þul *Kvenna I*[III] — Vol. 3. Þulur, *Kvenna heiti* (772)
  Skj: Anonyme digte og vers [XII]: IV. i. Kvenna heiti (AI, 659; BI, 661)
Þul *Kvenna I* 1[III] — Vol. 3. Þulur, *Kvenna heiti*, 1 (772)
  Skj: Anonyme digte og vers [XII]: IV. i. Kvenna heiti (AI, 659; BI, 661)
Þul *Kvenna II*[III] — Vol. 3. Þulur, *Kvenna heiti ókend* (959)
  Skj: Anonyme digte og vers [XII]: IV. yy. Kvenna heiti ókend (AI, 688; BI, 677-8)
Þul *Orma*[III] — Vol. 3. Þulur, *Orma heiti* (927)
  Skj: Anonyme digte og vers [XII]: IV. qq. Orma heiti (AI, 684-5; BI, 675)
Þul *Óðins*[III] — Vol. 3. Þulur, *Óðins nǫfn* (731)
  Skj: Anonyme digte og vers [XII]: IV. jj. Óðins nǫfn (AI, 680-2; BI, 672-3)
Þul *Sáðs*[III] — Vol. 3. Þulur, *Sáðs heiti* (985)
  Skj: Anonyme digte og vers [XII]: IV. ddd. Sáðs heiti (AI, 690; BI, 680)
Þul *Sea-kings* 1[III] — Vol. 3. Þulur, *Heiti for sea-kings*, 1 (988)
  Skj: Anonyme digte og vers [XII]: I. III. 1. Þulur: Forskellige: Søkongenavne (AI, 651; BI, 657)
Þul *Sjóvar*[III] — Vol. 3. Þulur, *Sjóvar heiti* (833)
  Skj: Anonyme digte og vers [XII]: IV. u. Sjóvar heiti (AI, 668-9; BI, 666)

Þul *Skipa*^{III} — Vol. 3. Þulur, *Skipa heiti* (861)
    Skj: Anonyme digte og vers [XII]: IV. z. Skipa heiti (AI, 672-4; BI, 668-9)
Þul *Spjóts*^{III} — Vol. 3. Þulur, *Spjóts heiti* (816)
    Skj: Anonyme digte og vers [XII]: IV. n. Spjóts heiti (AI, 665; BI, 664-5)
Þul *Spjóts* 1^{III} — Vol. 3. Þulur, *Spjóts heiti*, 1 (816)
    Skj: Anonyme digte og vers [XII]: IV. n. Spjóts heiti (AI, 665; BI, 664-5)
Þul *Sverða*^{III} — Vol. 3. Þulur, *Sverða heiti* (789)
    Skj: Anonyme digte og vers [XII]: IV. l. Sverða heiti (AI, 662-5; BI, 663-4)
Þul *Sækonunga*^{III} — Vol. 3. Þulur, *Sækonunga heiti* (677)
    Skj: Anonyme digte og vers [XII]: IV. a. Sækonunga heiti (AI, 653-4; BI, 658)
Þul *Trollkvenna*^{III} — Vol. 3. Þulur, *Trollkvenna heiti* (723)
    Skj: Anonyme digte og vers [XII]: IV. c. Trollkvenna heiti (AI, 655-6; BI, 659-60)
Þul *Tungls* 1^{III} — Vol. 3. Þulur, *Tungls heiti*, 1 (912)
    Skj: Anonyme digte og vers [XII]: IV. ll. Tungls heiti (AI, 682-3; BI, 674)
Þul *Vargs*^{III} — Vol. 3. Þulur, *Vargs heiti* (902)
    Skj: Anonyme digte og vers [XII]: IV. ee. Vargs heiti (AI, 677-8; BI, 670-1)
Þul *Veðra*^{III} — Vol. 3. Þulur, *Veðra heiti* (917)
    Skj: Anonyme digte og vers [XII]: IV. oo. Veðra heiti (AI, 683; BI, 674)
Þul *Waves*^{III} — Vol. 3. Þulur, *Heiti* for waves (996)
    Skj: Anonyme digte og vers [XII]: I. III. 4. Þulur: Forskellige: Bølgenavne (AI, 652; BI, 657-8)
Þul *Þorgþ I* 1^{III} — Vol. 3. Þulur, *Þorgrímsþula I*, 1 (670)
    Skj: Anonyme digte og vers [XII]: I. I. [a]. Þulur: Þórgrímsþula a 1 (AI, 649; BI, 656)
Þul *Þórs*^{III} — Vol. 3. Þulur, *Þórs heiti* (758)
    Skj: Anonyme digte og vers [XII]: IV. d. Þórs heiti (AI, 656-7; BI, 660)
Þul *Ǫrvar*^{III} — Vol. 3. Þulur, *Ǫrvar heiti* (818)
    Skj: Anonyme digte og vers [XII]: IV. o. Ǫrvar heiti (AI, 666; BI, 665)
Þul *Øxar* 1^{III} — Vol. 3. Þulur, *Øxar heiti*, 1 (813)
    Skj: Anonyme digte og vers [XII]: IV. m. Øxar heiti (AI, 665; BI, 664)
ǪgmEyb Lv (*Ǫrv*) — *Ǫrvar-Odds saga* (Ǫgmundr Eyþjófsbani, Lausavísur)
    See individual stanza(s) for *Skj* references
ǪlvH Lv (*HjǪ*) — *Hjálmþés saga ok Ǫlvis* (Ǫlvir Herrauðsson, Lausavísa)
    See individual stanza(s) for *Skj* references
Ǫlvǫr Lv (*Ǫrv*) — *Ǫrvar-Odds saga* (Ǫlvǫr, Lausavísa)
    See individual stanza(s) for *Skj* references
ǪrvOdd Lv — Ǫrvar-Oddr, Lausavísur
    See individual stanza(s) for *Skj* references
ǪrvOdd *Ævdr* (*Ǫrv*) — *Ǫrvar-Odds saga* (Ǫrvar-Oddr, *Ævidrápa*)
    Skj: Anonyme digte og vers [XIII]: E. 10. Vers af Fornaldarsagaer: Af Ǫrvar-Oddsaga IX (AII, 306-19; BII, 324-39)

Sigla for Manuscript Collections

Adv — Advocates' Library, National Library of Scotland, Edinburgh
AM — The Arnamagnæan Collection, Den arnamagnæanske håndskriftsamling, Nordisk forskningsinstitut, University of Copenhagen and Stofnun Árna Magnússonar í íslenskum fræðum, Reykjavík
AMAcc — Den arnamagnæanske håndskriftsamling: Accessoria
Berlin MS Germ. — Berlin, Staatsbibliothek: Manuscripta germanica
BLAdd — British Library, London: Additional Manuscripts
BN Lat. — Bibliothèque Nationale, Paris: Latin Manuscripts
BSG — Bibliothèque Sainte-Geneviève, Paris
DG — Delagardiska samlingen, Uppsala universitetsbibliotek
DKNVSB — Det Kongelige Norske Videnskabers Selskabs Bibliotek, Universitetsbiblioteket i Trondheim
Engestr — Engeströmska samlingen, Kungliga biblioteket, Stockholm
GKS — Den gamle kongelige samling, Det kongelige bibliotek, Copenhagen and Stofnun Árna Magnússonar í íslenskum fræðum, Reykjavík
Holm — Kungliga biblioteket, Stockholm
ÍB — Safn Hins íslenska bókmenntafélags deildar þess í Kaupmannahöfn, Landsbókasafn Íslands, Reykjavík
ÍBR — Handritasafn Reykjavíkurdeildar Hins íslenska bókmenntafélags, Landsbókasafn Íslands, Reykjavík
Ihre — Ihreska handskriftssamlingen, Uppsala Universitetsbibliotek
JS — Safn Jóns Sigurðssonar, Landsbókasafn Íslands, Reykjavík
Kall — Kalls samling, Det kongelige bibliotek, Copenhagen
KBAdd — Det kongelige bibliotek, Additamenta, Det kongelige bibliotek, Copenhagen and Stofnun Árna Magnússonar í íslenskum fræðum, Reykjavík
Lbs — Handritasafn Landsbókasafns Íslands
NKS — Den nye kongelige samling, Det kongelige bibliotek, Copenhagen and Stofnun Árna Magnússonar í íslenskum fræðum, Reykjavík
NRA — Riksarkivet, Oslo
OsloUB — Universitetsbiblioteket i Oslo
Rask — Rasmus Rasks samling, Den arnamagnæanske samling, Copenhagen
SÁM — Stofnun Árna Magnússonar á Íslandi
TCD — Trinity College Library, Dublin
Thott — Thotts samling, Det kongelige bibliotek, Copenhagen
Traj — Universiteitsbibliotheek, Rijksuniversiteit te Utrecht
UppsUB — Uppsala universitetsbibliotek

Sigla for Manuscripts used in the Editions of this Volume

6^x — AM 6 fol^x
7 — Holm perg 7 4°
9^x — AM 9 fol^x
11^x — AM 11 fol^x
27^x — JS 27 fol^x
30^x — Holm papp 30 4^{ox}
56^x — Holm papp 56 fol^x
58^x — Holm papp 58 fol^x
105^x — AM 105 fol^x
109a I^x — AM 109 a I 8^{ox}
109a II^x — AM 109 a II 8^{ox}
109a III^x — AM 109 a III 8^{ox}
114^x — AM 114 fol^x
147 — AM 147 4° (Heynesbók)
152 — AM 152 fol
164h^x — AM 164 h fol^x
173^x — AM 173 fol^x
194c^x — AM 194 c fol^x
203^x — AM 203 fol^x
281^x — AM 281 4^{ox}
285^x — AM 285 4^{ox}
335 — AM 335 4°
340^x — AM 340 4^{ox}
342^x — AM 342 4^{ox}
343a — AM 343 a 4°
344a — AM 344 a 4°
361^x — AM 361 4^{ox}
437^x — AM 437 4^{ox}
439^x — AM 439 4^{ox}
440^x — AM 440 4^{ox}
471 — AM 471 4°
510 — AM 510 4°
552q^x — AM 552 q 4^{ox}
554h b^x — AM 554 h b 4^{ox}
560c^x — AM 560 c 4^{ox}
567IV — AM 567 IV 4°
567XIa — AM 567 XI a 4°
567XIVg — AM 567 XIV g 4°
568^x — AM 568 4^{ox}
577 — AM 577 4°
586 — AM 586 4°

587c^x — AM 587 c 4°^{x}
589f — AM 589 f 4°
590a^x — AM 590 a 4°^{x}
590b-c^x — AM 590 b-c 4°^{x}
591e^x — AM 591 e 4°^{x}
597b^x — AM 597 b 4°^{x}
603 — AM 603 4°
762^x — AM 762 4°^{x}
1006^x — GKS 1006 fol^x
1824b — NKS 1824 b 4°
2845 — GKS 2845 4°
A — AM 748 I b 4°
C — AM 748 II 4°
Flat — GKS 1005 fol (Flateyjarbók)
Hb — AM 544 4° (Hauksbók)
Holm6 — Holm perg 6 4°
Holm10 VI — Holm perg 10 VI 8°
ÍB65^x — ÍB 65 4°^{x}
ÍBR5^x — ÍBR 5 fol^x (Vigrabók)
LR — *Literatura Runica* in Worm 1636 (for text of Anon *Krm*)
Mb — AM 445 b 4° (Melabók)
papp6^x — Holm papp 6 4°^{x}
papp11^x — Holm papp 11 8°^{x}
papp17^x — Holm papp 17 4°^{x}
papp25^x — Holm papp 25 8°^{x}
papp32^x — Holm papp 32 4°^{x}
R — GKS 2367 4° (Codex Regius)
R702^x — UppsUB R 702^x
R715^x — UppsUB R715^x
R693^x — UppsUB R 693^x
Rask87^x — Rask 87 8°^{x}
Sk — AM 104 fol^x (Skarðsárbók)
St — AM 107 fol^x (Sturlubók)
T^x — Traj 1374^x (Codex Trajectinus)
U — DG 11 (Codex Upsaliensis)
W — AM 242 fol (Codex Wormianus)
Þb106^x — AM 106 fol^x (Þórðarbók)

Sigla for Sagas, *Þættir* and Compendia

Alex — *Alexanders saga*
Án — *Áns saga bogsveigis*
Ásm — *Ásmundar saga kappabana*
Auð — *Auðunar þáttr vestfirzka*
Band — *Bandamanna saga*
Barth — *Bartholómeuss saga postula*
Bev — *Bevers saga*
BjH — *Bjarnar saga Hítdœlakappa*
Bós — *Bósa saga ok Herrauðs*
Bret — *Breta saga*
Bær — *Bærings saga fagra*
Eg — *Egils saga Skallagrímssonar*
EgÁsm — *Egils saga einhenda ok Ásmundar berserkjabana*
Eindr — *Eindriða þáttr ilbreiðs*
Eir — *Eiríks saga rauða*
Elís — *Elíss saga ok Rósamundar*
EVíð — *Eiríks saga víðfǫrla*
Eyrb — *Eyrbyggja saga*
Fbr — *Fóstbrœðra saga*
Finnb — *Finnboga saga ramma*
Flat — *Flateyjarbók*
Flj — *Fljótsdæla saga*
Flóv — *Flóvents saga*
Fornk — *Fornkonunga saga (Sǫgubrot af Fornkonungum)*
Frið — *Friðþjófs saga ins frækna*
Gautr — *Gautreks saga*
Geir — *Geirmundar þáttr heljarskinns*
GHr — *Gǫngu-Hrólfs saga*
Gísl — *Gísla saga Súrssonar*
Gr — *Grettis saga Ásmundarsonar*
Greg — *Gregors saga páfa*
GrL — *Gríms saga loðinkinna*
GunnK — *Gunnars saga Keldagnúpsfífls*
Gylf — *Gylfaginning*
Hák — *Hákonar saga Hákonarsonar*
Hálf — *Hálfs saga ok Hálfsrekka*
HálfdEyst — *Hálfdanar saga Eysteinssonar*
Hálfds — *Hálfdanar saga svarta*
Hallfr — *Hallfreðar saga*
Harð — *Harðar saga*
Hb — *Hauksbók*

Heiðr — *Hervarar saga ok Heiðreks*
HG — *Hrólfs saga Gautrekssonar*
HHárf — *Haralds saga hárfagra (in Heimskringla)*
HjǪ — *Hjálmþés saga ok Ǫlvis*
Hkr — *Heimskringla*
Hrólf — *Hrólfs saga kraka*
Ht — *Háttatal*
Íslb — *Íslendingabók*
Jvs — *Jómsvíkinga saga*
Ket — *Ketils saga hœngs*
Kgs — *Konungs skuggsjá*
Kjaln — *Kjalnesinga saga*
Konr — *Konráðs saga Keisarasonar*
Korm — *Kormaks saga*
Krók — *Króka-Refs saga*
LaufE — *Laufás Edda*
Ldn — *Landnámabók*
Mág — *Máguss saga jarls*
Mberf — *Magnúss saga berfœtts (in compilations)*
Mork — *Morkinskinna*
Nik — *Nikuláss saga erkibyskups*
Nj — *Njáls saga*
Norn — *Nornagests þáttr*
ÓH — *Óláfs saga helga in sérstaka/Separate saga of S. Óláfr*
ÓHHkr — *Óláfs saga helga (in Heimskringla)*
Orkn — *Orkneyinga saga*
OStór — *Orms þáttr Stórólfssonar*
ÓT — *Óláfs saga Tryggvasonar in mesta/Greatest Saga of Óláfr Tryggvason*
Part — *Partalópa saga*
Ragn — *Ragnars saga loðbrókar*
RagnSon — *Ragnars sona þáttr*
Rauð — *Rauðúlfs þáttr*
Skm — *Skáldskaparmál*
SnE — *Snorra Edda*
Snegl — *Sneglu-Halla þáttr*
StSt — *Sturlaugs saga starfsama*
Stu — *Sturlunga saga*
Styrb — *Styrbjarnar þáttr Svíakappa*
Sv — *Sverris saga*
Sǫrla — *Sǫrla þáttr*
TGT — *The Third Grammatical Treatise*
Trój — *Trójumanna saga*

Vígl — *Víglundar saga*
Vikt — *Viktors saga ok Blávuss*
Vilm — *Vilmundar saga viðútan*
VSj — *Vilhjálms saga sjóðs*
Vǫls — *Vǫlsunga saga*
Yng — *Ynglinga saga*
Yngv — *Yngvars saga víðfǫrla*
Þiðr — *Þiðreks saga af Bern*
ÞJ — *Þjalar-Jóns saga*
Þórð — *Þórðar saga hreðu*
ÞórlJ — *Þórleifs þáttr jarlsskálds*
ÞorstBm — *Þorsteins saga bæjarmagns*
ÞorstVík — *Þorsteins saga Víkingssonar*
Ǫgm — *Ǫgmundar þáttr dytts ok Gunnars helmings*
Ǫrv — *Ǫrvar-Odds saga*

Technical Terms

Old-Norse Icelandic Technical Terms

aðalhending, 'noble rhyme, chief rhyme', combination of two syllables participating in full internal rhyme (identical vowels and postvocalic environment) within a skaldic poetic line. Normally *aðalhending* occurs in even lines (so ll. 2, 4, 6 and 8) of a *dróttkvætt* or *hrynhent* stanza

áttmælt, 'eight-times spoken', a *dróttkvætt* stanza in which each of the eight lines contains a separate clause

bálkr, 'section', a longer poem containing narrative sections

bálkarlag, 'sections' metre' (?), a regularised *fornyrðislag* with two alliterating staves in the odd lines and the main stave placed in metrical position 1 in the even lines, as in *dróttkvætt*

bragarmál, poetic diction characterised by cliticisation, i.e. the suffixation of unstressed particles and pronouns with loss of vowel

drápa, long encomiastic skaldic poem with *stef* (see below)

dróttkvætt, 'court poetry', the most common metre used in skaldic poetry, comprising stanzas of eight hexasyllabic lines, regular alliteration and *hendingar* (*skothending* in odd lines and *aðalhending* in even ones)

erfidrápa, 'memorial poem', encomium commemorating a deceased person

ferskeytt, 'square metre', a four-line *ríma* stanza, comprising two couplets, each sharing alliteration, while two odd and two even lines share end rhyme abab

flokkr, long skaldic poem without *stef*

fornyrðislag, 'old story metre', Old Norse development of the common Germanic alliterative long-line

galdralag, 'incantations' metre', a variant of *ljóðaháttr* with verbal repetition and an additional full line with internal alliteration

greppaminni, 'poets' reminder', *dróttkvætt* variant in which each line in the first *helmingr* of a stanza consists of an independent question that is answered in the corresponding line of the second *helmingr*

Haðarlag, 'Hǫðr's metre', regularised *málaháttr* lines with internal rhyme (*skothending* in odd lines and *aðalhending* in even ones)

hagmælt, 'skilfully spoken', *fornyrðislag* with internal rhyme (*skothending* in odd lines and *aðalhending* in even ones)

háttlausa, 'formless', a kind of *dróttkvætt* lacking internal rhyme

háttr, metre, verse-form (lit. 'mode, manner')

heiti, poetic synonym, an alternative and often descriptive term or name for a frequently-occurring object or person mentioned in skaldic poetry, e.g. *skævaðr* 'high-strider' for 'horse', *Yggr*, an alternative name for the god Óðinn

helmingr (pl. *helmingar*), a half-stanza normally of four lines

hending (pl. *hendingar*), lit. 'catching', a syllable participating, with one other, in full internal rhyme (*aðalhending*) or partial rhyme (*skothending*) within a line of a skaldic stanza

hrynhent, 'flowing rhymed', a skaldic metre, and an expanded version of *dróttkvætt* in which each line contains eight syllables

hǫfuðstafr, 'head (main) stave', chief alliterating stave fixed in initial position of even lines of regular *dróttkvætt* and *hrynhent* stanzas

kenning, a nominal periphrasis, consisting of a base-word and one or more determinants

kviðlingr, a snippet of poetry, usually no more than two lines

kviðuháttr, 'poems' form' (?), a skaldic metre (a variant of *fornyrðislag*) in which the odd lines consist of three syllables and the even lines of four syllables

lausavísa (pl. *lausavísur*), 'loose stanza', a separate stanza or part thereof which does not belong to a long poem and which is normally presented as an integral part of a prose narrative

ljóðaháttr, 'songs' metre', a six-line metre in which ll. 1-2 and 4-5 alliterate, while ll. 3 and 6 alliterate internally

málaháttr, 'speeches' metre', an extended form of *fornyrðislag* with five metrical positions rather than four

mannjafnaðr, 'comparison of men', formal or semi-formal comparison of the merits of two or more men, often in poetry

níð, shaming slander or abuse, often in poetic form, typically containing implications of cowardice and/or passive male homosexuality (cf. *mannjafnaðr* and *senna*)

ofljóst, 'too transparent, excessively clear', play on words, punning, using homonyms

Ragnars háttr, 'Ragnarr's metre', a *dróttkvætt* variant characterised by a lack of internal rhymes in the odd lines and by alliteration in metrical position 2 rather than position 1 in the even lines

rekit, 'extended, driven' (?), an extended kenning with more than two determinants (cf. *tvíkent*)

ríma (pl. *rímur*), late medieval and modern Icelandic narrative poetry, characterised by complex metrical form indebted to both skaldic and eddic verse (see *ferskeytt* above), end rhyme, division into several cantos; subject matter is mainly indebted to existing romances and *fornaldarsögur*

runhent, 'end-rhymed' (?), skaldic metres employing end rhyme

senna, 'flyting', poetic debate between two persons evaluating each other's merits, usually accompanied by insults

skothending, 'inserted rhyme' (?), combination of two syllables with different vowels and similar postvocalic environments participating in a form of internal rhyme within a skaldic line. Normally *skothending* occurs in odd lines (so ll. 1, 3, 5, and 7) of a *dróttkvætt* or *hrynhent* stanza

Starkaðar lag, 'Starkaðr's metre', *fornyrðislag* with two alliterating staves in odd lines and anacrusis in even lines

stef, refrain of a skaldic *drápa*

stikki, a kind of poem, e.g. *Sǫrlastikki*

stikkalag, 'needle's metre', metre in which the main stave in even lines falls on a syllable other than the first

tvíkent, 'doubly modified', a kenning with two determinants (cf. *rekit*)

tøglag, 'journey metre', a variant of *fornyrðislag* in which the even lines have *aðalhending* and the odd may have *skothending*

vísa (pl. *vísur*), a skaldic stanza, in the plural often a term used of a long poem lacking a refrain (e.g. Sigvatr's *Bersǫglisvísur*)

þáttr, 'strand', a smaller, independent narrative usually embedded in or added to a saga

þula (pl. *þulur*), a list of poetic synonyms (*heiti*) in metrical form

ævikviða, 'life poem', retrospective autobiographical poem in which a speaker, often on the point of death, looks back on the course of his life and his achievements

Other Technical Terms

adynaton, figure of speech by which an impossible or unlikely situation is used for emphasis

anacrusis, an unstressed syllable at the beginning of a verse line

base-word, member of a kenning (see list above) that is modified by a qualifier, called the determinant

catalectic, of a line of poetry, lacking a final syllable in the last foot

chiastic, characterized by chiasmus, a grammatical figure by which the order of words in one of two parallel clauses is inverted in the other

cliticise, to add an enclitic syllable to a word (see enclitic below)

Craigie's Law, the observation of Sir William Craigie (1900) that even *dróttkvætt* lines in which metrical positions 1 and 2 are occupied by two stressed syllables cannot tolerate a long-stemmed nomen (noun, adjective, infinitive) in metrical positions 3 or 4

desyllabification, the process whereby syllabic liquids and nasals develop an excrescent vowel, in Icelandic usually involving the addition of [u] before [r]

determinant, qualifier of a base-word in a kenning, consisting either of a noun or name in the genitive or of the first element of a compound

dip, a metrically unstressed syllable

editio princeps, first edition

enclitic, monosyllabic word, usually a particle, verb or pronoun, added as a suffix to another word (see also cliticise and *bragarmál* in the list above)

enclitic position, post-position (as opposed to proclitic position) enjambement, the carrying over of a group of syntactically related words from one verse unit (e.g. a half-line) to the next

epenthesis (epenthetic, adj.), a sound, usually a vowel, inserted between two others (see excrescent)

excrescent, a sound, usually a vowel, inserted between two others (see epenthesis)

fit, a part or section of a poem or song, a canto

floruit, the period during which a person 'flourished'

fornaldarsögur (sg. *fornaldarsaga*), 'sagas of ancient time', a modern term for legendary or heroic sagas, usually set in Scandinavia before the settlement of Iceland

hypermetrical, a poetic line containing more syllables (metrical positions) than is normal for the metre in question

hypometrical, a poetic line containing fewer syllables (metrical positions) than is normal for the metre in question

hysteron proteron, rhetorical figure in which that which should logically come last is mentioned first for purposes of emphasis

Íslendingasögur (sg. *Íslendingasaga*), 'sagas of Icelanders', 'family sagas', usually set in Iceland during the first century or so of settlement, concerning the lives of Icelandic families

lectio difficilior, more difficult reading, sometimes preferred to a *lectio facilior* by editors, on the basis that if corruption occurs it is more likely to replace rare usages by common ones than the reverse

lectio facilior, easier reading; see *lectio difficilior*

lift, a metrically stressed syllable

litotes, understatement, in which an affirmative is expressed by negating its opposite

long-line, the basic unit of alliterative poetry in the common Germanic verse-form, including Old Norse, consisting of two half-lines, bound in pairs by alliteration on metrically stressed syllables, one or two in the first half-line and one on the first lift (the *hǫfuðstafr*) of the second

metonomy, the substitution of a word referring to an attribute or adjunct for the whole thing that is meant

neutralisation, a metrical situation in which two short syllables occupy one unstressed metrical position in a line

pars pro toto, 'part for whole', a figure of speech in which part of something is used to refer to the whole thing

pleonastic, syllable, word, or phrase that is superfluous

proclitic position, pre-position (as opposed to enclitic position)

prosimetrum, text composed partly in prose, partly in verse

referent, word expressing the unmentioned cognitive meaning value of a kenning, e.g. the referent of the kenning *logi fjarðar* 'flame of the fjord' is 'gold'

resolution, two short syllables occupying one fully stressed metrical position in a line

riddarasögur (sg. *riddarasaga*), 'sagas of knights', romances either translated from French and other European languages or with indigenous plots

samtíðarsögur (sg. *samtíðarsaga*), 'contemporary sagas', sagas written about events in Iceland during the twelfth and thirteenth centuries

siglum (pl. sigla), abbreviation, usually a combination of alphanumerical symbols, used to designate a specific manuscript and/or the collection in which it is found

stanza, a group of poetic lines, arranged according to a regular scheme; one of a series of such groups, which together make up a poem

stemma (pl. stemmata), a diagram representing a reconstruction of the relationships between the surviving and postulated witnesses to a text

synecdoche, a figure of speech in which a semantically narrower term is substituted for a broader one, or vice versa; it commonly consists of *pars pro toto* (see above)

terminus ante quem, the latest date at which something could have occurred or might occur (in contrast to a *terminus post quem*, the earliest date at which something could occur)

tmesis, the separation of a word or compound into two parts, with another word or words between them

The Contributors

Hannah Burrows is a Lecturer in Scandinavian Studies at the University of Aberdeen, and an Honorary Associate of the Medieval and Early Modern Centre, The University of Sydney. Her research interests and publications focus on Old Norse literature and culture, including riddles, poetry and literary-legal relations. She is Bibliography Editor for *Skaldic Poetry of the Scandinavian Middle Ages*.

Margaret Clunies Ross is an Emeritus Professor of English and Honorary Professor in the Medieval and Early Modern Centre of The University of Sydney. She is also an Honorary Research Associate of the Department of Anglo-Saxon, Norse and Celtic at the University of Cambridge and an Adjunct Professor in the School of Humanities within the Faculty of Arts at the University of Adelaide. Among her recent publications are *A History of Old Norse Poetry and Poetics* (2005, paperback 2011), *The Cambridge Introduction to the Old Norse-Icelandic Saga* (2010) and (with Jonas Wellendorf) *The Fourth Grammatical Treatise* (2014). She is one of the General Editors of *Skaldic Poetry of the Scandinavian Middle Ages* and Volume Editor of *SkP* VII and VIII.

Kari Ellen Gade is Provost Professor of Germanic Studies and Adjunct Professor of English at Indiana University, Bloomington. She is the author of *The Structure of Old Norse Dróttkvætt Poetry* (1995) and (with Theodore M. Andersson) *Morkinskinna: The Earliest Icelandic Chronicle of the Norwegian Kings (1030-1157)* (2000). Her research interests are in Old Norse language, literature, culture and history, together with Germanic Philology and metrics. She is one of the General Editors of *Skaldic Poetry of the Scandinavian Middle Ages* and Volume Editor of *SkP* II and (in collaboration with Edith Marold) *SkP* III.

Richard L. Harris is Professor of Old English and Old Icelandic in the Department of English at the University of Saskatchewan, where he has worked since 1973. He first undertook research on *Hjálmþés saga* in the mid-1960s when editing that saga at Háskóli Íslands. He published *A Chorus of Grammars. The Correspondence of George Hickes and his Collaborators on the* Thesaurus Linguarum Septentrionalium (1992) and, for the past decade, has studied paroemiological approaches to the reading of the Old Icelandic sagas (see "Jafnan segir inn ríkri ráð': Proverbial Allusion and the Implied Proverb in Fóstbrœðra saga' in *New Norse Studies: Essays on the Literature and Culture of Medieval Scandinavia* (2015). His Concordance to the Proverbs and Proverbial Materials of the Old Icelandic Sagas can be accessed online.

Wilhelm Heizmann is Professor of Scandinavian Studies at the Ludwig-Maximilians-University of Munich. His research and teaching interests are in the fields of Old Norse-Icelandic literature, Germanic mythology and religion, Germanic antiquity studies, runology, medieval medical and botanical literature, and late antique and medieval iconography. His publications include *Wörterbuch der Pflanzennamen im Altwestnordischen* (1993), (with Rudolf Simek) *Mythological Women: Studies in Memory of Lotte Motz 1922-1997* (2002), (with Heinrich Beck and Klaus Böldl) *Analecta Septentrionalia: Beiträge zur nordgermanischen Kultur- und Literaturgeschichte* (2009) and (with Morten Axboe) *Die Goldbrakteaten der Völkerwanderungzeit – Auswertung und Neufunde* (2011).

Peter Jorgensen is Emeritus Professor of Germanic Languages and Linguistics at the University of Georgia. His research has focused on the editing and translating of Old Norse texts, (e.g. *Tristrams saga ok Isöndar*, exempla from Middle English and Latin sources), the Bear's Son Folktale, Icelandic saga forgeries, computer-assisted instruction in German, linguistics, and medieval German pilgrimage literature. His publications include *The Story of Jonatas* (1997), *Valla-Ljóts Saga* (1991) and most recently 'The *Life of St. Basil* in Iceland', *Gripla* (2015).

Beatrice La Farge is Research Associate for the project *Edda-Kommentar* at the Institut für Skandinavistik, University of Frankfurt. She is one of the authors of the multi-volume *Kommentar zu den Liedern der Edda* (1996-) and, with John Tucker, author of *Glossary to the Poetic Edda* (1992).

Philip Lavender is a post-doctoral fellow at the University of Gothenburg, where his research project is a study of saga forgery in the seventeenth and eighteenth centuries, funded by a Marie Skłodowska-Curie Individual Fellowship. He is a graduate of the University of Oxford, where he studied English Literature and Medieval Studies (BA 2004, MPhil 2006), and was awarded a PhD at the University of Copenhagen (2015) for a study of *Illuga saga Gríðarfóstra*. His research interests include legendary and romantic sagas, post-medieval *rímur*, Scandinavian intellectual history and the reception of Nordic literature. Some of these interests were taken up in a recent research project at the University of Copenhagen on the reception of Saxo Grammaticus' work in post-Reformation Iceland funded by the Carlsberg Foundation.

Rory McTurk is Professor Emeritus of Icelandic Studies at the University of Leeds. He is the author of *Studies in* Ragnars saga loðbrókar *and its Major Scandinavian Analogues* (1991) and of *Chaucer and the Norse and Celtic Worlds* (2005). He is the editor of the Blackwell *Companion to Old Norse-Icelandic Literature and Culture*

(2005) and has published numerous articles on Old Norse-Icelandic literature and related subjects.

Russell Poole is Distinguished University Professor, emeritus, in the Department of English at Western University (University of Western Ontario), Canada. His research centres upon skaldic and other medieval poetry in Scandinavia and the British Isles. His publications include *Viking Poems on War and Peace* (1991), *Old English Wisdom Poetry* (1998), and the edited volume *Skaldsagas* (2000). He has also collaborated in two co-edited volumes: *Verbal Encounters: Anglo-Saxon and Old Norse studies for Roberta Frank* (2004), with Antonina Harbus, and *Egil the Viking Poet* (2015), with Laurence De Looze, Jón Karl Helgason and Torfi H. Tulinius. He is current Editor-in-Chief of *Viking and Medieval Scandinavia*.

Hubert Seelow retired recently from the Professorship of Scandinavian Studies (Nordische Philologie) in the Department of German and Comparative Studies of the University of Erlangen-Nuremberg (Friedrich-Alexander-Universität Erlangen-Nürnberg). His research interests and publications focus on medieval and post-medieval Icelandic manuscripts and literature. He has published a text edition of *Hálfs saga ok Hálfsrekka* (1981) and is author of *Die isländischen Übersetzungen der Deutschen Volksbücher* (1989).

†Desmond Slay (1927-2004), much of whose academic life was spent at the University of Aberystwyth, was a philologist whose meticulous studies of Icelandic texts and manuscripts included a study of the manuscript tradition of *Hrólfs saga kraka* and a diplomatic edition of that saga (both 1960), as well as facsimile editions of several important codices, including the Codex Scardensis (*Skarðsbók*), whose whereabouts in Britain he was instrumental in discovering.

INTRODUCTION[1]

1. *Skaldic Poetry of the Scandinavian Middle Ages* – a New Edition

This two-part volume is the fifth to be published of nine planned volumes of *Skaldic Poetry of the Scandinavian Middle Ages* (*SkP*), and it is Volume VIII in the overall sequence (*SkP* VII appeared in 2007, *SkP* II in 2009, *SkP* I in 2012 and *SkP* III in 2017). The series consists of eight volumes of text and a ninth containing indices and a bibliography of items cited in the editions. The aim of this new edition, which is discussed in detail in Section 2 in the General Introduction to the series (published in *SkP* I, xxvii-xxxix), is to provide a critical edition, with accompanying English translation and notes, of the corpus of Scandinavian poetry from the Middle Ages, excluding only the Poetic Edda and closely related poetry, and the *rímur*.

The edition is based on a thorough assessment of all known manuscript evidence and on a review of previous editions and commentaries, including Finnur Jónsson's *Den norsk-islandske skjaldedigtning* (*Skj* A and B), which has been the standard edition of the corpus since the early twentieth century. The interpretation of individual stanzas and the layout of the corpus differ in many instances from those of *Skj*, often reflecting a more conservative approach to the manuscript sources, and *Skj* references (titles, dates, page numbers) are provided throughout the present edition for purposes of comparison. *SkP* is available in book form and as an electronic edition. The electronic edition is fully searchable and includes images of most manuscript texts used in the edition, along with transcriptions of the main manuscript text for each stanza and of other select manuscripts.

Whereas Finnur Jónsson was able to produce his edition single-handedly, current academic conditions make it difficult for one scholar to undertake such Herculean tasks. This edition is thus the outcome of a group effort, directed by six General Editors: Margaret Clunies Ross, Kari Ellen Gade, Guðrún Nordal, Edith Marold, Diana Whaley and Tarrin Wills. Editorial work on individual poems and fragments has been carried out by a consortium of Old Norse scholars, who have

---

[1] This Volume Introduction is by Margaret Clunies Ross, except for Section 6, which is the work of Kari Ellen Gade. Section 1 is a revised version of Section 1 of the Introduction to *SkP* VII, also written by Margaret Clunies Ross, and Section 9 is a revised version of Section 10 of *SkP* VII. All other sections are specific to Volume VIII.

specialist expertise in the field of skaldic poetry. These editors' work is individually acknowledged in this and the other seven volumes of edited poetic texts. One or more of the General Editors are responsible for the overall supervision of each volume as Volume Editor(s); Margaret Clunies Ross is Volume Editor for *SkP* VIII. Tarrin Wills is responsible for the electronic edition (comprising all nine volumes), and Hannah Burrows is in charge of Volume IX, comprising the bibliography and indices. She also checks the bibliographical information for each published volume.

2. The Icelandic *fornaldarsaga*

The term *fornaldarsaga* (pl. *fornaldarsögur*) 'saga of the ancient time', or mythical-heroic saga, refers to a sub-genre of the medieval Icelandic saga. Depending on the classification one adopts, the *fornaldarsaga* sub-genre includes approximately twenty-five sagas (cf. Torfi H. Tulinius 2005, 448; Clunies Ross 2010a, 31; or about thirty-five, according to the *Stories for All Time: the Icelandic fornaldarsögur* database).[2] Twenty-one of these are represented in this edition, although two of them are sometimes regarded as *riddarasögur* 'sagas of knights' or romances, namely *Máguss saga jarls* 'The Saga of Jarl Mágus' (*Mág*) and *Þjalar-Jóns saga* 'The Saga of File-Jón' (*ÞJ*). Each of these two sagas displays some characteristics of the *fornaldarsaga*, however, including a few stanzas of poetry, unlike the *riddarasaga* sub-genre, which normally contains no verse. Poetry is an important component of the Icelandic *fornaldarsaga*, being found in about eighty percent of the corpus, and in a proportion varying from a low of one to three stanzas per saga to a high of 141 in the later manuscripts of *Ǫrvar-Odds saga* 'The Saga of Arrow-Oddr' (*Ǫrv*).

The term *fornaldarsaga* is not of medieval origin but was created by the Danish philologist Carl Christian Rafn (1795-1864) in the early nineteenth century, when, in 1829-30, he published a collection of thirty-one texts in three volumes that he called *Fornaldar Sögur Nordrlanda* 'Sagas of the Ancient Time of the Northern Lands' (*FSN*). Most of the narratives Rafn brought together have a number of characteristics in common that differentiate them from other sub-groups of the Icelandic saga. Firstly they are set in the prehistoric period, the *fornǫld* 'ancient time', and before the settlement of Iceland (c. 870-930 AD). Their protagonists may sometimes be claimed as ancestors of Icelanders from the historical period. Second, the geographical settings of *fornaldarsögur* are either in mainland Scandinavia, usually either Norway or Sweden, or in some more exotic location, such as the place called Bjarmaland in several sagas, which is usually identified with Permia, an area on the Kola Peninsula in the vicinity of the White Sea in northwest Russia. Thirdly, the *fornaldarsaga* world admits of a greater number of paranormal

---

[2] Accessed 16 November 2016. Hereafter this website will be abbreviated as *Stories for All Time*.

beings and happenings than one usually finds in some other kinds of saga literature, although this distinction is by no means hard and fast. Fourthly, and importantly for this edition, the majority of the *fornaldarsǫgur* contain poetry, and most of it is in eddic metres (*fornyrðislag*, *ljóðaháttr* and *málaháttr* for the most part), although variants of *dróttkvætt* are used in some sagas, most notably in *Ragnars saga loðbrókar* 'The Saga of Ragnarr Hairy-breeches' (*Ragn*) and in the anonymous poem *Krákumál* 'Speeches of the Crow' (Anon *Krm*). The metres of *fornaldarsaga* poetry are discussed in Section 6 below.

Various attempts have been made to distinguish sub-categories within the *fornaldarsaga*, the best-known being that of Helga Reuschel (1933), who identified three sub-categories of *fornaldarsaga*: heroic sagas, viking sagas and sagas of adventure. Hermann Pálsson (1985b), on the other hand, identified only two categories: heroic legends and adventure tales. While it may not be possible or desirable to establish hard-and-fast distinctions between groups of *fornaldarsǫgur* (Lönnroth 2003), it can be seen that the majority of these sagas that incorporate a good deal of poetry are heroic sagas, which depend on legends that are recorded in many cases in other early Germanic literary traditions and in the *Gesta Danorum* 'History of the Danes' (c. 1200) of Saxo Grammaticus.[3] Sagas of this type include *Gautreks saga* 'The Saga of Gautrekr' (*Gautr*), *Hálfs saga ok Hálfsrekka* 'The Saga of Hálfr and Hálfr's champions' (*Hálf*), *Hervarar saga ok Heiðreks* 'The Saga of Hervǫr and Heiðrekr' (*Heiðr*), *Hrólfs saga kraka* 'The Saga of Hrólfr Pole-ladder' (*Hrólf*), *Ragn* and *Vǫlsunga saga* 'The Saga of the Vǫlsungar' (*Vǫls*).

In some of the poetry in this group of sagas clear thematic and verbal parallels can be established with comparable verse in other languages, as, for example, between the prose narrative and stanzas recorded in *Ásmundar saga kappabana* 'The Saga of Ásmundr, Slayer of Champions' (*Ásm*), the Old High German *Hildebrandslied* 'Lay of Hildebrand' and Book VII of Saxo's *Gesta Danorum*. Likewise, incidents described in some heroic *fornaldarsǫgur* are attested indirectly by early Norse skaldic poetry, a case in point being the fire-kenning *bani Hǫalfs* 'slayer of Hálfr' recorded in the late ninth- or early tenth-century poem *Ynglingatal* 'Enumeration of the Ynglingar' (Þjóð *Yt* 6/7[1]), in an allusion to the hall-burning of the legendary king Hálfr and his men, as told in *Hálf*.

On the other hand, sagas set in the Viking Age, like *Friðþjófs saga ins frœkna* 'The Saga of Friðþjófr the Bold' (*Frið*), and more fantastic adventures involving mistaken identity, shape-shifting, bridal quests and similar motifs, such as we find

---

[3] In Volume VIII and in all subsequent volumes of *SkP* references to the *Gesta Danorum* are to the edition *Saxo* 2015, which has a Latin text and facing English translation. In earlier volumes of *SkP* the edition *Saxo* 2005 has been cited, often together with the English translation and commentary of Fisher and Davidson 1979-80.

in *Hjálmþés saga ok Ǫlvis* 'The Saga of Hjálmþér and Ǫlvir' (*HjǪ*), *Mág*, and *Sturlaugs saga starfsama* 'The Saga of Sturlaugr the Industrious' (*StSt*), have no parallels in cognate early Germanic literatures or earlier Old Norse witnesses and are not likely to be of very great age.

The so-called Hrafnista group of *fornaldarsögur* (named for the Norwegian island from which the family of the Hrafnistumenn is said to have come), *Áns saga bogsveigis* 'The Saga of Án Bow-bender' (*Án*), *Gríms saga loðinkinna* 'The Saga of Grímr Hairy-cheek' (*GrL*), *Ketils saga hœngs* 'The Saga of Ketill Salmon' (*Ket*) and *Ǫrvar-Odds saga* 'The Saga of Arrow-Oddr' (*Ǫrv*), forms a specific unit within the *fornaldarsaga* corpus and owes its cohesion as a group both to internal genealogical links between the protagonists, to thematic and geographical parallels, and to external links claimed with Icelandic families of the settlement age. *Ǫrv*, while belonging within the Hrafnista group, also has characteristics of both the heroic group and the fantastic adventure type of saga.

Although the earliest extant manuscript witnesses to the *fornaldarsaga* genre date from the early fourteenth century (see Section 4 below), there are several kinds of evidence that support the idea that this sub-genre of the saga may have been among the first to develop in Iceland during the twelfth and early thirteenth centuries. This was a period of intense interest among Western European writers in constructing the legendary past of their own communities, as witness Geoffrey of Monmouth's *De gestis Britonum* 'Concerning the deeds of the Britons' (c. 1136), clearly known to some Icelanders in the twelfth century (see Section 3 below), and the *Gesta Danorum* of Saxo Grammaticus, completed c. 1200 and, by Saxo's own admission, based in part on 'their packed store of historical treasures' (*quorum thesaurus historicarum rerum pignoribus refertos*) that his Icelandic informants had made available to him (*Saxo* 2015, I, Pr. 1. 4, pp. 6-7). Indeed, although Saxo's treatment of his sources is different from the treatment of similar subjects found in *fornaldarsögur*, the many parallels between them are significant. They seem to indicate that the combination of heroic poetry with a prose narrative frame had become a viable means for the literary expression of the subject of legendary prehistory, whether in Latin or a vernacular language, by about 1200 (cf. Torfi H. Tulinius 2002, 48-69). Around the same time sagas with subjects from the historical period after the ninth century were evolving along parallel lines, but in those cases writers were combining prose with skaldic rather than eddic poetry in what would become the sub-genres of the kings' sagas (*konungasögur*) and the sagas of Icelanders (*Íslendingasögur*).

A description of entertainment at a wedding feast at the Icelandic farm Reykjahólar in the year 1119 is found in the contemporary saga (*samtíðarsaga*) *Þorgils saga ok Hafliða* 'The Saga of Þorgils and Hafliði' (Brown 1952, 17-18, 72-3, 75-6), composed more than one hundred years after the event it purports to describe, and for that reason regarded with scepticism by some scholars (e.g. von

See 1981c). If the colourful details of this description can be trusted (Clunies Ross 2010a, 18-20) – and one might think such detail would be unlikely to have been invented – at least one of the entertainments there was a *fornaldarsaga* about the legendary hero Hrómundr Gripsson, which included many stanzas (*ok margar vísur með*). There is no extant medieval version of this saga, but Hrómundr's story survives in *rímur* (*Griplur*) from the fifteenth century and in a seventeenth-century *fornaldarsaga* version probably based on the *rímur*. The narrator of *Þorgils saga* adds that King Sverrir of Norway (r. 1177-1202) was entertained with this story, and it is further said that 'he called such lying stories the most entertaining' (*ok kallaði hann slíkar lygisǫgur skemtiligastar*). At the same time, the narrator states, some people are able to trace their genealogies to Hrómundr Gripsson, and presumably those people, like the descendants of the Hrafnistumenn, had good reason to consider the stories about their ancestors to hold at least a modicum of truth.

The description of the Reykjahólar wedding entertainment suggests that some form of the *fornaldarsaga*, incorporating both prose and verse, was being performed before an audience in the early twelfth century, presumably presented and transmitted orally. Another kind of evidence to support the idea that moves were afoot to link poetry and prose in a kind of legendary history comes from the presumed literary development during the twelfth and thirteenth centuries of the corpus of poetry now referred to as the Poetic (or Elder) Edda (cf. Larrington, Quinn and Schorn 2016). This term refers in the first instance to poems in alliterative verse with pre-Christian mythological and legendary subjects recorded in compilations with little or only a small amount of prose contextualisation. There are in fact only two such compilations extant, the more important being the late thirteenth-century Codex Regius of the Poetic Edda, GKS 2365 4°, of c. 1270, the other being the early fourteenth-century fragment AM 748 I a 4°, of c. 1325. Other poems of similar type were recorded in manuscripts containing versions of Snorri Sturluson's *Edda* and in the historical compilations *Hauksbók* and *Flateyjarbók* (for details of the preservation contexts of poetry in eddic metres, see Clunies Ross 2016).

It has been argued (Lindblad 1954; 1980) that the Codex Regius collection of eddic poetry had a complex prehistory and may have been in process for some decades during the thirteenth century before it achieved the form in which we know it. The idea that collections of mythological and heroic poetry may have been brought together over a period of some years has also been extended to include a surmise that Snorri Sturluson may have had access to such a collection of mythological poems when he composed the *Gylfaginning* 'The Delusion of Gylfi' (*Gylf*) section of his *Edda* (*SnE*) in the 1220s. Drawing attention to the way in which *fornaldarsögur* such as *Vǫls* create a prosimetrum comprising a great deal of eddic poetry linked by means of a relatively superficial prose narrative, Anne Holtsmark (1965c) suggested that both the evolution of the *fornaldarsaga* and the gathering together of eddic poems in a compilation may have been parallel developments, with the origin of each lying in the desire to amplify in prose the unspoken but generally understood context of the action of these traditional poems, especially those based on heroic legend.

In the Codex Regius of the Poetic Edda, the explanatory prose links between individual poems and groups of stanzas (termed in German *Begleitprosa*) are much more numerous in the heroic section than in the first part of the collection devoted to mythological poems, where longer explanatory prose passages are confined to *Grímnismál* (*Grí*), *Lokasenna* (*Lok*) and *Vǫlundarkviða* (*Vǫl*). On the evidence of the somewhat sketchy provision of prose narratives in some of the *fornaldarsögur* that include heroic poetry, notably *Vǫls*, *Hálf* and *Heiðr*, it seems plausible to suggest that these sagas developed in much the same way as the Codex Regius collection, but that the impulse to strengthen narrative links between groups of stanzas and whole poems eventually brought about a more balanced kind of prosimetrum in which poetry and prose were better integrated.

Most of the extant manuscripts in which *fornaldarsögur* have been recorded are of quite late date, the majority of them being post-medieval. This makes it difficult to provide authoritative statements about the early history of the sub-genre and the ways in which it developed during the thirteenth and fourteenth centuries. It is also difficult to gauge the relative age of individual sagas, as their texts often exist in several different versions. However, it is clear, where we possess manuscripts of a particular saga of varying age, that both the poetry and the prose underwent change as time went on in response to the changing tastes and interests of the patrons for whom the sagas were being copied or reworked and the capacities of the scribes who wrote them down. It is possible to detect certain themes and changes of emphasis in later versions of a text like *Ǫrv*, for example, which point to new kinds of reception as the tastes of audiences changed (cf. Arnold 2010; Lassen 2009). Recent research into the *fornaldarsögur* has begun to investigate the nature of the sponsorship and likely audiences of these sagas and how the tastes and social expectations of their sponsors may have influenced their reworking into significant compilations (cf. Orning 2012; 2017). What is certain is that most *fornaldarsögur* retained and even increased their popularity in Iceland after the Middle Ages, and this is attested by the very large number of extant paper manuscripts from the fifteenth to the nineteenth centuries (for details see the web site *Stories for All Time*).

As far as the poetry in these sagas is concerned, it is also of varying age in many cases, and is also likely to have been reworked in the process of scribal copying. It is clear from the presence of late, non-metrical linguistic forms in many manuscripts that late- and post-medieval scribes often did not understand the requirements of Old Norse metres and introduced contemporary linguistic features into the texts they were copying or composing (see Sections 6 and 8 below). In several sagas certain groups of stanzas stand out clearly as individual long poems, as in *Heiðr* and *Hálf*, though not all the stanzas within these long poems are necessarily of equal age. In some cases metrical analysis (see Section 6 below) can reveal those parts of the verse component of individual sagas that are earlier than other parts. In other cases it can be seen that certain manuscripts, usually later ones, amplified their poetic texts with the addition of many more stanzas than earlier manuscripts contained. The most striking case of this kind is found in *Ǫrv*. By contrast, there are cases where one can see that a redactor is likely to have cut out stanzas that were in his exemplar. This is the case with the mid-seventeenth-century manuscript of *Gautr*, Holm papp 11 8^{ox} (papp11^x), which omits all but six stanzas of the poetry ascribed to Starkaðr, but retains in the prose text the introductory formula *svá segir Starkaðr* 'so says Starkaðr' in places where the stanzas would be expected to appear in the text, thus indicating that they were probably there in the copyist's exemplar.

3. The poetry in this volume

The poetry in this volume includes all extant poetry that is judged to be of medieval origin in manuscripts of twenty-one *fornaldarsögur*. In addition the volume includes the two poems named *Merlínusspá I-II* 'The Prophecies of Merlin I-II' (GunnLeif Merl I-II), attributed in *Hauksbók*'s version of *Breta saga* 'The Saga of the British' (*Bret*) to the Icelandic monk Gunnlaugr Leifsson (GunnLeif, d. 1218 or 1219). *Bret* is not a *fornaldarsaga*, strictly speaking, but its position as an Old Norse version of Geoffrey of Monmouth's *De gestis Britonum* (or *Historia regum Britanniae* 'History of the kings of Britain') can be understood as creating a legendary history for the British in a manner similar to the Old Icelandic *fornaldarsaga*'s recreation of prehistoric Scandinavian history. In that context, Gunnlaugr's poetic versions of a prose section of Geoffrey's *Historia*, called *Prophetiae Merlini* 'Prophecies of Merlin', find a place in this volume.

The poem *Skaufhala bálkr* '*Bálkr* about Tassel-tail' (Svart *Skauf*), whose author is presented here as the little-known Svartr á Hofstöðum (Svart, d. 1392), is also included in Volume VIII. This poem occurs outside a *fornaldarsaga* context, but is included here as its subject is in part a parody of the *ævikviða* 'life poem' genre, which is found attributed to a number of the protagonists of *fornaldarsögur*, often on the point of death (see the discussion in Section 7.1 below). In Svart *Skauf* the speaker of the poem is a broken-down old fox whose days are numbered, and who reviews his hard life in the presence of his wife, the vixen. The poem shows the probable influence both of the beast fable and the *fornaldarsaga* genre in its tragi-comic imitation of the heroic life.

As is the case with the poetry recorded within sagas of Icelanders, forthcoming in Volume V, the poetry in *fornaldarsögur* is mostly attributed to named speakers who are also characters in the saga narrative, in contrast to the anonymity of the sagas themselves. While the identities of a few such speakers are independently attested from sources outside the *fornaldarsaga* texts, the majority cannot be traced elsewhere and indeed quite a few such speakers clearly belong to the world of myth or fantasy. The editorial policy of *SkP* is to treat all the poetry in this volume, and in Volume V, as the creation of the characters to whom it is attributed and these attributions are retained for convenience in this edition, whether credible or not. The case of Starkaðr gamli 'the Old' Stórvirksson (StarkSt) is a partial exception to editorial practice here, because he is provided with a skald biography and treated (at least in part) as if he had had an historical existence, even though, like the other characters represented as composing and reciting poetry in *fornaldarsögur*, Starkaðr is a figure of legend. However, several external medieval Icelandic sources, like *Skáldatal* 'List of Skalds', the *Háttatal* 'Enumeration of Verse-Forms' section (SnSt Ht^{III}) of *SnE* and the *Third Grammatical Treatise* (*TGT*) treat him as a human poet, so, following this emic classification, he is given a skald biography in this edition. Notwithstanding Starkaðr's status in these Icelandic sources and in Book VI of Saxo Grammaticus's *Gesta Danorum*, the poem *Víkarsbálkr* 'Víkarr's Section' (StarkSt *Vík*), attributed to Starkaðr, which is only recorded in manuscripts of *Gautr*, is edited with other stanzas from that saga in keeping with the general practice of this edition.

Another somewhat anomalous poem in this edition is *Krm*, which is classified in *SkP* as anonymous, even though one can legitimately interpret the manuscript witnesses to it as implying that it was considered to be the composition of the dying hero Ragnarr loðbrók. This poem appears as an integral part of *Ragn* in only one manuscript (AM 147 4° of c. 1400-1500), where it is presented as the utterance of the dying Ragnarr in King Ælle's snake-pit. In other manuscripts it has either been recorded outside a saga context or, in two cases, immediately follows *Ragn* as a kind of appendix. In the present edition it has been associated with the poetry from *Ragn* and *Ragnars sona þáttr* 'The Tale of the Sons of Ragnarr' (*RagnSon*), but edited as a separate item.

4. Manuscripts

The vast majority of extant manuscripts containing Icelandic *fornaldarsögur* are post-medieval and date predominantly from the seventeenth to the late nineteenth centuries. They thus bear witness to the continuing popularity of these stories and indigenous romances (*riddarasögur*) among the Icelandic population and to the vitality of scribal traditions of hand-copying in Iceland (Driscoll 1997, 4-6). The database *Stories for All Time* provides the most up-to-date details of currently known manuscripts of each *fornaldarsaga*, with information on the manuscripts' contents, material condition, provenance and ownership (if known).

The Introductions to individual editions of each *fornaldarsaga* in this volume provide information about known manuscripts of each text and the current and previous editors' discussions of the likely relationships between them, where possible providing a stemma of the extant manuscripts. The reader is referred to these discussions. Unlike the situation with other kinds of Old Icelandic vernacular texts containing poetry, it is often not possible to establish a definitive stemma for individual *fornaldarsǫgur*, because in many cases there is either only one or no parchment or vellum manuscript extant from earlier than the fifteenth century. Instead, there are many post-medieval paper manuscripts that are often likely to descend from a common original, either the one extant medieval manuscript or another medieval exemplar, now lost.

Rather than discuss the manuscript witnesses for each text in this volume one by one, it has seemed more useful to describe here some general characteristics of *fornaldarsaga* manuscripts and then to discuss some of the principal early witnesses in some detail. Most *fornaldarsǫgur* have been preserved in compilations rather than as single items, often together with the same group of companion texts. There are two obvious reasons for such repeated groupings, the first being that one compiler has copied from an earlier exemplar which contained a similar set of sagas, while the second is based on contemporary assumptions that the subject-matter and – particularly – the protagonists of two or more sagas were members of the same extended legendary family, with which the sponsors of such compilations may have felt a connection. This explains, for example, the consistent co-presence of sagas of the Hrafnistumenn in several major compilations of the fifteenth century (e.g. AM 343 a 4° (343a), AM 471 4° (471)) as well as the co-presence of *Gautr* with *Hrólfs saga Gautrekssonar* 'The Saga of Hrólfr Gautreksson' (*HG*) (in, for example, AM 152 fol (152) and Holm papp 11 8^{ox} (papp11^x)) and *StSt* with the saga of his supposed son, Gǫngu-Hrólfr, in *Gǫngu-Hrólfs saga* 'The Saga of Walker-Hrólfr' (*GHr*) (AM 589 f 4° (589f)). The genealogical basis for the arrangement of sagas within compilations can be deduced from many manuscripts.

Most of the *fornaldarsǫgur* in Volume VIII are extant in at least one parchment or vellum manuscript from either the fourteenth or the fifteenth century. However, there are a small number that do not appear in any manuscript from before 1500, including *HjǪ*, *Hrólf* and the independent poem Svart *Skauf*. In some cases, sagas exist in two versions, one probably later than the other, with one of these versions extant only in paper manuscripts. This is the case with the B version of *Frið*, for example. The possible connection of alternative versions of *fornaldarsǫgur* with the evolution of the *ríma* form is discussed below in Section 7.3.

4.1. Manuscripts of fourteenth-century date containing *fornaldarsögur*

The earliest extant manuscript to contain any *fornaldarsögur* is AM 544 4°, known as *Hauksbók* (*Hb*) because it was written for and in part by the Icelandic lawman Haukr Erlendsson (d. 1334). This compilation, which includes many religious and historical texts as well as various sagas, has been described as 'an entire private library, which Haukr, with assistance, wrote for himself' (Stefán Karlsson 1993, 271). All three of the items of interest to the present edition, *Bret* (in unique combination with *Merl I-II*), *Heiðr* and *RagnSon*, occur within the section of the compilation that Haukr is thought to have written himself between 1302-10 (Stefán Karlsson 1964b). This manuscript provides the only texts of *RagnSon* and *Merl I-II*, and a distinctive, often abbreviated, text of *Heiðr*. A facsimile of *Hb* is Hb 1960, and an edition of the whole manuscript is Hb 1892-6; see further the Introductions to *SkP* I, clxvi, II, lxii-lxiii. Separate discussions of the manuscript witnesses to the three above items can be found in their respective Introductions in this volume.

After *Hauksbók*, the second oldest compilation containing *fornaldarsögur* is Holm perg 7 4° (7) of c. 1300-25, originally part of a single codex with AM 580 4° (580), of roughly similar date. Both manuscripts are of Icelandic provenance, though their exact origins are unknown. Ms. 580 contains texts of three *riddarasögur*, *Elíss saga ok Rósamundar* 'The Saga of Elís and Rósamunda' (*Elís*), *Bærings saga* 'The Saga of Bæringr' (*Bær*) and *Flóvents saga* 'The Saga of Flóvent' (*Flóv*), followed by a fragment of *Mág* and the rubric for *HG*, while 7 contains texts of *Konráðs saga keisarasonar* 'The Saga of Konráðr, the Emperor's son' (*Konr*) and *HG*, followed by *Jómsvíkinga saga* 'The Saga of the Jómsvíkingar' (*Jvs*), *Ásm*, *Ǫrv* and the first few chapters of *Egils saga Skallagrímssonar* 'The Saga of Egill Skallagrímsson' (*Eg*). Because of its relatively early date, this manuscript is of considerable importance for the textual history of *Ǫrv*, as it differs in many respects from the later manuscripts of this saga, a matter discussed in detail in the edition in this volume. It is also the only early manuscript to contain the poetry of *Ásm*, as the other pre-1500 text (AM 586 4°) contains no stanzas.

Another relatively early manuscript containing a text of *Ǫrv* is AM 344 a 4° (344a), dated between 1350-1400. Interestingly, this Icelandic manuscript was previously bound together with a text of *Alexanders saga* 'The Saga of Alexander' (*Alex*), perhaps because both works include tales of exotic travel and conquest. Árni Magnússon acquired the codex containing both manuscripts in Norway in 1689 and separated them, and the part containing *Alex*, dated to c. 1280, was later given the siglum AM 519 a 4° (for the facsimile of this manuscript, see Jón Helgason 1966c; de Leeuw van Weenen 2009). The 344a text of *Ǫrv*, whose scribe and provenance are unknown, provides a version of the saga that differs considerably both in its prose and verse components from that of ms. 7, and is thus likely to derive from an exemplar different from that of 7.

The great historical compilation *Flateyjarbók* 'Book of Flatey' (GKS 1005 fol, *Flat*) contains two of the texts edited here, *OStór* and *Sǫrla þáttr* 'The Tale of Sǫrli' (*Sǫrla*), both as additions to the so-called *Greatest Saga* of the Norwegian king Óláfr Tryggvason (*ÓT*). The sole text of *Sǫrla* is in this manuscript, together with the earliest text of *OStór*. The section of the compilation in which these two *þættir* occur is usually dated c. 1382-7. For a fuller description of this codex, see the Introductions to *SkP* I, clxi-clxii, II, lx. There is a facsimile of the manuscript (*Flat* 1930) and an edition of the whole text (*Flat* 1860-8, I-III). Manuscripts of *OStór* and *Sǫrla* are discussed further in the Introductions to those texts below.

From roughly the same period, of the late fourteenth or the very early fifteenth century, comes the Icelandic manuscript NKS 1824 b 4° (1824b), which contains the sole medieval witness to *Vǫls* on fols 1r-51r (the ultimate source of all later paper manuscripts of this saga) and the only complete text of the Y version of *Ragn* (fols 51r-79r), followed by stanzas 1-22/5 of *Krm* (minus st. 16) as a separate appendix. This valuable manuscript is dated to c. 1400-25 or more recently (so *Stories for All Time*) to 1380-1420. The arrangement of the two sagas in this manuscript in a sequence followed by *Krm* is unique in the corpus and probably indicates that whoever had these texts copied in this way was fully aware of the supposed connection between the legendary Vǫlsungar and the family of Ragnarr loðbrók through his second wife Áslaug, who appears in both sagas (see the discussion of this idea in the Introductions to *Ragn* and *Krm* and in Section 7.1 below). The two sagas were edited together by Magnus Olsen (Olsen 1906-8). Ms. 1824b was sent to King Fredrik III of Denmark in the mid-seventeenth century by Bishop Brynjólfur Sveinsson of Skálholt.

Further texts of *fornaldarsögur* are found in manuscripts from the very late fourteenth century or the turn of the fifteenth. These include a fragment of *GHr* in AM 567 XI a 4° from c. 1350-1400, a text of *StSt* from AM 335 4° of c. 1400 (from 1390-1410 according to *Stories for All Time*) and a text of *ÞJ* in a manuscript compilation of *riddarasögur* in Holm perg 6 4° from c. 1375-1425.

4.2. Fifteenth-century manuscripts containing *fornaldarsögur*

A number of large compilations of *fornaldarsögur* date from the fifteenth century and indicate the continuing, and possibly growing, popularity of this kind of saga, along with *riddarasögur*, during this period. There have been several recent studies of some of these compilations, made with an eye to understanding both their context of production and the interests and motivation of the presumably wealthy Icelanders who commissioned them. Relatively few of these manuscripts date from the first half of the century, most being from the mid-century up to c. 1500.

Of perhaps earliest date in the fifteenth century is GKS 2845 4° (2845) of c. 1450 or earlier (1440-60 according to *Stories for All Time*). This moderately decorated Icelandic compilation contains a majority of *fornaldarsögur*. It begins with a single example of the *Íslendingasaga* genre, *Bandamanna saga* 'The Saga of the Confederates' (*Band*), and is then followed by *Norna-Gests þáttr* 'The Tale of Norna-Gestr' (*Norn*), *OStór*, *Rauðúlfs þáttr* 'The Tale of Rauðúlfr' (*Rauð*), *Hálf*, *GHr*, *Yngvars saga víðfǫrla* 'The Saga of Yngvarr The Widely travelled' (*Yngv*), *Eiríks saga víðfǫrla* 'The Saga of Eiríkr The Widely travelled' (*EVíð*) and *Heiðr*, the last-named lacking its conclusion. Thus four sagas edited in this volume appear in 2845. It contains the only medieval text of *Hálf*, all paper copies deriving from it, and one of the chief witnesses to the text of *Heiðr*, while its text of *OStór* is the second oldest after *Flat*. This manuscript was brought from Iceland to the king of Denmark, Christian V, by Þormóður Torfason (Torfæus) in 1662. Its provenance has been much discussed; it probably derives from the west or northwest of Iceland (see *Hálf* 1981, 106 and the facsimile edition by Jón Helgason 1955b, ix-x).

A number of compilations comprising *fornaldarsögur* and *riddarasögur* date from the second half of the fifteenth century. One of the earliest and most significant, dated between 1450 and 1475, is AM 343 a 4° (343a). The relationship of this manuscript to others produced in Iceland about this time has been much discussed, most authoritatively in recent decades by Sanders (2000) in the introduction to his facsimile edition of a manuscript collection of *riddarasögur*, Holm perg 7 fol, now in the Royal Library, Stockholm. Building on the work of earlier scholars, Sanders argued that a cluster of manuscripts, including Holm perg 7 fol, AM 81 a fol and a manuscript of *Konungs skuggsjá* 'The King's Mirror' (*Kgs*), AM 243 a fol, all emanated from the same book-producing milieu about the same time, and he suggested (Sanders 2000, 41, 44-8) that might have been located at the church-farm Möðruvellir, now called Möðruvellir *fram*, in the south of Eyjafjörður, close to the Benedictine monastery of Munkaþverá. He also identified the main hand of 343a as belonging to this milieu, possibly the same as the main hand of Holm perg 7, describing the manuscript as 'principally written in one hand, with quite frequent variations and what could appear to be occasional interruptions by other hands' (Sanders 2000, 42).

Ms. 343a contains fifteen items, most of them *fornaldarsögur* (9) or *riddarasögur* (5). Five of the texts edited in Volume VIII are present here: *Ket* (54r-57v), *GrL* (57v-59v), *Ǫrv* (59v-81v), *Án* (81v-87r) and two leaves of *Bós* (103v-104v). The four sagas of the Hrafnistumenn are arranged in correct genealogical order, Grímr being presented as Ketill's son, Oddr as Grímr's son, and Án more distantly related through the descendants of Hrafnhildr, daughter of Ketill hœngr. Ms. 343a constitutes the base manuscript for the present edition and the earliest and usually the best text of both *Ket* and *GrL*; it is the only parchment manuscript of *Án* extant, all other witnesses dating from the seventeenth century or later. As noted above, there are two earlier manuscripts of *Ǫrv*, 7 and 344a, both with shorter texts that are different in many ways from the much fuller versions of 343a and the similar AM 471 4° (471), to be described below. The differences affect both the prose and the poetry and are discussed in detail in the edition of *Ǫrv* in this volume. Unfortunately, only two leaves of *Bós* are present in this compilation, and they contain no poetry.

The manuscript AM 471 4° (471) is slightly later than 343a, being dated 1450-1500. It contains three sagas of the Hrafnistumenn, *Ket* (fols 49r-56v), *GrL* (fols 57r-60v) and *Ǫrv* (61r-96v). The layout and decoration of this manuscript are good, though some leaves of the original are missing and have been substituted with passages of later origin. The texts of all three of these sagas are very similar, though not identical, to those of the same sagas in 343a. They sometimes have better readings than those in 343a. The other texts in 471 include three late sagas of Icelanders (*Þórðar saga hreðu* 'The Saga of Þórðr the Menace' (*Þórð*), *Króka-Refs saga* 'The Saga of Refr the Sly' (*Krók*) and *Kjalnesinga saga* 'The Saga of the people of Kjalarnes' (*Kjaln*)) and the *riddarasaga Viktors saga ok Blávuss* 'The Saga of Viktor and Blávus' (*Vikt*). The manuscript's provenance is uncertain, although Jónas Kristjánsson (1964, xxxix-xlvi) argued for the farm Hvílft in Önundarfjörður in northwest Iceland on the basis of the similarity of its hand to that of a diploma issued there in 1475. Árni Magnússon obtained 471 from a Magnús Magnússon á Eyri í Seyðisfjörður in eastern Iceland, according to a slip in the manuscript.

The manuscript AM 586 4° (586), dated to c. 1450-99, includes a number of late medieval romances and the *fornaldarsögur Bós* (12v-19r), a fragment of *Hálfdanar saga Eysteinssonar* 'The Saga of Hálfdan Eysteinsson' (*HálfdEyst*) (25v-26v), and another fragment of *Ásm* (33r-33v), which contains no poetry. The principal value of this manuscript to the present edition is that it contains the earliest complete text of *Bós*, which appears in the manuscript followed by *Vilmundar saga viðutan* 'The Saga of Vilmundr from Outside' (*Vilm*) (19r-25r), a *riddarasaga* whose protagonist, Vilmundr, is claimed as Bósi's grandson. There is a facsimile (Loth 1977) of this compilation and of AM 589 f 4° (589f) of c. 1450-99, together with other fragments (AM 589 a-f 4°) that were previously part of a larger codex. Fragment 589f contains texts of *StSt* (1r-13r), followed by the saga of his supposed son, Gǫngu-Hrólfr (*GHr*) (13r-36v). Both sagas are partially defective in this manuscript.

4.3. Manuscripts of *fornaldarsögur* from after 1500

A relatively small number of parchment or vellum manuscripts containing *fornaldarsögur* survive from the first part of the sixteenth century, when animal skins were still being used for writing books, later to be replaced by paper. Two of these are AM 152 fol (152), dated to between 1500-25 and AM 510 4° (510) of c.

1550 (more narrowly 1540-60, according to *Stories for All Time*). The codex 512 is a finely produced manuscript, written in two columns to the page, with red rubrics and coloured initials. It contains one of the main witnesses to the *Íslendingasaga Grettis saga Ásmundarsonar* 'The Saga of Grettir Ásmundarson' (*Gr*) as its first item, followed by a mixture of *fornaldarsögur* (7) and *riddarasögur* (3), as well as *Þórð*. Of the sagas edited in Volume VIII of *SkP*, 512 contains *GHr* (98r-116r), *Mág* (159v-196v) and *Gautr* (196v-201v). This manuscript has the best text of *Mág*, and the best and earliest text of the longer version of *Gautr*. It contains a number of marginalia and other writings about its ownership before it was donated to Árni Magnússon (Jón Helgason 1958, 74-5; Stefán Karlsson 1970c) and includes a statement at the top of fol. 46v (over part of *Gr*) that *þessa sögu hefir skrifað bróðir Bjarnar Þorleifssonar* 'Björn Þorleifsson's brother [Þorsteinn] has written this saga'. The Þorleifssynir lived for the most part at Reykjahólar in Breiðafjörður (see Jóhanna Katrín Friðriksdóttir 2014, 90-2).

The manuscript AM 510 4° (510) contains eight items, two of which are *Íslendingasögur* (*Víglundar saga* 'The Saga of Víglundr' (*Vígl*) and *Finnboga saga ramma* 'The Saga of Finnbogi the Strong' (*Finnb*)), while one, *Jvs*, defies classification, though it is usually categorised as a historical saga with legendary overtones. There are two *riddarasögur* and three *fornaldarsögur*, *Bós* (8v-21r), *Þorsteins saga bæjarmagns* 'The Saga of Þorsteinn Town-Strength' (*ÞorstBm*) (32v-38v) and *Frið* (91v-96r). *ÞorstBm* contains no poetry. This text of *Frið* is the earliest and most complete of the A2 version of the saga (see the Introduction to that saga). The manuscript was written by one Ari Jónsson and one of his sons, either Jón or Tómas (Tumas) Arason, from Súgandafjörður in the northwest of Iceland (information from *Stories for All Time*; cf. Stefán Karlsson 1970d). Árni Magnússon obtained it from Jón Þorkelsson, and he got it from Ingibjörg Pálsdóttir á Eyri í Seyðisfjörður.

Significant paper manuscripts that bear witness to the various versions of *fornaldarsögur* with poetic content are described in the individual Introductions to the editions of the corpus of Volume VIII. A small number of the most important for the present edition, all from the seventeenth century, are mentioned here. The paper manuscript AM 590 b-c 4^{ox} (590b-c^x) is of unknown origin though of Icelandic provenance, and dates from c. 1600-1700. It contains one of the two main manuscripts of the longer version of *Gautr* (1r-10r) followed by a text of the saga of Gautrekr's supposed son, Hrólfr, *HG* (10r-44r). Another important witness to *Gautr* is Holm papp 11 8^{ox} (papp11^x), of 1630-58, which contains the same two sagas in the same order, *Gautr* followed by *HG*. Finally, the manuscript UppsUB R 715^x (R715^x) of c. 1650 (1630-58 according to *Stories for All Time*) deserves mention, as it contains one of the most important texts (the U version) of *Heiðr* (1r-37v) and a text of *Bós* (41r-64r), together with some Humanist poetry and the post-medieval saga *Úlfs saga Uggasonar* 'The Saga of Úlfr Uggason' (cf. Love 2013,

69). This manuscript was brought from Iceland to Sweden by Jón (or Jónas) Rugman in 1658, and was eventually donated to Uppsala University Library with the rest of the collection of the Swedish scholar Petter Salan in 1717.

5. Editions

Individual editions of the sagas included in this volume are discussed in the pages below. It is the purpose of this section to provide an overview of the state of scholarship with regard to editions of Icelandic *fornaldarsögur*, with special reference to the poetry transmitted in them. The reception history of Icelandic *fornaldarsögur* is unlike that of other saga types, in that they were studied and became popular very early in the European Enlightenment, mainly in Sweden and Denmark. They were considered by many people to be historically respectable sources that could be drawn on to confirm the status of Sweden (or Denmark) as the true foundation of early Scandinavian culture. Thus there was a push among Swedish and Danish scholars to obtain manuscripts of these sagas, and, with the invaluable help of Icelandic assistants, to produce editions of them, often accompanied by a Scandinavian vernacular or Latin translation. Many of these editions were among the first examples of medieval Icelandic writings to become known to the European world outside Scandinavia during the seventeenth and eighteenth centuries.

The very first edition of any Icelandic saga was Olaus Verelius' edition of *Gautr* (*Gautr* 1664), which he followed up with an edition of *Bós* in 1666 (*Bós* 1666), and with an edition of *Heiðr* (*Heiðr* 1672) in 1672. Other seventeenth-century editions included texts of Anon *Krm* (Worm 1636), of *OStór* and *Sǫrla* in the 1689 Skálholt edition of *ÓT* (*ÓT* 1689) and Olof Rudbeck's 1697 edition of *Ket* and *GrL* (Rudbeck 1697). Many a *fornaldarsaga* saw its *editio princeps* in the eighteenth century: *HjǪ* (Johan Fredrich Peringskiöld, *HjǪ* 1720), *Ásm* (Peringskiöld 1722), *Hálf*, *Ragn* and *Vǫls* in Erik J. Björner's *Nordiske Kämpa Dater* (Björner 1737) and *RagnSon* (*RagnSon* 1773 in Langebek *et al.* 1772-1878). These editions were pioneer works, but they were often based on manuscripts that are not regarded today as suitable foundations for editions.

The nineteenth century was distinguished both by the first publication of saga series, in which editions of the *fornaldarsögur* as a genre made their appearance, and, as the century progressed, by the first scholarly editions of these texts that began to evaluate the merits of the various versions of each saga to the extent that they were then known. C. C. Rafn's *FSN*, published in three volumes between 1829-30, defined the genre, gave it a name and published texts of thirty-five works, a few of which were not sagas strictly speaking. Later in the century and into the twentieth century, other collected editions of *fornaldarsögur* appeared, many (e.g.

Valdimar Ásmundarson 1885-9, *FSGJ*) aimed at the Icelandic reading public, others (e.g. *SUGNL*) for a wider Scandinavian readership.

The heyday of scholarly editing of *fornaldarsögur* was the period from c. 1885-1914. A number of these sagas were edited for the first time during these years in either diplomatic or critical editions (mostly the former), taking account of manuscript variants and producing either parallel text editions from the most significant manuscripts (e.g. *Ǫrv* 1888, *Gautr* 1900) or separate editions of a particular branch of the text (e.g. Ludvig Larsson's edition of *Frið* 1901). It is no coincidence that it was in this period (1903) that Andreas Heusler and Wilhelm Ranisch produced their anthology of *fornaldarsaga* poetry, *Eddica Minora* 'The Lesser Eddic Poetry' (*Edd. Min.*).

After the early twentieth century new editions of *fornaldarsögur* declined in number, consequent upon a flagging of general scholarly interest in the *fornaldarsögur* as a genre and a parallel increase of interest in sagas of Icelanders and kings' sagas. Very few new scholarly editions of *fornaldarsögur* appeared after 1914, with the exception of *Hálf* 1981 (Seelow), *Heiðr* 1924 (Jón Helgason) and *Heiðr* 1960 (Christopher Tolkien), *Hrólf* 1960 (Slay), *StSt* 1969 (Zitzelsberger), Glazyrina 1996 (*StSt*) and *Vǫls* 1965 (Finch). In addition a small number of editions appeared as unpublished doctoral theses: *Ket* and *GrL* (Anderson 1990), *HjǪ* 1970 (by R. L. Harris), *Mág* 1963 (by Dodsworth) and *Sǫrla* (Barwell 1976). There were also two editions of these texts in Modern Icelandic (*Bós* 1996 (Sverrir Tómasson) and *Ragn* 1985 (Örnólfur Thorsson)).

During recent decades (c.1990 to the present) there has been a distinct revival of interest in *fornaldarsögur*, along with *riddarasögur* (romances), as works of literature, together with the study of the material evidence for their reception and transmission in the late Middle Ages and beyond. The *Stories for All Time* project has assembled a great deal of valuable information about manuscripts, editions, studies and other sources for these sagas, and has so far inspired a small number of new editions, mostly of sagas that do not contain poetry, like *Illuga saga Gríðarfóstra* 'The Saga of Illugi, Gríður's Foster-Son' (Lavender 2015a) and a collaborative electronic edition of *Hrólf* (Driscoll *et al.* 2013), available on the *Stories for All Time* database. Although a number of very interesting studies of *fornaldarsögur* have appeared in the last twenty years, almost no work has been undertaken on the poetry (an exception is Love 2012). It is to be hoped that the present volume will lead to a revival of interest in the verse as well as the prose of these sagas.

It is important that new editions of these texts be undertaken now that scholars have a greater sympathy for late medieval and post-medieval Icelandic manuscripts and a greater understanding of the processes of oral transmission and the many reasons, social, intellectual and material, for why manuscript versions of *fornaldarsögur* may vary. Many of the late nineteenth- and early twentieth-century editions, excellent though they are in many respects, are based on assumptions about textual transmission that have been called into question in recent decades.

Processes of amplification and retraction of both poetry and prose components such as we find in the extant versions of many *fornaldarsögur* were treated by earlier editors as instances of interpolation (or less commonly excision) from an existing, static original text. This approach is reflected in the way in which many earlier editors divided and reordered the poetry from these sagas as it appears in manuscripts in order to express their own views of what in the poetry was authentic and what was later interpolation (cf. Clunies Ross 2013, 184-7). The editions of Finnur Jónsson (*Skj*) and E. A. Kock (*Skald*) are cases in point. Because of the divisions and rearrangements of the *fornaldarsaga* poetry in their editions, it is often very difficult for readers to understand the ways in which the poetry is presented in the various manuscript witnesses.

In *Edd. Min.*, their influential anthology of poetry from certain *fornaldarsögur*, Heusler and Ranisch likewise had no compunction in separating poetry transmitted in the same saga into different categories, depending on their ideas of what constituted ancient poetry and their ideas of its age (see further Section 7.1 below). Their conviction that only certain genres of poetry were authentic and old led them to omit a certain proportion of the poetry in *fornaldarsögur*, on the ground that *eine merklich Kluft trennt diese Schreiberversuche selbst von Dichtungen wie dem Hróksliede und Útsteins Kampfstrophen* 'a marked gap separates these authorial attempts [the poetry they omitted] from poems like the lay of Hrókr and Útsteinn's battle stanzas' (*Edd. Min.* iii). While the present edition recognises the rationale for invoking such a distinction, as can be seen from the normalisation practices described below in Section 8, it also recognises that many *fornaldarsögur* show evidence of continuing reworking, expansion and occasionally retraction of older material, which makes it difficult to use a fixed chronology as the most important criterion for inclusion in such a volume.

6. Metre

As pointed out in Sections 2 (above) and 8 (below), much of the poetry edited in the present volume is metrically irregular, and it is often difficult to put a label on the metre in which a stanza is composed because the same stanza may consist of half-lines in *fornyrðislag*, *kviðuháttr*, *málaháttr* and *ljóðaháttr*. Hence the present section will not attempt to assign each stanza and poem to a specific metre, but rather try to give an overview of the metrical developments that can be detected within this poetic corpus and offer tentative explanations for the plethora of metres the stanzas display.

Because the manuscripts in which the poetry is preserved are young (see Section 4 above), the extant manuscripts have usually gone through several stages of reworking, with individual scribes often miscopying or changing the text to incorporate later linguistic forms and new metrical features. Sometimes such changes are fairly easy to detect. For example, even though scribes still recognised a form such as the negative clitic *-at* appended to a finite verb, they would routinely modernise and replace the clitic with the negation *eigi/ei* or *ekki*. Syntactic simplification, especially the insertion of personal pronouns, is also extremely common. The following line from *Hálf* serves to illustrate this: *Hálf* 57/1 *Bað hann ekki við dauða*.[4] This Type A3*-line is hypermetrical (*málaháttr*), but if we delete the pronoun *hann* 'he' and replace the negation *ekki* 'not' with the clitic *-at*, the line becomes a regular Type A3 *fornyrðislag* line: *Baðat við dauða*. Sometimes a scribe would change a word in an odd half-line, which would result in another change in the following, even half-line. In the earliest manuscript (603) of *Svart Skauf*, for example, st. 3/7-8 reads as follows: *þrír yrmlingar | og þeira dóttir* (Types D, aA2). In the later manuscript of the same poem, Rask87[x], the alliterating numeral *þrír* 'three' has been replaced by the adjective *armastir* 'the most miserable', probably to achieve double alliteration in an odd line, which prompted the insertion of the numeral *ein* 'one' in the even line to preserve the alliteration between the two half-lines. The new long-line, *armastir yrmlingar | og ein þeira dóttir*, defies metrical classification.

It is clear that, at least during the fourteenth century, alliteration was losing its structuring power and had been reduced to a mere adornment. Words belonging to lexico-grammatical categories that normally would be too weakly stressed to alliterate, such as the conjunction *at* 'that', are used in stressed positions, as in *Heiðr* 36/3-4 **at** *þér skuluð* | **all**ir liggja (Types A2k, A2). Often alliteration is found on the second rather than on the first lift, as in *Frið* 30/1-2 *Hafa skal ek* **b**aug | ór **b**eggja **h**öndum (Types E, aA), and there is an increasing amount of double alliteration in even lines (e.g. *Hálf* 17/1-2 **Ás**mundr **h**efir | **o**ss **u**m **u**nnit). In some cases, such double alliterations are demonstrably scribal, as in Svart *Skauf* 5/4 where ms. 603 reads *sem eftir sitja* (Type aA2), which has been changed to *sem eftir eru* (a *ljóðaháttr* half-line) in the younger manuscript Rask87[x]. To be sure, alliteration on the second lift in odd and even lines, double alliteration in even lines and, occasionally, alliteration on words that ought to be weakly stressed all occur in the poetry in the Poetic Edda as well (see Suzuki 2014, 339-41), but by no means with the frequency encountered in the *fornaldarsögur* poetry. In some cases alliteration is found in even lines only, and there is no alliteration between the two half-lines, as in *HjǪ* 38/1-4 *Statt upp, Hástigi, | ok gef rúm gestum | mönnum velbornum | furðu farmóðum*, and in other instances we appear to be dealing with rhythmical prose, with or without

---

[4] Here and in the following, alliterating letters are emphasised (bolded). For the metrical types referred to in this section, see the overview in the General Introduction to *SkP* I, liii-liv.

alliteration: *Heiðr* 116 *Eigi gera Húnar oss felmtraða,* | *né hornbogar yðar*; *HjǪ* 22/1-4 *Hver ertu,* | *þrifnust fljóða,* | *hýrlunduð með kinn* | *ok fagra lokka*?

As far as phonetic changes are concerned, the change that had the greatest impact on metre was desyllabification of final -*r* after a consonant (-*r* > -*ur* | C-), which took place during the fourteenth century, although the overt representation of excrescent -*u*- only gradually becomes widespread in the manuscripts (see *ANG* §161). Desyllabification added new syllables and new metrical positions to a line, which can be illustrated by *Ǫrv* 54/1 *Gekk skarpr Þórðr*. This is a catalectic *kviðuháttr* Type C-line with three metrical positions, but if *skarpr* is desyllabified to *skarpur*, we achieve a *fornyrðislag* Type B-line (*Gekk skarpur Þórðr*), if *Þórðr* rather than *skarpr* is desyllabified, the line becomes a *fornyrðislag* Type C-line (*Gekk skarpr Þórður*), and if both words are desyllabified, the line turns into a *málaháttr* Type aA-line with anacrusis (*Gekk skarpur Þórður*). After desyllabification, a *fornyrðislag* B-line, such as GunnLeif *Merl I* 9/5 *Hét yngva vinr*, would be transformed into a *ljóðaháttr* half-line, *Hét yngva vinur*, ending in a short-stemmed disyllable, as would an E/D4-line such as *Merl I* 39/6 *mannfjǫlða kemr* (> *mannfjǫlða kemur*). In the poetic corpus edited in the present volume, clear instances of desyllabification can be confirmed for Svart *Skauf* (also corroborated by the date of this poem), and for the stanzas attributed to Hreggviðr in *Gǫngu-Hrólfs saga* (*GHr* sts 1-3), which must also date from the fourteenth century.

Below follows a brief outline of the metres used in the poetry edited in this volume, namely, *dróttkvætt* with variants, *fornyrðislag*, *kviðuháttr*, *málaháttr* and *ljóðaháttr* (for a more detailed discussion, see Section 4 of the General Introduction in *SkP* I, li-lxvii). Two stanzas, *Frið* 9 and *Sǫrla* 1, are composed in *runhent* and *Haðarlag* respectively (see *SkP* I, lix-lx, lxiv-lxv, lxvii).

Dróttkvætt

A *dróttkvætt* stanza consists of eight lines that are usually divided metrically and syntactically into two four-line half-stanzas (*helmingar*), and each *dróttkvætt* line consists of six metrical positions, with two alliterative staves in the odd lines alliterating with the first stressed syllable (*hǫfuðstafr* 'main stave') in the following even line (see *SkP* I, lx-lxi, lxv-lxvii). Each line ends in a cadence – a long syllable followed by an enclitic short syllable – and each line contains two internal rhymes (*hendingar*) that consist of different vowels and similar post-vocalic environment (*skothending*) in odd lines and similar vowels and post-vocalic environment (*aðalhending*) in even lines. The second *hending* in each line always falls on the long syllable in the cadence. Consider the following couplet (internal rhymes are italicised):

ÓStór 7/1-2
*Ann*at var, þá er *inn*i.
*Orm*r at Hildar st*orm*i

Very few of the stanzas edited in this volume are composed in regular *dróttkvætt* (e.g. *Gautr* 7, *ÞJ* 1-2); rather, they show irregularities in the distribution and quality of internal rhymes found in the *dróttkvætt* variants *háttlausa* 'formless' (SnSt *Ht* 67^{III}) and *munnvǫrp* 'mouth-throwings' (SnSt *Ht* 66^{III}). See, e.g. *Án* 1, 3, *Frið* 2-3, 5-7, 10, 12-13, 15, 28-9, 31, 33, 37, *OStór* 2, 4-8, 11. All stanzas in *Ragn* (and *RagnSon* st. 1), aside from sts 38-40, which are in *fornyrðislag*, are in variants of *dróttkvætt*, and these stanzas constitute the bulk of the stanzas with six metrical positions. Anon *Krm* (*Ragn*) is very regular metrically (aside from the use of internal rhyme, see Introduction to Anon *Krm*), and, judging from the metrical types and metrical fillers used in that poem, it was not composed by the same poet(s) who composed the other stanzas in *Ragn* (which is also supported by the manuscript evidence; see Introduction to Anon *Krm*).

Fornyrðislag

This is the Norse variant of the Germanic long-line, in which each half-line has four metrical positions and alliteration – one or two staves in the odd lines alliterating with (usually) the first stressed syllable in the even line, which has one alliterative stave as in *dróttkvætt* (see *SkP* I, lii-lv, lxiv-lxvii):

> GunnLeif *Merl II* 7/1-2
> Illr es annarr; | allir svelta

The bulk of the poetry in the *fornaldarsögur* is based on *fornyrðislag*, but in many cases the metre is highly irregular, and we often find catalectic lines and *kviðuháttr* lines, *málaháttr* lines, and *ljóðaháttr* half-lines interspersed with *fornyrðislag*. Of the longer poems, GunnLeif *Merl I* and *II* 1-61, 68 are in *fornyrðislag*, as is most of Starkaðr's *Víkarsbálkr* (*Gautr* 9-24, 33-41), Ǫrvar-Oddr's so-called *Ævidrápa* (*Ǫrv* 71-141) and Svart *Skauf*, although the latter also contains quite a few hypermetrical lines and some hypometrical lines, and shows clear signs of a late date of composition. Some of the odd *fornyrðislag* lines in GunnLeif *Merl I-II* are rather peculiar, because they are characterised by a tendency for the second alliteration in Types E and B (and C2) to fall on the second lift rather than the first, as in *Merl I* 31/1 *stór verða rǫk* (see also *Merl I* 38/1, 52/7, 86/1, 91/7, 96/1, 101/7, *Merl II* 4/5, 44/5). This is unusual in such an early poem, and it could be a conscious choice by Gunnlaugr (placing additional stress right before the metrical caesura) and also explain why he switches to catalectic *kviðuháttr* at the end of *Merl II* (sts 62-7). Both *Merl I* (st. 43/5, 7) and *Merl II* (sts 46/5, 7, 9, 11, 47/3) also contain *kviðuháttr* lines interspersed with *fornyrðislag*.

Kviðuháttr

This metre is a variant of *fornyrðislag* in which all odd lines are catalectic and have three metrical positions, while the even lines have four metrical positions and the same structure as even *fornyrðislag* lines (see *SkP* I, lx, lxv-lxvii):

Gautr 26/1-2
Átti sér
erfivörðu

There are no separate poems in *kviðuháttr* edited in the present volume, but GunnLeif *Merl* II 62-7 and part of Starkaðr's *Vík* (*Gautr* 25-32) are in *kviðuháttr*. Like *Merl* I-II, the latter also has *kviðuháttr* lines mixed with *fornyrðislag* (sts 9/1, 3, 10/7, 11/1, 14/3, 18/3, 23/3, 35/3, 37/3, 5, 7, 38/7, 40/3, 41/3, 7). Other stanzas in *kviðuháttr* are *Hrólf* 7 and *Ǫrv* 37, and, as mentioned above, many of the stanzas in *fornyrðislag* contain *kviðuháttr* lines.

Málaháttr

Málaháttr is an expanded variant of *fornyrðislag* with five (rarely six) metrical positions and alliteration usually falling as in *fornyrðislag*, although the main stave in even lines may occur further back than the first stressed syllable (see *SkP* I, lv-lvii):

Ket 5/5-6
Friðmálum mæla | mun ek eigi við Finn ragan

The metre is characterised by an increase in the inventory of lines with anacrusis and by more syllables both in anacrusis and in internal dips, many of which carry secondary stress. Because of the scribes' (and poets') tendency to insert additional words into poetic lines (see above) and linguistic changes taking place during the fourteenth century, such as desyllabification of final *-r* (see above), many of the lines which earlier may have been *fornyrðislag* or *kviðuháttr* lines were turned into *málaháttr* during manuscript transmission. Hence, even though there are very few stanzas in the present corpus that are composed in fairly 'pure' *málaháttr* (see, e.g. *HjǪ* 8-9, 17, 20, 24, 30, 40-42b, 44, 46, *Ket* 5, 14-15, 17, 26, 34-41), *málaháttr* lines in general abound in poetry from the *fornaldarsögur*.

Ljóðaháttr

This metre, which is unique to Scandinavia, is characterised by the sequence of two alliterative half-lines, with alliteration as in *fornyrðislag*, *kviðuháttr* and *málaháttr*, followed by a full line with (usually) internal alliteration. The full line ends either in a monosyllable or in a disyllable with a short stem, unless the line-final word is a compound (see *SkP* I, lvi-lvii):

Gautr 3/1-3
Allar vættir, | er í jörðu búa,
vilja Fjölmóðar fé fara

A good deal of scholarly attention has been devoted to the structure of the full line (cf. Sievers 1879, 353-72; 1893, 83-9; Heusler 1956, 239-40; overview in von See

1967, 54-5; Suzuki 2014, 577-625), but so far without yielding a satisfactory description of the metrical structure of *ljóðaháttr* half-lines, which is very free (cf. Sievers 1879, 372-4; 1893, 89-90; Heusler 1956, 236-9; Suzuki 2014, 665-739). In general, all metrical types found in *fornyrðislag*, *kviðuháttr* and *málaháttr* odd and even half-lines can also occur in odd and even *ljóðaháttr* half-lines, but in addition, this metre allows half-lines that have no correspondence in the other Old Norse alliterative metres, such as lines consisting only of two syllables (*Hávm* 76/1 (*NK* 29) *Deyr fé* 'Cattle dies'), lines that are longer than in other metres (*Hávm* 108/4 (*NK* 33) *ef ec Gunnlaðar né nytac* 'if I do not enjoy Gunnlǫð'), and, above all, half-lines that contain an abundance of short-stemmed, stressed disyllables that mirror the line-end of full lines, such as *Hávm* 15/1 (*NK* 19) *Þagalt oc hugalt* lit. 'silent and thoughtful', *Vafþr* 10/4 (*NK* 46) *ofrmælgi mikil* 'abundant chatter', *Vafþr* 23/4 (*NK* 48) *himin hverfa* 'travel the sky', *Hávm* 18/4 (*NK* 19) *hverio geði* 'what kind of sense' and *Vafþr* 8/5 (*NK* 46) *hefi ec lengi farit* 'I have travelled for a long time' (see also *Gautr* 3/2 *er í jörðu búa* above). Most of these disyllables were likely resolved, and if so, many are in violation of the rule that the second lift in alliterative half-lines ought not to resolve.

There are around sixty stanzas in *ljóðaháttr* consisting of two half-lines plus a full line in the poetic corpus from the *fornaldarsögur*, and almost half of those stanzas come from Gestumblindi's *Heiðreks gátur* (*Heiðr* 48-53, 55-63, 65-73, 77, 79, 81). The remaining *ljóðaháttr* stanzas are found in *Gautr* (sts 1-6), *HjǪ* (sts 4-5, 10-11) and *Ket* (sts 4, 13, 16, 18, 22-3, 27-33). All of these sequences of *ljóðaháttr* stanzas are recited in connection with gnomic poetry (*Heiðr*) and encounters between a protagonist and supernatural beings (*HjǪ*, *Ket*; cf. the so-called Hrímgerðarmál in *HHj* 12-30); in the satirical Dalafíflar episode with semi-proverbial content in *Gautr*, the metre may have been used consciously to underscore the parody that plays out.

What seems to have escaped attention, however, is that a number of lines in the *fornaldarsögur* poetry (and in such late poetry as Svart *Skauf*) that are often regarded as metrically irregular are similar in structure to *ljóðaháttr* half-lines, and particularly to the lines with two short stressed syllables given above. Consider the following lines, which will have to suffice as examples of this: *Frið* 1/3 *gamanferðum*, *GrL* 7/5 *nauðig gefin*, *Hálf* 3/8 *granir þínar*, *Heiðr* 111/5 *Þar opt Gotar*, *HjǪ* 32/6 *þeir sem beztir eru*, *HjǪ* 29/8 *búaz mega*, *Ket* 20/6 *á hólm til sela*; cf. Svart *Skauf* 1/3 *leingi búið*, 24/3 *upp og ofan*, 21/6 *ferlíki mikið*, 31/7 *rifið af þönum*, 10/7 *en að höndum kominn*, 12/3 *sem seggir munu*, 41/4 *hart til bana*.

It would appear, then, that the development that took place linguistically and in the course of the written and oral transmission of the stanzas in the *fornaldarsögur* (i.e. syllables added through desyllabification of final -*r*, insertion of personal pronouns, negations, etc.) not only served to relax metrical rules, but the lines that were generated through these changes could easily be accommodated by metrical patterns that already existed, such as those found in the hypermetrical *málaháttr* and in the *ljóðaháttr* half-lines. The new patterns most likely reinforced the use of these metrical types and contributed to later poets availing themselves of them in their poetic compositions when they augmented the corpus of *fornaldarsögur* poetry, often creating a mixture of metres within one poem.

The question is whether metrical analysis, despite all uncertainties, can tell us anything about the unity of the longer poems in the *fornaldarsögur* and about the age of the poetry these sagas contain. In the following, we shall take a brief look at two longer poems, Starkaðr's *Vík* (*Gautr* sts 9-41) and Ǫrvar-Oddr's *Ævdr* (*Ǫrv* sts 71-141), as well as the poetry in *Ásmundar saga kappabana* (*Ásm* sts 1-6, 7-10), and attempt to shed some light on these issues.

The first sixteen stanzas of *Vík* (*Vík* 1-16 (*Gautr* 9-24)) are composed in fairly regular *fornyrðislag* with some lines in *kviðuháttr* (see above). That is also the case with the last eight stanzas (*Vík* 25-33 (*Gautr* 33-41)), although the final stanza (*Gautr* 41) is metrically highly irregular, and *Gautr* 24 and 33 also contain metrically suspect lines. The middle section of the poem, *Gautr* 25-32, is composed in *kviðuháttr*, however, and earlier editors have considered these stanzas interpolations in *Vík*, particularly because they are found in only one manuscript (ms. 590b-c^x; see 'Introduction to *Vík* 17-24 (*Gautr* 25-32)' and Section 2 above). The *kviðuháttr* section of *Vík* is metrically very regular, and verbal echoes from such longer *kviðuháttr* poems as Þjóðólfr's *Ynglingatal* (Þjóð *Yt*^{I}) and *Nóregs konungatal* (Anon *Nkt*^{II}), show that the poet who composed these stanzas must have been familiar with this type of genealogical poetry: *Gautr* 27/7 echoes *Nkt* 39/5^{II} *sá réð einn* and *Gautr* 28/1, 30/1, 32/1 echoes Þjóð *Yt* 26/5^I *Réð Ǫleifr*. Hence the *kviðuháttr* stanzas in *Vík* appear to have been composed by one poet, and it is likely that they belonged to the same poem. If we look at the transitional stanzas between the sections in *fornyrðislag* and the *kviðuháttr* part, *Gautr* 24 and 33, both stanzas contain lines that are metrically suspect: st. 24/1 *Sneidda ek honum* is a *ljóðaháttr* half-line, and st. 33/2 *valamálm* is a *kviðuháttr* odd line with suspended resolution in metrical positions 1-2. In addition, st. 33/7 is repeated as st. 34/1. *Vík* appears to end in *medias res* (see Note to *Gautr* 41 [All]), and the last stanza is also highly irregular: l. 2 *er mik sjá* is catalectic and there is no alliteration between ll. 1 and 2; l. 3 *ljótan skolt* is *kviðuháttr*, as is l. 7 *hrjúfan háls*, and l. 6 *hár úlfgrátt* is also catalectic. From a metrical point of view, then, it looks as though the extant *Vík* indeed consisted of at least two poems, one (or more) in *fornyrðislag* and one in *kviðuháttr*, and that these poems were sewn together at a later stage by someone who composed *Gautr* 24 and 33 to bridge the gaps, and who possibly added a final stanza (*Gautr* 41) to conclude the poem.

The seventy-one stanzas of Ǫrvar-Oddr's *Ævdr* (*Ǫrv* sts 71-141) are distributed unevenly across the manuscript witnesses and not all appear in all manuscripts (see 'Introduction to ǪrvOdd *Ævidrápa* 1-71 (*Ǫrv* sts 71-141)' and the table there). All stanzas are composed in *fornyrðislag*, but whereas *Ǫrv* 71-123 are fairly regular metrically, sts 124-33 display metrical features that distinguish them from the earlier and later stanzas in the poem. In sts 71-123 there are lines that correspond structurally to *ljóðaháttr* half-lines (e.g. sts 81/6, 90/4), but a section of the poem that is preserved only in the younger manuscripts, *Ǫrv* 124-33 (see Note to *Ǫrv* 124 [All]), abounds in metrical irregularities, beginning with st. 124, in which ll. 5-8 (see Note there) appear to have been adapted from *HHund II* 43. There is a wealth of hypermetrical aA-lines (*Ǫrv* 126/3, 127/4, 128/8, 129/4, 132/7), one hypermetrical D*-line (*Ǫrv* 133/7), *ljóðaháttr* half-lines (e.g. *Ǫrv* 125/2, 126/2, 132/8, 133/6) and hypometrical lines (e.g. *Ǫrv* 125/1, 126/5, 127/2, 130/7, 133/1, 5), some of whose metricity may be restored if we assume desyllabification. Other lines are simply unmetrical: st. 131/5 *félaga hans níu*, st. 132/4 *gekk skegg af flagði*, and there is no alliteration between ll. 1-2 in st. 129. *Ǫrv* 134-41 are again quite regular metrically, displaying none of the features that characterise *Ǫrv* 124-33. There can be no doubt that we are dealing with different poets and different layers of transmission here, and even if we take textual corruption into account (a few manuscripts show significant variants), it is quite unlikely that *Ǫrv* 71-123/134-41 and *Ǫrv* 123-33 were composed at the same time.

Ásmundar saga kappabana (*Ásm*) contains ten stanzas (*Ásm* sts 1-10) allegedly composed by the two half-brothers Ásmundr (*Ásm* sts 7-10) and Hildibrandr (the so-called 'Hildibrandr's Death song'; *Ásm* sts 1-6), and all stanzas are preserved in one vellum manuscript, ms. 7 (see Introduction to the saga). All stanzas are composed in *fornyrðislag*. *Ásm* sts 1-6 are extremely tight and regular metrically, and they clearly belong to the same poem. Stanza 4 contains an echo from the Old High German *Hildebrandslied* (see Note to st. 4/1-2), and st. 5/1-2 echoes *Sigsk* 65/1-2. Metrically, sts 1-6 bear all the marks of belonging to an older poem (see also Introduction to the saga). The remaining stanzas (*Ásm* sts 7-10) are composed in *fornyrðislag* as well, but they are by no means as regular metrically as sts 1-6. Stanzas 7/2 and 8/5 are *ljóðaháttr* half-lines, st. 7/3-4 are texually corrupt and cannot be restored, sts 8/1 and 9/3 are in *málaháttr* (Types B* and C*), and st. 10/2 is hypometrical. Hence we can only conclude that the stanzas in *Ásm* were composed at different times and by at least two different poets. While sts 1-6 must belong to one older poem, sts 7-10 display features that are younger, and they must have been composed at a later point in time.

We see, then, that in some instances close metrical analysis may yield valuable information about the unity and the age of the poetry in the *fornaldarsögur*, despite the metrical difficulties compounded by the young manuscripts and textual corruption. Yet it is equally clear that the use of metrical criteria for establishing dates and provenance for this poetic corpus will in most cases prove futile.

7. Structure, style and diction of *fornaldarsaga* poetry

7.1. Genres of *fornaldarsaga* poetry

The editors of *Edd. Min.* drew the chronological borderline for inclusion in their anthology of *fornaldarsaga* poetry at the end of the thirteenth century in order to distinguish eddic poetry that still followed the metrical and stylistic rules of older Icelandic verse from later poetry that did not. They also invoked other selection criteria. One of their main tests for inclusion of longer poems or groups of *lausavísur* 'freestanding stanzas' in *Edd. Min.* was whether the poetry conformed to poetic genres (*Gattungen*) that Heusler and Ranisch regarded as characteristic of the verse that belonged *in eine Familie* 'in one and the same family' with the heroic poetry of the Poetic Edda (*Edd. Min.* iii). The contents of *Edd. Min.* are arranged both in terms of their subject-matter and in terms of the stylistic types to which the editors judged they belonged. In the year before *Edd. Min.* appeared, Heusler (1902) had published a long article on the importance of dialogue poetry in Germanic narrative verse, an article that still commands attention today, so it is not surprising that one of the criteria invoked for classifying the poetry in *Edd. Min.* was whether it was primarily dialogic, monologic or involved third-person narrative.

Another criterion employed in *Edd. Min.* was whether a poem could be classified as a *Lied*, a German word sometimes translated into English as 'lay', with the connotation of having originated from an oral tradition as a heroic song- or ballad-like poem of some length. This is a concept that owes a lot to the nineteenth-century idea that heroic songs were the foundation of a Germanic national literature (Heusler 1905; de Vries 1963, 44-71). Poems identified as *lieder* were given pride of place as the first ten items in *Edd. Min.* By contrast, various groups of *lausavísur* and even dialogue poems that reflected 'no epic story' (*keine epische Fabel, Edd. Min.* iv), like the *mannjafnaðr* 'comparison of men' from *Ǫrv*, were accorded an implicitly lesser status, as were various other poetic genres, like dance stanzas, prophecies, riddles and curses. While a modern attempt to identify the various kinds of *fornaldarsaga* poetry follows Heusler and Ranisch in making use of several of their analytical criteria, it pays greater attention to the role the poetry plays in the saga in which it is embedded, though noting that there are some poems within *fornaldarsǫgur*, like *Útsteinskviða* 'Poem of Útsteinn' (Útsteinn *Útkv*) in *Hálf*, that have hardly any points of connection with the narrative of the prose saga and some sagas, like *Hrólf*, that contain very little poetry, where one might have expected a good deal.

There have been relatively few recent critical studies of the conceptual and stylistic building blocks of *fornaldarsaga* poetry in comparison to the poetry of the Poetic Edda, the heroic group in particular. Aside from Heusler (1902), many earlier literary surveys, such as de Vries (1964-7), have tended to see similarities between poetry in *fornaldarsögur* and the verse of the Poetic Edda in terms of specific literary influence from one text to another, rather than in terms of repeatedly used structural and conceptual features. Recently, however, valuable detailed work has been contributed to form the basis of such an analysis by the editors of the Frankfurt-based *Kommentar zu den Liedern der Edda* (*Kommentar* 1997-) and two recent chapters by Schorn (2016a and b) have begun to explore this field.

There are obvious similarities between the Poetic Edda corpus and *fornaldarsögur* poetry on many levels, metrical, thematic and lexical, but there are also differences. Among the similarities is the use of a dialogic narrative frame within which to energise a great variety of narratives of conflict. The dialogue form is a very plastic medium in *fornaldarsögur*, as it is in Saxo (Friis-Jensen 1987, 59), and Heusler was right to draw attention to its probable antiquity as a literary form in Germanic poetry and to its great malleability in *fornaldarsögur*. In *Heiðr* alone, for example, three very different groups of stanzas make use of the dialogue format: the encounter between Hervǫr and her dead father Angantýr amidst the grave mounds of Samsø, the riddles of Gestumblindi and the ancient battle of the Goths and the Huns. Dialogue is also the preferred literary mode even for the presentation of the topic of armed conflict between legendary heroes, like the fight on Samsø (Old Norse Sámsey) between Ǫrvar-Oddr, his companion Hjálmarr and a group of twelve berserks (*Ǫrv* 5-12), recorded in manuscripts of both *Heiðr* and *Ǫrv*. The literary effect of the use of dialogue here, in which each of the heroes expresses his view of the battle, is to give the event a personalised quality that would be difficult to achieve through third-person narrative. Another such example, from *Hálf*, is the focalisation provided by dialogue to the topic of the burning of the Hálfsrekkar inside an enemy hall, as described in the exchange between the foolish King Hálfr, who is blind to imminent danger, and his wise retainer Innsteinn in *Innsteinskviða* 'Poem of Innsteinn' (Innsteinn *Innkv*).

Dialogue is also the medium of choice, unsurprisingly, for verbal combats between rivals that do not (quite) escalate into physical conflict. These are designated *mannjafnaðr* 'comparison of men' and *senna* 'quarrel, flyting' in Old Norse and employ a number of standard formulae in which the speakers challenge their rivals in terms of their physical courage, manly accomplishments and social status (cf. Harris 1979; Clover 1980; Bax and Padmos 1983). Here *fornaldarsaga* poetry is as rich as, if not richer than, the examples found in the Poetic Edda (*Hárbarðsljóð* (*Hárb*), *Lok*, the flytings between Atli and Hrímgerðr in *Helgakviða Hjǫrvarðssonar* (*HHj*) and between the giantess Hyndla and the goddess Freyja in *Hyndluljóð* (*Hyndl*)). Instances in *fornaldarsögur* include *Útkv* (*Hálf*), the *mannjafnaðr* between Ǫrvar-Oddr and two rivals as well as Oddr's exchange with a pagan priestess in Bjálkaland (*Ǫrv*), *sennur* between Ketill hœngr and the Saami king Gusi(r), between Ketill and a troll-woman, Forað, and between Ketill and a viking, Framarr (*Ket*); a *senna* between Ketill's son Grímr and two troll-women (*GrL*); and various exchanges of the heroes Hjálmþér and Ǫlvir with apparently hostile supernatural creatures in *HjǪ*. This use of verbal dialogue of a usually agonistic kind between *fornaldarsaga* heroes and the denizens of the supernatural worlds they inhabit reflects the dominance of themes of Otherworld encounters in this sub-genre of the Icelandic saga.

While the extent of the use of dialogue in *fornaldarsaga* poetry is remarkable, the presence of first-person monologue in this corpus is even more so. By contrast with the Poetic Edda, where monologue is often attributed to female speakers, particularly in the elegiac poetry attributed to the women of the Nibelung households (Guðrún Gjúkadóttir, Brynhildr Buðladóttir, Oddrún Atlasystir), the first-person monologue in *fornaldarsǫgur* is an almost exclusively male medium. Many of the examples of monologue in these sagas are of a particular kind, usually termed *ævikviða*, literally 'life poem' or poetic autobiography, a term not attested, however, in *ONP*. (The term *ævidrápa* is sometimes used in scholarly discussion, especially as applied to Ǫrvar-Oddr's monologue, but it is technically incorrect, as this and the other *fornaldarsaga* monologues only occasionally contain refrains, a defining characteristic of a *drápa*.)

Edd. Min. described such *ævikviður* as *monologischen Rückblickslieder* 'monologic retrospective lays', referring to the characteristic positioning of *ævikviður* at crucial times of a character's life, usually when he is on the point of death and looking back on the events that shaped it, hence the frequent inclusion of the term 'death song' in descriptions of this poetic kind (cf. Marold 2005b). Heusler (1902, 199-200, 232) called these poems 'situation poems' (*situationslieder*) and identified them as unique to Old Norse and to Saxo. Among the poems of this type are Hjálmarr's death song in *Ǫrv*, also partially recorded in *Heiðr* (*Ǫrv* 13-29), Ǫrvar-Oddr's own lengthy *ævikviða* (*Ǫrv* 71-141), Hildibrandr's death song in *Ásm* (*Ásm* 1-6), *Krm*, attributed to the dying Ragnarr loðbrók, Ásbjǫrn's *ævikviða* in *OStór* (*OStór* 4-12), and, in an *Íslendingasaga* with many similarities to the *fornaldarsaga*, both the *ævikviður* attributed to Grettir Ásmundarson in *Gr* (Grett *Ævkv I* 1-3^V and *II* 1-4^V (*Gr* 22-4 and 39-42) as well as the *Hallmundarkviða* 'Poem of Hallmundr' (HallmGr *Hallkv*1-6^V (*Gr* 51-6)) in the same saga. Svart *Skauf* has already been mentioned in Section 3 as, in part, a parody of an *ævikviða*. The *Víkarsbálkr* 'Víkarr's Section' of *Gautr* arguably constitutes Starkaðr's *ævikviða* although in its present form the stanzas are divided and presented as *lausavísur* within the saga text. It may also be possible to classify *Hrókskviða* 'Poem of Hrókr' (Hróksv *Hrkv*) in *Hálf* as a kind of *ævikviða*: although the speaker Hrókr is not on the point of death, he has been subject to great misfortune, which, however, has a happy ending, when the woman who overhears his monologue agrees to marry him. Most of these poems are in *fornyrðislag*, though the two *ævikviður* from *Gr* are in *kviðuháttr* and *Krm* and Ásb *Ævkv* are in variants of *dróttkvætt*. The latter two have another feature in common that is not found in the other poems of this genre: each has a single-line refrain at the beginning of the majority of its stanzas.

The *ævikviða* displays consistent structural and thematic components. (1) The speaker is mortally wounded (or in danger of death) and (2) his impending death inspires him to compose a poem, (3) looking back at the many significant events of his life (or sometimes (3a) focusing on the circumstances in which he got his death wound), normally highlighting a series of martial exploits in which he has engaged alone or with others. (4) The poem is presented as a first-person narrative of what 'I' or 'we' did and experienced. (5) The speaker of the *ævikviða* usually has an audience (i.e. the poem is a monologue but not a soliloquy), and this audience is quite often female (cf. *Sonatorrek* 'Hard Loss of Sons' (Egill St^V) in *Eg*). (6) The speaker enjoins his audience to write down his poem, often on a rune stave (*Eg*, *Gr*) or to commemorate him on some other form of lasting memorial (*Ǫrv*; cf. *Beowulf* 2792-2808 (*Beowulf* 2008, 95-6)). (7) The speaker dies at the moment when or very shortly after he finishes uttering the poem. (8) Sometimes the speaker is abnormally long-lived (e.g. Starkaðr and Ǫrvar-Oddr, cf. Norna-Gestr and the Old English Wīdsīð), thus allowing his many exploits to be told at very great length.

The evidence of the various manuscript versions of the *ævikviður* in *fornaldarsögur* indicates that they became a very popular kind of poetry in Iceland in the later Middle Ages. During the fourteenth and fifteenth centuries some of them were subject to a good deal of scribal amplification and reworking, as can be seen from later manuscripts. It may be plausibly suggested that they fulfilled the need to amplify the characters of heroic figures in these sagas along similar lines to the treatment of the heroes of romance and legend in other vernacular literatures of the European High Middle Ages. Saxo Grammaticus's knowledge of similar death songs, like Hildiger's in Book VII (*Saxo* 2015, I, vii. 9. 14-15, pp. 506-9) and Starkatherus's in Book VIII (*Saxo* 2015, I, viii. 8. 3-8. 11, pp. 560-71), indicates that such vernacular poetic kinds existed already, or were in process of evolution, in the late twelfth century.

There are other examples of monologue poetry in *fornaldarsögur* that do not conform to the *ævikviða* model. Typically, the speakers' poetic monologues are interspersed with prose, in which the reactions of their audiences are noted, making it difficult to determine whether these were original longer poems with prose links added later or original *lausavísur* combined in a prosimetrum. Several examples of prophetic declamations by *vǫlur* 'prophetesses' (cf. *Vǫluspá* (*Vsp*) and *Hyndl* in the Poetic Edda) occur in *Hrólf* (*Hrólf* 2-5), *Ǫrv* (*Ǫrv* 1-3) and *OStór* (*OStór* 1), the last-named probably an imitation of the *Ǫrv* stanzas, while the *Buslubœn* 'Busla's curse' (*Busl*) in *Bós* is the sole example of its kind. These are the only monologic poems in the corpus in which the speakers are female. There is also a small group of prophecies uttered by male speakers, including Bragi Lv 1a^{IV} and 1b, the latter stanza in *Hálf*, Mágus jarl in *Mág* 1-3, and a variety of supernatural beings that predict the fates of members of the family of King Hálfr Hjǫrleifsson in *Hálf*. These last include a *þurs* 'giant' (Anon *Hálf* 1), a mountain in the shape of a man (Anon *Hálf* 2) and a *marmennill* 'merman' (*Hálf* 6-16). The Bragi figure here (cf. Lindow 2006), as well as the other supernatural beings in *Hálf*, act as agents of natural order in the uncertain world of human conflict depicted in this saga (cf. Torfi H. Tulinius 2002, 115-16). The monologue of the *trémaðr* 'wooden man' (*Ragn* 38-40) at the end of *Ragn* fulfils a similar function. Likewise, the prophecies of the *spámaðr* 'prophet' Merlin, as expressed in the two long poems *Merl I* and *II*, convey a sense of overarching destiny to the jumble of pseudo-historical and legendary events recounted in these works.

The poetry in some *fornaldarsǫgur* does not fit easily into the categories discussed above. In the probably late *Frið*, for example, there is great variability between the two main versions of the saga, and frequent disparity between them in terms of the content and sequencing of the stanzas they contain. Most of the stanzas are first-person narrative accounts of events, persons and personal feelings attributed to the protagonist, Friðþjófr, himself, but these are presented in the saga as *lausavísur*. There is a long sequence of stanzas, which might once have been part of a longer poem, in which Friðþjófr describes a storm at sea on the way from Norway to Orkney brought on by two troll-women who threaten him, his companions and his ship, Elliði, with destruction. These stanzas interweave several themes: of the power of the storm and the supernatural forces that cause it; of Friðþjófr's love for the beautiful Ingibjǫrg, which is thwarted by his enemies (who have set the troll-women on him), and of the difference between the perils of the sea and the soft life among women back in Norway. Such a mixture of elements of romance, the supernatural and the sensational must have appealed to a fourteenth-century Icelandic audience, just as it appealed to European Romantic tastes in the nineteenth century.

An especially difficult saga to fit into any kind of pattern is *Ragn*. Like *Frið*, its poetry consists exclusively of *lausavísur* and these form small groups depending on the identity of their fictive speakers. Most of the stanzas are spoken by Ragnarr and his wives and sons. They describe actions, mostly fights, in which the father and sons had been involved or in which they met their deaths, and they are partly retrospective, beginning with Ragnarr's account of his slaying of a serpent from which he got his nickname *loðbrók* 'Hairy-breeches' and won his first wife, Þóra. There is an admixture of dialogue between Ragnarr and his second wife Kráka/Áslaug, but the primary impression conveyed by the stanzas as a whole is of a family history of warfare and then vengeance, orchestrated by Ragnarr's second wife, now called Áslaug/Randalín, for the deaths in battle of her sons and stepsons. Two stanzas (*Ragn* 26-7) present Ragnarr's own account of his impending death in the Northumbrian King Ælle's snake-pit, with wording reminiscent of sts 24 and 28 of *Krm*, but the death song form is merely incipient here. At the end of its Y version the saga concludes with a group of six almost *mannjafnaðr*-like stanzas (*Ragn* 32-7) exchanged by two wandering ex-warriors loyal to Ragnarr and his sons and, finally, there is the eerie monologue of the *trémaðr*, who stands forlornly on the island of Samsø where he was once set up as the recipient of sacrifice by the sons of Loðbrók (or Loðbróka, see *Ragn* 39, second Note to l. 4). The saga thus has a dying fall, suggesting the end of a glorious, heroic era in which Ragnarr and his family played important roles.

The social resonance in Iceland of the legend of Ragnarr, his sons and various wives perhaps offers a clue to the nature and structure of the saga and its poetry. It is well known that it came to be believed that Áslaug, Ragnarr's second wife, who plays an important part in *Ragn* and in *RagnSon*, was the daughter of the legendary heroic couple Sigurðr Fáfnisbani and Brynhildr Buðladóttir, and that through her a number of important Icelandic families descended (Ólafia Einarsdóttir 1964, 62-8). Ari Þorgilsson includes mention of her (though he does not give her actual name) in his own family tree at the end of his *Íslendingabók* 'Book of the Icelanders' (*Íslb*) of c. 1122-33 (*ÍF* 1, 28) and he mentions the killing of King Eadmund of East Anglia in 869/870 by Ívarr Ragnarsson in the same work. Thus the story of Ragnarr and his wives and sons had an important position between legend and history for an Icelandic audience and this in-between status may be reflected particularly in the saga's poetry, in which all but the *trémaðr*'s monologue is in a version of the court metre, *dróttkvætt*, and, like stanzas in historical sagas, presented as *lausavísur*. *Krm* is also in a version of *dróttkvætt*, as has been mentioned earlier.

7.2. Poetic Diction

Below the level of the genres of poetry to be found in *fornaldarsögur* it is possible to identify particular types of conventional scenes or settings, such as battle scenes, sea voyages, or meetings between a hero and a supernatural being, and, within such scenes, smaller compositional units, such as meeting or challenge formulas or lists of heroes. On the whole particular types of scene are expressed stylistically by means of particular levels of poetic diction, ranging from a high style, often characterised by the use of kennings (and less commonly *heiti*), through a medium to plain style, appropriate to narratives recounting heroic action, to a low style, employing vocabulary whose register includes terms of abuse or references to menial household tasks. Very many of these units of composition and their accompanying levels of diction are also evident in the corpus of the Poetic Edda, especially in the heroic poems, where correspondences are frequent. Lexical parallels with the Helgi poems (*Helgakviða Hundingsbana I* and *II* (*HHund I*, *HHund II*) and *HHj*) are particularly evident and this has been detailed both in the Notes to the editions in this volume and in many places in *Kommentar*, Volumes IV-VI.

Generally speaking, the diction of *fornaldarsaga* poetry descriptive of battles, single combat or other forms of fighting between human heroes resembles that of poems of the Codex Regius collection like *Atlakviða* (*Akv*) and *Hamðismál* (*Hamð*): the style is largely straightforward, employing a heroic vocabulary that emphasises themes of courage in the face of death, loyalty, prudence and a desire for fame. The poem often called *Hlǫðskviða* from *Heiðr* (*Heiðr* 87-119), the dialogue between King Hálfr and Innsteinn (*Innkv*, *Hálf* 14-37), and the combat between Hjálmarr and Ǫrvar-Oddr and twelve berserks on the island of Samsø (*Ǫrv* 5-12) use this register. Much of the descriptive vocabulary of these poems highlights the material accompaniments of the heroic life: emphasis falls on mead- or ale-drinking in the hall, gold rings, weapons and armour. There are some kennings, especially for the topics of ruler and weapons, but they are not especially frequent.

A variation on the pattern of a hero's physical fight with one or more human opponents is the *mannjafnaðr* 'comparison of men' and the *senna* 'flyting', in which verbal duelling replaces actual physical aggression. Appropriately, as the fighting is with words, not deeds, the opponents glorify their own acts of bravery in a register that is medium to high, while vilifying their opponents in the language of abuse, with frequent terms of insult or reference to demeaning activities, like lolling around in the kitchen or having sexual intercourse with maid-servants. *Ǫrv* 34-58 is the main example of this type in the *fornaldarsaga* corpus.

Fornaldarsaga poetry based on the compositional unit of an encounter between a human hero and a supernatural being is usually classifiable as a *senna* and employs a kind of diction that combines a vocabulary descriptive of extreme physical aggression on the part of the otherworld being and, on the part of the hero figure, taunting and abuse directed towards the aggressor. Unsurprisingly, a low register is often employed in these exchanges, though we also find a few kennings, especially for giantesses. Unlike human-to-human combat, in which both parties are male, many of the encounters of this type are between male heroes and giantesses or troll-women. The examples of this type are plentiful: *GrL* 1-5 (Grímr, Feima and Kleima); *Ket* 14-24 (Ketill and Forað); *HjǪ* 3-10 (Hjálmþér and Vargeisa), *HjǪ* 11-21 (Hjálmþér, Ǫlvir and various sea-ogresses); *StSt* 1-2 (Sturlaugr and pagan priestesses); *Ǫrv* 59-70 (the Bjálkaland episode, Oddr versus Gyðja). In the last two examples, the paganism of the hero's opponents is stressed, though it is not an issue elsewhere. One apparent exception to the male to female paradigm of this group is the combat between Ketill hœngr and the Saami ruler Gusi in *Ket* 3-12; it could be argued, however, that here Gusi's status as a member of an 'outsider' ethnic group puts him on the same level as troll-women and other supernatural females.

A variation on the meeting between a hero and a supernatural being is the encounter between a heroic figure and foolish country folk in *Gautr* 1-6, the

Dalafíflar 'Valley-fools' episode, where the stanzas are all spoken by the Dalafíflar, whose register is appropriately low, employing everyday vocabulary and semi-proverbial sayings. Another variation on the same basic pattern, with an interesting inversion of the gender stereotyping of the base format, is the encounter between Hervǫr and her father, the *draugr* 'revenant' Angantýr, in *Heiðr* 25-47. Here the diction emphasises both the design for terror of the setting, describing opening grave mounds, strange noises and burning fires, and at the same time Hervǫr's resolve to obtain the cursed sword Tyrfingr, referred to in several repeated kennings (*Heiðr* 36/9, 39/2 and 45/4).

It has been mentioned already in Section 7.1 that the *ævikviða* within the *fornaldarsaga* corpus displays consistent structural and thematic features. These shape the ways in which some of the compositional units described in the present section actually function. Because the *ævikviða* is always retrospective, and because the speaker is invariably a former fighting man, it is inevitable that *ævikviður* relate accounts of battles that took place long ago, which the speaker recollects, if not in tranquillity, then at the point of acceptance of his fate. This is the basic situation which the poet of *Krm* capitalises on with his insistent refrain *Hjuggu vér með hjörvi* 'We hewed with the sword' through stanzas full of descriptions of bloody battles, slain enemies (many named) and places (also named) where the battles occurred. This pattern can also be seen, with variations, in *Ásm* 1-6 (Hildibrandr's death song), *ÓStór* 4-12 (Ásbjörn's *ævikviða*), *Ǫrv* 13-29 (Hjálmarr's death song), Ǫrvar-Oddr's *Ævidrápa* (*Ǫrv* 71-141) and Starkaðr's *Víkarsbálkr* (*Gautr* 9-41).

In terms of diction, the poetry in *Frið* and *Ragn* deserves special mention, as it did in Section 7.1 above. In both cases the stanzas appear in the sagas as groups of *lausavísur* rather than as long poems. In *Frið*, however, the stanzas numbered 2-18 in the present edition display certain features of a long poem, in that they are thematically interconnected. The vivid descriptions of Friðþjófr, his men and the semi-animate ship Elliði, struggling against the power of the rough, cold sea, conveyed through the use of descriptive adjectives (*svellvífaðar Sólundar* 'the ice-covered Sula islands' 3/7, 8; *hrímfaxaðar hrannir* 'the rime-maned waves' 6/1, 3) and a number of kennings (e.g. 8/4 *brekka svana* 'the hillside of swans [WAVE]'), are interwoven with equally affecting references to Friðþjófr's love for Ingibjǫrg, whom he has been forced to leave behind, and his fears that she will be married off to King Hringr. The storm at sea, which has been caused by two troll-women, is sexualised as the destructive being Rán, who tries to drag seafarers down to her bed on the sea floor, and this scenario is contrasted with Friðþjófr's heart-felt but frustrated fantasies of having intercourse with Ingibjǫrg (this is made explicit in *Frið* 11). Whoever composed this sequence of *lausavísur* implicitly and very effectively turned the compositional unit of the encounter of the hero with otherworld beings on its head and combined it with a romantic interest that is absent from most earlier *fornaldarsögur*.

The diction of *Ragn*, like its structure and metrical form, stands out from the other sagas of the *fornaldarsaga* corpus, though some of the remarks to be made about it apply also to *Krm*, and suggest that the subjects of both works, Ragnarr loðbrók, his wives and his sons, hold the key to understanding why *Ragn* is so different from other *fornaldarsögur*. It is the assumed status of Ragnarr as a king and progenitor of many well-known Icelanders of the historical period that has probably influenced the composers of both *Ragn* and *Krm* to adapt a prestigious and courtly metrical form (variants of *dróttkvætt*) and a high stylistic register employing many kennings and other circumlocutions.

The distribution of kennings in *Ragn* shows clearly how these literary ornaments are used to aggrandise the hero, Ragnarr, and his son, Sigurðr ormr-í-augu 'Snake-in-eye', through whom some Icelandic families claimed descent. The first cluster of kennings, for the serpent that Ragnarr slew in his youth, occurs in st. 1. In the stanzas (2-6) that describe how Ragnarr and Kráka (later revealed as Áslaug) first meet, Kráka's language is simple and unadorned, while Ragnarr's is characterised by his use of several kennings for 'king' to describe himself (3a/2, 3; 4/7, 8). Later (sts 8-10) there is another kenning-cluster around the subject of the preternaturally bright eyes of Sigurðr, a trait often associated with dominance and rulership (cf. Marold 1998a). Several of the kennings emphasise Sigurðr's descent through his mother's family as *niðr Buðla* 'the descendant of Buðli' (9/7). The importance of Áslaug in the rest of the saga and its stanzas is conveyed more by their emphasis on her role as a whetter of her sons to take revenge for the various misfortunes that have befallen them than by specific ornaments of diction.

It remains to comment more generally on the use of the kenning in *fornaldarsaga* poetry. (Kennings in the corpus as a whole are discussed in the General Introduction to *SkP* I, lxx-lxxxv and in Section 7, 'Poetic Diction' of the Introduction to *SkP* III.) Almost all kennings in *fornaldarsögur* are of the simple variety; *tvíkent* 'doubly modified' or 'doubly paraphrased' kennings are encountered infrequently but *rekit* 'driven, i.e. extended' kennings never. Most kenning referents are for the usual topics of skaldic verse, including warrior, prince/king, giant/troll and giantess/troll-woman, battle, weapons, ships and the sea. Within these kennings, poets used a number of mythological or legendary base-words and determinants: valkyrie-names are quite frequent as constituents of battle-kennings, for example (see the Index of Mythical, Biblical and Legendary Names). There are also a number of woman-kennings, particularly in the later poetry.

A large number of kennings in *fornaldarsögur* conform to standard kenning patterns, and the notes to individual editions usually refer to Meissner's categories for comparison. However, in some probably later texts, certain irregularities are found, at least in terms of classical skaldic diction. These may involve an unusual choice of either base-word or determinant (e.g. *veigarskorð* 'the prop of drink [WOMAN]', *ÞJ* 1/3, where *skorð* 'prop' is often found in *rímur* as the base-word of a woman-kenning, but less often in skaldic verse), or the use of a word in an unusual sense (e.g. *mellur Hrungnis* 'the female lovers of Hrungnir [GIANTESSES]', *GrL* 5/6), where *mella* means 'giantess' in earlier Icelandic, but obviously must have a different sense here, as this kenning as a whole denotes a giantess).

In general, kennings in *fornaldarsaga* poetry function as literary devices to raise the stylistic register and emphasise dramatic or otherwise important parts of the poetic narrative. They are by no means evenly distributed throughout the corpus, but cluster in groups corresponding to high points of a saga narrative or a group of stanzas. This kind of clustering is also exemplified in the two *Merlínusspá* poems by Gunnlaugr Leifsson, which we are able to date to the late twelfth or very early thirteenth century, based on what is known of the author's life. While much of Gunnlaugr's narrative follows Geoffrey of Monmouth's Latin prose text rather closely and is straightforwardly direct in style, he uses a sprinkling of kennings throughout, especially those for ruler, (generous) man and prophet on the one hand, and battle, weapons and armour on the other, to focus upon the many actors and events in Geoffrey's history of Britain. As Russell Poole observes in his edition in this volume, there are two places, one in each poem, where Gunnlaugr abandons his restrained use of kennings, and piles them on thickly, together with a series of short clauses describing battle scenes, in *Merl I* 65-9 and *Merl II* 33-6. Here he is undoubtedly following traditional skaldic practices.

One final issue in the study of poetic diction in *fornaldarsögur* concerns the question of whether *fornaldarsaga* poets directly imitated existing Old Norse poems in other, and presumably earlier, text corpora. It has often been claimed (and details of individual arguments will be found in the notes to this edition) that some poetry shows the direct influence of specific works in the corpus outside the *fornaldarsögur*; for example, the influence of *Vsp* upon *Merl* and of RvHbreiðm *Hl*[III] upon *Krm*. Some of these arguments are plausible and may be significant for several reasons: of dating, provenance and authorial intention. Others are harder to evaluate, as stylistic similarities, even extending to similarities in vocabulary, may be part of a more general influence of similar compositional units or themes upon different poets and not the result of the specific influence of one poem upon another.

7.3. *Fornaldarsaga* poetry and *rímur*

There is considerable evidence in several of the *fornaldarsögur* whose poetry is edited in this volume of the similarities between the poetry in late examples of this saga type and the new narrative poetic genre of the *rímur* 'rhymes' (sg. *ríma*), which made their appearance in Iceland during the fourteenth century (Davíð Erlingsson 1987; Jorgensen 1993). The first recorded *ríma* is the mid-fourteenth-century *Óláfs ríma Haraldssonar* in *Flateyjarbók*, attributed to the poet Einarr Gilsson, who was also the composer of several skaldic poems (see his Biography in Volume IV of

SkP). Though most of the early *rímur* were not recorded in writing until the sixteenth century and later, their popularity appears to have taken off quickly. In a number of cases of both *riddarasögur* and *fornaldarsögur*, *rímur* versions of these saga narratives came into being, and it has been suggested that in some cases, where more than one version of a *fornaldarsaga* exists, the reworking of the saga may have been inspired by the existence of *rímur* on the same subject.

As with some of the fourteenth-century poetry edited in *SkP* VII, there is ample evidence of the influence of the vocabulary of *rímur* on the poetry of *fornaldarsögur*, and the *ríma* influence may also be responsible for the greater interest in topics of romantic love detectable in the poetry of later sagas like *HjǪ* (albeit in a parodic mode), *ÞJ* and *Frið*. Where early *rímur* have been recorded (cf. Finnur Jónsson 1905-22; Björn K. Þórólfsson 1934), it is possible to compare their presentation of a narrative with that of the corresponding saga. Many of these parallels have been pointed out in the Notes to the editions of, for example, *HjǪ* and *Frið*. Generally speaking, the *rímur* style allows for a greater expansiveness and a greater degree of repetition than do eddic or skaldic verse-forms. In terms of vocabulary it is hard to tell whether new words that appear in both *rímur* and late sagas (e.g. *beigla* 'lumber about' *Ket* 24/9; *klén* 'nice' *HjǪ* 6/6) show the influence of one genre on the other or simply the use by poets in both media of a newly available linguistic resource. There are other instances, however, observed in both Volume VII and this volume, in which a probably late stanza shows a changed usage in the formation of kennings corresponding to the ways in which certain kenning patterns are formed in *rímur* (examples are given above in Section 7.2). In such cases the influence of *rímur* upon the poetry of *fornaldarsögur* seems probable.

7.4. The relationship between poetry and prose in *fornaldarsögur*

The interweaving of poetry and prose in Icelandic sagas is often referred to by the term *prosimetrum*, which indicates a text partly composed in prose and partly in verse. However, the relationship between the two component parts in Icelandic texts is not equal, either in quantity, distribution or, arguably, in age. There has been a great deal of debate about how the verse relates to the prose, and whether one gave rise to the other, as has already been discussed in Section 2 of this Introduction. In various of the separate editions of *fornaldarsögur* in this volume editors have suggested that some of the poetry probably had its origins in compositions likely to be older than the prose narratives in which they have been embedded. Such claims are based on the presence of archaic linguistic forms or older conventions of *bragarmál* in some of the manuscript versions, which point to exemplars from earlier than the period 1250-1300, to which these editions are normalised. Other criteria that can be invoked to attest to the age and independence of some *fornaldarsaga* poetry from the prose sagas in which they have been recorded draw on the undoubtedly independent presence of poetry with comparable subjects in Saxo's *Gesta Danorum*, which often has an astonishing similarity to some of the poetry in Icelandic *fornaldarsaga prosimetra*. There is, then, strong evidence that some, though by no means all, of the poetry recorded in *fornaldarsögur* was originally older than the prosimetrical sagas themselves, and presumably based on earlier, orally transmitted compositions.

Another interesting question, that arises when Saxo's Latin poems are compared with their Old Icelandic counterparts, is whether the poetry is used in a similar way in Saxo's prose to its use in *fornaldarsögur*. Again, the evidence suggests that this is the case, not only with regard to the similar genres and literary modes employed (dialogue, monologue, *mannjafnaðr*, *senna* and *ævikviða* are all represented in both), but also to the ways in which the poetry and the prose are deployed in the *prosimetrum*. Frequently in both cases the poetry offers dramatic intensification of the narrative action, especially in cases where it is concentrated in particular scenes. Characters from the human world meet with Otherworld counterparts, as several times in sagas such as *Ket*, *GrL* and *HjǪ*, and exchange emotionally charged, usually hostile, stanzas. These exchanges are not evenly distributed through the saga prose, however, but clustered in concentrated bursts. In other examples, where dramatic monologue is dominant, the poetry has been compared in its emotive and action-retarding effect to 'the arias of a nineteenth-century opera' (Lönnroth 1971, 7).

It has of course been argued by many scholars that one of the functions of poetry in the *prosimetra* of the *Íslendingasögur* is very similar, in that the apparently objective saga prose is set off by stanzas that reveal the inner thoughts and motivations of the saga characters. While this is undoubtedly partly true, there is a much greater intensification of the dramatic element in *fornaldarsaga* poetry, mainly because the poetic medium is different: in *Íslendingasögur*, skaldic *lausavísur* are the main vehicle for the characters' private thoughts, and these by their very nature have their expressive limitations, while in most *fornaldarsögur* the use of dialogue, monologue and non-skaldic verse-forms allows a much more extensive development of emotional, even sometimes melodramatic postures on the part of the characters.[5]

It is evident from the editions in this volume that the relationship between poetry and prose in *fornaldarsögur* was an evolving one, and that changing tastes of the patrons and redactors of these sagas could alter the balance between the two elements and their relative positioning in the saga narratives. Different tendencies are apparent, pulling in different directions: towards the almost independent long

---

[5] An obvious exception to this generalisation about *Íslendingasögur* is *Eg*, but there the long poems were arguably extra-textual in the earliest versions of that saga.

poetic form of Ǫrvar-Oddr's *ævikviða* in the fifteenth-century manuscripts 343a and 471, placed as it is almost at the end of the saga, to the fragmentation of Starkaðr's *ævikviða* into groups of *lausavísur* cited like stanzas in historical sagas, with explanatory passages of prose, in the longer version of *Gautr*. Much still remains to be explored and analysed in connection with the *fornaldarsaga prosimetrum*, including the question of how it compares with the role of prose and poetry in other types of Icelandic saga narrative.

8. Normalisation

The question of how and to what chronological standard to normalise poetry in manuscripts of *fornaldarsögur* is a vexed one, to which there is no fully satisfying answer. There are several reasons for this, including the fact that most of the poetry in these sagas has been recorded in manuscripts of the fourteenth century or later, sometimes much later. Although we may suspect that some of this poetry is old, perhaps very old, we do not know in most cases exactly how old it is. A similar situation exists with the corpus of the Poetic Edda, but there at least the manuscript witnesses are of reasonably early date.

Much of the poetry in the *fornaldarsaga* corpus is metrically irregular and difficult to date using either linguistic or metrical criteria (see Section 6 above). As a good deal of it is in *fornyrðislag* or *málaháttr* it has probably been readily subject to changes, both in oral and written tradition, in scribal transmission and through the scribes' introduction of more modern linguistic forms. There are some instances in which criteria can be invoked (e. g. linguistic, metrical, lexicographical) to suggest that the poetry is considerably older than the prose context in which it has been recorded (e.g. the various archaic features of the text of *Ásm* in 7, mentioned in its Introduction), and others where criteria indicate that the poetry is likely to be quite young, but rarely can we be precise about its age. Furthermore, in some cases it is probable that narratives similar to certain *fornaldarsögur* were extant by the late twelfth or early thirteenth centuries (e.g. Snorri Sturluson (*Skm*, *SnE* 1998, I, 58-9) probably knew a version of the saga of Hrólfr kraki), but we do not know whether they took a similar form to that in which we know them now, either with regard to the poetry or the prose.

In the face of this uncertainty, while at the same time wishing to offer a reasonably conservative text of the poetry in *fornaldarsögur*, it has seemed best to adopt a 'neutral' dating for this poetry to the period 1250-1300, allowing for the possibility (discussed in the Introductions and Notes to specific editions) that some of it may be earlier and some later than the second half of the thirteenth century. The General Editors decided against normalising to a fourteenth-century standard, as in parts of Volume VII (though many of the extant texts probably date from that period), because it would be far more intrusive than normalising to the half-century immediately before 1300. This decision means that some poetry in this volume is probably presented as linguistically older than it really is, while some may be normalised to a linguistic standard some years younger than the probable date of composition. For purposes of comparison, Finnur Jónsson (*Skj*) and E. A. Kock (*Skald*) place their editions of *fornaldarsaga* poetry within the thirteenth century without further specification, but tend to normalise to the standard of its first half, 1200-50, not the second.

There are four exceptions to the principle outlined above, and these are provided by Bragi Lv 1b (*Hálf* 78), *Hrólf* 10-11 and GunnLeif *Merl I-II*, on the one hand, and Svart *Skauf* on the other. In the first three instances there is reason to normalise to the period before 1250, while in the fourth external evidence indicates a dating in the fourteenth century. In the case of Bragi's *lausavísa*, a date of composition consistent with his supposed *floruit* in the late ninth century is assumed. The fragments *Hrólf* 10-11 are cited in *SnE*, which is usually dated to the 1220s, and the fragments are likely to be earlier than that. Although *Merl* occurs in *Hb* as an appendage to *Bret*, its authorship is known and it may be dated with considerable certainty to c. 1200, give or take a decade or two. Thus the text of *Merl* has been normalised to the period pre-1250 (see *SkP* I, xliv-l for details for that period). With regard to Svart *Skauf*, although the precise identity of the poet, Svartr á Hofstöðum, is probable rather than certain, both external evidence and metrical and linguistic evidence from the poem itself indicate a dating in the fourteenth century. Thus this poem has been normalised to the period after 1300 (for details of normalisation of fourteenth-century poetry, see *SkP* VII, lxv-lxvii).

The general principles of normalisation adopted in *SkP* have been set out in the General Introduction in Volume I (*SkP* I, xliv-li). There it is explained that normalisation occurs either on metrical grounds or as a consequence of linguistic changes. Both *Skj* B and *Skald* normalise metrically to a pre-1250 standard and silently change the orthography of the manuscripts from free-standing uncliticised forms of verbs, pronouns, conjunctions and relative particles, which frequently render a verse line hypermetrical, to the corresponding cliticised forms. Some examples, all from sts 34-7 of *Ket*, show the differences between this edition and the practices of *Skj*: *hefi ek* 'I have' 34/7 (*hefk, Skj* B); *villr ertu* 'you are confused' 35/5 (*villr ert, Skj* B); *máttir þú eigi bíta* 'you are unable to bite' 36/4 (*máttira bíta, Skj* B); *þar er bragnar hjuggusk* 'where warriors exchanged blows' 37/8 (*þars bragnar hjoggusk, Skj* B).

The General Editors decided not to use contracted forms of these and similar word combinations in order to restore metrical and alliterative regularity to poetry edited to the 1250-1300 standard or to change the word order of manuscript witnesses to achieve the same effect. Both *Skj* B and *Skald* usually do both. The procedure adopted in this volume has been to leave the poems as they are, but to point out metrical and alliterative irregularities in the Notes, and to use the variant apparatus as much as possible to show how the scribes have altered earlier forms to later ones. However, if one or other of the manuscripts has the 'correct' reading, which would restore either metrical or alliterative regularity, it has then been regarded as appropriate to emend or normalise, with explanations given in the Notes.

With regard to normalisations resulting from linguistic changes in the period 1250-1300, the most obvious are those that took place in stressed syllables in Icelandic, where *ǿ* coalesced with *á*, *ǿ* with *æ* and *ǫ* with *ø*, represented orthographically as *ö* (*ANG* §§107, 115.2, 120). All these changes are reflected in the spellings used in the present volume. Other changes are mentioned in the General Introduction to *SkP* (*SkP* I, l).

Proper names (including personal names and place names) provide a special problem for normalisation, because they need to be presented in the Introduction, Translation and sometimes in the Notes as well as in the Text of a stanza or poem. The General Editors decided to adopt the 1250-1300 forms of proper names in both the Text and Prose order, but to normalise to a 1200-50 standard everywhere else, as is done in other *SkP* volumes. So this means that forms like Hervör and Ölvir are used in the Text and Prose order, but Hervǫr and Ǫlvir in other places.

9. How to use this edition

SkP is intended for a variety of users: for students and scholars of Old Norse and other medieval European languages and literatures, for scholars in cognate disciplines such as history, archaeology, the history of religion, and comparative literature, and for users whose primary interest is in Old Norse poetry. In view of its likely augmented readership, *SkP* contains a greater proportion of introductory and explanatory material than most previous editions, certainly in comparison with *Skj*, where it is minimal. Most of the explanatory material is to be found in the skald Biographies, which appear at the head of the *oeuvre* of named skalds whose authorship of poetry is known;[6] in the Introductions to poems; in the Context sections, which indicate the wider prose context(s) in which a stanza or set of stanzas have been preserved; and in the Notes to each stanza.

Each poem, single stanza (*lausavísa*) or fragment has a distinct designation and siglum in *SkP*, which in many cases is different from that used in *Skj* and in the list at the beginning of *Lexicon Poeticum* 1931 (*LP*). The new sigla are designed to be

---

[6] There are only three skald Biographies in Volume VIII, Gunnlaugr Leifsson (GunnLeif), Starkaðr gamli Stórvirksson (StarkSt) and Svartr á Hofstöðum (Svart). The bulk of the poetry in Volume VIII is anonymous, though attributed in the prose texts to individual characters in the narratives.

more consistent and transparent and to reflect reconstructions of poems that differ at some points from those in *Skj*. In Volumes V and VIII the new sigla for sagas have two parts: there is one part combining the abbreviated saga title (e.g. *Heiðr*) with the number of a particular stanza in the whole sequence of stanzas in that saga (e.g. *Heiðr* 80). This is prefaced by abbreviated information conveying the identity of the speaker of the stanza in question, according to the saga, and other information (e.g. whether the stanza is a *lausavísa* or a part of a named poem and where it comes in the sequence of stanzas attributed to that speaker). Thus *Heiðr* 80 combines with the more detailed information Gestumblindi *Heiðreks gátur* 33 to give the full siglum Gestumbl *Heiðr* 33 (*Heiðr* 80). Usually when stanzas from Volume VIII sagas are cited in cross-references in this volume (most commonly in Notes), the abbreviated siglum (e.g. *Heiðr* 80) is given; however, sometimes, where it is important to indicate the identity of the speaker or the name of the poem, the full siglum appears. A comparative table of sigla used in *SkP*, *Skj* and *LP* is included in the prefatory material of this volume, as of each volume of *SkP*.

The text of each poem, single stanza or fragment has been established by its editor on the foundation of a main or base manuscript, judged by the editor to be the best or (in some cases) the only witness to the probable original. The orthography of the text will have been normalised to the standard appropriate to its probable date of origin.[7] Any emended text, that is, letters or words that have no manuscript attestation, is given in italics. Where editors have omitted letters or words that are present in the manuscript(s), the symbol * appears in the text and prose order. On the matter of emendation, this edition is more conservative than most of its predecessors, avoiding emendation as far as reasonably possible, though previous editors' conjectures may be mentioned in the Notes. Normalisations are not regarded as emendations, and they are therefore not marked in italics in the printed text.

Since stanzas are written out continuously, as if prose, in medieval (and some post-medieval) manuscripts, the lineation is partly editorial, though normally unproblematic, as are the stanza divisions; any problems are discussed in Introductions and Notes. Stanzas are printed with the two *helmingar* or half-stanzas side by side, except where the metre is *fornyrðislag*, *ljóðaháttr* or *málaháttr*, in which case the stanzas are printed in long-lines.

---

[7] A full discussion of normalisation in the edition as a whole is given in Section 3.2 in the General Introduction to *SkP* I, while Section 8 of the present Introduction covers the period 1250-1300, to which the poetry in Volume VIII has been normalised. Section 9 in the Introduction to *SkP* VII covers the fourteenth century. The actual orthography of most base manuscripts for each poem or stanza can be seen in the transcripts available in the electronic edition, where images of the manuscripts are also available.

Below the stanza is the same text rendered in a prose order, and underneath that is an English translation. The translation provides a version as close as reasonably possible to the sense of the Old Norse text. Unlike most other translations of skaldic poetry, those in *SkP* give kennings their full sense values, that is, both base-word and determinant are translated and the referent, not being part of the actual text but implicit in it, is given within square brackets, and normally in small capitals (e.g. 'the stallion of the wave [SHIP]'). Referents of one category of kennings, the so-called *sannkenningar* and *viðkenningar*, which both paraphrase individuals, are given in lower case preceded by an = sign, in order to indicate that these referents are literally equivalent to the periphrasis of base-word and determinant within the text. For example, 'the son of Óðinn' is designated [= Þórr] and 'Hjálmarr's killer' is [= Tyrfingr]. Angle brackets within the English translation are used to provide the generic sense value of Old Norse mythological and legendary names, such as Hildr <valkyrie> and Hálfr <legendary king>, or alternative poetic names for mythological beings, such as Viðurr <= Óðinn>. In the latter case, an = sign appears to the left of the 'normal' name.

The editorial apparatus allows the reader to compare the edited version of the main manuscript with the text in other manuscript witnesses. The *Mss* listing gives the main manuscript first in bold type, followed by the other manuscript witnesses ordered primarily on the basis of the assumed stemma (if one can be determined), each with folio or page number in round brackets immediately following. Paper manuscripts are distinguished from those of parchment or vellum by having a superscript [x] after the manuscript siglum. Abbreviated reference to the prose source represented by each group of manuscripts is given in italics within round brackets immediately after the group, and where the stanza is found in more than one prose source the groups of manuscripts are separated by semi-colons.

All significant manuscript variants, but not simple orthographical variants, are given in the *Readings* line. They are given in normalised orthography unless the non-normalised manuscript reading is ambiguous, difficult to interpret or of particular interest or significance, in which case it is placed within inverted commas. Where variants are given, the lemma (the reading of the text and normally that of the main manuscript) is given first, followed by the readings of the other manuscripts, separated from the lemma by a colon. The lemma is shown in the same normalised form as in the text, and if this differs significantly from the manuscript form, the manuscript spelling is added in round brackets and within inverted commas (e.g. þars ('þar er'):). In cases where the editor has not followed the main manuscript, the variant reading selected for the text is in first place as the lemma, followed by a colon and the formula '*so* X', to indicate that the lemma is not the reading of the main manuscript.

The *Editions* line lists all significant previous editions of the text, beginning with *Skj*, *Skald* and (where applicable) *NN* and/or *FF*, finishing with *Edd. Min.*,

NK and *ÍF Edd.* (if applicable); the text's designation in *Skj* B is specified, comprising the poet's name (if any) as given there, the title of the poem, stanza or fragment and equivalent stanza number. Editions of prose sources containing the stanza are then listed, and followed by other editions, usually in chronological order, with date of publication and relevant page number. The editions are followed, in round brackets, by abbreviated references to the relevant text or saga within a compilation (if applicable), and by the chapter in which the stanza occurs. Chapter numbers are omitted if chapter divisions are too unstable in the source in question. If a stanza is found in more than one prose source, the editions of the individual prose sources are grouped together and separated by semi-colons. Where there are separate editions of the poem in question, these are listed last.

The *Context* sections are summaries of the prose context(s) in which a stanza or a set of stanzas have been preserved, those in *SkP* VIII being drawn mostly from the relevant *fornaldarsögur*. Sometimes, as is the case with Svart *Skauf*, there is no prose context. It should be emphasised that the Contexts represent understandings, on the part of medieval authors and compilers, of the stanzas and the circumstances to which they were thought to refer.

The *Notes* are intended to address significant linguistic, metrical, lexicographical and above all interpretative issues as well as questions of a broader contextual nature. Although the editors do not aim to give a comprehensive history of scholarship and previous editorial practice, significant editorial interpretations and emendations are discussed and evaluated in the Notes.

A sample stanza with graphic explanations of the main features of the edition appears in the endpapers to all *SkP* volumes. Abbreviated sigla for manuscripts, and sigla for sagas, *þættir* and compendia are listed and explained in the prefatory material to this volume; see also Section 4 above. Also listed are general abbreviations (aside from standard ones such as e.g. and cf.) and technical terms that may be unfamiliar to the reader. Abbreviated references to all editions and secondary works cited are expanded in the Bibliography at the end of the volume.

POETRY IN *FORNALDARSÖGUR*: THE CORPUS

Áns saga bogsveigis

Edited by Beatrice La Farge

Introduction

Áns saga bogsveigis 'The Saga of Án Bow-bender' (*Án*) is a *fornaldarsaga* associated with the *Hrafnistumannasögur* 'sagas of the men of Hrafnista' (for this group, see Introduction to stanzas from *Ket* and *GrL* and, for the intricacies of the genealogical connections between Án and the other Hrafnistumenn, Hughes 1976, 212-15). It is set in Norway in the time preceding the unification of regional kingdoms under a single ruler. It tells the story of Án, a young good-for-nothing with enormous physical strength. In his youth he meets a dwarf, Litr, whom he forces to give him a great bow and five arrows that always hit their target. When he reaches adulthood, his brother Þórir takes him to the court of King Ingjaldr, where he earns himself the nickname *bogsveigir* 'Bow-bender' because he cannot get his bow through the doorway of the royal hall. However, he later becomes involved in hostilities with the king because he kills the latter's two half-brothers, as a consequence of which he is outlawed. The ensuing feud is eventually settled by Án's son Þórir háleggr 'Long-leg', who kills Ingjaldr.

The earliest extant recension of *Án* is preserved in the fifteenth-century ms. AM 343 a 4° (343a) of c. 1450-75, although scholars have dated the original saga to 'not later than 1300' (*LH* II, 818). The hero of the saga, Án bogsveigir, is however probably identical with a figure named Ano sagittarius 'Ano the Archer' mentioned by Saxo Grammaticus (c. 1200), who is a protagonist in a story which shares some motifs, plot structure and names with the saga (*Saxo* 2015, I, vi, 4. 8-11, pp. 372-5; cf. Hughes 1972, 1-2, 81-93, 104-8; Hughes 1976). A figure with the synonymous name Án skyti 'Án the Archer' is also mentioned in *Hkr* (on this and on motifs, etc. common to this saga and other Old Norse texts see Hughes *loc. cit.*).

There is only one surviving parchment ms. of the saga, AM 343 a 4° (343a), and the forty-six extant paper mss all ultimately derive from it (Campbell 1993, 16; Ólafur Halldórsson 1973, 74). Chief among them are AM 109 a I 8°ˣ (109a Iˣ, C17th); AM 173 folˣ (173ˣ, c. 1700); AM 340 4°ˣ (340ˣ, C17th); AM 560 c 4°ˣ (560cˣ, c. 1700-1725) and AM 395 folˣ (C18th). Ms. 343a supplies the best text of the five stanzas contained in the saga and is used here as the base ms., while readings from 109a Iˣ are also given. An eight-fit *ríma* (*Áns ríma bogsveigis*) was composed in the fifteenth century, apparently based on a longer version of the saga than the one preserved in 343a (Ólafur Halldórsson 1973, 74-5, 81-2). This *ríma* appears to have been used by the redactor or scribe of the oldest saga ms., and a second version of the saga exists which in turn is based upon the *ríma* (Ólafur Halldórsson 1973, 60, 81). In the nineteenth century two further *rímur* about Án were composed, and these are based upon the text of the saga as it appears in Rafn's *FSN* edition of 1829 (Hughes 1976, 197-8).

Since the *ríma* from the fifteenth century corresponds closely to the saga as it appears in 343a, it is possible to say that the version of the saga used by the *ríma* poet contained all of the stanzas we know from the saga with the exception of *Án* 4 (Ólafur Halldórsson 1973, 76, 79). But although the *ríma* is based upon the saga, the adaptation of the material and text of the saga to the *ríma* form makes it impossible to draw conclusions about the wording of the saga text used (Ólafur Halldórsson 1973, 79, 81). Thus the wording of the passages in the *ríma* which correspond to the stanzas from the saga we know provides no basis for emendation of lines in the stanzas which appear faulty or incomplete (cf. Notes to *Án* 2).

The five stanzas edited here are preserved only in *Án*, where they are all spoken by Án as *lausavísur*, each in a different situation and in chs 4 or 5. They therefore appear below in the same order as they appear in the saga. The stanzas are diverse in character and in metre: *Án* 1 and 3 are composed in irregular variants of *dróttkvætt*; *Án* 2 may originally have been in *ljóðaháttr* (Ólafur Halldórsson 1973, 80 n.); *Án* 4 and 5 are in *fornyrðislag*. The character of *Án* 2 and 5 has led some scholars to conclude that *Án* 2 may originally have been a love stanza spoken by a woman (cf. st. 2 Note to [All]), whilst it has been suggested that *Án* 5 may in fact be a riddle (cf. Notes to this stanza).

The following editions have been cited: *FSN* 2, 334, 336-7, 341, 343, *FSGJ* 2, 376, 378-9, 383, 385; *Edd. Min.* lxxxiv, lxxxvii-viii, 97, 104.

Án (Án Lv 1)

1. Skeldi mér sem skyldi
   skelkinn maðr við belki;
   við máttak þá vætki
   vinna; svei þeim æ manni.
   Varð í fang at fallaz;
   feldum eldsmat nökkut
   honum synjaðak heiðri;
   svei þeim æ manni.

Skelkinn maðr skeldi mér við belki sem skyldi; máttak þá vinna vætki við; svei þeim manni æ. Varð at fallaz í fang; feldum eldsmat nökkut; synjaðak honum heiðri; svei þeim manni æ.

The man fond of mockery dashed me against the wall as he should; I was able to put up no resistance then; fie upon that man forever. It was necessary to grapple with each other; we [I] felled fire-nourishment [FIRE-WOOD] in some way; I deprived him of honour; fie upon that man forever.

Mss: **343a**(83r), 109a I[x](5v) (*Án*).

Readings: [2] maðr: niðr 109a I[x]   [3] þá: þótt 109a I[x]   [4] svei: snar 109a I[x]; æ: á 109a I[x]   [6] -mat nökkut: sinns at mikit 109a I[x]   [8] svei þeim æ manni: sneri þeim at manni 109a I[x].

Editions: *Skj*: Anonyme digte og vers [XIII], E. 11. *Vers af Fornaldarsagaer: Af Áns saga bogsveigis* 1: AII, 319, BII, 339, *Skald* II, 182, *NN* §§1482-3, 2611; *FSN* 2, 334, *FSGJ* 2, 376.

Context: Án speaks this stanza after a wrestling match with a man named Bjǫrn inn sterki 'the Strong', a retainer of King Ingjaldr who has made fun of Án. In the first round Bjǫrn lifts Án up and casts him to the ground so that his shoulders land in the fire and his feet strike the beam in the wall (*bálkr*). Since Án is wearing a long loden coat he suffers no burns. In the second round Án swings Bjǫrn to and fro as if Bjǫrn were a small child and then slings him into the fire where he suffers severe burns.

Notes: [All]: The metre of this stanza is an irregular variant of *dróttkvætt*. Finnur Jónsson and Kock regard the inf. *vinna* as the first word of the final half-line in the first *helmingr*, so that there is a full stop before the sentence *svei þeim æ manni* (*Skj* B, *Skald*; on their alterations of the wording cf. the Note to ll. 4, 8 below). They thus regard the words *við máttak þá vætki | vinna; svei þeim æ manni* as a long-line with alliteration on <v>; this division of ll. 3-4 has a basis in most of the mss. The sentence *svei þeim æ manni* occurs again at the end of the second *helmingr*, where it is preceded by the sentence *honum synjaðak heiðri* 'I deprived him of honour'. In that sentence the words *honum* and *heiðri* seem to alliterate, with emphatic alliteration on the pers. pron. *honum*: 'him I deprived of honour'. In this case the words *honum ... manni* could not be a long-line with alliteration on <s>: *honum synjaðak heiðri; | svei þeim æ manni*. Previous eds (Finnur Jónsson, Kock) have emended the text by supplying or suggesting various words beginning with <h> at the beginning of the final half-line, so that the final long-line of the stanza would read: *honum synjaðak heiðri | heldr; svei þeim æ manni* 'I rather deprived him of honour ... ' (*Skj* B); *honum synjaðak heiðri | hála; svei þeim æ manni* 'I guilefully deprived him of honour ... ' (*Skald*); *honum synjaðak heiðri | harðla; svei þeim æ manni* 'I very much deprived him of honour ... ' (*NN* §2611). On Kock's further emendation of the final half-line of the stanza cf. the Note to ll. 4, 8. If the text is not emended in the ways Finnur Jónsson or Kock suggest, one could regard the two sentences *við máttak þá vætki vinna; | svei þeim æ manni* at the end of the first *helmingr* and the two sentences *honum synjaðak heiðri; | svei þeim æ manni* at the end of the second *helmingr* as two full-lines respectively, albeit the final line of each *helmingr* (*svei þeim æ manni*) contains no words which alliterate. Finnur Jónsson and Kock present the stanza as one in *fornyrðislag* or *málaháttr*, but the pre-requisite for this is their addition of a word beginning with <h> before the words *svei þeim æ manni* at the end of the stanza (see above). The present edn follows the ms. tradition in presenting the first *helmingr* as four half-lines with six metrical positions (l. 4 has seven), with the inf. *vinna* as the first word of l. 4. Given the probable double alliteration on <h> in l. 7 *honum synjaðak heiðri*, the refrain in l. 8 has no alliteration and only five metrical positions. — [1] *sem skyldi* 'as he should': In most previous eds the verb *skyldi* 'should' is emended to *skyldit* 'should not', presumably because it is thought that the stanza should indicate that Án is stronger than Bjǫrn and thus that Bjǫrn should not have overcome Án in the first round of the wrestling match. However, the prose exchange between Án and King Ingjaldr after the first round of the match suggests otherwise (*FSGJ* 2, 375): *Konungr mælti þá: 'Eigi þykkir mér þú, Án, jafnsterkr sem þú lézt.' Án mælti: 'Sá þykki mér, konungr, sterkari, er fyrri fellr'* 'Then the king said: "It doesn't seem to me as if you were as strong as you said, Án." Án said: "The one who falls first seems to me the stronger of the two, king"'. — [2] *skelkinn* 'fond of mockery': This word is interpreted by Finnur

Jónsson (*Skj* B) as meaning *spottelysten* 'given to mockery, malicious' (cf. the verb *skelkja* 'mock' and the noun *skelkr* 'mockery'). *LP*: 2. *skelkinn*, 2. *skelkja*, 2. *skelkr* suggests that both the adj. *skelkinn* and the verb *skelkja* are related to the noun *skálkr* 'servant, rogue'. There are homonyms to most of these words: *LP*: 1. *skelkinn* 'fearful', 1. *skelkja* 'frighten', 1. *skelkr* 'fright, fear'. Both *skelkinn* 'fearful' and *skelkinn* 'given to mockery' apparently occur only once each (*LP*: 1.-2. *skelkinn*); the sense 'mocking' makes better sense in this stanza than the sense 'fearful'. — [4, 8] *svei þeim manni æ* 'fie upon that man forever': This curse occurs like a refrain in the same form at the end of each *helmingr*. Finnur Jónsson (*Skj* B) and Guðni Jónsson (*FSGJ*) both omit the adv. *æ* 'forever' in l. 4 but retain it in l. 8, presumably because the adv. produces a seven-syllable line in l. 4. Kock proceeds on the assumption that the curse in l. 4 is repeated in identical form in l. 8 (*NN* §§1482, 2611); however, he regards the reading *þeim æ* as a way of writing *þeima* or *þema*, a variant of the m. sg. dat. form *þessom* of the demonstrative pron. *sjá* 'this' (*NN* §2611; *ANG* §470). — [5] *at fallaz í fang* 'to grapple with each other': These words can be translated lit. as 'to let oneself fall into a [wrestling] grip'. They refer to grappling with one's opponent in the wrestling match, not, as Kock thinks (*NN* §1483), to Björn's fall (death) during the wrestling match. The construction *verða at* + inf. means 'must, be forced, obliged to (do sth.)'. Since there is no explicit subject in this sentence it is unclear whether the pret. indic. verb *varð* is the 1st pers. sg. or the 3rd pers. sg. In the first case the speaker, Án, would be the putative subject. In the second case the putative subject could be 'he' (= Bjǫrn), and this is the interpretation favoured by Finnur Jónsson (*Skj* B) and Kock (*Skald*; *NN* §1483). The 3rd pers. sg. could however also be understood as a general statement about the situation, from the perspective of Án: 'one was obliged to let oneself fall into a grip' or 'it was necessary to let oneself fall into a grip'. If *varð at* is understood in this latter, non-personal sense, the phrase *fallaz í fang* could also be interpreted in a reciprocal sense (m. v.): 'fall into each other's grip', i.e. 'grapple, wrestle with each other': thus 'it was necessary to grapple with each other'. — [6] *felldum eldsmat nǫkkut* 'we [I] felled fire-nourishment [FIRE-WOOD] in some way': The n. sg. *nǫkkut* is used adverbially here. Depending upon how the 1st pers. pl. verb form *felldum* is interpreted, the line either refers to the fact that each man threw his opponent into the fire, or, if Án is speaking of himself in the 1st pers. pl., which seems more likely from the prose context, to the fact that Án caused Björn to be burned by pitching him into the fire. The kenning *eldsmatr* 'fire-nourishment' refers to Björn and metaphorically equates him with fire-wood.

Introduction to st. 2

Án speaks this stanza during a journey undertaken by King Ingjaldr to meet with his half-brothers, ostensibly in order to reach an agreement with them about sharing the kingdom inherited from their father (*FSGJ* 2, 377-9). Án and his brother Þórir accompany the king and his men, although Án suspects that the king has evil designs on his half-brothers. Þórir had previously served Ingjaldr's brother, King Óláfr, and had received from him a fine sword called Þegn 'Freeman', as a consequence of which he himself was given the nickname *þegn* (*FSGJ* 2, 368-9).

Án (Án Lv 2)

2. Vel þér, selja;   stendr þú sjó nær
      laufguð harla vel.
   Maðr skekkr af þér   morgindöggvar,
   en ek at þegni þrey   nátt sem dag.

Vel þér, selja; þú stendr nær sjó, laufguð harla vel. Maðr skekkr morgindöggvar af þér, en ek þrey at þegni nátt sem dag.

It is well for you, willow-tree; you stand near the sea, very well covered with leaves. One shakes the morning dews off you, but I yearn for a freeman night and day.

Mss: **343a**(83r), 109a I[x](6v) (*Án*).

Readings: [1] selja: 'seirna' 109a I[x]   [2] stendr þú sjó nær: víst svá stendr þó svá næri 109a I[x]   [3] laufguð harla vel: laufi vaxið 109a I[x]   [4] Maðr: margt 109a I[x];   af þér: á þik 109a I[x]   [5] -döggvar: dögginn 109a I[x]   [6] þrey: þreyi 109a I[x].

Editions: *Skj*: Anonyme digte og vers [XIII], E. 11. *Vers af Fornaldarsagaer: Af Áns saga bogsveigis* 2: AII, 319, BII, 339; *Skald* II, 182; *FSN* 2, 336, *FSGJ* 2, 378; *Edd. Min.* 104.

Context: The king has just ordered his men to set up a 'harbour mark' (*hafnarmerki*) at the spot where the expedition is resting. Since Án speaks this stanza immediately thereafter the word *selja* 'sallow, willow-tree' appears to refer to the harbour-mark, whose good location, healthy condition and usefulness are contrasted with the longing for a *þegn* expressed by the speaker (cf. *Edd. Min.* lxxxvii; Läffler 1912, 7-9; Liestøl 1945, 82).

Notes: [All]: The stanza appears to express a conventional contrast familiar from love poetry, in which a speaker contrasts a natural phenomenon with his or her inner longing; cf. *Skí* 4 and the C13th Middle English song 'Fowles in þe friþe' 'Birds in the wood'. Several scholars have considered the stanza may originally have been a love-poem spoken by a woman (*Edd. Min.* lxxxvii-viii; Läffler 1912, 7, 13, 61; Liestøl 1945, 85-92; Ólafur Halldórsson 1973, 80). However, this is not how it is interpreted in *Án* because there the stanza is spoken by a man, Án himself, about his longing for a *þegn*. In the context of the saga the word *þegn* 'freeman, man' could have several meanings: it might refer to the sword of that name owned by Án's brother Þórir, but *þegn* is also a very common term for 'man' in poetry (cf. *LP*: *þegn*), and Án claims to be using the word to refer to his brother Þórir by his nickname, which is also *þegn*. In *Án* a discussion about the meaning of the stanza follows and highlights its homoerotic implications and the ambiguities of the word *þegn* within the saga (*FSGJ* 2, 378-9; cf. Hughes 1976, 199 n.; Läffler 1912, 8): Þórir mælti: '*Eigi skaltu þess þurfa, því at ek mun gefa þér sverðit Þegn.' Án segir: 'Ekki þrey ek at þeim þegni.' Ketill sagði þar: 'Ek ætla, at þú þreyir at karlmanni nokkorum, ok viltu serða hann,' ok gerðu þeir at þessu gys mikit ok dáraskap. 'Eigi er svá,' sagði Án, 'ekki þrey ek at þeim þegni, ek þrey at Þóri þegn, bróður mínum, því at hann er svá grunnhygginn, at hann trúir konungi þessum, en ek veit, at hann mun honum at bana verða'* 'Þórir spoke: "You shall not have need of that [i.e. to long for *þegn*], for I will give you the sword Þegn." Án says: "I do not long for that *þegn*." Then Ketill [one of the king's retainers] said: "I think that you are yearning for some man, and you want to fuck him," and they made much mockery and sport of this. "That is not so," said Án, "I do not yearn for such a man, I suffer for my brother Þórir the follower [*þegn*] of the king, because he is so shallow-minded that he trusts this king, but I know that he [the king] will become his killer"'. Án's foreboding proves true, for the king eventually kills Þórir with the latter's own sword Þegn (*FSGJ* 2, 394). — [All]: In 340^x the stanza is very different and has clearly been influenced by the *ríma* tradition; for the text, see *Edd. Min.* 104 and notes there. — [1-3]: In *Áns rímur bogsveigis* III 6/1-2 there are two lines which correspond in content to this passage (Ólafur Halldórsson 1973, 110): *Vel þier selia vidi nær | vaxen laufe goda* 'It is well for you, willow-tree near the sea, grown with good foliage'. In the four-line *ríma* stanza in *ferskeytt* metre the two lines of a couplet share alliteration, whilst the two odd and the two even lines share end rhyme (abab; cf. Vésteinn Ólason 1982, 57). Since *Án* 2/3 is much shorter than the other lines and contains no two words that alliterate with one another, several eds emend l. 3 on the basis of the line *vaxen laufe goda* in the *ríma* (cf. Note to l. 3 below). Heusler and Ranisch and Läffler also emend the word *sjó* 'sea' to *víði* and thus implicitly assume that ll. 1-2 and 3-4 share alliteration on <v>, though their interpretations of *víði* differ. Heusler and Ranisch (*Edd. Min.*) treat *víði* as from *víðir*, a poetic word for 'sea', while Läffler (1912, 2-3, 5) understands it as the dat. sg. of *víðir* 'willow' (cf. ModGer. *Weide* and ModEngl. *withy*). Läffler argues that the scribe of 343a misunderstood *víði* 'willow' in his exemplar as the homonym *víði* 'sea' and substituted the more usual word *sjó*. The reconstructed line would thus read: *Vel þér selja! | Stendr þú víði nær* 'It is well for you, [female] willow-tree (*selja*)! You stand near a [male] willow-tree (*víðir*)' and would thus provide a heightened contrast between the proximity of the female and male willow trees on the one hand and the (presumed) lonely woman speaker, who longs for the man she loves, on the other (Läffler 1912, 13, 24-61). Such a reconstruction is purely hypothetical, because, as Ólafur Halldórsson (1973, 74-5, 79-80) points out, the *ríma* stanza cannot provide any evidence about whether the *ríma* poet knew the stanza from the saga in a different form from the one we know from 343a: the *ríma* poet doubtless changed the word *sjó* 'sea' to *víði* 'sea' to provide alliteration between ll. 1 and 2 of his stanza in conformity with the *ríma* metre. The *ríma* thus provides no adequate basis for emendation of the stanza from the saga (cf. also Note to st. 2/3 below). — [2] *þú stendr nær sjó* 'you stand near the sea': Finnur Jónsson (*Skj* B) and Kock (*Skald*) omit the pers. pron. *þú* 'you' but retain the word *sjór/sær* and change the one-syllable dat. form *sjó* to the two-syllable form *sævi*, presumably in order to obtain a four-syllable half-line and to provide an unaccented syllable between the two monosyllabic words *sjó* and *nær* (cf. Läffler 1912, 3, 61-3). Guðni Jónsson (*FSGJ*) prints the two-syllable dat. form *sævi* as well, although he also retains *þú*. In any case the dat. form *sjó* is perfectly acceptable from the point of view of grammar, since both the case-ending [i] and the stem consonant [w] are dropped in later Icelandic (cf. *ANG* §365). — [3] *laufguð harla vel* 'very well covered with leaves': Neither the 343a nor 109a I[x] text of this line has alliteration. *Skj* B and *Skald* adopt an emended amalgam of the two texts, *laufi vaxin vel* 'well grown with foliage', presuming the stanza to be in the metre *ljóðaháttr* and influenced by the text of the corresponding passage in *Áns rímur bogsveigis* (III, 6-7, Ólafur Halldórsson 1973, 110): *vaxen laufe goda* 'grown with good foliage'. Läffler (1912, 7, 14, 61) on the other hand proceeds from the assumption that the stanza is in *fornyrðislag* and emends l. 3 to: *ok ert harla vel | vaxin laufi* 'and you are very well grown with foliage'. Heusler and Ranisch suggest a similiar reconstruction in *Edd. Min.* 104 n.: *vel of vaxin | vænu laufi* 'well grown with beautiful foliage'. Ólafur Halldórsson (1973, 79-80) regards the word *vaxen* in the *ríma* as an attempt on the part of the poet to adapt the stanza he found in the version of the saga he used by supplying a word to alliterate with words in l. 1 of the *ríma* st. III, 6 in accord with *ferskeytt* metre. — [5] *morgindöggvar* 'the morning dews': For the positive associations of dew cf. *Vsp* 19/5-6, *Vafþr* 45/4-6, *HHj* 28/5-6. — [6-7] *en ek þrey at þegni nátt sem dag* 'but I yearn for a freeman night and day': Finnur Jónsson and Kock assume that the stanza was originally composed in *ljóðaháttr* (cf. Note to l. 3); they regard the words *nátt sem dag* 'night and day' as a later addition or omit them to produce a full-line without a caesura that reads: *en ek at þegni þrey* 'but I long for a man' (cf. Ólafur Halldórsson 1973, 80 n.). These lines are reminiscent of GSúrs Lv 5/5-6[V] (*Gísl* 7).

Án (Án Lv 3)

3. Því betr mér þykkir, Drekkum alt af uxa
   ef þá skal valr falla ennigeira hlenni;
   nær vér fráligra færum vera mun snarpra sverða
   fót at geira móti. svipun, ef ek skal ráða.

Þykkir mér því betr, ef valr skal þá falla, nær vér færum fráligra fót at móti geira. Drekkum alt af hlenni ennigeira uxa; mun vera svipun snarpra sverða, ef ek skal ráða.

It will seem to me so much better, if then the slain are to fall, when we quickly betake our feet to the meeting of spears [BATTLE]. Let us drink fully from the resounding sea (?) of the forehead-spears of oxen [HORNS > DRINK]; there will be a swinging of sharp swords [BATTLE], if I am to have my way.

Mss: **343a**(83v), 109a I[x](6v-7r) (*Án*).

Readings: [1] Því betr mér þykkir: Því betr \mér/ þykkir 343a, því þykkir betr 109a I^x   [2] þá: þá *possibly corrected from* þó 343a, þú 109a I^x   [3] fráligra: fraligar 109a I^x   [4] fót: fór 109a I^x; móti: mæri 109a I^x   [6] -geira: 'ge[...]' 109a I^x.

Editions: *Skj*: Anonyme digte og vers [XIII], E. 11. *Vers af Fornaldarsagaer: Af Áns saga bogsveigis* 3: AII, 320, BII, 339, *Skald* II, 182, *NN* §§1484, 3291; *FSN* 2, 337, *FSGJ* 2, 379.

Context: Án speaks this stanza when King Ingjaldr and his followers have arrived in the territories of Ingjaldr's half-brothers. Ingjaldr has announced that his half-brothers are not willing to settle the matter of their inheritance peacefully and that it will therefore be necessary to do battle against them. Many of Ingjaldr's followers now wish they had remained at home. The king orders that they all be provided with drinks, so that they become more eager to go on. Án proclaims his willingness to fight in the stanza he speaks as he has been given a large oxhorn filled with drink.

Notes: [All]: The metre of this stanza, like that of st. 1, is an irregular variant of *dróttkvætt*. It is ornamented with three kennings, an unusually high number for a *fornaldarsaga* stanza. — [2] *ef valr skal þá falla* 'if then the slain are to fall': This subordinate clause is proleptic, since warriors become *valr* 'the slain' when they fall in battle. — [5-6] *af hlenni ennigeira uxa* 'from the resounding sea (?) of the forehead-spears of oxen [HORNS > DRINK]': *Ennigeirar uxa* 'the forehead-spears of oxen' is clearly a kenning for drinking horns, and it is presumed that *hlenni* must here denote some kind of liquid, in order to produce a kenning for alcoholic drink similar to Egill Lv 6/3-4^V (*Eg* 10) *ýring atgeira ýrar* 'moisture of the spears of the [female] aurochs' (cf. *ÍF* 2, 110 n.). In the construction *drekkum ... af ... hlenni* the form *hlenni* must be dat. sg. The only Old Norse word with the stem *hlenn-* is *hlenni* 'robber, thief', but the dat. sg. of this word is *hlenna* and in any case it does not fit the context. Finnur Jónsson (*Skj* B) offers no explanation of the word here (cf. *LP*: *hlenni*; *Skj* B). Kock suggests that there may be an etymological connection between the word *hlenni* here and such Old English words as *hlyn* (m. 'sound, noise, din'; *NN* §1484). Since many Old Norse words whose etymological meaning is 'noise, din' are used to denote the sea or a wave, Kock suggests that *hlenni ennigeira uxa* is a kenning for drink of the type 'resounding sea/wave of the drinking horn' (cf. *Meissner* 432). Hughes (1972, 221 n. 36) emends *hlenni* to *hlemi*, which he appears to interpret as a word meaning 'noise' (1972, 46). The word *hlenni* remains obscure, but the meaning of the kenning and the passage as a whole is clear.

Án (Án Lv 4)

4. Þat muntu finna,   er þú flór mokar,
   at þú eigi ert   Án bogsveigir.
   Þú ert brauðsveigir   heldr en bogsveigir
   ostasveigir   en eigi * álmsveigir.

Muntu finna þat, er þú mokar flór, at þú ert eigi Án bogsveigir. Þú ert brauðsveigir, heldr en bogsveigir, ostasveigir, en eigi * álmsveigir.

You will find that out, when you muck out the floor, that you are not Án bogsveigir ('Bow-bender'). You are a bread-bender rather than bow-bender, a cheese-bender, but not a bow-bender.

Mss: 343a(84r), 109a I[x](9r) (*Án*).

Readings: [8] en eigi * álmsveigir: 'en eigi b alm sueigir' 343a, en ek heiti álmsveigir 109a I[x].

Editions: *Skj*: Anonyme digte og vers [XIII], E. 11. *Vers af Fornaldarsagaer: Af Áns saga bogsveigis* 4: AII, 320, BII, 339; *Skald* II, 182; *FSN* 2, 341; *FSGJ* 2, 383; *Edd. Min.* 97.

Context: Án speaks this stanza when he confronts King Ingjaldr's man Ketill, who is making advances to a young girl by pretending to be Án. Án turns up just at the right moment and seizes Ketill by the forelock. Before he mishandles Ketill by pulling out his hair, tarring him, putting out one of his eyes and castrating him, Án speaks this stanza, in which he makes it clear that Ketill is only fit to perform the most menial farmyard or kitchen tasks, not to be a warrior like Án.

Notes: [All]: This stanza is in the metre *fornyrðislag*. Both the stanza itself and the surrounding prose passage contain several examples of word-play (*FSGJ* 2, 382-4; Hughes 1972, 222 nn. 37-8). — [All]: The demeaning characterisation of Ketill as a *brauðsveigir* 'bread-bender' (i.e. 'kneader of bread') and an *ostasveigir* 'cheese-bender' has many parallels in Old Norse literature, e.g. in a stanza from *LaufE* (Anon (*LaufE*) 5[III]), in which a man-servant is called an *ostmýgir* 'oppressor of cheese' and a *saupstríðir* 'tormentor of buttermilk', while the maid-servant for whom he pines is called *brauðgýgr* 'ogress of bread' (i.e. 'woman who consumes bread') and *saurug flot-Gríðr* 'the filthy Gríðr <giantess> of fat' (i.e. a woman who consumes the fat that swims on the surface of the soup); cf. *Edd. Min.* lxxxiv and *LP*: *flotgríðr*). Heusler and Ranisch also cite a parallel from Saxo (*Saxo* 2015, I, vi, 9. 14, pp. 436-7). Cf. the hostile exchange between Kormákr and Narfi in *Korm* ch. 4, in the course of which Kormákr refers to his opponent as *Áli orfa* 'Áli <sea-king> of the scythe-handle' (KormQ Lv 12/1[V] (*Korm* 13), *ÍF* 8, 216). — [2] *er þú mokar flór* 'when you muck out the floor': The word *flórr* (not used elsewhere in Old Norse poetry) designates the passageway in the middle of a cow barn between the two rows of stalls for the individual cows where their dung and urine collect (Valtýr Guðmundsson 1889, 135; Stigum and Kristján Eldjárn et al. 1959, 399- 401). The verb *moka* 'muck out, shovel, cleanse by shovelling' occurs in Bjhít Lv 3/2,

4ᵛ (*BjH* 3), a derogatory *lausavísa* in which Bjǫrn says that his beloved Oddný told her husband *ganga at moka kvíar innan* 'to go and muck out from inside the pens'; cf. *BjH* ch. 12 (*ÍF* 3, 140). — [8] *en eigi * álmsveigir* 'but not a bow-bender': Ms. 343a reads *en eigi b álmsveigir*. Apparently the scribe first wrote an abbreviation for the word *bogsveigir*, which occurs in the previous line of the stanza, before he wrote the synonymous word *álmsveigir*, which alliterates with *ostasveigir* and is thus clearly correct. The word *álmr* 'elm' is often used metonymically for 'bow', since bows were made of elm-wood (*LP*: *almr* 2; Falk 1914b, 92).

Án (Án Lv 5)

5. Meyjar spurðu,   er mik fundu,
    hvíthaddaðar: 'hvaðan komt*u* ferfaldr?'
    En ek svaraða   silki-Gunni
    heldr hæðinni: 'hvaðan er logn úti?'

Hvíthaddaðar meyjar spurðu, er mik fundu: 'hvaðan komt*u* ferfaldr?' En ek svaraða heldr hæðinni silki-Gunni: 'hvaðan er logn úti?'

The fair-haired maidens asked, when they met me: 'Where did you come from, fourfold?' But I answered the rather mocking silk-Gunnr <valkyrie> [WOMAN]: 'Where does the calm outside come from?'

Mss: **343a**(84r), 109a Iˣ(10r) (*Án*).

Readings: [3] -haddaðar: *so* 109a Iˣ, 'haddaraðar' 343a   [4] komt*u*: 'komti' 343a, komst 109a Iˣ.

Editions: *Skj*: Anonyme digte og vers [XIII], E. 11. *Vers af Fornaldarsagaer: Af Áns saga bogsveigis* 5: AII, 320, BII, 340, *Skald* II, 182; *FSN* 2, 343, *FSGJ* 2, 385; *Edd. Min.* 97.

Context: Án stays the summer with a farmer whose daughter is named Drífa 'Snowstorm', the girl to whom Ketill was previously making advances (cf. Context to st. 4). Án is wearing four layers of clothing and is neither well-dressed nor good-looking. One day he meets Drífa outdoors. She is in the company of three other girls and is not only very pretty but also very elegantly dressed. Drífa and her companions make fun of Án's garb, and Drífa asks him: '*Hvaðan gekktu at nú, ferfaldr?*' '*Frá smiðum,*' *sagði Án* '"From where did you come now, fourfold?" "From work," said Án'. The farmer orders the girls to stop making fun of Án, and then Án recapitulates his exchange with the girls in this stanza, which probably plays on the name Drífa; cf. Note to l. 8 below.

Notes: [All]: The metre of this stanza is *fornyrðislag*. — [All]: According to Ólafur Haldórsson (1973, 81), this stanza originated as a riddle about a rainbow and a billow on the sea in calm weather, presumably because there are similarities in diction between it and some of the riddles in *Heiðr* and because ll. 3-4 and 8 may carry double meanings (see Notes to l. 3 and l. 8 below). Ólafur suggested that the author of the saga may have been inspired by the word *ferfaldr* 'fourfold' (l. 4) in the original stanza (where it would refer to the colours of the rainbow) to invent the motif of Án's four layers of clothing. This hypothesis is attractive but cannot be verified. It is more likely that some of the terms used in the stanza to refer to the young women draw on associations with riddles for natural phenomena in order to play on the basic (common noun) sense of the name Drífa. — [3] *hvíthaddaðar* 'fair-haired': This reading from 109a I[x] and other mss is certainly correct; 343a has *hvíthaddaraðar*. The form *-haddaðr* '-haired' is attested in other virtually synonymous compounds, which are used as epithets of girls and young women: e.g. *bjarthaddað man* 'bright-haired maiden', *Gríp* 33/6 (*NK* 169), *bjarthadduð brúðr* 'bright-haired woman', GunnLeif *Merl I* 77/7-8 and *brúðir bleikhaddaðar* 'pale-haired women', Gestumbl *Heiðr* 17/1-2 (*Heiðr* 64). There is a particular similarity between the last-named riddle and the stanza from *Án* in that this stanza poses a question or questions, and the second question (ostensibly) concerns a natural phenomenon (*logn*, see Note to l. 8), as Gestumbl *Heiðr* 17 (the answer to the riddle is 'swans') and several other riddles in *Heiðr* do. — [4] *komt*u 'did you come': The reading *komti* (343a) is meaningless, the reading *komst* in 109a I[x] is 2nd pers. sg. indic. m. v. of *koma*; the question *hvaðan komst, ferfaldr* may also be translated 'Where did you escape from, fourfold?' (cf. the expression *komask af* 'escape (with one's life)'). Previous eds have emended the reading *komti* (343a) to *komtu* 'did you come' (2nd pers. sg. pret. tense of *koma* + enclitic pers. pron. *þú*, cf. the form *gekktu* (2nd pers. sg. pret. tense of *ganga* + *þú*) in the corresponding prose passage quoted above in Context). The emendation *komtu* differs from the reading *komti* only in the number of minims and is thus paleographically plausible. — [6] *silki-Gunni* 'silk-Gunnr <valkyrie> [WOMAN]': The woman-kenning *silki-Gunnr* is also attested in VíglÞ Lv 1/2[V] (*Vígl* 3). The earliest kenning of this kind with *silki* as a determinant is found in a stanza ascribed to Kormákr (KormQ Lv 32/6[V] (*Korm* 51)): *silki-Nanna* 'silk-Nanna <goddess>'. — [8] *hvaðan er logn úti* 'where does the calm outside come from?': This question is Án's answer to Drífa's query 'Where do you come from?' (l. 4). Heusler and Ranisch (*Edd. Min.* lxxiv) think that it is a nonsense question posed by Án in jest. Finnur Jónsson on the other hand proposed that Án's question is a riddling and oblique allusion to the name Drífa, which, as a common noun, means 'snow-storm', and adduces the cpd *logndrífa* 'snowfall in calm weather' (*Fritzner: logndrífa*) as evidence for his interpretation (*LH* II, 145 and n. 4; *Skj* B). In this case the question *hvaðan er logn úti* mirrors Drífa's query: (Drífa) 'Where do you come from?'; (Án) 'Where does Drífa (i.e. where do you) come from?' In the context of the saga the correspondence between the adv. *úti* 'outside' in the prose passage (*þat var einn dag, at Án mætti úti Drífu karlsdóttur* 'It happened one day that Án met Drífa, the daughter of the farmer, outside') and the adv. *úti* in the stanza could be an indication that Finnur Jónsson is correct in supposing that the word *logn* 'calm' alludes to Drífa. In this case the appearance of the adv. *úti* would not merely serve a rhythmical purpose in the line but would be an indication that Án is asking Drífa where she comes from and not posing a question about the origin of a weather phenomenon. The form of the question is reminiscent of several posed by Óðinn in *Vafþr*, e.g. sts 20/4-6, 22/4-6, 24/4-6, 26/4-6, 36/4-6, 46/4-6.

Ásmundar saga kappabana

Edited by Peter Jorgensen

Introduction

Ásmundar saga kappabana 'The Saga of Ásmundr, Slayer of Champions' (*Ásm*) is a short *fornaldarsaga*, thought to have been composed c. 1300, although parts of the tale are considerably older. The story is related to that told in the ninth-century Old High German *Hildebrandslied* 'Lay of Hildebrand' (de Boor 1923, 1926; Kolk 1967; Gutenbrunner 1976) and a version of the Old Norse stanzas was probably used by Saxo Grammaticus in Book VII of his *Gesta Danorum* (*Saxo* 2015, I, vii. 9. 14-19, pp. 506-13; Friis-Jensen 1987, 59). Saxo's Latin version probably goes back to a source common to it and *Ásm*, which relates the following story. In the saga Hildr, daughter of the Swedish king Buðli, marries Helgi, prince of the Huns, and bears Hildibrandr, who becomes a famous if overbearing champion of the Hunnish king. After Danish attacks on Sweden, Hildr is carried off and married to Áki, a powerful warrior in Denmark, eventually bearing a second son, Ásmundr, who attains fame as a warrior. In order to win the hand of Æsa, daughter of the Danish king Álfr, Ásmundr must avenge the death of her father at the hands of the Huns. Æsa aids Ásmundr in acquiring the second of two special swords forged for King Buðli, who had had the weapon sunk beneath the waves near Agnafit upon learning that it would bring death to his grandsons. Ásmundr then aids the people of Saxland, oppressed by Hildibrandr, by duelling with ever-increasing numbers of Huns. The Hunnish champion, aware that he was Ásmundr's half-brother, had been reluctant to battle against him, but upon learning that his bravest warriors had been defeated, a berserk rage overcomes him, causing him to slay his own son, and he rushes off to fight against his half-brother. Ásmundr mortally wounds Hildibrandr and returns to marry Æsa.

Ásm is preserved in two vellum mss, Holm perg 7 4° (7) of the first quarter of the fourteenth century and AM 586 4° (586) of the second half of the fifteenth century, but the latter has lost all the stanzas in a lacuna. For this reason, 7 is the base and only ms. used in this edition. Both 7 and 586 go back to a common source, and forms like *of* (1/5), *þanns* (6/4), *synjaðak* (4/6) and *talðir* (3/3), as well as the use of the free-standing definite article (*in* 3/2, *inir* 3/4, *inn* 4/1, 10/1), indicate the stanzas to be indebted to a much older, written tradition.

Of the ten stanzas in *Ásm*, seven contain eight lines, sts 3 and 4 each contain six lines, and st. 6 comprises four lines. The metre is *fornyrðislag*, with each line containing two stressed and, quite often, two unstressed syllables. Each odd line contains one stave alliterating with the first stressed syllable of the following line.

The saga and its stanzas, together and separately, have been edited a number of times. The first edition of the saga is Peringskiöld (1722), followed by *FSN* 2, 461-87,

Detter (1891, 79-100), Valdimar Ásmundarson (1885-9, 2, 337-56) and *FSGJ* 1, 385-408. The stanzas have been edited separately in *Skj* and *Skald*, as well as in *CPB* I, 190-2, *Edd. Min.* 53-4 and 87, Halvorsen (1951) and *NK* 313-14 (sts 1-6 only).

Introduction to sts 1-6

The following six stanzas, which may originally have been from an independent poem sometimes referred to as 'Hildibrandr's Death song', are said to have been recited by Hildibrandr as he lay dying. Poems reviewing their lives are said to have been recited by several *fornaldarsaga* heroes, like Hjálmarr and Ǫrvar-Oddr, just before they die. These stanzas correspond, though with much elaboration on Saxo's part, to *Saxo* 2015, I, vii. 9. 14-15, pp. 506-9.

Hildibrandr (Hildibrandr Lv 1)

1. Mjök er vandgætt, hvé verða skal
   um borinn öðrum at banaorði.
   Þik Drótt um bar af Danmörku
   en mik sjálfan á Svíþjóðu.

Mjök er vandgætt, hvé skal verða um borinn öðrum at banaorði. Drótt um bar þik af Danmörku en mik sjálfan á Svíþjóðu.

It is very difficult to deal with how one must be born to become the slayer of another. Drótt gave birth to you in Denmark and to me myself in Sweden.

Mss.: 7(43r) (*Ásm*).

Editions: *Skj*: Anonyme digte og vers [XIII], E. 12. *Vers af Fornaldarsagaer: Af Ásmundar saga kappabana* I 1: AII, 320, BII, 340, *Skald* II, 183, *FF* §31, *NN* §2994C; Peringskiöld 1722, 21 (ch. 9), *FSN* 2, 484-5 (ch. 9), Detter 1891, 98, *FSGJ* 1, 405 (ch. 9) (*Ásm*); *CPB* I, 190, Halvorsen 1951, 11; *Edd. Min.* 53, *NK* 313.

Context: After Ásmundr has slain a succession of Hildibrandr's best warriors, Hildibrandr breaks into a berserk rage, slays his own son, and meets Ásmundr at the River Rhine. Hildibrandr's sword breaks on his adversary's helmet and flies into the Rhine. Mortally wounded, he utters a poem of six stanzas.

Notes: [1] *vandgætt* 'difficult to deal with': This cpd adj. has only one attested usage in prose, notably in *Hallfr* (*Hallfr* 1977, 52-3), where King Óláfr Tryggvason says to Hallfreðr that the sword he is giving him will be *vandgætt* because it has no sheath. Here Hildibrandr may mean that his fate, of being the killer of his half-brother, is a situation that is difficult to handle. — [3, 5]: In both ll. 3 and 5, the first element of the ms.'s *of borinn* 'be born' and *of bar* 'bore' has been normalised to *um*, to conform to Old Norse usage of the period after 1250. The untranslatable pleonastic particle *of* occurs most commonly in early poetic texts, and its presence here suggests a lengthy transmission history for this stanza. — [5-6]: These lines are similar to *Saxo* 2015, I, vii. 9. 14, ll. 9-11, pp. 506-8: '*Danica te tellus, me Sueticus edidit orbis,* | *Drot tibi maternum quondam distenderat uber. Hac genitrice tibi pariter collacteus exto*' 'Danish territory bore you, | Sweden me. Once Drot extended a mother's | breast to you; I too sucked milk from her teat.' — [5] *Drótt*: Name of the mother of both Ásmundr and Hildibrandr; she is consistently called Hildr in the saga prose, but always Drota or Drot in Saxo, which would indicate that the prose was added a considerable time after the stanzas were composed. — [6] *af* 'in': Lit. 'from'. Several eds (e.g. *Edd. Min.*, *Skald*) often emend *af* to *í* or *á* to better reflect events in the story. If an emendation is necessary, it could be either *á*, which would better parallel l. 8, or *í* for both lines, which would be the more common form.

Hildibrandr (Hildibrandr Lv 2)

2. Tveir váru þeir,   tír*argjarnir,
    Buðlanautar;   nú er brotinn annarr.
    Svá höfðu dvergar   dauðir smíðat,
    sem engi mun   áðr né síðan.

Þeir váru tveir, tír*argjarnir, Buðlanautar; nú er annarr brotinn. Dvergar dauðir höfðu smíðat svá, sem engi mun áðr né síðan.

They were two, eager for fame, treasures of Buðli <legendary king>; now one is broken. Dwarfs [now] dead had forged [them] in such a way that no one could before or since.

Ms.: 7(43r) (*Ásm*).

Reading: [2] tír*ar: 'tyrvir' 7.

Editions: *Skj*: Anonyme digte og vers [XIII], E. 12. *Vers af Fornaldarsagaer: Af Ásmundar saga kappabana* I 2: AII, 320-1, BII, 340, *Skald* II, 183, *FF* §32; Peringskiöld 1722, 21-2 (ch. 9), *FSN* 2, 485 (ch. 9), Detter 1891, 99, *FSGJ* 1, 405-6 (ch. 9) (*Ásm*); *CPB* I, 191, Halvorsen 1951, 12; *Edd. Min.* 53, *NK* 314.

Notes: [All]: The reference is to two swords, forged by Alíus and Olíus, two dwarfs who visit King Buðli and who each fashion a sword for him. The king finds fault with that of Olíus and commands him to make another. Olíus does so and predicts that it will bring death to the king's grandsons, whereupon the dwarfs disappear. — [2] *tír*ar-* 'for fame': The ms. reads 'tyrvar', which does not correspond to a known Old Norse word. Most eds emend. Kock (*FF* §32), drawing on the parallel phrase *tírargjarn* 'eager for glory' (Hfr *Óldr* 6/8[1]), offers the emendation to *tírar* 'for fame' adopted here. — [6] *dauðir* '[now] dead': *Skj* B emends to *Dáinsleif* 'Dáinn's legacy', the name of a sword forged by dwarfs, that belonged to the hero Hǫgni (*SnE* 1998, I, 72), while Kock (*Skald*; cf. *FF* §32) emends to *dáðgir* 'dynamic', but neither emendation has any ms. support.

Hildibrandr (Hildibrandr Lv 3)

3. Stendr mér at höfði   hlíf in brotna.
    Eru þar taldir   tigir in*ir* átta
    manna þeira,   er ek at morði varð.

In brotna hlíf stendr at höfði mér. In*ir* átta tigir manna, þeira er ek varð at morði, eru taldir þar.

The broken shield stands by my head. Eighty men, of whom I was the slayer, are counted there.

Ms.: 7(43r) (*Ásm*).

Reading: [4] in*ir*: 'ens' 7.

Editions: *Skj*: Anonyme digte og vers [XIII], E. 12. *Vers af Fornaldarsagaer: Af Ásmundar saga kappabana* I 3: AII, 321, BII, 340, *Skald* II, 183; Peringskiöld 1722, 22 (ch. 9), *FSN* 2, 485 (ch. 9), Detter 1891, 99, *FSGJ* 1, 406 (ch. 9) (*Ásm*); *CPB* II, 191, Halvorsen 1951, 13; *Edd. Min.* 54, *NK* 314.

Notes: [All]: Some eds (e.g. *FSGJ*) collapse sts 3 and 4, which both have only six lines, into a single stanza of twelve lines. Alternatively, to complete an eight-line stanza for each, *Edd. Min.* posits two missing lines between ll. 2 and 3 in st. 3 and two missing lines between ll. 4 and 6 in st. 4. — [1-2]: These lines are mirrored in *Saxo* 2015, I, vii. 9. 15, ll. 1, 4, pp. 508-9: *Ad caput affixus clypeus mihi Sueticus astat*, 'By my head stands fixed a Swedish shield', which depicts *proceres pugilesque subactos* 'princes destroyed, champions overthrown'. The reference to a shield painted or otherwise inscribed with images (or possibly names) of dead warriors suggests an affinity with the Carolingian and early Scandinavian pictorial poem or ekphrasis (cf. Clunies Ross 2007; Fuglesang 2007). — [4] *in*ir *átta tigir* 'eighty': Lit. 'the eight tens'. *Skj* B, *Skald* and *Edd. Min.* emend *tigir* to *tigar* (gen. sg.) to agree with 7's 'ens'. Here it is assumed that the scribe mistook the abbreviation symbol for <-ir> for a long <s>.

Hildibrandr (Hildibrandr Lv 4)

4. Liggr þar inn svási   sonr at höfði
    eptir, erfingi,   er ek eiga gat;
    óviljandi   aldrs synjaðak.

Inn svási sonr liggr þar eptir at höfði, erfingi, er ek gat eiga; óviljandi synjaðak aldrs.

The beloved son lies there behind at my head, the heir whom I begot; unwillingly I deprived [him] of life.

Ms.: 7(43r) (*Ásm*).

Editions: *Skj*: Anonyme digte og vers [XIII], E. 12. *Vers af Fornaldarsagaer: Af Ásmundar saga kappabana* I 4: AII, 321, BII, 340-1, *Skald* II, 183, *FF* §33; Peringskiöld 1722, 22 (ch. 9), *FSN* 2, 485 (ch. 9), Detter 1891, 99, *FSGJ* 1, 406 (ch. 9) (*Ásm*); *CPB* I, 191, Halvorsen 1951, 13; *Edd. Min.* 54, *NK* 314.

Notes: [All]: This stanza shows close similarities both to the Old High German *Hildebrandslied* and to parts of Saxo's poem. — [1-2] *inn svási sonr* 'the beloved son': The poetic adj. *sváss* 'agreeable, pleasant, gracious, dear' occurs exclusively in eddic poetry (cf. *LP*: *sváss*); when applied to persons (family members, the gods) it means 'dear, beloved, gracious'. It is cognate with Goth. *swēs* 'own', OE *swǣs* 'dear, own', OHG *swās* 'dear', Lat. *suus* 'belonging to oneself, one's own' and a number of other Indo-European languages (cf. *AEW*: *sváss*). This phrase bears a striking similarity to the *suâsat chind* 'beloved son, boy' of *Hildebrandslied* l. 53a (cf. Halvorsen 1951, 14). The phrase *sonr at höfði* (l. 2) may indicate that this episode too was depicted on the father's shield, as it is said to be in Saxo, meaning that the saga prose no longer understood the original story. Thus it may rather be a reference to the dead body of Hildibrandr's son, lying beside his dying father. The lines in Saxo (*Saxo 2015*, I, vii. 9. 15, ll. 6-10, pp. 508-9) are *medioxima nati | Illita conspicuo species celamine constat, | Cui manus hec cursum mete uitalis ademit. | Vnicus hic nobis heres erat, una paterni | Cura animi superoque datus solamine matri* 'there stands the likeness | of my son, whose course of life this hand brought to | its boundary. He was my only heir, the one | concern of his father's mind, given by the gods | to comfort his mother.' — [3]: Here, as with *Skj* B and *Skald*, *eptir* in the sense 'after, behind' is construed with *liggr* 'lies' in l. 1, but other eds (e.g. Detter, *Edd. Min.*, *NK* and *FSGJ*) understand the line as a cpd noun *eptirerfingi* lit. 'inheritor after sby' with a sense similar to Saxo's *unicus heres* 'only heir'.

Hildibrandr (Hildibrandr Lv 5)

5. Bið ek þik, bróðir,   bænar einnar,
   einnar bænar   eigi þú synja.
   Mik skaltu verja   váðum þínum,
   sem fjörsbani   fár annars mun.

Ek bið þik, bróðir, einnar bænar, einnar bænar, synja þú eigi. Skaltu verja mik váðum þínum, sem fár fjörsbani annars mun.

I ask you one favour, brother, one favour, do not deny me [that]. You must wrap me in your garments, as no life-slayer of another [man] would do.

Ms.: 7(43r) (*Ásm*).

Editions: *Skj*: Anonyme digte og vers [XIII], E. 12. *Vers af Fornaldarsagaer: Af Ásmundar saga kappabana* I 5: AII, 321, BII, 341, *Skald* II, 183; Peringskiöld 1722, 22 (ch. 9), *FSN* 2, 485-6 (ch. 9), Detter 1891, 99, *FSGJ* 1, 406 (ch. 9) (*Ásm*); *CPB* I, 191, Halvorsen 1951, 15; *Edd. Min.* 54, *NK* 314.

Note: [8] *fár* 'no': Lit. 'few', a mild litotes.

Hildibrandr (Hildibrandr Lv 6)

6. Nú verð ek liggja   lífs andvan*i*,
     mæki undaðr,   *þeim* er magna*r* sár.

Ek verð nú liggja andvan*i* lífs, undaðr mæki, *þeim* er magna*r* sár.

Now I must lie bereft of life, wounded by a sword, the one that increases wounds.

Ms.: 7(43r) (*Ásm*).

Readings: [2] andvan*i*: andvana 7   [4] *þeim* er: þannz 7;   magna*r*: magna 7.

Editions: *Skj*: Anonyme digte og vers [XIII], E. 12. Vers af Fornaldarsagaer: Af Ásmundar saga kappabana I 6: AII, 321, BII, 341, *Skald* II, 183, *NN* §796; Peringskiöld 1722, 22 (ch. 9), *FSN* 2, 486 (ch. 9), Detter 1891, 99, *FSGJ* 1, 406 (ch. 9) (*Ásm*); *CPB* I, 191, Halvorsen 1951, 16; *Edd. Min.* 54, *NK* 314.

Notes: [All]: This *helmingr* is sometimes treated as part of the previous stanza, giving a twelve-line stanza (so *FSGJ*), or as the second half of an eight-line stanza, although there is no indication in the ms. of missing texts (so *Edd. Min.*). — [2] *andvan*i 'bereft': The ms. reads *andvana*, but it is necessary to emend in order to give an adj. in the m. nom. sg. in agreement with *ek* 'I' (l. 1). — [3-4]: These lines refer to the dwarf-forged sword destined to bring death to King Buðli's grandsons (see st. 2 Note to [All]). — [4] *þeim er magna*r 'the one that increases': Both emendation of the ms.'s *þannz magna* and normalisation is required here. The final -*z* of *þannz* is a cliticised form of the rel. particle *es*, common in poetry from before 1200. This has been normalised to *er*, following the practice of normalizing all *SkP* VIII texts to the standard of 1250-1300. *Þann* (m. acc. sg.) must be emended to *þeim* (m. dat. sg.) to agree with *mæki* 'sword' (l. 3), while the verb should be 3rd pers. sg. pres. indic., not 3rd pers. pl., hence *magnar*, not *magna*. The majority of eds adopt the emendations preferred here, while *Skald* keeps *þanns* and emends *magna* to *manga* (cf. *NN* §796), claiming a meaning for the verb 'maim, mutilate', though that sense is unattested in Old Norse, where the meaning seems rather to be 'trade, barter, haggle' (*AEW*, *CVC*, *Fritzner*: *manga*); according to *Edd. Min.* 54 n. to 6/8, this suggested interpretation goes back to Möbius (1877, 325); it is interpreted as an unidentified p. n. in *CPB* I, 191.

Introduction to sts 7-10

In *Ásm* several lines of prose text follow Hildbrandr's *lausavísur*, and describe his death and Ásmundr's journey to ask for the hand of Æsa in fagra 'the Fair'. The two groups of stanzas are separated by only slightly more text in Saxo. The stanzas are again in *fornyrðislag*.

Ásmundr (Ásmk Lv 1)

7. Lítt varði mik   laga þeira,
   at †mik manns einskis   ofyr kvæði†,
   þá er mik til kappa   kuru Húnmegir
   átta sinnum   fyr jöfurs ríki.

Lítt varði mik laga þeira, at †mik manns einskis ofyr kvæði†, þá er Húnmegir kuru mik átta sinnum til kappa fyr ríki jöfurs.

I little expected of their laws that …, when the Huns chose me for contests eight times before the king's realm.

Mss.: 7(43r) (*Ásm*).

Editions: *Skj*: Anonyme digte og vers [XIII], E. 12. *Vers af Fornaldarsagaer: Af Ásmundar saga kappabana* II 1: AII, 321, BII, 341, *Skald* II, 183; Peringskiöld 1722, 22-3 (ch. 10), *FSN* 2, 486 (ch. 10), Detter, 1891, 99, *FSGJ* 1, 407 (ch. 10) (*Ásm*); *CPB* I, 191, Halvorsen 1951, 18; *Edd. Min.* 87.

Context: Entering the hall where Æsa is, Ásmundr utters this and the following three stanzas, which retrospectively celebrate his own prowess in a series of single combats with multiple opponents and, in the last of these, his encounter with Hildibrandr.

Notes: [All]: In both the saga prose (ch. 8) and Saxo it is stated that Ásmundr (called Haldanus by Saxo) takes on an ever-increasing number of Hildibrandr's men in a series of single combats (from one to eleven men at a time) over a period of eight days. It is this act of prowess that persuades Hildibrandr to fight Ásmundr himself, even though he knows the latter is his half-brother. This incident is also the subject of the following three stanzas. — [All]: Aside from issues of sense (see Note to ll. 3-4 below), ll. 2-4 of this stanza present a number of metrical irregularities, which suggest textual corruption; l. 2 is hypometrical, or has suspended resolution in metrical positions 1-2; l. 3 is hypermetrical and alliteration falls in metrical position 3 (if the line is construed as Type C), which is not possible, and l. 4 is hypometrical. — [3-4]: Almost as many emendations have been proposed for these lines as there have been eds, though none have been convincing. The ms.'s 'ofyr' is not an Old Norse word. *Skj* B's proposed emendation of ll. 3-4 to *at mik engum | øfra kvæði*, translated as *at man vilde sige, at jeg ingen kunde overgå* 'that one would say that I could not outmatch anyone' is the most plausible of these, although it does not fit well with the sense of ll. 1-2. For further suggestions, see *Edd. Min.* 87 n. — [5] *til kappa* 'for contests': Gen. pl. of *kapp* 'contest', not gen. sg. of *kappi* 'champion'.

Ásmundr (Ásmk Lv 2)

8. Börðumz einn við einn   en endr við tvá,
fimm ok fjóra   fletmegninga,
sex ok við sjau   senn á velli,
einn *o*k við átta,   þó ek enn lifi.

Börðumz einn við einn en endr við tvá, fimm ok fjóra fletmegninga, sex ok við sjau senn á velli *o*k einn við átta, þó ek lifi enn.

We [I] fought one against one and again against two, five and four hall-fighters, six and against seven at a time on the field, and one against eight, yet I am still alive.

Ms.: 7(43r) (*Ásm*).

Reading: [7] *o*k: ek 7.

Editions: *Skj*: Anonyme digte og vers [XIII], E. 12. *Vers af Fornaldarsagaer: Af Ásmundar saga kappabana* II 2: AII, 321, BII, 341, *Skald* II, 183, *NN* §797; Peringskiöld 1722, 23 (ch. 10), *FSN* 2, 486 (ch. 10), Detter 1891, 98, *FSGJ* 1, 407 (ch. 10) (*Ásm*); *CPB* I, 191, Halvorsen 1951, 19; *Edd. Min.* 87.

Context: As for the previous stanza.

Notes: [All]: Cf. Egill Lv 42/1-2^V (*Eg* 122). The corresponding lines in Saxo's poem are surprisingly close to those in this stanza and the beginning of st. 9 (*Saxo* 2015, I, vii. 9. 18, ll. 5-10, pp. 510-11: *Vnum quando duosque, | Tres ac quatuor, et mox | Quinos indeque senos, | Post septem, simul octo, | Vndenos quoque solus | Victor Marte subegi* 'when I subdued in battle | one alone, then two, | three and four, and soon | five followed by six, | seven, eight together, | then eleven single-handed'. — [4] *fletmegninga* 'hall-fighters': This cpd noun is a *hap. leg*. The first element is *flet* 'raised platform along the wall of a hall where the benches are and where people sleep, hall (*pars pro toto*)', but the meaning of the second must be inferred from the context and possible etymology. *LP*: *fletmegningr* suggests that the noun may mean 'incompetent, unwarlike man', with the implied sense of someone who has only the strength (*megin*) to sit on a bench in the hall or possibly someone who derives strength from being at home. On the other hand Kock (*NN* §797) postulates that the cpd is equivalent in meaning to OE *fletwerod* 'hall-troop', *fletsittend(e)* 'sitter in the hall' (*Beowulf* 476, 1788, 2022). — [7] *ok* 'and': Ms. *ek* 'I' makes relatively poor sense and may be a case of dittography, anticipating the following line, while the minor emendation to *ok* gives good sense and syntax and matches ll. 3 and 5.

Ásmundr (Ásmk Lv 3)

9. Þá hvarflaði   hugr í brjósti,
   er menn ellifu   ofrkapp buðu,
   áðr mér í svefni   sögðu dísir,
   at ek hjörleik þann   heyja skyldak.

Þá hvarflaði hugr í brjósti, er ellifu menn buðu ofrkapp, áðr dísir sögðu mér í svefni, at ek skyldak heyja þann hjörleik.

Then courage wavered in my breast when eleven men offered violence, until *dísir* <minor female deities> said to me in my sleep that I should engage in that sword play [BATTLE].

Ms.: 7(43r) (*Ásm*).

Editions: *Skj*: Anonyme digte og vers [XIII], E. 12. *Vers af Fornaldarsagaer: Af Ásmundar saga kappabana* II 3: AII, 321, BII, 341-2, *Skald* II, 184; Peringskiöld 1722, 23 (ch. 10), *FSN* 2, 486 (ch. 10), Detter 1891, 98, *FSGJ* 1, 407-8 (ch. 10) (*Ásm*); *CPB* I, 191, Halvorsen 1951, 19; *Edd. Min.* 87.

Context: According to ch. 8 of *Ásm*, Ásmundr almost loses his nerve when Hildibrandr decides to send eleven men against him. However, on the night before the contest, Ásmundr has a dream, in which armed women stand over him and identify themselves as his *spádísir*, supernatural prophetesses, possibly to be identified with valkyries. The women tell him not to fear the eleven men, saying that they will protect him in the fight.

Note: [8] *skyldak* 'I should': The ms. form with cliticised pers. pron. *ek* 'I', usually characteristic of Old Norse from before 1200, has not been normalised to the post-1200 form *skylda ek*, as it is needed to give a metrical Type A-line. This and other early forms remaining in 7 probably indicate that the poetry already existed in written form in one or more older mss.

Ásmundr (Ásmk Lv 4)

10. Þá kom inn hári   Hildibrandr,
    Húnakappi;   hann var mér ómakr.
    Ok ek markaða   meðan á hánum
    herkumbl harðlig   fyr hjálm neðan.

Þá kom inn hári Hildibrandr Húnakappi; hann var mér ómakr. Ok ek markaða meðan á hánum harðlig herkumbl fyr hjálm neðan.

Then came the grey-haired Hildibrandr, champion of the Huns; he was not easy for me to deal with. And meanwhile I marked on him hard war tokens [WOUNDS] beneath his helmet.

Ms.: 7(43r) (*Ásm*).

Editions: *Skj*: Anonyme digte og vers [XIII], E. 12. *Vers af Fornaldarsagaer: Af Ásmundar saga kappabana* II 4: AII, 322, BII, 342, *Skald* II, 184; Peringskiöld 1722, 23 (ch. 10), *FSN* 2, 487 (ch. 10), Detter 1891, 100, *FSGJ* 1, 408 (ch. 10) (*Ásm*); *CPB* I, 192, Halvorsen 1951, 20; *Edd. Min.* 87.

Context: According to the saga, after Hildibrandr hears that Ásmundr has disposed of the eleven men, he flies into a berserk rage, and sets out for the River Rhine to meet him.

Notes: [2] *Hildibrandr*: The line as it stands in the ms. is hypometrical, but if excrescent -*u*- were added in *Hildibrand*[*u*]*r*, the metre would be restored. — [3] *Húnakappi* 'champion of the Huns': According to *Skj* A, the final <i> of this word is absent, but it appears legible to this ed. — [4] *ómakr* 'not easy to deal with': Lit. 'unequal'; cf. *makara* 'more equal, more agreeable', KormQ Lv 9/5^V (*Korm* 9). — [6] *meðan* 'meanwhile': Emended by *Skj* B and *Skald* to *mæki* 'with a sword'. — [7-8]: The wording here is grimly playful. The cpd *herkumbl* usually refers to a token or mark on a helmet and can also be a *heiti* for helmet; see Þul *Hjálms* 2/2^{III}, *Hálf* 9/3. A *herkuml* beneath the helmet, however, is in the wrong place and hence is a wound to the face.

Bósa saga

Edited by Wilhelm Heizmann

Introduction

Buslubœn 'Busla's Curse' (*Busl*), transmitted within *Bósa saga ok Herrauðs konungs* 'The Saga of Bósi and King Herrauðr' (*Bós*), consists of nine stanzas in *fornyrðislag*, arranged into three unevenly distributed groups (7:1:1). Bósi's foster-mother, Busla, speaks the stanzas and directs them at King Hringr of East Götaland (ON Gautland) in Sweden, who wishes to execute both Bósi and his own legitimate son, Herrauðr, because Bósi had killed the king's preferred bastard son, Sjóðr 'Purse'.

Contrary to the conventions of the 'saga of adventure' (ModGer. *Abenteuersaga*) genre (see Introduction, Section 2 for this and other sub-generic distinctions), where one usually finds no poetry, *Buslubœn* is initially transmitted within mss containing *Bós*, a saga probably composed in the fourteenth century. Only in the post-medieval period is *Busl* recorded separately. Unlike the poetry in heroic and viking sagas (ModGer. *Helden-* and *Wikingersagas*), the *Busl* stanzas do not function to legitimise the narrative with metrically bound ancient lore, but operate as curse stanzas. Even though the saga and the poem (*Busl* 2/1) apply the euphemistic term *bœn* 'boon, plea, prayer' to the stanzas, this noun should be considered synonymous with *forbœnir* 'maledictions' or 'curses'.

Bós is transmitted in two versions which differ from one another so extensively that they could be classified as belonging to separate genres. While the earlier *Bós* may be spoken of as an *Abenteuersaga*, the younger version (which survives only in paper mss from the middle of the seventeenth century onwards and probably came into existence during post-Reformation times) falls into the *Märchensaga* genre of fabulous and legendary kind. However, the younger *Bós* displays some characteristics which are likely to be based on a more original version of the saga (*Bós* 1893, lxxiii-lxxv). Two *rímur* cycles exist alongside the two versions of the saga. The content of each has been recast according to the tastes of the time. The younger *Bósa rímur* stem from the Icelandic poet, Guðmundur Bergþórsson (1657-1705). The older *rímur* are transmitted only as fragments in just two sixteenth- or seventeenth-century mss and may well have been composed around the turn of the sixteenth century. The older *rímur* follow the older *Bós* to a great extent, though they do share some traits with the younger *Bós*, which was influenced by the *rímur* (cf. *Bós* 1893, lxvi-lxx).

Bósa saga attracted scholarly attention rather early. It was utilised as a putative source for the glory of early Swedish history during the acrimonious conflict between Sweden and Denmark over primacy in the North. The 1666 *editio princeps* (*Bós* 1666) published in Uppsala by the Swedish Royal Antiquarian, Olaus Verelius, is among the earliest editions of Old Norse literature. Its scholarly worth is insignificant though, as it is based on a textually irrelevant paper ms. in the possession of Verelius' Icelandic assistant, Jón Rugman. The first, and up to now only, edition that meets modern critical standards (with some reservations), stems from Otto Luitpold Jiriczek, who in 1893 published both versions of the saga as well as excerpts from the older *rímur*. The latter were published by him in their entirety in 1894 (for a new edition of the older *Bósa rímur* cf. Ólafur Halldórsson 1974). The saga also appears in the *FSN* and *FSGJ* collected editions of *fornaldarsögur*, as well as in that of Valdimar Ásmundarson (1885-9), while *Bós* 1996 is a Modern Icelandic edition by Sverrir Tómasson with a useful and extensive Afterword and partial glossary (*Bós* 1996, 48-79).

Jiriczek's edition of the older version of *Bós* (*Bós* 1893) accounts for all four extant vellum mss as well as two paper mss. The vellum mss in question are the following: AM 586 4° (586, Jiriczek's A, of c. 1450-1500), AM 343 a 4° (343a, Jiriczek's B, of c. 1450-75), AM 510 4° (510, Jiriczek's C, of c. 1550) and AM 577 4° (577, Jiriczek's D, of c. 1450-1500). Of these, 343a includes only two leaves of *Bós*, neither of which include stanzas of *Busl*, while there is one leaf missing from 577. The two paper mss, which fill in the gaps in the fragments, are AM 340 4^{ox} (340^x, Jiriczek's b, of c. 1600-1700) and AM 361 4^{ox} fols 10r-15v (361^x, Jiriczek's d, of c. 1600-1700). Beyond these, Jiriczek documents further paper mss, which in his opinion possess no critical value and therefore remain unconsidered. Unknown to him was a large group of paper mss of the saga located in various Icelandic and other collections. To this day these mss have not even been examined to see which version they contain. They are: AM 361 4^{ox} fols 1r-9v (c. 1600-1700), AM 591 f 4^{ox} (c. 1600-1700), AM 1039 4^{ox} (c. 1600-1700; *olim* Addit 89 c 4^{ox}), BLAdd 11108^x (c. 1700-1800), GKS 1006 fol^x (c. 1600-1700), Holm 13 4^{ox} (c. 1600-1700), Lbs 272 fol^x (c. 1700), Lbs 423 fol^x (c. 1700-1800), Lbs 1491 4^{ox} (1880-1905), Lbs 1767 4^{ox} (1857-63), Lbs 1943 4^{ox} (1877-8), UppsUB R 715 8^{ox} (R715^x, of c. 1650).

A critical edition of *Busl* from the older *Bós* was published separately by Andreas Heusler and Wilhelm Ranisch in their edition of the *Eddica Minora* from 1903 (*Edd. Min.* 126-8). Like Jiriczek, they elected to use 586 as their base ms. The same goes for the present edition; however, for the variant apparatus all mss known to the editor were inspected, although they are not reproduced in their entirety here. Only the vellum mss and the paper mss which descend from them have received comprehensive treatment.

The prose narrative in which *Busl* is embedded divides the order of stanzas into three sections of unequal size. The saga itself makes reference to this tripartition (*Bós* 1893, 18): *Busla lét þá frammi annan þriðjung bænarinnar* 'Busla uttered the second third of the plea'. Comparable to this is the threefold structure named in *Þorleifs þáttr jarlsskálds* 'The Tale of Þorleifr the Jarl's Poet' (*ÞorlJ*). *ÞorlJ* transmits only a single *helmingr* of the abusive stanzas, called *Jarlsníð* 'Níð against the jarl', imbued with magical force, that the Icelandic skald, Þorleifr jarlsskáld Rauðfeldarson, directed at the Norwegian Hákon jarl Sigurðarson (see Þjsk *Jarl*; *Flat* 1860-8, I, 212; cf. Almqvist 1965-74, I, 186-205). Here the second section of that poem has its own name, *Þokuvísur* 'Fog-*vísur*', while in *Busl* it is the final stanza that is called *Syrpuvísa* 'Syrpa-

vísa'. For the sense of the term *Syrpa*, we find documented meanings of both 'whore, ugly old woman', and 'document of mixed contents, potpourri' (*AEW*: *syrpa*; Sigfús Blöndal 1920-4, 699). The first explanation is preferable in the present instance. The designation 'Syrpa-*vísa*' is likewise attested in the *Filipórímur* (Wisén 1881, I, 21, 3), in an Icelandic marriage poem from the second half of the eighteenth century (Ólafur Davíðsson 1894, 89), and in the form *Syrpuvers hið forna* 'the ancient Syrpa-*vísa*' in two paper mss from the second half of the nineteenth century beside two young versions of *Busl* dubbed 'apocryphal' by Jiriczek (*Bós* 1893, 141-4). These instances do not, however, throw any light on the exact meaning of the term (*Edd. Min.* c).

The saga repeatedly suggests that the extant stanzas constitute only a portion of a longer original poem. At the start of the first two thirds, the prose text states that they are only a beginning (*Bós* 1893, 15, cf. 18): *en þó er þetta upphaf á henni*, and the prose introduction to the final stanza hints at a larger context (*Bós* 1893, 19): *ok er þetta þar í nærri endanum* 'and near the end it is said as follows'. The extent to which this assertion actually applies cannot be verified. We do not know if we are dealing with the fragmentary transmission of stanzas which were once more numerous than they are now. However we should not overlook places where the saga contradicts itself. On the one hand, it verbosely advises that the stanzas are not suitable for Christians on account of *mörg orð ok ill* 'many vile words' (*Bós* 1893, 15), but the stanzas are then immediately conveyed anyway.

An additional point of significance in the transmission of *Busl* is the fact that immediately after the end of *Busl* 9 a series of runes is presented in the mss. Runes are frequently mentioned in other literary texts (cf. Björn Magnússon Ólsen 1883; Finnur Jónsson 1910; Dillmann 1996), but runic characters themselves are never employed in the ms. transmission. Here, however, *Busl* 9 states that the king has to guess the names of six warriors 'unbound' (*óbundin*), i.e. unconcealed, which are apparently hidden within a row of runes, consisting of six groups of six runic characters, and these runes are depicted in detail in the mss, albeit with some variation (images in Bæksted 1942, 217-19). For a discussion of their likely meaning, see *Busl* 9 Note to [All].

In spite of its obscurity, the runic riddle of *Bos* possesses considerable importance. It requires the medium of script, as the runic formula cannot be recited in its 'bound' form. Moreover, the final stanza of *Busl* also states that Busla will 'show' (*sýna*) six warriors to the king. This suggests that *Busl* may have had at least a certain form of half-literacy, since the runes that accompanied it required the runic script, and may have been followed by some kind of instructions for carving magical runes.

Speculation over an original form of *Busl* seems to have little purpose, as it ultimately gets lost in the anonymity of the genre, which has produced numerous similar curse formulae (cf. *Edd. Min.* ic-c). In the extant form of the riddle stanza some of its terminology, such as *sál* 'soul' (9/9) and *víti* 'punishment' (9/10), is identifiable as Christian. Likewise, words such as *fortala* 'discuss, curse' (2/8) and *klárr* 'nag' (6/4) suggest a relatively young age. Finally, a series of analogous scenes from diverse eddic poems, and especially the similarity to curse stanzas transmitted by Saxo (*Saxo* 2015, I,

i. 8. 11, pp. 62-3), speak to this dating. In the words of Heusler and Ranisch (*Edd. Min.* c), *Busl* is described most saliently as *ausweitende und steigernde Nachbildung volkstümlicher Verwünschungsformeln* (*incantationes haereticae*) 'extended and augmented emulation of popular curse formulas' or rather *freie Variation über ein Thema des praktischen Aberglaubens, ausgeführt mit Hilfe alter Gedichtstellen* 'free variation on a theme of practical superstition accomplished with the aid of ancient poetry'.

Busla (Busla *Busl* 1)

1. Hér liggr Hringr konungr hilmir Gauta
    einráðastr allra manna.
    Ætlar þú son þinn sjálfr at myrða;
    þau munu fádæmi fréttaz víða.

Hér liggr Hringr konungr, hilmir Gauta, einráðastr allra manna. Þú ætlar sjálfr at myrða son þinn; þau fádæmi munu fréttaz víða.

Here lies King Hringr, ruler of the Gautar, the most stubborn of all men. You yourself intend to murder your son; these shocking events will be heard far and wide.

Mss: **586**(14r), 577(53r-v), 510(11r), 340^x(270), 361^x(11r) (*Bós*).

Readings: [6] at: *om*. 340^x [7] fá-: sjálf 577, 361^x [8] fréttaz: spyrjaz 577, 361^x.

Editions: *Skj*: Anonyme digte og vers [XIII], E. 14. *Vers af Fornaldarsagaer: Af Bósasaga* 1: AII, 330, BII, 350-1, *Skald* II, 189; *Bós* 1666, 18, *FSN* 3, 202, *Bós* 1893, 16, *FSGJ* 3, 291, *Bós* 1996, 12; *Edd. Min.* 123.

Context: Bósi, a farmer's son, is to be executed along with the king's legitimate son, Herrauðr, Bósi's blood-brother, on account of the former's slaying of the king's bastard son, Sjóðr. Herrauðr joined with Bósi against his own father, King Hringr of East Götaland. The night before the execution, Bósi's sorcerous foster-mother, Busla, appears. In her youth she had been Bósi's father's lover. She appears in the king's bed-chamber and is ultimately successful in dissuading him from his plan. She achieves this goal by reciting a total of nine curse stanzas. They begin with two stanzas that outline the scenario, and then the curses are pronounced.

Notes: [1] *Hringr konungr* 'King Hringr': Legendary kings of this name appear frequently in the *fornaldarsögur*. — [2] *Gauta* 'of the Gautar': The Gautar (OSwed. *Gøtar*) or people from Götaland are the eponymous inhabitants of the Swedish heartland (OWN *Gautland*), as well as the areas of Västergötland and Östergötland, which were probably conquered c. 600 by the Svear. The tribal name is first attested by Procopius during the middle of the sixth century in the form *Gautoí* (Andersson 1998b).

Busla (Busla *Busl* 2)

2. Heyr þú bæn Buslu;   brátt mun hon sungin,
svá at heyraz skal   um heim allan
ok óþörf öllum,   þeim sem á heyra,
en þeim þó fjandligust,   sem ek vil fortala.

Heyr þú bæn Buslu; hon mun sungin brátt, svá at skal heyraz um allan heim ok öllum óþörf, þeim sem á heyra, en þó fjandligust þeim, sem ek vil fortala.

Hear Busla's plea; it will soon be sung, so that it will be heard over the whole world, and harmful for all those who hear [it], but yet most ruinous for that one whom I wish to curse.

Mss: **586**(14r), 577(53v), 510(11r), 340ˣ(270-271), 361ˣ(11r) (*Bós*).

Readings: [2] brátt mun hon: hun mun brátt 577, brátt mun 510;   sungin: sungin verða 510 [3] at: *om*. 340ˣ;   skal: skal *corrected from* 'ma' *or* 'man' 510   [6] þeim: *om*. 510;   sem: *so* 577, 510, 340ˣ, 361ˣ, *om*. 586   [7] þó: *om*. 510.

Editions: *Skj*: Anonyme digte og vers [XIII], E. 14. *Vers af Fornaldarsagaer: Af Bósasaga* 2: AII, 330, BII, 350-1, *Skald* II, 189; *Bós* 1666, 18, *FSN* 3, 203, *Bós* 1893, 16, *FSGJ* 3, 291-2, *Bós* 1996, 12-13; *Edd. Min*. 123.

Notes: [All]: The second opening stanza stresses the danger of the curses, whose harmful effect generally applies to all who hear them. However, in this case they mainly affect the king, against whom the curses are directed. — [All]: The word choices *óþörf* 'harmful, ill' (l. 5), *fjandligust* 'very baleful, most ruinous' (l. 7) and *fortala* 'curse' (l. 8) point emphatically toward the vilifying nature of the stanzas to come. — [1] *Buslu* (gen. sg.) 'Busla's': The name is attested in Old Norse only here. The appellative *busla* is used in Modern Icelandic with the meaning 'whore' (Sigfús Blöndal 1920-4, 121) or 'slob, slovenly person' (cf. *Bós* 1996, 72) and probably belongs etymologically to the IE root **bhu* 'inflate, swell' (*ÍO*: 1 *busla*). — [2] *hon mun sungin brátt* 'it will soon be sung': Here 'sing' probably indicates an etymological root shared by the Old Norse word for 'magic, magical song' (*galdr*). Related are ON *gala* 'sing, cry out, pronounce a magical incantation', OE, OHG *galan* 'sing' (*AEW*: *gala*), which scholarship suggests hints at a magical song sung in falsetto voice (cf. Wesche 1940, 40-5; *ARG* I, 304-5).

Busla (Busla *Busl* 3)

3. Villiz vættir,   verði ódæmi,
   hristiz hamrar,   heimr sturliz,
   vestni veðrátta,   verði ódæmi,
   nema þú, Hringr konungr,   Herrauð friðir
   ok honum Bósa   bjargir veitir.

Vættir villiz, ódæmi verði, hamrar hristiz, heimr sturliz, veðrátta vestni, ódæmi verði, nema þú, Hringr konungr, veitir Herrauð friðir ok honum Bósa bjargir.

May spirit beings become lost, may the monstrous become reality, may the cliffs falter, may the world become disturbed, may the weather become chaotic, may the monstrous become reality, unless you, King Hringr, make peace with Herrauðr and grant freedom to Bósi.

Mss: **586**(14r), 577(53v), 510(11r), 340^x(271), 361^x(11r) (*Bós*).

Readings: [6] ódæmi: 'orðe' 340^x [7] konungr: *om.* 510, 340^x, 361^x [8] friðir: friði 577, 'fryer' 340^x [9] honum Bósa: Bögubósa 577, 361^x [10] veitir: veiti 577.

Editions: *Skj*: Anonyme digte og vers [XIII], E. 14. *Vers af Fornaldarsagaer: Af Bósasaga* 3: AII, 330, BII, 351, *Skald* II, 189; *Bós* 1666, 18, *FSN* 3, 203, *Bós* 1893, 16, *FSGJ* 3, 292, *Bós* 1996, 13; *Edd. Min.* 123-4.

Notes: [All]: In stanzas three to six, three different areas are named in which the curse exerts its power: Nature will fall into chaos, the king's body will be battered and contact with the outside world will be cut off, as travelling in ships and horseback riding will be rendered impossible. These four stanzas are bound together through refrain-like repetition in the four final lines of each, in which both prisoners are named in reverse order. All four are longer than the normal eight lines of a *fornyrðislag* stanza, st. 3 having ten lines and sts 4-6 having twelve. — [1] *vættir villiz* 'may spirit beings become lost': *Vættir* (archaic Engl. 'wights') are lesser mythological beings (cf. Dillmann 2007). Like *landvættir* 'guardian spirits of a country' they are evidently attributed a protective function. These beings are meant to be so confused by Busla's magic that they lose their orientation. The goal of this operation is to provoke them in this manner against the king. There is a comparable passage in *Eg* (*ÍF* 2, 170-1), in which Egill forces the *landvættir* to drive King Eiríkr blóðøx 'Bloodaxe' and his wife, Gunnhildr, out of Norway by setting up an insult-pole (*níðstǫng*, cf. Almqvist 1965-74, I, 89-118). A stanza which has wording similar to *Busl* 3 is located at the end of the so-called *Allra flagða þula* 'Reckoning of all trolls' in *VSj* (Loth 1962-5, 4, 66-8; the stanza is at p. 68). — [9] *Bósa* 'to Bósi': Relation to OE *Bōsa*, OS *Bōso*, Old Frankish *Boso*, OHG *Buoso* as well as the m. name *Bosi* in a Danish runic inscription (*DRI* 268) is uncertain (cf. *AEW*: *bósi*), as is the etymology. Sverrir Tómasson (*Bós* 1996, 51) discusses the possibility that the name may originally have referred to *þann sem klappaði kvið og rass* 'someone who stroked the belly and arse', which would have been appropriate to Bósi's role as a womaniser in the saga. Ms. 577 regularly provides the form Bögu-Bósi, abbreviated to 'bb' or 'bba' for the protagonist's name. Baga 'bent, twisted' was the nickname of Bósi's shield-maiden mother Brynhildr, which she acquired as a result of serious injuries Bósi's viking father had inflicted on her in a fight in their youth. The idea that the name Bósi is an abbreviation for [Giovanni] Boccaccio, author of the *Decameron*, and known for his outspoken narratives, seems far-fetched (Jørgensen 1997, 104-5).

Busla (Busla *Busl* 4)

4. Svá skal ek þjarma   þér at brjósti,
    at hjarta þitt   höggormar gnagi,
    en eyru þín   aldrigi heyri,
    ok augu þín   úthverf snúiz,
    nema þú Bósa   björg um veitir
    ok honum Herrauð   heipt upp gefir.

Ek skal þjarma þér svá at brjósti, at höggormar gnagi hjarta þitt, en eyru þín heyri aldrigi, ok augu þín snúiz úthverf, nema þú um veitir Bósa björg ok gefir honum Herrauð upp heipt.

I shall so oppress your breast as though adders are gnawing at your heart, and your ears shall never hear [again], and your eyes shall turn outwards, unless you grant Bósi freedom and forego your hatred towards Herrauðr.

Mss: **586**(14r), 577(53v), 510(11r), 340^x(271), 361^x(11r) (*Bós*).

Readings: [1] ek: þik 577, 361^x [2] þér: *so* 577, 510, 340^x, 361^x, þat 586   [7] ok: enn 577, 361^x [9] Bósa: Bögubósa 577, '[...] bosa' 510   [11] honum: *om.* 577, 510, 340^x, 361^x.

Editions: *Skj*: Anonyme digte og vers [XIII], E. 14. *Vers af Fornaldarsagaer: Af Bósasaga* 4: AII, 330-1, BII, 351, *Skald* II, 189, *NN* § 793; *Bós* 1666, 18-19, *FSN* 3, 203-4, *Bós* 1893, 16-17, *FSGJ* 3, 292, *Bós* 1996, 13; *Edd. Min.* 124.

Notes: [All]: The curse in this stanza is directed at the bodily welfare of the king. He will endure not only pains, but he will simultaneously be locked within himself to the extent that his eyes and ears, two vital sensory organs, will cease to function. — [3-4] *at höggormar gnagi hjarta þitt* 'as though adders are gnawing at your heart': In this way King Gunnarr perishes in the snake pit according to the Nordic transmission of the Nibelung tradition (cf. *Vǫls* ch. 39, Olsen 1906-8, 101 and *Oddrgr* st. 32). Both *Skj* B and *Skald* emend *höggormar* (nom. pl.) to *höggormr* (nom. sg.) to make l. 4 metrical (Type A2k).

Busla (Busla *Busl* 5)

5. Ef þú siglir,   slitni reiði,
   en af stýri   stökkvi krókar,
   rifni reflar,   reki segl ofan,
   en aktaumar   allir slitni,
   nema þú Herrauð   heipt upp gefir
   ok svá Bósa   biðir til sátta.

Ef þú siglir, slitni reiði, en krókar stökkvi af stýri, reflar rifni, segl reki ofan, en allir aktaumar slitni, nema þú gefir Herrauð upp heipt ok biðir Bósa svá til sátta.

If you are sailing, may the rigging tear, and the clamps spring from the steering rudder, your canvas be torn to tatters, the sail fall down, and the braces all break, unless you forego your hatred towards Herrauðr and likewise grant forgiveness to Bósi.

Mss: 586(14r-v), 577(53v), 510(11r), 340^x(271), 361^x(11r) (*Bós*).

Readings: [3] en: *om.* 577;   af: ef 577, 361^x;   stýri: stýrir 577, 361^x [6] reki: rekiz 510 [7] ak-: akt 577   [11] ok: enn 577;   svá: *om.* 577;   Bósa: Bögubósa 577, 510, 340^x [12] sátta: 'sætta' 577, 340^x, 361^x.

Editions: *Skj*: Anonyme digte og vers [XIII], E. 14. *Vers af Fornaldarsagaer: Af Bósasaga* 5: AII, 331, BII, 351, *Skald* II, 189; *Bós* 1666, 19, *FSN* 3, 204, *Bós* 1893, 17, *FSGJ* 3, 293, *Bós* 1996, 13; *Edd. Min.* 124.

Notes: [All]: The curse is now directed against the king's ability to travel and begins with the realm of seafaring. — [2-3] *en krókar stökkvi af stýri* 'and the clamps spring from the steering rudder': These lines refer to the stern rudder. In this context the clamps are attached to the rudder. Were they to spring off, the rudder would become dislodged from the stern (Falk 1912, 77). — [7] *aktaumar* 'the braces': The rope by means of which the sail is controlled (Falk 1912, 64-5; cf. Þul *Skipa* 10/3^{III}).

Busla (Busla *Busl* 6)

6. Ef þú ríðr,   raskiz taumar,
   heltiz hestar,   en hrumiz klárar,
   en götur allar   ok gagnstígar
   troðiz allar   í tröllhendr fyrir þér,
   nema þú Bósa   bjargir veitir
   ok Herrauð   heipt upp gefir.

Ef þú ríðr, raskiz taumar, hestar heltiz, en hrumiz klárar, en allar götur ok allar gagnstígar troðiz fyrir þér í tröllhendr, nema þú veitir Bósa bjargir ok gefir Herrauð upp heipt.

If you ride, may the reins become tangled, the horses limp, the nags become decrepit, and on all roads and through-routes may you be driven into the hands of trolls, unless you grant Bósi freedom and forego your hatred against Herrauðr.

Mss: 586(14v), 577(53v), 510(11r), 340˟(271), 361˟(11r) (*Bós*).

Readings: [3] hestar: hestr 510 [6] ok: *so* 510, '[...]' 586, en 577, 340˟, 361˟ [7] allar: tvéfaldar 577, 361˟ [8] í tröllhendr: í trölla hendr 510, 340˟; fyrir þér: *om.* 340˟ [9] Bósa: Bögubósa 577 [10] bjargir veitir: 'bi vm w̄ vei.' 577 [12] heipt: 'hei' 577, heyptir 340˟.

Editions: *Skj*: Anonyme digte og vers [XIII], E. 14. *Vers af Fornaldarsagaer: Af Bósasaga* 6: AII, 331, BII, 352, *Skald* II, 190; *Bós* 1666, 19, *FSN* 3, 204-5, *Bós* 1893, 17, *FSGJ* 3, 293, *Bós* 1996, 14; *Edd. Min.* 124.

Notes: [All]: This stanza has a number of metrical irregularities. Lines 1 and 11 are hypometrical, while l. 8 in the form of the majority of mss is unmetrical, though the version of 510 and 340˟ is metrical. — [All]: By means of this stanza, the king's opportunities to travel throughout the land on horseback are intended to be diminished or rendered impossible. — [8] *í tröllhendr* 'into the hands of trolls': In saga literature the etymologically uncertain ON *trǫll* (*AEW*: *troll/trǫll*) often signifies cave-dwelling, anthropomorphic creatures of abnormal size and ugliness who are equipped with magical abilities (cf. Schulz 2004, 45-6; Arnold 2005).

Busla (Busla *Busl* 7)

7. Sé þér í hvílu   sem í hálmeldi
   en í hásæti   sem á hafbáru.
   Þó skal þér seinna   sýnu verra,
   en, ef þú vilt við meyjar   manns gaman hafa,
   villiz þú þá vegarins;   eða viltu þulu lengri?

Sé þér í hvílu sem í hálmeldi en í hásæti sem á hafbáru. Þó skal þér seinna sýnu verra, en, ef þú vilt hafa gaman manns við meyjar, villiz þú þá vegarins; eða viltu lengri þulu?

May it be for you in your bed as if [you were] in burning straw and on your high-seat like on a churning sea. Yet later may it be a great deal worse for you, and if you wish to have a man's pleasure with girls, may you then lose your way: or do you desire a longer rigmarole?

Mss: 586(14v), 577(53v), 510(11r), 340˟(271), 361˟(11r) (*Bós*).

Readings: [2] hálm-: strá 340˟ [5] seinna: síðarr 577, 510, 340˟, 361˟ [6] verra: vera 577 [7] en: *om.* 577, 361˟; við: vita 510 [9] villiz þú: villr ert þú 577, 361˟; þá: *om.* 577, 361˟, þá *added above the line* 510 [10] eða: *om.* 577, 361˟.

Editions: *Skj*: Anonyme digte og vers [XIII], E. 14. *Vers af Fornaldarsagaer: Af Bósasaga* 7: AII, 331, BII, 352, *Skald* II, 190; *Bós* 1666, 19-20, *FSN* 3, 205, *Bós* 1893, 18, *FSGJ* 3, 293-4, *Bós* 1996, 14; *Edd. Min.* 124.

Notes: [All]: In the seventh stanza it is made manifest before the king that he will find no peace within his own four walls. The curses of sts 3-7 finally culminate in the threat of sexual deviance. — [3] *hásæti* 'your high-seat': The raised seat of the prince in the hall. It is comparable to OE *heahsetl* and OHG *hohsedal*. The term *ǫndvegi* or *ǫndugi* is limited exclusively to Old Norse and above all to the *Íslendingasögur* (cf. Beck 2000). — [9] *villiz þú þá vegarins* 'you will then lose your way': The additional line immediately after l. 9 in ms. 510 and several later mss clarifies what is meant by this 'confusion': ms. 510 has *ok far í rassinn* 'and make your way into the arse'! This is the only place in Old Norse literature where heterosexual anal intercourse, which here is certainly portrayed as abnormal, is explicitly mentioned. In the context of *níð*, the sexual practices referred to more often allude to homosexual intercourse between men implicitly rather than explicitly (cf. below st. 8/6). — [10] *eða viltu lengri þulu* 'or do you desire a longer rigmarole': This can be compared to *HHund I* 43/8 (*NK* 137) *vill þú tǫlo lengri*? 'do you desire further speech'?, and *Hyndl* 31, 34, 36, 39 (*NK* 293-4) *viltu enn lengra*? 'do you desire more'?; cf. Anon (*Stu*) 23[IV]. The use of *þula* 'rigmarole' here is comparable with the word's other two uses in skaldic poetry (SnH Lv 7/2[II] and Anon *Mhkv* 11/3[III]) to refer to lists of synonyms or list-like verse. For further discussion, see Introduction to the *Þulur* in *SkP* III.

Busla (Busla *Busl* 8)

8. Tröll ok álfar ok töfrnornir,
búar, bergrisar brenni þínar hallir.
Hati þik hrímþussar, hestar streði þik,
stráin stangi þik, en stormar æri þik,
ok vei verði þér, nema þú vilja minn gjorir.

Tröll ok álfar ok töfrnornir, búar, bergrisar brenni hallir þínar. Hrímþussar hati þik, hestar streði þik, stráin stangi þik, en stormar æri þik, ok verði þér vei, nema þú gjorir vilja minn.

May trolls and elves and magic-Norns, supernatural inhabitants and mountain giants burn your halls. May frost giants loathe you, stallions violate you, straw prick you and storms bewilder you; and harm will come to you unless you do my bidding.

Mss: **586**(14v), 577(53v), 510(11v), 340[x](271-272), 361[x](11r) (*Bós*).

Readings: [2] töfr-: taufra 577, töfra 361[x]   [4] brenni: brenn 577, 361[x]   [5] þik: *om.* 577, 361[x]   [6] hestar streði þik: 'heller þínar' 577, 361[x];   streði: tróði 340[x]   [8] en: *om.* 577, 361[x]; stormar: stofnar 577, 361[x], stjörnur 510, stormur 340[x];   æri: angri 577, 361[x]   [9] ok: *om.* 577; vei verði þér: verði þér vei 577   [10] vilja: vili 577.

Editions: *Skj*: Anonyme digte og vers [XIII], E. 14. *Vers af Fornaldarsagaer: Af Bósasaga* 8: AII, 331-2, BII, 352, *Skald* II, 190; *Bós* 1666, 20-1, *FSN* 3, 205-6, *Bós* 1893, 18, *FSGJ* 3, 294, *Bós* 1996, 14-15; *Edd. Min.* 124.

Context: A passage of prose now intervenes in *Bós* after st. 7 and before st. 8. It tells that the king remains implacable and insults Busla by calling her a *vættr*, a word which can be understood in the sense of 'witch' in this context. Busla's magic causes the king to be stuck fast to the bed and the servant boys kept asleep. Thus she can begin to recite the poetry that begins the second section of the curse, in which an entire army of demons is invoked to rise up against the king.

Notes: [1] *álfar* 'elves': Mythical beings akin to the Æsir who receive cult worship (*álfablót* 'sacrifice to the elves') (Kuhn 1973; Shippey 2005b). Younger sources, as here in *Bós*, emphasise the demonic aspects of elves (Grimm 1875-8, 2, 381-2; Turville-Petre 1964, 232; Shippey 2005b, 166-8). — [2] *töfrnornir* 'magic-Norns': A *hap. leg.* While the Norns appear elsewhere as a threesome of fatal women (Dillmann 2002a), here they seem to present a younger development in which the Norns are included in a series of other baleful mythical creatures. Here the saga uses the word *töfr* n. pl., a concept initially applied to equipment and instruments used for magic, but then later for sorcery in general (cf. Wesche 1940, 5-17; Dillmann 2006, 130-2; *AEW*: *taufr*). — [3] *búar* 'supernatural inhabitants': Lit. 'inhabitants'. The inhabitants of mountains (*bergbúar*) and hills or mounds (*haugbúar*). These may include the dead as well as lesser mythological beings. — [3] *bergrisar* 'mountain giants': Old Norse tradition differentiates between several types of giants (cf. Schulz 2004, 29-37). *Jǫtunn*, *þurs* and *risi* are old words and are attested in all Germanic languages. *Trǫll* is attested only in Scandinavian languages and with a younger dating. Apart from some giants who are connected to the gods in Old Norse mythology by marriage or blood, the giants are generally regarded as threatening. They are demonised as forces of chaos and embody the forces of nature. The group of the mountain giants is attested in the eddic poem *Grott* (st. 9), but is otherwise mentioned relatively seldom. The mountain giants were probably first established as a separate group by Snorri Sturluson in *Gylf* (Schulz 2004, 44-5). — [5] *hrímþussar* 'frost giants': In *Gylf* frost giants appear as the archetypal embodiment of the giant race. Their lineage leads directly to the eldest humanoid primordial being, Ymir, who is licked out of the primordial frost by the cow, Auðhumla, and reproduces hermaphroditically with himself (*SnE* 2005, 11; cf. Schulz 2004, 43, 65-8). — [6] *hestar streði þik* 'may stallions violate you': Counted among the gravest insults in Old Norse society is the suggestion of passive homosexuality (cf. Meulengracht Sørensen 1983, 18-20; Almqvist 2002, 141; Price 2005, 254-6). It culminates not infrequently in the accusation of having changed sexes. Thus an anonymous Icelandic mocking verse in *Hkr* (*ÍF* 27, 270-1) about the Danish king, Haraldr Gormsson, and his jarl, Birgir, depicted the two men as stallion and mare (Anon (*ÓTHkr*) 1[1]; cf. Almqvist 1965-74, I, 119-85). Although the matter might generally remain at the level of obscene imagery, the line in *Busl* takes it to excess with the threat of real, repeated rape by stallions. On the verb *streða* 'screw', as a key word in the context of *níð*, cf. Meulengracht Sørensen (1983, 17-20) and Price (2005, 253).

Busla (Busla *Busl* 9)

9. Komi hér seggir sex;   seg þú mér nöfn þeirra
   öll óbundin;   ek mun þér sýna.
   Getr þú ei ráðit,   svá at mér rétt þikki,
   þá skulu þik hundar   í hel gnaga,
   en sál þín   sökkvi í víti.

Sex seggir komi hér; seg þú mér nöfn þeirra öll óbundin; ek mun sýna þér. Getr þú ei ráðit, svá at mér þikki rétt, þá skulu hundar gnaga þik í hel, en sál þín sökkvi í víti.

Let six warriors come here; tell me all their names without concealment; I will show [them] to you. If you cannot guess, so that it seems correct to me, then let dogs gnaw you to death and your soul sink to punishment.

Mss: 586(14v), 577(54r), 510(11v), 361ˣ(11v) (*Bós*).

Readings: [4] mun: skal 577, 361ˣ   [6] at: *om.* 510;   mér: *om.* 577, 361ˣ;   þikki: 'þike' 510 [10] sökkvi: sökkva 577, 361ˣ;   í víti: 'i v' 577.

Editions: *Skj*: Anonyme digte og vers [XIII], E. 14. *Vers af Fornaldarsagaer: Af Bósasaga* 9: AII, 332, BII, 352-3, *Skald* II, 190; *Bós* 1666, 21, *FSN* 3, 206, *Bós* 1893, 19, *FSGJ* 3, 295, *Bós* 1996, 15; *Edd. Min.* 125.

Context: The king partially gives in by agreeing to grant Herrauðr his life, but insists on maintaining his hostility to Bósi. This is not enough for Busla, and thus there now follows the crucial and decisive final third section, the 'Syrpa-*vísa*' (for this name, cf. Introduction).

Notes: [All]: Here the king is confronted with a riddle before which he must ultimately capitulate. It involves guessing the names of six warriors, apparently by decoding the six runes r. o. þ. k. m. u. which appear immediately after *Busl* 9 in all the older mss, followed by the runic letters i, s, t, i and l, each written six times over. The six warriors are to be understood as the six runes above, whose meaning the king is supposed to unlock. The six times repeated runes are a variant of the so-called *þistill-mistill-kistill* formula, which is frequently attested from various runic objects (cf. Heizmann 1998, 519-20), the oldest example of which is located on the Danish runestone from Gørlev c. 800 (*DRI* 239). It is likely that the formula was originally a curse associated with burial rituals, whose purpose was to banish the dead into the grave (*NIyR* 4, 177-8). — [8-9] *þá skulu hundar gnaga þik í hel* 'then let dogs gnaw you to death': I.e. 'let dogs chew on you until you die'. Cf. ModDan. *ihjæl*, ModNorw. *ihjel* 'to death' and Anon *Mhkv* 8/2ᴵᴵᴵ (see Note there). — [9-10] *en sál þín sökkvi í víti* 'and your soul sink to punishment': The implication is that this is punishment for King Hringr's soul in the Christian Hell.

Breta saga

Gunnlaugr Leifsson

Biography

Gunnlaugr Leifsson (GunnLeif, d. 1218 or 1219) was a monk at the Benedictine house of Þingeyrar, a monastery near the shores of Húnaflói, in northern Iceland, that maintained close relations with the seat of the bishop at Hólar (Turville-Petre 1953, 135). Nothing is known concerning Gunnlaugr's place of birth, upbringing or social origins. He was regarded in his own time as a man of singular Latin learning (*LH* II, 394-5) and worked in a distinguished historiographic and hagiographic milieu (de Vries 1964-7, II, 246). In a rare personal anecdote, perhaps apocryphal, Arngrímr Brandsson, a Benedictine monk and abbot at Þingeyrar (d. 1361 or 1362), tells that Gunnlaugr attempted to recite his new history of Saint Ambrose at the church at Hólar but was rebuffed by Bishop Guðmundr Arason (*LH* II, 394-5; Ciklamini 2008, 1). The two men were evidently on good terms at an earlier stage, however (Ciklamini 2004, 66), and, while bishop at Hólar, Guðmundr commissioned Gunnlaugr to prepare a life of Jón helgi 'the Saint' Ǫgmundarson and an account of portents and miracles pertaining to Þorlákr Þórhallsson, both in Latin (*LH* II, 394-5).

Works ascribed to Gunnlaugr that survive in one form or other include the Latin life of Jón helgi, represented by a close Icelandic translation; the account of Þorlákr's miracles; a Latin expansion of Gunnlaugr's Þingeyrar colleague Oddr Snorrason's life of King Óláfr Tryggvason, extant in the shape of excerpts translated into Icelandic; an Icelandic original version of *Þorvalds þáttr víðforla* 'The Tale of Þorvaldr the Far-traveller' that may at one time have formed part of the life of Óláfr; and a now entirely lost life of Saint Ambrose (*LH* II, 394-403; Turville-Petre 1953, 194-200; Bekker-Nielsen 1958; de Vries 1964-7, II, 245-7; Würth 1998, 205-6; Ciklamini 2004, 66; Katrín Axelsdóttir 2005). The only work ascribed to Gunnlaugr that appears to survive in a relatively complete state is *Merlínusspá* 'The Prophecies of Merlin' (*Merl I* and *II*). It is also the sole medieval instance of a direct verse translation into Icelandic from Latin prose (Würth 1998, 206).

Merlínusspá I

Edited by Russell Poole

Introduction

Uniquely extant in Hauksbók (Hb, AM 544 4°), *Merlínusspá* 'The Prophecies of Merlin' (GunnLeif *Merl*) is preserved as two separate poems (termed here *Merl I* and

Merl II) that form part of *Breta saga* 'The Saga of the British' (*Bret*), a rendering of *De gestis Britonum* 'Concerning the deeds of the Britons' (*DGB*: formerly known as *Historia regum Britanniae* 'History of the kings of Britain') (Halvorsen 1959, 22-3; cf. Lönnroth 1965, 83). The present Introduction is pertinent to both parts of *Merl* and their relationship is discussed below. The author of *Merl* is identified in Hb as follows (*Bret* 1848-9, II, 12, here normalised): *Hér eptir hefir Guðlaugr munkr ort kvæði, þat er heitir Merlínusspá* 'In accordance with this, Guðlaugr the monk has composed a poem called *Merlínusspá*'. The reading *Guðlaugr* found in Hb appears to result from later over-writing of original *Gunnlaugr* (*Bret* 1848-9, II, 13 n. 9). The section of Hb where *Merl* occurs was written by Haukr Erlendsson himself in the first decade of the fourteenth century (Stefán Karlsson 1964b; cf. Johansson 2005, 111); the text of *Merl* begins on fol. 49r and ends on fol. 53r. The AM 573 4° redaction of *Bret* corroborates the ascription of *Merl* to Gunnlaugr but omits the text, observing (*Bret* 1848-9, II, 13 n. 11): *kunna margir menn þat kvæði* 'many people know that poem', where *kunna* is assumed to mean 'know by heart' (Jakob Benediktsson 1966, 556). The attribution to Gunnlaugr has never been seriously questioned in scholarship (though for a suggestion, on insufficient evidence, that part of the text was composed by an imitator of Gunnlaugr rather than Gunnlaugr himself, see Horst 2006).

Gunnlaugr is thought to have completed *Merl* c. 1200 (for somewhat earlier suggested datings see Leach 1921, 138; Sveinbjörn Rafnsson 1999, 391). The poem represents an Icelandic rendering of a prose narrative by Geoffrey of Monmouth entitled the *Prophetiae Merlini* 'Prophecies of Merlin', which is now best known to us as a section of the *DGB*. The *DGB* probably assumed its finally published and transmitted form at some point in late 1137 or in 1138 (cf. Tatlock 1950, 433-7; Gransden 1974, 201; Wright 1985, ix-xvi; Reeve and Wright 2007, vii). The text-within-a-text constituted by the *Prophecies* occupies *DGB* VII chs 3 and 4 in the edition of Griscom (1929), corresponding to chs 111-17 of the edition of Faral (1929) and of Reeve and Wright (2007, 142-59; the page and line numbers of the latter edition are used in the ensuing discussion and Notes). The *Prophecies* are thought to have been separately issued by Geoffrey in 1135 (Wille 2015, iv).

In the narrative of *DGB*, the *Prophecies* are prompted by the attempts of Vortigernus, king of the Britons, to build a mountain-top fortification against the invading Saxons. The builders find that the foundations they build one day have mysteriously disappeared by the next. The king seeks the advice of wise men who counsel him to have the mortar mixed with the blood of a child without a father (*iuuenem sine patre*: Reeve and Wright 2007, 137). Questing for such a child, the king's envoys discover Merlin, whose father was an incubus. Rather than be killed as the treacherous wise men propose, Merlin discloses the presence of two serpents that are responsible for undermining the foundations and goes on to reveal at great length what they portend for the Britons. These prophecies cover aspects of British history and legend starting with the wars between the Anglo-Saxons and the Britons (*Prophecies* 1 to 8, as numbered in Wright 1988), continuing with the Norman Conquest and the

Plantagenet kings (9 to 12) and finally projecting onward to events that lay in the future from Geoffrey's viewpoint so as to conclude with the end of the world (13 to 74). The last historical event definitely verifiable in the *Prophecies* is the drowning of Henry I's heir apparent and some of his other offspring in the year 1120 (Tatlock 1950, 403). Thereafter the events described bear no clear relation to known historical events, though see *Merl I* 53 and 54, Notes to [All]. Geoffrey's distinctive use of an intermittent allegory, where rulers are represented by one or more animal figures (lion, lynx, boar, fox, wolf, serpent or combinations thereof), renders the content of the *Prophecies* highly cryptic and enigmatic (Taylor 1911, 4, 11). Many readers will wholeheartedly concur with Tatlock (1950, 416), who describes the *Prophecies* as 'imaginative to the point of lunacy' – 'much of them it is hard to believe ever had any intelligible meaning for anyone'. While such strictures are partly justifiable, and will have been concurred in by at least a few medieval readers, the importance of the prophecies of Merlin and the numerous vaticinatory texts composed under its influence in the workings of society, both English and European, right down to the early modern period, is well documented (see e.g. Aurell 2007, 391; Dobin 1990, 25, 51; Curley 1984, 335-6; Fraiolo 1982). The reign of Henry II saw particularly intense scrutiny of the text with an eye to signs and portents (see e.g. Warren 1978, 25). The redactor of the AM 573 4° version of *Bret* notes this fact (*Bret* 1848-9, II, 13): *Sv spá hefir oft síðan af hinum uitrvztvm mönnum á Einglandi rannsökuð uerið* 'That prophecy has often since been inquired into by the wisest men in England'. Gunnlaugr enjoins readers of his adaptation to scrutinise it in the same light (see *Merl I* 101). Towards this end, perhaps, he appears to put the credentials of the *Prophecies* on their best footing by vouching for Merlin's Christian status and by adducing only the Old Testament prophets Daniel and David as analogues rather than the Sibyls and other non-Scriptural figures adduced by some European commentators.

Symptomatic of its extraordinary popularity and rapid dissemination, the *DGB* survives in over 200 mss, of which about fifty belong to the twelfth century; in addition, over eighty mss of the *Prophecies*, separate from *DGB*, are extant (Veysseyre and Wille 2008, 93). It is not known how and in what form Geoffrey's work reached Iceland. A Lincoln connection has been tentatively suggested by Leach (1921, 138-9) on circumstantial grounds. The bishop of Lincoln, Alexander the Magnificent (1123-43), as dedicatee of Geoffrey's separate publication of the *Prophecies*, received the first copy of it from Geoffrey (Wright 1984, 1) and it could have been copied and made available to readers there, among them members of the celebrated cathedral school at Lincoln. This school had Icelanders among its international band of students, notably, around 1160, Þorlákr Þorhallsson, later bishop at Skálholt 1178-93, and his successor in the see Páll Jónsson (Orri Vésteinsson 2000b, 154). The intense interest in the *Prophecies* in England during the reign of Henry II, prompted not least by the king's antagonism toward Thomas Becket, coincided with an era of conflict over leadership policies and the limits of ecclesiastical jurisdiction in Iceland (cf. Helgi Þorláksson 2005, 146; Guðrún P. Helgadóttir 1987, xii-xiv). Prominent in the debate was

Guðmundr Arason, a celebrated priest and later bishop of Hólar (1203-37). Close relations with this see were maintained by Gunnlaugr's institution of Þingeyrar, near the shores of Húnaflói (Turville-Petre 1953, 135). The most noteworthy honour accorded to Guðmundr prior to his election as bishop was the procession led by Karl, abbot of Þingeyrar, and Gunnlaugr to greet him on his visit to the monastery in 1199 (Ciklamini 2004, 66). Gunnlaugr for his part was regarded in his own time as a man of singular Latin learning (ÍF 15, cclxxxiii). He is known to have been entrusted by Guðmundr with commissions for writings pertaining to S. Þorlákr and Bishop Jón Ǫgmundarson, both in Latin (Turville-Petre 1953, 198-9). More than this, Guðmundr actively provided some of the content by sending Gunnlaugr accounts of portents and miracles relating to S. Þorlákr. Given this relationship between Guðmundr and Gunnlaugr, the former might well have been responsible for commissioning Gunnlaugr's translation of the *Prophecies*. As Crick (2011, 76) notes, 'Merlin was a matter for bishops and popes' and Guðmundr might well have aspired to an episcopal role long before his election.

Alternative possibilities exist as to the character of Gunnlaugr's source ms.:

1) He might have based himself on a ms. of *DGB*. This assumption would be favoured by the fact that, codicologically speaking, the unique attestation of *Merl* occurs within the Hb redaction of *Bret*, the Icelandic prose translation of the *DGB*, and is placed in a context corresponding to that of the prophecies in *DGB*. In the Hb redaction the poem is preceded by a brief paragraph mentioning the poet Gunnlaugr, which, although apparently an interpolation, in fact does not preclude the presence of a non-Gunnlaugr text of the prophecy in Haukr's source. In the other extant redaction of *Bret*, that of AM 573 4° (fol. 45r), the situation is similar. An advantage of this hypothesis is that it obviates the need to posit two importations of Geoffrey material to Iceland: first, a separate copy of the *Prophecies* for Gunnlaugr to translate; second, at some unknown time, a copy of the complete *DGB* which, whether directly or through intermediaries, yielded the extant redactions of *Bret*. On the other hand, this application of Ockham's razor is far from conclusive, since while we know that large quantities of learned books were brought to Iceland in the relevant period we have very little by way of precise inventories from which to gauge patterns of acquisition. Moreover, as we shall see later, it would be difficult to prove that Gunnlaugr personally had access to the full *DGB*.

2) Gunnlaugr might have worked from a separate ms. of the *Prophecies*. Within this scenario there are again two possibilities to be distinguished. He might have used a copy of the *Prophecies* that derived from the full *DGB*. Alternatively, he might have had recourse to a copy of the *Libellus Merlini* 'The Booklet of Merlin', an early version of the *Prophecies* that appears, as noted, to have been separately issued by 1135. Evidence for its separateness takes three forms. Ordericus Vitalis quotes the equivalent of *DGB* chs 113:72-115:108 in his *Historia ecclesiastica* 'Ecclesiastical History' (1135), stating that they emanate from a *Merlini libellus* (Reeve and Wright 2007, viii-ix; contrast Tatlock 1950, 418-21). In some mss the *Prophecies* are separately dedicated to Bishop

Alexander. Finally, Geoffrey states that he accessed the *Prophecies* in a British-language source distinct from the one purportedly used for *DGB* (Reeve and Wright 2007, 142-3). While this claim, as applied to the *Prophecies* as a whole, is no doubt spurious, he may have had access to a Brittonic source or sources for at least some of his material (Faletra 2012, 306, 309).

In considering the rival claims of the two possible source types within scenario 2, we can refer to the study of manuscript affiliations carried out by Michael D. Reeve (in Reeve and Wright 2007). Reeve posits a separate text of the *Prophecies*, called Π, which he equates with the *Libellus*. As he recognises, not all complete mss of the *Prophecies* descend from this text: some appear to have had an incomplete ancestor that was later supplemented from *DGB* (Reeve and Wright 2007, xxix). In order to determine which separate copies of the *Prophecies* descend from Π and were not extracted from *DGB*, Reeve singles out two of Ordericus' readings, 113:74 *ipsius* 'of the same' for *albi draconis* 'of the white serpent' and 114:92 *translateralibus* 'adjacent peoples' for *collateralibus* 'adjacent peoples' (Reeve and Wright 2007, xxix). To judge from *Merl I* 47/6: *snáks ins hvíta* 'of the white snake', Gunnlaugr's source ms. would have contained *albi draconis* 'of the white dragon'. The status of the other decisive reading, at 114:92, cannot be determined, since it is not represented in the extant text of *Merl*. This diagnostic, taken at face value, would indicate that Gunnlaugr's source ms. belonged not with Π but with the Ω group, where Ω = a no longer extant ms. of *DGB* that is posited as the common source of most of the non-Π ms. classes (Reeve and Wright 2007, l). That might well be correct, but the reservation must be made that Gunnlaugr so often uses *heiti* and kennings instead of pronominal forms of reference that this reading falls short of proof that he is here following a ms. of the Ω class. The same applies to the other readings characteristic of Ω that we find apparently reflected in *Merl*. These include *septem* 'seven' for *octo* 'eight' in ch. 112.52-3 and *tria* 'three' for *quattuor* 'four' in ch. 116.188 (respectively *Merl I* 33/3 and *II* 27/1); numerals are a frequent source of error in the transmission of *DGB* and coincident error is always possible. Additionally, a sentence at 116:174 which is omitted by the Ω group but represented in Π (and hence in Ordericus) does not appear in *Merl* (see *Merl II* 19 Note to [All]); once again, however, such silence might be due to coincident error, since on his own admission Gunnlaugr omits some tracts of text and moreover losses of portions of the text of *Merl* in transmission subsequent to him are likely to have occurred. For further readings that might be interpreted as indicating the detailed affiliations of Gunnlaugr's copy-text see *Merl I* 28, *I* 29, *I* 41, *I* 45, *I* 54, Notes to [All], *Merl II* 25 and *II* 48, Notes to [All]. In sum, the textual evidence, taken in isolation, is scarcely conclusive as to which class of mss Gunnlaugr's source belonged to (cf. Tétrel 2010, 496). At the same time, the weight of evidence points us in the direction of the Ω group.

In deciding whether his copy-text confined itself to the *Prophecies*, included the whole of *DGB* or lay somewhere in between these extremes, we should note that Gunnlaugr appears to have had some knowledge of the contents of certain parts of

DGB outside the *Prophecies*, notably Books IX-XI but also Books V and VI (cf. J. S. Eysteinsson 1953-7). This does not necessarily prove, however, that he had access to *DGB per se*. From the time of their first publication the *Prophecies* were immediately copied, glossed, annotated and translated, sometimes alongside the complete *DGB* and sometimes separately. The *Prophecies* are one of a very few secular texts of the twelfth century to have become the subject of commentaries written by contemporary scholars and many text-plus-commentary compilations on the *Prophecies* were produced before the end of the twelfth century. Instances are the twelfth-century mss Lincoln Cathedral Ms. A. 46 (Taylor 1911, 87-8; Crick 1991, 85-7) and Paris BN Lat. 14465, the latter of which adds the chapters of *DGB* that precede the *Prophecies* from 105.489 to the end of 108 so as to explain their historical background (Reeve and Wright 2007, xxx). Most of the commentaries so far studied contain a digest of information about Arthur (ultimately stemming from *DGB* IX-XI). Gunnlaugr could have obtained his supplementary material from such a source. Gunnlaugr seems likely, on other evidence, to have availed himself of a copy with annotation or commentary of some kind: see *Merl I* 9/5 and *I* 56 Notes to [All]. In the present state of scholarship, with not all commentaries and annotated versions edited, it is not feasible to reach a firm conclusion on this question. Complicating the matter is the lack of scholarly agreement as to whether the translation of *DGB* into *Bret* preceded that of *Merl* (Turville-Petre 1953, 202), or *vice versa* (*Hb* 1892-6, cxi; Paasche 1957, 323); in its extant shape *Bret* is a much altered version of the original translation (Kalinke 2009, 218; Tétrel 2010, 493-5) and offers no clear indications as to the *floruit* or identity of the translator (Würth 1998, 56).

Aside from *DGB* and commentaries on this work, Gunnlaugr appears to have made sporadic use of a few other sources. He refers on occasion to Bede's *Historia Ecclesiastica* 'Ecclesiastical History' (*HE*; on Gunnlaugr's knowledge of Bede, cf. *LH* II, 402; J. S. Eysteinsson 1953-7, 102, 110), to Henry of Huntingdon's *Historia Anglorum* 'History of the English' (*HA*), published in different versions from c. 1131 down to c. 1155 (*HA* 1996, lxx-lxxvii; on knowledge of Henry in twelfth-century Denmark see Gelting 2007, 106), and to William of Malmesbury's *Gesta regum Anglorum* 'Deeds of the kings of the English', published c. 1125 (Mynors *et al.* 1998-9, II, xxiv; on Gunnlaugr's possible access to William, cf. J. S. Eysteinsson 1953-7, 102, 110). On these possible references see *Merl I* 2, *I* 4, *I* 5 and I 50, Notes to [All], and Note to *I* 49/4. Additionally, *Merl* seems to reflect an awareness of contemporary beast epic. This emerging genre was available from the mid-twelfth century in the shape of the *Ysengrimus*, a Latin epic poem that featured lengthy dialogue passages. It prompted the production of vernacular texts such as the *Roman de Renart*, which contains a series of short episodes centred on the fox's hoodwinking of various other animals (Mann 2009, 17-19). These texts proliferate between 1150 and 1200 (Mann 1987, 3) and some of their distinctive features appear in *Merl II* 37-45, the passage that deals with Geoffrey's fox king. For Gunnlaugr's knowledge of vernacular Old Norse literature see below.

So far as we can judge from the extant text of *Merl*, Gunnlaugr's translation of the *Prophecies per se* follows Geoffrey's text with remarkable closeness and accuracy (cf. *LH* II, 173). This appears to arise from the nature of the text: as prophetic material, Merlin's vaticination was treated as tantamount to sacred, and scribes and translators seem to have taken care to preserve the precise wording or sense whenever possible (cf. Blacker 2005, 10). To facilitate comparison, this edition cites both text and translation from Reeve and Wright (2007) for all relevant passages; in those instances where their translation is somewhat free, masking the accuracy of the rendition in *Merl*, a more literal version has been substituted (marked by the use of 'cf.' before the page reference to Reeve and Wright). It must be borne in mind, however, that a definitive edition of *DGB*, using all extant mss, has yet to be attempted; indeed, even with a complete account of the paradosis the exact wording of Gunnlaugr's source text is likely to remain indeterminate. The same difficulty applies to any attempt to show that his translation has value for the textual criticism of *DGB* (for an investigation of this kind into the prose of *Bret*, see van Hamel 1936), but see Note to *Merl I* 54/4 for a possible instance of Gunnlaugr's text reflecting an otherwise unknown superior reading. Exceptions to Gunnlaugr's fidelity to *DGB* consist of material added from the other sources noted above, along with material he freely composed, comprising introductions and conclusions to each Part and two matched battle descriptions, each placed approximately centrally within its Part. Some of the apocalyptic material in Merlin's prophecy is supplanted by a brief homily attacking vanity and urging contempt of the world (*Merl II* 52-7): Gunnlaugr expressly states in *Merl II* 50 that he will omit many prophecies on account of their length and distasteful content. In some cases, however, it is difficult, as noted above, to decide whether the absence of these materials reflects deliberate omission on Gunnlaugr's part or casual loss in subsequent transmission.

Gunnlaugr chose verse as the medium for his translation, and specifically the *fornyrðislag* metre, varied with use of *kviðuháttr* at the close of *Merl II*. The choice of verse rather than prose may have been prompted by a persisting tradition, fostered by William of Newburgh among other commentators (Curley 1982, 221-2), that Geoffrey had a vernacular source in poetic form. The choice of *fornyrðislag* rather than other metres may be owing to the existence of several well-known Icelandic poems of prophecy in that verse-form, notably *Vsp* but also *Gríp* and *Hyndl*. For a systematic study of the relationship between *Merl* and *Vsp*, see Horst (2010); for the view that *Vsp* was based on *Merl*, instead of the other way around, as has been the standard assumption in scholarship and in this edition, see Sveinbjörn Rafnsson (1999). It happens that both *Merl* and *Vsp* occur in Hb; see Simek (1991) and Johansson (2005) for opinions on the textual relationship between them in that ms. On the other hand, *Vsp* should not be seen as Gunnlaugr's unique model (cf. Horst 2010); verbal parallels have been detected not merely between *Merl* and *Vsp* but also between *Merl* and such other eddic poems as the *Helgakviða* sequence and *Gríp*: see Notes to *Merl I* 10/6, *I* 66/3, *I* 77/8, *Merl II* 2/7-8, *II* 24/1, *II* 35/7, *II* 36/6, *II* 51/6, *II* 54/1, 3, *II* 59/2 and *II* 61/1. (For possible allusions to *Hávm* see Notes to *Merl I* 103/1-2 and *II* 24/4.) These proposed stylistic parallels have been explained as due to Gunnlaugr's direct borrowing from specific poems (de Vries 1964-7, II, 75-6), but, given the broadly generic nature of the verbal resemblances, most are better explained on the basis that he was simply using a general eddic style such as we also see in the early twelfth-century Gísl *Magnkv*[II] and the mid-twelfth-century Ív *Sig*[II]; for a verbal parallel with Gísl *Magnkv* see Note to *Merl I* 67/9. The occasional use of ten- and twelve-line stanzas rather than the standard eight is also best explained as resulting from a general awareness of eddic style rather than indebtedness to any one specific poem. It has been claimed (Turville-Petre 1953, 200) that, as used by Gunnlaugr, the *fornyrðislag* metre is regularised more than is typical of poems in this verse-form in the Poetic Edda, and this observation, if tenable, suggests his independent command of the medium. Complementarily, Gunnlaugr incorporates some skaldic stylisms, especially in the expanded battle descriptions, which feature an array of *heiti* and kennings on martial themes that considerably surpasses the incidence of such features to be found in more strictly eddic poetry (*LH* II, 173-4; de Vries 1964-7, II, 76). Here once again it is easier to see a general resemblance to twelfth- and thirteenth-century skaldic style, as represented by such works as RvHbreið *Hl*[III], SnSt *Ht*[III] and Anon *Krm* (*Ragn*), than an indebtedness to specific poems. As to possible influence of *Merl* on other poems, the most salient candidate is *Ht*: the length of *Merl I*, at 103 stanzas, is closely comparable with that of *Ht*, at 102 stanzas, and commonalities of certain distinctive kennings for body parts between the two works (Guðrún Nordal 2001, 242, 308) might further indicate some emulation of Gunnlaugr on Snorri's part. Another important element in the poem is the characteristic vocabulary of homiletic and related literature (see e.g. Notes to *Merl I* 54/4, *I* 87/1, *II* 53/1-4, *II* 55/8, *II* 65/1).

As to structure, *Merl* is made up of two linked poems. The Part designated *Merl I* in this edition contains Geoffrey's chs 105.494 to 115.146 (inclusive), covering events from the lead-up to Merlin's utterances down to the massacre at London narrated in Prophecy 30. The Part designated *Merl II* in this edition continues from chs 116.1 to 117.304, covering events from the emergence of the three springs at Winchester in Prophecy 31 down to the end of the world concluded in Prophecy 74. Each Part is complete as an independent poem, having its own introduction and conclusion (*Hb* 1892-6, cxi). In *Merl I* the introduction consists of nine stanzas that provide information on the historical background, including Merlin, and the conclusion consists of Gunnlaugr's freely composed apologia for Geoffrey's allegorical method. In *Merl II* the introduction consists of four stanzas of explanation about Merlin and the nature of the ensuing poem and the conclusion consists of Gunnlaugr's freely composed peroration. Of the two Parts, *Merl I* is the more informative on the historical background and on Merlin, whereas *Merl II* carries the more elaborate conclusion and peroration. Linking these two Parts are stanzas *I* 93 and 94, where Gunnlaugr speaks of further prophecies that he has evidently already rendered and means to issue as a separate installment (*Merl II*). When he says that he has compiled 'some' of the prophecies (*I* 93/7-8), this should be seen not as indicating that the preparation of Part

II is still in progress but rather that other prophecies have been deliberately excluded from the project, as he duly states in *II* 50 (and cf. *II* 62). From the internal evidence, then, we can draw the conclusion that Gunnlaugr published his translation in the form of two installments, having first prepared the entire poem. Even so, the renewed introduction of Merlin at the start of *Merl II* is odd. Gunnlaugr may simply have felt that his audience needed a quick reminder about Merlin's role, but the stanzas read more like an introduction *de novo* for the benefit of an audience that had not previously heard of Merlin. This feature, along with the reverse-order sequencing of the Parts in Hb, on which see below, has prompted suggestions that Gunnlaugr wrote and published the Parts of his translation project in reverse-chronological order (*Bret* 1848-9, II, 71 n. 8; cf. *LH* II, 173; de Vries 1964-7, II, 75; Sveinbjörn Rafnsson 1994, 736; Guðrún Nordal 2001, 88). The likelihood of that is reduced by the factors reviewed above, notably the pivotal role played by *Merl I* 93-4. On the other hand, it is conceivable that Gunnlaugr might have done a pre-publication limited issue of Part II in booklet form. If such were the case, we could suggest speculatively that the natural person to submit it to would have been Guðmundr Arason in his known capacity (noted above) as Gunnlaugr's patron or commissioner for other works. The motive could have been to solicit vetting and clearance prior to full publication of either Part (Poole 2009, 310-15). The solicitation of prior approval before full publication would be comparable to and perhaps emulative of that pursued by Ari Þorgilsson (1067-1148) in his preparation of *Íslb* (on Ari, see *ÍF* 1, 3; Andersson 1985, 200; cf. *LH* II, 397) and would have been all the more important when debate raged in England and Europe as to whether Merlin should be seen as Christian or pagan (cf. Crick 2011, 77). The use of booklets is indicated elsewhere in Old Icelandic manuscript production (Lindblad 1954, 326) and there is abundant parallel evidence from medieval England (Robinson 1978, 231-2; Hanna 1996, 21-34).

As noted, a very strange feature of the transmission of *Merl* is that, as presented in Hb and in all editions up until now, the two Parts appear in reverse order, so that the chronologically posterior part of the *Prophecies*, as sequenced in Geoffrey's *DGB* (VII 4 in Griscom 1929), is placed before the chronologically prior part (VII 3 in Griscom 1929) (*Hb* 1892-6, cxi; Jón Helgason 1960a, xix; Turville-Petre 1953, 200-2). This transposition of Parts could once again be accounted for on the basis that from the outset the translation lived in two separate booklets, each containing one Part, and that the vagaries of distribution and perhaps also factors of individual interest and taste meant that some readers saw Part II ahead of Part I. It would then be possible for a copyist, perhaps Haukr himself, to copy the booklets in the incorrect order, either inadvertently (cf. *Merl* 2012, 16) or as an artifact of the timing of availability. For the possible use of booklets elsewhere in Hb see the discussion by Gatch (1978, 55) of the two Ælfric sermons excerpted and adapted within it (described by Jón Helgason 1960a, xiii).

In addition to this reversal of Parts, *Merl* as extant represents a substantially damaged state of the poem composed by Gunnlaugr (Würth 1998, 81). The damage takes various forms. Chronologically first, and hypothetical rather than conclusively proven, are possible lacunae in the text of *Merl* that might have originated either memorially or scribally (see *I* 51 and *II* 48 Notes to [All]). *Merl II* is very much shorter, at 68 stanzas, than *Merl I*, at 103 – a disproportion that could have been caused by loss of text: for evidence of one quite extensive possible lacuna, extending to perhaps as many as fifteen stanzas, see *Merl II* 48 Note to [All]. On a smaller scale, *Merl* on several occasions lacks substantive material corresponding to individual clauses and sentences within the *Prophecies*. The variability of stanza length in *Merl* – normally eight lines but intermittently expanded to ten or twelve lines – opens the possibility that lines have been lost in transmission without leaving any detectable gaps in the Icelandic text, considered in isolation from *DGB*. Admittedly, as noted above, it can be difficult on occasion to distinguish between possible deliberate omission of material on Gunnlaugr's part and loss in subsequent transmission. Another form of damage is specifically scribal. Although Haukr appears to have been a careful copyist, he commits evident errors from time to time, some corrected in his own hand but a significant number of others not detected (*Hb* 1892-6, xxxvi; see Notes to *Merl I* 21/5, *I* 35/5, *I* 36/2, *I* 38/5-6, *I* 44/1, *I* 79/7, *I* 81/7, *I* 84/4, *Merl II* 52/3, *II* 64/3, *II* 65/5, and *II* 66/7). Finally, massive damage has arisen thanks to conditions of preservation and curation of the codex (Jón Helgason 1960a, xxiv-xxv). The ink was already badly faded when Björn Jónsson of Skarðsá (1574-1655) gained access to the ms. During the time that Bishop Brynjólfur Sveinsson had the ms. on loan (approximately 1660-70), he had the ink refreshed where fading was compromising legibility. Refreshing on the folios containing *Merl* is said to have been done in part by Brynjólfur himself and in part by two legal officials (*lögmenn*), Sigurður Björnsson and Sigurður Jónsson (*Handrit.is*, accessed 05/07/2015). The incidence of refreshing is visible in the facsimile edition (Jón Helgason 1960a) and is thoroughly documented in the diplomatic transcription (*Hb* 1892-6, 272-83; cf. *Skj* A). Intermittent traces of the older ink beneath the refreshing indicate that not all the restoration was accurate (for instances see *Merl II* 6/1, *II* 14/3, *II* 16/1, 4, *II* 20/7, *II* 28/9, *II* 36/2, *II* 38/2, *II* 65/4); with access to new technology it is possible that further readings may be recovered, notably at *Merl I* 8/9-10. Thanks to some subsequent washing out of ink on the ms. pages, possibly in the course of attempted recovery of readings, a few words are now wholly illegible or barely legible, and at these points (indicated in the apparatus) Jón Sigurðsson's edition (*Bret* 1848-9), supported by *Hb* 1892-6 and *Skj* A, becomes the primary, if not wholly reliable, witness to the text.

In the progress towards a modern edition the earliest known transcripts are due to Björn Jónsson. Although his autograph draft is lost, copies of copies of it survive (Jón Helgason 1960a, xxxii). He was unable to read any portions that are now illegible and his transcription, at least as preserved, contains obvious errors. Subsequent to Björn, and sometimes with the benefit of reference to these copies, several other attempts were made at partial transcriptions from Hb, but they do not add to our knowledge of the text (Jón Helgason 1960a, xxxv; Lavender 2006, 132-3) and are not cited in the present edition (for a partial listing of these mss see *Merl* 2012, 54-5). The decisive step toward an edition was made by Jón Sigurðsson, who transcribed and published virtually the entire poem and added the Latin text of *DGB* (using Giles 1844) for comparison. In the present edition, as noted, a few readings from Jón are cited selectively in places where Hb is now illegible, and designated 'Hb*JS*'. He incorporated in his edition some emendations contributed by Hallgrim (Hallgrímur) Scheving, schoolmaster at Bessastaðir, in the form of personal communications to Jón (cf. Jón Helgason 1960a, xxxvi). Scheving's decisive contribution was to demonstrate that Gunnlaugr's fidelity to *DGB*, sentence by sentence and sometimes word by word, could be of material assistance in attempts to repair damaged passages; for instances of emendations proposed by Scheving that deserve renewed consideration see Notes to *Merl I* 70/2, *II* 17/1-2 and *II* 31/8. Finnur Jónsson largely adopted Jón's edition in *Skj*, with some new readings, emendations and interpretations. The posthumous edition of E. A. Kock (*Skald*) bases itself almost entirely on *Skj*, and it is clear from the mere scattering of notes in *NN* and *FF* and the lack of evident recourse to the ms., *Bret* or *DGB* that Kock never seriously engaged with this poem. The edition by Simone Horst (*Merl* 2012), with German translation, examines the ms. afresh and also considers select passages from *DGB* but fails to take proper account of a number of key matters: the metrics of the poem, the distinctive orthography of Hb, the contribution of *Bret* 1848-9 to the establishment of the text and current textual scholarship on *DGB*. In the present edition the two Parts are published in the order of their narrative chronology for the first time, a few further readings are recovered from Hb (see especially the Notes to *I* 72/6 and *II* 39/3), a number of new emendations and interpretations are proposed, the contribution of *Bret* is reassessed, systematic comparison with *DGB* is made stanza by stanza and *DGB* and *Merl* itself are explicated where necessary by reference to British historiography.

Merl has seldom been translated in other than excerpts. Aside from the editions, namely *Bret* 1848-9 and *Skj* B (into Danish), *Merl* 2012 (into German) and the present edition, there is only the translation into German by Stefanie Würth (1996, 98-120).

1. Nú skalk flotnum,   þats forðum vas,
   — hlýði fróðir mér   fyrðar — segja,
   at buðlungr sat   Bretlandi at;
   hét vellskati   Vortígernus.

Hlýði mér fróðir fyrðar; nú skalk segja flotnum, þats vas forðum, at buðlungr sat at Bretlandi; vellskati hét Vortígernus.

Listen to me, wise men; now I shall tell men what once was, that a king resided in Britain; the generous man was called Vortigern.

Ms.: **Hb**(50v) (*Bret*).

Editions: *Skj*: Gunnlaugr Leifsson, *Merlínússpá II* 1: AII, 22, BII, 24, *Skald* II, 15; *Bret* 1848-9, II, 39 (*Bret* st. 69); *Hb* 1892-6, 277; *Merl* 2012, 129-30.

Note: [All]: Vortigern was remembered in tradition, not necessarily accurately, as the C5th British leader who authorised the first settlement of the Saxon invaders in eastern Britain (Hunter Blair 1963, 161-4; Bromwich 1978, 386-7). Geoffrey's much elaborated account of his rise to power occurs in *DGB* VI.

2. Jǫrð vas forðum   fyrr kend Bretum,
   sús Englum es   eignuð síðan,
   þvíat in enska þjóð   áðan vélti
   breks ósama   brezka lýði.

Jǫrð, sús es eignuð Englum síðan, vas fyrr kend Bretum forðum, þvíat in enska þjóð vélti áðan brezka lýði ósama breks.

The land, which has since been assigned to the English, was previously called after the Britons in former days, for the English people beforehand deceived the British people, [who were] averse to the extortion of land.

Ms.: **Hb**(50v) (*Bret*).

Editions: *Skj*: Gunnlaugr Leifsson, *Merlínússpá II* 2: AII, 22, BII, 24; *Skald* II, 15; *Bret* 1848-9, II, 39 (*Bret* st. 70); *Hb* 1892-6, 277; *Merl* 2012, 130.

Notes: [All]: The notion of deception derives from the tradition that when Vortigern invited a select corps of Saxons to protect his kingdom they seized the opportunity to conquer the country, despite oaths to the contrary (Bede *HE* I, 15: Colgrave and Mynors 1969, 50-1; cf. Henry of Huntingdon, largely quoting Bede, in *HA* 1996, 80-1). — [2] *fyrr* 'previously': A refreshed reading, emended to *frið* 'beautiful' in *Skj* B, followed by *Skald* and *Merl* 2012. A cpd *fyrkend* 'named for' is proposed in *Bret* 1848-9, but without parallel attestations. The text is admittedly somewhat laborious in articulating the chronology, but emendation is not strictly necessary. — [2] *kend* 'called after': A possible alternative interpretation is 'belonged to', but this sub-sense has only one attestation in skaldic poetry (Anon *Brúðv* 27/8[VII]). — [7] *ósama breks* '[who were] averse to the extortion of land': I.e. the Britons did not authorise the Angles' seizure of land. Rather, they were tricked by false assurances from the new arrivals. The adj. *ósamr* occurs only once elsewhere (*ONP*: *ósamr*), and is explained as 'unwilling, disinclined' or similar (*LP*, *Fritzner*: *ósamr*; *CVC*: *úsamr*). The word *brek* seems to have had a specialised sense, in relation to land claims, of 'strenuous insistence, exorbitance, rapacity or fraudulence in claiming' (cf. *CVC*, *Fritzner*, *ONP*: *brek*) and this probably pertains in the present context. *Bret* translates as *haardføre* 'resistant, intransigent', but this seems to be a purely *ad hoc* explanation. Finnur Jónsson explains as 'living peacefully' (*Skj* B, *LP*: *brek*), but this does not capture the specific meaning of *brek* and is belied by subsequent characterisations of the Britons as given to faction-fighting (see especially *I* 35). *Merl* 2012 renders *brek* as *Begehren* 'desire' (noun), which seems too mild and, once again, does not reflect the specialised sense of *brek*.

3. Ok láð þeira   með liði miklu
    sjǫlf eignaðisk   í sǫgum fornum.
    Ok, þars kristnir kœnir byggja,
    áðr tók heiðin þjóð hallir smíða.

Ok í fornum sǫgum eignaðisk sjǫlf láð þeira með miklu liði. Ok, þars kœnir kristnir byggja, tók heiðin þjóð áðr smíða hallir.

And according to the ancient stories, they themselves took possession of their land with a great army. And where wise Christians settle, heathen people had previously taken to constructing halls.

Ms.: **Hb**(50v) (*Bret*).

Reading: [6] kœnir: 'kiænir' Hb.

Editions: *Skj*: Gunnlaugr Leifsson, *Merlínússpá II* 3: AII, 22, BII, 24, *Skald* II, 15; *Bret* 1848-9, II, 39-40 (*Bret* st. 71); *Hb* 1892-6, 277; *Merl* 2012, 131.

Notes: [3] *sjǫlf* 'they themselves': The adj. *sjǫlf* is f. nom. sg. referring back to *in enska þjóð* 'the English people' in l. 5 of the previous stanza. — [6] *kœnir* 'wise': This is an emendation of the unrefreshed ms. reading 'kiænir', first suggested in *Bret* 1848-9 and adopted by all subsequent eds, including the present one. Possibly, however, it has supplanted an original *kirkjur* 'churches', with *byggja* used in the sense of 'occupy, frequent' (cf. *Fritzner*: *byggja* 2; *ONP*: *byggja* 3), which would yield a noun contrastive with *hallir* 'halls'. Cf. *Merl I* 23/2.

4. Es áttbogi   enskrar þjóðar
    saxneskr sagaðr   í sǫgum fornum.
    Þaðan eflðusk þeir til þrimu geira
    landi at ræna   lofðung Breta.

Áttbogi enskrar þjóðar es sagaðr saxneskr í fornum sǫgum. Þaðan eflðusk þeir til þrimu geira at ræna lofðung Breta landi.

The lineage of the English people is said in ancient stories to be Saxon. From there they strengthened themselves for the clash of spears [BATTLE] to deprive the king of the Britons of the land.

Ms.: **Hb**(50v) (*Bret*).

Editions: *Skj*: Gunnlaugr Leifsson, *Merlínússpá II* 4: AII, 22, BII, 24-5, *Skald* II, 15, *NN* §3258; *Bret* 1848-9, II, 40 (*Bret* st. 72); *Hb* 1892-6, 277; *Merl* 2012, 131-2.

Notes: [All]: For Gunnlaugr's source here, cf. *Merl I* 2 Note to [All]. — [3] *sagaðr* 'said': This is a by-form of the usual p. p. *sagðr* (*LP*: *segja*). — [5] *þaðan* 'from there': With the implicit notion of the continental homeland of the Saxons. Kock argues for a sense 'thereafter' (*NN* §3258A, followed by *Merl* 2012), and this is definitely possible (cf. Heggstad *et al.* 2008: 4. *þaðan*).

5. En hers jaðarr   halda máttit
    brezkri jǫrðu   né bauga fjǫlð.
    Alt fór inn heiðni   herr it eystra
    eldi ok jarni   eylands jaðar.

En jaðarr hers máttit halda brezkri jǫrðu né fjǫlð bauga. Inn heiðni herr fór alt it eystra, jaðar eylands, eldi ok jarni.

And the leader of the army [RULER = Vortigern] could not hold the British land nor the mass of treasures. The heathen army overran the edge of the island, all the east, with fire and iron.

Ms.: **Hb**(50v) (*Bret*).

Editions: *Skj*: Gunnlaugr Leifsson, *Merlínússpá II* 5: AII, 22, BII, 25, *Skald* II, 15; *Bret* 1848-9, II, 40 (*Bret* st. 73); *Hb* 1892-6, 277; *Merl* 2012, 132.

Notes: [All]: This stanza possibly represents an inference from one or both of the following in *DGB* 105: *Vortegirnus ... duci eorum Hengisto dedit agros plurimos in Lindiseia regione* (Reeve and Wright 2007, 127.299-300) 'Vortigern ... gave their leader Hengest extensive lands in the region of Lindsey' (Reeve and Wright 2007, 126) or [*Saxones*] *urbem Lundoniae primitus adeuntes ceperunt. Ceperunt deinde Eboracum et Lindocolinum nec non et Guintoniam, quasque prouincias deuastantes* (Reeve and Wright 2007, 137.494-5) '[The Saxons] went first to London, which they took. Next they took York, Lincoln and Winchester and laid waste to all regions' (Reeve and Wright 2007, 136). But the more likely source, at least for ll. 5-8, is Bede (*HE* I 15: Colgrave and Mynors 1969, 50-1), who locates the incursions generically *in orientali parte insulae* 'in the eastern part of the island', cited by Henry of Huntingdon (*HA* 1996, 78-9). — [5-6] *alt it eystra* 'all the east': Lit. 'all the eastern [edge]'. An adverbial phrase, modifying *fór* 'overran', whose acc. object is *jaðar* 'edge'. *Bret* 1848-9 paraphrases loosely here: *over Öens hele östlige Bred* 'over the island's entire eastern margin' (similarly *Skj* B), obscuring the syntax. Cf. *Merl I* 73/7-8 for adverbial constructions with comp. and sup. adjectives of direction. *Merl* 2012 appears to presuppose movement towards the east rather than along the eastern side: *fuhr ... ganz nach Osten bis an den Rand der Insel* 'drove all the way to the east up to the edge of the island'. — [5] *fór* 'overran': For this sense of *fara*, see *LP*: *fara* A4. — [8]: Double alliteration on vowels in even lines, where one of them is <j>, as seen here, occurs rarely as an apparent licence, starting in the late C12th. See Note to Eyv *Hál* 10/2-3[1].

6. En hertogi   hœlis leitar;
   gerisk traustan turn   tyggi at smíða.
   Ok þangat til   þeirar gerðar
   samnar mǫrgum   mildingr smiðum.

En hertogi leitar hœlis; tyggi gerisk at smíða traustan turn. Ok mildingr samnar mǫrgum smiðum þangat til þeirar gerðar.

But the duke searches for a stronghold; the lord sets about building a trusty tower. And the king assembles many craftsmen there for that work.

Ms.: **Hb**(50v-51r) (*Bret*).

Editions: *Skj*: Gunnlaugr Leifsson, *Merlínússpá II* 6: AII, 22, BII, 25, *Skald* II, 16; *Bret* 1848-9, II, 40 (*Bret* st. 74); *Hb* 1892-6, 277; *Merl* 2012, 132-3.

Notes: [All]: This and the following stanza derive from the following in *DGB* 106 (Reeve and Wright 2007, 137.499-503): *Vocatis denique magis suis, consuluit illos iussitque dicere quid faceret. Qui dixerunt ut aedificaret sibi turrim fortissimam quae sibi tutamen foret, cum ceteras munitiones amisisset … Venit tandem ad montem Erir, ubi coadunatis ex diuersis patriis caementariis iussit turrim construere* 'Finally he summoned and consulted his magicians, commanding them to tell him what to do. They said that he should build a very strong tower as a refuge, since he had lost his other fortresses … he came at last to Mount Snowdon, where he gathered stonemasons from various regions and ordered them to build the tower' (Reeve and Wright 2007, 136). — [1] *hertogi* 'the duke': I.e. Vortigern. — [5-6] *til þeirar gerðar* 'for that work': The placement of prep. and noun phrase in enjambement is a poetic licence used sporadically in *Merl* (cf. Notes to *I* 47/3, 4, *I* 63/6, 7, *II* 7/10, and *II* 12/3).

7. Kómu til smíðar   spakir vǫlundar
   — þats ýtum sagt —   uppi í fjalli.
   En, þats drengir   á degi gerðu,
   sá þess engan stað   annan morgin.

Spakir vǫlundar kómu til smíðar uppi í fjalli; þats sagt ýtum. En, þats drengir gerðu á degi, sá þess engan stað annan morgin.

Skilful builders came to the work up on the mountain; that is told to men. But what the men achieved by day, nowhere was it to be seen the next morning.

Ms.: **Hb**(51r) (*Bret*).

Editions: *Skj*: Gunnlaugr Leifsson, *Merlínússpá II* 7: AII, 23, BII, 25, *Skald* II, 16; *Bret* 1848-9, II, 40-1 (*Bret* st. 75); *Hb* 1892-6, 277; *Merl* 2012, 133.

Notes: [All]: See Note to st. 6. In part Gunnlaugr's source appears to be *DGB* 106 (Reeve and Wright 2007, 137.503-6): *Conuenientes itaque lapidarii coeperunt eam fundare. Sed quicquid una die operabantur, absorbebat tellus illud in altera, ita ut nescirent quorsum opus suum euanesceret* 'They met and began to lay foundations. But whatever they accomplished one day would be swallowed up by the ground the next day, so that they had no idea where it had gone' (cf. Reeve and Wright 2007, 136). In view of *in altera* [*die*] 'the next day', it seems likely that sts 7 and 8 may additionally draw on material now extant in the First Variant Version: cf. *DGB* 108 (cf. Wright 1988, 100): *Volens enim turrim edificare, non possunt fundamenta eius in loco isto consistere quin quod in die construitur in nocte a terra deuoretur* 'Attempting to build a tower, they could not lay its foundation in that place since whatever was built during the day was engulfed by the earth during the night'. It is clearer in this version, as also in Gunnlaugr's stanza, that the disappearance of the foundations happens during the night, not on the following day. — [2] *vǫlundar* 'builders': The name of the archetypal legendary smith Vǫlundr is occasionally used of craftsmen and skilled artisans in general (*LP*: *Vǫlundr*). — [3]: A conventional expression that may evoke oral delivery. Cf. *Merl I* 22/2-3. — [7] *sá þess engan stað* 'nowhere was it to be seen': Lit. 'of this [one] saw nowhere', an impersonal construction with gen. of the object.

8.   Kalla lét fylkir   fróða seggi;
      frá gunnþorinn   gramr hvat olli,
      es gǫrla hvarf   grundvǫllr sá brott,
      se*m grund gǫmul   gleypði steina
      eða †hamloðin   harmin seldi†.

Fylkir lét kalla fróða seggi; gunnþorinn gramr frá hvat olli, es sá grundvǫllr hvarf gǫrla brott, se*m gǫmul grund gleypði steina eða †hamloðin harmin seldi†.

The king had wise men summoned; the battle-bold lord inquired what was the cause, when that foundation completely vanished, as if the ancient earth swallowed stones or … .

Ms.: **Hb**(51r) (*Bret*).

Readings: [2] seggi: *refreshed as* 'seti' Hb   [7] se*m grund: seimgrund Hb.

Editions: *Skj*: Gunnlaugr Leifsson, *Merlínússpá II* 8: AII, 23, BII, 25, *Skald* II, 16, *NN* §1282; *Bret* 1848-9, II, 41 (*Bret* st. 76); *Hb* 1892-6, 277; *Merl* 2012, 133-5.

Notes: [All]: Cf. St. 7 for *DGB*. Also *DGB* 106 (Reeve and Wright 2007, 137.506-7): *Cumque id Vortegirno nunciatum fuisset, consuluit iterum magos suos ut causam rei indicarent* 'When Vortigern was informed of this, he again consulted his magicians in order to find out what was causing it' (Reeve and Wright 2007, 136). — [7] *se*m grund* 'as if the earth': Emended in *Bret* 1848-9 (followed by *Skj* B and *Skald*) from ms.

seimgrund (refreshed). — [9-10]: No satisfactory explanation of the obelised words has so far been proposed. They occur in a heavily refreshed passage in Hb. Scheving proposed *eða hám glóða garmi seldi* 'or gave to the lofty wolf of embers [FIRE]'. This scarcely makes sense, in the apparent absence of an appropriate grammatical subject, and is rejected in *Bret* 1848-9, although the translation there retains the idea of fire. *Skj* B prints *hamloðin | har ... eldi* and offers no translation. Kock (*NN* §1282) compares *harmin*, the apparent ms. reading, with ME *harmin*, ModSwed. *hermelin* 'ermine', but this word has no cognate in Old Norse and the motif as a whole has no counterpart in Geoffrey's text (cf. *Merl* 2012).

9. Einn vas maðr sá,   es myrkva frétt
    fyr skata skýrum   skynja kunni.
    Hét yngva vinr   Ambrósíus,
    en inn ágæti   ǫðru nafni
    Merlínus sá   maðr kallaðisk.

Sá maðr vas einn, es kunni skynja myrkva frétt fyr skýrum skata. Vinr yngva hét Ambrósíus, en sá inn ágæti maðr kallaðisk ǫðru nafni Merlínus.

That man was [the] only [one], who could explain the obscure portent to the wise king. The friend of the king was called Ambrosius but that excellent man was known by another name, Merlin.

Ms.: **Hb**(51r) (*Bret*).

Editions: *Skj*: Gunnlaugr Leifsson, *Merlínússpá II* 9: AII, 23, BII, 25-6, *Skald* II, 16, *NN* §§2164, 3142, 3258B; *Bret* 1848-9, II, 41-2 (*Bret* st. 77); *Hb* 1892-6, 277; *Merl* 2012, 135-6.

Notes: [All]: For the source, see *Merl I* 10 Note to [All]. — [2] *frétt* 'portent': 'Intelligence, report, enquiring of men or gods about the future' (*CVC, Fritzner: frétt*; cf. *NN* §3258). — [3] *skýrum* 'wise': So *Bret* 1848-9 and *Skj* B. Kock (*NN* §3142, followed by *Merl* 2012) sees it as awkward to attribute wisdom to Vortigern, who has expressed himself baffled by the portent, and proposes that *skýrum* instead be taken adverbially, meaning 'clearly'. But the adj. may allude to Vortigern's reputation for wisdom as he assumes power (cf. *DGB* VI: Reeve and Wright 2007, 120-1); cf. the similar application of the adj. *spǫkum* 'sagacious' to him in *I* 11/8. — [5-8]: Word order follows *Bret* 1848-9 and *Skj* B (cf. *Merl* 2012). Kock (*NN* §2164) proposes a word order *en sá maðr kallaðisk ǫðru nafni inn ágæti Merlínus* 'but that man was called by another name the excellent Merlin', but the combination *sá inn* needs no special explanation. — [5] *vinr yngva* 'the friend of the king': J. S. Eysteinsson (1953-7, 96-7) points out the conventional nature of this phrase, comparing e.g. *I* 10/2, *I* 11/8 and *I* 20/1. Geoffrey's presentation of Merlin as the son of an incubus (Reeve and Wright 2007, 138-9) troubled some commentators, as in effect associating his prophecy with diabolic powers (Crick 2011, 77); Gunnlaugr may be following their lead by normalising his nature and social status.

10. Þat kvað valda   verdags hǫtuðr,
     at þar undir vas   ólítit vatn.
     Bauð grund grafa   gumna stjóri;
     reynisk spaklig   spámanns saga.

Hǫtuðr verdags kvað þat valda, at ólítit vatn vas þar undir. Stjóri gumna bauð grafa grund; saga spámanns reynisk spaklig.

The hater of the sea-day [GOLD > GENEROUS MAN = Merlin] said the cause was that a not small lake lay underneath. The commander of men [RULER = Vortigern] ordered the ground to be dug up; the prophet's account turns out to be percipient.

Ms.: **Hb**(51r) (*Bret*).

Editions: *Skj*: Gunnlaugr Leifsson, *Merlínússpá II* 10: AII, 23, BII, 26; *Skald* II, 16; *Bret* 1848-9, II, 42 (*Bret* st. 78); *Hb* 1892-6, 277-8; *Merl* 2012, 136-7.

Notes: [All]: Cf. *DGB* 108 (Reeve and Wright 2007, 141.565-9): '*Tunc ait Merlinus, qui et Ambrosius dicebatur: "Domine mi rex, uoca operarios tuos et iube fodere terram, et inuenies stagnum sub ea quod turrim stare non permittit." Quod cum factum fuisset, repertum est stagnum sub terra, quod eam instabilem fecerat*' 'Then Merlinus, who was also called Ambrosius, said, "My lord King, call your workmen and set them digging up the ground; you will find a pool beneath it which prevents the tower from standing." This was done and a pool was discovered beneath the ground, which made it unstable' (cf. Reeve and Wright 2007, 140). — [6]: De Vries (1964-7, II, 75 n. 181) compares *Gríp* 1/6. — [7] *reynisk* 'turns out': Pres. historic tense. See Note to *I* 15/5.

11. Ok inn fróði halr   frétti lofða,
     hvat und vatni   væri niðri.
     Ok, es engi þat   annarr vissi,
     sagði fylki   fleinþollr spǫkum:

Ok inn fróði halr frétti lofða, hvat væri niðri und vatni. Ok, es engi annarr vissi þat, sagði fleinþollr spǫkum fylki:

And the wise man asked people what was further down beneath the lake. And, when nobody else knew that, the spear-fir [WARRIOR = Merlin] said to the sagacious king:

Ms.: **Hb**(51r) (*Bret*).

Editions: *Skj*: Gunnlaugr Leifsson, *Merlínússpá II* 11: AII, 23, BII, 26; *Skald* II, 16, *NN* §3142; *Bret* 1848-9, II, 42 (*Bret* st. 79); *Hb* 1892-6, 278; *Merl* 2012, 137.

Notes: [All]: Cf. *DGB* 108 (Reeve and Wright 2007, 141.559-65): *Ammirans continuo rex super uerbis illius iussit uenire magos et coram Merlino sedere. Quibus ait Merlinus: '... Dicite michi quid sub fundamento latet ...' Expauescentes autem magi conticuerunt* 'Amazed at what he said, the king ordered the magicians to come and sit before Merlin. To them Merlin said: "... Tell me what is hidden beneath the foundations ..." The magicians were cowed into silence' (Reeve and Wright 2007, 140). — [8] *fleinþollr* 'the spear-fir [WARRIOR = Merlin]': Cf. Sturl *Hrafn* 11/5[II] and Note. — [8] *spǫkum* 'sagacious': Kock (*NN* §3142, followed by *Merl* 2012) instead proposes that *spǫkum* be construed adverbially, i.e. 'sagaciously', parallel to *skýrum*, taken as 'wisely' in *I* 9/3: see Note there.

12. 'Sofa þar í dimmu   djúpi niðri
    tvennir ormar   tveim hellum í.
    Þeir eru lindar   lands ólíkir;
    sék rauða seil   rás ok hvíta.

'Tvennir ormar sofa þar í dimmu djúpi niðri í tveim hellum. Þeir lindar lands eru ólíkir; sék rauða ok hvíta seil rás.

'Two snakes sleep there in the dark depth down in two caves. Those girdles of the land [SNAKES] are unlike [one another]; I see a red and a white rope of the earth [SNAKE].

Ms.: **Hb**(51r) (*Bret*).

Editions: *Skj*: Gunnlaugr Leifsson, *Merlínússpá II* 12: AII, 23, BII, 26, *Skald* II, 16; *Bret* 1848-9, II, 42-3 (*Bret* st. 80); *Hb* 1892-6, 278; *Merl* 2012, 137-8.

Notes: [All]: Cf. *DGB* 108 and 111 (Reeve and Wright 2007, 141.573-4, cf. 145.25-6): *et uidebis in fundo duos concauos lapides et in illis duos dracones dormientes ... quorum unus erat albus et alius rubeus* 'and at the bottom you will see two hollow rocks with two dragons asleep in them ..., one white, one red' (Reeve and Wright 2007, 140, cf. 144). Gunnlaugr interprets the 'hollow rocks' as caves. The decasyllabic version of the Anglo-Norman *Verse Prophecies of Merlin* also uses this interpretation (Blacker 2005, 80), but probably this agreement arises through independent anticipation of Prophecy 1 (see *I* 21 Note to [All]). — [7-8] *seil rás* 'a rope of the earth [SNAKE]': This, together with *lindar lands* 'girdles of the land' (ll. 5-6), is the first of several snake-kennings Gunnlaugr employs that implicitly compare a snake to a rope, thong, girdle or fetter. In the analysis of *Meissner* 114-15, the defining phrase 'of the land' or similar used in association with these base-words might mean either 'living on the ground' or 'encircling the earth', in the latter case with their basis in the story of the Miðgarðsormr or World Serpent. — [8] *rás* 'of the earth': This *heiti* for 'land, earth' occurs uniquely in *Merl*. Cf. *I* 21/2 and *LP*: *rá*. The word is little-known in Icelandic (*CVC*: *rá* n. 'landmark') and not attested by Fritzner or *ONP*, though it occurs in Modern

Norwegian and Swedish dialects in the sense 'boundary' (*AEW*: *rá*). Possibly Gunnlaugr knew it from no longer extant skaldic poems.

13.   'Lát grund grafa,   gera skorninga,'
        sagði Merlínus   menja deili.
        'Veitið vatni,   ok vitið síðan,
        hvat spát hafi   spillir bauga,
        — þat es nýlunda —   niðr ór fjalli.'

'Lát grafa grund, gera skorninga,' sagði Merlínus deili menja. 'Veitið vatni niðr ór fjalli ok vitið síðan, hvat spillir bauga hafi spát; þat es nýlunda.'

'Have the earth dug, form channels,' Merlin said to the sharer of neck-rings [GENEROUS MAN = Vortigern]. 'Drain the lake down from the mountain and then find out what the despoiler of rings [GENEROUS MAN = Merlin] has prophesied; that is a novelty.'

Ms.: **Hb**(51r) (*Bret*).

Editions: *Skj*: Gunnlaugr Leifsson, *Merlínússpá II* 13: AII, 23-4, BII, 26, *Skald* II, 16-17; *Bret* 1848-9, II, 43 (*Bret* st. 81); *Hb* 1892-6, 278; *Merl* 2012, 138-9.

Notes: [All]: Cf. *DGB* 108 (Reeve and Wright 2007, 141.573): *Praecipe hauriri stagnum per riuulos* 'Order the pool to be drained through channels' (cf. Reeve and Wright 2007, 140). — [2] *skorninga* 'channels': A *hap. leg.* in poetry (*LP*: *skorningr*). The word is attested only three times in prose (*ONP*: *skorningr*), all in the meaning of 'strip of cloth' (*CVC*: *skorningr*); the general sense is 'cutting'. — [5-10]: Complex word order occurs intermittently in *Merl*. See for example *I* 54/9-12 and *I* 63/5-8. — [5-6] *veitið ... vitið* 'drain ... find out': As noted by *Merl* 2012, this is 2nd pers. pl., contrasting with the sg. *lát* 'let' used in l. 1. The interpretation of *Merl* 2012 is that Merlin turns from addressing Vortigernus to addressing his workmen. More likely, however, is that implicitly Vortigernus is the speaker of ll. 5-10, as indicated by the following sentence in *DGB* (see *I* 14, Note to [All]).

14.   Gerðu greppar,   þats gumnum bauð;
        varð vatni niðr   veitt ór fjalli.
        Ok seimgefendr   snáka þekðu
        tryggðarlausa,   sem Týr firum
        hafði Hristar   hugspár sagat.

Greppar gerðu, þats bauð gumnum; varð vatni veitt niðr ór fjalli. Ok seimgefendr þekðu tryggðarlausa snáka, sem hugspár Týr Hristar hafði sagat firum.

Men did as he ordered them; the lake was drained down from the mountain. And the givers of treasure [GENEROUS MEN] could see the treacherous snakes, just as the prophetic-minded Týr <god> of Hrist <valkyrie> [WARRIOR = Merlin] had said to men.

Ms.: **Hb**(51r) (*Bret*).

Editions: *Skj*: Gunnlaugr Leifsson, *Merlínússpá II* 14: AII, 24, BII, 27, *Skald* II, 17; *Bret* 1848-9, II, 43 (*Bret* st. 82); *Hb* 1892-6, 278; *Merl* 2012, 139.

Notes: [All]: Cf. *DGB* 108 (Reeve and Wright 2007, 141.575): *Credidit rex uerbis eius quia uerum dixerat de stagno et iussit illud hauriri* 'Because he had been right about the pool, the king believed him and ordered it to be drained' (cf. Reeve and Wright 2007, 140). — [2] *gumnum* 'them': Lit. 'men'. — [8, 9] *Týr Hristar* 'the Týr <god> of Hrist <valkyrie> [WARRIOR = Merlin]': The name of the valkyrie, Hrist, functions, like the more common valkyrie-name Hildr, as a replacement for the concept 'battle', to create a warrior-kenning, with the base-word the name of the god Týr; cf. *Meissner* 273. — [10] *sagat* 'said': See Note to *I* 4/3.

15. Ok drjúgligir   drekar vǫknuðu;
    gerðusk báðir   brott úr rúmi.
    Rennask síðan   snart at móti
    fróns fásýnir   frœknir baugar.

Ok drjúgligir drekar vǫknuðu; báðir gerðusk brott úr rúmi. Fásýnir frœknir baugar fróns rennask síðan snart at móti.

And the mighty serpents woke; both moved away from their resting-places. The rarely-seen ferocious rings of the earth [SNAKES] then swiftly run towards each other.

Ms.: **Hb**(51r) (*Bret*).

Editions: *Skj*: Gunnlaugr Leifsson, *Merlínússpá II* 15: AII, 24, BII, 27, *Skald* II, 17; *Bret* 1848-9, II, 43-4 (*Bret* st. 83); *Hb* 1892-6, 278; *Merl* 2012, 140.

Notes: [All]: Cf. *DGB* 111 (Reeve and Wright 2007, 145.27): *Cumque alter alteri appropinquasset* 'As they neared each other' (Reeve and Wright 2007, 144). Gunnlaugr elaborates on this description. — [5] *rennask* 'run': For a discussion of the pres. historic tense in this passage, see Poole (1991, 36-44).

16. Gerisk sókn mikil   snáka tveggja;
    gapa grimmliga   grundar belti.
    Hǫggvask hœknir   hauðrs gyrðingar,
    blásask eitri á   ok blǫm eldi.

Mikil sókn snáka tveggja gerisk; belti grundar gapa grimmliga. Hœknir gyrðingar hauðrs hǫggvask, blásask eitri ok blǫm eldi á.

A great fight commences between the two snakes; the belts of the ground [SNAKES] gape savagely. The vicious girdles of the earth [SNAKES] strike each other, blow venom and blue fire on each other.

Ms.: **Hb**(51r) (*Bret*).

Editions: *Skj*: Gunnlaugr Leifsson, *Merlínússpá II* 16: AII, 24, BII, 27, *Skald* II, 17; *Bret* 1848-9, II, 44 (*Bret* st. 84); *Hb* 1892-6, 278; *Merl* 2012, 140.

Notes: [All]: Cf. *DGB* 111 (Reeve and Wright 2007, 145.27-8): *commiserunt diram pugnam et ignem anhelitu procreabant* 'they fought a terrible battle and created fire with their breath' (Reeve and Wright 2007, 144). Gunnlaugr goes beyond *DGB* in specifying the emission of venom and the colour of the flame (on the latter see Note to l. 8 below). — [5] *hœknir* 'vicious': A *hap. leg.*, whose meaning and origin are uncertain but whose core sense has been stated as 'greedy' (*LP*: *hœkinn*; cf. *CVC*: *hækinn*). Finnur Jónsson translates with a query as *kraftig* 'powerfully' in *Skj* B; *Merl* 2012 has *heftig* 'violently'. But if the etymological connection with *hákr* conjectured in *LP* is correct, the meaning might rather be 'vicious, relentless'; cf. the *ONP* citation (*ÍF* 12, 303): *Var hann því kallaðr Þorkell hákr, at hann eirði hvárki í orðum né verkum, við hvern sem hann átti* 'He was called Þorkell *hákr* because he never spared anyone in words or deeds with whom he had dealings'. The word *hákr* is attested only in nicknames; for (inconclusive) conjectures as to its core meaning and etymology see *AEW*: *hákr*. — [8] *blǫm eldi* 'blue fire': The reference is probably to the blue flame emitted on combustion of sulphur. In a fragment of *Barth* extant in the mid-C13th Norwegian ms. AM 237 b fol (Loth 1969, 233), the phrase *blár loge* 'blue flame' is used to translate Lat. *flamma sulphurea* 'sulphurous flame' (cf. *ONP*: *blár* 3; Loth 1969, 221).

17. Forflótti vas   fránn inn rauði;
    bar inn ljósi hann   liðr at bakka.
    En hann hagliga   hrøkkr at móti;
    elti hann inn hvíta   hugtrúr dreka.

Inn rauði fránn vas forflótti; inn ljósi liðr bar hann at bakka. En hann hrøkkr hagliga at móti; hugtrúr elti hann inn hvíta dreka.

The red serpent took flight, the white snake drove it to the bank. But it [the red snake] nimbly twists to resist; valiant, it pursued the white serpent.

Ms.: **Hb**(51r) (*Bret*).

Editions: *Skj*: Gunnlaugr Leifsson, *Merlínússpá II* 17: AII, 24, BII, 27; *Skald* II, 17; *Bret* 1848-9, II, 44 (*Bret* st. 85); *Hb* 1892-6, 278; *Merl* 2012, 141.

Notes: [All]: Cf. *DGB* 111 (Reeve and Wright 2007, 145.28-30): *Praeualebat autem albus draco rubeumque usque ad extremitatem lacus fugabat. At ille, cum se expulsum doluisset, impetum fecit in album ipsumque retro ire coegit* 'The white dragon began to get the upper hand and drove the red to the edge of the pool. But it was irked at being driven back and attacked the white, forcing it back in turn' (Reeve and Wright 2007, 144). — [2] *fránn* 'serpent': This rare *heiti*, attested solely in C12th or later religious poetry, derives from the adj. *fránn* 'flashing' (*LP*: *fránn*). — [4] *liðr* 'the snake': A variant form of the more common *linnr* m. 'snake' (cf. *I* 18/4 below and *LP*: 2. *liðr* m.)

18. Þeir víg gera   vatns farveg í,
    ok lengi hvatt   linnar berjask.
    Mega ormar þar   ýmsir meira
    ok ýmsir þar   undan leggja.

Þeir gera víg í farveg vatns, ok linnar berjask lengi hvatt. Ýmsir ormar mega þar meira ok ýmsir leggja þar undan.

They wage battle in the lake's outlet and the snakes fight each other fiercely for a long time. Now one snake, now the other has the advantage there; now one, now the other takes refuge there.

Ms.: **Hb**(51r) (*Bret*).

Reading: [7] þar: þeir Hb.

Editions: *Skj*: Gunnlaugr Leifsson, *Merlínússpá II* 18: AII, 24, BII, 27; *Skald* II, 17; *Bret* 1848-9, II, 44-5 (*Bret* st. 86); *Hb* 1892-6, 278; *Merl* 2012, 141-2.

Notes: [All]: Cf. *DGB* 111 (Reeve and Wright 2007, 145.30-1): *Ipsis ergo in hunc modum pugnantibus* 'As they fought in this way' (cf. Reeve and Wright 2007, 144). — [2] *farveg vatns* 'the lake's outlet': Referring to the *skorningar* 'channels' mentioned in *I* 13/2. The noun *farvegr*, lit. 'route of travel', is in prose predominantly used of the course of a river (*Fritzner*: *farvegr* 2; *ONP*: *farvegr*) but this is its sole attestation in that sense in poetry (*LP*: *farvegr*). — [7] *þar* 'there': Emended in this edn from ms. *þeir* 'they' (not refreshed) for the sake of sense and parallelism with l. 5.

19. 'Seg, Merlínus,'   kvað menbroti,
    '— est þú fróðari   fyrðum ǫðrum —,
    hvat tákna mun   tveggja orma
    ógurligt víg   aldar bǫrnum.'

'Seg, Merlínus,' kvað menbroti, '— þú est fróðari ǫðrum fyrðum —, hvat ógurligt víg tveggja orma mun tákna bǫrnum aldar.'

'Say, Merlin,' said the neck-ring breaker [GENEROUS MAN = Vortigern], '— you are wiser than other men —, what the fearsome battle of the two snakes will mean for the children of men.'

Ms.: **Hb**(51r) (*Bret*).

Editions: *Skj*: Gunnlaugr Leifsson, *Merlínússpá II* 19: AII, 24, BII, 27-8; *Skald* II, 17; *Bret* 1848-9, II, 45 (*Bret* st. 87); *Hb* 1892-6, 278; *Merl* 2012, 142.

Note: [All]: Cf. *DGB* 111 (Reeve and Wright 2007, 145.31-2): *praecepit rex Ambrosio Merlino dicere quid proelium draconum portendebat* 'the king commanded Ambrosius Merlin to tell him what the battle of the serpents presaged' (cf. Reeve and Wright 2007, 144).

20.   Grét gumna vinr,   es hann greiða bað
    þengill gǫfugr   þessa hegju.
    Ok eptir þat   aldar snytrir
    rǫkstælta spá   rekkum sagði.

Vinr gumna grét, es gǫfugr þengill bað hann greiða þessa hegju. Ok eptir þat sagði snytrir aldar rekkum rǫkstælta spá.

The friend of men wept when the noble king bade him explain this happening. And after that the teacher of the people [PROPHET = Merlin] spoke well-grounded prophecy to the men.

Ms.: **Hb**(51r) (*Bret*).

Editions: *Skj*: Gunnlaugr Leifsson, *Merlínússpá II* 20: AII, 24, BII, 28; *Skald* II, 17; *Bret* 1848-9, II, 45-6 (*Bret* st. 88); *Hb* 1892-6, 278; *Merl* 2012, 143.

Notes: [All]: Cf. *DGB* 111 (Reeve and Wright 2007, 145.32-3): *Mox ille, in fletum erumpens, spiritum hausit prophetiae et ait* 'He burst into tears and was inspired to prophesy thus' (Reeve and Wright 2007, 144). Gunnlaugr's added characterisations of the prophet ('teacher of the people') and the prophecy ('well-grounded') may be part of his determined advocacy of the material's veracity, seen most explicitly in *I* 95-102. — [7] *rǫkstælta spá* 'well-grounded prophecy': Cf. *LP*: *rǫkstæltr*; this would mean literally 'prophecy reinforced by signs'; cf. Note to *II* 3/7.

21. 'Táknar inn rauði   rás fagrsili,'
    kvað bjóðr bragar,   'brezka lýði,
    en inn hvíti *n*aðr   ina heið*nu* þjóð,
    es byggja mun   brezkar jarðir.

'Inn rauði fagrsili rás,' kvað bjóðr bragar, 'táknar brezka lýði, en inn hvíti *n*aðr ina heið*nu* þjóð, es mun byggja brezkar jarðir.

'The red fine rope of the earth [SNAKE],' said the offerer of poetry [POET = Merlin], 'stands for the British people, and the white snake for the heathen folk who will settle the British lands.

Ms.: **Hb**(51r) (*Bret*).

Readings: [5] *n*aðr: maðr Hb [6] heið*nu*: heiðna Hb.

Editions: *Skj*: Gunnlaugr Leifsson, *Merlínússpá II* 21: AII, 24-5, BII, 28, *Skald* II, 17; *Bret* 1848-9, II, 46 (*Bret* st. 89); *Hb* 1892-6, 278; *Merl* 2012, 143-4.

Notes: [All]: Cf. *DGB* 112 (Reeve and Wright 2007, 145.34-6; cf. Wright 1988, 102, prophecy 1): *Cauernas ipsius occupabit albus draco, qui Saxones quos inuitasti significat. Rubeus uero gentem designat Britanniae, quae ab albo opprimetur* 'Its caves will be taken by the white dragon, which symbolises the Saxons whom you have summoned. The red represents the people of Britain, whom the white will oppress' (Reeve and Wright 2007, 144). Gunnlaugr rationalises the 'caves' as 'lands'. — [2] *fagrsili rás* 'the fine rope of the earth [SNAKE]': See Note to *I* 12/8. The cpd *fagrsili* is a *hap. leg*. — [5] *n*aðr 'snake': Emended by *Bret* 1848-9, followed by all subsequent eds, from ms. *maðr* 'man' (not refreshed). Cf. *I* 32/2.

22. 'Es harmr mikill   holðum *at* segja;
    segik sigr hafa   snák inn hvíta.
    Láð mun leggjask   ok lýða fjǫlð;
    munu dreyrgar ár   ór dǫlum falla.

'Mikill harmr es *at* segja hǫlðum; segik inn hvíta snák hafa sigr. Láð mun leggjask ok fjǫlð lýða; dreyrgar ár munu falla ór dǫlum.

'A great sorrow is to be told to men; I say the white snake has the victory. The land and the multitude of people will be subjugated; blood-stained rivers will fall from the valleys.

Ms.: **Hb**(51r) (*Bret*).

Reading: [2] *at* segja: segja Hb.

Editions: *Skj*: Gunnlaugr Leifsson, *Merlínússpá II* 22: AII, 25, BII, 28; *Skald* II, 18; *Bret* 1848-9, II, 46 (*Bret* st. 90); *Hb* 1892-6, 278; *Merl* 2012, 144.

Notes: [All]: Cf. *DGB* 112 (Reeve and Wright 2007, 145.34, 36-7; cf. Wright 1988, 102, prophecy 1): *Vae rubeo draconi; nam exterminatio eius festinat … Montes itaque eius ut ualles aequabuntur, et flumina uallium sanguine manabunt* 'Alas for the red dragon, its end is near … Its mountains will be levelled with the valleys, and the rivers in the valleys will flow with blood' (Reeve and Wright 2007, 144). Gunnlaugr's handling of *Montes … aequabuntur* is consistent with his tendency to rationalise the allegory. — [2] at *segja* 'to be told': The prep. *at* is supplied in this edn to clarify the syntax. The inf. *segja* is passive in function though active in form.

23. 'Farask mun krístni,   kirkjur falla;
    sás harmr hǫfugr;   herr es í landi.
    Þá mun enn eflask   in auma þjóð;
    áðr es harðla hnekt   hennar kosti.

'Krístni mun farask, kirkjur falla; sás hǫfugr harmr; herr es í landi. Þá mun in auma þjóð enn eflask; kosti hennar es áðr harðla hnekt.

'Christianity will vanish, churches collapse; that is a grievous sorrow; the [invading] army is in the land. Then the miserable people will gain strength once more; prior to that their welfare is sorely checked.

Ms.: **Hb**(51r) (*Bret*).

Editions: *Skj*: Gunnlaugr Leifsson, *Merlínússpá II* 23: AII, 25, BII, 28; *Skald* II, 18; *Bret* 1848-9, II, 46 (*Bret* st. 91); *Hb* 1892-6, 278; *Merl* 2012, 144-5.

Note: [All]: Cf. *DGB* 112 (Reeve and Wright 2007, 145.38-9; cf. Wright 1988, 102, prophecies 1 and 2): *Cultus religionis delebitur, et ruina ecclesiarum patebit. Praeualebit tandem oppressa et saeuiciae exterorum resistet* 'Religious observance will be destroyed and churches stand in ruins. At last the oppressed will rise up and resist the foreigners' fury' (Reeve and Wright 2007, 144).

24. 'Mun þar í líki   lofðungr koma
    — sás vegligastr —   villigaltar.
    Hann fulltingir   fárǫðum her
    ok und fótum trøðr   ferðir Saxa.

'Lofðungr mun koma þar í líki villigaltar; sás vegligastr. Hann fulltingir fárǫðum her ok trøðr ferðir Saxa und fótum.

'A king will come there in the likeness of a wild boar; he is the most glorious. He will help the bewildered army and will tread the armies of the Saxons underfoot.

Ms.: **Hb**(51r) (*Bret*).

Editions: *Skj*: Gunnlaugr Leifsson, *Merlínússpá II* 24: AII, 25, BII, 28-9; *Skald* II, 18; *Bret* 1848-9, II, 47 (*Bret* st. 92); *Hb* 1892-6, 278; *Merl* 2012, 145.

Notes: [All]: Cf. *DGB* 112 (Reeve and Wright 2007, 145.39-40; cf. Wright 1988, 102, prophecy 2): *Aper etenim Cornubiae succursum praestabit et colla eorum sub pedibus suis conculcabit* 'The boar of Cornwall will lend his aid and trample the foreigners' necks beneath his feet' (Reeve and Wright 2007, 144). The reference is to King Arthur. Gunnlaugr rationalises the animal allegory by describing the king as in a boar's likeness rather than an actual boar. Geoffrey's reference to Cornwall is omitted. — [3]: J. S. Eysteinsson (1953-7, 99) argues that this recognition of Arthur's key role amongst British kings must stem from *DGB* proper (IX-XI), not the *Prophecies* in isolation; but see Introduction on Gunnlaugr's possible use of commentary material.

25. 'Fersk undir hann   foldu grœnni
    ok eyja fjǫlð   í úthafi,
    Íra ok Engla   ok Út-Skota,
    víðum lǫndum   valskra þjóða,
    Nóregs síðu   ok Norðr-Dana.

'Fersk undir hann grœnni foldu ok fjǫlð eyja í úthafi, Íra ok Engla ok Út-Skota, víðum lǫndum valskra þjóða, síðu Nóregs ok Norðr-Dana.

'Under him is brought the green land and a multitude of islands in the outer ocean, of the Irish and the English and the outlying Scots, extensive territories of the French people, the coast of Norway and [lands] of the northern Danes.

Ms.: **Hb**(51r) (*Bret*).

Editions: *Skj*: Gunnlaugr Leifsson, *Merlínússpá II* 25: AII, 25, BII, 29; *Skald* II, 18; *Bret* 1848-9, II, 4 (*Bret* st. 93); *Hb* 1892-6, 278; *Merl* 2012, 145-6.

Notes: [All]: Cf. *DGB* 112 (Reeve and Wright 2007, 145.41; cf. Wright 1988, 102, prophecy 2): *Insule occeani potestati ipsius subdentur, et Gallicanos saltus possidebit* 'The islands of the ocean will fall under his sway and he will occupy the glades of France' (Reeve and Wright 2007, 144). As noted by J. S. Eysteinsson (1953-7, 99), Gunnlaugr appears to draw on a wider knowledge of legends of Arthur's conquests than this Latin sentence would supply, taken on its own, and shows interest in the North Atlantic and Scandinavian regions. This, along with the mention of the Romans in *I* 26, could have been derived direct from *DGB* IX-XI (see Introduction). It could also, however, with much greater convenience have been derived from a commentary. Alain de Flandres, for instance, annotates as follows (Wille 2015, 161): *Hyberniam namque, Islandiam, Scotiam, Orcadum insulas, Gothlandiam, Norguegiam, Datiamque sub iugum misit et suo subiecit imperio* 'For he subjugated Ireland, Iceland, Scotland, the Orkney islands,

Gotland, Norway and Denmark and subjected them to his imperial rule' (cf. Hammer 1935, 26, and, for another commentary with similar content, Hammer 1935, 8). Arthurian incursions into Scandinavian territories would not necessarily have been judged improbable or incongruous by Gunnlaugr's audience; Haukr Erlendsson makes occasional changes to the text of *Bret* 'in order to reveal connections with Scandinavian history, particularly with Norwegian royal dynasties' (Tétrel 2010, 494). On the other hand, there is no mention in *Merl*, at least as extant, of Iceland, which both Geoffrey and the commentators included in Arthur's dominions (cf. Tatlock 1950, 107). Gunnlaugr appears to correct the designation of Denmark and Norway as islands, which again is a designation in Geoffrey that is reproduced by the commentators (cf. Tatlock 1950, 107), instead placing them in explicit parallel (Denmark) or implicit parallel (Norway) with France. — [1] *fersk* 'is brought': This verb governs the dat. case of *grœnni foldu* 'the green land' (l. 2), *fjǫlð* 'a multitude' (l. 3), *víðum lǫndum* 'extensive territories' (l. 5) and *síðu* 'the coast' (l. 9). The concatenation of gen. pl. nouns makes it difficult to determine which of these territories are assigned to which peoples. — [4] *úthafi* 'the outer ocean': A *hap. leg.* in poetry; prose attestations are confined to learned and religious texts (*Fritzner, ONP*: *úthaf*). — [6] *Út-Skota* 'the outlying Scots': I.e. the Scots on outlying islands. A *hap. leg.*; for the formation cf. *útþrœnskr* 'belonging to outer Þrándheimr', as contrasted with *innþrœnskr* 'belonging to inner Þrándheimr' (*Fritzner*: *útþrœnskr*). — [8] *Norðr-Dana* 'of the northern Danes': A *hap. leg.*, and it is not altogether clear which group of Danes might be referred to. The rhetorical thrust is to emphasise the far-flung nature of Arthur's conquests.

26. 'Ok Rúmverjar   ræsi ugga;
     megut reisa þeir   rǫnd við stilli.
     Mart veitk annat   of menbrota,
     en óglǫgt sék   ørlǫg konungs.

'Ok Rúmverjar ugga ræsi; þeir megut reisa rǫnd við stilli. Veitk mart annat of menbrota, en ørlǫg konungs sék óglǫgt.

'And the Romans will fear the king; they will not be able to raise a shield against the lord. I know much else about the breaker of neck-rings [GENEROUS MAN = Arthur], but the fate of the king I see indistinctly.

Ms.: **Hb**(51r) (*Bret*).

Editions: *Skj*: Gunnlaugr Leifsson, *Merlínússpá II* 26: AII, 25, BII, 29; *Skald* II, 18; *Bret* 1848-9, II, 47 (*Bret* st. 94); *Hb* 1892-6, 278; *Merl* 2012, 146-7.

Notes: [All]: Cf. *DGB* 112 (Reeve and Wright 2007, 145.42; cf. Wright 1988, 102, prophecy 2): *Tremebit Romulea domus saeuiciam ipsius, et exitus eius dubius erit* 'The house of Romulus will tremble before his rage, and his end shall be unknown' (cf. Reeve and Wright 2007, 144). Gunnlaugr adds the claim to know more about Arthur

(J. S. Eysteinsson 1953-7, 99). — [3-4] *reisa rǫnd við* 'raise a shield against': Meaning 'be capable of resisting' (*CVC*: *reisa*). Cf. Note to *II* 37/3-4.

27. 'Hann munu tígna   tungur lýða;
    sá mun gramr vera   gumnum tíðastr.
    Ey mun uppi   ǫðlings frami
    ok hans hróðr fara   með himinskautum.

'Tungur lýða munu tígna hann; sá gramr mun vera tíðastr gumnum. Frami ǫðlings mun ey uppi ok hróðr hans fara með himinskautum.

'The tongues of men will honour him; that king will be the most renowned among men. The lord's prowess will always be remembered and his glory will travel to the corners of heaven.

Ms.: **Hb**(51r) (*Bret*).

Editions: *Skj*: Gunnlaugr Leifsson, *Merlínússpá II* 27: AII, 25, BII, 29; *Skald* II, 18; *Bret* 1848-9, II, 47-8 (*Bret* st. 95); *Hb* 1892-6, 278; *Merl* 2012, 147-8.

Notes: [All]: Cf. *DGB* 112 (Reeve and Wright 2007, 145.42-3; cf. Wright 1988, 102, prophecy 2): *In ore populorum celebrabitur, et actus eius cibus erit narrantibus* 'He will be celebrated in the mouth of the nations and his deeds will feed those who tell them' (Reeve and Wright 2007, 144). The extension of the 'mouth' motif to 'food' and the allusion to tellers of stories on Arthurian themes is not represented in *Merl*. — [1] *tígna* 'honour': This verb, along with its cognates *tíginn* 'revered, honoured' and *tígn* 'honour', is distinctive of late religious poetry (*LP*: *tígna*); similarly in prose, attestations are most frequent in learned texts (*ONP*: *tígna*). — [5] *mun ey uppi* 'will always be remembered': The formula *vera uppi* in this context means 'live in the memory, be remembered' (cf. *Fritzner*: *vera uppi* b, Arn *Hryn* 15/1[II], *Gríp* 23/5, 41/3). — [8] *himinskautum* 'the corners of heaven': *Himinskaut* is a largely poetic word, with only one prose attestation (cf. *ONP*: *himinskaut*). The phrase *með himinskautum* occurs only here and in *Hyndl* 14/8, also a passage in praise of a king. Cf. also *Gríp* 10/8 and SnSt *Ht* 95/8[III].

28. 'Ok ǫttungar   ins ítra grams
    laða at lofðungi   landi ok þegnum.
    En eptir þat   orms ins hvíta
    verðr meira vald   en verit hafði.

'Ok ǫttungar ins ítra grams laða landi ok þegnum at lofðungi. En eptir þat verðr vald ins hvíta orms meira en hafði verit.

'And the descendants of the illustrious king will attract land and subjects to the ruler. But after that the power of the white snake will become greater than it had been.

Ms.: **Hb**(51r) (*Bret*).

Editions: *Skj*: Gunnlaugr Leifsson, *Merlínússpá II* 28: AII, 25, BII, 29; *Skald* II, 18; *Bret* 1848-9, II, 48 (*Bret* st. 96); *Hb* 1892-6, 278-9; *Merl* 2012, 148.

Notes: [All]: Cf. *DGB* 112 (Reeve and Wright 2007, 145.43-4; cf. Wright 1988, 102, prophecy 3): *Sex posteri eius sequentur sceptrum, sed post ipsos exsurget Germanicus uermis* 'His six successors will wield the sceptre, but after them the German [i.e. Germanic] worm will rise' (Reeve and Wright 2007, 144). The idea of 'six' is absent from *Merl*. The variant reading *sed*, for *sex*, is found in mss O and G (Reeve and Wright 2007, 145; cf. xlv and xlvii for identifications of these mss); Gunnlaugr's copy-text may have been related to them, but polygenetic error is also thinkable (Reeve and Wright 2007, xviii). Equivalents of the term 'sceptre' do not occur in *Merl* (cf. *I* 33). In reckoning with an increase in territorial sway on the part of Arthur's successors, Gunnlaugr may have drawn on the narrative in *DGB* XI (J. S. Eysteinsson 1953-7, 100; for text see Reeve and Wright 2007, 254-5). — [3-4] *laða landi ok þegnum at lofðungi* 'will attract land and subjects to the ruler': Among possible explanations for sg. 'ruler' here are that it alludes to Arthur's status as perpetual king (cryptically referred to in *I* 26/7-8) or that it is used *pars pro toto* for 'royal line/dynasty'.

29. 'Honum fulltingir   Fenrir sjóvar,
    þeims Affríkar   útan fylgja.
    Verðr kristnibrot   of kyni þjóðar;
    þó munu sjalfir   síðar nøkkvi
    enskir lýðir   allir skírask.

'Fenrir sjóvar fulltingir honum, þeims Affríkar fylgja útan. Verðr kristnibrot of kyni þjóðar; þó munu sjalfir enskir lýðir allir skírask nøkkvi síðar.

'The Fenrir <mythical wolf> of the sea, which Africans follow from overseas, will help it. There will be a breakdown of Christianity among the kindred of the people; yet the English people will themselves all be baptised somewhat later.

Ms.: **Hb**(51r-v) (*Bret*).

Editions: *Skj*: Gunnlaugr Leifsson, *Merlínússpá II* 29: AII, 25-6, BII, 29-30; *Skald* II, 18; *Bret* 1848-9, II, 48 (*Bret* st. 97); *Hb* 1892-6, 279; *Merl* 2012, 148-9.

Notes: [All]: Cf. *DGB* 112 (Reeve and Wright 2007, 145.45-6; cf. Wright 1988, 102, prophecy 3): *Sublimabit illum aequoreus lupus, quem Affricana nemora comitabuntur. Delebitur iterum religio* 'It [the Germanic worm] will be raised by a wolf from the sea, who will be accompanied by the forests of Africa. Religion will be destroyed again' (Reeve and Wright 2007, 144). The events prophesied here are narrated in *DGB* XI:

the Saxons call for assistance from Gormundus, the king of the Africans, who has just subdued Ireland and therefore can be called the 'wolf from the sea'; he brings an army composed of 160,000 Africans (J. S. Eysteinsson 1953-7, 100; for text see Reeve and Wright 2007, 256-7; on Geoffrey's sources for the story of Gormundus see Tatlock 1950, 135-8). The first sentence is absent from some mss of *DGB* (Reeve and Wright 2007, 145) but must have been available to Gunnlaugr. Gunnlaugr rationalises the figurative 'the forests of Africa' and adds the idea that despite the breakdown of religion the English will in due course be baptised, as foreshadowed in *DGB* XI (cf. Reeve and Wright 2007, 258-9; J. S. Eysteinsson 1953-7, 100) and fully narrated in Bede *HE* I, 23-6 and Henry of Huntingdon *HA* Book III. — [1] *honum* 'it': The antecedent is *orms ins hvíta* 'of the white snake' (*I* 28/6). — [2] *Fenrir* 'the Fenrir <mythical wolf>': This is the mythical wolf, son of Loki and the giantess Angrboða, especially associated with Ragnarǫk in Old Norse eschatology, where he fights against Óðinn and kills him (cf. *SnE* 2005, 25-7, 50). — [5] *kristnibrot* 'a breakdown of Christianity': A *hap. leg.* in poetry (*LP*: *kristnibrot*) and not cited by *ONP*.

30. 'Líðr byskups stóll Lundúnum ór
  í ina breiðu borg Kantara.
  Ok langa tígn Légíónum
  taka mun in mæta Menelógía.

'Stóll byskups líðr ór Lundúnum í ina breiðu Kantaraborg. Ok in mæta Menelógía mun taka langa tígn Légíónum.

'The bishop's seat will move from London to the broad Canterbury. And the splendid Menelogia will take over the long-held distinction of Caerleon.

Ms.: **Hb**(51v) (*Bret*).

Editions: *Skj*: Gunnlaugr Leifsson, *Merlínússpá II* 30: AII, 26, BII, 30, *Skald* II, 19; *Bret* 1848-9, II, 48-9 (*Bret* st. 98); *Hb* 1892-6, 279; *Merl* 2012, 149-50.

Notes: [All]: Cf. *DGB* 112 (Reeve and Wright 2007, 145.46-7, 48-9; cf. Wright 1988, 102, prophecy 3): *et transmutacio primarum sedium fiet. Dignitas Lundoniae adornabit Doroberniam ... Meneuia pallio Vrbis Legionum induetur* 'and archbishoprics will be displaced. London's honour will adorn Canterbury ... St David's [*sic*] will wear the pallium of Caerleon' (Reeve and Wright 2007, 144). London is described by Geoffrey as the seat of an archbishop in Romano-British times (*DGB* VI: Reeve and Wright 2007, 112-13; cf. Tatlock 1950, 264). The existence of a see of Caerleon and its pre-eminence in Britain before the arrival of the Saxons appear to be inventions on Geoffrey's part (Tatlock 1950, 264-5, 266). Geoffrey recounts the death of David, archbishop of Caerleon, at Menevia (Welsh *Mynyw*), subsequently St Davids (Welsh *Tyddewi*) in *DGB* XI (Reeve and Wright 2007, 254-5). The prophecy appears to foreshadow the expression of Welsh aspirations to restore this see to the status of an archbishopric (cf. Tatlock 1950, 266, 415; Curley 1982, 220, 223; see *II* 16 Note to [All]). As noted in *Bret* 1848-9, two other locations mentioned in Geoffrey's text, York and Ireland, are not represented in *Merl*, at least as extant. — [4] *Kantaraborg* 'Canterbury': Lit. 'city of the Kentish people'. *Kantaraborg* is the normal Old Norse name for Canterbury, here as elsewhere with the elements reversed in order to conform to the requirements of alliteration; cf. Ótt *Hfl* 10/4¹ and Note there. — [6] *Légíónum* 'of Caerleon': Latin 'of the legions'. Gunnlaugr retains the Latin gen. pl. form. — [8] *Menelógía* 'Menelogia': In the form *menologion*, pl. *menologia* this is a term for a Greek Orthodox calendar of saints' lives (*OED*: *menologion*), but here evidently used in error for the perhaps unfamiliar p. n. *Menevia*, 'St Davids'. The error is unlikely to be Gunnlaugr's, given the general high level of his Latinity. As the reading is unrefreshed it can be added to the list of probable errors already present in *Hb*. *Bret* 1848-9 emends to *Menevia* accordingly but *Skj* B retains, as do *Merl* 2012 and the present edn. (*LP*, presumably in error also, records the Latin name as *Menovia*.)

31. 'Stór verða rǫk,   rignir blóði,
hár snarpr at þat   sultr mannkyni.
En inn rauði snákr   eflisk síðan;
fær hann af miklu   mátt erfiði.

'Stór rǫk verða, rignir blóði, snarpr sultr hár mannkyni at þat. En inn rauði snákr eflisk síðan; hann fær mátt af miklu erfiði.

'Great wonders will occur, it will rain with blood, acute famine will thereupon afflict mankind. But the red snake gathers strength afterwards; he will acquire power from great exertion.

Ms.: **Hb**(51v) (*Bret*).

Editions: *Skj*: Gunnlaugr Leifsson, *Merlínússpá II* 31: AII, 26, BII, 30, *Skald* II, 19; *Bret* 1848-9, II, 49 (*Bret* st. 99); *Hb* 1892-6, 279; *Merl* 2012, 150-1.

Notes: [All]: Cf. *DGB* 112 (Reeve and Wright 2007, 147.50-1; cf. Wright 1988, 102, prophecies 3 and 4): *Pluet sanguineus imber, et dira fames mortales afficiet. His superuenientibus, dolebit rubeus sed emenso labore uigebit* 'A rain of blood will fall, and a terrible famine will afflict mortals. The red dragon will lament as these occur, but will recover its strength once the travail is over' (cf. Reeve and Wright 2007, 146). This prophecy alludes to events narrated in *DGB* XI (Reeve and Wright 2007, 256-7). — [3] *hár* 'will afflict': From *há* 'afflict, plague', a weak verb, attested only twice in poetry (*LP*: *háa*) and not at all in prose (*ONP*) but familiar in Modern Icelandic (*AEW*: *há*). — [6] *eflisk síðan* 'gathers strength afterwards': This is the reading of Hb (not refreshed) and it is retained by *Bret* 1848-9, *Merl* 2012 and this edn. Other eds have seen the lack of alliteration as pointing to a problem with the text. *Skj* B, followed by *Skald*, emends to *síðan eflisk* with the objective of restoring alliteration on <s> on the *hǫfuðstafr* 'head-stave'; the alliteration created in this way, however, would then cause difficulties in l. 5, where it would fall in a prohibited position, the second lift in a Type B-line. Given that demonstrable errors in the Hb text occur elsewhere (see Introduction), it may be that *eflisk* has supplanted some other word.

32.   'Líðr nauðr yfir   naðr inn hvíta;
      es hans kyn kvalit   ok konur ristnar.
      Rǽntr es hann borgum   ok búi mǫrgu,
      fé hvers konar,   foldu grœnni;
      eru grimmliga   gumnar drepnir.

'Nauðr líðr yfir inn hvíta naðr; kyn hans es kvalit ok konur ristnar. Hann es rǽntr borgum ok mǫrgu búi, fé hvers konar, grœnni foldu; gumnar eru grimmliga drepnir.

'Hardship will overwhelm the white snake; his kindred will be tormented and his women lacerated. He will be robbed of cities and many an estate, property of every kind, the green land; men will be slaughtered savagely.

Mss.: **Hb**(51v) (*Bret*).

Editions: *Skj*: Gunnlaugr Leifsson, *Merlínússpá II* 32: AII, 26, BII, 30, *Skald* II, 19; *Bret* 1848-9, II, 49 (*Bret* st. 100); *Hb* 1892-6, 279; *Merl* 2012, 151.

Notes: [All]: Cf. *DGB* 112 (Reeve and Wright 2007, 147.51-5; cf. Wright 1988, 102, prophecy 4): *Tunc infortunium albi festinabit et aedificia ortulorum eius diruentur … Ventres matrum secabuntur, et infantes abortiui erunt. Erit ingens supplicium hominum ut indigenae restituantur* 'Then the misfortune of the white will be hastened and the buildings in its gardens be destroyed … Mothers' bellies will be cut open and infants aborted. People will suffer greatly in order that the natives be restored' (Reeve and Wright 2007, 146). The prophecy refers to the reconquest of the Britons led by King Caduallo recounted in *DGB* XI (Reeve and Wright 2007, 272-3). — [4] *ok konur ristnar* 'and his women lacerated': Gunnlaugr characteristically slightly tones down the reference to murderous abortion. — [5-8]: Gunnlaugr expands on the implications for land and property, as occasionally elsewhere: cf. *I* 41 Note to [All], *I* 42 Note to [All], *I* 62 Note to [All]. — [5] *hann* 'he': Omitted in *Skald* for metrical reasons.

33.   'Hníga fyr brezkum   bragninga kon
      siklingar sjau,   sigri numnir.
      Ok heilagr verðr   herja deilir
      einn af enskum   ǫðlingum sjau.

'Sjau siklingar, numnir sigri, hníga fyr brezkum kon bragninga. Ok deilir herja, einn af sjau enskum ǫðlingum, verðr heilagr.

'Seven kings, deprived of victory, will fall before the British scion of kings [KING = Caduallo]. And the commander of armies [LEADER = S. Oswald], one of the seven English lords, will become a saint.

Ms.: **Hb**(51v) (*Bret*).

Editions: *Skj*: Gunnlaugr Leifsson, *Merlínússpá II* 33: AII, 26, BII, 30, *Skald* II, 19; *Bret* 1848-9, II, 50 (*Bret* st. 101); *Hb* 1892-6, 279; *Merl* 2012, 152.

Note: [All]: Cf. *DGB* 112 (Reeve and Wright 2007, 147.52-3; cf. Wright 1988, 102, prophecy 4): *Septem sceptrigeri perimentur, et unus eorum sanctificabitur* 'Seven sceptre-bearers will be killed, and one of them will become a saint' (cf. Reeve and Wright 2007, 146). Gunnlaugr treats this sentence separately from its neighbours, which are covered in *I* 32. His translation is evidently based on the reading *septem* 'seven', not the variant *octo* 'eight' that occurs in the Π group of mss (Reeve and Wright 2007, 147); see Introduction. The prophecy refers to the death of S. Oswald, narrated in *DGB* XI (Reeve and Wright 2007, 272-3). Caduallo (variant spelling *Cadwallon*), king of Gwynedd in North Wales (rendered by Geoffrey as *Venedotia*) in the first third of the C7th, formed an alliance with Penda of Mercia to overthrow the Anglo-Saxon royal dynasty of Northumbria, but was defeated and killed by Oswald of Northumbria in 633. Oswald met his death at Penda's hands in 641 (Stenton 1971, 80-2).

34. 'Sá, es slíkt gerir,   mun sjalfr taka
    eirmann á sik,   aldar stjóri;
    ok of hǫ hliði   hilmir síðan
    eirhesti á   ítarligr sitr.
    Gætir Lundúna   lofsæll konungr.

'Sá stjóri aldar, es gerir slíkt, mun sjalfr taka eirmann á sik; ok hilmir sitr síðan ítarligr á eirhesti of hǫ hliði. Lofsæll konungr gætir Lundúna.

'That ruler of the people [KING = Caduallo] who does this will take a copper form upon himself, and thenceforward the ruler will sit in splendour on a copper horse above the high gate. The renowned king will watch over London.

Ms.: **Hb**(51v) (*Bret*).

Editions: *Skj*: Gunnlaugr Leifsson, *Merlínússpá II* 34: AII, 26, BII, 30-1, *Skald* II, 19; *Bret* 1848-9, II, 50 (*Bret* st. 102); *Hb* 1892-6, 279; *Merl* 2012, 152-3.

Notes: [All]: Cf. *DGB* 112 (Reeve and Wright 2007, 147.55-6; cf. Wright 1988, 102, prophecy 4): *Qui faciet haec aeneum uirum induet et per multa tempora super aeneum equum portas Londoniae seruabit* 'He who achieves this will don a man of bronze and for many years guard the gates of London upon a bronze steed' (Reeve and Wright 2007, 146). This prophecy alludes to the placing of the body of King Caduallo inside a bronze effigy, narrated in *DGB* XI (Reeve and Wright 2007, 276-7). The effigy combined with its mount would have made up an equestrian statue (cf. Tatlock 1950, 375). — [3] *eirmann* 'a copper form': Lit. 'copper man'. The word is a *hap. leg.* (*LP*, *ONP*: *eirmaðr*). — [7] *eirhesti* 'a copper horse': The word is attested only here and in *Bret* (*ONP*: *eirhestr*). — [9-10]: The <G> in *Gætir* is majuscule in the ms., presumably to indicate that in the belief of the copyist a new stanza began at this point. But the grouping of the narrative material speaks for the division of stanzas adopted here and by all previous eds.

35. 'Þá gerisk þat   of þjóð Breta,
    es þeim enn hefir   áðr of grandat,
    at þeir sjalfir s*íz*t sáttir verða.
    Deila þeir of veldi ok of víða fold;
    eru kappsamar   kindir brezkar.

'Þá gerisk þat of þjóð Breta, es hefir enn áðr of grandat þeim, at þeir sjalfir verða s*íz*t sáttir. Þeir deila of veldi ok of víða fold; brezkar kindir eru kappsamar.

'Then it will come about for the British people, as has also harmed them in the past, that they themselves will not at all be in harmony. They will compete for power and for the wide territory; the British peoples will be in rivalry.

Ms.: **Hb**(51v) (*Bret*).

Reading: [5] s*íz*t: 'sitz' Hb.

Editions: *Skj*: Gunnlaugr Leifsson, *Merlínússpá II* 35: AII, 26-7, BII, 31, *Skald* II, 19; *Bret* 1848-9, II, 50-1 (*Bret* st. 103); *Hb* 1892-6, 279; *Merl* 2012, 153-4.

Notes: [All]: Cf. *DGB* 112 (Reeve and Wright 2007, 147.56-7; cf. Wright 1988, 103, prophecy 5): *Exin in proprios mores reuertetur rubeus draco et in se ipsum saeuire laborabit* 'Then the red dragon will return to its old ways and strive to tear at itself' (Reeve and Wright 2007, 146). Gunnlaugr elaborates on the cryptic allusion to internecine conflict in Geoffrey's text and rationalises the allegory, on the lines seen in *DGB* XI (J. S. Eysteinsson 1953-7, 101-2; for text see Reeve and Wright 2007, 276-7) and Bede *HE* I, 22 (Colgrave and Mynors 1969, 66-9). According to Geoffrey in *DGB* XI, Cadualadrus (Cadwallader, referred to by Bede as *Ciedwalla*) succeeds Caduallo as king but falls sick, whereupon the Britons fight among themselves and suffer famine and pestilence. — [5] s*íz*t 'not at all': Emended in *Bret* 1848-9 (followed by *Skj* B, *Skald* and *Merl* 2012) from ms. 'sitz' (not refreshed). Given that the spelling <z> in C14th usage, including Haukr's own orthography, can denote either *st* or *ts*, 'sitz' may have originated in an erroneous expansion of *síz*. — [7-10]: All eds treat these lines as the conclusion of st. 35. In Hb <D> of *deila* is clearly majuscule, indicating the copyist's understanding of the stanza division, but the disposition of narrative materials suggests that he was mistaken on this score. See Note to *I* 34/9-10.

36. 'Kemr bardagi   buðlungs himins
     ákafr of her,   ári steypir.
     Kvelr inn harði   helverkr fira;
     megut dauðan her   dróttir hylja.
     Líðr sultr ok sótt   at sigrviðum
     — missir manna —   mǫrg stríð hǫfug.

'Ákafr bardagi buðlungs himins kemr of her, steypir ári. Inn harði helverkr kvelr fira; dróttir megut hylja dauðan her. Sultr ok sótt líðr at sigrviðum, mǫrg hǫfug stríð; missir manna.

'The violent scourge of the king of heaven [= God] will come over the people, will ruin the harvest. The harsh torment of Hell will afflict men; men will not be able to bury the dead people. Hunger and sickness will advance on victory-trees [WARRIORS], [and] many grievous hardships; there is loss of men.

Ms.: **Hb**(51v) (*Bret*).

Reading: [2] buðlungs: buðlung Hb.

Editions: *Skj*: Gunnlaugr Leifsson, *Merlínússpá II* 36: AII, 27, BII, 31, *Skald* II, 19, *FF* §63; *Bret* 1848-9, II, 51 (*Bret* st. 104); *Hb* 1892-6, 279; *Merl* 2012, 154-5.

Notes: [All]: Cf. *DGB* 112 (Reeve and Wright 2007, 147.58-9; cf. Wright 1988, 103, prophecy 5): *Superueniet itaque ultio Tonantis, quia omnis ager colonos decipiet. Arripiet mortalitas populum cunctasque nationes euacuabit* 'Upon it will come the retribution of the Thunderer, for every field will disappoint its cultivators. Pestilence will smite the people and empty every region' (Reeve and Wright 2007, 146). — [1] *bardagi* 'the scourge': This sense of the word, which normally means 'battle' (see further Note to l. 10), occurs chiefly in learned and religious texts. The word is not otherwise attested in poetry except in Bjbp *Jóms* 7/2[1], where it refers to a battle. — [2] *buðlungs* 'of the king': Emended in *Skj* B, followed by *Skald*, *Merl* 2012 and this edn, for ms. *buðlung* (not refreshed). — [9-12]: A composite subject, with sg. verb governed by the first component of the subject, as happens sporadically elsewhere in *Merl* (cf. *NS* §66). Kock (*FF* §63) notes the parallel construction in ll. 9 and 12. — [10] *sigrviðum* 'victory-trees [WARRIORS]': Gunnlaugr appears to ironise the plight of the Britons, who having waxed excessively bellicose now find themselves defeated by God's *bardagi*, understood as 'scourge' (l. 1) but with overtones of the other familiar sense, 'warfare'. Cf. their description as *þingdjarfa* 'battle-daring' in *I* 37/3. — [11] *missir* 'there is loss': This edn follows *Skj* B, with which Kock concurs (*FF* §63); on this construal *missir* is a verb, used impersonally (cf. *LP*: *missa* 2). *Merl* 2012 instead construes *missir* as the nom. sg. of the noun *missir* 'loss', as suggested in *LP*: *missir*, which may equally well be the correct solution.

37. 'Láð mun*u* láta   þeirs lifa eptir;
    ferr in þingdjarfa   þjóð ór landi.
    Býr blezaðr gramr   — sás brezkr jǫfurr —
    skip sín á brott,   ok hann skjótla verðr
    taliðr tírgǫfugr   í tolfta hǫll
    sæll með sælum   settr guðs vinum.

'Þeirs lifa eptir mun*u* láta láð; in þingdjarfa þjóð ferr ór landi. Blezaðr gramr — sás brezkr jǫfurr — býr skip sín á brott, ok hann verðr skjótla taliðr tírgǫfugr settr í tolfta hǫll sæll með sælum vinum guðs.

'Those who survive will abandon the land; the battle-daring people will go from the territory. A blessed king — he is the British leader — prepares his ships for departure and he will soon become reckoned glorious, seated in the twelfth hall, blessed among the blessed friends of God.

Ms.: **Hb**(51v) (*Bret*).

Reading: [1] mun*u*: mun Hb.

Editions: *Skj*: Gunnlaugr Leifsson, *Merlínússpá II* 37: AII, 27, BII, 31, *Skald* II, 19-20; *Bret* 1848-9, II, 51 (*Bret* st. 105); *Hb* 1892-6, 279; *Merl* 2012, 155.

Notes: [All]: Cf. *DGB* 112 (Reeve and Wright 2007, 147.59-61; cf. Wright 1988, 103, prophecy 5): *Residui natale solum deserent et exteras culturas seminabunt. Rex benedictus parabit nauigium et in aula duodecimi inter beatos annumerabitur* 'The survivors will leave their native soil and sow in foreign fields. A blessed king will prepare a fleet and will be numbered among the saints in the palace of the twelfth' (cf. Reeve and Wright 2007, 146). This prophecy alludes to the exodus of the British people from their native land to settle in Armorica (Brittany). They are accompanied by King Cadualadrus, who after eleven years of exile contemplates a re-settlement of Britain but is summoned by an angelic voice to go to Rome to do penance in advance of eventual sanctification, as narrated in *DGB* XI (Reeve and Wright 2007, 276-81). — [1] *mun*u 'will': Emended in *Bret* 1848-9, followed by all subsequent eds, from ms. *mun*. — [10] *í tolfta* 'in the twelfth': This apparently nonsensical expression must ultimately be due to an incorrect reading *.xii.* (expanded to *duodecimi* 'of the twelfth') in Geoffrey's text, supplanting original *xri or *xti, i.e. *Christi* 'of Christ', in reference to the *caelestis regni aula* 'palace of the heavenly kingdom' mentioned in *DGB* XI (206.586: Reeve and Wright 2007, 281). The commentaries attempt to explain in *ad hoc* fashion, e.g. (Hammer 1940, 416): *in aula duodecimi, id est in ecclesia beati Petri apostoli* 'in the hall of the twelfth, i.e. in the church of St Peter the apostle' and 'King Cadwaladre ... was buried in the chirche of xij. Apostolles. and is a seint' (Eckhardt 1982, 73). Emended to *tólpti í* and construed as 'twelfth in [the hall]' in *Skj* B, followed by *Skald*, on the basis of an incorrect interpretation of *.xii.* as *duodecimus* 'twelfth' in *Bret* 1848-9. In a hybrid approach, *Merl* 2012 reads *í tólpta hǫll* but translates, in combination with *hann skjótla* *verðr taliðr*, as *der Edle wird bald als zwölfter gerechnet in der Halle* 'the noble one will soon be reckoned as twelfth in the hall', but this is ruled out by considerations of syntax and word order.

38. 'Svá tœmir láð   lýða bǫrnum,
    — drífr hryggr heðan   herr ór landi —
    at sk*ógar* þar   skjótla vaxa,
    es ársamir   akrar vǫru
    fyrr með fyrðum   á fold Breta.

'Svá tœmir láð bǫrnum lýða — hryggr herr drífr heðan ór landi —, at sk*ógar* vaxa skjótla þar, es fyrr vǫru ársamir akrar með fyrðum á fold Breta.

'Thus the land will be emptied of the children of men [MANKIND] — the grieving people will stream from here out of the land — so that the forests will quickly grow there where previously among men there were fertile fields in the land of the Britons.

Ms.: **Hb**(51v) (*Bret*).

Reading: [5] sk*ógar*: skjótla Hb.

Editions: *Skj*: Gunnlaugr Leifsson, *Merlínússpá II* 38: AII, 27, BII, 31-2; *Skald* II, 20; *Bret* 1848-9, II, 52 (*Bret* st. 106); *Hb* 1892-6, 279; *Merl* 2012, 156.

Notes: [All]: Cf. *DGB* 112 (Reeve and Wright 2007, 147.61-2; cf. Wright 1988, 103, prophecy 5): *Erit miseranda regni desolatio, et areae messium in fruticosos saltus redibunt* 'There will be grievous desolation in the kingdom and the threshing-floors for harvest will revert to fruitful glades' (Reeve and Wright 2007, 146). This passage would make better sense if *in infructuosos* 'in unfruitful', the reading of ms. H of the First Variant Version were adopted (Wright 1988, 103), thus correcting an obvious haplography. This is done by e.g. the Anglo-Norman decasyllabic translation: *lande senz fruit* 'fruitless scrub' (Blacker 2005, 35) and Alain de Flandres (Wille 2015, 128). Implicitly, at least, Gunnlaugr's *skógar* 'forests' are unfruitful: it is unclear whether he knew such a reading or has rationalised the text on his own initiative. Geoffrey explains in *DGB* XI that the famine and plague are so severe that the Saxons cannot survive in Britain any better than the Britons (Reeve and Wright 2007, 278-9). Gunnlaugr interweaves motifs from the source passage corresponding to *I* 36. — [1] *tœmir* 'will be emptied': The verb is used impersonally. This is one of only two attestations in poetry, both in C12th or later texts (*LP*: *tœma*). — [4] *herr* 'people': *Merl* 2012 reads acc. sg. *her*, treats *drífr* as transitive and construes *hryggr* as the subject (adj. for noun), yielding a translation *traurig drängt er (man?) die Menge von hier aus dem Land* 'sorrowful he (one?) expels the multitude from here out of the land'. But this fits poorly with *DGB* and leaves the identity of the person described as *hryggr* 'sorrowful' unexplained; moreover, the required sense of *drífa* is attested in only a single dubious instance (*ONP*: *drífa* B *út* 2).

Geminate <r> is frequently simplified in Hb (*Hb* 1892-6, xliii). — [5] *skógar* 'forests': Emended by *Bret* 1848-9, followed by all eds, for ms. *skjótla* 'quickly' (not refreshed), an anticipation of the next line. Also possible would be the reverse order *skjótla … skógar*.

39. 'Þá mun inn hvíti   hjarlþvengr fara
     snót saxneska   snarráðr laða.
     Ok með miklum   mannfjǫlða kemr
     fjarðbyggs Skǫgul   fold at byggja.

'Þá mun inn hvíti hjarlþvengr fara snarráðr laða saxneska snót. Ok Skǫgul fjarðbyggs kemr með miklum mannfjǫlða at byggja fold.

'Then the white thong of the earth [SNAKE] will travel, with swift resolution, to invite the Saxon woman. And the Skǫgul <valkyrie> of fjord-barley [JEWEL (*steinn* 'stone') > WOMAN] will come with a great multitude of men to settle the land.

Ms.: **Hb**(51v) (*Bret*).

Editions: *Skj*: Gunnlaugr Leifsson, *Merlínússpá II* 39: AII, 27, BII, 32, *Skald* II, 20; *Bret* 1848-9, II, 52 (*Bret* st. 107); *Hb* 1892-6, 279; *Merl* 2012, 157.

Notes: [All]: Cf. *DGB* 112 (Reeve and Wright 2007, 147.63; cf. Wright 1985, 75, prophecy 6): *Exurget iterum albus draco et filiam Germaniae inuitabit* 'The white dragon will rise again and summon Germany's daughter' (Reeve and Wright 2007, 146). The absence of this sentence from the text of the *Prophecies* in the First Variant Version of *DGB* (Wright 1988, 103) misled J. S. Eysteinsson (1953-7, 102) into supposing Gunnlaugr derived the motif of the Saxon woman from *DGB* XI. Geoffrey tells in *DGB* XI that the Saxons who survived the hardships summoned more immigrants from Germania (Reeve and Wright 2007, 278-9); the *filia Germaniae* is evidently a representation of these people. By contrast, Gunnlaugr's rather specific-sounding phrase, *snót saxneska*, along with the second *helmingr*, suggests that he interpreted the representation as referring to a specific woman, perhaps prompted by Geoffrey's account of the key role in the invasion played by Hengest's daughter Ronwein in *DGB* VI (Reeve and Wright 2007, 128-31). — [7] *Skǫgul fjarðbyggs* 'the Skǫgul <valkyrie> of fjord-barley [JEWEL (*steinn* 'stone') > WOMAN]': The determinant of the first level of this kenning is understood by *ofljóst* to refer to a jewel or precious stone, given that 'fjord-barley' refers metaphorically to a stone standing in the water of a fjord; cf. *Meissner* 90 for this group of stone-kennings.

40. 'Mun sáð koma   sinni ǫðru
    útlent yfir   óra garða.
    En s*a*mt yfir   á svǫlum barmi
    eylands þrumir   ormr inn rauði;
    færr hann lítit   af landinu.

'Mun útlent sáð koma ǫðru sinni yfir garða óra. En inn rauði ormr þrumir s*a*mt yfir á svǫlum barmi eylands; hann færr lítit af landinu.

'Foreign seed will come a second time over our precincts. And still the red snake remains on the cool fringe of the island; he will gain little from the land.

Ms.: **Hb**(51v) (*Bret*).

Reading: [5] s*a*mt: sumt Hb.

Editions: *Skj*: Gunnlaugr Leifsson, *Merlínússpá II* 40: AII, 27, BII, 32, *Skald* II, 20; *Bret* 1848-9, II, 52 (*Bret* st. 108); *Hb* 1892-6, 279; *Merl* 2012, 157-8.

Notes: [All]: Cf. *DGB* 112 (Reeve and Wright 2007, 147.63-4; cf. Wright 1988, 103, prophecy 6): *Replebuntur iterum ortuli nostri alieno semine, et in extremitate stagni languebit rubeus* 'Our gardens will be filled again with foreign seed and the red dragon will languish at the pool's edge'. This prophecy alludes to the restriction of British occupation to Wales, narrated in *DGB* XI (Reeve and Wright 2007, 280-1). Gunnlaugr replaces the symbolic pool with the literal island and appears to freely add the notion that the British king will gain little from his occupation of Wales, in a theme of land use and productivity that appears occasionally elsewhere; for other instances see Note to *I* 32/5-8. *DGB* speaks disparagingly about the British dynasties in Wales but does not address this specific point (Reeve and Wright 2007, 280-1). — [5] s*a*mt 'still': Emended in this edn from ms. *sumt* 'some' (not refreshed), which *Bret* 1848-9, *Skj* B and *Merl* 2012 retain but without translation (also retained in *Skald*). The sense is 'continuously' (*CVC*: *samr*; Fritzner: *samr* 4). — [9-10]: Previous eds have placed these lines at the beginning of *I* 41, but they are clearly integral to the present stanza, just as they are clearly extraneous to the subject-matter of *I* 41. The stanza division in Hb, signalled by rubricated majuscule <F> initial in *færr*, is likely to be erroneous; for the reverse error, cf. *I* 34/9-10 and *I* 35/7-10.

41. Þá kórónask   kapps hvítdreki,
    ok saxneskir   seggir ríkja.
    En eirjǫfurr   ofan at stíga
    verðr af brǫttum   borgararmi.

Þá kórónask hvítdreki kapps, ok saxneskir seggir ríkja. En eirjǫfurr verðr at stíga ofan af brǫttum borgararmi.

Then the white serpent of belligerence will be crowned and Saxon men will rule. And the copper lord has to climb down from the sheer city wall.

Ms.: **Hb**(51v) (*Bret*).

Editions: *Skj*: Gunnlaugr Leifsson, *Merlínússpá II* 41: AII, 27-8, BII, 32; *Skald* II, 20; *Bret* 1848-9, II, 53 (*Bret* st. 109); *Hb* 1892-6, 279); *Merl* 2012, 158.

Notes: [All]: Cf. *DGB* 112 (Reeve and Wright 2007, 147.65; cf. Wright 1988, 103, prophecy 7): *Exin coronabitur Germanicus uermis et aeneus princeps humabitur* 'Then the Germanic worm will be crowned, and the prince of bronze buried' (Reeve and Wright 2007, 146). Gunnlaugr's elaboration on the passing of the bronze prince raises the question of whether his copy-text contained the variant reading *humiliabitur* 'will be humbled', found in mss O and M, as also in mss a, H and R of the First Variant Version and the commentary by Alain de Flandres (Wille 2015, 129), rather than the standard reading *humabitur* 'will be buried' (Reeve and Wright 2007, 147, Wright 1988, 103). Alain explains the bronze horseman allegorically, as representing the British people (Wille 2015, 129), and Gunnlaugr's understanding, in speaking of this figure climbing down, may have been similar. — [5] *eirjǫfurr* 'the copper lord': Referring to the effigy of Caduallo mentioned in st. 34. — [8] *borgararmi* 'city wall': Printed separately as *borgar armi* by all previous eds, but the cpd form *borgararmr*, referring especially to the outer wall of a fortress or city, is standard (*ONP*: *borgararmr*).

42. 'Eru laufviðar   ljósum fjǫtri
    takmǫrk gefin   í tali ára.
    Munat hann ríkja   of in rǫmmu skǫp
    né því inu fagra   fróni ráða.

'Takmǫrk eru gefin ljósum fjǫtri laufviðar í tali ára. Hann munat ríkja of in rǫmmu skǫp né ráða því inu fagra fróni.

'Limits are set to the white fetter of the leafy tree [SNAKE] as to number of years. He will not govern the mighty fates nor rule that fair land.

Ms.: **Hb**(51v) (*Bret*).

Editions: *Skj*: Gunnlaugr Leifsson, *Merlínússpá II* 42: AII, 28, BII, 32; *Skald* II, 20; *Bret* 1848-9, II, 53 (*Bret* st. 110); *Hb* 1892-6, 279-80; *Merl* 2012, 159.

Notes: [All]: Cf. *DGB* 112 (Reeve and Wright 2007, 147.66; cf. Wright 1988, 103, prophecy 7): *Terminus illi positus est quem transuolare nequibit* 'A limit has been set for the white dragon beyond which it will not be able to fly' (Reeve and Wright 2007, 146). Gunnlaugr partially rationalises this prophecy of the Norman Conquest by explicitly mentioning rule over the land (cf. Note to *I* 32/5-8) and additionally invokes the concept of an over-ruling Fate (*skǫp*: cf. *Fritzner*: *skǫp*), as also in *I* 49/8. The Norman Conquest itself is narrated in *I* 46-8. — [1-2] *ljósum fjǫtri laufviðar* 'to the white fetter of the leafy tree [SNAKE]': The determinant of this snake-kenning belongs to a miscellaneous group that refers to the environment in which the snake lives, here the woods (cf. *Meissner* 115 and the similar snake-kenning in *I* 44/4).

43. 'Vera mun* ára   í aga miklum
    fimtán tigi   foldar belti.
    En tírœð   tíri gǫfgaðr
    hundruð þrjú   hann mun sitja
    Lundúnum at   ok lýða fjǫlð.

'Belti foldar mun* vera í miklum aga fimtán tigi ára. En hann mun sitja at Lundúnum þrjú hundruð tírœð gǫfgaðr tíri, ok fjǫlð lýða.

'The belt of the earth [SNAKE] will be in great strife for fifteen decades. But for three hundred years, counted decimally, he will reign in London, endued with glory, and a multitude of people [with him].'

Ms.: **Hb**(51v) (*Bret*).

Reading: [1] mun*: munu Hb.

Editions: *Skj*: Gunnlaugr Leifsson, *Merlínússpá II* 43: AII, 28, BII, 32-3, *Skald* II, 20, *NN* §102; *Bret* 1848-9, II, 53 (*Bret* st. 111); *Hb* 1892-6, 280; *Merl* 2012, 159-60.

Notes: [All]: Cf. *DGB* 113 (Reeve and Wright 2007, 147.66-7; cf. Wright 1988, 103, prophecy 7): *centum namque quinquaginta annis in inquietudine et subiectione manebit, ter centum uero insidebit* 'for a hundred and fifty years it will endure harassment and submission, but for three hundred it will be in occupation' (Reeve and Wright 2007, 146). Gunnlaugr adds the idea of a multitude of people living under the sway of the white snake. — [1] *mun** 'will': Emended in this edn from Hb *munu*. Also emended to *mun* in *Skj* B (followed by *Skald*), but perhaps tentatively, since the translation in *Skj* B (albeit rather loose) presupposes retention of a pl. verb to match the pl. subject 'snakes': *vil der være stor strid mellem ormene* 'there will be great strife between the snakes'. Kock does not comment on the matter. *Bret* 1848-9 had retained *munu* with a similar translation and it is retained without comment in *Hb* 1892-6. *Merl* 2012 would also retain, noting that *belti* 'belt', as a n. noun, could be either sg. or pl. But a pl. in l. 1 followed by sg. *hann* in l. 8 would be odd and the evidence of *DGB* speaks against it. — [5] *tírœð* 'counted decimally': In contradistinction to the 'long hundred' = 120. Cf. SnSt *Ht* 100/3[III] and Note. — [8] *ok* 'and': Kock (*NN* §102) points out a fondness on Gunnlaugr's part for complex subjects with sg. verb after the first subject component. See Note to *I* 36/9-12.

44. 'Þá mun g*rimm*um   ganga at móti
     landnyrðingr hvass   lundar fjǫtri
     ok blóma þá   á brott reka,
     es vestrœnir   vindar grœddu.

'Þá mun hvass landnyrðingr ganga at móti g*rimm*um fjǫtri lundar ok reka þá blóma á brott, es vestrœnir vindar grœddu.

'Then a sharp northeast wind will come against the savage fetter of the grove [SNAKE], and drive away the flowers that the westerly winds fostered.

Ms.: **Hb**(51v) (*Bret*).

Reading: [1] g*rimm*um: gumnum Hb.

Editions: *Skj*: Gunnlaugr Leifsson, *Merlínússpá II* 44: AII, 28, BII, 33, *Skald* II, 20-1, *NN* §102; *Bret* 1848-9, II, 54 (*Bret* st. 112); *Hb* 1892-6, 280; *Merl* 2012, 160-1.

Notes: [All]: Cf. *DGB* 113 (Reeve and Wright 2007, 147.68-9; cf. Wright 1988, 103, prophecy 8): *Tunc exurget in illum aquilo et flores quos zephyrus procreauit eripiet* 'Then the north wind will rise against it and blow away the flowers the western breeze has nurtured' (Reeve and Wright 2007, 146). This prophecy alludes to Viking raids in England. — [1] *þá* 'then': *Merl* 2012 interprets the ms. reading as *þat* 'that' and translates *Das wird den Menschen und der Fessel des Waldes* [= *der Schlange*] *wie ein scharfer Nordostwind entgegenwehen* 'That will blow against men and the fetter of the grove [= the snake] like a bitter northeast wind', but this involves the introduction of *wie* 'like, as'. — [1] g*rimm*um 'savage': Emended in this edn from ms. *gumnum* 'to men' (not refreshed), which is retained in all previous eds. *Bret* 1848-9 and *Skj* B leave *gumnum* untranslated (despite a statement to the contrary regarding *Skj* B in *Merl* 2012) but appear to have construed it as an appositional expansion to *fjǫtri lundar* 'the fetter of the grove [SNAKE]'; this, although advocated by Kock (*NN* §102), leads to an awkward discrepancy between pl. and sg. The other cases discussed by Kock are not syntactically parallel. *Merl* 2012 instead posits a double object but is obliged to add *und* 'and' to the translation (see Note to l. 1 above). The emendation g*rimm*um is palaeographically straightforward and removes these difficulties. Gunnlaugr uses the adj. *grimmr* 'savage' and adv. *grimmliga* 'savagely' elsewhere (*I* 16/3, *I* 32/9, *I* 48/2, *I* 64/5, *II* 28/6) and it fits well with Geoffrey's ascription of *saeuicia* 'savagery' to the white serpent in 112.39 (Reeve and Wright 2007, 147). See Introduction for apparent errors in the Hb text. — [3] *landnyrðingr* 'a northeast wind': This term is explained as originating with reference to the western coast of Norway (*LP*: *landnorðr* lit. 'land-north', north-east). Cf. *Merl I* 84/2. For scholarly discussion of this system of orientation see Stefán Einarsson (1944), Haugen (1957), Jackson (1998), Wanner (2009, 49-50). *DGB* has simply 'a north wind'.

45. 'Mun gull glóa   guðs húsum á,
en lǫgðis veðr   lægir þeygi.
Mun trautt taka   tálsamr dreki
híð sín mega,   þvíat honum nálgask
víti fyr vélar,   þats hann verðr bera.

'Gull mun glóa á húsum guðs, en veðr lǫgðis lægir þeygi. Tálsamr dreki mun trautt mega taka híð sín, þvíat víti nálgask honum fyr vélar, þats hann verðr bera.

'Gold will shine in God's houses, but the storm of the sword [BATTLE] will not cease. The treacherous dragon will scarcely manage to reach its lairs, since retributions for its machinations will come upon it, that it will have to endure.

Ms.: **Hb**(51v) (*Bret*).

Editions: *Skj*: Gunnlaugr Leifsson, *Merlínússpá II* 45: AII, 28, BII, 33, *Skald* II, 21; *Bret* 1848-9, II, 54 (*Bret* st. 113); *Hb* 1892-6, 280; *Merl* 2012, 161-2.

Notes: [All]: Cf. *DGB* 113 (Reeve and Wright 2007, 147.69-71; cf. Wright 1988, 103, prophecy 8): *Erit deauratio in templis, nec acumen gladiorum cessabit. Vix obtinebit cauernas suas Germanicus draco, quia ultio prodicionis eius superueniet* 'There will be gilding in the temples, nor will the sharpness of sword-blades decline. The Germanic dragon will be hard put to keep possession of its caves, since retribution will be visited on its treason' (cf. Reeve and Wright 2007, 146). Gunnlaugr renders *cauernas* 'caves' as *híð* 'lairs', here differing from his interpretation of the earlier occurrence of *cauernas* as 'lands' (see *I* 21 Note to [All]). He seems to have had the majority reading *draco* 'dragon' in his source ms., not the minority variant *vermis* 'worm, serpent' (cf. Reeve and Wright 2007, 147). The mention of enriched decoration of churches might relate to the very large endowments to religious foundations from Cnut and, later in the C11th, Edward the Confessor. The treachery Geoffrey alludes to might be both the generalised perfidy of the Saxons, as seen from a British perspective, and the more specific perceived failure of Earl Harold Godwineson to keep his oath to Duke William, as interpreted by, for instance, the C12th commentator John of Cornwall (Curley 1982, 237; on Harold's oath see Stenton 1971, 577-8). — [1] *gull mun glóa* 'gold will shine': A poetic commonplace; cf. SnSt *Ht* 72/1, 2^{III}. — [7] *híð sín* 'its lairs': *Skj* B erroneously has the sg., *sit leje* 'his lair'. The pl. of the ms. and all other eds accords with Geoffrey's *cavernas* 'caves'. — [10] *hann* 'it': Omitted in *Skald*.

46. 'Fá mun hann uppgang   afarlitla stund;
     hnekkir hǫnum   hringserkjat lið.
     Kømr sunnan sú   sveit of ægi,
     es hann ríki mun   ræna miklu.

'Hann mun fá uppgang afarlitla stund; hringserkjat lið hnekkir hǫnum. Sú sveit kømr sunnan of ægi, es mun ræna hann miklu ríki.

'He will obtain success for a very short time; the mail-shirted army will check him. That band will come from the south across the sea, which will rob him of his great kingdom.

Ms.: **Hb**(51v) (*Bret*).

Editions: *Skj*: Gunnlaugr Leifsson, *Merlínússpá II* 46: AII, 28, BII, 33; *Skald* II, 21; *Bret* 1848-9, II, 54 (*Bret* st. 114); *Hb* 1892-6, 280; *Merl* 2012, 162-3.

Notes: [All]: Cf. *DGB* 113 (Reeve and Wright 2007, 147.72-3; cf. Wright 1988, 103, prophecy 9): *Vigebit tandem paulisper, sed decimatio Neustriae nocebit. Populus namque in ligno et ferreis tunicis superueniet, qui uindictam de nequitia ipsius sumet* 'Then it will prosper for a short time, but the decimation visited on it by Normandy will injure it. A people will come in wood and tunics of iron to take vengeance on its wickedness' (cf. Reeve and Wright 2007, 146). This and the ensuing prophecies resume the theme of the Norman Conquest. Between the coronation of Edward the Confessor, the first member of the native Anglo-Saxon royal dynasty to rule since Æthelred II, in 1043 (Stenton 1971, 423) and the Norman Conquest in 1066 only twenty-three years elapsed, hence Geoffrey's *paulisper*. Gunnlaugr postpones mention of the alleged decimation perpetrated by Normandy upon the Saxons until st. *I* 48 and in general plays down the Norman identification. He may have preferred to focus on the Breton component of the invasion force, which is also covered by the vague phrase *sunnan of ægi* 'from the south across the sea': cf. *I* 47/3. He conveys the idea of 'wood', Geoffrey's rather cryptic reference to the Norman longships, by using the more explicit phrase *of ægi* 'across the sea' (l. 6). — [1] *uppgang* 'success': A *hap. leg.* in poetry. — [2] *afarlitla* 'very short': The intensive adv. *afar* is attested chiefly in learned prose and in C12th or later verse (*LP*: *afar-*; *ONP*: *afar*). — [4] *hringserkjat* 'mail-shirted': A *hap. leg.*

47. 'Sá mun lofðungr,   es liði stýrir,
     brátt brezkum her   byggva jarðir.
     Mun sáð tekit   snáks ins hvíta
     endr ór órum   aldingǫrðum.

'Sá lofðungr, es stýrir liði, mun brátt byggva jarðir brezkum her. Sáð ins hvíta snáks mun tekit endr ór aldingǫrðum órum.

'The lord who leads the army will swiftly settle the lands with British people. The white snake's seed will be taken once more out of our orchards.

Ms.: **Hb**(51v) (*Bret*).

Reading: [7] ó*ru*m: ófám Hb.

Editions: *Skj*: Gunnlaugr Leifsson, *Merlínússpá II* 47: AII, 28, BII, 33, *Skald* II, 21, *NN* §103; *Bret* 1848-9, II, 55 (*Bret* st. 115); *Hb* 1892-6, 280; *Merl* 2012, 163.

Notes: [All]: Cf. *DGB* 113 (Reeve and Wright 2007, 147.73-4; cf. Wright 1988, 103, prophecy 9): *Restaurabit pristinis incolis mansiones, et ruina alienigenarum patebit. Germen albi draconis ex ortulis nostris abradetur* 'They [the people from Normandy] will restore the original inhabitants to their dwellings, and the ruin of the foreigners will be plain to see. The seed of the white dragon will disappear from our gardens' (Reeve and Wright 2007, 146). Gunnlaugr appears to have worked from a source ms. that contained the reading *albi draconis* 'of the white dragon', characteristic of the Ω group of mss (Reeve and Wright 2007, 147); see Introduction. With the phrase *Sá lofðungr, es stýrir liði* 'The lord who leads the army' Gunnlaugr makes more explicit reference to William the Conqueror than does Geoffrey. Geoffrey's notion of a Breton resumption of residency in Britain may be owed in part to an awareness that William brought over a large Breton contingent as part of his army, with the support of the Breton aristocracy (cf. Stenton 1971, 594). Many Breton lords and their followers were given lands in England during the two decades after the Conquest (Stenton 1971, 629). — [3-4] *byggva … brezkum her* 'settle … with British people': This edn follows the construal implied by *Bret* 1848-9, with *brezkum her* in the instr. dat.; similarly *Merl* 2012. The meaning of *byggva* here is 'cause the land to become settled' (*Fritzner*: *byggja* 5; *ONP*: *byggja* 8; cf. *LP*: *byggva* 2). Gunnlaugr makes frequent use of constructions in which a noun in dat./instr. function appears without a prep. such as *með* (cf. *Í* 63/6-7; *NS* §§104, 105, 108, and 110). *Skj* B translates less precisely as *give landet til det brittiske folk* 'give the land to the British people'. Kock (*NN* §103) takes *brezkum her* in apposition to *liði*, evidently positing a sense 'The lord who leads the army, the British people, will promptly settle the land', but this is to ignore not merely the applicable sub-sense of *byggva* but also Geoffrey's text, where the idea is that the land is re-settled by the original inhabitants; such a structure of variation, with the intervening adv. *brátt*, would be hard to parallel in Old West Norse poetry. — [7] *órum* 'our': Emended in this edn from ms. *ófám* 'not few' (refreshed). Cf. the Latin; also *garða óra* (*I* 40/4), translating *ortuli nostri*. — [8] *aldingǫrðum* 'orchards': Elsewhere in poetry found only in Anon *Pl* 24/7[VII].

48. 'Þá mun hann gjalda   grimmra ráða;
     es hans tíundat   tálaukit kyn.
     Verðr hann grœna   *grund at vi*nna,
     ok hann upp frá því   aldri ríkir.
     Tekr hann svá fyr svik   sárar hefnðir.

'Þá mun hann gjalda grimmra ráða; tálaukit kyn hans es tíundat. Hann verðr *at vi*nna grœna *grund*, ok hann ríkir aldri upp frá því. Svá tekr hann sárar hefnðir fyr svik.

'Then he will pay for his savage actions; his treacherous kindred will be decimated. He will have to work the green earth and from that time onwards he will reign no more. Thus he will incur grievous retributions for his treachery.

Ms.: **Hb**(51v) (*Bret*).

Readings: [6] *grund at vi*nna: '[…]nna' Hb, grund at vinna Hb*JS*.

Editions: *Skj*: Gunnlaugr Leifsson, *Merlínússpá II* 48: AII, 28, BII, 33-4, *Skald* II, 21; *Bret* 1848-9, II, 55 (*Bret* st. 116); *Hb* 1892-6, 280; *Merl* 2012, 164.

Notes: [All]: Cf. *DGB* 113 (Reeve and Wright 2007, 147.75-6; cf. Wright 1988, 103, prophecy 9): *et reliquiae generationis eius decimabuntur. Iugum perpetuae seruitutis ferent matremque suam ligonibus et aratris uulnerabunt* 'And the remnants of its generation will be decimated. They will bear the yoke of unending slavery and wound their mother with hoes and ploughs' (Reeve and Wright 2007, 146). Under the Conqueror's rule the leading English landowners, both secular and ecclesiastical, were supplanted by Normans (Stenton 1971, 680-1). This subjugation of the English was a key element in what Curley (1982, 219) terms 'the supposed progressive unfolding of the *spes Britannorum*' ('hope of the Britons'). Gunnlaugr tones down the maternal imagery and the notion of slavery but plays up the treachery of the white snake, i.e. the Saxon occupiers of Britain. — [6]: See Introduction for readings no longer visible in Hb that could be read by earlier eds. — [7] *hann* 'he': Omitted in *Skald*.

49. 'Ríkir enn at þat   ormar *tve*nnir;
     missir annarr þar   aldrs fyr skeyti,
     en annarr mun   aptr of hverfa
     und skugga nafns   at skǫpum vinna.

'Ríkir enn at þat ormar *tve*nnir; annarr missir þar aldrs fyr skeyti, en annarr mun of hverfa aptr und skugga nafns at vinna skǫpum.

'After that two more snakes will rule; one will lose his life there to an arrow, but the other will return under the cover of a name to contend against the fates.

Ms.: **Hb**(51v) (*Bret*).

Readings: [2] *tve*nnir: '[...]nnir' Hb, tvennir Hb*JS*.

Editions: *Skj*: Gunnlaugr Leifsson, *Merlínússpá II* 49: AII, 29, BII, 34, *Skald* II, 21; *Bret* 1848-9, II, 55 (*Bret* st. 117); *Hb* 1892-6, 280; *Merl* 2012, 164-5.

Notes: [All]: Cf. *DGB* 113 (Reeve and Wright 2007, 147.76-8; cf. Wright 1988, 104, prophecy 10): *Succedent duo dracones, quorum alter inuidiae spiculo suffocabitur, alter uero sub umbra nominis redibit* 'Two dragons will succeed, one of which will be suffocated by the arrow of envy, while the other will return beneath the shadow of a name' (Reeve and Wright 2007, 146). This prophecy appears to allude to two of the sons of William the Conqueror, William Rufus, who succeeded his father as King of England in 1087, and Robert Curthose, Duke of Normandy, who early in William Rufus's reign made a return to Normandy from the Crusades and competed with him for the throne; among the commentators to offer this interpretation is John of Cornwall (Curley 1982, 237). — [2] *ormar* 'snakes': Gunnlaugr thus translates Geoffrey's allegorical *dracones* 'dragons', which, despite appearances, are not to be equated with either the Germanic white snake or the British red snake whose hostilities are described earlier in the poem. — [4] *skeyti* 'an arrow': Taken literally in *Merl*; the notion of *invidia* 'envy' is absent. This indeed fits well with the manner of death of William Rufus and may point to Gunnlaugr's familiarity with the accounts of either Henry of Huntingdon (*HA* 1996, 446-7: *Ubi Walterus Tirel cum sagitta ceruo intendens regem percussit inscius* 'There Walter Tirel, aiming at a stag, accidentally hit the king with an arrow') or William of Malmesbury (Mynors *et al.* 1998-9, I, 504-5: *sagitta pectus ... traiectus* 'pierced ... by an arrow in the breast' and cf. Mynors *et al.* 1998-9, I, 574-5). — [7] *und skugga nafns* 'under the cover of a name': The phrase *sub umbra nominis*, translated by Thorpe as 'under the cover of authority' (1966, 174), is also handled literally by Gunnlaugr. It is translated in error as *under skyggens navn* 'under the name of a shadow' in *Skj* B (contrast *LP*: *skuggi*; also *Bret* 1848-9). For an explication of the Latin phrase, which disparages weak leaders who hide behind a great name or reputation, see Feeney (1986). Robert Curthose was in name the heir apparent to power over England as well as Normandy, being the elder son, but in reality subordinate to William Rufus, whom William the Conqueror had designated as successor to the throne in England (Stenton 1971, 608, 620). — [8] *at vinna skǫpum* 'to contend against the fates': To resist the fates was an *adynaton* in Old Norse (cf. *Gríp* 53/2, *Am* 48/3). This element in the characterisation of Robert Curthose appears to be derived not from *DGB* but from the following account in William of Malmesbury (Mynors *et al.* 1998-9, I, 706-7): *... sed nullo impetrato ad bellum publicum uenit, ultimam fortunam experturus. Qua illum infelici pede prosequente ...* ' ... he was reduced to overt war, to try a last throw with Fortune. But she pursued him with hostile intent ...'. Such a passage might have appealed to Gunnlaugr, who had already invoked *skǫp* 'fate' in *I* 42/6. Related in substance but not so close in wording is Henry of Huntingdon, who speaks of divine determination to thwart Robert's wishes and efforts (*HA* 1996, 452-5, s. a. 1106).

50. 'Þá mun ríkja   réttlætis dýr,
    þats eyverskir   ormar hræðask.
    Ok fyr sunnan sæ   sjalfir ugga
    víz rammligir   valskir turnar.

'Þá mun dýr réttlætis ríkja, þats eyverskir ormar hræðask. Ok sjalfir valskir turnar víz rammligir ugga fyr sunnan sæ.

'Then the beast of justice will rule, which the island-dwelling serpents will dread. And south across the sea the French towers themselves, redoubtable on every side, will be fearful.

Ms.: **Hb**(51v) (*Bret*).

Editions: *Skj*: Gunnlaugr Leifsson, *Merlínússpá II* 50: AII, 29, BII, 34, *Skald* II, 21, *NN* §3217; *Bret* 1848-9, II, 56 (*Bret* st. 118); *Hb* 1892-6, 280; *Merl* 2012, 165.

Notes: [All]: Cf. *DGB* 113 (Reeve and Wright 2007, 147.78-9; cf. Wright 1988, 104, prophecy 11): *Succedet leo iusticiae, ad cuius rugitum Gallicanae turres et insulani dracones tremebunt* 'They will be succeeded by the lion of justice, at whose roar the towers of France and the island dragons will tremble' (cf. Reeve and Wright 2007, 146). The reference is to Henry I (c. 1068/1069 - 1 December 1135), the fourth son of William the Conqueror, who succeeded to the throne in 1100 and campaigned extensively in France and Normandy. The soubriquet 'Lion of Justice' refers to his judicial and financial reforms (cf. the account of William of Malmesbury: Mynors *et al.* 1998-9, I, 742-3, and 798-9). The expression 'island dragons', translated literally by Gunnlaugr, refers to 'all British rulers of the islands belonging to Wales, Scotland and Ireland' (Curley 1982, 241). For Henry's Welsh campaign of 1114 see Poole (1955, 287). — [2] *réttlætis* 'of justice': This noun is characteristic of C12th and later religious poetry and learned prose texts. — [7] *víz* 'on every side': Equivalent to *víðs*. For discussion of this adverbial usage, see *NN* §3217.

51. 'Þá mun gull snarat   af grasi mǫrgu;
    flýtr ór klaufum   kalfs ættar silfr.
    Eru fagrbúin   fljóð í landi;
    verðrat snótum   siðbót at því.

'Þá mun gull snarat af mǫrgu grasi; silfr flýtr ór klaufum ættar kalfs. Fagrbúin fljóð eru í landi; siðbót verðrat snótum at því.

'Then gold will be wrung from many a herb; silver will flow from the hooves of the kindred of the calf [CATTLE]. There will be finely dressed women in the land; there will not be moral reform for the ladies on account of that.

Ms.: **Hb**(51v-52r) (*Bret*).

Editions: *Skj*: Gunnlaugr Leifsson, *Merlínússpá II* 51: AII, 29, BII, 34, *Skald* II, 21; *Bret* 1848-9, II, 56 (*Bret* st. 119); *Hb* 1892-6, 280; *Merl* 2012, 166.

Note: [All]: Cf. *DGB* 113 (Reeve and Wright 2007, 147.79-81; cf. Wright 1988, 104, prophecy 11): *In diebus eius aurum ex lilio et urtica extorquebitur et argentum ex ungulis mugientium manabit. Calamistrati uaria uellera uestibunt, et exterior habitus interiora signabit* 'In his time gold will be wrung from the lily and the nettle, and silver shall drip from the hooves of lowing cattle. Men with curled hair will wear fleeces of varied hue, and their outer apparel will betray their inner selves' (Reeve and Wright 2007, 146). The allegory here seems to reflect various aspects of Henry I's reign, including his zeal for taxation, which raised much money from wealthy owners of rural land (Hollister 2003, 356-7), and his creation of *novi homines* 'new men' to serve as officials (Green 2009, 242-3). Gunnlaugr subsumes the lily and the nettle under *gras* 'herb'. In the second *helmingr* Gunnlaugr diverges markedly from Geoffrey, attributing the irregularities of attire and appearance and by implication the vanity they betoken not to the new men but to women and adding information to the effect that there was no reform of women's morals. This material he could have derived from Henry of Huntingdon (*HA* 1996, 484-5), who links the king to sexual licence on two fronts. He sharply criticises the king's licensing clerics to keep concubines: *Verum rex decepit eos simplicitate Willielmi archiepiscopi. Concesserunt namque regi justiciam de uxoribus sacerdotum ... Accepit enim rex pecuniam infinitam de presbiteris, et redemit eos* 'But the king deceived them through Archbishop William's simplicity. For they granted the king jurisdiction on the matter of priests' wives ... For the king took vast sums of money from the priests, and released them' (for commentary on Henry's policy here see Poole 1955, 183). Henry of Huntingdon also inveighs against the king's personal promiscuity (*HA* 1996, 700-1): *Luxuria quoque, quia mulierum dicioni regis more Salomonis continue subiacebat* 'And debauchery, since he was at all times subject to the power of women, after the manner of King Solomon'. William of Malmesbury, by contrast, exonerates Henry from sexual misconduct (Mynors *et al.* 1998-9, I, 744-5). Missing from the text of *Merl* is any counterpart to the three sentences relating to Henry's harsh hunting laws that follow in Geoffrey, to the effect that the paws of barking dogs will be cut off, wild beasts will enjoy peace and men will suffer punishment (Reeve and Wright 2007, 146-7). Given that Gunnlaugr is in other respects following Geoffrey closely here and there are no known lacunae at this point in the ms. tradition of *DGB*, it is possible that stanzas have been lost from *Merl*.

52. 'Sprett es í miðju   mótpenningum;
     mun gǫrst gleðu   glatask ránsemi.
     Tennr munu gylðis   trausti numnar,
     ok léons vargar   verða at fiskum
     hvassir hvelpar   hvaltúnum í.

'Sprett es í miðju mótpenningum; ránsemi gleðu mun gǫrst glatask. Tennr gylðis munu numnar trausti, ok vargar léons, hvassir hvelpar, verða at fiskum í hvaltúnum.

'There will be a split down the middle of stamped pennies; the thieving ways of the kite will completely come to a stop. The wolf's teeth will be deprived of their strength, and the lion's wolves, keen cubs, will become fish in the whale-enclosures [SEA].

Ms.: **Hb**(52r) (*Bret*).

Readings: [3] gleðu: gleði Hb   [7] léons: léo Hb.

Editions: *Skj*: Gunnlaugr Leifsson, *Merlínússpá II* 52: AII, 29, BII, 34; *Skald* II, 21-2; *Bret* 1848-9, II, 56-7 (*Bret* st. 120); *Hb* 1892-6, 280; *Merl* 2012, 166-7.

Notes: [All]: Cf. *DGB* 113 (Reeve and Wright 2007, 146-7.83-6; cf. Wright 1988, 104, prophecy 11): *Findetur forma commercii; dimidium rotundum erit. Peribit miluorum rapacitas, et dentes luporum hebetabuntur. Catuli leonis in aequoreos pisces transformabuntur, et aquila eius super montem Arauium nidificabit* 'The shape for trading will be split: the half will be circular. The greed of kites will be ended, and the teeth of wolves blunted. The lion's cubs will become fishes of the sea, and his eagle will nest on mount Aravius' (cf. Reeve and Wright 2007, 146). The reference of the first sentence is to a currency reform contemplated by Henry I which has occasioned much confusion in the sources. John of Worcester, writing 1118 or earlier, and following him Symeon of Durham, in his *Historia de Regibus* 'History of the Kings', writing probably in 1129 or earlier, appear to have the correct story: they state under the year 1108 that, 'since pennies were often rejected because bent and broken, Henry I made several orders about them, one being that circular halfpence should be coined' (Tatlock 1950, 404). This new issue was stamped with an outer circle to guard against the practice of clipping (Poole 1955, 415). A somewhat different story is told by William of Malmesbury (Mynors *et al.* 1998-9, I, 742-3): *Cum nummos fractos, licet boni argenti, a uenditoribus non recipi audisset, omnes uel frangi uel incidi precepit* 'Having heard that broken coins, although made of good silver, were not being accepted in payment, he gave orders that all coins alike should be broken or cut'. Gunnlaugr's account seems to reflect this less accurate version but he understands that the coins were stamped. More general information on Henry's measures against corrupt money-lenders and merchants, characterised as kites and wolves in Geoffrey's allegory, is contained in William (*loc. cit.*) and Henry of Huntingdon (*HA* 1996, 474-5). The last historical event that can be identified with certainty in the *Prophecies* is the drowning of Henry I's children, including the heir-apparent William Adelin, collectively referred to in the allegory as the lion's cubs, in 1120 in the wreck of the White Ship (cf. Henry of Huntingdon, *HA* 1996, 466-7; Taylor 1911, 13; Tatlock 1950, 403). By the eagle, Geoffrey refers to the Empress Matilda, but he describes her taking refuge on a mountain – this and the eagle motif in apparent reference to her marriage to Henry IV, the German emperor, in 1114 (Curley 1982, 242-3) – and there is no apparent awareness that she was subsequently active in English politics in dispute with her cousin Stephen of Blois for the English crown. Gunnlaugr treats the *catuli leonis* 'lion's cubs' as part and parcel of the evil forces that the Beast of Justice (Henry I) has checked, a shift from Geoffrey's version of the story that might reflect influence from the chroniclers' condemnations of the drowned passengers and crew as variously sodomites (Henry of Huntingdon) or drunkards (William of Malmesbury) that brought the wrath of God upon themselves. *Merl* as extant contains no mention of the eagle. This might be simply a matter of accidental loss of text subsequent to Gunnlaugr but it is conceivable that the mention was deliberately by-passed by Gunnlaugr or his source, as contradicting known recent history. — [1-2]: *Bret* 1848-9 explains this as a reference to the custom of dividing coins as a token of allegiance, apparently in ignorance of the various C12th accounts mentioned above (see Note to [All]). Finnur Jónsson explains *mótpenningum* correctly as *præget mønt* 'stamped coins' (*LP*: *mótpenningr*). The explication in *Merl* 2012 is unclear and seems to reflect some chronological confusion. The noun *mótpenningr* is a *hap. leg.* and may be a neologism on Gunnlaugr's part; *ONP*: *mót* 1 cites two instances from C14th prose texts of the simplex in reference to marks or stamps on silver coins. The noun *mótmark* 'stamp-mark' and verb *mótmarka* 'mark with a stamp' appear first in the latter half of the C13th in Norwegian contexts (*ONP*: *mótmark*, *mótmarka*). — [3] *gleð*u 'of the kite': Emended from ms. *gleði* 'gladness' (not refreshed) in *Skj* B (followed by *Skald*). In *Bret* 1848-9 an otherwise unattested m. by-form of *gleða* (**gleðr*?) is proposed. *Merl* 2012 retains *gleði*, translating this in combination with *ránsemi* as *das Vergnügen am Rauben* 'pleasure in robbery'. Gunnlaugr no doubt rendered Geoffrey's animal lore accurately but in subsequent transmission of *Merl* the phrase was possibly misinterpreted in this way. — [7] *vargar léo*ns 'the lion's wolves': Emended from ms. 'leó vargar' (not refreshed) in the present edn. This yields a free-standing noun with initial *v*-, needed to carry alliteration with *verða* in l. 8. Presupposed is Gunnlaugr's use of a double form of the gen. case of *léo*, i.e. *léons* beside *léonis*. For the form cf. GSvert *Hrafndr* 4/7[IV], *ljóns* 'of the lion'. The nom. pl. *hvelpar* 'cubs', rendering Geoffrey's *catuli*, is construed as standing in apposition to *vargar*. The solutions adopted by previous eds do not reckon with the deficiency in alliteration. *Bret* has *léo-vargar* 'Lövevargens' ('of the lion-wolf'), evidently interpreted as a sg., governing *hvassir hvelpar*, thus 'the keen cubs of the lion-wolf', an analysis also adopted by *Merl* 2012 (independently?), while *Skj* B (followed by *Skald*) emends to *léo-varga* 'of the lion-wolves'. Use of the potentially pejorative word *vargr* 'wolf, outcast' in relation to the children of Henry I may be explained as reflecting the censorious attitude to them displayed by the chroniclers (on which see Note to [All]). For attestations of the latter meaning in skaldic poetry cf. Mark *Eirdr* 6/1[II], ÞSjár *Þórdr*

2/1¹, Eskál *Vell* 7/6¹. The handling of vowel quantities in the borrowed word *léó* is uncertain. *LP* has *léó*, perhaps reflecting the fact that a long first vowel is metrically required in *II* 57/7. But contrast *Skj* B, *CVC*, *Fritzner*: *leó*, while *Skald* has *léo-*. The second vowel appears to be short in Anon *Pl* 23/2^(VII) and Svtjúg Lv 1/8¹. Perhaps this foreign word could be flexibly treated to achieve correct metre, or alternatively the present attestation could represent an anticipation of ModIcel. monosyllabic *ljón* (for possible parallel instances see *ONP*: *ljón* sb. m., *ljón* sb. n.). The vowel quantities in Latin and Greek are short followed by long (Lewis and Short 1879: *leō*; Liddell and Scott 1940: λέων).

53. 'Verðr meinliga   mæki brugðit;
     sék blóði ben   blása móður;
     líðr mart hǫfugt   of lýða kyn.
     Rýðr varðar blóð   Venedócíam,
     ok síðan sex   snarpir lifra
     kynsmenn drepa   Kórínéus.

'Mæki verðr meinliga brugðit; sék ben blása blóði móður; mart hǫfugt líðr of kyn lýða. Blóð varðar rýðr Venedócíam, ok síðan drepa snarpir kynsmenn Kórínéus sex lifra.

'The sword will be drawn with ill intent; I see the wound spurt with the mother's blood. Much hardship will come over the race of men. The blood of the woman will redden Venedotia and then bold kinsmen of Corineus will slay six brothers.

Ms.: **Hb**(52r) (*Bret*).

Editions: *Skj*: Gunnlaugr Leifsson, *Merlínússpá II* 53: AII, 29, BII, 34-5; *Skald* II, 22; *Bret* 1848-9, II, 57 (*Bret* st. 121); *Hb* 1892-6, 280; *Merl* 2012, 168.

Notes: [All]: Cf. *DGB* 113 (Reeve and Wright 2007, 147.86-149.87; cf. Wright 1988, 104, prophecy 11): *Venedocia rubebit materno sanguine, et domus Corinei sex fratres interficiet* 'Venedotia will run red with a mother's blood, and the house of Corineus kill six brothers' (Reeve and Wright 2007, 146, 148). The historical status of this prophecy is difficult to assess. The first clause of the prophecy possibly extrapolates Geoffrey's awareness of growing unrest against Henry I in Wales (Poole 1955, 290-1; cf. Curley 1982, 223) into the immediate future. The Lat. *Venedocia* corresponds to Welsh *Gwynedd*, the kingdom in North Wales. The mention of the house of Corineus, i.e. the successors of the legendary first ruler of Cornwall (cf. *DGB* I: Reeve and Wright 2007, 28-9) in the second clause of the prophecy might then personify Cornish involvement in this imagined conflict. But confused records exist concerning an atrocity in Cornwall, committed against Normans and datable to some time between 1100 and 1129 (Padel 1984, 20-7), that matches the account and hence gives the prophecy historic status. — [3-4]: To judge by their subject-matter, these lines may have originally belonged after ll. 5-6 and have come in here by way of anticipation. Previous eds signal the difficulty by placing ll. 5-6 in parentheses. — [6] *lýða* 'of men': *Skj* A has *liða*, probably by dittography, for clear 'lyda' in Hb (cf. *Bret* 1848-9 and *Skj* B). — [8] *Venedóciam* 'Venedotia': Gunnlaugr uses the Latin first declension acc. sg. form. *Merl* 2012 states that no such name exists in the British Isles and looks to Brittany for referents, but see Note to [All]. — [9-12]: The word order is somewhat convoluted, since *sex* 'six' must be taken, for sense and match with Geoffrey's text, with *lifra* 'brothers', not *snarpir kynsmenn* 'bold kinsmen' (contrast *Bret* 1848-9).

54. 'Þá munu gumnar   gráta á nóttum
    ok þjóð gera   þægjar bœnir.
    Þá munu holðar   til himins kosta;
    fá it langa líf   lofðar nýtir.

'Þá gumnar munu gráta á nóttum ok þjóð gera þægjar bœnir. Þá munu holðar kosta til himins; nýtir lofðar fá it langa líf.

'Then men will weep at night and people will say acceptable prayers. Then men will strive after heaven; worthy men will obtain the long life.

Ms.: **Hb**(52r) (*Bret*).

Editions: *Skj*: Gunnlaugr Leifsson, *Merlínússpá II* 54: AII, 29, BII, 35, *Skald* II, 22; *Bret* 1848-9, II, 57-8 (*Bret* st. 122); *Hb* 1892-6, 280; *Merl* 2012, 169.

Notes: [All]: Cf. *DGB* 113 (Reeve and Wright 2007, 149.87-9; cf. Wright 1988, 104, prophecies 12 and 13): *Nocturnis lacrimis madebit insula, unde omnes ad omnia prouocabuntur. Nitentur posteri transuolare superna, sed fauor nouorum sublimabitur* 'The island shall be soaked in nightly tears, and so all men will be provoked to all things. Their progeny will try to fly beyond the heavens, but the favour of new men will be raised up' (Reeve and Wright 2007, 148). The prophecy describes the reaction of the British people to the atrocities described in the previous stanza. Following this, two paragraphs of prophecy in Geoffrey's text (13, except for its first sentence, and 14) have no counterpart in *Merl* (cf. *Bret* 1848-9), possibly because of loss of stanzas in the transmission of *Merl*. There is likewise no counterpart in *Merl* to the added sentence *Vae tibi Neustria, quia cerebrum leonis in te ... a patrio solo eliminabitur* 'Woe to thee, Neustria [Normandy], ... for the brain of the lion in thee ... will be banished from its native soil' found in mss Y and G, whose claims to authenticity remain unresolved (Reeve and Wright 2007, 149 n. to l. 88). — [4] *þægjar bœnir* 'acceptable prayers': The adj. *þægr* is characteristic of homiletic prose texts, used (sometimes in collocation with *bœnir*) to mean 'acceptable to God' (*ONP*: *þægr*) and this also appears to be the sense in which it is used in poetry (contrast *LP*: *þægr*); cf. *I* 59/8. — [4] *bœnir* 'prayers': This reading in *Merl* deviates markedly from *omnia* 'all things', the reading of all mss of *DGB* so far collated. Various possible explanations can be suggested. It may represent an innovation on Gunnlaugr's part, either made freely in order to improve the sense or because he read *omnia* as some form of *oratio* 'prayer'. Possibly too, however, the reading occurred in his source ms., whether through scribal emendation or even as a superior reading originating in the archetype. Universal prayer on the part of the nation was not unknown in English history. In 1009, a state of national emergency was declared by Archbishop Wulfstan, requiring that everyone go to church barefoot and make their confession, fast for three days and distribute the surplus food as alms – an initative with precedents in earlier Carolingian and Anglo-Saxon practice (Keynes 2008, 184-8; Cubitt 2013, 69). Gunnlaugr (or Geoffrey, if the reading was his) could have extrapolated from such an event. By contrast, the commentaries interpret *omnia* 'all things' as 'all kinds of expedients to combat evil' (cf. Hammer 1935, 16; Blacker 1996, 39-40, 2005, 61; Wille 2015, 160-1). — [7-8]: If *nýtir* 'worthy' is correct, Gunnlaugr appears to sidestep Geoffrey's politically charged comment about 'new men' (see Note to *I* 51 [All]) in favour of a pious sentiment that 'worthy men' go on to the eternal (lit. 'long') life in heaven.

55. 'Enn mun*u* í skógi   skœðir síðan
     vargar vakna   veiða í borgum.
     Þeir munu sína   sjalfir dolga
     fella eða fjǫtra;   fáir munu verða,
     þeirs treystask þeim   telja at móti.

'Enn mun*u* skœðir vargar síðan vakna í skógi, veiða í borgum. Þeir munu sjalfir fella eða fjǫtra dolga sína; fáir munu verða, þeirs telja treystask at móti þeim.

'Then once more will vicious wolves awaken in the forest, hunt in the cities. They will themselves kill or shackle their foes; few will there be, who have confidence to complain against them.

Ms.: **Hb**(52r) (*Bret*).

Reading: [1] mun*u*: mun Hb.

Editions: *Skj*: Gunnlaugr Leifsson, *Merlínússpá II* 55: AII, 29, BII, 35, *Skald* II, 22; *Bret* 1848-9, II, 58 (*Bret* st. 123); *Hb* 1892-6, 280; *Merl* 2012, 169-70.

Notes: [All]: Cf. *DGB* 114 (Reeve and Wright 2007, 149.94-7; cf. Wright 1988, 104-5, prophecy 15): *Euigilabunt regentis catuli et postpositis nemoribus infra moenia ciuitatum uenabuntur. Stragem non minimam ex obstantibus facient et linguas taurorum abscident. Colla rugientium onerabunt catenis* 'The cubs of the ruler will awake, leave the forests and hunt within city walls. They will do great slaughter among those who oppose them and cut out the tongues of bulls. They will load with chains the necks of those who roar' (cf. Reeve and Wright 2007, 148). From this point onward, after the two preceding transitional stanzas, Geoffrey's prophecies (and Gunnlaugr's adaptation of them) have no historical or pseudo-historical referent but merely hint in vague and portentous language at possible future events affecting the British people, conceived on the basis of both the deep and the recent past. While it is possible that Gunnlaugr had knowledge from Henry of Huntingdon or William of Malmesbury concerning the Anarchy (i.e. the conflict between Stephen and Matilda for the crown of England following the death of Henry I), it is not reflected in his adaptation, but see *I* 56 Note to [All] for an indication that he took the reign of Henry II into account. Geoffrey appears to refer back in this prophecy to the *catuli leonis* 'lion's cubs' of prophecy 11 (corresponding to *I* 52 in Gunnlaugr's rendering). *Merl* paraphrases loosely here and, at least as extant, does not include a rendering of the final sentence of prophecy 15. — [1] *mun*u 'will': Emended in *Skj* B and subsequent eds from ms. *mun*, to gain concord with pl. *vargar* in l. 3. — [3] *vargar* 'wolves': Gunnlaugr appears to replace Geoffrey's prediction of insurrection on the part of the king's children with a less specific vision of an uprising by outlaws, 'outlaw' being another sense of *vargr* in Old Norse. But possibly he is referring back to the progeny of the *léons vargar* 'the lion's wolves' mentioned in *I* 52/9. — [9-10]: The syntax and meaning here are not entirely certain. Both *treystask* and *telja* can be finite (3rd pers. pl. pres. indic.) or inf. Adopted in this edn is the interpretation by *Bret* 1848-9, which treats *treystask* as the finite verb and *telja* as the inf. (*treystask telja at móti þeim*), translating *faae kun ville vove mod dem at före Ordet* 'only a few will venture to bring the word against them'. For *telja* in this sense see *CVC*: *telja* III; *Fritzner*: *telja* 3. Finnur Jónsson wavers in his interpretation: *Skj* B translates *det vil være få som vover at imødegå dem* 'there will be few that venture to oppose them' (cf. *Merl* 2012), leaving the meaning of *telja* unclear, whereas *LP*: *telja* 4 gives *telja treystask at móti* as *som siger at de tröster sig til modstand* 'who say that they have confidence to resist [them]' and *LP*: *treysta* 3 has *treystask telja móti e-m* (the latter in agreement with *Bret* 1848-9). Gunnlaugr seems not to reproduce *DGB* with his customary closeness in this passage but Geoffrey's mention of severed tongues might have prompted this evocation of fears of outspokenness.

56. 'Einn sitr nýtastr Néústríe
 Englandi at auðar skelfir.
 Þó 'ro siklingar sunnan komnir
 fimm eða fleiri foldu at ráða.

'Einn nýtastr skelfir auðar Néústríe sitr at Englandi. Þó 'ro fimm eða fleiri siklingar komnir sunnan at ráða foldu.

'The one worthiest shaker of riches [GENEROUS MAN] of Neustria will preside over England. Yet five kings or more have come from the south to rule the land.

Ms.: **Hb**(52r) (*Bret*).

Reading: [5] 'ro: om. Hb.

Editions: *Skj*: Gunnlaugr Leifsson, *Merlínússpá II* 56: AII, 30, BII, 35, *Skald* II, 22, *NN* §3143; *Bret* 1848-9, II, 58 (*Bret* st. 124); *Hb* 1892-6, 280; *Merl* 2012, 170-1.

Notes: [All]: This stanza may represent a rationalisation of and extrapolation from Geoffrey's prophecy 16 (Reeve and Wright 2007, 149.97-9; cf. Wright 1988, 105): *Exin de primo in quartum, de quarto in tercium, de tercio in secundum rotabitur pollex in oleo* 'Then from the first to the fourth, from the fourth to the third, from the third to the second, the thumb shall roll in oil' (Reeve and Wright 2007, 148). This enigmatic passage presumably refers to the anointing of successive Norman kings, as recognised in some of the commentaries (Hammer 1935, 30). But other commentators were bewildered by this passage, as emerges e.g. from the explication *pollex in oleo, hoc est non difficultate, sed gratia quasi* (Hammer 1940, 418) 'thumb in oil, i.e. not with difficulty but as if with pleasure', and Gunnlaugr could well have shared their bewilderment. Instead Gunnlaugr, or more probably his source ms., appears to extrapolate from the passage so as to praise Henry II (r. 1133-89); this interpretation may have been assisted by annotation or commentary of the kind we find in John of Cornwall's version of the *Prophetiae Merlini*. John speaks of *quartum seu quintum* 'the fourth or the fifth' in the sequence of kings (Curley 1982, 234), where Gunnlaugr speaks of 'five or more', and this shared vagueness as to the exact number of Norman kings (down to John's and Gunnlaugr's source's respective times of writing?) may reflect the fact that Henry I's son and designated successor William Adelin, who perished in the White Ship (see *I* 52 Note to [All]) but had been crowned previously, was sometimes counted as the fourth, with Stephen then taken to be the fifth (Curley 1982, 244; cf. Faletra 2012, 333) and Henry II the sixth; the list could be stretched to a seventh after the advanced coronation of Henry II's son (also Henry) in 1170 (Poole 1955, 212-13). — [1] *einn nýtastr* 'the one worthiest': That is to say, 'worthiest of all'. On this idiom see *NN* §3143A. The idea seems to be that the current ruler (Henry II) surpasses the previous kings of the Norman dynasty, a sentiment no doubt reflecting the political position of Gunnlaugr's source, in the light of Henry's conduct subsequent to the death of Thomas Becket in 1170. Some of the commentaries take the same view of Henry, e.g. (Hammer 1940, 419): *sed in aetate sua stabilis et perfectus erit per clara merita, fama praeconante de eo* 'but in his old age he will be stable and perfect through his manifest merits, with fame proclaiming about him'. — [2] *Néústríe* 'of Neustria': Here Gunnlaugr uses the Latin first declension gen. sg. form, no doubt with dissyllabic realisation of <eu> (cf. *I* 61/9); thus emendation to *Neustríe ór* (*Bret* 1848-9, followed by *Skj* B) is unnecessary (cf. *NN* §3143B). Neustria is Geoffrey's standard pseudonym for Normandy and is always retained by Gunnlaugr. — [5] 'ro 'have': Lit. 'are'. Supplied in *Bret* 1848-9 and *Skj* B. Kock (*NN* §3143C), tacitly followed by *Merl* 2012, instead construes ll. 5-8 as *Þó ráða fimm eða fleiri siklingar, sunnan komnir, at foldu*, translated as *dock styra i landet fem eller flera söderifrån komna furstar* 'Yet five or more rulers, come from the south, reign in the land'. But if *at* functions as a postponed prep. it should occupy a metrical rise, which is impossible as the line stands in the ms.

57. 'Sá bjartar brýtr   borgir Íra
    ok foldar til   fellir skóga.
    Gerir ræsir eitt   ríki margra;
    tekr léónis   lávarðr hǫfuð.

'Sá brýtr bjartar borgir Íra ok fellir skóga til foldar. Ræsir gerir eitt ríki margra; lávarðr tekr hǫfuð léónis.

'He will destroy the splendid cities of the Irish and fell the forests to the ground. The leader will create one kingdom out of many; the lord will take on the head of a lion.

Ms.: **Hb**(52r) (*Bret*).

Reading: [8] lávarðr: lávarð Hb.

Editions: *Skj*: Gunnlaugr Leifsson, *Merlínússpá II* 57: AII, 30, BII, 35, *Skald* II, 22, *NN* §3143B; *Bret* 1848-9, II, 59 (*Bret* st. 125); *Hb* 1892-6, 280; *Merl* 2012, 171.

Notes: [All]: Cf. *DGB* 114 (Reeve and Wright 2007, 149.99-100; cf. Wright 1988, 105, prophecy 17): *Sextus Hiberniae moenia subuertet et nemora in planiciem mutabit. Diuersas portiones in unum reducet et capite leonis coronabitur* 'The sixth will overthrow the city walls of Ireland and turn its forests into a plain. He will reduce various shares to one and be crowned with the lion's head' (Reeve and Wright 2007, 148). This prophecy relates to the strong Norman king referred to in st. 56. Henry II did indeed successfully invade Ireland in 1171, lending credence to Geoffrey's prophecy. — [7] *léónis* 'of a lion': Realised trisyllabically (cf. *NN* §3143). Printed as *leónis* in *Skj* B, but *LP*: *léó* tacitly adjusts to *léónis*. See Note to *I* 52/7 on vowel quantities in this word. Gunnlaugr uses the Latin form of the gen., as sporadically elsewhere; cf. *I* 30/6. — [8] *lávarðr* 'lord': Emended from ms. *lávarð* (unrefreshed) by *Bret* 1848-9 and subsequent eds.

58. 'Es í reiðingu   ráð þjóðkonungs
    inn fyrra hlut   fylkis ævi.
    En inn øfri aldr   auðvarpaðar
    líkar helgum   himinstilli vel.

'Ráð þjóðkonungs es í reiðingu inn fyrra hlut ævi fylkis. En inn øfri aldr auðvarpaðar líkar helgum himinstilli vel.

'The behaviour of the mighty king will waver for the first part of the leader's life. But the later life of the wealth-flinger [GENEROUS MAN] will please the holy ruler of heaven [= God] well.

Ms.: **Hb**(52r) (*Bret*).

Editions: *Skj*: Gunnlaugr Leifsson, *Merlínússpá II* 58: AII, 30, BII, 35-6, *Skald* II, 22; *Bret* 1848-9, II, 59 (*Bret* st. 126); *Hb* 1892-6, 280; *Merl* 2012, 172.

Note: [All]: Cf. *DGB* 114 (Reeve and Wright 2007, 149.101-2; cf. Wright 1988, 105, prophecy 17): *Principium eius uago affectui succumbet, sed finis ipsius ad superos conuolabit* 'His beginning will be weakened by uncertain desires, but his end will ascend to the heavens' (cf. Reeve and Wright 2007, 148).

59. 'Mun hann byskupa   borgum skrýða
     ok helgan stað   hefja margan.
     Tígnar borgir   tvær pallío;
     gefr hann þýjum Krists   þægjar hnossir.

'Hann mun skrýða byskupa borgum ok hefja margan helgan stað. Tígnar tvær borgir pallío; hann gefr þýjum Krists þægjar hnossir.

'He will endue bishops with cities and elevate many a holy place. He will honour two cities with the pallium; he will give acceptable treasures to the servant-women of Christ.

Ms.: **Hb**(52r) (*Bret*).

Editions: *Skj*: Gunnlaugr Leifsson, *Merlínússpá II* 59: AII, 30, BII, 36, *Skald* II, 22; *Bret* 1848-9, II, 59 (*Bret* st. 127); *Hb* 1892-6, 280; *Merl* 2012, 172-3.

Notes: [All]: Cf. *DGB* 114 (Reeve and Wright 2007, 149.102-4; cf. Wright 1988, 105, prophecy 17): *Renouabit namque beatorum sedes per patrias et pastores in congruis locis locabit. Duas urbes duobus palliis induet et uirginea munera uirginibus donabit* 'For he shall rebuild the homes of the saints throughout his lands and place shepherds in appropriate places. He will dress two cities in two pallia and give virginal gifts to virgins' (cf. Reeve and Wright 2007, 148). 'Shepherds' here equates to bishops (cf. Note to *II* 16/5). Whether Geoffrey means a renewal of the *pallia* held by York and Canterbury or the bestowal of *pallia* on two new sees is unclear. — [1-2]: In this edn the ms. reading *borgum* 'cities' (not refreshed) is retained. The resulting sentence reads: *hann mun skrýða byskupa borgum* 'he will endue bishops with cities', with *byskupa* construed as acc. pl., corresponding to *DGB*'s *pastores* 'shepherds'. Extended uses of *skrýða* relating to appurtenances other than clothing are characteristic of 'learned style' and are attested in *Fritzner*: *skrýða*, ONP: *skrýða*. Also to be noted is Geoffrey's use of *induet* 'will dress' in the immediate context, *skrýða* being the standard translation for Lat. *induere*. To present meritorious persons with a city has its purported precedent in Arthur (*DGB* IX 157: Reeve and Wright 2007, 214-15) but in Geoffrey's time would have been especially appropriate when a prelate was the recipient. Episcopal migrations from small sequestered villages to the major urban centre in the diocese had been set in train in 1049-50 and were accelerated by Archbishop Lanfranc's council at London in 1075; thus the bishops of Lichfield, Selsey and Sherborne were called on to move their seats to the appropriate towns of Chester, Chichester and Salisbury respectively (Barrow

1956, 61; Stenton 1965, 227). Remigius, the first post-conquest bishop of Lincoln, maintained a seat at Stow St Mary, a few miles north-west of Lincoln, without a seat in Lincoln itself, whereas the second bishop, Robert de Bloet (1094-1123), acceded to the new rules by taking up residence in the city proper. Of his successors, Bishop Alexander, Geoffrey's patron, used land granted by Henry I (Woodfield and Woodfield 1981-2, 1) towards an 'aggrandisement' of the complex of cathedral, palace and precinct (Coulson 2003, 199). Geoffrey's talk of placing bishops in appropriate places seems to chime in with these developments, cf. the commentary *in congruis locis, in metropolitanis civitatibus* 'in appropriate places, in metropolitan cities' (Hammer 1940, 419). Gunnlaugr's choice of phrasing makes the idea of episcopal distinction somewhat more explicit and brings the language closer to an Arthurian presentation of an entire city rather than merely land within it (for a later instance of this motif see Kalinke 2009, 227). *Bret* 1848-9, followed by subsequent eds, interprets ms. *borgum* as *borg um*, with *um* construed as the completive particle with inf. *skrýða* 'endue' and *byskupa* construed as gen. pl. The sense is then taken to be 'he will adorn the city of bishops'. — [1] *hann* 'he': Again a reference to the strong Norman king first mentioned in *I* 56. — [6] *pallíó* 'with the pallium': Latin 2nd declension ablative sg. Compare Note to *I* 56/2. — [7] *þýjum Krists* 'to the servant-women of Christ': This phrase probably translates the *uirginibus* 'to virgins' of Geoffrey's text. The word *virgo* 'virgin' is a common expression for 'nun' in the C12th (Freeman 2015, 268). Finnur Jónsson (*LP*: *þý*) considered Gunnlaugr may have had female saints in mind, but he could equally have been thinking of nuns. — [8] *þægjar hnossir* 'acceptable treasures': The identical phrase appears in the undatable fragment Anon *Stríðk* 1[III]. Whereas Gunnlaugr's usage of the adj. is in accord with its standard meaning of 'acceptable [in the sight of God or God's servants]' (cf. *I* 54/4), the more general sense of 'delightful' has been proposed for the latter poem, with its decidedly secular and irreverent tone; but possibly the standard sense of *þægr* is operative there as well and the poet can be seen as engaged in a travesty of the moral ethos that it embodies.

60. 'Verðr af slíku   sverðéls hǫtuðr
    himna ferðar   hugþekkr grami.
    Ok at þetta líf   þingdjarfr konungr
    talið es tyggja   tungls með englum.

'Hǫtuðr sverðéls verðr hugþekkr grami ferðar himna af slíku. Ok þingdjarfr konungr es talið at þetta líf með englum tyggja tungls.

'The hater of the sword-storm [BATTLE > HOLY MAN] will be dear to the lord of the host of the heavens [ANGELS > = God] because of such [deeds]. And the king bold in encounters will be counted after this life with the angels of the lord of the moon [= God].

Ms.: **Hb**(52r) (*Bret*).

Reading: [7] tyggja: 'tigia' Hb.

Editions: *Skj*: Gunnlaugr Leifsson, *Merlínússpá II* 60: AII, 30, BII, 36, *Skald* II, 23; *Bret* 1848-9, II, 60 (*Bret* st. 128); *Hb* 1892-6, 280; *Merl* 2012, 173-4.

Notes: [All]: Cf. *DGB* 114 (Reeve and Wright 2007, 149.104-5; cf. Wright 1988, 105, prophecy 17): *Promerebitur inde fauorem Tonantis et inter beatos collocabitur* 'For this he will earn the favour of the Thunderer and be numbered among the blessed' (Reeve and Wright 2007, 148). — [2] *hǫtuðr sverðéls* 'the hater of the sword-storm [BATTLE > HOLY MAN]': This phrase, as it stands in the ms., is most straightforwardly explained as a kenning meaning literally somebody who hates warfare, and this might seem appropriate for an evidently saintly king (*LP*: *hǫtuðr*, cf. *Merl* 2012). In l. 6, however, the same person is described as *þingdjarfr* 'bold in encounters', which would normally mean bellicose encounters, and that might be regarded as indicating an interpretation of the kenning in l. 2 as 'warrior' (so *Bret* 1848-9 and *Skj* B). Saintly kings such as Oswald, referred to earlier in the poem (*I* 33/5-6), are not necessarily averse to battle – indeed Oswald is described as a leader in warfare. It is true that the adj. *þingdjarfr* appears in a somewhat similar context in *I* 37/3 (see Note there) and can be explained in both instances as an ornamental epithet without close reference to the immediate situation. But another possibility, broached in *LP*: *hǫtuðr*, is that the reading *hǫtuðr* is a simple error for *hvǫtuðr* 'whetter', a *heiti* that occurs once elsewhere in *Merl* (*I* 94/11); *Meissner* 321 appears to incline to this solution and it is adopted in *Skald*. A similar difficulty arises in Anon *Pl* 29/3[VII]. — [5] *at þetta líf* 'after this life': The use of *at* appears irregular. Gunnlaugr may have taken Geoffrey's *inde* 'for this' in the sense 'thenceforward', as is assumed in *Skj* B, but attestations of *at* in the sense of 'after' are not precisely parallel, as they involve constructions of the type *at jǫfur dauðan* 'after the lord's death', lit. 'at/with the lord dead', *at gram fallinn* 'after the king's fall', lit. 'at/with the king fallen': see *ONP*: *at* II. B. Possibly Gunnlaugr's usage mingles this sense of *at* with *at* with the dat. in the sense of 'because of': see *ONP*: *at* I D 12. — [7] *tyggja* 'lord': Normalised in *Bret* 1848-9 (followed by subsequent eds) from ms. 'tigia' (not refreshed), with spelling *tiggja* in *Bret* 1848-9 and *Merl* 2012.

61. 'Glíkt mun gaup*u* grams jóð vesa;
 vill þat sinni þjóð sjalfri steypa.
 En af þeim sǫkum þermlask bæði
 Íra ok Engla auðgrar jarðar
 Néústría ok numin tígnum.

'Jóð grams mun vesa glíkt gaup*u*; þat vill steypa þjóð sinni sjalfri. En af þeim sǫkum þermlask Néústría auðgrar jarðar bæði Íra ok Engla, ok numin tígnum.

'The king's son will resemble a lynx; it will wish to destroy its own people. And for those reasons Neustria will be stripped of the rich land of both the Irish and the English and deprived of honours.

Ms.: **Hb**(52r) (*Bret*).

Readings: [1] gaup*u*: gaupa Hb   [6] þermlask: þremlask Hb.

Editions: *Skj*: Gunnlaugr Leifsson, *Merlínússpá II* 61: AII, 30, BII, 36, *Skald* II, 23, *NN* §§104, 3143B, 3258C; *Bret* 1848-9, II, 60 (*Bret* st. 129); *Hb* 1892-6, 280-1; *Merl* 2012, 174-5.

Notes: [All]: Cf. *DGB* 115 (Reeve and Wright 2007, 149.105-7; cf. Wright 1988, 105, prophecy 18): *Egredietur ex eo linx penetrans omnia, quae ruinae propriae gentis imminebit. Per illam enim utramque insulam amittet Neustria et pristina dignitate spoliabitur* 'From him will emerge a lynx, which will penetrate through everything and threaten to destroy its own people. Because of it Normandy will lose both islands and be stripped of its former honour' (Reeve and Wright 2007, 148). The lynx appears as a simile rather than allegorically in *Merl* and the idea that the lynx's preternaturally acute sight enables it to see through into the viscera of animals, hinted at in *DGB*, is not carried over. — [1] *gaup*u 'a lynx': Emended in *Skj* B, followed by subsequent eds, from ms. *gaupa* (not refreshed), the nom. form. *Bret* 1848-9 retains *gaupa* without explanation, but the oblique form is required. — [3] *þat* 'it': Omitted in *Skald*. — [6] *þermlask* 'will be stripped': *Þermlask* is normalised from the metathesised ms. form *þremlask* in *Skj* B (followed by *Skald* and *Merl* 2012) and in this edn. This edn follows *Skj* B (cf. *Skald* and *Merl* 2012) in deleting the pron. *hann* which appears after *þremlask* in the ms. — [9] *Néústría*: Evidently realised as four syllables. See Note on *I* 56/2. Emended to *Neustríe* 'of Neustria', presumably intended as governing *auðgrar jarðar* 'of the rich land', in *Skald*: see Note to l. 10; *Merl* 2012 also translates as gen., but retains the ms. form. — [10] *ok numin tígnum* 'and deprived of honours': Finnur Jónsson reads *numinn*, referring back to the lynx-like king – *og han berøvet sin hæder* 'and he [will be] deprived of his honour' (*Skj* B, cf. *NN* §3258C; *Merl* 2012) – but the sense and adherence to the Latin are improved if we interpret the ms. form *numin* as f. nom. sg., agreeing with *Neustría*, which is the subject of the clause. Kock doubts (*NN* §104, cf. §3258C) that the names of countries can function as grammatical subjects, but fails to take account of the Latin. Cities and nations, like individual persons, could be thought of as possessing honours (cf. *I* 30/5, *I* 59/5).

62. 'En eptir þat   óðals á vit
    fara fráliga   fyrðar brezkir.
    Þó es illa áðr   ært í landi;
    eru ósáttar   enskar þjóðir.

'En brezkir fyrðar fara fráliga eptir þat á vit óðals. Þó es ært illa áðr í landi; enskar þjóðir eru ósáttar.

'But the British people will go back swiftly after that to their ancestral land. Yet there has been a poor harvest previously in the land; the English peoples will be at odds with one another.

Ms.: **Hb**(52r) (*Bret*).

Editions: *Skj*: Gunnlaugr Leifsson, *Merlínússpá II* 62: AII, 30, BII, 36, *Skald* II, 23; *Bret* 1848-9, II, 60 (*Bret* st. 130); *Hb* 1892-6, 281; *Merl* 2012, 175.

Note: [All]: Cf. *DGB* 115 (Reeve and Wright 2007, 149.107-8; cf. Wright 1988, 105, prophecy 19): *Deinde reuertentur ciues in insulam; nam discidium alienigenarum orietur* 'Then the natives will return to the island; for strife will break out among the foreigners' (Reeve and Wright 2007, 148). Here Geoffrey seems to envisage a return by the Bretons (living in Armorica, across the English Channel), to the British Isles, taking advantage of discord among the English. Their initial migration to Brittany is alluded to in *I* 37. The idea of the poor harvest is added by Gunnlaugr; see Note to *I* 32/5-8.

63. 'Ríðr inn prúði   til Peritónis ár
    hvítum hesti   hvatr ǫldurmaðr.
    Ok hvítum þar   hann markar staf
    aldrœn*n* yfir   ó kvernar hús.

'Inn prúði, hvatr ǫldurmaðr, ríðr hvítum hesti til ár Peritónis. Ok hann, aldrœn*n*, markar þar hvítum staf hús kvernar yfir ó.

'The splendid man, a bold lord, will ride a white horse to the river Periron. And there he, the aged [man], will mark out a mill-house above the river with a white staff.

Ms.: **Hb**(52r) (*Bret*).

Reading: [7] aldrœn*n*: aldrœn Hb.

Editions: *Skj*: Gunnlaugr Leifsson, *Merlínússpá II* 63: AII, 30-1, BII, 36-7, *Skald* II, 23; *Bret* 1848-9, II, 61 (*Bret* st. 131); *Hb* 1892-6, 281; *Merl* 2012, 176.

Notes: [All]: Cf. *DGB* 115 (Reeve and Wright 2007, 149.108-10; cf. Wright 1988, 105, prophecy 19): *Niueus quoque senex in niueo equo fluuium Perironis diuertet et cum candida uirga molendinum super ipsum metabitur* 'A snow-white old man on a snow-white horse will divert the river Periron and with a white rod measure out a mill on its bank' (cf. Reeve and Wright 2007, 148). The *Book of Llan Dav*, c. 1150, locates *Aper Periron* not far from the town of Monmouth as a branch of the Cadlan (Curley 1982, 244, citing Williams 1955, xxxvi-xxxvii); some of the commentaries also place it near Monmouth (e.g. Hammer 1940, 419). The C10th *Armes Prydein* 'The Prophecy of Britain' describes a confrontation between the Welsh and the steward of an English king, possibly Æthelstan, at this location (Curley 1982, 225-6; Faletra 2008, 134). However, it is possible that Geoffrey is alluding by means of this anecdote about a snow-white old man to the rapid rise of the Cistercians, a monastic order distinguished by its members' wearing of white robes. The order gained institutional definition with the *Carta caritatis* of Stephen Harding, confirmed by Pope Calixtus II in 1119 (Poole 1955, 187), and rapidly became very popular in England (Barrow 1956, 105). The earliest known reference to the adoption of white clothing by the Cistercians occurs in a letter of Peter the Venerable (1092/94-1156), abbot of Cluny, to Bernard of Clairvaux (Burton 2006, 10). The reference to a water mill may also be suggestive, as the typical Cistercian monastery straddled a mill-race, an artificial stream diverted from a nearby river to provide power for grain milling and other technologies as well as running water for domestic purposes (Hansen [n. d.], accessed 03/09/2015; cf. Bostan *et al.* 2012, 187; Woods 2005, 33). The Cistercians' founding of Tintern Abbey, not far from Monmouth, occurred early enough for Geoffrey to have been able to allude to it in the separate *Libellus Merlini* as well as the subsequent *DGB*. — [1, 2] *ríðr ... til* 'rides ... to': Possibly a misinterpretation of *divertet* 'will divert' (applying to the course of the river). — [2] *Peritónis* 'Periron': This reading agrees with that of ms. R of the First Variant Version, viz. *Peritonis* for majority *Perironis* (Wright 1988, 105), but may be a case of coincident error, given that confusion of <r> and <t> is frequent. The form *Peritónis* is a Latin gen. (cf. *léónis* in *I* 57/7), and Gunnlaugr seems to have taken it over as a gen. of definition specifying the river denoted generically by the common noun *ár* (gen. case). — [4] *ǫldurmaðr* 'lord': This term, adopted from OE/Early ME *ealdormann, aldormann* (*LP*: *ǫldurmaðr*, but not noted by Hofmann 1955) or Middle Low German (*AEW*: *ǫldurmaðr*), occurs in later C12th skaldic poetry, notably Bjbp *Jóms* 11/2[I] and Anon *Pl* 13/4[VII], evidently in the sense of 'leader'; see Notes to those two locations. Gunnlaugr may have used it in awareness of English terminology, but it was also current in reference to Old Testament patriarchs (*ONP*: *ǫldurmaðr*) and was subsequently applied to Norwegian guild leaders (*Fritzner*: *ǫldurmaðr*), perhaps influenced by ME *alderman*. At some point it appears to have become associated with *aldr* 'age, old age' (*ONP*: *ǫldurmaðr*, citing Kolsrud 1952, 110): *Prestbiter þyðiz olldur madr at voro máli. þviat hann skylldi sua vera at uiti ok uisdomi* 'Priest is translated as *ǫldurmaðr* in our language because he should be such in knowledge and wisdom'. Possibly this had already occurred at Gunnlaugr's time. — [6, 7] *hvítum staf* 'with a white staff': See Note to *I* 47/3-4. — [7] *aldrænn* 'the aged [man]': In this edn the adj. is taken as in apposition with *hann* 'he' and referring back to the man mentioned in the first *helmingr*. The emendation to *-rænn* is minor, since geminate <n> is frequently not shown in Hb (*Hb* 1892-6, xliii). In previous eds the adj. is construed as n. pl., qualifying *hús*, also construed as n. pl., but this deviates from Geoffrey's text, where it is the *niveus* 'snow-white' man who is described as 'old' (*senex*), not the mill-house, which in the logic of the passage is presumably not old, since it awaits construction, and is clearly sg., not pl.

64. 'Kalla mun Kónan   Káðvaládr*us*
    ok skilfinga*   Skotlandi af.
    Rýkr af grimmu   Gǫndlar éli;
    verðr it mikla   malmþing háit.

'Káðvaládr*us* mun kalla Kónan ok skilfinga* af Skotlandi. Rýkr af grimmu éli Gǫndlar; it mikla malmþing verðr háit.

'Cadwallader will summon Conan and kings from Scotland. Smoke will rise from the savage storm of Gǫndul <valkyrie> [BATTLE]; the great metal-encounter [BATTLE] will be waged.

Ms.: **Hb**(52r) (*Bret*).

Readings: [2] Káðvaládr*us*: Káðvaladría Hb   [3] skilfinga*: skilfingar Hb.

Editions: *Skj*: Gunnlaugr Leifsson, *Merlínússpá II* 64: AII, 31, BII, 37, *Skald* II, 23; *Bret* 1848-9, II, 61 (*Bret* st. 132); *Hb* 1892-6, 281; *Merl* 2012, 177-8.

Notes: [All]: Cf. *DGB* 115 (Reeve and Wright 2007, 149.110-11; cf. Wright 1988, 105, prophecy 20): *Cadualadrus Conanum uocabit et Albaniam in societate accipiet* 'Cadualadrus will summon Conanus and make Scotland his ally' (Reeve and Wright 2007, 148). This predicts the expulsion of the foreigners and the restoration of Welsh hegemony under the ancestral British king Cadualadrus (Taylor 1911, 90). He was assisted by a pan-Celtic alliance. One participant in it was Brittany, among whose rulers Conanus was a favourite name, harking back to Conanus Meriadocus (Welsh *Cynan Meiriadoc*), who figures in *DGB* as a leader in the conquest of the territory that became Brittany; Tatlock (1950, 158) remarks that 'Conanus ... is an obvious symbol for Brittany'. The other participant was Scotland (Tatlock 1950, 414 n. 45; Bromwich 1978, 320-1). According to *DGB* XI (Reeve and Wright 2007, 278-9), Cadualadrus was remembered as the last native king to rule Britain before the Saxon monarchy; Geoffrey envisages his return in the style of Arthur. The identification of this Cadualadrus with a C7th king of Gwynedd proposed by *Merl* 2012 does not fit this scenario. In *Armes Prydein*, from which Geoffrey derives this prophecy, Cadwallader and Conan appear as prophesied saviours of the Britons (Faletra 2008, 134). As if to signal the importance of this juncture, Gunnlaugr amplifies Geoffrey's text with a battle excursus. — [2] *Káðvaládr*us 'Cadwallader': Emended in *Bret* 1848-9 (followed by subsequent eds) from ms. *Káðvaladría* (not refreshed); the spelling perhaps results from a misunderstanding of this word as a national instead of a pers. n. *Bret* 1848-9 appears to make *Kónan* the subject and *Káðvaládrús* the object, but this, if not simply an artifact of word inversion, deviates unnecessarily from Geoffrey's text. — [3] *skilfinga** 'kings': Emended in *Bret* 1848-9 (followed by subsequent eds) from ms. *skilfingar* (not refreshed).

65. 'Svífr it hvassa   hagl tvíviðar
    — hnígr hǫlða lið —   hart af strengjum.
    En geyst hinig   gaflok fara;
    megut Skǫglar ský   við skotum halda.

'It hvassa hagl tvíviðar svífr hart af strengjum; lið hǫlða hnígr. En gaflok fara geyst hinig; ský Skǫglar megut halda við skotum.

'The cutting hail of the bow [ARROWS] flies hard from the strings; the troop of men sinks down. And javelins travel this way ferociously; the clouds of Skǫgul <valkyrie> [SHIELDS] cannot withstand the volleys.

Ms.: **Hb**(52r) (*Bret*).

Editions: *Skj*: Gunnlaugr Leifsson, *Merlínússpá II* 65: AII, 31, BII, 37, *Skald* II, 23; *Bret* 1848-9, II, 61-2 (*Bret* st. 133); *Hb* 1892-6, 281; *Merl* 2012, 178.

Notes: [All]: Battle commonplaces without a substantive source in Geoffrey's text (cf. *Bret* 1848-9). These extend from this stanza to st. 69. Although all the events described in these stanzas are represented as taking place in the future, the present tense has been used in their translation to convey a sense of immediacy. — [2] *tvíviðar* 'of the bow': Cf. Þul *Boga* l. 2^{III} and Eil *Þdr* 20/5^{III}. — [6] *gaflok* 'javelins': Sometimes spelt *gaflak*; word for a light spear, cf. Þul *Spjóts* 1. 7^{III}.

66. 'Bresta brynjur,   bíta malmar,
    eru dreyrfáið   dǫrr á lopti,
    fleinn á flaugun,   folk í dreyra,
    bíldr í benjum,   broddar á skildi,
    hjalmr á hǫfði,   hlíf fyr brjósti,
    geirr á gangi,   guðr í vexti.

'Bresta brynjur, malmar bíta, dreyrfáið dǫrr eru á lopti, fleinn á flaugun, folk í dreyra, bíldr í benjum, broddar á skildi, hjalmr á hǫfði, hlíf fyr brjósti, geirr á gangi, guðr í vexti.

'Mail-shirts split, weapons bite; blood-stained darts are in the air, the spear in flight, the army in blood, the arrow in wounds, spear-points in the shield, the helmet on the head, the shield before the breast, the spear in motion, battle on the increase.

Ms.: **Hb**(52r) (*Bret*).

Reading: [5] flein*n* á: fleina Hb.

Editions: *Skj*: Gunnlaugr Leifsson, *Merlínússpá II* 66: AII, 31, BII, 37, *Skald* II, 23; *Bret* 1848-9, II, 62 (*Bret* st. 134); *Hb* 1892-6, 281; *Merl* 2012, 178-80.

Notes: [3, 4] *dreyrfáið dǫrr* 'blood-stained darts': This appears in the form *dreyrfáðir dǫrir* in *Bret* 1848-9, without explanation or apparent warrant, probably through a misunderstanding of the declension of *darr* n. with nom./acc. pl. *dǫrr* (cf. *LP*: *darr*). — [3] *dreyrfáið* 'blood-stained': De Vries (1964-7, II, 75 n. 180) compares *HHj* 9/6. — [5] *fleinn á* 'the spear in': Emended by *Bret* 1848-9, followed by *Skj* B and *Skald*, for ms. *fleina* 'of spears' (not refreshed), to maintain parallelism in the catalogue commencing in l. 3. *Merl* 2012 retains the ms. reading but at the cost of sense and syntax. — [8] *broddar* 'spear-points': So in Hb, with superscript *-ar* contraction (not refreshed). *Bret* 1848-9, *Skj* B, *Skald* and *Merl* 2012 read *broddr*, which would fit better with the surrounding sg. nouns.

67. 'Hittisk targa   ok inn togni hjǫrr,
    hjalmr ok hneitir,   hlíf ok ǫrvar,
    brynja in brezka   ok brandr roðinn,
    manns mǫttug hǫnd   ok meðalkafli,
    hvítmýlingar   ok hǫlða brjóst.

'Targa ok inn togni hjǫrr hittisk, hjalmr ok hneitir, hlíf ok ǫrvar, in brezka brynja ok roðinn brandr, mǫttug hǫnd manns ok meðalkafli, hvítmýlingar ok brjóst hǫlða.

'Shield and the drawn sword meet, helmet and sword, shield and arrows, the British mail-shirt and red-stained sword, a man's strong hand and a sword-grip, white-muzzled arrows and the breasts of men.

Ms.: **Hb**(52r) (*Bret*).

Editions: *Skj*: Gunnlaugr Leifsson, *Merlínússpá II* 67: AII, 31, BII, 37; *Skald* II, 23-4; *Bret* 1848-9, II, 62 (*Bret* st. 135); *Hb* 1892-6, 281; *Merl* 2012, 180.

Notes: [1] *hittisk* 'meet': This verb applies to all the double subjects of the stanza. — [3] *hneitir* 'sword': Lit. 'cutter, striker'. Cf. *Þul Sverða* 2/7[III]. As a proper noun, Hneitir was the name of S. Óláfr's sword; see ESk *Geisl* 43/1[VII] and Note to [All]. — [8] *meðalkafli* 'a sword-grip': Or 'sword-hilt'. Strictly that part of the sword handle between the two hilt-plates; cf. *Þul Sverða* 12/6[III]. — [9] *hvítmýlingar* 'white-muzzled arrows': Cf. *Gísl Magnkv* 13/7[II] and *Þul Ǫrvar* 1/2[III].

68. 'Hrapa hræva gǫr,   hátt gjalla spjǫr,
    es malmþrima   mest á hjarli.
    Verðr einn við einn   valkǫstr hlaðinn;
    munu blóðgar ár   af bjǫðum falla,
    en vígroða   verpr á hlýrni.

'Gǫr hræva hrapa, spjǫr gjalla hátt, malmþrima es mest á hjarli. Einn valkǫstr verðr hlaðinn við einn; blóðgar ár munu falla af bjǫðum, en vígroða verpr á hlýrni.

'Heaps of corpses tumble, spears scream loudly, the weapon-tumult [BATTLE] is greatest on the earth. One pile of slain is built up beside another; bloody rivers will fall from the lands, and the redness of battle is cast up into heaven.

Ms.: **Hb**(52r) (*Bret*).

Editions: *Skj*: Gunnlaugr Leifsson, *Merlínússpá II* 68: AII, 31, BII, 37-8, *Skald* II, 24, *NN* §2406; *Bret* 1848-9, II, 62-3 (*Bret* st. 136); *Hb* 1892-6, 281; *Merl* 2012, 180-2.

Notes: [All]: Cf. *DGB* 115 (Reeve and Wright 2007, 149.111-12; cf. Wright 1988, 105, prophecy 20): *tunc flumina sanguine manabunt* 'then the rivers will flow with blood' (Reeve and Wright 2007, 148). Gunnlaugr reverses the order of this and the following clause from *DGB* (see *I* 69 Note to [All]). The rest of the material represents battle commonplaces in skaldic style. — [1-2]: The end-rhyme is reminiscent of *runhent* but, aside from *I* 69/5-6, Gunnlaugr does not maintain the treatment consistently; a more thorough-going attempt is seen in *II* 36. — [9] *en* 'and': Treated as *enn* 'once more', introducing a new sentence, in *Skald*, but this violates the word order in independent clauses. — [9] *vígroða* 'the redness of battle': For the full array of attestations of this and related compounds see *Kommentar* IV, 726-7. It is usually interpreted as a red glow in the sky, portending battle (*Bret* 1848-9; *Skj* B; *LP*, *LT*: *vígroði*; cf. *NN* §2406 *stridens glöd* 'glow of battle'). Given the context in *Merl*, an additional connotation might be that blood spatters the heavens: cf. Anon *Darr* 1/4^V(*Nj* 53) *rignir blóði* 'it rains with blood'.

69. 'Falla fyrðar   í fleindrífu;
    verðr enskri þjóð   aldrspell skipat.
    Es vǫllr roðinn   en víg boðin;
    hlýtr hǫvan sigr   helmingr Breta.

'Fyrðar falla í fleindrífu; aldrspell verðr skipat enskri þjóð. Vǫllr es roðinn en víg boðin; helmingr Breta hlýtr hǫvan sigr.

'Men will fall in the arrow-blizzard [BATTLE]; loss of life will be allotted for the English people. The field will be stained red and killing proffered; the force of Britons will win a great victory.

Ms.: **Hb**(52r) (*Bret*).

Editions: *Skj*: Gunnlaugr Leifsson, *Merlínússpá II* 69: AII, 31, BII, 38, *Skald* II, 24; *Bret* 1848-9, II, 63 (*Bret* st. 137); Hb 1892-6, 281; *Merl* 2012, 182.

Notes: [All]: Cf. *DGB* 115 (Reeve and Wright 2007, 149.111; cf. Wright 1988, 105, prophecy 20): *Tunc erit strages alienigenarum* 'Then there will be a slaughter of foreigners' (cf. Reeve and Wright 2007, 148). — [6] *en* 'and': Lines 5-6 comprise two parallel clauses joined by *en* 'and'. *Merl* 2012 interprets as adv. *enn*, translated as *wiederum* 'again'. This reading is ruled out, however, as l. 6 would then require a finite verb in metrical position 2. — [6] *víg* 'killing': The *heiti* can mean either 'killing' or 'battle' and it is often difficult to distinguish between these senses (cf. *LP*: *víg*), but context in this passage seems to suggest the former. *Bret* 1848-9 has *Slagmarken den röde bedækkes af Döde* 'the red battlefield is covered with the dead' (an atypically free translation, perhaps intended to match the end-rhyme in the original) and *Skj* B *mandefald sker* 'slaughter of men occurs'.

70. 'Yppir fjǫllum   fljót*t* Valbre*t*a;
    munu Brútus þau   bera kórónu.
    Grœnask ǫflgar   eikr Kornbreta;
    fagnar slíku   fús Kambría.

'Yppir fljót*t* fjǫllum Valbre*t*a; þau munu bera kórónu Brútus. Ǫflgar eikr Kornbreta grœnask; fús Kambría fagnar slíku.

'The mountains of French Britons will be swiftly raised up; they will bear the crown of Brutus. The mighty oaks of the Cornish Britons will grow green; eager Cambria rejoices at that.

Ms.: **Hb**(52r) (*Bret*).

Readings: [2] fljót*t*: 'fljot' Hb;   Valbre*t*a: valbreka Hb.

Editions: *Skj*: Gunnlaugr Leifsson, *Merlínússpá II* 70: AII, 31-2, BII, 38, *Skald* II, 24; *Bret* 1848-9, II, 63 (*Bret* st. 138); *Hb* 1892-6, 281; *Merl* 2012, 182-3.

Notes: [All]: Cf. *DGB* 115 (Reeve and Wright 2007, 149.112-13; cf. Wright 1988, 105, prophecy 20): *tunc erumpent Armorici montes et diademate Bruti coronabuntur. Replebitur Kambria laeticia, et robora Cornubiae uirescent* 'then the hills of Brittany will burst forth and be crowned with Brutus' diadem. Wales will be filled with rejoicing and the Cornish oaks will flourish' (cf. Reeve and Wright 2007, 148). Geoffrey envisages an assumption of monarchical power in the British Isles on the part of the returning Bretons (cf. *I* 63) to the satisfaction of the British still resident in Wales and Cornwall. — [1] *yppir* 'will be … raised up': Lit. 'there is … a raising': From *yppa* 'raise, lift up', used impersonally. — [2] *Valbre*t*a* 'of French Britons': Meaning 'Bretons, Armoricans', in apparent contrast to *Kornbreta* (gen. pl.) 'Cornish Britons' in l. 6. Emended by Scheving (as reported in *Bret* 1848-9) from ms. *valbreka* (not refreshed). Confusion between letters *c* and *t* is not uncommon and this emendation gives excellent agreement with Geoffrey's text, since the phrase *fjǫllum Valbreta* corresponds neatly to *Armorici montes*. For the formation, compare *Kornbretar* 'Cornish Bretons' (cf. *II* 16/2), paraphrasing Geoffrey's *Cornubiae*. Both may have been nonce-terms devised by Gunnlaugr, but *Val-* 'French' was a long-established element in the cpd *Valland* 'France', properly 'Normandy and the lower Seine region' (Foote 1975, 69) but extendable to other regions (cf. Sigv *Víkv* 6^1, Note to l. 5). *Bret* 1848-9 and *Skj* B (the latter followed by *Skald* and *Merl* 2012) retain the ms. reading and explain it as part of a kenning *fljót valbreka* 'river of the corpse-wave [BLOOD]'. In *Bret* 1848-9, ll. 1-2 are translated *Fjelden hæver Valflodens Ström* 'the stream of the corpse-flood raises the mountains' (cf. *Skj* B and *LP*: *fljót*). But this does not sit well with Finnur's construal of *yppir* as impersonal (cf. *LP*: *yppa*) and altogether the sense is both inferior in itself and discrepant from the Latin, which has nothing to say about rivers raising mountains. For discussion of evident errors in Hb see Introduction. — [3] *Brútus* 'of Brutus': Latin nom. form, used with gen. function (cf. *I* 53/12, *I* 72/4). Brutus is mentioned by virtue of his supposed status as the eponymous founder of the British people, as implied in the next stanza (cf. *DGB* I 21.459-60: Reeve and Wright 2007, 28-9); the Bretons are said to take on his crown because it is they who are asserting ancient British rights on behalf of all British peoples. — [6] *Kornbreta* 'of the Cornish Britons': This is the first explicit naming of the Cornish people (or Cornwall) in *Merl* as extant.

71. 'Eyðisk eyjar   it enska nafn;
     mun hon Anglía   eigi kǫlluð.
     Hlýtr hon at halda heiti inu forna;
     kend es við Brútum Brítannía.

'It enska nafn eyjar eyðisk; hon mun eigi kǫlluð Anglía. Hon hlýtr at halda inu forna heiti; es kend Brítannía við Brútum.

'The English name of the island is expunged; it will not be called Anglia. It gets to retain the old name; it is called Britain after Brutus.

Ms.: **Hb**(52r) (*Bret*).

Editions: *Skj*: Gunnlaugr Leifsson, *Merlínússpá II* 71: AII, 32, BII, 38, *Skald* II, 24; *Bret* 1848-9, II, 63-4 (*Bret* st. 139); *Hb* 1892-6, 281; *Merl* 2012, 183.

Notes: [All]: Cf. *DGB* 115 (Reeve and Wright 2007, 149.114; cf. Wright 1988, 105, prophecy 20): *Nomine Bruti uocabitur insula, et nuncupatio extraneorum peribit* 'The island will be called by Brutus' name and the naming conferred on it by the foreigners will perish' (cf. Reeve and Wright 2007, 148). — [7-8]: The idea is familiar, but Gunnlaugr may have taken it either from a commentary or perhaps directly from *DGB* I (21.459-60: Reeve and Wright 2007, 28-9). He spells out more explicitly than Geoffrey that this represents a reversion to the ancient name.

72. 'Mun villigǫltr   vígdjarfr koma
ór kynstórri   Kónánus ætt
sá vigra konr   Vallandi á.
Hǫggr yngva sonr   eikr ór skógi;
þó mun hilmir   hollr smáviði.

'Villigǫltr, sá konr vigra, mun koma vígdjarfr ór kynstórri ætt Kónánus á Vallandi. Sonr yngva hǫggr eikr ór skógi; þó mun hilmir hollr smáviði.

'A wild boar, that scion of pigs, will issue, daring in combat, from the mighty lineage of Conan in France. The prince's son hews down oaks from the forest; yet the ruler will be kindly to small trees.

Ms.: **Hb**(52r) (*Bret*).

Readings: [4] Kónánus: 'Kominus' Hb   [5] vigra: 'viga-' Hb.

Editions: *Skj*: Gunnlaugr Leifsson, *Merlínússpá II* 72: AII, 32, BII, 38, *Skald* II, 24; *Bret* 1848-9, II, 64 (*Bret* st. 140); *Hb* 1892-6, 281; *Merl* 2012, 184-5.

Notes: [All]: Cf. *DGB* 115 (Reeve and Wright 2007, 149.114-17; cf. Wright 1988, 105-6, prophecy 21): *Ex Conano procedet aper bellicosus, qui infra Gallicana nemora acumen dentium suorum exercebit. Truncabit namque quaeque maiora robora, minoribus uero tutelam praestabit* 'From Conanus will come forth a warlike boar, who will exercise the sharpness of his tusks on the forests of France. He will cut short all the tallest trees, but give protection to the smaller' (cf. Reeve and Wright 2007, 148). Geoffrey envisages the resurgent British monarchy gaining power in France. Gunnlaugr amplifies on the glory of the boar king's lineage, probably with Arthur, the greatest of the boar kings, in mind: cf. *I* 24/4. — [4] *Kónánus* 'of Conan': Emended by *Bret* 1848-9, followed by subsequent eds, for ms. 'Kominus' (refreshed). The reference is to Conan Meriadoc: see *I* 64 Note to [All]. — [5] *konr vigra* 'scion of pigs': The latter word is emended in this edn from ms. 'viga-' (refreshed). The *heiti vigrir* 'boar' occurs in Þul *Galtar* 1/7[III]; see Note there; cf. *LP*: *vigr*, where an etymology based on *med tænder som spyd* 'with spear-like teeth' is tentatively suggested. Scheving (reported in *Bret* 1848-9) emended the words *viga konr* more drastically to *vígtǫnnum* 'with battle tusks', guided by the wording of *DGB*. This solution was adopted in *Bret* 1848-9 and *Skj* B and may well be correct. Other possibilities, however, are that Gunnlaugr omitted the mention of tusks, as he evidently does in *II* 30/5-8, perhaps in order to rationalise the allegory, or that there is a lacuna after l. 6, in which the boar's tusks could have been mentioned. In *Skald* 'viga-' is read as *víga*, without explanation: *Merl* 2012 adopts this reading, translating *konr víga* as *Mann der Kämpfe* [= *dieser Krieger*] 'man of battles [= this warrior]', but such a periphrasis would be unidiomatic; also, *konr* as a *heiti* for 'man' in general is very rarely attested as against the numerous attestations in the sense of 'scion, descendant, heir' (*LP*: *konr*). — [6] *Vallandi* 'France': This is the hitherto unrecognised ms. reading (refreshed). Above the first vowel, which as refreshed might be either <a> or ‹i›, is a stroke sloping downwards and rightwards that appears to have been part of an original ‹a›. A pen stroke runs across the ‹lld› of *valldi*, descending rightwards somewhat to merge with ‹d›. It is distinct from the ascender of ‹d›, as is shown by comparison with *I* 35/7 *veldi* and *I* 66/8 *skildi*, and might be interpreted as a mark of contraction, thus 'landi'. A similar pen stroke, reaching leftwards from the ascender of ‹d› so as to cross the ‹l› or occasionally placed above both ‹l› and ‹d›, is seen in such refreshed readings as *II* 13/2 'landi', *II* 15/4 'Bretlands', *II* 19/4 'landreki' and *II* 31/4 'landher'. This stroke can usually but not always be distinguished from the stroke seen elsewhere in association with preceding ‹l› or ‹ll› which is merely a run-in to the ‹d›, and where no contraction is involved (e.g. *I* 38/10). Sometimes, however, the abbreviated form of *land* lacks any mark of contraction, as in the refreshed readings *II* 1/6 and *II* 2/2, and this may have been the norm in the original hand (cf. *I* 12/6, *I* 23/4, *I* 28/4 and *I* 37/4). Regardless of how the pen stroke is interpreted, then, expansion to -*landi* seems secure and there are no indications that the refreshing is other than accurate on this occasion. Earlier eds, not recognising the reading, are led into tentative emendations. Scheving is reported in *Bret* 1848-9, without further explanation, as conjecturing *valdastar* 'mightiest' or *vildastar* 'choicest', in reference to the *eikr* (f. acc. pl.). *Bret* 1848-9 emends to *valskar* 'French', likewise qualifying *eikr*. Finnur Jónsson reads *villdi a* (*Skj* A) and emends to *vildjá..* (*sic*: left untranslated), with ellipses to show that the line was metrically deficient (*Skj* B, followed by *Skald* and *Merl* 2012).

73. 'Munu Rábítar ræsi ugga
  út í heimi ok Affríkar.
  Fǫr mun vísi víðlendr gera
  á it ýtra œgr Ispáníam.

'Rábítar ok Affríkar munu ugga ræsi út í heimi. Œgr, víðlendr vísi mun gera fǫr á it ýtra Ispáníam.

'The Arabs and Africans will fear the leader out in the world. The awe-inspiring leader with extensive territories will make an expedition to Spain on its farther side.

Ms.: **Hb**(52r) (*Bret*).

Editions: *Skj*: Gunnlaugr Leifsson, *Merlínússpá II* 73: AII, 32, BII, 38-9, *Skald* II, 24; *Bret* 1848-9, II, 64-5 (*Bret* st. 141); *Hb* 1892-6, 281; *Merl* 2012, 185-6.

Notes: [All]: Cf. *DGB* 115 (Reeve and Wright 2007, 149.117-18; cf. Wright 1988, 106, prophecy 21): *Tremebunt illum Arabes et Affricani; nam impetum cursus sui in ulteriorem Hispaniam protendet* 'The Arabs and Africans will tremble before him; for his charge will carry him all the way to the further regions of Spain' (cf. Reeve and Wright 2007, 148). Geoffrey appears to envisage an Arthur-like British conqueror (cf. sts 24-7); he repeats the boar-king allegorisation used of Arthur. — [1] *Rábítar* 'the Arabs': This name is found only here in poetry; it is also of rare occurrence in prose sources (*ONP*). — [7-8]: The word order here is rather convoluted by Gunnlaugr's standards, with the interweaving of the adj. *œgr* 'awe-inspiring', part of the noun phrase, with adverbial phrases attaching to the verb phrase. The syntax is not altogether resolved. It would seem, however, that the prep. *á* 'on' governs *Ispáníam* 'Spain' (a Latin first declension acc. sg., to be scanned as four syllables (contrast *Bret* 1848-9). This leaves *it ýtra* fulfilling an adverbial function, lit. 'on the outer side', or 'on the farther side', as seen from a British or Scandinavian perspective: to judge from the mention of Arabs and Africans in ll. 1 and 4 respectively, the southern side is intended. Comparable are the following passages: Þjsk *Jarl* 1/1¹ and Ív *Sig* 32/3ᴵᴵ (see Notes there). Also probably to be thus construed is Mark *Eirdr* 22/6ᴵᴵ (though see Note there and *LP*: *ýtri*). Translations in other eds obscure the syntax, apparently ignoring the f. gender of *Ispáníam*: *Bret* 1848-9 has *til det fjerne Hispania* 'to distant Spain', *Skj B til det fjærnere Spanien* 'to the further [regions of?] Spain', *Merl* 2012 *zum äußeren Spanien* 'to outer Spain'. Also obscured in these eds is the fact that the antecedent of *œgr* 'awe-inspiring' is *vísi* 'leader', not *fǫr* 'expedition'.

74. 'Sitr ept hilmi   hafr at lǫndum;
    hans esat skilja   skap frá vífni.
    Berr hann á hǫfði   horn ór gulli;
    es skegg skata   skapat ór silfri.

'Hafr sitr ept hilmi at lǫndum; skap hans esat skilja frá vífni. Hann berr á hǫfði horn ór gulli; skegg skata es skapat ór silfri.'

'A he-goat will preside over the lands after the king; his temperament cannot be separated from desire for women. He will bear on his head horns of gold; the leader's beard will be formed from silver.'

Ms.: **Hb**(52r) (*Bret*).

Editions: *Skj*: Gunnlaugr Leifsson, *Merlínússpá II* 74: AII, 32, BII, 39, *Skald* II, 24; *Bret* 1848-9, II, 65 (*Bret* st. 142); *Hb* 1892-6, 281; *Merl* 2012, 186-7.

Notes: [All]: Cf. *DGB* 115 (Reeve and Wright 2007, 149.118-51.119; cf. Wright 1988, 106, prophecy 22): *Succedet hircus Venerii Castri, aurea habens cornua et argenteam barbam* 'The goat of the Fortress of Venus, with golden horns and a silver beard, will succeed him' (cf. Reeve and Wright 2007, 148-50). The reference to Venus in *DGB* is not taken up explicitly in *Merl*, at least as extant (cf. *I* 76 Note to [All]), but the concept of her castle is conveyed indirectly in the words *kastra kvensemi* 'castles of desire for women' (*I* 76/5-6). — [3-4]: The sense is that the king cannot be prevailed on (e.g. by his counsellors) to give up his predilection for women – an accusation frequently made against Henry I by churchmen and other contemporaries (see *I* 51 Note to [All]). *Merl* 2012 would instead modify the normally accepted ms. reading *hans erat* to *hann sérat*, translating *er versteht es nicht* 'he does not understand it', but the required sense of *sjá* seems to occur only in combination with prepositions (*LP*: *séa*; Fritzner: *sjá*).

75. 'Blæs Mistar vinr   ór nǫsum †tiossa†
    þoku þvílíkri,   at þekr of ey.
    Friðr *es* of fylkis   fastr lífdaga;
    brestr eigi þá   ár í landi.

'Vinr Mistar blæs ór nǫsum †tiossa† þoku þvílíkri, at þekr of ey. Friðr *es* fastr of lífdaga fylkis; ár brestr eigi þá í landi.

'The friend of Mist <valkyrie> [WARRIOR] blows such a fog out of his nostrils ... that it covers the island. Peace is fixed throughout the king's lifetime; prosperity does not fail then in the land.

Ms.: **Hb**(52r) (*Bret*).

Readings: [2] *ór*: ok Hb   [5] Friðr *es*: Friðr Hb.

Editions: *Skj*: Gunnlaugr Leifsson, *Merlínússpá II* 75: AII, 32, BII, 39, *Skald* II, 24-5, *NN* §105; *Bret* 1848-9, II, 65 (*Bret* st. 143); *Hb* 1892-6, 281; *Merl* 2012, 187-8.

Notes: [All]: Cf. *DGB* 115, prophecies 22 and 23 (Reeve and Wright 2007, 151.119-22; cf. Wright 1988, 106): *qui ex naribus suis tantam efflabit nebulam quanta tota superficies insulae obumbrabitur. Pax erit in tempore suo et ubertate glebae multiplicabuntur segetes* 'who will breathe forth from his nostrils a cloud which will cover the whole surface of the island. There will be peace in his time and the rich soil will increase its crops' (Reeve and Wright 2007, 150). — [1] *vinr Mistar* 'the friend of Mist <valkyrie> [WARRIOR]': By introducing a warrior-kenning where Geoffrey has *qui* 'who', Gunnlaugr emphasises the human represented by the allegorical goat-king of *I* 74. The absence of alliteration suggests, however, that *Mist* might have replaced some other *heiti*. Finnur Jónsson tentatively suggests *Njǫrðr* (*LP*: *Mist*). Kock (*NN* §105) proposes *Nipt* 'sister, female relative' as a valkyrie-*heiti*, but this is highly doubtful (see Þul *Ásynja* 5/3-4[III] and Note there). It is also possible that this passage is more extensively damaged: see Notes to l. 2. — [2] *ór* 'out of': Emended from ms. *ok* (not refreshed) in *Bret* 1848-9, followed by subsequent eds. — [2] †*tiossa*† '...': This ms. reading (not refreshed) has not so far been explained or convincingly emended; *DGB* supplies no guidance at this point. *Skj* B emends to *brúsa* 'of the he-goat'. *Bret* 1848-9 already interprets it in that sense (*af Bukkenæsen*) but without emendation; *CVC* has the entry *tjossi* 'he goat (?)', citing the present passage as the unique attestation, but it does not feature in *Fritzner* or *ONP* and is no doubt a mere ghost-word. Kock (*NN* §105; *Skald*), followed by *Merl* 2012, emends to acc. *tjǫssu, taken as in apposition to *þoku* 'fog' and glossed as 'wave'. He bases his case on inference from West Germanic words denoting 'heavy wave, sea-swell', but no such word is attested in Old Norse and Kock does not clarify how such a sense would relate to the context. — [5] es 'is': Added in *Skj* B, followed by subsequent eds.

76. 'Þá munu *á* foldu   fǫgr víf draga;
     blístrar meyjum   metnuðr í spor.
     Munu kvensemi   kastra smíðuð;
     svíkr gumna vin   girnð in ranga.

'Þá munu fǫgr víf draga *á* foldu; metnuðr blístrar í spor meyjum. Kastra kvensemi munu smíðuð; in ranga girnð svíkr vin gumna.

'Then beautiful women will make their way on the ground: pride hisses in the maidens' trail. Castles of desire for women will be built; the wrongful concupiscence betrays the friend of men [RULER].

Ms.: **Hb**(52v) (*Bret*).

Reading: [1] *á* foldu: foldu Hb.

Editions: *Skj*: Gunnlaugr Leifsson, *Merlínússpá II* 76: AII, 32, BII, 39, *Skald* II, 25; *Bret* 1848-9, II, 65-6 (*Bret* st. 144); *Hb* 1892-6, 281; *Merl* 2012, 188-9.

Notes: [All]: Cf. *DGB* 115 (Reeve and Wright 2007, 151.122-4; cf. Wright 1988, 106, prophecy 23): *Mulieres incessu serpentes fient, et omnis gressus earum superbia replebitur. Renouabuntur castra Veneris, nec cessabunt sagittae Cupidinis uulnerare* 'Women in their movement will become snakes and their every step will be filled with pride. The Fortress of Venus will be renewed, and Cupid's arrows will not fail to wound' (cf. Reeve and Wright 2007, 150). Geoffrey's *castra Veneris* is rendered more generically by Gunnlaugr as *kastra kvensemi* 'castles of desire for women' (cf. *I* 74 Note to [All]), and he rationalises the reference to Cupid's arrows. The word *kvensemi* (or *kvennsemi*) 'desire, lust for women' occurs chiefly in learned texts (*ONP*: kvensemi, cf. kvensamr; *Fritzner*: kvennsemi, cf. kvennsamr). The target of disapproval here may be the developing cult of love that was to reach its apogee in the later C12th at the courts of aristocratic women such as Eleanor of Aquitaine and Ermengarde of Narbonne (see Cheyette 2001, 237-8, 244-5); Gunnlaugr and his audience could have known of the ethos at Ermengarde's court from Rv Lv 15, 16, 17, 19, 20, 21, 25[II]. — [1-2]: A difficult passage which has resisted definitive solution. This edn follows *Skj* B (also *Skald* and *Merl* 2012) in adding prep. *á* 'on' before *foldu* 'land'. This solution represents a refinement of *Bret* 1848-9, which tentatively supplies prep. *um* 'around' before *foldu*. It results in the sentence *Þá munu fǫgr víf draga á foldu* 'Then beautiful women will make their way on the ground'. The idea would be that the women move along the ground in the manner of snakes, as stated by Geoffrey. In the sense 'move oneself', however, the reflexive *dragask* would be expected rather than active *draga* (*CVC*: draga), though see *Fritzner*: draga 18; *LP*: draga 12 for rare and uncertain attestations in this sense. An alternative interpretation of the ms. text that avoids emendation would be to regard it as a late C13th or C14th garbling that has effaced Gunnlaugr's original. Here ms. *foldu* would be interpreted as *fǫldu* 'headdress', a f. counterpart of *faldr* 'headdress' (only one example extant in *ONP* but clearly attested in Bbreiðv Lv 3/3^V (*Eyrb* 28), KormQ Lv 49/2^V (*Korm* 70), and KormQ Lv 60/5^V (*Korm* 81)). Then *draga* would have the sense 'wear' (*ONP*: *draga* A4), attested in translation texts from the mid to late C13th. The resulting sentence would read *Þá munu fǫgr víf draga fǫldu* 'Then beautiful women will wear headdress[es]'. Women sporting headdresses of varying grades of showiness were emblematic of pride in medieval literature, the *locus classicus* in Old Norse being *Rþ* 29/1 (Dronke 1997, 168, 227). — [3] *blístrar* 'hisses': The application of the verb *blístra* in context remains unclear. Attested senses include 'make a strong blowing noise (of uncertain type), whistle, hiss, snort, sniff' (so *ONP*: *blístra*); in the present context 'hiss' is tentatively selected, in view of Geoffrey's allusion to snakes, which Gunnlaugr otherwise seems to have passed over, at least to judge from the present state of the text. *Bret* 1848-9 translates as *hvisler* 'hisses', followed by *Skj* B, while *Merl* 2012 has *pfeift* 'whistles'. Meanwhile the idiom *blístra í spor*, glossed in *ONP*: *blístra* as 'to sniff in somebody's tracks [to no avail]', 'to whistle for somebody in vain' (cf. also *ÍF* 8, 227 n. 3, *ÍF* 30, 38 n. 3), also needs to be taken into account. Conceivably Gunnlaugr could have in mind verses where the speaker is an intimidated or outwitted male lover (e.g. Bjbp *Jóms*^{I} and Steinarr *Woman*^{III}). In *DGB*, however, it is overweening behaviour on the part of women themselves that is under attack, not the allegorised pride of someone sniffing in vain in their tracks. Admittedly it is uncertain whether Gunnlaugr has resumed his close adherence to the Latin by this point or whether the rendering might be looser and more euphemistic (cf. Note on ll. 1-2); *replebitur* 'will be filled' is semantically remote from *blístrar*, though for another somewhat loose translation of *replebitur* see *I* 70/8. An alternative approach would see the problem as lying with a disruption of the text: *blístrar* could have arisen through error for original **miklask* (3rd pers. sg. pres. ind. of *miklask* 'be augmented, increased'), thus **metnuðr miklask í spor meyjum* 'pride is augmented in the maidens' tracks', where **miklask* would loosely render *replebitur*. The noun *metnuðr* occurs in collocation with *miklask* in Anon *Hsv*^{VII} 30, as a variant reading for *magnask* (*LP*: *mikla*), and with *þróask* 'swell' in *Hávm* 79/4. In prose usage *mikill* 'great' and its sup. *mesti* 'greatest' are frequent collocates of *metnuðr* (*ONP*: *metnuðr*). For the idea of something springing up from the footsteps of a woman, cf. *II* 12/3-4. — [6] *kastra* 'castles': Latin 2nd declension n. nom. pl.

77. 'Verðr at blóði   brunnr inn fagri;
     þós á grundu   gnótt hvers konar.
     En á holmi   hildingar tveir
     berjask of brúði   bjarthaddaða;
     sús í víðri   Vaðbatúli.

'Inn fagri brunnr verðr at blóði; þós gnótt hvers konar á grundu. En tveir hildingar berjask á holmi of bjarthaddaða brúði; sús í víðri Vaðbatúli.

'The fine spring turns to blood; yet there is every kind of bounty on the earth. And two leaders fight on an island over a bright-haired woman; she is in broad Vadum batuli.

Ms.: **Hb**(52v) (*Bret*).

Editions: *Skj*: Gunnlaugr Leifsson, *Merlínússpá II* 77: AII, 32-3, BII, 39, *Skald* II, 25; *Bret* 1848-9, II, 66 (*Bret* st. 145); *Hb* 1892-6, 281; *Merl* 2012, 189-90.

Notes: [All]: Cf. *DGB* 115 (Reeve and Wright 2007, 151.124-6; cf. Wright 1988, 106, prophecy 23): *Fons Annae uertetur in sanguinem, et duo reges duellum propter leaenam de Vado Baculi committent. Omnis humus luxuriabit, et humanitas fornicari non desinet* 'The spring of Anna will turn to blood, and two kings will fight a duel over the lioness of Stafford. All the soil will be rank, and mankind will not cease to fornicate' (cf. Reeve and Wright 2007, 150). The name Anna (with a common variant reading 'Amne') is not mentioned elsewhere in *DGB* and has not been identified; Gunnlaugr translates generically. *Merl* 2012, 190 states that this p. n. cannot be identified with any actual city, but in fact Geoffrey's *Vadum baculi* is no more than a thin disguise for the English p. n. Stafford, rendered folk-etymologically as 'ford of the stave' (cf. *gué de bastun* 'Ford of the Staff' in the Anglo-Norman decasyllabic version; Blacker 2005, 41). Gunnlaugr seems to have recognised that a ford was involved, translating Lat. *vado* with the vernacular cognate *vað* 'ford', but not to have understood the allusion in *Baculi*. The town of Stafford (OE *æt Stæfforda*) in the West Midlands, site of major fortifying works in the Anglo-Saxon period under Queen Æthelflæd, assumed renewed importance under the Normans, with the construction of a castle (Stenton 1971, 605); Geoffrey appears to be extrapolating from that history into continuing prominence for this settlement under British rule in an imagined future. It is possible that the key role of Æthelflæd, Lady of the Mercians, at Stafford in the early C10th prompted his evocation of a 'lioness' associated with that locality (Tatlock 1950, 27-8), as the culmination of his animadversions on women and their power over men earlier in the same prophecy. Although Gunnlaugr's rendering apparently reduces the lioness to a simple 'bride' (i.e. 'woman'), he may be continuing the theme of destructive female pride in his own way: see Note to ll. 7-8 below. *Merl* lacks the reference to fornication; also the duel is 'nativised' into a *hólmganga*, a ritualised single combat classically fought on an island. — [7-8] *bjarthaddaða brúði* 'a bright-haired woman': De Vries (1964-7, II, 75 n. 181) compares *Gríp* 33/6; the adj. is attested only in these two poems. In *Gríp* the 'bright-haired maiden' is none other than Brynhildr, who proves to be the death of Sigurðr. — [10] *víðri Vaðbatúli* 'broad Vadum batuli': See Note to [All] above for the probable etymology of this p. n. The element 'batúli' is merely a variant spelling for *bacúlí* 'of a stave/staff'. The adj. *víðr* is probably an ornamental epithet, with precedents in Ótt *Hfl* 10/4¹ and Ótt *Knútdr* 5/5¹, where the adj. describing a town is *breiðr* 'broad' in both cases.

78. 'Sjá þessi rǫk   þrennar aldir,
    — þó es lýða ráð   ljótt fyr dróttni —
    unz landrekar   Lundúnum í
    grafnir ór grundu   gumnum vitrask.

'Þrennar aldir sjá rǫk þessi — þó es ráð lýða ljótt fyr dróttni —, unz landrekar grafnir ór grundu í Lundúnum vitrask gumnum.

'Three ages witness these wonders — yet the conduct of men is odious before the Lord —, until kings disinterred from the ground in London are revealed to men.

Ms.: **Hb**(52v) (*Bret*).

Editions: *Skj*: Gunnlaugr Leifsson, *Merlínússpá II* 78: AII, 33, BII, 39-40, *Skald* II, 25; *Bret* 1848-9, II, 66 (*Bret* st. 146); *Hb* 1892-6, 281-2; *Merl* 2012, 190.

Notes: [All]: Cf. *DGB* 115 (Reeve and Wright 2007, 151.126-7; cf. Wright 1988, 106, prophecy 24): *Omnia haec tria saecula uidebunt donec sepulti reges in urbe Lundoniarum propalabuntur* 'Three generations will witness all this until the kings buried in the city of London are revealed' (Reeve and Wright 2007, 150). With this motif of exhumation, Geoffrey partially reprises the Cadwallader story told in *DGB* XI (Reeve and Wright 2007, 278-9). — [5-8]: The syntax and meaning of these lines could be interpreted in at least two different ways. Previous eds have inserted explanatory phrases to clarify their understanding of the lines. *Bret* 1848-9 inserts an explanatory phrase: *indtil Konger i London begravne stige op af Jorden og aabenbares* 'until kings buried in London rise up from the earth and show themselves'. Similarly *Skj* B (*indtil konger begravede i London viser sig for folk, (stegne) op af jorden* 'until kings buried in London reveal themselves to men, (risen) up from the earth') and *Merl* 2012. But the phrases 'rise up', 'risen up' have no counterpart in Gunnlaugr and are not strictly necessary for sense. The present edn adopts the view that *grafnir ór grundu* 'disinterred from the ground' (l. 7) is a phrase qualifying *landrekar* 'kings' (l. 5) and further specified by the adverbial phrase *í Lundúnum* 'in London' (l. 6), while the statement *vitrask gumnum* 'are revealed to men' (l. 8) translates Geoffrey's Lat. *propalabuntur* 'are revealed'. Another possible interpretation rearranges the syntax of ll. 5-8 as *unz landrekar grafnir í Lundúnum vitrask gumnum ór grundu* 'until kings buried in London reveal themselves to men from the ground'. This has the disadvantage of requiring the phrase *grafnir ór grundu* to be split, and it is further from the sense of Geoffrey's Latin text.

79. 'Kømr árgalli   enn inn mikli
    ok meinliga   manndauðr of her;
    eyðask borgir   við bragna tjón.
    Es *nauðr* mikil   nýtra manna;
    flýr margr á brott maðr ór landi.

'Enn kømr inn mikli árgalli ok manndauðr meinliga of her; borgir eyðask við tjón bragna. Es mikil *nauðr* nýtra manna; margr maðr flýr á brott ór landi.

'Once more there will come a great failure of the harvest and mortality [with it], hurtfully over the people; cities will be devastated with the loss of men. There will be great adversity for valiant men; many a man will flee away from the land.

Ms.: **Hb**(52v) (*Bret*).

Reading: [7] *nauðr*: auðn Hb.

Editions: *Skj*: Gunnlaugr Leifsson, *Merlínússpá II* 79: AII, 33, BII, 40, *Skald* II, 25; *Bret* 1848-9, II, 66-7 (*Bret* st. 147); *Hb* 1892-6, 282; *Merl* 2012, 190-1.

Notes: [All]: Cf. *DGB* 115 (Reeve and Wright 2007, 151.127-8; cf. Wright 1988, 106, prophecy 25): *Redibit iterum fames, redibit mortalitas; et desolationem urbium dolebunt ciues* 'Hunger will return, plague will return, and the natives will lament the desolation of their cities' (cf. Reeve and Wright 2007, 150). — [7] n*au*ðr 'adversity': Emended, so as to supply alliteration, from ms. *auðn* (not refreshed) to *nauð* by Scheving (reported in and followed by *Bret* 1848-9, from which it is subsequently accepted by *Skj* B and *Skald*); *nauð*, however, is a later form for *nauðr* (*LP*: *nauðr*), which is adopted in this edn. *Merl* 2012 retains the reading of the ms., *auðn* 'wilderness, desert, devastation', which fits well for sense within a context of failures of harvest (cf. the cognate *eyddar* 'devastated' in *I* 80/9), but *auðn* is used elsewhere in relation to land, not people, and does not provide an alliterating line, as alliteration cannot fall on *mikil* in l. 7. — [8] *nýtra manna* 'for valiant men': Lit. 'of valiant men'; subjective gen., following *Skj* B: *nød blandt dygtige mænd* 'adversity among valiant men'. Interpreted in *Bret* 1848-9 as *Nödklager af Borgerne* 'cries of calamity from the citizens'.

80. 'Kømr kaupskapar   kappgóðr þinig
    villigalti   virðum samna,
    þeims af fróni   flýðu áðan.
    Lætr hann byggva þá brezkar jarðir,
    borgir eyddar,   ból góligust.

'Kappgóðr villigalti kaupskapar kømr þinig samna virðum, þeims flýðu áðan af fróni. Hann lætr þá byggva brezkar jarðir, eyddar borgir, góligust ból.

'The wild boar of commerce, exceedingly good, will come there to gather men who had previously fled from the land. He causes them to settle the British lands, the devastated cities, the choicest estates.

Ms.: **Hb**(52v) (*Bret*).

Reading: [6] flýðu: flýði Hb.

Editions: *Skj*: Gunnlaugr Leifsson, *Merlínússpá II* 80: AII, 33, BII, 40, *Skald* II, 25, *NN* §3258D; *Bret* 1848-9, II, 67 (*Bret* st. 148); *Hb* 1892-6, 282; *Merl* 2012, 191-2.

Notes: [All]: Cf. *DGB* 115 (Reeve and Wright 2007, 151.128-9; cf. Wright 1988, 106, prophecy 26): *Superueniet aper commercii, qui dispersos greges ad amissam pascuam reuocabit* 'The boar of commerce will arrive and call the scattered flocks back to their lost pasture' (Reeve and Wright 2007, 150). This is a third salvific boar-king in Geoffrey's series. Gunnlaugr rationalises the allegory by replacing 'flocks' with 'men' and expanding 'pasture' to include the concept of 'cities'. — [2] *kappgóðr* 'exceedingly good': A *hap. leg.*, which, in the absence of any counterpart in the Latin, resists definitive interpretation. Difficulty is caused by the variety in uses of *kapp-* in the other compounds where this is the initial element, along with the fact that some of them are also *hap. leg.* The interpretation tentatively adopted in this edn is due to *Bret* 1848-9 and *Skj* B, which take *kapp-* as an intensifier, thus 'very good', but varies on it by introducing the concept of 'exceeding' or 'outdoing' inherent in the sense of *kapp* 'contest, ardour' (see *CVC*, Fritzner, *ONP*: *kapp*). Against this, *NN* §3258D, followed by *Merl* 2012, proposes the interpretation 'able in competition'. Gunnlaugr goes beyond *DGB* so as to introduce the word *kapp*, either as simplex or compounded, in three other instances: *I* 41/2 *hvítdreki kapps* 'the white serpent of belligerence', *I* 92/1 *mǫnnum kapps* 'to men of bravery' and *II* 9/3-4 *í kappsauðga borg* 'in the exceedingly prosperous city'. They demonstrate that he was capable of using the word in both the key meanings in contention here. Kock is only able to discount the latter meaning by basing himself on a highly select subset of *kapp-* compounds that exhibit the former meaning; *Merl* 2012 does not elaborate on this aspect. Also, in context the characterisation of the boar-king as 'able in competition' would seem to have little relevance, whereas his being described as 'exceedingly good' can be taken as borne out by the restoration of his people to their former fortunes; in effect, he will be a 'good king' memorable as outdoing other kings in terms of 'goodness', a decided contrast to the bad leadership described in the preceding stanzas and also a polar opposite of a subsequent ruler, the *asni illingar* 'ass of evil' (*I* 87/1-2). The specific aspects of his goodness are further spelt out in the following stanzas. — [4] *samna* 'to gather': In *Skj* B emended to *samnar* 'gathers' (followed by *Skald*), but the inf. can be understood as following on loosely from *kømr* 'comes' (cf. *Bret* 1848-9 and, apparently independently, *Merl* 2012). — [6] *flýðu* 'fled': Emended from ms. *flýði* in *Skj* B to give a verb in the 3rd pers. pl. pret. indic., followed by subsequent eds. *Bret* 1848-9 retains the ms. reading without comment. — [10] *góligust ból* 'the choicest estates': Cf. Anon (*Mberf*) 2/2^{II} *ból, þats ek veit gólast* 'the farm, which I find the best'.

81. 'Mun hans brjóst vesa   brǫgnum fœzla,
    þeims fátt hafa   fjár með hǫndum.
    Ok in tállausa   tunga hilmis
    sløkkvir þorsta   þjóðans liði.

'Brjóst hans mun vesa fœzla brǫgnum, þeims hafa fátt fjár með hǫndum. Ok in tállausa tunga hilmis sløkkvir þorsta liði þjóðans.

'His breast will be sustenance for men who have little property at their disposal. And the ruler's tongue, free of deception, will slake thirst for the following of the lord.

Ms.: **Hb**(52v) (*Bret*).

Reading: [7] þorsta: 'þiosta' Hb.

Editions: *Skj*: Gunnlaugr Leifsson, *Merlínússpá II* 81: AII, 33, BII, 40, *Skald* II, 25; *Bret* 1848-9, II, 67 (*Bret* st. 149); *Hb* 1892-6, 282; *Merl* 2012, 192.

Notes: [All]: Cf. *DGB* 115 (Reeve and Wright 2007, 151.130; cf. Wright 1988, 106, prophecy 26): *Pectus eius cibus erit egentibus, et lingua eius sedabit sicientes* 'His breast shall be food for the needy and his tongue drink for the thirsty' (Reeve and Wright 2007, 150). Geoffrey continues his prophecies regarding the 'boar of commerce'. Gunnlaugr adds the idea of the ruler's tongue being free from deceit; for other additions relating to deceit and treachery cf. *I* 48 Note to [All] and *II* 25 Note to [All]. — [7] þorsta 'thirst': Emended in *Bret* 1848-9 (followed by subsequent eds) from ms. 'þiosta' (not refreshed), with point of deletion under the <i>.

82. 'Falla ór orða   almærri vǫk
    dynjandi ár   dróttar stýris.
    Þær munu dǫggva   dýrar jarðir
    geðs í glæstum   gollorheimi
    ok þurrar kverkr   þjóðar margrar.

'Dynjandi ár falla ór almærri vǫk orða stýris dróttar. Þær munu dǫggva dýrar jarðir geðs í glæstum gollorheimi ok þurrar kverkr margrar þjóðar.

'Resounding rivers will fall from the much-famed gap of words [MOUTH] of the ruler of the entourage [PRINCE]. They will spread dew on the beloved lands of the mind [HEARTS] in the splendid home of the pericardium [BREAST] and on the dry throats of many a people.

Ms.: **Hb**(52v) (*Bret*).

Editions: *Skj*: Gunnlaugr Leifsson, *Merlínússpá II* 82: AII, 33, BII, 40, *Skald* II, 25; *Bret* 1848-9, II, 67-8 (*Bret* st. 150); *Hb* 1892-6, 282; *Merl* 2012, 193.

Notes: [All]: Cf. *DGB* 115 (Reeve and Wright 2007, 151.130-1; cf. Wright 1988, 106, prophecy 26): *Ex ore ipsius procedent flumina, quae arentes hominum fauces rigabunt* 'Out of his mouth will issue rivers to moisten the parched throats of men' (Reeve and Wright 2007, 150). Geoffrey continues his prophecies regarding the 'boar of commerce'. The source material for sts 81 and 82 is somewhat amplified in *Merl*, evidently so as to explicate the allegory. — [6-7] *dýrar jarðir geðs* 'the beloved lands of the mind [HEARTS]': In *Bret* 1848-9 and *Skj* B, the latter followed by *Merl* 2012, *geðs* 'of the mind' is grouped with *gollorheimi* 'in the home of the pericardium' (*Skj* B has *sjælens hjærteverden* 'heart-world of the soul'), but there it is redundant, whereas it is positively required as a determinant for *jarðir* 'lands', to generate a kenning for a part of the body, as is evident from the parallelism with *kverkr* 'throats' in l. 9. Cf. *II* 35/6, where *gollorhallir* 'halls of the pericardium', a parallel formation, signifies 'breasts'. — [8] *gollor-* 'pericardium': The membrane enclosing the heart (*OED: pericardium*). Thus the breast can be termed the 'home of the pericardium'. Attestations of the word are restricted to literary usage. In poetry the word occurs only here and in *Þul Hugar ok hjarta*[III]. The two prose attestations cited by *ONP: gollurr* are from *SnE* mss, and occur in discussions of *heiti* for 'heart'; in one of these passages *gollorr* is itself understood as such a *heiti* (cf. *CVC: gollurr*; Fritzner, *LP*, *AEW: gollorr*; also Guðrún Nordal 2001, 255-6).

83. 'Upp renn síðan   — sék þat fyrir —
    traust í turni   tré Lundúna;
    þrír eru kvistir   þeim lundi á,
    en hann laufi þekr   land með hringum.

'Traust tré renn upp síðan í turni Lundúna; sék þat fyrir. Þrír kvistir eru á þeim lundi, en hann þekr laufi land með hringum.

'A sturdy tree will shoot up then in the tower of London: I foresee that. There are three branches on that tree and with its foliage it completely shelters the land.

Ms.: **Hb**(52v) (*Bret*).

Editions: *Skj*: Gunnlaugr Leifsson, *Merlínússpá II* 83: AII, 33, BII, 41; *Skald* II, 25-6; *Bret* 1848-9, II, 68 (*Bret* st. 151); *Hb* 1892-6, 282; *Merl* 2012, 193-4.

Notes: [All]: Cf. *DGB* 115 (Reeve and Wright 2007, 151.131-3; cf. Wright 1988, 106, prophecy 27): *Exin super turrim Lundoniarum procreabitur arbor, quae tribus solummodo ramis contenta superficiem tocius insulae latitudine foliorum obumbrabit* 'Then a tree will sprout above the tower of London, whose three branches in themselves will shade the surface of the entire island with the breadth of their foliage' (cf. Reeve and Wright 2007, 150). — [8] *með hringum* 'completely': A common idiom (*CVC: hringr*). Comparable is *II* 13/8.

84. 'Kømr þar af lœgi   landnyrðingr hvass;
    lýstr hann illum byl   ei*nn* af stofni.
    Þar munu kvistir,   es þruma eptir,
    þess rúm taka;   þat sék gǫrla.

'Hvass landnyrðingr kømr þar af lœgi; hann lýstr ei*nn* af stofni illum byl. Kvistir, es þruma eptir, munu taka rúm þess þar; sék þat gǫrla.

'A sharp northeast wind will come there from the sea; it will knock one [branch] from the trunk with a malevolent gust. The branches that remain afterwards will take up its space there; I see that clearly.

Ms.: **Hb**(52v) (*Bret*).

Reading: [4] ei*nn*: eik Hb.

Editions: *Skj*: Gunnlaugr Leifsson, *Merlínússpá II* 84: AII, 34, BII, 41; *Skald* II, 26; *Bret* 1848-9, II, 68 (*Bret* st. 152); *Hb* 1892-6, 282; *Merl* 2012, 194-5.

Notes: [All]: Cf. *DGB* 115 (Reeve and Wright 2007, 151.134-5; cf. Wright 1988, 106-7, prophecies 27 and 28): *Huic aduersarius Boreas superueniet atque iniquo flatu suo tercium illi ramum eripiet. Duo uero residui locum extirpati occupabunt* 'The North wind will come as its enemy and with its cruel blast will rip off the third branch. The remaining two will take the place of the one that has been removed' (cf. Reeve and Wright 2007, 150). Here Geoffrey re-uses his earlier prophecy of Viking raids in England, not altogether incongruously since sporadic raiding from Scandinavia continued through his life-time. Raids carried out in England and Scotland by Eysteinn Haraldsson of Norway in the 1150s are alluded to in ESk *Run*[II] and ESk *Eystdr*[II]; for historical commentary see A. B. Taylor (1965) and references there. — [2] *hvass landnyrðingr* 'a sharp northeast wind': Exactly the same line occurs at *Merl* I 44/3. See Note there. — [4] *einn* 'one': Emended in *Skj* B, followed by *Skald*, from ms. *eik* 'oak' (not refreshed). This, despite speculations in *Merl* 2012 concerning the possible presence of three oaks, is necessary for sense. — [8]: A free addition on Gunnlaugr's part, emulating vernacular prophetic poems such as *Vsp* and *Gríp*. Cf. *I* 89/4 and 6.

85. 'Hylja þeir alla   ey með laufi,
    unz annarr þar   ǫðrum bœgir
    ok eyðir hans   ǫllu laufi;
    tekr hann þrjú rúm   þrekstórr hafa.

'Þeir hylja alla ey með laufi, unz annarr bœgir ǫðrum þar ok eyðir ǫllu laufi hans; þrekstórr tekr hann hafa þrjú rúm.

'They will cover the entire island with foliage until one [branch] subdues the other there and destroys all its foliage; very vigorous it will commence to have the three places.

Ms.: **Hb**(52v) (*Bret*).

Editions: *Skj*: Gunnlaugr Leifsson, *Merlínússpá II* 85: AII, 34, BII, 41; *Skald* II, 26; *Bret* 1848-9, II, 68-9 (*Bret* st. 153); *Hb* 1892-6, 282; *Merl* 2012, 195.

Notes: [All]: Cf. *DGB* 115 (Reeve and Wright 2007, 151.135-7; cf. Wright 1988, 107, prophecy 28): *donec alter alterum foliorum multitudine adnichilabit. Deinde uero locum duorum optinebit ipse* 'until one chokes the other with its abundant foliage. Then it will occupy the place of the first two' (cf. Reeve and Wright 2007, 150). — [5] *ok eyðir* 'and destroys': Normalised in *Skald* from ms. *ok hann eyðir* 'and he destroys' for metrical reasons. *Hann* is retained by *Bret* 1848-9, *Skj* B and *Merl* 2012.

86. 'Ok hann síðan þekr   þykku laufi
    einn of alla   eybarms fjǫru.
    Megut þá fljúga   foglar í landi,
    þvíat hann œgir þeim,   en hann enn til sín
    laðar fogla fljótt   ferð útlendra.

'Ok síðan þekr hann einn þykku laufi of alla fjǫru eybarms. Foglar megut þá fljúga í landi, þvíat hann œgir þeim, en hann laðar enn ferð útlendra fogla fljótt til sín.

'And then it alone will cover with its dense foliage the entire foreshore of the island's fringe. The birds within the land will then be unable to fly, because he will frighten them, but yet he will quickly entice a host of foreign birds to himself.

Ms.: **Hb**(52v) (*Bret*).

Editions: *Skj*: Gunnlaugr Leifsson, *Merlínússpá II* 86: AII, 34, BII, 41; *Skald* II, 26; *Bret* 1848-9, II, 69 (*Bret* st. 154); *Hb* 1892-6, 282; *Merl* 2012, 195-6.

Notes: [All]: Cf. *DGB* 115 (Reeve and Wright 2007, 151.137-9; cf. Wright 1988, 107, prophecy 28): *et uolucres exterarum regionum sustentabit. Patriis uolatilibus nociuus habebitur; nam timore umbrae eius liberos uolatus amittent* 'and feed birds from foreign lands. It will prove harmful to native birds; for they will not be able to fly freely in fear of its shadow' (Reeve and Wright 2007, 150). — [4] *eybarms* 'of the island's fringe': The ms. reading (not refreshed) has been taken as *eykarms* by earlier eds, but the letter read as k could be either <b> or <k>. Cf. *barmi eylands* 'fringe of the island' in *I* 40/6-7. The cpd *eybarmr* 'the island-edge' appears in Angantýr Lv 3/4 (*Heiðr* 32). *Bret* 1848-9 adopts *eybarms* as an emendation. This is also contemplated by Finnur Jónsson (*LP*: *eybarmr*) but not adopted in *Skj* B, where *eykarmr* is retained and translated as *hele strandbreddens kyst* 'the whole shore of the beach' (cf. *LP*: *eykarmr*). But such a sense is inappropriate to the context and the supposed underlying kenning pattern is weakly attested (*Meissner* 92; contrast *LP*: *eylúðr*). *Skald* and *Merl* 2012 retain *eykarms* without comment.

87. 'Þá mun illingar   asni ríkja;
      sás fljótr taka   fé gullsmiða.
      Es lofða vinr   latr at hefna
      gylðis barna   gramr ránsemi.

'Þá mun asni illingar ríkja; sás fljótr taka fé gullsmiða. Gramr vinr lofða es latr at hefna ránsemi barna gylðis.

'Then will the ass of evil reign; he will be quick to take the property of goldsmiths. The fierce friend of men [RULER] will be slow to avenge the rapacity of the children of the wolf [WOLVES].

Ms.: **Hb**(52v) (*Bret*).

Editions: *Skj*: Gunnlaugr Leifsson, *Merlínússpá II* 87: AII, 34, BII, 41, *Skald* II, 26, *FF* §64; *Bret* 1848-9, II, 69 (*Bret* st. 155); *Hb* 1892-6, 282; *Merl* 2012, 196-7.

Notes: [All]: Cf. *DGB* 115 (Reeve and Wright 2007, 151.139-40; cf. Wright 1988, 107, prophecy 29): *Succedet asinus nequitiae, in fabricatores auri uelox sed in luporum rapacitatem piger* 'The ass of wickedness is his successor, swift against makers of gold but slow against the rapacity of wolves' (cf. Reeve and Wright 2007, 150). — [1] *illingar* 'of evil': Attestations of this word mostly occur in homiletic and other religious contexts (*CVC*: *illing*; *Fritzner*: *illing*, cf. *illingr*; *ONP*: *illing*). — [8] *gramr* 'fierce': Construed here as an adj. qualifying *vinr* 'friend': cf. *II* 35/5. But the word is difficult to place convincingly; Finnur Jónsson (*Skj* B) treats it as a predicative adj., though his Danish translation renders it as an adverbial phrase *med grusomhed* 'with ferocity'; similarly *Merl* 2012. Kock (*FF* §64) would construe it as *gramr* 'king', in apposition to *vinr* 'friend' – basing himself, as often, on West Germanic verse style. An alternative approach might be to emend to *grams* 'fierce' or even *grás* 'grey', gen. sg. agreeing with *gylðis* 'wolf'.

88. 'Ok á hans dǫgum   harðla brenna
      ófs rammligar   eikr ór skógum.
      Enn á lítlum   lindar kvistum
      vex ǫrliga   akarn í lundi.

'Ok á dǫgum hans brenna ófs rammligar eikr ór skógum harðla. Enn vex akarn ǫrliga á lítlum kvistum lindar í lundi.

'And in his days exceedingly mighty oaks from the forests will burn fiercely. Once more an acorn will grow rapidly on the slender twigs of the lime-tree in the grove.

Ms.: **Hb**(52v) (*Bret*).

Editions: *Skj*: Gunnlaugr Leifsson, *Merlínússpá II* 88: AII, 34, BII, 42, *Skald* II, 26; *Bret* 1848-9, II, 69-70 (*Bret* st. 156); *Hb* 1892-6, 282; *Merl* 2012, 197.

Notes: [All]: Cf. *DGB* 116 (Reeve and Wright 2007, 151.140-1; cf. Wright 1988, 107, prophecy 30): *In diebus illis ardebunt quercus per nemora et in ramis tiliarum nascentur glandes* 'In those days oak trees will burn in the forests and acorns will grow on the branches of lindens' (cf. Reeve and Wright 2007, 150). — [8] *enn* 'once more': This edn follows the interpretation of *Skald* as the adv. *enn* 'once more', as the word carries full stress in a Type A-line, and the conj. *en* 'but' (so *Skj* B) cannot do that. Moreover, there is no contrast in sense between the two sentences.

89. 'Ok Ránar vegr renn of ósa
 Sábrínus sjau; sék þat fyrir.
 En Óskarǫ́ — þat es undr mikit —
 mun mánuðr sjau mǫ́ttug vella.
 Gervisk fiskum fjǫrtjón at því,
 e*n* ór sjǫlfum þeim snákar verða.

'Ok vegr Ránar renn of sjau ósa Sábrínus; sék þat fyrir. En Óskarǫ́ mun vella mǫ́ttug sjau mánuðr; þat es mikit undr. Fjǫrtjón gervisk fiskum at því, e*n* snákar verða ór sjǫlfum þeim.

'And the path of Rán <sea-goddess> [SEA] will run through seven mouths of the Severn; I foresee that. And the river Usk will boil powerfully for seven months; that is a great marvel. Loss of life for the fish will come of that, and snakes will be engendered out of them.

Ms.: **Hb**(52v) (*Bret*).

Readings: [2] *ósa*: 'asa' Hb [11] e*n*: er Hb.

Editions: *Skj*: Gunnlaugr Leifsson, *Merlínússpá II* 89: AII, 35, BII, 42, *Skald* II, 26, *NN* §3258E; *Bret* 1848-9, II, 70 (*Bret* st. 157); *Hb* 1892-6, 282; *Merl* 2012, 197-8.

Notes: [All]: Cf. *DGB* 116 (Reeve and Wright 2007, 151.141-3; cf. Wright 1988, 107, prophecy 30): *Sabrinum mare per septem hostia discurret, et fluuius Oscae per septem menses feruebit. Pisces illius calore morientur, et ex eis procreabuntur serpentes* 'The Severn sea will flow out through seven channels and the river Usk will boil for seven months. The heat will kill its fish and from them snakes will be procreated' (cf. Reeve and Wright 2007, 150). The Bristol Channel was formerly known as the Severn Sea (cf. Welsh *Mǫ́r Hafren*). — [1] *vegr Ránar* 'the path of Rán <sea-goddess> [SEA]': Possibly Gunnlaugr misunderstands Lat. *mare* as referring to the open sea rather than to the Severn estuary. — [2] *ósa* 'mouths': Emended in *Bret* 1848-9, followed by subsequent eds, from ms. 'asa' (not refreshed). — [3] *Sábrínus* 'the Severn': Nom. sg. form used as gen. — [5] *Óskarǫ́* 'the river Usk': Rises in Brecon, Wales and flows into the sea at

Newport, some fifty kilometres from the mouth of the Severn. — [11] *en* 'and': Emended from ms. *er* 'which' (not refreshed) in *NN* §3258E, *Skald* (printed as *enn*); not so *Bret* 1848-9, *Skj* B or *Merl* 2012, and the reading could perhaps stand, giving the sense 'when' or 'because', but cf. *men* 'but' in the translation in *Skj* B and *doch* 'but, however' in *Merl* 2012. For discussion of probable errors in Hb see Introduction.

90. 'Munu Bádónis borgar verða
 — líðr mart yfir — laugar kaldar.
 Ok hennar vǫtn heilnæm firum
 gera þá dauða drjúgt mannkyni.

'Laugar borgar Bádónis munu verða kaldar; mart líðr yfir. Ok vǫtn hennar, heilnæm firum, gera þá dauða drjúgt mannkyni.

'The baths of the city of Bath will become cold: many a thing will come to pass. And her waters, beneficial to men, will then cause deaths relentlessly for mankind.

Ms.: **Hb**(52v) (*Bret*).

Editions: *Skj*: Gunnlaugr Leifsson, *Merlínússpá II* 90: AII, 34, BII, 42, *Skald* II, 26-7; *Bret* 1848-9, II, 70 (*Bret* st. 158); *Hb* 1892-6, 282; *Merl* 2012, 198-9.

Notes: [All]:]: Cf. *DGB* 116 (Reeve and Wright 2007, 151.143-4; cf. Wright 1988, 107, prophecy 30): *Frigebunt Badonis balnea, et salubres aquae eorum mortem generabunt* 'The springs of Bath will run cold and their healing waters will bring death' (Reeve and Wright 2007, 150). — [1] *Bádónis* 'of Bath': A gen. of definition, retaining the Latin inflection: cf. *II* 63/2. — [6] *heilnæm* 'beneficial': Attestations of this adj., along with its derivatives of identical meaning, *heilnæmiligr* and *heilnæmligr*, are almost entirely confined to late texts containing learned material (*ONP*: *heilnæmr, heilnæmiligr, heilnæmligr*).

91. 'Verðr tuttugu tjón þúsunda
 ljóna ferðar Lundúnum í.
 Þeir munu drengir drepnir allir;
 gerir karla tjón Tems at blóði.

'Tjón tuttugu þúsunda ferðar ljóna verðr í Lundúnum. Þeir drengir munu allir drepnir; tjón karla gerir Tems at blóði.

'The loss of twenty thousand of the host of men will come to pass in London. Those men will all be slain; the loss of men will turn the Thames to blood.

Ms.: **Hb**(52v) (*Bret*).

Editions: *Skj*: Gunnlaugr Leifsson, *Merlínússpá II* 91: AII, 35, BII, 42, *Skald* II, 27, *NN* §3144; *Bret* 1848-9, II, 70-1 (*Bret* st. 159); *Hb* 1892-6, 282; *Merl* 2012, 199.

Notes: [All]: The stanza divisions for *I* 91, 92, and 93, as printed in this edn, following *Bret* 1848-9 and *Skj* B, are uncertain. Hb has a capital <V> with red colouring at *I* 91/1, a small <m> with no colouring at *I* 92/1, a capital <E> with red at *I* 91/5 and a small <h> without colouring at *I* 93/1. It might be that Gunnlaugr had only two stanzas here, each of 12 lines, but *I* 92/5-8 would be awkward to sever from the previous *helmingr* and similar stanza division errors have been detected elsewhere in the ms. (see Notes to *I* 34/9-10 and *I* 35/7-10). Cf. *DGB* 116 (Reeve and Wright 2007, 151.144-5; cf. Wright 1988, 107, prophecy 30): *Lundonia necem uiginti miliorum lugebit, et Tamensis in sanguinem mutabitur* 'London will grieve for the demise of twenty thousand, and the Thames will turn to blood' (Reeve and Wright 2007, 150). — [7] *tjón karla* 'the loss of men': Kock (*NN* §3144; *Skald*) would reverse the order of these two nouns in the line so as to create a Type C-line with alliteration in the metrical position 2.

92. 'Munu kapps mǫnnum   kvánfǫng boðin:
     eru ekkjur þar   orðnar margar.
     En á kǫldum   kall þeira næst
     menn Mundíu   montum heyra.'

'Kvánfǫng munu boðin mǫnnum kapps: margar eru orðnar ekkjur þar. En menn heyra kall þeira næst á kǫldum montum Mundíu.'

'Marriages will be offered to men of bravery: many [women] have become widows there. But men will hear their cry afterwards on the cold mountains of the Alps.'

Ms.: **Hb**(52v) (*Bret*).

Editions: *Skj*: Gunnlaugr Leifsson, *Merlínússpá II* 92: AII, 35, BII, 42; *Skald* II, 27; *Bret* 1848-9, II, 71 (*Bret* st. 160); *Hb* 1892-6, 282; *Merl* 2012, 200-1.

Notes: [All]: Cf. *DGB* 116 (Reeve and Wright 2007, 151.145-6; cf. Wright 1988, 107, prophecy 30): *Cucullati ad nuptias prouocabuntur, et clamor eorum in montibus Alpium audietur* 'The wearers of cowls will be challenged to marry, and their complaint will be heard in the mountains of the Alps' (Reeve and Wright 2007, 150). The comment about widows appears to be Gunnlaugr's innovation. — [1] *mǫnnum kapps* 'to men of bravery': That is to say, 'to warriors'. *Bret* 1848-9, *Skj* and *Skald* retain this ms. reading, but a word equivalent in sense to *kápumǫnnum 'cowled men' (for which see *Fritzner*, *ONP*: *kápumaðr*) would be expected, rendering *cucullati* 'those with cowls', i.e. 'monks' (*Hb* 1892-6, cxii; cf. *Skj* B); cf. the Anglo-Norman decasyllabic rendering: *Mungiu orra le cri des cuvelez* 'Montgieu will hear the cries of the cowled ones' (Blacker 2005, 43). *Bret* 1848-9 translates accordingly without altering the text: *de kuttoklædte Mænd* 'the cowl-clad men', i.e. 'monks', followed by *Skj* B. The word *kápumǫnnum* is introduced into the text by emendation in *Merl* 2012, but this is precluded by metrical considerations, since it would yield a hypermetrical *málaháttr* line and the metre of *Merl I* is otherwise regular. Alternatively, Gunnlaugr might be imagined as having first written lines that included the word *kápumǫnnum* or a synonym thereof in a different metrical context but then, whether as a result of his own self-censorship or advice from his mentors, altering it to the conveniently similar *kapps mǫnnum* in order to tone down the notion of forced marriages of monks into a scenario of warriors being offered marriage. The explanation that these marriages arise because the number of widows is so large could be seen as part of this revision. It is unclear whether he intends the *kall* 'cry' to be attributed to men or widows; the punctuation adopted in this edn preserves the logic of *DGB*, where it is the men. — [7] *á kǫldum montum Mundíu* 'on the cold mountains of the Alps': Here *DGB* has *montibus Alpium* 'on the mountains of the Alps'. The name Mundía used by Gunnlaugr (and also recorded in Sigv Lv 18/1[1]; see Note there) can be traced back to **Montgiu* = French *Mont Joux* < Lat. *Mons Jovis*, lit. 'mountain of Jove', 'Great S. Bernard'; the Latin name derives from the presence of a Roman temple to Jupiter Poeninus at the site (Meissner 1903, 193-4, cf. *LP: Mundio*). It would have been known from pilgrimage itineraries (Meissner 1903, 193-4 and references there given) but it was early generalised, as in the present stanza, so as to denote the Alps as a whole (Meissner 1903, 196).

93. Hér munk létta   ljóð at semja
    ok spásǫgu   spillis bauga.
    Þó eru fleiri orð   ins fróða manns;
    hefk sumt af þeim   samit í kvæði.

Hér munk létta at semja ljóð ok spásǫgu spillis bauga. Þó eru fleiri orð ins fróða manns; hefk samit sumt af þeim í kvæði.

Here I will leave off composing the song and the prophetic tale of the destroyer of rings [GENEROUS MAN = Merlin]. Yet there are more words of the wise man; I have arranged some of them in a poem.

Ms.: **Hb**(52v) (*Bret*).

Editions: *Skj*: Gunnlaugr Leifsson, *Merlínússpá II* 93: AII, 35, BII, 43, *Skald* II, 27; *Bret* 1848-9, II, 71 (*Bret* st. 161); *Hb* 1892-6, 282; *Merl* 2012, 201-2.

Note: [All]: At this point Gunnlaugr suspends his rendering of the *Prophecies*. For the significance of this and the following stanza, see the Introduction.

94. Þau eru ǫnnur ljóð   upp frá þessum;
      †alvisk† eigi   auðs be*r*draugar
      — biðk þjóðir þess —   við þenna brag,
      þó at ek mynt hafa   mál at hætti,
      þeims spár fyrir   spjǫllum rakði
      malmþings hvǫtuðr,   í mǫrgum stað.

Þau eru ǫnnur ljóð upp frá þessum; be*r*draugar auðs †alvisk† eigi við þenna brag — biðk þjóðir þess —, þó at ek hafa mynt mál í mǫrgum stað at hætti, þeims hvǫtuðr malmþings rakði fyrir spár spjǫllum.

There are other songs following on from these; may bearing logs of wealth [MEN] not … with this poem — this I ask of people —, although I have formed my sayings in many a place after the style in which the whetter of the metal-meeting [BATTLE > WARRIOR = Merlin] recited prophecies in speeches.

Mss.: **Hb**(52v) (*Bret*).

Reading: [4] be*r*-: ben Hb.

Editions: Skj: Gunnlaugr Leifsson, *Merlínússpá II* 94: AII, 35, BII, 43, *Skald* II, 27, *NN* §3258F; *Bret* 1848-9, II, 71-2 (*Bret* st. 162); *Hb* 1892-6, 282-3; *Merl* 2012, 202-3.

Notes: [1-2]: Here Gunnlaugr is referring in anticipation to *Merl II* (*Bret* 1848-9, II, 71 n. 8; see Introduction). — [3] †*alvisk*† '…': Possibly 'be vexed' (?). This ms. reading (not refreshed) is obscure, though the general sense is apparent from the context. The reading is tentatively retained in *Bret* 1848-9 with the gloss *laste* 'blame' and Scheving's proposed emendation to *ylfisk* 'be worried', i.e. 'harassed' (*CVC: ylfa*), is rejected. In *Skj* B *abbisk* 'become incensed at, vexed with' is conjectured (cf. *CVC, LP, ONP: abbask; Fritzner: abbast*), and followed by *Merl* 2012, and that remains the most plausible solution. Kock's suggestion *ǫlvisk* 'grow drunk' (*NN* §3258F) is ruled out by the context. — [4] *be*r-- 'bearing': Emended in *Skj* B, followed by *Skald* and *Merl* 2012, from ms. *ben* (refreshed). A determinant *ben* 'wound' would be difficult to explain in combination with *auðs* 'wealth' (gen.). For a similar confusion of *ber-*, *ben-*, cf. *LP: berdraugr* and Glúmr Lv 1/2[I] and Note there. — [4] *-draugar* 'logs': The interpretation of this *heiti* remains uncertain. *Meissner* 264-5 cites the interpretation as 'wood', therefore 'tree', in *Orms Eddu-brot* (*SnE* 1848-87, II, 497), but notes that *draugr* is not attested in this general sense and instead posits, following Neckel (1914), an agentive noun with the meaning 'one who carries or draws', from a verb **driuga* 'lead, carry out', as the base-word for this and similar kennings (but cf. *AEW: draugr* 2).

95. Viti bragnar þat,   þeirs bók lesa,
    hvé at spjǫllum sé   spámanns farit,
    ok kynni þat   kjaldýrs viðum,
    hverr fyrða sé   framsýnna hǫttr
    mǫl at rekja,   þaus menn vitut.

Bragnar, þeirs lesa bók, viti þat, hvé sé farit at spjǫllum spámanns, ok kynni þat viðum kjaldýrs, hverr hǫttr framsýnna fyrða sé at rekja mǫl, þaus menn vitut.

May men, who read the book, know that, how the prophet's sayings have been rendered, and teach that to trees of the keel-beast [SHIP > SEAFARERS], what the style of prophetic persons is in narrating matters that men do not know.

Ms.: **Hb**(52v) (*Bret*).

Readings: [5] kynni: kunni Hb   [6] kjal-: kal Hb   [8] hǫttr: hǫttu *corrected from* 'hǫttr' *during the process of refreshing* Hb.

Editions: *Skj*: Gunnlaugr Leifsson, *Merlínússpá II* 95: AII, 35, BII, 43, *Skald* II, 27; *Bret* 1848-9, II, 72 (*Bret* st. 163); *Hb* 1892-6, 283; *Merl* 2012, 203-4.

Notes: [5] *kynni* 'teach': Emended in *Skj* B, followed by *Skald* and *Merl* 2012, from ms. *kunni* (refreshed). — [6] *kjaldýrs* 'of the keel-beast [SHIP]': Obscure but probably a kenning for 'ship'. The determinant *kal-* is difficult to explain as it stands. A first element *kal-* in compounds occurs in *kalreip* 'rope on a ship that prevents the sail from flapping', but is unlikely to be relevant, since it depends on the (Modern Icelandic) idiom *segl kelur* 'the sail loses the wind', lit. 'the sail cools' (*LP*: *kalreip*), thus a 'rope [to prevent] "cooling"'. Instead ms. *kal-* appears to represent a miswriting for (or conceivably a reduced form of) *kjal-*, combinative form of *kjǫlr* 'keel'. Thus 'of the keel-beast [SHIP]'. The late kenning *meiðar kjaldúks* 'trees of the keel-cloth' (EGils *Guðkv* 20/3-4[IV]) may represent an imitation of Gunnlaugr. — [8] *hǫttr* 'style': The word, as used here, does not have its more usual meaning of metrical form or stanza-form (despite Sveinbjörn Rafnsson 1994, 737) but instead relates, as the context shows, to figurative language. Comparable in sense is *hætti* in *I* 94/10.

96. Lesi sálma, spjǫll   lesi spámanna,
    lesi bjartar þeir   bœkr ok roðla,
    ok finni þat,   at inn fróði halr
    hefr horskliga   hagat spásǫgu,
    sem fyr hǫnum   fyrðar helgir.

Lesi sálma, lesi spjǫll spámanna, lesi þeir bjartar bœkr ok roðla, ok finni þat, at inn fróði halr hefr hagat spásǫgu horskliga, sem helgir fyrðar fyr hǫnum.

Let them read the psalms, read the sayings of the prophets, let them read bright books and rolls, and discover that the wise man has devised his prophecy sagaciously, like holy men before him.

Ms.: **Hb**(52v) (*Bret*).

Editions: *Skj*: Gunnlaugr Leifsson, *Merlínússpá II* 96: AII, 35, BII, 43, *Skald* II, 27; *Bret* 1848-9, II, 72-3 (*Bret* st. 164); *Hb* 1892-6, 283; *Merl* 2012, 204-5.

Notes: [All]: For admonitions on the correct interpretation of prophecy similar to those advanced in this and the ensuing stanzas, cf. *Stjórn* (Unger 1862, 30): *Spamanna bøkr ok postolanna ritningar uerda mǫrgum sua myrkar ok uskilianligar. sem þær se meðr nǫckurum þokum edr skyflokum skyggdar ok huldar. enn þa uerda þær uel skiliandi monnum sua sem nytsamligh sannleiks skúúr. ef þær eru medr margfalldri ok uitrligri tracteran talaðr ok skynsamliga skyrðar* 'The books of the prophets and the writings of the apostles are to many so obscure and unintelligible as if they were shadowed and hidden by fogs or cloud-banks yet then they become fully intelligible to men just like beneficent showers of truth, if they are recounted with manifold and wise exegesis and explicated with discrimination'. — [1-2] *lesi spjǫll spámanna* 'read the sayings of the prophets': Previous eds have treated each line as a syntactic unit but a *spjǫll sálma* 'sayings of psalms' makes inferior sense and leaves the gen. *spámanna* hanging: *Skj* B, following *Bret* 1848-9, ignores the difficulty, translating *lese profeterne* 'read the prophets'; *Merl* 2012 supplies *die Reden* 'the speeches', translating the initial *vísuorð* as follows: *Sie mögen die Reden der Psalmen lesen, sie mögen [die Reden] der Propheten lesen* 'they can read the sayings of the psalms, they can read [the sayings] of the prophets'. — [4] *roðla* 'rolls': I.e. scrolls, or rolls of parchment. Apparently a *hap. leg.* in Old Norse (not cited in *Fritzner*; *ONP*: *roðull* notes it only as a 'poetic word') and distinct from *rǫðull* 'sun'. Finnur Jónsson correctly explains it as a loan-word, ultimately from Lat. *rotulus* 'small wheel' (*LH* II, 174; cf. *LP*: *roðull*), implicitly correcting *Bret* 1848-9, which reads *rǫðlar* 'suns', interpreted as 'holy men' (so also *CVC*: *röðull*). In post-classical Latin *rotulus* assumed the sense of 'a scroll of parchment' and was adopted into Old French (*role, rolle*, from the end of the C12th), Anglo-Norman and ME (*rouel, rolle*).

97. Virði engi   þat vitlausu,
    þótt hann hoddskǫtum   heiti gæfi
    viðar eða vatna   eða veðrs mikils
    eða alls konar   orma eða dýra.
    Táknar eðli   taldrar skepnu
    spjǫrráðanda   spjǫll eða kosti.

Virði engi þat vitlausu, þótt hann gæfi hoddskǫtum heiti viðar eða vatna eða veðrs mikils eða alls konar orma eða dýra. Eðli taldrar skepnu táknar spjǫll eða kosti spjǫrráðanda.

Let nobody think it nonsense if he gives treasure-chieftains [RULERS] the name of a wood or lakes or a great storm or all kinds of serpents or beasts. The nature of the creature described signifies the flaws or strengths of the wielders of the spear [WARRIORS].

Ms.: **Hb**(52v) (*Bret*).

Editions: *Skj*: Gunnlaugr Leifsson, *Merlínússpá II* 97: AII, 35-6, BII, 43-4, *Skald* II, 27; *Bret* 1848-9, II, 73 (*Bret* st. 165); *Hb* 1892-6, 283; *Merl* 2012, 205.

Notes: [All]: Here, following up on the preceding stanza, Gunnlaugr succinctly explains Geoffrey's system of allegory and foreshadows that some members of his audience might find it nonsensical. — [3]: The pron. *hann* is omitted in *Skj* B and *Skald* for metrical reasons. — [3] *hoddskǫtum* 'treasure-chieftains [RULERS]': Attested only here and in *II* 29/5. — [5] *viðar* 'of a wood': Conceivably the gen. pl. *viða* 'of woods/trees' should be read here, for better match with *vatna* and because *Merl* refers to a variety of trees, e.g. oaks and linden-trees; *Bret* 1848-9 has 'tree' and *Skj* B, followed by *Merl* 2012, has 'trees', but without emendation. Gunnlaugr may also be referring to woods or forests collectively, with e.g. *viðr inn danski* 'Danish wood' (*II* 15/6) in mind. — [5] *vatna* 'lakes': It is not clear which prophecies are referred to here, unless Gunnlaugr was thinking of the idealisation of the boar of commerce as a refreshing stream (*I* 82-3) or of the inundation of the mouths of the Severn (*I* 89/2-3). — [6]: Cf. the mentions of the *landnyrðingr* 'northeast wind' in *I* 44/3, *I* 84/2.

98. Segir Dáníel   drauma sína
marghátta ða   merkjum studda.
Kvezk drjúglig sjá   dýr á jǫrðu,
þaus tǫknuðu   tyggja ríki,
þaus á hauðri   hófusk síðan.

Dáníel segir marghátta ða drauma sína, studda merkjum. Kvezk sjá drjúglig dýr á jǫrðu, þaus tǫknuðu ríki tyggja, þaus hófusk síðan á hauðri.

Daniel tells his diverse dreams, supported by miracles. He says that he sees mighty animals on earth that signified the realms of kings that later came into being on earth.

Ms.: **Hb**(52v) (*Bret*).

Editions: *Skj*: Gunnlaugr Leifsson, *Merlínússpá II* 98: AII, 36, BII, 44, *Skald* II, 28; *Bret* 1848-9, II, 73 (*Bret* st. 166); *Hb* 1892-6, 283; *Merl* 2012, 206.

Notes: [All]: See Dan. VII.3-12 for evocation of animal figures in a political allegory (cf. Taylor 1911, 25-6). Greatly augmenting the biblical prophet's substantial reputation, beyond the information contained in Scripture, was the *Somniale* ascribed to Daniel. This pseudonymous early medieval compilation, consisting of a list of dream-symbols, underlay much dream symbolism in Icelandic literature, both medieval and more recent

(Turville-Petre 1972b, 45-6), and incorporated many mentions of animals seen in dreams. Text and translation of an Old English version are included in Liuzza (2011, 80-123). — [5] *drjúglig* 'mighty': cf. *I* 15/1. Finnur Jónsson (*LP*) understands as 'great' in both these cases, also citing Ótt *Hfl* 6/1¹ *drjúgligr ótti* 'great terror'. Citations in *ONP* show a range of other meanings in prose, including 'substantial, effective, solid'.

99. Rekr inn dýri   Dávíð konungr
    margfalda spǫ́,   ok mælir svá:
    'Fjǫll munu fagna   ok inn fríði skógr,
    en skœðar ár   skella lófum,
    ok dalir ymna   dróttni syngja.'

Inn dýri Dávíð konungr rekr margfalda spǫ́, ok mælir svá: 'Fjǫll ok inn fríði skógr munu fagna, en skœðar ár skella lófum, ok dalir syngja ymna dróttni.'

The noble King David utters manifold prophecy and speaks thus: 'The mountains and the fair forest will rejoice, and dangerous rivers clap their hands and the valleys sing hymns to the Lord.'

Ms.: **Hb**(52v) (*Bret*).

Editions: *Skj*: Gunnlaugr Leifsson, *Merlínússpá II* 99: AII, 36, BII, 44; *Skald* II, 28; *Bret* 1848-9, II, 73-4 (*Bret* st. 167); *Hb* 1892-6, 283; *Merl* 2012, 206-7.

Notes: [All]: Cf. Ps. XCVII.8: *Flumina plaudent manu simul montes laudabunt* 'The rivers shall clap their hands, the mountains shall rejoice together'. The mentions of the 'forest' and the 'valleys' seem to represent free variation; for the concept of forest as speaker, cf. *II* 15/5-8. The psalms of David were regarded as prophesying the coming of the Messiah, but this would not have been the totality of their perceived relevance to an Icelandic audience; *Sv* (*ÍF* 30, 152) represents King Sverrir himself as claiming that the prophecies of the *psálmaskáldit* 'the poet of the psalms', i.e. King David, have come true in Sverrir's own days. — [3] *margfalda* 'manifold': The adj. *margfaldr* is commonly used with sg. nouns (*ONP*: *margfaldr*) in a variety of senses that include 'manifold, plentiful, abundant, abounding' (cf. *Fritzner*: *margfaldr*); *Skj* B has *mangedobbelt* 'multiplied' (cf. *CVC*: *margfaldr*). *Bret* 1848-9 instead opts for *ypperlig* 'superb, excellent', but the existence of so general a sense would be hard to support.

100. Hirtisk hǫlðar   at hæða bœkr;
    nemi skynsemi   ok skili gǫrla,
    hvat táknat mun   í tǫlu þessi;
    esat enn liðin   ǫll spásaga;
    þó eru mǫrgum myrk   mǫl própheta.

Hirtisk hǫlðar at hæða bœkr; nemi skynsemi ok skili gǫrla, hvat mun táknat í þessi tǫlu; ǫll spásaga esat enn liðin; þó eru mǫl própheta myrk mǫrgum.

Let men be chary of scorning books; let them learn wisdom and understand fully what is signified in this narration; the entire prophecy has not yet come to pass; yet the words of the prophets are obscure to many.

Ms.: **Hb**(52v-53r) (*Bret*).

Editions: *Skj*: Gunnlaugr Leifsson, *Merlínússpá II* 100: AII, 36, BII, 44, *Skald* II, 28; *Bret* 1848-9, II, 74 (*Bret* st. 168); *Hb* 1892-6, 283; *Merl* 2012, 207.

Note: [All]: For the advocacy here, see *I* 101, Note to [All].

101. Frétti fyrðar,   þeirs á fold búa
    enn at óra   ævi liðna,
    hvat of her gerisk   ok huga leiði.
    Beri in nýju spjǫll   við spásǫgu;
    sé síðan þat,   hvé saman falli.

Frétti fyrðar, þeirs búa enn á fold at liðna ævi óra, hvat gerisk of her ok leiði huga. Beri in nýju spjǫll við spásǫgu; sé síðan þat, hvé falli saman.

Let men who remain on earth after our lifetime has passed find out what becomes of men and pay heed. Let them compare the new tidings with the prophecy; then let them see how the two coincide.

Ms.: **Hb**(53r) (*Bret*).

Editions: *Skj*: Gunnlaugr Leifsson, *Merlínússpá II* 101: AII, 36, BII, 44-5, *Skald* II, 28; *Bret* 1848-9, II, 74-5 (*Bret* st. 169); *Hb* 1892-6, 283; *Merl* 2012, 208.

Note: [All]: Gunnlaugr's sentiment here, that the *Prophecies* would be borne out in the fullness of time, was one shared by people in the medieval and even early modern British Isles, especially in Wales (Taylor 1911, 103-4). See Introduction on this topic.

102. Varð sú in enska   ætt fyr stundu
     veldis missa;   nús valskr konungr.
     Þós þeygi enn   þeira hætti
     liðit af láði,   né lýðs Breta
     hvǫssum mæki   hjarl eignaðisk.

Sú in enska ætt varð missa veldis fyr stundu; nús valskr konungr. Þós þeygi enn hætti þeira liðit af láði, né eignaðisk hjarl lýðs Breta hvǫssum mæki.

The English people had to lose their dominion some time ago; now there is a French king. Yet their character has still in no way vanished from the land, neither has the land of the people of the British been taken over by the sharp sword.

Ms.: **Hb**(53r) (*Bret*).

Editions: *Skj*: Gunnlaugr Leifsson, *Merlínússpá II* 102: AII, 36, BII, 45; *Skald* II, 28; *Bret* 1848-9, II, 75 (*Bret* st. 170); *Hb* 1892-6, 283; *Merl* 2012, 208-9.

Notes: [All]: Gunnlaugr appears to refer to two developments that might be seen as prophesied by Merlin and due for fulfilment: 1) the obliteration of the English race and culture from Britain, 2) the conquest of Wales by the descendants of the Norman dynasty. Although a full conquest of Wales did not occur until some decades after the turn of the thirteenth century, i.e. after the probable date of composition of *Merl*, such a development must have seemed inevitable and indeed imminent from much earlier (Thomas 2008, 62-3). — [4] *nú es valskr konungr* 'now there is a French king': As noted in *Merl* 2012, the reference is to the Plantagenet dynasty of the House of Anjou, though which of the Angevin kings, Henry II (r. 1154-89), Richard I (r. 1189-99) and John (r. 1199-1216), Gunnlaugr had in mind is uncertain.

103. Heilir allir,   þeirs hlýtt hafa,
     fleinvarpaðir   frœði þessu.
     Geri gótt gumar   en glati illu,
     bíði bráða   bót afruna,
     hafi hylli guðs   ok himinríki.

Heilir allir fleinvarpaðir, þeirs hafa hlýtt þessu frœði. Gumar geri gótt en glati illu, bíði bráða bót afruna, hafi hylli guðs ok himinríki.

Hail all barb-throwers [WARRIORS] who have listened to this lore. Let men do good and shun evil, experience a speedy remedy for their errors, have the grace of God and the heavenly kingdom.

Ms.: **Hb**(53r) (*Bret*).

Editions: *Skj*: Gunnlaugr Leifsson, *Merlínússpá II* 103: AII, 36, BII, 45; *Skald* II, 28; *Bret* 1848-9, II, 75 (*Bret* st. 171); *Hb* 1892-6, 283; *Merl* 2012, 209-10.

Notes: [1-2]: Turville-Petre (1953, 201) compares these lines with *Hávm* 164/5-8. — [3] *fleinvarpaðir* 'barb-throwers [MEN]': A *hap. leg.* — [6] *en* 'and': *Merl* 2012 has *enn*, but perhaps as a slip, since the translation is *aber* 'but'. — [10]: After this line, as noted in *Merl* 2012, the word *Amen* appears, probably as a scribal addition.

Merlínusspá II

Edited by Russell Poole

1. Ráðumk segja   sun*d*báls viðum
   spár spakligar   spámanns gǫfugs,
   þess's á breiðu   Bretlandi *sat*;
   hét Merlínus   margvitr gumi.

Ráðumk segja viðum sun*d*báls spakligar spár gǫfugs spámanns, þess's *sat* á breiðu Bretlandi; margvitr gumi hét Merlínus.

I resolve to tell the trees of the channel-fire [GOLD > MEN] the wise prophecies of the noble prophet, who resided in extensive Britain; the man wise in many things was called Merlin.

Ms.: **Hb**(49r) (*Bret*).

Readings: [2] sun*d*báls: 'svnbals' Hb   [6] *sat*: *om.* Hb.

Editions: *Skj*: Gunnlaugr Leifsson, *Merlínússpá I* 1: AII, 10, BII, 10, *Skald* II, 6; *Bret* 1848-9, II, 14 (*Bret* st. 1); *Hb* 1892-6, 272; *Merl* 2012, 64-6.

Notes: [2] sun*d*báls 'of the channel-fire [GOLD]': Ms. 'svnbals' (refreshed) is explained in *Bret* 1848-9 as representing *sundbáls*, to which *Skj* B emends (followed by *Skald*, *Merl* 2012 and this edn). — [6] sat 'resided': Added in *Bret* 1848-9, following scribal emendations in transcriptions of Hb (the transcriptions concerned are not specified, but 'sat' is added in AM 281 4°, 82r and in the margin of AM 597b 4°, 30r), and in turn followed by all subsequent eds. The line is metrically deficient as it stands in Hb.

2. Sagðr vas lýðum   ok landrekum
   myrk* at ráða   mǫrg rǫk fyrir.
   Kærr vas hann krist*n*u   kyn*n*i þjóðar;
   vasat á moldu   maðr vitrari.

Sagðr vas at ráða mǫrg myrk* rǫk fyrir lýðum ok landrekum. Hann vas kærr krist*n*u kyn*n*i þjóðar; vitrari maðr vasat á moldu.

He was said to interpret many obscure signs before the people and rulers. He was dear to the Christian family of people; there was not a wiser man on earth.

Ms.: **Hb**(49r) (*Bret*).

Readings: [1] Sagðr: 'Sagði' *refreshed from* Sagðr Hb   [3] myrk*: myrkt Hb   [5, 6] krist*nu* kyn*n*i: kristin kyni Hb.

Editions: *Skj*: Gunnlaugr Leifsson, *Merlínússpá I* 2: AII, 11, BII, 10, *Skald* II, 6, *NN* §§90, 91; *Bret* 1848-9, II, 14 (*Bret* st. 2); *Hb* 1892-6, 272; *Merl* 2012, 66-7.

Notes: [1] *sagðr vas* 'he was said': *Merl* 2012 adopts the refreshed reading *sagði* '[he] said', but this is to put too much faith in the refresher, when traces of earlier <r> are still visible. Instead of the ms.'s 'var' (normalised here to *vas*), *Merl* 2012 reads *við*, translated as *im Hinblick auf* 'in respect of'. But the refresher's abbreviation directly above ms. <v>, interpreted as '-ið' by *Merl* 2012, is followed to the right by a clearly legible unrefreshed abbreviation for '-ar', as is in fact conceded by *Merl* 2012. — [3] *myrk** 'obscure': Emended by Scheving (followed in *Bret* 1848-9 and *Skj* B) from ms. *myrkt* (refreshed). Kock (*NN* §90; *Skald*) treats *myrkt* and *mǫrg rǫk* as in apposition (*Han sades spå ... om dunkla ting, om mångt, som skulle ske* 'he was said to prophesy ... about obscure matters, about many things that were destined to occur'), but, while this construal is not impossible, Kock (as often: cf. Note to ll. 5-6 below) assumes that apposition is a more prevalent stylistic feature in skaldic poetry than in fact is the case; also, the sense and syntax yielded by Scheving's emendation are clearly superior. Conceivable, with *Merl* 2012, would be retention of *myrkt* in the sense 'darkly', taken with the verb, thus *at ráða myrkt mǫrg rǫk* 'to interpret darkly many signs'. But this would seem an odd disparagement of the popular prophet who is being praised in this very context and, once again, relies overmuch on the accuracy of the refresher. Cf *I* 9/1-4 and *I* 100/9-10. — [5-6]: These lines emphasise that Merlin is beloved of Christians, probably a point it would have been important for Gunnlaugr to establish, when contemporary commentators were apt to fret about Merlin's diabolic pedigree (Crick 2011, 77). The ms. reading *kristin* (refreshed) is emended to *kristnu* by Scheving, followed in *Bret* 1848-9, *Skj* B, *Merl* 2012 and this edn. In this edn the ms.'s 'kyni' is emended to *kynni*, dat. sg. of the n. noun *kynni* in the sense 'family, stock, lineage' (*Fritzner: kynni* 2); geminate <n> is not necessarily shown in Haukr's orthography (*Hb* 1892-6, xiii). These minor adjustments produce two metrical A-lines. *Skj* B on the other hand, presumably to improve the metre of l. 5, transposes *kristnu* and *kyni*, followed by *Merl* 2012, but this leaves l. 6 metrically deficient. Kock (*NN* §91) instead proposes to read *kristni, í kyni*, interpreting ll. 5-6 as *han var de kristne kär, var omtyckt ibland folket* 'he was dear to the Christians, was well-regarded amongst the people'. But the double construction, mixing uses of dat. case with and without prepositions, militates against this solution. — [7-8]: De Vries (1964-7, II, 75 n. 181) compares *Gríp* 52/5-6.

3. Leita ýtir   orð at vanda
    — viti flotnar þat —   frœðis þessa.
    Heldr fýsumk nú   fornra minna
    miðsamlig rǫk   mǫnnum segja.

Ýtir leita at vanda orð þessa frœðis; flotnar viti þat. Heldr fýsumk nú segja mǫnnum miðsamlig rǫk fornra minna.

Men seek to elaborate on the words of this lore; let people realise that. Rather, I now hasten to tell men of momentous signs from ancient memories.

Ms.: **Hb**(49r) (*Bret*).

Editions: *Skj*: Gunnlaugr Leifsson, *Merlínússpá I* 3: AII, 11, BII, 11, *Skald* II, 7, *NN* §92, *FF* §62; *Bret* 1848-9, II, 14-15 (*Bret* st. 5); *Hb* 1892-6, 272; *Merl* 2012, 67-8.

Notes: [1]: This edn follows Kock (*NN* §92; *Skald*; cf. *Merl* 2012) in retaining the ms. readings *ýtir leita* (refreshed), 'men seek'. Emendation to *leitiga ýtum* 'I do not seek ... for men', with *Bret* 1848-9 (followed in *Skj* B), is unnecessary. — [2] *at vanda orð* 'to elaborate on the words': The inf. *vanda* can be glossed as either 'make elaborately, take care over, elaborate on' (*CVC*: *vanda* I 2; Fritzner: *vanda* 3) or 'make difficulties concerning, baulk at, object to' (*CVC*: *vanda* II 2; Fritzner: *vanda* 1, 2). The former is the only usage documented for poetry in *LP*: *vanda* and is that adopted here, as in *Bret* 1848-9 (*söge pyntelige Ord* 'seek out embellished diction') and *Skj* B (identical). Gunnlaugr may possibly be noting the inclination of other poets to produce elaborate renderings of the *Prophecies*, thereby perhaps anticipating the attitude to obscurity exhibited by the C14th composer of *Lilja* (Anon *Lil* 98[VII]), which expresses disapproval of poetry composed in an elaborate (*vandan*) style. Kock's interpretation, *noggrant återjiva* 'render exactly', is derived from the same sub-sense of *vanda*. Although the sense 'make difficulties concerning' is otherwise undocumented in poetry up to and including Gunnlaugr's time, a case could perhaps be made for it insofar as Geoffrey's material was undoubtedly objected to by some contemporaries. External to *Merl*, scepticism concerning Geoffrey's historiography culminates in the strenuous objections expressed by William of Newburgh (b. 1135/6, d. in or after 1198). In his *Historia rerum Anglicarum*, apparently composed between 1196 and 1198 (cf. Taylor 2004), William writes (Liebermann and Pauli 1885, 225): *Qui etiam maiori ausu cuiusdam Merlini divinationes fallacissimas, quibus utique de proprio plurimum adiecit, dum eas in Latinum transfunderet, tanquam authenticas et inmobili veritate subnixas prophetias vulgavit* 'Furthermore, with greater temerity he promulgated the utterly false predictions of a certain Merlin, to which assuredly he added more of his own, then rendered them into Latin, as if they were authentic prophecies founded on an unwavering veracity'. Gunnlaugr's parenthesis *flotnar viti þat* 'let people realise that' (l. 3) could be understood as the poet's honest disclosure and advance warning to his audience that such objections have been raised. At the same time, he differentiates his own attitude from that of the persons who would make difficulties by stating that he means to launch right into his account. — [7] *miðsamlig rök* 'momentous signs': Both words in this phrase offer difficulties of interpretation. In its draft article on *rǫk* ONP proposes the following main senses: 1. *ophav, oprindelse, grund, argument, bevis*; 2. *tegn, under, åbenbaring*; 3. *forhold, hændelse, begivenhed* '1. beginning, origin, cause, argument, proof; 2. sign, wonder, revelation; 3. condition, event'. While this might suggest a variety of possible senses in *II* 3/7, the presence of *rǫk* in *II* 2/4 limits the options, if we assume that the same sense applies in both stanzas, which seems likeliest. Here sense 2. 'sign' is selected. The adj. *miðsamligr* (here n. pl., agreeing with *rǫk*) is not attested elsewhere and any explanation can only be tentative. Compounds, either adjectives or adverbs, with the final element *-samlig-* are numerous (cf. *Fritzner* IV: *samliga* and *samligr*). The attestations show that the first element in such compounds is typically if not invariably a noun rather than an adj. or verb. On that basis, in this edn the first element in *miðsamlig* is interpreted as *mið* 'middle-point', in one of its derived senses of 'pointer, mark, sign, indicator, indication, guidance' (cf. *ONP: mið (hafa mið); Fritzner: II mið*). Particularly relevant is the attestation (Unger 1874, 304; cf. *CVC, ONP: mið*) *kváðu þeir lítil mið at Páli ok kenningum hans* 'they said that there was little guidance [to be had] from Paul and his teachings', i.e. the teachings were 'little to be relied on'. Comparable senses can be inferred from the verb *miða* 'mark, indicate, point to, enable someone to gauge' (*CVC: miða; Fritzner: miða* 1). Signs (*rǫk*) that are *miðsamlig* would on this logic be 'indicative, pregnant, momentous', from a basic sense of 'pointing to', where the thing pointed to is the shape of the future. The same thinking can be seen in *Merl I* 100/3-8: *nemi skynsemi ok skili gǫrla, hvat mun táknat í þessi tǫlu – spásaga esat ǫll enn liðin* 'let them learn wisdom and understand fully what is signified in this narration – the entire prophecy has not yet come to pass'. The following stanza, *I* 101/7-10, enjoins the audience to compare recent events with the prophecies to see that they do indeed coincide, i.e. to see how the prophecies point to and are borne out by subsequent events. Suggestions by previous eds about the meaning of *miðsamligr* differ widely. *Bret* 1848-9 translates it as *mindeværdig* 'memorable', followed by *Merl* 2012 (though there the gloss is misleadingly ascribed to *LP* (1860): *miðsamligr*), but this is purely *ad hoc*, since there is no connection between the attested senses of the Icelandic words *mið*, *miða* and the concept of memorability. Finnur Jónsson explains as *passende* 'fitting', from a literal *rammende midten* 'hitting the midpoint' (*LP*: *miðsamligr*), but such a sense seems too vague to measure up to the demands of the context. Kock (*FF* §62) translates ll. 5-8 as *själv önskar skalden ivrigt att för folket tälja en välbehaglig följd av forna minnen* 'for his part the skald wishes earnestly to give men a pleasing series of ancient memories', where *miðsamlig* is glossed as *välbehaglig* 'pleasing'. This gloss rests upon a posited derivation of *miðsamligr* from MHG *mitesam* 'affable, friendly'; in support Kock adduces other foreign words in *Merl*, but these are not properly speaking comparable and in any case the notion of 'affable', even stretched to 'pleasing', scarcely fits the context.

4. Ljós mun lýðum   ljóðbók vesa;
    þós í frœði   flest at ráða,
    þats fyrir jǫfurr   ǫldum sagði
    brezkri þjóðu;   nú skal brag kveða.

Ljóðbók mun vesa ljós lýðum; þós flest at ráða í frœði, þats jǫfurr sagði brezkri þjóðu fyrir ǫldum; nú skal kveða brag.

The song-book will be clear to men; yet most [of it] is to be interpreted by means of wisdom that ages ago the leader imparted to the British people; now the poem shall be recited.

Ms.: **Hb**(49r) (*Bret*).

Reading: [2] ljóðbók: ljóðborg Hb.

Editions: *Skj*: Gunnlaugr Leifsson, *Merlínússpá I* 4: AII, 11, BII, 11, *Skald* II, 7, *NN* §93; *Bret* 1848-9, II, 15 (*Bret* st. 4); *Hb* 1892-6, 272; *Merl* 2012, 68-70.

Notes: [All]: Here Gunnlaugr concludes his introduction. — [2] *ljóðbók* 'song-book': Emended in this edn from ms. *ljóðborg* 'city of song' (refreshed). Such a cpd would normally be construed as a kenning meaning 'mouth, chest' and similar, but the sense required by context is 'poem', as posited in *Bret* 1848-9 and *Skj* B. Gunnlaugr refers elsewhere to the parts of this poem as *bók* (*I* 95/2, *II* 63/3) or *bœkr*, the latter collocated with adj. *bjartar* 'bright' (*I* 96/3-4), corresponding to *ljós* 'clear' here. Cf. *ljóðabók* 'book of lays' (*CVC*, *ONP*: *ljóðabók*). Possibly Latin titles such as Herbert of Bosham's well-known *Liber melorum* 'Book of songs/harmonies', written shortly after 1186 (cf. Smalley 1973, 79), suggested this expression. — [5, 6] *fyrir ǫldum* 'ages ago': This interpretation follows *Skj* B. Kock, followed by *Merl* 2012, objects to the complicated word order and instead proposes, with parallels from West Germanic poetry, that *ǫldum* and *brezkri þjóðu* (l. 6) should be read as in apposition (*NN* §93): *vad fursten forutsagt för människorna, för det bretonska folket* 'what the leader prophesied before men, before the British people'. But Gunnlaugr occasionally uses complex word orders (cf. *I* 13/5-10, *I* 54/9-12, *I* 63/5-8), whereas the typically West Germanic style of variation imputed to him by Kock is nowhere unmistakably exemplified. — [5] *jǫfurr* 'the leader': There is nothing in *DGB* to justify reference to Merlin as *jǫfurr*, a *heiti* whose attestations relate specifically to leaders and rulers (*LP*: *jǫfurr*), but possibly the use of this *heiti* reflects influence from Geoffrey's later *Vita Merlini*, which narrates the life of Merlin Caledonius (also known as Silvestris) (Poole 2014, 23-4). Crick (2011, 70-1) comments that often medieval commentators failed to discriminate between Merlin Caledonius and Merlin Ambrosius, and Merlinian prophecy circulated without precise attribution. For a probable instance of this confusion see Curley (1982, 220); Gunnlaugr might have drawn upon such a commentary. For references to Merlin Caledonius as king see Clarke's edn of *Vita Merlini* (1973, 52-3). — [8] *skal* 'shall': The verb is impersonal. Emendation to *skalk* 'I shall', with *Merl* 2012, is unnecessary.

5. 'V*ella* í víðri   Vintónía
    — þats borgar nafn —   brunnar þrennir.
    Þeir munu láði   lœkjum skipta
    þrír óglíkir   í þrjá staði.

'Þrennir brunnar v*ella* í víðri Vintónía; þats nafn borgar. Þeir þrír óglíkir munu skipta láði lœkjum í þrjá staði.

'Triple springs will well up in broad Winchester; that is the name of the city. Those three, [each] unlike [the others], will divide the land with their streams into three parts.

Ms.: **Hb**(49r) (*Bret*).

Reading: [1] V*ella*: 'Sar er' *apparently corrected from* 'Varu' Hb.

Editions: *Skj*: Gunnlaugr Leifsson, *Merlínússpá I* 5: AII, 11, BII, 11, *Skald* II, 7; *Bret* 1848-9, II, 15-16 (*Bret* st. 5); *Hb* 1892-6, 272; *Merl* 2012, 70-1.

Notes: [All]: Cf. *DGB* 116 (Reeve and Wright 2007, 151.147-8; cf. Wright 1988, 107, prophecy 31): *Tres fontes in urbe Guintonia erumpent, quorum riuuli insulam in tres portiones secabunt* 'Three springs will well up in the city of Winchester, and their streams will cut the island in three' (cf. Reeve and Wright 2007, 150). — [1] *v*ella 'will well up': In Hb the text is refreshed as 'Sar er' but the traces of initial majuscule <V> are visible; Finnur Jónsson (*Hb* 1892-6, 272) interprets these indications as *Váru*. This reading seems unlikely to originate with Gunnlaugr, however, since pres. (for future), not pret., is called for by the remainder of the stanza; in transmission the pret. could have encroached from the preceding stanza. Additionally, *váru* would denote a steady state rather than a development that divides the lands within which the city is built into three, as required by the remainder of the stanza. In the present edn emendation to *vella* 'well up' is proposed to solve these difficulties and as the obvious vernacular rendition of Geoffrey's *erumpent*; cf. its use in *I* 89/8. *Bret* 1848-9, followed by *Skj* B and *Skald*, emends to *vaxa* 'grow, increase', but this verb is not attested in relation to springs. *Merl* 2012 proposes *Þar eru* 'There are' but this, besides being vague and unidiomatic in itself, does not fit with the idea of a sudden break-out required by *DGB*. — [2] *Vintónía* 'Winchester': Winchester was a major royal and ecclesiastical centre under the Normans, continuing its prominent role in the late Anglo-Saxon period.

6. 'Einn es brunna   beztr at reyna;
    eykr auðstǫfum   aldr, ef drekka.
    Né sótt hǫfug   sœkir hǫlða,
    þás bergt hafa   beisku vatni.

'Einn brunna es beztr at reyna; eykr aldr auðstǫfum, ef drekka. Né sœkir hǫfug sótt hǫlða, þás hafa bergt beisku vatni.

'One of the springs is best to try; it will increase the life-span for wealth-staves [MEN], if they drink it. Nor will grievous sickness afflict men who have tasted the bitter water.

Ms.: **Hb**(49r) (*Bret*).

Editions: *Skj*: Gunnlaugr Leifsson, Merlínússpá I 6: AII, 11, BII, 11, *Skald* II, 7; *Edns*: Bret 1848-9, II, 16 (*Bret* st. 6); *Hb* 1892-6, 272; *Merl* 2012, 71.

Note: [All]: Cf. *DGB* 116 (Reeve and Wright 2007, 151.148-9; cf. Wright 1988, 107, prophecy 31): *Qui bibet de uno diuturniori uita fruetur nec superuenienti languore grauabitur* 'Whoever drinks from the first will enjoy a longer life, nor be weighed down by disease' (cf. Reeve and Wright 2007, 150).

7. 'Illr es annarr;   allir svelta,
    þeirs af bekk*i*   bergja drekku.
    Þós inn þriðja   þyngst at reyna;
    deyja þeir allir,   es þar drekka af;
    né hræ guma   hyljask foldu.

'Annarr es illr; allir svelta, þeirs bergja drekku af bekk*i*. Þós inn þriðja þyngst at reyna; allir deyja, þeir es þar drekka af; né hyljask hræ guma foldu.

'The second is bad; all those who taste a drink from the stream will die. Yet the third is most grievous to try; all those who drink from it will die; nor will men's corpses be covered with earth.

Ms.: **Hb**(49r) (*Bret*).

Reading: [3] bekk*i*: bekkjar Hb.

Editions: *Skj*: Gunnlaugr Leifsson, Merlínússpá I 7: AII, 11, BII, 11, *Skald* II, 7; *Bret* 1848-9, II, 16 (*Bret* st. 7); *Hb* 1892-6, 272; *Merl* 2012, 71-2.

Notes: [All]: Cf. *DGB* 116 (Reeve and Wright 2007, 151.149-51; cf. Wright 1988, 107, prophecy 31): *Qui bibet de altero indeficienti fame peribit, et in facie ipsius pallor et horror sedebit. Qui bibet de tercio subita morte periclitabitur, nec corpus ipsius subire poterit sepulchrum* 'Whoever drinks from the second will die of a thirst that cannot be quenched, and a ghastly pallor will appear on his face. Whoever drinks from the third will die a sudden death, and no one will be able to bury his body' (Reeve and Wright 2007, 150). The notion of *pallor et horror* is not represented in *Merl*. — [3-4] *bergja drekku af bekki* 'taste a drink from the stream': The refreshed reading *bekkjar* is emended to *bekki* 'stream' (dat. sg.) in this edn. Bret, Skj B, Skald and Merl 2012 have *bergja af drekku bekkjar* 'taste a drink of the stream', lit. 'taste from a drink of the stream'. But the emendation provides a better fit with the attestations of *bergja* in *ONP*: *bergja* 1, where the prep. *af* represents the source of the thing tasted rather than the thing itself. — [9] *guma* (gen. pl.) 'men's': This form is not uncommon, beside *gumna*; cf. *ANG* §401.3. Gen. pl. *guma* also occurs at *II* 16/10 and *II* 35/5.

8.   'Vilja hǫlðar   hylja brunna,
      þás flestum hal   fjǫrspell gera.
      En, þats lýðir   á lǫg bera,
      alt verðr at ǫðru, en áðr séi:
      grund at grjóti,   grjót at vatni,
      viðr at ǫsku,   en af ǫsku vatn.

'Hǫlðar vilja hylja brunna, þás gera flestum hal fjǫrspell. En, þats lýðir bera á lǫg, verðr alt at ǫðru, en áðr séi: grund at grjóti, grjót at vatni, viðr at ǫsku, en vatn af ǫsku.

'Men will want to cover up the springs that cause death for most people. But all that men carry to the water will turn to something other than it was previously: earth to stone, stone to water, wood to ash, and water from ash.

Ms.: **Hb**(49r) (*Bret*).

Readings: [5] þat*s*: þat Hb   [11] ǫsk*u*: ǫsk Hb   [12] a*f*: at Hb.

Editions: *Skj*: Gunnlaugr Leifsson, *Merlínússpá I* 8: AII, 11-12, BII, 12, *Skald* II, 7; *Bret* 1848-9, II, 16-17 (*Bret* st. 8); *Hb* 1892-6, 272; *Merl* 2012, 72-3.

Notes: [All]: Cf. *DGB* 116 (Reeve and Wright 2007, 151.151-5; cf. Wright 1988, 107, prophecy 31): *Tantam ingluuiem uitare uolentes, diuersis tegumentis eam occultare nitentur. Quaecunque ergo moles superposita fuerit formam alterius corporis recipiet. Terra namque in lapides, lapides in limpham, lignum in cineres, cinis in aquam, si superiecta fuerint, uertentur* 'To escape this menace, they will try to hide it under various things. Whatever is placed upon it will assume a different form. If earth is put over the spring, it will become stones, stones become water, wood become ash and ash become water' (Reeve and Wright 2007, 150). — [5] *þats* 'that': Lit. 'that which'. Emended in *Skj* B (followed by *Skald* and *Merl* 2012, the latter reading *er*) from ms. *þat* (refreshed). — [10] *vatni* 'water': *Viði* 'wood' might be expected, to preserve the pattern, but the reading *limpham* 'water' rather than *lignem* 'wood' is the dominant one in the witnesses of *DGB* (Reeve and Wright 2007, 151; cf. Wright 1988, 107) and is no doubt what stood in Gunnlaugr's source. — [12] *af* 'from': Emended in *Bret* 1848-9 (followed by subsequent eds) from ms. *at* (not refreshed), to improve the logic of the list.

9.   'Farit es at meyju   margfróðastri
     í kappsauðga   Knútsskógar borg,
     at hon lækningar   leiti þjóðum
     ok firri menn   fári slíku.

'Farit es at margfróðastri meyju í kappsauðga borg Knútsskógar, at hon leiti þjóðum lækningar ok firri menn slíku fári.

'A maiden most wise about many things will be approached in the exceedingly prosperous city of Canute's wood, so that she may seek remedies for the people and rescue men from such peril.

Ms.: **Hb**(49r) (*Bret*).

Editions: *Skj*: Gunnlaugr Leifsson, *Merlínússpá I* 9: AII, 12, BII, 12, *Skald* II, 7; *Bret* 1848-9, II, 17 (*Bret* st. 9); *Hb* 1892-6, 272; *Merl* 2012, 74.

Notes: [All]: Cf. *DGB* 116 (Reeve and Wright 2007, 151.155-6; cf. Wright 1988, 108, prophecy 32): *Ad haec ex urbe canuti nemoris eliminabitur puella ut medelae curam adhibeat* 'At this, a girl will be sent forth from the city of the hoary forest to bring curing medicine' (cf. Reeve and Wright 2007, 150). The city Geoffrey had in mind, though not identified in previous scholarship, is probably Lichfield (OE *Liccidfeld*), which was founded close to and partially takes its name from the Romano-British settlement *Letocetum* 'Grey forest' (cf. Watts 2004, 372; for this location see also Stenton 1970, 259). In Anglo-Latin the adj. form *canutus/kanutus* is used to mean 'grey', in parallel with the classical Latin form *canus*. Gunnlaugr appears to infer a connection with the name Knútr, no doubt via the Anglo-Norman (Latinised) form of this name, *Canutus/Kanutus*, and this is also done by some modern scholars, e.g. Faral (1929, II, 60), followed by Thorpe (1966, 177) and *Merl* 2012. Tatlock (1950, 77) lists the location as unknown. *DGB* shows a keen interest, some of it reflected by *Merl*, in the vicissitudes and rival claims of dioceses and diocesan cities; cf. (e.g.) *I* 30 (London, Canterbury, Carlisle, St Davids), *II* 5-8 (Winchester) and *II* 16-18 (Winchester and St Davids). A reference to Lichfield can be explained in those terms: already the seat of a bishop, the city had in Offa's time been proposed as the seat of the southern archbishop. It was briefly and very controversially the seat of an archbishop under Hygeberht from 787 to 799 (officially dissolved in 803), as a result of opposition on the part of Offa, King of Mercia, to domination by Canterbury (Stenton 1971, 217-18; Kirby 2000, 142; Brooks 1996, 118-19). In the late C11th Lichfield lost its bishop (though not its cathedral status) to Chester, as part of reforms proposed by Lanfranc (see Note to *I* 59/2); nevertheless its fortunes were reviving in Geoffrey's time, with the construction of a Norman cathedral (cf. Barrow 1956, 63). Gunnlaugr's added assertion of the status of 'Canute's wood' as an exceedingly prosperous centre (l. 3) rather than a mere rural retreat, augmenting Geoffrey's claim for its salvific influence on Winchester, may be seen as a piece of advocacy for the city fully in keeping with C12th

English practice: cf. *II* 16 Note to [All]. — [3] *kappsauðga* 'exceedingly prosperous': See Note to *II* 80/2. — [6] *þjóðum* 'for the people': This ms. reading (not refreshed) is retained in *Skald*, *Merl* 2012 and this edn. Emended in *Bret* 1848-9 and *Skj* B to *fyrðum* 'men', but the notion may be that the three springs and their streams have divided the land into three 'peoples'. — [7] *ok firri* 'and rescue': Normalised in *Skj* B (followed by *Skald* and this edn) from ms. *ok hon firri* 'and she rescue'. — [8] *slíku* 'such': Finnur Jónsson takes the unrefreshed ms. reading to be *miklu* 'great' in *Skj* A (followed by *Skald*), with the comment *sål. sikkert* 'definitely thus'. But in *Bret* 1848-9, *Hb* 1892-6 and *Skj* B it is read as *slíku*, and inspection of the ms., which is very indistinct at this point, suggests that that reading is correct. *Merl* 2012 erroneously prints *sliku*.

10.   'Tekr hon at reyna   ok at ráða fjǫlð;
     tekr hon íþróttir   allar fremja.
     Andar síðan   snót á brunna,
     ok brúð*r* þurra   báða gervir.

'Hon tekr at reyna ok at ráða fjǫlð; hon tekr fremja allar íþróttir. Snót andar síðan á brunna, ok brúð*r* gervir báða þurra.

'She will start to test and devise a great many [remedies]; she will start practising all her arts. Then the woman will breathe on the springs and the lady will make them both dry.

Ms.: **Hb**(49r) (*Bret*).

Reading: [7] ok brúð*r* þurra: 'ok hon brúðþurra' Hb.

Editions: *Skj*: Gunnlaugr Leifsson, *Merlínússpá I* 10: AII, 12, BII, 12; *Skald* II, 7; *Bret* 1848-9, II, 17 (*Bret* st. 10); *Hb* 1892-6, 272; *Merl* 2012, 75-6.

Notes: [All]: Cf. *DGB* 116 (Reeve and Wright 2007, 151.156-7; cf. Wright 1988, 108, prophecy 32): *Quae ut omnes artes inierit, solo anhelitu suo fontes nociuos siccabit* 'After she has tried all her arts, she will dry up the deadly springs with her breath alone' (Reeve and Wright 2007, 150). — [1] *reyna* 'to test': This reading and gloss are accepted by all eds but *LP*: *reyna* 3 glosses as *tyde* 'interpret' (contrast *Skj* B's *prøve* 'test') and suggests that the reading may have arisen in error for *rýna* 'enquire (into), investigate'. But emendation (or re-interpretation of the ms. reading) is not called for, inasmuch as in ll. 1-2 Gunnlaugr appears to amplify the idea in *DGB* that the woman is trying all her arts, i.e. those of healing, as requested by the inhabitants of Winchester, rather than enquiring into the causes of the crisis. — [3] *hon* 'she': Omitted in *Skald*. — [3] *íþróttir* 'arts': The word is used here, as repeatedly in *Hsv*[VII], to mean not 'feats' or 'accomplishments', in the sense of something to be exhibited, as in older skaldic poetry, but rather 'useful skills'. — [7] *ok brúðr … þurra* 'and the lady … dry': Emended in this edn from ms. 'ok hon brvðþurra' (not refreshed). This emendation assumes two *heiti* for 'woman', *snót* in l. 6 and *brúðr* in l. 7, referring to the same person in coordinate clauses, rather than the f. pron. *hon* 'she' at the second mention. However, departures from expected (prose) usage on this point are paralleled in skaldic poetry including Gunnlaugr's own: cf. the coordinate clauses in *II* 11/1-4, where *hon* 'she' is used in the first clause and *brúðar* 'the woman's' in the second, and in *II* 11/5-8, where *hon* and *kona* 'the woman' are seemingly in apposition, expressing the subject of the first clause, and *man* 'the maiden' in the second. For an alternation of the same *heiti*, *brúðr* and *snót*, see also *Gríp* 45 and 46. Omission of nom. *-r*, as apparently here, occurs sporadically in Hb (e.g. *lávarð* for *lávarðr* in *II* 57/8). *Bret* 1848-9 retains without emendation, translating ll. 7-8 as *og dem begge brat udtörrer* 'and dries them both out instantly', without explaining how *bruð*- would equate in sense or grammatical function to *brat* 'instantly'. Other suggestions require the postulation of unattested idioms or lexical items: *Skj* B (followed by *Skald*) emends to *ok hon brauðþurra* 'and she [makes them] dry as bread', while *Merl* 2012 retains *bruðþurra, apparently interpreting as 'so dry as to be hard to eat', but aside from the implausibility of such a formation the logic is hard to follow, since there is no question of the springs serving as food.

11. 'Hon þá drekkr   it dýra vatn,
    ok máttr við þat   magnask brúðar.
    Berr hon í hœgri   hendi sinni,
    kynstór kona,   Kolídónis skóg,
    en í lófa man   Lundúna borg.

'Hon drekkr þá it dýra vatn, ok máttr brúðar magnask við þat. Hon, kynstór kona, berr skóg Kolídónis í hœgri hendi sinni, en man Lundúna borg í lófa.

'She will then drink the precious water and the woman's strength will increase with that. She, the woman of high lineage, will bear the forest of Colidon in her right hand and the maiden [will bear] the city of London in her palm.

Ms.: **Hb**(49r-v) (*Bret*).

Editions: *Skj*: Gunnlaugr Leifsson, *Merlínússpá I* 11: AII, 12, BII, 12, *Skald* II, 8, *NN* §§94, 1281; *Bret* 1848-9, II, 18 (*Bret* st. 11); *Hb* 1892-6, 272; *Merl* 2012, 76-7.

Notes: [All]: Cf. *DGB* 116 (Reeve and Wright 2007, 151.157-153.159; cf. Wright 1988, 108, prophecy 33): *Exin, ut sese salubri liquore refecerit, gestabit in dextera sua nemus Colidonis, in sinistra uero murorum Lundoniae propugnacula* 'Next, refreshing herself with healing water, she will bear in her right hand the forest of Colidon and in her left the battlements of London's walls' (Reeve and Wright 2007, 150-2). — [5] *hon … berr* 'she … will bear': *Skj* B deletes *hon*, but Kock (*NN* §94) defends the parallelism of noun and pronominal, pointing out internal inconsistencies in the treatment of pron. subjects in *Skj* B. Cf. Note to *II* 10/7. — [8] *Kolídónis* 'of Colidon': Gunnlaugr retains the Latin gen. sg. Cf. *I* 63/2. The identity of the forest is unknown (cf. Tatlock

1950, 16-17). — [9] *man* 'the maiden': The difficulties raised by this reading have not so far been satisfactorily resolved. This edn follows Kock (*NN* §1281; *Skald*) in retaining ms. *man* (not refreshed), construed as a noun, 'maiden', in parallel structure with *kona* 'woman' in l. 7; so too *Merl* 2012. For the syntax cf. Note to *II* 10/7. The reading *man* is also retained in *Bret* 1848-9, which translates l. 9 as *i den hule Haand* 'in the cupped hand', with a note explaining that this interpretation is prompted by the Latin. No such sense of *man* is attested (unless an otherwise unknown *heiti* for 'hand' from Lat. *manus*, Fr. *main* is to be posited), but a mention of the maiden's left hand would indeed be expected, so as to complement that of her right hand, as presupposed by both the Latin and l. 5 of the present stanza. *Skj* B emends to *mun*, presumably understood as an auxiliary verb with assumed *bera*.

12. 'Gengr hon síðan gótt frón yfir,
    svát *ór* sporum snótar sprettr upp logi.
    Með rǫmmum reyk Rúténéos
    sá vekr ok ver*ð* verþjóðu gerr.

'Hon gengr síðan yfir gótt frón, svát logi sprettr upp *ór* sporum snótar. Sá vekr Rúténéos með rǫmmum reyk ok gerr ver*ð* verþjóðu.

'Then she will walk over the good land, so that flame springs up from the footsteps of the woman. It will wake up the Ruteni with the powerful smoke, and make a meal for the sea-people.

Ms.: **Hb**(49v) (*Bret*).

Readings: [3] *ór* sporum: sporum Hb [7] ver*ð*: 'verkn' Hb.

Editions: *Skj*: Gunnlaugr Leifsson, *Merlínússpá I* 12: AII, 12, BII, 12-13, *Skald* II, 8, *NN* §§95, 607, 2992A; *Bret* 1848-9, II, 18 (*Bret* st. 12); *Hb* 1892-6, 273; *Merl* 2012, 77-8.

Notes: [All]: Cf. *DGB* 116 (Reeve and Wright 2007, 153.159-61; cf. Wright 1988, 108, prophecy 33): *Quacumque incedet passus sulphureos faciet, qui dupplici flamma fumabunt. Fumus ille excitabit Rutenos et cibum submarinis conficiet* 'Wherever she goes, she will leave tracks of sulphur, which will burn with a double flame. That smoke will arouse the Flemings and provide food for the people beneath the sea' (cf. Reeve and Wright 2007, 152). The expression *submarini* 'people beneath the sea' is an elegant variation referring to the Ruteni. Cf. II 23 Note to [All]. For the ethnic designation *Ruteni*, denoting peoples inhabiting Flanders, Geoffrey states his authority as Julius Caesar in *De bello gallico* (*DGB* 54.1-2: Reeve and Wright 2007, 68-9). Gunnlaugr does not carry over Geoffrey's mention of sulphur but adds the characterisation of the smoke as powerful, which could be based on local knowledge of the choking or suffocating odour of sulphur dioxide, released naturally by volcanic activity. In mentioning the *Ruteni*, Geoffrey appears to allude to the presence of Flemish mercenaries in England in royal Anglo-Norman service from William the Conqueror onwards (on which see Poole

1955, 135). The flame will arouse the Ruteni and provide them with food inasmuch as warfare calls up mercenaries and secures them a livelihood; for a similar expression, cf. *actus eius cibus erit narrantibus* 'his deeds will feed those who tell them' (*I* 28 Note to [All]). Often the younger sons of knightly families and trained for warfare, these mercenaries stood to earn a better living in England, where many of them settled, than at home. Under Henry I, probably between 1107 and 1111, entire communities of Flemish immigrants were transferred to the Welsh marches from central England, where their possession of land had led to grievances (Oksanen 2008, 264-5) that Geoffrey appears to reflect. — [2] *gótt frón* 'the good land': Gunnlaugr adds this idea. — [3] *ór sporum* 'from the footsteps': The prep. *ór* is added by *Skj* B (followed by *Skald*, *Merl* 2012 and this edn). *Bret* 1848-9 supplies *at*. — [7] *verð* 'a meal': Emended from ms. 'verkn' (refreshed) by Finnur Jónsson (*Skj* B), on the basis of a conjecture in *Bret* 1848-9. Kock prefers to emend to *verk*, taken in the sense 'suffering' (*NN* §95; *Skald*, followed by *Merl* 2012), but evidently without taking account of *DGB*. — [8] *verþjóðu* 'the sea-people': This is the meaning to be inferred from *DGB* (so *Skj* B) but, as pointed out in *Bret* 1848-9, where instances are given, the cpd would normally be understood as 'mankind', with first element *verr* 'man'. Kock (*NN* §95; cf. *NN* §§607 and 2992A, followed by *Merl* 2012) rejects the sense 'sea-people' out of hand, listing parallel formations in West Germanic poetry, but overlooks *DGB* and also *Merl II* 23/3, where the context requires that *verþjóðu* be glossed as 'sea-people' (cf. Finnur Jónsson 1924a, 329-30). The reference, in both Geoffrey and Gunnlaugr, is presumably to the exposure of the Flemish coastal counties, which lay below sea level, to frequent inundations from the onset of the so-called Great Reclamation Period in the C12th (Augustyn 1995, 12-13). Many of the Flemish mercenaries came from this region (Oksanen 2008, 265). In choosing the *heiti ver*, conventionally used to mean 'sea' in poetry but lit. 'hunting or fishing ground' (Fritzner: *ver* 1), Gunnlaugr may be rationalising Geoffrey's talk of 'submarine' people. A Flemish coastal fishing industry flourished at his time, with backing from the larger towns and ports (Tys and Pieters 2009, 91-4).

13. 'Gerisk ógurligt   óp í landi,
    es gull-Skǫgul   grætr hástǫfum.
    Ok þjóta tekr   þjóð með henni
    innan of alla   ey með hringum.

'Ógurligt óp gerisk í landi, es gull-Skǫgul grætr hástǫfum. Ok þjóð tekr þjóta með henni innan of alla ey með hringum.

'A terrible cry will be made in the land, when the Skǫgul <valkyrie> of gold [WOMAN] weeps loudly. And people therein will start wailing with her throughout the entire island.

Ms.: **Hb**(49v) (*Bret*).

Editions: *Skj*: Gunnlaugr Leifsson, *Merlínússpá I* 13: AII, 12, BII, 13, *Skald* II, 8; *Bret* 1848-9, II, 18-19 (*Bret* st. 13); *Hb* 1892-6, 273; *Merl* 2012, 78-9.

Notes: [All]: Cf. *DGB* 116 (Reeve and Wright 2007, 153.161-2; cf. Wright 1988, 108, prophecy 33): *Lacrimis miserandis manabit ipsa et clamore horrido replebit insulam* 'She will be drenched with pitiful tears and fill the island with a terrible cry' (Reeve and Wright 2007, 152). Gunnlaugr appears to rationalise this account by attributing the cries of lamentation to the people as a whole rather than to one preternaturally loud woman. — [8] *með hringum* 'throughout': See Note to *I* 83/8.

14. 'Hj*ǫ*rtr drepr hana,   hinns tvenna fimm
    hv*a*ssa hausi   hornkv*i*stu berr.
    En hafa kórónu   kvistir fjórir,
    en sex aðrir   sjalfir verða
    at vísundar   verstum hornum.

'Hj*ǫ*rtr drepr hana, hinns berr tvenna fimm hv*a*ssa hornkv*i*stu hausi. En fjórir kvistir hafa kórónu, en sex aðrir verða sjalfir at verstum hornum vísundar.

'A hart will slay her, he who bears twice five sharp antler-branches on his head. And four branches will have a crown while the other six for their part will turn into the worst horns of a bison.

Ms.: **Hb**(49v) (*Bret*).

Readings: [1] Hj*ǫ*rtr: 'hrottr' Hb   [3] hv*a*ssa: 'kræsa' *or* 'hræsa' Hb   [4] -kv*i*stu: '-kvstu' Hb.

Editions: *Skj*: Gunnlaugr Leifsson, *Merlínússpá I* 14: AII, 12-13, BII, 13, *Skald* II, 8, *NN* §§96, 2992A, 3004; *Bret* 1848-9, II, 19 (*Bret* st. 14); *Hb* 1892-6, 273; *Merl* 2012, 79-80.

Notes: [All]: Cf. *DGB* 116 (Reeve and Wright 2007, 153.162-4; cf. Wright 1988, 108, prophecy 34): *Interficiet eam ceruus decem ramorum, quorum quatuor aurea diademata gestabunt, sex uero residui in cornua bubalorum uertentur* 'She will be killed by a stag with ten branches, four of which will wear golden crowns, while the remaining six will become the horns of buffaloes' (Reeve and Wright 2007, 152). — [1] *hjǫrtr* 'a hart': Emended from ms. 'hrottr' (refreshed) in *Bret* 1848-9 (followed by *Skj* B), with reference to *DGB*. — [3] *hv*assa 'sharp': Emended in this edn from the refreshed and uncertain ms. reading 'kræsa' or 'hræsa'. This adj. yields good sense and is rather a favourite with Gunnlaugr. Use of *hausi* without a prep. would be consistent with Gunnlaugr's use of the bare dat./instr.: see Note to *I* 47/3-4. *Bret* 1848-9 and *Skj* B emend to *hræs á* 'of a corpse on' (cf. *LP*: *hræ*), but this makes little sense in context. Kock (*NN* §96; *Skald*; cf. *NN* §2992A and 3004, followed by *Merl* 2012) posits an adj. **hrœrr* 'quick', qualifying *hjǫrtr*, inferred from West Germanic (putatively cognate with ModGer. *rühren* 'move'), but this, even if sustainable philologically, would give inferior sense. — [4] *hornkv*istu 'antler-branches': Cf. Kock (*NN* §96), correcting *Skj*

B's *horngrene* 'horn-branches' (cf. *LP*: *hornkvistr*). — [4] *-kvistu* '-branches': The emendation was first suggested by *Bret* 1848-9 and adopted by subsequent eds. — [5] *en* 'and': Omitted in *Bret* 1848-9, *Skj* B and *Skald*, presumably because *en* occurs again at the head of l. 7. *Merl* 2012 prints the second *en* as *enn* (properly 'again, once more') but translates *aber* 'but', without comment. — [7]: The quantity of the <i> in *vísundr* appears to have been variable. In its present metrical position it is required to be long, although *Skj* B and *Skald* give this example as short. The vowel is short in Sigv *ErfÓl* 3/8[I] and Arn *Magndr* 6/4[II]. *LP*, *AEW*: *visundr* both give the vowel as short, perhaps in view of the word's West Germanic cognates, while *ONP* and most other dictionaries of medieval and modern Icelandic have it as long. — [10] *verstum* 'worst': This adj. is introduced by Gunnlaugr and is perhaps mostly determined by metrical and alliterative requirements, since the horns of European bison are not specially long, though certainly sharp and capable of use as weapons (Stöcker and Dietrich 1996, 182).

15. 'Þeir þjótandi   þr*já*r of hrœra
     búnir at berjask   Bretlands eyjar.
     Þá mun vakna   viðr inn danski
     ok manns rǫddu   mæla sjalfri.

'Þjótandi, búnir at berjask, of hrœra þeir þr*já*r eyjar Bretlands. Þá mun inn danski viðr vakna ok mæla sjalfri rǫddu manns.

'Wailing, prepared to fight, they will stir up the three islands of Britain. Then the Danish wood will awake and speak with a man's actual voice.

Ms.: **Hb**(49v) (*Bret*).

Reading: [2] þr*já*r: þrír Hb.

Editions: *Skj*: Gunnlaugr Leifsson, *Merlínússpá I* 15: AII, 13, BII, 13, *Skald* II, 8; *Bret* 1848-9, II, 19 (*Bret* st. 15); *Hb* 1892-6, 273; *Merl* 2012, 80-1.

Notes: [All]: Cf. *DGB* 116 (Reeve and Wright 2007, 153.164-6; cf. Wright 1988, 108, prophecies 34 and 35): *quae nefando sonitu tres insulas Britanniae commouebunt. Excitabitur Daneum nemus et in humanam uocem erumpens clamabit* 'which stir up Britain's three islands with their dreadful sound. The Daneian Forest will awaken and shout in a human voice' (cf. Reeve and Wright 2007, 152). — [1] *þeir* 'they': Presumably the referent is loosely understood as the people of the island (sg.), who are mentioned as wailing in *II* 13/5-8. — [2] *þrjár* 'three': Emended from ms. *þrír* (refreshed), the m. nom. pl. form, in *Bret* 1848-9, followed by all subsequent eds. — [3]: Gunnlaugr makes Geoffrey's implications of ensuing battle explicit. — [6] *inn danski viðr* 'the Danish wood': Possibly to be identified as the Forest of Dean, located in the western part of Gloucestershire (see *CPB* I, 156; Poole 1987, 276; Townend 1998, 29-31); cf. Ótt *Knútdr* 10/8[I] and Note there. Geoffrey's reference to this wood may reflect its status as the centre of iron-working to equip military expeditions (Poole

1955, 81-2). The reading *danorum* 'of the Danes' is found in the R ms. of the First Variant Version (Wright 1988, 108), as noted by *Merl* 2012; cf. the Anglo-Norman decasyllabic rendering (Blacker 2005, 44) *les bois de Danemarche* 'the woods of Denmark'. But Gunnlaugr does not appear to be basing himself on R, which contains many erroneous readings not reflected by *Merl*, or indeed on the First Variant Version in general: see *I* 39 Note to [All]. He might have found the reading included as a variant in his source ms. (cf. *I* 41 Note to [All], *II* 25 Note to [All]) or instead have adapted Lat. *daneum* or a different variant reading such as *danerium* independently, perhaps aware of Óttarr svarti's reference to a locality in England as *Danaskógar* (*Ótt Knútdr* 8/8[1]). For an identification of this locality as the Forest of Dean see *CPB* I, 156, Poole (1987, 276). For interpretation of Latin place names on Gunnlaugr's part, cf. *II* 9 Note to [All]. — [8] *sjalfri* 'actual': This adj. is translated as *saalunde* 'thus' (referring to the ensuing speech) in *Bret* 1848-9 and left unaccounted for in *Skj* B; *Merl* 2012 translates *und selbst mit der Stimme eines Menschen sprechen* 'and itself speak with the voice of a man'. But *sjalfri* is dat., qualifying *rǫddu* 'voice', and should be construed in the sense of 'very, actual' (cf. *CVC*: *sjálfr*). Gunnlaugr's translation thereby emphasises the miraculous nature of the event more than is expressed in the Latin.

16. '"Kom Kambría   með Kornbretum,
       seg Vintóni: 'Vǫllr þik *gleyp*ir.
       Fœr hirðis sjǫt   hinig, es le*gg*ja
       lung at láði;   munu liðir allir
       hǫfði fylgja;   þats hjǫlp guma.'

'"Kom Kambría með Kornbretum, seg Vintóni: 'Vǫllr *gleyp*ir þik. Fœr sjǫt hirðis hinig, es lung le*gg*ja at láði; allir liðir munu fylgja hǫfði; þats hjǫlp guma.'

'"Come Cambria, along with the Cornish Britons, say to Winchester: 'The plain will swallow you up. Move the shepherd's settlement here, where ships make for the land; all limbs will follow the head; that is the salvation of men.'

Ms.: **Hb**(49v) (*Bret*).

Readings: [1] Kambría: cimbria *corrected from* cambría *during the process of refreshing* Hb   [3] Vintóni: vontoni Hb   [4] *gleyp*ir: skýfir *corrected from* gleypir *during the process of refreshing* Hb   [6] le*gg*ja: lengra Hb.

Editions: *Skj*: Gunnlaugr Leifsson, *Merlínússpá I* 16: AII, 13, BII, 13, *Skald* II, 8; *Bret* 1848-9, II, 20 (*Bret* st. 16); *Hb* 1892-6, 273; *Merl* 2012, 81-2.

Notes: [All]: Cf. *DGB* 116 (Reeve and Wright 2007, 153.166-8; cf. Wright 1988, 108, prophecy 35): *accede, Kambria, et iunge lateri tuo Cornubiam, et dic Guintoniae 'absorbebit te tellus; transfer sedem pastoris ubi naues applicant, et cetera membra caput sequantur'* 'Come, Wales, and join Cornwall at your side, and say to Winchester, "The earth will swallow you up; move the seat of your shepherd to the place where ships make landfall, and let the remaining limbs follow the head"' (cf. Reeve and Wright 2007, 152). Geoffrey's prophecy expresses Welsh aspirations to restore the see of St Davids to metropolitan status (Tatlock 1950, 405; Poole 1955, 296; Barrow 1956, 220; Brooke 1961, 212); the key to this kind of advocacy was to present the preferred location as no mere rural retreat but the major urban centre within its diocese, hence the mention of ships, with its implication that St Davids was a port as well as a city (see Note to *I* 59/2). Winchester may have been the target of this campaign insofar as its bishop traditionally filled the post of Chancellor of England and hence commanded significant secular power. The allegory here is probably based on the literal fact that the city of Winchester is notoriously built upon unstable ground. Channels of the river Itchen come close to the Cathedral, causing periodic flooding of the crypt. The admonition for the limbs to follow the head has its ultimate source in the Aesopian fabulist Babrius 134: 'Fable of the Snake and his Tail' (Perry 1984, 174-5), where the tail insists on replacing the head as leader but, having then blindly led the snake into a stony pit, is obliged to beg the head to save the snake by resuming its customary role; Gunnlaugr goes beyond Geoffrey in spelling out that this is mankind's salvation, as stated by Babrius, because symbolically the tail represents the irrational and has to be subordinated to the head, which represents the rational. He therefore either knew the fable independently of *DGB* or found this amplification in a commentary on *DGB*. In Geoffrey's allegory the limbs would represent the regions dependent upon Winchester, which, with numerous estates, was the richest diocese in England. — [1, 3, 5] *kom ... seg ... fær* 'come ... say ... move': The extrametrical suffixed pronouns *kompú* (l. 1), *segþú* (l. 3) and *færþú* (l. 5) have been deleted in the present edn to reduce the hypermetrical lines that otherwise result. *Skj* B and *Skald* delete those in ll. 3 and 5. — [1] *Kambría* 'Cambria': Refreshed as 'cimbria', and reported thus in *Bret* 1848-9 and *Skj* A, but the *a* is visible beneath the refreshing. — [3] *Vintóni* 'Winchester': Emended in *Bret* 1848-9 (followed by all subsequent eds) from ms. 'vontoni' (refreshed). This form, without final *-a*, is irregular and perhaps used for metrical reasons, but might also be an artefact of the refreshing. — [4] gl*ey*p*ir* 'will swallow': Refreshed as *skýfir* 'will cut', but the original reading is still partially visible, as noted by Scheving, who restored accordingly, followed by *Bret* 1848-9, *Skj* B and *Skald*. *Merl* 2012 retains *skýfir*, understood in the sense of *verstosse* 'disown/expel', but this scarcely makes sense in context and ignores the textual history. — [5] *hirðis* 'the shepherd's': Rendering Lat. *pastoris* 'of the shepherd', a standard expression for 'bishop' (Smalley 1973, 34). See *I* 59 Note to [All]. — [7] *leggja* 'make': Emended by Scheving (followed by *Bret* 1848-9, *Skj* B and *Skald*) for ms. *lengra* (refreshed). *Merl* 2012 would retain *lengra*, translating in combination with *lung* as *das lange Schiff* 'the long ship', but this, besides ignoring the comp. degree of the adj., disregards the clear testimony of the Latin (*naues applicant* 'ships make landfall') and leaves the clause without a finite verb, which is supplied in the German translation in parentheses as *kommt* 'comes'.

17. 'En sæti *hans*   sund*dýr* fagna;
    hans mun stóll vesa   yfir stoðum tvennum.
    Þó hefr gumnum   grandat mǫrgum
    hvítrar ullar   hvers kyns litir.

'En sund*dýr* fagna sæt*i hans*; stóll hans mun vesa yfir tvennum stoðum. Þó hefr litir hvers kyns hvítrar ullar grandat mǫrgum gumnum.

'But his seats gladden sound-animals [SHIPS]; his throne will rest on two columns. Yet dyes of every kind for white wool have harmed many men.

Ms.: **Hb**(49v) (*Bret*).

Reading: [1, 2] En sæt*i hans* sund*dýr* fagna: 'En sætaz svndi fagna' Hb.

Editions: *Skj*: Gunnlaugr Leifsson, *Merlínússpá I* 17: AII, 13, BII, 13-14; *Skald* II, 8; *Bret* 1848-9, II, 20 (*Bret* st. 17); *Hb* 1892-6, 273; *Merl* 2012, 83-4.

Notes: [All]: Cf. *DGB* 116 (Reeve and Wright 2007, 153.169-72; cf. Wright 1988, 108, prophecies 35 and 36): "'*candor lanarum nocuit atque tincturae ipsarum diuersitas; uae periurae genti, quia urbs inclita propter eam ruet. Gaudebunt naues augmentatione tanta, et unum ex duobus fiet*'" "'The whiteness of wool and the many colours it has been dyed have done you harm; woe to the treacherous people on whose account a famous city will fall." The ships will rejoice at this great increment and two will become one' (Reeve and Wright 2007, 152). Winchester was by Geoffrey's time the base for a flourishing wool industry (see Leach 1900b, 134-5; Page 1912b, 36-44). For the privileges of cloth makers and their growing unpopularity see Poole (1955, 84-6). Geoffrey seems to single out the commune of the city for suspicion of potential disloyalty, against either the king or the bishop, whose vassals they would have been. Gunnlaugr focuses on the dyeing of wool, to which special privileges attached. The sentences beginning respectively *candor* and *gaudebunt* are reversed in the text of *Merl* as extant, and several other sentences are omitted. — [1-2]: Emended by Scheving (followed by *Bret* 1848-9) from ms. 'En sætaz svndi fagna' (refreshed). The three-fold emendation here is necessary to create sense in an incoherent passage and fits well with *DGB*, which describes ships, i.e. their passengers, rejoicing in the augmentation of the see of St Davids through the addition of Winchester. The conjectured reading *sæti* 'seats' (i.e. 'sees'), construed as pl. because of the pl. verb *fagna* 'rejoice', conforms admirably to this logic. Gunnlaugr uses *sund* 'sea' as a kenning determinant twice elsewhere (*II* 1/2, *II* 31/2, the latter in the ship-kenning *sundraukn* 'the beasts of burden of the sea'); for the postulated second element *dýr* 'animal', cf. *kjaldýr* 'keel beast' (*I* 95/6). Skj B (followed by *Skald* and *Merl* 2012) emends to *sætré* 'timbers of the sea [SHIPS]', while retaining *sundi*, interpreted as 'voyage', and explains the whole clause as 'the timbers of the sea [SHIPS] rejoice in the voyage'. But that fits poorly with *DGB*. — [3] *hans* 'his': Omitted in *Skald*. — [4] *tvennum stoðum* 'two columns': Presumably another reference to the combined revenues of the bishoprics of Winchester and St Davids. *Stóll* (sg.) 'throne' apparently clashes with pl. *sæti* 'seats', but the logic is presumably that, to paraphrase *DGB*, the two sees have become one. — [8] *litir* 'dyes': Emended in *Merl* 2012 to *litr* 'dye', so as to create concord with the sg. verb *hefr* (lit. 'has'). But this is unnecessary, since often the sg. of the verb is used when a pl. subject is placed later in the clause (*NS* §66b Anm. 3); moreover, the emendation would introduce a trisyllabic line at a point in the poem where such lines do not otherwise occur.

18. 'Borg mun falla,   — veitk bana þjóðum —
     þvíat hon eiðrofa   áðr of gerðisk.
     Munu griðbítar   gǫrla drepnir;
     geldr Vintóna   vándra manna.

'Borg mun falla, þvíat hon áðr of gerðisk eiðrofa; veitk bana þjóðum. Griðbítar munu gǫrla drepnir; Vintóna geldr vándra manna.

'The city will fall, because it had previously perjured itself; I know of death for the people. The breakers of the truce will [be] comprehensively put to death; Winchester will pay for the wicked men.

Ms.: **Hb**(49v) (*Bret*).

Reading: [2] bana: bana *corrected from* 'kana' Hb.

Editions: *Skj*: Gunnlaugr Leifsson, *Merlínússpá I* 18: AII, 13, BII, 14; *Skald* II, 8; *Bret* 1848-9, II, 20-1 (*Bret* st. 18); *Hb* 1892-6, 273; *Merl* 2012, 84.

Notes: [All]: Cf. *DGB* 116 (Reeve and Wright 2007, 153.168-9; cf. Wright 1988, 108, prophecy 35): "'*festinat namque dies qua ciues ob scelera periurii peribunt*'" "'The day is at hand when your citizens will perish because of their crimes of betrayal'" (Reeve and Wright 2007, 152). This concludes the speech from the Forest of Dean in *DGB*. In *Merl* motifs from prophecies 35 and 36 are intermixed here and in *II* 19; it is not clear where the Forest's speech is regarded as ending, but since Gunnlaugr's use of 2nd pers. sg. forms is confined to *II* 16 the placement of quotation marks in this edn follows *Skald* and *Merl* 2012, which treat only *II* 16 as direct speech. *Bret* 1848-9 and *Skj* B do not use quotation marks in this passage. — [2] *veitk* 'I know': Gunnlaugr's addition. — [7-8]: The verb *gjalda* with gen. denotes the cause for which payment is made or suffering incurred (*CVC*: *gjalda* 2; *Fritzner*: *gjalda* 6). The English idiom 'pay for' covers both of these senses. — [7] *Vintóna* 'Winchester': This is the reading of the ms. (not refreshed). It would be tempting to emend to *Vintónía*, by analogy with *II* 5/2 and forms in Geoffrey's text, as is done in *Merl* 2012, but such a form would produce an unmetrical line and there are parallels elsewhere for Gunnlaugr's use of variant forms, e.g. *Kónan* (*I* 64/1) vs. *Kónánus* (gen.) (*I* 72/2).

19. 'Mun bjarnígull   borg upp gera;
    smíðar hæsta   họll landreki.
    Hana mun remma   ríkr oddviti
    fimm hundruðum   fagra turna.

'Bjarnígull mun gera upp borg; landreki smíðar hæsta họll. Ríkr oddviti mun remma hana fimm hundruðum fagra turna.

'A hedgehog will restore the city; the ruler will build the highest hall. The mighty leader will strengthen it with five hundred fine towers.

Ms.: **Hb**(49v) (*Bret*).

Editions: *Skj*: Gunnlaugr Leifsson, *Merlínússpá I* 19: AII, 13-14, BII, 14-15; *Skald* II, 9; *Bret* 1848-9, II, 21 (*Bret* st. 19); *Hb* 1892-6, 273; *Merl* 2012, 85.

Notes: [All]: Cf. *DGB* 116 (Reeve and Wright 2007, 153.172, 173-4; cf. Wright 1988, 108, prophecy 36): *Reaedificabit eam hericius … Adiciet palacium ingens et sexcentis turribus illud uallabit* 'The city will be rebuilt by a hedgehog … He will add a huge palace and will fortify it with six hundred towers' (cf. Reeve and Wright 2007, 152). This prophecy appears to be an extrapolation from an upsurge of castle-building and circumvallation in Geoffrey's time (cf. Eales 2003, 50); for castle-building and re-building at Winchester contemporary with Geoffrey see Kenyon (2005, 31). The elements of *DGB*'s prophecy 36, 1) rebuilding of Winchester, 2) possession of apples, 3) bolstering of defences at London, 4) concealment of apples at London, are redistributed in *Merl* between *II* 19 and 21 in the order 1, 3, 2, 4. Possibly st. 21 originally preceded st. 20. *Merl*, in common with the Ω class of mss, omits a sentence of prophecy found in the Π class (Reeve and Wright 2007, ix, 153). — [1] *bjarnígull* 'a hedgehog': A *hap. leg.* in poetry; prose occurrences are rare and confined to learned contexts, as are also those of the simplex *ígull* (see *ONP*: *ígull*). — [7] *fimm hundruðum* 'with five hundred': No doubt Gunnlaugr's copy-text had .d. '500', not .dc. '600', parallel to ms. H of the First Variant Version (Wright 1988, 108) but most probably through coincident error, as arises frequently with numerals.

20. 'Þat Lundúnum   líkar illa;
    eykr hon þrimr hlutum   þykka veggi.
    Kostar hon kepp*a*   við konungíðnir;
    *fe*rr suðr of fjall   frægð af smíði,
    e*n** Te*m*s of borg   tekr at geisa.

'Þat líkar Lundúnum illa; hon eykr þykka veggi þrimr hlutum. Hon kostar kepp*a* við konungíðnir; frægð af smíði *fe*rr suðr of fjall, e*n** Te*m*s tekr at geisa of borg.

'That will displease London; she will increase her thick walls threefold. She will attempt to compete with the king's exploits; news of the work will travel south over the mountain and the Thames will start to surge around the city.

Ms.: **Hb**(49v) (*Bret*).

Readings: [5] kepp*a*: keppir Hb   [7] *ferr*: 'mer' *apparently corrected from* 'ferr'(?) *during the process of refreshing* Hb   [9] e*n* Te*m*s*: 'eyr teins' Hb.

Editions: *Skj*: Gunnlaugr Leifsson, *Merlínússpá I* 20: AII, 14, BII, 14, *Skald* II, 9; *Bret* 1848-9, II, 21-2 (*Bret* st. 20); *Hb* 1892-6, 273; *Merl* 2012, 85-6.

Notes: [All]: Cf. *DGB* 116 (Reeve and Wright 2007, 153.174-6; cf. Wright 1988, 109, prophecy 37): *Inuidebit ergo Lundonia et muros suos tripliciter augebit. Circuibit eam undique Tamensis fluuius, et rumor operis transcendet Alpes* 'London will be filled with envy and will increase its walls threefold. The Thames will encircle the city, and fame of this feat will travel beyond the Alps' (cf. Reeve and Wright 2007, 152). London and Winchester were increasingly in competition in Geoffrey's time as royal and administrative centres. — [5-6]: This idea is made more explicit than in *DGB*, as would have been necessary if st. 21 had originally preceded st. 20 (see Note to *II* 19 [All]). — [5] *kepp*a 'to compete': Emended in *Skj* B (followed by *Skald*) from ms. *keppir* (refreshed) '[he] competes'. *Merl* 2012 retains *keppir*, evidently construing *kostar* as a noun but without explaining its sense and function. — [6] *konungíðnir* 'the king's exploits': A *hap. leg.* Compounds with initial *konung-*, as distinct from *konungs-* and *konunga-*, are sparsely attested in Old Norse (*ONP*). — [7] *fjall* 'the mountain': The sg. *fjall*, as used in *Merl*, often corresponds to Lat. *montes* 'mountains' and other pl. forms in *DGB* (cf. *II* 39/1, *II* 41/2). — [9] e*n* Te*m*s* 'and the Thames': Emended in *Bret* 1848-9, followed by all subsequent eds, from ms. 'eyr teins' (refreshed).

21. 'En it horska dýr   hlezk aldini
     harðla góðu,   þvís hilmir velr.
     Koma foglar þar   fljúgandi til
     af *vi*ð*um* víða   vitja epla.

'En it horska dýr hlezk harðla góðu aldini, þvís hilmir velr. Foglar koma þar fljúgandi til, víða af *vi*ð*um*, vitja epla.

'And the wise beast will load himself with very good fruit, which the king selects. There birds will come flying up, far and wide from the woods, to visit the apples.

Ms.: **Hb**(49v) (*Bret*).

Reading: [7] *vi*ð*um*: 'vogvm' Hb.

Editions: *Skj*: Gunnlaugr Leifsson, *Merlínússpá I* 21: AII, 14, BII, 14, *Skald* II, 9; *Bret* 1848-9, II, 22 (*Bret* st. 21); *Hb* 1892-6, 273; *Merl* 2012, 86-7.

Notes: [All]: Cf. *DGB* 116 (Reeve and Wright 2007, 153.172-3; cf. Wright 1988, 108, prophecy 36): *oneratus pomis, ad quorum odorem diuersorum nemorum conuolabunt uolucres* 'laden with apples, to whose fragrance the birds will flock from various forests' (cf. Reeve and Wright 2007, 152). — [1-4]: The 'wise beast' and the 'king' are one and the same, both nouns referring back to the hedgehog-king of *II* 19/1 (also *II* 22/1); cf. his designation as *landreki* 'ruler' in 19/4. — [2] *hlezk … aldini* 'will load himself … with fruit': *Merl* 2012 seeks a source for this motif in the *Physiologus* (Curley 2009, 24), which describes the hedgehog as collecting food for his young by rolling in fallen grapes so that they are skewered by his quills; to be noted, though, is that the fruit collected by the hedgehog-king is identified in *DGB* and, following him, *Merl*, as apples. — [7] *viðum* 'woods': Emended in this edn from ms. 'vogvm' (refreshed), in view of *DGB*'s 'forests'. *Bret* 1848-9 seems to interpret 'vogvm' as *vágum*, normally 'bays' (dat. pl.) but here understood as 'depths', with *viða* construed as 'forests' (gen. pl.): thus 'depths of forests', but that is scarcely possible. *Skj* B, followed by *Skald* and *Merl* 2012, has *vegum* 'ways', deviating from the sense of *DGB*.

22. 'En bjarnígull   býr of vélar;
      leynir hann eplum   Lundúnum í.
      Grefr í grundu   gǫtur háligar
      fýstr til fengjar   fláráðugt dýr.

'En bjarnígull býr of vélar; hann leynir eplum í Lundúnum. Fláráðugt dýr, fýstr til fengjar, grefr háligar gǫtur í grundu.

'But the hedgehog will engineer contrivances; he will hide the apples in London. The treacherous beast, eager for booty, will dig lofty passages in the ground.

Ms.: **Hb**(49v) (*Bret*).

Editions: *Skj*: Gunnlaugr Leifsson, *Merlínússpá I* 22: AII, 14, BII, 14-15; *Skald* II, 9; *Bret* 1848-9, II, 22 (*Bret* st. 22); *Hb* 1892-6, 273; *Merl* 2012, 87-8.

Notes: [All]: Cf. *DGB* 116 (Reeve and Wright 2007, 153.176-7; cf. Wright 1988, 109, prophecy 37): *Occultabit infra illam hericius poma sua et subterraneas uias machinabitur* 'The hedgehog will hide his apples there and devise pathways beneath the earth' (cf. Reeve and Wright 2007, 152). Gunnlaugr plays up the notion of the hedgehog-king's perfidy, on lines similar to his characterisation of the fox-king (*II* 27-45). — [1] *býr* 'will engineer': For this sense of *búa* + *um* cf. *ONP*: *búa um*. — [3] *hann* 'he': Omitted in *Skald*. — [6] *háligar* 'lofty': For this tentative translation, cf. *Skj* B. As noted by Finnur Jónsson in *LP*: *hǫligr*, the meaning of this sparsely attested adj. in context is not entirely clear. It represents Gunnlaugr's free addition to the account in *DGB*. Possibly the general meaning is 'capacious, commodious'; possibly too, however, the reading has arisen in error for *hagligar* 'artful' (*Fritzner*: *hagligr* 1; *LP*: *hagligr* 1; *ONP*: *hagligr*), whose inclusion in the text would bring out the meaning of *machinabitur* 'will devise, engineer' more fully. For *háligr* and *hagligr* as variant readings see Hbreiðm Lv 1/3^(II). — [7]: The idea of the hedgehog-king's eagerness for plunder is another of Gunnlaugr's additions.

23. 'Þá mun*u* ór moldu   mæla steinar
    ok verþjóðar   vél upp koma.
    Ey mun víðask,   en Valir skjalfa,
    ok sær saman   sœkja fíkjum,
    svát millim landa   mál of heyri.

'Þá mun*u* steinar mæla ór moldu ok vél verþjóðar koma upp. Ey mun víðask, en Valir skjalfa, ok sær sœkja saman fíkjum, svát mál of heyri millim landa.

'Then stones will speak from the earth and the machinations of the sea-people be revealed. The island will be widened, and the French will tremble, and the sea will come together greatly so that speech can be heard between the lands.

Ms.: Hb(49v) (*Bret*).

Reading: [1] mun*u*: mun Hb.

Editions: *Skj*: Gunnlaugr Leifsson, *Merlínússpá I* 23: AII, 14, BII, 15, *Skald* II, 9; *Bret* 1848-9, II, 23 (*Bret* st. 23); *Hb* 1892-6, 273; *Merl* 2012, 88-9.

Notes: [All]: Cf. *DGB* 116 (Reeve and Wright 2007, 153.177-81; cf. Wright 1988, 109, prophecy 38): *In tempore illo loquentur lapides et mare quo ad Galliam nauigatur infra breue spacium contrahetur. In utraque ripa audietur homo ab homine, et solidum insulae dilatabitur. Reuelabuntur occulta submarinorum, et Gallia prae timore tremebit* 'At that time stones will speak and the sea where one sails to France will become a narrow strait. Men on opposite shores will be within earshot and the island's surface will grow larger. The secrets of the people beneath the sea will be revealed, and France will tremble in fear' (cf. Reeve and Wright 2007, 152). Gunnlaugr appears to alter the sequence of ideas in *DGB* by associating the revelations concerning the *submarini* 'people beneath the sea' with the capacity of stones to speak rather than with the drying up of the English Channel. Through his re-use of the *heiti verþjóð*, Gunnlaugr clearly identifies Geoffrey's *submarini* with the sea-people mentioned in *II* 12/8; they are presumably the *Ruteni* 'Flemings', who were frequently accused of machinations in respect of both trade and mercenary service. — [1] mun*u* 'will': Emended in *Skald*, followed by *Merl* 2012 and the present edn; *Bret* 1848-9 and *Skj* B retain the ms. reading *mun* 'will' (sg.). The sg. form is possible, when a composite subject (including both sg. and pl.) follows, but is less likely here. — [5] *víðask* 'be widened': A *hap leg.* in poetry. *Bret* 1848-9 notes the rarity of this verb; both the other two attestations are from texts concerned with Bishop Þorlákr (*ONP*: *víða*). — [7-8] *ok sær sœkja saman fíkjum* 'and the sea will come together greatly': I.e. 'the sea will shrink considerably'. These lines seem to refer to the narrowing of the English Channel, as mentioned in *DGB*'s *mare ... breue spacium contrahetur* (see Note to [All] above), translated lit. 'the sea ... will be drawn together in a small space'.

24. 'Kemr ór skógi   Kalatério
     fogl fljúgand*i*,   sás fira villir.
     Flýgr of nǫttum,   nýsir gǫrla;
     kallar hegr*i*   hvern fogl til *s*ín;
     es um tvívetri   tálráð samit.

'Fogl kemr fljúgand*i* ór skógi Kalatério, sás villir fira. Flýgr of nǫttum, nýsir gǫrla; hegr*i* kallar hvern fogl til *s*ín; tálráð es samit um tvívetri.

'From the forest of Calaterium a bird will come flying that will lead men astray. It will fly at night, spy thoroughly; the heron will call every bird to itself; treachery will be devised over a two-year span.

Ms.: **Hb**(49v) (*Bret*).

Readings: [3] fljúgand*i*: fljúganda Hb   [7] hegr*i*: hegra Hb   [8] *s*ín: þín Hb.

Editions: *Skj*: Gunnlaugr Leifsson, *Merlínússpá I* 24: AII, 14, BII, 15, *Skald* II, 9; *Bret* 1848-9, II, 23-4 (*Bret* st. 24); *Hb* 1892-6, 273-4; *Merl* 2012, 89-90.

Notes: [All]: Cf. *DGB* 116 (Reeve and Wright 2007, 153.181-3; cf. Wright 1988, 109, prophecy 39): *Post haec ex Calaterio nemore procedet ardea, quae insulam per biennium circumuolabit. Nocturno clamore conuocabit uolatilia et omne genus uolucrum associabit sibi* 'Afterwards a heron will emerge from the forest of Calaterium and will circle the island for two years. It will summon the birds of the air with its cry at night and assemble all their species' (cf. Reeve and Wright 2007, 152). Gunnlaugr partially rationalises the prophecy of a charismatic new leader and adds the notion of his treachery. The forest of Calaterium is unidentified but evidently located in Albania (Scotland), as appears from *DGB* III (Reeve and Wright 2007, 50-1; cf. Tatlock 1950, 17-18). — [1, 3]: De Vries (1964-7, II, 75 n. 179) compares *Vsp* 66/2. — [3] *fljúgand*i 'flying': Emended from ms. *fljúganda* (refreshed) in *Bret* 1848-9, followed by subsequent eds. — [4] *sás villir fira* 'that will lead men astray': This is Gunnlaugr's amplification of *DGB*, perhaps in allusion to the notion of the heron seen in *Hávm* 13/1-3 (*NK* 19): *Óminnis hegri heitir, | sá er yfir ǫldrom þrumir, | hann stelr geði guma* 'He is called the heron of forgetfulness, who hovers over the ale-feasts; he steals the wits of men'. How the heron gained this reputation is unclear (Evans 1986, 80). Dronke (1984, 54-5) notes a traditional association of this bird with vomiting and flapping around as if drunk, but it is hard to see why such behaviours would 'lead men astray', as required by the context in *Hávm* and *Merl*. Invective against drunkenness on Gunnlaugr's part is seen again in *II* 56-7. In modern times the Black-crowned Night

Heron (*nátthegri, Nycticorax nycticorax*) is an occasional visitor and resident in Iceland (Gunnlaugur Pétursson 2006). — [6]: The idea of the heron acting as a spy (or scout?) is introduced by Gunnlaugr. — [7] *hegr*i 'the heron': Emended from ms. *hegra* (refreshed) in *Bret* 1848-9, followed by *Skj* B and *Skald*. This is a rarely attested word in Old Norse; outside *Merl* there are only two attestations in poetry (*LP*: *hegri*) and in all four prose citations in *ONP* it is used as a nickname rather than a common noun; of the two men thus designated, one is a C12th Norwegian and the other an early settler in Iceland. *Merl* 2012 retains *hegra* without explanation of this form. — [8] *sín* 'itself': Emended from ms. *þín* (refreshed) in *Bret* 1848-9, followed by subsequent eds.

25. 'Flykkjask foglar;   fara þeir í sæði;
    eyða þeir ǫkrum   ok aldini.
    Sultr verðr ok sótt   — sék mart fyrir —
    manndauðr mikill;   mein gengr of þjóð.

'Foglar flykkjask; þeir fara í sæði; þeir eyða ǫkrum ok aldini. Sultr verðr, ok sótt, manndauðr mikill; sék mart fyrir; mein gengr of þjóð.

'The birds will flock together; they will go into the crops; they will devastate the fields and fruit. Famine will develop, also sickness, great mortality of men; I see many things to come; harm will afflict the people.

Ms.: **Hb**(49v) (*Bret*).

Editions: *Skj*: Gunnlaugr Leifsson, *Merlínússpá I* 25: AII, 15, BII, 15, *Skald* II, 9, *FF* §63; *Bret* 1848-9, II, 24 (*Bret* st. 25); *Hb* 1892-6, 274; *Merl* 2012, 90.

Notes: [All]: Cf. *DGB* 116 (Reeve and Wright 2007, 153.183-5; cf. Wright 1988, 109, prophecies 39 and 40): *In culturas mortalium irruent et omnia grana messium deuorabunt. Sequetur fames populum atque dira mortalitas famem* 'They will fall upon men's crops and eat all the grains of corn. The people will be afflicted by hunger and after that by a deadly plague' (Reeve and Wright 2007, 152). For *grana* 'grains' a variant reading is *genera* 'kinds' (Reeve and Wright 2007, 153, Wright 1988, 109) and the expansion of the Latin seen in *Merl* could be interpreted as an attempt to incorporate the sense of both readings by mentioning the different types of produce. Ms. D of the First Variant Version has *genera* in the main text and *grana* noted in the margin as a variant (Wright 1988, 109), and Gunnlaugr's source ms. may have been similar in this respect. — [2, 3] *þeir* 'they': Omitted in *Skald* in both lines. — [5]: This edn follows Kock (*FF* §63) in its analysis of the components of the subject; *Skj* B, apparently followed by *Merl* 2012, takes *manndauðr* as the subject of *gengr*, with *mein* in apposition, but that, as Kock notes, is less consonant with poetic style. — [8] *þjóð* 'the people': *Merl* 2012 would retain the refresher's reading *þjóðir*, but, as noted in *Hb* 1892-6, the contraction sign for *-ir* arises from misinterpretation of the loop in preceding *-ð-*.

26. 'En fogl ept þat   ferr vestr í dal,
þanns Gálábes   gumnar kalla.
Hann mun hefjask   *í it* hæsta fjall,
ok þar uppi   í eikr limu*m*
*h*reið*r*ask *h*egri;   hann *es* fogla verstr.

'En fogl ferr vestr í dal ept þat, þanns gumnar kalla Gálábes. Hann mun hefjask *í it* hæsta fjall, ok *h*egri *h*reið*r*ask þar uppi í limu*m* eikr; hann *es* verstr fogla.

'But after that the bird will go westwards into the valley that people call Galabes. It [the valley] will raise itself into the highest mountain and up there the heron will nest on the branches of an oak; it is the worst of birds.

Ms.: **Hb**(49v) (*Bret*).

Readings: [6] *í it*: '[…]' Hb, í it Hb*JS*   [8] limu*m*: '-limv' Hb   [9] *h*reið*r*ask: 'treiðr[…]' Hb; *h*egri: '[…]' Hb, hegri Hb*JS*   [10] *es*: 'a' Hb.

Editions: *Skj*: Gunnlaugr Leifsson, *Merlínússpá I* 26: AII, 15, BII, 15, *Skald* II, 9-10; *Bret* 1848-9, II, 24-5 (*Bret* st. 26); *Hb* 1892-6, 274; *Merl* 2012, 90-1.

Notes: [All]: Cf. *DGB* 116 (Reeve and Wright 2007, 153.185-3; cf. Wright 1988, 109, prophecy 40): *At cum calamitas tanta cessauerit, adibit detestabilis ales uallem Galahes atque eam in excelsum montem leuabit. In cacumine quoque ipsius plantabit quercum atque infra ramos nidificabit* 'When this great calamity is over, the accursed bird will visit the valley of Galahes and raise it into a lofty mountain. At the summit the heron will plant an oak and nest in its branches' (cf. Reeve and Wright 2007, 152). In *Merl* the heron is not credited with planting the oak, merely with nesting in it. — [3] *Gálábes*: This is the reading of some mss of Geoffrey, against majority *Galahes* (Wright 1988, 109, cf. 111), and therefore presumably stood in Gunnlaugr's source. — [6, 9]: See Introduction for readings no longer visible in Hb that could be read by earlier eds. — [8] *limum* 'the branches': Emended in this edn from ms. 'limv' (refreshed). Use of the pl. form is suggested by Geoffrey's *ramos* 'branches'. *Skj* B (followed by *Skald*) emends to *limi* 'branch', perhaps in view of actual nesting behaviour on the part of herons, but *LP*: *eikrlim* notes *limum* as a possible alternative. *Bret* 1848-9 retains *limu*, apparently as an acc. pl., translating as *kviste* 'branches', but dat. would be required syntactically, since the context requires a point of rest, not motion towards. *Merl* 2012 would also retain, interpreting *limu* 'branch' as sg. for pl.; this dat. sg. form is however not attested. — [9] *h*reiðrask 'will nest': Emended in *Skj* B (followed by *Skald* and *Merl* 2012) from ms. 'treiðr[…]' (partially refreshed); cf. *h*reiðri 'nest' in *II* 27/2. *Bret* 1848-9 takes the ms. reading to be 'treiðr' and explains as a form of *treðr* 'treads', the 3rd pers. sg. pres. indic. of *treðja* 'tread'. — [10] *es* 'is': Emended from ms. 'a' (refreshed) in *Bret* 1848-9, followed by subsequent eds.

27. 'Þrjá klekr hann unga   því hreiðri í;
     eigi es hegra kyn   hugþekkt firum.
     Þars vargr ok bjǫrn   ok at vísu refr
     slœgr ok sínum   sjaldan verr alinn.

'Hann klekr þrjá unga í því hreiðri; kyn hegra es eigi hugþekkt firum. Þars vargr ok bjǫrn ok at vísu refr slœgr ok sjaldan alinn verr sínum.

'It will hatch three young in that nest; the offspring of the heron is not loved by men. A wolf will be there, also a bear and assuredly a fox sly and seldom born [one] worse to its own [kind].

Ms.: **Hb**(49v) (*Bret*).

Editions: *Skj*: Gunnlaugr Leifsson, *Merlínússpá I* 27: AII, 15, BII, 15-16; *Skald* II, 10; *Bret* 1848-9, II, 25 (*Bret* st. 27); *Hb* 1892-6, 274; *Merl* 2012, 91-2.

Notes: [All]: Cf. *DGB* 116 (Reeve and Wright 2007, 153.188-9; cf. Wright 1988, 109, prophecy 41): *Tria oua procreabuntur in nido, ex quibus uulpes et lupus et ursus egredientur* 'In the nest it will lay three eggs, from which will hatch a fox, a wolf and a bear' (Reeve and Wright 2007, 152). Gunnlaugr does not show awareness of the variant *quattuor* 'four' found in some mss (Reeve and Wright 2007, 153): see Introduction. In the ensuing stanzas Gunnlaugr somewhat amplifies Geoffrey's story of the fox; some details of Gunnlaugr's characterisation and kenning diction are very similar to those in *Skaufhala bálkr* (Svart *Skauf*); see further *II* 28/8, 9 and Notes there. — [1] *klekr* 'will hatch': The verb *klekja* 'hatch' is attested only here in poetry. Its prose occurrences are confined to learned texts (*ONP*: *klekja*). — [1] *hann* 'it': Omitted in *Skald*. — [3-4]: Gunnlaugr again amplifies on the nature of the heron, taking his cue from *detestabilis ales* 'accursed bird' in *DGB* 116 (see *II* 26 Note to [All]).

28. 'Vaxa þar allir   upp brœðr saman;
     erut gjarnir þeir   gótt at vinna.
     Refr á móður   ræðr grimmliga;
     tapar henni sá   týnir sauða;
     es grenbúi   gjarn á ríki.

'Allir brœðr vaxa þar upp saman; þeir erut gjarnir at vinna gótt. Refr ræðr grimmliga á móður; sá týnir sauða tapar henni; grenbúi es gjarn á ríki.

'The brothers will all grow up together there; they will not be eager to do good. The fox will attack its mother savagely; that destroyer of sheep [FOX] will kill her; the lair-dweller [FOX] will be eager for power.

Ms.: **Hb**(49v-50r) (*Bret*).

Reading: [3] er*u*t: erat Hb.

Editions: *Skj*: Gunnlaugr Leifsson, *Merlínússpá I* 28: AII, 15, BII, 16, *Skald* II, 10, *NN* §2741; *Bret* 1848-9, II, 25-6 (*Bret* st. 28); Hb 1892-6, 274; *Merl* 2012, 92-3.

Notes: [All]: Cf. *DGB* 116 (Reeve and Wright 2007, 153.189; cf. Wright 1988, 109, prophecy 41): *Deuorabit uulpes matrem* 'The fox will devour its mother' (Reeve and Wright 2007, 152). Gunnlaugr considerably amplifies Geoffrey's text. — [3] *er*ut 'are not': Emended from ms. *erat* (refreshed) in *Bret* 1848-9 (*eru-at*) and apparently independently by Kock (*NN* §2741; *Skald*), followed by *Merl* 2012. Retained in *Skj* B, but the sg. verb does not agree with the immediately following pl. adj. and pron. Contrast the cases mentioned in the Note to *I* 36/9-12. — [8]: Attested kennings for 'fox' are few (*Meissner* 111), but the three that occur in this poem (see l. 9 here and *II* 39/3) have a parallel in Svart *Skauf*, where there are a number of nickname-like compounds for 'fox' and 'vixen', together with two kennings, *grenlægja* 'the lair-lier [VIXEN]' (4/2, 5/1) and *sauðbítr* 'the sheep-biter [FOX]' (18/6). — [9]: The kenning *grenbúi* 'lair-dweller [FOX]' is a *hap. leg.*; see Note to l. 8. The noun *gren* 'lair' was most commonly associated with foxes and the expression *sem melrakka í greni* 'like a fox in its lair' occurs frequently in relation to a humiliating capture or death (*ONP*: *gren*).

29. 'Brœðr vill hann sína   beita vélum;
     tekr horshǫfuð   hildingr á sik.
     En hoddskata   hræðask báðir;
     flýja barmar   brott ór landi.

'Hann vill beita brœðr sína vélum; hildingr tekr horshǫfuð á sik. En báðir hræðask hoddskata; barmar flýja brott ór landi.

'It will attack its brothers with tricks; the ruler will put on a horse's head. And both [brothers] will fear the treasure-chieftain [MAN]; the brothers will flee from the land.

Ms.: **Hb**(50r) (*Bret*).

Editions: *Skj*: Gunnlaugr Leifsson, *Merlínússpá I* 29: AII, 15, BII, 16, *Skald* II, 10; *Bret* 1848-9, II, 26 (*Bret* st. 29); *Hb* 1892-6, 274; *Merl* 2012, 93.

Notes: [All]: Cf. *DGB* 116 (Reeve and Wright 2007, 153.189-91; cf. Wright 1988, 109, prophecy 41): *et asininum caput gestabit. Monstro igitur assumpto, terrebit fratres suos ipsosque in Neustriam fugabit* 'and wear the head of an ass. Taking on the form of a monster, therefore, it will frighten its brothers and drive them off to Normandy' (cf. Reeve and Wright 2007, 152). Gunnlaugr omits the mention of Neustria (Normandy) as the brothers' place of refuge, perhaps because the wild boar whose aid they enlist in the following stanza is more to be associated with Cornwall. Cf. Note to *II* 31/7-8. — [1] *hann* 'it': Omitted in *Skald*.

30. 'Ok suðr sk*ulu þeir*   sveitar leita;
    vekr vargr ok bjǫrn   villigalta.
    En galti þeim   gengi sínu
    heitr hvatliga,   þvít hann hug trúir.

'Ok *þeir* sk*ulu* leita sveitar suðr; vargr ok bjǫrn vekr villigalta. En galti heitr þeim gengi sínu hvatliga, þvít hann trúir hug.

'And they will have to seek for an army in the south; the wolf and the bear will rouse a wild boar. And the boar will promise them his support with alacrity, since he trusts in his [own] courage.

Ms.: **Hb**(50r) (*Bret*).

Reading: [1] sk*ulu þeir*: skal Hb.

Editions: *Skj*: Gunnlaugr Leifsson, Merlínússpá I 30: AII, 15-16, BII, 16, *Skald* II, 10, *NN* §97; *Bret* 1848-9, II, 26 (*Bret* st. 30); *Hb* 1892-6, 274; *Merl* 2012, 93-4.

Notes: [All]: Cf. *DGB* 116 (Reeve and Wright 2007, 153.191-2; cf. Wright 1988, 109, prophecy 42): *At ipsi excitabunt aprum dentosum in illa et nauigio reuecti cum uulpe congredientur* 'They will stir up a tusked boar against it and sail back with a fleet to fight the fox' (Reeve and Wright 2007, 152). Gunnlaugr expands on the characterisation of the boar, introducing indirect speech and an element of irony, since the boar, despite his trust in his own courage, will emerge as rather a pathetic figure. — [1]: Emended in *NN* §97 (cf. *Skald*) from ms. *skal* (refreshed) to *skulu* 'must'. While syntactically speaking *skal* might be used impersonally, as in *Bret* 1848-9 and *Skj* B (followed by *Merl* 2012), the line as it stands in the ms. is metrically deficient and *skal* for *skulu* could have arisen through abbreviation. In this edn *þeir* is added by analogy with *II* 31/3 and similar lines, with its antecedent in *barmar* 'brothers' in *II* 29/7. In *Bret* 1848-9 ms. *ok* (refreshed) is emended to *í*, which is accepted in *Skj* B with further emendation of *suðr* to *suðri*, which might also be right; *Merl* 2012 rejects this further emendation. — [8] *hann* 'he': Omitted in *Skald*.

31. 'Þeir snarliga   sundraukn búa;
    dragask lítinn þeir   landher saman.
    Gnýr es manna,   gengr lið róa;
    hylr Hǫgna sjǫt   †herkorn† skipa.

'Þeir búa sundraukn snarliga; þeir dragask lítinn landher saman. Es gnýr manna, lið gengr róa; †herkorn† skipa hylr sjǫt Hǫgna.

'They will rapidly equip the draught animals of the sea [SHIPS]; they will bring a small land-army together. There will be a commotion of men, the army will set to rowing; †...† of ships covers the seat of Hǫgni <sea-king> [SEA].

Ms.: **Hb**(50r) (*Bret*).

Editions: *Skj*: Gunnlaugr Leifsson, *Merlínússpá I* 31: AII, 16, BII, 16; *Skald* II, 10; *NN* §98; *Bret* 1848-9, II, 26-7 (*Bret* st. 31); *Hb* 1892-6, 274; *Merl* 2012, 95.

Notes: [All]: Stanzas *II* 31-6 are an amplification of the theme of voyage and battle, loosely adapted from *DGB* 116 (Reeve and Wright 2007, 152-3). — [5] *manna* 'of men': This is the ms. reading (cf. *Hb* 1892-6), but thanks to the refresher the final *-a* has become indistinct. *Bret* 1848-9 interpreted the word as *meirr*, translating *er meirr* as *voxer* 'increases'. *Merl* 2012 reads *meir* (presumably intending 'more', as adv.), without clarifying how this would work syntactically. — [7-8]: Not definitively resolved. (a) Scheving's conjecture (reported in *Bret* 1848-9) *Kornbreta* 'of the Cornish Britons' would combine with ms. *her*, interpreted as *herr* 'army' (since gemination is often not shown in Hb), to make superior sense if the kenning *sjǫt Hǫgna* 'the seat of Hǫgni <sea-king>' can be explained, not as 'sea' (*LP*: *sjǫt*, with the present occurrence as the sole attestation; cf. *Meissner* 93), but as 'ship' (cf. SnSt *Ht* 75/2^{III} *hafbekks* 'of the sea-bench [SHIP]'; *Meissner* 222). Gunnlaugr uses *sjǫt* once elsewhere (*II* 16/5), in relation to a bishop's seat. Thus emended, the line would fit well with the comment in l. 3 that the army is small; an army could be small yet still cover some ships, whereas the ships conveying it could scarcely be said to cover the sea. Other attempted solutions do not reckon with this necessary logic. (b) Finnur Jónsson (*LP*: *herkorn*), followed by *Merl* 2012, explains *herkorn* 'army-grain' *ad hoc* as an idiomatic expression for uncountable numbers. (c) Kock (*NN* §98; *Skald*) conjectures *herkorðr 'military force', on the basis of compounds in West Germanic, and interprets as *skeppens krigiska skara höljer havet* 'the ships' military force covers the sea'. Also in favour of Scheving's conjecture are the appropriateness of describing a Cornish army as sailing from the south to attack Wales, as required by *II* 32/1-3, and perhaps too the association of an earlier boar-king with Cornwall in *DGB* (cf. *I* 24 Note to [All]). Gunnlaugr could be seen as furthering the attention to Cornwall that is already a remarkable feature of *DGB* (Padel 1984).

32. 'Halda þeir sunnan   of svalan ægi
    Bretlands á vit;   búask til rómu.
    En refr hinig   með rekka lið
    ferr fráliga   fold at verja.

'Þeir halda sunnan of svalan ægi á vit Bretlands; búask til rómu. En refr ferr fráliga hinig at verja fold með lið rekka.

'They will hold their course from the south across the cold sea towards Wales; they will prepare for battle. But the fox will go there swiftly to defend the land with a band of men.

Ms.: **Hb**(50r) (*Bret*).

Editions: *Skj*: Gunnlaugr Leifsson, *Merlínússpá I* 32: AII, 16, BII, 16-17, *Skald* II, 10; *Bret* 1848-9, II, 27 (*Bret* st. 32); *Hb* 1892-6, 274; *Merl* 2012, 96.

Notes: [All]: See Note to *II* 31 [All]. — [3] *á vit Bretlands* 'towards Wales': Although *Bretland* otherwise refers to the whole of Britain, in this case it is likely to refer specifically to Wales, as the army is said to be coming from the south across the sea.

33. 'Hríð gerisk hjalma,   hlífar klofna;
     eru rammliga   randir kníðar.
     Gnesta geirar,   es guðr vakin;
     verðr víða lið   at vallroði.

'Hríð hjalma gerisk, hlífar klofna; randir eru kníðar rammliga. Geirar gnesta, guðr es vakin, lið verðr víða at vallroði.

'The storm of helmets [BATTLE] arises, shields are split; the shields are battered powerfully. Spears clatter, battle is awakened; far and wide the army is made to redden the battlefield.

Ms.: **Hb**(50r) (*Bret*).

Editions: *Skj*: Gunnlaugr Leifsson, *Merlínússpá I* 33: AII, 16, BII, 17, *Skald* II, 10; *Bret* 1848-9, II, 27 (*Bret* st. 33); *Hb* 1892-6, 274; *Merl* 2012, 96-7.

Notes: [All]: See Note to *II* 31 [All]. — [7-8] *lið verðr víða at vallroði* 'far and wide the army is made to redden the battlefield': Lit. 'the army far and wide is made into a field-reddening'. The cpd *vallroð* 'field-reddening', meaning 'slaughter', is a *hap. leg*.

34. 'Dregr él yfir   ógnar ljóma;
     gerir drjúgan dyn   dýrra malma.
     Gnýr es á glæstum   Gǫndlar himni
     ok í hǫrðum hlam   Hlakkar tjǫldum.
     Erut skjólsamar   Skǫglar kápur;
     hrýtr hagl boga   hlíf í gegnum.

'Él ljóma ógnar dregr yfir; gerir drjúgan dyn dýrra malma. Gnýr es á glæstum himni Gǫndlar ok hlam í hǫrðum tjǫldum Hlakkar. Kápur Skǫglar erut skjólsamar; hagl boga hrýtr í gegnum hlíf.

'A blizzard of the light of terror [SWORD > BATTLE] is blowing; it causes a mighty din of precious weapons. There is a clashing on the shining heaven of Gǫndul <valkyrie> [SHIELD] and a thudding against the tough awnings of Hlǫkk <valkyrie> [SHIELDS]. The capes of Skǫgul <valkyrie> [MAIL-SHIRTS] are not protective; the hail of bows [ARROWS] pierces through armour.

Ms.: **Hb**(50r) (*Bret*).

Readings: [9] Er*u*t: erat Hb   [12] hlíf í: 'hlift' *refreshed from* 'hlif i' Hb;   gegn*u*m: 'gegnari' Hb.

Editions: *Skj*: Gunnlaugr Leifsson, *Merlínússpá I* 34: AII, 16, BII, 17, *Skald* II, 10-11, *NN* §2567A; *Bret* 1848-9, II, 27-8 (*Bret* st. 34); *Hb* 1892-6, 274; *Merl* 2012, 97-9.

Notes: [All]: See Note to *II* 31 [All]. — [2] *ógnar ljóma* 'of the light of terror [SWORD]': De Vries (1964-7, II, 75 n. 180) compares *HHund I* 21/6. — [3-4] *drjúgan dyn dýrra malma* 'a mighty din of precious weapons': This phrase could be construed as a battle-kenning but is here taken as a literal description of the noise of battle, dependent on the metaphorical battle-kenning *él ljóma ógnar* 'a blizzard of the light of terror [SWORD > BATTLE]' (ll. 1-2), in which the base-word *él* 'blizzard' is said to blow and cause the din of weapons. — [9] *er*ut 'are not': Emended by Kock (*NN* §2567A; *Skald*; cf. *NN* §2741), followed by *Merl* 2012, from ms. *erað* (refreshed) to agree with pl. *kápur*. See Note to *II* 28/3. — [10] *kápur* 'capes': This noun appears rarely in skaldic poetry, but note the similar mail-shirt-kenning *kápa Skǫglar* 'the cloak of Skǫgul <valkyrie>' in Anon *Krm* 18/9. — [12] *hlíf í gegn*um 'through armour': The original reading of Hb, apparently *hlíf í*, is here assumed to be correct, following *Merl* 2012. The use of the sg. noun to denote armour in general is similar to sg. *himni* in the shield-kenning in l. 6. Previous eds, following *Bret* 1848-9, unnecessarily generate a pl. noun by emending to *hlífar* 'armour' (lit. 'items of armour'), where *hlífar* would be acc. pl. The emendation of ms. 'gegnari' to *gegnum* was made by *Bret* 1848-9 and has been adopted by all subsequent eds.

35. 'Grenja gránir   garmar slíðra;
    bítr fránn freki   ferð halsgerðar.
    Rýfr gramr guma   gollorhallir;
    bregðr benlogi   byggðum hjarna;
    eru brotnar mjǫk   borgir heila.

'Gránir garmar slíðra grenja; fránn freki halsgerðar bítr ferð. Gramr rýfr gollorhallir guma; benlogi bregðr byggðum hjarna; borgir heila eru mjǫk brotnar.

'The grey dogs of scabbards [SWORDS] growl; the piercing wolf of the neck-strap [SWORD] bites the army. The cruel one <sword> breaks men's halls of the pericardium [BREASTS]; the wound-flame [SWORD] topples the settlements of brains [HEADS]; the strongholds of brains [HEADS] are smashed to pieces.

Ms.: **Hb**(50r) (*Bret*).

Editions: *Skj*: Gunnlaugr Leifsson, *Merlínússpá I* 35: AII, 16-17, BII, 17, *Skald* II, 11; *Bret* 1848-9, II, 28 (*Bret* st. 35); *Hb* 1892-6, 274-5; *Merl* 2012, 99-100.

Notes: [All]: See Note to *II* 31 [All]. The verbs describing the action of the battle are chosen with regard to the base-words of each sword-kenning in ll. 1-4, creating a metaphorical congruence between them; thus 'dogs' growl and the 'wolf' bites. The substantivised adj. *gramr* 'the cruel one' (l. 5), taken here as a sword-*heiti*, is said to break men's breasts, with the rib-cage possibly in mind. In ll. 7-10 the sword-kennings again show a congruence between base-word and verb; the 'flame' topples heads, represented as tall buildings being engulfed by fire, and, using similar imagery, 'strongholds' are smashed to pieces. It is possible that Gunnlaugr had mythological referents in mind when he wrote of 'dogs' (*garmar*, l. 2) and a wolf (*freki*, lit. 'greedy one' or 'bold one', l. 3), because Garmr is the name of a mythical dog in eddic poetry (*Vsp* 44/1, 58/1; cf. *SnE* 2005, 34, 59), while Freki is the name of one of Óðinn's wolves (*SnE* 2005, 32; *Þul Vargs* 1/5^(III); cf. *Vsp* 44/2). *Gramr* (l. 5) may also be reminiscent of the name of the hero Sigurðr's sword (cf. *Reg* prose (*NK* 177) and *Þul Sverða* 1/5^(III). — [6]: This is the reading of the ms, here unrefreshed, reported by *Bret* 1848-9 and *Hb* 1892-6. The contraction for *-ir* is visible above and to the left of following *b-*. On grounds that remain unclear, *Merl* 2012 would read and retain the sg. form *gollorhall*, which, aside from being contrary to the ms. evidence, also disrupts the metre. For this type of kenning, compare Note to *I* 82/8. *Merl* 2012 incorrectly glosses *gollor-* as 'heart'. — [7] *benlogi* 'the wound-flame [SWORD]': De Vries (1964-7, II, 75 n. 180) compares *HHund I* 51/9.

36. 'Sék vé vaða,   verðr †mittt† skaða;
    syngr sára klungr   snyrtidrengjum.
    En á leið fara   lægjǫrn ara
    jóð ok ylgjar   enn til sylgjar;
    hrapa hernumin   hvártveggja bǫrn.

'Sék vé vaða, †mittt† verðr skaða; klungr sára syngr snyrtidrengjum. En lægjǫrn jóð ara ok ylgjar fara enn á leið til sylgjar; bǫrn hvártveggja hrapa hernumin.

'I see the standards advance, … will harm; the thorn of wounds [SWORD] sings to brave men. And the treacherous children of the eagle and the she-wolf go on their way to the drinking once more; the offspring of both will tumble down, taken in battle.

Ms.: **Hb**(50r) (*Bret*).

Reading: [10] hvártveggja: hvártveggi Hb.

Editions: *Skj*: Gunnlaugr Leifsson, *Merlínússpá I* 36: AII, 17, BII, 17, *Skald* II, 11, *NN* §2163D, E; *Bret* 1848-9, II, 28-9 (*Bret* st. 36); *Hb* 1892-6, 275; *Merl* 2012, 100-1.

Notes: [All]: See *II* 31 Note to [All]. Note the end-rhymes (ll. 1-2, 5-8) in this stanza, possibly imitated from such poems as Egill *Hfl*^(V)(*Eg*). As elsewhere in his battle descriptions, Gunnlaugr reaches for special stylistic devices associated with traditional skaldic poetry. — [2] †*mittt*†: Scheving conjectured *flýtt* 'speedily, hastily' from ms. 'mitt' (refreshed) and this suggestion was adopted in *Bret* 1848-9 and *Skj* B. *Hb* 1892-6 notes, however, that *flýtt* cannot have been the original reading of Hb. Kock (*NN*

§2163D; *Skald*) suggests, without reference to the ms., *mætt* (spelt *mǽtt* in *Skald*), apparently in the sense 'met', and also notes an OE *mittan* 'meet'. *Merl* 2012 follows in reading *mætt*, translated as *angetroffen* 'encountered'. But this proposal leaves the syntax problematic: the nom. forms *mættr* and *skaði* would be expected. — [3] *klungr sára* 'the thorn of wounds [SWORD]': Treated in *Merl* 2012 as an emendation but it is in fact the unrefreshed reading in Hb, first recognised by *Bret* 1848-9 and adopted by subsequent eds. — [6] *lægjǫrn* 'treacherous': De Vries (1964-7, II, 75 n. 179) compares *Vsp* 35/3. — [9] *hernumin* 'taken in battle': Ms. *hernumin* (refreshed) 'taken in battle' raises the difficulty that 'the children of the eagle and the wolf' are otherwise presented in the stanza as benefiting from the battle (by drinking blood), not actively fighting in it or suffering as a result of it, activities that would hardly constitute an expected element in the 'beasts-of-battle' type scene widely used in skaldic poetry. In the absence of a Latin analogue at this point a secure emendation has not so far been suggested. Scheving proposed *hræmunin*, explained as 'eager for corpses' (reported but not adopted in *Bret* 1848-9). *Skj* B emends to *hræfikin* 'corpse-greedy', which is suitable in terms of both metre and sense. Kock suggests *hrapa á hræ numin*, translated as *störta sig över de gripna liken* 'collapse over the captured bodies' (*NN* §2163E; *Skald*; followed by *Merl* 2012), but this fails for metrical reasons.

37. 'En refr gerir   ráða á galta;
    þvíat hann reisa mát   rǫnd við hánum,
    svá lætr dǫglingr,   sem hann dauðr séi;
    esat lík hulit   lofðungs Breta.

'En refr gerir ráða á galta; dǫglingr lætr svá, sem hann séi dauðr, þvíat hann mát reisa rǫnd við hánum; lík lofðungs Breta esat hulit.

'But the fox will prepare to attack the boar; the ruler [the fox] will act as if he were dead, because he [the fox] is unable to raise a shield against him [the boar]; the body of the prince of the Britons [the fox] will not be buried.

Ms.: **Hb**(50r) (*Bret*).

Editions: *Skj*: Gunnlaugr Leifsson, *Merlínússpá I* 37: AII, 17, BII, 17-18, *Skald* II, 11; *Bret* 1848-9, II, 29 (*Bret* st. 37); *Hb* 1892-6, 275; *Merl* 2012, 101-2.

Notes: [All]: Cf. *DGB* 116 (Reeve and Wright 2007, 153.192-155.193; cf. Wright 1988, 109, prophecy 42): *Quae cum certamen inierit, finget se defunctam et aprum in pietatem mouebit* 'When it enters into battle the fox will feign death and move the boar to pity' (cf. Reeve and Wright 2007, 152-4). — [1-6]: No fully satisfactory solution to the logical problems of this stanza has yet been devised. The principal difficulty is that the statement that the fox prepares to make an attack on the pig (ll. 1-2) is seemingly contradicted by the statement that he is not in a position to attack him (ll. 3-4): unable to handle a pitched battle, he must mount a different kind of attack, relying on his cunning (cf. *II* 39/3-4 and *II* 41/6). (For the idiom *ráða á* 'attack' cf. *II* 28/5-6 and *II* 38/6.) (a) For this reason *Skj* B (followed by *Skald*) emends ms. *gerir* (refreshed) 'will prepare' in l. 1 to *gerrat* 'does not prepare' and *Merl* 2012 emends *ráða á* 'attack' in line 2 to *ráð á* 'a plan against'. But these emendations seem to be a case of cutting the Gordian knot: it would be odd for Gunnlaugr to translate the affirmative statement in *DGB* (*Quae cum certamen inierit*) with a negative. Also, it is awkward to say (with *Skj* B) that the fox does not attack when in the next stanza (38/5-6) the contrary is said. (b) The tentative proposal in this edn is that the subordinate clause with initial *því at* constituted by ll. 3-4 be construed as preceding, not following, its main clause, thus linking ll. 3-4 onwards to ll. 5-6 rather than back to ll. 1-2. Then the gist of this and the ensuing stanza would be: 'The fox prepares to make an attack on the pig. As he cannot do so in a pitched battle, he feigns death and his body is left unburied so as to lure the pig to come and inspect it personally; then the fox is able to attack the pig by taking him by surprise'. An admitted weakness with this construal is that the examples of such reversal of clauses in *NS* §367b feature initial *með því at* rather than simple *því at*; *Merl* itself does not contain any instance of *því at* used in this way. (c) Thinkable, therefore, would be emendation of *því at* to *þóat, þótt* 'although', modifying the content of ll. 1-2. Similar are the construals in *Bret* 1848-9 and *Merl* 2012, which, retaining *gerir*, attempt to resolve the apparent contradiction with ll. 3-4 by translating *því at* as if it meant 'but' (*Bret* 1848-9) or *aber weil* 'but because' (*Merl* 2012); in both cases, adoption of *þóat/þótt* would produce better correspondence between text and translation. In *Merl* 2012, probably as a mere slip, *mátti* 'might' replaces *mát* 'is unable', lit. 'may not', against the evidence of the ms. and the metre, and is translated as 'might not', leaving the source of the negative unspecified. — [3] *hann* 'he': Omitted in *Skald*. — [3, 4] *reisa rǫnd við* 'raise a shield against': For the idiom cf. *I* 26/3-4. — [5-6]: The notion that the fox plays dead in order to ensnare its prey was familiar in the Middle Ages, with a *locus classicus* in the *Physiologus* (Curley 2009, 27; cf. *Merl* 2012, 102). — [5] *dǫglingr* 'the ruler': The allegory is rationalised; cf. *lofðungs Breta* 'of the prince of the Britons' in l. 8. — [6] *hann* 'he': Omitted in *Skald*. — [7]: For this sense of *hylja* cf. *I* 36/8, *II* 7/10.

38. 'En galti þat   *geng*r at reyna;
     blæss hann í andlit   ok í augu gram.
     En refr við þat   ræðr á galta;
     fær hann af hánum   fót inn vinstra
     hlust ina hœgri   *ok* hryggjar nes.

'En galti *geng*r at reyna þat; hann blæss í andlit ok í augu gram. En refr ræðr á galta við þat; hann fær inn vinstra fót af hánum, ina hœgri hlust *ok* nes hry*gg*jar.

'And the boar will go to test that; he will blow in the face and eyes of the ruler. But thereupon the fox will attack the boar; he will take from him the left foot, the right ear, and the headland of the back [TAIL].'

Ms.: **Hb**(50r) (*Bret*).

Readings: [2] *gengr*: 'egiar'(?) *apparently corrected from* gengr *during the process of refreshing* Hb [10] *ok*: firi Hb;   *hryggjar*: 'hrydiar' Hb.

Editions: *Skj*: Gunnlaugr Leifsson, *Merlínússpá I* 38: AII, 17, BII, 18, *Skald* II, 11, *NN* §2163F; *Bret* 1848-9, II, 29 (*Bret* st. 38); *Hb* 1892-6, 275; *Merl* 2012, 102-3.

Notes: [All]: Cf. *DGB* 116 (Reeve and Wright 2007, 155.193-6; cf. Wright 1988, 109, prophecy 42): *Mox adibit ipse cadauer et dum superstabit anhelabit in oculos eius et faciem. At ipsa, non oblita præteriti doli, mordebit sinistrum pedem ipsius totumque ex corpore euellet. Saltu quoque facto, eripiet ei dexteram aurem et caudam* 'It will at once approach the fox's body and, standing over it, will breathe into its eyes and face. But the fox, not forgetting its old cunning, will bite the boar's left foot and tear it from its body. Then, leaping up, it will bite off its right ear and tail' (cf. Reeve and Wright 2007, 154). — [2] gen*gr* 'will go': The refreshed reading in Hb has previously been taken as 'eggiar' (*Hb* 1892-6, 275; read as *eggjar* by *Bret* 1848-9 and *Merl* 2012) or emended variously to *girnisk* (*Skj* B) and *getr* (*NN* §2163F; *Skald*). But as refreshed the ms. seems to read 'egiar', with minuscule <g> and a contraction mark running above the three letters 'egi', rather than 'eggiar'. On this basis, emendation to (or more precisely restoration of) *gengr* is proposed in the present edn. The word *gengr* written with a mark of contraction above the second <g> is seen in the ms. text of *II* 25/8 and *II* 31/6. This solution is more economical than those of *Skj* B and *Skald* and gives good sense in context, corresponding to *DGB*'s *adibit* 'will approach', as contrasted with *eggjar*, which *Bret* 1848-9 is obliged to translate freely as *önsker* 'wishes', not otherwise an attested meaning of the verb (*ONP*: *eggja* 'sharpen, urge on, goad, incite'); *Merl* 2012 presupposes an otherwise undocumented intransitive use of *eggja*. — [3] *hann* 'he': Omitted in *Skald*. — [10] *ok* 'and': Emended in *Bret* 1848-9, followed by subsequent eds, from ms. *firi* (refreshed). — [10] *hryggjar* 'of the back': Emended in *Bret* 1848-9, followed by subsequent eds, from ms. 'hrydiar' (refreshed). — [10] *nes hryggjar* 'the headland of the back [TAIL]': This unusual kenning is clarified in *II* 40/7.

39. 'En í fjalli *fel*sk   fádyggt hǫfuð;
    hyggr færtǫpuðr   flærð at œxla.
    En villigǫltr   vargi ok birni
    segir sárliga   sorg ok missu.

'En fádyggt hǫfuð *fel*sk í fjalli; færtǫpuðr hyggr at œxla flærð. En villigǫltr segir vargi ok birni sárliga sorg ok missu.

'But the untrustworthy person will hide in the mountain; the sheep-destroyer [FOX] will intend to add to his deception. And the wild boar will tell the wolf and the bear of his grievous sorrow and loss.

Ms.: Hb(50r) (*Bret*).

Reading: [1] *fel*sk: næst Hb.

Editions: *Skj*: Gunnlaugr Leifsson, Merlínússpá I 39: AII, 17, BII, 18, *Skald* II, 11, *NN* §2163G; *Bret* 1848-9, II, 29-30 (*Bret* st. 39); *Hb* 1892-6, 275; *Merl* 2012, 103-5.

Notes: [All]: Cf. *DGB* 116 (Reeve and Wright 2007, 155.196-8; cf. Wright 1988, 109-10, prophecies 42 and 43): *et infra cauernas montium delitebit. Aper ergo illusus requiret lupum et ursum ut ei amissa membra restituant* 'and hide in the mountain-caves. The tricked boar will demand that the wolf and bear restore its lost limbs' (Reeve and Wright 2007, 154). — [1] fel*sk* 'will hide': Emended by Scheving (and adopted in *Bret* 1848-9 and *Skj* B) from ms. *næst* (refreshed). Cf. Note to *II* 36/9. The spelling of reflexive *-sk* as *-st* in Hb is exemplified by *hleðst* (= *hlezk*) in *II* 21/2 (*Hb* 1892-6, 273); thus change of ms. final <t> to <k> represents normalisation rather than emendation. Kock (*NN* §2163G; *Skald*), followed by *Merl* 2012, would emend the line to *es í fjalli næst*, with *næst* meaning 'then' (thus 'is then in the mountain'), but this does not take *DGB* into account. — [2] *hǫfuð* 'the person': Lit. 'head' (*CVC*: *hǫfuð* III). I.e. the fox. — [3] *fǽrtǫpuðr* 'the sheep-destroyer [FOX]': This is the hitherto unrecognised reading of Hb. With this kenning cf. *II* 28/8 *týnir sauða* 'that destroyer of sheep [FOX]' and Note there. For the agentive *tǫpuðr* see *LP*: *tǫpuðr*; Gunnlaugr uses its formative verb, *tapa* 'kill', in reference to the fox in *II* 28/7. Earlier eds read the ms. at this point as *þær* (or *þar*) *jǫfuðr*. *Bret* 1848-9 adopts *þar jǫfuðr*, translating the line as *der tænker han* 'there he thinks', which indicates that *jǫfuðr* is regarded as a *heiti* for 'king', like *jǫfurr*. *Skj* B and *NN* §2163G (cf. *Skald*) emend to *þar fóa* 'there the vixen' and *þar jǫfurr* ('there the ruler') respectively. Additionally *NN* §2163G (cf. *Skald*) transposes the word order in l. 4 in order to maintain correct alliteration. *Merl* 2012 proposes *lofuðr* 'praised', i.e. 'the leader', but without any supporting attestations for such a usage. — [4] *flærð* 'deception': Here *Bret* 1848-9 inexplicably reads *kun*, translated as *sin Slægt* 'his family', an error implicitly corrected in *Hb* 1892-6.

40. 'En hraustir brœðr   hugga galta;
     kveðask sár munu   sjalfir grœða.
     "Fara skulum báðir   fótar at leita
     hlustar ok hala þér;   hér bíð þú, galti!"

'En hraustir brœðr hugga galta; kveðask sjalfir munu grœða sár. "Skulum báðir fara at leita fótar hlustar ok hala þér; hér bíð þú, galti!"

'But the brave brothers will comfort the boar; they will say they themselves will heal its wounds. "We will both go to find your foot, ear, and tail; you wait here, boar!"

Ms.: **Hb**(50r) (*Bret*).

Editions: *Skj*: Gunnlaugr Leifsson, *Merlínússpá I* 40: AII, 17, BII, 18, *Skald* II, 11; *Bret* 1848-9, II, 30 (*Bret* st. 40); *Hb* 1892-6, 275; *Merl* 2012, 105.

Notes: [All]: Cf. *DGB* 116 (Reeve and Wright 2007, 155.198-200; cf. Wright 1988, 110, prophecy 43): *Qui ut causam inierint, promittent ei duos pedes et aures et caudam et ex eis porcina membra component. Acquiescet ipse promissamque restaurationem expectabit* 'Plotting together, they will promise it two feet and ears and a tail to replace the boar's members. The boar will consent and await their promised restitution' (cf. Reeve and Wright 2007, 154). *Merl* differs from Geoffrey in being consistent about the number of feet and ears to be replaced. Altogether, the treatment in *Merl* is notably free, especially in its incorporation of direct speech, and suggests that Gunnlaugr had contemporary beast epic in mind (see Introduction). — [8] *þú* 'you': Omitted in *Skald*.

41. 'En refr ofan   renn ór fjalli;
     ferr fárhugaðr   finna galta.
     Hann býðr sættir   af svikum einum;
     kvezk hann mart við svín   mæla vilja.

'En refr renn ofan ór fjalli; fárhugaðr ferr finna galta. Hann býðr sættir af svikum einum; hann kvezk vilja mæla mart við svín.

'But the fox will run down from the mountain; the baleful one will go to meet the boar. He will offer a settlement out of pure treachery; he will say he wishes to discuss many things with the pig.

Ms.: **Hb**(50r) (*Bret*).

Editions: *Skj*: Gunnlaugr Leifsson, *Merlínússpá I* 41: AII, 18, BII, 18, *Skald* II, 11-12; *Bret* 1848-9, II, 30 (*Bret* st. 41); *Hb* 1892-6, 275; *Merl* 2012, 105-6.

Notes: [All]: Cf. *DGB* 116 (Reeve and Wright 2007, 155.200-2; cf. Wright 1988, 110, prophecy 44): *Interim descendet uulpes de montibus et sese in lupum mutabit et quasi colloquium habitura cum apro adibit illum callide* 'Meanwhile the fox will come down from the mountains, transform itself into the wolf, cunningly approach as if to talk with the boar' (Reeve and Wright 2007, 154). The transformation of the fox into a wolf does not appear in *Merl*. — [7] *hann* 'he': Omitted in *Skald*.

42. "'Trú mér, galti!   *Munk* heill vesa;
    svík ek aldregi   svín í tryggðum.
    Fund skulum leggja   ok frið gera;
    skaltu einn gera   okkar í millim."

'"Trú mér, galti! *Munk* vesa heill; ek svík aldregi svín í tryggðum. Skulum leggja fund ok gera frið; skaltu einn gera í millim okkar."

'"Trust me, boar! I will be honourable; I will never deceive the pig in truces. We will set a meeting and devise a safe-conduct; you alone will determine between us two."

Ms.: **Hb**(50r) (*Bret*).

Reading: [2] *Munk*: ek ek man Hb.

Editions: *Skj*: Gunnlaugr Leifsson, *Merlínússpá I* 42: AII, 18, BII, 18-19, *Skald* II, 12, *NN* §2163A; *Bret* 1848-9, II, 31 (*Bret* st. 42); *Hb* 1892-6, 275; *Merl* 2012, 106.

Notes: [All]: Cf. *DGB* 116, as for *II* 41. — [1-2]: Kock (*NN* §2163A; *Skald*) suggests emendation of *trú* to *hlýð* 'hear', yielding alliteration with *heill*. — [2] munk 'I will': Corrected from ms. *ek ek man* (not refreshed) to *ek man* by *Bret* 1848-9 and *Merl* 2012. *Skj* B (followed by *Skald* and this edn) emends to *munk* 'I will'. — [7] *gera* 'determine': For this sense of *gera* see *CVC*: *göra* IV; *Fritzner*: *gera* 12. In a legal embellishment to Geoffrey's narrative, Gunnlaugr has the fox deceptively offering the boar sole judgement (*sjálfdæmi*) in the dispute between them.

43. 'Es fundr lagiðr   ok friðr samiðr;
    koma mildingar   málstefnu til.
    En á fundi þeim   flærðir reynask;
    banar hertoga   brezkr landreki.

'Fundr es lagiðr ok friðr samiðr; mildingar koma til málstefnu. En flærðir reynask á þeim fundi; brezkr landreki banar hertoga.

'A meeting will be set and a safe-conduct concluded; the leaders will come to the council. But at that meeting treacheries will come to pass; the British ruler will slay the war-leader.

Ms.: **Hb**(50r) (*Bret*).

Editions: *Skj*: Gunnlaugr Leifsson, *Merlínússpá I* 43, 45/1-4: AII, 18, BII, 19, *Skald* II, 12; *Bret* 1848-9, II, 31 (*Bret* st. 43); *Hb* 1892-6, 275; *Merl* 2012, 107.

Notes: [All]: Cf. *DGB* 116 (Reeve and Wright 2007, 155.202; cf. Wright 1988, 110, prophecy 44): *et ipsum totum deuorabit* 'and will eat him whole' (cf. Reeve and Wright 2007, 154). Here the usurping fox, disguised as the wolf, consumes the boar-king: Geoffrey's animal symbolism is rationalised in *Merl*. Gunnlaugr also elaborates on the establishment of the truce, both here and in the preceding stanza. — [4] *málstefnu* 'the council': The sole attestation of this cpd in poetry. Cf. *mæltrar stefnu* 'appointed meeting' in Halli XI *Fl* 3/4[II], a poem that exhibits a similar interest in procedures concerning truces and meetings.

44.   'Ok svíns at þat   á sik hami
      brigðr ok brœðra   bíðr slœgliga.
      En, es þeir koma   kosti at fœra,
      bítr hann báða tvá   ok banar hlýrum.

'Ok brigðr á sik hami svíns at þat ok bíðr brœðra slœgliga. En, es þeir koma at fœra kosti, bítr hann báða tvá ok banar hlýrum.

'And with that he will take on the form of the boar and wait slyly for the brothers. But when they come to bring their offerings he will bite both of them and will slay the siblings.

Ms.: **Hb**(50r) (*Bret*).

Editions: *Skj*: Gunnlaugr Leifsson, *Merlínússpá I* 45/5-8: AII, 8, BII, 19, *Skald* II, 12; *Bret* 1848-9, II, 31-2 (*Bret* st. 45); *Hb* 1892-6, 275; *Merl* 2012, 108.

Notes: [All]: Cf. *DGB* 116 (Reeve and Wright 2007, 155.202-4; cf. Wright 1988, 110, prophecy 44): *Exin transuertet sese in aprum et quasi sine membris expectabit germanos. Sed et ipsos postquam aduenerint subito dente interficiet* 'Next it will disguise itself as the boar and as if without its members await its brothers. But when they arrive, it will swiftly bite them also to death' (cf. Reeve and Wright 2007, 154). In other words, the fox, now *de facto* a king, takes on the semblance of the deposed and assassinated boar-king in order to dispose of its brothers, the bear and the wolf. This stanza and *II* 45 appear in reverse order in Hb, followed by *Bret* 1848-9, *Skj* B and *Skald*, but the announcement of the end of the *saga þengils* 'story of the king' in *II* 45/5-8 should logically come at the point when indeed nothing remains to be added to his story. The reversal of stanza-order can be explained on the basis of eye-skip from one *helmingr*-initial *ok* to another, followed by retrospective insertion of the missing stanza (Poole 2009, 316-17; cf. *Merl* 2012). — [6] *kosti* 'their offerings': Referring to the substitutes for the boar's missing body parts that the wolf and bear have promised to bring. — [7] *hann* 'he': Omitted in *Skald*.

45. 'Ok á sjalfan sik   síðan festir
    lépards hǫfuð   lofðungr at þat.
    Ræðr hann lýðum   ok lofða fjǫlð;
    þar þrýtr þessa   þengils sǫgu.

'Ok lofðungr festir síðan hǫfuð lépards á sik sjalfan at þat. Hann ræðr lýðum ok fjǫlð lofða; þar þrýtr þessa sǫgu þengils.

'And with that the ruler will then fix a leopard's head on himself. He will rule over peoples and a multitude of men; there is the end of this story of the king.

Ms.: **Hb**(50r) (*Bret*).

Editions: *Skj*: Gunnlaugr Leifsson, *Merlínússpá I* 44: AII, 18, BII, 19, *Skald* II, 12; *Bret* 1848-9, II, 31 (*Bret* st. 44); *Hb* 1892-6, 275; *Merl* 2012, 108-9.

Notes: [All]: For discussion of the stanza order see *II* 44 Note to [All]. Cf. *DGB* 116 (Reeve and Wright 2007, 155.204; cf. Wright 1988, 110, prophecy 44): *atque capite leonis coronabitur* 'and be crowned with a lion's head' (Reeve and Wright 2007, 154). Having destroyed its rivals while in the semblance of a boar, the fox-king makes his final transformation – to a lion. — [3] *léparðs* 'a leopard's': Geoffrey clearly specifies a lion but, in common with much medieval literature and heraldry, Gunnlaugr does not seem to distinguish lions from leopards consistently. In the *Second-family Bestiary*, from the later C12th, Pliny is cited as stating (*Historia naturalis* 8.17.42-3) that the lion mates with the female pard, or the pard with the lioness, and from each coupling degenerate young are created. It is this irregular union of lion and pard that was regarded as making the leopard a 'bad lion' (Clark 2006, 122-3 and n. 22). — [5-8]: The episode is rounded off in an approximation of saga style (Poole 2009, 317).

46. 'Es á hans dǫgum   hǫggormr alinn,
    sás fyrðum vill   fjǫrspell gera.
    Svá es hann langr,   at of Lundúnir
    heiðar hvalr   hring of mælir
    ok svá óðr,   at urðar sigðr
    umlíðendr   alla gleypir.

'Hǫggormr es alinn á dǫgum hans, sás vill gera fyrðum fjǫrspell. Hann es svá langr, at hvalr heiðar of mælir hring of Lundúnir, ok svá óðr, at sigðr urðar gleypir alla umlíðendr.

'In his days a serpent will be born who will bring about an end to life for men. It is so long that the whale of the heath [SNAKE] will measure a circle around London and so ferocious that the sickle of the cairn [SNAKE] will devour all passers-by.

Ms.: **Hb**(50r) (*Bret*).

Editions: *Skj*: Gunnlaugr Leifsson, *Merlínússpá I* 46: AII, 18, BII, 19, *Skald* II, 12, *NN* §§2163B, 2820; *Bret* 1848-9, II, 32 (*Bret* st. 46); *Hb* 1892-6, 275-6; *Merl* 2012, 109-10.

Notes: [All]: Cf. *DGB* 116 (Reeve and Wright 2007, 155.204-6; cf. Wright 1988, 110, prophecy 45): *In diebus eius nascetur serpens, quae neci mortalium imminebit. Longitudine sua circuibit Lundoniam et quosque pretereuntes deuorabit* 'In its time will be born a snake which will threaten men with death. It will coil itself around London and devour all who pass by' (Reeve and Wright 2007, 154). — [7]: A trisyllabic line, like ll. 9 and 11. Kock suggests (*NN* §§2163B; *Skald*) filling out l. 7 with initial *at*, shifted from the previous line, to yield regular *fornyrðislag* metre. But this unnecessarily complicates the word order and obscures the sense. He further suggests filling out l. 9 with *es hann*, on the analogy of l. 5 and would regularise l. 11 into *fornyrðislag* by reading *umlíðanda*. But the occurrence of three short lines in the one stanza militates against emendation, and it may be that Gunnlaugr is foreshadowing the sequence of *kviðuháttr* stanzas from *II* 62 onwards that concludes *Merl II*. — [10] *sigðr urðar* 'the sickle of the cairn [SNAKE]': A snake-kenning employing *urð* 'cairn, pile of stones' as an alternative to more common determinants such as words for 'earth' and 'ground'; cf. *Meissner* 113-14.

47. 'Hann Kambríe   kallar sveitir
    ok Norðhumru   nánar hjarðir.
    Ok ótrautt   Tems at þurru
    drengs dolgþorins drekka lýðir.

'Hann kallar sveitir Kambríe ok hjarðir nánar Norðhumru. Ok lýðir dolgþorins drengs drekka ótrautt Tems at þurru.

'It will summon the bands of Cambria and the herds near Northumbria. And without reluctance the people of the battle-resolute warrior will drink the Thames dry.

Ms.: **Hb**(50r) (*Bret*).

Editions: *Skj*: Gunnlaugr Leifsson, *Merlínússpá I* 47: AII, 18, BII, 19-20, *Skald* II, 12, *NN* §2163B; *Bret* 1848-9, II, 32 (*Bret* st. 47); *Hb* 1892-6, 276; *Merl* 2012, 110-11.

Notes: [All]: Cf. *DGB* 116 (Reeve and Wright 2007, 155.208-9; cf. Wright 1988, 110, prophecy 46): *Associabit sibi greges Albanorum et Kambriae, qui Tamensem potando siccabunt* 'It will ally itself to the flocks of Scotland and Wales, which will drink the Thames dry' (Reeve and Wright 2007, 154). The previous sentence in Geoffrey's text is not represented in *Merl*. — [3-4] *hjarðir nánar Norðhumru* 'the herds near Northumbria': Presumably the Scots. Gunnlaugr does not use a name corresponding to Geoffrey's *Albania* 'Scotland' (cf. *I* 64/4, where he translates Geoffrey's *Albania* with *Skotland*). — [5] *ótrautt* 'without reluctance': Kock suggests (*NN* §§2163B; *Skald*) reading *ótrauðla*, adv. with similar meaning, so as to restore regular *fornyrðislag*, but see Note to *II* 46/11. — [6] *at þurru* 'dry': For this use of the prep. *at* with adj. to denote the result of an action, see *CVC*: *at* with dat. C VII; *ONP*: *at* I with dat. D 14. — [7] *dolgþorins drengs* 'of the battle-resolute warrior': Referring back to the serpent-king of *II* 46/1 (represented by *hann* 'it' in 47/1), with a characteristic rationalisation of the allegory on Gunnlaugr's part; *Merl* 2012 unnecessarily posits some other antecedent.

48. 'Verða síðar   á sama landi
    léparðar sjau   linni bornir.
    Þeir hafa brúsa   bǫlgjǫrn hǫfuð;
    eru dáðlausir   dǫglings synir.

'Sjau léparðar verða bornir linni síðar á sama landi. Þeir hafa bǫlgjǫrn hǫfuð brúsa; synir dǫglings eru dáðlausir.'

'Seven leopards will be born to the snake later in that same land. They will have the baleful heads of he-goats; the king's sons will be bereft of [noble] deeds.'

Ms.: **Hb**(50r) (*Bret*).

Reading: [3] léparðar: 'lǫpartar' Hb.

Editions: *Skj*: Gunnlaugr Leifsson, *Merlínússpá I* 48: AII, 19, BII, 20, *Skald* II, 12-13, *NN* §1281; *Bret* 1848-9, II, 33 (*Bret* st. 48); *Hb* 1892-6, 276; *Merl* 2012, 111-12.

Notes: [All]: Cf. *DGB* 116 (Reeve and Wright 2007, 157.228-9; cf. Wright 1988, 111, prophecy 53): *Egredientur ex eo septem leones capitibus hircorum turpati* 'From it will emerge seven lions, disfigured with the heads of goats' (Reeve and Wright 2007, 156). Prophecies 47 to 52 inclusive are not represented in *Merl*; for the possibility that there is an extensive lacuna at this point in Hb see *Merl* 2012, 39-44). — [3] *léparðar* 'leopards': Emended thus in *Skald* from ms. 'lǫpartar' (printed as *lœpartar* in *Skj* B, but contrast *LP*: *léparðr*). Again Geoffrey has 'lion' here: for Gunnlaugr's confusion of leopards and lions, see Note to *II* 45/3. — [5] *brúsa* 'of he-goats': This edn follows Kock (*NN* §1281; cf. *Merl* 2012), who construes *brúsa* as gen. pl. rather than sg. (cf. Geoffrey's text and contrast *Skj* B). — [7] *dáðlausir* 'bereft of [noble] deeds': This edn follows Kock (*NN* §1281), who compares *II* 64/5 *drýgjum dáð* 'let us practise [good] deeds'. Finnur Jónsson explains as 'without renowned deeds' (*LP*: *dáðlauss*; cf. *Merl* 2012), and that might also be correct.

49. 'Þeir flest taka   fljóða sveita
    hervígssamir   ok hóra mengi.
    Ok sameignar   sín*ar kvánir
    gera geirvanir;   geigr es í slíku.'

'Hervígssamir taka þeir flest sveita fljóða ok mengi hóra. Ok geirvanir gera kvánir sín*ar sameignar; geigr es í slíku.'

'Belligerent, they will take most bands of women and a multitude of whores. And the spear-accustomed ones will have their women in common; peril lies in that.'

Ms.: **Hb**(50r) (*Bret*).

Reading: [6] sín*ar: sinnar Hb.

Editions: *Skj*: Gunnlaugr Leifsson, *Merlínússpá I* 49: AII, 19, BII, 20, *Skald* II, 13, *NN* §99; *Bret* 1848-9, II, 33 (*Bret* st. 49); *Hb* 1892-6, 276; *Merl* 2012, 112-13.

Notes: [All]: Cf. *DGB* 116 (Reeve and Wright 2007, 157.229-30; cf. Wright 1988, 111, prophecy 53): *Fetore narium mulieres corrumpent et proprias communes facient* 'By the stench of their nostrils they will corrupt women and make the women of individual men into women shared in common' (cf. Reeve and Wright 2007, 156). Gunnlaugr adds the final summative statement of moral condemnation. — [3] *hervígssamir* 'belligerent': This edn follows Kock (*NN* §99; *Skald*; cf. *Merl* 2012), who notes that ms. *hervígssamir* (a *hap. leg.*) makes good sense, has close analogues in formation and meaning and is in parallel structure with *geirvanir* 'the spear-accustomed ones' in l. 7. Earlier eds deviate from the ms. reading. *Bret* 1848-9 has *hervígs ramir*, translated as *de kampstærke Mænd* 'the battle-strong men'. Given that *ramir* is not signalled as an emendation, perhaps Jón Sigurðsson read <r> where other eds have seen <s>, but occasionally he emends tacitly (cf. *II* 39/4). In *Skj* B the line is further emended to *rammir horvegs* 'strong of snot-way [NOSTRIL]', explained as meaning *med stinkende næsebor* 'with stinking nostrils', so as to enhance the correspondence with *DGB*. The ms. reading appears in *LP* (*LP*: *hervíg*) but with the comment that it is erroneous. Finnur's emendation is ingenious, and possibly right, despite Kock's strictures (made in ignorance of *DGB*), but it would be characteristic of Gunnlaugr to tone down such offensive material. Cf. *II* 50/5-6. — [5] *sameignar* 'in common': *Merl* 2012 appears to posit a less overtly sexual reference, but Gunnlaugr is simply translating *DGB* at this point. — [6] *sín*ar* 'their': Emended in *Skj* B (followed by *Skald*, *Merl* 2012 and this edn) from ms. *sinnar* (refreshed).

50. Langt es at tína,   þats lofða vinr
    of aldar far   ýtum sagði.
    Es fæst í því   fagrt at heyra;
    lætk líða þat   ok lok segja.

Es langt at tína, þats vinr lofða sagði ýtum of far aldar. Fæst es fagrt at heyra í því; lætk þat líða ok segja lok.

It is long to compile what the friend of the people told men concerning the course of the age. Very little of it is pleasant to hear; I will let it go by and tell the conclusion.

Ms.: **Hb**(50v) (*Bret*).

Editions: *Skj*: Gunnlaugr Leifsson, *Merlínússpá I* 50: AII, 19, BII, 20, *Skald* II, 13; *Bret* 1848-9, II, 33 (*Bret* st. 50); *Hb* 1892-6, 276; *Merl* 2012, 113.

Notes: [All]: From this point in *Merl* the use of the prophecies in *DGB* becomes more selective. Cf. *I* 93/7-8, which states that *sumt* 'some' of the prophecies to be found in Gunnlaugr's source are translated, but not all of them. — [2] *vinr lofða* 'the friend of the people': The reference is to Merlin; cf. *vinr gumna* 'the friend of the people' in *I* 20/1. — [5-6]: Perhaps in particular an allusion to prophecy 54, which describes a battle between a dragon and a naked giant (Reeve and Wright 2007, 156-7); similar motifs occur in subsequent prophecies.

51. 'Verðr á foldu,'   kvað inn fróði halr,
    'styrjǫld mikil,   stórar ógnir,
    víg ok vélar,   vargǫld ok kǫld
    hrími hvers konar   hjǫrtu lýða.

'Mikil styrjǫld verðr á foldu, stórar ógnir, víg ok vélar, vargǫld ok hjǫrtu lýða kǫld hrími hvers konar,' kvað inn fróði halr.

'A great war will come to pass on the earth, great terrors, battle and treacheries, the time of the wolf and hearts of men [will grow] cold with frost of every kind,' said the wise man.

Ms.: **Hb**(50v) (*Bret*).

Editions: *Skj*: Gunnlaugr Leifsson, *Merlínússpá I* 51: AII, 19, BII, 20, *Skald* II, 13; *Bret* 1848-9, II, 34; (*Bret* st. 51); *Hb* 1892-6, 276; *Merl* 2012, 113-14.

Notes: [6] *vargǫld* 'the time of the wolf': De Vries (1964-7, II, 75 n. 179) compares *Vsp* 45/9. — [6, 8] *hjǫrtu ... kǫld* 'hearts ... cold': The interpretation here follows that implicit in *Skj* B, with the verb *verða* 'will grow' understood from *verðr* in l. 1, the adj. *kǫld* construed as nom. pl. from *kaldr* 'cold' qualifying the n. nom. pl. *hjǫrtu* 'hearts' and the noun *hrími* 'with frost' construed as an instr. dat. from *hrím* 'frost'. *Bret* 1848-9 (also *Merl* 2012, presumably independently) appears to construe *kǫld* as an otherwise unattested noun 'cold', in parallel with *vargǫld*, etc., but that leads to deficient syntax, with *hjǫrtu* seemingly understood as a virtual dat. *i Hjerter* 'in hearts'. Similarly *Merl* 2012 *im Herzen* 'in hearts', but there *hrími* is construed as the nom. of the weak m. noun corresponding to n. *hrím*. — [7]: This line is in the metre *málaháttr*.

52. 'Þá munu gleymask   gálausir menn,
     ok sællífir   seggir drekka,
     leita at fagna   ok við fé una,
     vell at œxla   ok vegsmuni.

'Þá munu gálausir menn gleymask, ok sællífir seggir drekka, leita at fagna ok una við fé, at œxla vell ok vegsmuni.

'Then feckless men will make merry, and pleasure-seeking men take to drink, seek to rejoice and take pleasure in property, to increase their gold and distinctions.

Ms.: **Hb**(50v) (*Bret*).

Editions: *Skj*: Gunnlaugr Leifsson, *Merlínússpá I* 52: AII, 19, BII, 20-1, *Skald* II, 13; *Bret* 1848-9, II, 34 (*Bret* st. 52); *Hb* 1892-6, 276; *Merl* 2012, 114-15.

Notes: [1-4]: For the homiletic tone and content, cf. *HómÍsl* (*HómÍsl* 1993, 39): *þetta líf eGiar galausa meN til ofáts oc ofdryckio* 'this life encourages feckless men to over-eating and excessive drinking'. — [1] *gleymask* 'make merry': Attestations of *gleyma* in this sense are rare, the dominant sense being 'forget' (*ONP*: *gleyma*), as in *II* 66/6. — [8] *vegsmuni* 'distinctions': The cpd *vegsmunir* 'distinctions, honours' (pl.) is attested only here in poetry and rarely in prose (*ONP*: *vegsmunr*).

53. 'Hagr gerisk hǫlða   hættr í mǫrgu;
     munat fyrða ráð   fag*r*t at reyna.
     Dyljask drjúgum   dr*a*ums ívaðendr;
     við sjalfa sik   sjásk ekki at.

'Hagr hǫlða gerisk hættr í mǫrgu; munat fag*r*t at reyna ráð fyrða. Ívaðendr dr*a*ums dyljask drjúgum; sjásk ekki at við sik sjalfa.

'The state of men will become perilous in many ways; it will not be good to test the conduct of men. Wanderers in a dream, they will be massively deluded; they will not take heed about themselves.

Ms.: **Hb**(50v) (*Bret*).

Readings: [4] fag*r*t: fagr Hb   [6] dr*a*ums: 'dráms' Hb.

Editions: *Skj*: Gunnlaugr Leifsson, *Merlínússpá I* 53: AII, 19, BII, 21, *Skald* II, 13; *Bret* 1848-9, II, 34 (*Bret* st. 53); *Hb* 1892-6, 276; *Merl* 2012, 115.

Notes: [4] *fag*r*t* 'good': Emended in *Bret* 1848-9, followed by all subsequent eds, from ms. *fagr* (refreshed). — [4] *reyna* 'test': This verb is attested in relation to God's testing of Job and Abraham in *HómÍsl* (*HómÍsl* 1993, 29, 43; cf. *ONP*: *reyna*), and the sense is probably similar here. — [6] *dr*a*ums* 'in a dream': Lit. 'of a dream'. Emended in *Bret*

1848-9, followed by all subsequent eds, from ms. 'dráms' (refreshed). — [6] *ívaðendr* 'wanderers': A *hap. leg.*

54. 'Verst es í heimi; veitat sonr fǫður;
slíta þeir sifjum svá synir við feðr.
Kannask engi við kunna menn
né nána frændr Nirðir bauga.

'Verst es í heimi; sonr veitat fǫður; þeir synir slíta svá sifjum við feðr. Engi kannask við kunna menn né [kanna] Nirðir bauga nána frændr.

'It will be worst in the world; the son will not know the father; the sons will thus break the bonds of kinship with fathers. No one will recognise familiar people, nor will the Nirðir <gods> of rings [MEN] [recognise] any kinsmen.

Ms.: **Hb**(50v) (*Bret*).

Editions: *Skj*: Gunnlaugr Leifsson, *Merlínússpá I* 54: AII, 19, BII, 21, *Skald* II, 13, *NN* §100; *Bret* 1848-9, II, 34-5 (*Bret* st. 54); *Hb* 1892-6, 276; *Merl* 2012, 115-17.

Notes: [All]: Cf. *DGB* 116 (Reeve and Wright 2007, 157.230; cf. Wright 1988, 111, prophecy 53): *Nesciet pater filium proprium* 'A father will not recognise his own son' (cf. Reeve and Wright 2007, 156). — [1] *verst es í heimi* 'it will be worst in the world': De Vries (1964-7, II, 75 n. 179) compares *Vsp* 45/5. — [3-4]: The difficulties posed by these lines have not so far been satisfactorily resolved. This edn follows *Skj* B (*Bret* 1848-9 reads similarly but with emendation of *feðr* to *feðra*) in adhering to the ms. readings (refreshed). The placement of *svá* is difficult, however, since regardless of whether it is assigned to l. 3 (with *Bret* 1848-9, also *Merl* 2012) or l. 4 (with *Skj* B) it generates an extra potentially alliterating syllable. Moreover, ll. 3-4 seem curiously repetitive of ll. 1-2. Kock suggests (*NN* §100) that *svá synir* may represent a misunderstanding of the adj. *svásir*, used substantivally, and proposes the emendation *slíta þeir sifjum,* | *svásir, við feðga*, translated as *och frändskap slita de, de nära, med far och son* 'they sever kinship ties, the near and dear, between father and son' (*Skald* is similar, with omission of *þeir*). He notes that ON *svás*, OE *swǽs* was particularly used with nouns denoting 'close blood-relative' (cf. *Ásm* 4/1-2), the latter often in collocation with *gesibb*, corresponding to *sifjum* here, a noun that denotes relationships by marriage (as noted by *Merl* 2012). De Vries (1964-7, II, 75 n. 179) compares l. 3 with *Vsp* 45/4.

55. 'Hǫfugt es at heyra, þats of her gerisk;
    lifa fénaðar fyrðar lífi.
    Hyggja á þennan þrágjarnan heim
    ok hvers konar hafna gœzku.

'Hǫfugt es at heyra, þats gerisk of her; fyrðar lifa lífi fénaðar. Hyggja á þennan þrágjarnan heim ok hafna hvers konar gœzku.

'It is grievous to hear what becomes of the people; men will live the life of beasts. They will think of this obdurate world and forsake goodness of every kind.

Ms.: Hb(50v) (*Bret*).

Editions: *Skj*: Gunnlaugr Leifsson, *Merlínússpá I* 55: AII, 20, BII, 21, *Skald* II, 13; *Bret* 1848-9, II, 35 (*Bret* st. 55); *Hb* 1892-6, 276; *Merl* 2012, 117.

Notes: [All]: Cf. *DGB* 116 (Reeve and Wright 2007, 157.230-1; cf. Wright 1988, 111, prophecy 53): *quia more pecudum lasciuient* 'because they will rut like animals' (Reeve and Wright 2007, 156). Gunnlaugr characteristically tones down this sexual reference. — [6] *þrágjarnan heim* 'obdurate world': The sole attestation of this adj. where it is not used in relation to persons (*ONP*: *þrágjarn*). — [8] *hafna* 'forsake': This verb occurs frequently in homiletic writings in the sense of Lat. *contemnere* 'disregard, despise', in relation to God or a virtuous life (*ONP*: *hafna*). — [8] *gœzku* 'goodness': The noun *gœzka* in this sense occurs frequently in homiletic writings (*ONP*: *gózka*).

56. 'Mun it hvíta silfr hǫldum granda,
    ok gull gera gumna blinda.
    Himni hafna en á hauðr séa;
    svíkr ofdrykkja ýta mengi.

'It hvíta silfr mun granda hǫldum, ok gull gera gumna blinda. Hafna himni en séa á hauðr; ofdrykkja svíkr mengi ýta.

'The white silver will harm men, and gold make men blind. They will forsake heaven and look on the earth; excessive drinking will undo a multitude of men.

Ms.: **Hb**(50v) (*Bret*).

Editions: *Skj*: Gunnlaugr Leifsson, *Merlínússpá I* 56: AII, 20, BII, 21, *Skald* II, 13; *Bret* 1848-9, II, 35 (*Bret* st. 56); *Hb* 1892-6, 276; *Merl* 2012, 118.

Notes: [All]: Cf. *DGB* 116 (Reeve and Wright 2007, 159.285-; cf. Wright 1988, 114, prophecy 71): *Fulgor auri oculos intuentium excaecabit. Candebit argentum in circuitu et diuersa torcularia uexabit. Imposito uino, inebriabuntur mortales postpositoque caelo in terram respicient* 'The glint of gold will blind the eyes of those who behold it. Silver will gleam as it passes round and trouble various wine-presses. When the wine has been served, mortals befuddled with drink will neglect the heavens and gaze at the ground' (cf. Reeve and Wright 2007, 158). From this point Geoffrey draws upon the dire cosmological prodigies and the astrologer's prophecies in Lucan's *Pharsalia* I 522-695 (Tatlock 1950, 405-6, citing Rydberg 1881). Whereas Geoffrey constructs a progression from the circulation of the silver cup to the drunkenness of the company and their neglect of the heavens in favour of earthly things, Gunnlaugr appears to treat drunkenness as a separate issue, obscuring its relation to the silver of the cup: for a later instance of invective against silver cf. *Nik* (Unger 1877 II, 101): *silfrpenningar blinduðu þin augu steypandi þik fram i þvilika glæpsku* 'silver pennies blinded your eyes, plunging you into such sin [i.e. avarice]'. — [6] *en séa á hauðr* 'and look on the earth': Meaning that people will concentrate on earthly things at the expense of the spiritual dimension to life.

57. 'Lifir in danska   drótt at holdi,
    gerir eyvit sér   ǫlðri at móti.
    Því munu in tígnu   tíðmǫrk himins
    ljósi sínu   frá lýð snúa.

'In danska drótt lifir at holdi, gerir eyvit sér at móti ǫlðri. Því munu in tígnu tíðmǫrk himins snúa ljósi sínu frá lýð.

'The Danish people will live on meat, do nothing to resist ale-drinking. Therefore the glorious time-markers of heaven [HEAVENLY BODIES] will turn their light away from the nation.

Ms.: **Hb**(50v) (*Bret*).

Reading: [4] ǫlðri: ǫlð Hb.

Editions: *Skj*: Gunnlaugr Leifsson, *Merlínússpá I* 57: AII, 20, BII, 21-2, *Skald* II, 13-14; *Bret* 1848-9, II, 35 (*Bret* st. 57); *Hb* 1892-6, 276; *Merl* 2012, 118-19.

Notes: [All]: Cf. *DGB* 116 (Reeve and Wright 2007, 159.287-8; cf. Wright 1988, 114, prophecy 72): *Ab eis uultus auertent sydera et solitum cursum confundent* 'The planets will look away from men and disrupt their customary paths' (cf. Reeve and Wright 2007, 158). — [1-2] *in danska drótt* 'the Danish people': The apparently anti-Danish polemics are Gunnlaugr's contribution; the foundation of a metropolitan see in Norway in 1153 severed older allegiances of the Icelandic bishoprics with Lund in what was then Denmark (cf. Foote 1975, 73). However, the adj. *dansk* may sometimes apply to Scandinavians generally, especially in the phrase *dǫnsk tunga* 'Danish tongue', which acquired the generalised meaning 'Scandinavian language' at least as early as the C11th (cf. Sigv *Víkv* 15/8[1] and Note; see also *SnE* 1998, I, 52, 80). — [4] *ǫlðri* 'ale-drinking': Emended from ms. *ǫlð* (refreshed) (Poole 2009, 312). The Hb text features regular use of superscript contraction for <ri>, e.g. in *eit<ri>* (fol. 51r l. 16), which could easily be obscured by refreshing. For the sentiment, compare *ofdrykkja* 'excessive drinking' (*II*

56/7); also *II* 52/3-4. The ms. reading is retained in *Bret* 1848-9, *Skj* B and *Skald*, evidently in the sense of 'people'; in *Skj* B ll. 3-4 are translated loosely as *og gör intet mod sig selv (sine lyster)* 'and does nothing against itself (its pleasures)' (*Bret* 1848-9 similarly). *Merl* 2012 also retains the ms. reading, but with translation of *ǫlð* as *Schicksal* 'fate', which is hard to account for unless by confusion with *ørlǫg* 'fate'.

58. 'En grund ept þat   gróða hafnar;
    né skúr ofan   ór skýjum kemr.
    Sól ok máni   sjǫlf annan veg
    fara fagrskǫpuð,   en þau fyrr hafi.

'En grund hafnar gróða ept þat; né kemr skúr ofan ór skýjum. Sól ok máni sjǫlf, fagrskǫpuð, fara annan veg, en þau fyrr hafi.

'But the earth will lose its fecundity after that; nor will the shower descend from the clouds. The sun and the moon themselves, beautifully created, will take a different path from the one they have [taken] previously.

Ms.: **Hb**(50v) (*Bret*).

Editions: *Skj*: Gunnlaugr Leifsson, *Merlínússpá I* 58: AII, 20, BII, 22; *Skald* II, 14; *Bret* 1848-9, II, 35-6 (*Bret* st. 58); *Hb* 1892-6, 276; *Merl* 2012, 119-20.

Notes: [All]: Gunnlaugr appears to be summarising Geoffrey's description of the disruption of the heavenly bodies in prophecies 72 and 73, especially 72 (Reeve and Wright 2007, 159.288-9): *Arebunt segetes his indignantibus, et humor conuexi negabitur* 'Because of their wrath crops will wither and moisture from the sky will be denied' (cf. Reeve and Wright 2007, 158; cf. Wright 1988, 114). — [7] *fagrskǫpuð* 'beautifully created': A *hap. leg.* in poetry; the sole prose attestation occurs in *Kgs* (Holm-Olsen 1983, 98; cf. *ONP*: *fagrskapaðr*). — [8] *þau* 'they': Omitted in *Skald*.

59. 'Ok þar á hlýrni   heiðar stjǫrnur
    má marka því   moldar hvergi.
    Sumar fara ǫfgar,   sumar annan veg
    af inni gǫmlu   gǫngu sinni.

'Ok því má marka heiðar stjǫrnur þar á hlýrni hvergi moldar. Sumar fara ǫfgar, sumar annan veg af inni gǫmlu gǫngu sinni.

'And for that cause it will not be possible anywhere on earth to distinguish the bright stars there in heaven. Some will go backwards, some on a different path away from their ancient course.

Ms.: **Hb**(50v) (*Bret*).

Editions: *Skj*: Gunnlaugr Leifsson, *Merlínússpá I* 59: AII, 20, BII, 22; *Skald* II, 14; *Bret* 1848-9, II, 36 (*Bret* st. 59); *Hb* 1892-6, 276; *Merl* 2012, 120.

Notes: [All]: Briefly summarised from *DGB* 117, prophecy 73. — [2] *heiðar stjǫrnur* 'the bright stars': De Vries (1964-7, II, 75 n. 179) compares *Vsp* 57/4. — [3-4] *má marka … hvergi moldar* 'it will not be possible anywhere on earth to distinguish': An impersonal construction, lit. 'one can distinguish nowhere of earth'. The sense, in the context of ll. 5-8 and *II* 60/1-4, appears to be that the stars (and with them the sun and the moon, *II* 58/5-8), following perturbed courses, can no longer be identified or distinguished one from another, even if they are still visible. With that, human systems of time-keeping and navigation would collapse, an idea hinted at in *II* 57/6 *tíðmǫrk himins* 'time-markers of heaven'. Cf. the admonition to the would-be merchant in *Kgs* (Holm-Olsen 1983, 130): *Nemðu uandliga birting lopz oc gang himintvngla* 'Note carefully the illumination of the sky and the movement of the heavenly bodies'. *Skj* B translates *marka af* as *tage mærke af* 'take notice of, recognise', cf. *Bret* 1848-9 and *Merl* 2012. — [4] *hvergi moldar* 'anywhere on earth': Lit. 'nowhere of earth': A well attested usage, for the syntax of which see *Fritzner*: *hvergi* adv. 3; *CVC*, *LP*: *hvergi*. The line is so construed in *Skj* B. In *Bret* 1848-9, by contrast, *hvergi moldar* appears to be interpreted as 'nowhere in the firmament', but that is unlikely in view of the standard senses of *mold* 'earth'. *Merl* 2012 takes a radically different approach, construing *hvergi* as equivalent to *hverrgi* 'no one', taken as subject of *má* 'can', but a phrase *hver[r]gi moldar*, translated as *keiner auf der Erde* 'no one on Earth', is not otherwise attested.

60. 'Sumar sœkjask at,   en sumar firrask;
    bregða ljósi   ok litum fǫgrum.
    Berjask vindar   — þau eru veðr mikil —
    ok hljóm gera   meðal himintungla.

'Sumar sœkjask at, en sumar firrask; bregða ljósi ok fǫgrum litum. Vindar berjask ok gera hljóm meðal himintungla; þau eru veðr mikil.

'Some will approach each other and some draw away; change their light and their beautiful colours. The winds will contend and cause tumult between the heavenly bodies; those are great storms.

Ms.: **Hb**(50v) (*Bret*).

Editions: *Skj*: Gunnlaugr Leifsson, *Merlínússpá I* 60: AII, 20, BII, 22; *Skald* II, 14; *Bret* 1848-9, II, 36 (*Bret* st. 60); *Hb* 1892-6, 276; *Merl* 2012, 120-1.

Note: [All]: The first *helmingr* summarises *DGB* 117, prophecy 73 (see Note to *II* 58-9). The second *helmingr* is based on *DGB* 117 (Reeve and Wright 2007, 159.303-4; cf. Wright 1988, 115, prophecy 74): *Confligent uenti diro sufflamine et sonitum inter sidera conficient* 'The winds will contend with a terrible blast and make a din amongst the stars' (cf. Reeve and Wright 2007, 158).

61. 'Geisar geimi;   gengr hann upp í lopt;
slíkt es ógurligt   ýta bǫrnum.
Slíkt es ógurligt   upp at telja;
mun in forna mold   af firum verða.'

'Geimi geisar; hann gengr upp í lopt; slíkt es ógurligt bǫrnum ýta. Slíkt es ógurligt at telja upp; in forna mold mun verða af firum.'

'The sea will surge; it will go up into the sky; such [a thing] is terrifying for the children of men [MANKIND]. Such [a thing] is terrifying to recount; the ancient earth will be emptied of men.'

Ms.: **Hb**(50v) (*Bret*).

Editions: *Skj*: Gunnlaugr Leifsson, *Merlínússpá I* 61: AII, 20, BII, 22, *Skald* II, 14; *Bret* 1848-9, II, 36-7 (*Bret* st. 61); *Hb* 1892-6, 276; *Merl* 2012, 121.

Notes: [All]: Cf. *DGB* 117 (Reeve and Wright 2007, 159.302; cf. Wright 1988, 115, prophecy 74): *In ictu radii exurgent aequora* 'In the flash of its beam, the seas will rise' (Reeve and Wright 2007, 158). This marks a conclusion of the prophecies in *DGB*. — [1]: De Vries (1964-7, II, 75 n. 179) compares *Vsp* 57/5.

62. Væri mart   mǫnnum kynna
ór folkstafs   fornu kvæði.
Ek mun þó   þeygi fleira
Þróttar þings   þollum segja.

Mart væri kynna mǫnnum ór fornu kvæði folkstafs. Ek mun þó þeygi segja þollum þings Þróttar fleira.

There would be many things to inform men [about] from the old poem of the people-stave [LEADER = Merlin]. I will however not say more to the fir-trees of the assembly of Þróttr <= Óðinn> [BATTLE > WARRIORS].

Ms.: **Hb**(50v) (*Bret*).

Editions: *Skj*: Gunnlaugr Leifsson, *Merlínússpá I* 62: AII, 20-1, BII, 22-3, *Skald* II, 14; *Bret* 1848-9, II, 37 (*Bret* st. 62); *Hb* 1892-6, 276; *Merl* 2012, 122.

Notes: [All]: The consistent use of the *kviðuháttr* verse-form begins with this stanza and continues to the end of the poem. — [6] *þeygi* 'not': Emended in *Skald* to *eigi*, presumably to improve the alliteration, but unnecessarily, since in *kviðuháttr* *þó* (l. 3) can bear alliteration.

63. Þó hefk sagt   seggja kindum
    slíkt, es bók   brǫgnum kynnir.
    Nýti sér   njótar stála
    slíka sǫgn,   ok sésk fyrir.

Þó hefk sagt kindum seggja slíkt, es bók kynnir brǫgnum. Njótar stála nýti sér slíka sǫgn, ok sésk fyrir.

Yet I have told the children of men such [things] as the book teaches men. Let the users of weapons [WARRIORS] avail themselves of such sayings and take heed.

Ms.: **Hb**(50v) (*Bret*).

Editions: *Skj*: Gunnlaugr Leifsson, *Merlínússpá I* 63: AII, 21, BII, 23, *Skald* II, 14; *Bret* 1848-9, II, 37 (*Bret* st. 63); *Hb* 1892-6, 276-7; *Merl* 2012, 122-3.

64. Sjá*m* við synð   ok svikaráðum
    ok alls kyns   illum verkum.
    Drýgjum dǫ́ð,   dróttin elskum,
    hrindum ǫrt   illu ráði.

Sjá*m* við synð ok svikaráðum ok alls kyns illum verkum. Drýgjum dǫ́ð, elskum dróttin, hrindum ǫrt illu ráði.

Let us eschew sin and treacherous counsels and all kinds of evil deeds. Let us practise [good] works, love the Lord, reject evil counsel forthwith.

Ms.: **Hb**(50v) (*Bret*).

Reading: [1] Sjá*m*: sjá Hb.

Editions: *Skj*: Gunnlaugr Leifsson, *Merlínússpá I* 64: AII, 21, BII, 23, *Skald* II, 14, *NN* §2163C; *Bret* 1848-9, II, 37 (*Bret* st. 64); *Hb* 1892-6, 277; *Merl* 2012, 123.

Note: [1] *sjá*m *við* 'let us eschew': Sjá*m* is emended in *Skald* (cf. *NN* §2163C), followed by *Merl* 2012, from ms. *sjá* (not refreshed). The abbreviation for <m> could have been obscured by fading of the ink. *Bret* 1848-9 has *Sjá* við *synd* translated as *Agte sig for Synd* … 'Guard oneself from sin …', where *sjá* appears to be construed as an imp. Emended in *Skj* B to *sé*, apparently construed as if it were 3rd pers. pl. indic., continuing the usage of verbs in the previous stanza. *Skj* B translates as *De undgå synd* … 'They shun (or 'will shun') sin …'. The construals of the verb in both *Bret* 1848-9 and *Skj* B raise difficulties, for the 1st pers. pl. is called for in view of the other verbs in the stanza. The phrasal verb *sjá við* 'eschew' is a standard formulation in homiletic admonitions (cf. *HómNo* 87).

65. Skrjúpt es líf   lýða barna
und hreggská   heiðar tjaldi.
En lífs lau*n   líða eigi
góð eða ill   gumna mengis.

Skrjúpt es líf barna lýða und hreggská tjaldi heiðar. En lau*n lífs mengis gumna, góð eða ill, líða eigi.

Brittle is the life of the children of men [MANKIND] under the storm-worn awning of heaven [SKY/HEAVEN]. But the rewards, good or evil, of the life of the multitude of men [MANKIND] do not pass away.

Ms.: **Hb**(50v) (*Bret*).

Readings: [4] heiðar: hliðar *corrected from* heiðar *during the process of refreshing* Hb   [5] lau*n: lausn Hb.

Editions: *Skj*: Gunnlaugr Leifsson, *Merlínússpá I* 65: AII, 21, BII, 23, *Skald* II, 14; *Bret* 1848-9, II, 37-8 (*Bret* st. 65); *Hb* 1892-6, 277; *Merl* 2012, 124.

Notes: [1] *skrjúpt* 'brittle': The adj. *skrjúpr* is attested in poetry only here and in Anon (*FoGT*) 13/2[III], along with three prose attestations as a nickname (*ONP*: *skrjúpr*). The sense appears to be 'brittle, weak, lacking resilience, incapable of enduring' (*CVC*, *LP*: *skrjúpr*). — [4] *heiðar* 'of heaven': The reading adopted in this edn derives from *Bret* 1848-9 (followed by *Skj* B), where it is restored from ms. *hliðar* (refreshed); letter <e> is visible beneath refreshed <l>. The erroneous reading *hliðar* is retained (without reference to the ms.) in *Skald*, presumably interpreted as *hlíðar* 'of the hill-slope', and this is followed in *Merl* 2012, which glosses as *Abhangs* 'of the incline'. — [5] *lau*n* 'rewards': Emended from ms. *lausn* (not refreshed) in *Bret* 1848-9, followed by subsequent eds.

66. Gleðjumk ǫll   í góðum hug
ok við ván   vegs ok dýrðar.
Gætum góðs,   gleymum illu,
*e*flum opt   andar prýði.

Gleðjumk ǫll í góðum hug ok við ván vegs ok dýrðar. Gætum góðs, gleymum illu, *e*flum opt prýði andar.

Let us all rejoice in good heart and with the expectation of honour and renown. Let us heed the good, forget the bad, often strengthen the glory of the soul.

Ms.: **Hb**(50v) (*Bret*).

Reading: [7] *e*flum: 'oflum' Hb.

Editions: *Skj*: Gunnlaugr Leifsson, *Merlínússpá I* 66: AII, 21, BII, 23, *Skald* II, 14-15, *NN* §101; *Bret* 1848-9, II, 38 (*Bret* st. 66); *Hb* 1892-6, 277; *Merl* 2012, 125.

Notes: [7] *eflum* 'strengthen': Emended in *Skj* B, followed by *Skald*, *Merl* 2012 and this edn, from ms. 'oflum' (not refreshed); *eflum* is incorrectly read in *Bret* 1848-9. — [8] *prýði* 'glory': *Merl* 2012 reads *frýði*, emending to *prýði*, but the status of the latter as the ms. reading is not in doubt.

67. Biðjum opt   bragna stilli
     œztan eflð   ǫllu hjarta,
     at víðfrægr   virða stjóri
     dœgr ok dag   dróttar gæti.

Biðjum opt stilli bragna, œztan eflð, ǫllu hjarta, at víðfrægr stjóri virða gæti dróttar dœgr ok dag.

Let us often pray to the Lord of men [= God], highest power, with all our heart that the widely-renowned governor of men [= God] may watch over his following night and day.

Ms.: **Hb**(50v) (*Bret*).

Editions: *Skj*: Gunnlaugr Leifsson, *Merlínússpá I* 67: AII, 21, BII, 23-4, *Skald* II, 15, *NN* §§30, 2567B; *Bret* 1848-9, II, 38 (*Bret* st. 67); *Hb* 1892-6, 277; *Merl* 2012, 125-6.

Notes: [3]: The interpretation of this line is not definitively resolved. While collocation of the verb *efla* in the sense of 'support, strengthen' with expressions for 'God' and 'Christ' is well attested (*ONP*: *efla* A1, cf. D5), the form *eflð* remains obscure. (a) No noun *eflð* is attested in *CVC*, *Fritzner* or *ONP* and it may represent a neologism designed to meet the demands of the *kviðuháttr* verse-form. (b) An alternative but less likely explanation is as an otherwise unattested noun derived from *efla* 'strengthen', with the -ð suffix seen also in *efnð* 'fulfilment' (< *efna*) and *hefnð* 'revenge' (< *hefna*) and parallel to Goth. *-ōþu*, OHG *-ōd*. In contrast to Old Norse, where such nouns have acquired f. gender, they remain m. in Gothic and Old High German (Wright 1954, 174). The m. form of the adj. *œztan* 'highest' in Hb might represent a retention of the older gender but is more probably a rationalisation to reflect the conventionally m. gender of *guð* 'god' (originally a neuter). On this basis the ms. reading is tentatively retained here, but emendation to *œzta* 'highest', the f. form of the adj., agreeing with the presumed f. gender of *eflð*, as advocated by Kock (*NN* §2567B; *Skald*), and followed by *Merl* 2012, is an attractive option. In other respects the interpretation adopted in this edn is that of Kock (*NN* §2567B; *Skald*), who, followed by *Merl* 2012, interprets ll. 3 and 4 together: *æzta [sic] eflð, | ǫllu hjarta*, translating as *människors furste, den högsta styrkan* 'the lord of men, the greatest support'. The line has a possible source in Lat. *summa potentia*, part of the chant *O summa potentia o summa bonitas et laude digna Maria mitis et benigna* 'Oh highest power, oh highest goodness and merciful and beneficent Mary, worthy of praise' (Sankt Gallen, Stiftsbibliothek, 388, f. 471, sequence 2 (Can 204367i in Lacoste and Koláček [n. d.], accessed 11 July 2015). By contrast, *Bret* 1848-9, followed by *Skj* B, appears to construe *eflð* as a noun in the dat.

sg., translating den *ypperste om kraft* 'the highest in power' and *ypperste i kraft* 'highest in power' respectively; *LP*: *eflð* treats the ms. reading as corrupt but tentatively proposes *ypperst ved sin hjælpende kraft* 'highest in his supporting power'. — [7] *dægr* 'night': Finnur Jónsson explains as referring to half the duration of the twenty-four hour cycle, in this context the night (*LP*: *dægr*); cf. *ONP*: *dǿgr* 1, which is glossed 'period of 12 hours [of a day or a night]'. Kock (*NN* §30) alternatively proposes 'day after day', which may also be correct: *dag oc dægr* occurs in *Stjórn* (Unger 1862, 417) as a rendering of Lat. *per multos dies* (*ONP*: *dǿgr* 1).

68. Ok herþarfr   hrindi gǫrla
gumna liðs   grandi hverju,
svát til lífs   leiði gǫrva
þjóðar vǫrðr   þetta mengi.

Ok hrindi herþarfr gǫrla hverju grandi liðs gumna, svát vǫrðr þjóðar leiði gǫrva þetta mengi til lífs.

And may the one beneficent to his people utterly avert all harm to the host of men, so that the protector of the people [= God] may fully lead this multitude to life.

Ms.: **Hb**(50v) (*Bret*).

Editions: *Skj*: Gunnlaugr Leifsson, *Merlínússpá I* 68: AII, 21, BII, 24, *Skald* II, 15; *Bret* 1848-9, II, 38 (*Bret* st. 68); *Hb* 1892-6, 277; *Merl* 2012, 126-7.

Friðþjófs saga ins frækna

Edited by Margaret Clunies Ross

Introduction

Friðþjófs saga ins frækna 'The Saga of Friðþjófr the Bold' (*Frið*) is generally classified as a *fornaldarsaga* although it has a number of qualities that align it with indigenous *riddarasǫgur* 'sagas of knights', most notably its bridal-quest theme (cf. Kalinke 1990, 109-29; Mitchell 1991, 25-9). However, the saga's Norwegian and Orcadian setting in the Viking Age and the presence of a substantial quantity of poetry within the text mean that its classification fits better among the *fornaldarsǫgur*. There is also some overlap in subject matter with two other *fornaldarsǫgur*, *Gautr* and *ÞorstVík* (cf. *Frið* 1901, xviii-xix).

The saga begins with old King Beli of Sogn and his sons, Helgi and Hálfdan and their beautiful sister Ingibjǫrg. On the other side of Sognefjorden is the dwelling of an old commoner, Þorsteinn Víkingsson, who has a very promising son, Friðþjófr, who is in love with Ingibjǫrg, and she with him. Both Beli and Þorsteinn die early in the narrative and bequeath their inheritances to their sons. The brothers Helgi and Hálfdan go off to visit King Hringr in Ringerike, who has demanded tribute from them, and, while they are gone, leave Ingibjǫrg and her attendants at a sanctuary, Baldrshagi 'Baldr's pasture', where they consider she will be safe from Friðþjófr's attentions. However, he disregards the sanctity of the place and visits her there. To punish him, the brothers send him off on a long and dangerous sea voyage to collect tribute from the Orkney islands in his ship Elliði. While he is away, they burn down his farm and marry Ingibjǫrg to King Hringr. Upon his return to Norway, Friðþjófr goes straight to Baldrshagi, where he finds the brothers attending to pagan rites and he throws the Orkney tribute in Helgi's face, knocking out two of his teeth. He then recovers a ring he had given Ingibjǫrg and sets fire to the sanctuary. He is now a wanted man. He escapes back to the Orkneys but is declared an outlaw in Norway. Eventually, tiring of a life on the run, he returns in disguise to King Hringr's court, where he can be close to Ingibjǫrg, who recognises the ring he had once given her. Hringr makes Friðþjófr his heir, both in respect of his wife and his kingdom (the latter until his young sons are old enough to inherit), but, after Hringr's death, Helgi and Hálfdan fight Friðþjófr for possession of the kingdom. Friðþjófr kills Helgi while Hálfdan is spared to live as a subordinate under his rule.

Frið enjoyed an extraordinary popularity in Scandinavia and in Europe more generally during the nineteenth century (Wawn 2000, 117-32; Zernack 1997, 68-72) as the quintessential Viking adventure story, complete with heroic action, arduous sea voyages to exotic lands, romance and a good dash of the pagan supernatural. Bishop Esias Tegnér's Swedish epic poem, *Frithiofs saga*, published in 1825 and loosely based on the Old Icelandic saga, did much to sustain an interest in *Frið* that had already been aroused. The saga's poetry also contributed to its popularity, especially the sequence concerning the hero's hazardous voyage to Orkney (Wawn 2000, 130-1).

Frið is an anonymous work, now extant in two distinct redactions, a longer (B) and a shorter (A). All of the saga's modern editors have considered the shorter version (A) the older of the two. The relationship of the longer version to *Friðþjófs rímur* (*Frið* 1893, 92-133; Finnur Jónsson 1905-22, I, 411-54) has been debated. *Friðþjófs rímur* is a composition possibly of the early fifteenth century, and is extant in the unique ms. AM 604 4°^{x} of the first half of the sixteenth century (*Frið* 1893, xxxii). While it shows considerable similarities at certain points to the B text, it is unlikely, as Larsson (*Frið* 1901, xiii-xvii) suggested, to have been the basis for it; rather, both *rímur* and B redaction appear to have developed independently from a version that descended from the older A redaction (cf. Björn K. Þórólfsson 1934, 307-9).

Editors have expressed differing views of the likely age of composition of the shorter version of *Frið*, whose extant mss can in any case be divided into two branches, usually named A1 and A2. Larsson (*Frið* 1901, xix) puts the date of composition of A as between c. 1270 and 1400, while Falk (1890, 97) suggested a narrower dating to the end of the thirteenth or the beginning of the fourteenth century. The earliest ms. of the A1 version is the fragmentary Holm perg 10 VI 8° (Holm10 VI) of c. 1500-25, which comprises only three vellum leaves, while AM 568 4°^{x} (568^x) of c. 1600-50 is a copy of this text made when Holm10 VI was still intact, and is thus of great value in establishing the text of this branch of the A recension (*Frið* 1893, xxx-xxxi). The earliest ms. of the A2 version of the saga is AM 510 4° (510), a vellum ms. of c. 1550, which Wenz (*Frið* 1914, lxiv-lxxi) takes as the basis for his edition of the A text, arguing, against Larsson and Falk, that the A2 version is more representative of the A redaction than the A1 mss, from which the B redaction probably derived. Other mss belonging to the A2 redaction, but not directly descended from 510, are JS 27 fol^x (27^x) of c. 1670 (?), ÍB 121 4°^{x} (121^x) of 1796-7 and the eighteenth-century ms. BLAdd 4860 fol (4860^x), the latter two probably copies of 27^x (for Larsson's and Wenz's proposed stemmata, see respectively *Frið* 1893, xxxii and *Frið* 1914, lxv).

The B version of *Frið* exists in at least twenty mss, many more than the A version, and many of these are from the eighteenth and nineteenth centuries, thus attesting to the continuing popularity of *Frið* after the Middle Ages. Larsson (*Frið* 1893, xxvi) presents a stemma of the mss of the B redaction, from which it is apparent that there are two main branches of descent. The first, on which AM 109a II 8°^{x} (109a II^x), of 1660, is high, would have been used by Larsson as his main text if the ms. had not contained a large lacuna (cf. *Frið* 1893, xxiii). Two mss descend indirectly in this line, AM 342 4°^{x} (342^x) and Holm papp 17 4°^{x} (papp17^x), the former dated 1653, the latter 1671. The second branch of descent of the B redaction has as its main exemplar GKS 1006 fol^x (1006^x), a ms. dated c. 1600-1700 containing many sagas, for the most part written by Jón Erlendsson (1538-1672) (*Frið* 1893, xxiv-xxv). Other mss of the second branch include AM 172 b fol^x (172b^x) and AM173 fol^x (173^x), both copies of 1006^x by

Ásgeir Jónsson (*Frið* 1893, iv-v). Other mss of the B redaction include Berlin MS Germ 25 4^{ox} (Berlin25^x), ÍB 43 fol (43^x) and BLAdd 24972 4^{ox} (24972^x).

Following Rafn's (*FSN* 2, 61-100) publication of the longer redaction, based on 173^x, this ms. came to be reckoned the best witness of the B text, and was presented as main ms. by Finnur Jónsson in *Skj* A, though he also gives B-text readings there from papp17^x and 1006^x. However, Larsson (*Frið* 1893, iv-vi) had shown that 173^x was a copy of 1006^x and asserted the priority of papp17^x as the main ms. of B. Wenz (*Frið* 1914, xii-xiii), however, argued for the priority of 1006^x over papp17^x as the best witness to the B recension.

The earliest edition of *Frið* was in *Nordiska kämpa dater* (Björner 1737), based on the B recension ms. Holm papp 56^x (papp56^x), which is a copy of papp17^x. The saga next appeared in the second volume of Rafn's *FSN* (1829-30) and here versions of both recensions were published, B being represented by a text based on 173^x (*FSN* 2, 63-100), and A by a text based on 510 (*FSN* 2, 488-503). In volume 2 of his edition, Valdimar Ásmundarson (1885-9) gave a text of the A redaction from 27^x, arguing that it contained a better treatment of the poetry than 510. Ludvig Larsson produced two editions of *Frið* around the turn of the nineteenth century, a period that saw intensive study of the saga (e.g. Calaminus 1887; Falk 1890). Larsson's first edition (*Frið* 1893) presents diplomatic texts of both short and long versions, B being represented by the text of papp17^x (*Frið* 1893, 1-37) with variant readings from other B mss (109a II^x, 342^x, 1006^x, 43^x and ÍB 65 4^{ox} (ÍB65^x)). Larsson also gives 510's text of the A version (*Frið* 1893, 38-61), followed by that of 568^x on pp. 62-91, with the parallel fragmentary text of Holm10 VI (*Frið* 1893, 64-8, 75-80, 85-90). *Frið* 1893 also has a text of *Friðþjófs rímur* (*Frið* 1893, 92-133). Larsson's second edition (*Frið* 1901) is a critical, normalised edition of the saga's B recension based on papp17^x, with variant readings from the A recension based on 510 and 568^x. In 1914 Gustav Wenz published an edition of the A recension alone (*Frið* 1914) based on 510, with variant readings from 568^x, Holm10 VI and 27^x. Separate editions of twenty-one of the stanzas of *Frið* without the accompanying saga prose were published in 1903 by Heusler and Ranisch (*Edd. Min.* 97-103) and of thirty-nine stanzas by Finnur Jónsson in *Skj* A and B (1912-15). In *Skj* A Finnur bases his diplomatic text of the A redaction on 510, giving readings from Holm10 VI and 568^x, while basing his text of the B redaction on 173^x, but also giving readings from papp17^x and 1006^x. Where stanzas occur in both A and B redactions, 510 is usually used as base text, though Finnur often either emends the text or adopts material from the B redaction mss. Kock (*Skald*) does not give diplomatic readings and mostly follows Finnur's *Skj* B text.

Forty-one separate stanzas in total occur across the extant mss of *Frið*, but neither redaction, nor any one ms., contains all forty-one stanzas. There are twenty-nine individual stanzas in A recension mss, though not all A version mss contain all twenty-nine stanzas. Thirty-five stanzas are in B recension mss. Six stanzas (*Frið* 14, 20, 30, 31, 34 and 35) are in A texts alone, while eleven others (*Frið* 1, 2, 3, 5, 6, 13, 17, 28, 29, 33 and 36) are only in B recension mss. The remaining twenty-four stanzas (*Frið* 4, 7,

8, 9, 10, 11, 12, 15, 16, 18, 19, 21, 22, 23, 24, 25, 26, 27, 32, 37, 38, 39, 40 and 41) are extant in mss of both recensions. According to a list of correspondences (*Frið* 1901, xiv n. 1), there are twenty-one stanzas that show some correspondence with stanzas in *Friðþjófs rímur*, all of them with stanzas that occur in B redaction or AB redaction mss.

Editions cited in the present edition are as follows: *Skj* A and B, *Skald* and *NN*; Falk 1890 treated as an edition; *Frið* 1893, *Frið* 1901, *Frið* 1914 and *Edd. Min.* The present edition adopts the following procedures. In editing the twenty-four stanzas that occur in both A and B redactions, priority is given to the A text, as representing an earlier form of the saga, and 510 is used as the main ms., having the best text of this redaction. Ms. 510 is also used as best text for the six stanzas that occur only in A mss. Other A recension mss used in this edition are Holm10 VI (where available), 568[x] and 27[x]. B redaction mss used for this edition are papp17[x], 109a II[x], 1006[x] and 173[x], and the following is used selectively: ÍB65[x]. When stanzas are extant only in B redaction mss, papp17[x] is used as main ms. It should be observed here that the state of the ms. paradosis for a number of the stanzas in *Frið* makes editing very difficult. Even though the A redaction mss probably represent an earlier version of many of the stanzas, the mss are clearly often corrupted and sense is difficult to establish. The B redaction mss, on the other hand, while sometimes clearer in their general sense than the corresponding A texts, are probably sometimes at least simplifications of material that redactors did not understand. Hence the principle of the *lectio facilior* applies to a number of readings in B text mss.

The question of the normalisation of the stanzas from *Frið* is a complex one, given that the B redaction probably stems from the fifteenth century, even though its stanzas are likely to be based for the most part on versions of the A redaction, which is probably at least a century older. In keeping with the policy adopted by the editors of *SkP* to normalise all *fornaldarsaga* stanzas to the period 1250-1300, this standard has been adopted for all *Frið* stanzas, whether they occur in A, B or A and B mss. From a metrical point of view, the mss of *Frið* in both versions display the usual licences that characterise late Icelandic versification, including the inclusion of free-standing personal pronouns and non-cliticised forms of verbs. The metres used are often irregular in their observance (or lack of it) of regular alliteration and *hendingar*. The most common metre in the forty-one stanzas of *Frið* is *fornyrðislag*, followed by *málaháttr*. A number of stanzas are in irregular variants of *dróttkvætt*.

The editor should like to place on record her debt to Jonathan Grove of the University of Cambridge for passing on to her some notes and a trial edition of the first two stanzas that he had made towards an edition of *Frið*. He was the original editor of these stanzas but found he was too busy with other editing tasks to continue with them. The editor has incorporated as much as she could of his material in the present edition.

Friðþjófr (Friðþ Lv 1)

1. Þat mun ek segja   seggjum várum,
at görla mun farit   gamanferðum.
Skulu ei skatnar   til skips fara,
því at nú eru blæjur   á blik komnar.

Þat mun ek segja seggjum várum, at görla mun farit gamanferðum. Skatnar skulu ei fara til skips, því at blæjur eru nú komnar á blik.

I will tell that to our [my] warriors, that pleasure trips will be completely out of bounds. Men must not go to the ship, because bed-sheets have now been placed on the bleaching ground.

Mss: **papp17^x**(358r), 109a II^x(145v), 1006^x(581), 173^x(83r) (*Frið*).

Readings: [1] Þat: *om*. 1006^x, 173^x [2] seggjum várum: *deleted and supplied again in the following line* 173^x [5] Skulu: skulum 109a II^x [6] til skips: *so all others*, á skip papp17^x [7] því at: því *all*.

Editions: *Skj*: Anonyme digte og vers [XIII], E. 7. *Vers af Fornaldarsagaer: Af Friðþjófssaga ens frækna* I 1: AII, 269, BII, 292, *Skald* II, 153-4; Falk 1890, 70-1, *Frið* 1893, 9, *Frið* 1901, 12; *Edd. Min.* 97.

Context: Friðþjófr and his men have been visiting Ingibjǫrg and her female companions at Baldrshagi 'Baldr's pasture', while her brothers Helgi and Hálfdan are away. Friðþjófr tells Ingibjǫrg that, when her brothers return, she must spread linen sheets out to bleach on the rooftop of the highest building, called *dísarsalr* 'hall of the goddess', where he could see them from his farm at Framnes. The next morning he recites this stanza, and his men look across Sognefjorden and see that the roof of the hall is covered in white linen cloth.

Notes: [All]: This stanza and the two following (*Frið* 1, 2 and 3) are found only in B recension mss. The A text has neither the motif of the linen sheets nor the stanza itself (but see an apparent allusion in *Frið* 8/7-8). This stanza is in *fornyrðislag*. — [3-4]: Finnur Jónsson (*Skj*) and Kock (*Skald*) put the line division between *mun* and *farit*, producing a long-line comprising a regular Sievers Type B odd line plus a Type C2 even line with neutralisation (*farit*) and resolution (*gaman-*) in metrical positions 1-2. From the point of view of distribution of stress it is unlikely, however, that the auxiliary *mun* could receive full stress directly followed by the p. p. *farit* in an unstressed position after the metrical caesura. The lineation adopted here and in most eds results in an irregular Type B odd line followed by a hypometrical even line, unless we assume suspension of alliteration on the first element of the cpd (*gaman-*), which is rare but does occur in later poetry. — [3-4] *at görla mun farit gamanferðum* 'that pleasure trips will be completely out of bounds': Lit. 'that it will be completely at an end with respect to pleasure trips'. On the usage of the p. p. of *fara* 'go' with dat. object in this sense, see *LP*: *fara* B2. — [7] *því at* 'because': For the common loss of *at* after *svá* 'so that', *þó* 'although' and *því* 'because' in the C14th, see *NS* §265 Anm. 2b. — [7-8] *blæjur eru nú komnar á blik* 'bed-sheets have now been placed on the bleaching ground': Before the discovery of chlorine in the late C18th, sunlight was the principal bleaching agent for whitening flax-woven linen, for light energy causes a reaction in wet flax, producing a hydrogen peroxide solution that bleaches the fabric. Until well into the C20th in Scandinavia, after washing the household linen, women would set it out to whiten and dry off on a bleaching ground (ON *blik*; cf. ModDan. *bleg*, ModNorw. *bleik*, ModSwed. *blek*), usually a patch of grass beside the house (cf. Falk 1919, 40; Schlabow 1978, 76). Although conceived in the B text of *Frið* as a prearranged signal, the gesture of washing and whitening linen bed-sheets (*blæjur*) may well symbolise the termination of the intimacies understood to have been enjoyed between the women at Baldrshagi and the men of Framnes. Cf. *Oddrgr* 6/4, 25/8 and *Rþ* 23/9, where references to *blæjur* indicate sexual intimacy.

Introduction to sts 2-9

With *Frið* 2 begins a long series of stanzas describing Friðþjófr's perilous, stormy voyage on his ship Elliði from Norway to the Orkney islands, interlaced with reminiscences of his courtship of Ingibjǫrg. The stanzas, most of which are put in the mouth of Friðþjófr himself, alternate descriptions of the raging storm he and his men encounter with yearning for the women back home. They employ some common conventions of skaldic poetry, including the contrast between the tough man's life at sea and soft indoor amusements with women at home.

Friðþjófr (FriðÞ Lv 2)

2. Snyðja lét ek ór Sogni   Nú tekr hregg at herða;
    (en snótir mjaðar neyttu)   hafi dag brúðir góðan,
    bræddan byrjar sóta   þær er oss vilja unna,
    (í Baldrshaga miðjum).   þótt Elliða fylli.

Ek lét bræddan sóta byrjar snyðja ór Sogni, en snótir neyttu mjaðar í miðjum Baldrshaga. Nú tekr hregg at herða; hafi brúðir, þær er vilja unna oss, góðan dag, þótt Elliða fylli.

I made the tarred steed of the breeze [SHIP] speed out from Sogn, but the ladies were enjoying mead amidst Baldrshagi. Now a squall begins to strengthen; may those women who desire to love us have a happy life, although Elliði may founder.

Mss: **papp17^x**(358v), 109a II^x(146v), 1006^x(582), 173^x(83v-84r) (*Frið*).

Readings: [1] Snyðja: *so* 109a II^x, 1006^x, sindra papp17^x, 'sinda' 173^x [5] at: á 173^x [6] góðan: *so* 109a II^x, *om. with* fagran *inserted above the line in a later hand* papp17^x, *om.* 1006^x, 173^x [7] þær: þar 1006^x, 173^x;   er: *so all others*, 'ed' papp17^x [8] þótt: enn þótt 109a II^x;   fylli ('fille'): felli 1006^x, 173^x.

Editions: *Skj*: Anonyme digte og vers [XIII], E. 7. *Vers af Fornaldarsagaer: Af Friðþjófssaga ens frækna* I 2: AII, 269, BII, 292, *Skald* II, 154, *NN* §§1470, 2338Fa, 2385A, B; Falk 1890, 71, *Frið* 1893, 11, *Frið* 1901, 15.

Context: Helgi and Hálfdan punish Friðþjófr for his dalliance with their sister and his desecration of Baldrshagi (see Note to l. 4 below) by sending him to collect tribute from the Orkney islands, ostensibly so they can pay Ingibjǫrg's dowry to King Hringr, but actually so they can have Friðþjófr killed. As he sails out from Sognefjorden, Friðþjófr and his men encounter a storm caused by two witches (*seiðkonur*) in the pay of the brothers. Friðþjófr then speaks this stanza.

Notes: [All]: This stanza has no counterpart in the A redaction mss, but it is similar to *Friðþjófs rímur* III, 3/3-5/1 (*Frið* 1893, 108; Finnur Jónsson 1905-22, I, 426). The metre of *Frið* 2 is the variant form of *dróttkvætt* that Snorri Sturluson calls *munnvǫrp* 'mouth-throwings' (*SnE* 2007, 28-9), in which odd lines have no rhyme, and even lines have *skothending*. *Frið* 2 has several metrical irregularities; line 2 begins with an unstressed element (cf. *NN* §§2338Fa, 2385B, 1470), which Finnur Jónsson (*Skj* B) regularises by emendation, while l. 4 has no *hending*. Falk (1890, 71) points out other metrically irregular lines in *Frið* stanzas (6/4, 14/8, 28/4, 29/4 and 32/6) that contain the cpd *Baldrshagi* and/or the adj. *miðr*. *Brúðir* (l. 6) violates Craigie's Law. — [1] *snyðja* 'speed': This verb, often used of ships travelling fast (cf. SnSt Ht 77/1[III]), is the only variant to make sense here, as contrasted with papp17[x]'s *sindra* 'emit sparks' (which does not fit the context and is usually impersonal in usage) and 173[x]'s *sinda*, which Finnur Jónsson (*Skj* B) understands as *synda* 'swim'. *Snyðja* also appears in the *ríma* counterpart to ll. 1-2: 'Snyðja læt ek,' kvað snerpir málms, | 'snekkju barð úr Sogni' 'The sharpener of metal [WARRIOR] said, 'I make the ship's prow speed out from Sogn'. — [3] *bræddan* 'tarred': On the tarring of ships' hulls to protect them from water and other damage, see Falk (1912, 50-1) and Jesch (2001a, 144). — [4] *í miðjum Baldrshaga* 'amidst Baldrshagi': According to the A redaction of *Frið* (*Frið* 1914, 3), Baldrshagi 'Baldr's pasture' was the name of a *griðastaðr ok hof mikit* 'a place of peace and a great temple' near the residence of King Beli. The B redaction adds (*Frið* 1901, 1-2) that there was a large paling fence (*skíðgarðr*) around the sanctuary, and that inside many gods (presumably images of gods) were venerated, though Baldr was the most important of them. No injury was to be done to man or beast there and men and women should not have intercourse (*viðskipti*) there. *Frið*'s presentation of a temple dedicated to Baldr is unique in Old Norse literature, and there is little clear evidence to support this god's cult in Viking-Age Scandinavia. Theophoric place names incorporating the element Baldr are either non-existent or dubious in Norway (Olsen 1924, 169; Brink 2007a, 120-2) and *Frið*'s representation of his cult and cult house may be an antiquarian fiction (cf. Lindow 1997, 29 n., 132-3). — [6]: This line is too short in several mss, and was also so in papp17[x], where a later hand has added the adj. *fagran* 'fair, beautiful'. Most eds have preferred the adj. *góðan* 'happy, good', adopted from 109a[x] and found in several other B redaction mss. — [8] *Elliða* (acc.) 'Elliði': The name of Friðþjófr's ship, which he inherited from his father, Þorsteinn Víkingsson.

According to the B recension, Elliði was under an enchantment that allowed it to understand human speech (*Frið* 1901, 26), although no such magical qualities are mentioned in recension A. Larsson (*Frið* 1901, xviii) suggested that the account of Elliði's magical powers in B may have been borrowed from *ÞorstVík* ch. 21 (*FSGJ* 3, 57), which stated that the ship had a fair wind whenever it wanted to sail, and could practically understand human speech (*kunni hann náliga manns máli*). The noun *elliði* occurs as a ship-*heiti* in skaldic poetry (Þul *Skipa* 4/3^{III}, Eil *Þdr* 15/7^{III}, KormQ Lv 57/6^V (*Korm* 78/6). Other figures in Old Norse literature to own ships named Elliði include the legendary King Górr (*FSN* 2, 5; *Flat* 1860-8, I, 22), and the Icelandic settler Ketilbjǫrn inn gamli 'the Old' (*ÍF* 1, 384). *Sǫrla* (*Flat* 1860-8, I, 277) lists Elliði (presumably Górr's ship) as one of the three greatest longships of all time, together with Óláfr Tryggvason's Ormr inn langi 'the Long Serpent' and Gnóð (see below). The etymology of Elliði is uncertain, some scholars (Falk 1912, 88) deriving it from Old Slavonic, others considering it of native origin < *einliði* 'one that travels alone' (see Note to Þul *Skipa* 4/3^{III} for further discussion and *AEW*: *elliði*). Friðþjófr is not the only *fornaldarsaga* hero to have a named ship; Gnóð 'Rustling', which gave its name to its owner, Gnóðar-Ásmundr, is mentioned in *EgÁsm* and *GrL* (see Introduction to Anon *GnóðÁsm* 1^{III} for details). — [8] *fylli* (3rd pers. sg. pres. subj.) 'may founder': An impersonal use of *fylla* 'fill' with the acc. of that which fills with water, in a specific nautical sense (*Fritzner*: *fylla* 1; *CVC*: *fylla*) of a ship taking water. The line *þótt Elliða fylli* appears also in *Friðþjófs rímur* III, 4/4.

Friðþjófr (FriðÞ Lv 3)

3.   Mjǫk tekr sjór at svella;   Ei skal ek við ægi
    svá er nú drepit skýjum;   í ofviðri berjaz;
    því ráða galdrar gamlir,   látum Sólundir seggjum
    er gjálfr ór stað færiz.   svellvífaðar hlífa.

Sjór tekr mjǫk at svella; svá er nú drepit skýjum; gamlir galdrar ráða því, er gjálfr færiz ór stað. Ek skal ei berjaz við ægi í ofviðri; látum svellvífaðar Sólundir hlífa seggjum.

The sea begins to swell greatly; thus clouds are now louring; old spells cause the surge to be moved from its place. I will not fight against the ocean in the violent storm; let us make the ice-covered Sula islands protect the men.

Mss: **papp17**^{x}(358v), 109a II^x(146v), 1006^x(582), 173^x(84r), ÍB65^x(47r) (*Frið*).

Readings: [4] færiz: *so* ÍB65^x, færir papp17^x, 109a II^x, 1006^x, 173^x [7] Sólundir: *so* 173^x, 'sal vnder' *all others*   [8] svell-: 'sioll-' 109a II^x, 'sverll-' 1006^x, 'sverl-' 173^x.

Editions: *Skj*: Anonyme digte og vers [XIII], E. 7. Vers af Fornaldarsagaer: Af Friðþjófssaga ens frækna I 3: AII, 269, BII, 292, *Skald* II, 154, *NN* §§2338 Fb; Falk 1890, 71-2, *Frið* 1893, 11, *Frið* 1901, 16.

Context: In the B recension text Friðþjófr and his men steer their ship to the islands called Sólundir (ModNorw. Sulen), seeking protection from the storm. This incident is not mentioned in the A redaction.

Notes: [All]: This stanza is not in the A text. Its general sense is paralleled in *Friðþjófs rímur* III, 7-8 (*Frið* 1893, 108). The metre is an irregular form of *dróttkvætt*, comprising four couplets and virtually no *hendingar*, except in l. 8, where *aðalhending* occurs. Earlier eds (Falk 1890, 72; *Skj* B; *Skald*) have attempted to regularise ll. 3 and 7, where long and short vowels in open syllables (e.g. *ráða*, l. 3, *látum*, l. 7) appear to have begun to be confused. Finnur Jónsson (followed by *Skald*) also deletes all mss' initial *því* 'that' in l. 3 to regularise the metre. — [2] *svá er nú drepit skýjum* 'thus clouds are now louring': The expression is impersonal. The construction *skýjum er drepit* means that clouds hang low and heavily over the earth (cf. *LP*: *drepa* 3), lit. 'are knocked down'. — [4] *færiz* 'is moved': The expression *færa* (older *føra*) *ór stað* 'to move (sth.) from its place' requires a direct object if in active voice, and *gjálfr* 'the surge' may be either acc. or nom. Most mss read *færir* 'moves' 3rd pers. sg. pres. tense, but sense requires a passive construction, hence the preference here (so also *Frið* 1901, 16) for m. v. *færiz*. At least one younger ms., ÍB65[x], has the m. v. form. Finnur Jónsson (*Skj* B; so also *Skald*) keeps *færir*, but translates with a passive construction: *gamle galdre volder nu det, at havet bevæges stærkt* 'old spells now cause the sea to be strongly moved'. There is, however, no evidence of *færa* used impersonally with an acc. object. — [7] *Sólundir* 'the Sula islands': These islands, Indre and Ytre Sula, at the mouth of Sognefjorden, are currently in the municipality of Solund. The word is based on 173[x]'s reading, where 'ol' has been added above the line; this may be a scribal correction rather than a variant reading, seeing that 173[x] is a copy of 1006[x]. Sólund is listed among island names in Þul *Eyja* 5/3[III] and mentioned in KormǪ Lv 38/7[V] (*Korm* 57) and Bjhít Lv 9/4[V] (*BjH* 11). — [8] *svellvífaðar* 'ice-covered': This cpd adj. is a *hap. leg*. The first element *svell* 'ice, sheet of ice' (especially over land) is unproblematic, even though the scribes had difficulty with it. The second element appears to be the p. p. *-vífaðr* 'covered, wrapped' from the verb *vífa* 'come upon suddenly or by accident' (cf. *ÍO*: 1132). Exactly how the meaning of the p. p. derives from the inf. *vífa* is unclear; *ONP*: *vífa* gives five examples of this verb, all exemplifying the pres. part.

Friðþjófr (FriðÞ Lv 4)

4. Þat var forðum   á Framnesi;
   rera ek opt á tal   við Ingibjörgu.
   Nú skal ek sigla   í svölu veðri,
   láta létt und mér   lögdýr bruna.

Þat var forðum á Framnesi; ek rera opt á tal við Ingibjörgu. Nú skal ek sigla í svölu veðri, láta lögdýr bruna létt und mér.

It was long ago at Framnes; I often rowed to have conversation with Ingibjǫrg. Now I must sail in the cold storm, make the sea-animal [SHIP] speed easily beneath me.

Mss: **510**(93r), 568[x](100r), 27[x](134v), papp17[x](358v), 109a II[x](146v), 1006[x](582-583), 173[x](84r) (*Frið*).

Readings: [1] forðum: fyrri papp17[x], 109a II[x], fyrr 1006[x], 173[x]   [2] á Framnesi: 'a fra[...]' 568[x]   [3] rera ek opt: '[...]' 568[x], rædda ek oft 27[x], at reri ek papp17[x], 109a II[x], 1006[x], 173[x];   á tal: '[...] vit' 568[x], á vit papp17[x], 1006[x], 173[x], á 109a II[x]   [4] við Ingibjörgu: Ingibjargar 568[x]   [5] ek: *om.* 568[x], papp17[x], 109a II[x], 1006[x], 173[x]   [6] svölu: svöl- papp17[x], 109a II[x], 1006[x]   [7] láta: *so all others*, ok láta 510;   und mér ('under mier'): 'u[...]' 568[x], undan papp17[x], 109a II[x], 1006[x], 173[x]   [8] lög-: '[...]' 568[x], lang papp17[x], 109a II[x], 1006[x], 173[x];   bruna: '[...]runa' 568[x], hlaupa papp17[x], 109a II[x], 1006[x], 173[x].

Editions: *Skj*: Anonyme digte og vers [XIII], E. 7. *Vers af Fornaldarsagaer: Af Friðþjófssaga ens frækna* I 4: AII, 269-70, BII, 292, *Skald* II, 154; Falk 1890, 72, *Frið* 1893, 12, 43, 70, *Frið* 1901, 16-17, *Frið* 1914, 11-12; *Edd. Min.* 98.

Context: Shortly after a lull in the storm, the wind begins to freshen and Friðþjófr speaks this stanza.

Notes: [All]: This is the first stanza in the A redaction of *Frið* and the fourth in the B redaction, the first to appear in both redactions. Larsson (*Frið* 1901, xiv) detected a similarity with *Friðþjófs rímur* III, 12-13, but it is not very close. The stanza contrasts Friðþjófr's previously happy life courting Ingibjörg and his present privations at sea. The metre is *fornyrðislag*, although l. 4 is in *málaháttr*. Clear differences between the two redactions are apparent in ll. 1, 2, 3, 6, 7 and 8 (cf. Wenz's discussion in *Frið* 1914, lxxiii). — [2] *á Framnesi* 'at Framnes': In the A redaction, this p. n. is not mentioned in the prose text, but only in this stanza and *Frið* 25/2. In the B redaction, Framnes is named in the prose of the saga's first chapter (*Frið* 1901, 2) as the farm of Þorsteinn, Friðþjófr's father, which lay on the opposite side of Sognefjorden from King Beli's dwelling. — [3-4] *ek rera opt á tal við Ingibjörgu* 'I often rowed to have conversation with Ingibjǫrg': This is the reading of 510. There is a considerable variation in the ms. readings of these two lines, with the B recension mss favouring *rera ek opt á vit* 'I often rowed to pay a visit' in l. 3, followed by *við Ingibjörgu* 'to Ingibjǫrg' in l. 4. Ms. 568[x] alone has the gen. *Ingibjargar*, which has been adopted by *Edd. Min.*, *Skj* B and *Skald*, though the many lacunae in this ms. at this point make it difficult to recover the reading of l. 3, except that the word before *Ingibjargar* was *vit*. It may be that scribes confused *á vit* 'on a visit' which usually takes the gen. of the person or place visited, with the prep. *við* 'with, towards'. There also seems to have been some confusion about the main verb of l. 3, as between *rera ek* 'I rowed' and *rædda ek* 'I spoke' (so 27[x]), which was then reflected in the variation between *á vit* 'on a visit' and *á tal* 'for conversation'. — [8] *lögdýr* 'the sea-animal [SHIP]': The reading of 510 and 27[x], 568[x] having a lacuna. A regular ship-kenning with an animal name as base-word, cf. *Meissner* 208-12. The B redaction mss all have *langdýr* 'long animal', an inferior reading probably affected by the cpd *langskip* 'longship'; the second element *-dýr* 'animal', present in all mss except 568[x], signals a ship-kenning, however. The B mss also read *hlaupa* 'leap, jump', a verb that fits the metaphorical sense of the ship as an animal, but is the *lectio facilior* by comparison with the A mss' *bruna* 'speed, rush'. *Lögdýr* could be sg. or pl.: *Skj* B treats it as pl., but the speaker, Friðþjófr, is talking about his own actions sailing his own ship, Elliði, hence the sg. translation here. The saga prose does not state that Friðþjófr commanded more than one ship.

Friðþjófr (FriðÞ Lv 5)

5. Eigi sér til Alda
    — erum út á brim komnir
    frægir fylkis drengir —
    fyr gerningaveðri.

    Ok standa nú allir
    — eru Sólundir horfnar —
    átján menn í austri,
    er Elliða verja.

Sér eigi til Alda fyr gerningaveðri; erum komnir út á brim, frægir drengir fylkis. Ok allir átján menn, er verja Elliða, standa nú í austri; Sólundir eru horfnar.

Alden cannot be seen because of a sorcery-induced storm; we have come out on a rough sea, renowned warriors of a king. And all eighteen men, who defend Elliði, are now engaged in baling out; the Sula islands are out of sight.

Mss: **papp17**[x](358v), 109a II[x](146v-147r), 1006[x](583), 173[x](84v) (*Frið*).

Reading: [3] frægir: frægðar 1006[x], 173[x].

Editions: *Skj*: Anonyme digte og vers [XIII], E. 7. *Vers af Fornaldarsagaer: Af Friðþjófssaga ens frækna* I 5: AII, 270, BII, 293, *Skald* II, 154, *NN* §1471; Falk 1890, 72, *Frið* 1893, 12, *Frið* 1901, 17.

Context: As for *Frið* 4. Further out in the ocean, another enormous storm with great snow-drifts hits the ship and the men have to bale out furiously.

Notes: [All]: This stanza is not in the A redaction mss, though *Frið* 7, which is very similar to it in content, is present there. *Frið* 5 in the B mss may have been modelled on the pre-existing *Frið* 7. *Friðþjófs rímur* III, 14-15 present similar material. The metre is *háttlausa* 'lack of form', a variant of *dróttkvætt* lacking internal rhyme. — [1] *Alda* 'Alden': Aldi (ModNorw. Alden) is the name of an island in Sunnfjord, Sogn og Fjordane, west of Atløy; cf. *Þul Eyja* 2/8[III] and Note. This interpretation of all mss' 'allda' follows *Skj* B and *Skald*; previous eds (Falk 1890; *Frið* 1901) have understood the word as gen. pl. of *ǫld*, pl. *aldir* 'men, people', giving a sense 'One could not see people because of a sorcery-induced storm'. However, this interpretation is at odds with the sense of the second *helmingr* of this stanza. — [8] *verja* 'defend': The men 'defend' Elliði by continuing to bale out the water it has taken on; otherwise it might sink.

Friðþjófr (FriðÞ Lv 6)

6. Helgi veldr, at hrannir
hrímfaxaðar vaxa;
er ei, sem bjarta brúði
í Baldrshaga kyssim.

Ólíkt mun mér unna
Ingibjörg eða þengill;
heldr vilda ek hennar
hæfi at minni gæfu.

Helgi veldr, at hrímfaxaðar hrannir vaxa; er ei, sem kyssim bjarta brúði í Baldrshaga. Ingibjörg eða þengill mun unna mér ólíkt; ek vilda heldr hæfi hennar at gæfu minni.

Helgi is causing the rime-maned waves to grow; it is not as though we [I] were kissing the radiant woman in Baldrshaga. Ingibjǫrg and the king will love me differently; I would rather her situation [was] to my advantage.

Mss: **papp17ˣ**(358v), 109a IIˣ(147r), 1006ˣ(583), 173ˣ(84v) (*Frið*).

Editions: *Skj*: Anonyme digte og vers [XIII], E. 7. *Vers af Fornaldarsagaer: Af Friðþjófssaga ens frækna* I 6: AII, 270, BII, 293, *Skald* II, 154, *NN* §1472; Falk 1890, 72-3, *Frið* 1893, 12-13, *Frið* 1901, 18.

Context: As for *Frið* 5.

Notes: [All]: Like *Frið* 5, this stanza is not in the A redaction mss. This and the following stanza are in an irregular form of *munnvǫrp* 'mouth-throwings' metre. *Friðþjófs rímur* III, 16-17 are closely similar. Lines 3-4 are reminiscent of Anon *Krm* 13/7-8 (*Ragn*) *Varat, sem bjarta brúði | í bing hjá sér leggja* 'It was not like placing a fair maiden in a bed beside one' and 20/7-8 *Varat, sem unga ekkju | í ǫndvegi kyssa* 'It was not like kissing a young woman in the high seat' and may have been influenced by *Krm* or be simply drawing on the conventional Norse contrast between the tough man's life in battle or, as here, at sea, and the delights of affairs with women; cf. Anon *Sveinfl* 1/1-4¹. The close similarity of vocabulary may, however, suggest poetic influence rather than pure convention. — [1] *Helgi*: Name of the elder of the two sons of King Beli of Sogn. In the saga's B redaction he is said to have been a great *blótmaðr* 'sacrificer, idolater, heathen worshipper' (*Frið* 1901, 3). — [2] *hrímfaxaðar* 'rime-maned': This cpd adj. is a *hap. leg.* but causes no difficulty in understanding. The icy waves are likened to horses tossing their manes covered by hoar-frost. — [5-6] *Ingibjörg eða þengill mun unna mér ólíkt* 'Ingibjǫrg and the king will love me differently': This remark is a kind of litotes, to signal Friðþjófr's awareness that the king (presumably Helgi is meant though it is possible that the allusion is to King Hringr, Ingibjǫrg's intended) does not love him at all, though Ingibjǫrg does. The conj. *eða* (l. 6) must be understood here as meaning 'and' rather than its usual sense 'or'. — [8] *hæfi* 'situation': The meaning of this noun seems to be 'situation, position' in the sense of a situation that it is fitting for someone to be in (cf. *LP*: *hæfi*; Fritzner: *hæfi* 2; *ÍO*: 406).

Friðþjófr (Friðþ Lv 7)

7. Eigi um sér til Alda;
erum vestr í haf komnir;
allr þykki mér ægir,
sem ei*myrju hræri.

Hrynja hávar bárur,
haug verpa svanflaugar;
nú er Elliði orpinn
ákafligri báru.

Eigi um sér til Alda; erum komnir vestr í haf; allr ægir þykki mér, sem hræri ei*myrju. Hávar bárur hrynja, svanflaugar verpa haug; Elliði er nú orpinn ákafligri báru.

Alden cannot be seen; we have come westwards into the ocean; the whole sea seems to me as if it were alive with glowing coals. Towering waves topple down, swan-flights [WAVES] build up a mound; now Elliði is tossed in a furious roller.

Mss: 510(93r), 568[x](100v), 27[x](135r), papp17[x](359r), 109a II[x](147r), 1006[x](583), 173[x](84v-85r) (*Frið*).

Readings: [1] um sér: so 568[x], 27[x], of sjór 510, sér papp17[x], 109a II[x], 1006[x], 173[x]   [2] vestr: 'vest[...]' 568[x]; í: '[...]' 568[x]   [3] allr: allt 1006[x];   ægir: so 27[x], papp17[x], ægi 510, 109a II[x], 'ægier' 568[x], 'æe' 1006[x], 173[x]   [4] ei*myrju: 'einmyriu' 510, 'einmyria' 568[x], 'i einmyriu' 27[x], 'a einmyriu' papp17[x], 109a II[x], 1006[x], 173[x];   hræri: 'sæge' papp17[x], 'sæe' 109a II[x], 1006[x], 'se' 173[x]   [5] hávar: haf papp17[x], 109a II[x], 1006[x], 173[x]   [6] haug: '[...]aug' 568[x];   verpa: uppa 568[x];   -flaugar: so 27[x], papp17[x], 109a II[x], 1006[x], 173[x], 'flauger' 510, 'flaugan' 568[x]   [8] ákafligri: so 27[x], í ákafa 510, á ákafa 568[x], í örðugri papp17[x], 109a II[x], 1006[x], 173[x].

Editions: *Skj*: Anonyme digte og vers [XIII], E. 7. *Vers af Fornaldarsagaer: Af Friðþjófssaga ens frækna* I 7: AII, 270, BII, 293, *Skald* II, 154, *NN* §§1473, 3287; Falk 1890, 73, *Frið* 1893, 13, 44, 70, *Frið* 1901, 19, *Frið* 1914, 12.

Context: As for *Frið* 5 and 6.

Notes: [All]: The many variant readings of this stanza suggest the scribes had considerable difficulty in understanding some of its vocabulary, which powerfully evokes a storm at sea, viewed from the perspective of someone on board ship. Line 1 is exactly the same as *Frið* 5/1 in the B redaction mss. *Frið* 5 may well be a partial duplication of this stanza. — [1] *eigi um sér* 'cannot be seen': Several of the mss (568[x], 27[x], 510) read *of* rather than *um* here, but the text has been normalised to the later form of the pleonastic particle; see further Note to *Ásm* 1/3, 5. — [4] *sem hræri ei*myrju* 'as if it were alive with glowing coals': Lit. 'as if it were moving with live coal'. The allusion is presumably to phosphorescence playing on the surface of the sea. *Eimyrja* 'live coals, embers' occurs among fire names in *Þul Elds* 2/5[III], and in Hallm *Hallkv* 2/5[V] (*Bergb* 2). — [6] *svanflaugar* 'swan-flights [WAVES]': This cpd is a *hap. leg.* of uncertain meaning and status. It is not certain that it is a kenning, but cf. *Frið* 8/4 *í brekku svana* 'in the hillside of swans [WAVE]', whose status as a kenning is clear. With Larsson (*Frið* 1901, 19 n.) the cpd is understood here to mean 'waves', comparing the white crests of the towering waves to the wings of flying swans. The use of the abstract noun *flaug* 'flight' is unusual, however; Larsson (*Frið* 1901, *loc. cit.*) suggests the cpd may have an adjectival sense. Kock (*NN* §1473) proposes that *flaug* might have the sense 'place from where something flies', pointing to periphrases for the sea like OE *swanrād* 'swan-path', but there is no evidence to support this hypothesis. Edith Marold (pers. comm.) has suggested a minor emendation to *svan*laugar* 'swan-baths [SEA]', which would still produce an unusual kenning, but one that is less unusual than *svanflaugar*. Finnur Jónsson (*Skj* B) emends to *svanteigar* 'swan-fields [SEA]'. — [8] *ákafligri* 'furious': The reading of 27^x. The other A redaction mss have *í ákafa* or *á ákafa* (which is hypometrical) while the B mss read *í ǫrðugri* [*báru*] 'in a towering, rising [wave]'.

Friðþjófr (Friðþ Lv 8)

8.   Mjǫk drekkr á mik;   mær mun kløkkva,
     ef ek skal søkkva   í svana brekku,
     — austr er orðinn   í Elliða —
     þó lá blæja   á bliki nǫkkut.

Drekkr mjǫk á mik; mær mun kløkkva, ef ek skal søkkva í brekku svana, þó lá blæja nǫkkut á bliki; austr er orðinn í Elliða.

My ship is taking on a great deal of water; the young woman will sob, if I must sink in the hillside of swans [WAVE], although bed-linen lay ableaching somewhat; baling has taken place on board Elliði.

Mss: **510**(93r), 568^x(100v), 27^x(135r), papp17^x(359r), 109a II^x(147r), 1006^x(583), 173^x(85r) (*Frið*).

Readings: [2] mær: 'Mornun' 568^x, mærin papp17^x, 109a II^x, 1006^x, 173^x;   mun: *om*. 568^x [4] svana: 'sauna' 568^x, 27^x, 109a II^x [5] austr er orðinn: austr papp17^x, 109a II^x, 1006^x, 173^x [6] í Elliða: *om*. papp17^x, 109a II^x, 1006^x, 173^x [7] þó lá ('þola'): þó bo- 568^x, þar sem papp17^x, 109a II^x, 1006^x, 173^x;   blæja: *so* 568^x, 27^x, 'blærra' 510, blæjan papp17^x, 109a II^x, 1006^x, 173^x [8] á bliki nǫkkut: *so* 27^x, á blik nǫkkut 510, bliki mikit 568^x, lá á bliki papp17^x, 109a II^x, 1006^x, 173^x.

Editions: *Skj*: Anonyme digte og vers [XIII], E. 7. Vers af Fornaldarsagaer: Af Friðþjófssaga ens frækna I 8: AII, 270-1, BII, 293, *Skald* II, 154, *NN* §§2386, 2994A, 3193; Falk 1890, 73, *Frið* 1893, 13, 44, 71, *Frið* 1901, 20, *Frið* 1914, 12-13; *Edd. Min*. 98.

Context: A huge sea towers over the men in Elliði and they all bale out the ship furiously.

Notes: [All]: This stanza is in both A and B recensions, but ll. 5-8 differ considerably between them. The sense of the first four lines is paralleled in *Friðþjófs rímur* III, 20. In the B recension mss, ll. 5-6 are effectively absent, and *austr* (l. 5) is taken with the B mss' version of ll. 7-8, to mean 'east' (rather than 'baling'), these lines then having the sense *austr þar sem blæjan lá á bliki* '[the young woman will sob] in the east where the bed-linen lay ableaching'. This is unlikely to be the original sense of these lines, which is probably represented by the rather garbled text of the A redaction mss. The metre is *fornyrðislag*, with end rhyme in ll. 2-3. — [All] *þó lá blæja nökkut á bliki* 'although bed-linen lay ableaching somewhat': The sense of ll. 7-8 in the B mss is discussed in Note to [All] above. It is difficult to make sense of the A mss, but the lines must refer to the subject of *Frið* 1/7-8, q. v. *Edd. Min.* and Finnur Jónsson (*Skj* B) emend the n. *nökkut* (or *mikit* 'much, greatly' in 568ˣ) of the A mss to *nökkur* 'some' to agree with *blæja* 'bed-linen' (l. 7), Finnur translating *mange lagner lå til blegning* (*derfor traf F. ikke Ingeborg*) 'many bed-sheets lay ableaching (therefore F. did not meet Ingeborg)'. Kock, on the other hand, emends *blæja* (l. 7) to *blæju*, having understood *þó* as 'washed' (pret. of *þvá*) and *lá* (earlier *ló*) as 'wave'; cf. *NN* §2386. *Frið* 1901 combines the A and B mss' texts in ll. 5-8. — [1] *drekkr mjök á mik* 'my ship is taking on a great deal of water': The impersonal construction *drekkr á e-n* means 'one ships a sea, takes on a great deal of water over the sides of the ship'. — [4] *í brekku svana* 'in the hillside of swans [WAVE]': Possibly a sea-kenning, cf. ESk Frag 9/2ᴵᴵᴵ *strindar svana* 'of the land of swans [SEA]', but more likely a kenning for a wave, in which the base-word is a term for hill or mountain; cf. SnSt Ht 76/5, 8ᴵᴵᴵ *hríðfeld fjǫll svana* 'the stormy mountains of swans [WAVES]' and Ht 83/4ᴵᴵᴵ *svanfjalla* 'of swan-mountains [WAVES]', as well as st. 7/6 above.

Bjǫrn (Bjǫrn Lv 1)

9. Erat sem ekkja
á þik vili drekka,
björt baugvara
biði nær fara.

Sölt eru augu,
sitkak í laugu;
bálskorð arma,
bítr mér í hvarma.

Erat sem ekkja vili drekka á þik, björt baugvara biði fara nær. Augu eru sölt, sitkak í laugu; arma bálskorð, bítr mér í hvarma.

It it not as if a woman would want to drink to you, [or that] a bright ring-bearer [WOMAN] would ask [you] to come close. [My] eyes are salty, I am not sitting in a bath; prop of the fire of arms [(*lit.* 'fire-prop of arms') GOLD > WOMAN], my eye-lids are stinging.

Mss: **510**(93r), 568ˣ(100v), 27ˣ(135r), papp17ˣ(359r), 109a IIˣ(147r), 1006ˣ(584), 173ˣ(85r) (*Frið*).

Readings: [1] Erat: *so* 27ˣ, papp17ˣ, 109a IIˣ, 1006ˣ, 173ˣ, er em at 510, væra 568ˣ;   ekkja: *so* 568ˣ, papp17ˣ, 109a IIˣ, 1006ˣ, 173ˣ, ekki 510, 'ölga' 27ˣ   [2] á þik vili drekka: *so* papp17ˣ, 109a IIˣ, 1006ˣ, 173ˣ, 'at austur fir oss drekkie' 510, at ek drekka 568ˣ, 'aur at drecka' 27ˣ   [3] baugvara: 'baugvarit' 568ˣ, 27ˣ   [5] Sölt: 'so ilt' 568ˣ;   augu: nú 27ˣ   [6] sitkak ('sitka ek'): *so* 568ˣ, 'ef soka' 510, 'sickiu' 27ˣ, sikkuð papp17ˣ, 109a IIˣ, 1006ˣ, 173ˣ;   í laugu: ekki lógi 27ˣ   [7] bálskorð: 'bilskorðs' 510, 'bilskord' 568ˣ, 'bil skortt' 27ˣ, bil sterka papp17ˣ, 109a IIˣ, 1006ˣ, 173ˣ   [8] bítr: *so all others*, birtiz 510.

Editions: *Skj*: Anonyme digte og vers [XIII], E. 7. *Vers af Fornaldarsagaer: Af Friðþjófssaga ens frækna* I 9: AII, 271, BII, 293-4, *Skald* II, 154-5, *NN* §§1474, 2387; Falk 1890, 73-4, *Frið* 1893, 14, 44-5, 71, *Frið* 1901, 21, *Frið* 1914, 13; *Edd. Min.* 98.

Context: Friðþjófr's foster-brother Bjǫrn wonders whether the women of Sogn will weep over him, while the storm continues to rage. He speaks this stanza.

Notes: [All]: This is the only *runhent* stanza in *Frið*, though the end-rhyme of ll. 1-2 is not exact. The text is very difficult to make sense of in the A redaction mss, and not very easy in the others. It is clear that a great deal of scribal corruption has affected the stanza's transmission, with the consequence that there are a number of possible interpretations of the various readings in both redactions. Because the A mss are particularly hard to understand, readings from the B mss have been selected in ll. 1 and 2. Even so, the interpretation offered here is tentative. Line 7 is particularly difficult to understand. Kock (*NN* §1474) suggests a possible parallel between this stanza and *Krm* 20, in which some of the same vocabulary occurs (*ekkja* 'woman', *laug* 'bath'), and where a contrast is drawn between men fighting in battle and a woman bringing basins of warm water. The present stanza (in the reading offered here) seems to suggest that the bitter struggle at sea that Friðþjófr and his men now encounter has made them unattractive to the women back home, and this is consistent with Bjǫrn's expressed scepticism in the prose text of both redactions. — [2]: *Á þik vili drekka* is the reading of the B redaction mss. The text of the A mss is inconsistent, but may allude to the women of Baldrshagi situated east of where the men now are on their Orkney voyage. *Skj* B presents the following text of ll. 1-2: *Erat sem ekkja | austr á þik drekki ...* 'It is not as if a woman is drinking to you in the east ...'. — [3] *baugvara* 'a ring-bearer [WOMAN]': Or possibly 'a ring-adorner'. This *hap. leg.* cpd is treated as a woman-kenning, but the meaning of the second element is uncertain. Mss 568[x] and 27[x] have the p. p. *-varið* which would make better sense, if the second element derives from *verja* 'wrap, dress, adorn' (cf. *HHund* II 35/7, *NK* 158, *brúðr baugvarið* 'woman adorned with rings'), and this reading is adopted in *Skj* B and *Skald*, though the end-rhyme with *fara* (l. 4) is then lost. The cpd in *-vara* may be a secondary formation derived from *-varið*. — [4] *fara nær* 'to come close': Or possibly 'to come closer', as *nær* could be either positive or comp. degree of the adv. *nær*. *Skj* B emends the line to *biði vel fara* 'and wishes you a good journey'. *Frið* 1901, 21 n. suggests the phrase might mean 'wish you success'. — [6] *sitkak* 'I am not sitting': Both *Skj* B and *Skald* and this edn adopt 568[x]'s *sitkak* 'I am not sitting [in a bath]'. The B redaction mss read *sikkuð* 'sunken (?)' which may possibly be a form of the p. p. of an unrecorded **sikka* 'sink' (cf. Falk 1890, 74, who suggests a parallel with Norwegian dialect *sikka* 'sink'). However, this interpretation then requires *laug* to be understood in the extended sense of 'salt water, sea'. — [7-8]: The interpretation of these lines is uncertain. The first word or words of l. 7 have not been authoritatively explained, and most eds emend, following the B redaction, to either *bilar sterka arma* '[my] strong arms fail' (*Frið* 1901, 21) or *bilar styrk arma* 'the strength of my arms fails' (*Skj* B). The prose of the B text endorses the notion that baling the ship is hard work for the men's arms. Relying on the A text,

Wenz (*Frið* 1914, 13) has *bilskorð arma* but does not explain what it may mean. All known compounds in which *-skorð* 'prop, support' is the second element are women-kennings in which the first element denotes either ornament or clothing (cf. *LP*: *skorð*). Hence the *bil-* of the cpd's first element is anomalous, as the word's normal meaning is 'delay, moment'. *Edd. Min.* emends to *bálskorð* 'fire-prop', which, together with *arma* 'of arms', can be understood as an inverted, two-part woman-kenning, 'prop of the fire of arms' [GOLD > WOMAN]'. This seems the only feasible interpretation of the A mss' readings, and has been adopted here. Kock (*Skald*; *NN* §1474) has *Bil skortir arma*, in which Bil is a goddess-*heiti* (cf. *LP*: *Bil*) and *skortir* is an emendation, depending on 27ˣ's reading 'skortt', with the second <t> supposedly mistaken by the scribe for an <ir> abbreviation. Kock does not, however, explain what he thinks ll. 7-8 mean in this interpretation. In this edn the woman-kenning *arma bálskorð* is taken as a direct address to a woman, and the speaker complains of his miserable situation, not taking a warm bath, but being buffeted by salty seas, which are stinging his eyes. With *Skj* B, l. 8 is understood as an impersonal construction, *bítr mér í hvarma*, lit. 'it bites me on the eyelids, my eyes are stinging [with the salt sea]'. The alternative is to take the kenning (?) of l. 7 as the subject of the verb *bítr* 'bites' (l. 8), 'the woman bites me on the eyelids', but the scenario conjured up by this interpretation is either ludicrous or improbable, unless one imagines the hostile sea-deity Rán as the kenning referent (cf. *Frið* 11/5-6).

Ásmundr (Ásm Lv 1)

10. Þá var svarf um siglu,
    er sær of mér gnúði;
    ek varð einn með átta
    innanborðs at vinna.

    Dælla er til dyngju
    dagverð konum færa
    en Elliða ausa
    á úrigri báru.

Þá var svarf um siglu, er sær gnúði of mér; ek varð einn at vinna með átta innanborðs. Dælla er færa konum dagverð til dyngju en ausa Elliða á úrigri báru.

Then there was tumult around the mast, when the sea roared over me; I had to work alone [as if] with eight on board. It is more pleasant to bring women breakfast in their quarters than to bale out Ellidi on a spray-drenched wave.

Mss: **510**(93r), 568ˣ(100v), 27ˣ(135r), papp17ˣ(359r), 109a IIˣ(147r), 1006ˣ(584), 173ˣ(85r-87r) (*Frið*).

Readings: [1] Þá: Hér papp17ˣ, 109a IIˣ, 1006ˣ, 173ˣ;   var: varð papp17ˣ, 109a IIˣ, 1006ˣ, 173ˣ; svarf: snæfrt papp17ˣ, 109a IIˣ, 1006ˣ, 173ˣ;   um siglu: *so all others*, við siglu 510   [2] sær: sjór papp17ˣ, 109a IIˣ, 1006ˣ, 173ˣ;   of mér: um mik 568ˣ, á skip papp17ˣ, 109a IIˣ, 1006ˣ, 173ˣ; gnúði: glumði 568ˣ, 'hnúði' papp17ˣ, 1006ˣ, knúði 109a IIˣ, hrundi 173ˣ   [3] með: við papp17ˣ, 1006ˣ, 173ˣ, *om.* 109a IIˣ;   átta: átján 568ˣ   [5] Dælla: sælla 568ˣ;   er: var papp17ˣ, 109a IIˣ, 1006ˣ, 173ˣ   [6] dagverð: *so all others*, 'daugur uerd' 510;   færa: *so* 568ˣ, 27ˣ, papp17ˣ,

109a II^x, 173^x, at færa 510, færra 1006^x [7] en Elliða ausa: *so* 568^x, papp17^x, 109a II^x, 1006^x, 173^x, en sjó Elliða at ausa 510, en sæ Elliða ausa 27^x [8] úrigri: örðugri 568^x, papp17^x, 109a II^x, 173^x, 'arigre' 27^x, 'öruggri' 1006^x.

Editions: *Skj*: Anonyme digte og vers [XIII], E. 7. *Vers af Fornaldarsagaer: Af Friðþjófssaga ens frækna* I 10: AII, 271, BII, 294, *Skald* II, 155; Falk 1890, 74, *Frið* 1893, 14, 45, 71, *Frið* 1901, 21-2, *Frið* 1914, 13-14.

Context: Friðþjófr's second foster-brother Ásmundr comments on Bjǫrn's stanza and, having been encouraged to recite a verse himself, speaks this one.

Notes: [All]: This stanza follows a common skaldic pattern of contrasting the tough life of a man at sea with the soft life indoors spent with women. There is a good deal of variation in the readings of the various mss, but the gist of the stanza is clear in all. The metre is an irregular variant of *dróttkvætt* with rhymes in ll. 4 and 8. — [1] *svarf* 'tumult': The basic sense of this word is 'file dust', but, by extension, it seems to refer here to the tumult caused by sea-spray beating against the ship's mast; cf. Bjarni Frag 2/4^{III} and Note there. The B recension mss have *snæfrt*, n. sg. of the adj. *snæfr* 'narrow, tight, tough'. — [2] *gnúði* 'roared': Ms. 568^x has *glumði* 'dashed noisily, splashed', while 109a II^x has *knúði* 'drove onwards' and papp17^x and 1006^x have 'hnúði', possibly a scribal variant for *knúði*. Ms. 173^x has *hrundi* 'pushed, thrust', the reading adopted in *Frið* 1901. — [3]: The line is reminiscent of Egill Lv 42/1^V (*Eg* 122) and *Ásm* 8/1, 7. The B recension mss have *við átta* rather than *með átta*. Both versions seem to be drawing on an idiom that is also found in *Ket* 2/5-6, also in the context of baling out a ship on one's own: *ok í allan dag | einn jós ek við þrjá* 'and the whole day long alone I baled [as if] in competition with three'. The sense in each case is that the one man claims to do the work of several others on his own. Larsson (*Frið* 1901, 22 n.) translates *Ich musste für acht an bord arbeiten* 'I had to work for eight on board'. The B reading is adopted by *Frið* 1901, *Skj* B and *Skald*. — [3] *átta* 'eight': Ms. 568^x has *átján* 'eighteen', probably reflecting the statement in the prose text (B version and 568^x) that Friðþjófr and his men were a party of eighteen (*Frið* 1901, 13; *Frið* 1893, 69), although most A text mss put the number at thirteen (*Frið* 1914, 11). — [6] *dagverð* 'breakfast': The name of the first of two meals of the day in early Scandinavia (*dag* 'day' + *verðr* 'food, meal'), taken about nine in the morning after the initial farm-work had been done (cf. Foote and Wilson 1980, 167). — [7] *en ausa Elliða* 'than to bale out Elliði': *Skj* B and *Skald* adopt *at ausa* from 510. — [8] *á úrigri báru* 'on a spray-drenched wave': *Frið* 1901, *Skj* B and *Skald* all prefer the B redaction reading *á örðugri báru* 'on a towering wave' here with loss of internal rhyme, which is also found in the A ms. 568^x. This line also occurs in the B mss in *Frið* 7/8.

Friðþjófr (Friðþ Lv 9)

11. Sat ek á bólstri   í Baldrshaga;
    kvað, hvat ek kunna,   fyr konungs dóttur.
    Nú skal Ránar   ra*u*nbeð troða,
    en annarr mun   Ingibjargar.

Ek sat á bólstri í Baldrshaga; kvað, hvat ek kunna, fyr dóttur konungs. Nú skal troða ra*u*nbeð Ránar, en annarr mun Ingibjargar.

I sat on a cushion in Baldrshagi; I recited what I knew before the daughter of the king. Now I must tread the testing bed of Rán <sea-goddess> [SEA], but another will [tread the bed] of Ingibjǫrg.

Mss: 510(93r), 568[x](100v), 27[x](135r), papp17[x](359r), 109a II[x](147r), 1006[x](584), 173[x](85v) (*Frið*).

Readings: [3] kvað: kvað ek 568[x], 27[x], papp17[x], 109a II[x], 1006[x], 173[x]; hvat: þat papp17[x], 109a II[x], 1006[x], 173[x]   [4] konungs: kongs 568[x], 27[x], papp17[x]   [5] skal: skal ek kunna 568[x], skal ek 27[x], papp17[x], 109a II[x], 1006[x], 173[x];   Ránar: raunar papp17[x], 109a II[x], 1006[x], 173[x]   [6] ra*u*nbeð: 'ra[...] ban' 510, 'ranbed' 568[x], papp17[x], 109a II[x], 1006[x], 173[x], 'rannbed' 27[x]   [8] -bjargar: -björgu 1006[x].

Editions: *Skj*: Anonyme digte og vers [XIII], E. 7. Vers af Fornaldarsagaer: Af Friðþjófssaga ens frækna I 11: AII, 271-2, BII, 294, *Skald* II, 155, *FF* §47; Falk 1890, 74-5, *Frið* 1893, 15, 45, 72, *Frið* 1901, 22-3, *Frið* 1914, 14; *Edd. Min.* 98.

Context: Friðþjófr speaks another stanza, giving his view of the dire situation he is in.

Notes: [All]: This stanza, like the previous one, draws a contrast between the speaker's situation and happier days in female company, the difference being that Friðþjófr speaks as a privileged suitor, while his foster-brother, Ásmundr, can only think of menial tasks in the presence of women, like serving meals, something Friðþjófr teases him about in both prose versions of the saga. The stanza is in *fornyrðislag*. — [1] *á bólstri* 'on a cushion': According to *ONP*: *bolstr*, the first prose citation of this word dates from c. 1300. For the etymology, see *AEW*: *bolstr, bulstr*. For comparable usage, cf. *Sigsk* 48/1, *Guðr I* 15/2. The word-picture of Friðþjófr reclining on a cushion in Ingibjǫrg's quarters, with its suggestions of luxury and sexual intimacy, looks forward to the imagery of the second *helmingr*, in which similar sexual imagery evokes the watery embraces of Rán, a sea-deity who takes drowned men to her bed at the bottom of the ocean. — [3-4]: These lines may refer either to the recitation of poetry or to the singing of songs, the latter presumed by the translations in *Frið* 1901 and *Skj* B. — [5-6] *nú skal troða raunbeð Ránar* 'now I must tread the testing bed of Rán [SEA]': The specific wording of these lines is problematic, although their general sense is clear: Friðþjófr fears that he will drown, using an image of a lover mounting his partner's bed, which he contrasts with the situation of someone else, but not him, making love to Ingibjǫrg (ll. 7-8). The word *Ránar* 'of Rán', the sea-deity who takes to herself drowning men (cf. *SnE* 1998, I, 41), is present in l. 5 in the A mss 510, 568ˣ and 27ˣ, while in its place the B mss have *raunar* 'in truth, in reality', which appears to be a *lectio facilior*. However, l. 6 presents a further problem because the first word in 510 has a lacuna, probably of only one letter, and reads 'ra[…] ban', which does not correspond to the other A mss here (568ˣ has 'ranbed' and 27ˣ 'rannbed'), nor to the B mss, which have a similar reading. Thus one can either read (A version) *nú skal Ránar | raunbeð tróða* 'now I must tread the testing bed of Rán' (with emendation of *Ránbeð* to *raunbeð*, as suggested by Falk (1890, 75) on the ground that the A scribes must have been influenced by their writing of 'ran' in the previous line) or (B version) adopt *nú skal raunar | Ránbeð troða* 'now I must really tread the bed of Rán'. Both readings have their merits. The B version has the merit of not requiring emendation, but it includes the suspiciously facile *raunar* 'really'. The cpd *Ránbeð* 'Rán's bed', although not exactly paralleled elsewhere, is similar to Rv Lv 16/4ᴵᴵ *Ránheim* 'Rán's world [SEA]' and cf. SnH Lv 6/3ᴵᴵ *sitk at Ránar* 'I'm living at Rán's', supposedly uttered by the ghost of a drowned man. The readings of the A mss suggest that the first element of the cpd at the beginning of l. 6 was not *Rán-* but some other noun, and *raunbeð* 'testing bed, dangerous bed', as suggested by Falk and adopted in *Skj* B (cf. also *LP*: *raunbeð*) seems a reasonable emendation and is also adopted here. The concept of the sea and the sea-bed as Rán's is a skaldic commonplace and appears frequently in kennings for the sea (cf. *Meissner* 92); here the image is explicitly sexualised and contrasted with Friðþjófr's wished-for intercourse with Ingibjǫrg. The verb *troða* 'tread' suggests both sexual intercourse and menacing aggression, in line with similar senses in Þjóð *Yt* 3/6ᴵ, 20/2ᴵ and Egill *Hfl* 10/7-8ⱽ (*Eg* 43). *Skald* has adopted the reading of 27ˣ and some other A redaction mss, *rannbeð Ránar* 'the hall-bed of Rán'. This is also a possible reading.

Friðþjófr (FriðÞ Lv 10)

12. Þess hefk gangs of goldit;
    gekk mér en þér eigi
    með ambáttir átta
    Ingibjörg* at þinga.

    Saman höfum brenda bauga
    í Baldrshaga lagða;
    var þá vilgi fjarri
    vörðr Hálfdanar jarða.

Hefk of goldit þess gangs; Ingibjörg* gekk at þinga mér en eigi þér með átta ambáttir. Höfum lagða brenda bauga saman í Baldrshaga; vörðr jarða Hálfdanar var þá vilgi fjarri.

I have paid for this access; Ingibjǫrg went to meet me, but not you, with eight maidservants. We have placed together burnished [gold] rings in Baldrshagi; the guardian of the lands of Hálfdan <Norwegian king> [= Norway > RULER = Helgi?] was then very far away.

Mss: **510**(93r), 27ˣ(135r), papp17ˣ(359r), 109a IIˣ(147v), 1006ˣ(584), 173ˣ(85v) (*Frið*).

Readings: [1] gangs: gagns 27ˣ, papp17ˣ, 109a IIˣ, 1006ˣ, 173ˣ;   of: um 27ˣ, papp17ˣ, 109a IIˣ, 1006ˣ, 173ˣ   [2] gekk mér en þér eigi: so papp17ˣ, 109a IIˣ, 1006ˣ, 173ˣ, gekk mær þar 510, gekk mærin þær eigi 27[x]   [3] með: við papp17[x], 109a II[x], 1006[x], 173[x]   [4] Ingibjörg*: Ingibjörgu 510, Ingibjörga 27[x], Ingibjargar papp17[x], 109a II[x], 1006[x], 173[x];   at: *so* papp17[x], 109a II[x], 1006[x], 173[x], á 510, 27[x];   þinga: þingi papp17[x], 109a II[x], 1006[x], 173[x]   [5] Saman: samit 27[x];   brenda: brendra 27[x]   [6] lagða: *so* papp17[x], 109a II[x], 1006[x], 173[x], lagðar 510, 27[x]   [7] var þá: *so* papp17[x], 109a II[x], 1006[x], 173[x], 'varar' 510, 27[x];   vilgi: *so* 27[x], 'vigri' 510, 'vigli' papp17[x], 173[x], 'vigil' 109a II[x], 1006[x]   [8] vörðr: *so* papp17[x], 109a II[x], 1006[x], 173[x], verðr 510, varðs 27[x];   jarða: *so* papp17[x], 109a II[x], 173[x], garði 510, 27[x], jarðar 1006[x].

Editions: *Skj*: Anonyme digte og vers [XIII], E. 7. *Vers af Fornaldarsagaer: Af Friðþjófssaga ens frækna* I 12: AII, 272, BII, 294, *Skald* II, 155; Falk 1890, 75, *Frið* 1893, 15, 45-6, *Frið* 1901, 23-4, *Frið* 1914, 14.

Context: Friðþjófr speaks another stanza about his former life, seemingly addressed to his foster-brother Bjǫrn.

Notes: [All]: This irregular *dróttkvætt* stanza is lacking in ms. 568[x]. There are a number of places in it where 510's text is very hard to understand and recourse has been had to B recension readings in such cases. — [1] *hefk of goldit þess gangs* 'I have paid for this access': Friðþjófr presumably refers here to his access to Ingibjǫrg in Baldrshagi, which he has alluded to in the previous stanza, and for which the brothers Helgi and Hálfdan punished him by sending him to Orkney. Only ms. 510 reads *gangs* 'access, journey', and that not certainly, for the ms. reads 'ggs' with superscript <n> above the line across the second <g> and the <s>. Cf. *Guðr* I 26/5-6 (*NK* 206): *þess hefi ec gangs | goldit síðan* 'I have paid for this journey later'. All the other mss read *gagns* from *gagn* 'gain, advantage', which would give the sense 'I have paid for this advantage'. Both readings give good sense. — [2]: This is the reading of the B recension mss; there is no satisfactory reading of the A mss here. — [4] *Ingibjörg*_ 'Ingibjǫrg': All mss give oblique cases of this name, while the syntax indicates that it should be in nom. case. This emendation was first proposed by Falk (1890, 75). — [4] *þinga* 'meet': The B mss have *þingi*, dat. sg. of the noun *þing* 'meeting', preferred in *Skj* B, and a viable interpretation. — [5-6]: These lines appear to refer to an exchange of rings that Friðþjófr and Ingibjǫrg carried out at Baldrshagi; it is not mentioned in the prose of the A recension, but the B text (ch. 4) mentions a ring, an inheritance from his father, that Friðþjófr gives Ingibjǫrg, and the last line of this chapter indicates that they exchanged rings (*Frið* 1901, 11). — [7-8]: These lines are difficult to understand in both recensions, but particularly so in the A text. Falk (1890, 75) suggested that the A mss' *varar* might be a scribal error for *varat* 'was not', but this would make the line unmetrical. The B mss read *var þá* 'was then', and most eds, including the present one, have adopted this reading, understanding 'the guardian of the lands of Hálfdan was then very far away', 'the guardian of the lands of Hálfdan' being understood as a reference to one of the two brothers of Ingibjǫrg, who were called away to visit King Hringr, leaving Ingibjǫrg unguarded. An alternative view was expressed by Larsson (*Frið* 1901, 24 n.) who sees here a reference to the god Baldr in his sanctuary, understanding *vilgi* in its sense 'not at all', rather than as an intensifying adv. 'very' (cf. *Fritzner*: vilgi). This then gives the opposite sense 'the guardian of the lands of Hálfdan was not far away', that is, the deity was present in the sanctuary and saw to it that Friðþjófr was punished for breaking the tabu on conducting male-female relations in Baldrshagi. The problem with this interpretation is that the periphrasis 'the guardian of the lands of Hálfdan' (whichever Norwegian ruler this is meant to be) must be a ruler-kenning and is rather unlikely to be a kenning for the god Baldr, though in a late text this cannot be completely ruled out.

Friðþjófr (FriðÞ Lv 11)

13. Brustu báðir hálsar
    í báru hafs stórri;
    sukku sveinar fjórir
    í sæ ógrunnan.

Báðir hálsar brustu í stórri báru hafs; fjórir sveinar sukku í ógrunnan sæ.

Both sides of the bow broke apart in the enormous wave of the ocean; four men sank into the deep sea.

Mss: **papp17^x**(359r), 109a II^x(147v), 1006^x(585), 173^x(86r) (*Frið*).

Editions: *Skj*: Anonyme digte og vers [XIII], E. 7. Vers af Fornaldarsagaer: Af Friðþjófssaga ens frækna I 13: AII, 272, BII, 294; *Skald* II, 155; Falk 1890, 75, *Frið* 1893, 16, *Frið* 1901, 24.

Context: Friðþjófr speaks yet another stanza after an enormous wave has broken the bows of the ship and four men were washed overboard.

Notes: [All]: This *dróttkvætt helmingr* is extant only in the B redaction mss. It covers much the same ground as the first four lines of *Frið* 14, which is extant only in the A redaction mss. Thus it appears to be an alternative composition and suggests that the B redaction ms. tradition may have lost the equivalent of *Frið* 14. — [1] *hálsar* 'sides of the bow': The prose text of the B redaction explains (*Frið* 1901, 24): *Þá kom áfall svá mikit, at frá laust vígin ok hálsana báða* 'Then came such a heavy sea that the gunwale and both sides of the bow broke apart'. The noun *háls*, lit. 'neck', can refer to several different parts of a ship (cf. Þul *Skipa* 7/5^{III} and Note), but here seems most likely to denote the ends of the curved strakes running up to the prow. — [4] *í ógrunnan sæ* 'into the deep sea': The line is hypometrical, and both *Skj* B and *Skald* emend to *sæ enn ógrunna*, which provides an extra syllable, but produces a structurally irregular Type B-line.

Friðþjófr (FriðÞ Lv 12)

14. Nú hefr fjórum   um farit várum
    lögr lagsmönnum,   þeim er lifa skyldu.
    En Rán gætir   röskum drengjum,
    siðlaus kona,   sess ok rekkju.

Nú hefr lögr um farit fjórum lagsmönnum várum, þeim er skyldu lifa. En Rán, siðlaus kona, gætir sess ok rekkju röskum drengjum.

Now the sea has destroyed four of our comrades, who should have lived. But Rán <sea-goddess>, immoral woman, provides bench and bed for the brave fellows.

Mss: 510(93v), 27[x](135v) (*Frið*).

Reading: [5] gætir: býðr 27[x].

Editions: *Skj*: Anonyme digte og vers [XIII], E. 7. *Vers af Fornaldarsagaer: Af Friðþjófssaga ens frækna* I 13 b: AII, 272, BII, 294-5, *Skald* II, 155; Falk 1890, 75-6, *Frið* 1893, 46, *Frið* 1914, 15; *Edd. Min.* 99.

Context: As for *Frið* 13.

Notes: [All]: This stanza is only in 510 and later A redaction mss, though absent from 568[x], which gives a prose summary of the incident (see *Frið* 1914, 15). The first *helmingr* corresponds in subject matter to *Frið* 13, but the second *helmingr* reintroduces the notion of drowning seamen visiting the sea-deity Rán (see *Frið* 11/5-8 above), though here with a somewhat moralistic (and probably Christian) perspective. The stanza is regular *fornyrðislag*. — [2] *um farit* 'destroyed': The mss have here the more archaic *of farit*, with the same meaning. See Note to *Ásm* 1/3, 5. — [7] *siðlaus kona* 'immoral woman': This phrase may suggest Christian disapproval of pagan ideas, as well as a distasteful fascination with the idea of a necrophiliac Rán providing bed and board for dead sailors (cf. *Frið* 11/5-6 and Note).

Friðþjófr (FriðÞ Lv 13)

15. Þann skal hring um höggva,   Sjá skal gull á gestum,
    er Hálfdanar átti,   ef vér gistingar þurfum
    áðr oss tapi ægir,   — þat dugir rausnarrekkum —
    auðigr faðir, rauðan.   í Ránar sal miðjum.

Skal um höggva rauðan hring, þann er auðigr faðir Hálfdanar átti, áðr ægir tapi oss. Gull skal sjá á gestum, ef vér þurfum gistingar í miðjum sal Ránar; þat dugir rausnarrekkum.

The red-gold ring, which the wealthy father of Hálfdan owned, must be cut up, before the sea can destroy us. Gold must be visible on guests, if we need accommodation in the middle of Rán's <sea-goddess's> hall; that is fitting for men of splendour.

Mss: **510**(93v), 27[x](135v), papp17[x](359r), 109a II[x](148r), 1006[x](585), 173[x](86r) (*Frið*).

Readings: [1] hring um: *so* papp17[x], 109a II[x], 1006[x], 173[x], hringum 510, 27[x]   [2] Hálfdanar: *so* papp17[x], 109a II[x], 1006[x], 173[x], Hálfdan 510, 27[x];   átti: átti átti 27[x]   [3] áðr: áðr enn papp17[x], 109a II[x], 1006[x], 173[x];   tapi: *so* 27[x], papp17[x], 109a II[x], 'tapi[...]' 510, tapir 1006[x], 173[x]   [7] dugir: 'daugher' 27[x]   [8] sal: 'salnum' papp17[x], 109a II[x], 1006[x], 173[x].

Editions: *Skj*: Anonyme digte og vers [XIII], E. 7. *Vers af Fornaldarsagaer: Af Friðþjófssaga ens frækna* I 14: AII, 272-3, BII, 295, *Skald* II, 155; Falk 1890, 76, *Frið* 1893, 16, 46, *Frið* 1901, 25, *Frið* 1914, 15.

Context: The prose text of both redactions introduces the idea, attributed to Friðþjófr, that those about to travel to Rán should be well dressed and carry something made of gold about their persons. To this end Friðþjófr decides to cut the ring *Ingibjargarnaut* 'Ingibjǫrg's gift' into pieces so each man can have one. He then speaks *Frið* 15.

Notes: [All]: This stanza is an irregular *dróttkvætt*, rather than the *málaháttr* suggested by Wenz (*Frið* 1914, lxxii). *Aðalhendingar* are lacking in ll. 6 and 8, while l. 6 is hypermetrical when *vér* 'we', present in all mss, is included. *Skj* B and *Skald* regularise the metre here by deleting the pron. — [1, 4] *skal um hǫggva rauðan hring* 'the red-gold ring must be cut up': Lit., 'one must cut up the red ring'. — [3] *tapi* 'can destroy': The 3rd pers. sg. pres. subj. of *tapa* 'destroy, kill'. The scribe of 510 has erased a letter after *tapi-* and it is not now possible to say what it was. Finnur Jónsson (*Skj* A n.) suggested it might be a <d>. — [3] *ægir* 'the sea': It is possible that the personified Ægir, male sea-deity, supposedly the husband of Rán (cf. *SnE* 1998, I, 36, 40-1, 92-5) is intended here rather than the common noun *ægir* 'sea'. *Frið* 1901 and 1914 both treat the noun as a personification.

Friðþjófr (FriðÞ Lv 14)

16. Sé ek trollkonur   tvær á báru;
    þær hefir Helgi   hingat sendar.
    Þeim skal sníða   sundr í miðju
    hrygg Elliði,   áðr af hafi skríði.

Ek sé tvær trollkonur á báru; Helgi hefir sendar þær hingat. Elliði skal sníða þeim hrygg sundr í miðju, áðr skríði af hafi.

I see two troll-women on the wave; Helgi has sent them hither. Elliði must slice their spines asunder in the middle, before he glides from the ocean.

Mss: **510**(93v), 568[x](100v), 27[x](135v), papp17[x](359v), 109a II[x](148r), 1006[x](585-586), 173[x](86v) (*Frið*).

Readings: [2] á báru: 'a Ba[...]' 568[x]   [3] þær hefir: '[...]' 568[x]   [5] sníða: sigla 27[x]   [7] hrygg: hryggs 109a II[x], 173[x];   Elliði: 'E[...]' 568[x]   [8] áðr: '[...]' 568[x], áðr enn 109a II[x], 1006[x], 173[x];

af hafi: '[…]f hafe' 568^x, 'af fer' papp17^x, 'af fǫr' 109a II^x, 173^x, 'af fór' 1006^x;   skríði: skríðr papp17^x, 109a II^x, 1006^x, 173^x.

Editions: *Skj*: Anonyme digte og vers [XIII], E. 7. *Vers af Fornaldarsagaer: Af Friðþjófssaga ens frækna* I 15: AII, 273, BII, 295, *Skald* II, 155; Falk 1890, 76, *Frið* 1893, 17, 47, 72-3, *Frið* 1901, 26, *Frið* 1914, 16; *Edd. Min.* 99.

Context: The ship does not founder, as Friðþjófr expected, but enters a murky stretch of ocean where it is impossible to see the way forward. Friðþjófr climbs the mast and spies a huge whale circling the ship, preventing it from making land; he interprets this phenomenon as a product of Helgi's sorcery and says that he can also see two women riding on the whale's back. He directs the ship to be steered towards them aggressively and recites *Frið* 16.

Notes: [All]: This *fornyrðislag* stanza is in both redactions, though 568^x contains several lacunae. The motif of hostile troll-women attacking the hero's ship is paralleled in other *fornaldarsögur*, like *Ket* and *GrL*. See particularly *GrL* 1-5, a dialogue between Grímr loðinkinni 'Hairy-cheek' and the troll-women Feima and Kleima. In all these instances, the level of physical aggression expressed by the hero towards the troll-women is very high. In this stanza agonistic agency is, however, attributed to the ship Elliði, rather than the speaker of the stanza, Friðþjófr, and *Frið* 17, extant only in the B mss, elaborates this motif. — [5-7] *Elliði skal sníða þeim hrygg sundr í miðju* 'Elliði must slice their spines asunder in the middle': *Miðju* is here a substantivised adj., with *þeim* either a possessive dat. or the dat. pl. of the 3rd pers. pronoun, while *hrygg* (acc.) is the object of *sníða*. This means of destroying troll-women or giantesses, by breaking their backbones, is attributed to the god Þórr in the myth of his dealings with the giant Geirrøðr and his daughters Gjálp and Greip, both in Snorri Sturluson's prose narrative (*SnE* 1998, I, 25) and in Eil *Þdr* 15/7-8^{III}, where the kenning *hundfornan kjǫl hlátr-Elliða* 'the age-old keel of laughter-Elliði <ship> [BREAST > BACK]' may allude to this incident of Elliði's destruction of the two troll-women by slicing through their backbones. Alternatively, *elliði* may simply be a ship-*heiti* in Eil *Þdr* 15, as presented in *Þdr* 15/7-8^{III} and Note to ll. 7, 8, without specific reference to the *Frið* legend.

Friðþjófr (FriðÞ Lv 15)

17. Heill Elliði!   Hlauptu á báru,
    brjóttu í trollkonum   tennr ok enni,
    kinnr ok kjálka   í konu vándri,
    fót eða báða   í flagði þessu.

Heill Elliði! Hlauptu á báru, brjóttu tennr ok enni í trollkonum, kinnr ok kjálka í vándri konu, fót eða báða í þessu flagði.

Friðþjófs saga ins frœkna 215

Hail Elliði! Run on the wave, break teeth and foreheads of the troll-women, cheeks and jaw-bone of the wretched woman, one leg or both of this ogress.

Mss: **papp17^x**(359v), 109a II^x(148v), 1006^x(586), 173^x(86v) (*Frið*).

Readings: [3] trollkonum: trollkonu 173^x [5] kinnr: *so* 173^x, kinnar papp17^x, 109a II^x, 1006^x [8] flagði: *so all others*, flagð papp17^x.

Editions: *Skj*: Anonyme digte og vers [XIII], E. 7. *Vers af Fornaldarsagaer: Af Friðþjófssaga ens frœkna* I 16: AII, 273, BII, 295, *Skald* II, 155; Falk 1890, 77, *Frið* 1893, 17, *Frið* 1901, 27; *Edd. Min.* 99.

Context: Friðþjófr grabs hold of a pole (*forkr*) and runs forward to the ship's prow, reciting this stanza (only in the B redaction).

Notes: [All]: This stanza is a mixture of *fornyrðislag* (ll. 1, 3-7) and *málaháttr* (ll. 2, 8) and is extant only in the B redaction mss. It elaborates on the subject matter of *Frið* 16 and is part of an expanded treatment of the incident of Elliði's animated assault upon the two troll-women in the B redaction mss, which also includes the statement that, *svá er sagt* 'so it is said', the ship had the marvellous capacity of being able to understand human speech. This attribute is not mentioned in the A mss (see Note to *Frið* 2/8). — [5] *kinnr* 'cheeks': Most mss read *kinnar*, which is the gen. sg. of *kinn* 'cheek', whereas *kinnr* is the nom. and acc. pl.

Friðþjófr (Friðþ Lv 16)

18. Ek bar átta   til eldstóar
    dæsta drengi   í drifaveðri.
    Nú hefi ek segli á sand komit;
    erat hafs megin   hægt at reyna.

Ek bar átta drengi dæsta í drifaveðri til eldstóar. Nú hefi ek komit segli á sand; megin hafs erat hægt at reyna.

I carried eight fellows, exhausted in the storm of sea-spray, to a fireplace. Now I have brought the sail onto the beach; the power of the ocean is not easy to experience.

Mss: **510**(93v), 568^x(101r), 27^x(135v), papp17^x(359v), 109a II^x(148v), 1006^x(586), 173^x(87r) (*Frið*).

Readings: [1] átta: upp papp17^x, 109a II^x, 1006^x, 173^x [2] eldstóar: *so all others*, eldstaðar 510   [3] dæsta: *so* 568^x, 27^x, papp17^x, 1006^x, 173^x, '[…]sta' 510, 'dædsta' 109a II^x [4] drifa-: drifu papp17^x, 109a II^x, 1006^x, 173^x [5] hefi ek: hef ek 568^x, 27^x, papp17^x, 109a II^x, 1006^x, 173^x [6] á: '[…]' 568^x [7] erat ('er að'): *so* 568^x, er eigi 510, er ór 27^x, 'eij er' papp17^x, ei er 109a II^x, 1006^x, 173^x;   hafs megin: hafs megni 27^x, við hafs megin papp17^x, 109a II^x, 1006^x, 173^x [8] reyna: ríma 27^x.

Editions: *Skj*: Anonyme digte og vers [XIII], E. 7. *Vers af Fornaldarsagaer: Af Friðþjófssaga ens frækna* I 17: AII, 273, BII, 295, *Skald* II, 156; Falk 1890, 77-8, *Frið* 1893, 18-19, 48, 73, *Frið* 1901, 28, *Frið* 1914, 17; *Edd. Min.* 99.

Context: After the two troll-women have been killed, the sea calms down but Elliði is in bad shape and all the men who have survived the journey are exhausted. In the A text prose Friðþjófr carries them all to land, with Bjǫrn saving one. In the B recension, Friðþjófr saves eight, Bjǫrn two and Ásmundr one. In the A recension Friðþjófr recites *Frið* 18 and 19 in quick succession; in the B text *Frið* 19 is recited before they actually make land, and *Frið* 18 comes after they have reached the bay of Evie (ON Effjasund), a village in the north-west part of Mainland, the chief island of Orkney.

Notes: [All]: This stanza is in regular *fornyrðislag*. — [All]: The order of *Frið* 18 and 19 is reversed in the B redaction, with 19 preceding 18. In terms of the narrative sequence this is illogical, as *Frið* 19 clearly relates to the men's situation after they have come safely ashore, whereas *Frið* 18 describes Friðþjófr's heroic behaviour in bringing them to land. — [3] *dæsta* 'exhausted': The first two letters of this word in ms. 510 are rubbed and partly illegible. The first letter looks more like a <v> than a <d>, as earlier eds have thought, while the second may be a misshapen <æ>. This surmise is strengthened by 510's clear *væsta* (from *væstr* 'worn out by wet and exhaustion') at *Frið* 21/3 where exactly the same line is repeated. The majority of the mss from both redactions read *dæsta*.

Friðþjófr (FriðÞ Lv 17)

19. Þurfum ei, drengir, dauða at kvíða!
    Veri þjóðglaðir, þegnar mínir!
    Þat mun verða, ef vitu draumar,
    at ek eiga mun Ingibjörgu.

Drengir, þurfum ei at kvíða dauða! Veri þjóðglaðir, þegnar mínir! Þat mun verða, ef draumar vitu, at ek mun eiga Ingibjörgu.

Comrades, we do not need to be afraid of death! Be really happy, my retainers! It will come about, if dreams are indicative, that I will marry Ingibjǫrg.

Mss: **510**(93v), 568[x](101r), 27[x](135v), papp17[x](359v), 109a II[x](148v), 1006[x](586) (ll. 3-8), 173[x](87r) (ll. 3-8) (*Frið*).

Readings: [1] Þurfum: þurfu 568[x], þurfa 27[x], þurfið papp17[x], 109a II[x], *om.* 1006[x], 173[x] [3] Veri: verið 568[x], papp17[x], 109a II[x], 1006[x], 173[x]; þjóðglaðir: 'þolgoder' 568[x] [5] Þat mun verða: enn mun þat verða 27[x], þat mun vita papp17[x], þat 109a II[x], 1006[x], 173[x] [6] ef vitu draumar: 'ef vit[...] draumar' 568[x], mínir draumar papp17[x], ef vita várir draumar 109a II[x], ef vita draumar 1006[x], 173[x] [8] Ingibjörgu: 'biorgu' 27[x].

Editions: *Skj*: Anonyme digte og vers [XIII], E. 7. *Vers af Fornaldarsagaer: Af Friðþjófssaga ens frækna* I 18: AII, 273, BII, 295-6, *Skald* II, 156; Falk 1890, 77, *Frið* 1893, 18, 48, 73, *Frið* 1901, 27-8, *Frið* 1914, 17; *Edd. Min.* 99.

Context: As for *Frið* 18. The two stanzas are presented in reverse order in recension B mss.

Notes: [All]: This stanza is in regular *fornyrðislag*. There is a good deal of minor variation in the ms. paradosis for this stanza, and it is shortened in 1006[x] and 173[x], which omit ll. 1-2 and shorten l. 5. — [6] *ef draumar vitu* 'if dreams are indicative': That is, if there is anything to be learnt from dreams. On this sense of *vita*, see *LP*: *vita* 5.

Introduction to sts 20-4

The following five stanzas relate to the saga narrative of Friðþjófr's arrival in Orkney and his reception there by the jarl and his entourage.

Hallvarðr (Hallvarðr *Frag* 1)

20. Er á skála   skjól at sitja
    vestrvíkingi,   sem vera inni.
    Eru hraustari, þeir er hlunngota,
    drengir, ausa   í drifaveðri.

Er skjól á skála, sem vera inni, vestrvíkingi at sitja. Drengir, þeir er ausa hlunngota í drifaveðri, eru hraustari.

There is shelter from the hall, as a place of refuge inside, for the viking on a westward expedition to sit. Those men who bale the roller-steed [SHIP] in the storm of sea-spray are braver.

Mss: 510(93v), 568[x](101r), 27[x](135v) (*Frið*).

Readings: [1] Er á skála: so 27[x], Er at skála 510, '[...] at skal' 568[x]   [2] skjól: so 27[x], 'skól' 510, 'skio' 568[x];   sitja: drekka 568[x], 27[x]   [3] vestrvíkingi: so 27[x], vestrvíkingar 510, '[...]stur vykingur' 568[x]   [4] sem vera inni: so 568[x], 27[x], sem váru inni 510   [5] Eru: þó eru 568[x], 27[x]   [6] er: 'ed' 568[x];   -gota: so 568[x], 27[x], '-geta' 510   [7] ausa: '[...]sa' 568[x].

Editions: *Skj*: Anonyme digte og vers [XIII], E. 7. *Vers af Fornaldarsagaer: Af Friðþjófssaga ens frækna* I 19: AII, 274, BII, 296, *Skald* II, 156, *NN* §3288; Falk 1890, 78, *Frið* 1893, 48, 74, *Frið* 1914, 18; *Edd. Min.* 100.

Context: Friðþjófr and his men find themselves in the Orkney islands, near the residence of Angantýr jarl. In the B recension only this place is said to be Effja, modern Evie on Mainland. The place is not named in the A recension. The jarl's watchman is called Hallvarðr and he recites the following three stanzas (*Frið* 20, 21 and 22) in quick succession, telling what he sees.

Notes: [All]: This *fornyrðislag* stanza is only in the A recension mss. The first *helmingr* is difficult and the sense of l. 4 not entirely clear. Most eds, except for Wenz (*Frið* 1914, 18), emend l. 1 to *Erat á skala* 'There is not in the hall', but this is not necessary to achieve sense. The stanza contrasts the anticipated comfort of Friðþjófr and his men drinking in the shelter of the hall (where the speaker himself is) with the hard conditions of the men baling Elliði. — [2] *at sitja* 'to sit': Ms. 510 has this reading, against the other mss' *at drekka* 'to drink'. Both are possible though *sitja* may fit better with *vera* in the sense 'a place of refuge' (l. 4). — [3] *vestvíkingi* 'for the viking on a westward expedition': With *LP*: *vestvíkingr*, assumed to refer to a man who is a viking (here Friðþjófr) rather than a viking expedition (*vestvíking*, f.). — [4] *sem vera inni* 'as a place of refuge inside': The sense and syntax of this line is not clear. Finnur Jónsson (*Skj* B), the only ed. to offer a translation of it, writes *som der inde* 'like in that place', but the role of *vera* is not then explicit. It is possible that *vera* is not here the inf. of the verb 'be' but the noun *vera* 'existence, place of refuge', as in *Hávm* 26/3 (*NK* 21) *ef hann á sér í vá vero* 'if he [the foolish man] has a place of refuge for himself in the corner'. That is how it has been tentatively interpreted here. — [6] *hlunngota* 'the roller-steed [SHIP]': Cf. ÞjóðA Frag 1/6[II]. — [8] *í drifaveðri* 'in the storm of sea-spray': The same line is at *Frið* 18/4, *Frið* 21/4 and *Ǫrv* 86/4.

Hallvarðr (Hallvarðr *Frag* 2)

21. Sex sé ek ausa   en sjau róa
     dæsta drengi   í drifaveðri.
     Þat er gunnhvötum   glíkt í stafni,
     Friðþjófr er framm fellr við árar.

Ek sé sex dæsta drengi ausa en sjau róa í drifaveðri. Þat er glíkt gunnhvötum í stafni, er Friðþjófr fellr framm við árar.

I see six exhausted men baling and seven rowing in the storm of sea-spray. That is like [seeing] a battle-bold one in the prow, when Friðþjófr falls forward over the oars.

Mss: 510(93v), 568[x](101r), 27[x](136r), papp17[x](359v), 109a II[x](149r), 1006[x](587), 173[x](87v) (*Frið*).

Readings: [1] Sex: Menn papp17[x], 109a II[x], 1006[x], 173[x]   [2] en sjau róa: í meginveðri papp17[x], 109a II[x], 1006[x], 173[x]   [3] dæsta drengi: *so* 27[x], væsta drengi 510, 'd[...]ta dreinge' 568[x], sex á Elliða papp17[x], 109a II[x], 1006[x], 173[x]   [4] í drifaveðri: en sjau róa papp17[x], 109a II[x], 1006[x], 173[x]   [5] Þat: *so* papp17[x], 109a II[x], 1006[x], 173[x], þar 510   [7] Friðþjófr er framm: en Friðþjófr fram í 510, 'Friðþiofur er fell [...]' 568[x], Friðþjófr framm 27[x], Friðþjófi frækna papp17[x], Friðþjóf frækna 109a II[x], 1006[x], 173[x]   [8] fellr við árar: '[...] vit arar' 568[x], fellr á árar 27[x], 109a II[x].

Editions: Skj: Anonyme digte og vers [XIII], E. 7. *Vers af Fornaldarsagaer*: *Af Friðþjófssaga ens frækna* I 20: AII, 274, BII, 296, Skald II, 156; Falk 1890, 77, *Frið* 1893, 19, 49, 74, *Frið* 1901, 29, *Frið* 1914, 18; *Edd. Min.* 100.

Context: In the A redaction mss, this stanza follows *Frið* 20 with simply *Ok enn kvað hann* 'and again he [Hallvarðr] spoke'. In the B redaction this is the first of Hallvarðr's stanzas and is preceded by a prose passage describing the scene in Angantýr's hall, from where the watchman Hallvarðr can see the doings of Friðþjófr and his men.

Notes: [All]: There is considerable variation between the A and B redactions here, especially in the first *helmingr*, which in B has: *Menn sé ek ausa | í meginveðri | sex á Elliða | en sjau róa* 'I see six men on Elliði baling in the powerful storm and seven rowing'. Lines 3-4 of the A text are exactly the same as *Frið* 18/3-4 and l. 4 is the same as *Frið* 20/8. — [7-8]: No ms. has exactly this order of words, but all elements are present in one ms. or other. Most previous eds have emended to the text presented here in order to achieve metrical and syntactic regularity. Some of the scribal versions (e.g. 27ˣ) doubtless depend on the desyllabified form *Friðþjófur* to form a metrical line. The B redaction mss introduce the adj. *frækna* 'bold' in l. 7; this epithet characterises Friðþjófr in the B text and in later tradition, though it does not appear in the prose of the A redaction mss (but cf. Note to *Frið* 40/1). — [8] *fellr framm við árar* 'falls forward over the oars': That is, Friðþjófr bends forward to pull on the oars in the rough sea, and is likened to a bold man (or bold men) in the prow of a ship going into battle.

Hallvarðr (Hallvarðr *Frag* 3)

22.   Taktu af gólfi,   gangfögr kona,
      horn hólfanda;   hef ek af drukkit.
      Menn sé ek á mar,   þá er munu þurfa
      hreggmóðir liðs,   áðr höfn taki.

Gangfögr kona, taktu hólfanda horn af gólfi; ek hef drukkit af. Ek sé hreggmóðir menn á mar, þá er munu þurfa liðs, áðr taki höfn.

Nicely moving woman, take [this] upside down horn from the hall-floor; I have drained it. I see storm-weary men out at sea, who will need help before they reach the harbour.

Mss: **510**(93v-94r), 568ˣ(101r), 27ˣ(136r), papp17ˣ(360r), 109a IIˣ(149r), 1006ˣ(587), 173ˣ(87v) (*Frið*).

Readings: [1] Taktu: *so* 568ˣ, papp17ˣ, 109a IIˣ, 1006ˣ, 173ˣ, Gakk þú þú 510, Gakk þú 27ˣ;   af: *so* papp17ˣ, 109a IIˣ, 1006ˣ, 173ˣ, á 510, 568ˣ, 27ˣ   [2] gang-: *so all others*, 'ga' 510   [3] horn: *so all others*, á horni 510;   hólfanda: *so* 568ˣ, 1006ˣ, 173ˣ, haldandi 510, hvólfanda 27ˣ, papp17ˣ, hvólfandi 109a IIˣ   [4] af: ór 27ˣ   [6] þá: þeir papp17ˣ, 109a IIˣ, 1006ˣ, 173ˣ   [7] liðs: lið 568ˣ, 27ˣ, papp17ˣ, 109a IIˣ, 1006ˣ, 173ˣ   [8] áðr höfn taki: áðr höfnum nái 27ˣ.

Editions: *Skj*: Anonyme digte og vers [XIII], E. 7. *Vers af Fornaldarsagaer: Af Friðþjófssaga ens frækna* I 21: AII, 274, BII, 296, *Skald* II, 156; Falk 1890, 78-9, *Frið* 1893, 19-20, 49, 74, *Frið* 1901, 30, *Frið* 1914, 18-19; *Edd. Min.* 100.

Context: In the A text, Hallvarðr speaks this stanza to a cup-bearer (*byrlari*), in the B text to a woman who had previously given him a drinking-horn.

Notes: [All]: The prose context of the A text seems to contradict the stanza, in which Hallvarðr addresses himself to a woman, not a male cup-bearer. Some of the A redaction mss urge the woman to go onto the hall-floor to collect the speaker's empty horn, but the majority (including 568[x]) urge her to take it away. — [3] *hólfanda* '[turned] upside down': The younger form of the inflected pres. part. from *hólfa* 'capsize, turn upside down' has been retained here, rather than the older *hválfanda* or *hvalfanda* (see *LP*: *hvalfa*), which is favoured by *Edd. Min.*, *Skj* B and *Skald*. — [7] *liðs* 'help': Taken with *þurfa* 'need' which requires the gen. case of what is needed. Some eds (*Edd. Min.*; *Frið* 1914) prefer *lið*, the same word, in the sense 'people, host', which must then be taken in a rather awkward syntactic construction in apposition to *hreggmóðir* 'storm-weary'.

Friðþjófr (FriðÞ Lv 18)

23. Þér munuð ekki   oss um kúga,
     æðrufullir   eyjarskeggjar!
     Heldr mun ek ganga   en griða biðja
     einn til ógnar   við yðr tíu.

Þér munuð ekki um kúga oss, æðrufullir eyjarskeggjar! Ek mun heldr ganga einn til ógnar við yðr tíu en biðja griða.

You will not tyrannise over us, fearful island-beards! I will rather go alone to battle against you ten than sue for peace.

Mss: 510(94r), Holm10 VI(2r) (ll. 7-8), 568[x](101r), 27[x](136r), papp17[x](360r), 109a II[x](149r), 1006[x](587), 173[x](88r) (*Frið*).

Readings: [1] munuð: 'munu[...]' 568[x];   ekki: '[...]' 568[x], ei papp17[x], 109a II[x], 1006[x], 173[x]   [2] oss um kúga: oss kúgat geta papp17[x], 109a II[x], 1006[x], 173[x]   [6] biðja: '[...]ia' 568[x]   [7] einn: *so* 568[x], 27[x], papp17[x], 109a II[x], 173[x], en 510, 'eirn' 1006[x].

Editions: *Skj*: Anonyme digte og vers [XIII], E. 7. Vers af Fornaldarsagaer: Af Friðþjófssaga ens frækna I 22: AII, 274-5, BII, 296, *Skald* II, 156; Falk 1890, 79, *Frið* 1893, 20, 50, 75, *Frið* 1901, 31, *Frið* 1914, 20; *Edd. Min.* 100.

Context: The jarl asks Hallvarðr for information about the men he has seen and tells him to go and meet them at the seashore. However, a viking named Atli starts to cause trouble and is aggressive towards Friðþjófr, who responds with this stanza.

Notes: [All]: The stanza is fairly stable in all mss. The metre is *fornyrðislag*. The fragmentary ms. Holm10 VI records one and a half lines (ll. 7-8) of this stanza. It shows no significant variation from the other mss here. — [1] *þér* 'you': The younger form of the 2nd pers. pl. nom. pers. pron *ér*, present in all mss, has been retained here (cf. *ANG* §464 and Anm. 5, §465 Anm. 5); *Edd. Min.*, *Skj* B and *Skald* restore *ér* to achieve double alliteration. — [2] *um kúga oss* 'tyrannise over us': Ms. 510's reading *oss of kúga*, which contains the archaic pleonastic particle *of*, has been normalised to a standard appropriate to the period after 1250. Similar examples occur elsewhere in the *fornaldarsaga* corpus, suggesting that some of the extant mss are based on older exemplars; cf. *Ásm* 1/3, 5 and *Ǫrv* 138/8 and Notes there. — [4] *eyjarskeggjar* 'island-beards': A pejorative term, found also in *Heiðr* 19/4 and *Ǫrv* 106/6, in the latter case also about men from Orkney, apparently reflecting a mainland Scandinavian view that island-dwellers were rough and hairy. A political faction in Norway c. 1093 that rebelled against King Sverrir was called Eyjarskeggjar. This group came from Orkney and the Hebrides and attempted to install Sigurðr, the young alleged son of Magnús Erlingsson, on the throne of Norway (see *Sv* chs 119-20, *ÍF* 30, 180-6). — [8] *við yðr tíu* 'against you ten': According to the prose of the A recension (*Frið* 1914, 19) Atli and his companions were twelve; according to the B recension (*Frið* 1901, 30) they were ten in all.

Bjǫrn (Bjǫrn Lv 2)

24. Jósum vér, en yfir   fell ór sval*ri* báru,
    teitir á tvau borð   tíu dægr ok átta.
    Þat var kynför   kænna dreng*j*a,
    hversu vér fórum   með Friðþjófi.

Vér jósum teitir á tvau borð tíu dægr ok átta, en fell yfir ór sval*ri* báru. Þat var kynför kænna drengja, hversu vér fórum með Friðþjófi.

We baled in good spirits on two sides for eighteen days, and [water] cascaded on board from the cold wave. That was an extraordinary journey of skilful men, how we voyaged with Friðþjófr.

Mss: **510**(94r), papp17ˣ(360r) (ll. 1-4), 109a IIˣ(149v) (ll. 1-4), 1006ˣ(588) (ll. 1-4), 173ˣ(88r) (ll. 1-4) (*Frið*).

Readings: [1] en yfir: meðan papp17ˣ, 109a IIˣ, 1006ˣ, 173ˣ   [2] fell ór sval*ri* báru: fell ór svala báru 510, yfir gekk svölr papp17ˣ, 109a IIˣ, 1006ˣ, 173ˣ   [3] teitir á tvau borð: bragnar teitir papp17ˣ, 109a IIˣ, 1006ˣ, 173ˣ   [4] tíu dægr ok átta: á bæði borð papp17ˣ, 109a IIˣ, á bæði borð tíu dægr \tel ek/ ok átta papp17ˣ, á bæði borð tíu dægr ok átta 109a IIˣ, 173ˣ, á bæði 1006ˣ, á bæði tíu dægr ok átta 1006ˣ, á bæði born 173ˣ   [6] kænna drengja: 'kuena dreinga' 510.

Editions: *Skj*: Anonyme digte og vers [XIII], E. 7. Vers af Fornaldarsagaer: Af Friðþjófssaga ens frækna I 23: AII, 275, BII, 296-7, *Skald* II, 156, *FF* §37C; Falk 1890, 79, *Frið* 1893, 21, 50, *Frið* 1901, 32, *Frið* 1914, 20; *Edd. Min.* 101.

Context: Hallvarðr hastens to welcome Friðþjófr and his men after Atli's rough treatment, and brings them into the hall to meet the local jarl, who asks them about their journey. Bjǫrn explains in a stanza (but see Note to [All] below).

Notes: [All]: This stanza and the preceding prose are poorly recorded in the A recension mss, and the stanza itself is not present in either 568^x or 27^x. The B mss do not have ll. 5-8. Although the prose of the B recension mss attributes it to Friðþjófr's foster-brother Bjǫrn, the attribution in 510 (*Frið* 1893, 50) is simply *hann kvað vísu* 'he spoke a stanza', and the most natural interpretation of this prose context would be that Friðþjófr spoke this stanza. However, ll. 5-8 of the stanza itself indicate that the speaker was someone other than Friðþjófr. The fact that these lines are missing in the B mss may indicate some confusion in the ms. transmission as to the identity of the speaker of the stanza. At all events, this stanza is badly mangled in all mss, and the present text represents the best that can be made of the A version, which involves two minor emendations and a hypothetical interpretation of the *hap. leg. kynfǫr* (l. 5). The metre is a mixture of *fornyrðislag* and *málaháttr*. — [1-2] *en fell yfir ór sval*ri *báru* 'and [water] cascaded on board from the cold wave': Ms. 510 has *svala* but this adj. must be emended to give the f. dat. sg. form to agree with *báru*. The construction is difficult because there is no expressed subject of *fell* 'it fell', but here it has been understood to refer to the sea. Larsson (*Frið* 1901, 32 n.) proposes emending the A text to *fellu svalar bárur* 'the cold waves fell'. In his main text, however, he adopts words from the B text and marries them with an emended l. 2 to give *meðan | yfir gekk svǫlúr* 'while the cold spray went over' (so Larsson, *Frið* 1901, 32, who explains that *svǫlúr* is a combination of *svalr* 'cold' and *úr* 'fine rain, spray'). *Edd. Min.*, *Skj* B and *Skald* have followed this emendation, but keep *en yfir* in l. 1 from 510. — [5] *kynfǫr* 'an extraordinary journey': Larsson (*Frið* 1901, 32 n.) suggested this interpretation of this *hap. leg.* cpd (510 has 'kynuor'), with the first element *kyn-* meaning 'extraordinary, wonderful, marvellous'. This interpretation was adopted by *Edd. Min.* and *Skald*, but Finnur Jónsson emended to *kynfylgja*, which he translated as *slægtsnatur* 'the nature of the stock [of the brave men]'. — [6] *kænna drengja* 'of skilful men': An emendation of ms. 510's 'kuena dreinga', suggested by Larsson (*Frið* 1901, 32 n.) and adopted by all subsequent eds.

Introduction to sts 25-32

The following eight stanzas concern Friðþjófr's return to Norway with the Orkney tribute, his reaction to the burning down of his family farm and Ingibjǫrg's marriage to King Hringr, and his revenge on Helgi and Hálfdan by desecrating and burning down the sanctuary at Baldrshagi.

Friðþjófr (FriðÞ Lv 19)

25. Drukkum forðum   á Framnesi
    fræknir drengir   með föður mínum.
    Nú sé ek brendan   bæ þann vera;
    á ek öðlingum   ilt at gjalda.

Forðum drukkum fræknir drengir á Framnesi með föður mínum. Nú sé ek þann bæ vera brendan; ek á at gjalda öðlingum ilt.

Once we, bold warriors, drank at Framnes with my father. Now I see that farm is burnt; I have to pay back the princes for that evil deed.

Mss: 510(94v), Holm10 VI(2v), 568ˣ(101v), 27ˣ(137r), papp17ˣ(360v), 109a IIˣ(150r), 1006ˣ(589), 173ˣ(88v) (*Frið*).

Readings: [1] Drukkum: Drukku Holm10 VI, 568ˣ;   forðum: fyrr papp17ˣ, 109a IIˣ, 1006ˣ, 173ˣ   [2] á: '[…]' 568ˣ   [4] föður: feðr Holm10 VI   [7] á ek: '[…]' 568ˣ   [8] ilt: illt *written above the line* 510;   gjalda: launa papp17ˣ, 109a IIˣ, 1006ˣ, 173ˣ.

Editions: *Skj*: Anonyme digte og vers [XIII], E. 7. *Vers af Fornaldarsagaer: Af Friðþjófssaga ens frækna* I 24: AII, 275, BII, 297, *Skald* II, 156; Falk 1890, 79, *Frið* 1893, 22, 51-2, 79, *Frið* 1901, 34, *Frið* 1914, 22; *Edd. Min.* 101.

Context: After his stay with the jarl of Orkney, who refuses to pay tribute to the brothers Helgi and Hálfdan, but willingly gives money to Friðþjófr himself, the latter, with his men, returns to Norway, bringing Hallvarðr with them. There they find that Helgi and Hálfdan have burnt down the dwellings at Framnes and married Ingibjǫrg off to King Hringr. Friðþjófr recites this stanza after having seen the burnt ruins at Framnes.

Note: [All]: The metre of this stanza is regular *fornyrðislag*, as is that of the following stanza.

Friðþjófr (FriðÞ Lv 20)

26. Einn mun ek ganga   upp frá ströndu;
    þarf ek lítit lið   lofða at finna.
    Verpið eldi   í jöfra bæ,
    ef ek eigi kem   aptr at kveldi.

Ek mun ganga einn upp frá ströndu; ek þarf lítit lið at finna lofða. Verpið eldi í bæ jöfra, ef ek kem eigi aptr at kveldi.

I will go alone up from the shore; I need little company to find the rulers. Set fire to the compound of the princes if I do not come back this evening.

Mss: 510(94v), 568ˣ(101v), 27ˣ(137r), papp17ˣ(360v), 109a IIˣ(150r), 1006ˣ(589), 173ˣ(89r) (*Frið*).

Readings: [1] Einn: 'eirn' papp17ˣ, 1006ˣ, 173ˣ [2] upp frá ströndu: inn til bæjar papp17ˣ, 109a IIˣ, 1006ˣ, 173ˣ [4] lofða at finna: lofðunga finna papp17ˣ, 109a IIˣ, lofðunga at finna 1006ˣ, 173ˣ [5] Verpið: *so* papp17ˣ, 173ˣ, verpi þér 510, 27ˣ, 'verpit E[...]' 568ˣ, varpið 109a IIˣ, 1006ˣ [6] í jöfra bæ: '[...]' 568ˣ [7] ef ek eigi kem ('ef eg ei kemur'): *so* 568ˣ, 27ˣ, ef ek kem eigi 510, ef ek kem ekki papp17ˣ, 1006ˣ, 173ˣ, ef ek kom ekki 109a IIˣ.

Editions: *Skj*: Anonyme digte og vers [XIII], E. 7. *Vers af Fornaldarsagaer: Af Friðþjófssaga ens frækna* I 25: AII, 275, BII, 297, *Skald* II, 157, *FF* §48; Falk 1890, 79-80, *Frið* 1893, 23, 52, 80, *Frið* 1901, 34-5, *Frið* 1914, 23; *Edd. Min.* 101.

Context: Friðþjófr and his men learn that Helgi and Hálfdan and their entourage are at Baldrshagi engaged in sacrifice to the *dísir* (*at dísablóti*, so the B text; A text has *ok blótuðu* 'and they were sacrificing'). Friðþjófr decides to enter the sanctuary alone, and tells his men to keep watch, speaking this stanza.

Notes: [2] *upp frá ströndu* 'up from the shore': The B text has *inn til bæjar* '[I will go] in to the compound'. — [3] *ek þarf lítit lið* 'I need little company': A litotes, meaning 'I need no company'. Or 'I need little help'. There is probably a play here on the two meanings of *lið* 'people, company' and 'help'.

Friðþjófr (FriðÞ Lv 21)

27. Taktu við skatti,   skatna dróttinn,
    fremstum tönnum,   nema þú framar beiðir!
    Silfr er á botni   belgjar niðri,
    sem vit Björn höfum   báðir ráðit.

Taktu við skatti, dróttinn skatna, fremstum tönnum, nema þú beiðir framar! Silfr er niðri á botni belgjar, sem vit Björn höfum ráðit báðir.

Receive the tribute, lord of men [RULER = Helgi], together with your front teeth, unless you are asking for more! There is silver down at the bottom of the bag, which Bjǫrn and I have both collected.

Mss: 510(94v), 568ˣ(102r), 27ˣ(137r), papp17ˣ(360v), 109a IIˣ(150r), 1006ˣ(589), 173ˣ(89v) (*Frið*).

Readings: [1] skatti: 'skat[...]' 27ˣ [3] fremstum: fremstu papp17ˣ, 109a IIˣ, 1006ˣ, 173ˣ [4] nema: enn 27ˣ;   þú: *om.* papp17ˣ, 109a IIˣ;   framar: friðar 27ˣ;   beiðir: biðisk 27ˣ [6] niðri: þessa papp17ˣ, 109a IIˣ, 1006ˣ, 173ˣ [7] vit: vér 1006ˣ, 173ˣ [8] ráðit: *so all others*, um ráðit 510.

Editions: *Skj*: Anonyme digte og vers [XIII], E. 7. *Vers af Fornaldarsagaer: Af Friðþjófssaga ens frækna* I 26: AII, 275-6, BII, 297, *Skald* II, 157, *NN* §1475; Falk 1890, 80, *Frið* 1893, 24, 53, 81, *Frið* 1901, 35, *Frið* 1914, 24; *Edd. Min.* 101.

Context: Friðþjófr enters Baldrshagi and finds the two brothers and their wives engaged in their *blót* 'sacrifice', the men drinking and the women handling the icons representing pagan deities. Friðþjófr goes up to Helgi and hurls a purse containing the silver tribute from Orkney into his face, knocking out two of his teeth, after which he speaks this stanza. In the A text, he also sees the ring he has previously given Ingibjǫrg on the arm of Helgi's wife, and he tries to get hold of it, the upshot being that the icon she was handling falls into the fire and is burnt, while the ring is loosened from her arm. This development happens after the stanza has been recited in the B redaction mss.

Notes: [All]: Like *Frið* 25-6, this stanza is *fornyrðislag*. — [5-6] *niðri á botni belgjar* 'down at the bottom of the bag': The B redaction mss read *á botni* | *belgjar þessa* 'at the bottom of this bag', which makes as good or possibly better sense, and has been preferred by Larsson in *Frið* 1901.

Friðþjófr (FriðÞ Lv 22)

28. Helgi varð fyr hǫggi;
    hraut sjóðr á nef kauða;
    hneig Hálfdanar hlýri
    ór hásæti miðju.

    Þar varð Baldr at brenna,
    en baugi náða ek áðr;
    síðan frá eldi usla
    ódrjúgr dró ek bjúga.

Helgi varð fyr hǫggi; sjóðr hraut á nef kauða; hlýri Hálfdanar hneig ór miðju hásæti. Þar varð Baldr at brenna, en ek náða baugi áðr; síðan dró ek ódrjúgr bjúga usla frá eldi.

Helgi met with a blow; the purse struck on the wretch's nose; the brother of Hálfdan [= Helgi] fell from the middle of the high-seat. There Baldr <god> had to burn, but I grabbed the ring beforehand; afterwards I, not sluggish, pulled curved embers out of the fire.

Mss: **papp17**ˣ(360v), 109a IIˣ(150v), 1006ˣ(590), 173ˣ(89v) (*Frið*).

Reading: [6] náða: 'nana' 173ˣ.

Editions: *Skj*: Anonyme digte og vers [XIII], E. 7. *Vers af Fornaldarsagaer: Af Friðþjófssaga ens frækna* I 27: AII, 276, BII, 297, *Skald* II, 157, *NN* §§1476, 2388; Falk 1890, 80-2, *Frið* 1893, 25, *Frið* 1901, 36.

Context: Bjǫrn asks Friðþjófr, who has left the hall with the ring that has fallen from the arm of Helgi's wife, what has happened while he was inside, and Friðþjófr recites this stanza while holding up the ring.

Notes: [All]: This and the following stanza (*Frið* 29) are only in the B redaction mss. Two separate stanzas covering much the same ground (*Frið* 30 and 31) are only in the A redaction mss. This stanza is in an irregular *dróttkvætt*, with *hendingar* in ll. 2, 6 and 8, although l. 6 is problematic. — [3-4]: These lines tally with the prose text; in the A recension, the text simply states that Helgi *fell* ... *í óvit* 'lost ... consciousness' (*Frið* 1914, 23), while B has *en hann fell ór hásætinu í úvit* 'and he fell from the high-seat in an unconscious state' (*Frið* 1901, 35). — [5] *þar varð Baldr at brenna* 'there Baldr <god> had to burn': According to the prose texts, Friðþjófr was struggling with Helgi's wife, in order to get hold of his ring, which was on her arm, while she was heating the icon of Baldr in the fire. As Friðþjófr dragged her over to the door, the Baldr image, presumably made of wood, slipped from her grasp into the fire and was burnt. According to the B version prose text (*Frið* 1901, 36), such icons were anointed with some kind of grease or oil. This detail may be part of an antiquarian reconstruction. However, there is now archaeological evidence to support the presence of phosphates and lipids, which indicate the presence of fat, blood or meat, at ritual sites. Such lipids could derive from sacrificial animals or from practices such as smearing grease on icons. A well documented example is the Viking-Age ritual site of Götavi in the province of Närke, west of Stockholm (Lagerstedt 2008, 75-86 and 197-210). — [6]: This line is hypometrical (assuming cliticisation of *ek*) unless *en* is deleted and *áðr* is desyllabified to *áður*. *Skj* B, following a suggestion of Konráð Gíslason, changes the word order to *en baugi ek áðr náða* 'but I got hold of the ring first', but this line is unmetrical. — [7-8]: Understood here as an oblique reference to the piece of firewood (*eldskíða*) which the B text says that Friðþjófr used to set fire to Baldrshagi. Other eds resort to emendation to make sense of these two lines, but this is unnecessary. Larsson (*Frið* 1901) emends *ódrjúgr* to *údrjúga* and *bjúga* to *bjúgur*, translating *dann zog ich gebückt schnellverzehrte brennende holzscheite aus dem feuer* 'then I drew curved, quickly consumed burning logs of wood from the fire'. Finnur Jónsson (*Skj* B) inserts an *ok* in l. 7 between *eldi* and *usla* (cf. *Ǫrv* 101/7) while emending *ódrjúgr* 'not sluggish' (lit. 'not lasting') to *ódeigr* 'not timid, not faint-hearted', presenting the following translation: *siden slæbte jeg ufej den krumböjede kvinde fra ilden og flammeødelæggeslen* 'afterwards I, not timid, dragged the bent woman from the fire and the destruction of flames'. Falk (1890, 82) suggested emending *bjúga* (l. 8) to *ljúga*, 'lie, tell a lie' and implied a translation like 'I, inadequate in lying', with reference to Friðþjófr's relationship to Helgi and Hálfdan. Kock (*Skald*; *NN* §2388) follows *Skj* B in emending *ódrjúgr* to *ódeigr* and also emends *síðan* 'afterwards' (l. 7) to *þá* 'then'. — [8] *ódrjúgr* 'not sluggish': The usual sense of *ódrjúgr* appears to be 'insufficient, inadequate' (cf. *Fritzner*: *údrjúgr*), which does not fit the context here. The commoner adj. *drjúgr* usually means 'substantial, lasting'. Because the normal sense is inappropriate, eds have emended, as explained in the Note to ll. 7-8 above. Here, however, it is possible that the negated adj. has the sense 'not sluggish, quick' rather than 'insubstantial'.

Friðþjófr (FriðÞ Lv 23)

29. Stundum nú til strandar,
    — stórt ráðum vér síðan —
    því at blár logi baukar
    í Baldrshaga miðjum.

Stundum nú til strandar, því at blár logi baukar í miðjum Baldrshaga; vér ráðum stórt síðan.

Let us make now for the beach, because dark flame is rooting around in the middle of Baldrshagi; we will hatch great plans afterwards.

Mss: **papp17**^{x}(360v), 109a II^x(150v), 1006^x(590), 173^x(90r) (*Frið*).

Readings: [1] Stundum: *so* 173^x, Skundum papp17^x, 109a II^x, stundum *corrected from* skundum 1006^x;   nú: vér 173^x.

Editions: *Skj*: Anonyme digte og vers [XIII], E. 7. *Vers af Fornaldarsagaer: Af Friðþjófssaga ens frækna* I 28: AII, 276, BII, 298; *Skald* II, 157; Falk 1890, 81-2, *Frið* 1893, 25, *Frið* 1901, 37.

Context: The B redaction prose text reports (*Frið* 1901, 37): *Þat segja menn, at Friðþjófr hafi undit eldskiðu í næfrarnar, svá at salrinn logaði allr, ok kvað vísu* 'People say that Friðþjófr flung a log of firewood into the birch-bark shingles so that the whole hall was ablaze, and recited a stanza'. *Frið* 29 is that stanza.

Notes: [All]: This *helmingr* is only in the B redaction mss; Friðþjófr's act of setting the hall on fire is not mentioned in the A text. The metre is an irregular variant of *dróttkvætt*. — [2] *vér ráðum stórt síðan* 'we will hatch great plans afterwards': Lit. 'we will resolve greatly afterwards'. — [3] *baukar* 'is rooting around': *Bauka* is an uncommon verb in Old Icelandic (*ONP*: *bauka* gives only one late citation, from *Gr*) and there it means 'dig in the ground, rummage around' for food. ModIcel. *bauka* means 'busy oneself with sth., potter about'. It is used here of the effect of fire on a building.

Friðþjófr (FriðÞ Lv 24)

30. Hafa skal ek baug   ór beggja höndum
    ór svefnhúsi   seggja meið*ma*.
    Sá er hugr á mér   af *þ*eim hringi digrum;
    verðr þeim, er varðar   við lítilmagna.

Ek skal hafa baug ór svefnhúsi ór beggja höndum seggja meið*ma*. Sá hugr er á mér af *þ*eim digrum hringi; verðr þeim, er varðar við lítilmagna.

I am determined to have a ring out of the sleeping house from both arms of the men of treasures. That thought is upon me on account of that substantial ring; let it belong to the man who protects [it] from a weakling.

Mss: 510(94v), 27ˣ(137r) (*Frið*).

Readings: [2] ór beggja höndum: ór brendum 27ˣ [3] ór svefnhúsi: 'vr suennhusi' 510, bauð nú svefnhúsi Svölnis 27ˣ [4] seggja meiðma: 'segja meiðum' *with* segja *added in the right margin in the scribal hand* 510, sá er hugr á mér er digran 27ˣ [5] Sá er hugr á mér: ekki stóð ek unda senn 27ˣ [6] af þeim hringi digrum: 'af eim hringi digrum' 510, 'i ótla þar ä miklum' 27ˣ [7] verðr þeim er varðar: gramr skyli verðr 27ˣ [8] við lítilmagna: því er varðar 27ˣ.

Editions: *Skj*: Anonyme digte og vers [XIII], E. 7. *Vers af Fornaldarsagaer: Af Friðþjófssaga ens frækna* I 29: AII, 276, BII, 298, *Skald* II, 157, *NN* §§1476 Anm., 2597, 3194; Falk 1890, 80-1, *Frið* 1893, 53, *Frið* 1914, 24.

Context: In the A redaction, Friðþjófr speaks this stanza immediately after leaving the sanctuary at Baldrshagi. He holds up the ring he has rescued from Helgi's wife as he does so.

Notes: [All]: The metre of this stanza is problematical. Line 1 is hypometrical, and could be 'restored' by using pl. *bauga* or rearranging as *baug skal ek hafa* (Type A2k). Lines 2, 6-8 are *málaháttr* and ll. 3-5 *fornyrðislag*. — [All]: This and the following stanza (*Frið* 31) are only in A redaction mss, and not in all of those. These display numerous variant readings (see further *Frið* 1914, 24 nn.), most of which are very difficult to make sense of and differ quite widely from the text of 510. The stanza is not in 568ˣ. *Frið* 30-1 come shortly after *Frið* 27 in those mss that include *Frið* 30. As Falk observed (1890, 80-1) this stanza is illogically placed where it stands, as it appears to refer to the situation before Friðþjófr has snatched back his ring, not after it, as here. — [1-4]: Ms. 510's text is impossible to construe without some emendation. Finnur Jónsson (*Skj* B) emends in the following places in ll. 1-4: *beggja* (l. 2) to *brúðar* 'of the bride, woman', *svefnhúsi* ('suennhusi' 510) (l. 3) to *sumlhúsi* 'banqueting house', *seggja meiðum* (l. 4) to *seima meiða*, together with *brúðar* (l. 2), forming a woman-kenning, 'of the bride of trees of gold wires [MEN > WOMAN]'. The present edn takes up a suggestion of Wenz (*Frið* 1914, lxxviii) that *meiðum* (l. 4) may be a scribal error for some form of the noun *meiðm* 'treasure, valuables' (usually in pl.). The emendation to *seggja* (l. 4) is minor. — [2-4] *ór svefnhúsi ór beggja höndum seggja meið*ma 'out of the sleeping house from both arms of the men of treasures': The meaning of these lines is obscure. Here it is suggested that the cpd *svefnhús* 'sleeping house' (l. 3) may refer to the sanctuary dedicated to Baldr, while the 'men of treasures' may be a phrase referring to the idols of the pagan gods contained inside it. — [7-8]: The syntax of these lines is obscure; this edn follows Kock's proposed interpretation (*NN* §3194). The word *við* (l. 8) could be from the noun *viðr* 'tree, wood' or the prep. *við(r)* 'against, to, with', as it is understood here, even though a prep. in first position in a line would not normally bear alliteration.

Friðþjófr (FriðÞ Lv 25)

31. Gekk ek því frá garði
    grun*d*skjöldunga tveggja,
    at ek illsögur ætt*a*
    †i enni mina grandvær†.
    Nær var ek nála Gunni
    við gistingar fundinn;
    þat rak mik frá húsi
    heldur meir, en skyldi.

Ek gekk frá garði tveggja grun*d*skjöldunga, því at ek ætt*a* illsögur †i enni mina grandvær†. Ek var fundinn nær Gunni nála við gistingar; þat rak mik frá húsi heldur meir, en skyldi.

I went from the courtyard of the two princes of the land, because I might have malicious stories … . I was found near the Gunnr <valkyrie> of needles [WOMAN = Ingibjǫrg] at the night-lodgings; that drove me from the house rather more than it should have.

Mss: **510**(94v), 27ˣ(137r) (*Frið*).

Readings: [1] Gekk ek því: *so* 27ˣ, Gangandi fór ek 510   [2] grun*d*-: 'grun-' 510, 'grunn' 27ˣ   [3] illsögur ætt*a*: illsögur ætti 510, 'ill saungs eijra' 27ˣ   [4] †i enni mina grandvær†: 'j enni mina granduær' *with* '-uær' *corrected from* -'nær' 510, 'enn minna granam' 27ˣ   [5] nála: *so* 27ˣ, nála *corrected from* 'uala' 510   [6] við gistingar: undinn stingu 27ˣ;   fundinn: *so* 27ˣ, fundi 510   [7] frá: hér frá 27ˣ   [8] skyldi: fleira 27ˣ.

Editions: *Skj*: Anonyme digte og vers [XIII], E. 7. *Vers af Fornaldarsagaer: Af Friðþjófssaga ens frækna* I 30: AII, 276, BII, 298, *Skald* II, 157, *NN* §§1476 anm., 3195; Falk 1890, 82-3, *Frið* 1893, 53-4, *Frið* 1914, 25.

Context: In some of the A redaction mss, Friðþjófr speaks this stanza as he and Bjǫrn go to their ships, while looking back towards Baldrshagi.

Notes: [All]: Like *Frið* 30, *Frið* 31 is only in certain of the A redaction mss, including 510, and is again missing from 568ˣ. The metre is an irregular variant of *dróttkvætt*; only l. 8 has internal rhyme. The adv. *heldur* 'rather' (l. 8) requires desyllabification from mss' *heldr* in order to provide a metrically regular line; this suggests a date of composition post-1300. Stylistically noteworthy is the use of the woman-kenning *Gunnr nála* 'the Gunnr <valkyrie> of needles' in l. 5. This stanza, in which Friðþjófr reflects on the supposed misdemeanour of his dalliance with Ingibjǫrg, which happened before his voyage to Orkney and his return to Norway, seems misplaced where it occurs in some of the A mss. — [1]: Ms. 27ˣ's text is preferred here because it is syntactically and metrically superior to that of 510. — [2] *tveggja grun*d*skjöldunga* 'of the two princes of the land': Presumably a reference to the two brothers Helgi and Hálfdan. Finnur Jónsson (*Skj* B) emends to *gramr skjǫldunga* and construes *gramr* 'angry' as referring to Friðþjófr. — [3-4]: It is impossible to give a reliable interpretation of ll. 3-4. Most eds who have attempted one make major emendations (e.g. *Skj* B) which have little regard for the mss. Kock (*Skald*; *NN* §3195) emends *i enni mina grandvær* to *enn in minna grandvarr*. The adj. *grandvarr* 'guileless, upright' is a sensible suggestion for the last word in l. 4, but the rest of Kock's emended text is arbitrary.

Friðþjófr (Friðþ Lv 26)

32. Kysta ek unga Ingibjörgu,
   Belja dóttur, í Baldrshaga.
   Svá skulu árar á Elliða
   báðar brotna sem bogi Helga.

Ek kysta unga Ingibjörgu, dóttur Belja, í Baldrshaga. Svá skulu báðar árar á Elliða brotna sem bogi Helga.

I kissed the young Ingibjǫrg, daughter of Beli, in Baldrshagi. Both oars on Elliði shall break, just like Helgi's bow.

Mss: **510**(95r), 568[x](102r), 27[x](137v), papp17[x](361r), 109a II[x](150v), 1006[x](590-591), 173[x](90r) (*Frið*).

Readings: [5] skulu: '[...]' 568[x]   [6] á Elliða: Elliða báðar 27[x]   [7] báðar brotna: brotna sundr 27[x], báðar bresta papp17[x], 109a II[x], 1006[x], 173[x].

Editions: *Skj*: Anonyme digte og vers [XIII], E. 7. *Vers af Fornaldarsagaer: Af Friðþjófssaga ens frækna* I 31: AII, 276, BII, 298, *Skald* II, 157; Falk 1890, 83, *Frið* 1893, 26, 54, 81, *Frið* 1901, 38, *Frið* 1914, 25; *Edd. Min.* 101-2.

Context: Helgi regains consciousness (see *Frið* 28/3-4 and Note) and sets off with some men down to the harbour in pursuit of Friðþjófr. The latter has had all other ships scuttled, so Helgi cannot reach his enemy by boat. He takes aim at Friðþjófr with his bow, which breaks in two when he bends it with great force. Friðþjófr sees this, and bends forcefully over Elliði's oars, which also break. He then speaks this stanza.

Notes: [All]: This stanza is in both the A and B redaction mss. The metre is *fornyrðislag*. — [All]: In the absence of any rational explanation for the motif of the reciprocal breaking of bow and oars, it is tempting to understand it as symbolic of the two adversaries' frustration, Helgi's at being unable to reach Friðþjófr in order to kill him, Friðþjófr's at being unable to reach Ingibjǫrg. — [1-2]: Collocation of adj. *ungr* and the pers. n. *Ingibjǫrg* occurs also in *Frið* 35/3-4 and *Ǫrv* 18/3-4 and 22/1-2, though the Ingibjǫrg in question in *Ǫrv* is the daughter of a Swedish king. — [3] *Belja* 'of Beli': Name of the king of Sogn, father of Helgi, Hálfdan and Ingibjǫrg. In other places, a giant name, whose meaning is 'Roarer', notably name of a giant killed by the god Freyr (*Gylf, SnE* 2005, 31; cf. *AEW*: *Beli*). — [7] *brotna* 'break': The B redaction mss have *bresta* 'burst, break'.

Introduction to sts 33-5

The following three stanzas concern Friðþjófr's exile from Norway as an outlaw and his desire to return to Norway and visit King Hringr's court, where he can be near Ingibjǫrg.

Friðþjófr (FriðÞ Lv 27)

33. Sigldum vér ór Sogni; En nú tekr bál at brenna
     svá fórum vér næstum; í Baldrshaga miðjan;
     þá lék eldr it efra því mun ek vargr at vísu;
     í óðali váru. veit ek, því mun heitit.

Vér sigldum ór Sogni; svá fórum vér næstum; þá lék eldr it efra í óðali váru. En nú tekr bál at brenna *í* miðjan Baldrshaga; því mun ek vargr at vísu; ek veit, mun heitit því.

We sailed out of Sogn; we travelled that way last time; then fire played high above our family homestead. But now the conflagration begins to burn in the middle of Baldrshagi; for that reason I will certainly [be] an outlaw; I know it will be promised.

Mss: **papp17ˣ**(361r), 109a IIˣ(151r), 1006ˣ(591), 173ˣ(90v) (*Frið*).

Readings: [6] *í* Baldrshaga: Baldrshaga *all*   [7] því: þat 1006ˣ, 173ˣ;   at vísu: *so all others*, í véum *corrected from* at vísu *in a later hand* papp17ˣ.

Editions: *Skj*: Anonyme digte og vers [XIII], E. 7. Vers af Fornaldarsagaer: Af Friðþjófssaga ens frækna I 32: AII, 277, BII, 298-9, *Skald* II, 157, *NN* §§1477, 2831; Falk 1890, 83, *Frið* 1893, 26, *Frið* 1901, 39.

Context: Friðþjófr recites this stanza as he and his companions sail out of Sognefjorden.

Notes: [All]: This stanza is only in the B redaction mss, and is in an irregular variant of *dróttkvætt*. — [3] *þá lék eldr it efra* 'then fire played high above': Lit. 'then fire played higher up'. *It efra* is adverbial here, 'in the upper part, high above'. — [4] *óðali* 'family homestead': In early Norway, *óðal* 'allodial lands, patrimony, homestead' was the inalienable property of a family, inherited in the patriline (cf. Foote and Wilson 1980, 81-2). Here Friðþjófr, who should have enjoyed his father Þorsteinn's *óðal*, was forced to watch it burn. — [7] *vargr* 'an outlaw': Lit. 'a wolf'. The noun has a dual semantic significance, like the OE *wearg* 'wolf, accursed one, outlaw'. The phrase *vargr í véum* 'outcast in the sanctuaries' applies particularly to those who have broken the tabu of sanctuary, as is the case here, although the more usual crime so designated was that of killing at an assembly (Foote and Wilson 1980, 402). — [8] *mun heitit því* 'it will be promised': That is, the brothers Helgi and Hálfdan will bring Friðþjófr to court and declare him an outlaw.

Friðþjófr (FriðÞ Lv 28)

34. Mákat ek eiga   * Ingibjörgu,
     Belja dóttur,   í Baldrshaga.
     Því skal ek hitta   Hring at máli,
     hversu *er* fylkir   fagnar greppi.

Ek mákat eiga * Ingibjörgu, dóttur Belja í Baldrshaga. Því skal ek hitta Hring at máli, hversu *er* fylkir fagnar greppi.

I am not able to marry Ingibjǫrg, daughter of Beli, in Baldrshagi. For that reason I must meet Hringr for a talk, regardless of how the ruler will welcome the man.

Mss: 510(95r), 27[x](137v) (*Frið*).

Readings: [1] Mákat ('Makad'): 'Mætkat' 27[x];   eiga: *so* 27[x], hýrra 510   [2] * Ingibjörgu: 'enn hugar rædum' 510, í Ingibjörgi 27[x]   [4] í: *so* 27[x], ok 510   [5] Því skal ek hitta: *so* 27[x], þar skal ek hætta 510   [7] hversu *er*: hversu at 510, ok vita hvé 27[x].

Editions: *Skj*: Anonyme digte og vers [XIII], E. 7. *Vers af Fornaldarsagaer: Af Friðþjófssaga ens frœkna* II 1: AII, 277, BII, 299, *Skald* II, 158; Falk 1890, 83-4, *Frið* 1893, 55, *Frið* 1914, 26; *Edd. Min.* 102.

Context: After having been declared an outlaw, Friðþjófr spends some time as a viking but eventually, tiring of this lifestyle, he decides to part from his companions and visit the court of King Hringr, husband of Ingibjǫrg, to be near her. He informs Bjǫrn of this and speaks this stanza.

Notes: [All]: This *fornyrðislag* stanza is only in A redaction mss, and is absent from 568[x]. In *Skj* and *Skald* all the stanzas in the saga from this point on are treated as belonging to a separate section of the text (designated II) and are numbered from 1 to 7, *Frið* 34 being number 1. In 510 (95r, l. 9) a large ornate capital begins the section of the prose text immediately preceding *Frið* 34 (*Frið* 1914, 26, l. 7) and in 568[x] there is a large capital in the same place on fol. 102r, l. 23, indicating that this section of the saga may have been considered separate from that preceding. — [All]: This edn follows *Edd. Min.* and Wenz (*Frið* 1914) in on the whole preferring the version of this stanza represented by 27[x], rather than 510's version, which requires considerable emendation to make sense. Ms. 27's version is very similar to *Frið* 32/1-4. *Skj* B and *Skald* prefer the 510 version. — [1] *mákat* 'I am not able': The reading of 510, followed by *Edd. Min.* and this edn. Falk (1890) and Wenz (*Frið* 1914) present a version of 27[x]'s reading to give *Mátkat* 'I was not able'. Both *Skj* B and *Skald* emend the 510 reading to *mankat* 'I do not remember'. They construe this with 510's *hýrra* 'sweeter, more friendly' and an emended version of 510's l. 2 (see below). — [2] * *Ingibjörgu* 'Ingibjǫrg': Ms. 27's initial *í* has been deleted. *Skj* B, followed by *Skald*, emends 510's 'enn hugar rædum' to give *en hugazrædur*, which Finnur Jónsson construes, with l. 1, as *Intet husker jeg gladere end de fortrolige samtaler med Beles datter* 'I do not remember anything sweeter than the confidential conversations with Beli's daughter'. He relies on the existence of a cpd *hugazræða* 'confidential conversation', found in *Gríp* 14/2 (*NK* 166). — [7] *hversu* er 'regardless of how': Lit. 'however'. The *at* of 510's *hversu at* has been emended here to *er*, assuming this to be a late instance in which *at* is used synonymously with *er* (*NS* §267) to equate to *hversu er fylkir fagnar greppi* 'however the ruler will welcome the man'. — [8] *greppi* 'the man': Friðþjófr means himself. Cf. his use of the same noun to refer to himself in *Frið* 37/3.

Friðþjófr (FriðÞ Lv 29)

35. Vilda ek kjósa   konung í helju
    en unga mér   Ingibjörgu,
    drykkju mikla,   drengi káta,
    en Elliða   upp á hlunnum.

Ek vilda kjósa konung í helju, en mér unga Ingibjörgu, mikla drykkju, káta drengi, en Elliða upp á hlunnum.

I would wish to choose for the king [to be] in Hel, and young Ingibjǫrg for myself, great drinking, happy warriors, and Elliði up on rollers.

Mss.: 568ˣ(102r) (*Frið*).

Readings: [2] konung: kóng 568ˣ   [4] Ingibjörgu: 'J[...]gu' 568ˣ.

Editions: *Skj*: Anonyme digte og vers [XIII], E. 7. *Vers af Fornaldarsagaer: Af Friðjófssaga ens frækna* II 2: AII, 277, BII, 299, *Skald* II, 158; *Frið* 1893, 82, *Frið* 1914, 27 n.

Context: After Friðþjófr has told Bjǫrn of his desire to visit King Hringr, Bjǫrn expresses concern at the journey's potential danger. However, Friðþjófr is determined to go, and asks his men to take him there. In 568ˣ only, he speaks this stanza.

Notes: [All]: This *fornyrðislag* stanza is only in ms. 568ˣ. The text appears in the diplomatic version of 568ˣ in *Frið* 1893, in a note in *Frið* 1914 and in *Skj* and *Skald*. It is uncomplicated and succinct, expressing the classic desire of a viking hero looking forward to a well-earned rest with his girl, his drink and his fellows, and with his ship securely beached on shore, at least as that viking hero's state of mind is imagined by a late medieval poet. — [2] *konung* 'the king': The reading of the sole ms. has been normalised here from the late form *kóng* to the bisyllabic *konung* to conform to the general normalisation of the poetry in this volume to the period 1250-1300.

Introduction to sts 36-41

The final section of the saga includes six stanzas that focus on Friðþjófr's encounter with King Hringr and Ingibjǫrg, now married to the king. Friðþjófr approaches the court in disguise but the king soon sees through it and recognises his visitor, whom he treats with extraordinary generosity, to the extent that he eventually offers him both his wife and his position as ruler. Friðþjófr indicates that he will accept this only if Hringr is mortally ill, and in the prose text, as if to order, the king develops an illness and dies. The conclusion to the saga is told in the prose only: Helgi and Hálfdan hear of Friðþjófr's good fortune and hurry to deprive him of his new position. Friðþjófr kills Helgi but spares Hálfdan to be *hersir* in Sogn under him. He and Ingibjǫrg have two sons (B version) or many children (A version). Ingibjǫrg's feelings throughout this final section of the saga are rather negative, but she acquiesces in whatever Friðþjófr has in mind, though she hardly acts as a heroine of romance.

Friðþjófr (FriðÞ Lv 30)

36. Þá hét ek Friðþjófr,   er ek fór með víkingum,
    en Herþjófr,   er ek ekkjur grætta,
    Geirþjófr,   er ek gaflökum fleygða,
    Gunnþjófr,   er ek gekk at fylki,
    Eyþjófr,   er ek útsker rænta,
    Helþjófr,   er ek henta smáb*örn*,
    Valþjófr,   þá ek var æðri mönnum.
    Nú hef ek sveimat síðan   með saltkörlum,
    hjálpar þurfandi,   áðr en hingat kom.

Ek hét Friðþjófr, þá er ek fór með víkingum, en Herþjófr, er ek grætta ekkjur, Geirþjófr, er ek fleygða gaflökum, Gunnþjófr, er ek gekk at fylki, Eyþjófr, er ek rænta útsker, Helþjófr, er ek henta smáb*örn*, Valþjófr, þá ek var æðri mönnum. Nú hef ek sveimat síðan með saltkörlum, þurfandi hjálpar, áðr en kom hingat.

I was called Friðþjófr ('Peace-thief'), when I travelled with vikings, and Herþjófr ('Army-thief'), when I made widows weep, Geirþjófr ('Spear-thief'), when I let fly throwing spears, Gunnþjófr ('Battle-thief'), when I went towards the host, Eyþjófr ('Island-thief'), when I plundered outlying skerries, Helþjófr ('Hel-thief'), when I seized little children, Valþjófr ('Slain men-thief'), when I was higher than [other] men. Now I have since roamed around with salt burners, needing help, before I came here.

Mss: **papp17^x**(361v), 109a II^x(152r), 1006^x(593), 173^x(91r-92r) (*Frið*).

Readings: [2] ek: *so* 1006^x, 173^x, *om*. papp17^x, 109a II^x [8] fylki: 'flik' 109a II^x [12] -b*örn*: björnu papp17^x, 109a II^x, -bornu 1006^x, 173^x.

Editions: *Skj*: Anonyme digte og vers [XIII], E. 7. Vers af Fornaldarsagaer: Af Friðþjófssaga ens frækna II 3: AII, 277, BII, 299, *Skald* II, 158, *FF* §22, *NN* §2837; Falk 1890, 84-6, *Frið* 1893, 30, *Frið* 1901, 43; *Edd. Min.* 102.

Context: Friðþjófr approaches King Hringr's court disguised as a wayfarer in a shaggy cloak. He claims to be engaged in the burning of salt (*saltbrenna*). When he comes before the king, Hringr asks him his name, and this stanza forms the answer.

Notes: [All]: This stanza, together with the surrounding prose, is only in the B redaction mss. Metrically and stylistically, it is unlike all the other stanzas in *Frið*, and clearly belongs to an enumerative model, in which an individual, usually in disguise, tells about his many adventures by means of a long list of names he has acquired on account of them. The god Óðinn is the prototype of this kind of figure, and *Grí* 48-50, quoted by Snorri Sturluson with commentary in *Gylf* (*SnE* 2005, 21-2), is the prototypical poetic realisation of this motif. It is a moot point as to how ll. 5-14 of the text should be divided metrically, as here (with *Edd. Min.*, observing that *er ek* would normally be in dip) or after *er ek* (so *Frið* 1901 and *Skald*). Finnur Jónsson (*Skj* B) gives up on this question and places ll. 3-12 in square brackets, presumably to indicate that he sees them as a late interpolation. The stanza is a mixture of metres, *fornyrðislag*, *málaháttr* and *kviðuháttr*. — [All]: The Odinic model does not really suit the chivalrous character of Friðþjófr, as presented in the rest of the saga, both prose and poetry; however, the figure of the wandering hero in disguise is a conventional motif in other *fornaldarsögur*, such as *Ǫrv*, where the wanderer calls himself by a pseudonym (often *Víðfǫrull* 'Widely-travelled' or, in some mss of *Ǫrv*, *Næframaðr* 'Bark-man'). In *Frið* 36, the many names Friðþjófr calls himself are all based on the semantic sense of the second element of his name *-þjófr* 'thief', while the first elements vary appropriately according to the activities with which they are associated. Most of these activities are of a martial or aggressive nature, which does not fit particularly well with Friðþjófr's character in the saga. On names in *-þjófr*, see Bugge (1890, 225-36). — [1] *Friðþjófr* '("Peace-thief")': Some eds (so *Skj* B) emend the text here to *Valþjófr* (taking this name from l. 13), on the ground that Friðþjófr would not state his actual name in such a stanza, designed to keep King Hringr guessing about his identity. Later in the saga prose, however, Hringr is made to say that he knew who Friðþjófr was as soon as he saw him (*Frið* 1901, 47; *Frið* 1914, 31), so it may be unwise to apply modern-day rationality to the use of conventional motifs in saga literature. — [6] *gaflǫkum* 'throwing spears': Old Norse *gaflak*, first appearing in prose texts c. 1270 (cf. *ONP: gaflak*), is possibly derived from late OE *gafeluc* (cf. OFr. *javelot*, MHG *gabilot*) and refers to some kind of throwing spear or javelin (cf. *Þul Spjóts* l. 7[III] and Note there). For the etymology, see *OED: gavelock*. — [11-12] *Helþjófr, er ek henta smáb*örn** 'Helþjófr ("Hel-thief"), when I seized little children': Some eds (e.g. *Edd. Min.*) have adopted the reading of papp17[x] in l. 12 *smábjörnu* (other mss having *smáborno*) in the sense 'little bears', sensing a possible connection with the name *Húnþjófr*, which appears in a corresponding passage of *Friðþjófs rímur* (IV, 55, 3, *Frið* 1893, 123) and which could be understood to contain the element *húnn* 'bear cub' or 'boy, young man' (cf. *LP: húnn*). The slight emendation to *smáborn* 'little children' was proposed by Falk, and seems far more probable than the over-ingenious bear cub hypothesis. Both *Skj* B and *Skald* emend to *smábǫrnum* (dat. pl.), though *henda* 'catch, seize' takes the acc. — [13] *Valþjófr* '("Slain men-thief")':

The first element of this name is understood here to derive from *valr* 'the dead slain in battle', but it may possibly derive from *val* 'choice' or *val-* 'foreign' (cf. Bugge 1890, 230). On the name and its likely connotations in Anglo-Norman, see Edmonds (2015).

— [16] *með saltkörlum* 'with salt burners': In early Norway and Iceland, salt was often produced by boiling seawater or burning seaweed on the seashore (Foote and Wilson 1980, 164; Buckland 2008, 599-600). See also Anon (*HSig*) 4/1-4[II] for another reference in Old Norse poetry to the activity of burning seaweed to obtain salt.

Friðþjófr (FriðÞ Lv 31)

37. Nú skal þér um þakka;
    þú hefir prúðliga veitta
    — búinn er greppr at ganga —
    gisting ara nisti.

    Ek man Ingibjörgu
    æ, meðan vit lifum bæði;
    — hon siti heil — en hljótum
    hnoss fyr koss at senda.

Nú skal þér um þakka; þú hefir prúðliga veitta nisti ara gisting; greppr er búinn at ganga. Ek man Ingibjörgu æ, meðan vit bæði lifum; hon siti heil; en hljótum at senda hnoss fyr koss.

Now I must thank you; you have splendidly granted hospitality to the feeder of the eagle [WARRIOR = me]; the man is ready to depart. I will remember Ingibjǫrg for ever as long as we both shall live; may she remain well; and we are [I am] obliged to send a precious ornament instead of a kiss.

Mss: **510**(95v), Holm10 VI(3r), 568[x](103r), 27[x](138v-139r), papp17[x](362v), 1006[x](597), 173[x](93v) (*Frið*).

Readings: [1] skal: *so* Holm10 VI, 568[x], 27[x], skal ek 510, papp17[x], 1006[x], 173[x];   um þakka ('of þacka'): *so* Holm10 VI, 568[x], 27[x], papp17[x], 1006[x], 'of gistingt þacka' 510, 'ofþcka' 173[x]   [2] prúðliga: mest papp17[x], 1006[x], 173[x];   veitta: *so* Holm10 VI, 27[x], mik prísat vetra 510, '[...]' 568[x], of veitta papp17[x], 1006[x], 173[x]   [3] búinn: '[...]' 568[x];   greppr: garpr papp17[x], 1006[x], 173[x]   [4] gisting ara nisti: *so* 27[x], papp17[x], 1006[x], 173[x], gistingar visti 510, gisting ara Holm10 VI, 568[x]   [5] man: mun papp17[x], 1006[x], 173[x]   [6] æ meðan vit lifum bæði: meðan vit lifum bæði Holm10 VI, 27[x], 'med[...]ifum bæði' 568[x], æ meðan lifum bæði papp17[x], 1006[x], 173[x]   [7] hon siti heil: lifi hon heil papp17[x], 1006[x], 173[x];   en hljótum: *so* papp17[x], 1006[x], 173[x], með hnossir 510, ok hylli Holm10 VI, 568[x], 27[x]   [8] hnoss fyr koss at senda: *so* Holm10 VI, 568[x], 27[x], 1006[x], 173[x], hylli fyr koss at senda 510, hnoss fyrir marga koss at senda *with* marga *added in a later hand and* at senda *crossed through* papp17[x].

Editions: *Skj*: Anonyme digte og vers [XIII], E. 7. Vers af Fornaldarsagaer: Af Friðþjófssaga ens frækna II 4: AII, 278, BII, 299, *Skald* II, 158, *NN* §2389; Falk 1890, 86-7, *Frið* 1893, 34, 58, 86-7, *Frið* 1901, 48, *Frið* 1914, 31-2.

Context: After Friðþjófr has been with King Hringr and Ingibjǫrg for some time, and has been very well treated by the king, though rather disdainfully by Ingibjǫrg, he decides early one morning to announce his impending departure to Hringr with this stanza.

Notes: [All]: This stanza occurs in both A and B redaction mss (though it is omitted in 109a II^x). It and the following four stanzas are also in the oldest witness to the saga, the fragmentary Holm10 VI, which provides a better text here than 510, though for editorial consistency 510 is still presented as the primary ms. The metre is an irregular *dróttkvætt*, with internal rhyme in l. 4 and, with incorrect placement, in l. 8. — [All]: The gracious, even noble sentiment of this stanza and the next is in marked contrast to the hero's ferocious self-image presented in *Frið* 36. — [3] *greppr* 'man': Friðþjófr uses the same word of himself in *Frið* 34/8. The B redaction mss have *garpr* 'champion, hero' here. — [7-8] *en hljótum at senda hnoss fyr koss* 'and we are [I am] obliged to send a precious ornament instead of a kiss': Most eds adopt this text, which is a mixture of B (*en hljótum*) and AB readings. Clearly, the scribe of 510 had a garbled text, as the full rhyme *hnoss* : *koss* is likely to have been the original *aðalhending* of l. 8, and this is misplaced in 510, though both Holm10 VI and 568^x have it correctly. These two mss of the A redaction have *ok hylli* instead of the B text's *ok hljótum* 'and we are [I am] obliged'. If *hylli* is a verb (from *hylla* 'make friends with') rather than a noun (*hylli* 'favour, grace'), the A text could be construed thus: *hon siti heil ok hylli, at senda hnoss fyr koss* 'may she remain well and show friendship, by sending an ornament instead of a kiss'. This seems to be at variance with the understanding of the B text redactors, as the prose of the B text immediately after the stanza states that Friðþjófr threw his ring towards Ingibjǫrg and urged her to take it. This statement is not present in the A text and the sense of the A text in Holm10 VI and 568^x may well be the original.

Friðþjófr (FriðÞ Lv 32)

38. Bú þú, Hringr konungr,   heill ok lengi,
    æztr ǫðlinga   undir Ymis hausi.
    Gættu, vísir, vel   vífs ok landa;
    skulu vit Ingibjörg   aldri finnaz.

Bú þú, Hringr konungr, heill ok lengi, æztr ǫðlinga undir hausi Ymis. Vísir, gættu vel vífs ok landa; skulu vit Ingibjörg aldri finnaz.

May you live, King Hringr, fortunate and long, the foremost of princes beneath the skull of Ymir <giant> [SKY/HEAVEN]. Ruler, look after your wife and lands well; Ingibjǫrg and I must never meet [again].

Mss: **510**(96r), Holm10 VI(3v), 568^x(103r), 27^x(139r), papp17^x(362v), 1006^x(597), 173^x(94r) (*Frið*).

Readings: [1] Bú þú Hringr konungr: Hringr konungr 27^x   [2] heill ok lengi: heill vertu lengi 27^x   [3] ǫðlinga: *so* Holm10 VI, 568^x, 27^x, konungr ǫðlinga 510, buðlungr papp17^x, buðlunga 1006^x, 173^x   [4] Ymis: *so* Holm10 VI, 568^x, 27^x, Vendils 510, heims papp17^x, 1006^x, 173^x; hausi ('hosi'): *so* Holm10 VI, 27^x, skauti 510, papp17^x, 1006^x, 173^x, ljósi 568^x   [5] Gættu vísir: 'g[…]' 568^x.

Editions: *Skj*: Anonyme digte og vers [XIII], E. 7. *Vers af Fornaldarsagaer: Af Friðþjófssaga ens frækna* II 5: AII, 278, BII, 299-30, *Skald* II, 158, *FF*§49; Falk 1890, 87, *Frið* 1893, 35, 58-9, 87-8, *Frið* 1901, 49, *Frið* 1914, 32; *Edd. Min.* 102-3.

Context: King Hringr tries to dissuade Friðþjófr from leaving his court, but Friðþjófr indicates his resolve to leave in this stanza.

Notes: [All]: The stanza is in both A and B recension mss, with the exception of 109a II^x. The metre is *fornyrðislag*. — [4] *undir hausi Ymis* 'beneath the skull of Ymir <giant> [SKY/HEAVEN]': Most eds (*Edd. Min.*; *Skj* B; *Skald*; *Frið* 1914) have favoured this reading which is present in Holm10 VI ('hosi') and 27^x ('hause'). This kenning alludes to the Old Norse myth of how Óðinn and his brothers Vili and Vé fashion the sky out of the skull of the primaeval giant Ymir, whom they had killed (*Gylf*, *SnE* 2005, 12). The sky-kenning *hauss Ymis* occurs also in Arn *Magndr* 19/4^{II}, but not elsewhere in Old Norse poetry. Its use here may be a conscious archaism; most of the other mss support the notion of a sky-kenning, but avoid the mythological allusion. Ms. 510 has *skauti Vendils* 'the corner [district] of Vendill', presumably referring to the Swedish district of Vendel, north of Uppsala (on Vendill, see Þjóð *Yt* 15/8^I, Note to [All]). The reference to Vendel seems misplaced here and may indicate scribal misunderstanding. The B redaction mss have a *lectio facilior*, *undir skauti heims* 'beneath the corner of the world' [SKY], which has been adopted in *Frið* 1901. The use of the word *skaut* here relates to its meaning in the cpd *himinskaut* (often pl.) 'corner, surface of the heavens, sky', which depends on the idea that the sky is a kind of cloth held taut at its four corners by four dwarfs, representing each of the four cardinal directions (cf. *SnE* 2005, 12).

Hringr (Hringrk Lv 1)

39. Far þú eigi svá,   Friðþjófr, heðan,
     dýrstr döglinga,   í döprum hug.
     Mun ek þér gjafir þínar launa
     víst betr, en þik um varir sjálfan.

Far þú eigi svá heðan, Friðþjófr, dýrstr döglinga, í döprum hug. Ek mun víst launa þér gjafir þínar betr, en þik sjálfan um varir.

Do not go from here in this way, Friðþjófr, most splendid of princes, in a downcast mood. I will reward you for your gifts certainly better than you yourself expect.

Mss: 510(96r), Holm10 VI(3v), 568^x(103r), 27^x(139r), papp17^x(362v), 1006^x(597), 173^x(94r) (*Frið*).

Readings: [1] Far þú: '[…]' 568^x;   eigi: ei 568^x, 27^x, papp17^x, 1006^x, 173^x [3] döglinga: *so* Holm10 VI, 568^x, 27^x, drengr 510, döglingr papp17^x, 1006^x, 173^x [4] hug: *so all others*, huga 510   [5] Mun ek þér gjafir: *so* Holm10 VI, 27^x, mun ek gjafir 510, 'mun ek […]' 568^x, þér mun ek gjalda papp17^x, 1006^x, 173^x [6] launa: hnossir papp17^x, 1006^x, 173^x [7] víst betr: *so all others*, betr 510   [8] um: *om.* papp17[x], 1006[x], 173[x];   varir sjálfan: sjálfan varir Holm10 VI, 568[x].

Editions: *Skj*: Anonyme digte og vers [XIII], E. 7. *Vers af Fornaldarsagaer: Af Friðþjófssaga ens frækna* II 6: AII, 278, BII, 300, *Skald* II, 158; Falk 1890, 87, *Frið* 1893, 35, 59, 88, *Frið* 1901, 49-50, *Frið* 1914, 32-3; *Edd. Min.* 103.

Context: King Hringr replies immediately to *Frið* 38 with these words.

Notes: [All]: The stanza is in both A and B recension mss, with the exception of 109a II[x]. The metre is *fornyrðislag*. — [3] *dýrstr döglinga* 'most splendid of princes': Most eds, including this one, follow the wording of the A redaction mss (with the exception of 510), as it gives a metrically regular line. — [5-6]: With *Edd. Min.* and *Frið* 1914 this edn follows the wording of Holm10 VI and 27[x] rather than that of the B redaction mss, preferred by *Frið* 1901, *Skj* B and *Skald*: *þér mun ek gjalda | þínar hnossir* 'I will reward you for your precious objects' (*hnoss* is used of the ring Friðþjófr gives Ingibjǫrg in *Frið* 37/8). — [7-8] *betr, en þik sjálfan um varir* 'better than you yourself expect': The main ms. (510) here has the more archaic reading *of varir*, which has been normalised to *um varir* (see Note to *Ásm* 1/3, 5). The verb *vara* 'expect' is used impersonally, with acc. of the person who expects something and gen. of what is expected.

Hringr (Hringrk Lv 2)

40. Gef ek þér fræknum   Friðþjófr, konu
     ok alla með   eigu mína.

Friðþjófr, ek gef fræknum þér konu ok alla eigu mína með.

Friðþjófr, I give you, bold one, my wife and in addition all my possessions.

Mss: **510**(96r), Holm10 VI(3v), 568[x](103r), 27[x](139r), papp17[x](362v), 1006[x](597-598), 173[x](94r) (*Frið*).

Readings: [1] þér: *so all others, om.* 510; fræknum: frægum papp17[x], 1006[x], 173[x]   [2] Friðþjófr: *so* Holm10 VI, 568[x], 27[x], 173[x], Friðþjófi 510, papp17[x], Friðþjóf 1006[x]   [3] með: *om.* 510   [4] mína: 'm[…]' 568[x].

Editions: *Skj*: Anonyme digte og vers [XIII], E. 7. *Vers af Fornaldarsagaer: Af Friðþjófssaga ens frækna* II 7 a: AII, 278, BII, 300, *Skald* II, 158; Falk 1890, 87-8, *Frið* 1893, 35, 59, 89, *Frið* 1901, 50, *Frið* 1914, 33; *Edd. Min.* 103.

Context: King Hringr follows *Frið* 39 with this *helmingr*, introduced with *ok enn kvað hann* 'and again he said'.

Notes: [All]: The stanza is in both A and B recension mss, with the exception of 109a II[x]. The metre is *fornyrðislag*. Some eds (*Edd. Min.*, *Skj* and *Skald*) treat this half-stanza together with *Frið* 41 as a single stanza with two parts and two speakers, Hringr and Friðþjófr. — [1] *fræknum* 'bold one': The A redaction mss' reading is preferred over B's *frægum* 'famous', as *inn frækni* 'the Bold' appears to have been Friðþjófr's nickname, oddly something expressed in the B text's prose but not in A's; cf. Note to *Frið* 21/7-8. Nevertheless, the adj. appears here in the A mss. — [2] *Friðþjófr*: Following the reading of the majority of A recension mss, though not 510, the nom. case of the hero's name has been selected, giving a direct address. Other mss (510, papp17[x]) make the pers. n. in apposition to dat. *þér* and *fræknum* 'to you bold Friðþjófr', but this makes the line unmetrical.

Friðþjófr (FriðÞ Lv 33)

41. Mun ek þær gjafir   þiggja eigi,
      nema frægr hafi   fjörsótt tekit.

Ek mun eigi þiggja þær gjafir, nema frægr hafi tekit fjörsótt.

I will not accept those gifts, unless you, famous one, have contracted a life-threatening illness.

Mss: 510(96r), Holm10 VI(3v), 568[x](103r), 27[x](139r), papp17[x](362v), 1006[x](598), 173[x](94r) (*Frið*).

Readings: [1] Mun ek þær gjafir: '[…]un ek þær gjafir' 568[x], Þær mun ek ekki papp17[x], 'mun eg […] eige' 1006[x], mun ek ekki þær 173[x]   [2] þiggja eigi: þiggja ei Holm10 VI, þiggja gjafir papp17[x], þær gäfur þyggja 1006[x], 'gafr þiggja' 173[x]   [3] nema frægr hafi: *so* Holm10 VI, 568[x], nema þú hafir frægr 510, nema þú frægr hafir 27[x], nema þú fylkir papp17[x], 1006[x], 173[x]   [4] fjörsótt tekit: *so* Holm10 VI, 568[x], 27[x], fjörsótt *with* tekit *added in right margin in scribal hand* 510, fjörsóttar hafir papp17[x], fjörsótt hafir 1006[x], 173[x].

Editions: *Skj*: Anonyme digte og vers [XIII], E. 7. Vers af Fornaldarsagaer: Af Friðþjófssaga ens frækna II 7 b: AII, 279, BII, 300, *Skald* II, 159; Falk 1890, 88, *Frið* 1893, 35-6, 59, 89, *Frið* 1901, 50, *Frið* 1914, 33; *Edd. Min.* 103.

Context: Following King Hringr's extraordinarily generous offer in *Frið* 40, Friðþjófr responds with this qualified acceptance.

Notes: [All]: The stanza is in both A and B recension mss, with the exception of 109a II[x]. The metre is *fornyrðislag*. — [3]: The reading of Holm10 VI has been preferred here to that of 510, which is unmetrical unless *frægr* is desyllabified to *frægur*. — [4] *fjörsótt* 'a life-threatening illness': A *hap. leg.* but the meaning of the cpd is perfectly clear. In the prose text following this stanza, the king indicates that he is indeed ill and he dies shortly afterwards.

Starkaðr gamli Stórvirksson

Biography

Starkaðr inn gamli 'the Old' Stórvirksson (StarkSt) was a legendary Scandinavian hero, known to Danish, Norwegian, Icelandic and possibly Anglo-Saxon traditions. Some sources (e.g. Saxo Grammaticus (*Saxo* 2015, I, vi. 5. 2, pp. 378-9), one version of *Heiðr* and *Víkarsbálkr* (*Vík*) in *Gautr*) claim that he was born a giant with six or eight arms, which the god Þórr reduced to two by tearing off the remainder. Both in Saxo and in *Gautr*, Starkaðr is represented as a hero of prodigious strength and bravery, but influenced by the gods Óðinn and Þórr to commit acts of gross treachery, the best-known of which is his mock sacrifice of his friend, King Víkarr, at Óðinn's instigation. The mock sacrifice turns into the real thing, and, as a consequence, Starkaðr is repudiated by his warrior companions. Saxo and the Icelandic sources also know Starkaðr as a poet. *Skáldatal* (*SnE* 1848-87, III, 251, 259) heads its list of poets and their patrons with Starkaðr's name as that of the earliest poet whose identity people remember, adding that he composed about the kings of Denmark. In *Ht* Snorri Sturluson names a verse-form, *Starkaðar lag*, after Starkaðr (*SnE* 2007, 38), while in *TGT* Óláfr Þórðarson quotes a fragment (StarkSt Frag 1^{III}) which he attributes to him. In *Gautr* the autobiographical poem *Víkarsbálkr* 'Víkarr's Section' (*Vík*) is attributed to Starkaðr.

Gautreks saga

Edited by Margaret Clunies Ross

Introduction

Gautreks saga 'The Saga of Gautrekr' (*Gautr*) has been transmitted in two major Icelandic versions, a longer and a shorter. Ranisch (*Gautr* 1900, xviii-xl) argued for the first time that the shorter version is probably the older of the two, at least in its present form, and this view has been supported more recently by Chesnutt (2009). In the view of this editor, though, the case for the prior status of the shorter version has not been proven conclusively; both versions probably contain early elements, especially in the poetry, and both are likely to have been reworked by later compilers or editors.

The subject-matter of the shorter version (*Gautr* 1900, 50-73) is mainly about King Gauti of Götaland (Old Norse Gautland) in Sweden, his adventures among a group of backwoods peasants, the Dalafíflar 'Valley-fools', his son Gautrekr and the latter's dealings with a certain Gjafa-Refr 'Gifts-Refr (Refr = "Fox")', who eventually marries Gautrekr's daughter. This narrative is built up from oral traditions and fairytale elements (*Gautr* 1900, lix-lxxxiii; Mitchell 1991, 55-8) and may have been influenced by oriental animal fables that had made their way to Scandinavia (Wikander 1964). A version of the story of Refr must have been known to Saxo Grammaticus, writing at the end of the twelfth century (cf. *Saxo* 2015, I, viii. 16. 1-4, pp. 620-5). Confirmation that legends about Gautrekr are of some antiquity is also provided by RvHbreiðm *Hl* 55-6[III], which commemorate Gautrekr for his generosity, while *Hl* 54/1-4[III] seem to draw on the same sources as *Gautr* 8 (see Note there). The age of the shorter *Gautr* is debated, but cannot be later that its oldest ms. fragment, AM 567 XIV γ 4° (567XIV γ) of c. 1400, and, according to Chesnutt (2009, 96-7), is likely to be perhaps fifty years earlier. Various mss of the shorter version contain eight stanzas, six of them in the Dalafíflar section of the text, and the remaining two in the so-called *Gjafa-Refs þáttr* 'Tale of Gifts-Refr'. These stanzas are also found in mss of the longer version, except that *Gautr* 3 is only in 164h[x] and *Gautr* 8 is lacking in papp11[x]. These mss are described in more detail below.

The shorter version of *Gautr* is only loosely linked to the subject-matter of the longer version (*Gautr* 1900, 1-49), which deals primarily with the life-history of the legendary hero Starkaðr and his close but troubled relationship with his companion Víkarr, king of Agðir (Agder) in southern Norway, which culminates in Starkaðr's sacrifice of Víkarr to the god Óðinn. Manuscripts of the longer version use the two parts of the shorter version, the so-called *þættir* of the Dalafíflar and Gjafa-Refr, as an envelope to enclose the so-called *Víkars þáttr*. This latter is a prosimetrum based upon a poem of thirty-three stanzas in its longest manifestation, named in the prose text (*Gautr* 1900, 31) as *Víkarsbálkr* 'Víkarr's Section' (StarkSt *Vík*), which is distributed throughout the prose narrative to provide supporting evidence for Starkaðr's life-history. The stanzas are an autobiographical retrospective monologue, often referred to as an *ævikviða* 'life poem', attributed to Starkaðr, who, the saga audience is led to believe, composed *Vík* towards the end of his life. *Vík* is extant only in mss of the saga's longer version.

The longer version of *Gautr* is likely to have been put together from an existing version of the shorter *Gautr* and a version of *Víkars þáttr*, probably no earlier than some time in the fourteenth century. The oldest complete ms. of the longer version, the compilation AM 152 fol (152), is dated c. 1500-25 (on its scribes' identity, see Stefán Karlsson 1970a and Driscoll 1992, xiii n. 2), but there is also a single leaf of an earlier fragment from c. 1400 (see below). However, some version of Starkaðr's *ævikviða* is likely to have existed well before an unknown author created the prosimetrum we now know. The concept of Starkaðr as a poet informs several of the poems Saxo attributes to Starcatherus, including his death song (*Saxo* 2015, I, vi. 8. 4-9. 20, pp. 416-47), and is also in play in SnSt *Ht*[III], where a variant of *fornyrðislag* is named *Starkaðarlag* (*SnE* 2007, 38), in *TGT*, where a fragment of poetry (StarkSt Frag 1[III]), said to be in *bálkarlag* 'section's metre', is ascribed to Starkaðr, and in both versions of *Skáldatal*, where Starkaðr is represented as the first poet at the dawn of historical memory. As to the age and authenticity of the original Icelandic version of Starkaðr's poem, Ranisch was of the view that it is unlikely to have been older than the late eleventh or early twelfth century (*Gautr* 1900, cvi-cix), and drew some parallels in wording and title with Ívarr Ingimundarson's *Sigurðarbálkr* (Ív *Sig*[II]), datable to after its subject, Sigurðr slembidjákn's, death in 1139. Finnur Jónsson, on the other hand, thought the poem could not be older than the thirteenth century (*LH* II, 159). The present editor's view is that elements of the poem probably go back to an oral substrate, one that also informed Saxo's Latin version. Its age is difficult to determine. The poem has been reworked and probably added to (though compilers subtracted stanzas as well); some of the metrical irregularities of the stanzas in the form in which they are presented in the extant mss are clearly of late date and we see the common addition of personal pronouns and other forms that characterise fourteenth-century and later versions of *fornyrðislag* poetry and make its lines unmetrical (see further Section 6 of the Introduction to this volume).

In the prose of *Gautr*, the title *Víkarsbálkr* is applied specifically to the section of Starkaðr's poem that tells of the death of Víkarr (*Gautr* 1900, 31), but modern editors have applied it to all thirty-three stanzas in which Starkaðr recounts his life-history, even though not all of them have to do with Víkarr. The use of the term *bálkr* 'section, list, partition' in poem titles most likely refers to the fact that their subject-matter can be divided into distinct sections (see SnSt *Ht* 97[III], Note to [All]). Also significant is the fact that extant poem titles ending in -*bálkr* trace an individual protagonist's biography (Ív *Sig*[II]) or autobiography (StarkSt *Vík*, Svart *Skauf*).

There are many extant mss of *Gautr*, the majority of them post-medieval. The three main mss of the longer version are AM 152 fol (152), of c. 1500-25, AM 590 b-c 4[ox] (590b-c[x]) of c. 1600-1700, and Holm papp 11 8[ox] (papp11[x]) of c. 1650. In addition, there is a single leaf extant of the vellum ms. AM 567 XIV α 4° (567XIVα), which may have provided the exemplar for 590b-c[x] (Chesnutt 2009, 93). The oldest witness to the shorter version of *Gautr* is also fragmentary and also dates from c. 1400; this is AM 567 XIV γ 4° (567XIV γ). It contains the first four stanzas of *Gautr*. The other principal witnesses to the shorter text all date from the seventeenth century. They are AM 194 c fol[x] (194c[x]), written by Jón Erlendsson of Villingaholt (d. 1672), its sister ms. Holm papp 1 fol[x] (papp1[x]), and AM 164 h fol[x] (164h[x]), written by Björn Jónsson of Skarðsá (d. 1655). This last ms. is a conflation of the version of 152 and a no longer extant version of the shorter *Gautr* (on relations between the younger mss, see *Gautr* 1900, xiii-xvii; Chesnutt 2009, 95-7). In this ms. *Gjafa-Refs þáttr* comes before *Dalafífla þáttr*.

All editions of *Gautr* to date have been based on the longer version of the saga, except for that of Ranisch (*Gautr* 1900), which contains both versions; the longer version in *Gautr* 1900 is based on 590b-c[x], but with critical apparatus from other mss; the shorter has parallel texts of 194c[x], 164h[x] and, where it exists, 567XIV γ. The *editio princeps* of *Gautr* was that of Olaus Verelius (*Gautr* 1664) and this was in fact the first printed edition of any Icelandic saga in the original language. Verelius considered *Gautr* and other *fornaldarsögur* set in Sweden to be evidence of the antiquity of the Gothic (= Swedish) language and culture in Scandinavia, and undertook to publish editions of these 'Gothic' texts. His edition was based on papp11[x]. Rafn's edition (*FSN* 3, 1-190) was based on 590b-c^x, and he was followed in this by Valdimar Ásmundarson (1885-9, 3, 3-38), though in this latter case the editor made a collation of 590b-c^x with ÍBR 6 fol^x, dated 1680, and written by Magnús Jónsson. Guðni Jónsson's edition and reprints (*FSGJ* 4, 1-50) follow the same tradition of using 590b-c^x (for a fuller discussion, see Chesnutt 2009, 93-5).

The present edition of the stanzas in *Gautr* uses the principal ms. witnesses of both the longer and the shorter prose versions where appropriate, although, as mentioned earlier, the shorter version does not contain *Vík* and is thus of no use as a witness to the majority of the stanzas. Previous editors of the poetry (as distinct from the prosimetrum) have separated the stanzas that are in the shorter *Gautr* (but also in the longer version) from the stanzas of *Vík*. In *Edd. Min. Vík* appears as item V well before the other stanzas, which are a separate item XXII, entitled *Die Geizhalsstrophen* 'The Miser-stanzas'. In *Skj* and *Skald* the eight stanzas found in the shorter *Gautr* come first in the section entitled *Af Gautrekssaga*, and include the two stanzas in *Gjafa-Refs þáttr*, even though these come after *Vík* in the longer version of the saga. *Skj* and *Skald* then follow with *Vík*, thus producing an order that does not conform to any ms. However, for convenience, it has been retained in the present edition.

Introduction to sts 1-6

These stanzas are found in the Dalafíflar section of *Gautr* and are presented as the direct speech of King Gauti and the backwoods family he encounters when he loses his way in the forest while out hunting. This family is terrified of doing anything or having anything done to them which would diminish their material wealth or, when it comes to procreation, of doing anything to increase their number, holding that this would reduce each member's share of the wealth. After Gauti unexpectedly enters their house as an uninvited and unwelcome guest, his actions, directly or indirectly, cause most of the family members to commit suicide by hurling themselves off the *ætternisstapi* 'ancestral cliff'. He also causes them grief by having sexual relations with the only outgoing and talkative member of the family, Snotra 'Wise One', who becomes the mother of his son Gautrekr.

All six stanzas are spoken by the male characters in this episode. The metre is *ljóðaháttr* and there is considerable variation in the prose and verse texts of the various witnesses. This is likely to point to the circulation of oral variants. The stanzas promote a dead-pan pragmatism on the part of their speakers, which highlights their absurd overreaction to their supposed misfortunes.

Gauti (Gauti Lv 1)

1. Skúa tvá, er mér Skafnörtungr gaf,
    þvengjum er hann þá nam.
    Ills manns kveð ek aldri verða
    grandalausar gjafir.

Skúa tvá, er Skafnörtungr gaf mér, er hann nam þá þvengjum. Ek kveð gjafir ills manns verða aldri grandalausar.

The two shoes, which Skafnǫrtungr gave me, he took the laces from them. I say the gifts of an evil man are never without harm.

Mss: **590b-c**[x](2r), 152(197rb), papp11[x](3r), 567XIV γ(1r), 164h[x](3r) (*Gautr*).

Readings: [1] Skúa: skó 152, papp11[x], 164h[x]   [2] er: *om.* 567XIV γ, 164h[x];   Skafnörtungr gaf: gaf Skafnartungr gaf 152, gaf Skafnartungr *with* gaf *added above the line in a different hand* papp11[x], gaf Skafnartungr 567XIV γ, gaf Skafnörungr 164h[x]   [3] þvengjum er hann þá nam: *so* 152, papp11[x], þvengjum er hann þar nam 590b-c[x], þvengjum at hann þá nam 567XIV γ, þvengjum hann þá nam 164h[x]   [4] Ills manns: at ills manns 152, sjaldan verða 567XIV γ, 164h[x]   [5] kveð ek aldri verða: verða vands manns 567XIV γ, naums manns 164h[x].

Editions: *Skj*: Anonyme digte og vers [XIII], E. 13. *Vers af Fornaldarsagaer: Af Gautrekssaga* I 1: AII, 322, BII, 342, *Skald* II, 184, *NN* §§1934, 3292; *Gautr* 1664, 9-10, *FSN* 3, 9, *Gautr* 1900, 6, 53, *FSGJ* 4, 6; *Edd. Min.* 121.

Context: When King Gauti wakes up in the morning, having forced himself upon the Dalafíflar household overnight, he asks the head of the household, called Skafnartungr, Skafnörtungr or Skafnörungr in most versions of *Gautr*, for a pair of shoes, as he had lost his own during his adventure in the forest the previous day. The man's wordless response is to give him shoes but to pull out the laces first.

Notes: [1-3]: A trace of this motif also appears in Saxo's account of the hero Starkaðr's adventures. Saxo (*Saxo* 2015, I, vi. 5. 11, pp. 384-7) tells that Starkaðr travelled to Ireland, where the ruler was one Huglecus, who had the reputation for being so mean that, when he offered someone a pair of shoes, he first withdrew the laces, thereby turning the gift into an insult. — [2] *Skafnörtungr* 'Skafnǫrtungr': This man's name is written in several ways in the mss, both in the prose and the verse, though the first element, *skaf* 'peeled bark', is largely constant (though *Skapnartungr* occurs in the prose of 152, *Gautr* 1900, 6 n. 13). *Skaf* was bark peeled from trees and used to feed animals, especially goats; cf. Sigv Lv 26/4[I]. The second element in the cpd is written -*nörtungr*, -*nartungr* or -*nörungr*. The last of these forms probably derives from *nœra* (later *næra*) 'nourish, feed'; thus the cpd *skafnörungr* should mean 'bark-feeder'. The element -*nörtungr* may be related to the Icelandic nickname *nörtr* (*CVC*: *nörtr*; *AEW*: *nǫrtr*), which *AEW* connects to ModIcel. *narta* 'nibble', but Lind (1920-1, col. 270) prefers to regard *nörtr* as a form of *knörtr*, which he connects to ModNorw. *knart* 'a small, thick-set person'. In *Skj* B Finnur Jónsson glosses the name *Skafnörtungr* as *den, der ved at skrabe forminsker noget* 'someone who diminishes something by scraping at it', but this explanation is not very convincing. *Skafnörtungr* seems more likely to mean 'bark-nibbler', following the etymology proposed by *AEW*, perhaps an allusion to the man's rustic character. — [3] *er hann nam þá þvengjum* 'he took the laces from them': The verb *nema* 'take', when it means 'deprive, take away' takes the acc. of the thing or person deprived (here *þá* '[from] them', referring to the shoes (*skúa*, l. 1), and the dat. of the object removed (here 'the laces', *þvengjum*); cf. *Fritzner: nema*, v. 5. — [3] *er*: Untranslatable anaphoric particle, sometimes used in the second or third line of a *ljóðaháttr* stanza to produce a caesura between it and the preceding line (cf. *LT*: ²*er*). Kock (*NN* §3292) points out that this particle occurs three times in this group of stanzas, in *Gautr* 1/3, 2/2 and 3/5. *Skj* B deletes the particle in *Gautr* 1/3 and 3/5. — [4-6]: These lines appear quasi-proverbial; cf. *Hávm* 117/5-10 and 123/1-3.

Gillingr (Gill Lv 1)

2. Heimsliga   er ek veik hendi til,
       er ek kom við kinn konu.
   Lítil lyf kveða   höfð til lýða sona;
       af því var hann Gautrekr getinn.

Er ek veik hendi heimsliga til, er ek kom við kinn konu. Kveða lítil lyf höfð til sona lýða; hann Gautrekr var getinn af því.

I moved my hand foolishly, when I touched the woman's cheek. They say little substance is required for [to make] the sons of men; that fellow Gautrekr was begotten from that.

Mss: **590b-c**ˣ(2v), 152(197vb), papp11ˣ(3v), 567XIV γ(1v), 164hˣ(3v), 194cˣ(2r) (*Gautr*).

Readings: [1] Heimsliga: hendi minni 567XIV γ, 'bendi eyk' 164hˣ   [2] er ek veik hendi til: *so* 152, papp11ˣ, ek veik hendi til 590b-cˣ, 'ek glætda (?) heimskliga' 567XIV γ, 'glærada heimsliga' 164hˣ, vildi mér til 194cˣ   [3] er: ok 152, þá er 567XIV γ, 164hˣ, at 194cˣ;   ek: *om.* 164hˣ;   kinn konu: konu kinn 194cˣ   [4] Lítil: 'litid' 567XIV γ, 164hˣ, 194cˣ;   lyf: efni 194cˣ   [4, 5] kveða höfð til lýða sona: kveða lýða sonar 152, þat (?) kveða lýðir vera 567XIV γ, kveði til lýða þrífa 164hˣ, til lýða sona 194cˣ   [6] af því var hann Gautrekr getinn: *so* papp11ˣ, 164hˣ, af því var hann Gautrekr görr 590b-cˣ, því var hann Gautrekr getinn 152, en af því var þó Gautrekr getinn 567XIV γ, af því varð hann Gautrekr getinn 194cˣ.

Editions: *Skj*: Anonyme digte og vers [XIII], E. 13. *Vers af Fornaldarsagaer: Af Gautrekssaga* I 2: AII, 322, BII, 342, *Skald* II, 184, *NN* §3292; *Gautr* 1664, 13, *FSN* 3, 11, *Gautr* 1900, 8-9, 56-7, *FSGJ* 4, 8; *Edd. Min.* 121.

Context: After Skafnǫrtungr, his wife and their servant had passed over the family cliff, their children decide to avoid any temptation to sexual intercourse by wrapping themselves up in woollen clothing fastened with wooden pins. Snotra realises that she is pregnant and about to give birth, so she loosens her dress so she can be touched. While she pretends to be asleep, her brother Gillingr accidentally touches her cheek. Noticing her shape, he thinks this action had made her pregnant and speaks stanza 2.

Notes: [All]: Gillingr is a giant name in Old Norse myth (cf. *SnE* 1998, II, 462). For Gillingr, see also Þul *Jǫtna II* 2/5[III] and Note there. — [1] *heimsliga* 'foolishly': A common variant of *heimskliga* (cf. *ANG* §291.6); the latter spelling occurs in mss papp11[x], 567XIV γ and 194c[x]. — [2] *er*: See Note to *Gautr* 1/3. — [5] *kveða* 'they say': The reading of most mss; both *Skj* B and *Skald* emend to *kveð* 'I say', presumably for metrical reasons. — [6] *hann Gautrekr* 'that fellow Gautrekr': The use of the formula *hann* 'he' (or other pers. pron.) plus a pers. n. occurs infrequently in late medieval Icelandic poetry (*LP*: *hann*), although it is found reasonably often in prose texts and has become a common colloquial idiom in later Icelandic usage. It occurs in Anon *Lil* 43/2[VII] (see Note there) and 47/1, as well as Anon *Sól* 20/3[VII].

Fjǫlmóðr (Fjǫl Lv 1)

3. Allar vættir,   er í jörðu búa,
         vilja Fjölmóðar fé fara.
    Gulli mínu   er þeir glutruðu;
         skalat því * lengi lifa.

Allar vættir, er búa í jörðu, vilja fara fé Fjǫlmóðar. Er þeir glutruðu gulli mínu; skalat því * lengi lifa.

All creatures that live in the earth want to destroy Fjǫlmóðr's wealth. They have squandered my gold; because of that I shall not live any longer.

Ms.: **164h[x]**(3v) (*Gautr*).

Reading: [6] skalat því * lengi lifa: skalat því eigi lengi lifa 164h[x].

Editions: *Skj*: Anonyme digte og vers [XIII], E. 13. *Vers af Fornaldarsagaer: Af Gautrekssaga* I 3b: AII, 323, BII, 342, *Skald* II, 184, *NN* §3292; *Gautr* 1900, 9, 59; *Edd. Min.* 121.

Context: This stanza is only preserved in 164h[x], where it comes immediately before *Gautr* 4, both stanzas being spoken by another son of Skafnǫrtungr named Fjǫlmóðr. He is distraught because he has found two black snails crawling over his gold bars. He interprets the discoloration produced by their tracks as dents in the gold, which he thinks have diminished his wealth, and he tells his brothers of his loss in this stanza and *Gautr* 4. Afterwards he and his wife plunge over the family cliff.

Notes: [All]: This stanza is not present in all eds of stanzas from *Gautr*. In *Skj* A it is found after the variant readings for *Gautr* 4 (Finnur Jónsson's st. 3) as 3b, while in *Skj* B it is presented within parentheses as st. 3b. *Skald* also records it as 3b. In *Edd. Min.* it is given in prose format before the readings of *Gautr* 4 (= *Edd. Min.*'s st. 3). — [3]

Fjǫlmóðar 'Fjǫlmóðr's': Both *Skj* B and *Skald* emend to the gen. sg. *Fjǫlmóðs*, though *LP*: *Fjǫlmóðr* gives the gen. sg. in *-ar*. Both endings are possible grammatically (Heggstad *et al.* 2008: *-móðr*) and metrically. — [5] *er*: Another example of the pleonastic *er*, as in *Gautr* 1/3 and 2/2. — [6] *skalat því * lengi lifa* 'because of that I shall not live any longer': The ms. negates the verb with suffixed *-at*, which the scribe of 164h[x], Björn Jónsson, may not have recognised as a negation, and gives free-standing *eigi* as well.

Fjǫlmóðr (Fjǫl Lv 2)

4. Stuttir sniglar   átu steina fyr mér;
        nú vill oss hvetvetna há.
    Snauðr mun ek snópa,   þvíat sniglar hafa
        gull mitt allt grafit.

Stuttir sniglar átu steina fyr mér; nú vill hvetvetna há oss. Ek mun snópa snauðr, þvíat sniglar hafa grafit allt gull mitt.

Puny snails have eaten the stones off me; now everything possible will go wrong for us [me]. I will mooch about penniless, because the snails have dug into all my gold.

Mss: **152**(197vb), 590b-c[x](3r), papp11[x](3v), 567XIV γ(1v) (ll. 1-3), 164h[x](3v) (ll. 1-3) (*Gautr*).

Readings: [1] Stuttir sniglar: slíkir fuglar 567XIV γ, 'stor-sniglar' 164h[x]   [3] nú: *om.* 164h[x]; hvet-: hver- 590b-c[x], hvor- 164h[x];   -vetna: -vitna papp11[x];   há ('háá'): *so* 590b-c[x], papp11[x], hata *all others*.

Editions: *Skj*: Anonyme digte og vers [XIII], E. 13. Vers af Fornaldarsagaer: Af Gautrekssaga I 3: AII, 322-3, BII, 342, *Skald* II, 184; *Gautr* 1664, 14-15, *FSN* 3, 12, *Gautr* 1900, 9-10, 59, *FSGJ* 4, 9; *Edd. Min.* 121-2.

Context: As for *Gautr* 3.

Notes: [All]: The full stanza is in mss of the longer *Gautr*, while 567XIV γ and 164h[x] have only the first three lines, which, in 164h[x], follow immediately from *Gautr* 3. — [1] *stuttir sniglar* 'puny snails': The first word of 567XIV γ is hard to read, but may be (so *Gautr* 1900, 8 n. to l. 19; *Edd. Min.*) *slíkir* 'sleek' rather than *Skj* A's *svartir* 'black'. The existence of *slíkr* adj. 'sleek, smooth' beside the noun *slíkr* 'slime' (attested only in Bjhít *Grám* 1/4[V] (*BjH* 26)) is debatable. This ms.'s *fuglar* 'birds', instead of *sniglar* 'snails' does not fit with the prose text, nor does it alliterate. It is possible that this variant was influenced by the subject-matter of *Gautr* 5. — [2] *átu steina fyr mér* 'have eaten the stones off me': *Fyr mér* here, as in *Gautr* 6/2 *drap uxa fyrir mér* 'has killed the ox I own', expresses the concept 'to the disadvantage or disfavour of' (+ dat.) (*LP*: *fyr, fyrir* B4). — [2] *steina* 'stones': Precious stones, jewels. — [3] *há* 'go wrong': Based on the *lectio difficilior* of 590b-c[x], this is the impersonal verb with dat. object *oss* (so *LP*:

háa) rather than the other mss' *hata*, in the sense 'harm, destroy, spoil' (cf. *Fritzner*: *hata* v. 2).

Ímsigull (Íms Lv 1)

5. Þat var spell,   er spörr um vann
       á akri Ímsiguls.
    Axi var skatt,   ór var korn numit;
       þat mun æ Tötru ætt um trega.

Þat var spell, er spörr um vann á akri Ímsiguls. Axi var skatt, korn var ór numit; þat mun ætt Tötru æ um trega.

It was devastation that a sparrow caused on Ímsigull's field. An ear of corn was destroyed, the grain was taken from it; that will grieve Tǫtra's family for ever.

Mss: 567XIV γ(1v), 152(198ra), 590b-c^x(3r), papp11^x(4r), 164h^x(3v), 194c^x(2r) (ll. 1-2) (*Gautr*).

Readings: [1] spell: spells 152, spjöll papp11^x, 194c^x, sjell 164h^x [2] er: *om*. 152, ok 590b-c^x, papp11^x, 164h^x;   spörr: spörn papp11^x;   um: *so* 152, 590b-c^x, papp11^x, 164h^x, of 567XIV γ, *om*. 194c^x;   vann: gerði 194c^x [3] á: *om*. 164h^x;   Ímsiguls: heimsyguls 164h^x [5] ór: ok 152; numit: 'nuid' 164h^x [6] þat: því slíkt papp11^x;   mun: *so all others*, man 567XIV γ;   æ: 'a' 152, *om*. papp11^x, 164h^x, 'ockr faa' 194c^x;   Tötru ætt: *so* 152, 590b-c^x, Tötru 567XIV γ, ætt vór papp11^x, Tötru mög 164h^x, trega Hjötru 194c^x;   um trega: *so* 152, 590b-c^x, of trega 567XIV γ, trega papp11^x, tregaz 164h^x, vinkonu 194c^x.

Editions: *Skj*: Anonyme digte og vers [XIII], E. 13. *Vers af Fornaldarsagaer: Af Gautrekssaga* I 4: AII, 323, BII, 343, *Skald* II, 184; *Gautr* 1664, 15, *FSN* 3, 13, *Gautr* 1900, 10, 59-61, *FSGJ* 4, 10; *Edd. Min*. 122.

Context: Another brother, Ímsigull, was inspecting his cornfields when he noticed that a sparrow had plucked a single grain from one of the ears of corn. He thought this such serious damage that he decided to plunge over the family cliff, taking his wife with him. Before he did so he spoke this stanza.

Notes: [All]: The stanza is a rather amusing example of hyperbole, pointing up the ridiculous lack of proportion in the Skafnǫrtungr family's view of their trivial losses. Ms. 567XIV γ has been used as base ms. here, as it offers the most conservative text. — [2, 6] *um vann*; *um trega* 'caused; grieve': The later form (*um*) of the pleonastic particle *of* has been preferred in both these cases. On the normalisation of *of* to *um* in post-1250 texts, see *Ásm* 1/3, 5 and Note there. — [6] *ætt Tötru* 'Tǫtra's family': In *Gautr* Tǫtra 'Tatters, Rags' is the name of Skafnǫrtungr's wife. The Hjǫtra mentioned by 194c^x is the name of one of Snotra's sisters.

Gillingr (Gill Lv 2)

6. Ungr sveinn   drap uxa fyrir mér;
    þetta eru banvæn býsn.
Mun ek aldri   eiga síðan
    jafngóðan grip,
    þó ek gamall verða.

Ungr sveinn drap uxa fyrir mér; þetta eru banvæn býsn. Ek mun aldri síðan eiga jafngóðan grip, þó ek verða gamall.

The young boy has killed the ox I own; this is a deadly portent. I shall never afterwards own an equally fine treasure, though I grow old.

Mss: 152(198ra), 590b-c^x(3r), papp11^x(4r) (*Gautr*).

Readings: [3] þetta: *om.* 590b-c^x [5] síðan: *om.* papp11^x [6] -góðan: góligan 590b-c^x, -góðligan papp11^x [7] verða: verði *all.*

Editions: *Skj*: Anonyme digte og vers [XIII], E. 13. *Vers af Fornaldarsagaer: Af Gautrekssaga* I 5: AII, 323, BII, 343, *Skald* II, 184, *NN* §3293; *Gautr* 1664, 16, *FSN* 3, 13, *Gautr* 1900, 10, 60-1, *FSGJ* 4, 10; *Edd. Min.* 122.

Context: On one occasion Gillingr was watching Snotra's son Gautrekr, now seven years old, stab an ox to death. Gillingr uttered this stanza and afterwards passed over the family cliff.

Notes: [All]: This stanza is missing in mss of the shorter version of *Gautr*. Instead of the expected single long l. 6 of a *ljóðaháttr* stanza, it has two irregular lines. It is possible that l. 7 is a later addition, and that the original l. 6 was a regular *ljóðaháttr* line. Kock (*Skald*) deletes l. 7 and emends 590b-c^x's version of l. 6 to read *svá góligan grip* 'such a fine possession'. *Gautr* 1900 and *Edd. Min.* divide ll. 5-7 as follows: *mun ek aldri eiga | síðan jafngóligan | grip, þó ek gamall verða* 'I shall never afterwards own an equally fine possession, though I grow old'. The present edn follows the version of 152, though it is unmetrical. — [3] *þetta eru banvæn býsn* 'this is a deadly portent': There is lack of congruence between *þetta* (n. sg.) and *eru banvæn býsn*, where both verb and noun phrase are pl.; this is common after *þat* and *þetta* (cf. *NS* §68). — [7] *verða* 'grow': Normalised from all mss' *verði*, which already shows the falling together in *verði* of the 1st pers. sg. and 3rd pers. sg. pres. subj., as in Modern Icelandic (cf. *ANG* §536.1; Stefán Karlsson 2004, 29).

Introduction to sts 7-8

Gautr 7 and 8 are found in the so-called *Gjafa-Refs þáttr* which follows *Víkars þáttr* in the longer version of *Gautr* and the *Dalafífla þáttr* in the shorter version, except in 164h^x, where it precedes it. *Gautr* 7 is found in the mss of the longer version of *Gautr* and also in 164h[x], which is a conflation of both versions. *Gautr* 8 occurs in both longer (except for papp11[x]) and shorter versions of the saga. Thus these two stanzas come towards the end of the saga in most mss. The tale of Gjafa-Refr, like that of Auðunn in *Auð*, is a story of a poor young man who wins powerful friends and great rewards by presenting high-ranking men with a sequence of judiciously selected gifts. In this case, Refr's major patron is a certain Neri jarl, who is said in *Gautr* to be the son of King Víkarr, hence the tenuous link between *Víkars þáttr* and the narrative of Gjafa-Refr.

Neri (Neri *Frag* 1)

7. Skein inn skrautligi raunar;   Skarð erat skapligt orðit;
    skjöldr hekk áðr á tjöldum;   skjótt mun ek snauðr af auði,
    oss verðr opt af þessu   ef braut með gjöf gautar
    angr mest, er ek lít þangat.   grandlaust bera randir.

Inn skrautligi skein raunar; skjöldr hekk áðr á tjöldum; angr verðr oss opt mest af þessu, er ek lít þangat. Skarð erat orðit skapligt; ek mun skjótt snauðr af auði, ef gautar með gjöf bera randir braut grandlaust.

The splendid one really shone; the shield previously hung on the wall-hangings; sorrow often strikes us [me] most because of this, when I look over there. The gap has not happened suitably, I will quickly [be] stripped of wealth, if men with a gift carry away shields scot-free.

Mss: **590b-c[x]**(7v), 152(200va), papp11[x](10v), 164h[x](1v) (*Gautr*).

Readings: [3] af: at papp11[x], 164h[x]   [4] mest er ek lít: er horfum 164h[x]   [5] orðit: yrði 152, virði 164h[x]   [6] skjótt mun: þó skjótt yrði 164h[x];   af: at 164h[x]   [7] með: mik 152, 164h[x]   [8] grandlaust: gnauðlaust 164h[x];   randir: dauðr 164h[x].

Editions: *Skj*: Anonyme digte og vers [XIII], E. 13. *Vers af Fornaldarsagaer: Af Gautrekssaga* I 6: AII, 323, BII, 343, *Skald* II, 184, *NN* §§ 1485, 1486, 3294; *Gautr* 1664, 47, *FSN* 3, 42, *Gautr* 1900, 38, *FSGJ* 4, 38-9.

Context: According to the saga prose, Refr, an unpromising young man, is thrown out of his father's farm. In revenge he takes with him a fine ox and presents it to Neri jarl, who has a reputation for being so mean that he never receives a gift because he cannot bear to requite the giver. In spite of his reputation, Neri gives Refr hospitality overnight and is moved to present him with a shield, inlaid with gold, that hangs among numerous others that overlap along the walls of Neri's hall. When he returns to the hall the next day, Neri regrets this generous gesture. Looking up at the gap where the shield had been, he speaks this stanza.

Notes: [All]: This stanza is in *dróttkvætt*, regular except for l. 1. — [1-2]: In this edn and also in *Skj* B, *Gautr* 1900 and *FSGJ*, l. 2 has been treated as an independent clause; however, it is possible (so *Skald*; *NN* §3294) to construe *skjöldr* 'shield' (l. 2) with *inn skrautligi* 'the splendid' (l. 1) in the first clause, and take *hekk áðr á tjöldum* 'it hung previously on the wall-hangings' as a separate co-ordinate clause with the implied subject *skjöldr* 'shield'. — [2] *á tjöldum* 'on the wall-hangings': The noun *tjald* usually refers to an awning on a ship or a wall-hanging or tapestry in a hall. The prose text of *Gautr* states (*Gautr* 1900, 38): *Ǫll hǫll jarls var búin með skjǫlldum, svó at hverr tók annan, þar sem þeir vóru uppfestir* 'The whole of the jarl's hall was decorated with shields, so that each overlapped another where they were suspended'. — [5] *skarð* 'the gap': That is, the empty place where the shield Neri gave to Refr was formerly hanging. — [7] *gautar* 'men': Here understood as a poetic word for men; *Skj* B understands *Gautar* 'men from Götaland (ON Gautland)' in Sweden. Finnur Jónsson combines this interpretation with the emendation of *bera* 'carry' (l. 8) to *fara* 'go' and *randir* 'shields' (l. 8, acc. pl.) to *randa* 'of shields' (gen. pl.) to give the following sense: *ef Gautar randa fara braut grandlaust með gjǫf* 'if the Gautar of shields [WARRIORS] depart safely with the gift'. Neither emendation has support in the ms. readings. — [8] *grandlaust* 'scot-free': A more common meaning for *grandlauss* is 'guileless, sinless', but here the sense seems to be that people can get away with all sorts of things just because they offer a [small] gift.

Anonymous (Anon Gautr 1)

8. Ráð þykki mér   Refnefs vera
    nökkru verri,   en Neri kendi.
    Varpat sínu   á sæ féi
    Gautrekr, er gaf   gullhring Refi.

Ráð Refnefs þykki mér vera nökkru verri, en Neri kendi. Gautrekr varpat féi sínu á sæ, er gaf gullhring Refi.

Refnefr's advice seems to me somewhat worse than [what] Neri gave. Gautrekr did not cast his wealth into the sea when he gave Refr a gold ring.

Mss: 152(201rb), 590b-c[x](9v), 164h[x](2v), 194c[x](5r) (*Gautr*).

Readings: [1] Ráð: brögðótt ráð 152;   þykki: þótti 164h[x], 194c[x]   [2] Refnefs: Refnis 164h[x], 'Refsnefs' 194c[x]   [3] nökkru verri: nökkvi verri 590b-c[x], heldr ólík þeim 164h[x], þeim ólík 194c[x]   [4] en: né 590b-c[x], er 164h[x], 194c[x];   Neri kendi: *so* 194c[x], 'merkinnde' 152, 'merkendi' 590b-c[x], mér kendi 164h[x]   [5] Varpat sínu: *so* 590b-c[x], upp á sínu 152, verpi hann sínu 164h[x], varp ei sinn 194c[x]   [6] á sæ féi: *so* 590b-c[x], 'sęfe' 152, á sæ út fé 164h[x], úr sjó fekk 194c[x]   [7] Gautrekr: Gautrekr konungs 590b-c[x], Gullbaug 164h[x], 194c[x]   [8] gullhring: Gautrekr kongur 164h[x], Gautrek 194c[x];   Refi: Ref 164h[x], Refr 194c[x].

Editions: *Skj*: Anonyme digte og vers [XIII], E. 13. Vers af Fornaldarsagaer: Af Gautrekssaga I 7: AII, 323-4, BII, 343, Skald II, 185; FSN 3, 49, *Gautr* 1900, 45, 67, FSGJ 4, 46; *Edd. Min.* 96.

Context: On Neri's advice Refr visits a certain King Óláfr with some expensive gifts including a golden helmet and a byrnie. The king is with his fleet out at sea. His evil counsellor, named Refnefr 'Fox-nose', advises him against accepting the presents and makes off with them himself, diving down to the bottom of the sea, where Refr pursues him and recovers the byrnie, but not the helmet, surfacing in a state of exhaustion. The prose text then states *þá var þetta kveðit* 'then this was spoken', but does not name the speaker. *Edd. Min.* attributes the stanza to Refr himself.

Notes: [All]: The narrative underlying *Gautr* 8 is probably alluded to in RvHbreiðm *Hl* 53-4^{III}, which mentions a generous sea-king named Óláfr flinging a golden helmet into the sea. The association with Gautrekr is confirmed by the following two sts of *Hl*, which are about Gautrekr; see RvHbreiðm *Hl* 54^{III}, Note to ll. 1-4. — [All]: The stanza is in *fornyrðislag* metre, and there are many variant readings, some of which suggest scribal confusion, e.g. as with the name Neri in l. 4. — [1] *ráð* 'advice': Ms. 152 adds the adj. *brögðótt* 'cunning' before *ráð*, and this has been adopted by *Skj* B and *Skald*, but the adj. is extrametrical, and has been omitted by other eds (*Gautr* 1900, *Edd. Min.* and *FSGJ*). — [3] *nökkru* 'somewhat': Ms. 590b-c^{x}'s *nökkvi* is also an acceptable reading; cf. *ANG* §475.3 Anm. 1. — [5-8]: These lines hark back to an earlier episode in Gjafa-Refr's career, when Neri advises Refr to visit King Gautrekr, who has been in the habit of sitting on his dead wife's burial mound and flying his hawk from it. Normally, as the days wore on, the king ran out of objects to throw at the bird to bring it back, and at this point Refr, positioned behind Gautrekr, slipped a whetstone into the king's hand, which he successfully threw at the bird. Gautrekr did not bother to look to see who gave him the whetstone, instead slipping a gold ring into Refr's hand.

Introduction to Starkaðr gamli Stórvirksson, *Víkarsbálkr* (StarkSt *Vík* 1-33, *Gautr* 9-41)

As has already been mentioned in the general Introduction to *Gautr* stanzas, the title *Víkarsbálkr* 'Víkarr's Section' is only applied in mss of the prose saga to the group of stanzas (*Vík* 26-33) that deal with the latter part of the hero's life and the death of Víkarr (*Gautr* 1900, 31-3). However, it is possible that the title was applied in the Middle Ages to all the stanzas that appear piecemeal in *Víkars þáttr* and present a poetic autobiography of the hero Starkaðr. It is a reasonable but unprovable assumption that these *lausavísur* formed part of a long *ævikviða* that was broken up and distributed throughout the prose account of Starkaðr's life to provide poetic evidence for his achievements. This assumption presupposes the existence of a version or versions of the poem prior to that of the earliest ms. that contains the prosimetrum of *Víkars þáttr*. An alternative hypothesis is that stanzas of disparate origin were assembled to form Starkaðr's *ævikviða* at a time when the prose text began to take shape in the fourteenth century or gradually thereafter. The stanzas, many of which are presented in small groups of two or three, are introduced by formulae such as we also find in historical sagas, in this case most commonly *svá segir Starkaðr* 'thus Starkaðr says'. The stanzas are mostly narrated in the first person, as the words of Starkaðr himself, while the prose narrative in which they are embedded is in the third person. Many of the stanzas of *Vík* are in a mixture of *fornyrðislag* with *kviðuháttr*, both in odd and even lines, when the latter are rendered as catalectic lines.

Vík is absent from mss of the shorter version of *Gautr* because the whole of *Víkars þáttr* is absent from it. Thus only mss of the longer version of the saga are witnesses to the text of *Vík*, and they differ considerably in the number of stanzas they contain. The witness that contains the most stanzas (all thirty-three) is 590b-c^x, a seventeenth-century ms. probably copied from a medieval exemplar. Ms. papp11^x, of c. 1640, omits all but six stanzas of *Vík*, but, as Ranisch observed (*Gautr* 1900, ii), usually retains in the prose text the introductory formula *svá segir Gautrekr* where the stanzas would be expected to appear, thus revealing that many, perhaps most, of these stanzas were likely to have been present in its exemplar. The oldest ms. of the longer *Gautr*, 152 of c. 1500-25, omits fourteen stanzas, all of which are also omitted in papp11^x. A good proportion of the stanzas omitted by both papp11^x and 152 (*Vík* 17-25) were regarded by Ranisch as late interpolations (*Gautr* 1900, lxxxv-lxxxviii; *Edd. Min.* xxx-xxxi), and both Finnur Jónsson and Kock followed him in relegating these stanzas to an addendum to the text of *Vík* with discontinuous numbering of the component stanzas. This policy has not been followed in the present edition out of respect for the integrity of the ms. witnesses.

The following list indicates the distribution of the stanzas of *Vík* across the ms. witnesses.

Vík 1 (*Gautr* 9)	152, 590b-c^x, papp11^x	*Þá var ek ungr*
Vík 2 (*Gautr* 10)	152, 590b-c^x, papp11^x	*Herr tapaðiz*
Vík 3 (*Gautr* 11)	152, 590b-c^x, papp11^x	*Þá er Herþjófr*
Vík 4 (*Gautr* 12)	152, 590b-c^x, papp11^x	*Prévetran mik*
Vík 5 (*Gautr* 13)	152, 590b-c^x	*Afl gat ek ærit*
Vík 6 (*Gautr* 14)	152, 590b-c^x	*Unz Víkarr kom*
Vík 7 (*Gautr* 15)	152, 590b-c^x	*Hann mældi mik*
Vík 8 (*Gautr* 16)	152, 590b-c^x, papp11^x	*Þá safnaði*
Vík 9 (*Gautr* 17)	152, 590b-c^x, papp11^x	*Styr ok Steinþóri*
Vík 10 (*Gautr* 18)	152, 590b-c^x	*Svá komu vér*
Vík 11 (*Gautr* 19)	152, 590b-c^x	*Var Víkari*
Vík 12 (*Gautr* 20)	152, 590b-c^x	*Var Víkari*
Vík 13 (*Gautr* 21)	590b-c^x	*Vart þú eigi*
Vík 14 (*Gautr* 22)	590b-c^x	*Mik lét sverði*
Vík 15 (*Gautr* 23)	152, 590b-c^x	*Ok á síðu*
Vík 16 (*Gautr* 24)	152, 590b-c^x	*Sneidda ek honum*
Vík 17 (*Gautr* 25)	590b-c^x	*Lét þreksamr*
Vík 18 (*Gautr* 26)	590b-c^x	*Átti sér*
Vík 19 (*Gautr* 27)	590b-c^x	*Var sínkgjarn*
Vík 20 (*Gautr* 28)	590b-c^x	*Réð Friðþjófr*

Vík 21 (*Gautr* 29)	590b-c[x]	*Réðum um*
Vík 22 (*Gautr* 30)	590b-c[x]	*Réð Óláfr*
Vík 23 (*Gautr* 31)	590b-c[x]	*Gengum fram*
Vík 24 (*Gautr* 32)	590b-c[x]	*Réð Friðþjófr*
Vík 25 (*Gautr* 33)	590b-c[x]	*Mér gaf Víkarr*
Vík 26 (*Gautr* 34)	152, 590b-c[x]	*Fylgða ek fylki*
Vík 27 (*Gautr* 35)	152, 590b-c[x]	*Þess erendis*
Vík 28 (*Gautr* 36)	152, 590b-c[x]	*Skylda ek Víkar*
Vík 29 (*Gautr* 37)	152, 590b-c[x]	*Þaðan vappaða ek*
Vík 30 (*Gautr* 38)	152, 590b-c[x]	*Nú sótta ek*
Vík 31 (*Gautr* 39)	590b-c[x]	*Hér settu mik*
Vík 32 (*Gautr* 40)	590b-c[x]	*Sjá þykkjaz þeir*
Vík 33 (*Gautr* 41)	590b-c[x]	*Hlæja rekkar*

Starkaðr (StarkSt *Vík* 1)

9. Þá var ek ungr,   er inni brann
    frækna fjǫlð   með feðr …
    þjóðnær vági   fyr Þrumu innan.

Ek var ungr þá, er fjǫlð frækna brann inni með feðr … þjóðnær vági fyr innan Þrumu.

I was young then, when a crowd of bold men burnt inside with … father very near the bay inside of Tromøy.

Mss: **590b-c**[x](3v), 152(198rb), papp11[x](5r) (*Gautr*).

Readings: [2] er: at 152;   inni: inni er papp11[x]   [3] frækna: flokna 152, papp11[x];   fjǫlð: ferð 152   [5] -nær vági: so 152, 'nerunge' 590b-c[x], papp11[x]   [6] innan: 'menn annj' 152.

Editions: *Skj*: Anonyme digte og vers [XIII], E. 13. *Vers af Fornaldarsagaer: Af Gautrekssaga* II 1: AII, 324, BII, 343-4, *Skald* II, 185; *FSN* 3, 16, *Gautr* 1664, 20 (ll. 1-4), *Gautr* 1900, 13, *FSGJ* 4, 13; *Edd. Min.* 38.

Context: This stanza, immediately followed by *Vík* 2 (*Gautr* 10), comes at the end of the first chapter of *Víkars þáttr*, which gives an account of Starkaðr's family and of his father, Stórvirkr's, relationship with King Haraldr of Agder in southern Norway. It mentions that King Haraldr had given Stórvirkr the island of Þruma (Tromøy) in Agder, where the latter established a farm. It then tells how Stórvirkr abducted a woman named Unnr, the mother of Starkaðr and the daughter of Jarl Freki of Hálogaland, and how Jarl Freki's sons Fjǫri and Fýri burnt Stórvirkr and Unnr and their household inside their farmhouse. Starkaðr himself was fostered by King Haraldr. The stanza is introduced with the words *Svá segir Starkaðr frá* 'Starkaðr tells thus about [the events]'.

Notes: [All]: This stanza and *Vík* 2 (*Gautr* 10) are presented as a single stanza of fourteen lines by *Gautr* 1900 and *Edd. Min.*, but divided at the end of l. 6 of this stanza by *Skj* and *Skald*. That division has been followed here. Some text appears to be missing from ll. 4-5 of st. 1, where *þjóð* (l. 5) follows immediately after *feðr* (l. 4) in the mss, yet seems to belong alliteratively with ll. 5-6. An additional couplet may also be lacking to bring the stanza up to the conventional eight lines; alternatively, the combination of what is here given as two separate stanzas may be better regarded as one long stanza of irregular length. The metre is a mixture of *fornyrðislag* and *kviðuháttr* (ll. 1, 3). — [3] *frækna* 'of bold men': *Edd. Min.*, *Skj* B, *Skald* and *FSGJ* have preferred the reading *flotna* 'of seamen', which occurs in one ms., AM 194a fol^x, a ms. close to papp11^x but not wholly dependent on it (*Gautr* 1900, iv-v). — [4] ...: Although there is no break between *feðr* and *þjóð* in l. 5, metre and alliteration require another word than *þjóð* after *feðr* and all previous eds have added *mínum* 'my' after *feðr*, a conjecture that may well be correct. — [5] *þjóðnær vági* 'very near the bay': For reasons already discussed in Note to l. 4 and because the readings of 590b-c^x and papp11^x are garbled, this interpretation is tentative. *Skj* B and *Skald* treat *þjóðnær* as a cpd adv. meaning 'very near', in which the element *þjóð-* is an intensifier, 'very', and that interpretation is followed here. — [6] *Þrumu* 'Tromøy': An island in the Skagerrak, near Arendal, Aust-Agder, mentioned in Þul *Eyja* 3/8^{III} and ESk Lv 14/2^{III}.

Starkaðr (StarkSt *Vík* 2)

10. Herr tapaðiz   Haralds ins egðska
    ok menbrota   mágar véltu,
    Fjöri ok Fýri,   Freka arfþegar,
    Unnar brædr   eiðu minnar.

Herr Haralds ins egðska tapaðiz ok mágar, Fjöri ok Fýri, arfþegar Freka, brædr Unnar eiðu minnar, véltu menbrota.

The army of Haraldr inn egðski ('from Agder') perished and the kinsmen, Fjǫri and Fýri, heirs of Freki, brothers of my mother Unnr, betrayed the necklace-breaker [GENEROUS MAN = Stórvirkr].

Mss: **590b-c^x**(3v), 152(198rb), papp11^x(5r) (*Gautr*).

Readings: [1] Herr: hers papp11^x;   tapaðiz: *so* 152, 'hraudtudr' 590b-c^x, 'hrvdur' papp11^x [3] menbrota: 'menn breta' 590b-c^x, meinbrota papp11^x [5] Fjöri: Fjörvi papp11^x [6] arfþegar: *so* 152, arfþegar *with* 'arfa' *written in left margin and final* a *crossed through* 590b-c^x, arfþegar *preceded by* 'arfa' *crossed through* papp11^x [7] Unnar: 'unar' 152.

Editions: *Skj*: Anonyme digte og vers [XIII], E. 13. Vers af Fornaldarsagaer: Af Gautrekssaga II 2: AII, 324, BII, 344, *Skald* II, 185; *FSN* 3, 16-17, *Gautr* 1664, 20 (ll. 1-4), *Gautr* 1900, 13-14, *FSGJ* 4, 13; *Edd. Min.* 38.

Context: As for *Vík* 1 (*Gautr* 9). This stanza follows it without a break.

Notes: [1] *tapaðiz* 'perished': The readings of 590b-c^x and papp11^x do not offer a satisfactory alternative here, either metrically or in terms of sense, even though *Gautr* 1900 and *Edd. Min.* offer the cpd *herhrǫðuðr* or the emended *ok herhrǫðuðr*, which are construed with the last two lines of *Vík* 1 (*Gautr* 9), though no interpretation is offered. The cpd *hrǫtuðr* occurs as a fire-*heiti* in *Þul Elds* 1/7^{III} in the sense 'stumbling', possibly related to *hrata* 'stagger, tumble', but this does not seem either syntactically or lexically appropriate here. — [2] *Haralds ins egðska* 'of Haraldr inn egðski ("from Agder")': A Haraldr, king of Agder, termed Haraldr inn granrauði 'Haraldr Red-whiskers', is mentioned in *Yng* ch. 48 (*ÍF* 26, 79-80) as being killed by the Ynglingr ruler Guðrøðr, the subject of Þjóð *Yt* 25^I. Guðrøðr asked for Haraldr's daughter Ása in marriage but was refused. However, this man must be different from the Haraldr, father of Víkarr, in *Gautr*; see Context to *Vík* 3 (*Gautr* 11) below. — [3] *menbrota* 'the necklace-breaker [GENEROUS MAN = Stórvirkr]': A common kenning-type, whose referent is presumably Starkaðr's father, Stórvirkr. The cpd *menbroti* occurs also in two poems probably of the early C13th, Bjbp *Jóms* 42/3^I and GSvert1/2^{IV}. — [5] *Fjöri* 'Fjǫri': In some mss, here represented by papp11^x, this character's name is given as Fjörvi, a form adopted by *Skj* B and *Skald*. — [6] *arfþegar Freka* 'heirs of Freki': Freki, the father of Starkaðr's mother Unnr, is said in the prose text to be from Hålogaland in the north of Norway. The noun Freki, related to the adj. *frekr* 'ravenous', can be applied to a wolf (cf. *Vsp* 51/6), as well as to fire and warriors (cf. *LT: freki*). The cpd *arfþegi* 'heir', lit. 'inheritance receiver' also occurs in *Gautr* 16/3 and Ív *Sig* 30/7^{II}, a poem that Ranisch considered (*Gautr* 1900, cviii) may have been influenced by *Vík*, though the influence may well have gone the other way. — [7]: This line is in *kviðuháttr*. — [8] *eiðu* 'mother': An uncommon noun, largely poetic; *Skm* (*SnE* 1998, I, 108) explains *Eiða heitir móðir* '*Eiða* is a name for mother'. *Eiða* is cognate with Goth. *aiþei* and MHG *eide*, both meaning 'mother', OIr. *aite* 'father' (*AEW*: *eiða*).

Starkaðr (StarkSt *Vík* 3)

11. Þá * Herþjófr   Harald um vélti;
    sér ójafnan   sveik í trygðum,
    Egða dróttin   öndu rænti,
    en hans sonum   haptbönd sneri.

Þá * um vélti Herþjófr Harald; sveik ójafnan sér í trygðum, rænti dróttin Egða öndu, en sneri sonum hans haptbönd.

Then Herþjófr tricked Haraldr; he betrayed [a man] unequal to himself in his plighted oath, robbed the lord of the Egðir [= Haraldr] of life and twisted captive shackles for his sons.

Mss: **590b-c^x**(3v), 152(198va), papp11^x(5r) (*Gautr*).

Readings: [1] Þá *: þá er *all*;   Herþjófr ('Herþ.'): Herþjófi 152   [2] Harald: Haraldi 152
[5] dróttin: dróttni papp11ˣ   [6] öndu: auðnu 152   [8] haptbönd: haptland *or* hæptland *with* t *added above the line* papp11ˣ.

Editions: *Skj*: Anonyme digte og vers [XIII], E. 13. *Vers af Fornaldarsagaer: Af Gautrekssaga* II 3: AII, 324, BII, 344, *Skald* II, 185; *FSN* 3, 17, *Gautr* 1664, 21, *Gautr* 1900, 14, *FSGJ* 4, 14; *Edd. Min*. 38.

Context: This stanza and the immediately following *Vík* 4 (*Gautr* 12) follow a prose passage that tells that Herþjófr, king of Hordaland (ON Hǫrðaland), made a surprise night attack on King Haraldr of Agder and killed him in spite of his plighted oath (*drap hann í trygðum*), taking his son Víkarr as a hostage, as well as many other sons of powerful men.

Notes: [1] *þá* * 'then': This edn follows *Skj* B and *Skald* in deleting all mss' *er* and understanding ll. 1-2 as a main clause. This line is in *kviðuháttr*. — [1] *Herþjófr*: According to an earlier passage of *Gautr* (*Gautr* 1900, 11), Herþjófr was the son of a certain Húnþjófr, King of Hordaland, who was in turn the son of Friðþjófr the Bold and Ingibjǫrg the Fair, who are the protagonists of another *fornaldarsaga*, *Friðþjófs saga ins frœkna* 'The Saga of Friðþjófr the Bold' (*Frið*). For a discussion of the possible relations between these two sagas and their genealogical information, see *Gautr* 1900, lxxxix-xcii. — [8] *haptbönd* 'captive shackles': There is one other instance of this cpd in Old Norse poetry, *Hálf* 5/6, where *snúa* 'twist' co-occurs. The first element is *hapt* 'fetter, shackle', metaphorically 'restraint, curb'; cf. OE *hæft* 'bond, fetter', OHG *haft* 'fetter, captivity'.

Starkaðr (StarkSt *Vík* 4)

12. Þrévetran mik   þaðan af flutti
    Hrosshárs-Grani   til Hörðalands.
    Nam ek á Aski   upp at vaxa;
    sákat niðja   á níu vetrum.

Hrosshárs-Grani flutti mik þrévetran þaðan af til Hörðalands. Ek nam at vaxa upp á Aski; sákat niðja á níu vetrum.

Hrosshárs-Grani ('Horse-hair Grani') carried me off from there at the age of three years to Hordaland. I grew up at Ask; I did not see my kinsmen for nine winters.

Mss: 590b-cˣ(3v), 152(198va), papp11ˣ(5r) (*Gautr*).

Readings: [1] -vetran: *so* 152, papp11ˣ, -vetrun 590b-cˣ   [3] -Grani: 'granne' 152   [5] Aski: skipi 152   [7] sákat: Stórvirks papp11ˣ   [8] vetrum: sumrum 152, papp11ˣ.

Editions: *Skj*: Anonyme digte og vers [XIII], E. 13. *Vers af Fornaldarsagaer: Af Gautrekssaga* II 4: AII, 324-5, BII, 344, *Skald* II, 185; *FSN* 3, 17-18, *Gautr* 1664, 21, *Gautr* 1900, 14-15, *FSGJ* 4, 14; *Edd. Min.* 38.

Context: Following the information given in the Context to *Gautr* 11, the prose text goes on to mention one of the important men in King Herþjófr's army called Grani, or Hrosshárs-Grani; on this name, see Note to line 3 below. He lived on the island of Fenhring (now Askøy near Bergen; cf. Þul *Eyja* 4/4[III] and Note) off the coast of Hordaland at a farm called Askr. Grani abducted Starkaðr, who was then aged three, and took him home to Fenhring, where he stayed for nine years. *Gautr* 11 and 12 are introduced with *Svá segir Starkaðr* 'so says Starkaðr'.

Notes: [1] *þrévetran* 'at the age of three years': Lit. 'being three winters'. — [3] *Hrosshárs-Grani* 'Hrosshárs-Grani ("Horse-hair Grani")': Lit. 'Horse-hair's Grani'. Grani 'bewhiskered one' (*AEW*: *grani*) was the name of the legendary hero Sigurðr's horse. Later in the saga, the figure of Hrosshárs-Grani is revealed to be a manifestation of the god Óðinn (cf. Þul *Óðins* 4/7[III] and Note there). Óðinn is associated with horses in several contexts in Old Norse myth, and this may point to his connection with a horse cult (cf. Falk 1924; Simek 1993, 161, 293-4). — [5] *á Aski* 'at Askr': The farm Askr was presumably located at or near the modern village of Ask on the island of Askøy (ON Fenhring), immediately north-west of Bergen and now connected to the city by a bridge. — [8] *vetrum* 'winters': Years were usually measured in winters rather than summers in early Scandinavia, as in other Germanic cultures. *Sumrum* may have been chosen here by some scribes out of a false belief that the alliteration of ll. 7-8 was on <s> rather than <n>. The age of twelve (9+3) was considered the age of adulthood in early Scandinavia, though later medieval sources place it at sixteen (cf. *Grg* Ib, 22; Dennis *et al.* 1980-2000, II, 46).

Starkaðr (StarkSt *Vík* 5)

13. Afl gat ek ærit,   uxu tjálgur,
    langir leggir   ok ljótt höfuð.
    En hímaldi   af h*u*gsi sat,
    fás forvit*inn*   í fleti niðri.

Ek gat ærit afl, tjálgur uxu, langir leggir ok ljótt höfuð. En sat hímaldi af h*u*gsi, forvit*inn* fás í fleti niðri.

I gained plenty of strength, my branches grew, long legs and ugly head. But I was a layabout lost in thought, curious about little down on the hall-floor.

Mss: **590b-c**[x](3v), 152(198va) (*Gautr*).

Readings: [1] Afl: alf 152   [6] h*u*gsi: 'hagse' 590b-c[x], hagli 152   [7] fás: *om.* 152; forvit*inn*: forvitni *both*.

Editions: *Skj*: Anonyme digte og vers [XIII], E. 13. *Vers af Fornaldarsagaer: Af Gautrekssaga* II 5: AII, 325, BII, 344, *Skald* II, 185, *FF* §26, *NN* §2612; *FSN* 3, 18-19, *Gautr* 1900, 15, *FSGJ* 4, 15; *Edd. Min.* 38-9.

Context: The prose text continues to tell of the warlike activities of King Herþjófr and his construction of warning beacons on high ground to alert him to possible incursions of enemies. He had put Víkarr in charge of the beacons on Fenhring. One day Víkarr went over to Askr and found his foster-brother Starkaðr there, sleeping among the ashes by the hearth. Víkarr was amazed at how big Starkaðr had grown. He gave him weapons and clothes and they sailed off on Víkarr's ship. The three stanzas, *Gautr* 13, 14 and 15, are then introduced with the formula *Svá segir Starkaðr* 'So says Starkaðr'.

Notes: [All]: Starkaðr's representation of his great strength but ugly appearance, here and in *Vík* 33 (*Gautr* 41), is reminiscent of some of Egill Skallagrímsson's self-portraits (cf. Egill *Arbj* 7-9^V (*Eg* 103-5)). Both figures are Odinic heroes and poets, and invoke stereotypical physical traits associated with their vocation (cf. Clunies Ross 2001b, 44-6). In addition, as both the prose text and ll. 5-8 make clear, the young Starkaðr also conforms to the 'coal-biter' (*kolbítr*) stereotype, which is sometimes associated with a poet-hero (e.g. Grettir Ásmundarson in *Gr*). — [2] *tjálgur* 'branches': The noun *tjálgr* (alternative form *tjalga*) has the primary sense of 'branch, bough' (cf. *AEW*: *tjalga*), but both here and in *Vík* 33/5 (*Gautr* 41) is clearly a half-kenning referring to Starkaðr's long arms. A similar sense occurs in Sigv *ErfÓl* 25/7^1 *tjǫlgur handar* 'branches of the hand', a kenning for the arms. In both instances of the use of the word in *Vík*, there is likely to be an allusion to an attribute of Starkaðr, described in *Gautr* 40 as well as in Saxo's *Gesta Danorum*. See further *Vík* 32 (*Gautr* 40), Note to [All]. — [6] *af hugsi* 'lost in thought': Emendation from 590b-c^{x}'s meaningless 'hagse' is required, while 152's *hagli* 'hail' does not make sense in context, although some earlier commentators proposed a meaning of 'on a bundle of straw' from an emended *á* or *at halga* (cf. *LP*: *hagli*; *LP* (1860): *hagall*). The emendation to the indeclinable adj. *hugsi* 'thoughtful, meditative' has been adopted in *LP*, *Skj* B and in this edn, but Kock (*NN* §2612) argues for the otherwise unrecorded form *afhagsi*, which he claims means the same as *úhagr* 'without talent, clumsy, awkward'. — [7] *forvit*inn 'curious': An emendation, first proposed by Sveinbjörn Egilsson (*LP* (1860): *hagall*), of both mss' *forvitni* 'curiosity' which does not fit the syntax of ll. 7-8.

Starkaðr (StarkSt Vík 6)

14. Unz Víkarr kom   frá vita innan,
gísl Herþjófs,   gekk inn í sal.
Hann kendi mik,   hann kvaddi mik
upp at standa   ok andsvara.

Unz Víkarr, gísl Herþjófs, kom frá vita innan, gekk inn í sal. Hann kendi mik, hann kvaddi mik at standa upp ok andsvara.

Until Víkarr, the hostage of Herþjófr, came from inside the beacon, went into the hall. He recognised me, he called on me to get up and answer.

Mss: **590b-c**^{x}(3v), 152(198va) (*Gautr*).

Readings: [6] hann kvaddi: ok kvað 152   [7] at: *om.* 152   [8] and-: an- 152.

Editions: *Skj*: Anonyme digte og vers [XIII], E. 13. *Vers af Fornaldarsagaer: Af Gautrekssaga* II 6: AII, 325, BII, 344-5, *Skald* II, 185; *FSN* 3, 19, *Gautr* 1900, 16, *FSGJ* 4, 15; *Edd. Min.* 39.

Context: As for *Gautr* 13.

Notes: [1, 3] *Víkarr, gísl Herþjófs* 'Víkarr, the hostage of Herþjófr': The prose saga tells that the sons of many powerful men in Agder, including Víkarr, son of King Haraldr, were taken hostage after Haraldr's death. Víkarr and Starkaðr were foster-brothers, as Starkaðr had been taken into King Haraldr's household after his own father, Stórvirkr, had been killed. — [2] *frá vita innan* 'from inside the beacon': In the prose text immediately preceding *Gautr* 13-15 it is stated that Víkarr had been put in charge of warning beacons (in which fires could be lit) on Fenhring. *Skj* B and *Skald* understand Viti as a p. n. in the west of Norway (cf. *LP: viti* 3). — [3]: This line is in *kviðuháttr*.

Starkaðr (StarkSt Vík 7)

15. Hann mæl*d*i mik   mundum ok spönnum,
alla arma   til úlfliða,
…   …,
vaxit hári   á höku niðri.

Hann mæl*d*i mik mundum ok spönnum, alla arma til úlfliða, … vaxit hári á höku niðri.

He measured me with hands and hand-breadths, all my arms to the wrists … grown with hair down on my chin.

Mss: **590b-c**^{x}(3v), 152(198va) (*Gautr*).

Readings: [1] mæl*d*i: mælti *both*   [8] á: ok 152.

Editions: *Skj*: Anonyme digte og vers [XIII], E. 13. *Vers af Fornaldarsagaer: Af Gautrekssaga* II 7: AII, 325, BII, 345, *Skald* II, 185; *FSN* 3, 19, *Gautr* 1900, 16, *FSGJ* 4, 16; *Edd. Min.* 39.

Context: As for *Gautr* 13.

Notes: [All]: Immediately after the end of this stanza, the prose text offers the following gloss: *Hér segir Starkaðr frá því, at hann hafði þá skegg er hann var tólf vetra* 'Here Starkaðr tells that he already had a beard when he was twelve years old'. This explanation may have been given because the stanza itself was defective when the prose text was first composed; neither ms. has a full eight-line stanza, yet there is no lacuna in either for the missing lines (probably ll. 5-6 in the original version), which would have mentioned Starkaðr's precocious growth of beard. It is interesting that the explanatory prose gloss is also present in papp11[x], though the stanza is absent. — [1] *mældi* 'measured': Both mss have *mælti* 'spoke', but the context indicates that the verb must be *mældi*, 3rd pers. sg. pret. indic. of *mæla* 'measure'. — [2] *spönnum* (dat. pl.) 'handbreadths': As in Modern English and other Germanic languages, a span or handbreadth was originally the distance from the tip of the thumb to the tip of the little finger, or sometimes to the tip of the forefinger, when the hand is fully extended, a measure of length of about nine inches (cf. *OED*: *span*, n.[1]). — [3-4] *alla arma til úlfliða* 'all my arms to the wrists': I.e. 'my arms from the top down to the wrists'. There may be another allusion to Starkaðr's original six or eight arms here (see Note to *Gautr* 13/2 and *Gautr* 40 Note to [All]). — [4] *úlfliða* 'the wrists': Lit. 'the wolf-joints'. The cpd *úlfliðr* 'wolf-joint' (cf. Arn Frag 4/3[III]) is explained by Snorri Sturluson in *Gylf* (*SnE* 2005, 25), doubtless basing himself on popular etymology, as derived from the story of how the gods persuaded the wolf Fenrir to be bound with the fetter Gleipnir. Týr placed his hand in the wolf's mouth as a pledge of the gods' good faith, but, when they later refused to release the wolf, he bit Týr's hand off at the wrist, and that is why the wrist may be called *úlfliðr*. The first element in this cpd probably derives from *ǫln* 'forearm'; cf. Þul *á hendi* l. 5 and Note.

Starkaðr (StarkSt *Vík* 8)

16. Þá safnaði Sørkvi ok Gretti,
    Haralds arfþegi Hildigrími,
    Erp ok Úlfi, Áni ok Skúmi,
    Hróa ok Hrotta, Herbrands syni,

Arfþegi Haralds safnaði þá Sørkvi ok Gretti, Hildigrími, Erp ok Úlfi, Áni ok Skúmi, Hróa ok Hrotta, syni Herbrands,

Haraldr's heir [= Víkarr] then gathered Sørkvir and Grettir, Hildigrímr, Erpr and Úlfr, Án and Skúmr, Hrói and Hrotti, son of Herbrandr,

Mss: **590b-c[x]**(4r), 152(198va), papp11[x](5v) (*Gautr*).

Readings: [3] Haralds: Harald 152, papp11ˣ;   arfþegi: 'ok horfþegi' 152, ok arfþegi papp11ˣ [6] ok: *om.* 152;   Skúmi: *so* papp11ˣ, Skúmi *with* i *corrected from* u *above the line* 590b-cˣ, Skútu 152   [7] Hróa ok: ok Hróa 152;   Hróa: Hrók ok papp11ˣ.

Editions: *Skj*: Anonyme digte og vers [XIII], E. 13. *Vers af Fornaldarsagaer: Af Gautrekssaga* II 8: AII, 325, BII, 345, *Skald* II, 185-6; *FSN* 3, 19-20, *Gautr* 1664, 23, *Gautr* 1900, 16-17, *FSGJ* 4, 16; *Edd. Min.* 39.

Context: After Víkarr has got Starkaðr off the floor at Askr, he equips him with clothes and weapons and gathers a troop of champions (*kappar*) and duellists (*hólmgǫngumenn*). *Vík* 8 and 9 (*Gautr* 16 and 17) are then introduced with the words *Svá segir Starkaðr* 'So says Starkaðr'.

Note: [6] *Skúmi* 'Skúmr': This pers. n. is assumed to be the dat. sg. of *skúmr* 'brown gull, skua, chatterer, gossip', but some eds (*Gautr* 1900, *Edd. Min.*, *FSGJ*) prefer the form *Skúmu*, from the nom. sg. *Skúma* 'Dusky' (?). There is certainly evidence for the existence of *skúma* as a nickname; cf. Biography of the poet Þorleifr skúma in *SkP* I, where various forms of *skúma* and *skúmr* and their likely meanings are discussed.

Starkaðr (StarkSt *Vík* 9)

17. Styr ok Steinþóri   frá Staði norðan;
    þar var inn gamli   Gunnólfr blesi.
    Þá váru vér   þrettán saman;
    fær varliga   fríðri drengi.

Styr ok Steinþóri frá norðan Staði; inn gamli Gunnólfr blesi var þar. Þá váru vér þrettán saman; fær varliga fríðri drengi.

Styrr and Steinþórr from north of Stadlandet; the old Gunnólfr blesi ('Blaze') was there. We were then thirteen together; finer fellows are scarcely to be had.

Mss: **590b-cˣ**(4r), 152(198va), papp11ˣ(5v) (*Gautr*).

Readings: [1] -þóri: -þór 152   [2] Staði: stöðum 152   [7] varliga: valla papp11ˣ   [8] fríðri: fríðu 152, fríðari papp11ˣ.

Editions: *Skj*: Anonyme digte og vers [XIII], E. 13. *Vers af Fornaldarsagaer: Af Gautrekssaga* II 9: AII, 325, BII, 345, *Skald* II, 186; *FSN* 3, 20, *Gautr* 1664, 23, *Gautr* 1900, 17, *FSGJ* 4, 16-17; *Edd. Min.* 39.

Context: As for *Gautr* 16.

Notes: [All]: This stanza carries on syntactically from *Gautr* 16, completing the list of the twelve champions (*kappar*) Víkarr gathered together. Like the personal names in *Gautr* 16, the personal names in 17/1 are in the dat. sg., dependent on the verb *safnaði* 'gathered' in *Gautr* 16/1. — [2] *Staði* 'Stadlandet': A headland in Romsdal and a prominent landmark; cf. Óhelg Lv 4/2¹ and Note to Þloft *Tøgdr* 4/5¹. — [6] *þrettán* 'thirteen': That is, the twelve men named in *Gautr* 16-17 plus Víkarr, but presumably excluding the speaker, Starkaðr, from the count.

Starkaðr (StarkSt *Vík* 10)

18. Svá kómu vér   til konungs garða;
    hristum grindr,   hjuggum gætti,
    brutum borglokur,   brugðum sverðum,
    þar er sjautigir   seggir stóðu,
    kostum góðir,   fyr konungi.
    Þó var um aukit   öllum þrælum,
    verkalýðum   ok vatndrögum.

Svá kómu vér til garða konungs; hristum grindr, hjuggum gætti, brutum borglokur, brugðum sverðum, þar er sjautigir seggir, góðir kostum, stóðu fyr konungi. Þó var um aukit öllum þrælum, verkalýðum ok vatndrögum.

Thus we came to the king's courts; we shook the gates, we hewed the door-frames, we broke the fortress-locks, we drew our swords, where seventy warriors of good quality stood before the king. Beside that, the number was increased with all slaves, workpeople and water-bearers.

Mss: **590b-c**ˣ(4r), 152(198vb) (ll. 1-8, 11-14) (*Gautr*).

Readings: [5] borglokur: lokur 152   [6] brugðum: en brugðu 152   [7] sjautigir ('lxx'): 'lxx tigir' 152   [13] -lýðum: *so* 152, -lýð 590b-cˣ.

Editions: *Skj*: Anonyme digte og vers [XIII], E. 13. *Vers af Fornaldarsagaer: Af Gautrekssaga* II 10: AII, 325-6, BII, 345, *Skald* II, 186; *FSN* 3, 21, *Gautr* 1900, 17-18, *FSGJ* 4, 17; *Edd. Min.* 39-40.

Context: The prose paragraph between *Vík* 9 and 10 (*Gautr* 17 and 18) narrates how Víkarr and his troop of champions, intent on vengeance, seek out King Herþjófr. It tells how Herþjófr had a house fortified like a castle or stronghold (*kastali eða borg*) with seventy warriors at hand, as well as various servants and workmen. The warriors attack hard, causing the kind of damage detailed in the stanza that follows, put into the mouth of Starkaðr, *svá segir Starkaðr* 'so says Starkaðr'.

Notes: [All]: This stanza in 590b-cˣ is fourteen lines long, twelve in 152, where ll. 9-10 are missing. It can easily be seen how additional lines, describing the attack on Herþjófr and his *borg*, could have been added to an originally eight-lined stanza; alternatively, what the mss have may be a slightly shortened version of two original stanzas. There is a close correspondence between the wording of the stanza and the immediately preceding prose account. — [3]: This line is in *kviðuháttr*.

Starkaðr (StarkSt *Vík* 11)

19. Var Víkari   vant at fylgja,
þvíat fremstr ok fyrstr   í flokki stóð.
Hjuggum hjálma   með höfuðgnípum,
brynjur sníddum   ok brutum skjöldu.

Var vant at fylgja Víkari, þvíat stóð fremstr ok fyrstr í flokki. Hjuggum hjálma með höfuðgnípum, sníddum brynjur ok brutum skjöldu.

It was difficult to follow Víkarr, because he stood foremost and first in the troop. We hewed helmets with head-peaks, we cut mail-coats and broke shields.

Mss: **590b-c^x**(4r), 152(198vb) (*Gautr*).

Readings: [1] Var Víkari: Víkari er 152   [3] ok fyrstr: hann 152   [7] brynjur: brynjum 152; sníddum: sneiddu 152   [8] brutum: brutu 152; skjöldu: *so* 152, hjálma 590b-c^x.

Editions: *Skj*: Anonyme digte og vers [XIII], E. 13. *Vers af Fornaldarsagaer: Af Gautrekssaga* II 11: AII, 326, BII, 345-6, *Skald* II, 186; *FSN* 3, 21, *Gautr* 1900, 18, *FSGJ* 4, 18; *Edd. Min.* 40.

Context: A short prose paragraph summarises the outcome of the battle: Herþjófr's men put up a good fight, but Víkarr's select troop prevails in the end. The stanza is put into Starkaðr's mouth, with the usual *svá segir Starkaðr* 'so says Starkaðr' formula.

Note: [6] *með höfuðgnípum* 'with head-peaks': The cpd *höfuðgnípa* is a *hap. leg.* and its meaning is uncertain. Most interpretations have understood the phrase *með höfuðgnípum* to be a metaphorical way of referring to the tall heads of the warriors inside their helmets, as in *Skj* B's proposed translation *vi huggede hjælmene med (på) de høje hoveder* 'we hewed the helmets with (on) the high heads'. However, other senses are possible, including that *með* 'with' might have instrumental function, and refer to some kind of weapon, or that the 'head-peaks' were some kind of ornament or crest on top of the warriors' helmets. The C10th helmet from a chieftain's grave at Gjermundbu in Ringerike has a crest with a small spike on it (Graham-Campbell 1980, no. 271; Grieg 1947). Swedish helmets from the Vendel period also bore crests, often with protective images of boars surmounting them, as did several from Anglo-Saxon England dated from C7th-11th (Marzinzik 2007, 33-42; *Beowulf* ll. 303-6). In the Viking Age and later, the typical Scandinavian helmet is conical, as can be seen from the figures on the Bayeux Tapestry and other witnesses (cf. Steuer 1999, 337-8).

Starkaðr (StarkSt *Vík* 12)

20. Var Víkari   vegs um auðit,
      en Herþjófi   heiptir goldnar.
      Særðum seggi   en suma drápum;
      stóðkat ek fjarri,   þá er fell konungr.

Var Víkari um auðit vegs, en Herþjófi heiptir goldnar. Særðum seggi en drápum suma; ek stóðkat fjarri, þá er konungr fell.

Honour was ordained for Víkarr and hostilities repaid to Herþjófr. We wounded men and killed some; I was standing not far away when the king fell.

Mss: 590b-c^x(4r), 152(198vb) (*Gautr*).

Readings: [2] auðit: 'ath bid' 152   [4] heiptir: herför 152   [8] fell konungr: konungr fell 152.

Editions: *Skj*: Anonyme digte og vers [XIII], E. 13. *Vers af Fornaldarsagaer: Af Gautrekssaga* II 12: AII, 326, BII, 346, *Skald* II, 186; *FSN* 3, 22, *Gautr* 1900, 19, *FSGJ* 4, 18; *Edd. Min.* 40.

Context: A short prose passage tells that Starkaðr and Víkarr fought side by side against King Herþjófr and eventually killed him. The other champions also distinguished themselves in the fight, as Starkaðr is reported to have commemorated in this stanza, introduced with the usual *svá segir Starkaðr* 'so says Starkaðr' (so 590b-c^x, but *Starkaðr kvað* in 152).

Note: [4] *heiptir goldnar* 'hostilities repaid': A common formula in eddic poetry; cf. *Guðr II* 28/2, *Ív Sig* 31/8^{III}.

Starkaðr (StarkSt *Vík* 13)

21. Vart þú eigi   með Víkari
      austr í Væni   árdag snemma,
      þá er sóttu vér   Sísar á velli;
      þat var þrekvirki   þokks megnara.

Þú vart eigi með Víkari austr í Væni árdag snemma, þá er vér sóttu Sísar á velli; þat var þokks megnara þrekvirki.

You were not with Víkarr east on Vänern early in the day, when we attacked Sísarr on the [battle-]field; that was a still more powerful feat of strength.

Ms.: 590b-c^x(4r-v) (*Gautr*).

Reading: [1] eigi: ei 590b-c^x.

Editions: *Skj*: Anonyme digte og vers [XIII], E. 13. *Vers af Fornaldarsagaer: Af Gautrekssaga* II 13: AII, 326, BII, 346, *Skald* II, 186, *NN* §122; *FSN* 3, 23, *Gautr* 1900, 20, *FSGJ* 4, 20; *Edd. Min.* 40.

Context: After their victory over King Herþjófr, Víkarr and Starkaðr take over all the king's ships and sail east along the coast of Norway to Agder, where many men join them. Víkarr becomes the ruler of all the districts that Herþjófr had controlled, and embarks on viking raids every summer. One such took him and his men to Lake Vänern in Sweden, where they fought a fierce battle with King Sísarr of Kiev (ON Kænugarðr). Starkaðr fought hand-to-hand with Sísarr, who gave him two serious head wounds, broke his collarbone, and wounded him on one side above the hip. *Vík* 13, 14 and 15 (*Gautr* 21, 22 and 23) give a verse account of these events, introduced by *svá segir Starkaðr* 'so Starkaðr says'.

Notes: [All]: There is no obvious addressee (*þú* 'you' l. 1) for this stanza and the opening gambit 'you were not there at a dangerous encounter' where the speaker says he fought bravely is strongly reminiscent of the *mannjafnaðr* 'comparison of men' convention, such as we find it in *Ǫrv* 34-58. The implication is usually that the addressee is a coward. The stanza seems out of place in *Vík*, unless it and the following stanzas detailing Starkaðr's wounds have been drawn into *Vík* from a separate source. *Gautr* 21 and 22 are only in 590b-c^x, but *Gautr* 23 is also in 152. — [3] *í Væni* 'on Vänern': The largest lake in Sweden, in the southwest of the country. — [4] *árdag snemma* 'early in the day': *Árdag*, possibly acc. sg. of time, is an unparalleled form, beside *árdagar* m. pl. 'days of yore', often found in eddic poetry, as in *Vsp* 61/5-6 (cf. *LP*: *árdagar*). The meaning of *árdag* here in combination with *snemma* 'early' is unclear. Finnur Jónsson (*LP*: *árdagar*) suggests the composer of *Gautr* 21 may have misunderstood the meaning of the cpd to mean the morning or early part of the day, and that is the sense given here. *Edd. Min.* emends to *árdags* (gen. sg.) but this does not make the meaning clearer. — [6] *Sísar* 'Sísarr': Name for the ruler of Kiev (ON Kænugarðr), according to the prose text. The name itself is probably derived from Lat. *Caesar* (cf. *Gautr* 1900, ic) and perhaps reflects a generalised awareness of the princely status ascribed to the rulers of Kiev in the late Viking Age and later (cf. Melnikova 1996 for a discussion of such legends).

Starkaðr (StarkSt Vík 14)

22. Mik lét sverði   hann sárum höggvinn
    skarpeggjuðu   skjöld í gegnum,
    hjálm af höfði   en haus skorat
    ok kinnkjálka   klofinn í jaxla
    en it vinstra   viðbein látit.

Hann lét mik sárum höggvinn skarpeggjuðu sverði í gegnum skjöld, hjálm af höfði en haus skorat ok kinnkjálka klofinn í jaxla en it vinstra viðbein látit.

He caused me to be struck with wounds with a sharp-edged sword right through my shield, [he caused] the helmet [to be struck] from my head, and my skull broken, and my jawbone cloven to the molars, and my left collar-bone to be shattered.

Ms.: 590b-c^x(4v) (*Gautr*).

Reading: [2] höggvinn: 'högg hann' 590b-c^x.

Editions: *Skj*: Anonyme digte og vers [XIII], E. 13. *Vers af Fornaldarsagaer: Af Gautrekssaga* II 14: AII, 326, BII, 346, *Skald* II, 186; *FSN* 3, 23-4, *Gautr* 1900, 20, *FSGJ* 4, 20-1; *Edd. Min.* 40.

Context: As for *Gautr* 21. This and the following stanza list the various wounds Sísarr inflicts on Starkaðr.

Notes: [All]: This stanza has ten lines instead of the usual eight and the second line is corrupted. As there is only one ms. witness, it is not certain exactly what l. 2 contained, though it is likely to have included some form of the verb *höggva* 'strike, cut down [with a sharp weapon]' and some form of the noun *sár* 'wound', but the function of the twice-repeated *hann* is unclear and presumably a scribal error. *Skj* A gives the second word as *särmann* (ms. 'sär^m') but it seems more likely to stand for *sárum*. Editors have conjectured *lét mik sáru hǫggvinn* 'he had me cut down with a wound' (*FSN*; *Gautr* 1900; *Edd. Min.*; *FSGJ*) or *lét mik sáran hǫggvit* 'he had me cut [so that I was] wounded' (*Skj* B; *Skald*). The present edn has opted for a minimal emendation of the ms.'s 'högg hann' to *höggvinn* 'struck'. — [8] *látit* 'shattered': The ms. has 'lattid', and this ed. has followed *FSN*'s presumed reasoning in supposing that this form is the p. p. of *láta* in the sense 'shattered, exhausted, dead, lost'. All other eds have emended to *lamit* 'crushed'.

Starkaðr (StarkSt *Vík* 15)

23. Ok á síðu   sverði beitti
    mér öflugr   fyr mjöðm ofan,
    en í aðra   atgeir lagði
    köldum broddi,   svá at á kafi yddi;
    þau sér merki   á mér gróin.

Ok öflugr beitti sverði á síðu mér fyr ofan mjöðm, en lagði atgeir í aðra köldum broddi, svá at yddi á kafi; sér þau merki gróin á mér.

And the powerful one thrust his sword into my side above one hip and plunged his halberd into the other with its cold point, so that it penetrated right through [me]; those scars are visible healed on me.

Mss: **590b-c**[x](4v), 152(199ra) (*Gautr*).

Readings: [8] at: *om.* 152; yddi: stóð 152   [9] sér: *so* 152, sér þú 590b-c[x].

Editions: *Skj*: Anonyme digte og vers [XIII], E. 13. *Vers af Fornaldarsagaer: Af Gautrekssaga* II 15: AII, 326-7, BII, 346, *Skald* II, 186-7; *FSN* 3, 24, *Gautr* 1900, 21, *FSGJ* 4, 20-1; *Edd. Min.* 40.

Context: As for *Gautr* 21.

Notes: [All]: A stanza of ten lines rather than the standard eight. *Edd. Min.* and *Skj* B place the last two lines in parentheses. — [3]: This line is in *kviðuháttr*. — [3] *öflugr* 'the powerful one': The reading of both mss. *Skj* B and *Skald* emend to *öflugri* 'more powerful', doubtless to produce a more regular line, and construe it with *mér* 'more powerful than me'. — [8] *yddi á kafi* 'it penetrated right through [me]': The idiom *ydda á kafi* means that a weapon goes right through its victim and comes out the other side. *Yddi* is the *lectio difficilior* beside 152's *stóð* 'stood, was'. — [9] *sér* 'are visible': Understood as the 3rd pers. sg. of the pres. indic. of *sjá* 'see' used impersonally. It is also possible (and the scribe of 590b-c[x] must have thought so) that *sér* is 2nd pers. sg. pres. indic. 'you see'.

Starkaðr (StarkSt *Vík* 16)

24. Sneidda ek honum   síðu aðra
    bitrum brandi   um búk þveran.
    Svá ek af heiptum   hjörvi beittak,
    at alls megins   áðr kostaðak.

Ek sneidda aðra síðu honum bitrum brandi um þveran búk. Ek beittak svá hjörvi af heiptum, at kostaðak áðr alls megins.

I sliced off one side of him with my sharp blade right across the body. Thus I wielded my sword with such fury that I had already expended all my strength.

Mss: 590b-c^x(4v), 152(199ra) (*Gautr*).

Readings: [1] Sneidda: 'Snei[...]ec' 152   [3] bitrum: *so* 152, 'brutt med' 590b-c^x.

Editions: *Skj*: Anonyme digte og vers [XIII], E. 13. *Vers af Fornaldarsagaer: Af Gautrekssaga* II 16: AII, 327, BII, 346-7, *Skald* II, 187; *FSN* 3, 24-5, *Gautr* 1900, 21, *FSGJ* 4, 21; *Edd. Min.* 41.

Context: The single combat between Starkaðr and Sísarr continues, with Starkaðr striking back at Sísarr, slicing off part of his side and wounding him in one leg below the knee, finishing him off by hewing off the other leg at the ankle.

Introduction to *Vík* 17-24 (*Gautr* 25-32)

With *Vík* 17 (*Gautr* 25) begins what Ranisch (*Gautr* 1900, xxxiii-xxxvi, lxxxv-lxxxviii; *Edd. Min.* xxx-xxxi) followed by *Skj* and *Skald* have considered an interpolation in *Vík*, consisting of *Vík* 17-24 (*Gautr* 25-32). All these stanzas are in 590b-c^x alone. However, the surrounding prose text is also in 152 and papp11^x, and, in the latter, a few of the formulae introducing the stanzas as Starkaðr's utterances can be found, showing that these stanzas were not peculiar to the tradition represented by 590b-c^x. An alternative hypothesis to account for the absence of these stanzas in 152 and papp 11^x might then be that their scribes (or their scribes' exemplars) chose to exclude a set of stanzas that were available to them as well as to the compiler of 590b-c^x. For a discussion of the concept of interpolation in skaldic editing, see Introduction to *SkP* VIII, Section 5. The following principal reasons have been adduced for considering the stanzas as interpolations or at least as of differing origin from the rest of *Vík* (see further Section 6 of the Introduction). All but two (*Vík* 21/1-4 and 23, *Gautr* 29 and 31) are third-person narratives, whereas the majority of stanzas in *Vík* are in the first person, presented as Starkaðr's direct speech. *Gautr* 25-32, including most of *Gautr* 31, are in *kviðuháttr* metre, whereas the dominant metrical form of *Vík* is *fornyrðislag*, sometimes interspersed with *kviðuháttr* lines. Both the prose text and *Vík* 19 (*Gautr* 27) introduce the figure of Jarl Neri and the theme of his extreme miserliness, thus establishing a connection with the *Gjafa-Refs þáttr*. Neri is presented as one of Víkarr's two sons.

Starkaðr (StarkSt *Vík* 17)

25. Lét þreksamr   þriðja sinni
     Hildar leik   háðan verða,
     áðr Upplönd   unnin yrði
     ok Geirþjófr   um gefinn helju.

Þreksamr lét leik Hildar verða háðan þriðja sinni, áðr Upplönd yrði unnin ok Geirþjófr um gefinn helju.

The powerful one had the play of Hildr <valkyrie> [BATTLE] held for a third time before Opplandene could be won and Geirþjófr given over to death.

Ms.: 590b-c^x(4v) (*Gautr*).

Editions: *Skj*: Anonyme digte og vers [XIII], E. 13. *Vers af Fornaldarsagaer: Af Gautrekssaga* α 1: AII, 328-9, BII, 349, *Skald* II, 188; *FSN* 3, 25, *Gautr* 1900, 22, *FSGJ* 4, 22; *Edd. Min.* 41.

Context: The prose saga turns to Geirþjófr, the brother of Víkarr's adversary, King Herþjófr. Geirþjófr seeks revenge for Víkarr's killing of Herþjófr and assembles a huge fighting force in Upplǫnd (Opplandene), while Víkarr travels there with a large army to oppose him. A seventeen-day battle ensues, which Víkarr wins, and Geirþjófr is killed. Víkarr now becomes king of Upplǫnd and Þelamǫrk (Telemark), taking over the latter while its king, Friðþjófr, another brother of Herþjófr, is away. The stanza is introduced with the words: *Þess getr Starkaðr, at sú var hin þriðja orrosta Víkars konungs, er hann hafði unnit á Upplǫndum* 'Starkaðr reports that that was the third battle of King Víkarr, which he had fought in Opplandene'.

Notes: [All]: The stanza is in the metre *kviðuháttr*, a variant of *fornyrðislag* in which the odd lines consist of three, rather than four, metrical positions, and the even lines are regular *fornyrðislag*. For a discussion of the metre and its uses, see General Introduction in *SkP* I, Section 4.3. — [2] *þriðja sinni* 'for a third time': No other times are mentioned in either the prose or the poetry, suggesting that both may have been shortened. The prose introduction to this stanza also suggests the compiler may have been aware of the lack of information at his disposal to cover the content of this stanza.

Starkaðr (StarkSt *Vík* 18)

26. Átti sér   erfivörðu
    tírsamr tvá   tyggi alna.
    Hét hans son   Haraldr inn ellri;
    setti þann   at Þelamörku.

Tírsamr tyggi átti tvá erfivörðu alna sér. Inn ellri son hans hét Haraldr; setti þann at Þelamörku.

The fame-desiring ruler had two heirs born to him. The elder son of his was called Haraldr; he placed that one over Telemark.

Ms.: 590b-c^x(4v) (*Gautr*).

Editions: *Skj*: Anonyme digte og vers [XIII], E. 13. *Vers af Fornaldarsagaer: Af Gautrekssaga* α 2: AII, 329, BII, 349, *Skald* II, 188; *FSN* 3, 26, *Gautr* 1900, 23, *FSGJ* 4, 22-3; *Edd. Min.* 41.

Context: The prose text tells that Víkarr becomes a very powerful king. He marries an unnamed wife and has two sons, the elder Haraldr, the younger Neri. Neri was the wisest of men and gave good advice, but was so stingy (*svá var hann sínkr*) that he could never give anything away without immediately longing for it again. *Vík* 18 and 19 (*Gautr* 26 and 27) are then cited as Starkaðr's comment on these matters.

Notes: [2] *erfivörðu* 'heirs': The noun *erfivǫrðr* is not common in skaldic poetry, though it occurs twice in the late C12th Anon *Nkt* 3/7 and 13/4[II], but is found in several poems of the Poetic Edda (cf. *LP*: *erfivǫrðr*). — [5] *son* 'son': The ms. has 'sun'. Most eds restore the final <r> to give the nom. sg. case, but this is not necessary, as the nom. form without <r> is common (*ANG* §395.1).

Starkaðr (StarkSt *Vík* 19)

27. Var sínkgjarn   sagðr af gulli
    Neri jarl,   nýtr í ráðum,
    Víkars sonr   vanr í sóknum;
    sá réð einn   Upplendingum.

Neri jarl var sagðr sínkgjarn af gulli, nýtr í ráðum, sonr Víkars vanr í sóknum; sá réð einn Upplendingum.

Jarl Neri was said to be covetous of gold, capable in counsels, Víkarr's son, accustomed to fight; he ruled alone over the Upplendingar.

Ms.: **590b-c**[x](4v) (*Gautr*).

Reading: [7] einn: 'eirn' 590b-c[x].

Editions: *Skj*: Anonyme digte og vers [XIII], E. 13. Vers af Fornaldarsagaer: Af Gautrekssaga α 3: AII, 329, BII, 349, *Skald* II, 188; *FSN* 3, 26, *Gautr* 1900, 23, *FSGJ* 4, 23; *Edd. Min.* 41.

Notes: [1] *sínkgjarn* 'covetous': The adj. is more commonly simplified as *síngjarn* (see Fritzner: *síngjarn*), but the sole ms. of this stanza spells it *sínk-*, a spelling reflected in the prose text (*sínkr*). On the etymology, see *AEW*: *sínka*. Some eds (*Skj* B; *Skald*) use the form *síngjarn* here. — [7] *einn* 'alone': All eds have emended the ms.'s 'eirn', which is not an Old Norse word. — [8] *Upplendingum* 'over the Upplendingar': The Upplendingar, people from Opplandene (ON Upplǫnd), Norway, the region which Víkarr's opponents, Herþjófr and his brothers, are said to have ruled.

Starkaðr (StarkSt *Vík* 20)

28. Réð Friðþjófr   fyrst at senda
    heiptarboð   horskum jöfri,
    hvárt Víkarr   vildi gjalda
    hilmi skatt   eða her þola.

Friðþjófr réð fyrst at senda horskum jöfri heiptarboð, hvárt Víkarr vildi gjalda hilmi skatt eða þola her.

Friðþjófr first sent a message of hostility to the wise prince, [enquiring] whether Víkarr wanted to pay tribute to the ruler or suffer his army.

Ms.: **590b-c**[x](4v) (*Gautr*).

Reading: [1] Friðþjófr: 'Fridþ.' 590b-c[x].

Editions: *Skj*: Anonyme digte og vers [XIII], E. 13. *Vers af Fornaldarsagaer: Af Gautrekssaga* α 4: AII, 329, BII, 349, *Skald* II, 188; *FSN* 3, 27, *Gautr* 1900, 23-4, *FSGJ* 4, 23-4; *Edd. Min.* 41.

Context: This stanza is said to be Starkaðr's poetic summary of the situation described in a few lines of saga prose. Friðþjófr, having heard that his two brothers had been killed, returns to Opplandene and regains his kingdom from Víkarr. He then sends a message to Víkarr offering him the choice of paying tribute or facing an enemy attack.

Note: [1, 2] *réð ... at senda* 'sent': Here *réð* functions as an auxiliary with *senda* 'send'. For *réð* formulas in the sense 'rule', which characteristically begin a stanza or a *helmingr* see, e.g., st. 30/1 below, as well as Anon *Nkt* 8/1, 12/1, 16/5, 23/1, 28/5[II], etc. Cf. also Þjóð *Yt* 26/5[I] as well as the *kviðuháttr* stanza on the Rök stone (Run Ög136[VI] *Ræð Þiðrikr*). These formulas must have been a staple of the genealogical *kviðuháttr* tradition.

Starkaðr (StarkSt *Vík* 21)

29. Réðum um   ... lengi;
    urðum vit   ekki dælir.
    Þat kaus herr,   at konungr skyldi
    ríkr með her   rómu knýja.

Réðum um ... lengi; vit urðum ekki dælir. Herr kaus þat, at ríkr konungr skyldi knýja rómu með her.

We debated ... long; we were not easy to deal with. The army chose that the powerful king should press on with the battle with his troop.

Ms.: **590b-c**[x](4v) (*Gautr*).

Reading: [2] ... lengi: lengi 590b-c[x].

Editions: *Skj*: Anonyme digte og vers [XIII], E. 13. *Vers af Fornaldarsagaer: Af Gautrekssaga* α 5: AII, 329, BII, 349, *Skald* II, 188, *NN* §3295; *FSN* 3, 27, *Gautr* 1900, 24, *FSGJ* 4, 24; *Edd. Min.* 41.

Context: The saga prose indicates that Víkarr and his counsellors discussed at some length how to proceed.

Notes: [All]: The first *helmingr* of this stanza reverts to the 1st pers. pl. mode of narrative, like earlier stanzas of *Vík*, but the second continues with 3rd pers. narrative. *Vit* 'we' (l. 3) is 1st pers. dual, yet the pl. would be expected in this context. — [2] ... *lengi* '... long': There is no gap in the ms. between *um* (l. 1) and *lengi* but a word is clearly missing. It must be disyllabic with a long stem and begin with *r*- or a vowel. The expected sense would be 'we did not debate for long' or words to that effect.

Starkaðr (StarkSt *Vík* 22)

30. Réð Óláfr   austr inn skygni,
    sældargramr,   fyr Svíaríki.
    Hann bauð út   almenningi;
    mikill var hans   helmingr talinn.

Óláfr inn skygni réð austr, sældargramr, fyr Svíaríki. Hann bauð út almenningi; helmingr hans var talinn mikill.

Óláfr inn skygni ('the Sharp-sighted') ruled in the east, the prosperous ruler, over the kingdom of the Swedes. He ordered the conscripted army out; his division was reckoned great.

Ms.: **590b-c^x(5r)** (*Gautr*).

Editions: *Skj*: Anonyme digte og vers [XIII], E. 13. *Vers af Fornaldarsagaer: Af Gautrekssaga* α 6: AII, 329, BII, 350, *Skald* II, 188; *FSN* 3, 28, *Gautr* 1900, 24-5, *FSGJ* 4, 25; *Edd. Min.* 41-2.

Context: King Óláfr the Sharp-sighted of Nærríki (Närke) in Sweden swings his support behind King Víkarr, ordering a general levy of his kingdom to come out to fight. He draws up his forces in a wedge-shaped column. The stanza expresses Starkaðr's version of the event.

Notes: [1-2] *Óláfr inn skygni* 'Óláfr inn skygni ("the Sharp-sighted")': Named in *Yng* ch. 42 (*ÍF* 26, 73) as king of Närke. According to *Yng* his daughter Álof was the mother of Gauthildr, mother of the Ynglingr king Óláfr trételgja 'Wood-cutter' (cf. Þjóð *Yt* 21[1]). — [3] *sældargramr* 'the prosperous ruler': *Sældar*- gen. sg. of *sæld* 'bliss, prosperity' often occurs as the first element in compounds in the adjectival sense 'happy, blessed, prosperous'; cf. *Fritzner*: *sældarlíf* 'fortunate life', *sældarstaðr* 'place to spend a happy life'. — [4] *Svíaríki* 'the kingdom of the Swedes': That is, the territory of the Svíar around Lake Mälaren in contrast to the southwestern territory of the Götar. — [6]

almenningi 'the conscripted army': Cf. *ONP: almenning* 3) 'men (and equipment) subject to military levy' and Þjóð*A Har*5/5[II].

Starkaðr (StarkSt *Vík* 23)

31. Gengum fram   í glam vápna,
    konungsmenn   kapp*i* gnægðir.
    Þar var Úlfr   ok Erpr lítinn;
    hjó ek brynjulauss   báðum höndum.

Gengum fram í glam vápna, konungsmenn gnægðir kapp*i*. Úlfr var þar ok Erpr lítinn; ek hjó brynjulauss báðum höndum.

We advanced in the clash of weapons, the king's men endowed with vigour. Úlfr was there and Erpr lítinn ('the Small'); I hewed without a mail-coat with both hands.

Ms.: **590b-c**[x](5r) (*Gautr*).

Reading: [4] kapp*i*: kappa 590b-c[x].

Editions: *Skj*: Anonyme digte og vers [XIII], E. 13. *Vers af Fornaldarsagaer: Af Gautrekssaga* α 7: AII, 329, BII, 350, *Skald* II, 189; *FSN* 3, 28, *Gautr* 1900, 25, *FSGJ* 4, 25; *Edd. Min.* 42.

Context: The battle is joined and Víkarr's champions fight very well. Starkaðr fights using both hands and is not wearing a coat of mail. The stanza is introduced with the words *sem hér segir* 'as it says here'.

Notes: [All]: This stanza is metrically mixed, with ll. 1, 3 and 5 being in *kviðuháttr*, and l. 7 in *fornyrðislag*. — [4] *kappi* 'with vigour': The sole ms. has *kappa* but the dat. sg. of *kapp* n. 'power, vigour' is required rather than the dat. sg. of *kappi* m. 'champion'. — [5, 6] *Úlfr … ok Erpr* 'Úlfr … and Erpr': Two of King Víkarr's warriors, mentioned here in the prose text and earlier in *Vík* 8/5 (*Gautr* 16).

Starkaðr (StarkSt *Vík* 24)

32. Réð Friðþjófr   friðar at biðja,
    þvíat Víkarr   vægði ekki,
    ok Starkaðr   St*ó*rverksson
    almátt fram   allan lagði.

Friðþjófr réð at biðja friðar, þvíat Víkarr vægði ekki, ok Starkaðr St*ó*rverksson lagði fram allan almátt.

Friðþjófr had to sue for peace because Víkarr did not yield and Starkaðr Stórverksson exerted all his mighty strength.

Ms.: **590b-c^x**(5r) (*Gautr*).

Reading: [6] Stórverksson: 'Sörverkzson' 590b-c^x.

Editions: *Skj*: Anonyme digte og vers [XIII], E. 13. *Vers af Fornaldarsagaer: Af Gautrekssaga* α 8: AII, 329-30, BII, 350, *Skald* II, 189; *FSN* 3, 29, *Gautr* 1900, 25, *FSGJ* 4, 26; *Edd. Min.* 42.

Context: King Friðþjófr is finally forced to ask Víkarr for mercy because his army's battle formation has disintegrated. The stanza is introduced with the words *svá segir Starkaðr* 'so says Starkaðr'.

Notes: [All]: Although this stanza is found only in 590b-c^x, 152 reproduces in its prose text (fol 199rb) the clause *en hann vægði ekki* 'but he did not yield', suggesting that its compiler knew the stanza but chose not to cite it. It is curious that the speaker refers to himself and his deeds in the third person in ll. 5-8. This stanza is in *kviðuháttr* metre. — [6] *Stórverksson*: This line is hypometrical. The second element of this pers. n. is usually spelled *-virkr* in the mss' prose texts, but here the spelling of the sole ms. is followed, including the form *-son*. *Skj* B and *Skald* substitute the more common *sonr*, but the nom. form without <r> is common; cf. *ANG* §395.1 and *Gautr* 26, Note to l. 5.

Starkaðr (StarkSt *Vík* 25)

33. Mér gaf Víkarr   valamálm,
    hring inn rauða,   er ek á hendi ber,
    mér þrímerking,   en ek Þrumu honum;
    fylgða ek fylki   fimtán sumur.

Víkarr gaf mér valamálm, hring inn rauða, er ek ber á hendi, mér þrímerking, en ek [gaf] honum Þrumu; ek fylgða fylki fimtán sumur.

Víkarr gave me costly metal, the red [gold] ring, which I wear on my arm, [a ring] three marks in weight for me, and I [gave] him Tromøy; I followed the ruler for fifteen summers.

Ms.: **590b-c^x**(5v) (*Gautr*).

Editions: *Skj*: Anonyme digte og vers [XIII], E. 13. *Vers af Fornaldarsagaer: Af Gautrekssaga* II 17: AII, 327, BII, 347, *Skald* II, 187; *FSN* 3, 31, *Gautr* 1900, 28, *FSGJ* 4, 28; *Edd. Min.* 42.

Context: The prose narrative concludes its account of the conflict between Friðþjófr and Víkarr with the latter dominant. The beginning of the *Gjafa-Refs þáttr* is then woven into the narrative, which introduces its protagonists, Neri (already sketchily present) and Refr, while keeping sight of King Víkarr and his champion Starkaðr. It tells that their friendship was strengthened with mutual gift-giving: Víkarr gave Starkaðr a gold bracelet of three marks' weight and Starkaðr reciprocated by giving Víkarr the island of Tromøy (Þruma), which King Haraldr of Agder had once given his father Stórvirkr.

This stanza is then cited (in 590b-c^x alone) as evidence that Starkaðr stayed with Víkarr for fifteen summers *sem hann segir* 'as he says'.

Notes: [All]: The metre of this stanza is *fornyrðislag*, but l. 2 is hypometrical. — [2] *valamálm* 'costly metal': The same cpd occurs in *Hyndl* 9/2. The first element, *vala-*, may derive from the gen. pl. of *Valir* 'Celtic southerners, French people', in the sense 'exotic, foreign, costly' or from *velja* 'choose' (cf. *LP*: *valamálmr*), in the sense 'choice, selected'.

Starkaðr (StarkSt *Vík* 26)

34. Fylgða ek fylki,   þeim er framast vissak,
    — þá unða ek bezt   ævi minni —
    áðr fór †ór†   — en því flögð ollu —
    hinzta sinni   til Hörðalands.

Ek fylgða fylki, þeim er vissak framast — þá unða ek bezt ævi minni —, áðr fór †ór† hinzta sinni til Hörðalands; en flögð ollu því.

I followed the ruler, the one I knew [to be] most distinguished — then I enjoyed my life the best — before I went … for the last time to Hordaland; but demons caused that.

Mss: **590b-c^x**(6r), 152(199vb) (*Gautr*).

Readings: [2] þeim er: *om.* 152   [3] þá: þá þá 152   [5] †ór†: verr 152   [6] því: 'þun'(?) 152   [8] -lands: 'lannz' 152.

Editions: *Skj*: Anonyme digte og vers [XIII], E. 13. *Vers af Fornaldarsagaer: Af Gautrekssaga* II 18: AII, 327, BII, 347; *Skald* II, 187; *FSN* 3, 35, *Gautr* 1900, 31, *FSGJ* 4, 31-2; *Edd. Min.* 42.

Context: The five following stanzas, *Vík* 26-30 (*Gautr* 34-8), are cited without intervening prose in two mss, 152 and 590b-c^x, at the end of the long prose account of how Starkaðr was persuaded by his foster-father, Hrosshárs-Grani, who is now revealed as the god Óðinn, to sacrifice Víkarr to him by hanging his lord from a tree. After this event, Starkaðr was reviled in Hordaland and fled Norway, spending a long time at Uppsala with the kings Eiríkr and Alrekr. The prose text presents *Vík* 26-30 as part of Starkaðr's response to King Alrekr's request to him to tell his life story: *þá orti Starkaðr kvæði, þat er heitir Víkarsbálkr: þar segir svá frá drápi Víkars konungs* 'then Starkaðr composed the poem that is called Víkarr's section; there it says thus about the killing of King Víkarr' (the wording of 590b-c^x).

Notes: [All]: Aside from l. 5, which is corrupt, the metre of this stanza is *fornyrðislag*. — [All]: This stanza probably alludes to the story of Starkaðr's killing of Víkarr by hanging him from a tree and piercing him with a reed-stalk in lieu of a spear. The hanging was presented to Starkaðr by Hrosshárs-Grani as a symbolic act, but it became a real sacrifice when the reed inexplicably became a spear and the noose of animal guts became a strong band. The story is told with some variation both in *Gautr* (*Gautr* 1900, 28-31) and in Saxo's *Gesta Danorum* (*Saxo* 2015, I, vi. 5. 6-7, pp. 380-3). It is likely that the kernel of the narrative is old, though how old is not possible to determine. Other aspects of the story, such as the hero's patronage by both Þórr and Óðinn, and the gifts that each god bestows on him, are also well established in Old Norse literature; for a review, see Turville-Petre (1964, 205-11). — [1] *ek fylgða fylki* 'I followed the ruler': This line echoes *Vík* 25/7 (*Gautr* 33) and the two stanzas may well have followed one another in *Vík* (there is now a good deal of intervening prose between them). — [5] *áðr fór* †*órt* 'before I went ...': Most eds accept the conjecture *áðr fórum vér* 'before we went', based in part on 152's *verr*, though this would necessitate a change from the speaker's 1st pers. sg. discourse in the first *helmingr*. — [6] *en flögð ollu því* 'but demons caused that': The line is reminiscent of the intercalary clause *bǫnd ollu því* 'the powers caused that' in Þjóð *Haustl* 17/2[III], although *flǫgð* are lesser beings than the pre-Christian gods (*bǫnd*). Starkaðr is here attributing the cause of his dastardly sacrifice of his own leader to *flǫgð*, translated here as 'demons' rather than the more specific 'ogresses, troll-women'. As the noun can refer to male as well as female supernatural beings (cf. Ingimarr Lv 1/1[II]), and may do so here, given the context, female causative agents have not been written into the translation. — [7] *hinzta* 'last': Both mss have *inzta*, but the <h> has been restored to achieve regular alliteration. — [8] *til Hörðalands* 'to Hordaland': According to the prose text, Víkarr had sailed north from Agder to Hordaland with a large army when they encountered unfavourable winds near a group of small islands. They tried divination to find out when the wind would turn and were informed that Óðinn demanded a human sacrifice. They cast lots to discover who it was fated to be and all signs pointed to Víkarr.

Starkaðr (StarkSt *Vík* 27)

35. Þess eyrendis,   at mér Þórr um skóp
    níðings nafn,   nauð margskonar;
    hlaut ek óhróðingr ilt at vinna.

Þess eyrendis, at Þórr um skóp mér nafn níðings, margskonar nauð; ek hlaut óhróðingr at vinna ilt.

With this result, that Þórr shaped for me the name of traitor, distress of many kinds; inglorious, I was fated to perform evil deeds.

Mss: **590b-c^x**(6r), 152(199vb) (*Gautr*).

Readings: [2] at mér Þórr: *so but with repetition of the whole phrase* 152, at mér þar 590b-c^x.

Editions: *Skj*: Anonyme digte og vers [XIII], E. 13. *Vers af Fornaldarsagaer: Af Gautrekssaga* II 19: AII, 327, BII, 347; *Skald* II, 187; *FSN* 3, 35, *Gautr* 1900, 31, *FSGJ* 4, 32; *Edd. Min.* 42.

Context: As for *Vík* 26.

Notes: [All]: This stanza has only six lines in both mss but no gaps to indicate lacunae, and has other irregularities as well. Both syntax and sense suggest that the first line might originally have been part of a main clause, the rest of which is missing, while l. 3 changes to *kviðuháttr*, leading *Gautr* 1900 and *FSGJ* to adjust ll. 2-3 to *at Þórr um skóp | mér níðings nafn*. — [All]: Again, as in the previous stanza, Starkaðr attributes the cause of his apparently inexplicable behaviour, changing from loyal champion to treacherous king-killer, to supernatural powers, in this case the god Þórr. — [1] *þess eyrendis* 'with this result': One has to assume that this line is part of an otherwise unpreserved clause, which presumably related to the struggle between Óðinn and Þórr to govern Starkaðr's fate, as reported in the prose text and also in Saxo. In particular when Óðinn granted him to live for three human lifespans, Þórr countered that *hann skal vinna níðingsverk á hverjum mannzalldri* 'he will perform a *níðingr*'s deed in each human lifespan' (cf. *Gautr* 1900, 29). The particular *níðingsverk* in this case is Starkaðr's killing of Víkarr. The word *eyrendi* here means 'result, consequence' (of a particular message or action), as it does in some eddic poetry (cf. *LP*: *ørendi*), including *Þry* 10/1 (*NK* 112), *Hefir þú erindi sem erfiði?* 'Have you got a result for your trouble?' — [3]: The metre of this line is *kviðuháttr*. — [3] *nafn níðings* 'the name of traitor': The Old Norse noun *níðingr* has a semi-legal sense and encompasses the semantic range 'wretch, worthless man, traitor, apostate', terms that indicate that the person in question was both socially and morally undesirable (cf. Meulengracht Sørensen 1983, 31-2). The noun is strongly condemnatory, and derives from the noun *níð* 'insult, shaming slander', itself a term defined in both early Norwegian and Icelandic law codes (*NGL* I, 70; *Grg* II, 392). In Starkaðr's case, his crime is that of treachery towards his lord, King Víkarr, whom he killed unintentionally in what he was led by Óðinn to believe was a mock sacrifice.

Starkaðr (StarkSt *Vík* 28)

36. Skylda ek Víkar   í viði hávum,
     Geirþjófs bana,   goðum um signa.
     Lagða ek geiri   gram til hjarta;
     þat er mér hermast   handaverka.

Ek skylda um signa Víkar, bana Geirþjófs, goðum í hávum viði. Ek lagða geiri til hjarta gram; þat er mér hermast handaverka.

I was obliged to dedicate Víkarr, the slayer of Geirþjófr, to the gods on the high tree. I thrust with the spear to the ruler's heart; that is for me the most regrettable of the deeds of my hands.

Mss: 590b-c^x(6r), 152(199vb) (*Gautr*).

Readings: [2] í viði hávum: ná við hofum 152   [4] um: *om.* 152   [5] geiri: geir 152
[7] hermast: harmast 152.

Editions: *Skj*: Anonyme digte og vers [XIII], E. 13. *Vers af Fornaldarsagaer: Af Gautrekssaga* II 20: AII, 327-8, BII, 347, *Skald* II, 187; *FSN* 3, 35, *Gautr* 1900, 31-2, *FSGJ* 4, 32; *Edd. Min.* 42.

Context: As for *Gautr* 34.

Notes: [All]: Starkaðr again refers to external forces, though without specifying which they are, as the causes of his action in sacrificing Víkarr to the gods. The use of the verb *signa* 'dedicate, consecrate' (l. 4) indicates as much, as does the manner of the sacrifice, which follows the pattern that Óðinn is said to have established both for himself (cf. *Hávm* 138-41) and for those heroes that he took for himself; on this subject see Turville-Petre (1964, 43-8; *ARG* I, 409-12, II, 49-50; Simek 1993, 242, 249). Characteristic of Odinic sacrifices are the use of a spear to pierce the victim and the mode of sacrifice, hanging on a tree, which is attested both from medieval ethnographic literature, such as Adam of Bremen's account of the sacrifices at the temple at Uppsala (Schmeidler 1917, 259-60), and from texts like *Hávm*. — [3] *bana Geirþjófs* 'the slayer of Geirþjófr': Geirþjófr was one of three brothers, mentioned earlier in *Gautr*, with whom Víkarr fought for dominance over disputed territory. Geirþjófr is said to have been king of Opplandene; cf. *Gautr* 25/5-8. — [4] *signa* 'dedicate': Although this verb (ultimately from Lat. *signare* 'dedicate, consecrate') appears more frequently in late Christian skaldic poetry, it also occurs in eddic poems (*Sigrdr* 8/1, *Hyndl* 28/10), as well as in Egill Lv 5/8^V (*Eg* 9), in contexts that are probably early and not obviously Christian. — [7] *hermast* 'the most regrettable': Some eds adopt the spelling of 152, *harmast* (so *FSN*; *Gautr* 1900; *Edd. Min.*; *FSGJ*).

Starkaðr (StarkSt *Vík* 29)

37. Þaðan vappaðak   viltar brautir,
    Hörðum leiðr,   með huga illan,
    hringa vanr   ok hróðrkvæða,
    dróttinlauss,   dapr alls hugar.

Þaðan vappaðak viltar brautir, leiðr Hörðum, með illan huga, vanr hringa ok hróðrkvæða, dróttinlauss, dapr alls hugar.

From there I wandered bewildering ways, hateful to the Hǫrðar, with a dark mind, lacking in rings and poems of praise, lordless, depressed in my whole mind.

Mss: 590b-c^x(6v), 152(199vb-200ra) (*Gautr*).

Readings: [1] vappaðak: *so* 152, vappaði ek 590b-c^x   [2] brautir: götur ('gótr') 152   [5] hringa: hrings 152   [6] hróðr-: *so* 152, hróðs 590b-c^x.

Editions: *Skj*: Anonyme digte og vers [XIII], E. 13. *Vers af Fornaldarsagaer: Af Gautrekssaga* II 21: AII, 328, BII, 348, *Skald* II, 187; *FSN* 3, 35-6, *Gautr* 1900, 32, *FSGJ* 4, 32; *Edd. Min.* 43.

Context: As for *Vík* 26.

Notes: [All]: Lines 3, 5 and 7 are in *kviðuháttr* metre, the rest in *fornyrðislag* (but see Note to l. 1 below). — [All]: Starkaðr's self-depiction as a social outcast, depressed and lacking the most valuable benefits of a courtly life, especially material wealth, the opportunity to compose poetry and the company of a lord, is strongly reminiscent of similar self-presentation in the Old English poems *Deor*, ll. 35-41 and (without the poetry theme) *The Wanderer* ll. 20-9. — [1] *þaðan* 'from there': As Ranisch comments (*Gautr* 1900, 32 n.), this adv. may be a later addition to the line, because otherwise the line is hypometrical. — [1] *vappaðak* 'I wandered': The verb *vappa* 'wander aimlessly, go unsteadily' is uncommon in Old Norse, but cf. Egill Lv 39/7^V (*Eg* 69). — [2] *viltar brautir* 'bewildering ways': *Viltar* 'bewildering' is f. acc. pl. of an adj. formed from the p. p. of *villa* 'falsify, lead astray'. Ms. 152 has *götur* 'paths' where 579b-c^x has *brautir*. — [3] *leiðr Hörðum* 'hateful to the Hǫrðar': Starkaðr was hateful to the Hǫrðar, the people of Hordaland (ON Hǫrðaland), because it was there that he killed Víkarr. According to the prose text (*Gautr* 1900, 30): *ok af þessu verki varð hann fyrst landflótti af Hǫrðalandi* 'and because of this deed he was first banished from Hordaland'. — [5-6] *vanr hringa ok hróðrkvæða* 'lacking in rings and poems of praise': The cpd *hróðrkvæði* 'poem of praise' is a *hap. leg.*, although its two component elements are well attested. It is understood here as an example of the rhetorical figure *hysteron proteron*, in which that which should come last (rings as a reward for praise-poems) is put first, emphasising that Starkaðr neither has the opportunity to compose praise-poems nor to be rewarded for them. *LP*: *hróðrkvæði*, on the other hand, assumes the cpd refers to poetry or generally laudatory opinions expressed by others about Starkaðr, though this seems less likely given that Starkaðr's poetic skills are attested in a number of Old Norse sources and in Saxo (cf. Clunies Ross 2006a). It is also possible that *vanr hringa ok hróðrkvæða* could refer to a general lack of courtly culture in the environment in which Starkaðr found himself.

Starkaðr (StarkSt *Vík* 30)

38. Nú sótta ek   til Svíþjóðar,
       Ynglinga sjöt,   til Uppsala.
       Hér láta mik,   sem ek lengi mun,
       þöglan þul,   þjóðans synir.

Nú sótta ek sjöt Ynglinga, til Svíþjóðar, til Uppsala. Synir þjóðans láta mik hér þöglan þul, sem ek mun lengi.

I now sought the residence of the Ynglingar, [made my way] to Sweden, to Uppsala. The prince's sons allow me [to stay] here [as] a silent poet, as I shall [be] for a long time.

Mss: 590b-c^x(6v) (*Gautr*); 152(200ra).

Readings: [3] sjöt: 'sið' 152   [6] ek: *om.* 152.

Editions: *Skj*: Anonyme digte og vers [XIII], E. 13. *Vers af Fornaldarsagaer: Af Gautrekssaga* II 22: AII, 328, BII, 348, *Skald* II, 187, *FF* §27, *NN* §5; *FSN* 3, 36, *Gautr* 1900, 32, *FSGJ* 4, 33; *Edd. Min.* 43.

Context: As for *Gautr* 34.

Notes: [2] *til Svípjóðar* 'to Sweden': In Old Norse the name designated the region around Lake Mälaren in the east, not the whole of modern Sweden. — [3] *sjöt Ynglinga* 'the residence of the Ynglingar': The Ynglingar were the ancient ruling house of the Svíar, based in Old Uppsala, and celebrated in Þjóð Yt^I, which gives the names of twenty Swedish Ynglingar at Uppsala and six rulers over Norway. Legendary and historical sources claim that the Norwegian royal house that was dominant in the historical period descended from the Swedish dynasty. The pl. form *Ynglingar* appears only here in Old Norse poetry, although the sg. *ynglingr* 'ruler, prince' is more common; for a discussion, see Introduction to Þjóð Yt^I. — [5] *láta* 'allow': *Skj* B and *Skald* emend this, the reading of both mss, to *létu* 'they allowed', although the pres. tense makes good sense. — [6] *mun* 'shall [be]': The reading of both mss; some eds prefer the variant form *man* (common in Old Norwegian, cf. *ANG* §524.2) with the same sense (so *Gautr* 1900, *Edd. Min.* and *FSGJ*, following *FSN*). — [7] *pöglan þul* 'a silent poet': This line is in *kviðuháttr*. The adj. *þǫgull* 'silent, discreet' expresses a quality regarded as praiseworthy in early Nordic society, and is associated with the qualities of wisdom and discretion; cf. *Hávm* 6/4, 15/1. Here, however, the phrase *þǫgull þulr* implies a negation of a poet's normal function of praising his patron at court. The sense to be attributed to *þulr* here is debatable (see Halvorsen 1976a, and, most recently, Poole 2010a). Where it occurs in the Poetic Edda corpus it usually means 'wise man, sage' (cf. *LT*: *þulr*), and frequently refers to supernatural beings who have lived a long time, as Starkaðr also has (e.g. *Hávm* 5-6 (*NK* 39): *at három þul | hlæðu aldregi* 'never laugh at a hoary sage'). The noun's other possible meaning, 'poet', is (probably) supported by *Hávm* 111/1-2 (*NK* 34): *Mál er at þylia | þular stóli á* 'It is time to recite on the poet's [*or* sage's] seat' (at the beginning of the Loddfáfnir section of *Hávm*) and by two examples in the skaldic corpus, Rv Lv 29/1^II, where Rǫgnvaldr uses the word of himself, and HaukrV *Ísldr* 18/5^IV, where it is used of Þorleifr jarlsskáld. ON *þulr* and its cognate, OE *þyle* (cf. *Beowulf* ll. 1165, 1456, where it is used of Unferð, spokesman for the Danish king Hroðgar and formal challenger of Beowulf, and in vernacular glosses where it is given as equivalent to Lat. *orator* 'orator' or *scurra* 'buffoon, jester'), both seem to have covered the roles of 'spokesman, sage' and 'poet' at the courts of kings, and then perhaps in Old Norse to have later lost the sense of 'spokesman, sage', to judge by the two skaldic examples, which are of C12th date (or possibly later, in the case of *Ísldr*). Thus the external evidence could support either meaning in *Gautr* 38/7. The poem itself in its present form is probably no earlier than the two skaldic examples, but its creator could have been drawing on older material or he could have been consciously archaising. In support of the sense 'poet', Starkaðr refers to himself in the following stanza (*Gautr* 39/8) as *greppr jöfurs* 'the prince's poet', and this role is supported by external evidence, particularly from Saxo, where it is claimed (*Saxo* 2015, I, vi. 5. 6, pp. 382-3) that Óðinn made Starkaðr famous both for his strength of spirit and also for his poetry: *non solum animi fortitudine, sed etiam condendorum carminum peritia* 'not only for the strength of his spirit, but also for his knowledge of the songs needing to be composed' (ed.'s translation), the implication being that Óðinn endowed Starkaðr with the power of certain kinds of poetry, probably magical, in order to bring about Víkarr's death. Poole (2010a, 253-6) offers a review of the Old Norse representation of Starkaðr as a *þulr*.

Starkaðr (StarkSt *Vík* 31)

39. Hér settu mik   sveina milli,
    heldr hæðinn*a*   ok hvítbránn*a*.
    Skelkja skatnar   ok sk*au*p draga,
    ófs óframir,   at jöfurs greppi.

Hér settu mik milli sveina, heldr hæðinn*a* ok hvítbránn*a*. Skatnar skelkja ok draga sk*au*p, ófs óframir, at greppi jöfurs.

Here they set me between serving men, rather mocking and white-eyelashed. The fellows mock and, exceedingly cautious, hold the prince's poet up to ridicule.

Ms.: **590b-c**[x](6v) (*Gautr*).

Readings: [3] hæðinn*a*: hæðinn 590b-c[x]   [4] hvítbránn*a*: hvítbránn 590b-c[x]   [6] sk*au*p: 'skop' 590b-c[x].

Editions: *Skj*: Anonyme digte og vers [XIII], E. 13. Vers af Fornaldarsagaer: Af Gautrekssaga II 23: AII, 328, BII, 348, *Skald* II, 187, *FF* §28; *FSN* 3, 36-7, *Gautr* 1900, 33, *FSGJ* 4, 33; *Edd. Min.* 43.

Context: A short prose paragraph in 590b-c[x] separates *Vík* 30 (*Gautr* 38) from the final three stanzas of *Vík*, which are cited after this without prose intervention. The prose text first comments on Starkaðr's self-condemnation of his killing of Víkarr and then on his situation at Uppsala, where twelve berserks who were employed as mercenaries (*málamenn*) were very aggressive and mocking towards him. The prose text further states that Starkaðr was silent (*þǫgull*, cf. *Gautr* 37/7) – presumably not responding to their insults – but the berserks called him a reborn giant (*endrborinn jǫtunn*) and a traitor (*níðingr*), *svá sem hér segir* 'as it says here'.

Notes: [All]: The three final stanzas of *Vík* (at least as it occurs in 590b-c^x) are not found in either 152 or papp11^x. — [All]: There is some resemblance between *Vík* 31-3 (*Gautr* 39-41) and part of one of Starkatherus's poems in Saxo (*Saxo* 2015, I, vi. 9. 4, pp. 424-6), in which the aged hero contrasts his previously favourable reception at Fróði's court with his present despised position among the riff-raff in the hall. — [2] *sveina* 'serving men': *Sveinn* is probably used here in the sense 'servant, attendant' (cf. *Fritzner: sveinn* 4) rather than 'youth, lad', although the latter cannot be ruled out, especially if it has a pejorative edge. — [3-4] *heldr hæðinn*a *ok hvítbránn*a 'rather mocking and white-eyelashed': The two adjectives *hæðinn* 'mocking' and *hvítbránn* 'having white eyelashes' are in the m. nom. sg. in the only ms. of this stanza, but the noun *sveina* 'serving men' (l. 2), which they probably qualify, is m. acc. pl. For this reason, following *Edd. Min.* (reportedly following a suggestion of Axel Olrik), *Skj* B and *Skald*, this edn emends each adj. to m. acc. pl. It is not clear why the serving men should be described as having white eyelashes. However, *Án* 5 may throw some light on the matter, because the rare conjunction of *heldr* and *hæðinn* 'rather mocking' occurs there also in l. 7 (cf. *LP: hæðinn*), as does the adj. *hvíthaddaðr* 'fair-haired' (l. 3). The stanza describes how a group of girls mocks Án Bow-bender because of his outlandish clothing. It is possible that pale hair or eyelashes was somehow associated with mockery, though exactly how or why is unclear. — [6] *skaup* 'ridicule': With *Skj* B and *Skald*, this edn adopts *CPB*'s suggested emendation (*CPB* II, 548) of the ms.'s 'skop', which does not make sense in this context. — [7] *ófs óframir* 'exceedingly cautious': This edn understands this adjectival phrase, referring to Starkaðr's insulters, as ironic, possibly litotic. *Ófs* 'exceedingly' is often used as an intensifier with adjectives, while *óframr* 'cautious' is well attested (cf. Sigv *Berv* 15/3^II). Kock (*FF* §28) suggests *ófs óframir* means *som stora uslingar* 'as great villains'. The ms.'s 'óframer' is interpreted as *oframmir* by *Skj* B in the sense 'very strong', and the whole phrase understood to mean *stærke i deres overdrevne adfærd* 'strong in their exaggerated behaviour'. — [8] *greppi* 'poet': This noun sometimes means 'man' in poetry, but much more often is one of several terms for 'poet'; cf., among others, Bragi *Troll* 1/4^III, Þorn *Harkv* 18/3^I and Anon *Nkt* 1/3^II.

Starkaðr (StarkSt *Vík* 32)

40. Sjá þykkjaz þeir   á sjálfum mér
    jötunkuml   átta handa,
    er Hlórriði   fyr hamar norðan
    Hergríms bana   höndum rænti.

Þeir þykkjaz sjá jötunkuml átta handa á mér sjálfum, er Hlórriði rænti bana Hergríms höndum fyr norðan hamar.

They think they can see the giant-marks of the eight arms on myself where Hlórriði <= Þórr> tore off the arms of Hergrímr's slayer [= Starkaðr] north of the crag.

Ms.: **590b-c**^x(6v) (*Gautr*).

Editions: *Skj*: Anonyme digte og vers [XIII], E. 13. *Vers af Fornaldarsagaer: Af Gautrekssaga* II 24: AII, 328, BII, 348, *Skald* II, 188, *FF* §29; *FSN* 3, 37, *Gautr* 1900, 33, *FSGJ* 4, 34; *Edd. Min.* 43.

Context: As for *Gautr* 39.

Notes: [All]: This stanza refers to an episode in Starkaðr's early life, also probably alluded to in the use of the word *tjálgur* 'branches' in *Vík* 5/2 (*Gautr* 13). This episode is known to Saxo (*Saxo* 2015, I, vi. 5. 2, pp. 378-9) and the composer of the prose *Gautr* (*Gautr* 1900, 11-13), as well as to the composer of the redaction of *Heiðr* in UppsUB R715^x, though in each case the story is slightly different, the main difference being that in some accounts an older, additional generation of giantlike beings with the names of Starkaðr and Stórvirkr precedes that of the Starkaðr central to *Gautr* and *Vík*. Saxo reports that Starkaðr was thought to have been born a giant with six arms. The god Þórr cut off four of them to give Starkaðr human form. Line 4 of this stanza claims he originally had eight arms, and the beginning of *Heiðr* according to R715^x gives the same number (*Heiðr* 1924, 90; *Heiðr* 1960, 67), but attributes this peculiarity to the older Starkaðr Áludrengr (see below). Vetrl Lv 1/3^III lists Starkaðr as one of the giants that Þórr attacked and slew. Earlier in the prose text of *Gautr* (*Gautr* 1900, 12) the connection of Starkaðr's giant family with Þórr is established, though the motif of the god's tearing off Starkaðr's extra arms is not mentioned. It is told there that Starkaðr's father Stórvirkr was the son of an exceedingly wise giant named Starkaðr Áludrengr, and a woman named Álfhildr, daughter of King Álfr of Álfheimr, whom he abducted from her father. Þórr killed Starkaðr senior at the insistence of King Álfr because of this abduction. A similar account appears in the R715^x version of *Heiðr* (*Heiðr* 1924, 91; *Heiðr* 1960, 66-7). — [3]: This line is in *kviðuháttr*. — [3-4] *jötunkuml átta handa* 'the giant-marks of the eight arms': That is, the scars on his body where Þórr had torn off Starkaðr's superfluous arms. They are giant marks in that they indicate Starkaðr's giant nature; *jötunkuml* is a *hap. leg.* — [5-8]: This *helmingr* refers to an event in Starkaðr's life which is not attested elsewhere except in the R715^x version of *Heiðr*, and there it is associated with Starkaðr Áludrengr. Ms. R715^x tells that a certain Hergrímr hálftröll 'Half-troll' abducted a woman named Ǫgn Álfasprengi from Jǫtunheimar, while Starkaðr Áludrengr, to whom she had been betrothed, was away in the north beyond the rivers Élivágar (cf. *Vafþr* 31/1, *SnE* 2005, 9, 10). When Starkaðr returned he challenged Hergrímr to single combat for the woman. They fought *við inn efsta fors at Eiði* 'by the uppermost waterfall at Eið' and Starkaðr killed Hergrímr though he did not get back his betrothed, who committed suicide. It is not said that Þórr had anything to do with the Hergrímr episode, as ll. 5-8 of this stanza seem to imply. However, this narrative is very similar to another, told shortly after the first in the R715^x version of *Heiðr*, in which Þórr kills Starkaðr because he abducted another woman, Álfhildr, against her father's wishes. On this, see Note to [All] above. — [5] *Hlórriði* 'Hlórriði <= Þórr>': On this name for the god Þórr, see Note to Þul Þórs l. 5^III. — [6] *fyr norðan hamar* 'north of the crag': It is not certain whether this is a reference to a particular place or to a generalised rocky, northern setting appropriate to giants. *Skj* B and *Skald* capitalise Hamarr as a p. n. It is possible that R715ˣ's location of the fight between Starkaðr and Hergrímr as 'by the uppermost waterfall at Eið' refers to the same place; Eið 'isthmus' is a common p. n. (see Note to Sigv *Austv* 2/1¹).

Starkaðr (StarkSt *Vík* 33)

41. Hlæja rekkar, er mik sjá,
    ljótan skolt,   langa trjónu,
    hangar tjálgur, hár úlfgrátt,
    hrjúfan háls,   húð jótraða.

Rekkar, er sjá mik, hlæja ljótan skolt, langa trjónu, hangar tjálgur, úlfgrátt hár, hrjúfan háls, jótraða húð.

Men who see me laugh at [my] ugly snout, long muzzle, dangling branches, wolf-grey hair, scabby neck, scarred skin.

Ms.: 590b-cˣ(6v) (*Gautr*).

Reading: [5] hangar: haugar 590b-cˣ.

Editions: *Skj*: Anonyme digte og vers [XIII], E. 13. *Vers af Fornaldarsagaer: Af Gautrekssaga* II 25: AII, 328, BII, 348, *Skald* II, 188, *NN* §§2613, 3363; *FSN* 3, 37, *Gautr* 1900, 33, *FSGJ* 4, 34; *Edd. Min.* 43.

Context: As for *Gautr* 39.

Notes: [All]: This is the final stanza of *Vík*, according to 590b-cˣ, and it is in a mixture of *fornyrðislag* and *kviðuháttr*; ll. 1 and 5 are *fornyrðislag*, ll. 2 and 6 are hypometrical, while ll. 3 and 7 are *kviðuháttr*. Shortly after its citation the prose text in all mss of the longer *Gautr* brings the story of Starkaðr to a rather abrupt end, with a few summary remarks about his later career as a viking, in which he was always victorious. As a concluding stanza to Starkaðr's life-history, *Vík* 33 is rather unconvincing; it is a list of Starkaðr's repulsive physical traits, which one might expect to lead on to further stanzas describing his various adventures, but they do not, leaving one to speculate that there may have been more stanzas not used in the prose saga. — [All]: The list of Starkaðr's physical traits is strongly suggestive of the animal as much as the human. *Skoltr* (the younger form of *skolptr*) 'snout' (l. 3) and *trjóna* 'muzzle' (l. 4) suggest the long face of an animal, like a bear or a wolf; *skoltr* is used in two places in Old Norse poetry to refer to figure-heads on ships, possibly dragon heads (cf. HSt *Rst* 14/5¹ and Valg *Har* 10/5ᴵᴵ). The adj. *úlfgrár* 'wolf-grey' (l. 6) contributes to this picture, not only by indicating Starkaðr's age, but also by drawing a comparison with a wolf, an animal frequently symbolic of both physical aggression and the position of social outcast in Old Norse and other Germanic literature (cf. Hildr Lv1ᴵ and Jacoby 1974). The same adj. is used by Egill Skallagrímsson in *Arbj* 7/5^V (*Eg* 103) of his own grey head. Both Egill and Starkaðr are figures of great physical strength but also have supernatural connections; the animal qualities ascribed to them may be a way of symbolising the mixture of these two sources of their power (cf. Clunies Ross 2015, 83-4). — [1-2]: These two lines show metrical and alliterative irregularities. Both *Gautr* 1900 and *Edd. Min.* replace *rekkar* 'men' in l. 1 with *menn* 'men' to regularise both metre and alliteration, while *Skj* B addresses the metrical irregularity of l. 2 by indicating that words must be missing between *mik* 'me' and *sjá* 'see'. *Skald*, on the other hand, keeps *rekkar* in l. 1 and replaces *mik* 'me' in l. 2 with *raum*, from *raumr* 'large, ugly person, giant' (*NN* §2613). — [5] *hangar tjálgur* 'dangling branches': On the likely implications of the word *tjálgur* 'branches', see *Vík* 5/2 (*Gautr* 13) and Note. The proposed adj. *hangar* 'dangling' (from **hangr* 'hanging down', not otherwise attested) is an emendation of the ms.'s *haugar* 'mounds' which does not make sense in context. It was first proposed in *FSN* and has been adopted by all subsequent eds. — [8] *jótraða húð* 'scarred skin': Starkaðr mentions his scars of battle elsewhere in *Vík* 15/9-10 (*Gautr* 23).

Gríms saga loðinkinna

Edited by Beatrice La Farge

Introduction

Gríms saga loðinkinna 'The Saga of Grímr Hairy-cheek' (*GrL*) is a short *fornaldarsaga*, which continues the family history of Ketill hœngr 'Salmon' by recounting the adventures of his son, Grímr, by the giantess-like Hrafnhildr, daughter of a Saami man named Brúni. Together with *Ketils saga hœngs* (*Ket*), *Áns saga bogsveigis* (*Án*) 'Saga of Án Bow-bender' and *Ǫrvar-Odds saga* (*Ǫrv*) 'Saga of Arrow-Oddr', this group of *fornaldarsögur* is often referred to as the sagas of the Hrafnistumenn, because all of their protagonists are claimed in their sagas to have come from the island of Hrafnista (Ramsta), off the coast of Namdalen, Norway. Although in their extant forms none of these sagas are preserved in mss earlier than the fifteenth century (except for two versions of *Ǫrv*, Holm perg 7 4° and AM 344 4°), there is reason to assume that some at least of the subject-matter, including some of the poetry recorded in the sagas, is older. See Introductions to the stanzas from *Án*, *Ket* and *Ǫrv* for references to the Hrafnistumenn in other Old Norse sources. In line with the normalisation policy of this edition, the texts of the stanzas edited here are normalised to a standard appropriate to Icelandic of the period 1250-1300.

GrL is extant in two late medieval mss plus one fifteenth-century fragment of a single leaf, AM 567 IV 4° (567IV). The saga contains seven stanzas, all of which appear in the two oldest complete mss of the saga, AM 343 a 4° (343a) of c. 1450-75 and AM 471 4° (471) of c. 1450-1500. As 343a also provides the best readings, its text has been adopted as the base ms. for this edition. Readings are also given from 471 and occasionally, when it has the better text, adopted from there. There are, in addition, more than forty paper mss from the seventeenth century and later, some of whose readings have been cited from time to time in the Notes, chief among them GKS 1006 fol[x] (1006[x]), AM 173 fol[x] (173[x]), AM 340 4°[x] (340[x]), two codices from the seventeenth century bound together as AM 109 a 8°[x] (109a I[x] and 109a II[x]; cf. Anderson 1990, 2, 73-5, 145), and AM 342 4°[x] (342[x]). On the four redactions or ms. traditions and their oldest representatives see Introduction to *Ket*. The ms. NKS 1778 b 4°[x] contains stanzas which are radically different from those contained in other mss; however, it is uncertain whether they represent a genuine medieval tradition or were not perhaps composed by Björn Jónsson á Skarðsá (d. 1655; see Anderson 1990, 271-8, 426-8). A detailed discussion of the ms. tradition can be found in Anderson (1990, 1-13). Although not all seven stanzas appear in all the mss, the order in which they appear never varies.

The stanzas edited below are all composed in *fornyrðislag* metre. The first five stanzas constitute a hostile dialogue (*senna*) between Grímr and two beings described in the saga as troll-women (*tröllkonur*), Feima and Kleima, and has parallels in several other *fornaldarsögur*, as well as in *HHj* (cf. Introduction to sts 1-5 and Notes to *GrL* 1 and 5/8; cf. *HjǪ* ch. 12, *FSGJ* 4, 205-7; *Frið* ch. 3, *FSGJ* 3, 87-8). A similar hostile exchange appears in *Ket* ch. 5 (*FSGJ* 2, 168-72); here it is Grímr's father Ketill hœngr who sails away on a hunting and fishing expedition during a famine and meets a troll-woman, Forað, whom he kills with one of the arrows known as *Gusisnautar* 'Gusir's gifts'; it is with one of these same arrows that Grímr kills Kleima (*GrL* ch. 1, *FSGJ* 2, 188). *GrL* 6 and 7 are spoken by Grímr in an episode which also has parallels in *Ket* (see Introduction to sts 6-7). In the corresponding episodes in *Ket* Grímr's father Ketill also speaks several stanzas.

The following editions have been cited here: *FSN* 2, 145-6, 154-5, *FSGJ* 2, 186-8, Anderson 1990, 60-1, 66, 111-12, 121-2, 444-5, 448-9, 196; *Edd. Min.* 85, 96.

Introduction to sts 1-5

One year, when there is a famine, Grímr sails north to Finnmǫrk (Finnmark, land of the Saami) to fish and hunt. In the middle of the night, he is awakened by the sound of laughter. He goes down to the shore and finds two troll-women shaking the stem and the stern post of his boat as if they were going to pull it apart. These five stanzas contain insults and threats which Grímr loðinkinni and the troll-women Feima and Kleima hurl at one another in *GrL* ch. 1 (*FSGJ* 2, 186-8).

Grímr (Gríml Lv 1)

1. Hvat heita þær hrauns íbúur,
 er skaða vilja skipi mínu?
 Ykr hefik einar sénar
 ámátligastar at yfirlitum.

Hvat heita þær íbúur hrauns, er vilja skaða skipi mínu? Ykr einar hefik sénar ámátligastar at yfirlitum.

What are the names of those female inhabitants of the lava field [TROLL-WOMEN], who want to harm my ship? You two alone are the most overwhelming in appearance I have [ever] seen.

Mss: **343a**(58r), 471(57v) (*GrL*).

Editions: *Skj*: Anonyme digte og vers [XIII], E. 9. *Vers af Fornaldarsagaer: Af Gríms saga loðinkinna* I 1: AII, 287, BII, 308, *Skald* II, 163; *FSN* 2, 145, *FSGJ* 2, 186-7, Anderson 1990, 60, 111, 444; *Edd. Min.* 85.

Context: This stanza is introduced by the words: *Grímr mælti ok kvað vísu* 'Grímr spoke and uttered a stanza'.

Notes: [All]: The troll-women are described in a manner traditional for troll-women and giantesses: they are 'inhabitants of the lava-field' (cf. Note to l. 2) and are overwhelmingly hideous in appearance; cf. Schulz (2004, 147-53); *Ket* 16. They are furthermore not the only such beings in Old Norse literature who attack the ships of the hero: in a similar episode in *Ket* ch. 3 (*FSGJ* 2, 158) Grímr's father Ketill hœngr also sails to Finnmark; he too awakens when a troll-woman shakes the stem of his ship; in *HjQ* (*FSGJ* 4, 207) nine sea-ogresses tear the ships apart; in other sagas giants or giantesses attack ships at sea (*Frið*, *FSGJ* 3, 87; *Qrv* 1888, 44, 46); cf. *HHj* 13, 18-19, 23, 26. — [2] *þær íbúur hrauns* 'those female inhabitants of the lava field [TROLL-WOMEN]': This kenning is not attested elsewhere, but there are synonymous kennings for 'giant' in other texts: *hraunbúi* 'lava-dweller' (*Hym* 38/5, *HHj* 25/5), *hraundrengr* 'rock-gentleman' (Þjóð *Haustl* 17/6^III). While the f. *íbúa* 'female inhabitant' is a *hap. leg.*, the corresponding m. noun *íbúi* 'male inhabitant' is attested in *Greg* (Unger 1877, 1, 393). — [7] *ámátligastar* 'the most overwhelming': In poetry the adj. *ámátligr* is only used of giants and a valkyrie (*HHund I* 38/3) and occurs in a similar stanza in *HjQ*, in which the hero of that saga asks a giantess who she is (*HjQ* 11, *FSGJ* 4, 205); in Þul *Jǫtna I* 6/7^III it is also predicated of giants. *Ámátligr* is derived from the noun *máttr* 'might, strength' and the prefix *á-* has intensifying character, hence *ámátligr* can be translated as 'overwhelmingly strong'. It is sometimes interpreted as meaning 'abominable, frightful' (cf. Gering 1903: *á-mátlegr*; Heggstad *et al.* 2008: *ámátligr*; *ÍO*: *ámát(t)legur*).

Feima (Feima Lv 1)

2. Feima ek heiti;   fædd var ek norðarla,
    Hrímnis dóttir   ór háfjalli.
    Hér er systir mín   hálfu fremri
    Kleima at nafni   komin til sjóvar.

Ek heiti Feima; ek var fædd norðarla, dóttir Hrímnis, ór háfjalli. Hér er systir mín, hálfu fremri, Kleima at nafni, komin til sjóvar.

I am called Feima; I was born in northern parts, daughter of Hrímnir <giant>, from the high mountain. Here my sister, twice as courageous, Kleima by name, has come to the sea-shore.

Mss: **343a**(58r), 471(57v) (*GrL*).

Editions: *Skj*: Anonyme digte og vers [XIII], E. 9. *Vers af Fornaldarsagaer: Af Gríms saga loðinkinna I* 2: AII, 288, BII, 309; *Skald* II, 163-4; *FSN* 2, 145, *FSGJ* 2, 187, Anderson 1990, 60-1, 111, 444-5; *Edd. Min.* 85.

Context: In the saga this stanza follows *GrL* 1 and is introduced by the words: *Sú kvað vísu, er nær honum stóð* 'The one [i.e. the giantess] who stood near him spoke a stanza'.

Notes: [1-2]: With the exception of the name *Feima* these lines are identical in wording to *Ket* 17/1-2, in which the troll-woman Forað identifies herself (in a similar episode) in answer to a question put to her by Grímr's father Ketill. — [1] *Feima*: Several mss (1006[x], 173[x], 342[x], 109a II[x]) offer the reading *Finna* 'Saami woman', a variant which makes use of the associations between the north and the Finnar (Saami people), who were credited with magical powers (see Nesheim 1970, 7-14; cf. the power ascribed to the father of Feima and Kleima in *GrL* 4). Occasionally one and the same figure is described both as giant and Saami, for example the father of Snjófríðr 'Snow-Beauty' in *HHárf* ch. 35 (*ÍF* 26, 125-7). Snjófríðr herself is called *finna* in Anon *Mhkv* 11/6[III]. Nevertheless *Feima* is the preferred reading, not only because it occurs in the two oldest mss but also because it rhymes with *Kleima*, a name which only occurs here: there are several other Old Norse examples of siblings whose names rhyme with one another (cf. *Kommentar* III, 870 and a further example in *Gautr, FSGJ* 4, 4-5). The word *feima* occurs as a name in *Rþ* 25/6 (one of the daughters of Karl, the progenitor of the peasant class) and is used elsewhere as a poetic term for 'woman' (*LP*: *feima*). The etymology of the word is unclear (*AEW*: *feima*), but in *Skm* the word *feima* is said to connote shyness (*SnE* 1998, I, 107; cf. Note to Þul *Kvenna I* l. 4[III]). If the name *Feima* in *GrL* evokes such associations then it is manifestly ironic, since it stands in great contrast to the bold and 'forward' behaviour of the two giantesses, cf. Feima's description of her sister Kleima as *hálfu fremri* 'twice as courageous' (as herself). — [2, 4] *ek var fædd norðarla; ór háfjalli* 'I was born in northern parts; from the high mountain': An origin in the north and in the mountains is typical of giants, cf. such kennings for 'giant' as *bergbúi* 'mountain dweller' *Hym* 2/1 or *fjallbúi* (same meaning) in *Ǫrv* 89/1. — [3] *dóttir Hrímnis* 'daughter of Hrímnir <giant>': The name Hrímnir is well-attested as a common name for a giant; the earliest example occurs in the giantess-kenning *drós Hrímnis* 'woman of Hrímnir' in Eil *Þdr* 18/6[III]. Since the name *Hrímnir* is derived from *hrím* which can mean both '(hoar)frost' and 'soot', it is not clear whether *Hrímnir* means 'Frosty' or 'Sooty'; cf. Þul *Jǫtna I* 1/5[III]. See Note to *Ket* 13/1-3. — [7] *Kleima*: This name is considered to be etymologically related to the Old Norse verb *kleima* 'besmear, besmirch' (*HálfdEyst* ch. 16, *FSGJ* 4, 271), and to the synonymous verb *klæma* used figuratively in the sense 'shame, mock' (*AEW*: *kleima*; *ÍO*: *1 kleima*). In New Norwegian dialects the noun *kleima* denotes something 'sticky' or a person who is slow (cf. also the New Norwegian verb *kleima* 'stick'), while the noun *kleim* variously refers to a person who is 'forward' or 'clumsy' (cf. Ross 1895-1913: *kleim*; Aasen 2003: *kleima* and *Kleima*; *NO*: *I kleima* and *kleime*). In Modern Icelandic the noun *kleima* means 'blotch, scratch'. All of these words are pejorative; if the name *Kleima* was understood to mean anything (and not simply invented to rhyme with *Feima*), then it may perhaps have been interpreted as 'smear, blotch' (cf. the characterisation of the milkmaid Beyla in *Lok* 56).

Grímr (Gríml Lv 2)

3. Þrífiz hvárgi   Þjassa dóttir
    brúðir verstar;   brátt skal ek reiðaz.
    Rétt skal ek ykr,   áðr röðull skíni,
    vörgum senda   víst til bráðar.

Þrífiz hvárgi dóttir Þjassa, verstar brúðir; ek skal brátt reiðaz. Ek skal víst senda ykr rétt til bráðar vörgum, áðr röðull skíni.

May neither daughter of Þjazi <giant> [GIANTESS] thrive, the worst women; I shall fly into a rage quickly. I will certainly dispatch you two straight as meat for wolves before the sun shines.

Mss: 343a(58r), 471(57v) (*GrL*).

Readings: [5] Rétt skal ek ykr: *so* 471, ykr skal ek rétt 343a   [8] bráðar: bráða 471.

Editions: *Skj*: Anonyme digte og vers [XIII], E. 9. *Vers af Fornaldarsagaer: Af Gríms saga loðinkinna* I 3: AII, 288, BII, 309, *Skald* II, 164; *FSN* 2, 145-6, *FSGJ* 2, 187, Anderson 1990, 61, 111-12, 445; *Edd. Min.* 86.

Context: This stanza follows straight on from *GrL* 2 and is introduced by the remark: *Grímr kvað* 'Grímr spoke'.

Notes: [2] *Þjassa* 'of Þjazi <giant>': This name is written with <ss> (or <sss>) in all mss of *GrL*; such forms as *Þjassi* (nom.) are a later variant (c. 1250 and later, *ANG* §274.2) of *Þjazi*, the name of a giant whom the gods eventually kill after a series of hostile encounters or dealings with him related in Þjóð *Haustl* 1-13[III]; cf. *SnE* 1998, I, 1-2 and Bragi Frag 2[III]. In that myth Þjazi's daughter Skaði seeks to take vengeance for him. In *GrL* 2 Feima states that her father is named Hrímnir; when Grímr refers to her and her sister here as *(hvárgi) dóttir Þjassa* '(neither) daughter of Þjazi', this pers. n. stands for any giant name and is the determinant of a giantess-kenning. — [3] *brúðir* 'women': Several mss (1006[x], 173[x], 342[x], 109a II[x]) offer the reading *bornar* (p. p. f. pl. nom. 'born'), which makes equally good sense here: *bornar verstar* ('the worst ones [ever] born'). — [5]: MS 471's reading has been preferred here over that of 343a because the alliteration (on *rétt*) falls correctly on the first lift of a Type E-line, whereas it falls incorrectly on the second lift in 343a. — [8] *bráðar* 'meat': The reading *bráða* (gen. pl.) which appears in 471 and several other mss is equally acceptable here. *Bráð* occurs frequently in poetry both in the sg. and pl. with reference to the corpses of men or animals as booty for wolves or birds of prey (cf. *LP*: *bróð*).

Kleima (Kleima Lv 1)

4. Þat var fyrri,   at faðir okkarr
   burtu seiddi   báru hjarðir.
   Skuluð aldrigi,   nema sköp ráði,
   heilir heðan   heim um komaz.

Þat var fyrri, at faðir okkarr seiddi burtu hjarðir báru. Skuluð aldrigi um komaz heilir heim heðan, nema sköp ráði.

That happened earlier, that our father removed herds of the wave [FISH] by magic. You will never return home from here in one piece, unless fate determines it that way.

Mss: **343a**(58r), 471(57v) (*GrL*).

Reading: [5] aldrigi: aldri 471.

Editions: *Skj*: Anonyme digte og vers [XIII], E. 9. *Vers af Fornaldarsagaer: Af Gríms saga loðinkinna* I 4: AII, 288, BII, 309, *Skald* II, 164; *FSN* 2, 146; *FSGJ* 2, 188, Anderson 1990, 61, 112, 445; *Edd. Min.* 86.

Context: According to the saga, Grímr has travelled north to the place named Gandvíkr (the White Sea, north-west Russia) during a famine to hunt for food and has seen that there was plenty of fish and game to catch there, though, shortly after he arrived, it suddenly disappeared (*GrL* ch. 1, *FSGJ* 2, 186). It was after this that he encountered Feima and Kleima. They explain that their father, Hrímnir, has caused the fish to disappear by means of sorcery. Later, when Grímr has killed the giantesses and their parents, he finds not only a whale stranded on the shore there but in every bay (*GrL* ch. 2, *FSGJ* 2, 190, 194). Furthermore the giant Hrímnir turns out to be the brother of the wicked stepmother from Finnmark who has put an evil spell on Grímr's fiancée Lopthœna, who has disappeared mysteriously (*GrL* chs 1 and 2, *FSGJ* 2, 185, 193). This stanza is introduced by the remark *Kleima kvað* 'Kleima said'.

Notes: [3-4]: Some mss have the readings *braut undir sik | búsveina lið* or *braut under sik | búkalla lið* 'trampled down the troop of farmers' or *braut undir sik | búsveina* 'trampled down the farmers' suggesting that the giant Hrímnir conquered or attacked human settlements (cf. *HHj* 17). Although these readings make sense grammatically the reading of the older mss is preferable, since it accords better with the plot. — [4] *hjarðir báru* 'herds of the wave [FISH]': *Meissner* 116 interprets this kenning as a reference to swarms of herring; he and *LP*: *hjǫrð* adduce a supposedly similar kenning (*fjarðhjǫrð* 'fjord-livestock') of Eyv Lv 14/2^I (see Note there); but cf. *Hkr* (*ÍF* 26, 223-4 and n. to st. 104).

Grímr (Gríml Lv 3)

5. Skal ek ykr báðum   skjótliga heita
oddi ok eggju   í upphafi.
Munu þá reyna   Hrungnis mellur,
hvárt betr dugir   broddr eða krumma.

Ek skal heita ykr báðum oddi ok eggju skjótliga í upphafi. Mellur Hrungnis munu þá reyna, hvárt broddr eða krumma dugir betr.

I will quickly promise you both at the outset weapon-point and blade. The female lovers of Hrungnir <giant> [GIANTESSES] will discover then whether weapon-point or claw is more effective.

Mss: 343a(58r), 471(57v) (*GrL*).

Readings: [6] Hrungnis: Rögnis 471   [7] betr: *so* 471, betr at 343a.

Editions: *Skj*: Anonyme digte og vers [XIII], E. 9. *Vers af Fornaldarsagaer: Af Gríms saga loðinkinna* I 5: AII, 288, BII, 309, *Skald* II, 164, *NN* §2396; *FSN* 2, 146, *FSGJ* 2, 188, Anderson 1990, 61, 112; *Edd. Min.* 86.

Context: This stanza is introduced by *Grímr kvað* 'Grímr said'.

Notes: [2] *heita* 'promise': Kock (*NN* §2396) interprets this word, not as the strong verb 'name, promise', but rather as the weak verb 'heat, brew'. See Note to *Ket* 35/2. — [6] *Hrungnis* 'of Hrungnir <giant>': Both this and the reading *Rögnis* are plausible, but 343a's *Hrungnis* is probably preferable to the 471 variant, despite the fact that *Rögnis* provides the line with conventional alliteration (see below). *Hrungnir* is immediately recognizable as the name of a giant, and there are other examples of giantess-kennings with a word for 'woman' as base-word and the pers. n. of a giant as determinant (*Meissner* 398; *GrL* 3/2). Hrungnir is the name of a giant whom the god Þórr kills in single combat; the story is narrated in Þjóð *Haustl* 14-20^{III} and in *Skm* (*SnE* 1998, I, 20-2) and mentioned or alluded to in a number of other skaldic and eddic poems. If the reading *Hrungnis* is retained, the line appears to contain an example of alliteration between <r> and <hr>. There are parallels for this in eddic verse, e.g. *Hamð* 25/1-2 (*NK* 273) *Þá hraut við | inn reginkunngi* 'Then the one of divine descent/the very wise one roared'. In this case and others, where <hv> appears to alliterate with <v>, some eds think that the initial [h] was weakened, allowing poets to use words beginning with <hr> or <hv> to alliterate with <r> and <v> respectively (cf. Dronke 1969, 240-2; *Edd. Min.* 86 n.). *Sigrdr* 15/5-6 (*NK* 193) may provide an indication that the initial <h> of the name *Hrungnir* was no longer pronounced or that there was an alternative form of that name or even a different mythic entity named Rungnir: *á því hvéli, er snýz | undir reið Rungnis* 'On that wheel that turns beneath the wagon of Rungnir'. *Rǫgnir* is usually one of the god Óðinn's names (*LP*: *Rǫgnir*), but in a kenning for 'giant' in Þjóð *Haustl* 4/5^{III} it appears to be used in the sense 'lord, chief' (see *SnE* 1998, II, 502 gloss to *Rǫgnir*).

There are examples of erotic relationships between Óðinn and giantesses (e.g. between Óðinn and Gunnlǫð in *Hávm* 104-10 or between Óðinn and Skaði in *Eyv Hál* 2¹). Hence the expression *Rögnis mellur* 'Rǫgnir's [Óðinn's] female lovers' in 471 could be a kenning for 'giantesses'. This however seems less appropriate in *GrL*, where the realm of the giants plays a large part, whilst the gods are not mentioned. There is no example for the usage of the simplex *rǫgnir* 'lord, ruler' as a term for 'giant'. Hence it is unlikely that the expression in 471 should be interpreted as *mellur rögnis* 'the female lovers of the ruler' and as a kenning for 'giantess'. If the alliterating words in this line are not *reyna* and *Hrungnis* then the only alternative is alliteration between the modal verb *munu* and *mellur*. In this case the head-stave (*mellur*) would be in the second lift of the second half-line, rather than in the first lift, and the first nominal form of the second half-line (*Hrungnis*) would not alliterate. Eddic poetry provides numerous examples of this non-compliance with the 'rules' for alliteration (on these 'rules' cf. von See 1967, 2, 19-20).
— [6] *mellur Hrungnis* 'the female lovers of Hrungnir <giant> [GIANTESSES]': The word *mella* is used as a giantess-*heiti* in several skaldic poems, as a determinant in kennings for Þórr or for giants, e.g.: *dolgs mellu* 'of the enemy of the giantess [= Þórr]' (*Eyv Lv* 8/7-8¹); *mellu mǫgfellandi* 'the feller of the kinsman of the giantess [(*lit.* 'kinsman-feller of the giantess') GIANT > = Þórr]' (Steinunn Lv 2/3ⱽ). In the kenning *mellur Hrungnis* in this stanza and in *mellu grams hellis* '*mella* of the lord of the cave [GIANT > GIANTESS]' (EGils *Selv* 14/4ᴵⱽ), however, *mella* is the base-word of a giantess-kenning and thus cannot itself have been understood to mean 'giantess'; *mella hellis grams* is a designation for the sea-giantess Selkolla 'Seal-Head' (*Meissner* 398). Finnur Jónsson interprets *mella* in these two late instances as 'female lover' (*LP*: 1. *mella*). A passage in *Flj* ch. 5 (*ÍF* 11, 228) can be adduced to lend support to this interpretation: a giant refers to a human maiden he has abducted as his *melluefni* lit. 'material for a *mella*', by which he evidently means his future wife. — [8] *broddr eða krumma* 'weapon-point or claw': A reference to the 'weapons' of Grímr and the troll-women respectively, illustrating the difference between the 'civilised technology' employed by the human being Grímr and the 'primitive' method of combat employed by the giantesses, who fight with their bare hands; cf. *Ket* 26/1-2 and Note to [All]. The literal meaning of *krumma* or *krymma* is '[hand with] bent or crooked [fingers]'; in other texts it is used of the (large) hands of giants and also of the large and/or ugly hands of human beings (*ÞorstBm* ch. 7, *FSGJ* 4, 334; *Kjaln* ch. 15, *ÍF* 14, 35; *Mork*, *ÍF* 23, 156; *Vígl* ch. 21, *ÍF* 14, 113-14). The closest parallel to the stanza in *GrL* appears in *HHj*, in the part of the poem known as *Hrímgerðarmál* 'The Speech of Hrímgerðr': in *HHj* 22 (*NK* 145) the giantess Hrímgerðr threatens Atli, who holds watch in the bow of Helgi Hjǫrvarðsson's ship, with the words: *Atli, gacc þú á land, | ef afli treystiz, | ok hittomc í vík Varins, | rifia rétti | er þú munt, reccr, fá, | ef þú mér í krymmor kømr!* 'Atli, go on land, if you trust in your strength, and let us meet in the bay of Varinn; it is a straightening of the ribs that you will get, man, if you fall into my clutches'.

Introduction to sts 6-7

Grímr speaks these two stanzas after he and his supporters have killed the berserk Sørkvir and his eleven berserk companions in an encounter to which Sørkvir challenged Grímr after Grímr's twelve-year-old daughter Brynhildr has refused to marry him (*FSGJ* 2, 194-5). Þrǫstr (*GrL* 6/8) is the name of the man who bears Sørkvir's shield and holds it in front of him when Grímr strikes the first blow (*FSGJ* 2, 195-6). The episode is parallel to two similar episodes in *Ket* (see *FSGJ* 2, 167-8, 173-81) where Grímr's father Ketill hœngr does battle against two different unwanted suitors for the hand of his own daughter Hrafnhildr; in *GrL* 7 below Grímr expressly says that he is following the example of his father. The motif of the twelve berserks as opponents of the hero also appears in *Heiðr* and in *Ǫrv*, and there are verbal similarities between *GrL* 6 and three stanzas transmitted in these two sagas (*Ǫrv* 10) and the two stanzas named in the note on *GrL* 6/3-4. Heusler and Ranisch see this as evidence that *GrL* is borrowing from an older version of *Ǫrv*, which in turn was used in *Heiðr*: one of the twelve berserks in *Heiðr* is the unsuccessful suitor for the hand of a king's daughter; he challenges the successful suitor Hjálmarr to combat (*Heiðr* 1924, 4-12; cf. *Edd. Min.* xxxvii-ix, lviii-ix, lxxxiii-iv). Ǫrvar-Oddr is said to be the son of Grímr (cf. *Ket* ch. 5, *GrL* ch. 4, *Ǫrv* ch. 1, *FSGJ* 2, 181, 198, 202).

Grímr (Gríml Lv 4)

6. Hér höfum fellt   til foldar
   tírarlausa   tólf berserki.
   Þó var Sørkvir   þróttrammastr
   þeira seggja   en Þrǫstr annarr.

Hér höfum fellt tólf tírarlausa berserki til foldar. Þó var Sørkvir þróttrammastr þeira seggja, en Þrǫstr annarr.

Here we have felled twelve inglorious berserks to the ground. Yet Sørkvir was the most powerful in strength of those men, and Þrǫstr was the second.

Mss: **343a**(59v); 471(60r) (*GrL*).

Readings: [1] höfum: höfum vér 471   [3] tírar-: '[...]' 471   [6] þróttrammastr: þroska mestr 471   [8] Þröstr: 'þrausti' 471.

Editions: *Skj*: Anonyme digte og vers [XIII], E. 9. *Vers af Fornaldarsagaer: Af Gríms saga loðinkinna* II 1: AII, 288-9, BII, 309-10, *Skald* II, 164; *FSN* 2, 154-5, *FSGJ* 2, 196, Anderson 1990, 66, 121, 448; *Edd. Min.* 96.

Notes: [All]: In 471 this part of the saga is written in a C17th hand on pages inserted into the ms. (cf. Anderson 1990, 71-2, 117 n. 300). — [3-4] *tólf tírarlausa berserki* 'twelve inglorious berserks': The words *tírarlausir* and *tólf* also alliterate with one another in two stanzas from *Ǫrv*, *Ǫrv* 8/7-8 and *Ǫrv* 9/2-3, where they also refer to twelve berserks in a similar episode (see Introduction above).

Grímr (Gríml Lv 5)

7. Fyrst mun ek líkja   eptir feðr mínum;
    skal eigi mín dóttir,   nema skör höggviz,
    nauðig gefin   neinum manni
    guðvefs þella,   meðan Grímr lifir.

Fyrst ek mun líkja eptir feðr mínum; dóttir mín, þella guðvefs, skal eigi gefin neinum manni nauðig, meðan Grímr lifir, nema skör höggviz.

First I will follow the example of my father; my daughter, the fir-tree of costly fabric [WOMAN], shall not be given in marriage to any man against her will while Grímr is [I am] alive, unless my head is hewn off.

Mss: **343a**(59v), 471(60r) (*GrL*).

Reading: [2] feðr: föður 471.

Editions: *Skj*: Anonyme digte og vers [XIII], E. 9. *Vers af Fornaldarsagaer: Af Gríms saga loðinkinna* II 2: AII, 289, BII, 310, *Skald* II, 164; *FSN* 2, 155, *FSGJ* 2, 196, Anderson 1990, 66, 121-2, 449; *Edd. Min.* 96.

Notes: [All]: Four mss preserve this stanza in a form which is unequivocally complete: 343a, 471, 340[x] and 109a I[x]. It is not clear whether the readings from other mss are to be regarded as poetry or prose because ll. 4 and 6 are omitted and the remainder are highly irregular metrically. — [1] *fyrst* 'first': This word appears as *Fyst* in 343a; on the assimilation of [rs] to [ss] before another consonant and the shortening of [ss] to [s], see *ANG* §271.3. The assimilation in question took place by 1300, but there are some examples from around 1200, including the form *fyst*. — [3] *skal eigi* 'shall not': All previous eds with the exception of Anderson (1990, 449) replace the negative particle *eigi* or *ei* which appears in the mss of the saga with the enclitic negation *-a* or *-at*. — [4] *nema skör höggviz* 'unless my head is hewn off': The noun *skör* refers to the hair on one's head; here it is a synecdoche for the whole head.

Gǫngu-Hrólfs saga

Edited by Margaret Clunies Ross

Introduction

Gǫngu-Hrólfs saga 'The Saga of Walker-Hrólfr' (*GHr*) probably dates from the fourteenth century. It is a rollicking and rather archly told narrative of multiple adventures, involving the hero Hrólfr, who is so big and heavy no horse can bear him all day, hence he must walk everywhere (thus his nickname). According to the saga (*FSGJ* 3, 173), Hrólfr is a son of Sturlaugr, the hero of *Sturlaugs saga starfsama* 'The Saga of Sturlaugr the Industrious' (*StSt*) by his wife Ása. Sturlaugr is presented in *GHr* as the king of Hringaríki (Ringerike) in Norway, where Hrólfr grows up as an unpromising lad. However he comes good and his adventures take him to many exotic lands where he is involved in fights with magical and monstrous enemies of various kinds, and a quest for the woman who will be his bride, Ingigerðr, daughter of King Hreggviðr of Hólmgarðaríki (Novgorod). This king is killed by an aggressive viking sea-king, Eiríkr, early in the saga narrative, and interred in a burial mound (*haugr*). At several points in the narrative the king emerges from his *haugr* to show Hrólfr his favour and give him advice because he intends Hrólfr to marry his daughter after the hero has taken vengeance on Eiríkr and his men for the king's killing. On the last such occasion, after a major battle, Hrólfr visits the mound at night and encounters the king, who recites three stanzas. These are the only stanzas in the saga and are edited below. They probably date from the late fourteenth century, as they show many examples of desyllabification, a change usually dated to c. 1300. These are mentioned in the Notes.

GHr has been a very popular saga in Iceland and beyond. It exists in at least sixty-nine mss (see the list in the *Stories for All Time* database, accessed 14 September 2015), most of them post-medieval. There are also five different *rímur* of varying ages based on versions of the saga, the earliest of them recorded in the early seventeenth-century ms. AM 610 4° (cf. Björn K. Þórólfsson 1934, 495-6). To date, there is no critical edition of *GHr* that takes account of all ms. witnesses. Some time ago Gillian Fellows Jensen prepared material towards a critical edition but was not able to complete it. She has kindly made her draft notes available to the project, together with a draft stemma drawn up by Jonna Louis-Jensen.

There are several late medieval vellum mss of *GHr*, of which all but one are either fragments or are lacking parts of the text. Four mss date from the later fourteenth or the fifteenth century, GKS 2845 4° (2845) of c. 1450, AM 567 XI α 4° (567XI α) of c. 1350-1400, AM 567 XI β (567XI β) of c. 1400-1500, and AM 589 f 4° (589f), of c. 1450-1500. The last of these mss contains *StSt* followed by *GHr*. AM 152 fol (152) of c. 1500-25 is the only extant vellum ms. of *GHr* that contains the complete saga. This large ms. contains texts of eleven sagas, including *Íslendingasögur*, *fornaldarsögur* and *riddarasǫgur*, and is headed by *Grettis saga Ásmundarsonar* (see Introduction to Vol. VIII, Section 4 for further information on this and other mss listed here).

The relationship between the medieval mss of *GHr* has not been fully ascertained, partly because of the fragmentary or incomplete nature of the majority of them. In the present edition, readings are given from 589f, 152 and 567XI α. for all three stanzas. Fragment 567XI β does not contain the three stanzas. Two paper mss have also been consulted for the edition and their readings are mentioned selectively, where appropriate, in the Notes. These are AM 587 c 4^{ox} (587c^x) of 1655, probably written by Brynjólfur Jónsson á Efstalandi, and AM 591 e 4^{ox} (591e^x) of the second quarter of the seventeenth century, written by séra Ólafur Gíslason á Hofi í Vopnafirði. These two mss were also used by Finnur Jónsson in *Skj* A and B.

The first printed edition of *GHr* was published by C. C. Rafn in *FSN* 3, 235-364, based on 2845. Rafn also published part of the text in his *Antiquités Russes* (Rafn 1850-2, I, 230-3). There are editions of the saga in Valdimar Ásmundarson (1885-9, 3, 143-239), Bjarni Vilhjálmsson and Guðni Jónsson (1943-4, 2, 357-461) and *FSGJ* 3, 161-280. A facsimile edition of 2845 with a useful introduction on the history of the ms. was published by Jón Helgason (Jón Helgason 1955b), while Agnete Loth published a facsimile edition of 589f and other fragments (Loth 1977). In the present edition the editions of *FSN* and *FSGJ* are cited, together with the separate editions of the stanzas in *Skj* and *Skald*. The editors of *Edd. Min.* did not publish these stanzas on the ground that they were too young for inclusion in their anthology (*Edd. Min.* iii).

Hreggviðr (Hregg Lv 1)

1. Glez Hreggviðr   af góðri fǫr
   Hrólfs ins hugdjarfa   hingat til landa.
   Mun rekkr sá   ræsis hefna
   á Eiríki   ok ǫllum þeim.

Hreggviðr glez af góðri fǫr Hrólfs ins hugdjarfa hingat til landa. Sá rekkr mun hefna ræsis á Eiríki ok ǫllum þeim.

Hreggviðr rejoices in the good journey of Hrólfr the bold-hearted to these lands. That warrior will take vengeance for the ruler upon Eiríkr and them all.

Mss: **589f**(31v), 152(111rb), 567XI α(1r-v) (*GHr*).

Readings: [2] góðri: fregri 152   [3] hugdjarfa: *so* 152, 567XI α, 'hugd[...]arfa' 589f   [5] rekkr sá: vegliga 567XI α   [6] ræsis: vísir 567XI α; hefna: 'hefn[...]' 567XI α   [7] á Eiríki: '[...]ki' 567XI α.

Editions: *Skj*: Anonyme digte og vers [XIII], E. 15. *Vers af Fornaldarsagaer: Af Gǫngu-Hrólfssaga* 1: AII, 332, BII, 353, *Skald* II, 190; *FSN* 3, 333-4, *FSGJ* 3, 253 (*GHr*).

Context: Shortly after a decisive battle with many casualties, and while exhausted warriors are asleep, Hrólfr goes to where King Hreggviðr's horse, Dúlcifal, is standing, and mounts him, riding until he comes to Hreggviðr's burial mound. It is bright moonlight. He dismounts and goes up onto the mound, where he sees Hreggviðr sitting outside below the mound, turned towards the moon. The dead king speaks this and the following two stanzas without interruption.

Notes: [All]: The verse-form of all three of Hreggviðr's stanzas is *fornyrðislag* and their theme is vengeance. Each stanza begins with the same line, *Glez Hreggviðr* 'Hreggviðr rejoices'. Hreggviðr must be desyllabified as Hreggviður in each instance to achieve metrical regularity (Types D and C). Repetition of lines, whether at the beginning or end of the stanza or from one stanza to another, as here, seems often to characterise the poetry of *draugar* 'revenants' in Old Norse; in the *lausavísa* GunnHám Lv 14^V (*Nj* 29) spoken by the dead Gunnarr from his mound in *Njáls saga* (*Nj*), when urging his kinsmen to vengeance, the last two lines repeat the same words. — [4] *hingat til landa* 'to these lands': Lit. 'hither to lands'. — [5-6]: This edn follows the text of 589f and 152, while *Skj* B and *Skald* prefer a slightly modified version of 567XI α's *mun vegliga | vísir hefna* 'the prince will nobly take vengeance'. Both versions are acceptable if *rekkr* is desyllabified to *rekkur*. — [5] *sá rekkr* 'that warrior': Meaning Gǫngu-Hrólfr. — [7] *Eiríki* 'Eiríkr': The viking leader, described in the saga as a sea-king, who, together with his berserks and champions, defeated and killed Hreggviðr early in the saga narrative (*FSGJ* 3, 167-70).

Hreggviðr (Hregg Lv 2)

2. Glez Hreggviðr   af Gríms dauða,
   Þórðar ok þar með   þrjóta lífstundir.
   Mun flokkr sjá   fjanda minna
   fyrir Hrólfi   hníga verða.

Hreggviðr glez af dauða Gríms, ok lífstundir Þórðar þrjóta þar með. Sjá flokkr fjanda minna mun verða hníga fyrir Hrólfi.

Hreggviðr rejoices in the death of Gríms, and the hours of Þórðr's life are diminishing as well. That group of my enemies will come to fall before Hrólfr.

Mss: **589f**(31v), 152(111rb), 567XI α(1v) (*GHr*).

Readings: [1] Hreggviðr: *so* 152, 567XI α, 'h[...]' 589f   [2] af Gríms dauða: af Gríms af dauða 567XI α   [3] Þórðar ok þar með: þeim munu 567XI α   [4] þrjóta: þrotnar 567XI α   [5] Mun flokkr sjá: vera mun flokkr sjá 567XI α   [6] minna: *so* 152, 567XI α, 'm[...]' 589f   [7] Hrólfi: '[...]' 567XI α   [8] hníga: '[...]ga' 567XI α.

Editions: *Skj*: Anonyme digte og vers [XIII], E. 15. *Vers af Fornaldarsagaer: Af Gǫngu-Hrólfssaga* 2: AII, 332-3, BII, 353, *Skald* II, 190; *FSN* 3, 334, *FSGJ* 3, 253 (*GHr*).

Notes: [All]: Both *Skj* B and *Skald* prefer here a version of this stanza based in part on 591e[x] for l. 3, *Þórðar ok Brynjólfs*, and in part on 567XI α for l. 4 *þrotnar lífstundir*. They use 591e[x] again for l. 6 *falla hrǫnnum*. They regularise the metre of l. 7 by inserting an *ok* before *fyr Hrólfi*. Their text reads: *Glezk Hreggviðr | Gríms af dauða, | Þórðar ok Brynjólfs | þrotnar lífstundir; | mun flokkr sjá | falla hrǫnnum | ok fyr Hrólfi | hníga verða*, which *Skj* B translates as *Hreggvid glæder sig over Grims død. Tords og Brynjolfs levetid er sluttet; den skare vil falde flokkevis og segne for Hrolf* 'Hreggviðr rejoices over Grímr's death. Þórðr's and Brynjólfr's lives are finished; that troop will fall in flocks and sink before Hrólfr'. This composite text corresponds to no single ms. version, whereas that adopted by *FSN* and *FSGJ* at least has the merit of following two medieval mss, 589f and 152. — [2] *Gríms* 'of Grímr': According to ch. 2 of *GHr* (*FSGJ* 3, 166-7), Grímr, nicknamed *ægir*, was Eiríkr the viking's closest confidant. The saga narrator associates his nickname with that of the mythical Ægir, a sea-god or giant. Grímr was the foster-brother of Þórðr (see Note to l. 3) a completely evil figure, of unknown parentage, the practitioner of sorcery, shape-shifting and malicious deeds. — [3] *Þórðar* 'of Þórðr': A kinsman of Eiríkr the viking, from Hlésey (Læsø) in Denmark (*FSGJ* 3, 167). The Brynjólfr, mentioned in some versions of this stanza, such as 591e[x] (see Note to [All] above), is the name of another of Eiríkr's henchmen. — [5] *flokkr* 'group': This must be desyllabified to *flokkur* to produce a metrical line (Type B).

Hreggviðr (Hregg Lv 3)

3. Glez Hreggviðr,   þá er Hrólfr fær
   ungrar meyjar   Ingigerðar.
   Mun Hólmgarði   hilmir stýra,
   Sturlaugs sonr;   standi kvæði.

Hreggviðr glez, þá er Hrólfr fær ungrar meyjar Ingigerðar. Hilmir, sonr Sturlaugs, mun stýra Hólmgarði; standi kvæði.

Hreggviðr will rejoice when Hrólfr marries the young maiden Ingigerðr. The prince, son of Sturlaugr, will govern Novgorod; let the poem cease.

Mss: **589f**(31v), 152(111rb), 567XI α(1v) (*GHr*).

Readings: [2] þá er: þá at 567XI α, þá at 567XI α   [3] ungrar meyjar: *om.* 567XI α   [5] Mun: *so* 152, 'm[...]' 589f, mun þá 567XI α   [7] Sturlaugs: 'Stulaugs' 589f, 'Sturlugs' 152, stýra mun 567XI α;   sonr: vegr hans 567XI α   [8] standi kvæði: um lengi standa 567XI α.

Editions: *Skj*: Anonyme digte og vers [XIII], E. 15. *Vers af Fornaldarsagaer: Af Gǫngu-Hrólfssaga* 3: AII, 333, BII, 353, *Skald* II, 190; *FSN* 3, 334, *FSGJ* 3, 253-4 (*GHr*).

Notes: [2] *þá er* 'when': The particle *er* has been restored as a routine normalisation to 1250-1300 usage from 589f's *þá*, which shows C14th loss of *er* after *þá* (*NS* §261). This has also been added by *Skj* B and *Skald*. Line 2 requires the desyllabification of

Hrólfr to *Hrólfur* to be metrically correct. — [4] *Ingigerðar* 'Ingigerðr': The name of King Hreggviðr's daughter, who is rescued by Hrólfr from the machinations of the evil viking Eiríkr. — [7-8]: Ms. 567XI α has a different text of these lines, *vegr hans mun um lengi standa* 'his reputation will last for a long time'. A variant version of this clause is also found in 587c^x. — [7] *sonr* 'son': Requires desyllabification to *sonur* to be metrically correct.

Hálfs saga ok Hálfsrekka

Edited by Hubert Seelow

Introduction

Hálfs saga ok Hálfsrekka 'The saga of Hálfr and Hálfr's champions' (*Hálf*) is a *fornaldarsaga* which relates the story of the tragic fate of the Norwegian viking king Hálfr and his warriors. After eighteen summers of successful plundering in distant countries, they fall victim to a treacherous invitation in their own country, Norway. Hálfr's stepfather, Ásmundr, sets fire to the hall when his guests have fallen asleep after much heavy drinking; they succeed in breaking out of the burning building, but in the ensuing battle Hálfr and most of his champions are killed.

This story of Hálfr proper is preceded by a series of anecdotal accounts dealing mainly with Hálfr's ancestors, among them his father, Hjǫrleifr inn kvensami 'the Womaniser', and their adversaries, as well as a short chapter on a disastrous viking expedition conducted by Hálfr's elder brother, Hjǫrólfr. Following the main narrative, there is an account of how Hálfr's death was avenged and how his descendants settled in Iceland.

The main narrative is expressed through three longer poems in *fornyrðislag*, *Innsteinskviða* 'Poem of Innsteinn' (*Innkv*), *Útsteinskviða* 'Poem of Útsteinn' (*Útkv*) and *Hrókskviða* 'Poem of Hrókr' (*Hrkv*), connected by comparatively short prose paragraphs. The genealogical anecdotes at the beginning and end of the saga consist of prose with interspersed *lausavísur*, many of which convey prophecies that look forward to the main story or, in the case of Bragi Lv 1b (*Hálf* 78), further into historical times. The early part of the saga is distinguished by a number of prophetic utterances expressed by a range of supernatural beings, from a water-polluting spirit, to an animated mountain, to a merman, to an unknown voice. All these *lausavísur* contribute to a powerful sense that Hálfr's ancestors have violated natural laws in their quests for power and dominance through polygynous sexual liaisons (cf. Torfi H. Tulinius 2002, 115-18). The titles given to the three long poems in *Hálf* can be traced back to Heusler and Ranisch (*Edd. Min.*), who were followed by Andrews (*Hálf* 1909). In the course of the twentieth century their titles, or similar ones, have become standard among most scholars and editors. *Edd. Min.* uses the titles *Das Innsteinslied* 'The Poem of Innsteinn', *Das Hrókslied* 'The Poem of Hrókr' and *Útsteins Kampfstrophen (eine Lausavísurgruppe)* 'Útsteinn's Battle-stanzas (a group of *lausavísur*)' for the three stanza sequences. Such titles do not appear in the earliest ms. nor in early editions before *Edd. Min.*, although Björner (1737), who took his chapter titles from the paper ms. Holm papp 68 fol[x], makes explicit mention of Hrókr's poem at the beginning of chapter xvi (Björner 1737, 33). This may have influenced Vigfusson and Powell in their Introduction to an appendix to *CPB* II (1883, II, 547) entitled 'Spurious Epic Poetry', to refer to 'The Death Song of Rook the Black'.

The story of Hálfr's death is among the earliest documented traditions in Old Norse and must have been known already c. 900 because the kenning *bani Hǫalfs* 'slayer of Hálfr' [FIRE] appears in Þjóð *Yt* 6/7[1] (cf. *SnE* 1998, I, 39). On the other hand, references to the story both in these and other sources, such as *Ldn*, are quite stereotypical, and this suggests that the *Hálf* tradition cannot have been very rich in literary times. The anecdotal parts rely on genealogies and make use of many folklore motifs, such as the laughing sage, together with motifs taken from Norse myth and heroic legend. What was probably an older version of the saga, called there *Hróks saga svarta* 'Saga of Hrókr the Black', is mentioned in *Geirmundar þáttr heljarskinns* 'The Tale of Geirmundr the Dark-skinned' (*Geir*) in *Stu*. This version seems to have been extant already between c. 1220-80, although the text that has been preserved as *Hálf* (see below) probably dates from the fourteenth century.

There is only one vellum ms. of *Hálf*, GKS 2845 4° (2845), which dates from c. 1450 (see further Introduction to Vol. VIII, Section 4). This ms., which contains several other *fornaldarsögur*, is the basis for all published editions of the saga and its stanzas, including the present one. There are a great many later paper mss of this saga, all derived from 2845; fifty-six have so far been identified on the database *Stories for All Time*, accessed 4 January 2016.

There is a facsimile edition of 2845 by Jón Helgason (1955b). The first printed edition of the saga was by Erik J. Björner (1737), and C. C. Rafn edited it in *FSN* 2, 25-60. The first scholarly edition was that of Sophus Bugge (*Hálf* 1864), followed by that of A. Le Roy Andrews (*Hálf* 1909). It was also edited by Valdimar Ásmundarson (1885-9, 2, 21-46) and in *FSGJ* 2, 93-134. The present editor produced a diplomatic edition of the saga (*Hálf* 1981). The following editions of the saga have been cited here, along with the verse-only editions in *Skj* A and B, *Skald* and *Edd. Min.*: *Hálf* 1864, *Hálf* 1909, *FSGJ* and *Hálf* 1981.

Introduction to st. 1

The first, very brief section of *Hálf* describes the conflict between two petty kings in Norway named Alrekr and Ǫgvaldr. The stanza below, spoken by Alrekr, refers to the circumstances of his son Víkarr's conception and his father's premonition of Víkarr's ultimate fate as a sacrifice to Óðinn.

Alrekr (Alrekr Lv 1)

1. Geirhildr, getta, gott er öl þetta,
   ef því annmarkar öngvir fylgja.
   Ek sé hanga á háum gálga
   son þinn, kona, seldan Óðni.

Geirhildr, getta, þetta öl er gott, ef öngvir annmarkar fylgja því. Ek sé son þinn, kona, hanga á háum gálga, seldan Óðni.

Geirhildr, girl, this ale is good, if there are no faults connected with it. I see your son, woman, hanging on the high gallows, handed over to Óðinn.

Ms.: **2845**(32r) (*Hálf*).

Editions: Skj: Anonyme digte og vers [XIII], E. 6. *Vers af Fornaldarsagaer: Af Hálfssaga* I: AII, 256-7, BII, 276, *Skald* II, 144; *Hálf* 1864, 4, *Hálf* 1909, 71-2, *FSGJ* 2, 96, *Hálf* 1981, 108, 170; *Edd. Min.* 89.

Context: King Alrekr's two wives, Signý and Geirhildr, are on such bad terms that he feels he has to get rid of one of them. He arranges a beer-brewing contest, declaring that he will keep the one whose beer turns out the better. The stanza is introduced by the words: *Þær kepptuzt um ölgerðina. Signý hét á Freyju, en Geirhildr á Hött. Hann lagði fyrir dregg hráka sinn ok kvezt vilja fyrir tilkomu sína þat, er milli var kersins ok hennar, en þat reyndizt gott öl. Þá kvað Alrekr ...* 'They [the two women] competed in ale-brewing. Signý invoked Freyja and Geirhildr [invoked] Hǫttr [Óðinn]. He used his spittle as yeast and said that for his intervening he wanted what was between the [brewing] vessel and her, and the ale proved to be good. Then Alrekr said ...'. The stanza is followed by the words: *Á þeim misserum var fæddr Víkarr, son Alreks ok Geirhildar* 'During that year Víkarr, the son of Alrekr and Geirhildr, was born'.

Notes: [All]: The prose text makes it clear, before the introduction of this stanza, that Hǫttr 'Hood' (another name for Óðinn) had made a bargain with Geirhildr that he would help her to marry Alrekr but in return she had to promise to call upon him in all things. His role in brewing good ale by spitting into the brew is reminiscent of the myth of the gods' creation of the wise being Kvasir, precursor to the mead of poetry, out of their spittle (*SnE* 1998, I, 3; cf. Boberg 1966, 193 (M 201.3) and 36 (A 1211.3.1); Lassen 2011, 166-7). — [All]: It is not evident from the prose text that King Alrekr is aware of Geirhildr's pact with Óðinn, yet the stanza strongly implies his awareness both of the god's involvement and the ultimate fate of his son, Víkarr, who is elsewhere (notably in the longer version of *Gautreks saga*) a king of Agder (Agðir), sacrificed to Óðinn by his foster-brother Starkaðr, who hangs him from a tree and pierces him with a reed-stalk that turns into a spear (cf. StarkSt *Vík* 26 (*Gautr* 34) and Note to [All]). Both the composer of *Hálf* and his audience must have known the story of Víkarr's death, although it is not directly mentioned in either prose or poetry, and his parentage and circumstances are different here from what is given in *Gautr*. — [1]

getta 'girl': Probably a form of *genta* 'girl', whose earliest citation in *ONP* is c. 1362. The word forms a full end-rhyme with *þetta* 'this' (l. 2). Cf. ModNorw. *jente*, *AEW*: *genta*. It is not necessary to emend as some earlier eds have (for details, see *Hálf* 1981, 108).

2. (*Ragn* 2 is edited as **Anon** (*Ragn*) **8** (*Ragn* 38) in this volume.)

Introduction to sts 3-4

These two stanzas form an exchange between King Hjǫrleifr and a spirit being who is identified by the king's men as intent upon polluting the water they are about to draw from a spring. The king speaks *Hálf* 3 to the spirit and threatens him with a burning spear; in *Hálf* 4 the spirit retaliates by prophesying the end of the good fortune of Hjǫrleifr's wife Hildr. Although the second *helmingr* of this stanza is defective, the prophecy appears to concern Hildr, Hjǫrleifr and a fire, and this links the episode with the main saga narrative and looks forward to the scene at King Hreiðarr's court, where Hjǫrleifr is bound between two fires and only Hildr's quick-thinking help saves him from death.

Hjǫrleifr (Hjǫrleifr Lv 1)

3. Gakk þú frá brunni — glettzt lítt* við mik,
   þræll herfiligr — þíns innis til.
   Mun ek senda þér sveiðanda spjót,
   þat er gyrja mun granir þínar.

Gakk þú frá brunni til innis þíns; glettzt lítt* við mik, herfiligr þræll. Ek mun senda þér sveiðanda spjót, þat er mun gyrja granir þínar.

Go [away] from the spring to your abode; provoke me little, wretched scoundrel. I shall send you a burning spear, which will stain your whiskers.

Ms.: **2845**(33r) (*Hálf*).

Readings: [1] G*a*kk: Geck 2845   [2] glettzt lítt*: 'gletta líttu' 2845.

Editions. *Skj*: Anonyme digte og vers [XIII], E. 6. Vers af Fornaldarsagaer: Af Hálfssaga II 1: AII, 257, BII, 276, *Skald* II, 144, *NN* §§2379, 3286; *Hálf* 1864, 7, *Hálf* 1909, 79, *FSGJ* 2, 99, *Hálf* 1981, 110-11, 172; *Edd. Min.* 94.

Context: Returning from a viking expedition, King Hjǫrleifr, his wife Hildr in mjóa 'the Slender', and their retinue spend the night on their ship off the coast of southern Finnmǫrk (Finnmark). The men light a fire on the shore and two of them go to fetch water from a spring. The stanza is preceded by the words: *Þar sáu þeir brunnmiga ok sǫgðu Hjǫrleifi kóngi. Síðan heitir kóngr broddspjót í eldi ok skaut til hans. Kóngr kvað ...* 'There they saw a *brunnmigi* ('spring-pisser') and told king Hjǫrleifr. Then the king heats a pike in the fire and shot at him. The king said ...'. The stanza is followed by the words *Þá tóku þeir vatn, en þussinn skauzt inn í bjargit* 'Then they took water, but the giant slipped away into the rock'.

Notes: [All]: The concept of a being that pollutes springs or streams by urinating in them is attested in Scandinavian folklore (cf. *CVC*: *brunn-migi*). It is sometimes imagined as a fox spirit, although here the being is called *þuss* 'giant' or 'troll'. The cpd *brunnmigi* 'spring-pisser' appears only in the prose preceding this stanza and in Þul Grýlu 1/8^{III}, where most of the other *heiti* in the stanza are terms for foxes. — [2] *glettzt lítt**'provoke ... little': I.e. 'do not provoke'. In *NN* §2379 Kock prints *glettsk lítt* and, referring to *NN* §604, where he argues that both *fátt* and *lítt* are common negations, criticises those eds who substitute the negation contained in the ms. reading *líttu* by enclitic *-at* (so *Skj* B). Nevertheless in *Skald* Kock prints *gletzat*. — [6] *sveiðanda spjót* 'a burning spear': The final superscript *a* of *sveiðanda* is barely discernible in the ms. In *NN* §3286 Kock suggests that the *hap. leg. sveiðanda* is a pres. part. derived from a verb *sveiða* and must mean 'burning'; *Hálf* 1909 renders *sveiðanda spjót* with *einen glühenden Speer* 'a glowing spear'; *Edd. Min.* 148 translates *sveiða* as *sengen (oder angesengt sein?)* 'singe (or be singed?)'; *AEW*: *sveiða* as *brennen, schmerzen* 'burn, ache'; *LP*: *sveiða* as *beskrive en bue (?)* 'curve(?)'. — [7] *gyrja* 'stain': This verb is a *hap. leg.* and is thought to be related to *gor* 'half-digested stomach contents, cud of an animal', deriving from a root *g^{u}her-* 'hot, warm' (see Pokorny 1959, 493-5); the meaning 'singe, burn' seems equally possible.

Þurs (Anon *Hálf* 1)

4. Veit ekki görla   víf þitt, konungr,
    hvat hnekkja mun   hennar sælu.
    Óverðum þér   ...
    Hildr, Hjörleifi,   haltu nær loga.

Víf þitt, konungr, veit ekki görla, hvat mun hnekkja sælu hennar. Óverðum þér ... Hildr, Hjörleifi, haltu nær loga.

Your woman, king, does not quite know what will thwart her happiness. To you, undeserving ... Hildr, to Hjǫrleifr, move near the flame.

Ms.: 2845(33r) (*Hálf*).

Reading: [5] Óverðum þér: 'u uerdum þier' 2845.

Editions: *Skj*: Anonyme digte og vers [XIII], E. 6. Vers af Fornaldarsagaer: Af Hálfssaga II 2: AII, 257, BII, 277, Skald II, 144; *Hálf* 1864, 7, *Hálf* 1909, 79, FSGJ 2, 99, *Hálf* 1981, 111, 172; Edd. Min. 90.

Context: The stanza is preceded by the words: *Þá er þau sátu við eld, þá kvað þuss af bjargi annat ljóð* 'Then, when they sat by the fire, the giant recited another song from the rock'. The stanza is followed by the words: *Þá skaut Hjörleifr hinu sama spjóti í auga því trölli* 'Then Hjǫrleifr shot the same spear in that troll's eye'.

Note: [5-6]: The stanza may contain a prophecy of the end of Hildr's good fortune. It is clear that either l. 5 or l. 6 is missing, although there is no lacuna in the ms., but, as the meaning of the stanza's second *helmingr* remains obscure, it cannot be determined whether *Óverðum þér* 'To you, undeserving' should be positioned as l. 5 or as l. 6. Most other eds have emended the ms. reading in various ways and/or added text to fill the lacuna; *vér verðum þér* (*Hálf* 1864); *óverðum þér* [*eld mun sløkkva*] 'undeserving for you, [the fire will go out]' (*Edd. Min.*); *vér undum þér* (untranslated *Hálf* 1909, *FSGJ*); [*Hildr mun ást sýna*] *óverðum þér* '[Hildr will show] you, undeserving, [her love]' (*Skj* B). *Skald* treats l. 5 as missing and gives the present text of l. 5 as l. 6.

Introduction to st. 5

This is yet another prophetic stanza spoken by a supernatural being, in this case a mountain in the shape of a huge man, who plays no further part in the saga narrative. However, the elements of his prophecy are fulfilled in the same sequence in the saga as they occur in the stanza, thus providing a pattern for the remainder of Hjǫrleifr's life history, and suggesting that his aggressive and womanising behaviour is out of tune with the natural world, whose messengers convey a series of prophecies of doom, a subliminal message also expressed in *Hálf* 3 and 4.

Fjall (Anon *Hálf* 2)

5.   Ek sé Hringju   haug um orpinn,
    en Hera h*níga*   hvátinn spjóti.
    Sé ek Hjörleifi   h*a*ptbönd snúin,
    en Hreiðari   höggvinn gálga.

Ek sé haug um orpinn Hringju, en Hera h*níga* hvátinn spjóti. Ek sé h*a*ptbönd snúin Hjǫrleifi, en gálga höggvinn Hreiðari.

I see a burial mound thrown up for Hringja and [see] Heri fall dead, pierced by a spear. I see captive bonds twisted for Hjǫrleifr and gallows hewn for Hreiðarr.

Ms.: **2845**(33v) (*Hálf*).

Readings: [2] haug um: haugum 2845   [3] h*níga*: hingat 2845   [6] h*a*ptbönd: 'hauptbaund' 2845.

Editions: *Skj*: Anonyme digte og vers [XIII], E. 6. *Vers af Fornaldarsagaer: Af Hálfssaga* III: AII, 257, BII, 277, *Skald* II, 145, *NN* §2380; *Hálf* 1864, 8-9, *Hálf* 1909, 81, *FSGJ* 2, 100-1, *Hálf* 1981, 111-12, 173; *Edd. Min.* 90.

Context: Attending a kings' meeting at Konungahella (Kungälv, Bohuslän), Hjǫrleifr makes friends with King Hreiðarr of Sjáland (Sjælland) and his son Heri. Urged by Heri, Hreiðarr invites Hjǫrleifr to his home. There Hjǫrleifr sees Hreiðarr's daughter Hringja and marries her; then he sets out to travel back to Norway with his bride. The stanza is introduced by the words: *Í Jótlandshafi lá Hjörleifr í lognrétt, ok er hann fór í sólarupprás, sá hann í norðr koma upp ór sjónum mikit fjall ok jafnt vaxit sem mann. Þat kvað* ... 'In the Jutland sea [Kattegat and/or Skagerrak] Hjǫrleifr lay becalmed, and when he went forth at sunrise, he saw a big mountain come up from the sea in the north, shaped just like a man. It said ...'.

Notes: [1] *Hringju* 'for Hringja': The daughter of King Hreiðarr, to whom Hjǫrleifr is very briefly married. Shortly after the mountain man's recital of this stanza, the party's ships will not move, so men take to their oars. For reasons unspecified, Hringja falls ill and dies; her coffin is thrown overboard and travels very quickly back south to Denmark. Heri expresses the opinion that King Hjǫrleifr must have murdered Hringja, thus providing a motive for the hostilities that follow between the two parties. — [3] *Hera* 'Heri': The son of King Hreiðarr, killed by being thrust through with a spear (*Hálf* 1981, 176). — [3] *h*níga 'fall dead': Most previous eds, following *Hálf* 1864, have emended the ms. *hingat* 'hither, [to] here' to *hníga*, as it is difficult to fit *hingat* into the sense or syntax of the *helmingr*. However, in *NN* §2380 Kock argues that the ms. reading *hingat* makes perfect sense, as *hingat* can be synonymous with *hér*, and that the emendation *hníga* spoils the symmetrical structure of the stanza. His retention of the ms. reading here has not met with favour (cf. *Hálf* 1981, 111). — [5-6] *ek sé haptbǫnd snúin Hjǫrleifi* 'I see captive bonds twisted for Hjǫrleifr': This alludes to the same incident as is touched on in *Hálf* 4/5-8, in which Hjǫrleifr is captured, tied up with his own shoe thongs and placed between two fires (*Hálf* 1981, 176). For the idiom *snúa e-m haptbǫnd* 'to twist captive bonds for sby', see *Gautr* 11/8 and Note. — [7-8] *en gálga hǫggvinn Hreiðari* 'and gallows hewn for Hreiðarr': After Hjǫrleifr has been freed from his bonds by Hildr, he takes his revenge on the sleeping Hreiðarr by stabbing him in the chest and then stringing him up on a gallows meant for himself (*Hálf* 1981, 176).

Introduction to sts 6-12

The following seven stanzas or part-stanzas comprise the prophetic utterances of a *marmendill* or *marmennill* 'merman', who is fished up from the sea by two fishermen and forced to predict King Hjǫrleifr's fate.

Marmennill (Marm Lv 1)

6. Ek sé lýsa   langt suðr í haf;
    vill danskr konungr   dóttur hefna.
    Hann hefir úti   ótal skipa;
    býðr hann Hjörleifi   hólmstefnu til.

Ek sé lýsa langt suðr í haf; danskr konungr vill hefna dóttur. Hann hefir ótal skipa úti; hann býðr Hjörleifi til hólmstefnu.

I see a glitter a long way south in the sea; a Danish king wants to avenge his daughter. He sails with countless ships; he challenges Hjǫrleifr to a duel.

Ms.: 2845(33v-34r) (*Hálf*).

Editions: *Skj*: Anonyme digte og vers [XIII], E. 6. *Vers af Fornaldarsagaer: Af Hálfssaga* IV 1: AII, 257, BII, 277, *Skald* II, 145; *Hálf* 1864, 9-10, *Hálf* 1909, 83, *FSGJ* 2, 102, *Hálf* 1981, 112, 174; *Edd. Min.* 90-1.

Context: Two fishermen called Handir and Hrindir catch a merman (*marmendill*) and bring him to King Hjǫrleifr, who entrusts him to the care of one of the women at his court. One night, when the lights had been put out, Hjǫrleifr's wife Hildr prods her co-wife Æsa with a horn. The king slaps Hildr, but Æsa says it is the dog's fault, so he strikes the dog. The merman laughs, and, when asked by the king why he is laughing, he replies that the king has acted foolishly, as the two he has slapped would save his life. The king asks more questions, but the merman gives no answer. Then the king says he will take him back to sea and asks the merman to tell him what he needs to know. The stanza is introduced by the words: *Hann kvað, er hann fór til sjóvar* ... 'He said, when he went to the sea ...'.

Notes: [All]: The motif of the laughing sage is attested in a number of folklore sources (see Boberg 1966, 69 (D1318.2.1); Davíð Erlingsson 1980). Davíð Erlingsson (1980) finds both this and the motif of the otherworld spirit that pollutes waterways in Irish sources about the dealings of the hero Fergus mac Léite with the elf-people. — [1] *lýsa* 'a glitter': *Lýsa* is here a verb 'glitter, gleam' without a specified subject.

Marmennill (Marm Lv 2)

7. Varaztu víti,   ef þú vilt;
    vil ek aptr í sjó.

Varaztu víti, ef þú vilt; ek vil aptr í sjó.

Beware of disaster, if you want; I want to go back into the sea.

Ms.: 2845(34r) (*Hálf*).

Reading: [1] vít*i*: 'uítŕ' 2845.

Editions: *Skj*: Anonyme digte og vers [XIII], E. 6. *Vers af Fornaldarsagaer: Af Hálfssaga* IV 1: AII, 257, BII, 277, *Skald* II, 145; *Hálf* 1864, 10, *Hálf* 1909, 83, *FSGJ* 2, 102, *Hálf* 1981, 113, 174; *Edd. Min.* 91.

Notes: [All]: This incomplete stanza is a continuation of the merman's prophecy in the preceding stanza and may be looked upon as its concluding statement. In fact, *Skj*, *Skald*, and *Hálf* 1864 treat these three lines as part of the preceding stanza. — [1] *varaztu ví*ti 'beware of disaster': The final letter 'ŕ' in the ms. is probably to be read as an <í> (denoting [i]) corrected from an <r> rather than as an <r> corrected from an <í>. Some eds read *vitr* 'wise' (so *Hálf* 1864, *Skj* B), Finnur Jónsson translating *Tag dig, klog som du er, iagt, hvis du vil* 'Watch out for yourself, wise as you are, if you wish'. — [3]: This line is very similar to *Hálf* 12/4 *lát mik aptr í sjó* 'put me back into the sea'.

Marmennill (Marm Lv 3)

8. Sögu kann ek segja   sonum Háleygja
    vilgi góða,   ef þér vilið heyra.
    Hér ferr sunnan   Svarðar dóttir,
    um drifin dreyra,   frá Danmörku.

Ek kann segja sonum Háleygja vilgi góða sögu, ef þér vilið heyra. Hér ferr dóttir Svarðar, um drifin dreyra, sunnan frá Danmörku.

I can tell the sons of the Háleygir a story [which is] by no means good, if you want to hear it. Here Svǫrðr's daughter, drenched with blood, moves from the south from Denmark.

Ms.: 2845(34r) (*Hálf*).

Editions: *Skj*: Anonyme digte og vers [XIII], E. 6. *Vers af Fornaldarsagaer: Af Hálfssaga* IV 2: AII, 257, BII, 277, *Skald* II, 145; *Hálf* 1864, 10, *Hálf* 1909, 84, *FSGJ* 2, 102, *Hálf* 1981, 113-14, 174; *Edd. Min.* 91.

Context: The merman now speaks four prophetic stanzas with no intervening prose warning that the Danish king Hreiðarr is preparing to take vengeance for the death of his daughter Hringja, and that he will mount an attack on Hjǫrleifr's hall, from which Hjǫrleifr will escape and kill Hreiðarr's son Heri with a spear. The stanza is preceded by the words: *En er þeir reru þangat með hann, sem þeir höfðu hann upp dregit, þá kvað hann* … 'And as they rowed with him to the spot, where they had hauled him up, he said …'.

Notes: [2] *sonum Háleygja* 'the sons of the Háleygir': The pl. referent is used here, though the merman is in fact directing his remarks to Hjǫrleifr alone. Andrews (*Hálf* 1909, 84) comments on the fact that here Hjǫrleifr is linked with Háleygjaland

(Hålogaland, a district in northern Norway), as is his son Hálfr in *Hálf* 56/6. — [6] *dóttir Svarðar* 'Svǫrðr's daughter': The pers. n. Svǫrðr is otherwise unknown, but is likely to be the determinant of a kenning for a valkyrie or other female figure of war. *Skj* B substitutes *Hǫgna* 'of Hǫgni', thus producing a kenning for the valkyrie Hildr, whose name as a common noun also means 'battle'. This emendation, though unjustified by the ms. and non-alliterating, fits with the merman's apparent personification of Danish aggression moving from the south in the form of a warlike valkyrie or shield-maiden in *Hálf* 9/1-4 and again in *Hálf* 10/1-4. Andrews (*Hálf* 1909, 15-16, 84) attempts to show that an otherwise unknown pers. n. Svǫrðr might be a shortened, syncopated form of *Sigvarðr/Sigurðr*.

Marmennill (Marm Lv 4)

9. Hefir sér á höfði   hjálm upp spenntan,
   herkuml harðligt   Heðins af létta.
   Skammt mun sveinum   — sé þat, sem er —
   hildar at bíða   hér á ferli.

Hefir sér á höfði upp spenntan hjálm harðligt herkuml Heðins, af létta. Sveinum mun skammt at bíða hildar hér á ferli; sé þat, sem er.

On her head she has clasped with ease a helmet, the hard war token of Heðinn <legendary hero> [HELMET]. The lads will have to wait a short time for war to be on its way here. I see it as it is.

Ms.: 2845(34r) (*Hálf*).

Editions: *Skj*: Anonyme digte og vers [XIII], E. 6. *Vers af Fornaldarsagaer: Af Hálfssaga* IV 3: AII, 258, BII, 277-8, *Skald* II, 145; *Hálf* 1864, 10, *Hálf* 1909, 84-5, *FSGJ* 2, 103, *Hálf* 1981, 114, 174-5; *Edd. Min.* 91.

Notes: [3-4] *harðligt herkuml Heðins* 'the hard war token of Heðinn <legendary hero> [HELMET]': The meaning of *herkum(b)l* is 'war token' (*Fritzner: herkuml*), 'helmet' (*LP: herkum(b)l*). *Herkuml Heðins* 'the war token of Heðinn' has the character of a kenning, although not listed by *Meissner* as such. *Meissner* does, however, mention *herkumbl* as a *heiti* for 'helmet', and lists kennings in which a famous hero's headgear means 'helmet'. In *Ásm* 10/7, where the same expression is used in the pl., *herkumbl harðlig* 'hard war tokens', its meaning is clearly 'wounds', but even in this instance it is closely associated with a helmet. — [4] *af létta* 'with ease': Andrews (*Hálf* 1909, 84-5) suggests *á fléttum* 'on (her) plaits', which would be a nice parallel to *á höfði* in l. 1 and is very close to the ms. reading. Bugge (*Hálf* 1864, 10) and Wimmer (1875, 200) think that the reading of l. 4 must have been a version of a Hildr-kenning, like *Heðins of leika* 'Heðinn's playmate', i.e. Hildr; so do Finnur Jónsson (*Skj* B) and Heusler and Ranisch (cf. *Heðins of beðja* 'Heðinn's bed-mate' *Edd. Min.*). Patzig (1924) explains *af létta* by presupposing the existence of an otherwise unknown f. noun *aflétta*, meaning 'obliging female companion', derived from the adj. *afléttr* 'willing (to give things away)' (see Fritzner: *afléttr*).

Marmennill (Marm Lv 5)

10. Bresta mun baugröst,
    brá mær augum
    um heruð hingat
    hegna til þegna.

    Hafa skal hverr drengr
    hjörnjóts mörg spjót,
    áðr komi mikil fram
    málmahríð síðan.

Baugröst mun bresta, mær brá augum um heruð hingat til þegna hegna. Hverr drengr hjörnjóts skal hafa mörg spjót, áðr mikil málmahríð komi fram síðan.

The ring-path [SHIELD] will break, the girl flashed her eyes around the district hither to the men of the defenders. Each brave fellow of the sword-user [WARRIOR] must have many spears, before a great weapon-storm [BATTLE] will then ensue.

Ms.: 2845(34r) (*Hálf*).

Readings: [2] mær: mér 2845   [6] hjörnjóts: 'híor níot ok' 2845.

Editions: *Skj*: Anonyme digte og vers [XIII], E. 6. *Vers af Fornaldarsagaer: Af Hálfssaga* IV 4: AII, 258, BII, 278, *Skald* II, 145, *NN* §2381; *Hálf* 1864, 11, *Hálf* 1909, 85, *FSGJ* 2, 103, *Hálf* 1981, 114-15, 175; *Edd. Min.* 91.

Notes: [All]: This stanza is metrically highly irregular, with ll. 2-3 and 5 in *fornyrðislag*, and the remainder in various metres that Snorri Sturluson exemplified in SnSt Ht 74-8[III]; l. 4 is *tøglag*. — [1] *baugröst* 'the ring-path [SHIELD]': This is the only instance in which the kenning *baugröst* occurs. However, it belongs to a common pattern of shield-kennings, which alludes to the flat form of the shield (see Meissner 169-70). — [2] *mær* 'the girl': The ms. reads *mér* 'to me', which most eds emend as here. *Skj* B retains *mér* and emends *augum* to *fyr augu* 'before my eyes'. — [6] *hjörnjóts* 'of the sword-user [WARRIOR]': The ms. reads 'híor níot ok', where *ok* is represented by a Tironian nota resembling a <z>. This can easily be mistaken for a final <z> denoting the genitive ending <s> and vice versa. The kenning *hjörnjótr* means 'sword-owner, sword-user' or possibly 'sword-god', as Njótr is also one of Óðinn's names (see Meissner 261, 331-2; Þul Óðins 6/6[III] and Note). — [8] *málmahríð* 'a weapon-storm [BATTLE]': *Skj* B, *Skald*, *Hálf* 1909 and *Edd. Min.* emend to *málmhríð* with the same meaning but one fewer syllable to give a metrically regular line. In *NN* §2381 Kock expresses disapproval of the eds that needlessly change *málmahríð* to *málmhríð*, although *málmhríð* is printed in *Skald*. *Málmahríð* 'weapon-storm' is a kenning for 'fight, battle'. Meissner 180 lists it as *málmhríð* with three examples. There is evidence that kennings for 'man' can also be formed with *málm-* as well as *málma-* (see Meissner 312).

Marmennill (Marm Lv 6)

11. Þó mun*u* — ef þat er satt,   þá ferr illa —
    hafa allir alkeypt   ár, þá er kemr vár.

Þó allir mun*u* hafa alkeypt ár, þá er kemr vár; ef þat er satt, þá ferr illa.

Still all will have paid very dearly for the year when spring comes; if that is true, then things will turn out badly.

Ms.: 2845(34r) (*Hálf*).

Reading: [1] mun*u*: man 2845.

Editions: *Skj*: Anonyme digte og vers [XIII], E. 6. *Vers af Fornaldarsagaer: Af Hálfssaga* IV 5: AII, 258, BII, 278, *Skald* II, 145; *Hálf* 1864, 11, *Hálf* 1909, 86, *FSGJ* 2, 103, *Hálf* 1981, 115, 175; *Edd. Min.* 91.

Context: This four-line stanza is a continuation of the merman's prophecy in the preceding stanza and may be considered its concluding statement. It is followed by the words: *þá lét Hjörleifr kóngr hann utan borðs* 'Then king Hjǫrleifr put him overboard'.

Notes: [All]: The stanza is again highly irregular metrically, and *Þó munu* 'Still will' of l. 1 is extrametrical. — [1] *mun*u 'will': The ms. reading is *man*, written *m* with a clearly discernible superscript *n*; *Hálf* 1864, *Edd. Min.* and *FSGJ* all emend to *munu* 'will' (3rd pers. pl.), agreeing with *allir* 'all' in l. 3, as does the present edn. *Skj* B, *Skald* and *Hálf* 1909 read *mun*. — [2] *ferr* 'things will turn out': Lit. 'it will turn out' (3rd pers. sg. pres. indic. of *fara* 'go'). The ms. reads 'fer', taken as a spelling for *ferr* by *Edd. Min.*, *FSGJ* and this edn. *Skj* B and *Skald* emend to *fara*, while *Hálf* 1864 and *Hálf* 1909 prefer *fǫr* 'journey'.

Marmennill (Marm Lv 7)

12. Kalt vatn augum   en kvett tönnum,
    lérept líki,   lát mik aptr í sjó.
    Dregr mik engi   í degi síðan
    maðr upp í skip   af marabotnum.

Kalt vatn augum en kvett tönnum, lérept líki, lát mik aptr í sjó. Engi maðr dregr mik síðan í degi upp í skip af marabotnum.

Cold water for the eyes and a piece of meat for the teeth, linen for the body, put me back into the sea. No man will pull me then by daylight from the depths of the ocean up into a ship.

Ms.: 2845(34r) (*Hálf*).

Editions: *Skj*: Anonyme digte og vers [XIII], E. 6. *Vers af Fornaldarsagaer: Af Hálfssaga* IV 6: AII, 258, BII, 278, *Skald* II, 145, *NN* §3188; *Hálf* 1864, 11, *Hálf* 1909, 86, *FSGJ* 2, 103-4, *Hálf* 1981, 116, 175; *Edd. Min.* 91.

Context: The stanza is preceded by the words: *Þá tók einn maðr í hönd honum ok spurði: Hvat er manni bezt? Marmendill svarar* ... 'Then a man took him by the hand and asked: What is best for a man? The merman replies ...'. The stanza is followed by the words: *Kóngr gaf þeim Handi ok Hrindi land at búa á ok þar með þræl ok ambátt* 'The king gave Handir and Hrindir land to farm and with it a slave and a bondwoman'.

Notes: [2] *kvett* 'a piece of meat': There has been much discussion about the meaning of the word *kvett*: Konráð Gíslason (1866c) suggests the reading *kveitt*, p. p. of an otherwise unknown verb **kveita* used as an adj. (attributive to the n. noun *vatn* 'water' in l. 1) meaning 'lukewarm, tepid'. Both *Skj* B and *Skald* adopt the form *kveitt*, Finnur Jónsson translating it as *kuldslåt* 'lukewarm'. Fritzner (1885) reads *kvett* as *kvætt*, explaining it as an otherwise unknown Old Norse noun denoting 'resin, treegum' (ModDan. *kvade*) allegedly chewed by people in Scandinavia in the old days; Konráð Gíslason (1885) is mainly a reply to Fritzner's criticism of Konráð Gíslason (1866c). Eiríkr Magnússon (1895) points out that in Modern Icelandic there is a noun *kvetti* 'lean whale meat' and suggests the meaning 'piece of (whale) meat' for *kvett*. — [6] *síðan í degi* 'then by daylight': Kock (*NN* §3188) disapproves of Finnur Jónsson's translation (*Skj* B *siden* 'again') of *í degi síðan* and suggests *mera i dag* 'more today'. Cf. *Hálf* 25/8 and Note there. — [8] *af marabotnum* 'from the depths of the ocean': This cpd was normalised to *mararbotnum* in *Hálf* 1864 and most later eds, except for *Skald*. According to *ONP*: *marabotn, mararbotn* this cpd is in most cases written *marabotn*, as in 2845.

Introduction to st. 13

The following stanza, spoken by some unknown voice, is a prophecy warning of imminent danger, but it is not clear to whom it is addressed. It comes near the end of a chapter of prose (*Hálf* 1981, 176) in which hostilities between Kings Hjǫrleifr and Hreiðarr are described. First Hreiðarr makes a night raid into Hjǫrleifr's territory, during which Hreiðarr's son Heri is killed, and escapes with a great deal of booty, apparently including Hjǫrleifr's two wives, Æsa and Hildr. Hjǫrleifr retaliates with a night raid on Hreiðarr's dwelling, where he is himself captured, though saved by Hildr. He then kills Hreiðarr and escapes, taking back his two wives.

An Unknown Voice (Anon *Hálf* 3)

13. Minntiz Hreiðarr, hvar Hera fellduð;
    vá vakðiz þar fyrir vestrdyrum.
    Enn man hon sinna til sala þinna,
    byrsæl kona; bíð þú enn, konungr.

Hreiðarr minntiz, hvar fellduð Hera; vá vakðiz þar fyrir vestrdyrum. Enn man hon, byrsæl kona, sinna til sala þinna; bíð þú enn, konungr.

Hreiðarr remembered, where you slew Heri; woe was roused there before the western gate. Still she, the woman who is lucky in getting a fair wind, will travel to your hall; just you wait, king.

Ms.: 2845(34v) (*Hálf*).

Editions: *Skj*: Anonyme digte og vers [XIII], E. 6. Vers af Fornaldarsagaer: Af Hálfssaga V: AII, 258, BII, 278; *Skald* II, 145-6; *Hálf* 1864, 13, *Hálf* 1909, 89, *FSGJ* 2, 105, *Hálf* 1981, 116-17, 176; *Edd. Min.* 92.

Context: The stanza is preceded by the words: *Þann en sama aptan, er Hjǫrleifr kóngr kom, heyrði Hreiðarr kóngr kveðit* ... 'On the very evening, when King Hjǫrleifr came, King Hreiðarr heard a voice say ...'.

Notes: [All]: It is unclear to whom this stanza is addressed. While l. 1 speaks of Hreiðarr in the 3rd pers. and l. 2 addresses Hreiðarr's enemies, who killed his son Heri, in the 2nd pers. pl., ll. 3-8 seem to be directed to Hreiðarr himself. These apparent inconsistencies explain the emendations from *minntiz* '[he] remembered' (l. 1) and *fellduð* 'you (pl.) slew' (l. 2) by some eds in ll. 1-2 (cf. *Hálf* 1981, 116-17 for further detail). — [5, 7] *hon, byrsæl kona* 'she, the woman who is lucky in getting a fair wind': Lit. 'she, the fair wind-fortunate woman'. The identity of this woman is also unclear, though ll. 5-8 may reiterate the personification of warfare in the person of a valkyrie that occurs in several of the merman's stanzas. It is possible that the two *helmingar* of this stanza were once separate.

Introduction to *Innsteinskviða*, part 1 (*Hálf* 14-28)

The long poem called *Innsteinskviða* 'Poem of Innsteinn' (*Innkv*) (*Hálf* 14-37), falls into three parts, each separated by prose links. The first part comprises *Hálf* 14-28, the second *Hálf* 29-33, and the third *Hálf* 34-7. The poem's main subject, the night-time burning of a troop of warriors inside a hall by a treacherous opponent, finds a parallel in other heroic poetry, such as the Old English *Fight at Finnsburh* and the telling of the same tale in *Beowulf* ll. 1063-1159 (cf. *Beowulf* 2008, 180-91, 273-90). The first, and longest, part is cast in the form of a dialogue between King Hálfr, son of Hjǫrleifr, now a renowned leader with a specially tough but chivalrous warrior band, the Hálfsrekkar 'Hálfr's Champions', and his loyal follower and chief adviser, Innsteinn. The background narrative is told sparingly in the saga: after eighteen years of successful warfare, Hálfr and his men return to Hǫrðaland (Hordaland), where a certain King Ásmundr, who has married Hálfr's mother Hildr after Hjǫrleifr's death and fostered their two sons, swears oaths of loyalty to Hálfr and 'becomes his man' (*gerðiz hans maðr*), inviting him and half his champions to a feast. Innsteinn suspects Ásmundr's motives and tries to dissuade Hálfr from attending the feast, proposing instead that they should set fire to Ásmundr's hall, but Hálfr is reluctant to withdraw and insists on going, invoking the high standards of honourable heroic behaviour that he claims Ásmundr abides by, though Innsteinn (and the audience) know differently. Thus the dialogue between these two characters creates a gap between ideal and reality for the audience that imparts a sense of tragic foreboding to the poem. Even when Innsteinn reveals the contents of his three prophetic dreams, Hálfr tries to explain them away in a rational manner, reminiscent of a similarly rationalising dismissal of prophetic dreams in *Am* 11-29. Stanzas 14-28 are cited without prose interruption except for the designation of the speaker.

Innsteinn (Innsteinn *Innkv* 1)

14. Upp mundum vér   allir ganga,
    skatna beztir,   af skipum várum,
    láta brenna   bragninga sveit
    ok Ásmundar lið   aldri týna.

Vér, beztir skatna, mundum allir ganga upp af skipum várum, láta brenna sveit bragninga ok lið Ásmundar týna aldri.

We, the best of warriors, should all go up from our ships, let the band of men burn and [make] the troops of Ásmundr lose [their] lives.

Ms.: **2845**(35v) (*Hálf*).

Editions: *Skj*: Anonyme digte og vers [XIII], E. 6. *Vers af Fornaldarsagaer: Af Hálfssaga* VI 1: AII, 258-9, BII, 278-9, *Skald* II, 146; *Hálf* 1864, 16, *Hálf* 1909, 99, *FSGJ* 2, 108-9, *Hálf* 1981, 117, 179; *Edd. Min.* 33.

Context: This stanza is introduced by the words: *En annan morgin, er kóngr bjózt ok sagði at helmingr liðs skyldi eptir vera á skipum, Innsteinn kvað …* 'But the following morning, when the king made himself ready and said that half the troops were to remain aboard the ships, Innsteinn said …'.

Notes: [All]: Innsteinn makes no bones about proposing to subject Ásmundr to the same fate as he believes Ásmundr has in store for Hálfr and his men. — [3] *skatna* 'of warriors': The pl. of *skati* 'man, chieftain, prince' has most often the meaning 'warriors' (see *Meissner* 265-6). — [7] *Ásmundar* 'of Ásmundr': The saga prose gives no detail of where Ásmundr was king, merely that he married Hildr, widow of Hjǫrleifr, and fostered his two sons, one of whom was Hálfr. Thus Hálfr owes loyalty to Ásmundr as his stepfather and fosterer, which complicates the present situation.

Hálfr (Hálfr Innkv 1)

15. Vér skulum, hálfir   herjar þessa,
    sáttir sækja   frá sjó neðan.
    Ásmundr hefir   oss um boðna
    hringa rauða,   sem hafa viljum.

Vér, hálfir þessa herjar, skulum sækja sáttir neðan frá sjó. Ásmundr hefir oss rauða hringa um boðna, sem viljum hafa.

We, half of this host, shall go on good terms up from the sea. Ásmundr has offered us red rings, which we want to have.

Ms.: 2845(35v) (*Hálf*).

Editions: *Skj*: Anonyme digte og vers [XIII], E. 6. *Vers af Fornaldarsagaer: Af Hálfssaga* VI 2: AII, 259, BII, 279, *Skald* II, 146; *Hálf* 1864, 16, *Hálf* 1909, 100, *FSGJ* 2, 109, *Hálf* 1981, 179; *Edd. Min.* 33.

Context: This stanza is introduced by the words: *kóngr kvað* 'the king said'.

Innsteinn (Innsteinn *Innkv* 2)

16. Sér ekki þú allan   Ásmundar hug;
    hefir fylkir sá   flærð í brjósti.
    Mundir þú, þengill,   ef vér því réðim,
    mági þínum   mjök litt trúa.

Þú sér ekki allan hug Ásmundar; sá fylkir hefir flærð í brjósti. Þú, þengill, mundir trúa mági þínum mjök litt, ef vér réðim því.

You do not see Ásmundr's whole mind; this prince has falsehood in his breast. You, king, should trust your kinsman very little, if it were up to us [me].

Ms.: 2845(35v) (*Hálf*).

Editions: *Skj*: Anonyme digte og vers [XIII], E. 6. *Vers af Fornaldarsagaer: Af Hálfssaga* VI 3: AII, 259, BII, 279, *Skald* II, 146; *Hálf* 1864, 17, *Hálf* 1909, 100, *FSGJ* 2, 109, *Hálf* 1981, 117, 179; *Edd. Min.* 33.

Context: This stanza is introduced by the words: *Innsteinn kvað* 'Innsteinn said'.

Notes: [6] *ef vér réðim því* 'if it were up to us [me]': Lit. 'if we decided about that'. With earlier eds, the ms.'s *réðum* has been normalised to *réðim* (pret. subj.), which would have been normal in a text of the C13th in a concessive clause (cf. *ANG* §536.2), but in a C15th ms. reflects the later Icelandic use of the indic. ending in such circumstances. Similar are *Hálf* 60/4, 6. — [7] *mági* 'kinsman': *Mágr*, usually meaning 'brother-in-law, son-in-law, father-in-law', here refers to Hálfr's stepfather, Ásmundr.

Hálfr (Hálfr *Innkv* 2)

17. Ásmundr hefir   oss um unnit
      margar trygðir,   sem menn vitu.
      Mun ekki góðr konungr   ganga á sáttir,
      né gramr annan   í griðum véla.

Ásmundr hefir oss margar trygðir um unnit, sem menn vitu. Góðr konungr mun ekki ganga á sáttir, né [mun] gramr véla annan í griðum.

Ásmundr has made many pledges to us, as people know. A good king will not violate agreements, nor [will] a prince betray another [prince] in a time of truce.

Ms.: 2845(35v-36r) (*Hálf*).

Editions: *Skj*: Anonyme digte og vers [XIII], E. 6. *Vers af Fornaldarsagaer: Af Hálfssaga* VI 4: AII, 259, BII, 279, *Skald* II, 146; *Hálf* 1864, 17, *Hálf* 1909, 101, *FSGJ* 2, 110, *Hálf* 1981, 179-80; *Edd. Min.* 33.

Context: This stanza is introduced by the words: *kóngr kvað* 'the king said'.

Note: [8] *í griðum* 'in a time of truce': Lit. 'in truces'.

Innsteinn (Innsteinn *Innkv* 3)

18. Þér er orðinn   Óðinn til gramr,
      er þú Ásmundi   allvel trúir.
      Hann mun alla   oss um véla,
      nema þú vitrari   viðsjár fáir.

Óðinn er orðinn þér til gramr, er þú trúir Ásmundi allvel. Hann mun oss alla um véla, nema þú fáir vitrari viðsjár.

Óðinn has become too angry with you, since you trust Ásmundr so well. He will betray us all, unless you acquire wiser wariness.

Ms.: 2845(36r) (*Hálf*).

Editions: *Skj*: Anonyme digte og vers [XIII], E. 6. *Vers af Fornaldarsagaer: Af Hálfssaga* VI 5: AII, 259, BII, 279, *Skald* II, 146; *Hálf* 1864, 17, *Hálf* 1909, 101-2, *FSGJ* 2, 110, *Hálf* 1981, 117-18, 180; *Edd. Min.* 33-4.

Context: This stanza is introduced by the words: *Innsteinn kvað* 'Innsteinn said'.

Notes: [1-2] *Óðinn er orðinn þér til gramr* 'Óðinn has become too angry with you': Cf. *Heiðr* 112/4, *gramr er yðr Óðinn* 'Óðinn is angry with you'. Both here and in *Hálf* 35/5-6 Innsteinn invokes the name of the god Óðinn, who is widely represented in Old Norse myth, especially in *fornaldarsögur*, as the god of battle, who not only confers victory on his favourites, but may sometimes withdraw his favour from them (cf. Turville-Petre 1964, 52-4; Marold 1972, 27-8). Here Innsteinn suggests that the god will turn against Hálfr and the Hálfsrekkar because Hálfr allows himself to trust Ásmundr uncritically. In *Hálf* 35/5-8 Innsteinn interprets the Hálfsrekkar's defeat as Óðinn's evil doing. — [7] *vitrari* 'wiser': This word is hardly legible in the ms. and has been variously interpreted by earlier eds (see *Hálf* 1981, 117-18). Jón Helgason (1955b, xxii) suggested either 'uitrarí' or 'uittrarí' as possible readings, but inspection under ultra-violet light has shown that it cannot be 'uitrarí', as there are too many vertical pen strokes discernible. — [8] *viðsjár* 'wariness': The f. noun *viðsjá* 'wariness, cautiousness' is nowhere else used with the verb *fá* 'get, acquire' and may be either gen. sg. or acc. pl.. Finnur Jónsson (*LP*: *viðrsjó, viðsjó*) describes the meaning of the word as *ævnen, handlingen at tage sig i agt for* 'the capability, the act of being wary of', giving it a slightly more concrete nuance, which makes its use with the verb *fá* seem more plausible.

Hálfr (Hálfr Innkv 3)

19. Æ lystir þik   æðru at mæla;
    mun ekki sá konungr   sáttir rjúfa.
    Gull eigum þar   ok gersimar,
    hringa rauða   frá hans búum.

Þik lystir æ at mæla æðru; sá konungr mun ekki rjúfa sáttir. Eigum þar gull ok gersimar, rauða hringa frá búum hans.

You always wish to utter words of fear; this king will not break [our] agreement. There we are entitled to gold and jewels, red rings from his estates.

Ms.: **2845**(36r) (*Hálf*).

Editions: *Skj*: Anonyme digte og vers [XIII], E. 6. *Vers af Fornaldarsagaer: Af Hálfssaga* VI 6: AII, 259, BII, 279-80, *Skald* II, 146; *Hálf* 1864, 18, *Hálf* 1909, 102, *FSGJ* 2, 110-11, *Hálf* 1981, 118, 180; *Edd. Min.* 34.

Context: This stanza is introduced by the words: *kóngr kvað* 'the king said'.

Note: [2] *at mæla æðru* 'to utter words of fear': Lit. 'to speak fear'.

Innsteinn (Innsteinn *Innkv* 4)

20. Hálfr, dreymði mik — hygðu at slíku —,
     at logi léki um liði váru.
     Ilt væri þar ór at leysaz;
     hvat kv*eð*r þú, þengill, þann draum vita?

Hálfr, mik dreymði — hygðu at slíku —, at logi léki um liði váru. Þar væri ilt at leysaz ór; hvat kv*eð*r þú, þengill, þann draum vita?

Hálfr, I dreamed — be mindful of this — that a flame flickered around our troop. It would be difficult to escape from there; what do you say, king, that dream means?

Ms.: 2845(36r) (*Hálf*).

Reading: [7] kveðr: kvað 2845.

Editions: *Skj*: Anonyme digte og vers [XIII], E. 6. *Vers af Fornaldarsagaer: Af Hálfssaga* VI 7: AII, 259-60, BII, 280, *Skald* II, 146; *Hálf* 1864, 18, *Hálf* 1909, 102, *FSGJ* 2, 111, *Hálf* 1981, 118, 180; *Edd. Min.* 34.

Context: This stanza is introduced by the words: *Innsteinn kvað* 'Innsteinn said'.

Notes: [All]: Here and in two further stanzas (*Hálf* 22 and 24), Innsteinn tries to persuade Hálfr to abandon his proposed visit to Ásmundr by telling him of three foreboding dreams he has had. Their cumulative effect is underlined by the verbal repetition of Innsteinn's question to Hálfr about the meaning of these dreams in ll. 7-8 of each stanza. — [7] *hvat kveðr þú* 'what do you say': The ms. has *kvað*, 2nd pers. sg. pret. 'did you say' here and in *Hálf* 22/7 (where it is written out in full) and *Hálf* 24/7, so is unlikely to be a scribal error. At the same time the pret. in this context does not make sense, so all eds, beginning with Bugge (*Hálf* 1864), have emended to the 2nd pers. sg. pres. tense here and in the two other instances in which *kvað* occurs. *Hálf* 1981, 118. 180 retains the ms. form.

Hálfr (Hálfr Innkv 4)

21. Hrynja um herðar, þeim er hamalt fylkja
     grams verðungu, gyldnar brynjur.
     Þat mun á öxlum öðlings vinum
     ljóst at líta, sem logi brenni.

Gyldnar brynjur hrynja um herðar, þeim er fylkja hamalt verðungu grams. Þat mun ljóst at líta á öxlum vinum öðlings, sem logi brenni.

Gilded byrnies fall around the shoulders of those who draw up the prince's retinue in a wedge-shaped phalanx. A brightness will be clearly seen on the shoulders of the prince's friends, as if a flame were burning.

Ms.: **2845**(36r) (*Hálf*).

Editions: *Skj*: Anonyme digte og vers [XIII], E. 6. *Vers af Fornaldarsagaer: Af Hálfssaga* VI 8: AII, 260, BII, 280, *Skald* II, 147, *NN* §118, *FF* §25; *Hálf* 1864, 19, *Hálf* 1909, 104, *FSGJ* 2, 112, *Hálf* 1981, 181; *Edd. Min.* 34-5.

Context: This stanza is introduced by the words: *kóngr kvað* 'the king said'.

Notes: [All]: Following a suggestion by Svend Grundtvig, Bugge (*Hálf* 1864) altered the ms. sequence of stanzas at this point, interchanging *Hálf* 23 and *Hálf* 21. This change of sequence has been followed by all subsequent eds aside from *Hálf* 1981 and the present edn, which follow the ms. order. — [2] *fylkja hamalt* 'draw up in a wedge-shaped phalanx': The word *hamalt* occcurs only in the idiomatic expression *fylkja hamalt*, see *LP*: 1. *hamall*. In the ms. *fylkja* is written *fylgía*; see further *Hálf* 67/5, where *fylkti* is written *fylgdí*; see Note to ÞjóðA *Run* 1/4^{II}. Óðinn was reputed to have taught warriors how to *fylkja hamalt* (Beck 1998). — [5, 7] *þat mun ljóst at líta* 'a brightness will be clearly seen': Lit. 'It will be bright to look at'.

Innsteinn (Innsteinn *Innkv* 5)

22. Enn dreymði mik   öðru sinni;
    hugða ek á öxlum   elda brenna.
    Gruna tek ek nökkut,   at þat gott viti;
    hvat kv*eð*r þú, þengill,   *þann* draum vita?

Enn dreymði mik öðru sinni; ek hugða elda brenna á öxlum. Ek tek gruna nökkut, at þat viti gott; hvat kv*eð*r þú, þengill, *þann* draum vita?

I dreamed again a second time; I thought fires were burning on the shoulders [of our men]. I am becoming rather doubtful that this is a good omen; what do you say, king, that dream means?

Ms.: **2845**(36r) (*Hálf*).

Readings: [7] kv*eð*r: 'kuad' 2845   [8] *þann*: om. 2845.

Editions: *Skj*: Anonyme digte og vers [XIII], E. 6. *Vers af Fornaldarsagaer: Af Hálfssaga* VI 9: AII, 260, BII, 280, *Skald* II, 147; *Hálf* 1864, 19, *Hálf* 1909, 103-4, *FSGJ* 2, 111-12, *Hálf* 1981, 181; *Edd. Min.* 34.

Context: This stanza is introduced by the words: *Innsteinn kvað* 'Innsteinn said'.

Note: [3] *á öxlum* 'on the shoulders [of our men]': Finnur Jónsson (*Skj* B) interprets the phrase to refer to Innsteinn's own shoulders, but this seems a less likely interpretation than one that envisages fire affecting the whole group of men (cf. st. 21/6 *öðlings vinum* 'the prince's friends').

Hálfr (Hálfr Innkv 5)

23. Gefa mun ek hverjum   hj*á*l*m* ok brynju
    frækna drengja,   er fylgja mér.
    Þat mun at líta,   sem logi brenni
    skjöldungs liði   um skarar fjöllum.

Ek mun gefa hverjum frækna drengja, er fylgja mér, hj*á*l*m* ok brynju. Þat mun at líta, sem logi brenni um fjöllum skarar liði skjöldungs.

I shall give to each of the brave warriors who follow me a helmet and a byrnie. That will look as if a flame were burning around the mountains of hair [HEADS] of the prince's host.

Ms.: **2845**(36r) (*Hálf*).

Reading: [2] hj*á*l*m*: 'hiaml' 2845.

Editions: *Skj*: Anonyme digte og vers [XIII], E. 6. *Vers af Fornaldarsagaer: Af Hálfssaga* VI 10: AII, 260, BII, 280, *Skald* II, 146-7, *FF* §25; *Hálf* 1864, 18-19, *Hálf* 1909, 103, *FSGJ* 2, 111, *Hálf* 1981, 118, 181; *Edd. Min.* 34.

Context: This stanza is introduced by the words: *kóngr kvað* 'the king said'.

Notes: [All]: See *Hálf* 21, Note to [All]. — [2] hj*á*lm ok brynju 'a helmet and a byrnie': Bugge (*Hálf* 1864) emends the line to hjálm gullroðinn 'gold-covered helmet' because to his mind *ok brynju* is not consistent with the content of the second *helmingr*. — [3] *frækna* (gen. pl.) 'brave': The reading of the ms. *Hálf* 1909, *FSGJ* and *Edd. Min.* correct to *fræknra*, *Skj* B, *Skald* and *Hálf* 1981 retain *frækna*. Both forms are possible; cf. *ANG* §427.2. — [8] *um fjöllum skarar* 'around the mountains of hair [HEADS]': The ms. reads *of* (prep.) 'around' rather than *um*, but has been normalised to a 1250-1300 standard. The kenning *fjall skarar* 'mountain of hair' for 'head' is also used in ESk Frag 2/4^III; *háfiall scarar* 'high mountain of hair' for 'head' occurs in *Hym* 23/6 (*NK* 92).

Innsteinn (Innsteinn *Innkv* 6)

24. Þat dreymði mik   þriðja sinni,
    at vér í kaf niðr   komnir værim.
    Eiga mun allstórt   um at véla;
    hvat kve*ð*r þú, þengill,   þann draum vita?

Þat dreymði mik þriðja sinni, at vér værim komnir niðr í kaf. Allstórt mun eiga um at véla; hvat kve*ð*r þú, þengill, þann draum vita?

The third time I dreamed that we were deeply immersed in water. Something very great will have to be dealt with; what do you say, king, that dream means?

Ms.: 2845(36r) (*Hálf*).

Reading: [7] kveðr: kvað 2845.

Editions: *Skj*: Anonyme digte og vers [XIII], E. 6. *Vers af Fornaldarsagaer: Af Hálfssaga* VI 11: AII, 260, BII, 280-1, *Skald* II, 147; *Hálf* 1864, 19-20, *Hálf* 1909, 105, *FSGJ* 2, 112, *Hálf* 1981, 118, 181-2; *Edd. Min.* 35.

Context: This stanza is introduced by the words: *Innsteinn kvað* 'Innsteinn said'.

Notes: [4] *vér værim* 'we were': All previous eds have normalised the ms.'s *værum* to the pret. subj. 1st pers. pl. *værim*; cf. Note to *Hálf* 16/6. — [4, 3] *komnir niðr í kaf* 'deeply immersed in water': Lit. 'come down into the deep sea'. The noun *kaf* means what lies below the surface of the water, and refers to the deep sea or ocean. This prediction does not relate literally to a prospective drowning of Hálfr's men, unlike Innsteinn's two previous prophecies of death by fire, but seems to be a metaphor for death or dying. — [5-6] *allstórt mun eiga um at véla* 'something very great will have to be dealt with': An impersonal construction, lit. 'it will very greatly have to be done with' (cf. *LP*: *véla* 3).

Hálfr (Hálfr Innkv 6)

25. Fulllangt er sjá   fíflskapr talaðr;
    vera kveð ek ekki   undir slíku.
    Seg þú öngva,   svá at heyri,
    drauma þína   í degi síðan.

Sjá fíflskapr er fulllangt talaðr; ek kveð ekki vera undir slíku. Seg þú öngva drauma þína síðan í degi, svá at heyri.

This foolish talk has been going on for too long; I say there is nothing in such talk. Do not tell any of your dreams in an audible manner later this day.

Ms.: 2845(36r) (*Hálf*).

Editions: *Skj*: Anonyme digte og vers [XIII], E. 6. *Vers af Fornaldarsagaer: Af Hálfssaga* VI 12: AII, 260, BII, 281, *Skald* II, 147, *NN* §3188; *Hálf* 1864, 20, *Hálf* 1909, 105, *FSGJ* 2, 113, *Hálf* 1981, 118, 182; *Edd. Min.* 35.

Context: This stanza is introduced by the words: *kóngr kvað* 'the king said'.

Notes: [All]: Hálfr's mistrust and dismissal of Innsteinn's foreboding dreams must surely make him appear reckless in an Old Norse tradition in which prophetic dreams were regarded as important indicators of events to come (see, among others, Turville-Petre 1972b). This inference is confirmed correct by Innsteinn's generous suggestion below, (*Hálf* 26/7-8), that the warriors should absolve Hálfr from any blame for his words. — [6] *svá at heyri* 'in an audible manner': Lit. 'so that it can be heard'. — [8] *síðan í degi* 'later this day': Kock (*NN* §3188) disapproves of Finnur Jónsson's translation in *Skj* B, *aldrig mere ... nogen dag* 'never more ... any day' of *síðan í degi* and suggests *mera i dag* 'more today'. Cf. *Hálf* 12/6.

Innsteinn (Innsteinn *Innkv* 7)

26. Hlýði Hrókar   *í* her konung*s*
    orðum mínum,   Útsteinn þriði.
    Göngum allir   upp frá ströndu;
    kunnum ekki   konungs mál um þat.

Hrókar hlýði orðum mínum *í* her konung*s*, Útsteinn þriði. Göngum allir upp frá ströndu; kunnum ekki mál konungs um þat.

May the Hrókar in the king's host listen to my words, Útsteinn as the third one. Let us all go up from the shore; let us not hold the king's words at fault for that.

Ms.: **2845**(36r) (*Hálf*).

Readings: [2] *í* her konung*s*: ok her kóngr 2845.

Editions: *Skj*: Anonyme digte og vers [XIII], E. 6. *Vers af Fornaldarsagaer: Af Hálfssaga* VI 13: AII, 260-1, BII, 281; *Skald* II, 147; *Hálf* 1864, 20, *Hálf* 1909, 105-6, *FSGJ* 2, 113, *Hálf* 1981, 118-19, 182; *Edd. Min.* 35.

Context: This stanza is introduced by the words: *Innsteinn kvað* 'Innsteinn said'.

Notes: [1-4]: Innsteinn addresses the two Hrókar 'Rooks' (the brothers Hrókr inn svarti 'Rook the Black' and Hrókr inn hvíti 'Rook the White') and his own brother Útsteinn, referring to him as *þriði* 'the third one'. As the reading *ok her kóngr* in 2845 would suggest that Innsteinn addresses four persons, eds emend l. 2 to *ok herr konungs* (*Skj* B, *Skald*) or *í her konungs* (*Hálf* 1909, *FSGJ*, *Edd. Min.*). — [4] *Útsteinn*: Brother of Innsteinn. According to *Hálf* (*Hálf* 1981, 177) both brothers were called Steinn. The saga explains that Innsteinn, the older of the two, got his name from an incident that took place on the first expedition of the Hálfsrekkar, when, on a rainy night, he asked for a tent to shelter in. Hálfr rejected his request as inappropriate for tough warriors like the Hálfsrekkar, and from then on he was called Innsteinn 'Inside Steinn'. The younger Steinn was too young to go with the Hálfsrekkar on their first expedition, but turned up anyway and asked for passage on board ship; he was taken on and called Útsteinn 'Outside Steinn'.

Útsteinn (Útsteinn Innkv 1)

27. Konung látum vér   keppinn ráða,
     fyrr í fólki,   um farir várar.
     Hættum, bróðir,   svát honum líki,
     fjörvi okkru   með frömum vísi.

Vér látum keppinn konung, fyrr í fólki, ráða um farir várar. Hættum, bróðir, fjörvi okkru með frömum vísi, svát líki honum.

We will let the contentious king, at the head of the host, decide about our journeys. Let us, brother, risk our lives with the valiant leader in such a way as to please him.

Ms.: 2845(36r) (*Hálf*).

Readings: [3] fyrr í fólki: 'fyrí folki' 2845   [6] svát: svá 2845.

Editions: *Skj*: Anonyme digte og vers [XIII], E. 6. *Vers af Fornaldarsagaer: Af Hálfssaga* VI 14: AII, 261, BII, 281, *Skald* II, 147, *NN* §3189; *Hálf* 1864, 21, *Hálf* 1909, 106, *FSGJ* 2, 113-14, *Hálf* 1981, 119, 182; *Edd. Min.* 35.

Context: This stanza is introduced by the words: *Útsteinn kvað* 'Útsteinn said'.

Note: [3] *fyrr í fólki* 'at the head of the host': Editors print either *fyrr í fólki* (*Hálf* 1909) or *fyrir í fólki* (*Skj* B, *Skald*, *Edd. Min.*). The reading of 'fyrí folki' in 2845 as *fyrr í fólki* is supported by the fact that in the *Hálfs saga* text in 2845 there are two more instances where *fyrr* is written 'fyr'; see P. B. Taylor (1965) for a similar phrase, *fyrstr í fólki*, in *HHund I* 53/7 (*NK* 138) and *Hálf* (1981, 119).

Innsteinn (Innsteinn *Innkv* 8)

28. Hlítt hefir fylkir   í förum úti
     mínum ráðum   mörgu sinni.
     Nú kveð ek öngu,   er ek mæli,
     hlýða vilja,   sízt hingat kómum.

Fylkir hefir mörgu sinni hlítt ráðum mínum í förum úti. Nú kveð ek hlýða vilja öngu, er ek mæli, sízt kómum hingat.

The prince has many times trusted my advice while on journeys out at sea. Now I declare [him] unwilling to listen to anything I say since we have come here.

Ms.: 2845(36r) (*Hálf*).

Editions: *Skj*: Anonyme digte og vers [XIII], E. 6. *Vers af Fornaldarsagaer: Af Hálfssaga* VI 15: AII, 261, BII, 281, *Skald* II, 147; *Hálf* 1864, 21, *Hálf* 1909, 106, *FSGJ* 2, 114, *Hálf* 1981, 182-3; *Edd. Min.* 35.

Context: This stanza is introduced by the words: *Innsteinn kvað* 'Innsteinn said'.

Note: [8] *hingat* 'here': The line is *málaháttr* and hypermetrical but can be regularised by adopting the alternative form *higat*, as is done in *Edd. Min.*, *Skj* B and *Skald*.

Introduction to *Innsteinskviða*, part 2 (*Hálf* 29-33)

The second part of *Innkv* (*Hálf* 29-33) is separated from the first in the saga by a short prose passage describing the events in Ásmundr's hall where Hálfr and the Hálfsrekkar have been feasting. It takes the form of a monologue spoken by Innsteinn to encourage Hálfr and the other Hálfsrekkar to fight and to leave the burning hall. There are some discrepancies between the prose introduction and the stanzas of this part that are discussed in the Notes below.

Innsteinn (Innsteinn *Innkv* 9)

29. Rýkr um hauka   í höll konungs;
     ván er at *d*rjúpi   vax af söxum.
     Mál er gulli   ok gersimum,
     hjálmum skipta   með Hálfsrekkum.

Rýkr um hauka í höll konungs; ván er at vax *d*rjúpi af söxum. Mál er skipta hjálmum, gulli ok gersimum, með Hálfsrekkum.

There is smoke around the hawks in the king's hall; it is to be expected that wax will drip from the swords. It is time to share helmets, gold and treasures with Hálfr's champions.

Ms.: **2845**(36v) (*Hálf*).

Reading: [3] *d*rjúpi: rjúki 2845.

Editions: *Skj*: Anonyme digte og vers [XIII], E. 6. *Vers af Fornaldarsagaer: Af Hálfssaga* VII 1: AII, 261, BII, 282, *Skald* II, 147-8, *NN* §2836; *Hálf* 1864, 22, *Hálf* 1909, 107-8, *FSGJ* 2, 115, *Hálf* 1981, 123-4, 183; *Edd. Min.* 36.

Context: This stanza is preceded by a prose paragraph. Hálfr attends King Ásmundr's banquet with half his troops. When the guests have fallen asleep, Ásmundr and his men set fire to the hall. One of Hálfr's champions wakes up and, realising that the hall is filled with smoke, says: *Rjúka mun um hauka vára nú* 'Now there will be smoke around our hawks.' He then goes back to sleep. Another of Hálfr's men wakes up and, realising that the hall is on fire, says: *Drjúpa man nú vax af söxum* 'Now wax will drip from the swords'. He then lies down again. Then King Hálfr awakes. He rises, wakes up his men and orders them to take their arms. They attempt to get out by jumping against the walls. The stanza is introduced by the words: *Þá kvað Innsteinn* 'Then Innsteinn said'.

Notes: [All]: The stanza is spoken by Innsteinn and warns indirectly that the hall is on fire. In the prose text ll. 1-2 are attributed to one of the Hálfsrekkar, and ll. 3-4 to another, while the hortatory remarks of the second *helmingr* are attributed in the prose to King Hálfr, who in the poem seems not to have yet woken from his postprandial sleep. — [1] *rýkr um hauka* 'there is smoke around the hawks': Here and in several other instances in the *Hálf* stanzas, the noun *haukr* (and the cpd *haukmaðr*) is used metaphorically to apply, not to birds of prey, but to keen, bold warriors; cf. *Hálf* 54/2 and 64/2. This sense is not uncommon in Old Norse poetry; cf. *LP*: *haukr* 2, Arn *Hryn* 3/5[II] and Note there. — [3-4]: Munch (1852-63, I, i, 304 n. 1) suggests that wax, smeared on the warriors' weapons to prevent corrosion, will melt in the heat of the fire and drip down. It seems that sword blades may have been coated with a thin layer of wax to prevent them rusting. — [3] d*rjúpi* 'will drip': The ms.'s *rjúki* 'will smoke' is obviously influenced by *rýkr* 'there is smoke, it is smoking' in l. 1. The emendation *drjúpi*, first suggested by Bugge (*Hálf* 1864), is in accordance with the preceding prose, and has been followed by subsequent eds.

Innsteinn (Innsteinn *Innkv* 10)

30. Hins fýsi ek nú,   at Hálfr vaki,
    er ekki af eklu   eldar kynd*ir.
    Áttu, menbrjótr,   mági þínum
    grimmlunduðum   gjafir at launa.

Nú fýsi ek hins, at Hálfr vaki, eldar er ekki kynd*ir af eklu. Áttu, menbrjótr, at launa grimmlunduðum mági þínum gjafir.

Now I advise that Hálfr should wake up, the fires are not lit scantily. You, necklace-breaker [GENEROUS RULER], have to reward your cruel-minded kinsman for his gifts.

Ms.: **2845**(36v) (*Hálf*).

Reading: [4] kynd*ir: kyndnir 2845.

Editions: *Skj*: Anonyme digte og vers [XIII], E. 6. Vers af Fornaldarsagaer: Af Hálfssaga VII 2: AII, 261, BII, 282, *Skald* II, 148; *Hálf* 1864, 23, *Hálf* 1909, 107-8, *FSGJ* 2, 115, *Hálf* 1981, 183; *Edd. Min.* 36.

Notes: [All]: On the discrepancy between this stanza and the prose text, see *Hálf* 29, Note to [All]. — [2] *vaki* 'should wake up': Cf. Anon *Bjark* 1/5[III] *vaki æ ok vaki* 'wake now and wake'. This is one of the rare instances, where the verb *vaka* 'be awake' has the meaning of the inchoative verb *vakna* 'awaken, wake up'. See Fritzner: *vaka, vakna*. — [3] *er* 'are': Lit. 'is'. The subject of the verb (*eldar* 'fires') is pl., but the verb sg. It is not uncommon for the sg. of the 3rd pers. to be used with a pl. subject if the subject follows the verb or is separated from it by several words, as here; cf. *NS* §66 Anm. 3. — [3] *af eklu* 'scantily': Lit. 'from scarcity'. That is, there are a great many fires around. — [5-8]:

This *helmingr* is bitterly ironic in view of Hálfr's protestations in part 1 of *Innkv* that Ásmundr, his cruel-minded kinsman, was acting generously and peacefully in inviting him and the Hálfsrekkar to a feast.

Innsteinn (Innsteinn *Innkv* 11)

31. Hrindum heilir   hallar bjóri;
     nú taka súlur   í sundr þoka.
     Æ mun uppi,   með*an* öld lifir,
     Hálfsrekka för   til hertoga.

Hrindum heilir bjóri hallar; súlur taka nú þoka í sundr. För Hálfsrekka til hertoga mun æ uppi, með*an* öld lifir.

May we succeed in pushing [out] the gable wall of the hall; now the pillars begin to move asunder. The journey of Hálfr's champions to the army-commander will always be remembered, as long as mankind lives.

Ms.: 2845(36v) (*Hálf*).

Reading: [6] með*an*: með 2845.

Editions: *Skj*: Anonyme digte og vers [XIII], E. 6. *Vers af Fornaldarsagaer: Af Hálfssaga* VII 3: AII, 261, BII, 282, *Skald* II, 148; *Hálf* 1864, 23, *Hálf* 1909, 108, *FSGJ* 2, 115-16, *Hálf* 1981, 124, 184; *Edd. Min.* 36.

Notes: [1] *hrindum heilir* 'may we succeed in pushing': Lit. 'May we fortunate push'. The verb *hrinda* 'push, thrust' takes the dat. of what is pushed, here *bjóri hallar* 'the gable wall of the hall' (l. 2). Cf. *Hálf* 34/5 for a similar use of *heilir* plus verb. — [5-6]: These lines are a commonplace, expressing the enduring importance of notable events or achievements to human society. The same two lines are at *Vsp* 16/5-6 and the first is at *Heiðr* 119/5. — [8] *hertoga* 'to the army-commander': The reference here is presumably to Ásmundr, whereas in *Hálf* 35/2 the same term is used to refer to Hálfr. The cpd occurs as a *heiti* for king in Þul *Konunga* 2/2^{III}; see Note there.

Innsteinn (Innsteinn *Innkv* 12)

32. Hart skulum ganga   ok hliða ekki *;
     verðr vísis lið   at vega með söxum.
     Þeir skulu sjálfir á sér bera
     blóðgar benjar,   áðr braki létti.

Skulum ganga hart ok hliða ekki *; lið vísis verðr at vega með söxum. Þeir sjálfir skulu bera á sér blóðgar benjar, áðr braki létti.

We shall go [forth] fast and not give way; the prince's troop has to fight with swords. They themselves shall bear bloody wounds on their bodies before the din ceases.

Ms.: 2845(36v) (*Hálf*).

Reading: [2] *: við 2845.

Editions: *Skj*: Anonyme digte og vers [XIII], E. 6. *Vers af Fornaldarsagaer: Af Hálfssaga* VII 4: AII, 261-2, BII, 282, *Skald* II, 148; *Hálf* 1864, 23, *Hálf* 1909, 109, *FSGJ* 2, 116, *Hálf* 1981, 124, 184; *Edd. Min.* 36.

Notes: [2] *hliða ekki* * 'not give way': The ms.'s *hliða við* 'give way' is the only recorded instance of this verb being used with the prep. *við* in Old Norse, and most eds (except *Hálf* 1981) have omitted it, as is done here. The omission restores the line to metrical regularity. — [5] *þeir sjálfir* 'they themselves': This must refer to the enemies of the Hálfsrekkar, i.e. Ásmundr and his men. — [6] *á sér* 'on their bodies': Lit. 'on themselves'.

Innsteinn (Innsteinn *Innkv* 13)

33. Snúiz snarliga   snyrtidrengir
    út ór eldi   með auðbrota.
    Enginn er ýta,   sá er æ lifir;
    mun ekki baugbroti   við bana kvíða.

Snyrtidrengir snúiz snarliga út ór eldi með auðbrota. Er enginn ýta, sá er lifir æ; baugbroti mun ekki kvíða við bana.

May the gallant warriors turn quickly out of the fire with the treasure-breaker [GENEROUS RULER = Hálfr]. There is no man who lives forever; the ring-breaker [GENEROUS RULER = Hálfr] will not be apprehensive of death.

Ms.: 2845(36v) (*Hálf*).

Editions: *Skj*: Anonyme digte og vers [XIII], E. 6. *Vers af Fornaldarsagaer: Af Hálfssaga* VII 5: AII, 262, BII, 282-3, *Skald* II, 148; *Hálf* 1864, 24, *Hálf* 1909, 109, *FSGJ* 2, 116, *Hálf* 1981, 124, 184; *Edd. Min.* 37.

Note: [All]: The kennings *auðbroti* 'the treasure-breaker' (l. 4) and *baugbroti* 'the ring-breaker' (l. 7) are of a common type denoting a generous ruler; see *Meissner* 326-7. Both the compounds *auðbroti* and *snyrtidrengir* 'the gallant warriors' (l. 2) occur in the late C12th or early C13th Bjbp *Jóms* 10/5[1] and 39/2[1] respectively, describing the gallant behaviour of the Jómsvíkingar. The cpd *snyrtidrengr* also occurs at GunnLeif *Merl II* 36/4 and *Ǫrv* 99/7.

Introduction to *Innsteinskviða*, part 3 (*Hálf* 34-7)

The third and final section of *Innkv* (*Hálf* 34-7) is another monologue spoken by Innsteinn after Hálfr has fallen and the remainder of the Hálfsrekkar have come up from their ships and have fought courageously until many have been killed, ultimately including Innsteinn himself. The stanzas do not follow the course of the fight (so *Edd. Min.*, xxviii) but rather praise the heroic courage and loyalty of the Hálfsrekkar and reflect upon Innsteinn's own prudent heroism, as well as the inevitability of death. They present the situation in a more restrained manner than the stanzas recited before the fight and during the arousal of the warriors in the burning hall. The dominant motifs – loyalty, death and fame – have been touched upon already in the second part of the poem (*Hálf* 31 and 33), while Innsteinn's final elegaic reflection on his past life takes up a theme already announced in *Hálf* 28.

Innsteinn (Innsteinn *Innkv* 14)

34. Hér sá ek alla   einum fylgja
  jafnröskliga,   öðlings syni.
  Hittumz heilir,   þá heðan líðum;
  er eigi léttara   líf en dauði.

Hér sá ek alla fylgja einum, syni öðlings, jafnröskliga. Hittumz heilir, þá líðum heðan; líf er eigi léttara en dauði.

Here I saw that all followed one man, the son of a prince [PRINCE = Hálfr], with equal bravery. May we meet happily, when we pass from here; life is not easier than death.

Ms.: 2845(36v) (*Hálf*).

Editions: *Skj*: Anonyme digte og vers [XIII], E. 6. *Vers af Fornaldarsagaer: Af Hálfssaga* VII 6: AII, 262, BII, 283; *Skald* II, 148; *Hálf* 1864, 24, *Hálf* 1909, 110, *FSGJ* 2, 116-17, *Hálf* 1981, 125-6, 184-5; *Edd. Min.* 37.

Context: This stanza is preceded by a short prose passage. Having managed to get out of the fire, Hálfr and his band succumb to their enemies and are slain. The stanza is introduced by the words: *Innsteinn kvað, er kóngr var fallinn* … 'Innsteinn said, when the king had fallen …'.

Notes: [4] *syni öðlings* 'the son of a prince [PRINCE = Hálfr]': *Meissner* 360 lists the kenning *sonr öðlings* among those which emphasise a ruler's princely descent; cf. also *SkP* I, lxxix. Andrews (*Hálf* 1909, 110), who interprets *syni* as acc. pl., matching *alla* in l. 1, translates *alla syni öðlings* as *alle krieger* 'all warriors'. In this case, the meaning of the kenning *sonr öðlings* would be 'warrior'. — [5] *hittumz heilir* 'may we meet happily': Lit. 'May we meet happy'. See *Hálf* 31/1 and Note.

Innsteinn (Innsteinn *Innkv* 15)

35. Hrókr er fallinn   með hertoga,
 fraékn a*t* fótum   fólks oddvita.
 Eigum Óðni   ilt at gjalda,
 er hann slíkan konung   sigri rænti.

Hrókr er fallinn með hertoga, frækn a*t* fótum oddvita fólks. Eigum at gjalda Óðni ilt, er hann rænti slíkan konung sigri.

Hrókr has fallen with the army-commander, valiant at the feet of the leader of the army [KING = Hálfr]. We have to repay Óðinn for evil, as he deprived such a king of victory.

Ms.: 2845(36v) (*Hálf*).

Readings: [3] a*t*: 'a' 2845   [4] oddvita: 'odd uíttá' *with* 'uíttá' *probably corrected from* 'uíttí' 2845.

Editions: *Skj*: Anonyme digte og vers [XIII], E. 6. Vers af Fornaldarsagaer: Af Hálfssaga VII 7: AII, 262, BII, 283, *Skald* II, 148; *Hálf* 1864, 25, *Hálf* 1909, 110, *FSGJ* 2, 117, *Hálf* 1981, 126, 185; *Edd. Min.* 37.

Context: This stanza is preceded by a prose paragraph, describing how those of the Hálfsrekkar, who had stayed behind, come up from the ships. Many of them are killed. The battle continues until dark, before Innsteinn is slain. The stanza is introduced by the words: *Innsteinn kvað* 'Innsteinn said'.

Notes: [1] *Hrókr*: This must be Hrókr inn hvíti 'Rook the White', as the prose text later indicates that Rook the Black, though seriously wounded in the fight, escapes and is looked after by a poor peasant (*Hálf* 1981, 186). — [2] *hertoga* 'the army-commander': Here the reference of this cpd is to Hálfr. See the use of the same term in *Hálf* 31/8 to refer to Ásmundr. — [4] *oddvita fólks* 'of the leader of the army [KING = Hálfr]': Here *oddviti fólks* is interpreted as a single kenning denoting 'king, prince', although *oddviti* itself (lit. 'point-director') might be looked upon as a kenning, albeit very much faded. See *Meissner* 358-9, *LP*: oddviti and Note to *Ket* 3[b]/3. — [5-6] *eigum at gjalda Óðni illt* 'we have to repay Óðinn for evil': A similar sentiment is expressed much more aggressively in *Hrólf*, when Bǫðvarr bjarki rails against Óðinn after Hrólfr has been killed, saying that he would squeeze him like the tiniest mouse if he could find him (cf. *Hrólf* 1960, 122). A similar threat is recorded by Saxo (*Saxo* 2015, I, ii. 7. 27, pp. 138-9). Cf. *Bjarkamál* 7[III] and Note to [All] there. — [7] *hann* 'he': Omitted in *Skj* B, *Skald* and *Hálf* 1909, though this does not produce a metrically regular line, nor does the restoration of *konung* for the ms.'s *kóng* in the same line.

Innsteinn (Innsteinn *Innkv* 16)

36. Ek hefi úti   átján sumur
 fylgt fullhuga   flein at rjóða.
 Skal ek ekki annan   eiga dróttin
 gunnargjarnan,   né gamall verða.

Ek hefi fylgt fullhuga úti átján sumur at rjóða flein. Ek skal ekki eiga annan gunnargjarnan dróttin, né verða gamall.

I have followed the dauntless man out at sea for eighteen summers in order to redden the spear. I shall not have another battle-eager lord, nor become old.

Ms.: 2845(36v-37r) (*Hálf*).

Editions: *Skj*: Anonyme digte og vers [XIII], E. 6. *Vers af Fornaldarsagaer: Af Hálfssaga* VII 8: AII, 262, BII, 283, *Skald* II, 148; *Hálf* 1864, 25, *Hálf* 1909, 111, *FSGJ* 2, 117, *Hálf* 1981, 126-7, 185; *Edd. Min.* 37.

Innsteinn (Innsteinn *Innkv* 17)

37. Hér mun Innsteinn   til jarðar hníga,
 hoskr at höfði   hers oddvita.
 Þat munu seggir   at sögum gjöra,
 at Hálfr konungr   hlæjandi dó.

Hér mun Innsteinn hníga til jarðar, hoskr at höfði oddvita hers. Seggir munu gjöra þat at sögum, at Hálfr konungr dó hlæjandi.

Here Innsteinn will sink to the ground, prudent by the head of the leader of the army [KING = Hálfr]. Men will fashion it into tales that king Hálfr died laughing.

Ms.: 2845(37r) (*Hálf*).

Editions: *Skj*: Anonyme digte og vers [XIII], E. 6. *Vers af Fornaldarsagaer: Af Hálfssaga* VII 9: AII, 262, BII, 283, *Skald* II, 148; *Hálf* 1864, 25, *Hálf* 1909, 111, *FSGJ* 2, 118, *Hálf* 1981, 126-7, 185; *Edd. Min.* 37.

Notes: [2] *til jarðar* 'to the ground': Most eds have emended the ms. reading. *Skj* B and *Skald* have *at jǫrð*, *Hálf* 1909 has *jarðar*; *Edd. Min.* retains the ms. reading but suggests in a footnote that for metrical reasons *á jǫrð* might be preferable. — [3] *hoskr* 'prudent': Most eds (*Skj* B, *Skald*, *Hálf* 1864, *Hálf* 1909, *FSGJ*, *Edd. Min.*) normalise the ms.'s *hoskur* to *horskr*, although the form *hoskr* is well-documented; see also *Hálf* 53/4. On the idea that both wisdom and courage were required traits of an early Germanic hero see Kaske (1958). — [4] *oddvita hers* 'of the leader of the army [KING = Hálfr]': Cf. *Hálf* 35/4 *oddvita fólks* 'of the leader of the people [KING = Hálfr]' and Note. — [5-8]: Innsteinn's expressed awareness that people will turn the Hálfsrekkar's heroic last stand into tales (*at sögum*) signals his recognition of *Innkv*'s place within the tradition of the hall fight (cf. Introduction to *Innkv*, part 1). The conceit that those tales will portray Hálfr as dying laughing is strongly reminiscent of the final line of Anon *Krm* 29/8 (see Note there) in which the dying Ragnarr loðbrók exclaims *læjandi skal ek deyja* 'I'll die laughing'. Another hero who dies laughing, as his heart is cut from his body, is Hǫgni in *Akv* 24/1.

Introduction to st. 38

This stanza stands outside the following sequence that constitutes *Útsteinskviða* 'Poem of Útsteinn' (*Útkv*). In it Útsteinn, who has survived the burning and hall fight described in his dead brother, Innsteinn's, *Innkv*, expresses his pleasure that at least one man, himself, is still alive and, by implication, ready to take vengeance on Ásmundr. However, such a statement does not fit well with the following sequence of stanzas (*Hálf* 39-50) in which the superiority of the Hálfsrekkar is mentioned frequently, but not a final battle against Ásmundr. The content of this stanza provides no reason for its incorporation into *Útkv*, contrary to the practice of most eds, even though the prose text places it more or less as an introduction to that poem.

Útsteinn (Útsteinn Lv 1)

38. Hitt hlægir mik   helzt í máli:
     mun ekki Ásmundi   öll vá sofa.
     Þrír eru fallnir   af því liði
     Eynefs synir,   en einn lifir.

Hitt hlægir mik helzt í máli: öll vá mun ekki sofa Ásmundi. Þrír synir Eynefs eru fallnir af því liði, en einn lifir.

This makes me laugh especially about the matter: not all danger will be dormant for Ásmundr. Three sons of Eynefr <sea-king> [SEAFARERS] have fallen of this host, yet one lives.

Ms.: 2845(37r) (*Hálf*).

Editions: *Skj*: Anonyme digte og vers [XIII], E. 6. Vers af Fornaldarsagaer: Af Hálfssaga VIII 1: AII, 262-3, BII, 283-4, *Skald* II, 149; *Hálf* 1864, 26, *Hálf* 1909, 113-14, *FSGJ* 2, 119, *Hálf* 1981, 127-8, 186; *Edd. Min.* 71.

Context: This stanza is preceded by a prose paragraph: Útsteinn was staying with King Eysteinn of Denmark, whose counsellor Úlfr inn rauði 'the Red' had eight boisterous sons. They envied Útsteinn and treated him badly, so a dispute arose. First, though, Útsteinn told of King Hálfr's death. The stanza is introduced by the words: *Hann kvað þá* 'He then said'.

Notes: [3, 4] *mun ... sofa* 'will ... be dormant': Lit. 'will sleep'. The threat expressed in these lines suggests that Útsteinn is plotting vengeance against Ásmundr, though no known poetic account of this action exists. — [7] *þrír synir Eynefs* 'three sons of Eynefr <sea-king> [SEAFARERS]': A sea-king name, taking the various forms *Eynefr*, *Eynæfir* or *Eynefir* occurs in Þul *Sækonunga* 2/1^{III} and as the determinant in kennings for 'ship', like Bragi *Þórr* 2/3^{III}; see *Meissner* 220 and Finnur Jónsson (1934-5, 292). It is not clear which three seafarers (i.e. warriors) are referred to here, but the most likely are Útsteinn's brother Innsteinn, King Hálfr himself and Hrókr inn hvíti, the only ones of the Hálfsrekkar mentioned by name in *Innkv*.

Introduction to *Útsteinskviða* (*Hálf* 39-50)

The following twelve stanzas, in contrast to the preceding *Innkv*, do not correspond to any part of the prose saga of Hálfr and the Hálfsrekkar. Rather, like the following *Hrókskviða*, they describe an episode from the life of one of the surviving Hálfsrekkar at a foreign king's court. Although there is frequent mention of the bravery and heroic deeds of the Hálfsrekkar, no mention is made of their last fight against Ásmundr, but it is clear from certain references (e.g. *Hálf* 40/3-4, *Hálf* 43 and 46) that most of them are no longer alive. Considerably later in the prose saga, mention is made of how King Eysteinn and Útsteinn took part in a successful revenge expedition against Ásmundr, who is killed (cf. *Hálf* 1981, 197), but this is not referred to in *Útv*. The only connection with the main plot of the saga is the person of Útsteinn himself; the deeds of the Hálfsrekkar are of importance only to the extent that mention of them helps to emphasise their outstanding bravery in contrast to the implied cowardice of Úlfr and his sons.

Útkv comprises two parts. The first (*Hálf* 39-46) is a dialogue between Útsteinn and Úlfr inn rauði which resembles the Old Norse compositional unit *mannjafnaðr* 'comparison of men'. The prose text (cf. *Hálf* 1981, 186) speaks of a verbal dispute over drinking at a feast (*kappmæli við drykkju*) and that Úlfr egged Útsteinn on to this (*eggjaði hann*). If so, the first stanza of *Útkv*, in which Útsteinn already refers to a physical combat with weapons, must represent an advanced stage of the dispute with Úlfr which is widened to include his sons, who become Útsteinn's actual antagonists in the fight that apparently ensues offstage.

The second part of *Útkv* (*Hálf* 47-50) is played out after the conclusion of the battle between Útsteinn and the eight sons of Úlfr, who all lose their lives. Stanza 47 is spoken by Útsteinn as he returns from the fight; the first *helmingr* explains the situation, while the second is addressed to King Eysteinn, at whose court Útsteinn is staying. Until this point Eysteinn has been merely mentioned in the prose text (cf. *Hálf* 1981, 186) and has played no part in the verbal dispute between Útsteinn and Úlfr; here he abruptly takes over Úlfr's place as Útsteinn's discussant, even though he is not in fact hostile to him.

Útsteinn (Útsteinn *Útkv* 1)

39. Upp skulum rísa,   út skulum ganga
ok ramligar   randir knýja.
Hygg við hjálmum   hingat komnar
til Danmarkar   dísir várar.

Skulum rísa upp, skulum ganga út ok knýja ramligar randir. Hygg dísir várar komnar hingat til Danmarkar við hjálmum.

Let us arise, let us go out and bash our strong shields. I believe that our *dísir* have come here to Denmark with helmets.

Ms.: 2845(37r) (*Hálf*).

Reading: [7] Danmarkar: dan merkur 2845.

Editions: *Skj*: Anonyme digte og vers [XIII], E. 6. *Vers af Fornaldarsagaer: Af Hálfssaga* VIII 2: AII, 263, BII, 284, *Skald* II, 149; *Hálf* 1864, 26-7, *Hálf* 1909, 114, *FSGJ* 2, 119, *Hálf* 1981, 128, 187; *Edd. Min.* 71.

Context: The stanza is preceded by the sentence: *Útsteinn kvað, er Úlfr jafnaði sér við hann ok eggjaði hann* 'Útsteinn said, when Úlfr compared himself to him and provoked him'.

Note: [8]: *Dísir* is the name for female guardian spirits, often considered to safeguard the interests of a particular individual or his or her family (cf. Ström 1961, 192-4; Turville-Petre 1964, 221-7). The claim that they have 'come here to Denmark with helmets' probably indicates the warlike state of mind of the *dísir* rather than their actual provision of helmets to Útsteinn. These *dísir* behave very much like valkyries.

Úlfr (Úlfrauð *Útkv* 1)

40. Yðr munu dauðar   dísir allar;
heill kveð ek horfna   frá Hálfsrekkum.
Dreymði mik í morgin,   at megir várir
efri yrði,   hvar er vér mættuz.

Allar dísir munu yðr dauðar; ek kveð heill horfna frá Hálfsrekkum. Dreymði mik í morgin, at megir várir yrði efri, hvar er vér mættuz.

For you, all *dísir* will be dead; I say luck has deserted Hálfr's champions. I dreamed this morning that our [my] sons would prevail, wherever we should meet.

Ms.: 2845(37r) (*Hálf*).

Readings: [1] dauðar: 'daud ar' *with a small hole in the parchment between* 'daud' *and* 'ar' 2845 [4] Hálfs: hálf 2845.

Editions: *Skj*: Anonyme digte og vers [XIII], E. 6. *Vers af Fornaldarsagaer: Af Hálfssaga* VIII 3: AII, 263, BII, 284, *Skald* II, 149; *Hálf* 1864, 27, *Hálf* 1909, 114, *FSGJ* 2, 120, *Hálf* 1981, 187; *Edd. Min.* 71.

Context: This stanza is introduced by the words: *Úlfr kvað* 'Úlfr said'.

Notes: [3] *heill* 'luck': The idea that some individuals were favoured by luck or good fortune was a commonplace of Old Norse literature, and is expressed both in poetry as well as in prose sagas (cf. Hallberg 1973). In *Útkv* 9/5-8 (*Hálf* 50), Útsteinn attributes his success in life to Óðinn. — [7] *yrði efri* 'would prevail': Lit. 'would become uppermost'. Cf. *Hálf* 42/1. — [8] *vér* 'we': The ms. has *vér* 'we', but this leaves ll. 7-8 without alliteration, so previous eds (e.g. *Hálf* 1864, *Edd. Min.*, *Skj* B) have emended *vér mættuz* to *ér mættiz* 'wherever you (pl.) should meet', i.e. Útsteinn and Úlfr's sons.

Útsteinn (Útsteinn *Útkv* 2)

41. Sigrs vænti ek mér   sýnu betra,
    en Úlfr vili   æskja Steini.
    Yðr mun snimma   a*t* sverðtogi
    hauss um högginn   en háls roðinn.

Ek vænti mér sýnu betra sigrs, en Úlfr vili æskja Steini. Hauss yðr mun snimma um högginn en háls roðinn a*t* sverðtogi.

I expect for myself a much better victory than Úlfr may wish for Steinn. Your head will soon be struck off and your neck reddened at the sword-drawing [BATTLE].

Ms.: **2845**(37r) (*Hálf*).

Reading: [6] a*t*: 'a' 2845.

Editions: *Skj*: Anonyme digte og vers [XIII], E. 6. *Vers af Fornaldarsagaer: Af Hálfssaga* VIII 4: AII, 263, BII, 284, *Skald* II, 149; *Hálf* 1864, 27, *Hálf* 1909, 115, *FSGJ* 2, 120, *Hálf* 1981, 187; *Edd. Min.* 71.

Context: This stanza is introduced by the words: *Útsteinn kvað* 'Útsteinn said'.

Notes: [4] *Steini* 'for Steinn': That is, for himself, Útsteinn. On the names Innsteinn and Útsteinn, see *Hálf* 26/4 and Note there. — [6] *at sverðtogi* 'at the sword-drawing [BATTLE]': The kenning *sverðtog* for 'battle', listed by *Meissner* 192, occurs also in SnSt Ht 54/6[III]. The emendation of ms. 'a' to *at* reflects normal Old Norse usage when expressing the idea of location 'at' a battle. — [7] *högginn*: Given as *hǫgvinn* by *Skj* B, *Skald*, *Hálf* 1909 and *Edd. Min.*, *hǫggvinn* in *FSGJ*. Both forms of the p. p. are recorded (cf. *Fritzner*: *hǫggva*).

Úlfr (Úlfrauð Útkv 2)

42. Munu þeir efri verða,   Úlfs synir:
    Oddr ok Örnólfr,   Áti inn svarti,
    Börkr ok Brynjólfr,   Búi, Harðskafi,
    Rauðr inn rammi,   ef þú reynir til.

Þeir munu efri verða, synir Úlfs: Oddr ok Örnólfr, Áti inn svarti, Börkr ok Brynjólfr, Búi, Harðskafi, Rauðr inn rammi, ef þú reynir til.

They will prevail, Úlfr's sons: Oddr and Ǫrnólfr, Áti inn svarti ('the Black'), Bǫrkr and Brynjólfr, Búi, Harðskafi, Rauðr inn rammi ('the Strong'), if you make an attempt.

Ms.: **2845**(37v) (*Hálf*).

Editions: *Skj*: Anonyme digte og vers [XIII], E. 6. *Vers af Fornaldarsagaer: Af Hálfssaga* VIII 5: AII, 263, BII, 284, *Skald* II, 149, *FF* §40; *Hálf* 1864, 28, *Hálf* 1909, 115, *FSGJ* 2, 120, *Hálf* 1981, 187-8; *Edd. Min.* 72.

Context: This stanza is introduced by the words: *Úlfr kvað* 'Úlfr said'.

Notes: [1-2]: Both these lines are irregular metrically, l. 1 being hypermetrical, and l. 2 hypometrical. Previous eds have rearranged them in various ways in order to achieve metrical regularity; *Edd. Min.*, *Hálf* 1909 and *Skj* B have *Munu Úlfs synir | øfri verða*, while *Skald* has *Munu þeir øfri, | Úlfs synir, verða*, but this latter is unmetrical. — [8] *þú* 'you': Some eds (*Skj* B, *Skald* and *Hálf* 1909) omit this pron. for metrical reasons.

Útsteinn (Útsteinn *Útkv* 3)

43. Mundi ekki Steini   með Stara þykkja
    ógn at etja   við Úlfs sonu,
    þvíat ekki var   órum bróður
    við dritmenni þitt   dramb at setja.

Steini með Stara mundi ekki þykkja ógn at etja við sonu Úlfs, þvíat ekki var bróður órum at setja dramb við dritmenni þitt.

It would not seem a menace to Steinn together with Stari to fight against Úlfr's sons, for it was not characteristic of our [my] brother to subdue the arrogance of a shit like you.

Ms.: **2845**(37v) (*Hálf*).

Reading: [6] órum: várum 2845.

Editions: *Skj*: Anonyme digte og vers [XIII], E. 6. *Vers af Fornaldarsagaer: Af Hálfssaga* VIII 6: AII, 263, BII, 284-5, *Skald* II, 149, *NN* §§2382, 3197G; *Hálf* 1864, 28, *Hálf* 1909, 116, *FSGJ* 2, 121, *Hálf* 1981, 128, 188; *Edd. Min.* 72.

Context: Although the usual introductory phrase is missing, it is clear from the context that this stanza as well as the following three (*Hálf* 44-46) are spoken by Útsteinn.

Notes: [1, 2] *mundi ekki þykkja* 'it would not seem': I.e. 'if they were alive'. Both Innsteinn (the Steinn intended here) and Stari had died in the fight with Ásmundr and his men. — [2] *með* 'together with': Lit. 'with'. Bugge (*Hálf* 1864), following a suggestion of Guðbrandur Vigfússon, proposed an emendation to *né* 'nor' (as in l. 2 of the following stanza), and this emendation is adopted by *Skj* B and *Skald*. — [2] *Stara* 'Stari': Name of one of the Hálfsrekkar (see *Hálf* 1981, 177). It means 'starling' and is, like some of the other personal names of this warrior band (e.g. Haukr 'Hawk', Hrókr 'Rook'), a bird name. — [5-6]: As they stand (with alliteration on *v*-), l. 5 is unmetrical. That can be remedied by using the older variant form *órum* for *várum* 'our' in l. 6 (as adopted in *Edd. Min.* and *Skald*; cf. *ANG* §467.2) which gives vowel alliteration and two metrical lines (Types C and A2). — [7-8]: There has been some discussion as to the exact meaning of the phrase *at setja dramb við*, here translated as 'subdue the arrogance of'; see Hollander (1911, 59), and Kock (*NN* §§2382 and 3197G). — [7] *dritmenni þitt* 'a shit like you': The invective *dritmenni* is a *hap. leg.*, as is *ragmenni* 'cowardly wretches' in l. 4 of the following stanza (*Hálf* 44). However, *drit* 'shit, excrement' is attested as a simplex (*ONP*: *drit*) and the cpd *dritskegg* 'muck-beard' expresses a similarly pejorative sense. The use of poss. *þitt* instead of the pers. pron. after a noun of abuse in direct address is idiomatic in Old Norse (cf. *Fritzner*: *þinn*; *CVC*: *þinn*, sense B). *Þitt* is extrametrical here, and is probably a later addition to the line.

Útsteinn (Útsteinn *Útkv* 4)

44. Þótti ekki Hrókum   né Hálfdani
     raun at berjaz   við ragmenni,
     þá er vér fjórir   falla létum
     átta jarla   fyrir Ann*snesi.

Þótti ekki Hrókum né Hálfdani raun at berjaz við ragmenni, þá er vér fjórir létum átta jarla falla fyrir Ann*snesi.

It did not seem a trial to either the Hrókar or Hálfdan to fight against cowardly wretches, when we four slew eight jarls off Annsnes.

Ms.: **2845**(37v) (*Hálf*).

Reading: [8] Ann*snesi: 'annis nesi' 2845.

Editions: Skj: Anonyme digte og vers [XIII], E. 6. *Vers af Fornaldarsagaer: Af Hálfssaga* VIII 7: AII, 263-4, BII, 285, *Skald* II, 149; *Hálf* 1864, 28-9, *Hálf* 1909, 116, *FSGJ* 2, 121, *Hálf* 1981, 128, 188; *Edd. Min.* 72.

Notes: [All]: This stanza follows a format frequently found in the *mannjafnaðr*; the speaker refers to his own or his companions' bravery, implying that it is much greater than that of their cowardly opponents. Frequently a place, often legendary, is mentioned as the site of the battle. The information that the four Hálfsrekkar slew eight jarls implies that Úlfr's eight sons do not stand a chance either. — [1] *Hrókum* 'the Hrókar': Two brothers, members of the Hálfsrekkar, Hrókr inn svarti 'Rook the Black' and Hrókr inn hvíti 'Rook the White'. Cf. *Hálf* 26/1 and Note there. — [2] *Hálfdani* 'Hálfdan': The name of another of the Hálfsrekkar (cf. *Hálf* 1981, 177). — [4] *ragmenni* 'cowardly wretches': Like *dritmenni* in l. 7 of the previous stanza, *ragmenni* is a *hap. leg.*, but is self-evidently formed from the adj. *ragr* 'cowardly, unmanly' plus the n. noun *menni* 'people, men'. — [8] *fyrir Ann*snesi* 'off Annsnes': The ms. has 'annis nesi', which cannot be accommodated into a metrical line without resorting to tmesis. It is uncertain whether this word is a common noun *andnes, annes* 'headland, promontory' (cf. *LP*: *andnes*, and as in Anon *Vǫls* 1/3[1]) or a p. n., though the context suggests the latter.

Útsteinn (Útsteinn *Útkv* 5)

45. Fari Úlfs synir   út at berjaz,
    átta drengir   við eitt höfuð.
    Mun ekki stökkva,   þóat Steinn hafi
    færa nokkut   í flokki lið.

Fari synir Úlfs út at berjaz, átta drengir við eitt höfuð. Mun ekki stökkva, þóat Steinn hafi nokkut færa lið í flokki.

Let Úlfr's sons go outside to fight, eight men against one head. He [Steinn] will not flee, although Steinn has somewhat fewer people in his host.

Ms.: 2845(37v) (*Hálf*).

Reading: [6] þóat: þó 2845.

Editions: *Skj*: Anonyme digte og vers [XIII], E. 6. Vers af Fornaldarsagaer: Af Hálfssaga VIII 8: AII, 264, BII, 285, *Skald* II, 149; *Hálf* 1864, 29, *Hálf* 1909, 117, *FSGJ* 2, 121, *Hálf* 1981, 128, 188; *Edd. Min.* 72.

Notes: [All]: Útsteinn's call for the sons of Úlfr to come out and fight him brings the verbal warfare to an abrupt end. Lines 5-8 emphasise the apparent inequality of the combat through their use of understatement. — [4] *við eitt höfuð* 'against one head': That is, against one man, Útsteinn himself, who refers to himself in the 3rd pers. throughout this stanza. *Hǫfuð* 'head' is used here in the sense 'individual person or thing'; cf. *Fritzner*: *höfuð* 3.

Útsteinn (Útsteinn *Útkv* 6)

46. Hálfr, dreym*ði* mik,   hvatti, at ek berðumz,
     ok kvez mér frækn konungr   fylgja skyldu,
     — hefir mér gramr verit   góðr í draumi —
     hvar sem vér orrostu   eiga skyldum.

Dreym*ði* mik, Hálfr hvatti, at ek berðumz, ok frækn konungr kvez mér fylgja skyldu, hvar sem vér skyldum eiga orrostu; gramr hefir verit mér góðr í draumi.

I dreamed Hálfr urged that I should fight, and the valiant king said that he would follow me, wherever we [I] should have a battle; the prince has been good to me in my dream.

Ms.: **2845**(37v) (*Hálf*).

Readings: [1] dreym*ði*: 'dreym' *with* 'di' *added by another hand in the margin to the left of the following line* 2845   [7] hvar sem: hvar 2845.

Editions: *Skj*: Anonyme digte og vers [XIII], E. 6. *Vers af Fornaldarsagaer: Af Hálfssaga* VIII 9: AII, 264, BII, 285, *Skald* II, 150, *FF* §41; *Hálf* 1864, 29, *Hálf* 1909, 117, *FSGJ* 2, 121-2, *Hálf* 1981, 129, 188-9; *Edd. Min.* 72.

Notes: [All]: Útsteinn now reveals that he has had a dream in which his fallen leader Hálfr has appeared, urging him to fight, and offering his personal support. — [2] *at ek berðumz* 'that I should fight': For the inflectional ending of the m. v. verb form *berðumz* see *ANG* §544, especially §544.3.

Útsteinn (Útsteinn *Útkv* 7)

47. Nú em ek inn kominn   Úlfi at segja,
     at hans synir   höggnir liggja.
     Nú fari, Eysteinn,   ef ér vilið,
     fleiri at freista   við fleina við.

Nú em ek kominn inn at segja Úlfi, at synir hans liggja höggnir. Fari nú fleiri at freista við við fleina, Eysteinn, ef ér vilið.

Now I have come in to tell Úlfr that his sons lie slain. Now let more [men] go to try [their strength] against the tree of spears [WARRIOR = Útsteinn], Eysteinn, if you wish.

Ms.: **2845**(37v) (*Hálf*).

Readings: [6] ér: þér 2845;   vilið: vilit 2845.

Editions: *Skj*: Anonyme digte og vers [XIII], E. 6. *Vers af Fornaldarsagaer: Af Hálfssaga* VIII 10: AII, 264, BII, 285, *Skald* II, 150; *Hálf* 1864, 29-30, *Hálf* 1909, 117-18, *FSGJ* 2, 122, *Hálf* 1981, 131, 189; *Edd. Min.* 73.

Context: The stanza is preceded by a short prose paragraph: *Þá gengu þeir Úlfssynir ok Útsteinn út ok börðuzt. Hann drap alla Úlfssonu ok gekk síðan inn fyrir kóng ok kvað* 'Then Úlfr's sons and Útsteinn went outside and fought. He killed all Úlfr's sons and then went in before the king and said'.

Notes: [1] *em ek* 'I have': The ms. reads *er ek* 'I am', showing the generalisation of the 3rd pers. sg. form of the pres. tense of the verb *vera* 'be' to the 1st pers. sg. form, which is characteristic of C14th and later Icelandic. — [5-6]: There is no alliteration in these lines, and this is likely to have been caused by the introduction of the later form of the 2nd pers. pl. nom. pronoun *þér* rather than the older *ér* in l. 6. Most eds have normalised to the older form. — [5] *Eysteinn*: According to the prose text, Eysteinn is a Danish king and a kinsman of Útsteinn's (cf. *Hálf* 1981, 186). Útsteinn has taken refuge at his court. — [8] *við fleina* 'the tree of spears [WARRIOR = Útsteinn]': This warrior-kenning occurs only here, though the type is quite common; see *Meissner* 270.

Eysteinn (Eystk Útkv 1)

48.   Sjálft mun letja   slíks at freista;
         Hálfs eru rekkar   hverjum meiri.
         Þik veit ek manna   miklu fremstan,
         einn snjallastan,   er þú átta vátt.

Sjálft mun letja at freista slíks; rekkar Hálfs eru meiri hverjum. Ek veit þik miklu fremstan manna, einn snjallastan, er þú vátt átta.

It is self-evidently futile to try such a thing; Hálfr's champions are superior to everyone. I know you [to be] by far the foremost of men, one of the most valiant, because you slew eight men.

Ms.: 2845(37v) (*Hálf*).

Editions: *Skj*: Anonyme digte og vers [XIII], E. 6. Vers af Fornaldarsagaer: Af Hálfssaga VIII 11: AII, 264, BII, 285-6, *Skald* II, 150, *NN* §3190; *Hálf* 1864, 30, *Hálf* 1909, 118, *FSGJ* 2, 122, *Hálf* 1981, 131, 189; *Edd. Min.* 73.

Context: This stanza is introduced by the words: *Eysteinn kvað* 'Eysteinn said'.

Note: [1-2] *sjálft mun letja at freista slíks* 'it is self-evidently futile to try such a thing': Lit. 'it will dissuade itself from trying such'. The meaning of ll. 1-2 is difficult to grasp, particularly the sense of *sjálft* 'itself' in l. 1. Some eds have considered emending *sjálft* 'itself' to *sjálfr* m. nom. sg. 'self'. *Edd. Min.* in a footnote queries whether l. 1 should not read *sjálfr mun [ek] letja* 'I myself will dissuade', while Andrews (*Hálf* 1909) translates *gerade davon will ich abraten* 'I will just advise against it' but does not alter the text. Here it is proposed that *sjálft* means something like 'self-evidently' and refers back to Útsteinn's proposal in st. 47 that Eysteinn might consider bringing on more warriors for him to fight, since he has now finished off all the sons of Úlfr. Eysteinn's response recognizes the futility of such a move, given the evident superiority of the Hálfsrekkar as warriors.

Útsteinn (Útsteinn *Útkv* 8)

49. Alla mundak   Eysteins liða
     sverði beita   at sömu hófi,
     ef ek mér þarfir   þess verks sæi,
     eða ilt með oss   áðr um væri.

Mundak beita alla liða Eysteins sverði at sömu hófi, ef ek sæi mér þarfir þess verks, eða um væri ilt með oss áðr.

I would strike all the followers of Eysteinn with a sword in the same way, if I saw need for such an action or there had been hostility between us before.

Ms.: **2845**(37v) (*Hálf*).

Editions: *Skj*: Anonyme digte og vers [XIII], E. 6. *Vers af Fornaldarsagaer: Af Hálfssaga* VIII 12: AII, 264, BII, 286, *Skald* II, 150; *Hálf* 1864, 30, *Hálf* 1909, 118, *FSGJ* 2, 123, *Hálf* 1981, 189; *Edd. Min.* 73.

Note: [1] *mundak* 'I would': The ms. has the uncliticised *munda ek*, which makes the line unmetrical. The cliticised form has therefore been restored here.

Útsteinn (Útsteinn *Útkv* 9)

50. Magni fýsir engi   við mik at deila,
     þvíat mér var *u*ngum   aldr skapaðr.
     Ek hefi hjarta   hart í brjósti,
     sízt mér í æsku   Óðinn framði.

Engi fýsir at deila magni við mik, þvíat aldr var skapaðr mér *u*ngum. Ek hefi hart hjarta í brjósti, sízt Óðinn framði mér í æsku.

Nobody is eager to pit his strength against me, for a long life was fated to me as a young man. I have a firm heart in my breast, since Óðinn furthered it for me in my youth.

Ms.: **2845**(37v) (*Hálf*).

Reading: [3] *u*ngum: 'angum' 2845.

Editions: *Skj*: Anonyme digte og vers [XIII], E. 6. *Vers af Fornaldarsagaer: Af Hálfssaga* VIII 13: AII, 264, BII, 286, *Skald* II, 150, *NN* §3191; *Hálf* 1864, 30, *Hálf* 1909, 118-19, *FSGJ* 2, 123, *Hálf* 1981, 131, 190; *Edd. Min.* 73.

Notes: [All]: There are various metrical irregularities in ll. 1-4, the first two of which are *málaháttr* (for l. 1, see Note below). Line 2 could be made regular if the *at* in *at deila* were deleted, as is done in *Skj* B and *Skald*. Line 4 could also be restored to regularity if the expletive particle *of* or *um* were added as *aldr of um skapaðr*, a collocation that is common in Old Norse poetry; cf. *eino dœgri | mér var aldr um scapaðr* (*Skí* 13/4-5, *NK* 72) 'on one day my life was shaped'. — [1]: Most eds have altered this line to produce metrical regularity. *Skj* B adopts a suffixed negative verb *magni fýsit* instead of *magni fýsir engi*. *Edd. Min.* and Andrews (*Hálf* 1909) emend the ms.'s *magni* to *man(n)gi* 'nobody', *fýsir* to *fýsi* and delete *engi* 'nobody'. Kock (*NN* §3191) assumes similarly that l. 1 originally read *Mangi fýsir* 'No one is eager' and emends the text accordingly in *Skald*. He argues that when, at some point, *-ng-* got confused with *-gn-*, so that nom. *mangi* 'nobody' was understood as dat. *magni* 'strength', the line came to lack a negation and nom. *engi* 'nobody' was added to it. Since the ms. reading makes perfect sense and the phrase *deila magni* 'pit one's strength' is also used in Anon *Lil* 8/8[VII] (albeit with the younger dat. form *megni*), emendation seems unnecessary. — [3] u*ngum* 'young': All eds have emended the ms.'s 'angum', which is clearly a scribal error. — [5-8]: Útsteinn here expresses two commonplaces of Old Norse heroic poetry, that, as a man of courage, he has a hard heart (cf. Note to Anon *Mhkv* 7/1[III] and von See 1978), and that Óðinn, the Norse god most frequently associated with warfare, has promoted his warlike nature. Finnur Jónsson (*LP*: *fremja* 7) has suggested that *mér* 'for me' (l. 7) might be a mistake for *mik* 'me' (acc.) and that the sense of ll. 7-8 might be 'since Óðinn furthered me in my youth', as this would conform more closely to ideas that Óðinn helped and supported his chosen warriors, rather than strengthened their hearts, a notion that is not attested elsewhere.

Introduction to to *Hrókskviða* (*Hálf* 51-77)

Hrókskviða 'Poem of Hrókr' (*Hrkv*) is the longest cohesive sequence of stanzas in *Hálf*. It is a dramatic monologue uttered by Hrókr inn svarti 'Rook the Black', one of the Hálfsrekkar who has survived the hall fire and finds himself at the court of a foreign king, Haki, in Skåne (ON Skáney), where his true identity as a great warrior is unknown and he is paid little respect. The poem is addressed to the king's daughter Brynhildr, and the immediately preceding prose narrative describes the circumstances of its performance: while the men of the court were out hunting, and the women gathered nuts, Brynhildr comes upon a big man alone under a tree, and overhears him recite this poem. At the end of his performance (according to the prose text) she comes to realise the man's identity, and that Hrókr had been talking about himself and the deeds of the Hálfsrekkar, as well as of his love for her. Evidently the poem has the desired effect in that Hrókr is immediately elevated to a position of honour at court, married to Brynhildr, and is then able to dispatch troublesome rivals for her hand. Eventually he and Haki join up with other Hálfsrekkar and their supporters to kill King Ásmundr in revenge for the burning of Hálfr and his men.

Hrkv is an interesting combination of an *ævikviða* 'life poem' or autobiography, in which a speaker reviews his own life, often upon the point of death (though this is not the case here), with a retrospective encomium of the life and mores of Hálfr and his warrior band, the Hálfsrekkar. Stanzas 57-9 enumerate the rules that Hálfr established for his men to follow, a subject treated briefly in the prose text (*Hálf* 1981, 177-8), while sts 62-7 form a catalogue of the names of individual members of the Hálfsrekkar, largely corresponding (though not quite in the same order of naming) to a list given in ch. 5 of the prose text (*Hálf* 1981, 177-8).

The primary function of *Hrkv* within the plot of *Hálf* is its connection to the theme of revenge. Although only three sts (69-72) deal explicitly with this theme, the majority of stanzas in *Hrkv* bear upon Hrókr's ultimate goal of achieving revenge for his dead leader. By concealing his identity and having it revealed indirectly, Hrókr gains prestige at court, and this enables him to be considered a fitting wooer for Brynhildr. The unstinting praise of *Hrkv* for the bravery and nobility of Hálfr and the Hálfsrekkar has the effect of making it more urgent and more meaningful that revenge for their killing should be carried out, while Hrókr's marriage to Brynhildr assures him of the support of Haki on the revenge expedition against Ásmundr.

Another distinguishing characteristic of *Hrkv*, which is not paralleled elsewhere in *Hálf*, is its representation of the complexity of Hrókr's psychological states, his wishes, hopes and reflections on his life and fate, especially in sts 69, 70 and 74-6.

Hrókr (Hróksv Hrkv 1)

51. Nú mun segja   sonr Hámundar,
    hvert eðli var   okkart bræðra.
    Var minn faðir   miklu fremri,
    haukr görr at hug,   en Haki yðvarr.

Sonr Hámundar mun nú segja, hvert eðli okkart bræðra var. *Var minn faðir* haukr görr at hug, miklu fremri en Haki yðvarr.

Now the son of Hámundr [= Hrókr inn svarti] will tell, what the parentage of us two brothers was. My father was a real hawk in regard to courage, much superior to your Haki.

Ms.: **2845**(38r) (*Hálf*).

Reading: [5] *Var minn faðir*: minn var faðir 2845.

Editions: *Skj*: Anonyme digte og vers [XIII], E. 6. *Vers af Fornaldarsagaer: Af Hálfssaga* IX 1: AII, 265, BII, 286; *Skald* II, 150; *Hálf* 1864, 31, *Hálf* 1909, 120, *FSGJ* 2, 124, *Hálf* 1981, 133, 190; *Edd. Min.* 44.

Context: This stanza is introduced by the words: *Brynhildr kóngsdóttir sá, hvar maðr stórr stóð við eik eina. Hún heyrði, at hann kvað* 'Brynhildr the king's daughter saw where a tall man was standing by an oak tree. She heard that he said'.

Notes: [All]: There is more than a trace of the *mannjafnaðr* in this and the following stanza of *Hrkv*, in that Hrókr compares King Haki and later Vifill, his rival for Brynhildr's hand, unfavourably with himself and his father in terms of courage. — [2] *sonr Hámundar* 'the son of Hámundr [= Hrókr inn svarti]': The prose text claims (*Hálf* 1981, 177) that Hámundr inn frækni 'the Bold' was a *hersir*, a Norwegian district chieftain. His sister Gunnlǫð was married to Álfr jarl inn gamli 'the Old' from Hordaland (Hǫrðaland) and their two sons were the two brothers named Steinn, Innsteinn and Útsteinn. — [3-4]: In the phrase *eðli okkart bræðra* 'the parentage of us two brothers', it should be noted that grammatically *okkart* qualifies *eðli*, not *bræðra*. — [3] *eðli* 'parentage': The noun *eðli* has several possible meanings of which 'parentage' is one (cf. *ONP*: *eðli* 2 'origin, descent, extraction'). Other eds (cf. *Skj* B's *hvorledes vi brødre var i karakter* 'how we brothers were in character') understand *eðli* in the sense of 'nature, (true) character' (*ONP*: *eðli* 3), and this interpretation is also possible. — [5] *var minn faðir* 'my father was': The ms. has these words in the unusual order *minn var faðir*; as this order makes the line unmetrical, the line has been emended here, as with most eds, to give a metrical line. — [7] *haukr* 'hawk': On the comparison of brave warriors to hawks, see Note to *Hálf* 29/1. — [8] *Haki*: Here the name of a king in Skåne (Skáney), at whose court Hrókr has taken refuge. Elsewhere Haki 'Hook' is a sea-king name (Þul *Sækonunga* 2/7III, Þul *Sea-kings* 1/8III) or the name of a famous pirate, brother of the legendary Hagbarðr (see Anon (*FoGT*) 24/1III and Note there).

Hrókr (Hróksv Hrkv 2)

52. Vildi engi   við Vifil jafnaz,
     þó at Hámundar   hjarðar gætti.
     Sá ek öngan þar   svínahirði
     huglausara   en Heðins arfa.

Engi vildi jafnaz við Vifil, þó at gætti hjarðar Hámundar. Þar sá ek öngan svínahirði huglausara en arfa Heðins.

No one would want to compare himself with Vifill, even though he tended Hámundr's livestock. There I did not see any swineherd more faint-hearted than the heir of Heðinn [= Vifill].

Ms.: 2845(38r) (*Hálf*).

Reading: [7] huglausara: huglausari 2845.

Editions: *Skj*: Anonyme digte og vers [XIII], E. 6. *Vers af Fornaldarsagaer: Af Hálfssaga* IX 2: AII, 265, BII, 286-7, *Skald* II, 150; *Hálf* 1864, 31, *Hálf* 1909, 120, *FSGJ* 2, 124, *Hálf* 1981, 133, 190-1; *Edd. Min.* 44.

Notes: [All]: The clear implication of this refusal to compare man with man is that Vifill is so far beneath the normal standards that warriors must measure up to that even swineherds would show greater courage. Implicit here also is the notion that people not of the warrior class in early Scandinavia could not possess noble qualities. — [2] *Vifil* 'Vifill': According to the prose text (*Hálf* 1981, 190), Vifill was the son of Heðinn, a jarl of King Haki, and is referred to by his patronymic in l. 8. The name Vifill, etymologically 'Beetle' (*AEW*: *Vifill*) appears in other Old Norse texts (see *Hrólf* 3/1) while Heðinn is elsewhere the name of a legendary hero (see Bragi *Rdr* 10/6[III] and Note 1). The prose text indicates that Vifill had sought the hand of Brynhildr and that she had been promised to him before Hrókr's identity and superior claim had been established. — [7] *huglausara* 'more faint-hearted': Most earlier eds, with the exception of *Skj* B and *Hálf* 1981, have normalised the ms. reading to the earlier form of the comp. m. adj. ending in -*a*. Forms of the comp. m. adj. ending in -*i* are generally found in texts later than 1250-1300 (cf. *ANG* §435 Anm. 1).

Hrókr (Hróksv Hrkv 3)

53. Mín var ævi   miklu æðri,
     þá er vér Hálfi konungi   hoskum fylgðum.
     Bárum allir   eitt ráð saman
     ok herjuðum   hvert land yfir.

Ævi mín var miklu æðri, þá er vér fylgðum hoskum Hálfi konungi. Bárum allir eitt ráð saman ok herjuðum yfir hvert land.

My life was much superior, when we followed prudent king Hálfr. We all pursued the same strategy and harried throughout every land.

Ms.: **2845**(38r) (*Hálf*).

Editions: *Skj*: Anonyme digte og vers [XIII], E. 6. *Vers af Fornaldarsagaer: Af Hálfssaga* IX 3: AII, 265, BII, 287, *Skald* II, 150; *Hálf* 1864, 31-2, *Hálf* 1909, 120, *FSGJ* 2, 124-5, *Hálf* 1981, 191; *Edd. Min.* 44.

Note: [3]: This line is hypermetrical, even if the ms.'s late form *kóngi* (for *konungi* 'king') is retained. It is therefore likely that the word *kóngi* is a later addition, and that the line originally read *þá er vér Hálfi*, as has been emended by *Edd. Min.*, *Skj* B and *Skald*.

Hrókr (Hróksv Hrkv 4)

54. Höfðu vér allir   haukmanna lið,
hvar sem fróðhugaðr   frama kostaði.
Gengum vér í gegnum   með grá hjálma
fullstór öll   fóstrlönd níu.

Höfðu vér allir lið haukmanna, hvar sem fróðhugaðr kostaði frama. Vér gengum með grá hjálma í gegnum öll níu fullstór fóstrlönd.

We all had a host of hawk-like men, wherever the wise-minded one tried his luck. We went with grey helmets through all nine vast homelands.

Ms.: 2845(38r) (*Hálf*).

Editions: *Skj*: Anonyme digte og vers [XIII], E. 6. *Vers af Fornaldarsagaer: Af Hálfssaga* IX 4: AII, 265, BII, 287, *Skald* II, 151, *NN* §3192; *Hálf* 1864, 32, *Hálf* 1909, 120-1, *FSGJ* 2, 125, *Hálf* 1981, 133, 191; *Edd. Min.* 44.

Notes: [2] *lið* 'a host': Some eds (*Hálf* 1864; *Edd. Min.*; *Skj* B; *Skald*) replace the ms. reading *lið* by *lund* 'mind, temperament', probably because there is an adj. *hauklundaðr/hauklundr/hauklyndr* 'with a hawk-like temperament' (see *LP*: *hauklundaðr*), but it is not necessary to emend to obtain good sense. — [7-8] *í gegnum öll níu fullstór fóstrlönd* 'through all nine vast homelands': Here *fullstór* 'vast' is construed as a n. acc. pl. adj. agreeing with *níu fóstrlönd* 'nine homelands', as in *Hálf* 1864 and *FSGJ*. Other eds have emended one or both of these words because the line as it stands is hypometrical; *Edd. Min.* has *fullstórir menn* 'very powerful men', in apposition to *vér* 'we' (l. 5); *Skj* B has *fullstórir ǫll*, taking *fullstórir* with *vér* and *ǫll* with an emended *folklǫnd* (see below, Note to l. 8); *Skald* prints *fullstórum ǫll*, understanding *fullstórum* as 'very powerfully' (cf. *NN* §3192), while *Hálf* 1909 emends to *fullstóra ǫld*, which Andrews translates as *durch die große welt* 'through the vast world'. — [8] *fóstrlönd* 'homelands': Bugge's emendation *folklönd*, in which he is followed by *Skj* B and *Skald*, seems unnecessary; according to *Fritzner*: *fóstrland*, this noun is synonymous with *fóstrjörð*, which can simply mean 'land'. *Fóstrland* is used in poetry in the sense 'homeland, native land'; cf. Hharð Lv 10/6[II], Anon *Pl* 55/2[VII] and Anon *Líkn* 33/4[VII].

Hrókr (Hróksv Hrkv 5)

55. Hálf sá ek höggva   höndum báðum;
hafði ekki hilmir   hlífskjöld fyrir sér.
Finnr engi maðr,   þóat fari víða,
hæfra hjarta   ok hugprúðara.

Ek sá Hálf höggva báðum höndum; hilmir hafði ekki hlífskjöld fyrir sér. Engi maðr finnr hæfra ok hugprúðara hjarta, þóat fari víða.

I saw Hálfr strike with both hands; the prince did not have a protecting shield before himself. No man will find a braver and nobler heart, though he travel widely.

Ms.: **2845**(38r) (*Hálf*).

Reading: [6] þóat: þó 2845.

Editions: *Skj*: Anonyme digte og vers [XIII], E. 6. *Vers af Fornaldarsagaer: Af Hálfssaga* IX 5: AII, 265, BII, 287, *Skald* II, 151; *Hálf* 1864, 32, *Hálf* 1909, 121, *FSGJ* 2, 125, *Hálf* 1981, 191; *Edd. Min.* 45.

Note: [1-4]: The statement that Hálfr made no use of a shield and struck with both hands indicates his boldness bordering on foolhardiness (cf. the criticism parried in st. 56) in giving up the protection of a shield in order to wield his sword with both hands.

Hrókr (Hróksv Hrkv 6)

56. Mæla virðar,   þeir er vitu ekki,
     at Hálfs frami   heimsku sætti.
     Kann ekki sá   konung háleyskan,
     er heimsku þrótt honum eignaði.

Virðar, þeir er vitu ekki, mæla, at frami Hálfs sætti heimsku. Sá kann ekki háleyskan konung, er eignaði honum þrótt heimsku.

Those men, who do not know, say that Hálfr's courage amounted to foolishness. He does not know the king from Hålogaland, who ascribed the valour of foolishness to him.

Ms.: **2845**(38r) (*Hálf*).

Editions: *Skj*: Anonyme digte og vers [XIII], E. 6. *Vers af Fornaldarsagaer: Af Hálfssaga* IX 6: AII, 265, BII, 287, *Skald* II, 151; *Hálf* 1864, 32-3, *Hálf* 1909, 122, *FSGJ* 2, 125, *Hálf* 1981, 133, 191-2; *Edd. Min.* 45.

Notes: [All]: Cf. this justification of Hálfr's behaviour and his insistence on visiting Ásmundr when warned against it with Innsteinn's criticism in *Hálf* 18. Hálfr's valour of foolishness (*þrótt heimsku*) can be compared with the *ofermod* or reckless courage of other heroic leaders, e.g. the Anglo-Saxon *ealdormann* Byrhtnoð in the Old English poem *The Battle of Maldon*, l. 89 (Gordon 1937, 49). — [6] *háleyskan* 'from Hålogaland': Some eds (*Hálf* 1864; *Edd. Min.*; *Hálf* 1909; *FSGJ*) print *háleygskan*. The adj. *háleyskr* 'from Hålogaland' may be used here as a synonym for 'Norwegian, from Norway'. Hálfr's and his champions' associations with Hålogaland are also referred to in *Hálf* 8/2, though their precise connection with this part of northern Norway is unclear.

Hrókr (Hróksv Hrkv 7)

57. Bað hann ekki við dauða   drengi kvíða,
    né æðruorð   ekki mæla.
    Engi skyldi   jöfri fylgja,
    nema forlögum   fylkis heldi.

Hann bað drengi ekki kvíða við dauða, né mæla ekki æðruorð. Engi skyldi fylgja jöfri, nema heldi forlögum fylkis.

He bade the young warriors not to be apprehensive of death, nor to utter any word of fear. No one was to follow the prince, unless he shared the leader's fate.

Ms.: 2845(38r) (*Hálf*).

Editions: *Skj*: Anonyme digte og vers [XIII], E. 6. *Vers af Fornaldarsagaer: Af Hálfssaga* IX 7: AII, 266, BII, 287-8, *Skald* II, 151; *Hálf* 1864, 33, *Hálf* 1909, 122, *FSGJ* 2, 126, *Hálf* 1981, 133, 192; *Edd. Min.* 45.

Notes: [All]: With this stanza begins a list of the various rules and ethical standards King Hálfr expected of the Hálfsrekkar. It corresponds roughly to ch. 5 of the prose text (*Hálf* 1981, 178) that precedes the account of Hálfr's last stand. Other bands of warriors said to have lived by sets of rules laid down by their leader include the Jómsvíkingar (*Jvs* 1962, 17-18 and n. 3) and the Danes under Fróði III, according to Book V of Saxo's *Gesta Danorum* (*Saxo* 2015, I, v. 5. 1-6, pp. 314-19) as well as under Knútr Sveinsson (*Saxo* 2015, I, x. 18. 2-6, pp. 752-7 and see n. 90 on pp. 754-5). — [7-8]: The expression *at halda forlögum e-s* 'share the fate of sby' does not occur elsewhere; see *LP*: *forlǫg* and note to *forlǫg* in *Hálf* 1909.

Hrókr (Hróksv Hrkv 8)

58. Skyldi ekki stynja,   þó at stór hlyti
    sár í sóknum,   siklings vinir,
    né benjar sér   binda láta,
    fyrr en annars dags   jafnlengð kæmi.

Vinir siklings skyldi ekki stynja, þó at hlyti stór sár í sóknum, né láta sér binda benjar, fyrr en jafnlengð annars dags kæmi.

The friends of the king should not moan, even if they received great wounds in combat, nor have their wounds dressed, before the same time of the following day arrived.

Ms.: 2845(38r) (*Hálf*).

Editions: *Skj*: Anonyme digte og vers [XIII], E. 6. *Vers af Fornaldarsagaer: Af Hálfssaga* IX 8: AII, 266, BII, 288, *Skald* II, 151; *Hálf* 1864, 33, *Hálf* 1909, 123, *FSGJ* 2, 126, *Hálf* 1981, 192; *Edd. Min.* 45.

Note: [7-8] *fyrr en jafnlengð annars dags kæmi* 'before the same time of the following day arrived': That is, before twenty-four hours had elapsed. Presumably, the idea was to ensure the men were toughened by bearing the pain of their wounds before allowing them to be bound up.

Hrókr (Hróksv Hrkv 9)

59. Bað ekki hann í her höptu* græta,
 né manns konu mein at vinna.
 Mey bað hann hverja mundi kaupa,
 fögru gulli, at föður ráði.

Hann bað ekki græta höptu* í her, né at vinna konu manns mein. Hann bað kaupa hverja mey mundi, fögru gulli, at ráði föður.

He forbade [men] to make a female captive in the army weep nor to do harm to a man's wife. He ordered every girl to be bought for a bride-price, for fine gold, with the consent of her father.

Ms.: **2845**(38r) (*Hálf*).

Reading: [2] höptu*: hoptum 2845.

Editions: *Skj*: Anonyme digte og vers [XIII], E. 6. *Vers af Fornaldarsagaer: Af Hálfssaga* IX 9: AII, 266, BII, 288; *Skald* II, 151; *Hálf* 1864, 33, *Hálf* 1909, 123, *FSGJ* 2, 126, *Hálf* 1981, 192; *Edd. Min.* 45.

Notes: [All]: According to Andrews (*Hálf* 1909, 22-3), this stanza represents an idealised romantic attitude towards women which never obtained in the Viking Age. However, similar legislation to improve the position of women is mentioned amongst King Fróði's laws (*Saxo* 2015, I, v. 5. 3, pp. 316-17). — [1] *bað ekki* 'forbade': Earlier eds (*Edd. Min.*, *Skj* B, *Skald*) have replaced this and other verbs negated with *ekki* 'not' with the suffixed negative particle *-at*, here *baðat*. — [2] *höptu** 'a female captive': The emendation *höptu* (so also *Edd. Min.*, *Hálf* 1909 and *FSGJ*) is very close to the ms. reading, giving perfect sense to an otherwise incomprehensible line. The ms. reads *hoptum*. *Skj* B and *Skald* read *hapt*, m. acc. sg. of *haptr* 'male captive'.

Hrókr (Hróksv Hrkv 10)

60. Váru ekki svá margir   menn á skeiðum,
    at vér á flótta   fyrri* heldim,
    þó at miklu lið   minna hefðim,
    svá at ellifu   einum gegndi.

Váru ekki svá margir menn á skeiðum, at vér heldim á flótta fyrri*, þó at hefðim miklu minna lið, svá at ellifu gegndi einum.

There were not so many men on the warships that we would take to flight earlier, although we had a much smaller host, so that eleven encountered one.

Ms.: 2845(38r) (*Hálf*).

Readings: [4] fyrri*: fyrir 2845   [5] miklu: mikla 2845.

Editions: *Skj*: Anonyme digte og vers [XIII], E. 6. *Vers af Fornaldarsagaer: Af Hálfssaga* IX 10: AII, 266, BII, 288, *Skald* II, 151; *Hálf* 1864, 34, *Hálf* 1909, 123-4, *FSGJ* 2, 126-7, *Hálf* 1981, 133, 192-3; *Edd. Min.* 45.

Notes: [All]: According to the prose text (*Hálf* 1981, ch. 5, 178, l. 36), Hálfr never had more than sixty men on board his ship. — [4] *fyrri** 'earlier': The ms. has *fyrir* but this produces a hypometrical line; emending to *fyrri* 'earlier', as has been done by most earlier eds (*Edd. Min.*; *Skj* B; *Skald*), gives the required long-stemmed disyllabic word in metrical positions 1-2. — [4, 6] *heldim ... hefðim* 'would take ... had': Normalised to the pret. subj. forms where the ms., following C14th Icelandic practice, has generalised the indic. endings (cf. *ANG* §536.2; Björn K. Þórólfsson 1925, 54-6). — [5] *miklu* 'much': Lit. 'by much'. The ms. has *mikla*, which gives no sense. See *Fritzner*: *mikill* 3 for the usage of *miklu* with a comp. adj.

Hrókr (Hróksv Hrkv 11)

61. Höfðum vér allir   inn efra hlut,
    hvar sem Hildar ...   hlífar knúði.
    Einn vissa ek   jafnsnjallan gram,
    Sigurð konung   at sölum Gjúka.

Vér höfðum allir inn efra hlut, hvar sem ... Hildar knúði hlífar. Ek vissa einn jafnsnjallan gram, Sigurð konung at sölum Gjúka.

We all had the better share wherever ... of Hildr [BATTLE?] struck shields. I knew only one prince to have been equally valiant, King Sigurðr at Gjúki's halls.

Ms.: 2845(38r) (*Hálf*).

Editions: *Skj*: Anonyme digte og vers [XIII], E. 6. *Vers af Fornaldarsagaer: Af Hálfssaga* IX 11: AII, 266, BII, 288, *Skald* II, 151, *NN* §2383; *Hálf* 1864, 34, *Hálf* 1909, 124, *FSGJ* 2, 127, *Hálf* 1981, 134, 193; *Edd. Min.* 45-6.

Notes: [1-2] *vér höfðum allir inn efra hlut* 'we all had the better share': That is, 'we all gained victory'. — [3-4]: The problem with these lines concerns the probable kenning that underlies them. Because *hlíf* (l. 4) itself means 'shield' it cannot be construed with *Hildar* (l. 3) to give a shield-kenning. Most eds have therefore supposed that another word, forming a kenning with *Hildar* 'of Hildr', must have dropped out of l. 3, even though there is no lacuna in the ms. The following suggestions have been made: *Hálfr* 1864: *hvars Hildar él* | *Hálfr knúði* (but this is unmetrical); *Edd. Min.*: *hvar sem Hildar hlynr* | *hlífar knúði*; *Skj* B: *hvars Hildar él* | *hlífar knúði*; *Skald*: *hvar er Hildar hríð* | *hlífar knúði*. The following kennings have been proposed: *él Hildar* 'the storm of Hildr <valkyrie> [BATTLE]'; *hlynr Hildar* 'the maple of Hildr <valkyrie> [WARRIOR]' and *hríð Hildar* 'the storm of Hildr <valkyrie> [BATTLE]'. A sword-kenning like 'fire (*eldr*, *bál*) of Hildr' is also a possibility. — [7-8] *Sigurð konung at sǫlum Gjúka* 'King Sigurðr at Gjúki's halls': A reference to the legend of Sigurðr Fáfnisbani 'Slayer of Fáfnir' and his stay at the court of King Gjúki, where he formed a bond of blood-brotherhood with Gjúki's son Gunnarr and wooed his daughter Guðrún, as told in *Vǫls* and several poems of the Poetic Edda. — [8] *at sǫlum Gjúka* 'at Gjúki's halls': Cf. *Gríp* 43/4 (*NK* 170) *í sǫlom Giúca* 'in Gjúki's halls'.

Hrókr (Hróksv Hrkv 12)

62. Margir váru   menn á skeiðum
    góðir ok fræknir   með gram sjálfum:
    Börkr ok Brynjólfr,   Bölverkr ok Haki,
    Egill ok Erlingr,   Ásláks synir.

Margir góðir ok fræknir menn váru á skeiðum með gram sjálfum: Börkr ok Brynjólfr, Bölverkr ok Haki, Egill ok Erlingr, synir Ásláks.

Many good and brave men were on the warships with the prince himself: Bǫrkr ok Brynjólfr, Bǫlverkr and Haki, Egill and Erlingr, sons of Áslákr.

Ms.: **2845**(38r) (*Hálf*).

Editions: *Skj*: Anonyme digte og vers [XIII], E. 6. *Vers af Fornaldarsagaer: Af Hálfssaga* IX 12: AII, 266, BII, 288-9, *Skald* II, 152; *Hálf* 1864, 34, *Hálf* 1909, 124-5, *FSGJ* 2, 127, *Hálf* 1981, 193; *Edd. Min.* 46.

Note: [All]: The prose text (*Hálf* 1981, 177, ch. 5, ll. 13-14, 17-18) mentions all of the warriors named here, though in a slightly different order: *Áslákr hét ríkr bóndi. Hans synir váru þeir Egill ok Erlingr. Þeir váru ágætir menn.* … [*Þar váru*] *Börkr ok Brynjólfr, Bölverkr ok Haki* … 'Áslákr was the name of a powerful farmer. His sons were Egill and

Erlingr. They were fine men. ... [There were] Bǫrkr and Brynjólfr, Bǫlverkr and Haki ...'.

Hrókr (Hróksv Hrkv 13)

63. Mest váru mér   manna hugðir
    Hrókr, bróðir minn,   ok Hálfr konungr,
    Styrr ok Steinar,   sterkir báðir,
    snarráðir menn,   synir Gunnlaðar.

Mest hugðir manna mér váru Hrókr, bróðir minn, ok Hálfr konungr, Styrr ok Steinar, báðir sterkir, snarráðir menn, synir Gunnlaðar.

Most friendly of [all] men towards me were Hrókr, my brother, and King Hálfr, Styrr and [the two] Steinar, both strong, resolute men, the sons of Gunnlǫð.

Ms.: **2845**(38r) (*Hálf*).

Editions: *Skj*: Anonyme digte og vers [XIII], E. 6. *Vers af Fornaldarsagaer: Af Hálfssaga* IX 13: AII, 267, BII, 289, *Skald* II, 152; *Hálf* 1864, 34-5, *Hálf* 1909, 125, *FSGJ* 2, 127-8, *Hálf* 1981, 134, 193; *Edd. Min.* 46.

Notes: [1-2] *mest hugðir manna mér* 'most friendly of [all] men towards me': On the meaning of this phrase, see *Fritzner: hugaðr* 2. Andrews (*Hálf* 1909) misunderstands the idiom to mean *Ich schätzte am meisten von der mannschaft* ... 'I treasured most from the men ...'. Finnur Jónsson (*Skj* B) emends *mest* (l. 1) to *bezt* 'best' and translates *mine bedste venner* 'my best friends'. In *LP*: *hugaðr*, Finnur quotes this example under two separate senses of the adj. 'courageous' and 'friendly'. — [3] *Hrókr*: That is, Hrókr inn hvíti 'Rook the White'. — [5-6]: Some eds have rearranged these lines, to conform better to the prose text, which mentions a *Styrr hinn sterki* 'the Strong' (*Hálf* 1981, 177, ch. 5, l. 17); *Hálf* 1864 has *Styrr hinn sterki ok Steinar báðir*, while *Edd. Min.* and *Hálf* 1909 have *Styrr enn sterki, Steinar báðir*, *Hálf* 1909 omitting the comma. — [5] *Steinar* '[the two] Steinar': That is, the two brothers each named Steinn 'Stone', Innsteinn and Útsteinn; see *Hálf* 26, Note to l. 4. — [8] *synir Gunnlaðar* 'the sons of Gunnlǫð': Gunnlǫð is named as the mother of the two Steinar in the prose text (*Hálf* 1981, 177, ch. 5, ll. 3-5). She was married to Álfr inn gamli 'the Old', jarl of Hordaland (Hǫrðaland), and was the sister of the district chieftain Hámundr inn frækni 'the Bold', the father of the two men named Hrókr 'Rook'. Thus the 'Stones' were first cousins of the 'Rooks'. The pers. n. Gunnlǫð is uncommon (Lind 1905-15, 416-17), but occurs in a mythological context in *Hávm* 105-10 and *SnE* (*SnE* 1998, I, 4) as the name of the daughter of the giant Suttungr, who allowed Óðinn to gain possession of the mead of poetry; cf. Steinþ Frag 1/2^{III} and Note. It is also the name given to the daughter of Hrókr inn svarti and Brynhildr Hakadóttir (see *Hálf* 75, Note to [All]).

Hrókr (Hróksv Hrkv 14)

64. Hringr ok Hálfdan,   haukar báðir,
    réttir dómendr,   * Dagr inn prúði,
    Stari ok Steingrímr,   Styrr ok Gauti;
    finnr þú aldri   fríðari drengi.

Hringr ok Hálfdan, báðir haukar, réttir dómendr, * Dagr inn prúði, Stari ok Steingrímr, Styrr ok Gauti; þú finnr aldri fríðari drengi.

Hringr and Hálfdan, both hawks, just judges, Dagr inn prúði ('the Courageous'), Stari and Steingrímr, Styrr and Gauti; you will never find finer lads.

Ms.: **2845**(38v) (*Hálf*).

Reading: [4] * Dagr inn prúði: Dana þjóðar Dagr hinn pruði 2845.

Editions: *Skj*: Anonyme digte og vers [XIII], E. 6. *Vers af Fornaldarsagaer: Af Hálfssaga* IX 14: AII, 267, BII, 289, *Skald* II, 152; *Hálf* 1864, 35, *Hálf* 1909, 125, *FSGJ* 2, 128, *Hálf* 1981, 134, 193-4; *Edd. Min.* 46.

Notes: [All]: In the ms. this stanza consists of nine lines. Most eds regard the words *Dana þjóðar* 'of the people of the Danes' (l. 4) which do not seem to make much sense in the context, as a surplus line and cut it out. That has also been done here. *Skj* B prints the line within square brackets, while *Edd. Min.* keeps part of the line as *dómendr Dana*, but deletes *réttir* 'just' (l. 3) and *þjóðar* 'of the people' (l. 4). — [2] *haukar* 'hawks': For the sense of *haukr* as 'brave young man' see Note to *Hálf* 29/1. — [5-6]: The names in this line correspond to those in the prose text (*Hálf* 1981, 177-8), except that Stúfr is named there instead of Styrr (l. 6). This is probably an error in the verse text, as Styrr has already been named in l. 5 of the previous stanza. *Edd. Min.* and *Hálf* 1909 here emend *Styrr* to *Stúfr*.

Hrókr (Hróksv Hrkv 15)

65. Valr ok Haukr   í víkingu,
    báðir fræknir   buðlungs vinir.
    Fáir mundu þeim   fylkis rekkum
    hæfir þykkja   ór Hakaveldi.

Valr ok Haukr í víkingu, báðir fræknir vinir buðlungs. Fáir ór Hakaveldi mundu þykkja hæfir þeim rekkum fylkis.

Valr and Haukr on a viking expedition, both valiant friends of the king. Few from Haki's realm would seem to match these champions of the prince.

Ms.: **2845**(38v) (*Hálf*).

Editions: *Skj*: Anonyme digte og vers [XIII], E. 6. *Vers af Fornaldarsagaer: Af Hálfssaga* IX 15: AII, 267, BII, 289, *Skald* II, 152; *Hálf* 1864, 35, *Hálf* 1909, 126, *FSGJ* 2, 128, *Hálf* 1981, 134, 194; *Edd. Min.* 46.

Notes: [All]: There is no finite verb in the first *helmingr*. — [1] *Valr ok Haukr* 'Valr and Haukr': Their names mean 'Falcon' and 'Hawk' respectively, thus denoting their bravery; cf. Note to *Hálf* 29/1. They are named as brothers in the prose text (*Hálf* 1981, ch. 5, 177, ll. 16-17). — [7] *hæfir* 'to match': From the adj. *hæfr* 'fit, proper, useful'. *Hálf* 1864 and later eds emend to *hæfri* 'braver [than]'. — [8] *Hakaveldi* 'Haki's realm': Similar to such compounds as *Danaveldi* 'the realm of the Danes' (cf. ÞjóðA *Magn* 12/4^{III} and Note), although defined in this instance by the control over territory of one man rather than an ethnic group, the term *Hakaveldi* refers to the realm controlled by King Haki, who is said in the prose text of *Hálf* to rule over the province of Skåne, which was part of greater Denmark in the Middle Ages.

Hrókr (Hróksv Hrkv 16)

66. Hvergi þótti ek   í því liði
     opt aukvisi   ættar minnar.
     Mik kváðu þeir   mann snarpastan,
     þvíat hverr öðrum   hróðrs leitaði.

Ek þótti hvergi opt aukvisi ættar minnar í því liði. Þeir kváðu mik snarpastan mann, þvíat hverr leitaði öðrum hróðrs.

I was by no means often thought to be a degenerate [member] of my family in that troop. They called me the most dashing man, for each sought for praise for the other.

Ms.: 2845(38v) (*Hálf*).

Editions: *Skj*: Anonyme digte og vers [XIII], E. 6. *Vers af Fornaldarsagaer: Af Hálfssaga* IX 16: AII, 267, BII, 289, *Skald* II, 152, *FF* §30; *Hálf* 1864, 36, *Hálf* 1909, 126, *FSGJ* 2, 128-9, *Hálf* 1981, 194; *Edd. Min.* 46.

Notes: [1-4]: Hrókr understates his considerable merits, 'I was by no means often thought to be a degenerate member of my family', i.e. 'I was never thought a degenerate family member'. This statement probably reflects upon a semi-proverbial formula *einn er aukvisi hverrar ættar* 'there is one degenerate in every family' (cf. *Fritzner*: *aukvisi*). — [3] *aukvisi* 'a degenerate': The ms. reads 'audkuisi', denoting an alternative form of the noun *aukvisi*, *auðkvisi* 'degenerate, weakling'. On the etymology, see Falk (1928b, 341-2) and *AEW*: *aukvisal aukvisi*. — [7-8] *þvíat hverr leitaði öðrum hróðrs* 'for each sought for praise for the other': I.e. 'each [member of Hrókr's family] sought to praise the other', meaning that they were generous towards each other and not jealous of each other's reputation.

Hrókr (Hróksv Hrkv 17)

67. Vá bar Vémundr, er vega þorði,
    — Björn ok Bersi — fyrir buðlungi.
    Fylkði sínu sá framligast
    lofðungr liði, meðan lifa mátti.

Vémundr, er vega þorði, bar vá fyrir buðlungi — Björn ok Bersi —. Sá lofðungr fylkði liði sínu framligast, meðan mátti lifa.

Vémundr, who dared to fight, endured danger for the prince [and so did] Bjǫrn and Bersi. That king drew up his troops most excellently, as long as he lived.

Ms.: **2845**(38v) (*Hálf*).

Editions: *Skj*: Anonyme digte og vers [XIII], E. 6. *Vers af Fornaldarsagaer: Af Hálfssaga* IX 17: AII, 267, BII, 289, *Skald* II, 152; *Hálf* 1864, 36, *Hálf* 1909, 126-7, *FSGJ* 2, 129, *Hálf* 1981, 134-5, 194; *Edd. Min.* 47.

Notes: [1] *vá* 'danger': In the saga prose, ch. 5, it says: *Vémundr hét merkismaðr Hálfs kóngs* 'Vémundr was the name of King Hálfr's standard-bearer' (*Hálf* 1981, 177, l. 15). Following Bugge (*Hálf* 1864), eds have taken heed of this, substituting the ms. reading *vo* with *vé* 'standard', construing 'Vémundr ... bore the standard before the prince'. However, there are two other places (*Hálf* 13/3 and 38/4) where ms. 'vo' represents *vá* 'danger' and it is thus preferable to retain the ms. reading *Vémundr, er vega þorði, bar vá fyrir buðlungi* 'Vémundr, who dared to fight, endured danger for [or 'before'] the prince'; cf. Björn K. Þórólfsson (1925, xi-xii). — [2] *vega* 'to fight': Or 'to kill'. — [4] *Björn ok Bersi* 'Bjǫrn and Bersi': Both these personal names mean 'Bear'. Because the prose text mentions *Bárðr ok Björn* (*Hálf* 1981, ch. 5, 178, l. 19) but not *Björn ok Bersi*, as here, some eds have written Bersi out of the stanza (so *Hálf* 1864; *Skj* B). — [5] *fylkði* 'drew up': From *fylkja* 'draw up, assemble [troops]'. The verb is written *fylgdí* in 2845; cf. *Hálf* 21/2, where *fylkja* is written *fylgía*. — [8] *meðan mátti lifa* 'as long as he lived': Lit. 'while he was allowed to live'.

Hrókr (Hróksv Hrkv 18)

68. Naut ekki svá aldrs, sem skyldi,
    frækn landreki við frama dáðir.
    Tólf vetra nam tiggi at herja,
    en þá var þengill þrítugr, er dó.

Frækn landreki naut ekki aldrs svá, sem skyldi, við dáðir frama. Tiggi nam at herja tólf vetra, en þengill var þrítugr, þá er dó.

The valiant land-ruler did not enjoy as long a life as he should have done with deeds of fame. The prince started harrying at the age of twelve and the king was thirty when he died.

Ms.: 2845(38v) (*Hálf*).

Editions: *Skj*: Anonyme digte og vers [XIII], E. 6. *Vers af Fornaldarsagaer: Af Hálfssaga* IX 18: AII, 267, BII, 290, *Skald* II, 152; *Hálf* 1864, 36-7, *Hálf* 1909, 127, *FSGJ* 2, 129, *Hálf* 1981, 194-5; *Edd. Min.* 47.

Note: [5-8]: The information that Hálfr was twelve years old when he began his viking career is in the prose text (*Hálf* 1981, ch. 5, 177, ll. 1-3). From a statement in the same chapter (*Hálf* 1981, ch. 5, 178, l. 33) that he carried on harrying for eighteen years (cf. *Hálf* 36/1-4), it can be deduced that he was thirty years old when he died. The age of twelve seems to have been regarded as traditionally the age of majority for Viking-Age rulers, like Óláfr Haraldsson (cf. Foote and Wilson 1980, 116).

Hrókr (Hróksv Hrkv 19)

69. Slíkt kennir mér   at sofa lítit
    marga grímu   ok mjök vaka:
    er bróðir minn   brenna skyldi
    kvikr í eldi   með konungs rekkum.

Slíkt kennir mér at sofa lítit marga grímu ok vaka mjök: er bróðir minn skyldi brenna kvikr í eldi með rekkum konungs.

This causes me to sleep little many a night and wake much: that my brother should burn alive in the fire with the king's champions.

Ms.: 2845(38v) (*Hálf*).

Editions: *Skj*: Anonyme digte og vers [XIII], E. 6. *Vers af Fornaldarsagaer: Af Hálfssaga* IX 19: AII, 267, BII, 290, *Skald* II, 152; *Hálf* 1864, 37, *Hálf* 1909, 128, *FSGJ* 2, 129, *Hálf* 1981, 195; *Edd. Min.* 47.

Notes: [All]: With this stanza Hrókr begins to express his feelings of grief for the loss of his brother and his king, and his desire to take vengeance for their deaths. — [1-2]: Similar phrasing in MBerf Lv 3/5, 8^{II} is attributed to a man's desire for a woman. — [3] *marga grímu* 'many a night': The noun *gríma* 'mask, cowl' has the transferred sense of 'night' in poetry; cf. Þul *Dœgra* 1/5^{III} and Note there; also *Heiðr* 22/4.

Hrókr (Hróksv Hrkv 20)

70. Sá hefir dagr um mik   daprastr komit
    miklu í heimi,   svá at menn vitu.
    *Una þykkjumz vér   al*dri* síðan,
    at fylgja máttum*a*   fræ*n*dum hollum.

Sá dagr hefir komit um mik, miklu daprastr í heimi, svát menn vitu. Síðan þykkjumz vér al*dri* *una, at máttum*a* fylgja hollum fræ*n*dum.

That day has come upon me, the very saddest in the world, as far as men know. We [I] think that we [I] shall never be happy again that we were [I was] not able to follow [my] loyal kinsmen.

Ms.: **2845**(38v) (*Hálf*).

Readings: [5] *Una: Muna 2845   [6] al*dri*: allir 2845   [7] máttum*a*: máttum 2845 [8] fræ*n*dum: fræðum 2845.

Editions: *Skj*: Anonyme digte og vers [XIII], E. 6. *Vers af Fornaldarsagaer: Af Hálfssaga* IX 20: AII, 268, BII, 290, *Skald* II, 152-3, *NN* §2384; *Hálf* 1864, 37, *Hálf* 1909, 128, *FSGJ* 2, 130, *Hálf* 1981, 135, 195; *Edd. Min.* 47.

Notes: [5-8]: The second *helmingr* of this stanza is difficult to understand without considerable emendation, and it lacks alliteration in ll. 5-6. The word *allir* 'all' in l. 6 shows that it is vocalic alliteration that is lacking, and so earlier eds have sought to emend *muna* 'remember' (l. 5) to *una* 'be happy' and *allir* 'all' to *aldri* 'never', giving the sense 'we think that we shall never be happy again'. In the present edn, as in others (e.g. *Skj* B), the pl. number is taken to refer to Hrókr himself, since almost all the other Hálfsrekkar are dead. Bugge (*Hálf* 1864) and *Skj* B further emend the verb *máttum* 'we were able' in l. 7 to the negated *máttuma* 'we were not able' on grounds of sense, given that the cause of Hrókr's sadness appears to be his inability to follow his loyal kinsmen. This edn has also adopted the emendation to *máttuma*. — [8] *frændum* 'kinsmen': Emended by all eds from ms. *fræðum*, which does not fit the context.

Hrókr (Hróksv Hrkv 21)

71. Alls mundi mér   angrs léttara,
    ef ek Hálf*s* konungs   hefna mættak,
    svá at Ásmundi   eggfrán*um* hjör,
    bana baug*b*rjót*s*,   brjóst rauf*aðak.

Mér mundi léttara alls angrs, ef ek mættak hefna Hálf*s* konungs, svá at rauf*aðak brjóst Ásmundi, bana baug*b*rjóts, eggfrán*um* hjör.

I would be eased of all grief, if I could avenge King Hálfr, so that I would pierce the breast of Ásmundr, slayer of the ring-breaker [GENEROUS RULER = Hálfr], with a sharp-edged sword.

Ms.: 2845(38v) (*Hálf*).

Readings: [3] Hálfs: hálf 2845   [6] eggfránum: egg fránan 2845   [7] baug*b*rjóts: baug spjót 2845   [8] rauf*aðak: 'rraufgadag' 2845.

Editions: *Skj*: Anonyme digte og vers [XIII], E. 6. *Vers af Fornaldarsagaer: Af Hálfssaga* IX 21: AII, 268, BII, 290, *Skald* II, 153; *Hálf* 1864, 37-8, *Hálf* 1909, 128-9, *FSGJ* 2, 130, *Hálf* 1981, 135, 195; *Edd. Min.* 47.

Notes: [1-2] *mér mundi léttara alls angrs* 'I would be eased of all grief': Lit. 'to me it would be lighter in respect of all grief'. — [6] *eggfránum* 'sharp-edged': The ms. reading cannot be correct, as the context requires a dat. instr.; this cpd adj. occurs also in Þórðh Lv 10/4^V (*Þórð* 10), again collocated with *hjǫrr* 'sword'. — [7] *baug*brjóts 'of the ring-breaker [GENEROUS RULER = Hálfr]': The element *baug-* 'ring' does not normally occur with terms for 'spear'; *baugbrjótr* 'ring-breaker' is a common kenning for 'man' (see Meissner 330-1) and cf. *Hálf* 33/7 *baugbroti* 'ring-breaker'. This emendation was first suggested by Bugge (*Hálf* 1864) and has been followed by all subsequent eds.

Hrókr (Hróksv Hrkv 22)

72. Hefnt mun verða   Hálfs ins frækna,
     því at þeir gǫfgan gram   í griðum véltu.
     Olli morði   ok mannskaða
     Ásmundr konungr   illu heilli.

Hálfs ins frækna mun verða hefnt, því at þeir véltu gǫfgan gram í griðum. Ásmundr konungr olli morði ok mannskaða illu heilli.

Hálfr the valiant will be avenged, for they betrayed the noble king in a time of truce. Through an evil fate, King Ásmundr caused murder and loss of life.

Ms.: 2845(38v) (*Hálf*).

Editions: *Skj*: Anonyme digte og vers [XIII], E. 6. *Vers af Fornaldarsagaer: Af Hálfssaga* IX 22: AII, 268, BII, 290, *Skald* II, 153; *Hálf* 1864, 38, *Hálf* 1909, 129, *FSGJ* 2, 130, *Hálf* 1981, 195-6; *Edd. Min.* 47-8.

Note: [4] *véltu ... í griðum* 'betrayed ... in a time of truce': Lit. 'betrayed in truces'. Cf. *Hálf* 17/8. In the sg. the noun *grið* means 'right of domicile, home', but in the pl. 'truce, peace'.

Hrókr (Hróksv Hrkv 23)

73. Þá mun reyna   ok raun gefa,
    ef vit Sveinn komum   saman í rómu,
    hvárir í vígi   verða hæfri,
    Hámundar burr   eða Haka þegnar.

Þá mun reyna ok raun gefa, ef vit Sveinn komum saman í rómu, hvárir verða hæfri í vígi, Hámundar burr eða þegnar Haka.

Then it will be experienced and put to the test, if Sveinn and I clash in battle, who will prove to be more courageous in fighting, the son of Hámundr [= Hrókr inn svarti] or Haki's men.

Ms.: **2845**(38v) (*Hálf*).

Editions: *Skj*: Anonyme digte og vers [XIII], E. 6. *Vers af Fornaldarsagaer: Af Hálfssaga* IX 23: AII, 268, BII, 291, *Skald* II, 153; *Hálf* 1864, 38, *Hálf* 1909, 129, *FSGJ* 2, 130-1, *Hálf* 1981, 196; *Edd. Min.* 48.

Notes: [All]: According to the prose text (*Hálf* 1981, ch. 10, 190), King Sveinn inn sigrsæli 'the Victorious' asked King Haki for the hand of his daughter Brynhildr, but Haki refused him. Sveinn then swore an oath that he would kill both the man who married Brynhildr and her father as well. Heðinn, a jarl of King Haki, then put himself forward as a suitor, together with his son Vifill. Haki promised Brynhildr to Vifill on condition that he defended the country against Sveinn. — [3] *vit Sveinn* 'Sveinn and I': The ms. has here 'uid sueín', which can be understood as *við Svein* 'against Sveinn' or as *vit Sveinn* 'Sveinn and I' (with *vit* the 2nd pers. dual nom. pers. pron.). In the former reading, the syntax *ef komum saman við Svein í rómu* 'if we come together against Sveinn in battle' requires an otherwise unattested *koma saman við e-n*, so some eds (*Skj* B; *Skald*) have adopted the second alternative, which is also adopted here. — [5] *hvárir* 'who': I.e. 'which of the two parties'.

Hrókr (Hróksv Hrkv 24)

74. Segi ek svá kveðit   snotru vífi,
    at ek Brynhildar   biðja mundak,
    ef vita þættumz,   at vildi hon
    Hróki unna,   Hámundar bur.

Ek segi svá kveðit snotru vífi, at ek mundak biðja Brynhildar, ef þættumz vita, at hon vildi unna Hróki, bur Hámundar.

Thus I make known to the wise woman that I would ask for the hand of Brynhildr, if I thought that she could love Hrókr, son of Hámundr.

Ms.: 2845(38v) (*Hálf*).

Editions: *Skj*: Anonyme digte og vers [XIII], E. 6. *Vers af Fornaldarsagaer: Af Hálfssaga* IX 24: AII, 268, BII, 291, *Skald* II, 153; *Hálf* 1864, 38, *Hálf* 1909, 129-30, *FSGJ* 2, 131, *Hálf* 1981, 196; *Edd. Min.* 48.

Notes: [All]: It would appear from this and the following stanzas that Hrókr is very well aware that he is being overheard (as the prose text represents it) and that he knows who his audience is. — [1] *ek segi svá kveðit* 'thus I make known': Lit. 'I say [it is] thus made known'.

Hrókr (Hróksv Hrkv 25)

75. Ván væri mér   vitra manna,
    snarpra seggja,   ef vér saman ættum,
    því at ek fann ekki mey   margsvinnari
    hvergi landa   en Haka dóttur.

Væri mér ván vitra manna, snarpra seggja, ef vér ættum saman, því at ek fann ekki margsvinnari mey hvergi landa en dóttur Haka.

I would expect wise people, smart men, if we had offspring together, for I did not find a more intelligent girl in any country than the daughter of Haki [= Brynhildr].

Ms.: 2845(38v) (*Hálf*).

Editions: *Skj*: Anonyme digte og vers [XIII], E. 6. *Vers af Fornaldarsagaer: Af Hálfssaga* IX 25: AII, 268, BII, 291, *Skald* II, 153; *Hálf* 1864, 39, *Hálf* 1909, 130, *FSGJ* 2, 131, *Hálf* 1981, 196; *Edd. Min.* 48.

Notes: [All]: Hrókr's expectation of wise and smart descendants from a marriage with Brynhildr is doubtless to be understood in the light of the intelligence conveyed in the saga prose (*Hálf* 1981, ch. 11, 197, ll. 11-13) that *dóttir Hróks ins svarta ok Brynhildar var Gunnlǫð, móðir Hrómundar Gripssonar* 'the daughter of Hrókr the Black and Brynhildr was Gunnlǫð, the mother of Hrómundr Gripsson'. Hrómundr Gripsson is mentioned in a number of Old Icelandic texts (for details, see *Hálf* 1909, 131-2 n. 19) and was the subject of a saga, now lost in its medieval form, which was performed at a wedding at Reykjahólar in 1119 (Brown 1952, 18). According to Anon *Mhkv* 7/4[III], *Hrómundr þótti garpr ok slœgr* 'Hrómundr seemed bold and cunning'. — [5]: As it stands, this line is unmetrical, though it could be emended to give a metrical line (e.g. *þvít mey fannkat* or *þvít mey fannk ei*).

Hrókr (Hróksv Hrkv 26)

76. Fann ek aldri — þó hefik farit víða —
    hugþekkri mey   en Haka dóttur.
    Hon er at öllu,   sem ek æskja mun.

Ek fann aldri hugþekkri mey en dóttur Haka, þó hefik farit víða. Hon er at öllu, sem ek mun æskja.

I have never found a more endearing girl than the daughter of Haki [= Brynhildr], yet I have travelled widely. She is in every respect as I could wish.

Ms.: 2845(38v) (*Hálf*).

Editions: *Skj*: Anonyme digte og vers [XIII], E. 6. *Vers af Fornaldarsagaer: Af Hálfssaga* IX 26: AII, 268-9, BII, 291, *Skald* II, 153; *Hálf* 1864, 39, *Hálf* 1909, 130, *FSGJ* 2, 131-2, *Hálf* 1981, 135, 196; *Edd. Min.* 48.

Note: [All]: Consisting of only six lines, this stanza echoes the contents of the preceding one and may be an incompletely transmitted variation of it (see *Hálf* 1909, 130). Bugge (*Hálf* 1864) notes that the stanza seems superfluous and may be a later addition.

Hrókr (Hróksv Hrkv 27)

77. Hér þykki ek nú   í Hakaveldi
    hornungr vera   hverrar þjóðar.
    Allir eigu   innar at sitja
    hálfargir m*enn*   en Hálfsrekkar.

Ek þykki nú vera hornungr hverrar þjóðar hér í Hakaveldi. Allir hálfargir m*enn* eigu at sitja innar en Hálfsrekkar.

I now seem to be an outcast amongst all people here in Haki's realm. All half-cowardly men are entitled to sit futher inwards than Hálfr's champions.

Ms.: 2845(38v-39r) (*Hálf*).

Reading: [7] hálfargir m*enn*: 'halfar girmar' 2845.

Editions: *Skj*: Anonyme digte og vers [XIII], E. 6. *Vers af Fornaldarsagaer: Af Hálfssaga* IX 27: AII, 269, BII, 291, *Skald* II, 153; *Hálf* 1864, 39, *Hálf* 1909, 130-1, *FSGJ* 2, 132, *Hálf* 1981, 135, 197; *Edd. Min.* 48.

Notes: [2] *Hakaveldi* 'Haki's realm': See *Hálf* 65/8 and Note there. — [3] *hornungr* 'an outcast': Lit. 'someone relegated to the corner', a term often applied to an illegitimate son; cf. *Fritzner*, *ONP*: *hornungr*. — [6] *sitja innar* 'sit futher inwards': The expression relates to the arrangement of seating in a hall, where more favoured men were allowed to sit on benches closer to the central part of the hall floor where the fire was. — [7]

hálfargir m*enn* 'half-cowardly men': This emendation appears in *Skj* B and *Skald*, while *Edd. Min.*, *Hálf* 1909 and *FSGJ* emend to *hallar gumnar*, construing *allir gumnar hallar* 'all men in the hall'. *Hálf* 1864 emended to *Haka gumar* 'Haki's men'. The ms. here reads 'halfar girmar' (not 'halfargirmadr' as *Skj* A has it), with the superscript *-ar* symbol for the final syllable of each word. Probably the scribe's exemplar had a nasal stroke instead of an *-ar* abbreviation over the *m* of *menn*. The adj. *hálfargr* 'half-cowardly' occurs nowhere else in Old Norse.

Introduction to Bragi Lv 1b (*Hálf* 78)

This stanza, edited here by Margaret Clunies Ross, is extant in three separate prose sources, and is attributed to Bragi skáld 'Bragi the Poet' in all three: *Ldn*, *Geir* (in *Stu*), and *Hálf*. For a summary of the narrative in which the stanza is embedded, see *Introduction* to Lv 1a[IV].

In all sources this narrative, a version of a folktale type (cf. Boberg 1966, 183, K1921.3; Mitchell 1987; Thompson 1955-8 IV, K1921.1-3; H41.5) in which lower-class infants are substituted for royal or aristocratic ones, serves to give background to the *vitae* of the twins Geirmundr and Hámundr heljarskinn 'Dark-skin', who were both among the most important settlers in Iceland and had many high-ranking descendants. Whereas *Ldn* and *Geir* use this narrative to enhance Geirmundr's status in particular, its function in *Hálf* is to provide a fitting conclusion to a *fornaldarsaga* about the brothers' legendary ancestors.

The Bragi skáld of this narrative has been traditionally identified with Bragi inn gamli 'the Old' Boddason (see his Biography in Vol. III). His role (all versions) is that of a seer and moral adviser, and is comparable to that played by seeresses elsewhere in Old Icelandic literature; cf. *Vsp* and the *lítil vǫlva* 'little seeress' Þorbjǫrg in *Eir*. There is a particular similarity to an episode in *Hrólf* in which a *vǫlva* 'seeress' recites verses disclosing the true identity and whereabouts of two brothers whose father has been killed by King Fróði; there are verbal similarities between Bragi's stanza and Heiðr Lv 1 and 3 (*Hrólf* 2 and 4). Like a *vǫlva*, whose name derives from *vǫlr* 'wand, switch', Bragi has a rod (*sproti*) which he uses to emphasise his message and direct it to the queen. In all versions of the verse text he affirms the royal birth of Hámundr and Geirmundr, while confirming the slave stock of Leifr.

The textual relationship between the three prose sources' versions of the narrative is complex. It is described in detail in the Introduction to Lv 1a[IV]. This edn of Lv 1b is based upon 2845, while the Melabók (Mb) version has been taken as base text for Lv 1a[IV].

Unlike all the other stanzas from *Hálf*, which have been normalised to the Old Icelandic of the period 1250-1300, it is presumed that Bragi's stanza belongs to the period pre-1200 and has been normalised accordingly. The metre of the stanza is in a somewhat irregular version of *fornyrðislag*. There is considerable variation across the versions in ll. 1-2 and, in particular, ll. 7-8. Not all of the versions are regular metrically, and it is difficult to establish a stemma (or stemmata) that will give a basis for the variations of the final two lines, which presumably differ as a result of oral transmission.

Bragi (Bragi Lv 1b)

78. Tveir eru inni,   trúik bǫðum vel,
    Hámundr ok Geirmundr,   Hjǫrvi bornir;
    en Leifr þriði,   Loðhattar son;
    fœddirat þú   þann mǫg, kona.

Tveir eru inni, trúik bǫðum vel, Hámundr ok Geirmundr, bornir Hjǫrvi; en Leifr, son Loðhattar, þriði: fœddirat þú þann mǫg, kona.

There are two inside, I trust both well, Hámundr and Geirmundr, born to Hjǫrr; but Leifr, son of Loðhǫttr [is] the third; you did not give birth to that youth, woman.

Mss: **2845**(39v) (*Hálf*); Mb(2rb), St^x(26r), 105^x(27r), Sk^x(30v), Þb106^x(17v) (*Ldn*); 114^x(4v), 437^x(1v), 439^x(1r), 440^x(1v) (*Stu*).

Readings: [1] eru inni: *so* St^x, 105^x, Sk^x, 114^x, 437^x, 439^x, 440^x, eru 2845, 'roo inní' Mb, 'roa inne' Þb106^x;   inni: *om. all others*   [2] trúik bǫðum vel: *so all others*, ok trúik vel bǫðum 2845   [3] Hámundr ok Geirmundr: Hámir ok Geirmir 114^x, 437^x [4] bornir: búnir Mb, Þb106^x [6] Loðhattar: 'lo hattar' Mb;   son: 's.' Mb, sun 105^x, sonr 114^x, 437^x [7] fœddirat þú ('fœddir eigi þú'): fœð hann, kona Mb, fœðat þú þann, kona St^x, fœð þann, kona 105^x, fœðat þu þann kona *with* 'eða: "fædd" eigi þann cona' *added in left margin in scribal hand* Sk^x, fœðat þú eigi þann kona *with* 'eda fæddir ei þann kona' *added in margin in scribal hand* Þb106^x, fær þrælum þann 114^x, 437^x, fátt prýðir þann 439^x, fátt fríðir þann 440^x [8] þann mǫg kona: í fjǫrð mun hann verri Mb, fáir munu verri St^x, Sk^x, 'fiordar man hann verri' 105^x, 'fäer um vere' *with* '(Landnámabók segir fæd hann kona i fiord mun hann væri.)' *added in scribal hand* Þb106^x, fár mun in verri 114^x, 437^x, 439^x, 440^x.

Editions: *Skj*: Bragi enn gamli, 3. *Lausavísur* 1: AI, 5, BI, 5, *Skald* I, 3; *Hálf* 1981, 198 (*Hálf*); *Ldn* 1900, 38, 162, 239, *Ldn* 1921, 67, *ÍF 1*, I, 151 (*Ldn*); *Stu* 1878 I, 2, *Stu*1906 I, 1, *Stu*1946 I, 6, *Stu* 1988 I, 2 (*Stu*).

Context: While her husband is away, the wife of King Hjǫrr, son of Hálfr, has exchanged her dark-skinned twin sons for Leifr, the fair son of a slave-woman. Some time later Bragi, on a visit to the court, sees how the twins dominate the slave's son who has taken their place as a legitimate heir. Bragi discovers the true identity of the boys and reveals it to the queen, who is forced to confess the twins' identity to their father. See further Introduction to Lv 1a[IV].

Notes: [All]: The version of this stanza in *Hálf* differs considerably from that in the mss of *Ldn* and *Stu*, not only in ll. 7-8, where the greatest variation occurs across the mss, but in ll. 1-2 as well. For a text of the Mb version, and Notes on this and other witnesses, see Bragi Lv 1a[IV]. — [1-2]: The first two lines of this stanza in 2845 are clearly unmetrical, while the version of the other mss *tveir ró inni, | trúik bǫ́ðum vel* 'two are inside, I trust both well' is superior in sense and regular in metre and has been adopted here. The version of 2845, *tveir eru, | ok trúik vel bǫ́ðum* can be translated 'there are two, and I trust both well'. — [4] *bornir Hjǫrvi* 'born to Hjǫrr': There may also be a punning subsidiary sense here, 'born to the sword' (*hjǫrr* 'sword'), that is, born to belong to the warrior class. — [7] *fœddirat* '[you] did not give birth': The text has been normalised from the ms. 'fœddir eigi þú', which is unmetrical, by substituting the suffixed negative particle *-at* for the negative adv. *eigi* 'not'. — [7-8] *fœddirat þú þann mǫg, kona* 'you did not give birth to that youth, woman': The text of 2845 is quite different from that of the other witnesses, which differ considerably among themselves as well, although they all convey a similar message, that Leifr could not have been the child of a royal couple. For a discussion of the other versions, see Bragi Lv 1a[IV] and Notes.

Hervarar saga ok Heiðreks
Edited by Hannah Burrows

Introduction

Hervarar saga ok Heiðreks 'The Saga of Hervǫr and of Heiðrekr' (*Heiðr*) includes 121 stanzas or part-stanzas across its three main extant redactions (see further below). It has been a popular work, surviving in at least fifty-five manuscripts (most post-medieval) and inspiring several cycles of *rímur*, based more or less closely on the material of the saga (Love 2013, 263-73). It has been edited at least seventeen times and translated into at least twelve modern languages (*Stories for All Time* database, accessed 28 October 2015). Its poetry, in groups of stanzas or as long poems, has taken on a life, or lives, of its own; the reception histories of these groups are discussed in the relevant Introductions. Individually or between them, the redactions of the saga prose tell the following story.

The saga opens by describing the origins of the enchanted sword Tyrfingr, an object which provides a thread of continuity through the saga. We are then told of Arngrímr, a great lord in Garðaríki (Russia), who is given Tyrfingr by the king and later settles down with his wife Eyfura on the island of Bólm, said in some versions of the saga to have been in Hálogaland in northern Norway, but more probably to be identified with the island Bolmsö on Lake Bolmen, southern Sweden (*Heiðr* 1960, 2 n. 2). They have twelve sons, all berserks, the most notable of whom are Angantýr, the eldest, and Hjǫrvarðr. At a *heitstrenging* 'vow-making' one *jól* 'Yule', Hjǫrvarðr vows to marry the daughter of Ingjaldr, the Swedish king. However, he is challenged to a duel for her hand by Hjálmarr inn hugumstóri 'the Great-minded', and after a brief interlude in which Angantýr marries the daughter of the Swedish jarl Bjarmi, the twelve brothers fight Hjálmarr and his companion Ǫrvar-Oddr on the island of Samsø (ON Sámsey), a Danish island in the Kattegat, with Angantýr wielding Tyrfingr. Ǫrvar-Oddr, who owns an enchanted shirt into which no weapons can bite, is the sole survivor. This story is also found in *Ǫrv*, and poetry from this part of the saga, including some *lausavísur* and part of the so-called 'death song' of Hjálmarr, is edited in the present edition with the rest of the poetry from *Ǫrv*, where more stanzas are preserved. For details of the number and disposition of these stanzas in *Heiðr* mss, see the edition of *Ǫrv* and, in particular, Introductions to *Ǫrv* 5-12 and *Ǫrv* 13-29.

The saga then moves on to tell that Angantýr's widow gives birth to a girl, Hervǫr, who is brought up in the household of her maternal grandfather Bjarmi jarl. *Sterk sem karlar* 'as strong as men', she is something of a troublemaker, until she decides to visit her kinsmen's burial mound on Samsø to claim the treasure that was buried with them, in particular the sword Tyrfingr. She rouses the ghost of her dead father and they engage in a verse dialogue in which Angantýr eventually yields Tyrfingr to her, but not without warning that it will bring ruin to her family. Later she marries Hǫfundr, son of King Guðmundr of Glasisvellir, and they have two sons, Angantýr and Heiðrekr.

Heiðrekr grows up to be unruly and difficult, and one day turns up to a feast, uninvited and intent on causing trouble, and throws a rock with blind aim which strikes and kills his brother Angantýr. Their father Hǫfundr orders him into exile, but gives him six pieces of *heilræði* 'good advice' (which Heiðrekr immediately resolves to break) at the behest of Hervǫr, whose own parting gift to her son is Tyrfingr. Heiðrekr then puts himself into the service of King Haraldr of Reiðgotaland, gaining honour, wealth and the hand of the king's daughter, Helga, by whom he has a son, Angantýr. When Haraldr and Heiðrekr each want to sacrifice the other's son to relieve a famine, however, Heiðrekr raises an army against Haraldr, defeats him and takes over his rule, at which Helga kills herself. Heiðrekr fathers another son, Hlǫðr, after abducting Sifka, daughter of the Hunnish king Humli; Hlǫðr is fostered at his maternal grandfather's court. After various other exploits Heiðrekr sets out to defy his father's advice, and is eventually married to the daughter of the king of Garðaríki, who bears him a daughter, Hervǫr.

Heiðrekr, now a powerful, wealthy and popular king, sends for his enemy Gestumblindi to come and be reconciled with him, either by submitting to the judgement of his councillors or else by propounding a riddle Heiðrekr is unable to solve. Gestumblindi sacrifices to Óðinn for help with this dilemma, and the god switches places with Gestumblindi to propose a series of riddles, all of which Heiðrekr solves. In the end Óðinn reveals himself but wins the contest by asking what he himself said into the ear of his son Baldr at the latter's funeral pyre (cf. *Vafþr*). Heiðrekr attempts to attack Óðinn for this deception, but the god transforms himself into a hawk and escapes, cursing Heiðrekr to death at the hand of *inir verstu þrælar* 'the basest slaves' (*Heiðr* 1960, 44). Sure enough, this comes to pass, the slaves also stealing Tyrfingr. Angantýr Heiðreksson is received as Heiðrekr's successor, and quickly avenges his father, reclaiming Tyrfingr in the process.

The next section, which intersperses prose with verse more than anywhere else in the saga, relates how Hlǫðr Heiðreksson travels to claim his share of their father's inheritance from Angantýr. Angantýr promises him wealth and material goods, but says he has no title to the land, as an illegitimate son. Hlǫðr and his maternal grandfather and foster-father Humli raise an army of Huns (*Heiðr* 1960, 52): *svá mikinn, at aleyða var eptir í Húnalandi vígra manna* 'so vast that afterwards the land of the Huns was utterly despoiled of all its fighting men'. They meet the army of Hervǫr Heiðreksdóttir first; she is defeated and killed. Her foster-father Ormarr then rides to warn Angantýr, who stakes out a battlefield in the land of the Goths. Fighting continues for eight days, but eventually Angantýr slays Hlǫðr and Humli with Tyrfingr and the Hunnish army flees. The saga ends with tales of Angantýr's descendants and genealogies of Swedish kings.

There are four main groups of poetic stanzas in the saga. First, there is that relating to the duel on Samsø (which does not appear in the so-called H redaction of *Heiðr*; on the different redactions see further below), which is found in fuller form in *Ǫrv* and edited in *SkP* VIII with the rest of the poetry from that saga. Then there are thirty-five stanzas relating to the story of the first Hervǫr, many of them constituting a dialogue between her and her (now-dead) father Angantýr. Third is Gestumblindi's riddle-series (*Heiðreks gátur*), and finally there are the stanzas relating the battle of the Goths and the Huns. The character of the poetry in the saga and the issues surrounding it, including questions of metre and normalisation, are discussed more fully in the Introductions to individual groups of stanzas.

Dating of the *fornaldarsögur* is difficult, but *Heiðr* is thought to be among the oldest of the genre, partly on structural grounds: the integration of poetry and prose is somewhat awkward, with the prose often serving to contextualise the verse and advance the plot between poems, rather than being developed in itself as in the more fully-evolved sagas (Torfi H. Tulinius 2002, 23, 58). Torfi H. Tulinius (2002, 63, 234-89) places the saga as a whole in the first third of the thirteenth century. Almost all the poetry is generally accepted as older than the prose; dating issues are discussed further in the relevant Introductions.

Three extant redactions of *Heiðr* are recognised, as first posited by Sharovol'sky (1906; see Andrews 1914, Love 2013, 22 n. 25) and are now known as H (whose main ms. is Hauksbók, AM 544 4° (Hb), of c. 1302-10), R (main ms. GKS 2845 4° (2845), of c. 1450) and U (main ms. Upps UB R715^x (R715^x), of c. 1650). The relationship between these redactions, and with later mss, is complicated and has not yet been fully worked out (Love 2013, 37-8). Love's recent study (2013) contributes much to addressing the issue and provides a review of previous scholarly opinion and new stemmata for each redaction, considering in total forty-one mss (Love 2013, 318-27). The conventional designations H, R and U for the three redactions will be retained in this edition, though the *SkP* sigla Hb, 2845 and R715^x are used for the mss.

H and U are more closely related to one another than either is to R, sharing several major differences from the latter including wording, names, plot details and the addition of 'new' matter not to be found in R (*Heiðr* 1960, ix). The H redaction can claim the oldest ms. witness of the saga, Hb, where the text of the saga is in the hand of Haukr Erlendsson himself (*Heiðr* 1924, xvii). However, it is shorter and less detailed than the other redactions, and has been described as 'a drastic and by no means careful abridgement' of its exemplar (*Heiðr* 1960, xxx). Hb does not contain any of the stanzas from the first group of poetry in the other redactions, relating to the duel on Samsø, though it summarises the plot and refers the reader to *Ǫrv*. Moreover a lacuna in the ms. beginning part-way through the solution to the second of the *Heiðreks gátur* means that the end of the saga in the H redaction is lost. Two seventeenth-century paper mss (AM 281 4°^{x} (281^x) and AM 597 b 4°^{x} (597b^x)), apparently copied from Hb in a more complete condition (*Heiðr* 1873, 203; though see Love 2013, 193-4 for problematisation), preserve the riddle-match to its conclusion, but neither these nor any other later mss preserve more of the H redaction of the saga.

The primary ms. of R, 2845, is also damaged: there is a lacuna part-way through the text of *Heiðr*, and the end is missing (from part-way through the battle section). No later ms. contains a fuller version of the R redaction, but some suggest another now-lost version of it (*Heiðr* 1924, xii-xiii, xxiv-xxxviii; Love 2013, 27). Ms. 2845 contains a number of other *fornaldarsögur*, including *Hálf*, of which it is the oldest extant witness.

The U redaction is preserved complete, without lacunae, meaning it is the only version to contain the end of the saga. However, it now exists only in paper copies from the mid-seventeenth century and later, and the primary ms., R715^x (written probably before 1647 by one Páll Hallson at Gnúpufell (*Heiðr* 1924, xx-xxi)) has been criticised for textual problems (e.g. Heinrichs 1979, 2) – in the poetry in particular – and is covered with marginal annotations and corrections, both apparently conjectural and identifiably from other sources, many in the hand of Jón Rugman (*Heiðr* 1924, xxii). His name is abbreviated as JR in the Readings below.

The ms. AM 203 fol^x (203^x), a collection of several *fornaldarsögur* written by Jón Erlendsson of Villingaholt in south-west Iceland (d. 1672) (*Heiðr* 1924, xxix), is also worthy of note. For the text of *Heiðr*, an R-redaction exemplar was copied almost entirely, with the lacuna in R filled in from an H-redaction exemplar (Andrews 1914, 366; Love 2013, 28). A U-redaction ms. was also used for the fuller beginning of the text which R does not have, and at the end from the point where R breaks off. This exemplar is now lost, but seems to share a common original with R715^x (*Heiðr* 1960, xxx). Ms. 203^x therefore has independent textual value for the parts of the saga where it does not follow R. Where it differs in the U redaction from R715^x, it is usually closer to Hb than the latter is, and is therefore probably closer to their common ancestor (Hall 2005, 5).

Given the complicated ms. relations and that the preferred witnesses differ between prose and poetry (and between different groups of poetry), the mss of the saga are listed here by siglum without further attempt to designate redaction or relation. These issues are discussed more fully as they relate to the poetry in the Introductions to each group of stanzas. The following list draws on the *Stories for All Time* database (accessed 28 October 2015), *Heiðr* 1924, Love 2013, and *Handrit.is* (accessed 28 October 2015). Included here are mss that contain versions of the saga or substantial extracts from it; the riddles in particular often exist outside the saga context and those mss are not included here but discussed further in the Introduction to those stanzas:

AM 192 fol^x; AM 193 a fol^x; AM 202k fol^x (202k^x) (two versions); AM 203 fol^x (203^x); AM 395 fol^x; AM 281 4° (281^x); AM 345 4° (345); AM 354 4°^{x}; AM 355 4°^{x}; AM 359 a 4°^{x}; AM 359 b 4°^{x}; AM 544 4° (Hb); AM 582 4°^{x}; AM 591 k 4°^{x}; AM 597 b 4°^{x} (597b^x); AM 738 4°^{x}; AM 949 c 4°^{x}; AMAcc 5^x; BLAdd 4859^x; DKNVSB 4 m fol^x; GKS 2845 4to; Holm papp 105 fol^x; Holm papp 120 fol^x; Holm papp 15 4°^{x}; Holm papp 34 4°^{x}; Holm papp 62 4°^{x}; Holm papp 63 4°^{x}; Holm papp 79 VII 4°^{x}; JS 19 fol^x; JS 160 fol^x; JS 624 4°^{x}; Lbs 633 fol^x; Lbs 1500 4°^{x} (from Valdimar Ásmundarson 1885-9); Lbs 1849 8°^{x}; NKS 1151 fol^x; NKS 1189 fol^x; NKS 635 4°^{x}; NKS 1701 4°^{x}; NKS 1711 4°^{x}; NKS 1762 4°^{x}; NKS 1769 4°^{x}; NKS 331 8°^{x}; OsloUB 1159 8°^{x}; Rask 30^x;

Riksarkivet E 8630^x; UppsUB R 715^x (715^x); UppsUB R 757^x; UppsUB Westin 604 IV^x.

The *editio princeps* of *Heiðr* is by Olaus Verelius (*Heiðr* 1672), with facing Swedish translation and Latin commentary. It has been thought (e.g. *Heiðr* 1924, xxi-xxv) that ms. R715^x formed the basis for this edition, but Love (2013, 249-53) has recently made a compelling case that Verelius used instead or as well the ms. Riksarkivet E 8630^x, written by Jón Rugman c. 1660. The following paper mss take material from Verelius' edition: AMAcc 5^x, BLAdd 11108^x, Lbs 896 4^{ox}, Rask 21 a^x, AM 1020 4^{ox}, Kall 620 4^{ox}, UppsUB Waller ms se 568^x. Other editions are as follows: *Heiðr* 1785 (based on 345); *FSN* 1, 409-512 (based on 345) and 513-33 (based on Hb); Petersen and Thorarensen 1847 (based on Hb, supplemented by 2845); Rafn 1850-2, I, 109-211 (based on 345); *Heiðr* 1873; Valdimar Ásmundarson 1885-9, 1, 307-60; *Hb* 1892-6 (facsimile); Scharovol'sky 1906; *Heiðr* 1924 (normalised text of Hb and diplomatic texts of 2845 and R715^x); *FSGJ* 2, 1-71, Jón Helgason 1955b (facsimile); *Heiðr* 1956 (normalised after the R text of *Heiðr* 1924); Hb 1960 (facsimile); *Heiðr* 1960 (based on 2845); Labuda 1961, 175-230 (extracts); Kozák 2008. In the present edition *Heiðr* 1672, *FSN* 1, *Heiðr* 1873, *Heiðr* 1924, *FSGJ* and *Heiðr* 1960 are cited routinely unless otherwise stated. Normalised prose text of *Heiðr* in Old Norse is routinely cited from *Heiðr* 1960 (unless otherwise stated), but translations throughout are those of the present editor.

For stanzas 1-12 see the edition of *Ǫrvar-Odds saga* in this volume.

Introduction to sts 13-17

This group of stanzas is found only in the so-called R and U redactions of the saga, not the H redaction. The preceding prose (and Hb's text) explains that Hervǫr perpetrated various misdeeds, eventually running away and becoming a *stigamaðr* 'highwayman', until being returned home by Bjarmi jarl. One day, a servant she has maltreated taunts her about her parentage, claiming she is the daughter of *inn versti þræll* 'the lowest slave' (*Heiðr* 1960, 10). There is nothing in the rest of the saga to suggest this claim had any substance, and Hb does not mention this part of the plot. In these stanzas Hervǫr speaks first to the jarl, bringing the claim before him (Herv Lv 1 (*Heiðr* 13)), and when he refutes it (Bjarmij Lv 1 (*Heiðr* 14)) she expresses her desire to visit the grave of her real father, Angantýr, in order to claim her inheritance, and her intention to disguise herself as a man in order to do so (Herv Lv 2-3 (*Heiðr* 15-16)). She then goes to her mother to ask for help in disguising herself (Herv Lv 4 (*Heiðr* 17)).

The stanzas are edited in the editions of the saga listed in the main Introduction, and in *Skj*, *Skald* and Ettmüller (1861, 31-2). The main ms. is 2845. The metre is *fornyrðislag*.

Hervǫr (Herv Lv 1)

13. Áka ek várri   vegsemð hrósa,
    þótt hefði Fróðmars   fengit hylli.
    Fǫður hugðumz ek   fræknan eiga;
    nú er sagðr fyrir mér: svína hirðir.

Ek áka hrósa vegsemð várri, þótt hefði fengit hylli Fróðmars. Ek hugðumz eiga fræknan fǫður; nú er sagðr fyrir mér: hirðir svína.

I cannot praise our honour, though I might have gained Fróðmarr's favour. I thought myself to have a brave father; now it is said before me: a herder of swine.

Mss: 2845(64v), R715ˣ(11v) (*Heiðr*).

Readings: [1] Áka: ætla R715ˣ [2] vegsemð: *so* R715ˣ, 'vegsems' 2845 [3] hefði: *so* R715ˣ, hon 2845; Fróðmars: bratt manns R715ˣ [5] hugðumz: hugða R715ˣ [7] sagðr fyrir mér: mér hann sagðr R715ˣ.

Editions: *Skj*: Anonyme digte og vers [XIII], E. 5. *Vers af Fornaldarsagaer: Af Hervararsaga* I 1: AII, 242, BII, 262, *Skald* II, 136; *Heiðr* 1672, 85, *FSN* 1, 431, *Heiðr* 1873, 311-12, *Heiðr* 1924, 15, 102-3, *FSGJ* 2, 11, *Heiðr* 1960, 10; *Edd. Min.* 88.

Context: Hervǫr is enraged at the slave's claim that she is the illegitimate child of a slave and goes before Bjarmi jarl.

Note: [1-4]: It is unclear who Fróðmarr, a name only appearing in 2845, may be. At one point in the saga, the text of 2845 refers to a Fróðmarr, a jarl in England, as the foster-father of the second Hervǫr to appear in the story, Hervǫr Heiðreksdóttir. This too seems to be the result of confusion since the other mss have Ormarr here, backed up by another prose reference in the section about the battle of the Goths and Huns (though this occurs in the part of the saga lost from 2845 and thus appears only in the U redaction). It could be that the stanza originally related to this part of the story, however (*Heiðr* 1956, 75 n.). Ms. 2845 reads *hon* 'she' in place of *hefði* 'might have' in l. 3. This has been followed by several eds, necessitating the emendation of p. p. *fengit*, which both mss agree on, to pret. *fengi* (inf. *fá* 'get, gain, win'), giving the sense 'though she gained Fróðmarr's favour'. If this reading is correct, the *hon* must be Hervǫr's mother and Fróðmarr could possibly be the swineherd, if the stanza is spoken in irony (*Heiðr* 1956, 75 n.; *Heiðr* 1960, 91). See Hall (2005, 7-9) for an alternative theory following this reading. Ms. R715ˣ's reading avoids the problem, though it is still rather obscure in meaning (as well as being unmetrical): *Ætla ek várri vegsemð hrósa, þótt hefði bratt manns fengit hylli* 'I intend to praise our honour, though I/she might have soon gained a man's favour'. The reading preferred in the present edn is also adopted in *Skj* B.

Bjarmi jarl (Bjarmij Lv 1)

14. Logit er mart at þér   lítil of efni;
    frækn með fyrðum   var faðir þinn talðr.
    Stendr Angantýs   ausinn moldu
    salr í Sámsey   sunnanverðri.

Mart er logit at þér of lítil efni; faðir þinn var talðr frækn með fyrðum. Salr Angantýs, ausinn moldu, stendr í sunnanverðri Sámsey.

Greatly are you lied to, about little substance; your father was reckoned bold among warriors. Angantýr's hall, sprinkled with soil, stands in the southern part of Samsø.

Mss: 2845(64v), R715ˣ(11v) (*Heiðr*).

Readings: [2] lítil of: ef lítit *corrected from* 'ef lítil' *in the hand of JR* R715ˣ;   efni: *om.* 2845, er efni *corrected from* 'er' *in the margin in the hand of JR* R715ˣ   [3] frækn: *so* R715ˣ, frétt 2845; fyrðum: 'fyrðdum' *corrected from* 'frÿd' *above the line in the hand of JR* R715ˣ   [4] var: *om.* 2845, inserted above the line in the hand of JR R715ˣ   [5] Angantýs: Angantýr 2845.

Editions: *Skj*: Anonyme digte og vers [XIII], E. 5. *Vers af Fornaldarsagaer: Af Hervararsaga* I 2: AII, 243, BII, 262, *Skald* II, 136, *FF* § 44; *Heiðr* 1672, 86, *FSN* 1, 431, *Heiðr* 1873, 312, *Heiðr* 1924, 15-16, 103, *FSGJ* 2, 11-12, *Heiðr* 1960, 11; *Edd. Min.* 88.

Context: This stanza follows directly from the previous one, introduced by the words *Jarl kvað* 'The jarl said'.

Notes: [2] *of lítil efni* 'about little substance': Neither ms. has a completely satisfactory reading here, and it seems a word or words were missing from the end of the line in both versions, since R715ˣ's *efni* is added in the hand of the annotator, Jón Rugman (whose *ef lítit er efni* appears to be an attempt to make sense of something he did not understand). Nevertheless, as things stand this reading must be accepted, with *of* interpreted as a prep. + acc. 'about, of'; cf. Heggstad *et al.* 2008: *of* B. 8. '*om, over (om sak, emne)*' 'about (a matter, subject)'. *Heiðr* 1956, 11 gives the line as here, while *Heiðr* 1960 prefers the arrangement *of lítil efni*, which is hypermetrical, and translates 'with little substance', which would require a dat. object rather than the nom./acc. pl. here. *Skj* B prefers to omit *of*/*ef* and emend R715ˣ's *er* 'is', omitted in the present edn, to the pl.: *lítil eru efni*, translating *lidet (sandt) er deri* 'little (truth) is in it'; however, this seems unlikely as a scribal error and may be discounted. Kock construes *lítil of frétt*, perhaps 'little [is] news', from 2845, pointing out the contrast *mart er logit* with *lítil er frétt* (*FF* §44). However, *frétt* seems to belong to l. 3, corresponding to R715ˣ's *frækn* (which is to be preferred), which leads Kock to insert there a purely conjectural *framr* 'foremost'. — [7] *salr* 'hall': Here referring to Angantýr's grave-mound. — [7] *Sámsey* 'Samsø': A Danish island in the Kattegat.

Hervǫr (Herv Lv 2)

15. Nú fýsir mik, fóstri, at vitja
    framgenginna frænda minna.
    Auð mundu þeir eiga nógan;
    þann skal ek öðlaz, nema ek áðr förumz.

Nú fýsir mik, fóstri, at vitja framgenginna frænda minna. Þeir mundu eiga nógan auð; ek skal öðlaz þann, nema ek förumz áðr.

Now I am eager, foster-father, to visit my deceased kinsmen. They must own abundant wealth; I shall inherit it, unless I die first.

Mss: 2845(64v), R715^x(11v) (*Heiðr*).

Readings: [2] fóstri: 'ad fostri' R715^x [7] ek: í *corrected from* 'ek' *in the margin the hand of JR* R715^x [8] áðr: áðra R715^x; förumz: forkomi R715^x.

Editions: *Skj*: Anonyme digte og vers [XIII], E. 5. *Vers af Fornaldarsagaer: Af Hervararsaga* I 3: AII, 243, BII, 262-3, *Skald* II, 136; *Heiðr* 1672, 86, *FSN* 1, 431, *Heiðr* 1873, 312-13, *Heiðr* 1924, 16, 103, *FSGJ* 2, 12, *Heiðr* 1960, 11; *Edd. Min.* 88.

Context: The stanza is introduced by *Hon kvað* 'She said'.

Hervǫr (Herv Lv 3)

16. Skal skjótliga um skör búa
    blæjulíni áðr braut fari.
    Mikit býr í því, er á morgin skal
    skera bæði mér skyrtu ok ólpu.

Skal skjótliga búa blæjulíni um skör, áðr fari braut. Mikit býr í því, er á morgin skal skera mér bæði skyrtu ok ólpu.

[I] must quickly dress my hair with a head covering of coloured cloth, before I go away. Much depends on it, that both shirt and cloak shall be cut for me in the morning.

Mss: 2845(64v), R715^x(11v) (*Heiðr*).

Readings: [3] blæju-: bleiku R715^x [5] býr: skil R715^x;   í: ek *added above the line in the hand of JR* R715^x [6] er: *om.* R715^x [7] bæði: *om.* R715^x [8] skyrtu ok ólpu: *so* R715^x, ólpu ok skyrtu 2845.

Editions: *Skj*: Anonyme digte og vers [XIII], E. 5. *Vers af Fornaldarsagaer: Af Hervararsaga* I 4: AII, 243, BII, 263, *Skald* II, 137; *Heiðr* 1672, 86, *FSN* 1, 432, *Heiðr* 1873, 313, *Heiðr* 1924, 16, 103-4, *FSGJ* 2, 12, *Heiðr* 1960, 11; *Edd. Min.* 88.

Notes: [1-3]: Given that Hervǫr intends to disguise herself as a man, these lines are problematic in terms of sense, though the implication may be that she will bind up her hair to conceal it (*Heiðr* 1960, 11 n. 1). *Skj* B emends to *Skal skjótliga | af skǫr búa | blæju líni*, translating *Hurtigt skal slör-linet bort fra mit hoved* 'Quickly must the linen veil be taken from my head'. This suggestion gives good sense, that she is shedding her feminine trappings, and *af* could have been misread as *of* and rendered *um* by later scribes, but *búa af* is not attested in the sense 'take off', and no other eds have adopted this suggestion. — [1-2] *skal* '[I] must': This could alternatively be understood as an impersonal construction: 'My hair must quickly be dressed'. — [5-6]: The interpretation here takes *er* as introducing a rel. clause, referring to *því* (l. 5), i.e. 'much depends on [the fact] that both shirt and cloak shall be cut for me'. Alternatively, *því* could refer to the statement in the first *helmingr* (about the dressing of the hair), with *er* meaning 'because', with the sense 'Much depends on me dressing my hair, because…'. — [8] *ólpu* 'cloak': See Note to *Heiðr* 17/1.

Hervǫr (Herv Lv 4)

17. Bú þú mik at ǫllu,   sem þú hraðast kunnir,
    sannfróð kona,   sem þú son myndir.
    Satt eitt mun mér   í svefn bera;
    fæ ek ekki hér   yndi it næsta.

Bú þú mik at ǫllu, sem þú kunnir hraðast, sannfróð kona, sem þú myndir son. Satt eitt mun bera mér í svefn; fæ ek ekki hér yndi it næsta.

Dress me in all respects, as quickly as you can, truly-wise woman, as you would a son. The truth alone will be brought to me in a dream; I will not get happiness here in the near future.

Mss: **2845**(64v), R715[x](11v-12r) (*Heiðr*).

Readings: [1] Bú þú: breiða *corrected from* beiða *in the hand of JR* R715[x]; mik: *om.* R715[x]; at: Ertu at *corrected from* 'at' *in the hand of JR* R715[x]   [2] sem: of sem *corrected from* sem *in the margin in the hand of JR* R715[x]; þú: *om.* R715[x]; hraðast: so R715[x], 'h ͣtaz' 2845; kunnir: 'k̶u̶[…]ir' R715[x]   [3] -fróð: -fund 2845, -find R715[x]   [4] myndir: 'munþir' 2845, 'm̄dir' R715[x]   [5] Satt: so R715[x], fátt 2845   [7] ekki: ei R715[x]; hér: *om.* R715[x]   [8] yndi it: 'nid hid' *corrected from* '[…]d[…]' *in the hand of JR* R715[x].

Editions: *Skj*: Anonyme digte og vers [XIII], E. 5. Vers af Fornaldarsagaer: Af Hervararsaga I 5: AII, 243, BII, 263, *Skald* II, 137, *NN* §2831B(d); *Heiðr* 1672, 86, *FSN* 1, 431, *Heiðr* 1873, 313, *Heiðr* 1924, 16-17, 104, *FSGJ* 2, 12-13, *Heiðr* 1960, 11-12; *Edd. Min.* 89.

Context: Hervǫr goes to speak to her mother, named elsewhere in the R and U redactions as Sváfa; see Note to Herv Lv 8/4 (*Heiðr* 25).

Notes: [1-2]: Ms. R715[x] reads (after alteration in l. 2): *Ertu at ǫllu | of sem hraðast* 'You are in all things too hasty'. Verelius (*Heiðr* 1672, 86), who accepts this reading, attributes this and the following two lines to the jarl, and only the second *helmingr* to

Hervǫr, presumably on grounds of sense; there is no ms. support for this. — [1] *bú þú* 'dress': The annotator of R715[x], Jón Rugman, has altered the ms.'s *beiða* 'ask', which makes no sense in the context, to *breiða* 'broad', apparently attempting to connect it to *ólpu* 'cloak' in the previous stanza by demarcating the end of the stanza (as he sees it) with a vertical line. He then inserts *Ertu* 'You are' to begin the present stanza. — [2] *hraðast* 'as quickly as you can': Lit. 'quickest'. The long-line lacks alliteration and the text is not sound, 2845 appearing to read *hvatast* (so, e.g. *Heiðr* 1924, 16 n. 3; *Skj* A) though with an ambiguous abbreviation (*Heiðr* 1873, 313 n. 14); the meaning is similar. Rafn (*FSN* 1, 432) and Tolkien (*Heiðr* 1960, 11) take the reading *bráðast*, also implying 'speed, haste', from a C17th ms., AM 345 4[ox]. This, however, stems from a copy of 203[x] and has no independent textual value (*Heiðr* 1924, xliv-xlv); the reading may be a scribal conjecture to restore alliteration, but results in a hypermetrical line. *Skj* B, *Skald* and *Edd. Min.*, following Bugge (*Heiðr* 1873, 313), opt for *bezt* 'best'. Andrews (1920, 96) suggests that *bú* 'prepare' in l. 1 may be where the corruption lies, but does not suggest an alternative. — [3] *sannfróð* 'truly-wise': The emendation was first suggested by Ettmüller (1861, 32), and has since been followed by most other eds (the earlier *FSN* 1, 432 has *sannprúð* 'truly-magnificent'). Bugge (*Heiðr* 1873, 313) suggests *sannreynd* 'truly-proved', perhaps because the claim of Sváfa's infidelity which prompted Hervǫr's actions in this group of stanzas has been invalidated (*Heiðr* 14). — [4] *myndir* 'would': Emended to the pret. subj. form, as do *Skj* B and *Skald*; *mundir*, retained by *Heiðr* 1960 among others, is pret. indic. — [7-8]: Although *Heiðr* 13-17 are omitted in Hb, these lines are echoed in the prose as the direct speech of Hervǫr: *brott vil ek heðan, því at ekki fæ ek hér yndi* 'I wish to go away from here, because I will not get happiness here'. — [8]: Jón Rugman's attempts to emend the text in R715[x] (apparently to *nið it næsta* 'a son in the near future') have partially obscured the original reading, but it was likely close to the reading of 2845 (*Heiðr* 1924 suggests 'indit'). On the senses of *næri, næstr*, see *NN* §2831.

Introduction to sts 18-24

In disguise as a man and calling herself Hervarðr, Hervǫr Angantýsdóttir travels late one evening to Samsø (ON Sámsey), to seek out the burial mound of her father Angantýr. Her companions, a band of vikings whose leader she has become, refuse to go with her because they are afraid of the island's eerie reputation. These stanzas narrate Hervǫr's arrival on the island, and her subsequent conversation with a terrified shepherd.

These stanzas are sometimes considered together with the following group, *Heiðr* 25-48, as part of a long poem, often called 'The Waking of Angantýr' (see Introduction to *Heiðr* 25-47), and are presented as such in *CPB*, *Edd. Min.* and a number of translations including that by Larrington (2014, 268-73) (based on the present edition). Indeed, the present group sets the scene for and introduces the dialogue between Hervǫr and Angantýr which forms the major part of that poem (cf. e.g. *Vafþr* and *Skí*, which have similar introductory sections). In addition, there is verbal echoing across sts 18b-19 of the sort that happens in several places in *Heiðr* 25-48. The present stanzas are separated from the following group by a prose passage in all redactions of the saga, however. They have also been edited in *Skj* B II, 263-5, *Skald* II, 137-8 and Ettmüller (1861, 32), as well as in editions of the saga (see Introduction to *Heiðr*).

Hb, which is the main ms., paraphrases this group of stanzas in the immediately preceding prose, and presents the stanzas themselves one after the other with no intervening prose but an introductory statement (*Heiðr* 1924, 18): *Þetta er kveðit eftir viðræðu þeira* 'This is composed according to their conversation'. The other ms. witnesses, 2845 and R715[x], indicate the speaker before each stanza. Ms. 2845, and consequently other mss of the so-called R redaction, omits Anon (*Heiðr*) 1a (*Heiðr* 18a) (though rendering its contents into prose; see Note to [All]), and all of Herv Lv 6 (*Heiðr* 21) and Anon (*Heiðr*) 4 (*Heiðr* 24). It consequently reverses the order of Anon (*Heiðr*) 3 (*Heiðr* 22) and Herv Lv 7 (*Heiðr* 23) in order to maintain the alternation between the speakers, even though Hervǫr's injunction to the shepherd, not to be afraid of the supernatural burning fires, is clearly a response to his complaints. Hb places Anon (*Heiðr*) 4 (*Heiðr* 24) after Herv Lv 6 (*Heiðr* 21), but this cannot be correct: the shepherd's leaving must come at the end of the dialogue, not part-way through it. The metre is *fornyrðislag*.

(Anon *Heiðr* 1a)

18a. Hitt hefir mær ung   í Munarvági
við sólarsetr   segg at hjörðu.

Ung mær hefir hitt segg at hjörðu í Munarvági við sólarsetr.

The young woman has met a man tending his flock in Munarvágr at sunset.

Mss: **Hb**(73v), R715[x](12v) (*Heiðr*).

Readings: [1] Hitt hefir mær ung: mælti Hervarðr *corrected from* mæti Hervarð *in the hand of JR* R715[x] [2] Munarvági: unnar vági R715[x] [4] segg at hjörðu: snotr at máli *corrected from* settr máli *in the hand of JR* R715[x].

Editions: *Skj*: Anonyme digte og vers [XIII], E. 5. *Vers af Fornaldarsagaer: Af Hervararsaga* II 1/1-4: AII, 243, BII, 263, *Skald* II, 137; *Heiðr* 1672, 89, *FSN* 1, 518, *Heiðr* 1873, 211, *Heiðr* 1924, 18, 105, *Heiðr* 1960, 12; *Edd. Min.* 13 n.

Context: The present half-stanza is third-person narrative in Hb, but put into the mouth of the shepherd in R715[x] (see second Note to [All] below), introduced with *Fjárhirðir kvað vísu* 'The shepherd recited a stanza'.

Notes: [All]: Ms. 2845 does not contain this half-stanza, but the prose immediately preceding Anon *Heiðr* 1b (*Heiðr* 18b) contains the same essentials and some of the diction, perhaps suggesting a basis in a verse original (*Heiðr* 1960, 12): Hervarðr …

lendi í Munarvági í þann tíma, er sól settisk, ok hitti þar mann þann er hjǫrð helt
'Hervarðr ... landed in Munarvágr at the time when the sun was setting, and met there that man who tended a flock'. — [All]: While this half-stanza is third-person narrative in Hb, R715[x] attributes it to the shepherd, presenting a variant which may be rendered as follows:

> Mælti Hervarðr   í Unnarvági
> við solarsetr   snotr at máli.

Prose order: Hervarðr mælti, snotr at máli, í Unnarvági við solarsetr. *Translation*: Hervarðr spoke, wise in speech, in Unnarvági at sunset. — [2] *Munarvági* 'Munarvágr': Lit. 'Bay of Desire'. Also occurs in *Heiðr* 27/8 and *Ǫrv* 7/2. Always *Una-* (lit. 'Bay of Delight') or *Unnar-* (lit. 'Bay of Waves') in R715[x] (except on one occasion when it is *Munarheimr*: see Note to *Heiðr* 27/8). The p. n. Unavágr also occurs in *HHund I* 31/1; see further *Kommentar* IV, 274, but, as noted by Jón Helgason (*Heiðr* 1924, lxviii), alliteration in the relevant stanzas of *Heiðr* and *Ǫrv* confirm that *Munarvágr* is the correct form here. The location of the bay on Samsø, if a real place was intended, has not been identified.

Hirðir (Anon *Heiðr* 1b)

18b. Hverr er ein*n* saman   í ey kominn?
       Gakktu greiðliga   gistingar til.

Hverr er kominn ein*n* saman í ey? Gakktu greiðliga til gistingar.

Who has come alone onto the island? Go quickly to your lodging.

Mss: **Hb**(73v), 2845(65r), R715[x](12v) (*Heiðr*).

Readings: [1] Hverr: þú R715[x];   er: *so* 2845, *om.* Hb, ert R715[x];   ein*n*: ein Hb, ýta 2845, 'eirn' R715[x];   saman: *om.* 2845, 'með ofs' R715[x]   [2] í ey: eyna í R715[x];   kominn: *so* R715[x], komin Hb, 'kominnn' 2845   [3] greiðliga: sýsliga 2845, 'skiæliga' R715[x].

Editions: *Skj*: Anonyme digte og vers [XIII], E. 5. Vers af Fornaldarsagaer: Af Hervararsaga II 1/5-8: AII, 243, BII, 263, Skald II, 137; *Heiðr* 1672, 89, *Heiðr* 1924, 18, 105, *FSGJ* 2, 13, *Heiðr* 1960, 12; *Edd. Min.* 13.

Context: Although this half-stanza is clearly supposed to be spoken by the shepherd, Hb does not indicate a speaker in the prose. Ms. 2845 narrates that Hervǫr/Hervarðr encounters a shepherd, and introduces the *helmingr* with *Hann kvað* 'He said'. In R715[x] this half-stanza follows directly from the previous one.

Notes: [1-2]: Ms. R715[x]'s version reads: *Þú ert einn* [ms. 'eirn'] *með oss* [ms. 'ofs'] *eyna í kominn* 'You have come alone among us onto the island'. — [1-2]: Despite the description of the *mær ung* 'young woman' in l. 1 and the use of the f. forms *ein* and *komin* in Hb, the m. forms of the pron. *einn* and p. p. *kominn* have been used here, since the shepherd, who is the speaker, believes Hervǫr to be male; cf. *hverr* 'who' m. nom. sg. in l. 5 (which form is written in Hb) and subsequent stanzas spoken by the shepherd, where Hb as well as the other mss use m. forms to refer to Hervǫr. — [1] *einn saman* 'alone': *Skj* and *Skald* prefer 2845's reading, *ýta* 'of men'. — [3] *greiðliga* 'quickly': The present edn follows the emendation of other eds, supported in meaning by the reading of 2845, *sýsliga* 'busily, smartly, speedily'. Ms. R715ˣ's reading, 'skiælega', is not an Old Norse word. In his edn, based on this ms., Verelius (*Heiðr* 1672, 89) prints 'skiælega' and translates *snarlig* 'speedily'.

Hervǫr (Herv Lv 5)

19. Munkat ek ganga   gistingar til,
    því at ek engan kann   eyjarskeggja.
    Segðu hraðliga,   áðr heðan líðir:
    hvar eru Hjörvarði   haugar kendir?

Ek munkat ganga til gistingar, því at ek kann engan eyjarskeggja. Segðu hraðliga, áðr líðir heðan: hvar eru haugar kendir Hjörvarði?

I will not go to lodging, because I know no island-beard. Say quickly, before you pass from here: where are the mounds named after Hjǫrvarðr?

Mss: **Hb**(73v), 2845(65r) (ll. 3-6, 1-2, 7-8), R715ˣ(12v) (*Heiðr*).

Readings: [1] Munkat ek: Munka ek 2845, Mun ek ei R715ˣ   [3] engan: engi 2845, R715ˣ   [5] hraðliga: elligar 2845, R715ˣ   [6] heðan líðir: vit skiljum 2845, R715ˣ   [7] Hjörvarði: Hjörvarðs 2845, Hervarði R715ˣ   [8] kendir: 'kiende[...]' R715ˣ.

Editions: *Skj*: Anonyme digte og vers [XIII], E. 5. *Vers af Fornaldarsagaer: Af Hervararsaga* II 2: AII, 244, BII, 263, *Skald* II, 137; *Heiðr* 1672, 89, *FSN* 1, 433, 519, *Heiðr* 1873, 212, 314, *Heiðr* 1924, 19, 105, *FSGJ* 2, 13-14, *Heiðr* 1960, 12; *Edd. Min.* 13.

Context: The speaker is clearly Hervǫr, although this is indicated in the prose only in R715ˣ.

Notes: [1] *ek munkat ganga* 'I will not go': A similar half-line, *Munca ec ganga*, occurrs in *HHj* 23/1 (*NK* 145). — [1] *munkat ek* 'I will not': The appearance of the cliticised 1st pers. sg. pron. (along with the negative suffix) together with the free-standing form is typical of the late C13th and occurs frequently in the stanzas of this dialogue and elsewhere. — [4] *engan eyjarskeggja* 'no island-beard': The circumlocution *eyjarskeggi* presumably arises from a tendency, factual or stereotypical, for islanders to let their hair and beards grow rather unkempt (*LP*: *eyjarskeggi*). There are only two other instances of the word in poetry, both from *fornaldarsögur*: *Frið* 23/4 and *Ǫrv* 106/6; see further Note to *Frið* 23/4. — [5] *hraðliga* 'quickly': The other mss read *elligar* 'otherwise', which, taken in the sense 'rather, instead', offers an acceptable alternative in terms of meaning, but loses the alliteration with *heðan* in the following line. — [6] *áðr heðan líðir* 'before you pass from here': The reading of 2845 and R715ˣ, *áðr vit skiljum* 'before we two part', makes equally good sense but lacks alliteration. — [8] *kendir Hjörvarði* (m. dat. sg.) 'named afer Hjǫrvarðr': Hjǫrvarðr is named earlier in *Heiðr* as the oldest after Angantýr of Arngrímr's twelve sons, and in the R and U redactions of the saga it is he who challenges Hjálmarr inn hugumstóri 'the Great-minded' to the duel over the hand of Ingibjǫrg (cf. Hjálm Lv 8 (*Ǫrv* 18)), daughter of the Swedish king (named Ingjaldr in R, Yngvi in H and U), in which the brothers are killed. In the H redaction it is Angantýr himself who challenges, but, although in all versions of the saga it is he who ends up fighting Hjálmarr, the duel is twelve against twelve, not single combat, and it is definitely Hjǫrvarðr who is Hjálmarr's love-rival: he speaks of Ingibjǫrg in his 'death song' (*Ǫrv* 18), while Angantýr marries someone else soon after the challenge has been made (see also *Heiðr* 1960, xiii-xiv).

Hirðir (Anon *Heiðr* 2)

20. Spyrjattu at því;   spakr ert eigi,
vinr víkinga;   ertu vanfarinn.
Förum fráliga,   sem fætr toga;
allt er úti   ámátt firum.

Spyrjattu at því; ert eigi spakr, vinr víkinga; ertu vanfarinn. Förum fráliga, sem fætr toga; allt er ámátt firum úti.

Do not ask about that; you are not wise, friend of vikings; you are in great difficulties. Let's go quickly, [as fast] as our feet can take us; all is terrible for men outside.

Mss: **Hb**(73v-74r), 2845(65r), R715ˣ(12v) (*Heiðr*).

Readings: [1] Spyrjattu: 'Spiriat þu' R715ˣ   [2] ert: *so* R715ˣ, ertu Hb, 2845   [4] ertu: *so* 2845, þú ert Hb, R715ˣ   [5] fráliga: fljótliga R715ˣ   [6] fætr: *so* R715ˣ, 'okkr fo[...]' Hb, 2845   [7] allt: hallt *corrected from* allt *in the hand of JR* R715ˣ   [8] ámátt firum: hurfum heim báðir R715ˣ.

Editions: *Skj*: Anonyme digte og vers [XIII], E. 5. Vers af Fornaldarsagaer: Af Hervararsaga II 3: AII, 244, BII, 264, *Skald* II, 137; *Heiðr* 1672, 89, *FSN* 1, 433, 518, *Heiðr* 1873, 211-12, 314, *Heiðr* 1924, 19, 105-6, *FSGJ* 2, 14, *Heiðr* 1960, 13; *Edd. Min.* 13.

Context: The speaker is the shepherd, indicated by *Hann kvað* 'He said' in 2845 and *Fjárhirðir kvað* 'The shepherd said' in R715ˣ.

Notes: [6] *fætr* 'feet': Hb is damaged here and the letters difficult to make out with certainty. *Hb* 1892-6, 354 prints 'fǿtr'. — [7] *allt* 'all': In R715ˣ a later hand corrects to 'hallt' for the sake of alliteration with its l. 8; see following Note. — [8] *ámátt* 'terrible': *Hap. leg.*, formed from *máttr* 'might' and the intensifying prefix *á-* (on which see Falk 1928b, 345-50). Cf. *ámátligstar* 'the most overwhelming' GrL 1/7, and see Note there. The reading of R715ˣ, *hurfum heim báðir* 'let us both turn home', is unmetrical.

Hervǫr (Herv Lv 6)

21. Men bjóðum þér   máls at gjöldum;
    muna drengja vin   dælt at letja.
    Fær engi nú   svá fríðar hnossir
    fagra bauga,   at ek fara eigi.

Bjóðum þér men at gjöldum máls; muna dælt at letja vin drengja. Engi fær nú svá fríðar hnossir, fagra bauga, at ek fara eigi.

We [I] offer you a necklace as reward for your word; it will not be easy to hold back the friend of the valiant ones. None can give now such beautiful treasures, fair rings, that I will not go.

Mss: **Hb**(74r), R715^x(12v) (*Heiðr*).

Readings: [3] vin: var inn R715^x [4] letja: leita R715^x [5] Fær: fær þú R715^x; engi: ei R715^x; nú: nú *added above the line in the scribal hand* Hb, mér R715^x [6] svá: 'so' R715^x [7] fagra bauga: *om.* R715^x [8] ek fara eigi: ek ei fara at mínum vilja *corrected from* ek ei fara vilja *in the hand of JR* R715^x.

Editions: *Skj*: Anonyme digte og vers [XIII], E. 5. *Vers af Fornaldarsagaer: Af Hervararsaga* II 4: AII, 244, BII, 264, *Skald* II, 137; *Heiðr* 1672, 89-90, *FSN* 1, 519, *Heiðr* 1873, 212-13, *Heiðr* 1924, 19, 106, *Heiðr* 1960, 75; *Edd. Min.* 14.

Notes: [All]: In Hb's prose paraphrase of this stanza it is the shepherd who offers Hervǫr/Hervarðr the necklace to flee rather than continue with her mission. However, this makes little sense: it is much more likely that Hervǫr would offer the shepherd a reward for information than vice-versa. — [3]: The phrase *vinr drengja*, translated as 'the friend of warriors', appears as a kenning for 'ruler' in SnSt *Ht* 14/2^{III}, where it refers to King Hákon Hákonarson of Norway (r. 1217-63). It is not clear whether the phrase should be treated as a kenning here, where the implication is somewhat different, since 'ruler' would not be an appropriate referent for Hervǫr. On the meanings of *drengr* see Goetting (2006). — [3] *muna* 'will not': This form has the negative poetic suffix *-a*. The inf. *vera* 'be' is understood. — [5] *engi fær nú* 'none can give now': *Skj* B prefers R715^x's reading, *fær þú eigi mér* 'you cannot give me'. — [7-8]: Line 7 was originally omitted in R715^x, but corrected in a later hand to *at ek ei fara at mínum vilja* 'that I will not go according to my desire', which restores an eight-line stanza, though one which is metrically deficient and clearly secondary to the reading of the main ms.

Hirðir (Anon *Heiðr* 3)

22. Heimskr þykki mér,   sá er heðra ferr,
    maðr einn saman   myrkvar grímur.
    Hyrr er á sveimun;   haugar opnaz;
    brennr fold ok fen;   förum harðara.

Þykki mér heimskr, sá er ferr heðra, maðr einn saman myrkvar grímur. Hyrr er á sveimun; haugar opnaz; brennr fold ok fen; förum harðara.

He seems to me foolish, that one who travels here, the man alone in the murky night. Fire is flickering; mounds open; the earth burns, and the fen; let us go faster.

Mss: Hb(74r), 2845(65r), R715^x(12v) (*Heiðr*).

Readings: [2] sá: *so* 2845, R715^x, þá Hb;   heðra: heðan 2845, til hauga R715^x [3] maðr einn saman: 'all ein saman' R715^x [4] myrkvar: dökkvar R715^x [5] á: sá R715^x;   sveimun: 'sueīmoɴ' 2845, 'sueinū' R715^x [7] brennr: brenn 2845.

Editions: *Skj*: Anonyme digte og vers [XIII], E. 5. *Vers af Fornaldarsagaer: Af Hervararsaga* II 5: AII, 244, BII, 264, *Skald* II, 137; *Heiðr* 1672, 90, *FSN* 1, 434, 519, *Heiðr* 1873, 213, 315, *Heiðr* 1924, 20-1, 106, *FSGJ* 2, 14-15, *Heiðr* 1960, 13; *Edd. Min.* 14.

Context: The speaker is the shepherd, indicated in 2845 and R715^x.

Notes: [1] *heimskr* 'foolish': Hervǫr is again described as *heimskr* in Angantýr Lv 8/1 (*Heiðr* 41), on that occasion by her father, Angantýr. — [4] *myrkvar grímur* 'in the murky night': Lit. 'in the murky nights', acc. pl. of the passage of time. The reading of R715^x, *dökkvar grímur* 'in the dark night', makes sense but lacks alliteration. The sense 'night' for *gríma* is poetic (cf. Þul *Dægra* 1/3^{III} and Note); otherwise the term refers to a hood, face-covering or mask, or armour for a horse's upper body (*LP*, *CVC*: *gríma*). — [5] *á sveimun* 'flickering': *Hap. leg.* Cf. the verb *sveima* 'wander, move without fixed direction'. — [6] *haugar opnaz* 'mounds open': I.e. the burial mounds of Angantýr and his brothers. See Angantýr Lv 1 (*Heiðr* 29), Note to [All]. This line is also found in Angantýr Lv 3/2 (*Heiðr* 32), in a stanza which also mentions the fires burning on the island and warns Hervǫr to return to her ships.

Hervǫr (Herv Lv 7)

23. Hirðumat fælaz   við fnösun slíka,
    þótt um alla ey   eldar brenni.
    Látum okkr eigi   *liðna rekka*
    skjótla skelfa;   skulum við talaz.

Hirðumat fælaz við slíka fnösun, þótt eldar brenni um alla ey. Látum eigi *liðna rekka* skelfa okkr skjótla; skulum talaz við.

Let us not care to be frightened at such roaring, though fires may burn around all the island. Let us not allow dead men to frighten us quickly; we must talk about it.

Mss: Hb(74r), 2845(65r), R715[x](12v-13r) (*Heiðr*).

Readings: [1] Hirðumat fælaz: hirðum ei at fælaz 2845, hirðum ei fælaz R715[x]   [2] við fnösun slíka: við þrösun slíka 2845, *om*. R715[x]   [3, 4] þótt um alla ey eldar brenni: þótt eldar um eyna brenni R715[x]   [5] okkr eigi: *so* 2845, eigi okkr Hb, ei okkr R715[x]   [6] liðna rekka: rekka liðna Hb, lítit hræða 2845, lítit saka R715[x]   [7] skjótla skelfa: rekka slíka 2845, R715[x]   [8] skulum við talaz: ræðumz fleira við 2845, ok ræðum fleira R715[x].

Editions: *Skj*: Anonyme digte og vers [XIII], E. 5. *Vers af Fornaldarsagaer: Af Hervararsaga* II 6: AII, 244-5, BII, 264, *Skald* II, 137; *Heiðr* 1672, 90, *FSN* 1, 434, 519, *Heiðr* 1873, 213, 315, *Heiðr* 1924, 20-1, 106, *FSGJ* 2, 14, *Heiðr* 1960, 13; *Edd. Min.* 14.

Context: The speaker is Hervǫr, indicated in 2845 and R715[x].

Notes: [1-4]: Line 2 is omitted in R715[x], and Verelius (*Heiðr* 1672, 90) omits *um eyna* 'around the island', presumably so that the stanza has an even six lines. His edn thus reads *Hirdum ey fælast | þott elldar brenni* 'Let us not be frightened though fires burn'. In Herv Lv 13/1-4 (*Heiðr* 33) Hervǫr once again has to deny that she is frightened by the fires, in that instance to her father, Angantýr. — [2] *fnösun* 'roaring': I.e. of the fires. Ms. 2845's reading *þrösun* 'violent behaviour' lacks alliteration and is clearly an error. — [5-8]: The other mss offer different versions of this half-stanza, both less preferable. Ms. 2845 reads: *Látum okkr eigi | lítit hræða | rekka slíka | ræðumz fleira við* 'Let us not allow such men to frighten us little; we will speak further'; while R715[x] has the similar *Látum ei okkr | lítit saka | rekka slíka | ok ræðum fleira* 'Let us not allow such men to harm us little, and let us speak further'. Both 2845 and R715[x] display metrical irregularities; in the 2845 version ll. 5 and 8 are hypermetrical, while the R715[x] version requires the word *okkr* (l. 5) to be desyllabified. — [5] *eigi ... okkr* 'not ... us': Ms. 2845's reading is metrically preferable, and also chosen by other eds. — [6] liðna rekka 'dead men': The reversal of Hb's word-order is necessary to achieve alliteration on the first stressed syllable, an emendation also made by other eds.

(Anon *Heiðr* 4)

24. Var þá féhirðir   fljótr til skógar
     mjök frá máli   meyjar þessar;
     en harðsnúinn   hugr í brjósti
     um sakar slíkar   svellr Hervöru.

Féhirðir var þá mjök fljótr til skógar frá máli þessar meyjar; en harðsnúinn hugr svellr í brjósti Hervöru um slíkar sakar.

The shepherd then fled quickly towards the forest from the speech of this girl; but the steadfast heart swells in the breast of Hervǫr because of such things.

Mss: **Hb**(74r), R715ˣ(13r) (*Heiðr*).

Editions: *Skj*: Anonyme digte og vers [XIII], E. 5. *Vers af Fornaldarsagaer: Af Hervararsaga* II 7: AII, 245, BII, 264-5, *Skald* II, 137-8; *Heiðr* 1672, 90; *FSN* 1, 519, *Heiðr* 1873, 213-14, *Heiðr* 1924, 21, 107, *Heiðr* 1960, 77; *Edd. Min.* 14 n.

Notes: [All]: The H redaction places this stanza after Herv Lv 6 (*Heiðr* 21), but it must come after the dialogue between Hervǫr and the shepherd, not part way through. — [All]: The U redaction (which has slight variants) has this stanza spoken by the shepherd, with the prose introduction, *Féhirðir ... tók til hlaupa sem mest mátti hann ... ok kvað þetta* 'The shepherd ... took to his heels as fast as he could ... and recited this'. The stanza is clearly meant to be third-person narrative rather than speech, however. — [All]: *Edd. Min.* prints this stanza only in the notes. — [1, 2] *var þá mjök fljótr* 'then fled quickly': Lit. 'was then very fast'. — [5] *harðsnúinn* 'steadfast': Lit. 'hard-turned'.

Introduction to sts 25-47

This group of stanzas constitutes a dialogue between Hervǫr and the ghost of her dead father, Angantýr. At the mound on Samsø where Angantýr and his brothers have been buried following their defeat in a duel, Hervǫr summons them to waken and give her the sword Tyrfingr (Herv Lv 8-11 (*Heiðr* 25-8)). Initially, Angantýr is reluctant and attempts to dissuade her, first by telling her he does not have the sword (Angantýr Lv 1-2 (*Heiðr* 29-30)), then by warning her against the dangers of being on the island (Angantýr Lv 3 (*Heiðr* 32)), and, when Hervǫr still persists (Herv Lv 12-13 (*Heiðr* 31, 33)), finally by foreboding that Tyrfingr *mun spilla allri ætt þinni* 'will destroy all your family' (Angantýr Lv 4 (*Heiðr* 34)). Hervǫr stands firm, however, and Angantýr agrees to yield up the sword to her (Angantýr Lv 7-8 (*Heiðr* 39, 41)), with a grudging admiration for her courage (*Mey veit ek enga | moldar hvergi | at þann hjör þori | í hendr nema* 'I know no woman anywhere on the earth who would dare to take that sword in her hands', Angantýr Lv 7/5-8 (*Heiðr* 39)), but not without some final words of warning: *Takattu á eggjum, | eitr er í báðum* 'Do not touch the edges, poison is in both' (Angantýr Lv 10/5-6 (*Heiðr* 45)). Hervǫr herself comes across as fearless and resolute throughout, allowing signs of trepidation to be revealed only in the final stanza (Herv Lv 19/2, 4 (*Heiðr* 47)): *bráott fýsir mik ... heðan vil ek skjótla* 'I long to be away ... I wish to go from here quickly'. On other episodes in Old Norse literature involving revenants, burial mounds and treasure, see Chadwick (1946).

These dialogue stanzas have often been treated as part of an eddic-style long poem, sometimes together with the preceding seven stanzas describing the encounter between Hervǫr and the shepherd, which set the scene. This poem has been called *Hervararkviða* (apparently first recorded in the foreword and contents page of Dietrich 1864, vi-vii, although the stanzas appear in that work within their prose context) but is now well known to the English-speaking world as 'The Waking of Angantýr', a title which seems to have been used first by Ker (1896), following the edition and translation in *CPB* under the Anglicised title 'The Waking of Angantheow'. Following Verelius' 1672 edition of the saga, extracts of these stanzas (in Latin) were published in Bartholin (1689), and it first appeared as a poem in English translation (untitled) in 1705, based on Verelius' edition, in George Hickes's *Linguarum Vett. Septentrionalium Thesaurus Grammatico-Criticus et Archaeologicus* (Hickes 1703-5, II, I, 193-5). It became a popular subject for reworking, and appeared regularly from the eighteenth century onward under various titles and in various incarnations with varying fidelity to the original (see Burrows 2017), most extreme being M. G. Lewis's 'The Sword of Angantýr' (Lewis 1801, 32-41), a melodramatic interpretation in rhyming tetrametric quatrains in which Hervǫr is devoured by flames at the end.

The presentation of these stanzas in Hb lends extra support to the possibility that they were intended as a long poem. Herv Lv 8 (*Heiðr* 25) begins on a new line, with the rubric *vísur* 'verses' written in red at the end of the preceding line. The first word of the stanza, *Vaki* 'Waken', is also given a large red initial <V>. The end of the poetry is not marked, however: a short passage of prose describing Hervǫr's desertion by her terrified shipmates and later passage away follows on from the end of the final stanza.

Dating remains unresolved, although there has been some, if not complete, scholarly consensus on a date in the first half of the twelfth century (*Edd. Min.* xxi; Mundt 1990, 410). As the discussion above implies, most scholars have believed the stanzas to be 'unquestionably older than the saga' (*Heiðr* 1960, xi) and later set into the present narrative frame. Alaric Hall (2005, 7) has argued to the contrary, however (though not without reservation), that the poem 'was specifically composed for a narrative very like the *Heiðreks saga* we know ... and put into writing soon enough afterward that it was not substantially corrupted by oral transmission'.

The stanzas are extant in full or in part in all of the mss of *Heiðr* listed in the Introduction to the saga above, and separately in JS 112 8^{ox}. As well as their inclusion in the editions of the saga listed above, they have been edited by Finnur Jónsson (*Skj*) and Kock (*Skald*), by Heusler and Ranisch (*Edd. Min.* 13-20) and by Guðbrandur Vigfússon and York Powell (*CPB* I, 163-8), and appear in Ettmüller (1861, 32-3). All of these editions use Hb as the base text: it contains more stanzas of the dialogue than the other redactions and its readings are often preferable; consequently it has also been chosen as the main ms. here. The speaker of the verse is indicated in all mss every time there is a change of speaker, except once in Hb, which does not note that Herv Lv 12 (*Heiðr* 31) is Hervǫr's (it does, however, note that the following stanza is spoken by Angantýr). The metre is *fornyrðislag*.

Hervǫr (Herv Lv 8)

25. Vaki þú, Angantýr;   vekr þik Hervör,
eingadóttir   ykkr Sváfu.
Seldu mér ór haugi   hvassan mæki,
þann er Svafrlama   slógu dvergar.

Vaki þú, Angantýr; Hervör vekr þik, eingadóttir ykkr Sváfu. Seldu mér ór haugi hvassan mæki, þann er dvergar slógu Svafrlama.

Waken, Angantýr; Hervǫr wakes you, only daughter to you and Sváfa. Give me from the mound the sharp sword which dwarfs forged for Svafrlami.

Mss: Hb(74r), 2845(65r), R715ˣ(13r) (*Heiðr*).

Readings: [3] -dóttir: mǫgr *added above the line in the hand of JR* R715ˣ   [4] Sváfu: *so* 2845, R715ˣ, Tófu Hb   [5] mér: *om.* 2845   [6] hvassan: harðan R715ˣ   [7] Svafrlama: Sigrlama 2845.

Editions: Skj: Anonyme digte og vers [XIII], E. 5. *Vers af Fornaldarsagaer: Af Hervararsaga* III 1: AII, 245, BII, 265, *Skald* II, 138; *Heiðr* 1672, 91, *FSN* 1, 435, 519, *Heiðr* 1873, 214, 316, *Heiðr* 1924, 21, 107, *FSGJ* 2, 15, *Heiðr* 1960, 14; *Edd. Min.* 15.

Context: In all redactions of the saga a prose passage narrates Hervǫr's arrival at the mound of Angantýr and his brothers.

Notes: [1] *vaki þú, Angantýr* 'waken, Angantýr': Similar to *HHj* 24/1 (*NK* 145): *Vaki þú, Helgi* 'Waken, Helgi' and *Grott* 18/4-5 (*NK* 300): *Vaki þú, Fróði* 'Waken, Fróði'. — [3-4]: Cf. *Vǫl* 36/7-8 (*NK* 123) *eingadóttir | yccor beggia* 'only daughter to you both'. — [3] *-dóttir* 'daughter': In R715ˣ Jón Rugman has added *mǫgr* 'son' above, though without crossing out the original, presumably in reference to the fact that Hervǫr is here in disguise as a man. — [4] *Sváfu* 'Sváfa': Hervǫr's mother is named as Sváfa in 2845 and R715ˣ, both here and elsewhere in the saga (*Heiðr* 1924, 8, 96, 102). There is thus stronger evidence for this reading than for Hb's *Tófa*: in Hb this stanza is the only place the name Tófa appears for Hervǫr's mother; she is not mentioned by name elsewhere in the H redaction. The eds of *Edd. Min.* and *CPB* (*CPB* I, 164) however, choose to retain *Tófu*. — [6-8] *hvassan mæki, þann er dvergar slógu* 'the sharp sword which dwarfs forged': I.e. Tyrfingr. In Old Norse literature dwarfs were consistently portrayed as craftsmen. In Old Norse mythology, they were said to have made a variety of magical objects valuable to the gods (Simek 1993, 68); in the later traditions of the *fornaldarsögur* and *riddarasögur* they became more narrowly associated with the crafting of weapons (Motz 1977, 49). Cf. *Heiðr* 26/7-8, 33/7. — [6] *hvassan mæki* 'the sharp sword': This half-line also occurs in *Heiðr* 40/3 and, in the dat. case, *Heiðr* 88/6; see Note there. See also Note to *Heiðr* 38/6. — [8] *Svafrlama* 'Svafrlami': Called Sigrlami in the R redaction; in the H and U redactions Sigrlami is Svafrlami's father, and son of Óðinn. According to the saga, Svafr-/Sigrlami is king of Garðaríki (Russia; in H the name of his kingdom is not stated) and father of Eyfura, mother of

Angantýr. In H and U the viking Arngrímr attacks Sigrlami's kingdom, abducts Eyfura and steals Tyrfingr, using it to kill Sigrlami; in R the king appoints Arngrímr overseer of his kingdom, grants him Eyfura's hand in marriage and gives Tyrfingr to him (*Heiðr* 1924, 3-4, 93).

Hervǫr (Herv Lv 9)

26. Hervarðr, Hjörvarðr,   Hrani, Angantýr,
    vek ek yðr alla   undir viðar rótum,
    hjálmi ok með brynju,   hvössu sverði,
    rönd ok með reiði,   roðnum geiri.

Hervarðr, Hjörvarðr, Hrani, Angantýr, ek vek yðr alla undir rótum viðar, hjálmi ok með brynju, hvössu sverði, rönd ok með reiði, roðnum geiri.

Hervarðr, Hjǫrvarðr, Hrani, Angantýr, I wake you all under the roots of the tree, with helmet and with mail-shirt, with sharp sword, with shield and with war-gear, with decorated spear.

Mss: Hb(74r), 2845(65r), R715^x(13r) (*Heiðr*).

Readings: [1] Hervarðr: *so* 2845, Hervaðr ok Hb, 'hieruardur og' R715^x [2] Hrani: *so* 2845, 'hran' Hb, 'hrani og' R715^x [3] vek: *so* 2845, R715^x, vel Hb   [5] hjálmi: með hjálmi *corrected from* hjálmi *in the hand of JR* R715^x;   með: *om.* R715^x;   brynju: brynjum 2845   [6] hvössu: *so* R715^x, 'hvorsv' Hb, 'ha/sv' 2845   [7] reiði: *om.* 2845, reiða *corrected from* reiði *in the hand of JR* R715^x.

Editions: *Skj*: Anonyme digte og vers [XIII], E. 5. Vers af Fornaldarsagaer: Af Hervararsaga III 2: AII, 245, BII, 265, *Skald* II, 138, *NN* §3179; *Heiðr* 1672, 91, *FSN* 1, 434, 519-20, *Heiðr* 1873, 214-15, 316, *Heiðr* 1924, 22-3, 107-8, *FSGJ* 2, 15-16, *Heiðr* 1960, 14; *Edd. Min.* 15.

Notes: [1-2] *Hervarðr, Hjörvarðr, Hrani, Angantýr* 'Hervarðr, Hjǫrvarðr, Hrani, Angantýr': The four eldest of the sons of Arngrímr. These lines are repeated at the beginning of *Heiðr* 28 and also occur in *Ǫrv* 5/1-2. — [3] *yðr alla* 'you all': *Ǫrv* ch. 30 (*Ǫrv* 1888, 106) states that the brothers were buried all together under one mound. — [4]: A similar line occurs in *Ski* 35/5. — [5-8]: These lines are more likely to refer to Hervǫr herself (cf. *Heiðr* 37/5-8) than to the sons of Arngrímr, though either is possible since we are told that the latter were buried *með ǫllum vápnum* (*Heiðr* 1960, 10) 'with all their weapons'. Cf. *Heiðr* 88, which lists the weapons of Hervǫr's grandson, Hlǫðr Heiðreksson, with some similarity. — [8] *roðnum* 'decorated': Probably a variant form, required for alliteration, of *hroðinn*, p. p. of *hrjóða*, rather than *roðinn* 'reddened, smeared with blood, bleeding' (p. p. of *rjóða*). Cf. *LP* (1860): *hrjóða*. *Hrjóða* usually means 'clear, empty (of ships)', but could apparently also imply 'decorate, adorn, paint', cf. *réð hrjóða* 'painted' ÞjóðA *Magnfl* 18/5^{II} (and see Note there); *hroðit sigli*, probably 'adorned brooch' *Sigsk* 49/6 (*NK* 215); and the cpd *gullroðinn* 'gilt' (see *Fritzner*:

gullroðinn). Cf. also the Old English p. p. *hroden* 'adorned', e.g. *hroden hildecumbor* 'adorned battle-banner', *Beowulf* l. 1022 (*Beowulf* 2008, 36). Though it is conventional in Old Norse poetry to describe weapons reddened with blood, the meaning 'decorated' accords better with *Heiðr* 37/5, where Hervǫr is described with *grafinn geirr* 'graven spear', and makes better sense, since at this point in the saga she has not recently been involved in fighting or battle.

Hervǫr (Herv Lv 10)

27. Mjök eruð orðnir,   Arngríms synir,
     megir meingjarnir   at moldarauka,
     er engi skal   sona Eyfuru
     við mik mæla   í Munarvági.

Synir Arngríms, meingjarnir megir, eruð mjök orðnir at moldarauka, er engi sona Eyfuru skal mæla við mik í Munarvági.

Sons of Arngrímr, kinsmen keen on harm, you have greatly become the increase of the earth, since none of the sons of Eyfura will speak with me in Munarvágr.

Mss: **Hb**(74r), 2845(65r), R715^x(13r-v) (*Heiðr*).

Readings: [1] eruð: eru 2845;   orðnir: 'vordnir' R715^x [2] Arngríms: 'arngris' 2845 [3] megir: *so* R715^x, megir at Hb, megin 2845;   -gjarnir: *so* 2845, R715^x, samir Hb   [4] at: *so* 2845, R715^x, *om*. Hb   [5] er: at R715^x;   engi: engi *corrected from* gingi 2845;   skal: gjǫrir 2845, 'gior' R715^x [6] Eyfuru: 'Eÿuorn' R715^x [8] í: úr R715^x;   -vági: heimi R715^x.

Editions: *Skj*: Anonyme digte og vers [XIII], E. 5. *Vers af Fornaldarsagaer: Af Hervararsaga* III 3: AII, 245, BII, 265, *Skald* II, 138, *NN* §2374; *Heiðr* 1672, 91, *FSN* 1, 435, 520, *Heiðr* 1873, 215, 316, *Heiðr* 1924, 23, 108, *FSGJ* 2, 16, *Heiðr* 1960, 14; *Edd. Min.* 15.

Notes: [1, 4] *eruð mjök orðnir at moldarauka* 'you have greatly become the increase of the earth': I.e. 'your bodies have greatly rotted away'. — [1] *eruð* 'you are': The reading of Hb, and that chosen here and by other eds, has Hervǫr apostrophise the sons of Arngrímr. The reading of the other mss, *eru* 'they are', has her speak about them in the 3rd pers. — [3] *meingjarnir* 'keen on harm': Hb reads *meinsamir* 'harmful', an acceptable alternative and favoured by *Skj* B, *Skald* and *Edd. Min.*, but the other mss are in agreement on the reading preferred here. — [4] *moldarauka* 'the increase of the earth': A *hap. leg.* in poetry. — [6] *Eyfuru* 'of Eyfura': Arngrímr's wife, who also appears elsewhere in the saga. See Note to *Heiðr* 25/8. She is also named, as the mother of Arngrímr's sons, in *Ǫrv* 5/8 and *Hyndl* 24/3-4. — [8] *Munarvági* 'Munarvágr': See Note to *Heiðr* 18a/2. Ms. R715^x reads *Munarheimi* (lit. 'World of Desire') here; this p. n. occurs in *HHj* 1/4, although probably with figurative meaning. See further *Kommentar* IV, 417-19.

Hervǫr (Herv Lv 11)

28. Hervarðr, Hjörvarðr,   Hrani, Angantýr,
svá sé yðr öllum   innan rifja,
sem þér í maura   mornið haugi,
nema sverð selið,   þat er sló Dvalinn;
samira draugum   dýr vápn fela.

Hervarðr, Hjǫrvarðr, Hrani, Angantýr, svá sé yðr öllum innan rifja, sem þér mornið í maurahaugi, nema selið sverð, þat er Dvalinn sló; samira draugum fela dýr vápn.

Hervarðr, Hjǫrvarðr, Hrani, Angantýr, may it be to you all within your ribs as if you rot in an anthill, unless you give [me] the sword, which Dvalinn forged; it is not fitting for revenants to hide precious weapons.

Mss: **Hb**(74r), 2845(65r), R715^x(13v) (*Heiðr*).

Readings: [2] Hrani Angantýr: *so* 2845, 'rani angantyr' Hb, 'hrani og angantyr' R715^x [6] haugi: *so* 2845, hauga Hb, hangi R715^x [7] selið: *so* 2845, R715^x, selið mér Hb   [9] samira: *so* R715^x, samir eigi Hb, samir ei 2845   [10] dýr: dýrt 2845, R715^x;   vápn: upp R715^x;   fela: bera 2845.

Editions: *Skj*: Anonyme digte og vers [XIII], E. 5. *Vers af Fornaldarsagaer: Af Hervararsaga* III 4: AII, 246, BII, 265-6, *Skald* II, 138; *Heiðr* 1672, 91, *FSN* 1, 436, 520, *Heiðr* 1873, 215, 317, *Heiðr* 1924, 23-4, 108, *FSGJ* 2, 16, *Heiðr* 1960, 14-15; *Edd. Min.* 15.

Notes: [All]: In Herv Lv 14 (*Heiðr* 36) Hervǫr again threatens the brothers that they shall not be allowed to rest in peace if they refuse to give up Tyrfingr. — [1-2]: The repetition of these lines from Herv Lv 8 (*Heiðr* 26) is omitted by several eds, presumably in order to maintain an eight-line stanza, but *fornyrðislag* stanzas need not be a regular eight lines and the emendation would be against the evidence of all mss. — [5] *maura* (gen. pl.) 'ant-': This is the only occurrence of the word *maurr* 'ant' in poetry. — [6] *mornið* 'rot': The verb *morna* has few recorded examples in either poetry or prose. In prose it features in the phrase *morna ok þorna*, perhaps 'wither and dry out' (*CVC: morna*; cf. *Fritzner: þorna*). The only other poetic examples are *Oddrgr* 32/4 and *Skí* 31/5. Possibly derived from *morkna* 'rot', with loss of medial 'k' (*AEW: morna* 2; *LP* (1860), *Fritzner: morna*). — [7] *draugum* 'for revenants': See *Heiðr* 29, Note to All. — [8]: Dvalinn is a dwarf, named in the prose of *Heiðr* in the H and U redactions. See also Note to *Heiðr* 25/8. The name is a common one for dwarfs, occurring elsewhere in eddic poetry in *Vsp* 11/4, 14/1; *Hávm* 143/3; *Alv* 16/3; and *Fáfn* 13/6. — [10] *dýr vápn* 'precious weapons': Mss 2845 and R715^x have the sg. *dyrt vápn* '(the) precious weapon', implying a specific reference to Tyrfingr. — [10] *fela* 'to hide': Ms. 2845's reading, *bera* 'bear', is an acceptable alternative and favoured by *Skj* B, *Skald* and the eds following 2845, but the other mss agree on the reading chosen here, which might also be supported by comparison to Herv Lv 15/8 (*Heiðr* 38), in which Hervǫr also speaks of Angantýr hiding the sword (*at leyna* 'hide').

Angantýr (Angantýr Lv 1)

29. Hervör, dóttir,   hví kallar svá?
Full feiknstafa   ferr þú þér at illu.
Ær ertu orðin   ok örvita;
villhyggjandi,   vekr dauða menn.

Hervör, dóttir, hví kallar svá? Full feiknstafa ferr þú illu at þér. Ertu orðin ær ok örvita; villhyggjandi, vekr dauða menn.

Hervǫr, daughter, why do you call thus? Full of curses, you carry on to your detriment. You have become mad and unhinged; reasoning astray, you wake dead men.

Mss: Hb(74r), 2845(65r), R715ˣ(13v) (*Heiðr*).

Readings: [2] hví: hvat 2845   [4] þér: *om.* R715ˣ   [5] Ær: óð *corrected from* 'or' *in the hand of JR* R715ˣ   [8] vekr: vekr upp 2845, vekja R715ˣ;   dauða menn: *so* 2845, R715ˣ, menn dauða Hb.

Editions: *Skj*: Anonyme digte og vers [XIII], E. 5. *Vers af Fornaldarsagaer: Af Hervararsaga* III 5: AII, 246, BII, 266, *Skald* II, 138; *Heiðr* 1672, 92, *FSN* 1, 436, 520, *Heiðr* 1873, 215-16, 317, *Heiðr* 1924, 24, 108-9, *FSGJ* 2, 16-17, *Heiðr* 1960, 15; *Edd. Min.* 16.

Context: A prose interjection in R715ˣ reads (*Heiðr* 1924, 108): *I þui bili opnudust haugarnir, og var allt at sia sem logi eirn, ok þa var þetta kuedid i haugi Ganntyrs* 'At that moment the mounds opened, and everything was like a single flame to look at, and then this was said in Angantýr's mound'.

Notes: [All]: The *draugr* or animate, corporeal ghost of a deceased person, in particular the inhabitant of a burial mound (*LP*; *Fritzner*; *CVC*; cf. *haugbúi* 'mound-dweller') is a common figure in Old Norse literature. The revenant may remain inside the mysteriously-opened mound (see *Heiðr* 22/6), as Angantýr does here, or break out to interact with (often haunt) the living (see Chadwick 1946 for comprehensive examples and discussion). The recitation of verse is a characteristic commonly associated with *draugar* (*ibid.*, 61-5 and 106-18); for a situation similar to the present one, see *Nj* ch. 78, in which the mound of Gunnarr Hámundarson opens and he is heard to recite poetry (GunnHám Lv 14ⱽ (*Nj* 29)), although in that instance there is no-one involved in dialogue with him. SnSt *Ht* 30ᴵᴵᴵ exemplifies a metre called there *draughent*, though it is not clear whether this means 'ghost-rhymed' or 'trunk-rhymed' (see Note to [All] there). — [All]: A prose context similar to that given at this point in R715ˣ occurs slightly later in the exchange in the other mss, before Angantýr Lv 3 (*Heiðr* 32). That stanza does not appear in R715ˣ, however. — [4] *feiknstafa* 'of curses': Lit. 'of portentous or terrible staves', probably runes (cf. Anon *Sól* 60/6ⱽᴵᴵ, *Grí* 12/6 and *LT* 57), taken here with the sense 'something which causes evil', and according with Hervǫr's curse of the previous stanza. Cf. OE *fācenstæf* (pl. *fācenstafas*, *Beowulf* l. 1017) 'works of evil, acts of malice, treachery' (*DOE*). Some eds construe this line with the previous two, rather than with l. 4, as here, but in this stanza and elsewhere in the poem Angantýr seems to be more concerned with the broader fact that Hervǫr is there at all rather than the specific content of her speech. — [5-6] *ær ok ørvita* 'mad and unhinged': This pairing also occurs in the eddic poems *Lok* 21/1-2, *Oddrgr* 11/1-2 and *HHund II* 34/1-2. — [7] *villhyggjandi* 'reasoning astray': A *hap. leg.* Most other eds also treat as a cpd.

Angantýr (Angantýr Lv 2)

30. Grófat mik faðir   né frændr aðrir.
     Þeir hǫfðu Tyrfing   tveir, er lifðu;
     varð þó eigandi   einn um síðir.

Faðir grófat mik né aðrir frændr. Þeir tveir, er lifðu, hǫfðu Tyrfing; þó varð einn eigandi um síðir.

A father did not bury me, nor other kinsmen. The two who lived had Tyrfingr, though one became the owner in the end.

Mss: **Hb**(74r), 2845(65r), R715ˣ(13v) (*Heiðr*).

Readings: [1] Grófat mik: Gróf ei mik 2845, gróf mik ei R715ˣ;   faðir: *so* 2845, faðir niðr Hb, faðir *corrected from* faðir niðr R715ˣ   [5] varð þó: urðu 2845   [6] einn: *so* R715ˣ, ein Hb, enn 2845.

Editions: *Skj*: Anonyme digte og vers [XIII], E. 5. Vers af Fornaldarsagaer: Af Hervararsaga III 6: AII, 246, BII, 266, *Skald* II, 138; *Heiðr* 1672, 92, *FSN* 1, 436, 520, *Heiðr* 1873, 216, 317, *Heiðr* 1924, 24-5, 109, *FSGJ* 2, 17, *Heiðr* 1960, 15; *Edd. Min.* 16.

Notes: [All]: Two half-lines appear to have been lost from this stanza, probably after l. 2. Though *fornyrðislag* stanzas need not conform to an eight-line standard, there seems to be something missing from the sense. *Skj* B, *Skald* and *Edd. Min.* all indicate this by means of a dashed line or lines where the missing ones are presumed to be, while *Heiðr* 1960 mentions it in a note. Bugge (*Heiðr* 1873, 216 n.) proposed the missing lines to have implied *det var vore Banemænd (el. Fiender), som lagde os i Haug* 'it was our slayers (or enemies) who laid us in the mound'. — [1] *faðir grófat mik* 'a father did not bury me': *Ǫrv* ch. 27 (*Ǫrv* 1888, 101) relates the vow between the duelling parties that the victors should bury the slain with all of their weapons and other precious possessions. The line is unmetrical as it stands; changing the word order to *faðir grófat mik* would result in a metrical line but would go against the readings of all mss. Hb and R715ˣ at one time shared the reading *Grófat mik faðir niðr* 'A father did not bury me beneath', thus giving it some claim to authenticity, but the *niðr* has been crossed out in R715ˣ and is also unmetrical. — [3] *Tyrfing* 'Tyrfingr': The first appearance of the sword-name in the poetry of *Heiðr*. Tyrfingr appears as a *heiti* for sword in the *þulur* in *SnE* (Þul *Sverða* 7/6ᴵᴵᴵ; *SnE* 1998, I, 120) and is used with the meaning 'sword' in Arn *Harðr* 2/3ᴵᴵ. *LP*: Tyrfingr suggests derivation from *torf* 'turf', with *tyrfingr* meaning *jordfunden* 'found in the ground', a meaning which would be dependent on the context of these stanzas. It may alternatively be derived from the ethnic name *Tervingi* or from *tyrfi* 'resinous fir-tree' (see Falk 1914b, 62). *Ǫrv* 5/5 gives it as the pers. n. of one of the sons of Arngrímr. It is also used as a pers. n. in *Ǫrv* 27/3 and *Hyndl* 23/5. — [4-6]: Angantýr's words are ambiguous here. The 'two who lived' are Hjálmarr and Ǫrvar-Oddr (cf. ǪrvOdd Lv 3/6 (*Ǫrv* 10) *en vit tveir lifa* 'but we two will live'), though Hjálmarr only lived long enough to recite his death song, *Ǫrv* 14-29. Angantýr appears to be trying to mislead Hervǫr (and cf. her response in the following stanza, Herv Lv 12 (*Heiðr* 31)), implying that his slayers kept the sword and that the *einn* 'one' of l. 6 is Ǫrvar-Oddr. His words are not outright untruths, though, since Hjálmarr and Ǫrvar-Oddr did have the sword in the immediate aftermath of his death, before burying it with him, and the *einn* could apply to Angantýr himself.

Hervǫr (Herv Lv 12)

31. Segir þú eigi satt, — svá láti áss þik
heilan í haugi — sem þú hafir eigi
Tyrfing með þér. Trautt er þér at veita
arfa þínum einar bænir.

Þú segir eigi satt, sem hafir þú eigi Tyrfing með þér; svá láti áss þik heilan í haugi. Trautt er þér at veita arfa þínum einar bænir.

You do not speak truly, [you speak] as though you do not have Tyrfingr with you; so may the god leave you unharmed in the mound. You are reluctant to grant one boon to your heir.

Mss: **Hb**(74r), 2845(65r-v), R715ˣ(13v) (*Heiðr*).

Readings: [1] Segir: *so* 2845, seg Hb, 'seiger' R715ˣ; þú: 'þu' R715ˣ; eigi: *so* 2845, ein Hb, 'ey' R715ˣ; satt: *so* 2845, satt mér Hb, satt mér R715ˣ [2] áss: *so* R715ˣ, oss Hb, 2845 [3] haugi: haugi sitja 2845 [4] hafir: *so* R715ˣ, hefir Hb, hafir(?) 2845 [5] með þér: *om.* 2845 [6] Trautt: trauðr 2845; er þér: ertu 2845; at veita: *om.* 2845 [7] arfa: arf 2845, R715ˣ; þínum: at veita 2845, Angantýr R715ˣ [8] einar bænir: eingabarni 2845, R715ˣ.

Editions: *Skj*: Anonyme digte og vers [XIII], E. 5. Vers af Fornaldarsagaer: Af Hervararsaga III 7: AII, 246, BII, 266, *Skald* II, 138, *NN* §3182; *Heiðr* 1672, 92, *FSN* 1, 436-7, 520, *Heiðr* 1873, 216, 317-18, *Heiðr* 1924, 25, 109, *FSGJ* 2, 17, *Heiðr* 1960, 15; *Edd. Min.* 16.

Notes: [All]: This stanza poses problems of reconstruction in several places. Tolkien (*Heiðr* 1960, 15 n. 5) suggests there was originally a stop at the end of the first half-stanza; this is likely correct, but the extant ms. evidence now requires l. 5 to be taken with l. 4. See also following Notes. — [1]: Ms. R715ˣ has the reading chosen here (with *ei* for *eigi* 'not'), but this appears to have been crossed out in the hand of Jón Rugman. Ms. 2845 agrees with the first four words; Hb includes *mér* in l. 1, but this is extrametrical (see also Andrews 1920, 97). Kock (*Skald*) takes the reading of Hb, *Seg einsatt mér* 'Speak clearly to me', from the adj. *einsær* 'only choice' (*Fritzner, LP*: *einsær*). He points out in *NN* §3182 that *einsætt* appears elsewhere in poetry with the meaning 'evident, clear'; see e.g. Gamlkan *Has* 43/8^{VII}, *Nj* 16//2^V, Arngr *Gd* 15/6^{IV}. This is an acceptable alternative. The reading of the present edn is chosen since 2845 and R715^x are almost in agreement and the sense fits the context more closely: Angantýr has told an untruth in the previous stanza, saying he does not have Tyrfingr. — [4]: *Edd. Min.* ends the sentence after this line (see Note [All] above): *sem þú hafir eigi!* 'If you don't have [it]!'. — [5-6]: *Edd. Min.* rearranges these lines to read *trauðr ertu at veita* | *Tyrfing hvassan* 'you are reluctant to grant sharp Tyrfingr'. All mss agree that *Tyrfing* comes before the rest of the long-line, however, and *hvassan* is purely conjectural. — [7-8] *arfa þínum einar bænir* 'one boon to your heir': Hb's reading is completely acceptable as it stands. However, rather than *arfa*, dat. sg. of *arfi* 'heir', the other mss have *arf*, acc. sg. of *arfr* 'inheritance' in l. 7, thus making this the direct object, and *eingabarni* (dat. sg.) 'only child' the indirect object in l. 8. *Skj* and *Skald* compromise, printing *eingabarni* | *einar bænir*, making the clause read 'you are reluctant to grant one boon to your only child', but displacing *eingabarni* from its position in the stanza as the mss have it. Following on from their emended reading of the previous lines, the eds of *Edd. Min.* opt for *arfa þínum,* | *einga barni* 'to your heir, your only child'. There is no good reason not to accept the reading of the main ms., however. The line *einnar bænar* occurs as *Ásm* 5/3. In the pl., as here, *einn* takes on the meaning 'only, just, alone'.

Angantýr (Angantýr Lv 3)

32. Hnigin er helgrind,   haugar opnaz,
     allr er í eldi   eybarmr at sjá.
     Atalt er úti   um at lítaz;
     skyntu, mær, ef þú mátt,   til skipa þinna.

Helgrind er hnigin, haugar opnaz, allr eybarmr er at sjá í eldi. Úti er atalt at lítaz um; skyntu, mær, ef þú mátt, til skipa þinna.

Hel's gate is fallen, mounds open, one can see the whole island-edge on fire. Outside it is terrible to look around; hurry, girl, if you can, to your ships.

Mss: **Hb**(74r), 2845(65v) (*Heiðr*).

Readings: [3] allr: allt 2845   [4] -barmr: -grims 2845;   at: *om.* 2845.

Editions: *Skj*: Anonyme digte og vers [XIII], E. 5. *Vers af Fornaldarsagaer: Af Hervarasaga* III 8: AII, 246-7, BII, 266, *Skald* II, 138-9; *FSN* 1, 437, 520, *Heiðr* 1873, 217, 318, *Heiðr* 1924, 25-6, *FSGJ* 2, 17-18, *Heiðr* 1960, 16; *Edd. Min.* 17.

Context: A prose interjection in Hb and 2845, though differently worded in each, relates that the mound opens and fire burns all around.

Notes: [All]: See *Heiðr* 29, Note to [All]. — [1] *helgrind* 'Hel's gate': In Old Norse mythology Hel is both a being and a location. The gates of Hell (*portae inferi*) are also present in Christian imagery; see Matt. XVI.18. Cf. Anon *Sól* 39/4[VII] and Note. — [2]: Identical to *Heiðr* 22/6 (and see Note). Both stanzas mention supernatural fires and warn Hervǫr to hurry away. — [4] *eybarmr* 'the island-edge': See Note to GunnLeif *Merl I* 86/4, the only other occurrence of this cpd. Ms. 2845's variant, *gríms*, cannot be satisfactorily construed in Old Norse.

Hervǫr (Herv Lv 13)

33. Brenniðˌ eigi svá   bál á nóttum,
    at ek við elda   yðra fælumz.
    Skelfrat meyju   muntún hugar,
    þótt hon draug séi   í durum standa.

Brennið eigi svá bál á nóttum, at ek fælumz við elda yðra. Skelfrat muntún hugar meyju, þótt hon séi draug standa í durum.

You will not burn blazes at night in such a way that I will be frightened of your fires. The desire-enclosure of the mind [BREAST] of the girl will not tremble, though she sees a revenant stand in the doorway.

Mss: **Hb**(74r), 2845(65v) (*Heiðr*).

Readings: [1] Brennið: *so* 2845, Brenni þér Hb   [4] fælumz: hræðumz 2845   [7] séi: sjái *all* [8] í: fyri 2845.

Editions: *Skj*: Anonyme digte og vers [XIII], E. 5. *Vers af Fornaldarsagaer: Af Hervararsaga* III 9: AII, 247, BII, 266-7, *Skald* II, 139; *FSN* 1, 437, 520-1, *Heiðr* 1873, 217, 318, *Heiðr* 1924, 26, *FSGJ* 2, 18, *Heiðr* 1960, 16; *Edd. Min.* 17.

Notes: [1-4]: Similar in content to *Heiðr* 23/1-4, where Hervǫr urges the shepherd not to be frightened by the fires burning around the island. — [6] *muntún hugar* 'the desire-enclosure of the mind [BREAST]': As other eds have noted, *hugar* appears to be redundant to the meaning of the kenning. *Muntún* is a *hap. leg.* — [7] *draug* 'a revenant': See *Heiðr* 29 Note to [All]. — [7] *séi* 'sees': Normalised to the 1250-1300 standard form of the subj. of *sjá* 'see'; the mss. all have the later subj. form *sjái*.

Angantýr (Angantýr Lv 4)

34. Segi ek þér, Hervör,   — hlýttu til meðan,
    vísa dóttir, —   þat er verða mun.
    Sjá mun Tyrfingr,   ef þú trúa mættir,
    ætt þinni, mær,   allri spilla.

Ek segi þér, Hervör, þat er mun verða; hlýttu til meðan, dóttir vísa. Sjá Tyrfingr mun spilla allri ætt þinni, mær, ef þú mættir trúa.

I tell you, Hervǫr, what will happen; listen a while, daughter of a prince. That Tyrfingr will destroy all your family, girl, if you are able to believe it.

Mss: Hb(74r), 2845(65v), R715^x(13v) (*Heiðr*).

Readings: [2] meðan: enn 2845   [4] er: *om*. R715^x.

Editions: *Skj*: Anonyme digte og vers [XIII], E. 5. *Vers af Fornaldarsagaer: Af Hervararsaga* III 10: AII, 247, BII, 267, *Skald* II, 139; *Heiðr* 1672, 92, *FSN* 1, 438, 521, *Heiðr* 217-18, 318-19, *Heiðr* 1924, 26-7, 109, *FSGJ* 2, 18, *Heiðr* 1960, 16; *Edd. Min.* 17.

Notes: [All]: Tolkien (*Heiðr* 1960, 16 n. 3) is troubled that Angantýr, who 'is not yet persuaded to yield up the sword', should make this prophecy at this point in the poem, and suggests the stanza 'must be displaced' from a later point. However, since the stanza can be read as a warning and an explanation of his reluctance, there is no good reason to suppose rearrangement is necessary. — [All]: The eds of *CPB* (*CPB* I, 167) print this stanza only in the notes, calling it a 'duplicate' despite the fact that ll. 1-4 appear nowhere else in the dialogue and, though ll. 5-8 appear again in Angantýr Lv 9/5-8 (*Heiðr* 43), there is evidence to suggest that they were not originally part of that stanza (see Note there). — [5-8]: Cf. *Harð* ch. 15, in which Hǫrðr and his companions break into the mound of the viking Sóti in order to steal certain treasures buried with him. When they take a gold arm-ring, Sóti warns them in verse (Sóti Lv 2/7-10^V (*Harð* 10)) that it will cause the death of all its (male) owners.

Angantýr (Angantýr Lv 5)

35. Muntu son geta,   þann er síðan mun
    Tyrfing hafa   ok trúa magni.
    Þann munu Heiðrek   heita lýðar;
    sá mun ríkstr alinn   und röðuls tjaldi.

Muntu geta son, þann er mun hafa Tyrfing síðan ok trúa magni. Lýðar munu heita þann Heiðrek; sá mun alinn ríkstr und tjaldi röðuls.

You will give birth to a son, who will have Tyrfingr later, and trust in its might. People will call him Heiðrekr; he will be born most powerful under the tent of the sun [SKY/HEAVEN].

Mss: **Hb**(74r), 2845(65v), R715ˣ(13v) (*Heiðr*).

Readings: [2] síðan: *so* 2845, síð Hb, 'sydar' R715ˣ   [3] hafa: *so* 2845, R715ˣ, bera Hb   [4] magni: *so* 2845, R715ˣ, afli Hb   [5] munu: mun 2845, R715ˣ   [7] mun: *so* 2845, R715ˣ, man Hb   [8] und: undir 2845.

Editions: *Skj*: Anonyme digte og vers [XIII], E. 5. *Vers af Fornaldarsagaer: Af Hervararsaga* III 11: AII, 247, BII, 267, *Skald* II, 139; *Heiðr* 1672, 92, *FSN* 1, 438, 521, *Heiðr* 1873, 218, 319, *Heiðr* 1924, 27, 109-10, *FSGJ* 2, 19, *Heiðr* 1960, 16-17; *Edd. Min.* 17.

Notes: [All]: Angantýr's prophecy is fulfilled later in the saga when Hervǫr has a son, Heiðrekr, with Hǫfundr, son of King Guðmundr of Glasisvellir (on the latter see further *Heiðr* 1960, 84-6); Heiðrekr becomes a powerful and wealthy king through marriage alliances, inheritance and his own war-making. — [4] *magni* 'might': Hb's reading, *afli* 'power', is also acceptable but in the minority.

Hervǫr (Herv Lv 14)

36. Ek vígi svá   virða dauða,
     at þér skuluð   allir liggja
     dauðir með draugum,   í dys fúnir.
     Sel mér, Angantýr,   út ór haugi
     hlífum hættan,   Hjálmars bana.

Ek vígi dauða virða svá, at þér skuluð allir liggja dauðir með draugum, fúnir í dys. Sel mér, Angantýr, út ór haugi, bana Hjálmars, hættan hlífum.

I curse dead noblemen, so that you will all lie dead with the revenants, rotten in the cairn. Give me, Angantýr, out from the mound, the slayer of Hjálmarr [= Tyrfingr], dangerous to shields.

Mss: **Hb**(74r), R715ˣ(13v-14r) (ll. 1-4, 7-10) (*Heiðr*).

Readings: [1] vígi: 'ofkingi' *corrected from* 'of ingi' *or* of vígi *in the hand of JR* R715ˣ   [3] skuluð: þolið R715ˣ   [4] allir: aldri R715ˣ;   liggja: kyrrir *corrected from* kyrrir liggja *in the hand of JR* R715ˣ   [6] fúnir: 'fynir' Hb   [7] Sel mér: nema þú R715ˣ   [8] út ór haugi: selir mér Tyrfing R715ˣ.

Editions: *Skj*: Anonyme digte og vers [XIII], E. 5. *Vers af Fornaldarsagaer: Af Hervararsaga* III 12: AII, 247, BII, 267, *Skald* II, 139; *Heiðr* 1672, 92-3, *FSN* 1, 438, 521, *Heiðr* 1873, 218, *Heiðr* 1924, 28, 110, *Heiðr* 1960, 78; *Edd. Min.* 17-18.

Notes: [All]: R715ˣ presents an alternative version of this stanza, as follows:

Ek vígi svá   virða dauða,
at þér þolið   aldri kyrrir,
nema þú, Angantýr,   selir mér Tyrfing,
hlífum hættan,   Hjálmars bana.

Prose Order: Ek vígi svá dauða virða, at þér þolið aldri kyrrir, nema þú, Angantýr, selir mér Tyrfing, hættan hlífum, bana Hjálmars. *Translation*: I curse dead noblemen so that you will never rest quietly, unless you, Angantýr, give me Tyrfingr, dangerous to shields, slayer of Hjálmarr [= Tyrfingr]. This version lacks alliteration across ll. 3-6, making Hervǫr's words more a threat than a general curse. As here, the eds of *CPB* (I, 166) choose Hb's version (with the same emendation to *fúnir* 'rotten'), while the eds of *Edd. Min.* print ll. 1-8 from Hb (also with emendation to *fúnir* and changing *sel mér* 'give me' to *seldu* 'you give'), replacing ll. 9-10 with ll. 7-8 from what in the present edn is Herv Lv 15 (*Heiðr* 38). *Skj* B and *Skald* print ll. 1-4 from R715^x with ll. 7-10 from Hb. — [3-4]: These lines lack alliteration. — [10] *bana Hjálmars* 'the slayer of Hjálmarr [= Tyrfingr]': Hjálmarr inn hugumstóri 'the Great-minded' is Hjǫrvarðr's rival for the hand of Ingibjǫrg, daughter of the king of Sweden. Hjǫrvarðr challenges Hjálmarr to the duel which results in both of their deaths, as well as those of the other sons of Arngrímr. Just before his death Hjálmarr recites his so-called 'death song', Hjálm Lv 4-19 (*Ǫrv* 14-29). The first seven stanzas of this also appear in *Heiðr* (*Heiðr* 6-12), but in the present edition are edited with the poetry from *Ǫrv*. The kenning is also used in *Heiðr* 39/2 and 45/2.

Angantýr (Angantýr Lv 6)

37. Kveðkat ek þik, mær ung,   mǫnnum líka,
er þú um hauga   hvarfar á nóttum
grǫfnum geiri   ok með Gota málmi,
hjálmi ok með brynju,   fyrir hallar dyrr.

Ek kveðkat þik, ung mær, líka mǫnnum, er þú hvarfar um hauga á nóttum grǫfnum geiri ok með málmi Gota, hjálmi ok með brynju, fyrir dyrr hallar.

I would not declare you, young girl, [to be] like humans, when you wander around the mounds at night, with engraved spear and with the metal of the Goths, with helmet and with mail-shirt, before the doors of the hall.

Mss: **Hb**(74r), R715^x(14r) (*Heiðr*).

Readings: [1] Kveðkat: Kveð R715^x; þik: þik R715^x [3] er þú um: 'e[…] vm' *with* 'þú' *in the margin* R715^x [4] hvarfar: 'huarlar' R715^x [6] ok: *om.* R715^x [7] hjálmi: hjálm R715^x; með: *om.* R715^x.

Editions: *Skj*: Anonyme digte og vers [XIII], E. 5. *Vers af Fornaldarsagaer: Af Hervararsaga* III 13: AII, 247-8, BII, 267, *Skald* II, 139; *Heiðr* 1672, 93, *FSN* 1, 439, 521, *Heiðr* 1873, 218-19, *Heiðr* 1924, 28, 110, *Heiðr* 1960, 78; *Edd. Min.* 18.

Notes: [2] *mǫnnum* 'humans': The Old Norse masculine noun refers both to males specifically, perhaps here playing on the fact that Hervǫr is disguised as a man, and to humankind in general, implying there is something unnatural about her activities; cf. her response (referring to herself as *mennskr maðr* 'human being') in the following stanza. — [5-7]: The content of these lines is similar to *Heiðr* 26/5-8, although there is no direct verbal echo. — [6] *málmi Gota* 'the metal of the Goths': *Málmr* can be used to denote 'sword' in particular (*LP*) and is used as a *heiti* for 'sword' in Þul *Sverða* 3/5[III]. It can also denote weapons or armour more generally, as would fit the context here. Hervǫr is of Gothic descent on her father's side, and is hence equipped with her ancestral possessions. — [8] *hallar* 'of the hall': Refers to Angantýr's burial mound; cf. *Heiðr* 14/7 and Note.

Hervǫr (Herv Lv 15)

38. Maðr þóttumz ek   mennskr til þessa,
    áðr ek sali yðra   sækja réðak.
    Seldu mér ór haugi,   þann er hatar brynjur,
    dverga smíði;   dugira þér at leyna.

Ek þóttumz mennskr maðr til þessa, áðr ek réðak sækja sali yðra. Seldu mér ór haugi, þann er hatar brynjur, smíði dverga; dugira þér at leyna.

I thought myself a human being until this, before I resolved to seek your halls. Give me from the mound that which hates mail-shirts, smith-craft of dwarfs; it will not help you to hide it.

Mss: **Hb**(74r), 2845(65v), R715[x](14r) (*Heiðr*).

Readings: [1] þóttumz: þótt R715[x];   ek: þú *corrected from* þú mjök *in the hand of JR* R715[x] [2] til: *om.* 2845;   þessa: *so* 2845, 'þersa' Hb, forna *corrected from* þessa *in the margin in the hand of JR* R715[x]   [4] sækja: 'seka' 2845, tók R715[x];   réðak: hafðak 2845, kanna R715[x]   [7] dverga: hlífum 2845;   smíði: hættan 2845   [8] dugira þér ('dvgeræ þer'): Hjálmars bana 2845, dugir þér ei R715[x];   at leyna: *om.* 2845.

Editions: *Skj*: Anonyme digte og vers [XIII], E. 5. *Vers af Fornaldarsagaer: Af Hervararsaga* III 14: AII, 248, BII, 267-8, *Skald* II, 139; *Heiðr* 1672, 93, *FSN* 1, 439, 521, *Heiðr* 1873, 219, 319, *Heiðr* 1924, 28-9, 110, *FSGJ* 2, 19, *Heiðr* 1960, 17; *Edd. Min.* 18.

Notes: [1-2] *mennskr maðr* 'a human being': Plays on Angantýr's *Kveðkat ek þik ... mǫnnum líka* 'I would not declare you ... to be like humans' in ll. 1-2 of the previous stanza. — [3] *sali* 'halls': I.e. Angantýr's grave-mound; see Note to *Heiðr* 14/3. — [4] *réðak sækja* 'I resolved to seek': Ms. R715[x]'s reading, *tók kanna* 'I resolved to investigate', has basically the same sense but lacks alliteration. — [6] *þann er hatar brynjur* 'that which hates mail-shirts': I.e., destroys mail-shirts. This is not structurally a kenning, but cf. GSúrs Lv 19/7ᵛ (*Gísl* 22) *hatr brynju* 'the hatred of the mail-shirt [SWORD]'. The verb *hata* can mean both 'hate' and 'destroy, damage', either of which is appropriate here. The eds of *CPB* (*CPB*, I, 165) replace this line with *hvassan mæki* 'the sharp sword', which in the present edn occurs in *Heiðr* 25/6 and 40/3. — [7-8]: Ms. 2845 has here ll. 7-8 of the problematic *Heiðr* 36, a stanza otherwise omitted in that ms. Tolkien (*Heiðr* 1960, 79) suggests 2845's reading could be closer to the original arrangement, because of the echoing of *Hjálmars bani* in l. 2 of the following stanza (*Heiðr* 39). The eds of *Edd. Min.* also prefer 2845's reading for the present stanza. However, Hb and R715ˣ, with some minor variations, agree on the arrangement followed here. — [7] *smíði dverga* 'smith-craft of dwarfs': See Notes to *Heiðr* 25/6-8 and 28/8.

Angantýr (Angantýr Lv 7)

39. Liggr mér und herðum Hjálmars bani;
    allr er hann útan eldi sveipinn.
    Mey veit ek enga moldar hvergi,
    at þann hjör þori í hendr nema.

Bani Hjálmars liggr und herðum mér; útan er hann allr sveipinn eldi. Ek veit enga mey hvergi moldar, at þori nema þann hjör í hendr.

The slayer of Hjálmarr [= Tyrfingr] lies under my shoulders; on the outside it is all encircled by fire. I know no girl anywhere on earth who would dare to take that sword in her hands.

Mss: **Hb**(74r), 2845(65v), R715ˣ(14r) (*Heiðr*).

Readings: [1] Liggr: *so* 2845, R715ˣ, 'L[...]ggr' Hb; und: undir 2845, R715ˣ [4] sveipinn: *so* R715ˣ, sveipin Hb, 'sueífín' 2845 [5] enga: öngva 2845, R715ˣ [6] moldar: fyrir mold 2845, molda *corrected from* moldar *in the hand of JR* R715ˣ; hvergi: ofan 2845 [7] at: er R715ˣ; þann hjör: hjör þann 2845 [8] hendr: hönd 2845, 'handur' R715ˣ; nema: bera 2845, at nema R715ˣ.

Editions: *Skj*: Anonyme digte og vers [XIII], E. 5. *Vers af Fornaldarsagaer: Af Hervararsaga* III 15: AII, 248, BII, 268, Skald II, 139; *Heiðr* 1672, 93, *FSN* 1, 439, 521, *Heiðr* 1873, 219, 319-20, *Heiðr* 1924, 29, 111, *FSGJ* 2, 19, *Heiðr* 1960, 17; *Edd. Min.* 18.

Notes: [2]: See Notes to *Heiðr* 36/8 and 38/7-8. — [3-4]: These lines are also found in *Fáfn* 42/3-4, there referring to the location on the mountain Hindarfjall on which the valkyrie Sigrdrífa lies in an enchanted sleep until, in *Sigrdr*, she is awakened by Sigurðr Fáfnisbani. — [4]: See Note to *Heiðr* 45/6. — [5-6]: Cf., especially in light of 2845's reading, *Gríp* 22/1-2 (*NK* 167): *Mann veit ec engi | fyr mold ofan* 'I know no man on the earth [lit. 'above the earth', i.e. 'alive']'.

Hervǫr (Herv Lv 16)

40. Ek mun hirða   ok í hendr nema
     hvassan mæki,   ef ek hafa mættak.
     Uggi ek eigi   eld brennanda;
     þegar loga lægir, er ek lít yfir.

Ek mun hirða hvassan mæki ok nema í hendr, ef ek mættak hafa. Ek uggi eigi brennanda eld; loga lægir þegar, er ek lít yfir.

I will guard the sharp sword and take it in my hands, if I might have it. I do not fear the burning fire; the flame will subside as soon as I look upon it.

Mss: Hb(74r), 2845(65v), R715˟(14r) (*Heiðr*).

Readings: [1] mun: *so* 2845, R715˟, man Hb;   hirða: *so* 2845, R715˟, hirða segir hon Hb [2] hendr: hönd 2845, R715˟ [4] mættak: 'gnædi' R715˟ [5] Uggi: 'higg' R715˟ [7, 8] þegar loga lægir er ek lít yfir: þann er framliðnum fyrðum leikr um sjónir R715˟.

Editions: *Skj*: Anonyme digte og vers [XIII], E. 5. *Vers af Fornaldarsagaer: Af Hervararsaga* III 16: AII, 248, BII, 268, *Skald* II, 139; *Heiðr* 1672, 93-4, *FSN* 1, 440, 521, *Heiðr* 1873, 220, 320, *Heiðr* 1924, 29-30, 111, *FSGJ* 2, 20, *Heiðr* 1960, 17; *Edd. Min.* 18-19.

Notes: [1]: The stanza is interrupted at the end of this half-line in Hb with the attribution *segir hon* 'she says'. This is clearly not part of the verse and is indicated as separate from it in the ms. by the placing of a vertical stroke on either side of the interjection. — [2] *nema í hendr* 'take it in my hands': Echoes l. 8 of the previous stanza. The agreement of the other mss on the sg. *hönd* 'hand' is not enough to go against the main ms. here, since in 2845 this is a direct repetition of its reading, *hönd*, in l. 8 of the previous stanza, a reading rejected in the present edn. Andrews (1920, 97-8), however, argues for the 'poetic effect' created (in R715˟ only) by the use of the sg. form following the pl. in the previous stanza: 'Hervǫr asserts her readiness to take it in one hand, answering not only the expressed doubt as to her courage, but also any possible implication as to her strength'. — [3] *hvassan mæki* 'the sharp sword': This half-line also occurs in *Heiðr* 25/6 and, in the dat. case, *Heiðr* 88/6; see Note there. — [5-8]: In these lines Hervǫr responds to ll. 3-4 of the previous stanza: *allr er hann útan | eldi sveipinn* 'on the outside it is all encircled by fire'. — [7-8]: Ms. R715˟ offers *er framliðnum fyrðum | leikr um sjónir* 'which plays around the eyes of the deceased warriors', which is unmetrical. In the readings in *Skj* A Finnur Jónsson suggests that the reading may originally have been *er framm-liðnum | leikr fyr sjónum* 'which plays around the deceased before [my] sight', but this lacks alliteration. The variant is clearly secondary.

Angantýr (Angantýr Lv 8)

41. Heimsk ertu, Hervör,   hugar eigandi,
er þú at augum   í eld hrapar.
Heldr vil ek selja þér   sverð ór haugi,
mær in unga;   mákat ek þér synja.

Ertu heimsk, Hervör, eigandi hugar, er þú hrapar í eld at augum. Ek vil heldr selja þér sverð ór haugi, in unga mær; ek mákat synja þér.

You are foolish, Hervǫr, [but] in possession of courage, since you rush into the fire with your eyes open. I will rather give you the sword from the mound, young woman; I cannot refuse you.

Mss: Hb(74r), 2845(65v), R715ˣ(14r) (*Heiðr*).

Readings: [3] augum: 'augunn' R715ˣ   [5] Heldr vil ek: *so* 2845, R715ˣ, ek vil heldr Hb;   selja: sverð R715ˣ   [6] sverð: selja R715ˣ   [7] mær in: 'mærinn' 2845   [8] mákat: má 2845, mun R715ˣ; þér: þér ei 2845, þik ei R715ˣ; synja: leyna R715ˣ.

Editions: *Skj*: Anonyme digte og vers [XIII], E. 5. *Vers af Fornaldarsagaer: Af Hervararsaga* III 17: AII, 248, BII, 268, *Skald* II, 140, *NN* §2375; *Heiðr* 1672, 94, *FSN* 1, 440, 522, *Heiðr* 1873, 220, 320, *Heiðr* 1924, 30, 111, *FSGJ* 2, 20, *Heiðr* 1960, 18; *Edd. Min.* 19.

Notes: [1-2]: Kock (*NN* §2375) draws a contrast between these lines and *Hamð* 27/1-2 (*NK* 273): *hug hefðir þú, Hamðir, | ef þu hefðir hyggiandi* 'you would have had courage, Hamðir, if you had wisdom'. — [1] *heimsk* 'foolish': The word derives from *heimr* 'home' and implies inexperience or naivety (*AEW, LT*: *heimskr*). Cf. *Heiðr* 22/1, in which Hervǫr is described as *heimskr* (with the masculine inflection, since she is disguised as a man) by the shepherd. In *Skj* B Finnur emends to *heimsks*, to agree with *hugar*, and construes *Et dumt sind har du* 'You have a foolish mind' (though in *LP*: 2. *eiga* 8 he gives *hugar eigandi* and translates as *modig mand* 'a brave man', as Kock points out in *NN* §2375). Emendation is unnecessary, however, since the text makes sense as it stands. — [3-4] *þú hrapar í eld at augum* 'you rush into the fire with your eyes open': Idiomatic expression. — [5-6] *selja þér sverð* 'give you the sword': *Skj* B and *Skald* reverse the order of *selja* and *sverð*, which is the reading of R715ˣ, and avoid the heavy anacrusis in the B-line. This is not necessary, however, and the verbal echo in the following stanza perhaps indicates that the order retained here is original, and aesthetically preferable. — [8] *ek mákat synja þér* 'I cannot refuse you': Ms. R715ˣ has here *mun ek þik ei leyna* 'I will not hide (it) from you'.

Hervǫr (Herv Lv 17)

42. Vel gerðir þú,   víkinga niðr,
    er þú seldir mér   sverð ór haugi.
    Betr þykkjumz nú,   buðlungr, hafa,
    en ek Nóregi   næðak ǫllum.

Þú gerðir vel, niðr víkinga, er þú seldir mér sverð ór haugi. Þykkjumz hafa betr nú, buðlungr, en ek næðak ǫllum Nóregi.

You did well, son of vikings, when you gave me the sword from the mound. I feel better now, prince, than if I were to obtain all Norway.

Mss: **Hb**(74r), 2845(65v), R715ˣ(14r) (*Heiðr*).

Editions: *Skj*: Anonyme digte og vers [XIII], E. 5. *Vers af Fornaldarsagaer: Af Hervararsaga* III 18: AII, 248, BII, 268; *Skald* II, 140; *Heiðr* 1672, 94, *FSN* 1, 440, 522, *Heiðr* 1873, 220, 320-1, *Heiðr* 1924, 30-1, 111-12, *FSGJ* 2, 20-21, *Heiðr* 1960, 18; *Edd. Min.* 19.

Context: R715ˣ has a prose interjection before this stanza: *Þá var sverð í hendi Hervarar* 'Then the sword was in Hervǫr's hand'.

Note: [3-4]: Echoes ll. 5-6 of the previous stanza.

Angantýr (Angantýr Lv 9)

43. Veizt eigi þú,   — vesǫl ertu mála,
    fullfeikn kona —   hví þú fagna skalt.
    Sjá mun Tyrfingr,   ef þú trúa mættir,
    ætt þinni, mær,   allri spilla.

Þú veizt eigi, hví þú skalt fagna; ertu vesǫl mála, fullfeikn kona. Sjá Tyrfingr mun spilla allri ætt þinni, mær, ef þú mættir trúa.

You do not know why you must rejoice; you are wretched in your utterances, destructive woman. That Tyrfingr will destroy all your family, girl, if you are able to believe it.

Mss: **Hb**(74r-v) (ll. 1-4), 2845(65v), R715ˣ(14r) (*Heiðr*).

Readings: [2] vesǫl: 'ad vppsol' R715ˣ; ertu: ert 2845; mála: máls 2845   [3] fullfeikn: *so* 2845, fláráð Hb, R715ˣ   [4] hví: *so* 2845, hverju Hb, því R715ˣ; skalt: *so* 2845, R715ˣ, '[...]' Hb   [7] ætt: *so* R715ˣ, *om.* 2845   [8] spilla: skal Hb.

Editions: *Skj*: Anonyme digte og vers [XIII], E. 5. *Vers af Fornaldarsagaer: Af Hervararsaga* III 19: AII, 249, BII, 269; *Skald* II, 140; *Heiðr* 1672, 94, *FSN* 1, 441, 522, *Heiðr* 1873, 221, 321, *Heiðr* 1924, 31-2, 112, *FSGJ* 2, 21, *Heiðr* 1960, 18; *Edd. Min.* 19.

Notes: [3] *fullfeikn* 'destructive': Mss Hb and R715[x] read *fláráð* 'deceitful, false', but it is difficult to see why Angantýr should consider Hervǫr so. *Fullfeikn* also provides a verbal echo with *full feiknstafa* 'full of curses' in *Heiðr* 29/3. *Fláráð* is preferred in *Heiðr* 1873, 221 and *Edd. Min.*, however, while the eds of *CPB* (*CPB* I, 167) emend to *fáráð* and translate 'foolish'. *Skj* B and *Skald* print *fullfeikn*, as here. — [5-8]: Missing from Hb through damage to the fol. The text is supplied from the other mss and repeats ll. 5-8 of Angantýr Lv 4 (*Heiðr* 34) (see Note). The fact that the final word of the stanza is present in Hb and reads *skal* 'shall, must' (1st/3rd pers. sg. pres.) suggests that these lines were not the original ending to the stanza. — [7] *ætt* 'family': Probably omitted from 2845 by haplography; an abbreviation sign is used to represent *-ir* in the previous word, *mættir* 'are able'.

Hervǫr (Herv Lv 18)

44. Ek mun ganga   til gjálfrmara;
    nú er hilmis mær   í hugum góðum.
    Lítt ræki ek þat, lofðunga niðr,
    hvé synir mínir   síðan deila.

Ek mun ganga til gjálfrmara; nú er mær hilmis í góðum hugum. Ek ræki þat lítt, niðr lofðunga, hvé synir mínir deila síðan.

I will go to the sea-horses [SHIPS]; now the prince's girl is in good spirits. I care little, son of rulers, how my sons contend afterwards.

Mss: **Hb**(74v), 2845(65v) (ll. 1-7), R715[x](14v) (*Heiðr*).

Readings: [3] nú: mun *corrected from* nú *in the hand of JR* R715[x]; er hilmis: ei *corrected from* er hilmis *in the hand of JR* R715[x]   [4] hugum: huga 2845, hug R715[x]   [5] ræki ek: *so* 2845, R715[x], hræðumz Hb   [6] lofðunga: lofðunga *corrected from* lofðungit *in the scribal hand* Hb; niðr: vinr 2845, R715[x]   [7] hvé: hvat 2845, R715[x]; synir mínir: 's.' 2845.

Editions: *Skj*: Anonyme digte og vers [XIII], E. 5. *Vers af Fornaldarsagaer: Af Hervararsaga* III 20: AII, 249, BII, 269, *Skald* II, 140; *Heiðr* 1672, 94, *FSN* 1, 441, 522, *Heiðr* 1873, 221, 321, *Heiðr* 1924, 32, 112, *FSGJ* 2, 21, *Heiðr* 1960, 18-19; *Edd. Min.* 19.

Notes: [All]: A lacuna of one folio in 2845 begins part way through l. 7; the rest of the dialogue between Hervǫr and Angantýr is now lost from that ms. — [2] *gjálfrmara* 'the sea-horses [SHIPS]': Verelius emended (quite unnecessarily) to *-manna* 'sea-men, sailors' (*Heiðr* 1672, 94). Though this exact cpd *gjálfrmara* is unique in poetry, similar kennings occurr in *Pl* 48/8[VII] (*gjalfrhestr* 'sea-stallion'), *Bǫlv Hardr* 8/3[II] (*gjalfrstóð* 'surge-steed') and *HHund I* 30/7 (*gjalfrdýr* 'sea-beast'). — [5] *ek ræki* 'I care': Mss 2845 and R715[x] are in agreement on this reading, similarly preferred by *Skj* B and *Skald*, against Hb's *hræðumz* 'I fear', which also gives good sense. Either reading is possible metrically. — [7-8]: Hervǫr goes on to have two sons, the good-natured and popular

Angantýr and the trouble-making Heiðrekr, who is sent away to be fostered. There is no indication of sibling 'contention' until Heiðrekr kills his brother with an indiscriminately-thrown stone. Tyrfingr is not involved in that trouble. Tolkien (*Heiðr* 1960, xi) suggests a now-lost account of strife between them may have once existed. Hervǫr's grandsons, on the other hand, the sons of Heiðrekr, contend over their inheritance in what becomes a battle between nations, resulting in one brother slaying the other (cf. Schück 1918, 79; *Heiðr* 1960, xi and n. 3).

Angantýr (Angantýr Lv 10)

45. Þú skalt eiga   ok una lengi;
    hafðu á huldu   Hjálmars bana.
    Takattu á eggjum, eitr er í báðum;
    sá er manns mjötuðr meini verri.

Þú skalt eiga ok una lengi; hafðu bana Hjálmars á huldu. Takattu á eggjum, eitr er í báðum; sá er mjötuðr manns, verri meini.

You shall own and enjoy [it] for a long time; keep the slayer of Hjálmarr [= Tyrfingr] in its sheath. Do not touch the edges, poison is in both; that is the ruin of a man, worse than disease.

Mss: **Hb**(74v), R715[x](14v) (*Heiðr*).

Readings: [5] Takattu: taktu R715[x] [7] mjötuðr: mataðr R715[x] [8] meini: miklu R715[x].

Editions: *Skj*: Anonyme digte og vers [XIII], E. 5. *Vers af Fornaldarsagaer: Af Hervararsaga* III 21: AII, 249, BII, 269, *Skald* II, 140; *Heiðr* 1672, 95, *FSN* 1, 441, 522, *Heiðr* 1873, 221, *Heiðr* 1924, 32, 112, *FSGJ* 2, 21-2, *Heiðr* 1960, 19; *Edd. Min.* 19.

Notes: [All]: This stanza does not seem to follow on from the previous one and may be misplaced from elsewhere in the poem. — [All]: This stanza is followed in R715[x] by the following:

Ek mun hirða   ok í hönd nema
hvassan mæki,   er mik hafa látið.
Uggik eigi þat, úlfa grennir,
hvat synir mínir síðan telja.

Prose Order: Ek mun hirða hvassan mæki ok nema í hönd, er látið mik hafa. Uggik þat eigi, grennir úlfa, hvat synir mínir telja síðan. *Translation*: I will guard the sharp sword and take it in hand, when I am allowed to have it. I do not fear, feeder of wolves [WARRIOR], what my sons reckon later. This seems to be the result of scribal confusion, since it comprises slightly variant versions of ll. 1-5 of Herv Lv 16 (*Heiðr* 40) and ll. 7-8 of Herv Lv 18 (*Heiðr* 44), with only l. 6 being new. Cf. Andrews (1920, 98), who suggests the stanza to be genuine, noting that repetition occurs elsewhere in the dialogue between Hervǫr and Angantýr and that its restoration 'would preserve the alternation of stanzas between the two speakers'; this alternation is not completely regular, however, and repetition does not occur elsewhere in the rest of the dialogue between Hervǫr and Angantýr to the same extent. — [3] *á huldu* 'in its sheath': Can also mean 'in secret, in hiding', but likely refers to the legend related earlier in the saga that Tyrfingr will cause a man's death every time it is unsheathed. — [4]: See Note to *Heiðr* 36/8. — [6] *eitr* 'poison': Hjálm Lv 4/8 (*Ǫrv* 14), which appears in the R and U redactions of *Heiðr*, describes Tyrfingr's tip as *herðr í eitri* 'hardened in poison' (see also Note there). In *Ket* 36/7 the edges of a sword are said to be *eitrherðar* 'poison-hardened' (see Note there), while *eitrblandinn* 'mixed with poison' is used of sword-edges in *HjǪ* 20/5 (and similarly, though not a cpd, in *Hyndl* 49/7).

Angantýr (Angantýr Lv 11)

46. Far vel, dóttir,   fljótt gæfa ek þér
     tólf manna fjör,   ef þú trúa mættir,
     afl ok eljun,   alt it góða,
     þat er synir Arngríms at sik leifðu.

Far vel, dóttir, ek gæfa þér fljótt fjör tólf manna, ef þú mættir trúa, afl ok eljun, alt it góða, þat er synir Arngríms leifðu at sik.

Farewell, daughter, I would readily give you the life of twelve men, if you are able to believe it, strength and energy, all the good that the sons of Arngrímr left after them.

Mss: **Hb**(74v marg), R715[x](14v) (*Heiðr*).

Readings: [2] gæfa: gef R715[x]   [7] þat: *om.* R715[x]   [8] at sik: eptir R715[x].

Editions: *Skj*: Anonyme digte og vers [XIII], E. 5. *Vers af Fornaldarsagaer: Af Hervararsaga* III 22: AII, 249, BII, 269, *Skald* II, 140; *Heiðr* 1672, 95, *FSN* 1, 442, 522, *Heiðr* 1873, 222, *Heiðr* 1924, 32-3, 113, *FSGJ* 2, 22, *Heiðr* 1960, 19; *Edd. Min.* 20.

Notes: [3] *fjör tólf manna* 'the life of twelve men': The number twelve had a general significance since a duodecimal counting system was employed in medieval Scandinavia intermingled with a decimal system (Karker 1974), but this instance seems to refer specifically to the sons of Arngrímr. — [4] *ef þú mættir trúa* 'if you are able to believe it': The same half-line occurs in *Heiðr* 34/6 and 43/6 (but see Note to *Heiðr* 43/5-8). — [5] *afl ok eljun* 'strength and energy': The same alliterating half-line is used in *Rþ* 44/5 and Anon *Hsv* 117/1[VII].

Hervǫr (Herv Lv 19)

47. Búi þér allir   — brótt fýsir mik —
    heilir í haugi;   heðan vil ek skjótla.
    Helzt þóttumz nú   heima í millim,
    er mik umhverfis   eldar brunnu.

Búi þér allir heilir í haugi; fýsir mik brótt; ek vil heðan skjótla. Þóttumz nú helzt í millim heima, er eldar brunnu umhverfis mik.

Dwell, all of you, safe in the mound; I long to be away; I wish to go from here quickly. I thought myself now most of all to be between worlds, where fires burned all around me.

Mss: **Hb**(74v), R715ˣ(14v) (*Heiðr*).

Readings: [2] fýsir: mun R715ˣ;   mik: ek skjótla R715ˣ   [4] vil ek: fýsir mik R715ˣ;   skjótla: *om*. R715ˣ   [5] nú: ek R715ˣ   [6] millim: milli R715ˣ   [7] umhverfis: 'vmheerfis' R715ˣ.

Editions: *Skj*: Anonyme digte og vers [XIII], E. 5. *Vers af Fornaldarsagaer: Af Hervararsaga* III 23: AII, 250, BII, 269-70, *Skald* II, 140; *Heiðr* 1672, 95, *FSN* 1, 442, 522, *Heiðr* 1873, 222, *Heiðr* 1924, 33, 113, *FSGJ* 2, 22, *Heiðr* 1960, 19; *Edd. Min*. 20.

Note: [5-8]: Hervǫr finally admits she is disturbed by the supernatural fires, despite her earlier words to the contrary in *Heiðr* 23/1-4, 33/1-4 and 40/5-8.

Introduction to sts 48-85, *Heiðreks gátur*

The following group of thirty-eight stanzas comprises a collection of riddles sometimes referred to in modern scholarship as *Heiðreks gátur* 'Riddles of Heiðrekr' (Gestumbl Heiðr 1-37 (*Heiðr* 48-84)), plus one response (Heiðrekr, *Heiðr* 38 (*Heiðr* 85); the other responses are in prose). Within *Heiðr*, the riddles are set in the context of a contest between the eponymous Heiðrekr, now a powerful, wealthy and popular king, and a man whom he believes to be his enemy Gestumblindi. The name appears as *Gestr inn blindi* 'the blind stranger' in the U redaction, and Wessén (1924, 543-8) argues that *Gestumblindi* is a contraction of this (cf. *ÍO: Gestumblindi* and Note to Þul *Óðins* 7/8^(III)). The soubriquet would be an appropriate one for the one-eyed god Óðinn, whom Heiðrekr's opponent turns out to be; *Gestumblindi* also occurs as an Óðinn-*heiti* in Þul *Óðins* 7/8^(III). The corresponding name in Saxo (*Saxo* 2015, I, v. 10. 1, pp. 332-5) is Gestiblindus, a king of Götaland. As Gestumblindi is replaced by Óðinn in a wisdom-contest in *Heiðr*, Gestiblindus is replaced by a more able hero, Eiríkr, in a duel, in Saxo, but other details of the plot do not correspond to those of *Heiðr*.

In *Heiðr*, King Heiðrekr has called Gestumblindi to his court to submit to judgement for his crimes, but offers him the option of redeeming himself by propounding riddles, on the understanding that he will be pardoned if he is able to ask a question the king is unable to solve. Gestumblindi, knowing he has little chance of success, sacrifices to Óðinn – well known from other texts as a participant in poetic wisdom contests – and the god goes to Heiðrekr's court in his place. There is thus not a great deal of suspense as to the outcome during the propounding of the riddles, and eventually Óðinn wins by asking what would not now be considered a true riddle, since it relies on information known only to the questioner (on the so-called 'neck riddle' see Taylor 1951, 1): he asks what Óðinn – i.e. he himself – spoke into the ear of his son Baldr at the latter's funeral. Óðinn also uses this get-out clause in a wisdom contest with the giant Vafþrúðnir in the eddic poem *Vafþrúðnismál* (*Vafþr*).

The riddles themselves take various forms, but all are relatively simple, having between six and eight lines plus a two-line *fornyrðislag stef* at the end of the main part of the stanza: *Heiðrekr konungr | hyggðu at gátu*, 'King Heiðrekr, consider the riddle', usually heavily abbreviated or omitted altogether in the mss. Lines 1-4 of riddle 7/1-4 are *ljóðaháttr* half-lines, riddle 12 is a mixture of *ljóðaháttr* and *fornyrðislag*, 16 a mixture of *ljóðaháttr* and *málaháttr*, 17 and 29 a mixture of *fornyrðislag* and *málaháttr*, 37 is *málaháttr*, and 27-8, 31, 33 and 35 are *fornyrðislag*; the rest are *ljóðaháttr*. The objects described in each riddle never speak for themselves, as they do in many of the Old English Exeter Book riddles (ed. Krapp and Dobbie 1936), although several have a first-person speaker describing something seen or experienced. Also in contrast to the Old English riddles, the *Heiðr* riddles (except of course the last) are accompanied by their solutions, in the form of Heiðrekr's prose responses. The majority describe natural phenomena, although eight have man-made objects as solutions, and two, in addition to the Baldr-riddle, refer to mythological beings. Most are straightforwardly descriptive, though a few involve more complex word-play or poetic devices (e.g. *ofljóst*, riddle 35 (*Heiðr* 82), *greppaminni*, riddle 7 (*Heiðr* 54)) and one or two are somewhat obscure (e.g. 'a dead serpent on an ice-floe', riddle 25 (*Heiðr* 72)).

It is commonly stated that the *Heiðr* riddles are the only riddles among the entire Old Norse corpus; and moreover, that there is no mention in the sagas or other texts of riddles being asked, whereas parallel evidence exists for story-telling, poetry-reciting, and other forms of entertainment (*Heiðr* 1960, xix). It has also been suggested, partly for these reasons, that the riddles were composed specifically for the saga (Hall 2005, 10). However, an alternative case can be made. While it is true, and rather curious, that there is little other evidence for the propounding of riddles as riddles (ON *gátur*), they have close analogues in the eddic corpus and in wisdom poetry in particular (Burrows 2014), and some have parallels in riddles known from other cultures (e.g. 12 (*Heiðr* 59), 29 (*Heiðr* 76): see Notes to these riddles). Three quite separate riddles survive in a ms. from c. 1400 and are edited in *SkP* III (Anon *Gát* 1-3[III]). Moreover, although they have basic similarities the *Heiðr* riddles are rather eclectic as a group, giving the impression of having been gathered together from disparate sources.

The ms. transmission of the riddles is complex. Hb, the main ms. for the poetry in the early part of the saga, has a lacuna after the first three riddles, and the rest of the saga is lost. However, Hb, or selections from it, appears to have been copied (rather badly) when it was in a less-damaged state, and although this intermediary is now lost, two seventeenth-century paper copies of it, AM 281 4°ˣ (281ˣ) and AM 597b 4°ˣ (597bˣ), preserve the H redaction's version of the riddle-contest, a total of 36 riddles (all those edited here but 23; 10, 11, 13, 15, 31 and 34 are exclusive to the H redaction). Since these mss are late, and their common exemplar seems to have been a poor copy, 2845 is usually preferable where there is overlapping material and is the main ms. where this is the case. It contains only thirty of the riddles, however (omitting 7, 10, 11, 13, 15, 31 and 34). Ms. 203ˣ follows the order of the R redaction, but its text is also influenced by the H redaction for the first eight riddles as they appear in H, and thus has independent significance after the lacuna in Hb (*Heiðr* 1924, xxx). R715ˣ contains 28 riddles (omitting those 2845 omits, plus 29 and 35).

As well as the differing numbers of riddles between the redactions, they are also differently ordered. The H redaction has the most logical order, grouping riddles with similar beginnings together; R715ˣ and 2845 often place riddles with similar subject matter next to one another, but any pattern when the subject matter is different is difficult to discern. For this reason and because it contains the most riddles, H's ordering is followed here. The arrangement of the riddles in the three redactions is shown in the Table below (and cf. Burrows 2014). The table follows the order of the H redaction and this edition (so that 1 = Gestumbl *Heiðr* 1, 2 = Gestumbl *Heiðr* 2 and so forth) and indicates the order of the riddles in the other redactions in comparison. The symbol '✗' indicates that a riddle does not appear at all in that redaction.

TABLE 1
Disposition of riddles across the H, R and U redactions (from Burrows 2014)

H (281ˣ and 597bˣ; only first three in Hb)	R (2845)	U (R715ˣ)
1 Ale	1 Ale	1 Ale
2 Paths	2 Paths	2 Paths
3 Dew	3 Dew	3 Dew
4 Hammer	4 Hammer	4 Hammer
5 Fog	9 Bellows	22 Waves
6 Anchor	14 Spider	23 Waves
7 Raven, dew, fish, waterfall	✗	✗
8 Leek	8 Leek	21 Waves
9 Bellows	16 Obsidian	20 Ptarmigans
10 Hail	✗	✗
11 Dung beetle	✗	✗
12 Pregnant sow	17 Swan	14 Spider
13 Arrow	✗	✗
14 Spider	18 Angelica	8 Leek
15 Sun	✗	✗

16 Obsidian	25 Dead snake on an ice-floe	18 Angelica
17 Swan	32 Ítrekr & Andaðr	32 Ítrekr & Andaðr
18 Angelica	19 *Hnefatafl* pieces	19 *Hnefatafl* pieces
19 *Hnefatafl* pieces	30 Fire	26 *Húnn* in *hnefatafl*
20 Ptarmigans	5 Fog	16 Obsidian
21 Waves	26 *Húnn* in *hnefatafl*	30 Fire
22 Waves	27 Shield	5 Fog
✗	20 Ptarmigans	24 Waves
24 Waves	22 Waves	6 Anchor
25 Dead snake on an ice-floe	21 Waves	9 Bellows
26 *Húnn* in *hnefatafl*	23 Waves	17 Swan
27 Shield	28 Duck nesting in a skull	25 Dead snake on an ice-floe
28 Duck nesting in a skull	6 Anchor	28 Duck nesting in a skull
29 Cow	24 Waves	✗
30 Fire	33 Piglets	27 Shield
31 Horse & mare	✗	✗
32 Ítrekr & Andaðr	12 Pregnant sow	33 Piglets
33 Piglets	29 Cow	12 Pregnant sow
34 Embers	✗	✗
35 *ofljóst* riddle (natural phenomena)	35 *ofljóst* riddle (natural phenomena)	✗
36 Óðinn & Sleipnir	36 Óðinn & Sleipnir	36 Óðinn & Sleipnir
37 ? (Baldr riddle)	37 ? (Baldr riddle)	37 ? (Baldr riddle)

The riddles' later ms. history is also interesting. As 281^x and 597b^x show, the riddle episode was sometimes extracted and copied independently of the rest of the saga. In addition to the mss containing *Heiðr* noted in the Introduction to the saga, varying numbers of the riddles are found in: Adv 21 5 2^x, AM 65 a 8^{ox}, AM 167 b 3 8^{ox}, AM 738 4^{ox}, BLAdd 4866^x, BLAdd 4877^x, BLAdd 6121^x, BLAdd 11165^x, BLAdd 11174^x, BSG 3717^x, Holm papp 34 4^{ox} (including Latin translations), Lbs 214 4^{ox}, Lbs 522 4^{ox}, Lbs 631 4^{ox}, Lbs 636 4^{ox}, Lbs 756 4^{ox}, Lbs 818 4^{ox}, Lbs 1199 4^{ox}, Lbs 1562 4^{ox}, Lbs 1588 4^{ox}, NKS 1866 4^{ox}, NKS 1869 4^{ox}, NKS 1873 4^{ox}, NKS 1891 4^{ox}, OsloUB 310 4^{ox}, Oslo UB 547 4^{ox}, SÁM 51^x, SÁM 72^x, Thott 773 a fol^x, Thott 1492 4^{ox}, Thott 1499 4^{ox}, TCD 1027^x, and UppsUB R 692^x. They are often accompanied by the three *ofljóst* riddles Anon *Gát* 1-3^{III} and the poems of the so-called Poetic Edda. Although none of these later mss have independent value as textual witnesses for *Heiðreks gátur*, they demonstrate that the riddles were valued in their own right, often in learned contexts, which is also witnessed by the appearance of the first three lines of Gestumbl *Heiðr* 25 (*Heiðr* 72) in *TGT* and a commentary on the riddles (mostly following the version of the R redaction) written in 1641 by Björn Jónsson á Skarðsá, a scholar and annalist (the commentary is edited by Lavender 2015b).

The riddles have been edited in all the editions of *Heiðr* listed in the Introduction to the saga, in *Edd. Min.*, 106-20 and in Ettmüller 1861, 35-40 (based on *FSN* I, 409-512 and Petersen and Thorarensen 1847). *Skj* and *Skald* follow the order of the R redaction and present the additional riddles in the H redaction at the end.

Gestumblindi (Gestumbl *Heiðr* 1)

48. Hafa vildak þat,   er ek hafða í gær;
    vittu, hvat þat var:
    lýða lemill,   orða tefill,
    ok orða upphefill.
    Heiðrekr konungr,   hyggðu at gátu.

Vildak hafa þat, er ek hafða í gær; vittu, hvat þat var: lemill lýða, tefill orða, ok upphefill orða. Heiðrekr konungr, hyggðu at gátu.

I would wish to have what I had yesterday; find out what that was: crippler of people, hinderer of words, and instigator of words. King Heiðrekr, think about the riddle.

Mss: **Hb**(76v), 2845(70v), 281ˣ(99r), 597bˣ(49r), 203ˣ(101ra), R715ˣ(26v) (*Heiðr*).

Readings: [1] Hafa: '[…]afa' 281ˣ;   vildak: *so* 2845, ek þat vilda Hb, 597bˣ, ek þat vilda *corrected from* ek þat vildu 281ˣ, mundak 203ˣ, vil ek dag þat R715ˣ;   þat: *so* 2845, 203ˣ, R715ˣ, *om.* Hb, 281ˣ, 597bˣ   [2] er: *om.* 2845, 203ˣ, R715ˣ;   ek: *om.* 2845, 203ˣ, R715ˣ;   hafða í gær: í gær hafða 2845, 203ˣ, í gær hafðak R715ˣ   [3] vittu: *so* 2845, 203ˣ, R715ˣ, konungr gettu Hb, konungr gettu til 281ˣ, 597bˣ;   hvat: 'huort' R715ˣ;   var: verk R715ˣ   [4] lemill: 's(?)emill' 203ˣ, lemill *corrected from* 'lemin' *in the hand of JR* R715ˣ   [6] orða: *so* 2845, 281ˣ, 597bˣ, 203ˣ, ok orða Hb, R715ˣ   [7]: *abbrev. as* 'H: k:' R715ˣ.

Editions: *Skj*: Anonyme digte og vers [XIII], D. 5. *Heiðreks gátur* 1: AII, 221, BII, 240, *Skald* II, 124, *NN* §792; *Heiðr* 1672, 143, *FSN* 1, 465, 533, *Heiðr* 1873, 235, 333, *Heiðr* 1924, 57, 130, *FSGJ* 2, 37-8, *Heiðr* 1960, 32-3; *Edd. Min.* 106.

Context: See Introduction to *Heiðr* 48-85. Hb elaborates on the setting (*Heiðr* 1924, 56): *Var síðan stóll settr undir Gestumblinda, ok hugðu menn gótt til at heyra þar vitrleg orð* 'Then a stool was set under Gestumblindi, and men thought it good to hear wise words there'.

Notes: [All]: Heiðrekr's response reads (*Heiðr* 1960, 33): *Færi honum mungát! Þat lemr margra vit, ok margir eru þá margmálgari, er mungát ferr á, en sumum vefsk tungan, svá at ekki verðr at orði* 'Bring him ale! That cripples the wit of many, and many are more talkative, when ale goes in, but with some the tongue becomes tied, so that no words come to them'. It is probably significant that the first riddle concerns ale, which 'seems to be a requirement for a wisdom performance' (Lindow 2007b, 299) and is also consumed by Óðinn at the beginning of *Grí* and *Vafþr.* — [1]: Ms. R715[x] reads *hafa vil ek dag*, emended to *hafa vil eg i dag* 'I wish to have today' by Verelius (*Heiðr* 1672, 143). This is likely a misreading of *vildak* (*Heiðr* 1924, 130 n. 2), probably patterned on *í gær* 'yesterday' in l. 2. — [2]: Similar to Gestumbl *Heiðr* 3/2 (*Heiðr* 50). — [2] *ek* 'I': Describing the referent as something the riddler has experienced is a convention occurring in several riddling traditions of Indo-European origin (West 2007, 366-7). Cf. Gestumbl *Heiðr* 2, 3, 8-16, 25, 31, 33-5 (*Heiðr* 49, 50, 55-63, 72, 78, 80-2). — [4-5]: These lines lack alliteration, though they have end-rhyme which carries on into l. 6. Kock emends *lýða* 'of people' to *óða* 'of minds', noting (*NN* §792) that this corresponds semantically with Heiðrekr's prose response: *þat lemr margra vit* 'that paralyses the wit of many'. He also suggests in *NN* that *ýta* 'of men' would produce satisfactory alliteration and a similar meaning to the ms. readings, but without the correspondence with the prose. These are purely conjectural suggestions, however. *Lemill* 'crippler' and *tefill* 'hinderer' are *hap. leg.*, from *lemja* 'thrash, beat, disable' and *tefja* 'hinder' respectively. — [6] *upphefill* 'instigator': A *hap. leg.*, from *upphefja*, lit. 'raise up'.

Gestumblindi (Gestumbl *Heiðr* 2)

49. Heiman ek fór,   heiman ek för gerðak,
        sá ek á veg vega;
     vegr var undir   ok vegr yfir,
        ok vegr á alla vega.
     Heiðrekr konungr,   hyggðu at gátu.

Ek fór heiman, ek gerðak för heiman, ek sá vega á veg; vegr var undir ok vegr yfir, ok vegr á alla vega. Heiðrekr konungr, hyggðu at gátu.

I went from home, I made a journey from home, I saw ways on the way; a way was under and a way over, and a way on all ways. King Heiðrekr, think about the riddle.

Mss: **Hb**(76v), 2845(70v), 281[x](99r) (ll. 2-8), 597b[x](49r) (ll. 2-8), 203[x](101r), R715[x](26v) (*Heiðr*).

Readings: [1] fór: *om*. 2845, heiman fór 203[x]   [2] heiman: *so all others*, 'hemian' Hb;   för: ferr 597b[x], ferð 203[x];   gerðak: gerða 2845, í dag 281[x], 597b[x], gærdag R715[x]   [3] vega: *so* 2845, 281[x], 597b[x], R715[x], 'w[…]g[…]' Hb, 'vega war þenn' 203[x]   [4] undir: þeim vegr undir 2845, þar vegr undir R715[x]   [5] ok: *om*. R715[x];   vegr: *om*. 281[x], yfir 597b[x];   yfir: vegr í *corrected from* vegr *in the margin in another hand* 597b[x]   [6] ok: *om*. 281[x], R715[x];   á: var 281[x], um *corrected from* á *in the margin in another hand* 597b[x];   alla: *om*. 597b[x];   vega: vega *corrected from* vegr 2845, vegu 281[x], vegr 597b[x]   [8] hyggðu ('hygg þú'): *so* 2845, 597b[x], 203[x], 'h.' Hb, hygg 281[x], 'h:' R715[x];   gátu: gátum 2845, 'g:' R715[x].

Editions: *Skj*: Anonyme digte og vers [XIII], D. 5. Heiðreks gátur 2: AII, 221, BII, 240, *Skald* II, 124; *Heiðr* 1672, 143; *FSN* 1, 465-6, 533, *Heiðr* 1873, 236, 333-4, *Heiðr* 1924, 57-8, 131, *FSGJ* 2, 38, *Heiðr* 1960, 33; *Edd. Min*. 106-7.

Notes: [All]: King Heiðrekr's response reads (*Heiðr* 1960, 33): *þar fórtu yfir árbrú, ok var árvegr undir þér, en fuglar flugu yfir hǫfði þér ok hjá þér tveim megin, ok var þat þeira vegr* 'There you went over a river-bridge, and the river-way was under you, and birds flew over your head and next to you on both sides, and that was their way'. Hb adds (*Heiðr* 1924, 58): *þú sátt lax í ánni, ok var þat hans vegr* 'you saw a salmon in the river, and that was his way', but this is superfluous since the *árvegr* 'river-way' has already been mentioned. Tolkien (*Heiðr* 1960, 33 n. 3) suggests that l. 6 may refer to the 'Earth-way', so that each riddling-line refers to one of river, sky, earth. But as he also notes, there is no extant textual evidence for this possibility. — [1-2]: As Tolkien (*Heiðr* 1960, 33 n. 2) notes, these lines are paralleled in *Fj* 46/1-2 (Guðni Jónsson 1949-54, II, 533): *Hvaðan þú fórt, | hvaðan þú fǫr gerðir* 'From where have you come, | from where have you made your journey'?

Gestumblindi (Gestumbl *Heiðr* 3)

50. Hvat er þat drykkja,   er ek drakk í gær?
    Var þat ei vín né vatn,
mjǫðr né mungát,   né matar ekki;
þó gekk ek þorstalauss þaðan.
Heiðrekr konungr,   hyggðu at gátu.

Hvat drykkja er þat, er ek drakk í gær? Þat var ei vín né vatn, mjǫðr né mungát, né ekki matar; þó gekk ek þorstalauss þaðan. Heiðrekr konungr, hyggðu at gátu.

What kind of drink is that which I drank yesterday? It was not wine or water, mead or ale, or any kind of food; yet I went thirstless from there. King Heiðrekr, think about the riddle.

Mss: **2845**(70v), 281[x](99r), 597b[x](49r), 203[x](101va), R715[x](27r) (*Heiðr*).

Readings: [1] drykkja: *so* 281[x], 597b[x], drykk í *or* drykki 2845, drykkju 203[x], drykkjar R715[x]   [2] er: *om*. R715[x]   [3] Var þat ei: var þat ekki 281[x], 597b[x], varat þat 203[x]   [4] mjǫðr: *so* 281[x], 597b[x], 203[x], né enn heldr 2845, *om*. R715[x]; né: *om*. 2845   [5] ekki: nokkut R715[x]   [6] þó: *so* 281[x], 597b[x], 203[x], ok 2845, *om*. R715[x]; þorstalauss: *so* 281[x], 597b[x], 'þosta la/ss' 2845, 'þostlaust' 203[x], 'þosta laus' R715[x]; þaðan: *so all others*, 'þadad' 2845   [7]: *so* 203[x], *abbrev. as* 'h k̄' 2845, *abbrev. as* 'H: k:' 281[x], *abbrev. as* 'heidr K:' 597b[x], *abbrev. as* 'H k:' R715[x]   [8]: *so* 597b[x], 203[x], *abbrev. as* 'h þ at ḡ' 2845, *abbrev. as* 'h· þu: ad g·' 281[x], *abbrev. as* 'h: at gatu' R715[x].

Editions: *Skj*: Anonyme digte og vers [XIII], D. 5. *Heiðreks gátur* 3: AII, 221-2, BII, 240, *Skald* II, 125; *Heiðr* 1672, 144, *FSN* 1, 466, *Heiðr* 1873, 236-7, 334, *Heiðr* 1924, 58-9, 131, *FSGJ* 2, 38-9, *Heiðr* 1960, 33; *Edd. Min.* 107.

Notes: [All]: Heiðrekr's response reads (*Heiðr* 1960, 34): *þar lagðisk þú í forsælu, er dǫgg var fallin á grasi, ok kœldir svá varrir þínar ok stǫðvaðir svá þorsta þinn* 'There you laid yourself down in the shade, where dew had fallen on the grass, and you thus cooled your lips and so quenched your thirst'. The H redaction adds (*Heiðr* 1924, 59): *En ef þú ert sá Gestumblindi, sem ek ætlaða, þá ertu vitrari en ek hugða, því at ek hefi spurt orð þín óvitrleg, en geraz nú á leið spaklega* 'But if you are that Gestumblindi that I expected, you are wiser than I thought, because I have heard your words [to be] without wit, but they take now a wise course'. Cf. Gestumbl *Heiðr* 12 (*Heiðr* 59), whose solution begins with similar wording. — [All]: *Vsp* 45 (*NK* 53) states that Líf and Lífþrasir, the survivors of Ragnarǫk, will be nourished by *morgindǫgg* 'morning dew'. — [1] *hvat drykkja* 'what kind of drink': Lit. 'what of drinks'; cf. Gestumbl *Heiðr* 8-16/1 (*Heiðr* 55-63). — [2]: Similar to Gestumbl *Heiðr* 1/2 (*Heiðr* 48). — [4]: The reading of 281[x] and 597b[x] is preferred on metrical grounds over that of 2845, *né enn heldr mungát* 'nor yet ale either', in accordance with other eds. — [4] *mungát* 'ale': A maltose-based alcoholic drink. Although sometimes translated 'small beer' (*CVC*: *mungát*), *mungát* seems to have been a strong ale (see further Guerrero Rodríguez 2007, 33-8). — [6] *þorstalauss* 'thirstless': A *hap. leg.* in poetry.

Gestumblindi (Gestumbl *Heiðr* 4)

51. Hverr er sá inn hvelli,   er gengr harðar götur,
    ok hefir hann þær fyrr um farit?
    Mjök fast kyssir,   sá er hefr munna tvá
    ok á gulli einu gengr.
    Heiðrekr konungr,   hyggðu at gátu.

Hverr er sá inn hvelli, er gengr harðar götur ok hefir hann þær fyrr um farit? Mjök fast kyssir, sá er hefr tvá munna ok gengr á gulli einu. Heiðrekr konungr, hyggðu at gátu.

Who is that shrill one who walks on hard paths and he has travelled on them before? Very firmly [he] kisses, the one who has two mouths, and walks on gold alone. King Heiðrekr, think about the riddle.

Mss: **2845**(71r), R715[x](27r), 281[x](99r) (ll. 1-6), 597b[x](49r) (ll. 1-6), 203[x](102ra) (*Heiðr*).

Readings: [2] gengr: gengr um R715[x]   [3] þær fyrr: *so* 281[x], 597b[x], 203[x], fyrrum 2845, R715[x]   [5] sá er: sá R715[x], ok 281[x], 597b[x], 203[x]   [6] ok: sá er 281[x], 597b[x], 203[x];   gulli einu: 'gullheine' 281[x], 'gullheine' *corrected from* 'gullheinu' *in another hand* 597b[x]   [7-8]: *so* 203[x], *abbrev. as* 'h kr. h.' 2845, *abbrev. as* 'H k h: at g:' R715[x].

Editions: *Skj*: Anonyme digte og vers [XIII], D. 5. Heiðreks gátur 4: AII, 222, BII, 240-1, *Skald* II, 125; *Heiðr* 1672, 144, *FSN* 1, 467, *Heiðr* 1873, 238, 334, *Heiðr* 1924, 59-60, 131, *FSGJ* 2, 39, *Heiðr* 1960, 34; *Edd. Min.* 107.

Context: In the H redaction (including 203[x]), before propounding the riddle Gestumblindi says, in response to Heiðrekr's comment after the previous riddle (see Gestumbl *Heiðr* 3 (*Heiðr* 50) Note to [All]) (*Heiðr* 1924, 59): *þat er ván at mik þrjóti brátt, en þó vilda ek enn, at þér hlýðið* 'The expectation is that they [i.e. words] will fail me soon, but yet I still wish that you would listen'.

Notes: [All]: Heiðrekr's response reads (*Heiðr* 1960, 34): *þat er hamarr sá, er hafðr er at gullsmíð; hann kveðr hátt við, er hann kømr á harðan steðja, ok þat er hans gata* 'that is that hammer, which is used in goldsmithing; he shrieks loudly when he comes down onto the hard anvil, and that is his path'. — [1] *hverr er sá inn ...* 'who is that ...': Lit. 'Who is that, the ...'. This formula also begins the following two riddles, as well as Gestumbl *Heiðr* 30 (*Heiðr* 77). A similar formula occurs in *Lok* 44/1 (*NK* 105) *Hvat er þat ið litla* 'What is that, the little one'. The stanza, which is riddling in form, describes Freyr's servant Byggvir, who replies, identifying himself, in the following stanza. — [3] *þær fyrr* 'on them before': The reading of 281[x] and 597b[x] is preferred in accordance with most other eds. — [5] *tvá munna* 'two mouths': Archaeological finds and pictorial depictions across Scandinavia and the North from the C9th to C12th are consistent in revealing that hammers, both practical smiths' tools and ceremonial instruments, such as the so-called Thor's hammers, were symmetrical in the shape of a T or (particularly in symbolic depictions) an elongated cross. Each side of its double-head is described as a 'mouth' in the present riddle. See, for example, the depiction of Weland (ON Vǫlundr) on the front panel of the Franks Casket (Anglo-Saxon, C8th Northumbrian); that of Reginn the smith, foster-father of Sigurðr, on the church at Hylestad, Norway (c. 1200); the Viking Age tool-chest found at Mästermyr, Gotland, Sweden (e.g. Arwidsson and Berg 1983); for Thor's hammers see e.g. Staecker (1999), Perkins (2001); on finds of possible smiths' graves see e.g. Wallander (1989).

Gestumblindi (Gestumbl *Heiðr* 5)

52. Hverr er sá inn mikli,   er líðr mold yfir?
       Svelgr hann vötn ok við;
    glygg hann óaz,   en gumna eigi,
       ok yrkir á sól til saka.
    Heiðrekr konungr,   hyggðu at gátu.

Hverr er sá inn mikli, er líðr yfir mold? Hann svelgr vötn ok við; hann óaz glygg, en eigi gumna, ok yrkir á sól til saka. Heiðrekr konungr, hyggðu at gátu.

Who is that, the great one, who moves over the earth? He swallows lakes and wood; he fears the wind, but not men, and sets upon the sun to harm [it]. King Heiðrekr, think about the riddle.

Mss: **2845**(71v), R715[x](28v) (ll. 1-6), 281[x](99r), 597b[x](49r), 203[x](104va) (*Heiðr*).

Readings: [2] líðr: ferr 281[x], 597b[x], 203[x]   [3] Svelgr: 'sulgir' R715[x];   vötn: vatn R715[x];   við: viðu R715[x], veisur 281[x], 597b[x]   [4] glygg: *so* 281[x], 597b[x], 'glug' 2845, 203[x], 'glÿs' R715[x];   óaz ('oast'): óast *corrected from* 'öas[...]' *in the hand of JR* R715[x]   [5] gumna: dóma 281[x], 'goma' *corrected from* guma *in the margin in another hand* 597b^x;   eigi: 'eÿ' *corrected from* 'ei[…]' *in the hand of JR* R715^x, ei 281^x, 597b^x [6] ok yrkir á sól: 'og irkir a sol og irkja a sok' R715^x [7-8]: *abbrev. as* 'h k h a G' 2845, *abbrev. as* 'heidr·· k: higg at g.' 281^x, *abbrev. as* 'h. K h. þ ad g:' 597b^x, 'h. k. h ad G' 203^x.

Editions: *Skj*: Anonyme digte og vers [XIII], D. 5. *Heiðreks gátur* 15: AII, 224, BII, 243, *Skald* II, 126; *Heiðr* 1672, 147, *FSN* 1, 474-5, *Heiðr* 1873, 238-9, 338-9, *Heiðr* 1924, 60-1, 70, 135, *FSGJ* 2, 44, *Heiðr* 1960, 38; *Edd. Min.* 108.

Notes: [All]: Heiðrekr's response is (*Heiðr* 1960, 38-9): *þat er myrkvi; hann líðr yfir jǫrðina, svá at ekki sér fyrir honum ok eigi sól, en hann er af, þegar vind gerir á* 'that is fog: he moves over the earth, so that one cannot see because of him, and the sun cannot [be seen], but he is off, as soon as the wind gets up'. The H redaction (including 203^x) adds (*Heiðr* 1924, 61): *ok megu menn ekki at honum gera; hann drepr skíni sólar. En vélasamlega berr þú upp slíkar gátur ok vandmæli, hverr sem þú ert* 'and men cannot do anything with him; he kills the shining of the sun. But you offer up such riddles and difficult questions craftily, whoever you are'. — [2]: A similar phrase occurs in Gestumbl *Heiðr* 20/2 (*Heiðr* 67) and *Vafþr* 48/5. — [3] *við* 'wood': Mss 281^x and 597b^x have *veisur* 'pools, puddles, swamps' here. — [4, 5] *óaz … eigi* 'fears … not': In R715^x the original readings have been obscured by the corrector, in the first instance because of overwriting, in the second because of deletion.

Gestumblindi (Gestumbl *Heiðr* 6)

53. Hverr er sá inn mikli,   er mǫrgu ræðr,
        ok horfir til heljar hálfr?
    *Öldum bergr   en við jǫrð sakaz,
        ef hann hefir sér vel traustan vin.
    Heiðrekr konungr,   hyggðu at gátu.

Hverr er sá inn mikli, er ræðr mǫrgu, ok horfir hálfr til heljar? Bergr *öldum en sakaz við jǫrð, ef hann hefir sér vel traustan vin. Heiðrekr konungr, hyggðu at gátu.

Who is that, the great one, who governs much, and half [of him] turns to Hel? He protects men but contends with the earth, if he has for himself a well-trusted friend. King Heiðrekr, think about the riddle.

Mss: 2845(72r), R715^x(28v) (ll. 1-6), 281^x(99r), 597b^x(49v), 203^x(106ra) (*Heiðr*).

Readings: [1] sá: *om.* R715^x [3] ok: *om.* 203^x;   horfir: horfir *corrected from* hverfir *in the margin in another hand* 597b^x [4] *Öldum: hölðum 2845, 281^x, 597b^x, 203^x, ýtum R715^x;   bergr: heitir bergr R715^x, hann bergr 281^x, 597b^x, 203^x [5] en: *so all others*, ok 2845;   við: *so all others*, *om.* 2845;   jǫrð: jǫrðu R715^x, hjǫrð 281^x, 597b^x, 'suðrð' 203^x;   sakaz: 'salast' R715^x [6] hann: *om.* R715^x;   sér: '[…]' R715^x [7-8]: *abbrev. as* 'h k' 2845, *abbrev. as* 'heidr: k: higg ad' 281^x, *abbrev. as* 'h: Kongur h: þu ad etc' *corrected from* 'h: Kongur h: þu etc' *in the margin in another hand* 597b^x, *abbrev. as* 'h. k. h. þ. a. Gatu' 203^x.

Editions: *Skj*: Anonyme digte og vers [XIII], D. 5. *Heiðreks gátur* 23: AII, 225-6, BII, 244, *Skald* II, 127, *NN* §2361; *Heiðr* 1672, 148, *FSN* 1, 480, *Heiðr* 1873, 239-40, 341, *Heiðr* 1924, 61-2, 78, 136, *FSGJ* 2, 47, *Heiðr* 1960, 41-2; *Edd. Min.* 108.

Notes: [All]: Heiðrekr's response is (*Heiðr* 1960, 42): *þat er akkeri með góðum streng; ef fleinn hans er í grunni, þá bergr þat* 'that is an anchor with a good rope; if his fluke is in the bed [of the sea etc.], then it is safe'. The H redaction has a longer explanation and adds (*Heiðr* 1924, 62): *En mjǫk undrumz ek orðfimi þína ok vitrleik* 'But I wonder greatly at your word-skill and wisdom'. — [3] *til heljar* 'to Hel': See Note to *Heiðr* 32/1. Here in the sense 'to the realm of the dead' (*LP:1. hel, Hel 1*), i.e. the fluke (ON *fleinn*) fastens into the bed of a body of water (*grunnr* in the prose solution) pointing downwards. Cf. Gestumbl *Heiðr* 8/4-5 (*Heiðr* 55), which describes a leek pointing *á helvega* 'towards the roads to Hel' with its head. — [4]: Cf. Gestumbl *Heiðr* 27/4 (*Heiðr* 74). — [4] **öldum* 'men': All the mss have a word meaning 'men' here, *ýtum* in the case of R715ˣ and *hǫlðum* in all the others, which lacks alliteration with the following line. Mss 281ˣ and 597bˣ achieve the alliteration with *hjǫrð* 'herd' for *jǫrð* in l. 5, but this makes little sense. Most eds, as here, emend to *ǫldum*. Cf. *Hym* 22/2 (*NK* 92): *sá er ǫldom bergr* 'that one who protects men', referring to the god Þórr in his fight with Miðgarðsormr. Kock retains *hǫlðum* and emends *jǫrð* to *hjarl* 'land' (*Skald*; *NN* §2361), which produces the desired meaning but is without ms. justification.

Gestumblindi (Gestumbl *Heiðr* 7)

54. Hverr byggir há fjöll?   Hverr fellr í djúpa dali?
    Hverr andalauss lifir?   Hverr æva þegir?
    Heiðrekr konungr,   hyggðu at gátu.

Hverr byggir há fjöll? Hverr fellr í djúpa dali? Hverr lifir andalauss? Hverr þegir æva? Heiðrekr konungr, hyggðu at gátu.

Who lives on high mountains? Who falls in the deep dales? Who lives without breath? Who is never silent? King Heiðrekr, think about the riddle.

Mss: **281ˣ**(99r-v), 597bˣ(49v), 203ˣ(107ra) (*Heiðr*).

Readings: [4] æva: æva *corrected from* æra *in the margin in another hand* 597bˣ [5-6]: *abbrev. as* 'heidr k higg' 281ˣ, *abbrev. as* 'h: K: h:' 597bˣ, *abbrev. as* 'h. k. h. etc. etc.' 203ˣ.

Editions: *Skj*: Anonyme digte og vers [XIII], D. 5. *Heiðreks gátur* 31: AII, 227, BII, 246, *Skald* II, 128; *FSN* 1, 482, *Heiðr* 1873, 240-1, *Heiðr* 1924, 62-3, *Heiðr* 1960, 80; *Edd. Min.* 108-9.

Context: Before propounding this riddle Gestumblindi says (*Heiðr* 1924, 62): *ek em nú ok nálega þrotinn at gátum, en frekr er hverr til fjǫrsins* 'I am now nearly out of riddles, but everyone is greedy for life', referring to his agreement with Heiðrekr that he must propound a riddle the king cannot solve in order to save his life.

Notes: [All]: Heiðrekr's response is (*Heiðr* 1924, 63): *hrafn byggir jafnan á hám fjǫllum, en dǫgg fellr jafnan í djúpa dali, fiskr lifir andalauss, en þjótandi fors þegir aldri* 'the raven always lives on high mountains, and dew always falls in the deep dales, the fish lives without breath, and the rushing waterfall is never silent'. The combination *dǫgg* and *dalr* appears to be a commonplace; cf. *Vsp* 19/5-6; *Vafþr* 14/6. — [All]: Lines 1-4 are in the form *greppaminni* 'poets' reminder', which uses a question-and-answer format. Cf. RvHbreiðm *Hl* 45/1-4[III], SnSt *Ht* 40[III]. In these other examples, the first four half-lines consist of questions, and the second four of answers. These lines correspond structurally to *ljóðaháttr* half-lines. Heiðrekr's rhythmical prose response shows signs that it may once have been in verse (*Heiðr* 1960, 80 n. 2), or that it was composed later by someone without full knowledge of the rules of metrical composition (Gade pers. comm.). On *greppaminni* see Vésteinn Ólason (1969). — [3] *andalauss* 'without breath': Found elsewhere in poetry only in another of the riddles, Gestumbl *Heiðr* 9/5 (*Heiðr* 56), where it refers to a smith's bellows. In the present context, cf. *Gylf* (*SnE* 2005, 28), which gives *anda fisksins* 'breath of the fish' alongside several seemingly impossible constituent parts of the dwarf-made fetter Gleipnir, used to tie up the mythical wolf Fenrir.

Gestumblindi (Gestumbl *Heiðr* 8)

55. Hvat er þat undra, er ek úti sá
    fyrir Dellings durum?
Höfði sínu vísar á helvega,
    en fótum til sólar snýr.
Heiðrekr konungr, hyggðu at gátu.

Hvat undra er þat, er ek sá úti fyrir durum Dellings? Vísar höfði sínu á helvega, en snýr fótum til sólar. Heiðrekr konungr, hyggðu at gátu.

What is the wonder that I saw outside before Dellingr's doors? It points its head towards the roads to Hel, but with its feet turns towards the sun. King Heiðrekr, think about the riddle.

Mss: **2845**(71r) (ll. 1-2, 4-8), 281[x](99v), 597b[x](49v), 203[x](102va-103ra), R715[x](27v) (ll. 1, 4-6) (*Heiðr*).

Readings: [1] þat: *om.* 203[x]; undra: 'vý' R715[x] [2] sá: *so* 281[x], 597b[x], 203[x], *om.* 2845 [3] Dellings: döglings 281[x], 597b[x], 203[x] [5] á helvega: helju til 281[x], 597b[x] [6] fótum: fótum sínum R715[x] [7-8]: *so* 203[x], *abbrev. as* 'h k h' 2845, *abbrev. as* 'h: k[r]. h:' 281[x], *abbrev. as* 'h: K: h þu ad g' 597b[x].

Editions: *Skj*: Anonyme digte og vers [XIII], D. 5. *Heiðreks gátur* 7: AII, 222, BII, 241, *Skald* II, 125; *Heiðr* 1672, 146, *FSN* 1, 469, *Heiðr* 1873, 241-2, 335-6, *Heiðr* 1924, 62-3, 133, *FSGJ* 2, 40, *Heiðr* 1960, 35; *Edd. Min.* 109.

Context: In the H redaction, before propounding the riddle Gestumblindi says (*Heiðr* 1924, 63): *Vandaz mun nú ... ok veitka ek nú, hvat fyrir verðr* 'It will get difficult now ... and I do not know now what will happen'.

Notes: [All]: Heiðrekr's response reads (*Heiðr* 1960, 35): *þat er laukr; hǫfuð hans er fast í jǫrðu, en hann kvíslar, er hann vex upp* 'That is the leek; his head is fast in the ground, but he branches out when he grows up'. The H redaction's version (including 203ˣ) corresponds more closely to the riddle itself, however (*Heiðr* 1924, 63): *þat er laukr; hǫfuð hans horfir í jǫrð, en blǫðin í lopt* 'that is the leek; his head turns into the earth, but his leaves into the sky'. On the use of leeks as a food and medicinal plant in medieval Scandinavia, see Guðrún P. Helgadóttir (1981). — [1-3]: These opening lines also occur in Gestumbl *Heiðr* 9-16 (*Heiðr* 56-63). Although this is the first occurrence in the H redaction, because of the different arrangement of the riddles in the other redactions, the present stanza is the third occasion on which this formula is used in 2845 and the second in R715ˣ, hence the heavy abbreviation in those mss. — [1]: Cf. l. 104 of the Old English poem *Solomon and Saturn II* (Anlezark 2009, 84): *Ac hwæt is ðæt wundor ...* 'But what is that wonder ...'. The Old English passage has a riddle-like structure and describes old age. Such abstract concepts are not represented among the *Heiðr* riddles. — [1] *hvat undra er þat* 'what is the wonder that': Lit. 'What of wonders is it'. Cf. Gestumbl *Heiðr* 3/1 (*Heiðr* 50) and Note. — [2]: See Note to Gestumbl *Heiðr* 1/2 (*Heiðr* 48) above. — [3]: The same line is found in *Hávm* 160/3 (*NK* 140), where the dwarf Þjóðreyrir is said to sing *fyr Dellings durom*. The pers. n. is also that of a dwarf in *Fj* 34/5. In *Vafþr* 25/1-2, however, Dellingr (lit. 'the shining one') is said to be the father of Dagr 'day'. Snorri gives further information in *Gylf* (*SnE* 2005, 13), which says that Dellingr *var ... Ása ættir* 'was of the family of the Æsir', and was married to Jǫrð (lit. 'Earth'), mother of Dagr, the latter of whom *var ... ljóss ok fagr eptir faðerni sínu* 'was light and fair according to his father's nature'. Dellingr also occurs as a dwarf-name in the *þulur*, where it might represent a misinterpretation of the *Hávm* stanza: see further Note to Þul *Dverga* 3/7[III]. The H-redaction mss read *dǫglings* here; this derives from the name of another Dagr, not the personification of day but a legendary king, son of Hálfdan gamli 'the Old' and, according to *Skm* (*SnE* 1998, I, 103), *er Daglingar eru frá komnir* 'from whom the Daglingar [Dǫglingar] are descended'. *Dǫglingr* is frequently used as a poetic word for 'king', and it could be that receivers of the H redaction understood the line thus, perhaps in reference to Heiðrekr himself. This reading is given some extra credence by the witness of 203ˣ, which has independent value here; however, 203ˣ reads *Dellings* in every other instance of this line, and the agreement of 2845 and R715ˣ, and the correspondence with *Hávm* 160/3, point decisively to the conclusion that *Dellings* is the correct reading. It is favoured by almost all eds (including *Edd. Min.*, which otherwise often prefers the text of the H redaction). The sense, however, remains somewhat obscure. Finnur Jónsson (*LP*) and Tolkien (*Heiðr* 1960, 34 n. 1) surmised that the phrase must mean 'at sunrise', apparently based on the *Hávm* instance, a suggested interpretation of which is that the dwarf is singing to warn his people of the impending sunrise which would turn them to stone (*idem*).

'Dwarfs turn to stone at sunrise' is a folklore motif (Thompson 1955-8, F451.3.2.1), but for discussion and problematisation of the assumption see Acker (2002, 219). A spatial rather than temporal location seems more likely, perhaps in front of rocks or mountains (i.e. *úti* 'outside', as in l. 2), the traditional dwelling-places of dwarfs (Simek 1993, 68). The meaning of the line is not crucial to the interpretation of the riddle. — [4-5]: *Skald* construes *Hǫfði sínu | vísar á helvega*, while *Edd. Min.*, following *Heiðr* 1873 (241), prefers the H-redaction text *hǫfði sínu | vísar heliar til* (with emendation from ms. 'heliu') 'its head points towards Hel'. — [5] *helvega* 'the roads to Hel': The few other instances of this cpd in poetry are all also in eddic-style verse: see *Vsp* 47/6, 52/7; *Ǫrv* 122/8. There the word is used rather more literally, describing men travelling to the world of the dead.

Gestumblindi (Gestumbl *Heiðr* 9)

56. Hvat er þat undra,   er ek úti sá
        fyrir Dellings durum?
     Ókyrrir tveir   andalausir
        sára lauk suðu.
     Heiðrekr konungr,   hyggðu at gátu.

Hvat undra er þat, er ek sá úti fyrir durum Dellings? Ókyrrir tveir andalausir suðu lauk sára. Heiðrekr konungr, hyggðu at gátu.

What is the wonder that I saw outside before Dellingr's doors? Two unquiet things, without breath, cooked a leek of wounds [SWORD]. Kings Heiðrekr, think about the riddle.

Mss: **2845**(71r), 281[x](99v), 597b[x](49v), R715[x](28v) (ll. 1-6) (*Heiðr*).

Readings: [1] þat: *om*. 281[x], 597b[x]   [3] fyrir: *so* 597b[x], 'f' *all others*; Dellings: döglings 281[x], 597b[x], delling R715[x]   [4] Ókyrrir: *so* 281[x], 597b[x], ókvikvir 2845, ok ókyrrir *corrected from* 'oku okirrir' *in the hand of JR* R715[x];   tveir: *so* 597b[x], 'ii' 2845, 281[x], 'iij' R715[x]   [5] andalausir: 'anda L:' 597b[x]   [6] suðu: suðu *corrected from* 'sudur' *in another hand* 597b[x]   [7-8]: *abbrev. as* 'h k h at' 2845, *abbrev. as* 'h. k.' 281[x], *abbrev. as* 'h K. h:' 597b[x].

Editions: Skj: Anonyme digte og vers [XIII], D. 5. *Heiðreks gátur* 5: AII, 222, BII, 241, *Skald* II, 125; *Heiðr* 1672, 148, *FSN* 1, 468, *Heiðr* 1873, 242, 335, *Heiðr* 1924, 60-1, 64, 136, *FSGJ* 2, 39, *Heiðr* 1960, 34; *Edd. Min.* 109.

Notes: [All]: Heiðrekr's response is (*Heiðr* 1960, 34): *þat eru smiðbelgir; þeir hafa engan vind, nema þeim sé blásit, ok eru þeir dauðir sem annat smíði, en fyrir þeim má líkt smíða sverð sem annat* 'those are smith's bellows; they have no wind, unless they are inflated, and they are dead like other smith-craft [i.e. man-made objects], but because of them one can just as well forge a sword as any other thing'. — [All]: In the R redaction this stanza follows Gestumbl *Heiðr* 4 (*Heiðr* 51). Although this arrangement does not achieve the grouping of riddles with the same opening formula found in the H redaction and preferred in the present edn, it is a logical placing since both solutions refer to objects used in smith-craft. — [1-3]: See Note to *Heiðr* 55/1-3. This is the first occurrence of this repeated opening formula in 2845. — [1]: See Note to *Heiðr* 55/1. — [4] *ókyrrir* 'unquiet': A *hap. leg.* in poetry. The main ms. has here *ókvikvir* 'unliving', which is an acceptable alternative and favoured by *Skj* B, *Skald*, *FSGJ* and *Heiðr* 1960. However, the H-redaction texts and R715[x] are in agreement on the reading chosen here, which is also preferable in terms of sense, referring to the noise made by bellows and creating a more effective riddling paradox with l. 5, in that the object is 'unquiet' but *andalausir* 'without breath'. This reading is also preferred in *Edd. Min.* It corresponds less well with the solution given in 2845 (*eru þeir dauðir* 'they are dead'), but the argument is circular since the prose in the H-redaction texts and R715[x] does not specifically state the bellows are dead; indeed the prose in R715[x] repeats the word *ókyrrir* (*Heiðr* 1924, 137) – although this, equally, could be influenced by the verse. — [5] *andalausir* 'without breath': See Note to *Heiðr* 54/3. Plays on the fact that the bellows do have 'breath', but not of their own; rather only 'when they are inflated', as the solution suggests. Skall Lv 2/8[V] (*Eg* 3) describes bellows as *vindfrekr* 'greedy for wind'. — [6] *suðu lauk sára* 'cooked a leek of wounds [SWORD]': I.e. forged a sword. The verb *sjóða* means both 'cook, boil' and 'forge [weapons]' (*Fritzner, CVC, LP: sjóða*), presumably because steel is plunged into water during the tempering process (on this see Davidson 1962, 18-19). In the present contexts there is nice word-play with the idea of cooking juxtaposed with the kenning base-word *laukr* 'leek'. The same sword-kenning appears elsewhere, e.g. Anon *Liðs* 9/6[I], and as a cpd (*sárlaukr*) in Skúli *Svǫlðr* 2/8[III]. See also *Meissner* 152.

Gestumblindi (Gestumbl *Heiðr* 10)

57. Hvat er þat undra,   er ek úti sá
    fyrir Dellings durum?
Hvítir fljúgendr   hellu ljósta,
    en svartir í sand grafaz.
Heiðrekr konungr,   hyggðu at gátu.

Hvat undra er þat, er ek sá úti fyrir durum Dellings? Hvítir fljúgendr ljósta hellu, en svartir grafaz í sand. Heiðrekr konungr, hyggðu at gátu.

What is the wonder that I saw outside before Dellingr's doors? White flying ones strike the rock-slab, but black ones bury themselves in the sand. King Heiðrekr, think about the riddle.

Mss: 281[x](99v), 597b[x](49v) (*Heiðr*).

Readings: [1] undra: undra *inserted in the margin in another hand* 597b[x]   [2] ek: *inserted in the margin in another hand* 597b[x]   [3] fyrir: *so* 597b[x], 'f' 281[x];   Dellings: döglings 281[x], 'd:' 597b[x];

durum: 'd:' 597b[x]   [7-8]: *abbrev. as* 'h: k· hiğ ad.' 281[x], *abbrev. as* 'h. K h: ad þu' *corrected from* 'h. K h: þu' *in the margin in another hand* 597b[x].

Editions: *Skj*: Anonyme digte og vers [XIII], D. 5. Heiðreks gátur 32: AII, 227, BII, 246, *Skald* II, 128; *Heiðr* 1873, 242-3, *Heiðr* 1924, 64-5, *Heiðr* 1960, 80; *Edd. Min.* 109-10.

Notes: [All]: King Heiðrekr's response reads (*Heiðr* 1960, 80): *smækkask nú gáturnar, en þat er hagl ok regn, því at hagli lýstr á stræti, en regndropar søkkva í sand ok sœkja í jǫrð* 'the riddles now grow trivial, but that is hail and rain, because hail strikes upon the road, but raindrops sink into the sand and push on into the earth'. — [1]: See Note to *Heiðr* 55/1. — [3] *Dellings* 'Dellingr's': Emended in keeping with the occurrence of this recurring formula in other riddles; other eds do the same. See Note to *Heiðr* 55/3. — [4] *fljúgendr* 'flying ones': The participial adj. is a *hap. leg.* in poetry.

Gestumblindi (Gestumbl *Heiðr* 11)

58. *Hvat er þat undra,   er ek úti sá*
       fyrir Dellings durum?
     Svartan gǫlt ek sá   í sauri vaða,
       ok reis honum eigi burst á baki.
     Heiðrekr konungr,   hyggðu at gátu.

Hvat undra er þat, er ek sá úti fyrir durum Dellings? Ek sá svartan gǫlt vaða í sauri, ok burst reis eigi á baki honum. Heiðrekr konungr, hyggðu at gátu.

What is the wonder that I saw outside before Dellingr's doors? I saw a black boar wade in muck, but bristles did not rise on his back. King Heiðrekr, think about the riddle.

Mss: **597b[x]**(49v), 281[x](99v) (*Heiðr*).

Readings: [1-3]: *om.* 597b[x], 281[x]   [7-8]: *abbrev. as* 'h[c]: K: h:' 597b[x], *abbrev. as* 'heidr: k[r]' 281[x].

Editions: *Skj*: Anonyme digte og vers [XIII], D. 5. Heiðreks gátur 33: AII, 227, BII, 246, *Skald* II, 128; *Heiðr* 1873, 243, *Heiðr* 1924, 65, *Heiðr* 1960, 80; *Edd. Min.* 110.

Notes: [All]: Heiðrekr's response is (*Heiðr* 1960, 81): *þat er tordýfill, ok er nú mart til tínt, er tordýflar eru ríkra manna spurningar* 'that is the dung-beetle, and much has been recounted now, when dung-beetles are [the subject of] the questions of powerful men'. — [1-3]: Omitted in the mss, but the organising principle of the H redaction is to group riddles with a similar beginning together, and this comes in the midst of eight other riddles with this opening. See also Note to *Heiðr* 55/1-3. Other eds also insert this opening formula. — [1]: See Note to *Heiðr* 55/1. — [5] *sauri* 'muck': Puns on the two (related) meanings of *saurr* (*Fritzner*: *saurr* 1, 2): 'mud', fitting the boar context, and 'excrement', fitting the dung-beetle context. — [6] *burst* 'bristles': A *hap. leg.* in poetry. In the sense 'the bristles on a boar's back', as here, the f. sg. noun is used collectively (*ONP*: *burst* 1).

Gestumblindi (Gestumbl *Heiðr* 12)

59. Hvat er þat undra,   er ek úti sá
         fyrir Dellings durum?
     Tíu hefir tungur,   tuttugu augu,
     fjóra tigu fóta;   fram líðr sú vættr.
     Heiðrekr konungr,   hyggðu at gátu.

Hvat undra er þat, er ek sá úti fyrir durum Dellings? Hefir tíu tungur, tuttugu augu, fjóra tigu fóta; sú vættr líðr fram. Heiðrekr konungr, hyggðu at gátu.

What is the wonder that I saw outside before Dellingr's doors? It has ten tongues, twenty eyes, forty feet; that creature moves forward. King Heiðrekr, think about the riddle.

Mss: 2845(72r), 281^x(99v), 597b^x(49v), R715^x(29v) (ll. 1-6) (*Heiðr*).

Readings: [1, 2] undra er ek: undra er ek *inserted in the margin in another hand* 597b^x [2] sá: sá *inserted in the margin in another hand* 597b^x [3]: *abbrev. as* 'f d d' 2845, *abbrev. as* 'f dóg dÿrū' 281^x, *abbrev. as* 'fyr^r d: d·' 597b^x, *abbrev. as* 'f dillīg dÿrū' R715^x [4] hefir: hafði R715^x [7] fram: ferr 281^x, 597b^x; líðr: hart 281^x, 597b^x, gengr R715^x;   sú: 'so' R715^x;   vættr: 'v̄tur' R715^x [7-8]: *abbrev. as* 'heidr k̄ h g' 2845   [8-9]: *abbrev. as* 'heid: k. h.' 281^x, *abbrev. as* 'h^c: K h:' 597b^x.

Editions: *Skj*: Anonyme digte og vers [XIII], D. 5. *Heiðreks gátur* 26: AII, 226, BII, 245, *Skald* II, 127; *Heiðr* 1672, 151, *FSN* 1, 485, *Heiðr* 1873, 244, 342, *Heiðr* 1924, 66, 80, 139, *FSGJ* 2, 48-9, *Heiðr* 1960, 43; *Edd. Min.* 110.

Context: In the H redaction, before propounding the riddle, Gestumblindi says (*Heiðr* 1924, 65-6): *frest eru bǫls bezt, en margr maðr vill at meira leita ok séz því sumum yfir; sé ek nú ok, at allra útfœra verðr at leita* 'delays are the best of misfortunes, but many a man wishes to seek more and because of this some make mistakes; I also see now that all escape routes must be tried'.

Notes: [All]: Heiðrekr replies (*Heiðr* 1960, 43): *Ef þú ert sá Gestumblindi, sem ek hugða, þá ertu vitrari en ek ætlaða; en frá gyltinni segir þú nú úti í garðinum* 'If you are the Gestumblindi I thought [you were], then you are wiser than I expected; but you speak now of the sow out in the yard'. The prose then adds (*Heiðr* 1960, 43): *Þá lét konungr drepa gyltina, ok hafði hon níu grísi, sem Gestumblindi sagði. Nú grunar konung, hverr maðrinn mun vera* 'Then the king had the sow killed, and she had nine piglets [inside her], as Gestumblindi said. Now the king suspects who the man will be'. The H redaction is somewhat different, giving the solution and explanation first, then a longer exchange between Heiðrekr and Gestumblindi (*Heiðr* 1924, 66): *Þá mælti konungr: 'eigi veit ek nú, nema vitrir eigi nú hlut í, ok eigi veit ek, hvat manna þú ert.' Gestumblindi svarar: 'slíkr em ek, sem þú mátt sjá, ok vilda ek gjarna þiggja líf mitt ok vera lauss af þessum þrautum.' Konungr svarar: 'upp skaltu bera gátur, þar til er þik þrýtr ella mik at ráða.'* "Then the king said: "I don't understand now, unless wise men now have a part in this, and I don't know what sort of man you are." Gestumblindi answers: "I am such as you can see, and I would wish eagerly to receive my life and be free from these tasks." The king answers: "you must offer riddles until you fail, or I [fail] to interpret them.'" See also *Heiðr* 50 Note to [All]. — [All]: The solution makes this situation-specific and therefore not a true riddle, requiring foresight rather than logic to be solved. The riddle itself however could easily be answered generically 'a sow with nine piglets'; cf. Aldhelm's *Scrofa praegnans* (Ehwald 1919, 136). A similar feat occurs in a fragment by Pherecydes of Athens, where the seer Mopsus defeats his rival Calchas by correctly stating the number of piglets carried by a pregnant sow (in another version he divines the number of figs on a tree) (West 2007, 364). See also Taylor (1951, 28-31). — [All]: In the R redaction this riddle follows Gestumbl *Heiðr* 33 (*Heiðr* 80), also about a sow with piglets. — [All]: Lines 1-3 are *ljóðaháttr*, 4-9 *fornyrðislag*. — [1]: See Note to *Heiðr* 55/1. — [7] *vættr* 'creature': The word often denotes a supernatural being.

Gestumblindi (Gestumbl *Heiðr* 13)

60. Hvat er þat undra,   er ek úti sá
        fyrir Dellings durum?
     Ofarliga flýgr,   †armlod gellr,
        harðar eru hillm†.
     Heiðrekr konungr,   hyggðu at gátu.

Hvat undra er þat, er ek sá úti fyrir durum Dellings? Flýgr ofarliga, †armlod gellr, harðar eru hillm†. Heiðrekr konungr, hyggðu at gátu.

What is the wonder that I saw outside before Dellingr's doors? It flies high up ... King Heiðrekr, think about the riddle.

Mss: **281ˣ**(99v), 597bˣ(50r) (*Heiðr*).

Readings: [1-3]: *abbrev. as* 'hvᵈ er þ vndra etc.' 281ˣ, *abbrev. as* 'hvad er þad vndra eʳ' 597bˣ [4] Ofarliga: 'ovarlega' 281ˣ, 597bˣ   [7-8]: *abbrev. as* 'heid: k.' 281ˣ, *abbrev. as* 'h: K h:' 597bˣ.

Editions: *Skj*: Anonyme digte og vers [XIII], D. 5. *Heiðreks gátur* 34: AII, 227, BII, 246-7, *Skald* II, 128, *NN* §§2834, 3397C; *Heiðr* 1873, 244-5, *Heiðr* 1924, 67, *Heiðr* 1960, 81; *Edd. Min.* 111.

Context: See Note [All] to previous stanza.

Notes: [All]: Heiðrekr replies (*Heiðr* 1960, 81): *ǫr er þat* 'that is the arrow'. It is unfortunate that the solution is not more elaborate, as many of the others are, since that might help in reconstructing the stanza, which cannot be made sense of without emendation. The brevity of the solution might suggest that the stanza was already corrupt or difficult to interpret when it was set into its prose context. — [1]: See Note to *Heiðr* 55/1. — [4] *ofarliga* 'high up': The mss have 'ovarlega', which could be read *óvarliga* 'unwarily', but this gives less good sense (though is preferred by Ettmüller 1861, 37, with the gloss *unverhofft* 'unexpectedly'). Emendation of <v> to <f> is reasonable, since <f> would be pronounced [v] when intervocalic (see *ANG* §36, cf. §42), and is made by most other eds, following Bugge (*Heiðr* 1873; Bugge notes this was the suggestion of Svend Grundtvig). Kock (*Skald*) emends to *ofárliga* and in *NN* §2834 translates *mycket tidigt (resp. snabbt)* 'very early (or swiftly)', comparing *árflognir* (*NN* §3397C) 'early flyer', i.e. 'raven' (*LP*). Although the bird-of-prey imagery would fit well with what has been conjectured for the next line (see Note to l. 5), it is less clear why an arrow would be described as as early flier. The meaning 'swiftly' might make more sense in the present context, however, and is attested elsewhere in poetry, although the cpd (with the prefix *of-* 'too, excessively' (= 'very' in Kock's interpretation)) would be a *hap. leg.* — [5] †*armlod gellr*† '…': *Skj* B does not attempt reconstruction of these lines. The second word, *gellr*, is the 3rd pers. sg. pres. indic. of *gjalla* 'scream, shriek', but the first cannot be normalised to a known Old Norse word. Bugge (*Heiðr* 1873) suggested emendation to *arnhlióð* 'eagle-shriek', which has also been adopted (with variant spellings) in *Skald*, *Edd. Min.* and *Heiðr* 1960. This word is unattested but has a parallel in *varg(h)ljóð* 'wolf-howl' (Fritzner: *vargljóð*; *LP*: *varghljóð*), found in *HHund I* 41/3 (*NK* 136); Bugge (*Heiðr* 1873, 245 n. 2) also compares *vápnhljóð* 'weapon-sound', see e.g. Okík *Magn* 1/4^{II}. — [6] †*harðar eru hillm*†: Again *Skj* B does not attempt reconstruction. Kock (*Skald*; *NN* §2834) suggests *harðárr er um hjálm* '[it] is a harsh messenger about helmets', giving *illþræll* 'wicked slave', *hollvinr* 'loyal friend' and *ítrmaðr* 'glorious man' as parallels for the otherwise unattested cpd *harðárr*. The suggestions of other eds are purely conjectural.

Gestumblindi (Gestumbl *Heiðr* 14)

61. Hvat er þat undra, er ek úti sá
   fyrir Dellings durum?
   Fætr hefir átta en fjögur augu,
   ok berr ofar kné en kvið.
   Heiðrekr konungr, hyggðu at gátu.

Hvat er undra þat, er ek sá úti fyrir durum Dellings? Hefir átta fætr en fjögur augu, ok berr kné ofar en kvið. Heiðrekr konungr, hyggðu at gátu.

What is the wonder that I saw outside before Dellingr's doors? It has eight feet and four eyes, and bears its knees higher than its belly. King Heiðrekr, think about the riddle.

Mss: **2845**(71r), 281^x(99v) (ll. 1-6), 597b^x(50r), R715^x(27v) (ll. 1-6) (*Heiðr*).

Readings: [1] undra: *so* 281^x, 597b^x, R715^x, 'u' 2845   [2] er: at 281^x, at *inserted in the margin in another hand* 597b^x;   ek: er *inserted in the margin in another hand* 597b^x, *om.* R715^x;   úti sá: *so*

281ˣ, R715ˣ, 'u sa' 2845, úti sá *inserted in the margin in another hand* 597bˣ   [3]: *abbrev. as* 'f d' 2845, *abbrev. as* 'f Døgl dÿrū' 281ˣ, *abbrev. as* 'f̄ d d:' 597bˣ, *abbrev. as* 'f dellīgz dÿr' R715ˣ   [4] átta ('uíîî'): '5' R715ˣ   [5] fjögur augu: augu fjögur 281ˣ   [6] ok: *om.* 281ˣ, 597bˣ, R715ˣ; berr: berr þat 281ˣ, 597bˣ;   kné: 'hnie' R715ˣ   [7-8]: *abbrev. as* 'h k̄ h þ ā ḡ' 2845, *abbrev. as* 'h: K h:' 597bˣ.

Editions: *Skj*: Anonyme digte og vers [XIII], D. 5. *Heiðreks gátur* 6: AII, 222, BII, 241, *Skald* II, 125; *Heiðr* 1672, 146, *FSN* 1, 468, *Heiðr* 1873, 245, 335, *Heiðr* 1924, 61-2, 67, 133, *FSGJ* 2, 40, *Heiðr* 1960, 35; *Edd. Min.* 111.

Notes: [All]: Heiðrekr's response is (*Heiðr* 1960, 35): *Þat er kǫngurváfur* 'Those are spiders'. The H redaction includes more dialogue, hinting at Heiðrekr's suspicions (*Heiðr* 1924, 68): *er nú bæði, at þú hefir hǫttinn síðan, enda sér þú niðr undan fleira en flestir menn aðrir, er þú hugsar hvert skrípi jarðarinnar, en þat er kǫngurváfa* 'It is now both: that you have your hood low over your face, and yet that you see more than most other men from under it when you think of every weird creature on the earth; but that is the spider'. The hood was a favourite disguise of Óðinn's. — [1]: See Note to *Heiðr* 55/1.

Gestumblindi (Gestumbl *Heiðr* 15)

62. Hvat er þat undra,   er ek úti sá
        fyrir Dellings durum?
     Lýðum lýsir,   en log*a* gleypir
        ok keppaz um þat vargar ávalt.
     Heiðrekr konungr,   hyggðu at gátu.

Hvat er undra þat, er ek sá úti fyrir durum Dellings? Lýsir lýðum, en gleypir log*a*, ok vargar keppaz ávalt um þat. Heiðrekr konungr, hyggðu at gátu.

What is the wonder that I saw outside before Dellinǵs doors? It gives light to men, but swallows flame, and wolves always compete for it. King Heiðrekr, think about the riddle.

Mss: **281ˣ**(99v), 597bˣ(50r) (*Heiðr*).

Readings: [1-3]: *abbrev. as* 'hvᵈ er þ̄ er' 281ˣ, *abbrev. as* 'hvad eʳ þad eʳ' 597bˣ   [5] log*a*: logi 281ˣ, 597bˣ   [7-8] *abbrev. as* 'heidr: kʳ' 281ˣ, *abbrev. as* 'h K:' 597bˣ.

Editions: *Skj*: Anonyme digte og vers [XIII], D. 5. *Heiðreks gátur* 35: AII, 227-8, BII, 247, *Skald* II, 128; *Heiðr* 1873, 246, *Heiðr* 1924, 68, *Heiðr* 1960, 81; *Edd. Min.* 111-12.

Notes: [All]: Heiðrekr replies (*Heiðr* 1960, 81): *þat er sól; hon lýsir lǫnd ǫll ok skínn yfir alla menn, en Skalli ok Hatti heita vargar ... en annarr þeira ferr fyrir, en annarr eptir sólu* 'that is the sun; she illuminates all lands and shines over all men, and the wolves are called Skalli and Hatti ... and one of them goes before, and the other after the sun'. On these wolves see Note to l. 6. — [1-3]: The mss are ambiguous as to whether the opening formula is intended here (their readings could be an abbreviation of these lines, as in the previous stanzas), or whether the riddle is simply intended to read *Hvat er þat er lýðum lýsir...* 'What is it that gives light to men...'. Considering the heavy use of abbreviation in these lines elsewhere, and the H redaction's practice of grouping riddles with a similar beginning together, it is assumed here and by other eds that the formula should be understood. See also Note to *Heiðr* 58/1-3. — [1]: See Note to *Heiðr* 55/1. — [5] *log*a 'flame': The emendation was first suggested by Grundtvig (*Heiðr* 1873, 246 n. 6); however Bugge, who noted this, chose instead to print *lönd öll yfir* 'over all lands' as l. 5 of this stanza, based on the prose. The eds of *Edd. Min.* were the first to take up Grundtvig's proposal, and it is also adopted in *Heiðr* 1960. The paradox is apt and the sense preferable to the emendation of *Skj* B and *Skald, lǫgr* 'sea'. — [6]: This conceit is found in *Grí* 39 and *Gylf*, in both of which the wolves are called Skǫll and Hati rather than Skalli and Hatti as in the prose solution here. *Gylf* explains that the sun travels fast because she is being chased, specifying (*SnE* 2005, 14): *Hann [i.e Skǫll] hræðisk hon ok hann mun taka hana, en sá heitir Hati Hróðvitnisson er fyrir henni hleypr, ok vill hann taka tunglit, ok svá mun verða* 'She is afraid of him and he will catch her, and that one is called Hati Hróðvitnisson who runs before her, and he wishes to catch the moon, and so it will happen'. In *Vafþr* 47 it is the mythical wolf Fenrir who will swallow the sun at Ragnarǫk.

Gestumblindi (Gestumbl *Heiðr* 16)

63. Hvat er þat undra,   er ek úti sá
    fyrir Dellings durum?
    Horni harðara,   hrafni svartara,
    skjalli hvítara,   skapti réttara.
    Heiðrekr konungr,   hyggðu at gátu.

Hvat er undra þat, er ek sá úti fyrir durum Dellings? Horni harðara, hrafni svartara, skjalli hvítara, skapti réttara. Heiðrekr konungr, hyggðu at gátu.

What is the wonder that I saw outside before Delling's doors? [It is] harder than horn, blacker than the raven, whiter than the membrane of an egg, straighter than a shaft. King Heiðrekr, think about the riddle.

Mss: **2845**(71r), 281ˣ(100r), 597bˣ(50r), R715ˣ(28r) (ll. 1-7) (*Heiðr*).

Readings: [1-3]: *so* R715ˣ, *abbrev. as* 'huᵗ er þ u' 2845, *abbrev. as* 'hvad er þad vndre etc.' 281ˣ, 'hvad er þad undra fyr d d:' *corrected from* 'hvad er undra fyr d d:' *in the margin in a later hand* 597bˣ   [4] Horni: horni er R715ˣ   [6-7]: *lines reversed* 281ˣ, 597bˣ   [6] skjalli: *so* 281ˣ, 597bˣ, R715ˣ, skildi 2845   [8-9]: *abbrev. as* 'h k̄ h a Gā' 2845, 'heidr kʳ.' 281ˣ, *abbrev. as* 'h: Kongur: h.' 597bˣ.

Editions: *Skj*: Anonyme digte og vers [XIII], D. 5. *Heiðreks gátur* 8: AII, 222-3, BII, 241, *Skald* II, 125; *Heiðr* 1672, 147, *FSN* 1, 470, *Heiðr* 1873, 246-7, 336, *Heiðr* 1924, 63, 69, 135, *FSGJ* 2, 41, *Heiðr* 1960, 35; *Edd. Min.* 112.

Notes: [All]: Heiðrekr's response is (*Heiðr* 1960, 35-6): *Smækkask nú gáturnar, Gestumblindi; hvat þarf lengr yfir þessu at sitja? Þat er hrafntinna, ok skein á hana sólargeisli* 'The riddles now grow trivial, Gestumblindi; what is the need to sit longer over this? That is obsidian, and a sunbeam shines on it'. The H redaction (*Heiðr* 1924, 69) omits the initial comment (but cf. *Heiðr* 57, Note to [All]) where a similar observation is made), but adds *er lá í einu húsi* 'which lay in a house'. Obsidian is a dark-coloured glassy volcanic rock; Iceland is one of the best known locations in Europe for its occurrence. It features in late antique and medieval encyclopedias, such as Pliny the Elder's *Naturalis Historia* (XXXVI, 67; Eichholz 1962, 154-6) and Isidore of Seville's *Etymologiae* (XVI, iv, 21: Isidore, *Etym.* II). There is evidence that it was used as flint during the Viking Age (Hughes and Lucas 2009, 46); cf. *Heiðr* 77 and 81, about flint and embers in the hearth, respectively. Obsidian forms a very sharp edge and was also used as a cutting tool (Orri Vésteinsson 2000a, 169); it may further have been used for decorative or magical purposes, though the Icelandic evidence for the latter is from as late as the C19th (Hughes and Lucas 2009, 46). — [All]: Lines 1-3 are *ljóðaháttr*, 4-7 *málaháttr* and 8-9 *fornyrðislag*. — [1]: See Note to *Heiðr* 55/1. — [5] *hrafni* 'than the raven': The ON (and ModIcel.) *hrafntinna* 'obsidian' is lit. 'raven-flint'. — [6-7]: These lines are reversed in the H-redaction mss, which ordering is favoured by *Skj* and *Skald*, but the other mss agree on the ordering retained here. Either is acceptable. — [6] *skjalli* 'than the membrane of an egg': Cf. *Gylf* (*SnE* 2005, 19), which says that the water in the well of the norn Urðr *er svá heiligt at allir hlutir þeir sem þar koma í brunninn verða svá hvítir sem hinna sú er skjall heitir, er innan liggr við eggskurn* 'is so holy that all those things which come there into the well become as white as the membrane which is called *skjall*, which lies within the eggshell'; cf. also *skjallhvít lilja* 'the *skjall*-white lily', Árni *Gd* 68/2[IV]. Some medieval philosophers, including Martianus Capella, William of Conches and Peter Abelard, used the membrane of the egg to represent the air in 'cosmic egg' models of the universe (see further Dronke 1974, 79-99, 154-66). Ms. 2845 reads *skildi* 'shield'; the scribe may have been thinking of shields painted white or made from a light-coloured wood, references to which are not uncommon in Old Norse poetry. Cf. e.g. *sciold hvítastan* 'the whitest shield', *Akv* 7/9 (*NK* 241); *hvítra skjalda* 'white shields', Þhorn *Harkv* 8/2[I] and Note; Sigv *Nesv* 9/2, 3[I] and Note. On painted and decorated shields see Falk (1914b, 129-32, 145-8). The sunbeam in the solution is presumably the key to resolving this paradox, that the object can be both whiter than *skjall* and blacker than the raven, since obsidian has reflective properties.

Gestumblindi (Gestumbl *Heiðr* 17)

64. Báru brúðir   bleikhaddaðar,
    ambáttir tvær,   öl til skemmu.
    Vara þat höndum horfit   né hamri klappat;
    þó var fyrir eyjar útan   örðigr, sá er ker gerði.
    Heiðrekr konungr,   hyggðu at gátu.

Bleikhaddaðar brúðir, tvær ambáttir, báru öl til skemmu. Vara þat horfit höndum né klappat hamri; þó var örðigr, sá er ker gerði, fyrir útan eyjar. Heiðrekr konungr, hyggðu at gátu.

Pale-haired brides, two handmaids, bore ale to the storehouse. It was not turned by hand nor struck by hammer; yet outside the islands was that upright one who made the keg. King Heiðrekr, think about the riddle.

Mss: 2845(71r), 281ˣ(100r), 597bˣ(50r), R715ˣ(29r) (ll. 1-8) (*Heiðr*).

Readings: [4] öl: áðr R715ˣ [5] Vara: *so* 281ˣ, 597bˣ, ei var 2845, vóru R715ˣ;   þat: þeir R715ˣ; höndum: höndum *corrected from* 'hordum' *in a later hand* 597bˣ, 'lyndum' R715ˣ [6] né: 'nei' R715ˣ;   hamri: *so* 281ˣ, 'hmri at' 2845, hamra 597bˣ, 'harmi nei hamri' R715ˣ;   klappat: 'klap' R715ˣ [7] þó: þá 281ˣ, 597bˣ, R715ˣ;   var: er 281ˣ, 597bˣ, R715ˣ [8] örðigr: 'anoþigur' R715ˣ;   ker: *so* 281ˣ, 597bˣ, *om*. 2845, konungr R715ˣ   [9-10]: *abbrev. as* 'h k̄ h a Gatu' 2845, *abbrev. as* 'heid. k.' 281ˣ, *abbrev. as* 'h: Kongʳ h:' 597bˣ.

Editions: *Skj*: Anonyme digte og vers [XIII], D. 5. Heiðreks gátur 9: AII, 223, BII, 241-2, *Skald* II, 125; *NN* §3283; *Heiðr* 1672, 148, *FSN* 1, 470-1, *Heiðr* 1873, 247-8, 336, *Heiðr* 1924, 64, 69, 137, *FSGJ* 2, 41, *Heiðr* 1960, 36; *Edd. Min.* 112.

Context: In the H redaction, before Gestumblindi speaks this riddle Heiðrekr challenges him (*Heiðr* 1924, 69): *Eða kantu ekki á annan veg gátur upp at bera en hafa et sama upphaf at, þar sem mér virðiz þú fróðr maðr?* 'Do you not know another way to propound riddles than to have the same beginning, since I think you a wise man?'

Notes: [All]: Heiðrekr's response is (*Heiðr* 1960, 36): *þar fara svanbrúðir til hreiðrs síns ok verpa eggjum; skurm á eggi er eigi hǫndum gǫrt né hamri klappat, en svanr er fyrir eyjar útan ǫrðigr, sá er þær gátu eggin við* 'There female swans go to their nest and lay their eggs; the shell of the egg is not made by hands nor struck by hammer, but the swan outside the islands is upright, he with whom they produced the egg'. The H-redaction wording is quite different (and less preferable) (*Heiðr* 1924, 70): *þat eru æðar tvær þær er eggjum verpa; eggin eru eigi gǫr með hamri eða hǫndum, en þjónostumeyjar báru ǫlit í eggskurninni* 'It is two eider-ducks who lay their eggs; the eggs are not made with hammer or hands, but the servant-girls carried the ale in the eggshell'. Female eider-ducks do not have white plumage (cf. *bleikhaddaðr* 'pale-headed' l. 2); moreover, the *örðigr* 'upright [one]' in l. 8 seems appropriate to a swan's long neck and/or the action of a male swan guarding its territory. — [All]: Following Heiðrekr's challenge in the H redaction (see Context), there is a move away from the *Hvat er þat undra* formula of the previous nine riddles. This effect is lost in the other redactions, which do not group all the *undra* riddles together, nor do they have the prose challenge. In this stanza, ll. 1-4 and 9-10 are *fornyrðislag* and 5-8 are *málaháttr*. — [1] *brúðir* 'brides': In poetry the word can refer to women in general as well as more specifically 'brides' (*Fritzner, LP*: *brúðr*). Cf. *Heiðr* 71/1. — [2] *bleikhaddaðar* 'pale-haired': The cpd is a *hap. leg.*, but similar compounds in *-haddaðar* '-haired' are attested: see e.g. *Án* 5/3 *hvíthaddaðar* 'fair-haired' and Note. Cf. also *Heiðr* 68/4 *hadda bleika* (acc. pl.) 'pale hair', which describes an attribute of waves. — [4] *öl* 'ale': *Edd. Min.* suggests *ǫlker* 'ale-keg' here, which gives better sense and is also adopted in *Skald* (cf. *NN* §3283), but is without ms. justification (but cf. l. 8 and Note). — [4] *skemmu* 'storehouse': Plays on alternate meanings of *skemma*, 'storehouse' and 'bower', the former appropriate to an ale-keg, the latter appropriate to a bird's nest. — [8] *ker* 'keg': Not in the main ms. and makes the line hypermetrical, and most eds omit, but the keg is clearly what is being referred to rather than the ale inside. To include it here avoids the need for more drastic emendation (cf. Note to l. 4 *öl* above), and although R715ˣ's reading, *konungr* 'king', is clearly nonsensical (and ungrammatical), it at least supports there originally having been a word (perhaps beginning with k) here. *Heiðr* 1873 (247) retains, though omits the previous *sá er* 'that one', making the line more acceptable metrically.

Gestumblindi (Gestumbl *Heiðr* 18)

65. Hverjar eru þær rýgjar   á reginfjalli,
      elr við kván kona?
    Mær við meyju   mög um getr,
      ok eigut þær varðir vera.
    Heiðrekr konungr,   hyggðu at gátu.

Hverjar eru þær rýgjar á reginfjalli, kona elr við kván? Mær um getr mög við meyju, ok þær varðir eigut vera. Heiðrekr konungr, hyggðu at gátu.

Who are those women on the mighty mountain, woman begets with woman? A girl begets a son with a girl, and those women do not have husbands. King Heiðrekr, think about the riddle.

Mss: 2845(71r), 281ˣ(100r), 597bˣ(50r), R715ˣ(27v) (ll. 1-2, 5-6) (*Heiðr*).

Readings: [1] rýgjar: 'Ryger' 281ˣ, 'Rygier' 597bˣ, 'eygar' *corrected from* 'ey(?)i[...]' *in the hand of JR* R715ˣ [3] kona: 'kvona' 597bˣ [4] Mær: *so* 281ˣ, 597bˣ, þar 2845; við: *so* 281ˣ, 597bˣ, til 2845; meyju: *so* 281ˣ, 597bˣ, er 2845 [5] um: *om.* R715ˣ; getr: 'gietur of gonn' *corrected from* 'gietur yfir garn' *in the hand of JR* R715ˣ [6] ok: kvenna R715ˣ; eigut: eigi 281ˣ, 597bˣ, eigur R715ˣ; þær: þær þess 281ˣ, 597bˣ, þat R715ˣ; vera: at vera 281ˣ, 597bˣ [7-8]: *abbrev. as* 'h kr h' 2845, *abbrev. as* 'heidr: kʳ:' 281ˣ, *abbrev. as* 'h: K:' 597bˣ.

Editions: *Skj*: Anonyme digte og vers [XIII], D. 5. *Heiðreks gátur* 10: AII, 223, BII, 242, *Skald* II, 125; *Heiðr* 1672, 146, *FSN* 1, 471, *Heiðr* 1873, 248-9, 337, *Heiðr* 1924, 65, 70, 133-4, *FSGJ* 2, 42, *Heiðr* 1960, 36; *Edd. Min.* 113.

Context: In the H redaction, before propounding the riddle Gestumblindi says (*Heiðr* 1924, 70): *liðar verðr sá at leita, er lítit sax hefir ok mjǫk er fáfróðr, ok vilda ek enn tala fleira, eða* ... 'He who has a small short-sword and is very short of knowledge must seek the joint, but I would like to speak yet more, so ...'. (A similar proverb occurs in *Saxo* 2015, I, v. 3. 12, pp. 284-5). The implication is that Gestumblindi/Óðinn could seek the easiest way out, i.e. by propounding his unanswerable question (*Heiðr* 84), but that he is enjoying the contest and intends to prolong it.

Notes: [All]: Heiðrekr's response is (*Heiðr* 1960, 36): *þat eru hvannir tvær ok hvannarkálfr á milli þeira* 'That is two angelicas and a young angelica [lit. angelica-calf] between them'. Two species of angelica are native to Iceland: garden angelica (*angelica archangelica*) and wild angelica (*angelica sylvestris/sylvatica*). It was traditionally an important food and medicinal plant in Iceland and elsewhere in Scandinavia: on historical uses and for other references in Old Norse texts see Fosså (2006) and Guðrún P. Helgadóttir (1981). — [1] *hverjar eru þær* ... 'who are those ...': This opening formula, followed by a word meaning 'women' or similar, appears in the following six riddles, Gestumbl *Heiðr* 19-24 (*Heiðr* 66-71). — [1] *rýgjar* 'women': Plays with alternate meanings of the word: 'women' and 'giantesses' (*LP: rýgr*). Together with the *reginfjalli* 'mighty mountain' of l. 2, this creates two layers of imagery: both of angelica growing wild and of giantesses in their traditional dwelling-place. — [2] *reginfjalli* 'mighty mountain': A *hap. leg.* as a cpd. — [4-5]: Angelica's main method of reproduction is seeding; plants can self-seed (Garland 2004, 31). Vegetative reproduction of the various sub-species of angelica is not well-documented in modern sources, but there is substantial evidence that the plant will produce off-shoots in or after its second year, especially if it is cut back (e.g. Ojala 1985, 193; Grieve 1931; Garland 2004, 31-2; Small 2006, 164-5), perhaps particularly in cooler climates (Vashistha *et al.* 2009, 76; Billings 1974, 434). This latter habit seems to be what is meant by the imagery of the riddle and the solution. — [5]: The H-redaction reading is clearly superior here, metrically as well as in terms of effect, to 2845's *þar til er* 'until'. — [6]: The same line is found in *Heiðr* 68/6, where the solution is 'waves'. — [6] *varðir* (nom. sg. *vǫrð*) 'women': Poetic word (*ONP: vǫrð*).

Gestumblindi (Gestumbl *Heiðr* 19)

66. Hverjar eru þær drósir,   er um *dróttin sinn*
    vápnlausar vega?
    Inar jarpari   hlífa um alla daga,
    en inar fegri fara.
    Heiðrekr konungr,   hyggðu at gátu.

Hverjar eru þær drósir, er vega vápnlausar um dróttin sinn? Inar jarpari hlífa um alla daga, en inar fegri fara. Heiðrekr konungr, hyggðu at gátu.

Who are those girls, who fight weaponless around their lord? The darker ones protect [him] during all the days, but the fairer ones go forth [to attack]. King Heiðrekr, think about the riddle.

Mss: **2845**(71v), 281^x(100r), 597b^x(50r), R715^x(28r) (ll. 1-3, 5-6) (*Heiðr*).

Readings: [1] drósir: *so* R715^x, brúðir *all others*   [2] um: *so* 281^x, 597b^x, R715^x, *om.* 2845; dróttin sinn: sinn dróttinn *all*   [3] vápnlausar: *so* 281^x, 597b^x, R715^x, vápnlausan 2845   [4] jarpari: 'jorpsku' 281^x, 597b^x [5] hlífa: 'lifa' 281^x, 597b^x;   um: *om.* 281^x, 597b^x [6] fara: frýja 281^x, 597b^x, R715^x [7-8]: *abbrev. as* 'h k̄ h' 2845, *abbrev. as* 'heidr: k:' 281^x, *abbrev. as* 'h Kong^r' 597b^x.

Editions: *Skj*: Anonyme digte og vers [XIII], D. 5. *Heiðreks gátur* 13: AII, 223-4, BII, 242, *Skald* II, 126, *NN* §2833; *Heiðr* 1672, 147, *FSN* 1, 473, *Heiðr* 1873, 249, 338, *Heiðr* 1924, 68, 71, 134, *FSGJ* 2, 43, *Heiðr* 1960, 37-8; *Edd. Min.* 113.

Notes: [All]: Heiðrekr's response reads (*Heiðr* 1960, 38): *þat er hnettafl; inar døkkri verja hnefann, en hvítar sækja* 'that is *hnefatafl*; the darker defend the *hnefi*, but the white ones attack'. The H redaction reads (*Heiðr* 1924, 71): *þat er hneftafl; tǫflur drepaz vápnalausar um hnefann ok fylgja honum enar rauðu* 'that is *hneftafl*; the *tǫflur* kill each other without weapons around the *hnefi*, and the red ones escort him'. *Hnefatafl* (also called *hneftafl* or just *tafl* 'tables', an earlier and generic word for board-games) was a game played on a square grid with an odd number of rows per side, leaving a distinct centre square on which stood the *hnefi* or 'king' piece. The *hnefi* was surrounded by his defenders, outnumbered by the opposing attacking pieces, which started the game on the outer squares of the board, in a 2:1 ratio. The object for the defending side was for the king to reach the outer edge of the board, while the attacking side could win by capturing the *hnefi*. Evidence of the playing of the game has been found throughout Scandinavia and the British Isles, with analogues in other Northern European cultures. It is mentioned in several places in Old Norse literature, often as an indicator of the players' status, including in *Vsp* 8, which relates that the Æsir *tefldo* 'played *tafl*' in the Golden Age early in the world's history (*Vsp* 61 tells that their playing-pieces will be once again discovered in the new world after Ragnarǫk), and in Rv Lv 1/1^{II}, where the ability to play the game is listed among the *íþróttir* 'skills' of Rǫgnvaldr Kali Kolsson, jarl of Orkney. For further information see Helmfrid (2005), Bayless (2005), Murray (1913, 428-37; 1978, 58-64) and Fiske (1905). — [All]: Cf. *Heiðr* 73 and 79, which also refer to aspects of the game *tafl*. — [1] *drósir* 'girls': All mss except R715^x have *brúðir* 'women, brides'; cf. *Heiðr* 71/1, which lacks alliteration. *Skj* B, *Edd. Min.* and *Heiðr* 1960 emend to *snótir* 'ladies' (cf. *Heiðr* 68/1); this is without ms. support. *Skald* prefers *drósir*, as here. — [2] *sinn dróttin* 'their lord': Reversing the mss' order of these two words restores a metrical line, an emendation also made by *Skald*. — [3] *vápnlausar* 'weaponless': The main ms., 2845, reads *vápnlausan* m. acc. sg., agreeing with *dróttin*, meaning it is the lord who is weaponless. The other mss agree on the f. nom. pl. form, however, supported by the solution in the H redaction, and this is also culturally more plausible, since women did not normally carry weapons while a lord normally would.

Gestumblindi (Gestumbl *Heiðr* 20)

67. Hverjar eru þær leikur,   er líða lönd yfir
at forvitni föður?
Hvítan skjöld   þær um vetr bera,
en svartan um sumar.
Heiðrekr konungr,   hyggðu at gátu.

Hverjar eru þær leikur, er líða yfir lönd at forvitni föður? Þær bera hvítan skjöld um vetr, en svartan um sumar. Heiðrekr konungr, hyggðu at gátu.

Who are those playmates, who move over lands to the curiosity of their father? They bear a white shield in winter, but a black one in summer. King Heiðrekr, think about the riddle.

Mss: **2845**(71v) (ll. 1-2, 4-6), 281^x(100r), 597b^x(50r-v), R715^x(27v) (ll. 1-2, 4-8) (*Heiðr*).

Readings: [2] líða: fara R715^x [5] um: á 281^x, 597b^x; vetr: vetrum 281^x, 597b^x, haust R715^x; bera: við síðu bera 281^x [7-8]: *abbrev. as* 'heidr: k.' 281^x, *abbrev. as* 'h. k:' *corrected from* 'h.' *in the margin in another hand* 597b^x, *abbrev. as* 'H: k: h: at g:' R715^x.

Editions: *Skj*: Anonyme digte og vers [XIII], D. 5. *Heiðreks gátur* 18: AII, 224-5, BII, 243, *Skald* II, 126, *NN* §115; *Heiðr* 1672, 145, *FSN* 1, 477, *Heiðr* 1873, 250, 339-40, *Heiðr* 1924, 71-4, 133, *FSGJ* 2, 45, *Heiðr* 1960, 40; *Edd. Min.* 113-14.

Notes: [All]: Heiðrekr's response is (*Heiðr* 1960, 40): *Þat eru rjúpur; þær eru hvítar um vetr, en svartar um sumar* 'Those are ptarmigans; they are white during winter, but black during summer'. The ptarmigan (*Lagopus mutus*) is seasonally camouflaged, with white plumage (except for a black tail) in winter and brown in summer. — [1-3]: This question, with slight variation in each case, is asked in each of the next three riddles. — [1-2]: Cf. *Vafþr* 48/4-5 (*NK* 54) *hveriar ro þær meyiar, | er líða mar yfir* 'who are those maids, who move over the sea'. The referent here is obscure, but apparently refers to benevolent spirits, three in number (*Vafþr* 49/4, 1), whom Boer (1922, II, 58) suggested as counterparts of the three malevolent *þursa meyiar* 'giants' girls' of *Vsp* 8/6 (*NK* 2), who herald the onset of Ragnarǫk. See *Heiðr* 69, Note to l. 1 and *Heiðr* 70, Note to [All]. — [1] *leikur* 'playmates': *Leika* f. can overlap in meaning with the n. form, usually 'plaything' (*LP*: 2. *leika*, Fritzner: *leika* n.; cf. *leika* 'play'); for the f. form, which occurs here, Fritzner: *leika*, f. 1 suggests the additional meaning *pige* 'girl', which corresponds with other riddles with this opening formula. — [2]: *Hyndl* 42/3 (*NK* 295) states that at Ragnarǫk the ocean *líðr lǫnd yfir* 'will pass over lands'. — [3]: See Note to *Heiðr* 68/3. Who the *faðir* 'father' is in the present context is unclear; the expression may be formulaic; for discussion see Burrows (2013, 206-8). — [4-5]: These lines lack alliteration. Ms. R715^x's *haust* 'autumn' restores it, but makes a less good contrast with *sumar* 'summer' in line 6. Bugge (*Heiðr* 1873, 250 n. 5) notes that AM 738 fol, an R-redaction ms. with no independent value, reads *hávetr* 'high winter'; this is adopted in *Skj* B and *Skald*.

Gestumblindi (Gestumbl *Heiðr* 21)

68. Hverjar eru þær snótir,   er ganga syrgjandi
    at forvitni föður?
    Hadda bleika   hafa þær inar hvítföldnu,
    ok eigu*t* þær varðir vera.
    Heiðrekr konungr,   hyggðu at gátu.

Hverjar eru þær snótir, er ganga syrgjandi at forvitni föður? Þær hafa bleika hadda, inar hvítföldnu, ok þær varðir eigu*t* vera. Heiðrekr konungr, hyggðu at gátu.

Who are those ladies, who go sorrowing, to the curiosity of their father? They have pale hair, the white-hooded ones, and those women do not have husbands. King Heiðrekr, think about the riddle.

Mss: **2845**(72r) (ll. 1-6), 281^x(100r), 597b^x(50v), R715^x(27r-v) (*Heiðr*).

Readings: [1] snótir: *so* 281^x, 597b^x, meyjar 2845, snótir *corrected from* 'sueitir' *in the hand of JR* R715^x [2] syrgjandi: *so* 281^x, 597b^x, R715^x, margar saman 2845   [3] forvitni: 'f' 281^x, 597b^x, 'foru' R715^x;   föður: 'f' 281^x, 597b^x, R715^x [4] bleika: *so* 281^x, 597b^x, 'bleka' 2845, hafa R715^x [5] hafa: hvar 281^x, hverjar 597b^x, 'þær Blecka' R715^x;   þær: ok R715^x;   inar: eru R715^x;   hvítföldnu: *so* 281^x, 597b^x, 'huitfa/lldodo' 2845, hvítfaldnar R715^x [6] ok: *om*. R715^x;   eigu*t*: eigu 2845, eiga 281^x, 597b^x, eigur R715^x;   þær: þær þar 2845, í 281^x, 597b^x, 'þier' R715^x;   varðir: vindi 281^x, 597b^x;   vera: at vaka 281^x, vera at *corrected from* vaxera at *in the margin in another hand* 597b^x [7-8]: *abbrev. as* 'heid: k:' 281^x, *abbrev. as* 'h: k:' *corrected from* 'h:' *in the margin in another hand* 597b^x, *abbrev. as* 'H: h: at gatu' R715^x.

Editions: *Skj*: Anonyme digte og vers [XIII], D. 5. *Heiðreks gátur* 20: AII, 225, BII, 244, *Skald* II, 126, *NN* §115; *FSN* 1, 478, *Heiðr* 1873, 251, 340, *Heiðr* 1924, 72, 75, 132, *FSGJ* 2, 46, *Heiðr* 1960, 40; *Edd. Min*. 114.

Notes: [All]: Heiðrekr's response is (*Heiðr* 1960, 40): *Þat eru bylgjur, er svá heita* 'Those are the billows, that are so called'. The H redaction has the variant (*Heiðr* 1924, 72): *þat eru bylgjur, er heita Ægis meyjar* 'Those are the billows, which are called Ægir's girls'. This is the first of four riddles with the solution 'waves', which draw upon the mythological tradition that the waves can be personified as supernatural women, the nine daughters of the sea-being Ægir (cf. the common noun *ægir* 'ocean') and his wife Rán. The wave-maidens are named in *Skm* as Himinglæva 'heaven-bright one', Dúfa 'dip', Blóðughadda 'bloody-haired one', Hefring 'lifting one', Uðr 'wave', Hrǫnn 'wave', Bylgja 'billow', Bára 'bore, tidal wave', Kólga 'cold one' (*SnE* 1998, I, 36); later in *Skm* Snorri lists the names again, but Bára is replaced by Drǫfn 'turbid one' (*SnE* 1998, I, 95). Cf. *Þul Sjóvar* 4^{III} and Note [All], from which the translations here are taken; see also Þul *Waves* 1^{III}. This tradition is reflected in both skaldic and eddic poetry; see e.g. Snæbj Lv 1^{III}, ESk Frag 17^{III}, SnSt Ht 22^{III}, HHund I 28-9. The wave-maidens (like their mother, Rán) are always portrayed as hostile figures. — [1-2]: In 2845 the opening lines of this riddle and the following one (Gestumbl *Heiðr* 22/1-2 (*Heiðr* 69)) are reversed. This is followed, presumably on the grounds that 2845 is the main ms., by most eds, including *Skj* B, *Skald*, *FSGJ* and *Edd. Min.* However, all the other mss are in agreement on the arrangement followed here. — [3]: A difficult phrase, of which the implications are unclear. It also appears as l. 3 of the following two riddles. The preposition *at* seems to mean that the father's *forvitni* has somehow motivated the wave-maidens' actions in ll. 1-2. If *forvitni* is understood in its usual sense of 'curiosity', and if Ægir is the *faðir* 'father' in question, a desire to know more about the world may be implied; the Ægir portrayed in the frame story of *Skm* is certainly curious about the Æsir and their deeds. Alternatively, Finnur Jónsson (*LP*) suggested that here *forvitni* may mean *begærlidhed, ønske* 'covetousness, desire', and Clunies Ross (1994b, 175) thinks it probable that the sea was seen by early Scandinavian societies as 'an entity where male and female principles met and mingled', suggesting that 'as both waves and ocean are formed from the same substance, it might be expected that the male-female relationship would have been thought of as incestuous'. On the formula as a potential reflex of traditions about valkyries or other supernatural women, see Burrows (2013). — [4] *bleika hadda* 'pale hair': Lit. 'pale heads of hair'. Cf. *Heiðr* 64/2, where the adj. *bleikhaddaðar* 'pale-haired' is used of female swans. — [5-6]: The quality of being white-hooded describes both waves and young, marriageable women or brides. The juxtaposition of the latter image with l. 6 creates a riddling paradox. Part of the prose solution in the U redaction reads (*Heiðr* 1924, 132-3): *þær fylgia iafnann farmonnum og eru verlausar* 'they always follow seafarers and are without husbands', suggesting a now-lost variant l. 5. See further Burrows (2013, 202-4). — [5]: The same half-line is found in *Heiðr* 71/5, also a wave-riddle. These are the only two recorded instances of the adj. *hvítfaldinn* 'white-hooded'. On the significance of the *faldr* as a feminine garment see Perkins (1986-9b). — [6]: The same line is found Gestumbl *Heiðr* 18/7 (*Heiðr* 65), applied to wild angelica. The emendation is based on the reading there, and is also made by all other eds. The H redaction places this line as l. 6 of the following riddle (see Note), but the other mss agree on the present arrangement. In its place here, the H-redaction mss have l. 6 of Gestumbl *Heiðr* 23 (*Heiðr* 70), also a wave-riddle; this is a weaker combination in terms of sense.

Gestumblindi (Gestumbl *Heiðr* 22)

69. Hverjar eru þær meyjar,   er ganga margar saman
at forvitni föður?
Mörgum mönnum   hafa þær at meini orðit;
við þat munu þær sinn aldr ala.
Heiðrekr konungr,   hyggðu at gátu.

Hverjar eru þær meyjar, er ganga margar saman at forvitni föður? Þær hafa orðit mörgum mönnum at meini; þær munu ala aldr sinn við þat. Heiðrekr konungr, hyggðu at gátu.

Who are those girls, who go many together to the curiosity of their father? They have caused harm to many men; with that they must spend their lives. King Heiðrekr, think about the riddle.

Mss: 2845(71v-72r), 281ˣ(100r), 597bˣ(50v), R715ˣ(27r) (ll. 1-6) (*Heiðr*).

Readings: [1] meyjar: *so* 281ˣ, 597bˣ, R715ˣ, snótir 2845   [2] ganga margar: margar ganga 281ˣ, 'mar[...] ganga' 597bˣ;   saman: *so* 281ˣ, 597bˣ, R715ˣ, syrgjandi 2845   [3] forvitni: firða 281ˣ, 'f' 597bˣ;   föður: för 281ˣ, 'f' 597bˣ   [4] mönnum: hafa manni 281ˣ, 597bˣ, R715ˣ   [5] hafa: *om.* 281ˣ, 597bˣ, R715ˣ;   þær: *om.* R715ˣ;   orðit: komit 281ˣ, 597bˣ, R715ˣ   [6] við þat munu þær sinn aldr ala: *so* 2845, ok eiga þær þat varðar at vera 281ˣ, ok eiga þær þess varar at vera 597bˣ, við þat mun hvor sinn aldr ala R715ˣ   [7-8]: *abbrev. as* 'h k̄ h' 2845, *abbrev. as* 'heidr: k·' 281ˣ, *abbrev. as* 'h. kongr' etc:' 597bˣ.

Editions: *Skj*: Anonyme digte og vers [XIII], D. 5. Heiðreks gátur 19: AII, 225, BII, 243-4, *Skald* II, 126, *NN* §115; *Heiðr* 1672, 144, *FSN* 1, 478, *Heiðr* 1873, 251-2, 340, *Heiðr* 1924, 72-5, 132, *FSGJ* 2, 46, *Heiðr* 1960, 40; *Edd. Min.* 114.

Notes: [All]: Heiðrekr's response is (*Heiðr* 1960, 40): *Þat eru Hlés brúðir, er svá heita* 'Those are Hlér's brides, who are so called'. Hlér is given in *Skm* as an alternative name for Ægir (*SnE* 1998, I, 1), possibly reinforcing the suggestion that the relationship between Ægir and his daughters was seen as an incestuous one (see Note to *Heiðr* 68/3 above). On the other hand, the word *brúðir* may refer to women in general (see Note to *Heiðr* 64/1 and cf. *Heiðr* 71/1). The H redaction has (*Heiðr* 1924, 73): *þetta eru bárur sem áðan* 'These are waves as before'. — [1-2]: See the preceding riddle, *Heiðr* 68, Note to ll. 1-2. As there, the other mss are in agreement on the readings chosen here, although they are not those of the main ms. *Syrgjandi* 'sorrowing' in 2845 is extrametrical, but could have been influenced by the line edited here as *Heiðr* 68/2 (which follows the present stanza in 2845). — [1]: This half-line also occurs in the eddic poems *Vafþr* 48/4 and *Bdr* 12/5, both of which stanzas strongly resemble *Heiðr*'s wave-riddles and are, as here, posed by Óðinn in disguise. On the first instance, see Note to *Heiðr* 67/1-2. The second instance is a good candidate for another description of waves (*Bdr* 12/5-6, *NK* 279): *hveriar ro þær meyiar, | er at muni gráta | oc á himin verpa | hálsa scautom?* 'Who are those girls, who weep at desire and who cast to the sky the sheets of their necks?'. The question goes unanswered in *Bdr*, serving as the question that reveals Óðinn's true identity. See further Malm (2000), Burrows (2013, 210-13) and *Kommentar* III, 458-60. — [3]: Ms. 281ˣ has here 'ad firda før', not in itself a meaningful line, but cf. Gestumbl *Heiðr* 24/3 (*Heiðr* 71) *ok eiga eptir firði fǫr* 'and have a journey along the fjord', which presumably influenced the present reading. The other H-redaction ms., 597bˣ, is ambiguous, abbreviating 'ad f f', presumably *at forvitni föður*. — [6]: An almost identical line appears in Gestumbl *Heiðr* 30/6 (*Heiðr* 77), where it refers to fire waiting to be kindled in the hearth. The H redaction has l. 6 of the previous stanza, Gestumbl *Heiðr* 21 (*Heiðr* 68) (see Note). This is an acceptable variant in terms of sense, creating ambiguity in the cause and effect of the wavemaidens' actions (Burrows 2013, 203): 'perhaps they do not have husbands because they cause harm to men, or perhaps they cause harm to men because they do not want husbands'.

Gestumblindi (Gestumbl *Heiðr* 23)

70. Hverjar eru þær ekkjur,   er ganga allar saman
    at forvitni föður?
    Sjaldan blíðar eru þær   við seggja lið,
    ok eigu í vindi vaka.
    Heiðrekr konungr,   hyggðu at gátu.

Hverjar eru þær ekkjur, er ganga allar saman at forvitni föður? Þær eru sjaldan blíðar við lið seggja, ok eigu vaka í vindi. Heiðrekr konungr, hyggðu at gátu.

Who are those women, who go all together to the curiosity of their father? They are seldom gentle with the host of men, and have to stay awake in the wind. King Heiðrekr, think about the riddle.

Mss: **2845**(72r), R715ˣ(27r) (ll. 1-6) (*Heiðr*).

Readings: [2] allar: margar R715ˣ   [3] föður: *so* R715ˣ, 'f' 2845   [4] Sjaldan: 'skialldann' R715ˣ; blíðar eru þær: 'bliþir eru þær' 2845, eru þær blíðar R715ˣ   [6] eigu: eigu þær 2845, skulu R715ˣ; í: við R715ˣ; vindi: vind R715ˣ; vaka: taka R715ˣ   [7-8]: *abbrev. as* 'h k' 2845.

Editions: *Skj*: Anonyme digte og vers [XIII], D. 5. *Heiðreks gátur* 21: AII, 225, BII, 244, *Skald* II, 126-7, *NN* §115; *Heiðr* 1672, 144-5, *FSN* 1, 479, *Heiðr* 1873, 252, 341, *Heiðr* 1924, 76, 132, *FSGJ* 2, 46, *Heiðr* 1960, 41; *Edd. Min.* 115.

Notes: [All]: Heiðrekr's response reads (*Heiðr* 1960, 41): *Þat eru Ægis ekkjur, svá heita ǫldur* 'They are Ægir's women, as the waves are called'. The U redaction (*Heiðr* 1924, 132) has *þad eru Ægis dætur; þær ganga iij saman, er vindur vekur þær* 'That is Ægir's daughters; they go three together, when the wind wakes them'. Elsewhere Ægir is said to have had nine daughters (see *Heiðr* 68, Note to [All]), but three is also a significant number in Old Norse mythology and trios of supernatural women are found in e.g. *Vafþr* 48-9, *Vsp* 8, 20. The text might imply the women go in threes rather than that there are only three of them. Cf. Note to *Heiðr* 67/1-2. — [All]: *Edd. Min.* prints this as a separate stanza, but numbers it 22a, following the previous one, numbered 22. — [1] *ekkjur* 'women': In prose *ekkja* usually means 'widow', having originally been used for any unmarried woman (*CVC: ekkja*), but in poetry it can also be synonymous with 'woman' in general (*LP, Fritzner, CVC: ekkja*). — [4-5]: Very similar in meaning to *Heiðr* 69/4-5. — [4]: Ms. 2845's word order is preferable, but its 'bliþir' with the standard *-ir* abbreviation is not possible as a f. adj. — [6]: See *Heiðr* 68, Note to l. 6.

Gestumblindi (Gestumbl *Heiðr* 24)

71. Hverjar eru þær brúðir,   er ganga í brimskerjum,
    ok eiga eptir firði fǫr?
    Harðan beð   hafa þær inar hvítfǫldnu,
    ok leika í logni fátt.
    Heiðrekr konungr,   hyggðu at gátu.

Hverjar eru þær brúðir, er ganga í brimskerjum, ok eiga fǫr eptir firði? Þær hafa harðan beð, inar hvítfǫldnu, ok leika fátt í logni. Heiðrekr konungr, hyggðu at gátu.

Who are those brides, who walk in surf-skerries, and have a journey along the fjord? They have a hard bed, the white-hooded ones, and play little in the calm. King Heiðrekr, think about the riddle.

Mss: **2845**(72r) (ll. 1-6), 281ˣ(100r), 597bˣ(50v), R715ˣ(28v) (ll. 1-6) (*Heiðr*).

Readings: [2] í brimskerjum: 'i brim skerum' 2845, brimserkjum í 281ˣ, brimserkjum í *corrected from* 'brinserkjum i' *in another hand* 597bˣ, 'j brinserkjum' R715ˣ   [3] firði: firði *corrected from* friði *in another hand* 597bˣ, friði R715ˣ   [5] hafa: hafa *corrected from* hjá *in the margin in another hand* 597bˣ;   hvítfǫldnu: *so* 281ˣ, 597bˣ, 'huitfa/lldudu konur' 2845, 'huitfolldu konur' R715ˣ   [7-8]: *abbrev. as* 'heid: kʳ·' 281ˣ, *abbrev. as* 'h Kong' 597bˣ.

Editions: *Skj*: Anonyme digte og vers [XIII], D. 5. *Heiðreks gátur* 24: AII, 226, BII, 244-5, *Skald* II, 127; *Heiðr* 1672, 147, *FSN* 1, 481, *Heiðr* 1873, 252-3, 342, *Heiðr* 1924, 73, 79, 136, *FSGJ* 2, 48, *Heiðr* 1960, 42; *Edd. Min.* 115.

Notes: [All]: Heiðrekr's response is (*Heiðr* 1960, 42): *Þat eru bárur, en beðir þeira eru sker ok urðir, en þær verða lítt sénar í logni* 'Those are waves, and their beds are skerries and stones, but they are little seen in calm weather'. The H redaction has (*Heiðr* 1924, 73): *þat eru enn Ægis meyjar, ok fǫrlaz þér nú mjǫk framburðrinn ok muntu nú vilja þola dóm spekinga* 'Those are again Ægir's girls, and you grow very weak now in your delivery, and must now wish to suffer the judgement of wise men'. — [1] *brúðir* 'brides': See *Heiðr* 69, Note to [All] and *Heiðr* 64, Note to l. 1. — [2] *brimskerjum* 'surf-skerries': A *hap. leg.* Cf. Snæbj Lv 1/4, 2ᴵᴵᴵ, where the waves are referred to as *níu brúðir skerja* 'nine brides of the skerries'. Ms. 281ˣ's reading, *brimserkjum* 'surf-shirts' is a possible but less satisfactory variant. The reading of R715ˣ (though its prose refers to sker (*Heiðr* 1924, 136)) and the original reading of 597b[x] (prior to correction) is *brinserkjum* 'mail-shirts', otherwise unattested in Old Norse but cf. e.g. *brynstakkr* 'mail-jacket'. This does not make satisfactory sense in the context. On these variants see Burrows (2013, 208-9). — [5]: The same half-line is found in the earlier wave-riddle *Heiðr* 68/5 (see Note there).

Gestumblindi (Gestumbl *Heiðr* 25)

72. Fara ek sá   foldar moldbúa;
        á sat nár á nái;
     blindr reið blindum   brim*l*eiðar til;
        jór var andar vanr.
     Heiðrekr konungr,   hyggðu at gátu.

Ek sá moldbúa foldar fara; á sat nár á nái; blindr reið blindum til brim*l*eiðar; jór var vanr andar. Heiðrekr konungr, hyggðu at gátu.

I saw a soil-dweller <snake> of the earth travelling; a corpse sat on a corpse; a blind thing rode on a blind thing to the surf-way [SEA]; the steed was lacking in breath. King Heiðrekr, think about the riddle.

Mss: **2845**(71v), 281[x](100r), 597b[x](50v), R715[x](29r) (ll. 1-6) (*Heiðr*); A(8r), W(110) (*TGT*, ll. 1-3).

Readings: [1] ek sá: *so* 597b[x], A, W, 'ek søg' 2845, sá ek 281[x], er ek sá R715[x]   [2] -búa: '-kůa' 281[x]   [3] sat nár: *so* A, sat naðr 2845, 281[x], W, sat maðr 597b[x], 'satnadar' R715[x];   nái: ná 281[x], 597b[x], A, W, nú R715[x]   [4] reið: at R715[x]   [5] brim-: brim- *corrected from* brun- *in the margin in another hand* 597b[x], 'Bun-' *with* bein- *written above in another hand* R715[x];   -leiðar: reiðar *all*; til: 'ofda' *with* góð hestr *written above in another hand* R715[x]   [6] jór: *so all others*, þá jór 2845; var: er 281[x], 597b[x];   vanr: vani 281[x], 597b[x], vani *apparently corrected from* 'vař' *in another hand* R715[x]   [7-8]: *abbrev. as* 'h k' 2845, *abbrev. as* 'heid: k[t]' 281[x], *abbrev. as* 'h K:' 597b[x].

Editions: *Skj*: Anonyme digte og vers [XIII], D. 5. *Heiðreks gátur* 11: AII, 223, BII, 242, *Skald* II, 125; *Heiðr* 1672, 150, *FSN* 1, 472, *Heiðr* 1873, 253, 337, *Heiðr* 1924, 66, 74, 137, *FSGJ* 2, 42, *Heiðr* 1960, 37 (*Heiðr*), *TGT* 1884, 31, 232, *TGT* 1927, 180, *TGT* 1998, 232 (*TGT*); *Edd. Min.* 115-16.

Context: In the H redaction, before propounding this riddle, Gestumblindi says, in response to Heiðrekr's comment after the previous riddle (see *Heiðr* 72, Note to [All]) (*Heiðr* 1924, 73): *tregr em ek þess, en þó væntir mik, at þar komi nú skjótt* 'I am reluctant for that [i.e. submitting to the judgement of the counsellors], but yet I expect that it will now come quickly'. In *TGT*, ll. 1-3 illustrate the figure of *enigma*, defined (*TGT* 1884, 114): *Enigma ær myrkt sen vm leynda liking | lvtann*a, *se*m *h*er 'Enigma is obscure sense on account of the hidden likeness of things, as here'. Following quotation of the riddle we are told (*ibid.*): *þæskonar figvrv kǫllvm ver gátv, ok ær hon iafnan sett í skalldskap* 'this kind of figure we call *gáta* ['riddle'], and it is always rendered in poetry'.

Notes: [All]: Heiðrekr's response is (*Heiðr* 1960, 37): *þar fanntu hest dauðan á ísjaka ok orm dauðan á hestinum, ok rak þat allt saman eptir ánni* 'there you found a dead horse on an ice-floe and a dead snake on the horse, and all together that drifted along the river' (the ms. reads *ǫrn* 'eagle' for *orm* 'snake', but this is clearly an error). The H redaction reaches the same solution in more words, but both appear to overinterpret the riddle: the *jór* 'steed' is the ice-floe, the means of conveyance for the *moldbúi foldar* 'soil-dweller of the earth', rather than a literal dead horse, and so 'a dead serpent on an ice-floe' solves the riddle by itself (*Heiðr* 1873, 358 n.). The U redaction offers (*Heiðr* 1924, 137): *þar fanstu stein; hann mun hafa leigid i isiaka; steirn er molldbui; þetta muntu hafa rekid* [emended to *sied reka* in *Heiðr* 1672, 150] *allt samann a vatni; þar voru badir blindir og daudir* 'There you found a stone; it must have lain on an ice-floe; a stone is a soil-dweller; this you must have driven ['seen driven' with Verelius' emendation] all together on the water; there were both the blind and the dead'. Though disappointingly mundane compared to the other redactions, this alternative admittedly addresses the description provided in the riddle. — [1] *ek sá* 'I saw': See Note to *Heiðr* 48/1-2 above. — [2] *moldbúa foldar* 'a soil-dweller <snake> of the earth': *Moldbúi* 'soil-dweller' is also found in *Harð* 8/3^V, where it refers to a revenant inhabiting a mound, but cf. *heiðbúi* 'heath-dweller' and *steinbúi* 'soil-dweller' as snake-*heiti* in Þul *Orma* 3/4, 5^{III}. *Foldar* 'of the earth' seems somewhat redundant in meaning. The phrase is kenning-like in structure but cannot be fitted into any known kenning pattern. The referent is taken as a stone rather than a snake in the U redaction: see Note to [All] above. — [3]: All mss have two instances of *á* 'on' in this line; the first is likely pleonastic. No other eds have emended or commented on the problem. — [3] *nár* 'a corpse': The reading of the *TGT* ms. A is clearly superior and preferred by most eds, the other mss' *naðr* 'snake' is probably influenced by the solution, but retained in *FSGJ*. — [5] *brimleiðar* 'the surf-way [SEA]': All mss read *-reiðar* 'chariot'; this cpd, a ship-kenning, is found in Sturl *Hrafn* 3/6^{II} (and see Note), but makes no sense in the present context. *Skj* B and *Skald* also emend to *-leiðar* 'way', which cpd is found, with tmesis, in Sigv *Knútdr* 8/7, 8^I. *Edd. Min., FSGJ, Heiðr* 1873 (253 and 358 n.) and *Heiðr* 1960 (37 and n. 3) retain *-reiðar*, the latter two citing the Old English poetic word *brimrād* 'sea-road' as a possible influence for the sense 'sea', which has to be what is meant. OE *brimrād* is only found in two instances in *Andreas* (ll. 1259 and 1585) (*DOE*), though there are other compounds in *-rād* with similar meaning, e.g. *hranrād* 'whale-road, i.e. sea', *swanrād* 'swan-road, i.e. sea' (*DOE* Corpus). The word *reið* 'rode' in l. 4 and the horse-imagery may have influenced the copying here.

Gestumblindi (Gestumbl *Heiðr* 26)

73. Hvat er þat dýra, er drepr fé manna,
　　ok er jarni kringt útan?
　　Horn hefir átta, en höfuð ekki,
　　ok fylgja því margir mjök.
　　Heiðrekr konungr, hyggðu at gátu.

Hvat dýra er þat, er drepr fé manna, ok er kringt útan jarni? Hefir átta horn, en ekki höfuð, ok mjök margir fylgja því. Heiðrekr konungr, hyggðu at gátu.

What is the creature who slays men's flocks and is surrounded outside with iron? It has eight horns, but no head, and a great many follow it. King Heiðrekr, think about the riddle.

Mss: **2845**(71v), 281ˣ(100r), 597bˣ(50v), R715ˣ(28r) (ll. 1-6) (*Heiðr*).

Readings: [3] ok er jarni: *om*. R715ˣ;　　kringt: *so* 281ˣ, 597bˣ, kringr 2845, 'krinkt' R715ˣ [5] ekki: 'ejn' 597bˣ　　[6] fylgja: rennr 281ˣ, 597bˣ, 'filgur' R715ˣ;　　því: sem 281ˣ, *om*. 597bˣ, R715ˣ;　　margir: hann 281ˣ, 597bˣ, margr R715ˣ;　　mjök: má 281ˣ, 597bˣ, *om*. R715ˣ　　[7-8]: *abbrev. as* 'h k̄' 2845, *abbrev. as* 'heidr. kr' 281ˣ, *abbrev. as* 'hᶜ Kongʳ h.' 597bˣ.

Editions: *Skj*: Anonyme digte og vers [XIII], D. 5. Heiðreks gátur 16: AII, 224, BII, 243, *Skald* II, 126; *Heiðr* 1672, 147, *FSN* 1, 475-6, *Heiðr* 1873, 254, 339, *Heiðr* 1924, 71-2, 74-5, 134-5, *FSGJ* 2, 44, *Heiðr* 1960, 39; *Edd. Min.* 116.

Notes: [All]: Heiðrekr's response is (*Heiðr* 1960, 39): *Þat er húnn í hnettafli* 'That is the *húnn* [lit. 'bear-cub'] in *hnefatafl*. The H redaction adds (*Heiðr* 1924, 75): *hann heitir sem bjǫrn; hann rennr þegar er honum er kastat* 'he is called the same as a bear; he runs as soon as he is cast'. On *hnefatafl* see *Heiðr* 66, Note to [All]. There is some disagreement as to whether the *húnn* was a playing piece or a die. Fritzner: *húnn* cites this example, translating *terning* 'die', but *hnefatafl* is not thought to have been played with dice. However, the verb *kasta* 'cast' in the solution to the H redaction seems unlikely to be used of playing pieces (and cf. *verpa* 'throw', used with *húnn* in Þhorn *Harkv* 16/4¹; see also Note). If the *húnn* is indeed a die, the riddle may refer to the game *kvátrutafl* or Icelandic tables, a game similar to backgammon, rather than to *hnefatafl* (Helmfrid 2005, 11). On the other hand, the U redaction reads *þad er tafla* 'that is a playing piece'. — [All]: Cf. *Heiðr* 66 and 79, which also refer to aspects of the game *tafl*. — [2] *fé* 'flocks': The animal imagery suggests that 'flocks' is the surface meaning, but plays also on the meaning 'money, property', suggesting that the game could be played for monetary stakes. This meaning is brought to the fore by the solution in the U redaction, which includes (*Heiðr* 1924, 135): *hun ... rænir margann fie, þann er fie legur vid tafl* 'the *húnn* ... plunders money from many a one who lays down money on *tafl*'. A clause in *Grágás* (K§233) forbids the playing of board games for money or other property. — [4] *hefir átta horn* 'it has eight horns': If the solution is to be interpreted as 'die' (see Note to [All] above), this line puns on two meanings of *horn*, 'horns' and 'corners', referring to the eight corners on a six-faced die. It is less clear what this line would refer to if the solution is 'playing piece', although Murray (1978, 61) suggested the solution to be the *hnefi* or 'king'-piece, with the eight 'horns' being the eight defending pieces on a 7x7 board. — [6]: The H redaction has a variant half-line here: *ok rennr sem hann má* 'and runs as he can'. *Heiðr* 1873 (254) emends to *ok rennr, er renna má* 'and runs, when he can run'. This is adopted in *Edd. Min.* Although the line is corrupt in R715[x], its similarity to 2845's reading supports 2845's over that of the H-redaction mss.

Gestumblindi (Gestumbl *Heiðr* 27)

74. Hvat er þat dýra,   er Dönum hlífir,
     berr blóðugt bak,   en bergr firum,
     geirum mætir,   gefr líf sumum,
     leggr við lófa   lík sitt guma?
     Heiðrekr konungr,   hyggðu at gátu.

Hvat er þat dýra, er hlífir Dönum, berr blóðugt bak, en bergr firum, mætir geirum, gefr sumum líf, leggr lík sitt við lófa guma? Heiðrekr konungr, hyggðu at gátu.

What is that creature, that protects Danes, bears a bloody back, but saves men, meets spears, gives life to some, lays its body against the palm of a man? King Heiðrekr, think about the riddle.

Mss: **2845**(71v), 281[x](100v), 597b[x](50v), R715[x](29r-v) (ll. 1-8) (*Heiðr*).

Readings: [2] Dönum: danir R715[x]; hlífir: skemma R715[x]   [5] geirum mætir: *om.* 281[x], 597b[x]   [6] gefr: getr R715[x];   sumum: *so* 281[x], 597b[x], R715[x], firum 2845   [7] lófa: lofða 281[x], 597b[x]   [8] lík: líf 281[x];   guma: *so* R715[x], gumi *all others*   [9-10] *abbrev. as* 'h k' 2845, *abbrev. as* 'heidr: k'' 281[x], *abbrev. as* 'h K:' 597b[x].

Editions: *Skj*: Anonyme digte og vers [XIII], D. 5. *Heiðreks gátur* 17: AII, 224, BII, 243, *Skald* II, 126; *Heiðr* 1672, 150, *FSN* 1, 476, *Heiðr* 1873, 255, 339, *Heiðr* 1924, 72-3, 75, 138, *FSGJ* 2, 45, *Heiðr* 1960, 39; *Edd. Min.* 116.

Notes: [All]: Heiðrekr's response is (*Heiðr* 1960, 39): *Þat er skjǫldr; hann verðr opt blóðugr í bardǫgum ok hlífir vel þeim mǫnnum, er skjaldfimir eru* 'That is a shield; it often becomes bloody in battles and protects those men well who are deft with a shield'. — [1]: See Note to *Heiðr* 73/1. — [2] *hlífir Dönum* 'protects Danes': Ms. R715[x] has *Danir skemma* 'the Danes damage', although in the prose solution (*Heiðr* 1924, 138), *hann skeina Danir opt* 'the Danes scratch him often'. Either (*skemma* or *skeina*) provides an acceptable alternative. 'Danes' should perhaps be understood as men in general (*Heiðr* 1956, 81 n. to p. 45, l. 4). — [4]: Cf. *Heiðr* 53/4. — [6] *sumum* 'some': Preferable to 2845's *firum* 'men' to avoid repetition from l. 4. — [8] *guma* 'of a man': Only R715[x] has the gen. sg., which makes most sense and is adopted by most eds, as here. The other mss read *gumi* nom. sg., which could be construed 'a man lays his body against its palm'. Tolkien, who adopts this reading (*Heiðr* 1960, 39 and n. 3), surmises that 'R's text means that the inner side of the shield is called its *lófi* (palm, i.e. hollow inner side of the hand)', but there are no recorded instances of such a usage.

Gestumblindi (Gestumbl *Heiðr* 28)

75. Nær var forðum   nösgás vaxin,
     barngjörn, sú er bar bútimbr saman.
     Hlífðu henni   hálms bitskálmir;
     þó lá drykkjar   drynhraun yfir.
     Heiðrekr konungr,   hyggðu at gátu.

Nösgás var forðum nær vaxin, barngjörn, sú er bar saman bútimbr. Bitskálmir hálms hlífðu henni; þó lá drynhraun drykkjar yfir. Heiðrekr konungr, hyggðu at gátu.

Long ago, a nostrils-goose [DUCK] was nearly grown, child-eager, who brought house-timber together. Biting-swords of straw [OX TEETH] protected her; yet the bellowing lava-field of drink [OX SKULL] lay over. King Heiðrekr, think about the riddle.

Mss: 2845(72r) (ll. 1-8), 281ˣ(100v), 597bˣ(50v), R715ˣ(29r) (ll. 1-8) (*Heiðr*).

Readings: [1] Nær: *so* R715ˣ, mjök *all others*; forðum: fyrri forðum 597bˣ [2] nösgás: 'nanz gras' R715ˣ [3] barngjörn: 'Bar ggiar' R715ˣ; sú er bar: 'sueipar' R715ˣ [6] hálms: hálm 281ˣ, 597bˣ; bit-: bits 281ˣ, 597bˣ [7] drykkjar: 'drickiar' R715ˣ [8] drynhraun: 'drunraun' *corrected from* drynhraun *in the margin in another hand* 597bˣ, 'drin huarn' *apparently corrected from* 'dÿraun' *in the margin in the hand of JR* R715ˣ; yfir: dýra yfer *corrected from* yfer *in the margin in the hand of JR* R715ˣ [9-10]: abbrev. *as* 'heidr: kʳ' 281ˣ, abbrev. *as* 'h K.' 597bˣ.

Editions: *Skj*: Anonyme digte og vers [XIII], D. 5. *Heiðreks gátur* 22: AII, 225, BII, 244, *Skald* II, 127, *NN* §2360, 2594; *Heiðr* 1672, 150, *FSN* 1, 479-80, *Heiðr* 1873, 256, 341, *Heiðr* 1924, 76-7, 138, *FSGJ* 2, 47, *Heiðr* 1960, 41; *Edd. Min.* 116-17.

Notes: [All]: Heiðrekr's response is (*Heiðr* 1960, 41): *Þar hafði ǫnd búit hreiðr sitt í milli nautskjálka, ok lá haussinn ofan yfir* 'There a duck had built its nest between the jaw-bones of an ox, and the skull lay over above'. The H redaction gives (*Heiðr* 1924, 76): *Þá lá ǫnd á eggjum millum nautzkjálka, er þú hálmbitz skálmir kallar, en drynhraun hausinn, en bútimbr hreiðrit* 'There a duck lay on eggs between the jaw-bones of an ox, which you call 'biting-swords of straw', and the skull 'bellowing lava-field', and the nest 'house-timber'. — [All]: The solution is reminiscent of Judges XIV.8-14, where Samson eats from a honeycomb produced by a swarm of bees inside the skull of a lion, and later propounds the riddle *de comedente exivit cibus et de forte est egressa dulcedo* 'Out of the eater came forth food, and out of the strong came forth sweetness'. Life-from-death symbolism could be said to be present in this riddle, although there is no overt Christian context. — [1] *nær* 'nearly': Ms. R715ˣ's reading is preferred here for alliteration. Some younger mss and early eds give *nóg* 'enough' (see *Edd. Min.*, 116 n. 27.1). *Skj* B emends to *næsta* and translates *fuldt* 'fully'. Kock (*Skald*) emends to *nýt* 'newly' on (dubious) palaeographical grounds, suggesting that the four minims of his proposed original *nut* could have been transformed to *míoc* via *míc* (*NN* §2360). *Edd. Min.* suggests that the problem could be with *forðum* rather than the first word, but does not offer a convincing alternative. — [2] *nösgás* 'nostrils-goose [DUCK]': A *hap. leg.* The prose solution indicates that a duck is being referred to, and *Meissner* 112 considers the cpd a kenning. There is one other duck-kenning in the corpus, *bekkþiðurr* 'brook-capercaillie' in Egill Lv 2/5^V (*Eg* 5), where the meaning is also indicated by the prose context. — [3] *barngjörn* 'child-eager': A *hap. leg.* — [4] *bútimbr* 'house-timber': The only recorded instances of this cpd are here and in the prose solution in the H redaction. — [6] *bitskálmir hálms* 'biting-swords of straw [OX TEETH]': *Meissner* 133. A situation-specific kenning, referring to the teeth of a grazing animal. Cf. the teeth-kenning *hvítgeirar hvapta* 'the white spears of mouths [TEETH]', StjOdd *Geirdr* 9/7^V (*StjǫrnODr* 14), where the base-word is also a weapon. *Bitskǫlm* only appears here and in the prose in the H redaction. — [7-8] *drynhraun drykkjar* 'the bellowing lava-field of drink [OX SKULL]': Cf. GSúrs Lv 27/5^V (*Gísl* 30), where the head is referred to as *hraun kveifar* 'the lava-field of the cap'.

Gestumblindi (Gestumbl *Heiðr* 29)

76. Fjórir hanga,   fjórir ganga,
     tveir veg vísa,   tveir hundum varða,
     einn eptir drallr ok jafnan heldr saurugr.
     Heiðrekr konungr, hyggðu at gátu.

Fjórir hanga, fjórir ganga, tveir vísa veg, tveir varða hundum, einn drallar eptir ok jafnan heldr saurugr. Heiðrekr konungr, hyggðu at gátu.

Four hang, four go, two point the way, two ward off dogs, one trails after and [is] always rather dirty. King Heiðrekr, think about the riddle.

Mss: **2845**(72r-v), 281^x(100v), 597b^x(50v) (*Heiðr*).

Readings: [1] hanga: ganga 281^x, 597b^x [2] fjórir: fjórir *added in the margin in another hand* 597b^x; ganga: hanga 281^x, hanga *added in the margin in another hand* 597b^x [4] varða: verjast 281^x, 597b^x [5] einn: 'eirn' 281^x, 'eirn eirn' 597b^x [6] jafnan: optast 281^x, 597b^x; heldr: *om.* 281^x, 597b^x; saurugr: óhreinn 281^x, 597b^x [7-8]: *abbrev. as* 'h k̄' 2845, *abbrev. as* 'heidr: k̄' 281^x, *abbrev. as* 'h^c: Kong^r hygg ad gätu miñe' 597b^x.

Editions: *Skj*: Anonyme digte og vers [XIII], D. 5. Heiðreks gátur 27: AII, 226, BII, 245, *Skald* II, 127, *NN* §§2362, 3397C; *FSN* 1, 484, *Heiðr* 1873, 257, 343, *Heiðr* 1924, 77, 81, *FSGJ* 2, 49, *Heiðr* 1960, 43; *Edd. Min.* 117.

Notes: [All]: Heiðrekr's response is (*Heiðr* 1960, 43): *þat er kýr* 'That is a cow'. The H redaction expands (*Heiðr* 1924, 77): *hón hefir fjóra fœtr ok fjóra spena, tvau horn ok tvau augu, enn halinn drallar eptir* 'she has four legs and four teats, two horns and two eyes, but the tail trails after'. — [All]: Versions of this riddle are found across European tradition; Tomasek (1999, 261-2) claims that the Old Norse is the earliest recorded instance in the vernacular. A cosmological variation, in which heaven and earth, day and night, and sun and moon are the referents, can be found in classical tradition. For parallels and further references see Taylor (1951, 610-21). — [All]: In this stanza ll. 1-3 are *fornyrðislag* and ll. 4-6 *málaháttr*. Kock, however, presents the stanza as *ljóðaháttr* by emending the word order in l. 3 to *tveir vísa veg* (*Skald*; *NN* §3397) and in l. 5 substituting *hinstr* 'hindmost' for *eptir* (cf. *NN* §2362). — [5] *drallar eptir* 'trails after': *Dralla* is a *hap. leg.* in poetry and the only occurrence in prose appears to be in the solution to this riddle in the H redaction. Cf. *NO*: 1 *dralla*. Kock emends *eptir* to *hinstr* 'hindmost', to alliterate with *hundum* 'dogs' in l. 4 (*NN* §2362). — [6]: The H redaction has the variant line *ok optast óhreinn* 'most often unclean'. *Skald* gives *ok óhreinn opt* 'and often unclean', with rearranged word order for more regular *ljóðaháttr* (*NN* §3397; cf. Notes to ll. 3 and 5 above), though in *NN* §2362 Kock retains the H redaction's reading unemended.

Gestumblindi (Gestumbl *Heiðr* 30)

77. Hverr er sá inn eini,   er sefr í ösgrúa,
    ok af grjóti einu görr?
    Föður né móður   áat sá inn fagrgjarni;
    þar mun hann sinn aldr ala.
    Heiðrekr konungr,   hyggðu at gátu.

Hverr er sá inn eini, er sefr í ösgrúa, ok görr af grjóti einu? Sá inn fagrgjarni *áat* föður né móður; þar mun hann ala aldr sinn. Heiðrekr konungr, hyggðu at gátu.

Who is that, the lone one, who sleeps in the ash-grate, and is struck from stone alone? That bright-eager one has neither father nor mother; there he must spend his life. King Heiðrekr, think about the riddle.

Mss: **2845**(71v), 281ˣ(100v), 597bˣ(51r), R715ˣ(28r-v) (ll. 1-6) (*Heiðr*).

Readings: [2] ösgrúa: ösku grúa 281ˣ, 597bˣ   [3] ok: ok er 281ˣ, 597bˣ, R715ˣ; einu: eru 281ˣ, einu er *corrected from* einu *in the margin in another hand* 597bˣ, ok jarni R715ˣ;   görr: görðr R715ˣ   [4] né: ok 281ˣ, 597bˣ, R715ˣ   [5] áat: á 2845, R715ˣ, 'ugad' 281ˣ, eigat 597bˣ;   fagr-: fjár- 281ˣ, 597bˣ, fár- R715ˣ   [6] þar: 'so' R715ˣ   [7-8]: *abbrev. as* 'h k̄ h' 2845, *abbrev. as* 'heid: k.' 281ˣ, *abbrev. as* 'h: K.' 597bˣ.

Editions: *Skj*: Anonyme digte og vers [XIII], D. 5. *Heiðreks gátur* 14: AII, 224, BII, 242-3, *Skald* II, 126, *NN* §3176; *Heiðr* 1672, 147, *FSN* 1, 474, *Heiðr* 1873, 257-8, 338, *Heiðr* 1924, 69, 77, 135, *FSGJ* 2, 43, *Heiðr* 1960, 38; *Edd. Min.* 117-18.

Notes: [All]: Heiðrekr's response is (*Heiðr* 1960, 38): *Þat er eldr fólginn á arni, ok tekr ór tinnu* 'That is fire hidden in the hearth, and it starts from flint'. — [All]: Cf. *Heiðr* 81, about embers in the hearth. — [1]: See Note to *Heiðr* 51/1. — [2] *ösgrúa* 'the ash-grate': A *hap. leg.* The H-redaction reading *ösku grúa* 'ash grate' probably represents a later attempt to make sense of an unfamiliar word, but is unmetrical. The other mss are in agreement on the reading chosen here. — [3] *af grjóti einu* 'from stone alone': The U redaction appears to be unhappy with the accuracy of this claim, reading *af grjóti ok jarni* 'of stone and iron'. Flint needs to be struck with iron or steel to produce sparks to kindle fire, though there is no reason why the riddle should necessarily refer to both; cf. *Heiðr* 63, Note to [All], about obsidian, a flint-stone. — [5] *á̂at* 'has not': Mss 2845 and R715^x have the positive *á* 'has', but the poetic negative suffix is needed for sense and to complement the negating conjunction *né* 'nor' in l. 4 (cf. *Heiðr* 1873, 258; *Edd. Min.*; *Skj* B). Mss 281^x and 597b^x have the 3rd pers. pl. with negative suffix *eigat*, though the subject is sg. — [5] *fagrgjarni* 'bright-eager one': Unrecorded as an Old Norse word, but appropriate to fire waiting to be kindled. Ms. R715^{x}'s variant, *fárgjarni* 'damage-eager', is also an acceptable reading and is adopted by several eds. The H-redaction mss have *fjárgjarni* 'money-eager', which gives poor sense in the context. — [6]: An almost identical line is found in *Heiðr* 69/6, where it describes waves.

Gestumblindi (Gestumbl *Heiðr* 31)

78. Hest sá ek standa;   hýddi meri,
    dúði dyndil,   drap *h*laun und kvið.
    Ór skal draga   ok †gjöpta† at góða stund.
    Heiðrekr konungr,   hyggðu at gátu.

Ek sá hest standa; hýddi meri, dúði dyndil, *h*laun drap und kvið. Ór skal draga ok †gjöpta† at góða stund. Heiðrekr konungr, hyggðu at gátu.

I saw a stallion stand; it flogged a mare, shook the penis, buttock beat under belly. [It] shall draw out and … a good while. King Heiðrekr, think about the riddle.

Mss: **281^x**(100v), 597b^x(51r) (*Heiðr*).

Readings: [2] meri: meri *corrected from* manni *in the margin in another hand* 597b^x [3] dúði: 'daudt' 281^x, dauðr *corrected from* dúði *in the margin in another hand after correction from* 'dr[…]e' *in the scribal hand* 597b^x [4] *h*laun: laun *all*; und: undir 597b^x [5] draga: 'draga ~~skal draga~~' 597b^x [7-8]: *abbrev. as* 'heidr: k^r' 281^x, *abbrev. as* 'h K:' 597b^x.

Editions: *Skj*: Anonyme digte og vers [XIII], D. 5. Heiðreks gátur 36: AII, 228, BII, 247, *Skald* II, 128, *NN* §3284; *Heiðr* 1873, 258, *Heiðr* 1924, 78, *Heiðr* 1960, 81-2; *Edd. Min.* 118.

Notes: [All]: Heiðrekr's response is (*Heiðr* 1960, 82): *Hest þann kallar þú línvef, en skeið meri hans, en upp ok ofan skal hrista vefinn* 'You call that stallion linen cloth, and the weaver's rod his mare, and up and down the web shall be shaken'. Tolkien (*Heiðr* 1960,

82 n.) points out that the solution 'is obviously wrong: the "mare" is the web on the loom, which is alternately raised up and pressed down by the rod or slay'. In the prose following the riddle, before giving the solution Heiðrekr invites his courtiers to solve it, but they are unable to. The riddle's obvious sexual overtones perhaps explain its omission in the R and U redactions and its textual problems in the H-redaction mss. — [1] *ek sá* 'I saw': See Note to *Heiðr* 48/2 above. — [3] *dúði* 'shook': This reading is in the scribal hand in 597b^x, but is a correction to a now illegible original. — [3] *dyndil* 'penis': Cf. *Fritzner*: *dindill*; *LP*: *dyndill*. A *hap. leg.* in poetry and found in prose only as a nickname in three instances in the *Flat* version of *Hák* (the form *dyntill* is found in the versions of F and 81a). Perhaps cf. *ONP*: *dyrðill*, *dyðrill* 'short tail, stump of a tail' and Anon *Ól* 6/6^1 and Note. — [4] h*laun* 'buttock': A *hap. leg.* in poetry. The emendation is made by all eds. — [5-6]: 'Gjöpta' l. 6 is not a known Old Norse word. Neither *Skj* B nor *Heiðr* 1960 attempt reconstruction, and the suggestions of Kock (*Skald*; *NN* §3284), Bugge (*Heiðr* 1873) and *Edd. Min.* are conjectural and not particularly satisfactory.

Gestumblindi (Gestumbl *Heiðr* 32)

79. Hverjar eru þeir þegnar,   er ríða þingi at
    sáttir allir saman?
    Lýða sína   senda þeir lönd yfir
    at byggja bólstaði.
    Heiðrekr konungr,   hyggðu at gátu.

Hverjar eru þeir þegnar, er ríða allir saman sáttir at þingi? Þeir senda lýða sína yfir lönd at byggja bólstaði. Heiðrekr konungr, hyggðu at gátu.

Who are those thanes, who all ride together reconciled to the assembly? They send their men over lands to settle homesteads. King Heiðrekr, think about the riddle.

Mss: 2845(71v), 281^x(100v), 597b^x(51r), R715^x(28r) (ll. 1-6) (*Heiðr*).

Readings: [1] þegnar: 'þeguar' R715^x [2] ríða: ráða R715^x;   þingi: landi R715^x;   at: 'all' R715^x [3] sáttir allir: ok eru sextán 281^x, 597b^x [4] Lýða: lýdi 281^x, 597b^x;   sína: *om.* R715^x [5] lönd: land R715^x [6] byggja: sigra menn R715^x;   bólstaði: 'sierhuoria' R715^x [7-8]: *abbrev. as* 'h k' 2845, *abbrev. as* 'heidr: k:' 281^x, *abbrev. as* 'h K:' 597b^x.

Editions: *Skj*: Anonyme digte og vers [XIII], D. 5. Heiðreks gátur 12: AII, 223, BII, 242, *Skald* II, 125-6; *Heiðr* 1672, 146, *FSN* 1, 473, *Heiðr* 1873, 259, 337-8, *Heiðr* 1924, 67, 79, 134, *FSGJ* 2, 43, *Heiðr* 1960, 37; *Edd. Min.* 118.

Notes: [All]: Heiðrekr's response is (*Heiðr* 1960, 37): *þat er Ítrekr ok Andaðr, er þeir sitja at tafli sínu* 'That is Ítrekr and Andaðr, when they sit at their *tafl*-board'. The H redaction has (*Heiðr* 1924, 79): *þat er tafl Ítreks konungs* 'That is King Ítrekr's *tafl*'. On *tafl* or *hnefatafl* see *Heiðr* 66, Note to [All]. One Ítreksjóð (lit. 'offspring of Ítrekr') appears in Þul *Ása* I 1/8^III, names for Óðinn's sons (cf. *SnE* 1998, I, 113), suggesting Ítrekr is an Óðinn-name. An Anduðr or Qnduðr appears in a list of *heiti* for giants in the same text (*SnE* 1998, I, 111; Þul *Jǫtna* I 4/6^III). Further details of such a skill-contest have not survived, but are not dissimilar to the wisdom-contests between gods and giants in e.g. *Vafþr* or *Alv*. — [All]: Cf. *Heiðr* 66 and 73, which both also refer to aspects of the game *tafl*. — [1-2]: Ms. R715^x has these two lines (with a slight variation in l. 1) at the beginning of *Heiðr* 83. — [2] *at þingi* 'to the assembly': Ms. R715^x has the variant 'landi all', which does not make grammatical sense and lacks alliteration with l. 1. — [3]: The H redaction has: *ok eru sextán saman* 'and are sixteen together', which is adopted by *Edd. Min.* On a 7x7 *hnefatafl* board there would be sixteen attackers.

Gestumblindi (Gestumbl *Heiðr* 33)

80. Sá ek á sumri   sólbjörgum í
     verðung vaka,   vilgi teita.
     Drukku jarlar   öl þegjandi,
     en æpanda   ölker stóð.
     Heiðrekr konungr,   hyggðu at gátu.

Ek sá verðung vaka, vilgi teita, á sumri í sólbjörgum. Jarlar drukku öl þegjandi, en ölker stóð æpanda. Heiðrekr konungr, hyggðu at gátu.

I saw a retinue be wakeful, not at all happy, in summer at sunset. The jarls drank ale in silence, but the ale-keg stood squealing. King Heiðrekr, think about the riddle.

Mss: **2845**(72r), 281^x(100v), 597b^x(51r), R715^x(29v) (ll. 1-8) (*Heiðr*).

Readings: [1] Sá ek á: 'sá ek ur' *corrected from* 'săkur' *in the hand of JR* R715^x;   sumri: 'suerr' R715^x   [2] sólbjörgum: *so* 281^x, 597b^x, sól björg of 2845, 'selbiorgum' R715^x; í: *so* 281^x, 597b^x, á 2845, R715^x   [3] verðung: *so all others*, bað ek vel 2845;   vaka: lífa 2845   [4] vilgi: vígi 281^x, 597b^x;   teita: *so* 281^x, 597b^x, teiti 2845, 'slito' R715^x   [7] æpanda: æpandi 281^x, 597b^x, 'leipanda' R715^x   [8] stóð: stóðu 281^x, 597b^x, R715^x   [9-10]: *abbrev. as* 'h k' 2845, *abbrev. as* 'heidr: k^r' 281^x, *abbrev. as* 'h: K:' 597b^x.

Editions: *Skj*: Anonyme digte og vers [XIII], D. 5. *Heiðreks gátur* 25: AII, 226, BII, 245, *Skald* II, 127; *Heiðr* 1672, 151; *FSN* 1, 482; *Heiðr* 1873, 259-60, 342; *Heiðr* 1924, 79-80, 138-9; *FSGJ* 2, 48; *Heiðr* 1960, 42; *Edd. Min.* 118-19.

Notes: [All]: Heiðrekr's response is (*Heiðr* 1960, 42): *Þar drukku grísir gylti, en hon hrein við* 'There piglets drank from a sow, and she squealed at that'. The H redaction has rather more prose (*Heiðr* 1924, 80): *'þat er grísasýr; þá er grísir sjúga hana, þá hrínn hón, en þeir þegja; en eigi veit ek, hvat manna þú ert, er þvílíka hluti gerir svá mjúklega af lítlum efnum.' Ok nú biðr konungr í hljóði at byrgja skuli hallardyrrnar* '"that is a sow with piglets; when the piglets suck her, then she squeals, but they are silent; but I don't know what kind of man you are, when you make such things so adroitly from little material.' And now the king orders in secret that the hall-doors should be closed'. — [1] *ek sá* 'I saw': See Note to *Heiðr* 48/2 above. — [2] *sólbjörgum* 'sunset': Lit. 'sun-saving'. *Hap. leg.* — [3] *verðung* 'a retinue': This word is attested only in poetry. — [4] *vilgi* 'not at all': *Vilgi* can mean, depending on the context, either 'not at all' or the opposite, 'very much', and was likely chosen for its ambiguity. The former meaning has been chosen for the translation here since, in a nice juxtaposition of opposites and subversion of expectations, the silence of the drinking jarls (cf. *Akv* 2/1-4) and the squealing of the 'keg' imply unhappiness. On the other hand, suckling piglets are likely to be content, and so the word can be reinterpreted once the solution is known. — [8] *stóð* 'stood': This is the reading of 2845, while the other mss have the 3rd pers. pl. pret. indic. *stóðu*. The subject of the verb, *ölker* 'the ale-keg', being n., could be either sg. or pl. Ms. 2845's 3rd pers. sg. pret. indic. variant has been preferred here, even though it renders the line hypometrical, while *stóðu* would make it a metrical *fornyrðislag* line, like the rest of the stanza. However, a pl. subject and verb here make awkward sense, and go against the understanding of both prose explanations of the riddle's meaning. *Skj* B and *Skald* emend to *of stóð* to give a metrical line.

Gestumblindi (Gestumbl *Heiðr* 34)

81. Meyjar ek sá   moldu líkar,
    váru þeim at beðjum björg,
svartar ok sámar   í sólviðri,
    en þess at fegri, er færra um sér.
Heiðrekr konungr,   hyggðu at gátu.

Ek sá meyjar líkar moldu, björg váru at þeim beðjum, svartar ok sámar í sólviðri, en þess at fegri, er færra um sér. Heiðrekr konungr, hyggðu at gátu.

I saw girls like dust, rocks were beds to them. [They are] black and swarthy in sunny weather, but the brighter, the less is seen of them. King Heiðrekr, think about the riddle.

Mss: **281ˣ**(100v), 597bˣ(51r) (*Heiðr*).

Readings: [1] ek: eru 597bˣ [3] beðjum: *so* 597bˣ, beðinn 281ˣ [4] svartar: svartr 281ˣ, 597bˣ; sámar: samr 281ˣ, 597bˣ [7-8]: *abbrev. as* 'heidr: kʳ:' 281ˣ, *abbrev. as* 'hᶜ K:' 597bˣ.

Editions: *Skj*: Anonyme digte og vers [XIII], D. 5. Heiðreks gátur 37: AII, 228, BII, 247, *Skald* II, 128; *FSN* 1, 483, *Heiðr* 1873, 260, *Heiðr* 1924, 81, *Heiðr* 1960, 82; *Edd. Min.* 119.

Notes: [All]: Heiðrekr's response is (*Heiðr* 1960, 82): *þat eru glæðr fǫlnaðar á arni* 'those are embers grown pale in the hearth'. — [All]: Cf. *Heiðr* 77, which is about fire waiting to be kindled from flint in the hearth. — [5] *sólviðri* 'sunny weather': A *hap. leg.*, but many similar compounds with the first element *sól-* are attested. — [6] *þess at fegri* 'the brighter': The construction *þess* + comp. adj. (here *fegri* 'brighter') means 'the more (so)' (*CVC*: *þat*).

Gestumblindi (Gestumbl *Heiðr* 35)

82. Sat ek á segli,   sá ek dauða menn
    blóðshol* bera   í börk viðar.
    Heiðrekr konungr,   hyggðu at gátu.

Ek sat á segli, ek sá dauða menn bera blóðshol* í börk viðar. Heiðrekr konungr, hyggðu at gátu.

I sat on a sail, I saw dead men carry a blood vessel into the bark of a tree. King Heiðrekr, think about the riddle.

Mss: **2845**(72v) (ll. 1-4), 281ˣ(100v), 597bˣ(51r) (*Heiðr*).

Readings: [1] segli: segl 281ˣ, 597bˣ [3] blóðshol*: 'blo þ holld' 2845, 'blodzhollld' 281ˣ, 'blǫds holld' 597bˣ [4] börk: björk 281ˣ; viðar: *so* 281ˣ, 597bˣ, 'viddar' 2845 [5-6]: *abbrev. as* 'heidr k:' 281ˣ, *abbrev. as* 'hᶜ K:' 597bˣ.

Editions: *Skj*: Anonyme digte og vers [XIII], D. 5. Heiðreks gátur 28: AII, 226, BII, 245, *Skald* II, 127, *NN* §2363; *FSN* 1, 484-5, *Heiðr* 1873, 261, 343, *Heiðr* 1924, 81-2, *FSGJ* 2, 49-50, *Heiðr* 1960, 43-4; *Edd. Min.* 119.

Notes: [All]: Heiðrekr's response is (*Heiðr* 1960, 44): *Þar saztu á vegg ok sátt val bera æði í hamra* 'There you sat on a wall and saw a falcon bear an eider-duck into the crags'. The H redaction has (*Heiðr* 1924, 82): *þar saztu á vegg ok sáttu val fljúga ok bar æði í klóm sér* 'there you sat on a wall and saw a falcon fly and it carried an eider duck in its claws'. — [All]: The interpretation of this stanza relies on the poetic device *ofljóst* 'excessively clear', where a homonym of the intended referent is substituted by a circumlocutory phrase. — [1] *segli* 'a sail': The homonym *veggr* means both 'wall', as in the solution, and 'sail', as in the Text (see *LP*: *veggr* 2). — [2] *dauða menn* 'dead men': The homonym *valr* means both 'the slain' ('dead men') and 'falcon'. Anon *Gát* 1/4ᴵᴵᴵ, a riddle referring to several different types of birds, uses *eggdauða menn* 'men killed by the sword' (lit. 'sword-edge-dead men') for *valr*, giving a more exact synonym for 'slain'. AM 738 4toˣ, which has a copy of *Heiðr*'s riddles stemming indirectly from 2845 and is without independent value (*Heiðr* 1924, xv), reads 'eggdauda' for *dauða* (86r); this is less good metrically in the present context (cf. *Heiðr* 1873, 261 n. 3). — [3] *blóðshol** 'a blood vessel': Lit. 'blood's hole'. The homonym *æðr*, given in the solution, means both 'eider duck' and 'blood vessel', but the scribes do not seem to have understood this pun. The main ms. reads 'bloþ holld', which *Skj* and, following Finnur Jónsson, *FSGJ*, expand to *blóðugt* 'bloody' (as did Petersen and Thorarensen in 1847) giving 'bloody flesh', only loosely synonymous with 'vein'. The H redaction has *blóðs hold* 'flesh of blood(?)'. The emendation to *blóðshol*, which is tentatively adopted here, was first suggested in Rafn *et al.* 1850-2, I, 189 n. 7. It is accepted in *Heiðr* 1873, 261, *Edd.*

Min., *Skald* and *Heiðr* 1960 among others, although the word is not otherwise attested in Old Norse. The interpretation of Anon *Gát* 1/5[III] relies on the same pun on *æðr*; a similar play on words occurs in Anon (*FoGT*) 20/5-6[III]. — [4] *börk viðar* 'the bark of a tree': Editors have struggled to work out the substitution here, not helped by the fact that the R and H redactions have different solutions: *í hamra* 'into the crags' in R and *í klóm sér* 'in his claws' in H. There are no recorded instances of *hamarr* meaning 'bark' or anything else associated with trees. Following H, the eds of *CPB* (*CPB* I, 92) emend to *í björk kviðar* 'in the birch of the belly', as a kenning for talons, but this is improbable as a kenning-type (elsewhere talons are called stems or thorns of the feet, not the belly; see *Meissner*: 142-3) and fails to provide a homonym. Kock (*NN* §2363) suggests that the pun in the riddle is not on *viðr* 'wood' at all, but on *viða* 'mast' or 'high deck', and that the H redaction's response is the correct one, the pun in the answer being on *kló* 'claw' and *kló* 'clew (of a sail)', with the 'bark of the ship' being a kenning-like description of some part of the outside of a ship. There are tempting aspects to this theory, but the correspondence is not exact. — [4] *viðar* 'of a tree': Ms. 2845 has 'u' with a superscript 'i' above (followed by 'd' and the -*ar* abbreviation (superscript 'r')). Most eds expand to *virðar*, but this is the standard abbreviation for *við* ('uid') and it seems likely that this is what the scribe intended, doubling up on the consonant in error and/or for something to attach the second abbreviation sign to.

Gestumblindi (Gestumbl *Heiðr* 36)

83. Hverjar eru þeir tveir,   er tíu hafa fætr,
        augu þrjú, ok einn hala?
     Heiðrekr konungr,   hyggðu at gátu

Hverjar eru þeir tveir, er hafa tíu fætr, þrjú augu, ok einn hala? Heiðrekr konungr, hyggðu at gátu.

Who are those two, who have ten feet, three eyes, and one tail? King Heiðrekr, think about the riddle.

Mss: **2845**(72v), 281[x](100v) (ll. 1-3), 597b[x](51r), R715[x](29v-30r) (ll. 1-3) (*Heiðr*).

Readings: [1] tveir: tveir þegnar R715[x] [2] er: er ríða þingi at R715[x] [3] augu þrjú: þrjú augu R715[x]; ok: en 281[x], 597b[x] [4-5]: *abbrev. as* 'h' 2845, *abbrev. as* 'h K:' 597b[x].

Editions: *Skj*: Anonyme digte og vers [XIII], D. 5. *Heiðreks gátur* 29: AII, 227, BII, 245-6, *Skald* II, 127; *Heiðr* 1672, 152, *FSN* 1, 486, *Heiðr* 1873, 262, 343, *Heiðr* 1924, 82, 139, *FSGJ* 2, 50, *Heiðr* 1960, 44; *Edd. Min.* 119-20.

Notes: [All]: Heiðrekr's response is (*Heiðr* 1960, 44): *Þat er þá, er Óðinn ríðr Sleipni* 'That is when Óðinn rides Sleipnir'. The H redaction is more elaborate (*Heiðr* 1924, 82): *margs freistar þú nú, er þú finnr þau rǫk til framburðar við mik, er forðum váru; þat er þá er Óðinn reið hestinum Sleipni; hann hafði átta fœtr, en Óðinn tvá, en þeir hǫfðu þrjú augu, Sleipnir tvau en Óðinn eitt* 'You are really making a game of it now, when you find in your deliveries to me those wonders which happened in ancient times; that is when Óðinn rode the horse Sleipnir; he had eight feet, and Óðinn two, and they had three eyes, Sleipnir two and Óðinn one'. The story of Sleipnir's conception and birth is related in *Gylf* (see *SnE* 2005, 34-5), as is the story of Óðinn exchanging an eye for a drink from Mímir's well, the well of knowledge (see *SnE* 2005, 17), for which Snorri quotes *Vsp* 28/7-14. — [All]: Taylor (1951, 24-8) identifies a subset of a riddle (his collection is of riddles in English, though he cites worldwide parallels) which he terms 'The Odin Riddle', in which an 'unusual number of feet' forms part of the clue and the solution concerns a rider on horseback. He feels that the Old Norse example is a 'special application', however, rather than that other riddles of this type originate with it. — [1-2]: For R715ˣ's reading, cf. *Heiðr* 79/1-2.

Gestumblindi (Gestumbl *Heiðr* 37)

84. Hvat mælti Óðinn   í eyra Baldri,
     áðr hann væri á bál hafðr?

Hvat mælti Óðinn í eyra Baldri, áðr hann væri á bál hafðr?

What did Óðinn say into the ear of Baldr, before he was brought to the pyre?

Mss: **2845**(72v), 281ˣ(101r), 597bˣ(51r), R715ˣ(30r) (*Heiðr*).

Readings: [1] Óðinn: Óðinn *corrected from* Óðinn í R715ˣ   [2] Baldri: Baldrs 281ˣ, 597bˣ   [3] væri: var 281ˣ, 597bˣ, 'veri' R715ˣ;   bál: báli 597bˣ.

Editions: Skj: Anonyme digte og vers [XIII], D. 5. Heiðreks gátur 30: AII, 227, BII, 246, *Skald* II, 128, *NN* §3177; *Heiðr* 1672, 152, *FSN* 1, 487, *Heiðr* 1873, 262-3, 344, *Heiðr* 1924, 81, 140, *FSGJ* 2, 50, *Heiðr* 1960, 44; *Edd. Min.* 120.

Context: Before reciting the riddle, Gestumblindi says: *segðu þat þá fyrst, ef þú ert hverjum konungi vitrari* 'say first then, if you are wiser than every king'.

Notes: [All]: Cf. *Vafþr* 54/4-6, in which Óðinn asks the same question (differently worded, though the present l. 3 and *Vafþr* 54/4 are identical) to win a wisdom contest with the giant Vafþrúðnir (*NK* 55): *hvat mælti Óðinn | áðr á bál stigi | siálfr í eyra syni?* 'what did Óðinn himself say into the ear of his son before he ascended the pyre?'. — [All]: This question bears all the hallmarks of a 'neck riddle', according to Taylor's definition (1951, 1): an 'insoluble puzzle' whose answer is known only to the questioner and with which the protagonist hopes to 'save his neck'. — [All]: *Skj, Skald* and *FSGJ*, with varying levels of emendation (and conjecture, on Kock's part), attempt to make Gestumblindi's words of introduction to this stanza (see Context above) part of the verse, but they are not metrical. *Skj* B places the whole stanza in square brackets. — [3] *hafðr* 'brought': *Edd. Min.* gives *of borinn* 'borne', from paper mss, which produces an alliterating line; cf. *áðr á bál of bar* (*Vsp* 33/3); *áðr á bál um berr* (*Bdr* 11/7). *Áðr hann væri á bál of borinn* would be a metrical *ljóðaháttr* full line.

Heiðrekr (Heiðrekr *Heiðr* 1)

85. Undr ok argskap   ok alla bleyði!
     En engi vissi   þín þau orð
     útan þú einn,   ill vættr ok örm.

Undr ok argskap ok alla bleyði! En engi vissi þau orð þín útan þú einn, ill ok örm vættr.

Shame and depravity and all cowardice! But no one knew those words of yours except you alone, evil and wretched creature.

Mss: **597b**^{x}(51r), 281^x(101r) (*Heiðr*).

Readings: [6] örm: ormr *corrected from* örm *in the margin in another hand* 597b^x, ormr 281^x.

Editions: *Skj*: Anonyme digte og vers [XIII], D. 5. *Heiðreks gátur* 38: AII, 228, BII, 247, *Skald* II, 128, *NN* §2364; *FSN* 1, 487, *Heiðr* 1873, 263, *Heiðr* 1924, 83; *Edd. Min.* 120.

Context: Heiðrekr's response to Gestumblindi's unanswerable final question.

Notes: [All]: *Edd. Min.* does not treat this response as poetry, but all lines except l. 4 are metrical, though l. 6 has two alliterating staves. — [All]: Mss 2845 and R715^x have the prose response (*Heiðr* 1960, 44), *Þat veiztu einn, rǫg vættr!* 'You alone know that, depraved creature!'. Cf. *Lok* 57/1, 59/1, 61/1, 63/1 *Þegi þú, rǫg vættr!* 'Be silent, depraved creature!'. On the implications of the word *ragr* (and *argskapr* 'depravity' in l. 1) see Meulengracht Sørensen (1983, 18-20). — [3]: Kock (*Skald*, *NN*) rearranges to *En engi þau | þín orð vissi* 'but no one knows those words of yours' and so restores alliteration to the line. — [5] *örm* 'wretched': Kock (*Skald*, *NN*) emends to *rǫg* 'depraved', *som duger* 'which fits', as he says in *NN*, and is in line with 2845's prose reading, although traces of the metrical response are not present in this or the U redaction.

Introduction to st. 86

At this point in the saga King Heiðrekr has been killed by nine noble-born men he had enslaved, who also steal the sword Tyrfingr. This half-stanza in *málaháttr* is now presented as a genuine *lausavísa* in *Heiðr*, but there has been speculation that it could preserve much older Germanic traditions from central or south-eastern Europe (*Heiðr* 1960, xxiii). The place name Harvaðafjǫll referred to in l. 4 certainly points in this direction, being the sole attestation of the regular Germanic form for the Carpathian mountains (see further Note below). Ms. 2845 is the main ms.

(Anon *Heiðr* 5)

86. Þess galt hon gedda fyr Grafár ósi,
   er Heiðrekr var veginn und Harvaðafjöllum.

Hon gedda galt þess fyr ósi Grafár, er Heiðrekr var veginn und Harvaðafjöllum.

The pike paid for the fact that Heiðrekr was slain in front of the mouth of the Grafá, under Harvaðafjǫll.

Mss: 2845(73r), R715^x(30v), 203^x(109r) (*Heiðr*).

Readings: [1] Þess: þá R715^x, þessa 203^x; galt: *so* R715^x, 203^x, allt 2845; gedda: 'giedda' R715^x [2] Grafár: 'grafarr' 2845, 'Gropar' R715^x, 'Greipar' 203^x [3] er: at 203^x; Heiðrekr: Heiðrekr konungr R715^x; veginn: 'veiginn' R715^x [4] Harvaða-: *with æ written above the first* a 2845, 'hauada' R715^x, 'hǻrvada' 203^x.

Editions: *Skj*: Anonyme digte og vers [XIII], E. 5. *Vers af Fornaldarsagaer: Af Hervararsaga* IV: AII, 250, BII, 270, *Skald* 140; *FSN* 1, 489, *Heiðr* 1873, 265, 345, *Heiðr* 1924, 84, 141, *FSGJ* 2, 51, *Heiðr* 1960, 45 (*Heiðr*).

Context: Heiðrekr's son, Angantýr, on a quest to find his father's killers, encounters three fishermen on the river Grafá. Upon catching a fish, one of them uses a sword to cut off its head and recites this stanza, unwittingly revealing to Angantýr that the sword is Tyrfingr and the fisherman is one of Heiðrekr's killers. After nightfall Angantýr kills all the assailants and takes back Tyrfingr.

Notes: [1] *gedda* 'pike': *Esox lucius*. — [2] *Grafár* 'of the Grafá': This river has not been identified. — [4] *und Harvaðafjöllum* 'under Harvaðafjǫll': The Carpathian mountains, the largest mountain range in Europe, form an arc of c. 1500 km from the Czech Republic, through Slovakia, Poland, the Ukraine and Romania, to the Iron Gates gorge on the River Danube at the border between Romania and Serbia. The Old Norse word is regularly formed from the root *karpat-* via Grimm's Law, but the p. n. is not otherwise attested in its Germanic form (*Heiðr* 1960, xxiii and n. 2).

Introduction to sts 87-119

The section of *Heiðr* which contains this group of stanzas concerns the saga's fourth generation: Heiðrekr's sons, the half-brothers Hlǫðr and Angantýr. After defeating the Hunnish king Humli, Heiðrekr captured his daughter Sifka (*Heiðr* 1960, 26), *en at ǫðru sumri sendi hann hana heim, ok var hon þá með barni* 'but the next summer he sent her back home, and she was then with child'. The child is Hlǫðr, who is brought up by his maternal grandfather Humli at the court of the Huns. Angantýr's mother is the unnamed daughter of the King of Saxland (northern Germany), to whom Heiðrekr is legitimately married.

The following stanzas relate Hlǫðr's attempt to claim his share of the inheritance after Heiðrekr's death and Angantýr's accession as king of the Goths. After a couple of introductory stanzas, Hlǫðr's arrival at Angantýr's court, during Heiðrekr's funeral feast, is described in detail. The public nature of the claim, the impressiveness of both parties and the ceremony of the occasion are emphasised. Hlǫðr is aggressive in his demands from the start, giving no observance to the niceties of feasting (*til annars vér hingað fórum | en ǫl at drekka* 'we have come here for another reason than to drink ale', HlǫðH Lv 2 (*Heiðr* 94)), and immediately asking for half of his father's property. Angantýr refuses, instead offering him a third, but emphasising how much this would actually amount to (AngH Lv 2-5 (*Heiðr* 95-98)). Heiðrekr's foster-father, Gizurr Grýtingaliði 'Retainer of the Grýtingar', then speaks a stanza (GizGrý Lv 1 (*Heiðr* 99)) expressing his belief that this is a good offer for an illegitimate son.

At this point there is a jump in the action of the stanzas to Humli's court, where, as the saga prose explains, Hlǫðr has returned having turned down Angantýr's offer. Hlǫðr's foster-father Humli speaks of his intention to prepare for war (Humli Lv 1-2 (*Heiðr* 100-1)). The action then jumps forward again to a Gothic messenger, Ormarr, the foster-father of Hervǫr Heiðreksdóttir, who is leading a Gothic troop on behalf of Angantýr. The saga prose does much of the work in explaining that Ormarr first speaks to Hervǫr (Ormarr Lv 1 (*Heiðr* 102)), who instructs him to ride out to challenge the approaching Huns to battle, then to Angantýr some time later (Ormarr Lv 2-4 (*Heiðr* 103-5)), after the Huns have killed Hervǫr and caused much destruction in the land of the Goths. Angantýr then sends his retainer, Gizurr Grýtingaliði, to ride and challenge the Huns to battle once again (*Heiðr* 107-115). The prose tells of hard fighting on both sides, Hlǫðr's death at the hands of Angantýr, and the defeat of the Hunnish army. The final two stanzas express Angantýr's regret that Hlǫðr did not accept his initial offer, and speak of the curse which has brought the situation about (AngH Lv 10-11 (*Heiðr* 118-19)).

Like *Heiðr* 25-48, the stanzas have often been considered as a long poem, which has come to be known as *Hlǫðskviða* 'The Lay of Hlǫðr' or, in English, often 'The Battle of the Goths and the Huns'. It has been considered to be very old, at least in origin (e.g. *Heiðr* 1960, viii), and has been given a prominent place among eddic-style poetry not contained in the Codex Regius (GKS 2367 4°), for example being included in *Edd. Min.* and *ÍF Edd.* and in appendices to *NK*. In the saga setting, the verse is interspersed with narrative prose, which sometimes seems to contradict or to have misunderstood the content of the stanzas. Some of the stanzas are fragmentary and/or are now unmetrical, suggesting that certain parts of a presumed original have been lost in transmission.

Particularly in the later stanzas of this section of *Heiðr* there is some question of whether the fragments here set out as stanzas of verse should really be considered as poetry rather than prose interspersed with a few metrical lines. In some cases (e.g. sts 93, 96, 100, 103, 113) the word groups are mixtures of different metres (mostly *fornyrðislag* and *málaháttr*), interspersed with non-metrical lines or prose inserts (e.g. *gef ek þér* 'I give you', st. 96/5, 6, 7). In other cases, which are still set out and numbered as stanzas in this edition, the word groups do not have poetic form and are thus effectively prose (e.g. st. 116), though some are prose with alliterating staves (e.g. sts 106, 115). The position of this edition is conservative, based on conventional treatments in earlier editions, though not all editors have agreed on identifying each stanza as either verse or prose. However, the reader's attention is drawn to the ambiguity and fluidity of the situation and to what it may imply for the preservation and indeed the transmission and reworking of legendary poetic texts.

There have been many attempts to discover a historical basis for the events related here (cf. Reifergerste 1989), which are comprehensively discussed by Tolkien (1955-6, 162), where he concludes, 'the search for a definite, historical underlying event should be called off'. Certain correspondences with the Old English poem *Wīdsīð* suggest a widely known underlying legend (see e.g. Malone 1925; Tolkien 1955-6; Niles 1999; Notes to Anon (*Heiðr*) 6 (*Heiðr* 87)). There are also echoes in Book V of Saxo Grammaticus's *Gesta Danorum*, though in that version the Huns are at war with the Danes, led by Fróði (*Saxo* 2015, I, v. 7. 1-4, pp. 318-23; see also Jón Helgason 1967, 163-9). The battle between the brothers is the subject of RvHbreiðm *Hl* 44^{III}.

The stanzas are not preserved in any H-redaction mss. Ms. 2845 is the basis for eight of the first ten stanzas (it does not contain AngH Lv 1 (*Heiðr* 92) and only part of HlǫðH Lv 2 (*Heiðr* 93), for which the version of the other mss is preferable). The lacuna in this ms. occurs after AngH Lv 2 (*Heiðr* 95), and no more is preserved of the saga in 2845 or its copies. Shortly before this, part-way through HlǫðH Lv 2 (*Heiðr* 93), 203^x, which up to here has followed the R redaction, switches to its U-redaction exemplar (see Introduction to the saga above). It becomes the main ms. for the remaining stanzas. Most are also contained in R715^x, except as indicated in the Mss line.

As well as their inclusion in the editions of the saga listed in the Introduction, the stanzas have been edited in *Skj*, *Skald*, *Edd. Min.* 1-12, *NK* 302-12, *CPB*, I, 348-52 and *ÍF Edd.*, II, 416-30 (R and U versions printed separately; introduction pp. 168-75). Of these all but *CPB* are cited routinely. Since *FSN* is based only on 345, a copy of 203^x, it is usually excluded from consideration in the Notes below. A Modern Icelandic edition by Jón Helgason has a detailed introduction and some useful Notes (Jón Helgason 1967, 147-246).

(Anon *Heiðr* 6)

87. Ár kváðu Humla   fyrir her ráða,
    Gizur Gautum,   Gotum Angantý,
    Valdar Dönum,   en Völum Kíar;
    Alrekr inn frækni   enskri þjóðu.

Ár kváðu Humla ráða fyrir her, Gizur Gautum, Angantý Gotum, Valdar Dönum en Kíar Völum; Alrekr inn frækni enskri þjóðu.

Long ago they said Humli ruled over the people, Gizurr the Gautar, Angantýr the Goths, Valdarr the Danes, and Kíarr the Valir; Alrekr inn frœkni ('the Brave') [ruled] the English people.

Ms.: 2845(73r) (*Heiðr*).

Readings: [4] Angantý: 'ang' 2845   [8] enskri: enskri enskri 2845.

Editions: *Skj*: Anonyme digte og vers [XIII], E. 5. *Vers af Fornaldarsagaer: Af Hervararsaga* V 1: AII, 250, BII, 270, *Skald* II, 140-1; *FSN* 1, 490, *Heiðr* 1873, 265-6, *Heiðr* 1924, 85, *FSGJ* 2, 52, *Heiðr* 1960, 46 (*Heiðr*); *Edd. Min.* 105, *ÍF Edd.* II, 417.

Context: The stanza provides a temporal setting for the action of this part of the saga and is introduced (*Heiðr* 1960, 46): *Þá réðu þessir konungar lǫndum, sem hér segir* 'Then these kings ruled the lands, as it says here'. It precedes the introduction of Hlǫðr Heiðreksson, who was brought up in the court of King Humli, his maternal grandfather, mentioned in l. 1.

Notes: [All]: This stanza is not always counted as part of the entity designated *Hlǫðskviða* (see Introduction). — [All]: As has often been noted, this stanza bears some resemblance to the Old English poem *Wīdsīð*, which includes an eighteen-line catalogue of rulers and their peoples (ll. 18-35), e.g. (ll. 18-19) (Malone 1962, 23): *Ætla weold Hunum, Eormanric Gotum,* | *Becca Baningum, Burgendum Gifica* 'Attila ruled the Huns, Eormanric the Goths, Becca the Banings, Gifica the Burgundians'. Although Attila and Eormanric (ON Atli and Jǫrmunrekkr) are chosen as the 'archetypical' leaders of the Huns and Goths respectively (cf. Niles 1999, 182-8), later in the poem the narrator speaks of visiting *Heaþoric ond Sifecan, Hliþe ond Incgenþeow* (l. 116), which have been compared to *Heiðr*'s Heiðrekr, Sifka(?) (Hlǫðr's mother), Hlǫðr and Angantýr. On further connections with *Wīdsīð* see e.g. *Heiðr* 1960, xxv-xxviii, Malone (1925). — [2] *fyrir her* 'over the people': *Skj* B, *Skald*, *FSGJ*, *Heiðr* 1960 and *ÍF Edd.* adopt the reading *Húnum* 'the Huns', from a marginal addition in Holm papp 120 fol[x]. This ms. is a copy of Verelius' edn of *Heiðr* (*Heiðr* 1672) with extensive annotations, most of which demonstrably stem from a ms. of the same class as 203[x] (Andrews 1914, 83-5), by Guðmundur Ólafsson (1652-95), an Icelandic scribe based in Sweden (see Busch 2002, 14-27). This gives good sense, since Humli is indeed king of the Huns, although it is not necessary to emend here. — [3] *Gautum* 'the Gautar': People from Götaland

(ON Gautland), Sweden. — [4] *Gotum* 'the Goths': The Goths are not straightforward to place historically. Tacitus (*Germania* 1967, 473) places them *trans Lugios* 'beyond the Lugii', to the north and west of what is now Poland, but more influential in medieval times would have been the mid-sixth-century account of Jordanes' *Getica*, which places their origins in 'Scandza', in *Oceani arctoi salo posita insula magna ... haec a fronte posita est Vistulae fluminis* 'a great island situated in the northern ocean ... it is situated at the mouth of the river Vistula' (Mommsen 1882, §1, III). Whether Jordanes means Skåne or Scandinavia is not certain (Swanson 2006, 169), but the original audiences of *Heiðr* and presumably even the earliest projected audiences of *Hlǫðskviða*, would have understood the 'Goths' of heroic legend to have had an East Scandinavian connection. On the historical Goths see further Heather (1991 and 1998) and Wolfram (1990), and on the traditions about them found in heroic legends including *Hlǫðskviða* and the Old English poem *Wīdsīth* see Schramm (1998). — [4] *Angantý* 'Angantýr': One of the main protagonists of the action of the following stanzas and the last main section of *Heiðr*; great-grandson of Angantýr Arngrímsson, who features earlier in the saga and is one of the participants in the dialogue constituting *Heiðr* 25-47. — [5]: The same line is found in *Guðr II* 19/1, where Valdarr is one of the hopefuls attempting to win the hand of Guðrún after the death of Sigurðr. — [6]: In the prose introduction to *Vǫl* (*NK* 116) Ǫlrún, one of the three swan-maidens or valkyries married to Vǫlundr and his brothers (Ǫlrún is married to Egill) is said to be *Kíars dóttir af Vallandi* 'the daughter of Kíarr of Valland' (cf. *Vǫl* 15/3-4). The name Kíarr is apparently used as a generic term for 'ruler' in Edáð *Bdr* 2/4[1], and may derive from Lat. *cæsar* (*LP*: *Kíarr* (not in *AEW*)). — [7] *Alrekr inn frækni* 'Alrekr inn frækni ("the Brave")': Otherwise unknown as a ruler of England, but an Alrekr inn frækni is listed in a genealogy in *Flat* (1860-8, I, 25), said to be part of the dynasty *þat heitir Skilfinga ætt eðr Skiolldunga ætt* 'that is called the Skilfingar family or Skjǫldungar family', and Þjóð *Yt* 10/1[1] lists a Swedish king Alrekr (see Note there). The acc.-inf. construction used in ll. 2-6 switches here (for no clear reason) to the use of the nom. *Skald* emends l. 7 to the acc. *Alrek enn frækna* to maintain consistency.

(Anon *Heiðr* 7)

88. Hlöðr var þar borinn   í Húnalandi
    saxi ok með sverði,   síðri brynju,
    hjálmi hringreifðum,   h*v*össum mæki,
    mari veltömum   á mörk inni helgu.

Hlöðr var borinn þar í Húnalandi með saxi ok sverði, síðri brynju, hringreifðum hjálmi, h*v*össum mæki, mari veltömum á inni helgu mörk.

Hlǫðr was born there in the land of the Huns with short-sword and with sword, with long mailcoat, with ring-adorned helmet, with sharp sword, with a horse well tamed in the holy forest.

Ms.: 2845(73r) (*Heiðr*).

Reading: [6] h*v*össum: 'ha/ssum' 2845.

Editions: *Skj*: Anonyme digte og vers [XIII], E. 5. *Vers af Fornaldarsagaer: Af Hervararsaga* V 2: AII, 250, BII, 270, *Skald* II, 141, *NN* §1204C; *FSN* 1, 491, *Heiðr* 1873, 266, *Heiðr* 1924, 85-6, *FSGJ* 2, 53, *Heiðr* 1960, 46-7 (*Heiðr*); *Edd. Min.* 1, *NK* 302, *ÍF Edd.* II, 418.

Context: King Heiðrekr's second son, Hlǫðr, is introduced. The prose rationalises the stanza (*Heiðr* 1960, 46): *þat var fornt mál þann tíma, at maðr væri borinn með vápnum eða hestum* 'it was an old saying at that time, that a man was born with weapons or horses', explaining: *þat var til þess haft, at þat var mælt um þau vápn, er þá váru gǫr þann tíma, er maðrinn var fœddr, svá ok fé, kykvendi, yxn eða hestar, ef þat var þá fœtt; ok var þat allt fœrt saman til virðingar tignum mǫnnum* 'it was for this reason, that it was said about those weapons which were made at the time a man was born, and likewise of animals, cattle, oxen or horses, if they were born then; and that was all brought together to honour noble men'. The stanza is introduced *sem hér segir um Hlǫð Heiðreksson* 'as it says here about Hlǫðr Heiðreksson'.

Notes: [1-4]: Kock (*NN* §1204C) highlights the alternation between the use of the dat. instr. by itself (*saxi* 'with short-sword', *síðri brynju* 'with long mailcoat'; also attributes in ll. 5-7) and with the preposition *með* 'with' in l. 3. A similar effect occurs in HlǫðH Lv 2/7-12 (*Heiðr* 94). — [1] *Hlöðr* 'Hlǫðr': As a common noun the name means 'destroyer, slayer' (*LP*: *hlǫðr*; *AEW*: *hlǫðr* 1). — [3-8]: See Note to *Heiðr* 94/3-8. — [3-6]: These lines, listing Hlǫðr's weaponry, are reminiscent of Herv Lv 9/5-8 (*Heiðr* 26), which list Hervǫr's. — [3] *saxi* 'with short-sword': The *sax* was a short, single-edged sword (see Falk 1914b, 9-13). — [5] *hringreifðum* 'ring-adorned': *Hap. leg.* Possibly refers to a chain-mail cheek and neck guard such as found on the seventh-century helmet Valsgärde 6 (for description see Arwidsson 1934) or, probably, on the tenth-century helmet from Gjermundbu, Norway (Grieg 1947, 3-4), the only Viking-Age helmet so far found in Scandinavia. — [6]: The same half-line, except in the acc. case, occurs as Herv Lv 8/6 and 16/3 (*Heiðr* 25 and 40). Exactly what kind of sword was a *mækir* is unclear (Falk 1914b, 14-16). — [8]: Probably a reference to Myrkviðr, which is referred to as *því inu mæta hrísi* 'that excellent forest' in *Heiðr* 94/13-14 (on the p. n. see Note to those lines).

Introduction to sts 89-90

Wear has made the folio containing these stanzas difficult to read in 2845; 203^x, which is an R-redaction ms. at this point, has therefore also been used selectively.

(Anon *Heiðr* 8)

89. Hlöðr reið austan,   Heiðreks arfi;
    kom hann at garði,   þar er Gotar byggja,
    á Árheima   arfs at kveðja;
    þar drakk Angantýr   erfi Heiðreks *.

Hlöðr reið austan, arfi Heiðreks; hann kom at garði, þar er Gotar byggja, at kveðja arfs á Árheima; þar drakk Angantýr erfi Heiðreks *.

Hlǫðr rode from the east, Heiðrekr's heir; he came to the court where the Goths live, to ask for his inheritance at Árheimar; there Angantýr was drinking Heiðrekr's wake.

Mss: 2845(73v) (*Heiðr*); *also used selectively*: 203ˣ(109v) (*Heiðr*).

Readings: [2] Heiðreks arfi: *so* 203ˣ, 'Heid[…]' 2845   [4] byggja: *so* 203ˣ, 'bygdia' 2845   [8] Heiðreks *: Heiðreks konungs 2845.

Editions: *Skj*: Anonyme digte og vers [XIII], E. 5. Vers af Fornaldarsagaer: Af Hervararsaga V 3: AII, 250, BII, 270, *Skald* II, 141; *FSN* 1, 491, *Heiðr* 1873, 266, *Heiðr* 1924, 86, *FSGJ* 2, 53-4, *Heiðr* 1960, 47 (*Heiðr*); *Edd. Min.* 1, *NK* 302, *ÍF Edd.* II, 418.

Context: Hlǫðr learns of his father's death, and that his brother Angantýr has gained the kingdom of Reiðgotaland, home of the Goths. With the encouragement of his foster-father and maternal grandfather King Humli, Hlǫðr resolves to ride to claim his inheritance, at first *með góðum orðum* 'with good words'. The stanza is introduced: *sem hér segir* 'as it says here'.

Notes: [1, 6]: See Note to RvHbreiðm *Hl* 44/1-2ᴵᴵᴵ. — [1] *Hlöðr* 'Hlǫðr': See Note to Anon (*Heiðr*) 8/1 (*Heiðr* 88). — [4] *Gotar* 'Goths': See Note to *Heiðr* 87/4. — [5] *Árheima* 'Árheimar': Lit. 'River-homes'. Unknown outside *Heiðr*, where it occurs also in *Heiðr* 114/4 and in a few places in the prose (*Heiðr* 1960, 46-7, 53). It is said to be *á Danparstǫðum* (*Heiðr* 1960, 46) 'on the banks of the Dnieper', but the location has not been identified. — [8] *: The mss read *konungs* 'king's', but this is not metrical and all eds but *FSN*, *NK* and *ÍF Edd.* omit it.

(Anon *Heiðr* 9)

90a. Segg fann hann úti   fyrir sal hávum
     ok síðförlan   síðan kvaddi:

Hann fann segg úti fyrir hávum sal ok kvaddi síðan síðförlan:

He met a man outside in front of the high hall, and then greeted the one travelling late:

Mss: 2845(73v) (*Heiðr*); *also used selectively*: 203ˣ(110r) (*Heiðr*).

Readings: [3] síðförlan: *so* 203ˣ, 's[…]d[…]a/llann' 2845.

Editions: *Skj*: Anonyme digte og vers [XIII], E. 5. *Vers af Fornaldarsagaer: Af Hervararsaga* V 4/1-4: AII, 250-1, BII, 270, *Skald* II, 141; *FSN* 1, 492, *Heiðr* 1873, 267, *Heiðr* 1924, 86, 142, *FSGJ* 2, 54, *Heiðr* 1960, 47 (*Heiðr*); *Edd. Min.* 1-2, *NK* 302, *ÍF Edd.* II, 418.

Context: Hlǫðr and his troops arrive at Árheimar, *sem hér segir* 'as it says here'.

Notes: [All]: Other eds take this *helmingr* together with the following one, HlǫðH Lv 1 (*Heiðr* 90b), to form one eight-line stanza. — [All]: Ms. R715^x, in keeping with its tendency to omit narrative (i.e. non-dialogue) verse, does not contain this *helmingr*. See also *Heiðr* 90b Note to [All]. The appearance of a minor character for the protagonist to run into late at night in order to move the plot along and explain the setting is utilised elsewhere in the saga in the poetry leading up to Hervǫr's dialogue with her father Angantýr, *Heiðr* 18-24. — [1] *hann* 'he': *Skj* B and *Skald* omit on metrical grounds. — [3] *síðfǫrlan* 'the one travelling late': Only recorded once elsewhere, *Ket* 3a/3 *seggr síðfǫrull* 'man travelling late', but -*fǫrull* is also compounded with other words with similar meaning, e.g. Arn *Magndr* 11/6^I *allnǫttfǫrull* 'ever prowling by night', Rv Lv 5/3^{II} *kveldfǫrlastr karl* 'old man who was out and about most in the evening'. Kock emends the half-line to *ok síðfǫrull hann*, making *síðfǫrull* apply to Hlǫðr and *hann*, acc., to the man. In *FF* §16 he proposes the meaning *som färda[t]s vida, långvägafarande* 'who travels widely, far-travelling', arguing, by comparison to the Old English phrase *sīde and wīde* 'far and wide' that *síðfǫrull* is essentially synonymous with *víðfǫrull* 'far-travelled' (which occurs in, e.g. *Ǫrv* 133/7, *Ket* 21/2). This seems unlikely, however, as the context of the *síð*- compounds would suggest late-night travelling is an appropriate description.

Hlǫðr (HlǫðH Lv 1)

90b. Inn gakktu, seggr,   í sal hávan;
      bið mér Angantý*   andspjǫll bera!

Gakktu inn, seggr, í hávan sal; bið Angantý* bera mér andspjǫll!

Go in, man, into the high hall; bid Angantýr bring me answers!

Mss: **2845**(73v), R715^x(31r) (*Heiðr*); *also used selectively*: 203^x(110r) (*Heiðr*).

Readings: [3] Angantý*: 'A' 2845, Angantýrs R715^x.

Editions: *Skj*: Anonyme digte og vers [XIII], E. 5. *Vers af Fornaldarsagaer: Af Hervararsaga* V 4/5-8: AII, 250-1, BII, 270-1, *Skald* II, 141; *Heiðr* 1672, 161, *FSN* 1, 492, *Heiðr* 1873, 267, *Heiðr* 1924, 86, 142, *FSGJ* 2, 54, *Heiðr* 1960, 47 (*Heiðr*); *Edd. Min.* 1-2, *NK* 303, *ÍF Edd.* II, 418, 421.

Notes: [All]: Ms. R715^x, which omits *Heiðr* 90a, appends another *helmingr* after this one, presumably to produce an eight-line stanza: *andspjǫll ljá | orða tveggja | tveggja eðr þriggja | ef hann til vil* 'to grant me answers of two words, of two or three, if he wishes to'. — [2]: Echoes l. 2 of the previous *helmingr*. — [4]: The half-line also occurs in *Guðr I* 12/6. *Skj* B and *Skald* prefer *léa* 'grant' to *bera* 'bring', from R715^x's reading (via *Heiðr* 1672).

(**Anon** *Heiðr* 10)

91. Hér er Hlöðr kominn,   Heiðreks arfi,
    bróðir þinn   inn böðskái.
    Mikill er sá maðr ungr   á mars baki;
    vill nú, þjóðann,   við þik tala.

Hlöðr er kominn hér, arfi Heiðreks, inn böðskái bróðir þinn. Sá ungr maðr er mikill á mars baki; vill nú, þjóðann, tala við þik.

Hlǫðr has come here, Heiðrekr's heir, your brother, the battle-ready. That young man is mighty on horseback; he wishes now, prince, to talk with you.

Mss: 2845(73v), R715^x(31v) (*Heiðr*).

Readings: [2] Heiðreks: *so* R715^x, 'Heiðrr' 2845;   arfi: *so* R715^x, arfþegi 2845   [4] inn: *om.* R715^x;   böðskái: *so* R715^x, 'bedskái' 2845   [5] maðr ungr: mögr R715^x [7] nú: sá R715^x; þjóðann: þundr R715^x [8] tala: mæla R715^x.

Editions: *Skj*: Anonyme digte og vers [XIII], E. 5. *Vers af Fornaldarsagaer: Af Hervararsaga* V 5: AII, 251, BII, 271, *Skald* II, 141; *Heiðr* 1672, 161, *FSN* 1, 492, *Heiðr* 1873, 267, *FSGJ* 2, 54, *Heiðr* 1924, 87, 142, *Heiðr* 1960, 48 (*Heiðr*); *Edd. Min.* 2, *NK* 303, *ÍF Edd.* II, 419, 421.

Context: The prose text of the saga explains that the man goes in to the king's table and greets Angantýr with this stanza.

Notes: [1] *Hlöðr* 'Hlǫðr': See Note to *Heiðr* 88/1. — [2] *arfi* 'heir': Ms. R715^x's reading is preferable both metrically and because it echoes the same line in Anon (*Heiðr*) 8/2 (*Heiðr* 89), but 2845's *arfþegi* 'recipient of an inheritance' has the same sense and is preferred as the reading of the main ms. in *FSN*, *Heiðr* 1873, *Edd. Min.* and *NK*. — [4] *böðskái* 'battle-ready': *Hap. leg.* — [6]: Similar wording occurs in *Grí* 17/5, *Skí* 15/2, *Hamð* 14/4 and Eyv *Hák* 11/3^1.

(**Anon** *Heiðr* 11)

92. Rymr var í ranni,   rísu með góðum;
    vildi hverr heyra,   hvat Hlöðr mælti,
    ok þat er Angantýr   andsvör veitti.

Rymr var í ranni, rísu með góðum; hverr vildi heyra, hvat Hlöðr mælti, ok þat er Angantýr veitti andsvör.

There was uproar in the hall, they rose with the good [man]; each wished to hear what Hlǫðr said, and what Angantýr offered in answer.

Ms.: **2845**(73v) (*Heiðr*).

Editions: *Skj*: Anonyme digte og vers [XIII], E. 5. *Vers af Fornaldarsagaer: Af Hervararsaga* V 6: AII, 251, BII, 271, *Skald* II, 141, *FF* §17; *FSN* 1, 492, *Heiðr* 1873, 268, *Heiðr* 1924, 87, *FSGJ* 2, 55, *Heiðr* 1960, 48 (*Heiðr*); *Edd. Min.* 2, *NK* 303, *ÍF Edd.* II, 419.

Context: Angantýr gets up from the table and arms himself with mailcoat, shield and the sword Tyrfingr. A clamour arises in the hall, *sem hér segir* 'as it says here'.

Notes: [All]: *Edd. Min.* assumes two lines have been lost after ll. 1-2, but nothing is missing from the syntax or the sense of the stanza as it stands. — [1] *rymr var í ranni* 'there was uproar in the hall': A formulaic description: cf. Bragi *Rdr* 3/5[III] *Rósta varð í ranni* 'There was tumult in the hall', *Hamð* 23/1 (*NK* 272), *Styrr varð í ranni* 'There was uproar in the hall' and, in Old English, *Beowulf* l. 1302a (*Beowulf* 2008, 45), *Hrēam wearð on Heorote* 'There was uproar in Heorot'. — [6]: The line also occurs in *Sigsk* 17/2, 45/2 and (in the pl.) 50/4, and in *Ǫrv* 10/2.

Angantýr (AngH Lv 1)

93. Heill kom þú, Hlǫðr,   Heiðreks *arfi*,
    bróður minn,   gakk á bekk sitja.
    Drekkum Heiðreks   hollar veigar,
    fǫður okkrum,   fyrstum manna:
    vín eða mjǫð,   hvárt þér valdara þykkir.

Heill kom þú, Hlöðr, *arfi* Heiðreks, bróður minn, gakk á bekk sitja. Drekkum hollar veigar Heiðreks, fǫður okkrum, fyrstum manna: vín eða mjǫð, hvárt þykkir þér valdara.

Welcome, Hlǫðr, heir of Heiðrekr, my brother, go to sit on the bench. Let us drink draughts of Heiðrekr, offered with good will for our father, the first of men: wine or mead, whichever seems to you preferable.

Ms.: **R715ˣ**(31v) (*Heiðr*).

Reading: [2] *arfi*: 'fedurz' *corrected from* 'feduz' *in another hand* R715ˣ.

Editions: *Skj*: Anonyme digte og vers [XIII], E. 5. *Vers af Fornaldarsagaer: Af Hervararsaga* V 7: AII, 251, BII, 271, *Skald* II, 141; *Heiðr* 1672, 161, *Heiðr* 1873, 268, *Heiðr* 1924, 143, *Heiðr* 1960, 83 (*Heiðr*); *NK* 303, *ÍF Edd.* II, 421.

Context: See Context for previous stanza. Since that stanza is not included in R715ˣ, the present one follows directly from the prose that introduces *Heiðr* 92 in the R redaction.

Notes: [All]: The content of this stanza is related in prose in the R redaction, and it is omitted from *Edd. Min.* 2-3 n. 5 on the grounds that *die nicht alt sein können* 'they [the lines] cannot be old'. The stanza is metrically irregular, with ll. 1-2, 4-6 and 8 regular *fornyrðislag*, ll. 3, 7 and 9 hypometrical and l. 10 hypermetrical, a fact that could point to late composition. However, Love (2013, 159-60) argues on the principle of Occam's razor that it is more likely that an original stanza was recast into prose in R than original prose was recast into 'novel poetry' in U. Tolkien (*Heiðr* 1960, 83) feels that 'a distinction between "old" and "late" may be misleading if pressed'. — [2] *arfi* 'heir': The ms. reading is assumed to be intended to be *föðurs* 'father's' (*Skj* A; *Heiðr* 1672), but that reading would not make sense, since Hlǫðr is Heiðrekr's son, not the other way round. *NK* and *ÍF Edd*. emend the line to *Heiðreki fœddr* 'born of Heiðrekr'. The emendation followed here, proposed in *Skj* B and taken up in *Skald* and *Heiðr* 1960, is taken from Anon (*Heiðr*) 8/2 (*Heiðr* 89); cf. Anon (*Heiðr*) 10/2 (*Heiðr* 91) and Note. — [6] *hollar* 'offered with good will': *Skj* B and *Skald* emend to *hallar* 'of the hall', giving ll. 5-6 the meaning 'we will drink the draughts of Heiðrekr's hall'. — [10] *valdara* 'preferable': Comparative of *valdr* or *valiðr*, p. p. of *velja* 'choose' (cf. Jón Helgason 1967, 222-3). *Heiðr* 1672 retains the ms. reading, as here, but most eds emend to *vildara* 'more desirable', which has similar meaning but is an unnecessary change.

Hlǫðr (HlǫðH Lv 2)

94. Til annars vér hingat fórum   en öl at drekka,
  þiggja *af* þjóðan   þínar veigar,
  nema ek hálft hafa alt,   þat er Heiðrekr átti:
  al ok af oddi,   einum skatti,
  kú ok af kálfi,   kvern þjótandi,
  þý ok af þræli   ok þeirra börnum,
  hrísi því inu mæta,   er Myrkviðr heitir,
  gröf þá ina helgu,   er stendr á Gotþjóðu,
  stein þann inn fagra,   er stendr á stöðum Danpar,
  hálfar herborgir,   er Heiðrekr átti,
  lönd ok lýða   ok ljósa bauga.

Vér fórum hingat til annars en at drekka öl, þiggja veigar þínar *af* þjóðan, nema ek hafa hálft alt, þat er Heiðrekr átti: al ok af oddi, einum skatti, kú ok af kálfi, þjótandi kvern, þý ok af þræli ok þeirra börnum, því inu mæta hrísi, er heitir Myrkviðr, þá ina helgu gröf, er stendr á Gotþjóðu, þann inn fagra stein, er stendr á stöðum Danpar, hálfar herborgir, er Heiðrekr átti, lönd ok lýða ok ljósa bauga.

We have come here for another [reason] than to drink ale, to receive from the prince your draughts, unless I have half of all that Heiðrekr owned: of awl and of weapon-point, of singular treasure, of cow and of calf, of resounding handmill, of bondwoman and of slave, and of their children; of that excellent forest which is called Myrkviðr, that holy grave, which stands in the land of the Goths, that fair stone, which stands on the banks of the Dnieper, half the war-fortifications which Heiðrekr owned, lands and people and bright rings.

Mss: **R715^x**(31v), 2845(73v) (ll. 5-6, 9-10, 7-8, 11-22) (*Heiðr*); *also used selectively*: 203^x(110r) (ll. 5-22) (*Heiðr*).

Readings: [3] *a*f: ef R715^x [5] nema: hafa vil 203^x, 2845; hafa: *om.* 203^x, 2845 [6] Heiðrekr: 'Heid' R715^x, Heiðrek 203^x, 'heidrr' 2845 [7] al: *so* 2845, af al R715^x, 203^x; ok af: '[...]' 2845; ok: *so* 203^x, í R715^x; af: *om.* R715^x [9] ok: *so* 203^x, 2845, í R715^x [11] þý: *so* 203^x, 2845, því R715^x; ok: *so* 203^x, 2845, *om.* R715^x [12] börnum: *so* 203^x, bænum R715^x, barni 2845 [13] hrísi: hrís 2845; því: þat 2845; inu: it 2845; mæta: mæra *corrected from* mæta *in another hand* 203^x, meira 2845 [14] Myrkviðr: Mirkviðir 203^x, 2845; heitir: heita 203^x, 2845 [15] helgu: góðu 2845 [16] Gotþjóðu: 'got þióða' 203^x, 'gautu þiodar' 2845 [17] stein: *so* 2845, steininn R715^x, stein *corrected from* steininn *in another hand* 203^x; inn: *so* 203^x, 2845, *om.* R715^x; fagra: meira 2845 [18] Danpar: 'Dampnar' 203^x, 'damp ar' 2845 [19] herborgir: *so* 203^x, 'her bar' R715^x, hervaðir 2845*JH* [20] er: þær er 2845*JH*; átti: 'ati' 2845*JH* [21] lönd: *so* 2845, landa 203^x, landi 203^x; ok lýða: *om.* 2845.

Editions: *Skj*: Anonyme digte og vers [XIII], E. 5. Vers af Fornaldarsagaer: Af Hervararsaga V 8-9: AII, 251-2, BII, 271-2, *Skald* II, 141, *NN* §§1204, 2376, 2044; *Heiðr* 1672, 162, *FSN* 1, 493, *Heiðr* 1873, 268-70, *Heiðr* 1924, 87-8, 143-4, *FSGJ* 2, 55-6, *Heiðr* 1960, 48-9, 83 (*Heiðr*); *Edd. Min.* 3, *NK* 304, *ÍF Edd.* II, 419-20, 422.

Context: In the U redaction this stanza follows directly from the previous one. In R, which does not contain that stanza, Angantýr welcomes Hlǫðr in prose and invites him to drink; Hlǫðr replies that he has come for another reason (*Heiðr* 1960, 48) *en at kýla vǫmb vára* 'than to fill our bellies'.

Notes: [All]: This stanza is a mixture of *fornyrðislag* and *málaháttr*. The R redaction contains a somewhat different version of this stanza, without the first four lines (the content of which are rendered into prose), with lines in different order and with some variant readings. The R version is presented here as an alternate stanza:

Hafa vil ek hálft alt, þat er Heiðrekr átti:
kú ok af kálfi, kvern þjótandi,
al *ok af* oddi, einum skatti,
þý ok af þræli ok þeirra barni,
hrís þat it meira, er Myrkvið*r heit*ir,
gröf þá inu góðu, er stendr á Gota þjóðar,
stein þann inn meira, er stendr á stǫðum Danpar,
hálfar hervaðir, þær er Heiðrekr átti,
lönd *ok lýða* ok ljósa bauga.

Prose Order: Ek vil hafa hálft alt, þat er Heiðrekr átti: kú ok af kálfi, þjótandi kvern, al *ok af* oddi, einum skatti, þý ok af þræli ok þeirra barni, þat it meira hrís, er heit*ir* Myrkvið*r, þá inu góðu gröf, er stendr á Gota þjóðar, þann in meira stein, er stendr á stǫðum Danpar, hálfar herváðir, þær er Heiðrekr átti, lönd *ok lýða* ok ljósa bauga.

Translation: I wish to have half of all that Heiðrekr owned: of cow and of calf, of resounding handmill, of awl and of weapon-point, of singular treasure, of bondwoman and of slave, and of their child; that great forest which is called Myrkviðr, that good grave which stands in the land of the Goths, that great stone which stands on the banks of the Dnieper, half the war-garments which Heiðrekr owned, lands and people and bright rings. — [All]: Ms. 203[x], as 2845, does not contain ll. 1-4 and has the same l. 5 as 2845, but seems to become a U-redaction ms. from l. 7, as it follows the order of the lines in R715[x] rather than in 2845. *Skj* B and *Skald* do not print ll. 1-4 and prefer 2845's reading for l. 5, but subsequently follow the order of U without explanation. Jón Helgason (1967, 224) suggests that the scribe of 2845 confused *átti* at the end of l. 6 with *skatti* at the end of l. 8, copying ll. 9-10 after *átti* instead of *skatti*. — [All]: The unusual length of the stanza is demanded by the syntax, since the list is without a main verb after l. 5. The syntax of the list is inconsistent, however: in ll. 7-12 the first object is in the acc. case (parallel with *hálft alt* ...) and the second (with prep. *af* 'of, from') in the dat. case. Line 13 is also in the dat., but 15, 17, 19 and 21 switch back to the acc. Though the Old Norse constructions do not use the gen. case, ModE. 'of' has been used here for the Translation for the sake of idiom. Other eds, most of which take 2845 as the main ms., prefer to create two separate stanzas of eight and ten lines respectively (the second beginning at *hrís þat* (a variant of l. 13 in the present edn, or l. 9 of the R redaction). — [4] *af* 'from': Following a suggestion by Jón Helgason (*Heiðr* 1924, 143 n. 2), *Heiðr* 1960 emends the line to *þigg ek ei, þjóðann* 'I do not accept, prince' and *ÍF Edd*. II, 422 *þigga ek, þjóðann* 'I do not accept, prince'. However, the slightly less intrusive change *ef > af* gives good sense, assuming that *þiggja* is in apposition with *drekka* with the sense 'we have come here for another reason than to receive ...'. The emendation is also made in *Heiðr* 1672. — [5]: From this point 203[x] switches to copying from a U-redaction exemplar, and has independent textual value. — [7] *al ok af oddi* 'of awl and of weapon-point': Used *pars pro toto* for tools and weapons. *Alr* is a *hap. leg.* in poetry. — [8] *einum* 'singular': *LP*: *einn* 1 suggests the translation *en, udelt* 'whole, undivided', tentatively adopted in *Skj* B and *Heiðr* 1960. Bugge (*Heiðr* 1873, 269 n. 7), however, suggested *enestaaende, udmærket* 'unique, exceptional', which is perhaps preferable in terms of sense; cf. *DOE*: *ān* A5, *Beowulf* l. 1885 (*Beowulf* 2008, 63) *þat wæs ān cyning* 'that was an exceptional king'. — [11, 13] *gröf, stein* 'grave; stone': The *gröf* 'grave' is presumably a sacred or ritual place; the *steinn* 'stone' may be too (see *Heiðr* 1960, xxv). Kock (*NN* §§2376, 2044) compares MHG *stein* 'castle' and suggests that meaning here, but a sacred stone (*ARG* I, 347-9; cf. *Guðr III* 3/4) would be possible in the context (cf. *Heiðr* 1956, 85 n.) A boundary marker would also be plausible. — [13-14] *því inu mæta hrísi, er heitir Myrkviðr* 'that excellent forest, which is called Myrkviðr': Ms. 2845's reading, *meira* 'great' in place of *mæta* 'excellent', is assumed by most eds to be an error for *mæra* 'renowned'; cf. *Akv* 5/7-8 (*NK* 241) *hrís þat iþ mæra, | er meðr Myrcvið kalla* 'that renowned forest, which men call Myrkviðr'. *Hrís* usually means 'brushwood', but its sense is extended here and in the *Akv* instance (cf. *LP*: *hrís*). *Myrkviðr* is lit. 'dark forest' and can be both a specific p. n. and a generic term, used to refer to various border forests (Eggers 2002, 460-1) or forested areas; cf. Eskál *Vell* 26/3[1] and Note. Though 2845 and 203[x] agree on the pl. *Myrkviðir heita* 'are called Myrkviðir', the sg. is more likely in terms of sense and accords with instances of the p. n. elsewhere in the corpus, and is necessary to agree with the sg. l. 13. — [16] *Gotþjóðu* 'in the land of the Goths': The term can refer to either the people (cf. *Heiðr* 102/3) or land of the Goths, as here and in *Heiðr* 103/5 (*LP*: *Gotþjóð*). The p. n. also appears in *Ghv* 8/6 and 16/4. — [18] *stöðum Danpar* 'the banks of the Dnieper': The same stanza in *Akv* which echoes ll. 1-2 here (see Note to ll. 13-14) refers to *staði Danpar*, recently translated by Carolyne Larrington (2014, 205) as 'farms on the Dnieper'. The present translation, taking *stöðum* to be the dat. pl. of the f. noun *stǫð* 'landing place', follows Tolkien (1955-6, 157). The relation of the name *Danpr* to the Gothic name of the river Dnieper, appearing as *Danaper* in Jordanes' *Getica* (Mommsen 1882, §5, cf. *Danaber* §52), was first noted by P. A. Munch (1967 [1880], 174-5) and has since received general acceptance (Tolkien 1955-6, 157). — [19-20]: Wear to 2845 has made these lines very difficult to read; the Readings and Transcription have been taken from *Heiðr* 1924. — [21-22]: These lines are placed within square brackets in *Skj* B and omitted altogether in *Skald*, presumably to further increase the regularity of the stanza (cf. Note to [All] above), but they occur in all three mss (albeit partially in 2845). — [22] *ljósa bauga* 'bright rings': Repeated with poignant effect in AngH Lv 9/8 (*Heiðr* 117).

Angantýr (AngH Lv 2)

95. Bresta mun f*yr*r, bróðir, *in* blikhvíta lind,
    ok kaldr geir*r* koma við annan,
    ok margr gumi í gras hníga,
    en ek mun Humlung hálfan láta,
    eða Tyrfing í t*v*au deila.

F*yr*r mun *in* blikhvíta lind bresta, bróðir, ok kaldr geir*r* koma við annan, ok margr gumi hníga í gras, en ek mun láta hálfan Humlung, eða deila Tyrfing í t*v*au.

The white-gleaming shield will break, brother, and the cold spear clash with another, and many a man sink into the grass, before I will allow the Humlungr ('descendant of Humli') half, or divide Tyrfingr in two.

Mss: 2845(73v) (ll. 1-2, 5-10), 203[x](110r) (ll. 1-6, 9-10, 7-8), R715[x](31v-32r) (ll. 1-6, 9-10, 7-8) (*Heiðr*).

Readings: [1] Bresta: Bera *corrected from* 'Bressa' *in the margin in another hand* 203[x];   fyrr: for 2845, 'áðr' *with strikethrough in another hand* 203[x], áðr R715[x]   [2] *in* blikhvíta lind: lind in blikhvíta 2845, minn blikhvíta hönd 203[x], 'iij blikr huita lind' R715[x]   [3] kaldr: kaldar 203[x]; geirr: geir 203[x], R715[x]   [4] annan: annat 203[x]   [5] gumi: gumi *corrected from* gunni *in the margin in another hand* 203[x], gunni R715[x]   [7] en: *om*. 2845, áðr en 203[x], áðr er R715[x];   ek:

om. 203^x, R715^x;   mun: þér 203^x, R715^x;   Humlung: Humlungr 203^x, R715^x [8] láta: arf gefak *corrected from* 'arf gefa' *in another hand* 203^x, arf gefa R715^x [9] eða: *om.* R715^x [10] tvau: 'tau' 2845, 'midt' 203^x, 'tuennra' R715^x;   deila: 'deilik' *corrected from* deili *in another hand* 203^x, deili R715^x.

Editions: *Skj*: Anonyme digte og vers [XIII], E. 5. *Vers af Fornaldarsagaer: Af Hervararsaga* V 10: AII, 252, BII, 271-2, *Skald* II, 142; *Heiðr* 1672, 162, *FSN* 1, 493-4, *Heiðr* 1873, 270-1, *Heiðr* 1924, 88, 144, *FSGJ* 2, 56, *Heiðr* 1960, 49 (*Heiðr*); *Edd. Min.* 3-4, *NK* 304, *ÍF Edd.* II, 420, 422.

Context: In R Angantýr tells Hlǫðr he has no right to the land and is acting unjustly. In U the stanza is introduced simply, *Angantýr kvað* 'Angantýr said'.

Notes: [All]: This stanza poses various problems for, and has seen various attempts at, reconstruction. See Notes below. — [1] *fyrr* 'before': *Skj*, *Skald*, *FSN*, *Heiðr* 1873 and *Edd. Min.* omit, though all mss have a word here. *Fyrr* can, however, be accommodated in a line of Type A* (*málaháttr*). The emendation (2845 has 'for') was suggested by Suhm and Stefán Björnsson in their 1785 edn of the R text (based on ms. 345; *Heiðr* 1785, 190) and, probably independently, by Jón Helgason (*Heiðr* 1924, 88 n. 4). — [2-3]: Omitted in 2845; *Skj* and *Skald* insert these lines after the present ll. 5-6, but no ms. has this reading. — [2]: Ms. 2845's word order gives alliteration on the wrong syllable. Ms. R715^x doubtless reflects the word order presented here, with its 'iij' in the place of *in* 'the' likely a misreading of the minims. *Blikhvíta* 'white-gleaming' is a *hap. leg.*, but white or bright shields are a common motif in the corpus. See Note to *Heiðr* 63/6. — [3] *kaldr geir*r 'the cold spear': Tolkien (*Heiðr* 1960, 49 n. 3) compares *Beowulf* ll. 3021-2 (*Beowulf* 2008, 103) *gār morgenceald* 'morning-cold spear'. — [5-6]: *Edd. Min.* places these lines in square brackets, but they appear in all mss. — [7-10]: None of the mss' readings work perfectly as they stand, but the insertion of *en* to go with *fyrr* l. 1 (= *fyrr en* 'before') from 203^x and the emendation of ms. 'tau', with the line break after the 't', to *tvau* 'two' are the only changes necessary to 2845's reading, and that is presented here. *Skj* B and *FSGJ* also follow this order, though the former places ll. 7-8 in square brackets, while *Skald* omits them altogether. Both begin l. 9 *áðr ek* 'before I'. The U redaction reverses the order of the last two long-lines, but also presents variants, both compared to the R redaction and between the two U mss. Ms. 203^x gives the better reading: *áðr en Tyrfing | í mið* [ms, 'midt', 'tuenn ra' R715^x] *deilak, | eða þér, Humlungr, | hálfan arf gefak* 'before I divide Tyrfingr in the middle, or I give to you, Humlungr, half the inheritance'. The enclitic 1st pers. pronouns could well have been in the original stanza, but are editorial in the ms. *NK* and *Heiðr* 1960 follow U, emending *mið* 'middle' to *tvau* 'two', while *Edd. Min.* follows the order of U, but picks and chooses variants from 2845 to produce a composite reading. — [7] *Humlung* 'the Humlungr ("descendant of Humli")': I.e. Hlǫðr. Humli was his mother's father. — [9] *Tyrfing* 'Tyrfingr': See Notes to Angantýr Lv 2/3 (*Heiðr* 30) and *Þul Sverða* 7/6^{III}.

Angantýr (AngH Lv 3)

96. Ek mun bjóða þér   fagrar veigar,
fé ok fjölða meiðma,   sem þik fremst tíðir.
Tólf hundruð gef ek þér manna,   tólf hundruð gef ek þér mara,
tólf hundruð gef ek þér skálka,   þeirra er skjöld bera.

Ek mun bjóða þér fagrar veigar, fé ok fjölða meiðma, sem fremst tíðir þik. Ek gef þér tólf hundruð manna, ek gef þér tólf hundruð mara, ek gef þér tólf hundruð skálka, þeirra er bera skjöld.

I will offer you fair draughts, wealth and multitudes of riches, as is most desirable to you. I will give you twelve hundred men, I will give you twelve hundred horses, I will give you twelve hundred servants, who bear a shield.

Mss: **203ˣ**(110r), R715ˣ(32r) (*Heiðr*).

Readings: [2] veigar: 'aigar' *apparently corrected from* 'vigar' R715ˣ   [3] meiðma: 'meidna' 203ˣ, R715ˣ   [4] þik: ung 203ˣ, mik R715ˣ   [7] skálka: *so* R715ˣ, skálkur *corrected from* skálka *in the margin in another hand* 203ˣ.

Editions: *Skj*: Anonyme digte og vers [XIII], E. 5. *Vers af Fornaldarsagaer: Af Hervararsaga* V 11: AII, 252, BII, 272, *Skald* II, 142; *Heiðr* 1672, 162-3, *FSN* 1, 494, *Heiðr* 1873, 271-2, *Heiðr* 1924, 144-5, *FSGJ* 2, 56-7, *Heiðr* 1960, 50 (*Heiðr*); *Edd. Min.* 4-5, *NK* 305, *ÍF Edd.* II, 422-3.

Context: The stanza is introduced, *Ok enn kvað Angantýr* (*Heiðr* 1960, 49) 'And again Angantýr said'.

Notes: [1-4]: This *helmingr* is echoed in AngH Lv 9/1-4 (*Heiðr* 117), where Angantýr ruefully reflects on the consequences of Hlǫðr's refusal of his offer. Alliteration is lacking across ll. 1-2 of the present stanza. *Skj* B emends l. 2 to *bjartar vigrar* 'bright lances', which is followed by *Skald*, *FSGJ*, *Heiðr* 1960 and *ÍF Edd*. Bugge's suggestion, *bauga fagra* (*Heiðr* 1873), is noted by *Heiðr* 1924 and *Heiðr* 1960 and adopted by *Edd. Min.*, which offers other conjectures in the notes. None have any ms. support, however. AngH Lv 9/2 has (with alliteration) *basmir óskerðar* 'undiminished riches'. This reading is problematic in itself (see Note), and it could be that both stanzas originally had the same line, but that it has not been preserved intact in either (cf. *Heiðr* 1960, 50 n. 1). — [3] *meiðma* 'riches': A word found only in poetry in Old Norse, but cf. OE *máðum* 'a precious or valuable thing, treasure' (Bosworth and Toller 1898: *máðum*), which has wider usage. All eds but *FSN* emend to *meiðma*. — [4] *þik* 'to you': The emendation from the 1st to the 2nd pers. sg. acc. pron., which gives better sense, is made by eds except *Heiðr* 1672, *FSN*, *NK* and *ÍF Edd*. — [5-7]: The words *gef ek þér* 'I will give you' are extrametrical and superfluous to the sense, and are omitted by all other eds except *FSN* and *ÍF Edd*. (*Heiðr* 1672 retains in l. 5 but omits in the following lines), but they are retained here according to the principles of *SkP*.

Angantýr (AngH Lv 4)

97. Manni gef ek hverjum   margt at þiggja,
    annat æðra,   en hann á ráði.
    Mey gef ek hverjum   manni at þiggja;
    men spenni ek hverri   *meyju* at hálsi.

Ek gef hverjum manni margt at þiggja, annat æðra, en hann ráði á. Ek gef hverjum manni mey at þiggja; ek spenni men at hálsi hverri *meyju*.

I will give much to every man to receive, other, better than he could acquire. I will give a girl to every man to receive I will clasp a necklace around the neck of each girl.

Mss: **203**[x](110r-v), R715[x](32r) (*Heiðr*).

Readings: [2] margt: margt margt R715[x]   [4] en: 'eā' R715[x]; á ráði: *so* R715[x], 'a nÿdi' 203[x] [5] gef: *so* R715[x]   [6] manni: 'mani' *corrected from* margt *(struck through) in the margin in another hand* R715[x]   [7] men: meyju 203[x], 'mæn' *or* 'mæu' R715[x]; hverri: *om*. R715[x]   [8] *meyju*: men 203[x], meiri R715[x].

Editions: *Skj*: Anonyme digte og vers [XIII], E. 5. *Vers af Fornaldarsagaer: Af Hervararsaga* V 12: AII, 252-3, BII, 272, *Skald* II, 142, *FSN* 1, 494, *FF* §18; *Heiðr* 1672, 163, *Heiðr* 1873, 272, *Heiðr* 1924, 145, *FSGJ* 2, 57, *Heiðr* 1960, 50 (*Heiðr*); *Edd. Min.* 5, *NK* 305, *ÍF Edd.* II, 423.

Context: The stanza follows directly on from the previous one.

Notes: [4] *ráði á* 'could acquire': The reading of R715[x] is not certain (ms. 'ărădi') and the sense otherwise unattested, but deduced by Kock (*FF* §18, translated *anskaffa, skaffa fram, hitta på* 'find, obtain, come upon, acquire') by comparison with the attested *ráða af, avskaffa, jöra slut på* 'do away with, put an end to'. Cf. *Fritzner: ráða* 24. This reading is adopted by *Skald*, *NK* and *FSGJ* and tentatively adopted here on the ground that it requires less emendation than the alternatives. Jón Helgason (1967, 228), followed by *ÍF Edd.*, suggested *árnaði*, with similar meaning ('could gain'). *Heiðr* 1924 suggests *á at ráða*, followed by *Heiðr* 1960, which translates ll. 3-4 'nobler than all that he now possesses'. *Skj* B's suggestion, *áðr nyti* 'enjoyed previously', is based on 203[x] but still requires emendation. *Edd. Min.*'s *á kveði* 'could fix, determine' and *Heiðr* 1873's *áðr á* 'owns previously' are conjectural. — [7-8]: Ms. 203[x] has the words *men* 'necklace' and *meyju* 'girl' reversed (which produces the same meaning), but R715[x]'s garbled version suggests the order presented here, which has the additional advantages of being metrically better and supported by the pattern of the previous two lines. The emendation is also made by *Skj* B, *Skald*, *FSGJ* and *Edd. Min.*

Angantýr (AngH Lv 5)

98. Mun ek um þik sitjanda   silfri mæla,
     en ganganda þik   gulli steypa,
     svát á vega alla   velti baugar:
     þriðjung Gotþjóðar,   því skaltu einn ráða.

Ek mun mæla um þik sitjanda silfri, en steypa þik ganganda gulli, svát baugar velti á alla vega: þriðjung Gotþjóðar, því skaltu einn ráða.

I will measure you, sitting, with silver, and shower you, walking, in gold, so that rings roll in all directions: a third of the land of the Goths, that you alone shall rule.

Mss: **203**[x](110v), R715[x](32r) (*Heiðr*).

Readings: [2] mæla: 'vila' R715[x]   [3] ganganda: gangandi R715[x]   [5] vega: *so* R715[x], vegu 203[x]   [7] Gotþjóðar: Gotþjóða R715[x]   [8] einn: *so* R715[x], einn 203[x].

Editions: *Skj*: Anonyme digte og vers [XIII], E. 5. *Vers af Fornaldarsagaer: Af Hervararsaga* V 13: AII, 253, BII, 272, *Skald* II, 142; *Heiðr* 1672, 163, *FSN* 1, 494-5, *Heiðr* 1873, 272, *Heiðr* 1924, 145, *FSGJ* 2, 57, *Heiðr* 1960, 50 (*Heiðr*); *Edd. Min.* 5, *NK* 305, *ÍF Edd.* II, 423.

Context: The stanza follows directly on from the previous one.

Notes: [1-6]: Cf. e.g *Snegl* (*ÍF* 9, 290-2), where King Haraldr Guðinason (Godwinson) offers to reward Halli for a poem by pouring silver on his head, telling him he can keep what sticks. Halli smears tar on his head and forms his hair into a bowl shape, thus gaining rather more reward than the king intended. See also examples listed under *Fritzner: steypa* 4 and, on the syntactic construction, cf. *Þry* 10. — [3-4]: Jón Helgason (1967, 229) observes that the idea of showering gold on a man who is walking along is an unlikely scenario and though he retains the ms. reading in his edition, in his notes proposes (in ModIcel.) *en standanda þig / steypa gulli* 'and steep you, standing, in gold'. This is, of course, purely speculative. — [5] *svát* 'so that': The ms. form, *svá* 'so', reflects a later (C14th and after) practice in which *að* 'at' (here cliticised for metrical reasons) is omitted (see *SkP* VII, lxvii (§9.B.3); *NS* §265 Anm. 2b). — [7] *þriðjung* 'a third': See Note to GizGrý Lv 1/5 (*Heiðr* 99) on the inheritance of the *hornungr* 'bastard', as Hlǫðr is called there. The closest parallel to the situation described here appears to be in Langobardic law, which allowed an illegitimate son to inherit one third where there was one legitimate son, who inherited two thirds (Grimm 1899, 655-6). — [7] *Gotþjóðar* 'of the land of the Goths': The cpd can also mean 'people of the Goths', which would also be possible here. — [8]: Cf. *Guðr* II 26/5-6 (*NK* 228), where Grímhildr offers Guðrún various treasures as Atli's bride: *ein scaltu ráða | auði Buðla* 'you alone shall rule the wealth of Buðli'. — [8] *því* 'that': The precise referent for the n. demonstrative pron. is uncertain: it likely refers to all the items listed as a whole, but could possibly alternatively refer to *landi*, understood from *Gotþjóðar* if taken, as here, in the sense 'land of the Goths' (see previous Note).

Gizurr (GizGrý Lv 1)

99. Þetta er þiggjanda   þýjar barni,
barni þýja*r*,   þótt sé borinn konung*i*.
Þá hornungr   á haugi sat,
er ǫðlingr   arfi skipti.

Þetta er þiggjanda þýjar barni, barni þýja*r*, þótt sé borinn konung*i*. Þá sat hornungr á haugi, er ǫðlingr skipti arfi.

This is acceptable for a servant-woman's child, child of a servant-woman, though he may be born to a king. The bastard sat on the mound, when the prince was dividing the inheritance.

Mss: **203**[x](110v), R715[x](32r) (*Heiðr*).

Readings: [1] þiggjanda: þiggjandi R715[x]   [2] barni: barmi R715[x]   [3] barni: barmi R715[x]; þýjar: þýja 203[x], R715[x]   [4] konung*i*: konungr 203[x], 'k:' R715[x]   [5] hornungr: hornung R715[x]   [6] haugi: 'haag' R715[x]   [7] ǫðlingr: 'odligar' R715[x].

Editions: *Skj*: Anonyme digte og vers [XIII], E. 5. *Vers af Fornaldarsagaer: Af Hervararsaga* V 15: AII, 253, BII, 273, *Skald* II, 142; *Heiðr* 1672, 166, *FSN* 1, 495, *Heiðr* 1873, 273, *Heiðr* 1924, 145-6, *FSGJ* 2, 58, *Heiðr* 1960, 51 (*Heiðr*); *Edd. Min.* 5-6, *NK* 305-6, *ÍF Edd.* II, 423.

Context: According to the saga prose, Heiðrekr's elderly foster-father Gizurr Grýtingaliði 'Retainer of the Grýtingar' thinks the offer is too generous, and speaks the stanza (but see Note to l. 1 below).

Notes: [1] *þiggjanda* 'acceptable': The meaning of the stanza seems to contradict what is stated in the prose, that Gizurr thinks Angantýr *ofmikit bjóða* 'offers too much'. — [2-3]: Tolkien (*Heiðr* 1960, 51 n. 2) highlights the 'emphatic repetition' and draws comparison to *Sigsk* 17/6-7; Jón Helgason (1967, 230) notes also the example of *Ásm* 5/2-3. Gizurr's claim is insulting, and alludes to the fact that Hlǫðr's mother, Sifka, the daughter of the Hunnish king Humli, was captured in a raid by Heiðrekr and returned pregnant to her father. — [4] *konungi* 'to a king': The emendation to dat. case was first made by Suhm and Stefán Björnsson (*Heiðr* 1785, 194; *konge* is what is actually printed) and has been followed in *Heiðr* 1873 and *Heiðr* 1960. The mss' reading, *ok þótt sé borinn konungr* 'and though he may be born a king' is possible grammatically, but gives less good sense because though Hlǫðr's parents are both of royal status, he was conceived illegitimately. The reading of the mss is retained by *FSN*, *FSGJ*, *Edd. Min.*, *NK* and *ÍF Edd.*, and by *Skj* B although Finnur Jónsson gives the translation *selv om han er født som konge(sön)* 'though he may be born a king('s son)'. — [5-6]: As shepherds are associated with the practice of sitting on mounds (e.g. *Vsp* 42/1-4, *Skí* 11/1-2), some have interpreted Gizurr's remark as insulting to Hlǫðr (e.g. Jón Helgason 1967, 231; *ÍF Edd.*; cf. *Heiðr* 1960, 51 n. 3). However, the concept most likely relates to inheritance or succession; by implication, the mound would be that of Hlǫðr's (and Angantýr's) father, Heiðrekr. In the *Flat* redaction of *ÓH*, for example, a certain Bjǫrn, son of a deceased king Óláfr, sits on his father's mound when he reaches the age of twelve before claiming the kingdom from his uncle, acting as regent (*Flat* 1860-8, II, 70). The practice of sitting on royal burial mounds may also have been a more abstract symbol of kingship: in *HHárf* in *Hkr* (ch. 8, *ÍF* 26, 99-100), King Hrollaugr of Namdalen goes *upp á haug þann, er konungar váru vanir at sitja á* 'up onto that mound which kings were accustomed to sit on', and rolls down from the kings' seat to the jarls', as a sign of his subjection to Haraldr hárfagri. Ellis (1943, 105-11) provides examples and discussion of these and other incidents, including further connections to kingship and inheritance of other kinds. The implication seems to be that Hlǫðr's actions were an attempt at symbolic validation of his claim. — [5] *hornungr* 'bastard': Lit. 'the one in the corner', i.e. someone relegated to a marginal status, an outcast. In the Old Norwegian *Gulaþingslǫg* (§104; *NGL* I, 48-9) the *hornungr* is the son of a free woman who has not had the bride-price paid for her but the relationship has not been secret. He is entitled to the 'seventh inheritance', which includes moveable wealth and odal land. In the *Frostuþingslǫg*, the *hornungr* is defined as the son of a man who has lain with a free woman in the house (as opposed to outside it: *NGL* I, 228 (X, §47)), and also takes the 'seventh inheritance' (*NGL* I, 206 (VIII, §8)). In Old Icelandic law the *hornungr* is the child of a woman and the slave she has freed in order to marry; the *hornungr* is not a lawful heir (*Grg* Ia, 224 (§118)). On other uses and cognates see Frimannslund (1968, 71-4) and Magnús Már Lárusson (1968, 74-5). Here the sense seems to be generally pejorative rather than legally specific.

Humli (Humli Lv 1)

100. Sitja skulum vér í vetr   ok sælliga lifa,
    drekka ok dæma   dýrar veigar,
    kenna Húnum   vápn at búa,
    þau er djarfliga   skulum fram bera.

Vér skulum sitja í vetr ok lifa sælliga, drekka dýrar veigar ok dæma, kenna Húnum at búa vápn, þau er skulum bera fram djarfliga.

We shall sit during winter and live prosperously, drink costly draughts and make conversation, teach the Huns to prepare the weapons that we shall carry forth boldly.

Mss: **203[x]**(110v), R715[x](32v) (*Heiðr*).

Readings: [1] skulum: skulu R715[x];   vér: 'vær' R715[x]   [3] dæma: tæma *corrected from* dæma R715[x]   [5] Húnum: hverjum R715[x].

Editions: *Skj*: Anonyme digte og vers [XIII], E. 5. *Vers af Fornaldarsagaer: Af Hervararsaga* VI 1: AII, 253, BII, 273, *Skald* II, 142, *NN* §3184; *Heiðr* 1672, 166, *FSN* 1, 495-6, *Heiðr* 1873, 274, *Heiðr* 1924, 146, *FSGJ* 2, 58-9, *Heiðr* 1960, 51 (*Heiðr*); *Edd. Min.* 6, *NK* 306, *ÍF Edd.* II, 424.

Context: Hlǫðr returns home and tells his maternal grandfather, King Humli, that he has been refused an equal division of the inheritance. Humli grows angry at his daughter's son being called the son of a servant woman, and speaks the stanza.

Notes: [3]: The same line is found in *Rþ* 32/9, *Sigsk* 2/5 (both in the past tense) and *Ǫrv* 25/1 (in the 1st pers. pl. pret.). — [4]: The same line is found in *Hyndl* 50/6 and *HHund* II 46/2, and cf. *Heiðr* 97/2 *fagrar veigar* 'fair draughts'. — [5-6]: Alliteration is lacking. To restore, all eds emend *vápn* 'weapons' to *hervápn* 'war-weapons', on the basis of a reading in Holm papp. 120, a ms. which is not of independent value (but cf. *herlið* 'war-troop' in *Heiðr* 101/2). However, the line is still unmetrical unless *at* 'to' is deleted. — [7-8]: Again, these lines lack alliteration. *Skj* B emends *djarfliga* 'boldly' to *framliga* (translating *djǫrvt*), with similar meaning. *Heiðr* 1873 offers *frœknliga* 'valiantly', followed by *Edd. Min.*, *FSGJ* and *Heiðr* 1960, while *Skald* chooses to emend *fram* 'forth' in l. 8 to *dramb* 'arrogance'. These conjectures are all unsupported by ms. evidence.

Humli (Humli Lv 2)

101. Vel skulum þér, Hlöðr,   herlið búa
      ok framliga   hildi heyja
      með tólfvetra mengi   ok tvævetrum fola.
      Svá skal Húna   her um safna.

Hlöðr, skulum búa þér herlið vel ok heyja hildi framliga með mengi tólfvetra ok [með] tvævetrum [mengi] fola. Svá skal um safna her Húna.

We shall prepare the war-troop well for you, Hlǫðr, and wage war boldly, with a multitude of twelve-year-olds and [with] a two-year-old [multitude] of foals. Thus shall the army of the Huns be assembled.

Mss: **203ˣ**(110v), R715ˣ(32v) (*Heiðr*).

Readings: [1] skulum: skulum vér R715ˣ   [3] framliga: *so* R715ˣ, 'fránliga' 203ˣ   [4] hildi: *so* R715ˣ, hildir 203ˣ   [5] -vetra: vetra *corrected from* vetra gömlu *with* gömlu *underlined* 203ˣ, 'var goml' R715ˣ;   mengi: 'meiñge' 203ˣ, 'mñgi' R715ˣ   [7] Húna: 'hrvna' R715ˣ   [8] um: *so* R715ˣ, af 203ˣ;   safna: 'sanna' R715ˣ.

Editions: *Skj*: Anonyme digte og vers [XIII], E. 5. *Vers af Fornaldarsagaer: Af Hervararsaga* VI 2: AII, 253-4, BII, 273, *Skald* II, 142, *NN* §3185; *Heiðr* 1672, 166-7, *FSN* 1, 496, *Heiðr* 1873, 275, *Heiðr* 1924, 147, *FSGJ* 2, 59, *Heiðr* 1960, 52 (*Heiðr*); *Edd. Min.* 6, *NK* 306, *ÍF Edd.* II, 424.

Context: The stanza follows directly on from the previous one.

Notes: [3-4]: Previous eds have made various conjectural attempts at alliteration across these lines. Jón Helgason (1967, 232) highlights some other examples of this alliterative pattern in *fornyrðislag*, but only from later poetry. — [5-6]: The implication is that absolutely all resources will be drawn on, with warriors and horses utilised from the youngest possible age. Foote and Wilson (1980, 116) suggest 'there are some signs that in an earlier period [than extant written laws] boys of twelve were accepted as full-grown members of society'. — [5] *með tólfvetra mengi* 'with a multitude of twelve-year-olds': Both mss indicate the word *gömlu* 'old' after *tólfvetra* (lit. 'of twelve years'), but this has been deleted by means of underlining in 203ˣ. It makes an already hypermetrical line more so and is not required for sense. — [6] *ok [með] tvævetrum [mengi] fola* 'and [with] a two-year-old [multitude] of foals': The syntax of this line depends on understanding the noun *mengi* 'multitude' (dat.) from l. 5, here, however, qualified by the adj. *tvævetrum* 'two-year-old' (also dat.), with both *tólfvetra* 'of twelve-year-olds' and *fola* 'of foals' in the gen. pl.

Ormarr (Ormarr Lv 1)

102. Skal ek víst ríða   ok rönd bera,
     Go*tn*a þjóðum   gunni at heyja.

Ek skal víst ríða ok bera rönd, at heyja gunni þjóðum Go*tn*a.

I shall certainly ride and bear a shield, to wage war with the people of the Goths.

Mss: **203ˣ**(111r), R715ˣ(33v) (*Heiðr*).

Readings: [2] ok: *so* R715ˣ, í 203ˣ   [3] Go*tn*a: Gauta 203ˣ, R715ˣ   [4] at: *so* R715ˣ, *om.* 203ˣ.

Editions: *Skj*: Anonyme digte og vers [XIII], E. 5. Vers af Fornaldarsagaer: Af Hervararsaga VII 1: AII, 254, BII, 273, *Skald* II, 142; *Heiðr* 1672, 172, *FSN* 1, 497, *Heiðr* 1873, 277, *Heiðr* 1924, 148, *FSGJ* 2, 60, *Heiðr* 1960, 53 (*Heiðr*); *Edd. Min.* 7, *NK* 307, *ÍF Edd.* II, 425.

Context: In spring the Huns gather a vast army and ride to the land of the Goths. Hervǫr Heiðreksdóttir, half-sister of Angantýr and Hlǫðr, sees the approaching forces from the watchtower of her stronghold and has the trumpet blown to raise her army. She instructs her foster-father Ormarr to ride to meet the Huns and challenge them to battle, and Ormarr replies with this half-stanza.

Notes: [All]: *Edd. Min.* and *Heiðr* 1873 make purely conjectural suggestions loosely based on the surrounding prose to create an eight-line stanza. — [1-2] *ríða ok bera rönd* 'ride and bear a shield': Repeated in *Heiðr* 108/5-6 and 109/5-6. In those instances the scribes of both mss write *í* 'in' for *ok* 'and', as that of 203ˣ does here, but that reading makes no sense. — [3]: *ÍF Edd.* conjecturally adds *bjóða* 'invite, offer' to the end of the line, but this does not make it metrical. — [4]: The same line occurs in *HHund I* 52/6 and *HHund II* 23/3.

Ormarr (Ormarr Lv 2)

103. Sunnan em ek kominn   at segja spjöll þessi:
sviðin er öll   Myrkviðar heiðr,
drifin öll Gotþjóð   gumna blóði.

Ek em kominn sunnan at segja þessi spjöll: öll heiðr Myrkviðar er sviðin, öll Gotþjóð drifin blóði gumna.

I have come from the south to relate these words: all Myrkviðr's heath is scorched, all the land of the Goths sprayed with the blood of men.

Mss: **203ˣ**(111r-v), R715ˣ(34r) (*Heiðr*).

Readings: [2] segja: segir R715ˣ   [4] -viðar: viðar *corrected from* -heiðar *above the line in another hand* 203ˣ, *om.* R715ˣ;   heiðr: *so* R715ˣ, heiði 203ˣ   [5] drifin: drjúgum er R715ˣ   [6] gumna: gunna 203ˣ, R715ˣ.

Editions: *Skj*: Anonyme digte og vers [XIII], E. 5. *Vers af Fornaldarsagaer: Af Hervararsaga* VII 2: AII, 254, BII, 273-4, *Skald* II, 143; *Heiðr* 1672, 172, *FSN* 1, 499, *Heiðr* 1873, 279, *Heiðr* 1924, 149, *Heiðr* 1960, 53 (*Heiðr*); *Edd. Min.* 7, *NK* 307, *ÍF Edd.* II, 425.

Context: The Goths and Huns meet in battle. Eventually Hervǫr, the leader of the Goths, is killed, whereupon Ormarr and the rest of the troop flee. The Huns harry widely in the land of the Goths. Ormarr rides to Angantýr and speaks this stanza.

Notes: [3-4]: To restore alliteration *Skj* B, *Skald*, *Heiðr* 1960 and *Edd. Min.* all add *in mæra* 'the renowned' after *öll*, *Edd. Min.* placing *öll* in square brackets. There is no ms. support for this emendation here, but cf. *Heiðr* 94/1-2 *hrís þat it mæra, | er Myrkviðr heitir* 'that renowned forest, which is called Myrkviðr' (and see Note there). *ÍF Edd.* takes *Sviðin er ǫll Myrkheiðr* (see following Note) to be l. 3, assuming another l. 4 to be lost. — [4] *heiðr Myrkviðar* 'Myrkviðr's heath': Ms. 203ˣ's original reading was *Myrkheiðar heiðr* 'Myrkheiðr's heath'; the correction is in another hand. R715ˣ reads just 'Mirk heiðr', which *NK* follows, but if it is a p. n. it is not otherwise known or mentioned elsewhere (cf. Jón Helgason 1967, 234). *Heiðr* 1672 emends to *Mork oc heidar* 'borderland and heath'. — [5] *Gotþjóð* 'the land of the Goths': See Note to *Heiðr* 94/16.

Ormarr (Ormarr Lv 3)

104. Mey veit ek Heiðreks, ...
systur þína,   svigna til jarðar.
Hafa Húnar   hana felda,
ok marga aðra   y*ðra* þegna.

Ek veit mey Heiðreks, ... systur þína, svigna til jarðar. Húnar hafa felda hana, ok marga aðra þegna y*ðra*.

I know Heiðrekr's girl, ... your sister, to have sunk to the earth. The Huns have felled her, and many others of your men.

Mss: 203^x(111v), R715^x(34r) (*Heiðr*).

Readings: [4] svigna: 'singna' R715^x [8] y*ðra*: 'ydar' R715^x.

Editions: *Skj*: Anonyme digte og vers [XIII], E. 5. *Vers af Fornaldarsagaer: Af Hervararsaga* VII 3: AII, 254, BII, 273-4, *Skald* II, 143, *NN* §§3144, 3186; *Heiðr* 1672, 173, *FSN* 1, 499, *Heiðr* 1873, 279, *Heiðr* 1924, 150, *FSGJ* 2, 61-2, *Heiðr* 1960, 53-4; *Edd. Min.* 7-8, *NK* 308, *ÍF Edd.* II, 425-6.

Notes: [2]: Metrically, there must be something missing here, but neither ms. gives any indication either of what it may be or of a gap. All previous eds have made suggestions, but all are conjecture. — [4] *svigna* 'to have sunk': Lit. 'sunk'. *Svigna* is an inflected (f. acc. sg.) p. p. of the first class strong verb *svíga* 'sink', which is only attested in the p. p. The construction is acc.-inf. — [7] *marga aðra* 'many others': Kock (*Skald*; *NN* §3144) prefers for metrical reasons, but against ms. evidence, to reverse the word order.

Ormarr (Ormarr Lv 4)

105. Léttari gerðiz hon at *böð**   en við biðil ræða,
eða í bekk at fara   at brúðargangi.

Hon gerðiz léttari at *böð** en ræða við biðil, eða at fara í bekk at brúðargangi.

She became more at ease with battle than with talking with a suitor, or with going to the bench in the bridal procession.

Mss: 203^x(111v), R715^x(34r) (*Heiðr*).

Readings: [1] Léttari: 'Littare' 203^x, *om.* R715^x;   at: so R715^x, á 203^x;   *böð**: hauðri 203^x, 'badni' R715^x [3] eða í bekk at fara: 'ad leik j saīa' R715^x [4] at: en at R715^x;   brúðar-: lundr R715^x;   -gangi: gengu R715^x.

Editions: *Skj*: Anonyme digte og vers [XIII], E. 5. *Vers af Fornaldarsagaer: Af Hervararsaga* VII 4: AII, 254, BII, 274, *Skald* II, 143, *FF* §19; *Heiðr* 1672, 173, *FSN* 1, 499-500, *Heiðr* 1873, 280, *Heiðr* 1924, 150, *FSGJ* 2, 62, *Heiðr* 1960, 54 (*Heiðr*); *Edd. Min.* 8, *NK* 308, *ÍF Edd.* II, 426.

Context: The stanza follows directly on from the previous one.

Notes: [1]: *ÍF Edd.* emends to *lútari* 'more inclined'. — [3-4]: The mss have different readings here, and neither version is completely satisfactory. Kock (*Skald*; *FF* §19), possibly following *Heiðr* 1672 (which however does not offer a translation), emends R715[x]'s problematic reading to *ad leiki sara | en ad lundar geingu* 'to the play of wounds [BATTLE], than to the journey to the grove'. *NK* also follows R715[x], emending to *at leic ísarna | enn at lundar gǫngo* 'to the play of irons [BATTLE], than to the journey to the grove'. Either conjectured battle-kenning would be the only kenning in the group of stanzas about the Huns and Goths, though that fact does not make it an impossible occurrence here, especially given the relative infrequency of kennings in non-skaldic metres. — [4] *brúðargangi* 'the bridal procession': Though Tolkien (*Heiðr* 1960, 54 n. 2) confidently explains, 'the *brúðargangr* was the procession of the bride and ladies from the *brúðarhús* (bride's chamber) to the *stofa* [main room] ... for the feast', the word is not attested in Old Norse (either as a cpd or its separate components, cf. *ONP*: *brúðr*), though it is in later Icelandic (*OHá*: *brúðargangur*).

Angantýr (AngH Lv 6)

106. Óbróðurliga vartu leikin,   in ágæta systir!

Vartu leikin óbróðurliga, in ágæta systir!

You were treated in an unbrotherly way, excellent sister!

Mss: **203**[x](111v), R715[x](34r) (*Heiðr*).

Editions: *Skj*: Anonyme digte og vers [XIII], E. 5. *Vers af Fornaldarsagaer: Af Hervararsaga* VII 5: AII, 254, BII, 274, *Skald* II, 143; *Heiðr* 1672, 173, *FSN* 1, 500, *Heiðr* 1873, 280, *Heiðr* 1924, 150, *FSGJ* 2, 62, *Heiðr* 1960, 54 (*Heiðr*); *NK* 308, *ÍF Edd.* II, 426.

Context: When King Angantýr hears of the death of his sister (*Heiðr* 1960, 54), *brá hann grǫnum ok tók seint til orða* 'he drew back his lips and was slow to speak', but finally speaks these words.

Notes: [All]: These lines are prose, not poetry, although they contain alliterating staves. *Heiðr* 1672, *FSN* and *Heiðr* 1960 treat them as prose, while *Skj* B and *Skald* combine them with the four following lines here identified as st. 107, which are in *málaháttr*. — [1] *óbróðurliga* 'in an unbrotherly way': *Hap. leg.*

Angantýr (AngH Lv 7)

107. Mjök várum vér margir,   er vér mjöð drukkum;
  nú erum vér færri,   er vér fleiri skyldum.

Vér várum mjök margir, er vér drukkum mjöð; nú erum vér færri, er vér skyldum fleiri.

We were very many, when we drank mead; now we are fewer, when we should be more.

Mss: 203ˣ(111v), R715ˣ(34r) (*Heiðr*).

Reading: [2] mjöð: 'mod' R715ˣ.

Editions: *Skald* II, 143; *Heiðr* 1672, 173, *FSN* 1, 500, *Heiðr* 1873, 280, *Heiðr* 1924, 150, *FSGJ* 2, 62, *Heiðr* 1960, 54 (*Heiðr*); *Edd. Min.* 8, *NK* 308, *ÍF Edd.* II, 426.

Context: King Angantýr looks over his remaining forces and speaks the stanza.

Note: [All]: Jón Helgason (1967, 237) draws comparison with the exchange between King Haraldr hárfagri and Þjóðólfr ór Hvíni in ch. 26 of *Hkr* (*Hhárf*, *ÍF* 26, 127-8): Haraldr mutters a *helmingr* (Hhárf Lv 1¹) grumbling about the large number of warriors who have come to a feast at one of his estates, and Þjóðólfr replies in another *helmingr* (Þjóð Lv 1¹), observing that Haraldr did not consider the number of warriors too great when they were fighting battles on his behalf (l. 4 *vǫruma þá til margir* 'then we were not too many').

Angantýr (AngH Lv 8)

108. Sé ek eigi þann   í mínu liði,
  þótt ek biða   ok baugum kaupa,
  er muni ríða   *ok* rönd bera
  ok þei*rra* Húna   herlið finna.

Ek sé eigi þann í liði mínu, er muni ríða *ok* bera rönd ok finna herlið þei*rra* Húna, þótt ek biða ok kaupa baugum.

I do not see that one in my troop who would ride and bear a shield, and meet the war-troop of the Huns, though I should beg and bargain with rings.

Mss: 203ˣ(111v), R715ˣ(34r) (*Heiðr*).

Readings: [4] baugum: 'bugum' R715ˣ   [6] *ok*: í 203ˣ, R715ˣ; rönd: rand R715ˣ   [7] þei*rra*: þeir 203ˣ, R715ˣ   [8] finna: bera R715ˣ.

Editions: *Skj*: Anonyme digte og vers [XIII], E. 5. *Vers af Fornaldarsagaer: Af Hervararsaga* VII 6: AII, 254-5, BII, 274, *Skald* II, 143; *Heiðr* 1672, 173, *FSN* 1, 500, *Heiðr* 1873, 281, *Heiðr* 1924, 150-1, *FSGJ* 2, 62-3, *Heiðr* 1960, 54 (*Heiðr*); *Edd. Min.* 8, *NK* 308, *ÍF Edd.* II, 426.

Context: The stanza follows directly on from the previous one.

Notes: [1] *þann* 'that one': The reading of both mss, *þann* 'that one', gives good sense and syntax but lacks alliteration. All eds but *Heiðr* 1672, *FSN* and *ÍF Edd.* emend to *mann* 'a man' (*Edd. Min.* moves *mann* to be the first word of the stanza). *ÍF Edd.* emends to *þann mann* 'that man'. — [3, 4]: The two verbs in these lines, *biða* and *kaupa*, appear in the mss as *biði* and *kaupi*, with C14th endings of the 1st pers. pres. subj. of, respectively, *biðja* 'beg, request' and *kaupa* 'bargain, buy'. These have been normalized to forms suitable to the period 1250-1300 in accordance with the procedures of the rest of this volume. — [5-6] *ríða ok bera rönd* 'ride and bear a shield': Also found in *Heiðr* 103/1-2 (and see Note) and *Heiðr* 109/5-6. — [7-8]: *Skj* B and *Skald* emend to *ok þeim Húnum | herboð inna* 'and perform the war-summons to the Huns'. This seems to be partly based on Verelius' emendation of R715^x's problematic reading, *Oc þeim Hunum | Herbod bioda* (*Heiðr* 1672) 'and offer the war-summons to the Huns', but both mss have *herlið* 'war-troop' and 203^x's reading gives good sense as it stands.

Gizurr (GizGrý Lv 2)

109. Ek mun þik enskis   eyris krefja,
    né skjall*anda   skarfs ór gulli.
    Þó mun ek ríða   *ok* rönd bera
    Húna þjóðum   gunni at bjóða.

Ek mun krefja þik enskis eyris, né skjall*anda skarfs ór gulli. Þó mun ek ríða *ok* bera rönd at bjóða þjóðum Húna gunni.

I will demand from you nothing of silver, nor chinking coin of gold. Yet I will ride and bear a shield to offer battle to the people of the Huns.

Mss: 203^x(111v), R715^x(34r-v) (*Heiðr*).

Readings: [1] þik: *so* R715^x, þar 203^x [2] eyris: 'eirirs' R715^x [3] né ('nie'): nei R715^x; skjall*anda: 'skulldanda' 203^x, 'skiall danda' R715^x [4] skarfs: 'skafst' R715^x [6] ok: í 203^x, R715^x; rönd: rand R715^x [7] Húna: 'gotta' *apparently corrected from* 'guña' *in another hand* R715^x.

Editions: *Skj*: Anonyme digte og vers [XIII], E. 5. *Vers af Fornaldarsagaer: Af Hervararsaga* VII 7: AII, 255, BII, 274, *Skald* II, 143; *Heiðr* 1672, 173, *FSN* 1, 500-1, *Heiðr* 1873, 281, *Heiðr* 1924, 151, *FSGJ* 2, 63, *Heiðr* 1960, 54-5 (*Heiðr*); *Edd. Min.* 9, *NK* 308-9, *ÍF Edd.* II, 427.

Context: The stanza is introduced (*Heiðr* 1960, 54), *Gizurr gamli sagði* 'Gizurr the Old said'.

Notes: [3] *skjall*anda* 'chinking': Neither ms. gives an acceptable reading and all eds but *FSN* emend. The significance seems to be that the coin is weighty enough to make a ringing noise when cast against another surface: *Heiðr* 1873, 366 and, following it, *Heiðr* 1960, 55 n. 2 refer to an incident related by Saxo (*Saxo* 2015, I, viii. 16. 7, pp.

626-7) in which only coins which made enough noise to be heard by a tax-collector twelve rooms away would be counted towards the tribute paid by the Frisians. — [4] *skarfs* 'coin': A *hap. leg.* with this meaning (*LP*: *skarfr* 2; *AEW*: *skarfr* 2). The word may be related to MLG *scharf, scherf* 'half penny', late ON *skerfr* 'share, portion'. The homonym *skarfr* 'cormorant (*Phalacrocorax carbo*)' does not seem to be etymologically related (*AEW*: *skarfr* 1; *Fritzner*: *skarfr* 2). — [5-6] *ríða ok bera rönd* 'ride and bear a shield': Echoes *Heiðr* 103/1-2 (and see Note) and *Heiðr* 108/5-6. — [7-8]: As they stand, these lines lack alliteration. Following 202k^x, which is not an independent ms. witness, all eds emend *gunni* 'battle' to *herstaf*, a *hap. leg. Skj* B translates *krigsruner* 'war-runes', *Heiðr* 1960 'war-staff'. Ms. R715^x's readings ('gotta', presumably *Gota* 'of the Goths', apparently corrected from 'guña' in another hand) suggest that alliteration may have been on the *g-* of *gunni*, but neither of its alternatives offers a satisfactory solution: Gizurr is on the side of the Goths, and gen. pl. *gunna* 'of the battles' makes no sense. The abbreviation 'guña' is used elsewhere in the ms. where *gumna* 'of men' seems to be intended (cf. *Heiðr* 103/6), but again, this does not give good sense, though it is given in *NK*. Emending *gunni* to *hildi* 'to war' would solve the problem, but would go against both mss.

Gizurr (GizGrý Lv 3)

110. Hvar skal ek Húnum   hervíg kenna?

Hvar skal ek kenna Húnum hervíg?

Where shall I tell the Huns the battle is?

Mss: **203^x**(111v), R715^x(34v) (*Heiðr*).

Readings: [1] Hvar: hér R715^x;   ek: *om.* R715^x;   Húnum: 'hūiūm' R715^x.

Editions: *Skj*: Anonyme digte og vers [XIII], E. 5. *Vers af Fornaldarsagaer: Af Hervararsaga* VII 8: AII, 255, BII, 274, *Skald* II, 143; *Heiðr* 1672, 174, *FSN* 1, 501, *Heiðr* 1873, 282, *Heiðr* 1924, 151, *FSGJ* 2, 63, *Heiðr* 1960, 55 (*Heiðr*); *Edd. Min.* 9, *NK* 309, *ÍF Edd.* II, 427.

Context: The narrative explains that if a king marks out a designated place of battle, invaders cannot harry in his territory until the battle is decided. Gizurr arms himself and prepares to ride to call the Huns to battle, and speaks these lines.

Angantýr (AngH Lv 9)

111. Kendu at Dylgju   ok á Dúnheiði,
ok á þeim öllum   Jassarfjöllum.
Þar opt Gotar   gun*ni* háðu,
ok fagran sigr   frægir vágu.

Kendu at Dylgju ok á Dúnheiði, ok á öllum þeim Jassarfjöllum. Þar háðu Gotar opt gun*ni*, ok frægir vágu fagran sigr.

Tell [them] at Dylgja and on Dúnheiðr, and on all the Jassarfjǫll. There the Goths often waged war, and the renowned ones won a fine victory.

Mss: **203**[x](111v), R715[x](34v) (*Heiðr*).

Readings: [1] at: *so* R715[x], á 203[x]   [4] Jassar-: *so* R715[x], 'Josur-' *corrected from* Jassar *in another hand* 203[x]   [5] Þar: báru 203[x], bar R715[x]   [6] gun*ni*: geir 203[x], gun R715[x]   [8] vágu: *so* R715[x], fengu 203[x].

Editions: *Skj*: Anonyme digte og vers [XIII], E. 5. *Vers af Fornaldarsagaer: Af Hervararsaga* VII 9: AII, 255, BII, 274-5, *Skald* II, 143, *FF* §20; *Heiðr* 1672, 174, *FSN* 1, 501, *Heiðr* 1873, 282-3, *Heiðr* 1924, 152, *FSGJ* 2, 63-4, *Heiðr* 1960, 55 (*Heiðr*); *Edd. Min.* 9-10, *NK* 309, *ÍF Edd.* II, 427.

Context: The stanza is introduced, *Angantýr konungr kvað* 'King Angantýr said'.

Notes: [1-4]: Similar lines appear in Gizurr's speech to the Huns, GizGrý Lv 5/1-4 (*Heiðr* 113). — [1] *Dylgju* 'Dylgja': *Heiðr* 1924 reports correction to 'Dyngjo' in another hand, both here and to the same word in GizGrý Lv 5/1 (*Heiðr* 113), but in both places this has since been obscured by the binding of the ms. In the prose following *Heiðr* 113, Gizurr says (*Heiðr* 1924, 153), *taladi eg vid þa, og stefndi eg þeim a vigvoll a Dunheidi i Dyngiudolum* 'I spoke with them, and I summoned them to the battlefield on Dúnheiðr in Dyngjudalir', with the spelling 'Dingiu' occurring in both mss. Neither Dylgja nor Dyngja have been identified as place names. The f. noun *dylgja* means 'enmity' or 'battle' (cf. Note to BjHall *Kálffl* 8/2[1]), and Tolkien 'hesitantly' emends both stanzas and the prose to accommodate this interpretation (*Heiðr* 1960, 55-6 and xxiv). *Dyngja* f. means 'woman's chamber', 'heap' (ModIcel. 'shield volcano'), but neither of these meanings help resolve the mystery of what or where is meant. — [2] *Dúnheiði* 'Dúnheiðr': Again, the location has not been identified. The *Dún* is usually the Danube (cf. Þul *Á* 2/3[III] and Note; cf. Note to *Dýna* 'Dvina' in the same line), the cpd then literally meaning 'Danube-heath'. — [3]: Jón Helgason (1967, 240) notes this line *er ólíklegt til að vera rétt* 'is unlikely to be correct', like several eds (*Skj* B; *Heiðr* 1960; *Edd. Min.*) objecting to the idea of fighting *á* 'on' mountains as opposed to near or under them. *Heiðr* 1960 emends the line to *orrostu undir* and translates (together with l. 4) 'below the hills of Ash | shall you call them to fight'. His suggested line appears as GizGrý Lv 5/3 (*Heiðr* 113), the first four lines of which have echoes of the first four of this stanza. Other eds make various small emendations, but since the mss agree on the reading presented here, anything else remains conjecture. — [4] *Jassarfjǫllum* (dat. pl.) 'the Jassarfjǫll': Much (1889) identified these mountains with the range now known as Hrubý Jeseník (ModGer. *Gesenke*) in the Czech Republic, meaning '(High) Ash Mountains'. No more convincing identifications have been forthcoming.

Gizurr (GizGrý Lv 4)

112. Felmtr er yðru fylki,   feigr er yðarr vísir,
      gnæfar yðr gunnfani,   gramr er yðr Óðinn!

Fylki yðru er felmtr, vísir yðarr er feigr, gunnfani gnæfar yðr, Óðinn er gramr yðr!

Your troop is terrified, your ruler is doomed, the battle-standard flies high for you, Óðinn is angry with you!

Mss: 203^x(111v), R715^x(34v) (*Heiðr*).

Readings: [3] gnæfar: *so* R715^x, gnæfr 203^x;   -fani: *so* R715^x, -fari 203^x.

Editions: *Skj*: Anonyme digte og vers [XIII], E. 5. Vers af *Fornaldarsagaer: Af Hervararsaga* VII 10: AII, 255, BII, 275, *Skald* II, 143; *Heiðr* 1672, 174, *FSN* 1, 501, *Heiðr* 1873, 283, *Heiðr* 1924, 152, *FSGJ* 2, 64, *Heiðr* 1960, 56 (*Heiðr*); *Edd. Min.* 10, *NK* 309, *ÍF Edd.* II, 427.

Context: Gizurr rides to within earshot of the Huns and declaims the stanza in a loud voice.

Notes: [1] *felmtr* 'terrified': The mss' reading, 'feltur', represents an instance of loss of a consonant in a cluster of three which are not commonly found together (*ANG* §291). Cf. *Heiðr* 116/1. — [3]: *Gnæfa* must be intransitive here and *yðr* in the dat. The *gunnfani* 'battle-standard' referred to is presumably that of the Goths, raised in victory over the Huns. Cf. *Hárb* 40/3 (*NK* 84) *gnæfa gunnfana* 'to raise high battle-standards'. — [4]: The following stanza, *Heiðr* 113/7-8, also refers to the god Óðinn's role as decider of battles (see Note). Cf. also Innstein *Innvk* 31/1-2 (*Hálf* 18) *Þér er orðinn | Óðinn til gramr* 'Óðinn has become too angry with you', and Note to that stanza.

Gizurr (GizGrý Lv 5)

113. Býð ek yðr at Dylgju,   ok á Dúnheiði,
      orrustu undir   Jassarfjöllum;
      †hræsi yðr   at há hverju†
      ok láti svá Óðinn flein fljúga,   sem ek fyrir mæli!

Ek býð yðr orrustu at Dylgju ok á Dúnheiði undir Jassarfjöllum; †hræsi yðr at há hverju† ok láti Óðinn flein fljúga svá, sem ek mæli fyrir!

I offer you battle at Dylgja and on Dúnheiðr under Jassarfjǫll; ... and may Óðinn let the spear fly as I determine!

Mss: 203ˣ(111v), R715ˣ(34v-35r) (*Heiðr*).

Readings: [4] Jassar-: 'Josur-' *corrected from* Jassar *in the margin in another hand* 203ˣ, 'Jassa' R715ˣ [5] hræsi: hrósi *apparently corrected from an original blank space in another hand* R715ˣ [6] há: hái R715ˣ; hverju: hverjum R715ˣ.

Editions: *Skj*: Anonyme digte og vers [XIII], E. 5. *Vers af Fornaldarsagaer: Af Hervararsaga* VII 11: AII, 255, BII, 275, *Skald* II, 143, *NN* §2377, *FF* §22; *Heiðr* 1672, 174, *FSN* 1, 501-2, *Heiðr* 1873, 283-4, *Heiðr* 1924, 152-3, *FSGJ* 2, 64, *Heiðr* 1960, 56 (*Heiðr*); *Edd. Min.* 10, *NK* 309, *ÍF Edd.* II, 428.

Context: The stanza is introduced (*Heiðr* 1960, 56): *Ok enn* 'And again'.

Notes: [1-4]: Echoes, though not exactly, Angantýr's instructions to Gizurr in *Heiðr* 111. — [1-4]: On the place names, see Notes to *Heiðr* 111/1, 2 and 4. — [5-6]: Suggestions for emendations to these lines are varied and conjectural. — [7-8]: Cf. *Vsp* 24/1-2 (*NK* 6): *Fleygði Óðinn | oc í fólc um scaut* 'Óðinn let fly [a spear] and shot [it] into the troop'. There are a number of examples of Óðinn consecrating an enemy army to himself by shooting a spear over their troop, or of human participants consecrating an army to Óðinn by doing the same: see e.g. *Eyrb* ch. 44 (*ÍF* 4, 122): *En er flokkrinn Snorra gekk neðan skriðuna, þá skaut Steinþórr spjóti at fornum sið til heilla sér yfir flokk Snorra* 'And when Snorri's troop went up the scree, Steinþórr shot a spear over Snorri's troop for luck according to the ancient custom'. See also *ARG* II, 49 (§376), Turville-Petre (1964, 47). Line 7 is unmetrical with *svá Óðinn* being extrametrical.

Hlǫðr (HlǫðH Lv 3)

114. Taki þér Gizur ...
    mann Angantýs,   kominn af Árheimum!

Taki þér Gizur ... mann Angantýs, kominn af Árheimum!

Seize Gizurr ... Angantýr's man, come from Árheimar!

Mss: 203ˣ(112r), R715ˣ(35r) (*Heiðr*).

Editions: *Skj*: Anonyme digte og vers [XIII], E. 5. *Vers af Fornaldarsagaer: Af Hervararsaga* VII 12: AII, 255, BII, 275, *Skald* II, 144, *NN* §3144; *FSN* 1, 502, *Heiðr* 1873, 284, *Heiðr* 1924, 153, *FSGJ* 2, 64, *Heiðr* 1960, 56 (*Heiðr*); *Edd. Min.* 10-11, *NK* 310, *ÍF Edd.* II, 428.

Context: The stanza is introduced (*Heiðr* 1960, 56): *Þá Hlǫðr hafði heyrt orð Gizurar, þá kvað hann* 'When Hlǫðr had heard Gizurr's words, then he said'.

Notes: [1] *taki þér* 'seize': The *-ð* in the 2nd pers. pl. pres. indic. was dropped before *þér*. The pron. was originally *ér* (*takið ér*), but the *-ð* was reanalysed as the onset of the pron.

(cf. *ANG* §531.4a). Other eds (*Skj* B; *Skald*; *Heiðr* 1873; *Edd. Min.*) emend to *takið þér*, but this is unnecessary. — [2] ...: Neither ms. indicates that anything is missing here, but metrically ll. 3-4 must be part of the same long-line. Bugge's (*Heiðr* 1873, 284) suggestion to insert Gizurr's byname Grýtingaliða has been followed by all subsequent eds. — [3] *mann Angantýs* 'Angantýr's man': Kock (*Skald*; *NN* §3144) reverses the word order for alliterative purposes, but this makes the lines unmetrical since *mann* ought not stand in a lift.

Humli (Humli Lv 3)

115. Eigi skulum   árum spilla,
       þeim er fara   einir saman.

Skulum eigi spilla árum, þeim er fara einir saman.

We must not harm messengers, those who travel alone.

Mss: **203**^{x}(112r), R715^x(35r) (*Heiðr*).

Readings: [1] skulum: skulu R715^x [4] einir: einn R715^x.

Editions: *Skj*: Anonyme digte og vers [XIII], E. 5. Vers af *Fornaldarsagaer*: Af *Hervararsaga* VII 13: AII, 255-6, BII, 275, *Skald* II, 144, *NN* §3187; *FSN* 1, 502, *Heiðr* 1873, 284, *Heiðr* 1924, 153, *FSGJ* 2, 65, *Heiðr* 1960, 56 (*Heiðr*); *Edd. Min.* 11, *NK* 310, *ÍF Edd.* II, 428.

Context: The text is introduced (*Heiðr* 1960, 56): *Humli konungr sagði* 'King Humli said'.

Note: [All]: *Heiðr* 1960 and *Edd. Min.* present this text as prose. If regarded as a long-line, the text does display vocalic alliteration. *Skj* B and *Skald* (cf. *NN* §3187) make conjectural emendations in ll. 3-4 to restore alliteration.

Gizurr (GizGrý Lv 6)

116. Eigi gera Húnar oss felmtraða,   né hornbogar yðar.

Húnar gera eigi oss felmtraða, né hornbogar yðar.

The Huns do not make us frightened, nor [do] your horn bows.

Mss: R715^x(35r), **203**^{x}(112r) (*Heiðr*).

Readings: [1] Eigi: *so* R715^x, ekki 203^x;   gera ('gjöra'): *so* R715^x, gjörar 203^x;   felmtraða: *so* R715^x, vélaða 203^x.

Editions: *Heiðr* 1672, 175, *FSN* 1, 502, *Heiðr* 1873, 284, *Heiðr* 1924, 153, *FSGJ* 2, 65, *Heiðr* 1960, 56 (*Heiðr*); *Edd. Min.* 11, *NK* 310, *ÍF Edd.* II, 428.

Context: The couplet is introduced (*Heiðr* 1960, 56), *Gizurr mælti* 'Gizurr said'.

Notes: [All]: This fragment is presented as prose by all eds but *Heiðr* 1873 (with conjectural emendations), *NK* and the Modern Icelandic edn by Jón Helgason (1967, 243). As it stands l. 1 is metrically too long. — [1] *felmtraða* 'frightened': Cf. *Heiðr* 112/1 and Note. Ms. 203ˣ has *vélaða* 'betrayed, tricked', which does not give good sense. — [2] *hornbogar* 'horn bows': A *hap. leg.* in poetry, not recorded in *LP* since Finnur Jónsson does not include this fragment in *Skj*. *Kgs* (Holm-Olsen 1983, 61) explains that *hornbogar*, presumably bows made from or covered with horn (cf. *Fritzner: hornbogi*) are useful weapons for men on horseback. There is also an Old English cognate: cf. *Beowulf* 2437, *Judith* 220 and the *Paris Psalter* 75/3. Hornbogi appears as a proper name in *Þiðr* (*Þiðr* 1905-11, I, 139).

Gizurr (GizGrý Lv 7)

117. Sex ein eru   seggja fylki,
    í fylki hverju   fimm þúsundir,
    í þúsund hverri   þrettán *hundruð*,
    í hundraði hverju   halir fjórtaldir.

Eru ein sex fylki seggja, í hverju fylki fimm þúsundir, *í* hverri þúsund þrettán *hundruð*, í hverju hundraði fjórtaldir halir.

There are around six troops of warriors, in each troop [are] five thousand, in every thousand thirteen hundreds, in every hundred men four times counted.

Mss: **203ˣ**(112-112r), R715ˣ(35r) (*Heiðr*).

Readings: [1] Sex: *so* R715ˣ, 'v. c.' 203ˣ; ein: *so* R715ˣ, *om.* 203ˣ   [2] seggja: *so* R715ˣ, í 203ˣ   [3] í: *om.* R715ˣ   [5] í: *om.* 203ˣ, R715ˣ; þúsund hverri: hverri þúsand 203ˣ, hverri R715ˣ   [6] *hundruð*: manna *placed in parentheses in another hand* 203ˣ, manna R715ˣ   [7] í: *om.* R715ˣ   [8] halir: *so* R715ˣ, hals 203ˣ.

Editions: *Skj*: Anonyme digte og vers [XIII], E. 5. *Vers af Fornaldarsagaer: Af Hervararsaga* VII 14: AII, 256, BII, 275-6, *Skald* II, 144, *NN* §3144; *Heiðr* 1672, 175, *Heiðr* 1873, 286-7, *Heiðr* 1924, 153-4, *FSGJ* 2, 65, *Heiðr* 1960, 57 (*Heiðr*); *Edd. Min.* 11-12, *NK* 310, *ÍF Edd.* II, 429.

Context: Gizurr returns to Angantýr and reports that he has summoned the Huns to battle. Angantýr asks about the size of the Huns' forces. Gizurr replies (*Heiðr* 1960, 57), *Mikit er þeira mengi* 'Their multitude is great', and speaks this stanza.

Notes: [All]: *Heiðr* 1672, *Heiðr* 1873, *NK*, *ÍF Edd.* and Jón Helgason (1967, 243-4) present Gizurr's words, given in the Context above, as part of the stanza. — [All]: Cf. *Saxo* 2015, I, v. 8. 1 (7. 6), pp. 326-7. — [3] *hverri þúsund* 'every thousand': Ms. 203ˣ has the reverse word order and R715ˣ omits the word *þúsund* 'thousand' altogether. The order chosen here (and by *Heiðr* 1672, *Heiðr* 1873, *Skald*, *FSGJ*, *Heiðr* 1960 and

Edd. Min.) is supported by the pattern of ll. 3 and 7 and is metrically preferable (*NN* §3144). — [6] hundruð 'hundreds': The reading of the mss, *manna* 'of men' (with parentheses as signs of deletion in another hand in 203ˣ) would be distinctly underwhelming. The emendation (made by all eds) can be safely assumed on the basis of the pattern of repetition across ll. 2-3 and 4-5.

Angantýr (AngH Lv 10)

118. Bauð ek þér, bróðir,   basmir óskerðar,
    fé ok fjǫlð meiðma,   sem þik fremst tíddi.
    Nú hefr þú hvárki   hildar at gjǫldum
    ljósa bauga   né land ekki.

Ek bauð þér, bróðir, óskerðar basmir, fé ok fjǫlð meiðma, sem fremst tíddi þik. Nú hefr þú at gjǫldum hildar hvárki ljósa bauga né ekki land.

I offered you, brother, undivided riches, wealth and a multitude of treasures, as was most desirable to you. Now you have in reward for battle neither bright rings nor any land.

Mss: **203ˣ**(112v), R715ˣ(36r) (*Heiðr*).

Readings: [2] basmir: *blank space* 203ˣ, 'Basnir' R715ˣ;   óskerðar: óskir tvær 203ˣ, 'oskertar' R715ˣ   [3] meiðma: 'meidna' 203ˣ, R715ˣ   [4] þik: mik 203ˣ, R715ˣ.

Editions: *Skj*: Anonyme digte og vers [XIII], E. 5. *Vers af Fornaldarsagaer: Af Hervararsaga* VII 15: AII, 256, BII, 276, *Skald* II, 144, *NN* §2378; *Heiðr* 1672, 176, *FSN* 1, 508, *Heiðr* 1873, 289, *Heiðr* 1924, 155, *FSGJ* 2, 67, *Heiðr* 1960, 58 (*Heiðr*); *Edd. Min.* 12, *NK* 311-12, *ÍF Edd*. II, 430.

Context: Angantýr and his army march to Dúnheiðr and there is bitter fighting between the Goths and the Huns; a great many men are slain. After more than a week Angantýr comes to the forefront of the fighting (*Heiðr* 1960, 57), and *skiptusk þeir brœðr hǫggum við* 'the brothers dealt blows against each other', and Hlǫðr and King Humli are killed. Angantýr seeks out the body of his brother Hlǫðr, and speaks the stanza.

Notes: [1-4]: Echoes, with the exception of l. 2, *Heiðr* 97/1-4 (see Note there), where the same emendations need to be made to *þik* 'you' and *meiðma* 'treasures' (see Notes to those words). — [1]: Ms. 203ˣ leaves a blank space after *bróðir* 'brother' to the end of the ms. line. — [2] *óskerðar basmir* 'undivided riches': Both words are *hap. leg.* in poetry and clearly were not well understood by the scribes. All eds emend though *NK* retains R715ˣ's 'basnir'. *Óskerðr* 'undivided' is well attested in prose (cf. *ONP: óskerðr*), but *basmir* (f. pl.; sg. *bǫsm (?)) is otherwise unknown and the meaning is uncertain; Bugge (*Heiðr* 1873, 367) suggested it may refer to rings (see also *AEW: basmir*). On the suffixes in *-m-* rather than *-n-*, which are generally accepted, see *NN* §2378, which also posits a relation to OE *basu* 'purple, crimson', Sanskrit *bhās* 'shine'. *Heiðr* 97/2 has here *fagrar veigar* 'fair draughts', but this has its own problems; see Note there.

Angantýr (AngH Lv 11)

119. Bölvat er okkr, bróðir;   bani em ek þinn orðinn;
 þat mun æ uppi;   illr er dómr norna!

Bölvat er okkr, bróðir; ek em orðinn bani þinn; þat mun æ uppi; dómr norna er illr!

We are cursed, brother; I have become your slayer; that will always be remembered; the judgement of the norns is evil!

Mss: **203**ˣ(112v), R715ˣ(36r) (*Heiðr*).

Readings: [3] *æ*: enn 203ˣ, R715ˣ   [4] norna: norna *corrected from* '[...]rna' *(struck through) in another hand* R715ˣ.

Editions: *Skj*: Anonyme digte og vers [XIII], E. 5. *Vers af Fornaldarsagaer: Af Hervararsaga* VII 16: AII, 256, BII, 276, *Skald* II, 144; *Heiðr* 1672, 176-7, *FSN* 1, 508, *Heiðr* 1873, 289, *Heiðr* 1924, 155, *FSGJ* 2, 67, *Heiðr* 1960, 58 (*Heiðr*); *Edd. Min.* 12, *NK* 312, *ÍF Edd*. II, 430.

Context: The stanza is introduced (*Heiðr* 1960, 58), *Ok enn kvað hann* 'and he said again'.

Notes: [1] *bölvat er okkr* 'we are cursed': An impersonal construction with the p. p. of *bǫlva* 'curse', the 3rd pers. sg. pres. indic. of *vera* 'be' and the acc./dat. dual pers. pron. — [2]: Internecine slaughter is frequently mentioned in medieval sources as particularly heinous, and is the first mentioned catastrophe for the human world at Ragnarǫk in *Vsp* 45/1-2. The present conflict is foreshadowed in *Heiðr* 34 and 43, in which Angantýr Arngrímsson warns Hervǫr that the cursed sword Tyrfingr will *spilla allri ætt þinni* 'destroy all your family'. Angantýr and Hlǫðr Heiðrekssynir are Hervǫr's grandsons. — [3] *æ* 'always': Both mss read *enn* 'yet, still'. The emendation was first made by Bugge (*Heiðr* 1873) and has been followed by all subsequent eds except *NK* and *ÍF Edd*. The same line is found in *Vsp* 16/5, with *æ* in the Hb text, simply *þat mun uppi* 'that will be remembered' in Codex Regius (*NK* 4 and n.). Cf. also Anon *Nkt* 9/5-6ᴵᴵ *Þess mun æ* | *uppi lengi* '[Haraldr's name] will be remembered for a very long time'. — [4]: Both mss leave a blank space to the end of the ms. line after this stanza, and in 203ˣ l. 4 is written in slightly larger letters, as if perhaps written in later, though it is in the scribal hand. — [4] *norna* 'of the norns': The norns are supernatural females representing fate or destiny in Old Norse mythology; cf. *Hamð* 30/5-6 (*NK* 274) *qveld lifir maðr ecci* | *eptir qvið norna* 'a person doesn't live for a night after the norns' decree'. They need not always signify ill fate, as they do in the present stanza: *Gylf* (*SnE* 2005, 18) explains that there are both malevolent norns, who deal out unfortunate lives, and good norns, who shape good lives.

- Number of stanza in a poem or group of stanzas

- Text of stanza: the second *helmingr* is placed next to the first in skaldic metres; italics indicate emended/conjectured text not found in any manuscript (not shown here) and an asterisk indicates that text has been removed (not shown here)

- Stanza text rearranged in prose order

- Translation of stanza; kennings are translated literally and *heiti* comprising personal names are glossed in angle brackets (e.g. Mist <valkyrie>; not shown here)

- Kenning referents, listed from innermost kenning to outermost kenning

- List of manuscripts in which the stanza occurs, followed by the folio or page on which it is recorded; the main manuscript is in bold; manuscripts are grouped by prose work where relevant (here, *Snorra Edda*)

- Readings from manuscripts which differ from the main text (may run on from the list of manuscripts); readings are grouped by line (in square brackets) and the word or words in the main text which have variants

- Categorisation and number of the stanza in Finnur Jónsson's *Skjaldedigtning*, followed by other editions of the stanza with page references; editions are grouped by prose work where relevant

- Description of the prose context in which the stanza occurs, where relevant

- Notes to the stanza (normally starting on a new line); line number(s) are given in square brackets followed by the word or words to be discussed